MAN AND HIS MUSIC

THE STORY OF MUSICAL EXPERIENCE IN THE WEST

MAN AND HIS MUSIC

THE STORY OF MUSICAL EXPERIENCE IN THE WEST

ALEC HARMAN
with Anthony Milner
WILFRID MELLERS

BARRIE & JENKINS
LONDON

First published in 4 parts in 1957-9 by
Barrie & Rockliff Ltd

First published in a revised, single-volume edition in 1962 by
Barrie & Jenkins Ltd
289 Westbourne Grove, London W11 2QA
Reprinted in 1964, 1968, 1971, 1977, 1980; new edition 1988

British Library Cataloguing in Publication Data
Harman, Alec, *1917–*
Man and his music: the story of musical
experience in the West. – Rev. ed.
1. Western music, to 1987
I. Title II. Milner, Anthony III. Mellers, Wilfrid
780'.9

ISBN 0 7126 2001 X

Printed and bound in Great Britain by
Anchor Brendon Ltd, Tiptree, Essex

CONTENTS

II. OPERA, RITUAL, AND MYTH

PART IV
ROMANTICISM AND THE 20TH CENTURY
(from c. 1800)

I. INTROSPECTION AND NATIONALISM

II. INTROSPECTION AND ISOLATION

APPENDIXES

ILLUSTRATIONS

PLATES

IN THE TEXT

Plates I and IX are from A History of Music in Pictures, *edited by G. Kinsky, J. M. Dent (London) and E. P. Dutton (New York).*

PREFACE TO PARTS I AND II

In the Preface to Parts III and IV of this history Wilfrid Mellers remarks that a music historian should approach his task with both 'circumspection and humility'. He is undoubtedly right, for when one considers what is involved in such an undertaking one should be extremely chary of adding to what has already been achieved in this sphere; indeed, it is doubtful whether the attempt should ever be made unless one is convinced that the kind of history one has in mind is sufficiently distinctive to justify the writing of yet another.

In this series the authors have been guided by three chief aims, and we believe that it is in the combination of these aims that the distinctiveness of this particular history lies.

To begin with, we have tried to convey something of the feelings aroused in us by the music we write about and to give as many aesthetic judgments on individual works and composers as is possible in a work of this size and scope, for although we realize that such feelings and judgments are purely personal and that therefore it is hardly likely that everyone will agree with them, we believe that a history which does not seek to arouse a critical enthusiasm for each and every period and in which there are few or no aesthetic judgments to guide the taste of those less familiar with the music in question is not fulfilling one of its functions.

Our second aim has been to write a history that would be of use in both schools and universities, and while conscious that there is a marked difference in ability and attainment between the English fifth-former and the third-year university student, and that hence this history will provide more for the one and less for the other than is needed, we hope that both will find omething of value, even though what is found may only have an indirect bearing on their examinations.

But a history of music should do more than stimulate enthusiasm, or assess greatness, or pass aesthetic judgments; it should do more than present facts and reasonable deductions, or include well-chosen examples and quotations, or give accurate analyses of styles and techniques, important as all these are; it should also (to quote *The New Oxford History of*

Music) 'present music not as an isolated phenomenon or the work of a few outstanding composers, but as an art developing in constant association with every form of human culture and activity'. This has been our third aim, and in pursuing it we have tried, by giving what we hope is sufficient relevant information of a general nature, to set the stage, as it were, for each successive scene and (to continue the analogy) by outlining the principal characters involved (religion, painting, literature, etc.), to show in what ways and to what extent they influenced or were influenced by music.

This attempt to present music as an integral part of western civilization is essential, we believe, because all creative artists are influenced by the spiritual and intellectual environment in which they live, and so it follows that the more we know about a particular period the more we can enter into the creative minds of that period and hence appreciate more fully their aims and achievements. This may appear, and indeed is, obvious enough, but it is all too often forgotten, because each of us can enjoy and even be profoundly moved by a work of art knowing little or nothing about its creator or general background. Nevertheless, it remains true that every creative artist gains in significance when his work is related to the conditions in which it was created, whether he be someone whose name is a household word, like Mozart, or a comparatively obscure mediaeval composer, like Pérotin. Thus, knowing something of the rationalism, the sophisticated sentimentality, the polished elegance of society in the latter half of the eighteenth century, of the delicate sensuousness and exquisite refinement of Watteau's and Boucher's paintings, we marvel more than if we knew nothing of all this, not only at the utter perfection of Mozart's style and sense of structure but also at the undercurrents of emotion that pervade his work and which at times amount almost to romantic passion.

Compared to Mozart, Pérotin gains in significance to a much greater extent when we know something about his background because the time at which he lived and the style in which he wrote have far fewer points of contact for us today than is the case with the eighteenth century. At first hearing, his music may well sound bare, monotonous, even meaningless, but when it is realized that the systematization and reiteration of rhythmic patterns, which are the main features of Pérotin's style, not only represented a new development in music, but also reflected, as did the solutions to the structural problems of contemporary Gothic architecture, the intellectual awakening of the twelfth and thirteenth centuries, an awakening that was stimulated by the discovery, through Arab philosophers, of the works of Aristotle, and which led men like Peter Abelard and St. Thomas Aquinas to believe and teach that faith can only be wholly assured when founded on reason; when it is further realized that, apart from the octave, the fourth and fifth were the basic intervals because they were as satisfyingly sonorous to ears accustomed to unison singing and playing as thirds and sixths are to us; and, lastly, that the music was intended to be performed as an act of devotion in a cathedral rather than listened to as an aesthetic experience in a concert hall—then the significance of the man becomes apparent and, after adjusting our ears and minds in the light of what we have learnt, we can begin to understand, assess, and (because he was in fact a fine composer) enjoy his music, with its marked contrast between the lively, bouncy rhythmic figures in one part and the sustained or slower-moving notes in another.

But writing alone cannot give an adequate account of any period, especially with regard to the fine arts, and if there had been no considerations as to cost this history would have included many more reproductions, some of them coloured, of buildings, paintings, sculpture, etc. Nevertheless, we hope that all those who read it will want to discover more of the achievements in other fields and that some will wish to pursue in greater detail the development of the music itself.

It is obvious, however, that the greatest value from knowing something about the background of a particular art can only be obtained if one has experienced or has the opportunity of experiencing that art, and because much of the music written in the Middle Ages is so different from that which we normally hear and, moreover, is performed so infrequently I have included, in the first five chapters of Part I, a fair number of complete compositions, together with suggestions as to performance and with the original words freely translated. Further examples for these chapters, for Chapter 6, and for the chapters in Part II can be found in the list of Selected Music at the end of the book, where may also be found a list of Recommended Books and a Discography, this last compiled by

Nicholas Cohu, to whom I am most grateful.

Because it is seldom possible to be dogmatic about what was typical of England rather than, say, Scotland, especially in the Middle Ages, I have in most cases used the term 'British' when referring to the music of this Island in Part I. Admittedly the bulk of what has survived was written down, if not actually composed, by Englishmen, but this does not necessarily mean that the style or type of composition was peculiar to England; it must be remembered that the ability to write music was largely restricted to centres of learning such as monasteries and, later, universities and the Chapel Royal, of which centres there were, even proportionally, many more in England than in Scotland or Wales (St. Andrews', the oldest university after Oxford and Cambridge, did not open until 1412). Furthermore, in Scotland, where there was a flourishing musical tradition second only to that of England, the destruction of music, particularly of part-music, during the early years of the Reformation was far greater than elsewhere in Britain.

Part II is deliberately less well balanced than Part I, the reason being that late Renaissance music and baroque opera (which together comprise nearly four-fifths of Part II) have been performed and written about less often than have baroque instrumental and vocal music. This is particularly true of baroque opera, and I wish that I could have included at least one complete aria from A. Scarlatti's and Hasse's later works, as well as a complete chorus and dance by Rameau. The reader must therefore be referred to the list of Selected Music and to the Discography.

For Parts I and II, the main difference between this and previous editions is that the dates of composers have all been checked with the new *Grove's Dictionary;* the lists of Recommended Books and Selected Music and the Discography are also revised and updated. I wish to express my thanks to the publishers for making this improvement possible by their decision to produce this new edition.

Bath, 1988 ALEC HARMAN

PART I

MEDIAEVAL AND EARLY RENAISSANCE MUSIC

(*up to c. 1525*)

by ALEC HARMAN

I

MUSIC IN THE EARLY CHURCH: CHRISTIAN CHANT

MOST people would agree that it is perfectly natural and proper for music to have a place in Christian worship. Natural because music and religion have been associated from the earliest times, and proper because the Bible sanctions its use. But there would be and always has been far less general agreement as to the *kind* of music that is suitable in religious services. If the suggestion were made that hymn texts should be adapted to popular 'hits' and accompanied by a cinema organ, very few people would tolerate the idea for one moment. Yet this suggestion gives us some idea of the problem facing the early Christian leaders or Church Fathers, as they are usually called, for although the problem was not so serious during the first two centuries when persecution was severe and the number of Christians small, and music not only sustained the converted but was an aid to conversion, it became acute in the third, fourth, and fifth centuries when the Church expanded rapidly, especially after its official recognition in 313, and the host of new converts brought with them their own cultural and philosophical traditions. Then it was that the Church Fathers had not only to combat the infiltration of pagan ideas, but also to decide whether music, with its strong worldly associations, was in any way suited to take part in Christian worship. To understand their difficulties fully we must remember that music was an essential part of Greek and Roman entertainment, for from as early as the sixth century B.C. there had been an instrumental 'class' in the great Greek contests (of which the Olympic Games is now the most famous), and by the early centuries A.D. the Romans, who adopted most of the Greek forms of entertainment, but in a coarser and more spectacular manner, had caused music to be largely associated with debauchery and immorality of all kinds. Small wonder, then, that the Church authorities were in a quandary and felt it imperative to draw the line somewhere, but exactly where was another problem. Some insisted that all instruments should be excluded from the service, others admitted only those mentioned in the Bible, while still others allowed any instrument, regarding each symbolically—the trumpet, for instance, being the power of God's message, the drum the conquering of sin, the cymbals the soul thirsting for Christ, etc. The first of these three attitudes eventually won the day, with the result that the music composed for the Church during the first thousand years or so was sung unaccompanied. As regards singing, however, practically all the Church Fathers decided that it was a good thing; indeed, they would have flouted all natural instincts had they decided otherwise, but, like the old Greek philosophers, whose influence on them was considerable, they realized that music can either ennoble or debase man's moral fibre and that therefore all church music must be associated with devout words—another reason for the rejection of instruments. In the words of St. Basil [*c.* 330-387], "God blended the delight of melody with doctrines in order that through the pleasantness and softness of the sound we might unawares receive what was useful in words. . . . For this purpose these harmonious melodies of the Psalms have been designed for us."*

What were these harmonious melodies? Unfortunately we do not know, for they were not written down in any shape or form until about the sixth century, and not until the middle of the eleventh century was a system of musical notation invented—that is, a system of symbols which show the exact pitch of the notes, but not necessarily their values. Hence the original melodies, passed down orally from generation to generation, must have changed a great deal both from careless alteration and deliberate variation, particularly during the first four or five hundred years, before the Church began to organize her repertoire (see p. 8).

Although we know very little of the actual music of the early Church, we do know that psalm-singing was the core of its services, the core from which radiated most of the songs now usually called plainsong. This name comes from the Latin *cantus planus* and was used by some thirteenth-century theorists in order to distinguish between the 'plain' notes of these

* Quoted from O. Strunk, *Source Readings in Music History*, p. 65.

melodies, which had no definite values, and 'musica mensurata', in which the notes were 'measured', i.e. had exact values. A better name, however, and the one we shall use, is Christian chant, for plainsong can be and is used to describe any unmeasured music that consists of only one melodic line.

We also know that there were three main types of melody which are usually called syllabic, group, and melismatic or florid. These are distinguished by their underlay—that is, by the way the syllables of the text are fitted to the notes of the melody. Thus the syllabic type has mainly one note to each syllable. (An accented syllable here and elsewhere is shown by an acute accent. The notes printed small are sung lightly, Ex. 1):

Ex. 1. Hymn *Ut queant laxis* (1st verse)
Modern transcription.* (♪= MM c.120)
Ut quéant lá - xis re-so - ná - re fí-bris Mí - ra ge-stó - rum fá-mu-li tu-ó - rum,
Sól - - - ve pol-lú - ti lá - bi - i re - á - tum, Sánc - te Jo- án- nes.

The group type has from two to four notes to most syllables (Ex. 2):

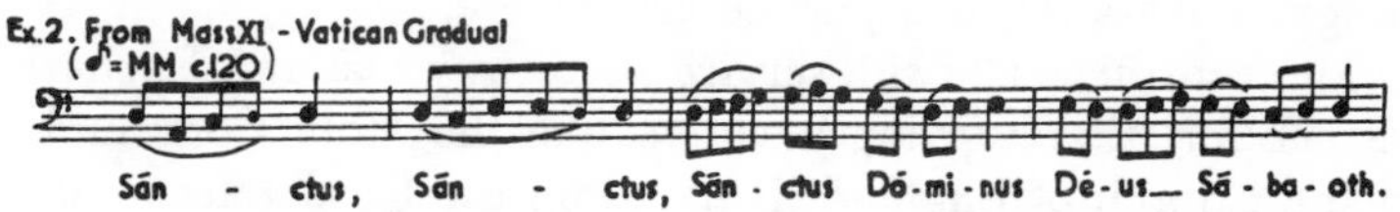
Ex. 2. From Mass XI - Vatican Gradual
(♪= MM c.120)
Sán - ctus, Sán - ctus, Sán - ctus Dó-mi-nus Dé-us Sá - ba - oth.

While in the melismatic type some syllables are sung to a great many notes (Ex. 3):

Ex. 3. From Mass III - Vatican Gradual (*Kyrie Deus sempiterne*) (♪= M.M.c.120)
(a)
Ký - ri - e e-lé-i-son.
Alleluia (sung at Mass on Easter Sunday)
(♪= MM c.120)
(b)
Al - le - lú - - ia

* See Plate III.

These three types, either separately or mixed, can be applied to any song that has ever been composed, and in general it is true to say that the first type is used when the text is regarded as more important than the music, while the third type shows the opposite point of view; in fact the 'alleluias', with their long flourishes on a single syllable, were really a contradiction of the official teaching that music was only permissible if directly associated with holy words, and were the first examples in Christian chant of the delight in singing for its own sake; the Church Fathers, however, duly pointed out that such singing praised God in a way no words could possibly express! Melismatic chant, however, was not the earliest type, being preceded by syllabic chant, and this provides one of the many examples of the so-called 'wave-theory' of art—the crests representing (in this case) a high degree of conscious elaboration and the troughs simplicity, either natural when the artist is unsure of or experimenting with his medium, or deliberate when he is pruning excessive ornamentation or trying to achieve a balance of expression. But the earliest Christian chants were simple not only because of this artistic wave progression, but also because the service itself had to be both simple and secret, owing to the ever-present threat of persecution which, under the Emperors Nero [37-68], Domitian [reigned 81-96], and Diocletian [reigned 283-305], was particularly severe.

The central act of the service or liturgy was the Eucharist (Greek for 'thanksgiving') which, like the Holy Communion in the Church of England, is based on the Gospel accounts of the Last Supper. At first this was held on the Jewish Sabbath (Saturday), but was later transferred to Sunday morning after 'vigils' or 'watches' had been held during the previous night. Although the Eucharist never lost its central position and importance, local variations of the service sprang up all over Christendom, both in ceremonial and musical performance, and it was not until the fourth century that any successful attempts at unification could be made. The reasons for this are twofold. Firstly, the division of the Roman Empire into eastern and western empires in 314 fostered existing liturgical differences between the eastern and western Churches and led to the formation of five main groups: the Syrian, Byzantine, and Egyptian in the east, where Greek remained the official language, and in the west the Roman (with its offshoot, the

Ambrosian) and Gallican (with its offshoot, the Mozarabic), in which Latin replaced Greek in the liturgy. This split encouraged a greater degree of unity within each group, but it is with the western groups only that we shall be concerned from now on. Secondly, the official toleration of Christianity in 313 by Constantine the Great [reigned 306-337] made public worship possible, and by thus openly exposing local variations stressed the need for greater uniformity. It also made possible the building of churches and encouraged elaboration of the service through the introduction of greater pomp and ceremonial, in the performance of which music took an active part, and the next five hundred years saw both a rapid development in the organization of the liturgy and the creation of most of the melodies we now call Christian chant.

We do not know who composed these melodies, but some of them were certainly adapted from Greek and Jewish sources and possibly from folk-song also. Which had the greater influence, Greek or Jewish music, was a bone of contention until recently, but although Greek was the accepted language in most of the churches during the early years—hence the words 'eucharist' and 'kyrie eleison' ('Lord have mercy' —originally a hymn to the Greek sun-god!), which were retained even after the Roman Church had changed over to Latin—and although the Church Fathers were greatly influenced by Greek thought, it now seems certain that Christian chant owes more to the Jewish synagogue than to the Greek temple. For one thing, the chant melodies as they have come down to us are much more closely allied to Jewish than to Greek music, and as the texts are nearly all taken from the psalms (which are of course Jewish, not Christian) it seems very probable that many of the psalm melodies themselves were adapted from those used in the synagogue. In fact, it has been shown that many such tunes sung to-day by Jewish communities who have been completely isolated since pre-Christian times are strikingly similar to those of the Christian Church. Furthermore, the different ways of singing the psalms were the same in both church and synagogue; these are now called direct, responsorial, and antiphonal psalmody. Direct psalmody means that part or the whole of a psalm is sung in syllabic style without any additional matter, the verses being alternately performed by either a soloist (cantor) and chorus, or else a divided chorus (men *versus* women and children in the early days). In responsorial psalmody the entire psalm was originally sung also in syllabic style by the cantor, while the congregation 'responded' after each verse with a single word like 'Alleluia', or 'Amen', or even a short phrase; later the music became more ornate and only a few verses were sung, while the 'response' grew longer and often preceded the psalm as well as being sung between each verse and at the end.

Antiphonal psalmody developed from direct psalmody, the distinction lying in the introduction of a short sentence which was sung before the psalm by the entire congregation, this new melody and text being known as the 'antiphon'. At important feasts this was sung both before and after the psalm and in some cases the psalm was omitted, the antiphon thus becoming an independent chant.

So far we have only dealt with chants based on the psalms, which are poetic in feeling but written in what we can call lyrical prose. The pure prose parts of the Bible, however, were recited by the priest in a manner borrowed from the synagogue and called 'cantillation'. This simply means chanting on a monotone or one note, but complete 'monotony' is avoided by the introduction of a few ascending or descending notes ('inflections') at the beginning, middle, or end of the phrase. Another important type of chant was the hymn, also of Jewish origin but influenced to some extent by Greek models. The first Christian hymns were written (in Greek) for the eastern churches, where they became extremely popular, and were eventually introduced into France by St. Hilary of Poitiers [d. *c*. 367]. St. Hilary's hymns were in Latin, and as all but one are lost, his younger contemporary, St. Ambrose, Bishop of Milan [339–97], is usually regarded as the father of western Christian hymnody. The Ambrosian hymn texts differed from those of all other chants in that they were not taken direct from the Bible, but are poetic paraphrases of Biblical passages written in a regular metrical pattern of short-long syllables, like Greek verse (see p. 29). They were meant for congregational singing and in fact were expressly written by St. Ambrose in order to strengthen the morale of his flock, who were being divided by an heretical sect. The music therefore, though it has not survived, must have been simple, with mainly one syllable to a note. This use of the hymn—which can be described as political in the sense that it was used to attack heresies and encourage orthodoxy—was one which lasted right through the early history of the Church; indeed, it was still a powerful weapon in the hands of Luther and others during the Reformation in the sixteenth century. Only four definitely authentic hymns by St. Ambrose have come down to us, of which three have been accorded places in the Roman Liturgy, but a great many more were written in imitation, and these are all called Ambrosian hymns, while the other chant melodies composed for and still used in Milan are called Ambrosian or Milanese chant.

As regards the chants of the other two western groups (excluding the Roman), the Gallican flourished (as its Latin name, *Gallicus*, implies) in Gaul, but its influence extended as far as Ireland, whose missionaries brought it to Britain in the late fifth century, where it was sung until Roman chant was introduced in 596 by St. Augustine [d. *c.* 604]. In Gaul itself, however, Gallican chant continued in use until it was banned by the Emperor Charlemagne [742-814], who decreed that it should be replaced by Roman chant. Mozarabic chant was sung in Spain, where, during the Moorish conquest from the eighth to the eleventh centuries, Christians were called 'Mozarabs' or 'would-be Arabs'. It had a longer life than Gallican chant, being farther from the authority of Rome, and partly as a result of this its liturgical practices often differed considerably (they actually danced during divine service in Toledo!); not until the eleventh century was it officially forbidden. Thus the chants of these three Christian provinces, northern Italy (Milan), Gaul, and Spain were ultimately replaced by that of Rome, and although this city was the obvious centre for western Christianity there is no reason to suppose that its chant, before the sixth century at any rate, was in any way superior to the others—in fact, in some ways Rome was conservative in its attitude to new ideas (a rôle she continued to play in later centuries) and, for example, antiphonal psalmody as well as hymn-singing were only admitted some time after they had become well established in Milan.

The reason why Roman chant eventually supplanted the other western chants was due to the organizing zeal of a number of Popes from Damasus I [366–84]—the patron of St. Jerome [*c.* 340–420], who was the translator of the official Latin Bible, the Vulgate—to Gregory III [d. 741], and to a lesser extent the Emperor Charlemagne. The most ardent organizer, however, was Gregory I [*c.* 540-604]. Elected Pope in 590, he intensified the efforts to establish a uniform liturgy and chant which would serve the whole of western Christendom, and by his death he had largely succeeded, for the classification and repertoire of Gregorian chant, as it was called in honour of him, have remained largely unchanged to this day. At present Gregorian chant consists of nearly 3,000 melodies, the great majority of which were selected and 'edited' under Gregory's authority and which the Church regarded and still regards as the only official ones. But the creative spark takes little account of officialdom, and although Gregory's reforms may have curbed they did not kill the urge of later composers to write new chants or embellish old ones, and while from the fifth century to the eighth may be called the Golden Age of Gregorian chant, there was also a Silver Age from the ninth to the twelfth centuries in which a whole host of new melodies and texts were composed.

This renewed creative impulse in the realm of Christian chant was no isolated event, but simply the result of a general flowering of the human mind and spirit that affected all human activity, and which manifested itself in the four Crusades, ending with the capture of Constantinople in 1204, the struggles for and against authority (Magna Carta, 1215), the final separation between the eastern and western Churches (1054), the Norman Conquest of England (1066), the organizing of communities into towns, the formation of guilds of craftsmen, the intensive study of classical literature and philosophy, the establishing of universities (Paris and Bologna, *c.* 1140; Oxford, early thirteenth century), the increasing use of the various vernaculars (e.g. Old English, Provençal, etc.), the beginnings of western science (a school of medicine was founded at Salerno, near Naples, *c.* 1000), the magnificent achievements of the Romanesque and Gothic architectural styles, the birth of European drama, the first blossoming of secular music (troubadours and trouvères), the rise of part-music, and so on. The culmination of this renaissance came in the twelfth and thirteenth centuries, but this takes us out of the realm of Gregorian chant and into the new and rapidly expanding territory of polyphony (Greek, *poly*=many; *phonos*=voice), and so discussion of it must wait until Chapter 2.

In all these different branches of human learning and action the Church was the dominating influence; it could make or mar a man's career and help or hinder the discovery of new knowledge; indeed, as a body the Church was an educational institution, research station, and library, and her buildings were places of worship, theatres, and opera houses. This may appear to be a sweeping claim, but we shall try to justify it by beginning at the heart of the Christian religion and then, so to speak, work outwards.

By the middle of the eleventh century the Eucharist had become enshrined in an elaborate ceremonial both spoken and sung which was eventually called the Mass and which has remained unchanged to the present day in the Roman Church. The various items of the Mass are divided up into two categories: the Proper, in which the texts of the items vary according to the day on which the Mass is celebrated; and the Ordinary, in which the texts are invariable, although they are not all sung at every celebration, the Gloria, for example, being omitted during Lent, and the Credo being only sung on Sundays and the more important feast days. The order and names of the sung items can best be shown as follows:

PROPER	ORDINARY
Introit	*Kyrie eleison* ('Lord have mercy')
	Gloria in excelsis Deo ('Glory to God in the highest')
Gradual	
Tract or Alleluia	*Credo in unum Deum* ('I believe in one God')
Offertory	*Sanctus, sanctus, sanctus* ('Holy, holy, holy')
	Agnus Dei ('Lamb of God')
Communion	*Ite missa est* ('Go, the congregation is dismissed') or *Benedicamus Domino* ('Let us praise the Lord')

The Proper of the Mass is the oldest part, and all the items are taken from or were originally connected with the psalms;

they thus represent the three types of psalmody mentioned earlier, the Tract being an example of direct psalmody, the Gradual and Alleluia of responsorial psalmody, and the remainder of antiphonal psalmody, except that in the Offertory and Communion the psalm verse has been dispensed with and therefore only the antiphon is sung. (In the Mass for the Dead or Requiem Mass however, the psalm verse is retained in the Offertory and Communion.) The items of the Ordinary were added to the service at various times from the sixth to the eleventh centuries, and except for the Ite missa est, which was nearly always sung to its original chants, have been set to music literally thousands of times from the thirteenth century onwards, for the simple reason that as the words never changed, composers were encouraged to write new settings which would be performed far more often than, say, a setting of an Introit text which was only sung once a year in memory of a particular saint; in fact, when we speak of a Mass by So-and-so we mean a composition based on the five main items of the Ordinary.

In addition to the Mass, short services called the Canonical Hours or Offices took place at various times of the day and night. These developed from the vigils held before the celebration of the Eucharist (see p. 4), and with the addition of other vigils adapted from the eastern churches became a complete and independent system by the fifth century, consisting of Nocturns, later called Matins (the original vigils), at midnight, Lauds at daybreak, Prime at 6 a.m., Terce at 9 a.m., Sext at midday, None between 2 and 3 p.m., Vespers at about 6 p.m., and Compline at 7 p.m., at each of which psalms, antiphons, and hymns were sung. Nowadays the Offices are rarely observed in their entirety except in monastic communities, and it was in such communities that they were first strictly organized and performed.

The founder of the first monastic order in the west was St. Benedict [*c*. 480-*c*. 547], although the seeds of monasticism had been sown in the days of persecution, when groups of Christians sought refuge in wild and lonely parts. This enforced isolation came to be regarded by many as the ideal expression of the Christian life, and even after Constantine's edict of 313 the number of such groups continued to grow all over Christendom. Some system of organization became essential, therefore, and St. Benedict, whose devoutness and self-denial were widely known, after establishing a monastery on Monte Cassino (destroyed, alas, in 1944, but since rebuilt as before), wrote the first monastic Rule in which the details of daily life and worship were laid down. The Benedictine Order eventually spread to the rest of Europe, and during the following seven centuries gave rise to a number of other dedicated brotherhoods, such as the Knights Templar, the Dominicans, and, perhaps most well-known of all, the Franciscans.

At first the monasteries were poor and the monks spent most of the daylight hours in manual labour in order to be self-supporting. Later, however, as the result of rich endowments, the intensive study of both Christian and classical authors was made possible and many monasteries became centres of learning; indeed, they were the only centres before the universities came into being. Here most of the more important earlier manuscripts were copied, annotated, or translated, a fact which disproves the common belief that interest in classical culture was first shown in the Renaissance, for the great secular awakening in the fifteenth century was largely prepared by the study and preservation of the ancient authors in the mediaeval monasteries. But such learning was by no means wholeheartedly approved of by the Church leaders, and such eminent men as St. Gregory, St. Benedict, and St. Augustine, bishop of Hippo [354–430], condemned it strongly; their views however, only affected Italian monasteries and explain the fact that not until the late Middle Ages did Italian scholarship compare favourably with that of other countries, although paradoxically enough the two men who most strongly advocated the study of classical literature and thought were both Romans. The first of these, Cassiodorus [*c.* 477–570], established a monastery on his own estate in the southern tip of Italy, where he insisted on the study of pagan works in order to confound pagan philosophy, and by thus subordinating secular knowledge to Christian theology set an example which most other monasteries outside Italy quickly followed. He also wrote many books, one of which, the *Institutiones*, contains an important section on music—in fact, he was one of the two most influential writers on this subject between the ancient Greek authors and the Middle Ages, the other being the second great Roman scholar, Boethius [*c.* 480-524]. Unlike Cassiodorus, Boethius valued knowledge for its own sake, not merely as a means to an end, and before he was brutally done to death at an early age on a false charge of treason, he had written voluminously on a wide variety of subjects, his most important work for our present purpose being *De Institutione Musice*. This is typical of its author's main purpose—namely, to transmit to Rome the wisdom and culture of ancient Greece, for it summarizes all that was then known of Greek musical theory, and such was its popularity and authority that it became the prime theoretical source for all mediaeval and most Renaissance musicians.

The amount of time, ink, and paper that has been spent in writing about Greek music in the last 1,000 years or so is past computing, but if we are to understand much of the mediaeval attitude to music as well as its practice, some of the more important aspects must be mentioned.

To begin with, music to the Greeks was largely a matter of speculation—that is, they were not so much concerned with melodies and intervals as with their effects on man or their imagined relationship with the heavenly bodies, each of which was supposed to emit a musical note as it revolved round the earth, and while they admitted that we never heard these notes they explained this awkward fact by maintaining that as they were always sounding in our ears we were therefore unconscious of them! This fantastic idea, known as 'the music of the spheres', was first put forward by Pythagoras [sixth century B.C.], who also claimed that man, as part of the Universe, was similarly constructed, the soul, mind, and body all being 'consonant' with each other, and such was his reputation and that of his advocate, Boethius, that not until the thirteenth century were these speculations seriously criticized, although they persisted in popular belief very much longer, as, for example, in Shakespeare's *The Merchant of Venice*, Act V, Scene 1, where Lorenzo informs Jessica that—

> There's not the smallest orb which thou behold'st
> But in his motion like an angel sings,
> Still quiring to the young-eyed cherubins :
> Such harmony is in immortal souls;
> But, whilst this muddy vesture of decay
> Doth grossly close it in, we cannot hear it.

On the other hand, most of the results of Pythagoras's mathematical investigations into music have remained to this day and are the basis of modern acoustics.

The belief that music affected man in different but very definite ways was much more fundamental, and explains why the study of it was such an essential part of Greek education, for each melody, rhythm, and instrument was thought to exert its own special influence on man's character, a belief which, as we have seen, the Church Fathers also subscribed to, and indeed so do we in a sense if we say that a major chord is brighter or happier than a minor one, or that a trumpet is martial, or an oboe mournful. The first great advocate of this doctrine was Plato [*c.* 427-347 B.C.], who associated each of the Greek 'modes', rhythms, and instruments with a definite emotional or moral effect. Thus the Mixolydian 'mode' made men sad, while the Dorian ennobled their minds; the rhythm short, long, long (⏑ – –) was suitable for drinking songs, but not heroic ballads; the aulos, a reed instrument of piercing tone, was only fit for feasts and virtuoso performances, while the kithara, an instrument of seven strings (in Plato's time) which were plucked, was regarded as more refined and moderate, and was in fact approved of by nearly all the Church Fathers, especially for music in the home, because King David was supposed to have played it. It is easy to dismiss the idea that music directly affects men's actions, but we would do well to remember, firstly, that Plato, to put it mildly, was no fool in matters concerning the human mind, and, secondly, that Greek music was entirely monophonic (*monos*=one): in other words, although a song might be sung simultaneously at different octaves, or varied slightly on an accompanying instrument, there was only one melodic line, and it is therefore only natural to expect—in fact, it has been proved conclusively—that in such a musical culture slight differences in melodic structure and rhythmic design expressed far more than they do to us, whose ears have become melodically dulled by incessant harmony, and limited harmony at that. Furthermore, the Greeks used intervals smaller than a semitone, as indeed do many Asiatic and other races today, thus increasing the flexibility and expressiveness of the vocal line. All this is important because European music was also entirely monophonic until the rise of part-music in the ninth century, and not until the thirteenth century did part-music begin to oust monophony to any great extent. This fact explains the seemingly incredible (to us) stories and legends concerning the power of music, from

Orpheus to the Pied Piper of Hamelin, and when we read of the kithara player of a certain Danish King in the twelfth century who boasted of his ability to drive his royal master into a raging madness and, on being challenged, succeeded so well that the King slew four men before being overpowered, we may allow for exaggeration, but should not dismiss the story as completely fantastic. After all, when comparatively sophisticated adolescents of the mid-twentieth century are transported into a state of near-ecstasy by the virtuosity of a jazz ensemble or the mellifluous tones of a male crooner it is perfectly credible that in an earlier and far less sophisticated age people were aroused to a high pitch of emotional excitement by music that we would regard as simple or even naïve.

We used the word 'mode' in the preceding paragraph and put it in inverted commas because we have no proof that Greek music was in fact modal, for by mode is usually meant an arrangement of notes within an octave which is regarded as having a distinct and separate existence from all other arrangements. Our major and minor scales for instance represent only four of the many modes possible (major, harmonic minor, ascending and descending melodic minor), another important one being this example of a pentatonic mode (*penta*=five) (Ex. 4)—

which is the oldest and most widely used, for it was known to the Chinese at least 2,000 years B.C., is found in many folk-songs all over the world, and is almost certainly the basis of a great many Gregorian chants, the gaps (*d'*-*f'* and *a'*-(*c''*) in our example)* being filled in later in most cases. However, when we talk about the modes in general we mean the twelve commonly recognized in the late fifteenth and sixteenth centuries. These were divided into six main modes called authentic, which range from the lowest and most important note—the final—to the octave above, and six dependent modes

* Throughout this book roman letters are used either when the exact position of the notes is immaterial (e.g. 'the perfect fifth C-G') or when they are qualified (e.g. 'middle C', 'violin A'); italicized letters refer to Helmholtz's pitch notation in which *c'*=middle C, *c''* and *c'''*=the octave and double octave above respectively, and *c*, *C* and C_1,=the octave, double octave and treble octave below respectively.

called plagal, each being 'part' of an authentic mode and ranging from the fourth below the final (the dominant) to the octave above (hence the prefix *Hypo-*, a Greek word meaning 'below'). Here are the twelve modes, the final of each being shown by a black semibreve (Ex. 5):

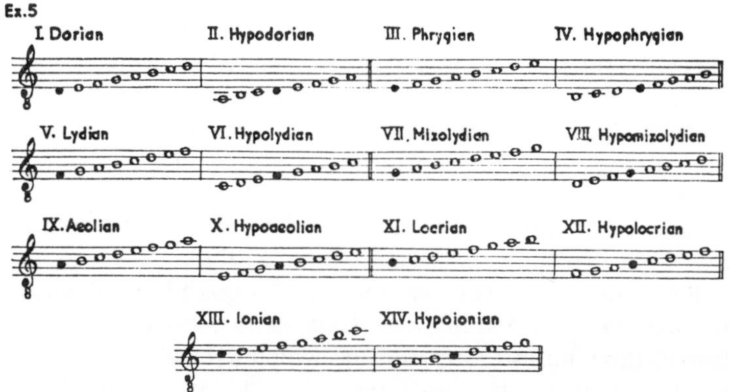

Modes XI and XII—Locrian and Hypolocrian—were not used in practice, as the important interval between final and dominant (B-F or F-B) is not a perfect fourth or fifth and was in fact called 'diabolus in musica'—'the devil in music').

Of these twelve modes, only the first eight (the 'ecclesiastical modes') were recognized and applied to Gregorian chant, and 'applied' is the word, for, as practically always happens in the realm of art, theory merely classifies and clarifies previous practice, and there seems little doubt that many chants composed before the eighth century (when the classification of melodies began as a result of Gregorian reform) were later altered in order to agree with the modal system. This system was not, as is sometimes supposed, taken over from the Greeks, nor did it achieve completion until the tenth century; moreover, the usual definition of 'mode' already given only applies to the tenth century and later, for it is almost certain that melodies were originally classified according to their *symbolical* significance—that is, their suitability for definite types of expression, praise or lamentation, for instance—because not only Greek (as we have seen), but Syrian, Jewish, and other chants went through a similar stage. Later the melodies achieved importance in their own right and were classified according to their *musical* significance: in other words, their melodic differences.

This would obviously necessitate melodic analysis, the first stage of which would be the recognition of certain characteristic groups of notes, and the frequency and position of one or more of these groups in any melody would distinguish it from other melodies. Analysis would also extend to the groups of notes themselves, and this would lead to a study of the scale in which the notes forming the groups were the most important, especially the notes which began or ended a melody, for in antiphonal psalmody—much the most popular of the three types of psalmody—the join between the antiphon and the psalm or vice versa was nearly always made easier by ending or beginning on the same note, and this led eventually to the classification of scales or modes according to their end note, i.e. their Final. In their attempts to organize the modes into some kind of system the mediaeval theorists, through the influence of the writings of Boethius and Cassiodorus, turned to Greek theory, their misinterpretation of which proved as fruitful as the misunderstanding of Greek drama by certain Italian gentlemen at the end of the sixteenth century. The confusion that reigned in the mediaeval camp concerning Greek theory is not surprising when we consider that even now we are unable to form a complete picture of how it worked in practice, for the simple reason that not only have a mere handful of melodies been preserved, but the theory itself changed at various times. It is clear to us, however, though it was not so 1,000 years ago, that the differences between Greek and mediaeval theory are greater than their similarities, as the following brief discussion will try to show.

The Greeks had only one important note and one important scale, which, like all their scales, was reckoned from top to bottom, the highest note to us being the lowest to them. This definition of pitch may have resulted from the way the kithara player tilted his instrument, the lowest sounding string (to us) being the highest in position, just as in the Italian method of writing lute music or 'tablature' in the sixteenth century, in which each string is represented by a horizontal line, the symbols representing the notes of the lowest string being placed on the top line, thus giving a clear, visual picture to the player, because the instrument was always held so that the lowest string was uppermost. On the other hand, it may be that the characteristics of highness to us were those of lowness to the

I Twelfth-century instruments. Chime-bells (top of main panel), harp (played by the central figure, King David), rebec, pan-pipes, recorder, vièle (bottom of panel, *L.* to *R.*), handbell, psaltery (bottom left inset), organistrum (bottom right inset). Illumination in a late twelfth-century English Psalter.

II Neumes. From the *De Harmonica Institutione* of Abbot Regino von Prüm (*c.* 900).

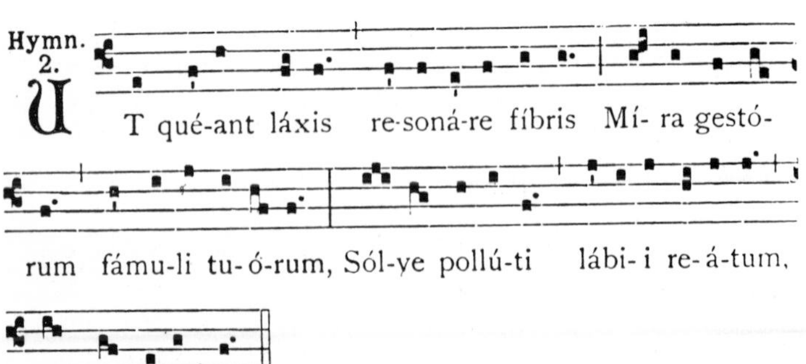
Hymn. 2.
UT qué-ant láxis re-soná-re fíbris Mí- ra gestó-
rum fámu-li tu-ó-rum, Sól-ve pollú-ti lábi- i re- á-tum,
Sáncte Jo-ánnes.

III Square notation. *Ut queant laxis* from *Liber Usualis* (see Ex. 1).

Greeks. The important note was *a*, called 'mese', the middle of a two-octave scale ranging from *a′* down to *A*, the central octave of which—*e′* down to *e*—was the important scale called Dorian, shown within square brackets in Ex. 6. (The black semibreve here and in the following examples is the mese.)

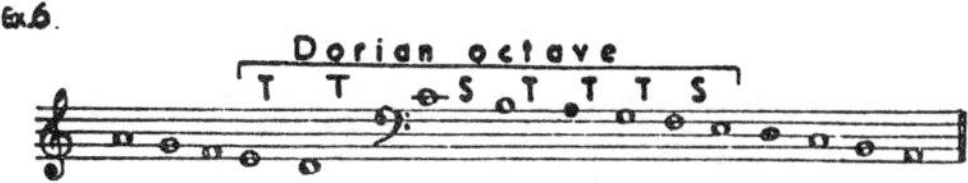

The Dorian scale, as can be seen, is built up of two tetrachords or four-note groups separated by a tone, each group consisting of the intervals tone, tone, semitone, thus: T, T, S/T/T, T, S.

By at least as early as the fourth century B.C. there were as many as six different Dorian scales, two diatonic (so called because they need no sharps or flats), three chromatic and one enharmonic. In both diatonic scales the semitone is the same size, but whereas in the commoner of the two scales the tones are all equal, in the other they are not. The most common chromatic scale consisted of the notes *e′*, *c*♯′, *c*♮′, *b*, *a*, *f*♯, *f*♮, *e*, while those of the enharmonic were *e′*, *c′*, *c**′, *b*, *a*, *f*, *f**, *e*, the asterisk standing for a quarter-tone. As regards the diatonic scale, it is worth noting that the order of the intervals is exactly the same as our *ascending* major scale, a fact which has provoked much speculation, particularly as the Greek idea of high and low was the opposite of ours.

All Greek diatonic melodies used the notes of the Dorian scale but they did not all, of course, keep to the octave range *e′*-*e*. Now if someone composed a song using these notes (Ex. 7)—

Ex.7
T T T S T T S

it is quite obvious that the relative position of the mese has changed; instead of being in the centre as it is in the Dorian scale, it is now near the top,* and as the mese was the most frequently used note in any composition, this new position to the melodically sensitive ear would give quite a different 'flavour' compared with a song which used the Dorian range.

* Unless otherwise indicated, 'high', 'low', 'ascending', 'descending', etc., are used in our sense, not the Greek.

As there are seven different notes in the scale there are clearly seven different positions for the mese, the highest being shown in Ex. 7, while the lowest is obviously this (Ex. 8):

Ex. 8

T T S T T T S T

If we put the two scales of Ex. 7 and 8 together, and add to Ex. 7 the low *A* (to which was given the magnificent name of Proslambanomenos, or 'the added') we get the complete diatonic scale shown in Ex. 6.

In actual practice, however, all the scales except the Dorian were transposed so that they lay within the Dorian octave *e′-e*, which was not only the average range of a man's voice (and it must be remembered that only men performed in public, whether at feasts, competitions, or in drama), but was also the range of the kithara, the earliest Greek type of which had six strings probably tuned pentatonically, thus (Ex. 9):

Ex. 9

In order to obtain the missing notes *c′* and *f* of the Dorian scale the kithara player had to 'stop' the two strings *b* and *e* by pressing on them firmly with his fingers. Now, when the scale in Ex. 7 was transposed up a fourth so that it ranged from *e′-e* the notes sung or played were these (Ex. 10)—

Ex. 10

T T T S T T S

Mixolydian *tonos* (transposed)

the relative position of the mese and the order of intervals being, of course, the same as in Ex. 7, while the notes *c′*, *b♭*, and *f* were stopped. Similarly the transposed scale of Ex. 8 was (Ex. 11)—

Ex. 11

T T S T T S T

Hypodorian *tonos* (transposed)

c′ and *f♯* being stopped, and so on with the remaining four scales. All these scales were called 'tonoi' (*tonos*=tightening) because two or more of the kithara's strings had to be stopped and hence tightened in order to produce all the notes. Each scale was given a name. Ex. 10, for instance, was called the Mixolydian tonos, and Ex. 11 the Hypodorian tonos, the order of the tonoi, from highest to lowest, being shown by the position of the mese in each scale, thus: Mixolydian (mese *d'*), Lydian (*c*♯'), Phrygian (*b*), Dorian (*a*), Hypolydian (*g*♯), Hypophrygian (*f*♯), and Hypodorian (*e*). (Notice that the hypotonoi are a fourth lower than the three main tonoi with which they are linked.)

It was these tonoi, these transposed scales all based on the Dorian scale, which represented actual Greek musical practice and which the mediaeval theorists mistakenly thought were modes. Moreover, they misinterpreted Boethius, for when he stated, as we have done, that the Mixolydian is the highest and the Hypodorian the lowest scale, he was referring to the position of the mese in the tonoi, but they thought, firstly, that he was referring to the untransposed scales (Exx. 7 and 8) because, having different octave ranges, they were more closely allied to mediaeval practice than were the tonoi, and, secondly, that he was judging the pitch of a scale by its lowest note (as they did), but that he used the words 'high' and 'low' in the Greek sense. Thus the order of the untransposed scales, if judged by their lowest note, is the exact opposite of the transposed scales—the tonoi, as a comparison of Exx. 7 and 8 with Exx. 10 and 11 will clearly show, the untransposed Mixolydian (Ex. 7) being the lowest and the Hypodorian (Ex. 8) being the highest; but if 'lowest' and 'highest' are interpreted in the Greek sense, then to the Greeks Ex. 7 was the highest and Ex. 8 the lowest scale. Thus when the Greek names were applied to the mediaeval modes round about A.D. 950 the highest mode was called Mixolydian (*g* up to *g'*), and the lowest Hypodorian (*A* up to *a*). Before the tenth century the modes had been called either 'Authentus Protus' ('First Leader'), 'Plaga Proti' ('Part of the First'), and so on with 'Deuterus', 'Tritus', and 'Tetrardus', or else 'Primus Tonus', 'Secundus Tonus', etc., up to 'Octavus Tonus'; this latter method we still use when we write Mode IV or Mode VIII instead of the more clumsy Hypophrygian or Hypomixolydian modes.

It may well be asked that, even allowing for mediaeval confusion concerning Greek theory, why is it that the modes bear so little resemblance to their namesakes in the untransposed Greek scales (compare the octave ranges in Ex. 12 with their equivalents in Ex. 13)? We do not know, but there are two possible answers, one theoretical and one practical. The theoretical explanation depends on the fact that in the untransposed Greek scales the mese is always the same note, *a*, while the octave ranges vary; thus the four main scales can be shown as follows (Ex. 12):

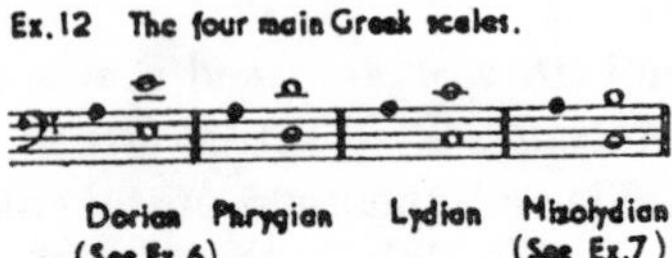

But to the early theorists it was not the mese but the octave range that was important, and hence they may have argued that in the Dorian octave for instance, as *e'* (to the Greeks) was the *lowest* note a fifth *below* the mese the equivalent effect to western ears would be obtained by making *d* the lowest note, for this (*to us*) is a fifth *below* the mese. Similarly, with the others; for example the lowest note (to the Greeks) in the Mixolydian scale was *b*, so that the equivalent to us would be *g*, hence the following, which of course tallies with Ex. 5 (Ex. 13):

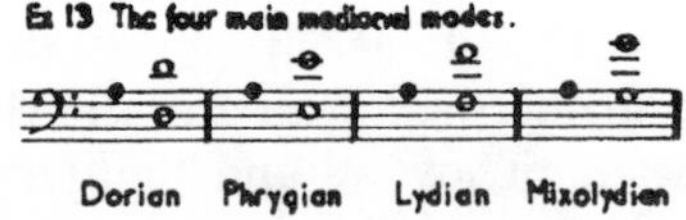

The second, practical, explanation depends on the fact that Eastern chants in Byzantium and Syria were based, at least as early as the sixth century, on a system of eight 'echoi' (*echos*='sound'). This system probably went through the same stages of evolution as those described on pp. 15-16, but had arrived at a series of scales classified according to their finals, before the west. These scales were divided up into four main echoi and four plagal, thus (the finals are given in brackets), Main echoi: I (*a*, less often *d*); II (*e*, less often *b*); III (*f*, less often *c'*); IV (*g*, less often *d'*); Plagal echoi: I (*d*); II (*e*); III (*f*); IV (*g*). By comparing these finals with those of the mediaeval modes it will be seen that the plagal echoi have the same finals, while the most common finals of the main echoi (except I) are also the same. (The fact that the numbering differs from that of the mediaeval modes is of no consequence.) In view of the great influence of eastern chant on western, it is extremely likely that the echoi played an important part in helping the western theorists to formulate their modal system, particularly as there were four plagal (=hypo) echoi, whereas the Greeks only had three, the Hypomixolydian being absent.

Considering that the only seats of learning before the rise of the universities in the twelfth and later centuries were the monasteries, it is not surprising to find that nearly all the early musical theorists were monks. The most important of these so far as information concerning Gregorian chant is concerned were Alcuin [753-804], Abbot of St. Martin's, Tours, a Yorkshireman and Charlemagne's chief spiritual, intellectual, and political adviser, Aurelian of Réomé [mid-ninth century], Hucbald of St. Amand [*c.* 840-930], Regino, Abbot of Prüm [d. 915], Odo, Abbot of Cluny [d. 942], Notker Labeo of St. Gall [d. 1022], Guido of Arezzo [991/2- after 1033], Berno of Reichenau [d. 1048], and Hermannus Contractus of Reichenau [1013-54]. (Note that the monastery at Arezzo is the only Italian one in this list.)

But the monasteries were not only places of learning; they were also centres of creative activity, and the "host of new melodies and texts" mentioned on p. 8 were composed so far as we know entirely by monks. These additions to the official collection of chants were called 'tropes' from a Greek word, which in its Latin form of *tropus* originally meant 'added melody'. The practice of inserting melismatic passages at certain places in some of the chants had been tolerated by the Church long before St. Gregory, but from the middle of the ninth century onwards not only new music was added to some of the official chants, but new words as well.

The most important and popular kind of trope was the 'sequence'. This came into being towards the end of the ninth century when the long melismas on the final syllable of 'Alleluia' were syllabically underlaid with a new text, partly in order to help the singer to memorize the notes and partly to allay the suspicion with which a number of churchmen had always regarded pure melody (see pp. 2, 4). These additions to the 'Alleluia' were not tropes in the original sense, because there was no new music, but the idea spread and was applied to other chants, notably the Kyrie, Gloria, Sanctus, Agnus Dei, and Benedicamus Domino chants. Thus, for instance, in Ex. 3, instead of 'Kyrie eleison', 'Kyrie Deus sempiterne eleison' ('Lord, everlasting God, have mercy') was sung, the added words being adapted to the melisma on the last syllable of 'Kyrie'. Later the added texts became long poems consisting of a number of couplets with a 'free' line at the beginning and end of the complete poem, and while each line of a couplet had an identical number of accented syllables, this number could vary from couplet to couplet. These poems were set to new music and so the sequence became a real trope.

As always in Christian chant, the words of the tropes were more important than the melodies, and hence the new texts always had a close connexion with those of the chants to which they were attached. The music, on the other hand, while sometimes being a kind of free variation on the chant melody, was more frequently entirely independent; moreover, it began to be less elaborate and more clear-cut, and there seems little doubt that much of it was influenced by music outside the Church, particularly instrumental music.

The main centres of trope composition were the monasteries of St. Martial at Limoges, and more especially of St. Gall in Switzerland, where two monks, Tuotilo [d. 915] and Notker Balbulus, or the 'Stammerer' [d. 912], wrote many examples, but did *not* invent the idea. Notker specialized in sequences, and while we know he was the author of many sequence texts we do not know who wrote the music, unless we assume that he composed the complete chant, a reasonable assumption and one that probably applies to all the other trope writers, such as the German Wipo [d. *c.* 1048], Hermannus Contractus, and the Frenchman Adam of St. Victor [d. 1177 or 1192]. Adam was particularly important, as he introduced rhyme into his sequences, and his six-line verses, each with the same number of accented syllables, are actually hymns; they became so popular and led to so many imitations that in the succeeding centuries the sequence threatened to overshadow the official body of Gregorian chant, a danger that was only averted by the drastic action of the Church in the sixteenth century, when the famous Council of Trent banned all tropes and sequences except four of the latter—namely, Wipo's *Victimae paschali laudes, immolent Christiani* ('Let Christians offer praises to the Easter victim'), the late twelfth-century anonymous *Veni Sancte Spiritus* ('Come, Holy Spirit'), *Dies Irae* ('Day of Wrath'), by Thomas of Celano [d. *c.* 1250], and *Lauda Sion salvatorem* ('Praise, O Zion, thy salvation'), by Thomas Aquinas [*c.* 1225-74]. A fifth sequence, the famous *Stabat Mater* by Jacopone da Todi [1230-1306], the great Franciscan poet, was admitted in 1727.

It would seem then that the great creative florescence of the Silver Age came to practically nothing so far as the official liturgy of the Church was concerned, yet in a tenth-century trope prefixed to the Introit for Easter is to be found the origin of a great secular art. This trope was a dramatization in dialogue form of the scene outside Christ's tomb between the Angel and the three Marys and begins:

ANGELUS: Quem quaeritis in sepulcro, O Christicolae?
MULIERES: Jesum Nazarenum crucifixum, O coelicola.

['ANGEL: Whom do ye seek in the tomb, O servants of Christ?']
['WOMEN: Jesus of Nazareth who was crucified, O celestial one.']

The complete trope takes about two minutes to perform, yet from this tiny seed stemmed the magnificent tree of European drama, a tree whose roots lie in the soil of Christian ceremonial not, as is sometimes stated, in Greek tragedy, although this too developed from religious rites. To this little scene others were quickly added describing the events both before and after the Resurrection until the whole formed a well-organized series of dramatic episodes. The idea soon spread and other parts of the Old and New Testaments and even the miracles of the saints were similarly treated, particularly the account of the Birth of Christ, the dramatization of which is still performed every Christmas all over the world. These dramatic presentations of Biblical stories are generally called 'liturgical dramas', an unfortunate title, as neither the tropes nor the scenes that developed from them were ever part of the liturgy; moreover, the word 'drama' is usually associated with the spoken word, whereas in actual fact the earliest examples were sung throughout. A more accurate name, and the one we shall use, is 'church operas', for this indicates both the place where they were originally performed and the fact that they are partially or wholly set to music. The texts of these church operas were taken from liturgical chants, tropes, or else (more rarely) added specially; the music was that associated with the chant and trope texts, while for the added passages it was either adapted from a chant melody, a popular song, or else newly composed. In the succeeding centuries these operas lost their symbolic simplicity and became increasingly complex and realistic, both in construction and in the use of costumes and scenery. Solos, ensembles, and choruses, processions and tableaux, and a greater degree of dramatic realism, together with an increasing use of the vernacular instead of Latin and of secular song instead of Gregorian chant, resulted in a spectacle so elaborate and, in the eyes of ecclesiastical authority, so worldly that in 1207 Pope Innocent III [1198–1216] passed an act forbidding performance in church, an act that was re-affirmed by Pope Gregory IX [1227-41]. Thus by the end of the thirteenth century church operas were taken over by professional actors, and the stage, originally the nave, later the steps of the church, now became the market-place. The subsequent history of the church operas which led to the Mystery and Miracle Plays of the fifteenth and sixteenth centuries will be dealt with in Chapter 5, but it is interesting to note that the musical development of the mediaeval church operas from short, simple chants in plainsong style to extended songs of widely differing character was essentially the same as that which took place in seventeenth-century opera.

But what is plainsong style? This, so far as Gregorian chant is concerned, is indeed a thorny problem to which there never will be a complete answer, because the early Christian composers did not write their melodies down; instead, they made them up in their heads and then taught them to their friends; and even when they did eventually put pen to parchment the symbols they used were chiefly an aid to the memory in showing the shape of a melody, not the exact manner of its performance; not until the thirteenth century in fact did a system of notation arise which was based on an exact distinction between notes of different value. In other words, not one Gregorian chant of the Golden or Silver Ages was written down in such a way as to give us a clear indication as to how it should be sung. Some people would say that this merely shows the backwardness of the composers, for after all the

Greeks had a notational system, and while admittedly this does not give us the value of the notes either, and only tells us their pitch, one would have thought that by A.D. 1000 somebody would have improved on it and invented a method that was foolproof. Such a view is perfectly justified if we assume that the attitude of the chant composers towards music was the same as our own today; but such an assumption would not only show an unwarrantable conceit and lack of imagination on our part, in that we would be judging according to the traditions in which we have been brought up, but also would take no account of a perfectly obvious explanation—namely, that the freedom in interpretation which a vague notation made possible was preferred for its own sake. Even the later attempts at writing the melodies down did not restrict this freedom; all they did was to define more and more precisely the actual pitch of the notes, not their values; and even those theorists who actually state that the melodies should be sung as a series of long and short notes and imply that the ratio between them is 2 : 1 do not suggest any means whatsoever to show this relationship.

The earliest attempts at writing the music of the chants down crystallized into a definite system just before Gregory's reform. This was no coincidence, but part and parcel of the urgent need for unifying the whole liturgy. This system used various symbols called 'neumes' (Greek, *neuma*='sign') which not only aided the memory by showing the general contours of the melody, but also indicated many of the finer shades of vocal expression, the technique of which, though it died out in Europe, is still practised in the East (see Plate II). Thus the neumes provided some sort of safeguard against the deliberate or careless alteration of the official chants, a real danger in a purely oral tradition. This safeguard, however, was plainly not strong enough to ensure that Gregorian chant retained its melodic purity no matter where it was sung, and from the eighth century to the eleventh century various systems of notation were tried, including the use of letters (as the Greeks had done), which, although they gave the exact pitch of a note, did not indicate the up-and-down movement of the music. It was this up-and-down movement that, in the tenth century, began to be shown more clearly by grouping the neumes round an imaginary line, the so-called 'heighted neumes'. The climax came in the eleventh century when Guido of Arezzo introduced a remarkable system which has made him famous ever since. The most important part of this system was that instead of one imaginary line a number of real lines, parallel to and equidistant from each other, were scratched on the parchment by a sharp-pointed instrument, these lines (except the two lowest) representing notes lying a third apart, just as the five-line stave we use today does. On or between these scratched lines Guido drew two red lines representing the notes *f* or *f*′, and two yellow lines representing the notes *c* or *c*′, and on or between any of these lines he placed the neumes, which therefore showed the exact pitch of the notes they represented. His complete system, which extended from the lowest note of the lowest mode (*A*-Hypodorian) to the highest note of the highest mode (*g*′-Mixolydian), was as follows (Ex. 14):

Ex. 14

(1) *g*′ ....
(2) *f* ————————————————————(red)
(3) *e*′ ....
(4) *c*′ — — — — — — — — — — — — —(yellow)
(5) *a* ....
(6) *f*′ — — — — — — — — — — — — —(red)
(7) *d* ....
(8) *c* ————————————————————(yellow)
(9) *B* ....
(10) *A* ....

(........ =scratched line, — — — — =scratched line drawn over in red or yellow ink, ———— =red or yellow line between two scratched ones. The bracketed numbers are added for reference.)

Of course, neither Guido nor anybody else used the complete system, but only a part of it when writing down a melody, for very few Gregorian chants exceed the range of an octave, and a great number have a much smaller range (this applies to nearly all early music, primitive songs, folks-songs, etc., and indeed to most voices in part-songs up to the seventeenth century); thus if he were notating the portion of the Kyrie given in Ex. 3, which ranges from *c* to *a*, he would only need to draw the lines (8) to (5). The whole point of the coloured lines was to catch the singer's eye and make the notes F or C stand out, and the reasons why these two particular notes were chosen were (*a*) that they occur more frequently and play a more important part in Gregorian melodies than any other notes, and (*b*) they are the only two notes in the diatonic scale which have a semitone beneath them. This latter reason in itself is remarkable enough, for by stressing the importance of a note because of its sub-semitonal approach Guido was not only ahead of his time, but was also at variance with modal practice, as this progression to an important note (e.g. E to F—the final of the Lydian mode) was the very one that was most avoided.

Guido also advocated the use of clefs—that is, letters placed on or between the scratched lines which provide the 'key' as to what note the line or space represents. We do not know how many or what letters he used, but in theory any of those between A and G were possible; twelfth- and thirteenth-century writers, however, tended to restrict the number to F and C only, representing the notes *f* and *c′*, and as soon as the importance of these two notes was clearly recognized the coloured lines, having served their purpose, fell into disuse; they were a nuisance anyway, as the writer always had to have red and yellow ink ready whenever he copied a chant. Our modern F and C clefs spring directly from the above two, as they represent exactly the same notes; the G clef, however, did not come into use until the late fifteenth century. As regards the number of lines, it was soon realized that three were sufficient to cover the entire range of Gregorian melodies, depending on the positions of the F or C clef, thus (Ex. 15):

Ex. 15

F (*A*) *to* C (*g′*)

But three lines did not cover the range of an octave, and although this could be overcome by moving the clefs about, it was obviously simpler to have a uniform stave of four lines all drawn in black or occasionally red ink. This in fact is the stave now used for all modern editions of Gregorian chant, and the notation of these editions is the same as that which developed from the neumes in the thirteenth century (see Plate III). This is called Square Notation, for obvious reasons, the two basic note shapes being the 'punctum' ■, and the 'virga' ◼ ; these were the only two notes that were used singly, but more often they were 'bound' together in different ways and with various other note shapes and called 'ligatures' (Latin, *ligare*='to bind'). These showed the singer the number of notes to be sung to a syllable (see Ex. 1, the syllables '*la*-xis', 'ges-*to*-rum', '*sol*-ve'), or the phrasing in a long melisma on a single syllable, or the manner of singing (see Ex. 1, where the middle note of the ligature on '*mi*-ra' is to be sung lightly).

So far so good; everyone agrees with the development and meaning of square notation up to this point. But once you breathe the words 'mensural' and 'accentual' the fat's in the fire with a vengeance and the flames that have been burning for nearly a century now show no signs of diminishing. The whole trouble revolves round the answers to two questions. Were the notes of Gregorian chant of equal duration? Were they unaccented? The monks of Solesmes, who represent the official attitude of the Roman Church today, reply 'Yes' to both questions. Another school of thought, usually called the Accentualists, replies 'Yes' to the first question and 'No' to the second. A third school—the Mensuralists—replies 'No' to both questions, at least the majority do. We shall not go into all the pros and cons of these three opposing interpretations, but as this matter is obviously a vital one some attempt at dealing with the problem must be made.

First of all we must define 'accentual' and 'mensural', both of which are used primarily in the discussion of poetry. Accentual means the classification of syllables as either strong or weak, stressed or unstressed, the lengths of the syllables being roughly the same. This is sometimes called 'qualitative' rhythm and is the basis of all early Jewish poetry. An accentual pattern may be either strict, in which an arrangement of strong and weak beats is repeated exactly in two or more lines (which need not necessarily be consecutive), as, for instance, in—

When he was dead and laid in grave,
  Her heart was struck with sorrow;
O mother, mother, make my bed,
  For I shall die tomorrow.

where alternate lines follow the patterns . .′ . .′ . .′ . .′ and . .′ . .′ . .′ . (. =weak syllable; .′ =strong syllable), or free, in which the number of strong syllables is the same in two or more lines but the number of weak syllables varies (as in Jewish poetry); for instance, these lines—

> Yes, I ken John Peel and Ruby too,
> Ranter and Ringwood, Bellman and True,
> From a find to a check, from a check to a view,

have this pattern

. . .′ . .′ . .′ . .′

.′ . . .′ . .′ . . .′

. . .′ . . .′ . . .′ . . .′

Mensural (or metrical) means the classification of syllables as either long or short. This is sometimes called 'quantitive' rhythm and is the basis of all classical Greek and Roman poetry, the ratio of long to short being theoretically 2 : 1. A metrical pattern may be strict or free as in accentual rhythm.

To these two definitions we shall add two facts. Firstly, that mediaeval Latin poetry from at least the fifth century onwards, and indeed European poetry in general, is predominantly accentual. Secondly, that as a result of this there has always been a tendency in European poetry, no matter what the language, to stress long syllables, and hence even the comparatively little metrical verse is also accentual.

To sum up, the text of every single Gregorian chant consists of accented and unaccented syllables, including the hymns of St. Ambrose and his imitators and those written under Byzantine (Greek) influence in the eighth century and later which are usually regarded as metrical. But the Solesmes interpretation of the melodies takes no account of this fact, for they maintain that all notes are both equal in length (except those at the ends of phrases and at certain other places) and also of equal stress, but that there is what they call a 'rhythmical ictus', marked in their editions by a short vertical dash beneath a note, this ictus being "felt and intimated by tone of voice rather than expressed by any material emphasis". Whether a note receives an ictus or not depends entirely on the position of the note in the melody, unless the chant is syllabic, in which case the accented syllables of the text have some influence on its position. In actual performance, however, the ictus has the effect of an accent—not, of course, a strong one, but no different from that in a smooth and sensitive rendering of, say, *Drink to me only*, hence the melodic accents are frequently at variance with those of the text. Although this interpretation of the melodies, together with various other vocal refinements, is undoubtedly effective and aesthetically satisfying for the bulk of Gregorian chant, it is most unlikely that it was used for the majority of hymns and sequences, particularly those intended for congregational use; furthermore, there is no historical evidence to prove that it was the only or even the ideal interpretation.

It is this failure to distinguish between the poetic texts of the hymns and sequences on the one hand and the prose chants on the other that is the chief weakness of the Solesmes school, for the former are popular in approach and written in either strict or free accentual and sometimes metrical patterns, and the melodies, which are mostly simple and syllabic, would therefore naturally follow the accentual patterns of the words, so naturally in fact that the theorists would not bother to mention it. Another weakness is the refusal to take into account the statements of several mediaeval theorists that note values were either long or short, and even though it is most unlikely that this was a universal practice, and even though we have proof that in the eleventh century at any rate there was a strong tendency towards evening the notes out, we do not know that this evening-out process represented the official interpretation or was generally accepted. What we do know, however, is that the way the hymns and sequences were performed varied in different parts of Europe and depended on purely local factors. For instance, St. Ambrose, if we assume that his hymns are metrical, most likely taught his flock to sing a long note to a long syllable; similarly the abbot of a monastery who happened to be a great admirer of Greek poetry might very well have insisted that all hymns and sequences be sung mensurally; but in both cases there would be an accentual pattern also. Here, for example, is a rhythmic version of the hymn *Ut queant laxis* which might well have been sung a thousand years ago; it should be compared with the Solesmes version on Plate III or the modern transcription in Ex. 1 (Ex. 16):

Ex. 16 Hymn *Ut queant laxis* (metrical accentual version)

Ut qué - ant lá - - xis re - so - ná - - re fí - - bris
Mí - - ra ge - - stó - - rum fá - mu - li tu - ó - - rum, Sól - - ve pol-
-lú - - ti lá - bi - i re - - á - - tum, Sán - - cte Jo - - án - - nes.

('Let Thine example, Holy John, remind us
Ere we can meetly sing thy deeds of wonder,
Hearts must be chastened, and the bonds that bind us
Broken asunder.')*

The prose chants are a more difficult problem, for the texts are not arranged in accentual patterns. Furthermore, they were sung by the choir, which consisted of trained singers, and it is therefore quite possible that the Solesmes manner of performance was practised in certain places during certain centuries. But again we must insist that there is no proof that this particular way of singing Gregorian chant was the official or even the most widely accepted one, and it is just as likely, indeed more likely, that chants in syllabic or group style would stress the notes set to accented syllables and possibly lengthen them also, depending on the factors mentioned on p. 30. The melismas, however, which are sung to only one syllable and were recognized as the most difficult parts of all Gregorian melody, were almost certainly sung in the Solesmes manner. The melisma in fact can be regarded as a miniature vocal fantasia or cadenza, a wordless and therefore rhythmically free outpouring of melody, the structure of which alone determines its rhythmical organization. But it was this very rhythmical freedom that the trope composers of the Silver Age destroyed, for by adding a text, particularly one arranged in accentual patterns as in the sequence, they turned the melismas into hymn tunes. This treatment of melismatic passages was continued by the polyphonic composers of the late twelfth and

* Quoted from *The New Oxford History of Music*, II, p. 291.

thirteenth centuries, as we shall see in Chapter 2, but instead of adding words they gave the notes exact values and eventually arranged them in regular groups.

To end this discussion on the performance of Gregorian chant, an observation must be made that is all too often forgotten—namely, that from the early Church Fathers to the Council of Trent in the sixteenth century it was the words, not the way the melodies were sung, that mattered most. It was the singing of biblical texts that was originally the main justification for including music in the Christian service, an attitude which virtually excluded instrumental music during the early centuries; it was the words of the tropes and sequences that the authorities objected to and ultimately banned (all but five), whether they were set to old or new music; it was because the words were largely unintelligible in the complex polyphonic settings of the mid-sixteenth century that caused the Council of Trent to advocate a simpler style and less elaborate presentation. Furthermore, the notation, as we have seen, was not concerned with values, only with pitch, and the various additional signs added to or above the neumes in some manuscripts from the ninth to the eleventh centuries that indicate such things as 'slower', 'quicker', 'longer', etc., not only stress this point, but provide interesting sidelights on purely local practices. Provided therefore that the melodies were those officially sanctioned, the Church did not concern itself unduly with the manner of performance, whether vocal or instrumental.

The use of instruments in accompanying Gregorian chant is another problem that will never be solved, for although the majority of the early Church Fathers objected strongly to instrumental participation in the service because of the close associations with pagan entertainments, there is no doubt that the organ at any rate was used in later centuries, particularly during the Silver Age of Gregorian chant. Other instruments, such as the kithara, trumpet, drum, etc., are also mentioned, but in most cases it is impossible to tell whether the writer is referring to actual performance in church or is being merely symbolic (see p. 2). We shall therefore leave detailed discussion of them until the next chapter, with the exception of the organ, the instrument that has always been most closely associated with Christian worship.

The first organ was invented and built by a Greek named Ktesibios [third century B.C.], who lived in Alexandria, a city then famous for its engineering skill, and rightly so if Ktesibios's organ is a typical example. This instrument consisted of an enclosed tank partially filled with water and divided into three interconnecting chambers. At the back of the organ was a handle which pumped air into the two side chambers, and so forced water from these into the central chamber, thus increasing the air pressure in the wind chest above. The pipes were placed above the wind chest and arranged in two or three ranks, one behind the other, so that each note had two or three pipes; in the latter case the pipes in the front rank were tuned two octaves above those in the back rank and those in the middle rank one octave above those in the back. Air was admitted to or cut off from the pipes by both sliders and valves. The sliders were strips of metal which moved horizontally beneath the mouths of the pipes; each represented a different note (not counting octave duplications) and therefore had two or three holes to correspond to the pipes. When the organist wanted to sound a note he pressed down a 'key' which pushed a slider along so that the holes came exactly below the mouths of the pipes and so made it possible for air to enter from the wind chest. When the key was released, a spring returned it and the slider back to their original positions. But even with a key pressed down the pipes would not speak unless one or more o the valves were open. These were placed at one side of the organ and each affected a complete rank of pipes, just as a modern organ-stop does; thus the player could vary both the pitch of a note by using only one rank at a time, and also its colour (timbre) by sounding the fundamental alone (back rank), or its octave (middle rank), or, if there were three ranks, its double octave (front rank), or any combination of these. This kind of organ was called the 'hydraulis' (Greek, *hydro* = 'water'; *aulos* = 'pipe'), and its loud, strident tone endeared it to the Romans, who increased its size and power and used it at their feasts, spectacles, and other orgies. This almost certainly explains why it was virtually never used in the western churches, for the organs mentioned from the ninth century onwards were all 'pneumatic' (Greek, *pneuma* = 'breath'), in which the wind to the pipes was transmitted straight from the bellows and hence lacked the constant wind pressure which the use of water gave to the hydraulis. They also lacked the key system of the hydraulis, for the sliders had to be pushed in and pulled out by direct manual labour, which in the larger organs was no mean task. Keys in fact were not rediscovered until the thirteenth century, an extraordinary example of how knowledge can disappear for long periods and one that is only surpassed by the gap between Archimedes of 'Eureka' fame [third century B.C.] and Copernicus in the sixteenth century, both of whom believed that the earth revolved round the sun. Some of these pneumatic organs must have been fearsome instruments, and a description of one built at Winchester about 950 states that it had 400 pipes, forty sliders (ten pipes to a slider), and twenty-six bellows which needed seventy men to operate them. The sliders were in two sets of twenty, each set having exactly the same notes and each requiring a player. There were no valves, so that if both organists pulled out a slider twenty pipes sounded simultaneously, and the resulting noise must have been indescribably ear-shattering!

There seems little doubt that instruments were at first used more frequently in churches outside Italy, particularly Germany and England, for, to adapt an old saying, 'While Rome's far away, the churchmen can play'. This, as we have seen, was true of Mozarabic chant and it was also true of British Gregorian chant, the chief collection of which was that originally practised at Salisbury or 'Sarum', to give it its Latinized form, and now known as the Sarum Use; later it spread to most parts of Britain until it was banned in 1547. The deviations of Sarum Use from the official Gregorian repertoire must have been deliberate to some extent, for a number of the chants differ considerably from those in the latter collection; and although such variations, as we have seen, were natural enough before the improved notation of the eleventh century there could have been no doubt after this as to what Rome considered to be the authentic melodies.

The most reliable way of transmitting these melodies before the advent of square notation was through trained singers who accompanied missions to various parts of Europe, and who either taught the newly converted how and what to sing or else refreshed the erring memories of those choirs already established.

These singers learned the repertoire in choir schools, the first of which was probably founded during the latter part of the fourth century. Later Gregory, as a natural outcome of his organizing bent, set aside two buildings in Rome, one housing the trained singers and clergy, the other being a school where orphans were taught to memorize the entire collection of Gregorian chant. This, of course, was not as large in Gregory's day as it is now, and it is a well-known fact that illiterates—which the orphans almost certainly were—have extremely good memories; even so, it was a long and arduous training, the same chant being sung over and over again until it was indeed unforgettable. Neither the use of neumes nor, later on, of lines and clefs helped much in learning a new song, because even with clefs the exact intervals represented by the lines and spaces vary according to the clef and to its position, and the labour of learning what these intervals were for all possible clefs and their positions and then reading the intervals at speed obviously demanded much more brainwork than in merely memorizing. The ordinary singer of today only has to learn the F and G clefs, whose positions on the stave never vary, if he or she wants to sing from staff notation, but many children find even this difficult enough to begin with. Admittedly the mediaeval singing masters used hand signs to indicate when a melody went up or down and by roughly how much, but these signs could not show the difference, for example, between a leap of a major or a minor third; in fact, they were only of any real use as a means of helping the memory over something imperfectly learned or partially forgotten, not as a means of teaching something completely new.

Once again, however, that remarkable monk, Guido of Arezzo, had a brilliant idea. He devised a method of teaching that enabled young boys, in his own words, "to sing an unknown melody before the third day, which by other methods would not have been possible in many weeks".* In modern terms, his method was this. He took the then well-known hymn to St. John, *Ut queant laxis* (see Ex. 1), the first six phrases of which begin on successive degrees of the scale, C, D, E, F, G, and A, and made his pupils memorize it so thoroughly that they could sing both the initial note of each phrase at will, and also the intervals between any of these notes. These six notes were later

* Quoted from O. Strunk, ibid., p. 124.

called the 'hexachord' (Greek, *hexa*='six'; *chordos*='tone'), and in order to cover the entire range of Gregorian chant Guido expanded them into a series of six overlapping hexachords, each hexachord being exactly similar in construction—the first six notes of our major scale in fact. Now, it is obvious that there are only two major scales that need no accidentals for their first six notes—namely, those beginning on C and G—but if we use a B♭ (which occurred in Gregorian chant long before Guido) then we get a third hexachord starting on F. Guido's complete system was built up from these three notes, each of which was the basis of two hexachords, thus (Ex. 17):

Ex. 17

														ut	*re*	*mi*	*fa*	—	*sol*	*la*
											ut	*re*	*mi*	*fa*	*sol*	*la*				
							ut	*re*	—	*mi*	*fa*	*sol*	*la*							
						ut	*re*	*mi*	*fa*	—	*sol*	*la*								
			ut	*re*	*mi*	*fa*	*sol*	*la*												
ut	*re*	*mi*	*fa*	*sol*	*la*															
G	*A*	*B*	*c*	*d*	*e*	*f*	*g*	*a*	*b♭*	*b♮*	*c'*	*d'*	*e'*	*f'*	*g'*	*a'*	*b♭'*	*b♮'*	*c''*	*d''*

The syllables *ut*, *re*, *mi*, etc., are those to which the initial notes of the six phrases in the hymn to St. John are set, and were used to help the pupil to distinguish between the different degrees of the scale. The most important interval in any hexachord is the semitone, or *mi-fa* progression (a fact which underlines what we said on p. 27), and even if the range of a melody necessitated changing from one hexachord to the one above or below, this progression was always sung in the same hexachord.

In order to see how the method actually worked we will imagine that we have to learn the part of the Kyrie given in Ex. 3, and that our only musical ability is that we can sing accurately any interval between any two notes in any hexachord. If we had to learn this melody by ear, then the first thing that happens is that our teacher sings it through for us. From this we should be able to find out how far away the last note is from the nearest semitone, which in this case is easy, because the third note from the end is a semitone above the last note. This is our clue, for it means that the final note can only be *mi*, the third note from the end being, of course, *fa*. We can now sing the entire melody, for although we may not be able to remember all the ups and downs, the teacher's hand-signs will tell us where they come and approximately how big the intervals are, and as all the notes will have the same relation to the last note as the hexachord syllables have to *mi* we shall sing these intervals not approximately, but exactly in tune. If we have to read the melody from notation, we first of all study the clef and discover what notes the lines and spaces represent, then look for the nearest semitone to the last note, E-F in this case, which of course means that E is *mi*. We can now sing the melody much more easily than in the first way because we can actually see when the melody goes up or down, instead of having to rely on the much vaguer gestures of our teacher; and although we do not know the exact intervals by looking at the notation (we are not musically intelligent enough for that!), we do know which note is *mi* and this gives us complete accuracy. Admittedly this second way involves knowing what the clefs mean, but this knowledge is only applied to the purely mechanical task of finding at our leisure what hexachord syllable should be given to the last note of the melody and not to the much more difficult one of remembering at speed exactly what the intervals are between the different lines and spaces while we are actually singing.

Guido's method of teaching spread all over Europe and is indeed the source of our present-day tonic sol-fa system, the only differences being the substitution of *doh* for *ut*, the addition of *te* for the seventh degree of the scale and of various other syllables for chromatic notes, and, most important of all, the linking of *doh* with the chief note of a scale, the tonic or key-note, whereas in the original system *ut* only represented the chief note in the Lydian and Mixolydian modes (F and G respectively). An offshoot of Guido's method was invented some years after his death in which each finger joint and tip of the hand represents a note, and by pointing to the appropriate part of his hand a teacher could impart a new melody much more quickly than by repeatedly singing it over. Later still a seventh hexachord beginning on *g′* was added to the original six, thus making the total range *G-e″*.

Guido claimed that he could teach boys a new song in three days, but if we assume that there were 1,000 different Gregorian melodies in his day then it looks as though the poor boys would be hard at it for about eight years! Actually it was not as bad as this, because most of the melodies are largely built up from a common pool of note groups (see p. 16), and once these were learnt they would be easily recognizable in a new chant. Thus chant composition was more a question of selecting a number of stock melodic fragments and arranging these in a new order rather than the invention of a completely original tune; in fact, the whole idea of originality in art is relatively modern and was quite foreign not only to the composers of Christian chant, but also to those of much later centuries, even including the eighteenth. This is a very important point to remember when studying or listening to early music, particularly mediaeval music, for to the mediaeval composer it was the way a composition was constructed that mattered most, not the parts of which it was constructed, just as in painting new colours were of minor importance compared to the way they were arranged on a manuscript, wall, or canvas. It was no accident, therefore, that of the three main visual arts—painting, sculpture, and architecture—it was architecture, the art in which structure is most important and clearly shown, that dominated the mediaeval scene. Moreover, the attitude towards music which the Church Fathers held—namely, that it was right and proper provided that it served devout ends and did not have a too obviously pagan association—was also applied to the erection of the first churches, known as basilicas, for it did not matter if the stones and pillars were taken from a Roman temple destroyed by the Huns, provided that actual statues of pagan gods were not used. Thus the interior of a completed church was often a most curious mixture of varied marbles and stones, pillars of unequal length and different designs, and (where the looters had been lucky) all kinds of gold and silver ornaments and mosaics (i.e. designs or pictures composed of small pieces of coloured glass or stone). But although the interiors of the basilicas varied greatly, their general plan was both more uniform and utilitarian, being T-shaped with a wooden roof and a central nave with supporting aisles on either side. In this contrast between having the same end in view (satisfying liturgical needs) and providing variety in the means to that end (the elaboration of basic material) the basilicas were like Christian chant, and it was again no coincidence that the next style of architecture—Romanesque—arose at the same time as the liturgical and chant reforms by Gregory and others, for Romanesque architecture parallels Gregorian chant in that it was originally simple and became international. Like Gregorian chant, too, Romanesque style became more ornamental during the Silver Age, but even so late an example as Durham Cathedral (eleventh to twelfth centuries) is simple (but what magnificent simplicity!) compared, say, to the thirteenth-century Gothic Cathedral at Lincoln (Plates IV and V). Gothic art, however, is more closely linked with polyphony than with Gregorian chant, the creation of which lost both its spontaneity and its purity of style after the twelfth century, and although we may disagree with the official Solesmes manner of singing many of the melodies, we owe them an enormous debt for their researches into and restoration of the original music, a labour that has revealed Gregorian chant as undoubtedly the finest single collection of melody ever created. Wonderfully supple and perfectly balanced, these melodies are not only historically important in that they provided the basis for nearly all liturgical music up to the seventeenth century, but are also as artistically and spiritually satisfying as most later compositions written for the Church.

PERFORMANCE

(See also pp. 6, 29-32.)

Ex. 1. Full choir. (N.B. It is most probable that the full choir sang only the simple chants such as psalms, 'Credo's, hymns, and sequences, the less simple ones being performed by a 'select choir' of not more than six singers.)

Ex. 2. The first 'Sanctus' is sung by a solo voice, the rest by the 'select choir'.

Ex. 3(a). The 'Kyrie', excluding the melisma on the final syllable, is sung by a solo voice, the melisma and 'eleison' being sung by the 'select choir'.

Ex. 3(b). The first phrase is sung by a solo voice, which is repeated, plus the long melisma on the last syllable, by the 'select choir'.

2

MUSIC IN THE EARLY CHURCH: THE BEGINNINGS OF PART-MUSIC

THE desire of the composers of the Silver Age to enrich Gregorian chant was not restricted only to the addition of words to old melodies or to the creation of new ones, but also found an outlet in the simultaneous combination of both old and new melodies, although in the earliest examples, which come from an anonymous treatise called *Musica enchiriadis* or *Musical Handbook* (*c.* 850), the new melodies mostly duplicate the old ones at the intervals of a fourth, fifth, or octave, or all three combined, above or below the main melody. This kind of part-music, the oldest that has come down to us, was called 'organum', but we do not know why for certain. The Latin word meant any kind of instrument, not only the organ, and it is possible therefore that this particular type of composition was originally instrumental. Some people believe that it sprang from the organ itself which, as we saw in Chapter 1, was introduced into Europe during the ninth century, for if two players on the same massive keyboard happened through design or accident to play a melody a fourth or fifth apart the effect may have been so attractive as to promote immediate vocal imitation. There is evidence, however, which makes it unlikely that the organ was the source of organum (see p. 41), and in any case the examples in *Musica enchiriadis* are all vocal, the main melody, which is either an original chant or else a sequence, being called the 'vox principalis', and the added melody the 'vox organalis'. There are two main kinds of organum, parallel and free. Parallel organum is either simple, with one added part moving in parallel fourths or fifths below the main melody, or two added parts moving in parallel octaves above and below the main melody, or composite, with one, two, or three parts doubling at the octave above and/or below the first of the simple types. In free organum the vox organalis moves in parallel, oblique, or contrary motion to the vox principalis. Here is an example taken from a commentary on the *Musical*

Handbook called *Scholia enchiriadis,* in which the first section (up to 'Domino') is in simple parallel organum at the fourth, while the second section is in free organum, the brackets marked 'a' showing oblique motion, and those marked 'b' contrary motion in the vox organalis (Ex. 18*):

Now, it is a well-known and obvious fact that it is impossible to classify anything that is not already fairly stable and well developed, whether it be an animal species or an artistic trend, and the fact that the authors of the two treatises mentioned could present organum in an ordered and rational manner means that it had been practised for some considerable time before. This rules out the organ theory and makes it likely that organum arose outside the Church, because if it did not then we should certainly have much more and clearer written evidence of its use in the service long before the middle of the ninth century. In fact, one theorist definitely refers to its 'popular' nature, and another implies that it was already quite familiar by about 900. As it is, however, the only distinct reference to part-song before *Musica enchiriadis* is by the Englishman, Bishop Aldhelm [640-709], but his account is too vague to be of much value.

Even if we assume that organum was popular in origin, we still do not know how it arose, although it is usually thought that parallel organum was practised first and that free organum was a later and more advanced development. However, it is much more likely that the two types grew more or less simultaneously from two different ways of performing a melody, both of which were known to the Greeks. In the first way, a melody was occasionally played or sung in octaves ('magadizing'), and it is not difficult to see how, in order to bring the melody within the comfortable range of male and female voices, consecutive octaves later became consecutive fourths or fifths, for the normal ranges of a bass, tenor, alto, and soprano are roughly a fourth or fifth apart. This kind of singing

* From O. Strunk, ibid., p. 130.

was classified as parallel organum by the mediaeval theorists. In the second way, a melody was sometimes freely and spontaneously varied, but complete chaos was avoided by everyone singing the same note at the beginnings and endings of phrases. This kind of singing was called 'heterophony' by the Greeks (*heteros* = 'other'), and from it free organum almost certainly developed, for this type of organum is essentially governed by beginning and ending on a unison, while the middle portion of the melody moves in consecutive fourths or fifths—according to the theorists at any rate. Actually it is very doubtful whether in fact organum was sung in as strict a succession of fourths or fifths as the mediaeval theorists make out, not only because it is quite likely that they simplified what was in practice much more varied in order to classify more easily, but also because the few examples that exist outside their treatises and which can be transcribed, while admittedly not earlier than the eleventh century, show a divergence from accepted theory. For instance, in the two-part organa contained in a manuscript fragment from Chartres, roughly 32 per cent. of the intervals are octaves or unisons, 20 per cent. are fourths, only 6 per cent. are fifths, and 28 per cent. *are thirds*; moreover, there are seven groups of three consecutive thirds.* Even so, the fourth, fifth, and octave were originally the only intervals which mediaeval ears accepted as fully concordant, other intervals being tolerated only if used as an approach to or as a contrast with these three, which even today textbooks call the 'perfect' concords, while thirds and sixths are classified as 'imperfect'.

These 'perfect' concords were the main ones used in all music up to the beginning of the fifteenth century, except that from *c.* 1150 the fourth, as a fundamental interval, was increasingly avoided, both in two-part compositions and as the lowest interval in three-part writing, until from *c.* 1225 on it was virtually restricted to the upper parts.

Why did the mediaeval musician regard these concords as more satisfactory than the 'imperfect' ones? The answer lies not in the primitiveness of the mediaeval ear, as is sometimes stated or implied, but to the exact opposite—the greater sensitivity to sound compared with our ears today. Before we justify this statement we must make a distinction between

* See *The New Oxford History of Music*, II, p. 284.

concord and discord on the one hand and consonance and dissonance on the other. The former are *musical* definitions of sound; the latter are *physiological*—that is, they depend on the pleasant or unpleasant effect of a sound on the ear regardless of musical context or fashion. Now, the mediaeval ear was no different from our own, for we know that like us they found the octave the most perfect consonance and the minor second the harshest dissonance. They also found, like us, that the fifth was the next most consonant sound, and then the fourth, and that the major second was less dissonant than the minor second. The difference between us lies in our respective attitudes towards thirds and sixths. We find them more satisfying than the octave, fifth, or fourth because they sound richer; but richness of sound (sonority) depends entirely on the amount of dissonance present, and we can prove scientifically that thirds and sixths are in fact more dissonant than the 'perfect' consonances. In other words, we accept as the most satisfying concords intervals which to mediaeval ears were too rich—i.e. too relatively dissonant—to be classed as wholly concordant, just as in some modern music today we judge as relatively concordant certain dissonant passages which would have been excruciatingly discordant to our grandfathers. The history of music, in fact, is also the history of aural development (which is not the same thing as aural progress), for the ear has constantly, though not continuously, accepted as concordant or relatively concordant sounds that in earlier times were ranked as discords. Thus the third and sixth, too rich for everyday mediaeval fare, became the staple diet from the Renaissance on, and the chord of the 'added sixth' (e.g. C–E–G–A), treated with great circumspection in the Renaissance, but with more freedom in the eighteenth and nineteenth centuries, provides a perfectly satisfactory and very popular final chord for many jazz pieces today. The important thing to remember is the musical tradition at any given moment in history; the earliest composers were brought up to music that was sung or played almost entirely in unison or in octaves, and hence they heard and judged any other interval far more acutely than we would, therefore the greater dissonance of the fifth and fourth compared to the octave, though slight to us, provided an increased richness of sound that was as satisfying to their ears as thirds and sixths are to our own. The fact that some compositions contain more thirds than was usual (as in the Chartres organa) is simply an indication of something we would have expected anyway—namely, that there was then as there have been ever since certain composers who were more experimental than their fellows, but this should not be allowed to distort the general picture.

The preponderance of fourths, fifths, and octaves in mediaeval part-music is justified by contemporary theorists on the grounds that Pythagoras had 'proved' that these intervals were consonant because they have simple ratios, e.g. $\frac{4}{3}$, $\frac{3}{2}$, and $\frac{2}{1}$ respectively. By 'simple' Pythagoras meant a ratio in which the denominator divides into the numerator either exactly ($\frac{2}{1}$) or else once or more with one part over ($\frac{4}{3}$, $\frac{3}{2}$), and by 'ratio' he meant, as we do today, the comparative speed of vibrations of two notes; thus $\frac{2}{1}$ means that the higher note of an octave vibrates twice as fast as the lower, $\frac{3}{2}$ means that the higher note of a fifth vibrates $1\frac{1}{2}$ times as fast as the lower, and so on. By taking four fifths, e.g. *c–g–d′–a′–e″* ($\frac{3}{2} \cdot \frac{3}{2} \cdot \frac{3}{2} \cdot \frac{3}{2} = \frac{81}{16}$), and subtracting two octaves, *c–c″* ($\frac{4}{1}$), Pythagoras arrived at a major third, *c″–e″*, with the ratio $\frac{81}{16} \cdot \frac{1}{4} = \frac{81}{64}$, a horrible fraction and by no means simple. The same applied to the minor third ratio, and therefore to their complements, the minor and major sixths, and so he stated that these are all dissonances. But he also found that the ratio of a second or whole tone is $\frac{9}{8}$, and that therefore this was also a consonant interval theoretically, whereas an eleventh (fourth plus octave) was theoretically a dissonance because its ratio is $\frac{8}{3}$ ($\frac{4}{3} \cdot \frac{2}{1}$)! But Pythagoras was primarily a mathematician who let his passion for numbers and neat calculations overrule his ear, with the result that his musical scale differs in several respects from that which exists naturally, as we shall see when we deal with scales and intervals in Part II.

As regards the two main ways of singing in parts—namely, the exact repetition of a melody at different pitches to suit different voices (parallel organum) and the simultaneous ornamentation of a melody (free organum)—it was, as we should expect, the latter which caught on, for the desire to ornament or vary given material is and always has been a much more powerful one than that which merely aims at duplication.

The most arresting thing about free organum is the use of

contrary motion, and although neither the ninth-century authors of *Musica enchiriadis* and *Scholia enchiriadis* nor Guido of Arezzo in the eleventh century specially stress this, Guido at any rate seems to prefer free to parallel organum, and some of the examples he gives not only employ contrary motion, but crossing of parts as well; furthermore, the collection of over 150 two-part organa from Winchester which are contemporary with Guido contain a number of passages in contrary motion, particularly at cadences. Thus one of the two essential characteristics of polyphony—melodic independence—had entered music, and round about 1100 the great theorist who is usually called John Cotton and described as an Englishman, but who was almost certainly a monk at the Flemish monastery of Affighem, near Liége, specifically recommended contrary motion and the crossing of parts. In so doing he advocated using all the concords, not just parallel fourths or fifths, as the theorists before him had done, but a mixture of unisons, fourths, fifths, and octaves, all the other intervals being regarded as discordant as before, and therefore only to be used as approaches to concords.

The second of the two essential characteristics of polyphony—rhythmic independence—can also be found in some of Guido's examples, where several notes of the chant melody or vox principalis are set against one note of the vox organalis, and although later practice reversed this procedure by setting several notes of the organalis to one of the principalis, the seed had been sown, and again we find John of Affighem strongly recommending what had previously only been allowed. But rhythmic independence inevitably demanded some kind of measuring system if the parts were to be sung or played as the composer wished. So long as the parts moved at the same time there was no difficulty in keeping together, but when, as happened at the beginning of the twelfth century, the chant melody was performed in long-drawn-out notes above which was added a florid organalis part, the problem of ensemble became serious. Admittedly the music was written in score with one part above the other, and the vertical alignment of the notes would give an approximate indication as to how many organalis notes were to be sung to one of the principalis, but the exact point at which the principalis changed from one 'held' note to the next (hence the later name, 'tenor', from the Latin *tenere* =

'to hold') can only have been decided by the choirmaster, assuming, of course, there was an 'exact point', because while accurate ensemble matters to us it may not have mattered to the early composers of organa, provided that certain 'rules' were observed, such as beginning and ending a phrase on a concord.

So far as we know, the earliest school of composers who wrote organa in which the two parts are rhythmically independent came from the monastery of St. Martial at Limoges during the first half of the twelfth century. This style of writing is usually called 'sustained-tone' from the way in which the notes of the chant were performed, but, as in the case of Gregorian chant, we do not know the exact values of these held notes nor those of the florid upper part, although it is probable that when the latter is set to words more or less syllabically it follows the rhythmic pattern of the text, and when it is melismatic with many notes to a syllable or else with no words at all it is performed freely in the Solesmes manner. Here is part of a St. Martial organum based on the *Benedicamus Domino* chant melody ordained to be sung at First Vespers on Solemn Feasts, a very popular melody with twelfth- and thirteenth-century composers. (The melody is given complete in Ex. 22) (Ex. 19*):

But not all St. Martial organa are written like this; in fact, Ex. 19 is rather exceptional in that both voices sing different

* Adapted from H. Gleason, *Examples of Music before 1400*, p. 33.

words, for usually the upper part has the same words as the lower, chant-bearing part, although this lower part was often performed by an instrument or by voice and instrument together. Moreover, there was another kind of organum in which the parts move together in note-against-note style. If the parts are melismatic, then the notes are presumably of roughly equal value, but if syllabic, then the notes probably follow the verbal rhythm, as in Ex. 20,* which is transcribed in triple time, although it sounds just as well in duple time:

Ex.20 Organum *Mira Lege*
(♩.=MM c.60)
St.Martial School
(c.1125)
Mi - ra le - ge mi - ro mo - do De - us for - mat ho - mi - nem.
By a law and in a fa-shion won-der-ful doth God make men,
Mi - re ma - gis hunc re - for - mat vi - de mi - rum or - di - nem.
But be-hold more won-der-ful this won-drous plan he forms a-gain.
Re - for - man - dis
Those who share this
mi - rus or - - do In hoc so - nat de - ca - cor
re - for - ma - tion Sound the lyre in ex - ul - ta
do.
tion.

* Adapted from H. Gleason, ibid., p. 31.

Four things should be noted about this very attractive little piece. Firstly, the predominance of contrary motion and the frequent crossing of parts. Secondly, the number of thirds and sixths that occur between the parts. Thirdly, the fact that the lower voice, the vox principalis, is not a borrowed chant, but a newly-composed melody—an important feature, as it led eventually to a quite distinct type of composition known as 'conductus' (see Chapter 4, p. 97). Fourthly, that each part has roughly the same number of notes. This note-against-note style was usually called 'discantus' by contemporary theorists, and later (*c.* 1300) the term 'punctus contra punctum' was applied to it, from which we get the word 'counterpoint'. Strictly speaking, counterpoint means the combination of two or more melodies which are more or less rhythmically identical, as in Ex. 20, but unfortunately it is often used as an alternative word for 'polyphony'. However, we shall use the word 'counterpoint' throughout this book to mean the combination of melodies that are only independent as regards their shape—that is, their movement up and down—while the word 'polyphony' will mean the combination of melodies that are rhythmically independent as well. Thus by the middle of the twelfth century there were two kinds of part-music or 'organum generale'—namely, the polyphonic 'organum speciale' (Ex. 19) and the contrapuntal 'discantus' (Ex. 20). (Whenever we use the word 'organum' in future we shall mean 'organum speciale'.)

The only other important school of composers which flourished in the first half of the twelfth century was that at the monastery of Santiago (St. James) de Compostela in the north-west corner of Spain, the only part of the country not conquered by the Moors. The organa of this school are clearly influenced by the earlier St. Martial compositions, but it can lay claim to the earliest composition in three distinct parts that we know. The existence of this school, however, does not alter the fact that from *c.* 1100 to *c.* 1400 France was the undoubted leader in European music, for during this period the French genius contributed more to the development and enrichment of music and exerted a greater influence than any other country, an achievement she has never repeated.

But this musical domination was no isolated feature; it was paralleled by the growing importance of France in European

IV Romanesque architecture: the nave, Durham Cathedral.

V Gothic architecture: the nave, Lincoln Cathedral.

VI Shawm—twelfth-century (Canterbury Cathedral).

VII Cornett. Detail of illumination in an early eleventh-century Anglo-Saxon Psalter.

VIII Transverse flute and harp. From *Hortus Deliciarum* by Abbess Herrad von Landsberg. Second half of the twelfth-century.

affairs, by the achievements of her scholars and craftsmen, and by the fact that Paris, during the twelfth and thirteenth centuries at any rate, was the intellectual centre of the world. Capital of France since the end of the tenth century, Paris had rapidly increased in size, importance, and beauty during the succeeding 300 years. Famous for her university, her teachers, and her architecture, it is small wonder that music too shared in her greatness, and the school of composers who made her musically pre-eminent among European capitals flourished at the same time as the erection of her most famous building, Notre Dame (1163-1257).

By the middle of the twelfth century the florid polyphonic organa of the St. Martial composers had made the introduction of a system in which notes had more definite values a crying necessity, and it is the great distinction of the Notre Dame School, as it is usually called, that it formulated the principles of such a system and put them into practice. This system is now known as 'modal rhythm' and consists of six metrical and accentual patterns which are almost certainly derived from the Greek poetic metres, for, as we have seen in Chapter 1 (p. 11), classical culture was assiduously studied in many monasteries, and this eventually led to what has been called the "Renaissance of the twelfth century". Here, then, are the six rhythmic modes reduced to modern note values, together with the Greek poetic metres and patterns (Ex. 21):

Ex. 21

Rhythmic Mode	Pattern	Greek name and	pattern
1.		Trochee	
2.		Iamb	
3.		Dactyl	
4.		Anapaest	
5.		Spondee	
6.		Tribrach	

By comparing the mediaeval and Greek patterns given above it is obvious that whereas in the Greek system only the first, second, and sixth patterns consist of ternary groupings, *all* the mediaeval patterns were so grouped, in France at any rate, for there seems little doubt that in twelfth-century England the third, fourth, and fifth modes were binary like the Greek patterns, but that this deviation from Continental practice disappeared towards the end of the century. Many reasons have been suggested as to why a ternary grouping was forced on rhythmic modes III-V, but it was probably due to the belief, held long before the twelfth century, that the number three was a symbol of perfection together with the strong desire for an ordered, logical system, a desire that affected all branches of learning during this period. Thus as the first rhythmic mode (the most common and probably the earliest in time) is naturally ternary, the naturally binary modes were altered so as to bring them into line, and as three cannot be divided into two equal whole numbers one of the short notes had to be doubled, hence, for example, ♩ ♫ became ♩. ♪ ♩. There were now therefore two basic note values, both derived from the notation of Gregorian chant (see Chapter 1, p. 28), the 'long', ꟷ which was either ternary as in the third, fourth, and fifth rhythmic modes, or binary as in the first and second modes, and the 'breve', ▪ (Latin *brevis*='short'), which was either normal and equalled a third of the ternary long, or else 'altered', when it doubled its value as in the third and fourth modes. These differences in value, however, are not explicitly shown in the notation, and the only way in which a composer could ensure that his music was performed in one particular rhythmic mode and not another was by grouping his notes into ligatures of two, three, or four notes and by arranging them in a certain order; for instance, a four-note ligature followed by a series of three-note ligatures indicates the sixth rhythmic mode, while a single note followed by a series of three-note ligatures indicates the third rhythmic mode, and so on, each mode being written down in a different way from the others. All this was admirably clear provided composers used only the six rhythmic patterns given above, but artistic creation never has been and never will be bound by a rigid set of rules, and composers therefore varied what might otherwise have become rhythmically monotonous pieces either by making a note longer than it would be normally or else by breaking it up into notes of smaller value; thus a binary long might become ternary, and a breve be divided into two. But despite the fact that modal rhythm makes no written distinction between the different note values, it was a tremendous step forward in the development of notation, for whereas the notation of Gregorian chant neither indicates nor implies exact note values, although such values were almost certainly applied in practice to syllabic chants, the notation of the Notre Dame School, while it too does not indicate differences in note values, definitely implies them by means of a well-ordered system.

The history of any art shows among other things that when one aspect of an art is being developed other aspects tend to suffer. This was certainly the case in the part-music of the late twelfth and early thirteenth centuries, for mainly as a result of their preoccupation with rhythm the melodies of the Notre Dame School were definitely inferior compared to those of Gregorian chant or of the contemporary trouvères and troubadours (see next chapter), just as the melodies of Stravinsky's early works are compared to those of Brahms or Wagner, and for the same reason. This melodic inferiority is particularly noticeable in three-part writing which became common round about the beginning of the thirteenth century, because it is obviously more difficult to add two interesting parts to a borrowed chant melody than one, especially when the ranges of the two parts are identical (as they normally were) and certain rules of concord and discord have to be observed. In theory the only concords were the unison, fourth (but see p. 42), fifth, and their octave duplications, although thirds and sixths were sanctioned by some theorists; in any case these last were certainly used in practice, as indeed was the tritone (e.g. B–F or F–B). Not until after *c.* 1425, however, were thirds and sixths generally recognized as essential constituents of part-music. In theory, all intervals on strong beats had to be concordant with the tenor, although what we would call accented appogiaturas were permissible provided they were short and resolved on to a concord, but in practice discordant intervals which are not appogiaturas and do not resolve on to concords also occur on strong beats, particularly in three-part writing, but it is unusual for both added parts to have different discordant notes with the tenor.

The inability or perhaps the disinclination of the Notre Dame composers to write continuous melodies resulted in their chopping up the added part or parts of an organum into short sections called 'ordines' (Latin, *ordo* = 'row' [of notes]), and it is worth noting that this constant interrupting of the melodic flow was an important characteristic also of the 'New Music' composed around 1600 and of the instrumental compositions of the mid-eighteenth century which preceded the symphonies and sonatas of Haydn and Mozart, the link between all three periods being that each followed and, to a greater or lesser degree, reacted against a tradition in which the melodic line was the dominant factor: Gregorian chant before 1200, Renaissance polyphony before 1600, and the Baroque operatic aria and instrumental fugue before 1750. The composers of the two later periods marked the end of their sections by cadences which consist of certain conventional chord progressions; such a procedure, of course, was out of the question for the Notre Dame composers, as harmonic considerations did not begin to enrich (and impoverish) music for another 250 years or so, and what they were largely concerned with was the interval between one accented note of an added part and the tenor, not with the effect of a succession of such intervals nor, in three-part compositions, with the simultaneous sound of all three notes; instead of cadences, they indicated the end of an ordo by drawing a short vertical line through the stave; this mark—the first ancestor of our modern system of rests—tells the performer to pause, usually for the duration of either a breve or a long, depending on the rhythmic mode. In three-part pieces the sections for the two added parts nearly always tally, thus making it easier for the singers to keep together, particularly if the normal notes of the mode are lengthened or broken up into smaller values. (The added part written immediately above the tenor in the original MS. was called 'duplum' and the part above this—if there was one—was called 'triplum'.)

Like the earlier St. Martial School, the Notre Dame composers wrote not only organa, but discanti as well. Both types of composition are divided into short sections (ordines) and both are based on a Gregorian melody in the tenor, this melody being only that portion originally sung by a soloist (cantor). Thus from the following *Benedicamus Domino* melody (the same as that used in Ex. 19) only the notes set to the first line of the text are used, the response, 'Deo gratias' being chanted in unison by selected members of the choir (Ex. 22):

Ex.22 Gregorian chant Benedicamus Domino
(Cantor) Be - ne - di-ca-mus Do - mi - no.
(Choir) De - o gra - ti - as.

The Notre Dame discanti, however, only use the melismatic portion of the soloist's section of the chant, e.g. that portion set to the word 'domino' in Ex. 22, and they are further distinguished from the organa in that the tenor also is written in modal rhythm. This means, of course, that the notes of the chant melody are sung very much faster than in organum, and in order perhaps to compensate for this and to make the length of the organum and discantus sections more equal, composers usually repeated the portion of the chant melody used in the latter. In the later Notre Dame pieces the discantus sections were called 'clausulae' (Latin, *clausula* = 'ending') because, as in Ex. 22, the part of the melody on which they are based usually comes at the end of a Gregorian chant.

The dominant characteristic of the Notre Dame composers was undoubtedly their ability to organize their material, for not only did they develop a system which gives the written notes both accent and metre, and divides their compositions into well-defined sections, but in their clausulae they frequently arranged the chant melody in the tenor so that it consists of a number of rhythmically identical patterns, and if the melody is repeated the pattern is usually altered in each repeat. This was not only the culmination of the Notre Dame School's pre-occupation with rhythm, but was also a very important innovation, because it eventually developed into the chief structural device of the fourteenth-century motet (see Chapter 5, p. 129). It also represents the highest intellectual achievement of the School, an achievement fully comparable with the new scholasticism and philosophy of men like Peter Abelard [1079-1142] and his pupil, John of Salisbury [*c.* 1115-80], and with the rise of independent thought fanned by the recently acquired knowledge of Arabian philosophy and science and, in Arabic translations, of the works of the great Greek philosopher, Aristotle [384-322 B.C.].

The two outstanding composers of the Notre Dame School are Léonin and Pérotin. The former flourished from about 1163 to about 1190 and can be regarded as the bridge between the St. Martial School and the fully developed style of Pérotin. Thus the notation of several of Léonin's early organa shows modal rhythm in its infancy, for the grouping of ligatures is less regular, the rhythmic patterns change more frequently, and the general melodic line is more fluid than in his later pieces. His discanti, however, are rhythmically much clearer, due to the fact that both parts are written in modal rhythm, although even here the ligatures often give no indication of the note values—in fact, in both the organa and the discanti of Léonin and his contemporaries the rules of concord and discord are often as much a guide to the performer as the grouping of the ligatures. (The tempo of Notre Dame organa and discanti was almost certainly quicker than that of Exx. 19 and 20, because when there is little difference in rhythm and texture, between melismatic and syllabically underlaid compositions, as in this case, it is more natural to sing the latter at a slower pace than the former. During the Renaissance, however, the distinction between the two styles became more pronounced, rhythm and texture being simpler in syllabic pieces than in melismatic, and hence the latter was almost certainly sung more slowly—see Chapter 6) (Ex. 23* opposite).

In the replica of the original opening given in Ex. 23, the short vertical stroke which marks the end of an ordo can clearly be seen in the upper part; in the transcription this is shown by a rest or comma. The tenor notes of the organum section have been written as breves, this being the conventional way of showing that they have no fixed value. They are based on the chant given in Ex. 22. The slurs in the upper part indicate the ligatures in the original, and the notes printed small should be sung lightly. The organum section contains numerous instances of broken modal rhythm, and particularly striking are the rapid scale passages in bars 6, 7, and 43, which appropriately enough were called 'currentes' (Latin, *currere*='to run') and which show clearly that this kind of music was performed by soloists in whom, moreover, a certain degree of virtuosity was expected. These soloists were members of the choir who, because of their natural ability and special training, were chosen to perform the polyphonic settings of the chant. This applies to all mediaeval part-music from the St. Martial School onwards, and it should be remembered that to perform a Notre Dame organum or indeed almost any composition before 1600 with a body of more than about twenty singers and instrumentalists is as indefensible as playing a Mozart symphony on a modern full-sized orchestra.

* Transcribed from MS. Florence, Bibliotica Medicea-Laurenziana, *plut. 29.I.* pp. 87vo, 88 (facsimile in W. Apel, *The Notation of Polyphonic Music: 900-1600*, 4th Ed., p. 247).

Ex·23 Organum Benedicamus Domino
In Leonin style
(c.1160)
(♩.=MMc.80)
[Duplum]
[Tenor]
[Be -
Be -
ne -
– ne –
- di -
- di -
- ca -
- ca -

EX. 23 (CONTD.)

45
50
-mus
-mus
[Discantus]
55
Do-
Do-
60
65
70
75
80
[repeat]
85
-mi - - - no.]
-mi - - - no.
90
(Select choir)
(etc. as in Ex.22)
De - o — gra - - [tias]

The discantus section of Ex. 23 is simpler and more consistent rhythmically than the organum section, but the chant notes in the tenor are not yet arranged in a definite, reiterated pattern. At bar 75, however, the chant is repeated and performed in shorter note values. The keen-eyed will notice that in bars 63 and 79 (the repeat) the tenor shows a local variation from the official version of the chant (Ex. 22), and that the last seven notes of the chant are missing from the end of the first statement (bar 74). Ex. 23 should be compared with that in *H.A.M.* (No. 29), which is in Léonin's later style, being more precise rhythmically and using a repeated pattern in the tenor of the last section (clausula).

Léonin's outstanding work is his *Magnus Liber Organi*, 'The Great Book of Organa' (i.e. organa generale), which consists of thirty-four pieces for the Canonical hours (see Chapter 1, p. 10) and fifty-nine for the Mass for the entire ecclesiastical year. Thus, for example, at First Vespers during Solemn Feasts, instead of singing the *Benedicamus Domino* chant in the traditional manner as shown in Ex. 22, a small choir (one to three voices per part and accompanied by suitable instruments) sang the polyphonic setting (organum and discantus) of the opening words, while the response ('Deo gratias') was chanted in unison by the select choir. This manner of performance also applied to Pérotin's organa and discanti (clausulae), which, however, differ from Léonin's in their greater rhythmic precision and clarity of notation. Pérotin and his contemporaries in fact re-wrote some of the pieces in the *Magnus Liber Organi*, shortening them and making their rhythmic patterns more consistent, and also composing a number of clausulae which were intended as substitutes for Léonin's discanti. In these clausulae, of which there are a great many, the arrangement of the chant melody in the tenor is developed in three main ways from Léonin's somewhat tentative beginnings. (1) The melody is organized in a reiterated rhythmic pattern which fits the notes of the melody exactly and which is maintained through all its repeats (see Ex. 26); hence it is identical in principle and construction with the 'ground bass' of the seventeenth and eighteenth centuries. (2) The pattern is altered when the melody repeats, as in this tenor part, for instance (Ex. 24*).

* Transcribed from MS. Florence, ibid., p. 175 (facsimile in Apel, ibid., p. 255).

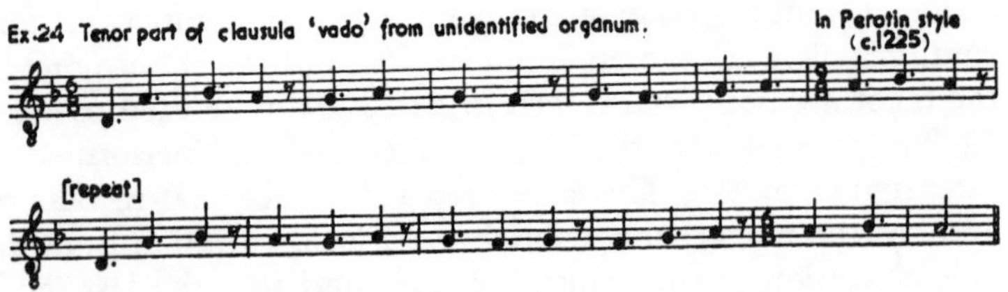

(3) The pattern is maintained, but does not fit the melody exactly, and so when the latter is repeated it is given a different rhythmic guise, as in Ex. 25, where Arabic numerals show the repeats of the rhythmic pattern and Roman numerals the repeats of the melody (Ex. 25*):

Here is a complete clausula of the Pérotin period which, being based on the same chant melody, was composed as a substitute for Léonin's discantus in Ex. 23. As in previous examples, slurs indicate the original ligatures and rests the ends of ordines, which in this case do not always tally between the two parts (Ex. 26† next page).

The thirteenth-century theorist known as Anonymous IV describes Léonin as "optimus organista" ("the greatest composer of organa") and Pérotin as "optimus discantor" ("the greatest composer of discanti [or clausulae]"); apart from this handsome compliment we know almost as little about Pérotin as about his predecessor, but it seems that he was at Notre Dame, possibly as a boy chorister, at about the same time as the choir of the Cathedral was completed in 1183, and he may have held the post of succentor or first bass in the choir

* Adapted from G. Reese, *Music in the Middle Ages*, pp. 301-2.
† Transcribed from MS. Florence, ibid., pp. 88vo, 89 (facsimile in Apel, ibid., p. 257).

from *c.* 1208 to 1238. Pérotin, however, was more than just a composer of clausulae, for he wrote organa as well, not only in two parts ('organa dupla') but in three and even four parts

('organa tripla' and 'quadrupla'); in fact, his three organa quadrupla represent the peak of this particular type of composition. Undoubtedly he added much to the greater clarity of rhythm and grasp of musical structure, but his melodies, as we might expect, are inferior to Léonin's, whose organum sections in particular, with their predominantly stepwise motion, broad sweep, and largely unorganized rhythmic patterns, show the still powerful influence of Gregorian chant. Pérotin's melodies, on the other hand, employ leaps more often, are divided into short sections, and show a high degree of rhythmic organization. Both composers wrote melodically sequential passages—that is, passages in which a group of notes is repeated at a higher or lower pitch (usually the latter), keeping their exact rhythmic patterns and general melodic shape, as, for instance, in bars 35-40 of Ex. 23. This device was not new, for it had been used in a number of Gregorian melodies, but not so frequently nor so extensively. It is a most satisfying device, as there are few things the ear enjoys more than recognizing a relationship with something already heard. Melodic sequence, in fact, is the simplest form of the two fundamentals of all music—unity and variety. The balance between these two has not, of course, remained the same in all periods. In Léonin's time variety predominated, but with Pérotin the pendulum swung the other way, and it is therefore no coincidence that, not content with unifying his freely composed parts (duplum, triplum, and quadruplum) by rhythmic means, he used an even more powerful device, imitation, so called because a musical phrase in one voice is later imitated in another, usually at the unison, fourth, fifth, or their octave combinations above or below the pitch of the original phrase. This device may have originated in England, but occurs fairly often in the three- and four-part compositions of Pérotin and his contemporaries; it is found in two forms. The first can be shown diagrammatically thus:

Triplum	Phrase A	Phrase B
Duplum	Phrase B	Phrase A

and is known as 'stimmtausch', which simply means 'voice-exchange'. It reappeared in the sixteenth century and was called 'contrappunto doppio' or 'double counterpoint', but on account of its difficulty if used extensively it occurs much less often than ordinary straightforward imitation which became common from the late fifteenth century onwards and which has its roots in the second of the two ways mentioned, thus:

Triplum	Phrase A	(Free part)
Duplum	(Free part)	Phrase A

Sometimes there is more than one imitated phrase, just as in stimmtausch there are sometimes more than two transposed phrases—in fact, in one of Pérotin's organa quadrupla there is a passage in which five phrases in the triplum part are imitated a fifth lower by the duplum part. This is the beginning of what we now call canon. Two examples of imitation will be found in bars 19-25 and 52-4 (indicated by ┌ ┐) of the following organum in Pérotin style. This fine example, with its dancing, changing rhythms and its sequential passages (bars 36-9 and 70-7), the second of which provides a most satisfying climax, when compared with Ex. 23, will give some idea of the enormous progress in rhythmic organization that took place in the sixty years or so that separates the two pieces (see Fig. 1) (Ex. 27*):

* Transcribed from MS. Wolfenbüttel Herzogliche Bibliothek, 1206, p. 7vo, 8 (facsimile in Apel, ibid., p. 233).

EX. 27 (CONTD.)

20
25
[cadential passage]
[Rhythmic mode II]
-dit
- dit
- dit
30
35
[Rhythmic mode III]
40
[Rhythmic mode I]

EX. 27 (CONTD.)

45

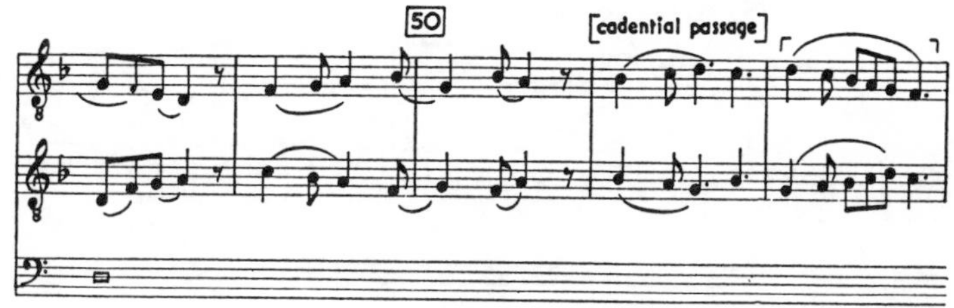
50
[cadential passage]

55
[Rhythmic mode I]
de
de
de

60
coe -
coe -
coe -

EX. 27 (CONTD.)

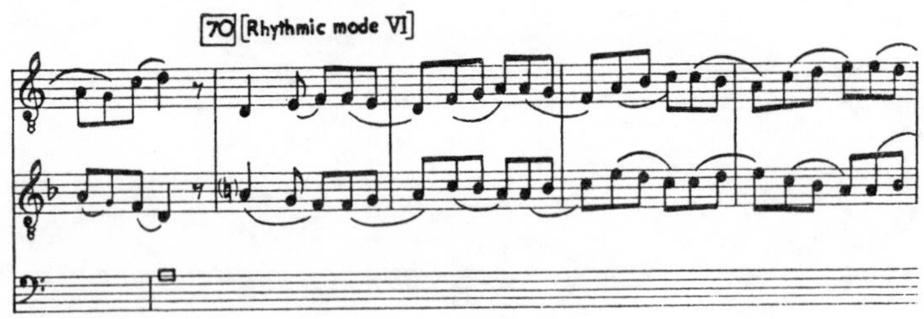

Fig. 1 Modal notation. The beginning of the organum *Descendit de coelis* (see Ex. 27 p. 61).

One of the main difficulties in trying to find out how mediaeval music should sound is the fact that as written down it does not tell us exactly how it was performed. (This indeed applies to nearly all music up to the middle of the eighteenth century.) Admittedly by Pérotin's time notation was much less ambiguous than previously, but there are two vital factors which we know took place in performance, but which are never shown in the MSS.—namely, improvisation and instrumentation. Improvisation meant that far from regarding the written music as unalterable, a trained singer was sometimes expected to add notes at various places, both to organa and discanti. Just where or how he improvised we do not know, but he might have 'filled in' a leap of a third or more with notes of shorter value, or ornamented a long note with a trill or grace note. Even the traditional chant melodies were embellished by the addition of improvised parts in the style of the older organum. To do this some of the choir stood round a lectern or reading desk on which was placed a large MS. chant-book, and while some sang the melody others improvised one or two parts above it at the fifth or octave. This kind of performance was later called 'discantus supra librum' or 'discant from the book', and it was still practised in the fifteenth and even the sixteenth centuries, though in a somewhat modified form, as we shall see. The ability to improvise was thus as essential to a singer as the ability to sight-read, and the practice of ornamenting organa and discanti in this way continued long after the actual composing of them had ceased in the second half of the thirteenth century.

Instrumental accompaniment was an even more essential part of any performance than improvisation, and although composers never specified the exact number or kind of instruments, this was because they were less instrumentally conscious than later centuries, and were content to leave the choice and size of the 'orchestra' to the choirmaster, who in turn would select his players according to the particular occasion and also to the material and money he had at his disposal.

Of the instruments we know to have been used in church the most traditional was the organ, but the great organ, because of its unwieldiness and loudness, was almost certainly restricted to doubling those portions of the simpler chants (e.g. psalm-tunes) that were sung in unison. There were, however, two smaller types of organ called the positive and the portative which became popular in the twelfth century. Both operated on the same clumsy slider principle as the large organ, but because the wind pressure was considerably lower and the sliders were therefore easier to push and pull and because the sound was much less loud than on the great organ, they were suitable for playing or doubling the sustained notes in both Léonin's and Pérotin's organa. The positive was small enough to move about, but had to be set down before it could be played, as it needed one person to work the bellows and another to operate the sliders. The portative, however, as its name implies, was carried and played at the same time by only one performer, one hand or arm pumping wind and the other hand playing the notes. In the thirteenth century a keyboard was added to both these instruments which greatly increased the speed of performance, but more of this in the next chapter.

Of more importance, so far as part-music was concerned, were the bowed instruments. These became popular in the twelfth century, probably because they were admirably suited to accompanying the tripping rhythm and melodies of Léonin's and Pérotin's music, for they were capable of both a sustained tone and a flexible technique. The two chief bowed instruments were the vièle* and the rebec, both of Arabian origin. The vièle, the more important of the two, was generally played sitting down, the instrument being held in a more or less vertical position resting on the lap; usually it had five strings, the lowest of which provided a drone or pedal note, the melody being played on the upper four strings (see Plates I and IX). The rebec was smaller, and was placed under the chin, rather like the violin today; it had either three or five melody strings and produced a shriller tone (see Plate I). Allied to the vièle is the organistrum or hurdy-gurdy (called 'vielle' in the fifteenth century), which was very popular from the tenth century until the advent of the improved portative and positive organs in the thirteenth century. It was a curious instrument, for it consisted of two melody strings tuned either in unison or an octave apart which were simultaneously stopped when one of a number of rods with flat bridges attached was turned so that the bridge came into contact with the strings; in addition there were from one to three lower strings which sounded as a drone. All the strings were vibrated by a wheel made tacky with resin, which was rotated at the lower end of the instrument. The earliest organistrum needed two players, one to turn the wheel and one to manipulate the rods (see Plate I).

The simplest stringed instrument was the monochord, said to have been invented by Pythagoras in order to demonstrate his system of musical intervals. Whether this is true or not it was certainly used for teaching scales and tunes from his day to *c.* 1500, and although we have no record of its being bowed before the fourteenth century it must have been affected by the popularity of the vièle and rebec long before this.

Wind instruments formed the next most important group used in church, of which the chief was the flute family. This included both the transverse flute, the forerunner of the modern type, and the recorder, with its smaller and shriller cousin, the flageolet. All the members of this family were known in the East long before Christianity, but do not appear to have been played in church before the twelfth century, when, as with bowed instruments, the increasing liveliness of church music probably encouraged their use (see Plates I and VIII).

* This is sometimes spelt 'vielle', but it is less ambiguous if this term is reserved for the organistrum (see text).

Reed instruments also took part, especially the strident-sounding shawm with its double reed, offspring of the Greek aulos and ancestor of the oboe, having, like the latter, only one tube, not two as in the aulos (see Plate VII). Another wind instrument, which may have originated in Britain (eleventh century?) was the cornett, a small horn made of wood with its tube either straight or slightly bent in which a number of holes were pierced, enabling a greater range of notes to be played than in the horn proper. Its tone blended excellently with voices and it remained popular both in and out of church until *c.* 1750 (see Plate VI).

We saw in Chapter 1 how the Greek kithara was tolerated and even approved of by the early Church Fathers, and therefore it is not surprising that other plucked instruments were widely used in church, the two chief being the harp and the psaltery. The harp, which goes back to at least 3000 B.C., probably made its first European appearance in Scandinavia or even possibly in England round about the sixth century. Like the modern type, the strings—of varying number—were arranged vertically to the sounding-board, but were tuned diatonically, so that although they could play in any mode, they were incapable of transposition, for this involves one or more sharps or flats; not till the end of the sixteenth century were harps tuned chromatically with each string representing a semitone and transposition therefore possible (see Plates I and VIII). The psaltery, also of very ancient origin, had various shapes, but the most common was that of an inverted triangle with the top cut off, the strings, usually ten in number, lying horizontally above the sounding-board (see Plate I).

In addition to all the above instruments which produced notes of definite pitch, there were a number of percussion instruments. These included bells (see Plate I) and small drums of various shapes and sizes, such as the tabor, cymbals, and possibly tambourines.

Many of the instruments used in church, especially those that were bowed or blown, were introduced into Europe from the East by the returning Crusaders, but their widespread participation in the service cannot be explained only by their ability to play the part-music of the twelfth century; it must also have meant that the Church authorities regarded instruments in a very different light from that of the early Christian leaders. There were, of course, exceptions among the former, and of these Aelred, Abbot of Rievaulx in Yorkshire [1109?–1166], seems to have been especially severe on the use of instruments and indeed on the performance of part-music in general, particularly the way it was executed, although in the following translation by William Prynne [1600–1669] from Aelred's *Speculum Charitatis* ('The Mirror of Charity') allowance must be made for the translator's puritanical exaggeration: "Whence hath the Church so many Organs and Musical Instruments? To what purpose, I pray you, is that terrible blowing of Belloes, expressing rather the crakes of Thunder than the sweetness of a voyce? To what purpose serves that contraction and inflection of the voyce? This man sings a base, that a small meane [i.e. middle part], another a treble, a fourth divides and cuts asunder, as it were, certaine middle notes [i.e. improvising]. One while the voyce is strained, anon it is remitted, now it is dashed, and then againe it is inlarged with a lowder sound. Sometimes, which is a shame to speake, it is enforced into a horse's neighings, sometimes, the masculine vigour being laid aside, it is sharpened into the shrilness of a woman's voyce; now and then it is writhed and retorted with a certain artifical circumvolution. . . . In the meantime, the common people standing by, trembling and astonished, admire the sound of the Organs, the noyse of the Cymballs and Musicall instruments, the harmony of the Pipes and Cornets."*

Another Englishman, the famous scholar John of Salisbury, also objected to the way vocal music was performed, remarking that if you heard "one of these enervating performances executed with all the devices of the art, you might think it a chorus of Sirens, but not of men, and you would be astonished at the singers facility, with which indeed neither that of the nightingale or parrot, nor of whatever else there may be that is more remarkable in this kind, can compare. For this facility is displayed in long ascents and descents, in the dividing or in the redoubling of notes, in the repetition of phrases, and the clashing of the voices, while, in all this, the high or even the highest notes of the scale are so mingled with the lower or lowest, that the ears are almost deprived of their power to distinguish."†

* Quoted from H. Davey, *History of English Music* (2nd Ed., 1921) pp. 16, 17.
† Quoted from H. E. Wooldridge, *Oxford History of Music*, I (2nd Ed., 1929), p. 290.

Despite these attacks and a few others like them, which incidentally may have been inspired by the incompetency of certain choirs or possibly their desire to show off, the Church as a whole did not object to the use of instruments nor to the new development in part-music provided these did not make a mockery of the service; in fact, it seems likely that the music of Léonin, Pérotin, and others, properly sung and accompanied by, say, a positive organ playing the tenor part, and vièles and harps doubling the upper part or parts, would have been regarded as a richer and worthier offering to the Almighty than if sung by voices alone. Indeed, to have been present at a celebration of High Mass on a feast day in Notre Dame must have provided a most profound experience both artistically and spiritually, with the fascinating blend of voices, organs, strings, wind, and percussion, and the immensely satisfying contrasts between the freely flowing Gregorian melodies, the wayward rhythm of the duplum part over the long tenor notes of a Léonin organum, and the throbbing waves of sound of a Pérotin clausula.

But Pérotin's achievement was no isolated phenomenon; the unity he brought through rhythmic organization, which reflected the attitude of the Notre Dame School as a whole, was inevitably part and parcel of the general artistic and intellectual outlook of the time. We have already mentioned the latter on p. 53, but the former was even more closely allied, for the Gothic style of architecture which arose at about the same time and in the same country that Léonin was active was also an expression, and the most outstanding one artistically, of the desire to unify (see Plate V). The oddly assorted pillars, the rounded and irregularly spaced arches, and almost haphazard ornamentation of the Romanesque style were replaced by regularly spaced and uniform columns made up of the clustered supports for the rib vaulting, which, like the arches, were pointed and so reached to a greater height than the rounded arch, allowing more light to enter the building, a practical consideration for northern countries, but one that did not affect the Romanesque architects working in their brilliant Mediterranean climate, with the result that Gothic architecture hardly affected Italy and Spain, the Romanesque style merging into the Renaissance during the fifteenth century. The greater height and constructional complexity of the nave imposed a severe strain on the outer walls, and in order to provide adequate support flying buttresses were invented. These consisted of massive tapering columns placed outside the church a few yards from the walls, but in line with the pillars inside which supported the nave; from these columns two half-arches 'flew' across the intervening space and strengthened the walls at the places where the maximum thrust from inside was exerted. The Gothic style was both more complex and yet more unified than Romanesque and represents a brilliant constructional and intellectual feat; moreover, its general character, in the twelfth century at any rate, was one of dignity and simplicity which was increased rather than diminished by the sculptured figures and stained-glass windows, for the figures were carved from the same stone as the portals, to ornament which was their chief function, and by being more formal than natural were able to blend with the main structure. The same was true of the stained-glass windows, and it did not matter if a shepherd, for instance, was depicted in a stiff and unnatural attitude, nor if he was surrounded by a multi-coloured flock of sheep, provided that the general design and colour scheme was satisfactory and in harmony with its surroundings when viewed from a distance. In gauging the colour effects, the Gothic artist used the technique of placing small pieces of, say, red and blue glass side by side in order that the eye, from some way away, would fuse them into a far richer colour than could be achieved by actually painting the glass purple, a technique rediscovered by the pointilliste painters some 700 years later.

Thus the clear-cut symmetry, simplicity, and unity of the early Gothic style with its ornamentation subordinated to the total effect, and the well-defined sections, incisive rhythms, simple melodies, and discreet instrumentation of Pérotin's music both show a distinct similarity in aim and achievement. Nevertheless, we must remember that his music—indeed, all part-music—constituted only a fraction of that performed in the church during the tenth to twelfth centuries, for it was obviously more difficult to sing than unison chanting or even extemporized organum, and was therefore only performed in the larger ecclesiastical establishments. Furthermore, the Church authorities as a body, and not only Aelred and John of Salisbury, may well have regarded it with less favour than the traditional method of performing the chant, because it not only obscured parts of the latter by either lengthening the notes so that the chant became unrecognizable or else chopping it up into short rhythmic patterns, but also because it was aesthetically inferior to the superbly wrought and wonderfully expressive Gregorian melodies, a view with which the present writer would agree, even though he finds much that is satisfying in Léonin's but more especially Pérotin's organa. Nor must we forget that the twelfth century produced a great many tropes and sequences together with a number of new melodies, and it was no accident that the organization of music into rhythmic patterns by the Notre Dame School took place at the same time as the introduction of regular metrical-accentual patterns into the sequence by Adam of St. Victor (see Chapter 1, p. 22). But although chant composition continued during the twelfth century, and indeed the thirteenth also, the melodies deteriorated in both quantity and quality, and it is to musicians outside the Church that we must look for the last spontaneous flowering of monophony.

PERFORMANCE

(See also pp. 54, 57, 65-70.)

The instruments mentioned below (and in the similar sections at the end of later chapters) are restricted to those likely to be available in amateur circles and which, if they are not direct descendants of, are roughly equivalent to the original ones; they are organ, violin, viola, 'cello, recorders, flute, oboe, bassoon, small drum, and triangle. The two last should not be used unless specifically mentioned in the details of performance given for each example. If the range of an instrument lies above that of a part as written, the notes should be, as they undoubtedly were in the Middle Ages, transposed up one or two octaves.

In accordance with mediaeval practice, no attempt is made at exact 'scoring', but details have been included in order to give some idea of the various ways in which the piece could have been performed originally.

The choice of instruments and the decision as to whether to double a voice by an instrument or to have two instruments playing the same part in unison or octaves should be dictated by four considerations:

(i) The fact that one of the main characteristics of mediaeval music is the differentiation of the parts through contrasts of timbre. Thus a two-part piece in which each part is of roughly the same range should not be sung by voices alone or played by two instruments of the same kind; in other words, if both parts are sung, then one or both of the voices should be doubled by an instrument; if the latter, then the instruments should have contrasting timbres.

(ii) The vertical sound of a piece must not be essentially altered. For instance, in Ex. 20 it would be wrong for a tenor to sing the upper part accompanied solely by a violin playing the lower part an octave higher, as this would result in the inversion of all the intervals, the less important fourth, for example, replacing the all-important fifth.

(iii) What instruments are at hand.

(iv) Individual taste.

Unless the contrary is specifically stated, there should not be more than three voices per part.

Ex. 18. Select choir with or without organ.

Ex. 19. *Upper part:* solo voice with or without instruments. *Lower part:* organ or 'cello with or without voices.

Ex. 20. Both of the parts should be sung, with instruments (except the organ) doubling one or both of them.

Ex. 22. Solo voice and select choir.

Ex. 23. *Upper part:* solo voice with or without instruments. *Lower part:* played by an organ (except in the discantus section) and/or 'cello with or without voices. A change of 'orchestration' in the discantus section is effective.

Ex. 26. Both parts should be sung by solo voices with instruments doubling one or both of them. (If an organ is used it should only play the lower part.)

Ex. 27. The triplum and duplum parts should be sung by solo voices with instruments doubling one or both of them. The tenor part should be played by an organ and/or 'cello with or without voices.

3

MUSIC OUTSIDE THE CHURCH: SOLO SONG AND DANCE MUSIC

Sweet sounds the viol
   Shriller the flute,
A lad and a maiden
   Sing to the lute.

He'll touch the harp for thee,
   She'll sing the air,
They will bring wine for thee,
   Choice wine and rare.*

THESE verses come from a tenth-century Latin poem, *Iam, dulcis amica, venito* ('Now, O sweet beloved, come'), which is, in the words of its translator, "the most famous and perhaps the oldest of the earlier mediaeval love songs".† It was certainly set to music at least three times, but, like nearly all settings before the eleventh century, the notation is impossible to transcribe because it is written in staffless neumes and, just as in Gregorian chant, not until after Guido's improvements can we get any clear idea of the melodies to which many of the mediaeval Latin lyrics were sung.

Of course, popular music, both instrumental and vocal, must always have existed, but none of it has survived before the ninth century; indeed, it is remarkable that even as early as this anyone took the trouble to write it down, for such music has always relied on the handing down from generation to generation of its repertoire, as was the case, for example, with British folk-songs, most of which were not written down until the end of the nineteenth century, and only then because of the interest of a few professional musicians.

It is a common belief that many of the mediaeval churchmen were gay dogs and as fond of wine, women, and song as any other man. Unlike most common beliefs, this is true, and it is as

* Translated from the Latin by Helen Waddell, *Mediaeval Latin Lyrics* (4th Ed.), p. 145.

† Ibid., p. 331.

well that it is, for if they who formed the bulk of the cultured, educated class had not been in love with the world as well as with their religion, literature (especially poetry) and to a lesser extent music would have been much the poorer; the only drawback is that as Latin was the accepted language in educated circles no songs in the vernacular were written down before the eleventh century.

The secular musicians of the tenth and eleventh centuries can be divided into two main groups: the educated group called 'goliards' which consisted of students, most of them young ecclesiastics who had not taken monastic or priestly vows, who wandered over Britain, France, and more especially Germany, and the largely uneducated group called 'jongleurs' in France, 'Gaukler' in Germany, and 'scops' and 'gleemen' in Britain.

The goliards, so called after a probably fictitious Bishop Golias, wrote in Latin and usually composed or arranged their own music. The subjects of their songs range from love songs, sometimes obscene, to spring songs, sometimes exquisite, from drinking songs, often coarse, to satirical songs, often bitter. These last, which were usually aimed at their religious superiors, eventually brought the wrath of the Church on their heads, and they were forbidden ecclesiastical protection and privileges.

The jongleurs and their confrères in Germany and Britain became increasingly active from the ninth century onwards. Unlike the goliards, they represent the continuation of the popular entertainers of earlier centuries, for both 'jongleur' and 'Gaukler' mean 'juggler'. Manual dexterity, however, was not the only accomplishment of these wandering vagabonds, and a competent jongleur danced, played several instruments, sang, performed tricks either himself or with trained animals, and was often an acrobat. Unlike the goliards, too, they sang what others had invented, and their songs were in the vernacular. Each year they attended 'refresher courses' during Lent (when they were forbidden to perform in public), and there they learned new songs and fresh tricks. Their scandalous behaviour exceeded even that of the goliards, and they were a constant thorn in the sides of both civil and ecclesiastical authority. A few of the more reputable ones, however, performed at society weddings and other aristocratic functions, and some even achieved the exalted position of being permanently attached to a feudal household. In Britain these resident musicians were called 'scops' while their less fortunate (or talented?) brethren—the gleemen—roamed the countryside. After the Norman Conquest in 1066 both classes were called 'minstrels'. We know less about these British entertainers than we do of their Continental counterparts, but so far as musical performance is concerned it seems likely that their repertoire was similar, consisting chiefly of the recital of heroic exploits. These were called 'chansons de geste' or 'songs of deeds' and sometimes contained as many as 10,000 lines, all roughly identical in metre and divided into sections of from twenty to fifty lines each. Only one of the melodies has survived, which is unfortunate but not surprising, as the music must have been extremely simple, easy to memorize, and therefore not worth writing down. The solitary example probably gives us the clue to most of the others, and it consists of a short phrase to which each line of the poem was sung with 'ouvert' (open) and 'clos' (closed) endings (see p. 81), the latter only being sung or played at the end of a section of the poem. Whether the jongleur accompanied himself while he sang or added free (extemporized) instrumental preludes, interludes, and postludes, or both, will probably never be known, but it may be that there was no fixed manner of performance and that the nature of the occasion and the singer's technical ability were the deciding factors.

Both goliards and jongleurs continued to flourish after the eleventh century, the former dying out in the early thirteenth century, when the number of universities grew and students became residential instead of wandering around Europe from one famous teacher to another. A number of goliard songs were called 'conducti', though exactly why is not clear. The name was probably first applied to tropes sung during processions when the priest was 'conducted' from one part of the church to another, but by the eleventh century this type of song embraced both secular and sacred subjects (though very few found a place in the liturgy) and conducti exist which express grief for the death of an archbishop, praise at the coronation of a king, a stern warning on the corrupt morals of ecclesiastical or courtly dignitaries, jubilation over a famous victory, political criticism, and even the delights of love. The conductus in fact can be regarded as an expansion of the hymn, which, as we saw in Chapter 1, had been used for moral and even political purposes during the early years of the Christian Church, particularly as a weapon with which to combat heresies (see Chapter 1, p. 7). Like many of the hymns, conductus poems are in Latin and are metrical, and the music was nearly always newly composed.

The jongleurs, before they were organized into guilds in the fourteenth century and therefore became 'respectable', received a new lease of life from their association with the first great flowering of secular art—the songs of the troubadours from Provence and their northern imitators, the trouvères.

Up to the end of the eleventh century music outside the Church was practised first of all by musicians from the lower classes (the jongleurs, etc.) and later by middle-class poet-composers (the goliards), but from *c.* 1080 to *c.* 1300 the aristocracy entered the field, and instead of devoting their time exclusively to hunting, fighting, and drinking they began to patronize the arts and letters; indeed, many of them went further and actually composed songs and even the music to which they were sung, but as learning and even the ability to write was not an essential part of a knight's education, some of the melodies were probably invented or adapted from existing ones by the more educated jongleurs, who may even have written down the poems which their noble masters made up in their heads. It is sometimes stated that all troubadours and trouvères were of high birth. This is not true, as some of the most famous were of very humble and, in at least one case, unknown parentage. The common factor running through this secular art was not so much the noble rank of the composers, although a great many of them were in fact out of the 'top drawer', particularly in the early years, but the refined way in which the sentiments of the poem (almost always about love) were expressed. Thus love to the troubadour and trouvère was a more disembodied emotion than it was to the goliard; woman was placed on a pedestal, largely due no doubt to the devotional enthusiasm accorded to the Virgin Mary, which reached its height in the early twelfth century, and hence a love song did not usually express the real feelings of the singer, but was an imaginative, artistic, and popular means of winning recognition. The difference in approach between the eager, impetuous, and passionate appeal contained in the last two verses of the goliard love song mentioned on p. 74 and given below, and the delicate, restrained, and tender lines of the anonymous trouvère poem which follows it are typical.

Dearest, delay not,
Ours love to learn,
I live not without thee,
Love's hour is come.

What boots delay, Love,
Since love must be?
Make no more stay, Love,
I wait for thee.*

Gentle heart could you love true,
Heart to whom my love I've tendered?
Night and day I think of you.
Gentle heart could you love true?
Live I cannot without you,
To your beauty I've surrendered.
Gentle heart could you love true,
Heart to whom my love I've tendered?†

Another difference between the goliard and the troubadour and trouvère poems is that those of the latter are usually constructed on one of several plans, particularly those of the trouvères. This is not surprising when we remember that the trouvères arose at about the same time and in the same part of France as the Notre Dame School, whose chief characteristic was, as we have seen, the ability to organize their material. Thus while the rhythm of the earlier troubadour melodies, like the syllabic Gregorian chants, almost certainly follows that of the texts or, if the song is fairly melismatic, was sung in a free manner, most of the trouvère songs and, as a result, the later troubadour songs as well were not only sung in modal rhythm, but were also cast into a number of moulds or forms. Admittedly the notation of many of these later songs does not definitely imply modal rhythm, for they are mainly syllabic and thus lack the well-organized ligature groupings of Pérotin and his contemporaries, but modal rhythm was in the air and secular composers could hardly have escaped its influence.

We are on much safer ground, however, when we come to the other intellectual aspect of troubadour and trouvère

* Helen Waddell, ibid., p. 147.
† G, Reese, *Music in the Middle Ages*, p. 222.

composition—namely, form—and as we have not the space to discuss in detail all the different kinds, we shall limit ourselves to the more important—the 'rotrouenge', the 'lai', the 'ballade', the 'virelai', and the 'rondeau', of which the last three became the chief forms of secular music in the fourteenth and fifteenth centuries.

The rotrouenge, possibly so called from the Latin ***retroientia***, or 'repetition', consists of two melodic phrases, the first of which is repeated a number of times, while the second is either sung once to the refrain (chorus), which is repeated at the end of each verse and which was usually sung by the audience, or else twice to a line of the verse plus the refrain. The most convenient way of showing this is alphabetically, small italicized letters representing the lines sung by the soloist and capital italicized letters representing the refrain. Thus the rotrouenge is either *a* (repeated) *B*, or *a* (repeated) *bB*. The musical form, on the other hand, is usually shown by roman capital letters, and in this case is either A (repeated) B, or A (repeated) BB. Here is a short and most attractive example of the latter type (*a a b B*) (only verses 1, 4, and 5 are given, and the refrain—here and elsewhere—is underlined) (Ex. 28*):

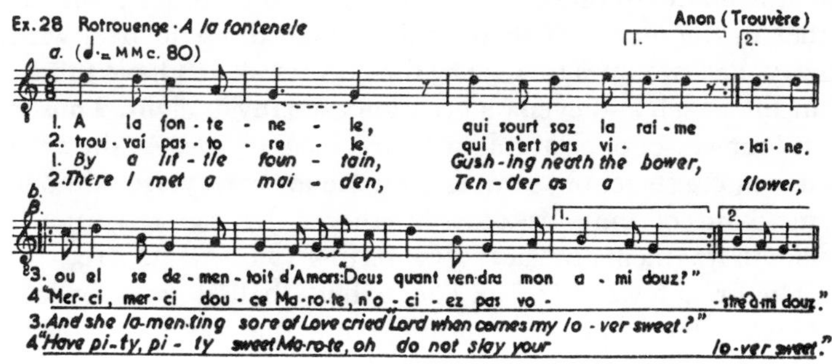

IV

Dites moi, Marote, seroiz vos m'amie?
A bele cotele ne faudroiz vos mie.
Et chainse et ride et peliçon avrez, se je ai vostre amor.

Merci, merci (etc.).

* From F. Gennrich, *Die altfranzösiche Rotrouenge*, p. 60 (see also G. Reese ibid., p. 220).

Tell me, O Marote, wilt love me alone, dear?
I a robe will give you for thy very own, dear,
A skirt, a furry cloak as well, and gold if I but have your love.

Have pity, pity (etc.).

V

Sire chevalier, ce ne di ge mie
C'onques a nul jor, fusse vostre amie;
Ainz ai a tel doné m'amor dont mi parent avront anor.

Merci, merci (etc.).

Knight, that you could win me I am not denying,
Nor that I might some day to your arms come flying,
But I do dearly love a man my father holds in high esteem.

Have pity, pity (etc.).

The melody of this song is in the Mixolydian mode, and although the modes exerted a strong influence on troubadour and trouvère melodies, many of the latter show a distinct and growing tendency towards our major and minor keys.

The lai has essentially the same structure as the sequence (see Chapter 1, pp. 21-2), from which it undoubtedly derived, for it is made up of a number of verses which differ from each other in the length of their lines. Unlike the sequence, which always has two lines to a verse, the lai verses often have three or four lines each and even on occasion as many as eight. Thus the first four verses of a lai might be *aa*, *bbbb*, *cc*, *ddd*. As the verses differ in construction, so does the tune for each verse, although some kind of unity is often preserved by the repetition of melodic fragments in each verse setting (see *H.A.M.*, 19, i).

The French word *ballade*, like 'ballet', 'ballad', and 'ballata', (see Chapter 5, p. 167), derives from the Latin verb *ballare* (='to dance'), and the first ballades were undoubtedly dance songs. As early as the thirteenth century, however, they lost their association with the dance and as a result became more complex. The simplest and probably the earliest type has the form *a a b*, i.e. with no refrain, but the commoner and probably later types do have a refrain, for this device was and still is a very popular one, not only because the ear enjoys repetition, but also because an audience usually welcomes an opportunity to join in. The most popular of the commoner types of ballade§ has the poetic form *ab ab cd E*, the musical form of which can be simplified to A A B, in which A=*ab* and B=*cd E*. The following song by the troubadour Andrieu contredit d'Arras [*c.* 1180-1248] is an example, and a remarkably fine one (Ex. 29):

One feature of the ballade, clearly shown in the above example, is the use of ouvert and clos cadences for the first section, the 'open' cadence ending on any note but the final of the mode, while the 'closed' cadence rounds off the section by ending on the final, the effect being the same as our imperfect and perfect cadences.

Although the most common form of the ballade is *ab ab cd E* there are in fact two other but infrequently used types, both of which begin and end with a refrain, a characteristic of the virelai also, with its form *A bb a A* or *AB cc ab AB*, in which the final refrain of a verse serves as the first refrain of the next verse, thus making the poem continuous. The name probably derives from *virer*, 'to turn', and 'lai', in the sense that it is a lai with verses of four lines and musical form B B A A with the A phrase 'turned' back to the beginning, as in this charming example (Ex. 30*):

Although the popular instrumental rondo of the seventeenth and eighteenth centuries with its A B A C A D . . . A structure has something in common with the mediaeval rondeau it is very unlikely that there is any connexion between the two. The simplest and earliest type of rondeau has the form *a A ab AB*, but the fondness for refrains which we noted in connexion with the ballade led to a later and commoner variety in which the complete refrain was sung at the beginning as well as at the

* Adapted from F. Gennrich, *Rondeaux, Virelais und Balladen*, Vol. I, p. 129.

end—*AB a A ab AB*. This is the form of the poem quoted on p. 78 and of the following very modern-sounding example (Ex.31*):

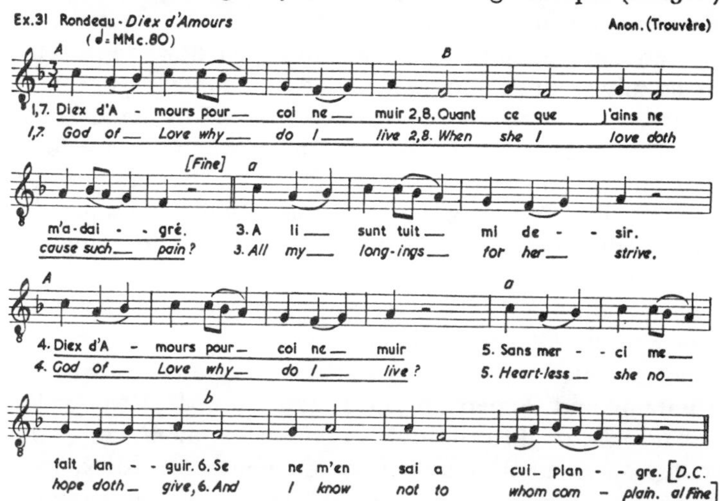

The forms of troubadour and trouvère song nearly all developed from ecclesiastical chant—in particular, the litany, the sequence, and the hymn—but the three most popular and lasting forms, the ballade, virelai, and rondeau, probably have their roots in an earlier dance-song which was purely secular and owed nothing to the Church. A number of the melodies, however, are clearly adapted from chants and are among the earliest examples of *contrafacta*—that is, songs in which the original sacred words are replaced by secular ones, or vice versa.

Although most of the mediaeval lyrics are concerned with love, they are by no means restricted to the worshipping from afar approach; thus there are 'albas', or 'dawn songs', in which a faithful friend stands watch for two lovers and warns them of the approach of day, 'chansons de toile', or 'spinning songs', in which an unhappy wife complains of her husband or a maiden pines for her absent sweetheart, and 'pastourelles', in which a knight woos a virtuous shepherdess who sometimes—as in Ex. 28—preserves her virtue! There are also songs which deal with other topics, such as mourning songs, satirical songs, and, more important, the 'sirventes', or 'songs of service', which often have a political or moral bias and are sometimes very outspoken in their comments on a particular nobleman (see Ex. 33).

* Adapted from F. Gennrich, ibid., Vol. I, p. 24.

One of the annoying things about mediaeval church music is the shroud of anonymity which covers nearly all its composers, but this is fortunately not the case with the troubadours and trouvères, as a great many names have come down to us. These are usually grouped into three periods: *c.* 1080–*c.* 1150, *c.* 1150–*c.* 1250, *c.* 1250–*c.* 1300, the trouvères being in the ascendant during the last two periods and the troubadours up to the early thirteenth century, although the latter might have sustained the high quality and spontaneity of their songs right through this century if it had not been for the crippling blow which the Church, in her zeal to exterminate heretics, dealt Provence during the twenty years' massacre and destruction known as the Albigensian Crusade (1209-29). Among the more important of these poet-musicians were Count Guillaume of Aquitaine and Poitiers [1071 – 1127], the earliest troubadour we know, Marcabru [fl. 1128 – 1150], a commoner and, oddly enough, a woman-hater, Bernart de Ventadorn [d. *c.* 1195], also a commoner and one of the greatest troubadour poets, Guiraut de Bornelh [d. *c.* 1200], who was called 'Master of the Troubadours' by his contemporaries, Guiraut Riquier [d. *c.* 1300], the last but by no means least of the troubadours, Blondel de Nesles [*c.* 1150-1200], the first of the trouvères, but who did *not* discover the dungeon into which his master Richard Cœur-de-Lion had been thrown by singing a song composed by the two of them, nor did he rescue him, Colin Muset [early thirteenth century], one of the educated jongleurs whose songs entitled him to be called a trouvère, Thibaut IV, King of Navarre [1201 – 1253], an unscrupulous monarch, but an inspired composer of love songs, Adam de la Halle [*c.* 1245 – *c.* 1288], another commoner and possibly the last of the trouvères, but more renowned and important for his part-music than for his solo songs (see Chapter 4, p. 117); he also either composed, or borrowed from folk-songs, or both, the music for *Li Gieus* [= *Le Jeu*] *de Robin et Marion*, a pastoral play with songs inserted in the dialogue. Only the songs have survived, but Adam can lay claim to have compiled the first secular opera. We could add other names of troubadours and trouvères, but to extend the list would not add to the delight which can be found in this often exquisite if sometimes stilted poetry and the charming, even ravishing melodies to which it is set.

It was natural enough for the Provençal troubadour movement to spread into northern France, and it was almost as natural for it to cross the frontier into Italy, but the effects were vastly different, for so far as we know French influence south of the Alps was confined to the poetic forms, not the music. Italian secular music, in fact, like secular learning, flourished much later than in other countries and for the same reason—the power and proximity of Rome. But singing was not confined to the liturgy only, and from at least the time of St. Francis of Assisi [1182-1226], whose famous *Hymn to the Sun* was certainly set to music now unfortunately lost, a number of songs with religious texts were composed, particularly during the late thirteenth and fourteenth centuries. During this period, as a result of political and religious upheavals and their attendant bloodshed, and of widespread outbreaks of the plague, bands of wandering penitents were formed who, as they journeyed about northern Italy, chastised themselves for their sins and sang hymns of praise called 'laude spirituali'. The form of many of these laude closely resembles the French virelai, and they also show the same tendency towards major and minor tonality, but the melodies, because they were sung by a group, and usually a marching group at that, are simpler and probably in binary rhythm. This lauda, for example, would be most exhilarating to march to (Ex. 32*):

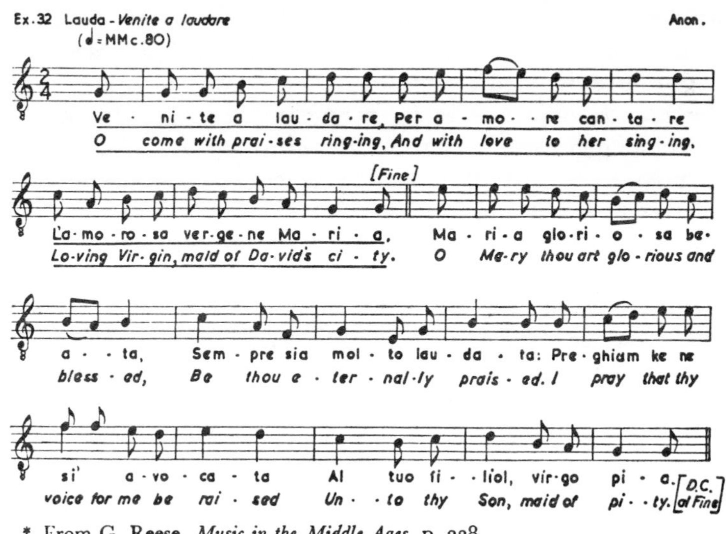
Ex. 32 Lauda - *Venite a laudare*
Anon.
(♩= MM c. 80)
Ve - ni - te a lau - da - re, Per a - mo - - re can - ta - re
O come with prai - ses ring-ing, And with love to her sing - ing.
[Fine]
L'a - mo - ro - sa ver - ge - ne Ma - ri - a. Ma - ri - a glo - ri - o - sa be -
Lo-ving Vir - gin, maid of Da - vid's ci - ty. O Me-ry thou art glo - rious and
a - - ta, Sem - pre sia mol - to lau - da - ta: Pre - ghiam ke ne
bless - ed, Be thou e - ter - nal - ly prais - ed. I pray that thy
si' a - vo - ca - ta Al tuo fi - - liol, vir - go pi - a.
voice for me be rai - sed Un - - to thy Son, maid of pi - - ty.
D.C. al Fine

* From G. Reese, *Music in the Middle Ages*, p. 238.

The penitential movement in Italy, with its practice of self-chastisement or flagellation, became almost a mania in the fourteenth century and invoked strong Papal action, as a result of which it had almost entirely disappeared by the end of the century; but the singing of devotional songs outside the church continued in popularity and prepared the way for the sixteenth-century oratorio. Before the authorities had banned the movement, however, it had caught on in Germany, where it was particularly rife during the terrible plagues of 1348 and later, known as the Black Death. These German penitential songs were called 'Geisslerlieder' or 'flagellation songs', and although the movement was banned at the same time as the Italian it persisted longer owing to the greater remoteness of Rome and the strong morbid streak in the German character.

German songs of course had existed long before the Geisslerlieder, but not until the latter half of the twelfth century did a definite group of song composers arise; these were the Minnesinger, or 'singers of chivalrous love', and it was the art of the troubadours that was their main inspiration, for in 1156 Frederick Barbarossa, or 'Redbeard' [1123-1190], Emperor of the Holy Roman Empire and leader of the Third Crusade, married Beatrix of Burgundy, who took with her to Germany a troubadour named Guiot of Provence, and it was almost certainly their influence that initiated the Minnesänger movement. The German composers, however, most of whom came from the south (Austria), did not slavishly imitate their French models, even though their best period, *c.* 1190-*c.* 1250, saw French influence at its strongest. The main reason for their independence was the difference between French and German verse, particularly the fact that the former was measured by the number of syllables in the line, while the latter was measured by the number of accents, which meant that the number of unaccented syllables could vary from line to line; thus the melodies were sung in either binary or ternary rhythm, depending on the position of the poetic accents, or else in free rhythm as in the more melismatic troubadour songs.

The forms used by the Minnesinger are less easily classifiable than their French counterparts, but apart from the 'leich', which corresponds to the French lai, the main musical one, capable of many variations within itself, is called 'bar' form and is the same as that of the ballade—A A B, the second section sometimes containing modified or complete repeats of the first section (see Ex. 33). The poetic types, on the other hand, are

Ex.33 Minnelied · Der kuninc Rodolp mynnet got
"Der Unvürzaghete"
(♩ = MM c.60)
a'
Der ku - ninc Ro - dolp myn - net got und ist an tru - wen
Der ku - ninc Ro - dolp rich - tet wol und haz - zet val - sche
King Ru - dolph loves Al - - migh - ty God his faith - ful - ness ne'er
King Ru - dolph judg - es right - eous - ly and hat - eth all false
a²
ste - te, Der ku - ninc Ro - dolp hat sich ma - ni - gen scan - den wol vür - sa - get.
re - te, Der ku - ninc Ro - dolp ist ein helt an_ tu - gen - den un - vür - tza - get.
break - ing; King Ru - dolph has re - sist - ed well ma - ny a de - vi - lish temp - ta - tion.
speak - ing; King Ru - dolph's brave and vir - tuous deeds de - - serve our ad - mi - - ra - tion.
b'
b²
Der ku - ninc Ro - dolp e - ret got und al - le wer - de vrou - wen, Der
King Ru - dolph ho - nours God and ev - 'ry maid of no - ble bear - ing; King
a'
ku - ninc Ro - dolp let sich dick ' in_ ho - en e - ren scou - wen. Ich
Ru - dolph oft re - - veals him - self in_ ac - tions fine and dar - - ing. I
c
gan ym wol, daz ym nach sy - ner mil - te heil ge - - scicht,___ Der
wish in mea - sure of his wealth that he may get his_ due,___ For
mei - ster syn - gen, gi - gen, sa - gen daz hort her gern und git yn drum - me nicht.
when the min - strels play or sing, he_ glad - ly hears, but gives them not a sou!

direct imitations of French models, and although love is still the predominant topic it is treated in an even more idealized and less personal way, the mystical trait in the German character finding its main outlet in songs of praise to the Virgin Mary, the ideal woman, thus transmuting the earthly passion of the earlier goliard poems. Epic songs and songs of a political or moral nature were also popular, the latter being the equivalent of the sirventes, and the following example by 'The Dauntless One' (whoever he may have been) has a decided sting in its tail. It also shows one of the more complex variations of bar form—a^1a^2 a^1a^2 b^1b^2 c, where $a^2=a^1$, but with a clos instead of an ouvert ending, and b^2 is derived from b^1 and a^1 (Ex. 33,* previous page).

Although the melody of the above example is clearly in the major mode, this is much rarer than in troubadour and trouvère songs, for Minnelied is not only more modal, but actually avoids the one mode, the Mixolydian, which of all the ecclesiastical modes comes closest to our major scale.

Among the more important Minnesinger there is one who has become widely known through the opera by Wagner which bears his name, Tannhauser [fl. mid-thirteenth century], who actually did take part in a Tournament of Song in 1207 together with another Minnesinger, Wolfram von Eschenbach [fl. *c.* 1200], the author of an epic poem called *Parzival* which Wagner used as the basis of his own opera of that name. Other Minnesinger include Neidhart von Reuenthal [*c.* 1180-*c.* 1240], Rumelant [fl. mid-thirteenth century], and Heinrich von Meissen [d. 1318], nicknamed Frauenlob because in a contest with another Minnesinger he strongly advocated the use of *Frau* (lady) instead of the more usual *Weib* (woman) when referring to the fair sex. With Frauenlob and his successors, such as Hugo von Montfort [1357–1423], the natural spontaneity of the movement diminished, although it must be remembered that much of their music which has come down to us was probably edited by the Meistersinger in the fifteenth and sixteenth centuries in order to conform to their rules; but more about them in Chapter 6. Undoubtedly the most outstanding Minnesinger is Walther von der Vogelweide [d. *c.* 1230], the model song composer for young David in Wagner's opera, *Die Meistersinger*. Born into the lower ranks of the nobility, Walther spent many years as a minstrel, singing songs of which he composed both words and music, and though most of the latter is fragmentary, enough remains to justify the very high regard of his contemporaries, and even to claim that artistically they are unequalled, let alone surpassed, by any German compositions before the late fifteenth century. Walther's ability to write his songs was by no means general among his fellow Minnesinger, for most of them had to dictate both poems and melodies to professional scribes in much the same way as some 'composers' of popular tunes do today.

* Adapted from F. L. Saran, *Die Jenaer Liederhandschrift*, Vol. II, p. 26.

Here is part of what is probably Walther's finest song, a Crusading song in which he prays for the deliverance of Jerusalem and ends with an exhortation to all men (Ex. 34*):

* Adapted from C. Bükler, *Untersuchungen zu den Melodien Walthers von der Vogelweide*, p. 79. (There are sixty more lines.)

So far we have traced the influence of the troubadour movement into northern France, eastwards into Italy, and north-eastwards into Germany. Now we will turn south into Spain, a country closely bound to France by cultural and political ties and where the visits of several troubadours, among them Guiraut de Bornelh and Guiraut Riquier, were mainly responsible for the rise of a native school of composers who wrote a large number of songs called 'cantigas', of which over 400 have survived. This number would certainly have been less had it not been for the enthusiasm of King Alfonso the Wise [reigned 1252–1284], who was responsible for their collection and who probably contributed some himself. Most of the cantigas, like the Italian laude, are religious but non-liturgical, being chiefly concerned with the miracles of the Virgin Mary, and this avoidance of the purely secular is a feature of Spanish music which persisted for several centuries, as we shall see. To be sure, there must have been popular songs and dances which owed nothing to religion both before and during the troubadour influence in the thirteenth century, but as usual they were either not written down or have since been lost.

The most common form of the cantigas is the same as the virelai, as in this delightful example. (Unfortunately, space does not permit the full story of the miracle to be told) (Ex. 35*).

Artistic movements, like armies, have always found it difficult to gain a foothold in Britain, and when, in 1152, Eleanor of Aquitaine married her countryman, Henry of Anjou, who later became Henry II of England [reigned 1154-1189], she was largely unsuccessful in her attempts to introduce troubadour song to the English Court, even though it is almost certain that the famous Bernart de Ventadorn himself paid a visit. Compared to the other European countries already mentioned, very few minstrel songs of the period have come down to us, mainly because the only language fit for literature, and therefore written by educated people, was the Norman-French of the trouvères, until the late thirteenth century, when it was gradually replaced by English (including Scots). Most of the songs that have survived are settings of religious texts in Latin, such as hymns to the Virgin or poems commemorating local saints like Thomas à Becket, whose murder was connived

* Transcribed from *Bulletin Hispanique*, Vol. XIII, Plate 10 (see also *The New Oxford History of Music*, Vol. II, p. 262).

at by Henry in 1170. Even the few purely secular songs in the vernacular often contain a moral (e.g. *Worldes blis*, *H.A.M.*,

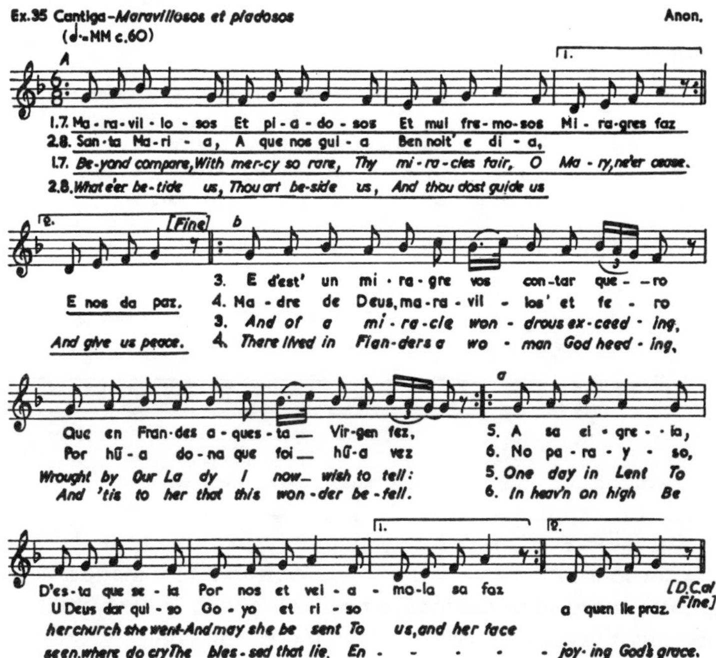

23B), but others express a more worldy sentiment, such as the plaintive longing of a lover for his mistress. The following charming example must have been typical of many others now unfortunately lost (Ex. 36* overleaf).

But the gay, springlike mood of mediaeval Britain was more truly reflected in her part-music (as we shall see in the next chapter) and her dances, for one has only to hum through Ex. 40C in *H.A.M.* to be struck by the vitality and freshness of this astonishingly modern-sounding piece with its fascinating three-part ending. The general name for mediaeval dances was 'estampie', and as they consist of a varying number of phrases each repeated twice (with ouvert and clos endings) they probably derived from the ecclesiastical sequence. (*H.A.M.*, 40B is a most attractive example.)

The instruments which played this dance music and which

* Adapted from J. Saltmarsh, 'Two Mediaeval Love Songs set to Music' *The Antiquaries Journal*, Vol. XV.

took part in the performances of solo song were many and varied, including all those mentioned in Chapter 2 except the great organ. The portative, however, and to a lesser degree the

positive, became exceedingly popular after the application of the keyboard in the early thirteenth century. This made a much greater speed of performance possible, and it is likely that the invention arose as a result of the increasing complexity of the upper parts in Pérotin's music and that of later composers. At first the sliders were replaced by pins, each with a button on the end which, when depressed by a finger, pushed open a valve and so admitted wind to the pipes. When the finger was lifted a spring automatically closed the valve. Soon afterwards the button was replaced by a wooden strip or key, hinged at one end, which when depressed operated the pin and valve as before. The great advantage of the key compared to the slider was that it was far less clumsy and therefore could be operated more quickly, and it was superior to the button in that it gave a larger surface for the finger to move on (see Plates X-XII).

The keyboard was obviously such a wonderful discovery, or rather rediscovery, that it cannot have been long before it was applied to a stringed instrument, and the one affected was the organistrum, which by the early thirteenth century had developed in two ways from that described in Chapter 2, p. 67. Firstly, it had become small enough for one player to turn the wheel and manipulate the bridges (Plate XII), and, secondly, the bridges had been replaced by sliding pieces of wood, each with two upright bits of wood (tangents.). When the sliders were pushed in the two tangents pressed against the two melody strings and 'stopped' them. It was soon discovered that if the sliders were pushed with sufficient force the impact of the tangents alone would cause the strings to sound—in other words, there was no need to excite the strings by means of the rosinned wheel. From this it was but a short step to constructing a tangent which would hit the string from below when a key was depressed. But this was only capable of playing a series of single notes, because there was only one string. When a number of strings were used the clavichord was born, but up till *c.* 1700 most of the strings still had more than one tangent and were thus called 'fretted' clavichords (see Chapter 6). The sound of this instrument was much softer and sweeter than the organistrum, and hence was only suitable (as it always has been) for intimate occasions. Its use in a church service would be quite out of the question.

Other instruments which so far as we know were used almost entirely outside the church were the lute, guitar, bagpipes, panpipes, horns, trumpets, and a few percussion instruments, such as castanets and triangles. The lute and guitar were plucked stringed instruments, the main difference between them lying in the shape of the body, the lute resembling a pear cut in half, while the guitar had a flat back and incurved ribs like the modern type, or the ukelele. The bagpipe, although it was known in the East before Christianity, achieved greater importance in Europe and has an unbroken history from Roman times to the present day. It was especially popular in the Middle Ages, and in fact it has been suggested that the sustained-tone organum of the twelfth and early thirteenth centuries was influenced by the instrument's characteristic drone. Panpipes too are still used today, though either as a toy or else by choir conductors or string players who have no piano handy. They have always consisted of a number of pipes bound together, each of different length and therefore of different pitch (see Plate I). The horn took its name from the material of which it was usually made, although wood and occasionally metal were sometimes used. Its chief function was in hunting and for signalling (see Plate IX). The same applies to the trumpet, and although both were known in various shapes and sizes in the East the trumpet appeared in Europe long before the horn, largely owing to its martial character, which the Romans fully exploited. Neither instrument could play more than two or three notes.

The songs of the troubadours and their imitators all over Europe were not only "the first great flowering of secular art", but also the last spontaneous outburst of monophony, the beauty, variety, and perfection of which has only recently begun to be appreciated, and it is high time that a selection of these songs with suitable translations was published separately as well as included in future editions of popular song-collections.

Up to the end of the twelfth century all part-music was composed for the church and all secular music was monophonic, but from *c.* 1200 onwards part-music was increasingly used for both sacred and secular purposes, while monophony declined. Moreover, the style of part-music in the thirteenth century was universal—in other words, there was no musical difference between a part-composition written for a saint's day, a secular song, and an instrumental dance for portative organ, vièle, and recorder. Of this style Pérotin was the founder.

PERFORMANCE

(See also pp. 76, 78.)

The songs of this period were almost certainly accompanied, usually by a plucked instrument, when originally sung, but as the modern equivalents (harp, lute, guitar) are not generally available they may be sung by a solo voice with a violin, viola, recorder, flute, or oboe doubling the refrain, when there is one. In Ex. 32 the refrain might well have been sung by a number of voices with the addition of some percussive instrument, such as a small drum or triangle.

4

THE ALL-EMBRACING STYLE OF THE THIRTEENTH CENTURY

"It may be granted that Mozart's religious feeling comes out most fully in his motets and they, together with the best of such pieces by other composers, may fittingly enough find a place in any but the most solemn services. But as for the Masses of Haydn, Mozart and Beethoven, I must confess my utter inability to understand how anyone immersed in prayer can listen to them, or listening to them, pray. . . . Haydn and Mozart wrote to please their patrons; Beethoven, with his 'Man, help thyself' and 'The starry heavens above us the moral law within us' was many a long league away from the old Catholic feeling. All three wrote first and foremost as modern composers, using every device they knew to add to the purely musical interest of their work. Sincere they were, but their sincerity was another thing from the profound naïve sincerity of the earlier men.

"The older music rolls along without a suggestion of display, lovely melody winding round lovely melody, and all combining to form a broad, sweeping, harmonious mass of tone that carries the spirit resistlessly with it. This is the true devotional music."*

There always have been and there probably always will be people whose attitude to church music makes them think, speak, or write in a manner similar to the above. It is the same kind of outlook that believes laughter in church to be irreverent and that to dress in one's best suit promotes piety. Such people lack the imagination to see that what is offensive to them may be quite acceptable to others, or that what is intolerable now may well have been completely satisfying in the past. On the other hand, there is a very common belief that at certain times in the past church music has been written which represents the ideal. The Catholic Church, for instance, states categorically

* From the *Morning Post*, quoted in R. Terry's *Catholic Church Music*, 1907, p. 50.

that Gregorian chant, and to a slightly lesser extent the masses and motets of Palestrina in the sixteenth century, are to be regarded as the highest attainments in this sphere, and that the farther more recent compositions stray from the atmosphere of these works the less suitable are they for the liturgy. The Catholic Church is not alone in this respect, for several other religious bodies have, at various periods in history, severely restricted the nature and use of church music. But what is important surely is not only what I personally feel to be a devout piece of music, which appeals to me both religiously and artistically, but also that I should tolerate and try to understand music which, while striking no chord in me, clearly means or has meant a great deal to others. In other words, any artistic creation is acceptable to God provided its creator has given of his best. What should not be tolerated is work that is slipshod or that is, with a tongue-in-the-cheek attitude, deliberately written in a style that is popularly regarded as suitable for church, but which is foreign to the creator's own. You may prefer the famous *Missa Papae Marcelli* of Palestrina to the *Missa Solemnis* of Beethoven, but that is no reason for saying that one is more religious than the other. You may find the use of a large orchestra in church objectionable, but to Beethoven this was the only way by which he could fully express all he had to say.

It is frequently forgotten when holding up Palestrina as a paragon composer of church music that not only was there very little difference in style between his sacred and secular work, but that he actually based some of his masses on secular pieces either by himself or others, even after this procedure had been condemned by ecclesiastical authority, and that in the *Missa Papae Marcelli*, which is usually regarded as a model church composition, he begins three of the movements with the first phrase of an extremely well-known French song. In so doing he was merely conforming, albeit unconsciously, to a tradition which stretched back to the early days of Christian chant (see Chapter 1, p. 5).

The differences between sacred and secular styles in the thirteenth century were far fewer, however, than in the sixteenth century—in fact, as the century progressed the musical distinction between the two completely disappeared. Round about 1200 there were three styles, organum, clausula, and conductus; the first two, which we have already described in Chapter 2, were used exclusively in the liturgy, but the third style was frequently used for secular texts, and even when sung in church was not so intimately connected with the liturgy as were organum and clausula.

The thirteenth-century conductus was so called because it had three features in common with the Latin songs of the same name mentioned in Chapter 3; these are metrical texts in Latin, syllabic underlay of the music, and the fact that, generally speaking, all the parts are newly composed. All these features distinguish the conductus from organum and clausula, in which the words are almost invariably in prose, with many notes to a syllable, and the tenor part is borrowed.

A further difference is that none of the parts in a conductus are arranged in repeated rhythmic patterns, and they all move together in the same rhythm, i.e. contrapuntally like a clausula, but unlike the polyphonic organum. It was also the first kind of part-music in which a composer could give completely free rein to his melodic invention. Sometimes, however, a composer would incorporate part of an existing clausula, with its rhythmically organized Gregorian tenor, into a conductus, probably because a word or even a syllable of his secular poem reminded him of part of a clausula set to the same word or syllable which he or someone else had already composed. This procedure is the reverse of that practised by Palestrina, for example (see above), but because something intimately connected with the liturgy was torn from its context and used in a secular work it too may well have caused a frown in high places.

The conductus was extremely popular from the time of Pérotin to about 1250, and it covered a similar range of subjects as those mentioned in Chapter 3. Here, for example, is a very fine one, possibly composed by Léonin, in which the poem expresses both grief and indignation at the murder of Thomas à Becket on 29th December 1170 (Ex. 37* overleaf).

Léonin (if it was he) was not the first to write in this style, for *Mira Lege* from the St. Martial School (Ex. 20) was, as we noted in Chapter 2, a forerunner of conductus style. The origin of this kind of composition, however, probably came from Britain or Scandinavia, for all British compositions of the late twelfth and early thirteenth centuries are less polyphonic and more

* Adapted from H. Gleason, *Examples of Music before 1400*, p. 43.

contrapuntal than those of the contemporary Notre Dame School, and, as we shall see, this preference for the more sonorous and full-blooded effect of all parts moving together was a characteristic of British music for some time to come. Another pointer in the same direction is the fact that thirds and sixths were used to a far greater extent in Britain than on the Continent, and these 'imperfect' concords were then, as they are today, richer in sound than the fourth, fifth, or octave.

The evidence that British music was different from Continental and that this difference was due mainly to the preference for the 'imperfect' concords, especially thirds, is fourfold. Firstly, an excerpt from a manuscript, *Descriptio Kambriae*, by a certain Gerald de Barri or, to give him his more usual Latinized name, Giraldus Cambrensis [*c.* 1147–1220], in which he describes his travels in Wales. The excerpt in question states that improvised singing in a number of different parts was a frequent practice with Welshmen, and that the same kind of singing, but in two parts only, was also heard in northern England. He stresses the fact that this kind of two-part singing was not general in Great Britain and suggests that it came from the Danes and Norwegians, who had frequently invaded our northern coasts. Gerald was a cultured, widely-travelled man who came from an aristocratic family and was well known in scholarly circles both abroad and at home; thus the singing he describes must have been markedly different from that on the Continent for him to single it out for special mention. Secondly, the thirteenth-century theorist known as Anonymous IV, who was probably an Englishman, states that major and minor thirds were esteemed the best consonances in the West of England, which would include Wales. Thirdly, the few examples of late twelfth- and thirteenth-century British part-music that have come down to us show a greater use of thirds and sixths than contemporary Continental pieces. And, fourthly, there exists a twelfth-century hymn, probably written in the Orkneys, which is almost entirely a succession of thirds (see *H.A.M.*, 25c). The Orkneys were a Norwegian possession from the ninth to the fifteenth centuries, and if Gerald's suggestion is correct then the singing he describes was almost certainly similar to that notated in this hymn.

The next example (Ex. 38,* p. 100) should be compared with Ex. 37.

This stirring, possibly processional, song, with its repeated first and last phrases in the lower part, is noteworthy not only because of the number of thirds it contains, but also because of its word-painting—that is, the composer has portrayed the sense of the words in his music. Thus in the third phrase, the line "Now are rich men trodden down" ("Dives nunc deprimitur"), both parts descend, and at the end of the piece the voices

* Adapted from A. Einstein, *A Short History of Music* (5th Ed.), p. 206.

have a whole 'flight' of notes on the word 'winging' ('fugatur'). Admittedly it was quite common (but entirely optional) to end a conductus with what was then called a 'cauda' ('tail'), but the fact that the poem ends with this word (perhaps a deliberate choice by the poet if he had a musical setting in mind) must clearly have influenced the composer.

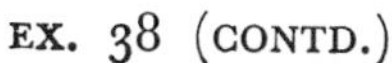

Redit aetas aurea was composed for and probably sung at the Coronation of Richard I (the Lion-hearted) in 1189, and its English origin is therefore certain. What is not so certain (and this applies to all conducti) is the way it should be transcribed, for the music, with its syllabic underlay and metrical verse, is not notated in modal rhythm, and hence gives the modern editor less help than in the case of organa. Despite this rhythmically vague notation, however, most scholars now agree that all conducti were in fact performed in one of the rhythmic modes, though the choice of which one is often difficult to decide.

Although the conductus was only popular during the first half of the thirteenth century on the Continent, it persisted in Britain in various modified forms up to *c.* 1450. The earliest of these modified forms was called 'gymel' (but the name was not used before the fifteenth century), which is an Anglicized abbreviation of the Latin 'cantus gemellus', or 'twin song', and its two parts move mostly in a succession of thirds and sixths. Later, in keeping with the British love of sonority, a third part was sometimes added, with the result that nearly every 'chord' contains a third or a sixth as compared to the fourths and fifths of Continental compositions (Ex. 39*).

* Transcribed from *Early English Harmony* (ed. Wooldridge), Vol. I, Plate 36.

Ex.39 Gymel style-Salve virgo virginum
Anon. Late 13th cent.
(𝅗𝅥 = 𝅘𝅥. = MM c.80)
1. Sal - ve vir - go vir - gi - num, Pa - rens ge - ni -
1. Hail, thou maid of maids most rare, Source of in - spi -
2. Sal - ve vir - go re - gi - a, Por - ta sa - lu -
2. Hail, thou maid of roy'l de - scent, Through whom we're re -
3. A - ve no - stra spe - i, Fi - nis et sa -
3. Wel - come thou, our hope al - ways, Sav'd and sin - ners
-to - ris: Sal - ve lu - men lu - mi - num, Ra - di - us splen
-ra - tion: Hail, thou light be - yond com - pare, Ray of con - so -
-ta - ris: Ve - rax ve - ri nes - ci - a Qui - a de - um
-cei - ved: True thou wert and in - no - cent, nor by sin de -
-lu - tis; A - ve per quam re - i Le - tan - tur eum
sing - eth: Wel - come thou, whose glo - rious rays Our sal - va - tion
-do - ris: Sal - ve flos con - val - li - um, Stil - la ve - ri
-la - tion: Hail, thou beau - teous flow'r so fair, Dew of our sal -
pa - ris: A - ve qui - a de - i - ta Pro - le fe - cun -
-cei - ved: Hail, for God om - ni - po - tent In thy womb con -
tu - is; A - ve spe - ci - e - i, De - cus et sa -
bring - eth; Wel - come thou, to whom all praise In our hearts we
ro - ris: No - stra spes in te.
-va - tion: Our hope is in thee,
-da - ris: No - stra spes in te.
-cei - ved: Our hope is in thee.
-lu - tis: No - stra spes in te.
ring - eth: Our hope is in thee.

There is little doubt that in the above hymn to the Virgin Mary the two lower voices are the original gymel, for they move almost entirely in thirds, but the topmost voice adds considerably to the sonority of the piece by frequently singing the fifth above the lowest note, and as a result nearly half the chords are full major or minor triads (i.e. chords consisting of the root, third, and fifth). In the original the words are placed beneath the lowest voice only, but they were meant to be sung by any or all of the parts.

Although the rich effect of the gymel sounds surprisingly modern to our harmonically-conditioned ears, and although the melodies are often charmingly fresh and simple, it is most probable that to a thirteenth-century Frenchman such music was out of date and not nearly so expressive, artistic, or subtle as the motet, which, from about 1225, was all the rage in France, its popularity being the main reason for the decline of the conductus.

The origin of the motet can be traced back to a few organa of the St. Martial School in which the two parts sing different words (see Ex. 19), a different text from the tenor being added to the florid upper part, probably as an aid to the singer (compare the origin of the sequence in Chapter 1, p. 21). That this idea was not adopted at first by the Notre Dame School may have been due to ecclesiastical objections that the words of the chant in the tenor would be obscured by the simultaneous rendering of a completely different text in the upper voice. In the early years of the thirteenth century, however, the idea was applied to the conductus which, being in the main a secular type, could not possibly have offended the authorities on religious grounds. The result was a class of composition now called 'conductus motet': conductus because none of the voices uses a borrowed melody and all move together in the same rhythm, motet because the upper part or parts have different words from the tenor.

The singing of two or more texts at the same time (polytextuality) was clearly popular with the Notre Dame and later composers, for, disregarding the admonishments of the clergy, they added different texts to the upper part or parts of some of their clausulae, thus producing the motet proper. The chant melodies in the tenor part of most clausulae are, as we saw in Chapter 2, arranged in repeated rhythmic patterns, and this feature is one of the main characteristics of most thirteenth-century motets, the other and more important being polytextuality. The name 'motet' comes from the Latin *motetus*, which in its turn was derived from the French word *mot* (='word'), and the part immediately above the tenor, which in organa was called duplum, was now called 'motetus' because new 'words' were added to it, and the name was soon applied to all compositions of this type.

Because the clausulae were an integral part of the liturgy, so were those motets in which new words were simply added to the upper voice or voices of the former. It was not long, however, before the motet became an independent type of composition, but it was still used liturgically, for it was still based on a Gregorian melody in the tenor while the words of the upper part or parts were poetic paraphrases of those of the chant. For instance, in Ex. 40 the tenor is taken from the Gradual sung during the Feast of the Assumption of the Blessed Virgin Mary which begins 'Propter veritatem', the notes in the tenor being those that are sung to the word 'veritatem' in the original chant. The words of the two upper parts are poems in honour of the Virgin—in fact, the fifth line in the motetus part, "And he didst raise thee up this day" ("Qui te assumpsit hodie"), refers specifically to the Assumption; thus the whole composition is a wonderfully subtle and expressive hymn of praise to Our Lady (Ex. 40*):

This is a more than usually interesting motet because, although the twice-stated tenor melody, unlike most, is not arranged in repeated rhythmic patterns, the two upper parts have very definite structures which have been shown by letters, the motetus being *ab bb ab ab* while the triplum is *AB CC AB AB*, which is identical with the troubadour and trouvère virelai (see Chapter 3, p. 81). Furthermore, the melody of the motetus has been lifted bodily from a troubadour song.

Although the actual intrusion of secular songs or song-forms into the liturgical motet is not very common, there is no doubt that the lyricism of the former considerably influenced the latter and contributed greatly to a musical style which made no distinction between sacred and secular; thus the only difference between a motet or conductus which portrays the joys of the blessed in Paradise and one which paints the delights of wine, women, and song in Paris (as in Ex. 41,† pp. 106-7) is the words.

* From Y. Rokseth, *Motets du XIIIe Siècle*, p. 10. † Adapted from *H.A.M.*, 33B.

Ex.40 Motet-Post partum virgo transisti-Ave regina-Veritatem
Anon. 13th. cent.
(Triplum)
(Motetus)
(Tenor)
Post par - tum vir - go man-sis-ti in - vi - o - la - ta
A vir - gin, though a child didst bear, O Ma - ry mild with-
A - ve re-gi - na glo - ri - e — et an - ge - lo - rum
To thee, O glo - rious queen, A - ve! — Who with the an - gels
[Ve - ri - ta -
Ma - ri - a, qui fi - li - um pe - pe - ri - sti cui- - us fi - li - a
out a flaw, Who bore a son in ho - ly fear, Of whom thou wert the
spe - cu - lum, que pe - pe - ri - sti do - mi - num tri - um - pha - to - rum
now art nigh. Thou bore our Je - su, who didst die To tri - umph o - ver
fu - i - sti; et par - tu tu - o fe - ci - sti stu - pe - re na - tu -
daugh - ter dear; And by thine act it doth ap-pear All things do gaze at
o - mni - um, qui te as - sum - psit ho - di - e ad e - the - re - um
earth and sky; And He didst raise thee up this day To see the heav'n - ly
— tem, ve - ri - ta -
-ra - li - a. Te pre - ca - mor ma - ter Chri - sti e - sto no - bis pro - pi - ti - a.
thee in awe. O Je - su's moth - er that thou'lt hear Our pray'rs to thee we thee im - plore.
tha - la - mum, et in san - cto - rum re - qui - e — fru - ens per - he - nne gau - di - um.
realms on high, E - ter - nal bliss to taste al - way, And e - ver with the blest to lie.
- tem.]

Ex.41 Motet - On parole - A Paris - Frèse nouvele
Anon. 13th.cent.
(Triplum)
(Motetus)
Tenor
On pa - ro - le de ba-tre et de van - ner Et de fo - ïr et de han-ner,
They speak of thresh-ing and of win-now-ing, Of dig - ging and of har-row-ing,
A Pa - ris soir et ma - - tin Truev' on
At Pa - ris, night or day - - time, One finds
Frè - - se nou - ve - - - - le! Mue - re fran - -
Fresh fine straw - - ber - - - - ries! Black-ber-ries,
Mais ces de-duis trop me des - plai - - - sent, Car il
But these sil - ly pas - times I spurn ay, For the
bon pain et bon cler vin, Bon - ne char
good bread and good clear wine, Good meat and
- ce, mue - re, mue - re fran - - - - ce! [Frè - - se nou - -
come buy my wild black - ber - - - - ries! Fresh fine straw - -
n'est si bon - ne vi - e Que d'est - re a ai - se
life that e'er doth me please Is the life of ease,
et bon pois - - son, De tou - - tes gui - ses com-pai -
good fish to eat, And a great ma - ny folk to
- ve - - - le! Mue - re fran - - ce, mue - re, mue - re,
- ber - - - ries! Black-ber-ries, come buy my wild black -

EX. 41 (CONTD.)

De bon cler vin et de cha - - pons, Et d'est - re a - - veue bons com -
With ca - pons fat and beau - jo - - - lais, And with good com - pa - ny
- gnons, Sens sou - - ti - - - - - e, grant
great. Spark-ling wit and joy
fran - - - - - ce! Frè - - - - se nou - -
- ber - - - - - ries! Fresh fine straw - -
- pai - gnons, Liés et joi - - ans, Chan-tans, truf - - fans et a - mo - rous,
al - way, So blithe and gay, sing-ing, cheat - - ing and a - mo - rous;
bau - - - dour, Biaus joi-aus da - - mes dou - - - nour,
is there, And ma-ny fine la - dies fair;
- ve - - - - le! Mue-re fran - - ce, mue-re, mue-re fran - -
- ber - - - - ries! Black-ber-ries, come buy my wild black - ber - - -
Et d'a - - - voir, quant c'on a mes-tier, Pour so - la - -
And to have, when we need so-lace, The fair of
Et si truev' on bien en - - - - - tre-deus
And some good times there are one finds when
- ce! Frè - - se nou - - ve - - - - le
- ries! Fresh fine straw - - ber - - - - ries
- cier Be - les da - mes a de - vis: Et tout ce truev'on a Pa - - ris.
face, Those la - dies ex - - ceed - ing kind: And all this in Pa - - ris you find.
De men - re feur pour ho - mes de - - si - - teus.
Food and drink can be shared by all poor men.
Mue - re fran - - - - ce, mue - re, mue - re fran - - - - - ce!]
Black-ber-ries, come buy my wild black - ber - - - - - ries!

The thirteenth-century motet has often been regarded as the most difficult type of composition to understand and appreciate in the whole history of western music before the twentieth century, not only because of the simultaneous performance of two or more different texts, sometimes in two different languages, e.g. French and Latin, but also because the actual sound of the music is bare, even harsh, when compared to the more sonorous, smoothly-flowing conductus.

The whole point of polytextuality, to begin with at any rate, was to enrich the chant by adding fresh words, usually in verse, which enshrined and expanded the meaning or purpose contained in the chant itself, as in Ex. 40; thus the authors of these added texts were stimulated by the same desire as that which prompted the writers of tropes and sequences. As for the largely incomprehensible jumble of words which inevitably results during a performance, two points should be borne in mind. Firstly, that this music, and in fact practically all music up to about 1600, was not intended for the general public; this applies to the liturgical as well as to the purely secular motet. In the former it was—and still is in cathedrals and monasteries—the act of worship expressed through the service that mattered, not the presence or absence of a congregation, and to the choirmen themselves and even to the officiating clergy the subtle technique in which two or three different texts simultaneously express the same sentiments would be fully intelligible and eminently satisfying. The same applies to the secular motet, which was always written for and performed by the cultured *élite* of society. The second point to remember is that the singing of different words at the same time has been a favourite and most dramatic operatic device from Mozart to the present day; in fact, operatic ensembles frequently go further than the average thirteenth-century motet because they express several different and often completely opposed sentiments, but as the audience knows roughly what these sentiments are from the previous action of the drama, it simply abandons itself to the total impression. Similarly in the thirteenth century; but it is also quite likely that when performing a motet like Ex. 40 or 41, particularly for the first time, only the tenor part was sung or played to begin with, then the tenor and motetus parts together, and finally the whole composition, with instruments either playing the unsung parts or else doubling the voices.

The manner of performance suggested above describes exactly the method by which a composer wrote a motet, for he first of all selected a melodic fragment, either from a chant or a secular song, and, having arranged the notes in repeated rhythmic patterns and decided on the number of repeats of the melody, he used this as his tenor, the basis of his composition. (The tenor of Ex. 41 may have been newly composed; if so, it was exceptional. On the other hand, it may have been a popular street-cry of the times.) Next he added the motetus, and finally the triplum. This is known as 'successive composition', and is clearly shown in Ex. 40, where both the upper parts are very attractive melodies, and if one were omitted the piece as a whole would not suffer greatly—in fact, to many ears it would gain, for it is between the upper parts that the most licence was allowed and the greatest dissonance occurs; in other words, provided that each upper part was concordant with the tenor at the beginning of every group of three 'beats', it did not matter what happened between the upper parts themselves. The concords were the unison, fifth, and their octaves (though some theorists included the major and minor thirds as well), and although a discord in the form of an accented passing note was permitted on the first 'beat', it had to resolve on to a concord. Thus the whole conception of polyphonic composition was very different from the normal one of today, which considers the sound of *all* the parts, both vertically as chords and horizontally as melodies. The thirteenth-century composer, indeed, enjoyed greater freedom than any composer between the fourteenth and twentieth centuries. Consecutive unisons, fifths, and octaves between the tenor and any other part were allowed because they were liked, while consecutive fourths, seconds, and sevenths between the upper parts were probably regarded as spicy discords which were subordinate to, while at the same time offsetting, the fundamental concords with the tenor.

So far we have only dealt with the purely liturgical and wholly secular motet. But there was another kind which seems positively blasphemous at first, for it combined both sacred and secular texts—for instance, a hymn to the Virgin Mary and a poem in which a lover yearns for his sweetheart (*H.A.M.*, 32B). Occasionally the two texts had nothing in common, but usually, as in the above instance, they were linked in the sense that they expressed much the same sentiments, only on different planes. This blending of sacred and secular was not peculiar to musicians, for once again we find an exact parallel in the architecture of the period, or, rather, the sculpture that formed an integral part of the magnificent Gothic cathedrals which reached their greatest perfection in France during the thirteenth century. As we saw in Chapter 2, the rigid, unnaturally-posed figures of the twelfth century were subordinated to the column they ornamented or to the design as a whole, but in the thirteenth century not only did decoration become increasingly rich and more widely used, but it also became more naturalistic. Figures became human, with smiling faces, tilted heads, expressive hands, and their clothing arranged in natural folds. The austere symbolic dignity of the earlier portrayals of Mary and the infant Jesus now gave way to the everyday picture of mother and child; humanity reflected divinity. Although the subject-matter, general treatment, and placing of the main pieces of sculpture were dictated by the Church, the less important or conspicuous places were apparently left to the carvers in wood and stone to do what they liked with, and it is in these places that one sees most clearly the increasing naturalism of the century. Animals, plants, mythological monsters, and fantastic—even grotesque—figures, half man, half beast, can be found tucked away in corners or high overhead, both inside and outside the cathedral.

Thus the thirteenth-century craftsmen and composers alike saw nothing incongruous or irreverent in associating things secular with things sacred, and both sculpture and motet represented what might well be called the 'art of analogy', in which the experiences and wonder of this world were used to help understand and partially reflect the glory of God; and it was no coincidence that this conception of the relationship between divinity and humanity was one of the main themes running through the works and teaching of the Church's most brilliant and saintly scholar, Thomas Aquinas.

The changes in the motet during the thirteenth century were not limited only to the use of the vernacular (French) or to the borrowings from earlier secular songs, for a casual comparison between Exx. 40 and 41 will show that the triplum part has become much more animated compared to the other parts during the twenty-five years or so which separates the two pieces—in other words, the tendency throughout the century was towards greater rhythmic independence of the parts.

The difference between the number of notes in the upper voices and in the tenor led to a new way of arranging the parts, for it was clearly wasteful to continue writing in score when the tenor had so few notes compared to the others, and parchment was very expensive. The most economical method was to write the parts separately and so use up as much of the page as possible, like this:

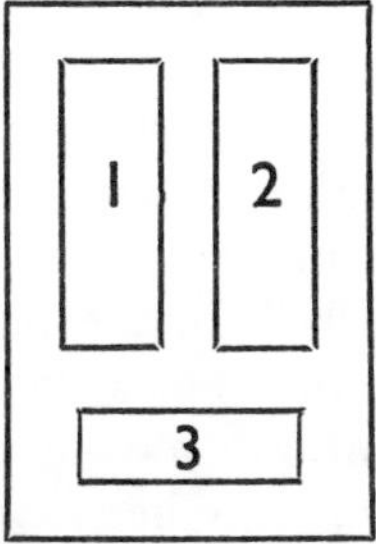

Where 1 is the triplum part, 2 the motetus, and 3 the tenor. If the motet was too long for a single page it was usually spread over two pages in this manner:

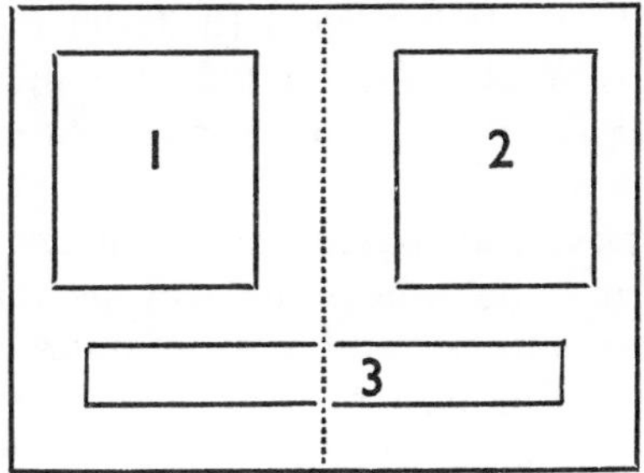

This separating of the parts on one or two pages (usually called 'choir-book' arrangement today or, in the fifteenth and sixteenth centuries, 'cantus collateralis', i.e. 'song [written] side by side' (see Chapter 6)—was used from about 1225 to about 1600 for practically all manuscript music except that written in conductus style, which was always written in score because all the voices have roughly the same number of notes.

The rhythmic independence of the parts in the motet is usually compensated by the repeated patterns in the tenor which give a basic rhythmic unity to the whole piece, and the more frequent but still fairly rare use of voice-exchange, an extreme example being the motet *Alle-psallite cum-luya* (*H.A.M.*, 33A), in which the two upper voices swop every phrase except the last. (The text, incidentally, is rather curious in that it consists of three tropes of the word 'Alleluya'.)

A more complex form of voice-exchange is the British 'rondellus', in which all three voices exchange phrases, but the most famous and remarkable piece of imitative writing is the so-called Reading Rota, *Sumer is icumen in*, which probably dates from the middle of the century. This six-part double canon is so well known that we shall not describe it in detail, but simply point out that technically it was far more ambitious than anything on the Continent until the fifteenth century, and that it cannot have been a flash in the pan, but must have been preceded by a number of other such pieces, which alas have not survived. It is ambitious, too, in its use of six voices, and this supports what has already been said about the British love of sonority.

The increasing animation of the upper voices, particularly the triplum, developed rapidly during the last half of the century, and reached its peak in the motets of a certain Petrus de Cruce (or Pierre de la Croix) [fl. latter half of thirteenth century], and as he played a vital part in altering the way in which music was written down we must first of all see what it was that he altered.

Up to about 1225 all part-music, with one exception, was written down in much the same way as that described in Chapter 2—that is to say, in groups of notes called 'ligatures' in which the alternations of long and short notes depend entirely on the arrangement of the ligatures. The exception was the conductus, in which ligatures could not be regularly used, because each syllable of the text corresponds roughly to one note. The same became true of the motet, and composers found it necessary to make clear to the singers which notes were long and which short; they therefore made two of the note shapes already in use in ligatures independent; these were the 'longa' (the 'virga' of Gregorian chant) and the 'brevis' (the 'punctum' of Gregorian chant). Later on (*c.* 1250), because composers wanted to write more flexible and expressive melodies, a shorter note value came into use, the 'semibrevis', with the shape ◆, also borrowed from Gregorian chant, but this (unlike the long and breve) had no independent existence and was regarded simply as a breve broken up, and hence could only be used in groups of two or three per breve unit. All these changes spelt the death of the old ligature groupings, and round about 1250 a theorist called Franco of Cologne [fl. *c.* 1250-after 1280] introduced a new notation in an admirable set of rules which he expounded in his *Ars Cantus Mensurabilis* ('The Art of Measured Song').

Franco's rules can be summarized as follows:

1. As in the older notation, the number three is the only perfect one.
2. There are four note shapes, the duplex longa, longa, brevis, and semibrevis, of which only the first three may be used singly.
3. The standard note value (tactus) is now the perfect breve, not the perfect long.
4. The double long has only one value, while the other three may each have two values, and these are reckoned by the perfect breve, thus (modern equivalents are placed in brackets):

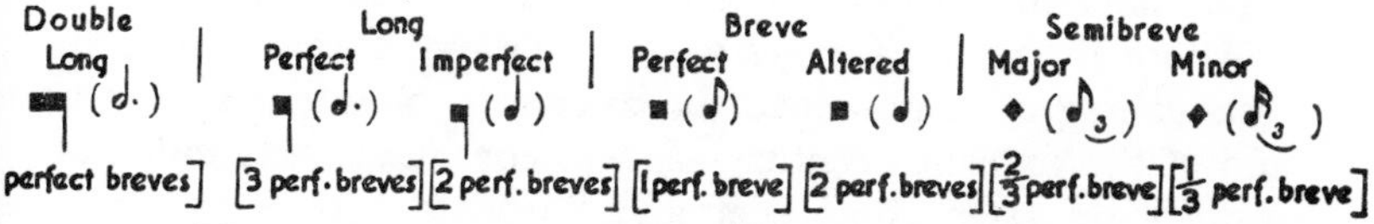

Double Long	Long: Perfect	Long: Imperfect	Breve: Perfect	Breve: Altered	Semibreve: Major	Semibreve: Minor
perfect breves]	[3 perf. breves]	[2 perf. breves]	[1 perf. breve]	[2 perf. breves]	[⅔ perf. breve]	[⅓ perf. breve]

(N.B.—Discounting the double long, only the perfect long and the perfect breve may be used singly, for an imperfect long must be followed or preceded by a perfect breve, and an altered breve must be preceded by a perfect breve.)

The values of the long (*L*), breve (*B*), and semibreve (*S*) depend on their position, e.g. (in modern notation and with bar lines):

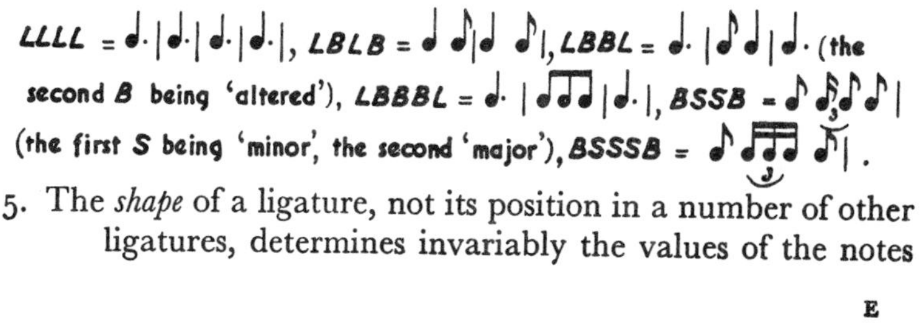

LLLL = | | | |, *LBLB* = | |, *LBBL* = | | (the second *B* being 'altered'), *LBBBL* = | | |, *BSSB* = | (the first *S* being 'minor', the second 'major'), *BSSSB* = | .

5. The *shape* of a ligature, not its position in a number of other ligatures, determines invariably the values of the notes

E

it contains, so that now the ligature ▝▖, for example, always means two perfect breves (♩♩), whereas before it could mean either *L B* (♩ ♪) or *L B* (♪♩), depending on whether it was written in the first or second rhythmic modes.

6. The vertical lines of haphazard length which marked off the ordines in the earlier notation and which stood for rests of varying duration are now replaced by lines of definite length which represent different rests (see Fig. 2).

While much of Franco's *Ars Cantus Mensurabilis*, like most theoretical works, simply summarizes previous practice, some of his rules are new and were clearly formulated in order to achieve a greater degree of consistency in notation—for example, his exact evaluations of ligatures and his rigid ternary division of the breve. As regards the latter, we have already seen that duple time almost certainly existed in the twelfth and thirteenth centuries in both monophony and part-music (see Chapter 2, pp. 49-50, and Chapter 3, pp. 85-86), and in fact there are a few pre-Franconian pieces that admit of no other interpretation; moreover, the very word '*semi*breve' must surely have meant that originally the breve was 'halved'.

Although the advantages of Franco's system outweighed its disadvantages—it remained the basis of all notation up to the end of the sixteenth century—it was continually expanded or pruned by later composers and theorists. To begin with, composers found that they needed a note smaller than the semibreve in order to be able to write more lively and quicker-moving melodies, particularly in the triplum part of their motets. To us the obvious solution would have been to invent a different note shape, but the idea of creating something completely new was largely foreign to the thirteenth-century mind; thus in the motet the most important part—the tenor—was borrowed, the upper voices were mostly made up of well-established melodic fragments, and even the note shapes themselves, the long, breve, and semibreve, had existed previously in Gregorian chant. What happened then was that round about 1280 certain composers, of whom Petrus de Cruce seems to have been the first and most important, continued to use the shape of the semibreve, but gave it values ranging from two-thirds of a breve (as with Franco) to one-seventh of a breve, and in order to show how many semibreves were meant to be sung in the time of a breve they marked off the groups by placing a long, or a breve, or a long or breve rest, or a ligature, or a dot at the beginning and end of each group. The dot in fact served much the same purpose as our modern bar-line, and although to our way of thinking it represents a real step forward in helping to make the notation clearer, in actual fact it did not remain in use for very long, for reasons which will become plain in the next chapter.

Another disadvantage of Franco's system was that it did not admit what we should call duple time, but only triple—in other words, a perfect long or breve could not be divided into two equal parts, but although duple time did not come into its own until the fourteenth century, Petronian notation (i.e. that used by Petrus de Cruce) prepared the way by, for example, making four semibreves equal a perfect breve, and the division of the latter into five or seven parts heralded the fall from power of the number three (*H.A.M.*, 34, 35; see Fig. 2*).

FIG. 2 Petronian notation. The last part of the motetus (left hand column) and duplum, and the complete tenor (bottom stave of both columns, right to left) from the motet *Garrit gallus—In nova fert. Le Roman de Fauvel.* (See Chapter 5.) Note the semibreve groupings by means of dots, rests, etc., and the semibreves with downward tails, e.g. motetus stave 1, 3rd note, stave 2, 5th note. The white ligatures in the tenor are red in the original. (See Ex. 51.)

* Facsimile in W. Apel, *The Notation of Polyphonic Music, 900-1600*, 4th Ed., p. 331.

Petrus de Cruce and his fellow composers wrote both sacred and secular motets, but the number of the latter was beginning to outstrip the former as the preference for secular song became stronger—a preference which reached its peak in the next century. Alongside this trend and to some extent linked with it was the growing independence of the composer, who, having established a musical style capable of enriching the liturgy on the one hand and courtly entertainments on the other, increasingly favoured the latter because it gave him more scope for experiments and was not subject to such dictatorial authority. His treatment of the words he set shows another side to his independence, for the subtlety and expressive qualities of his music began to assume greater importance than they had previously, and many late-thirteenth-century motets disregard the natural accents of the text in a most flagrant manner, largely owing to the rapid groups of semibreves syllabically underlaid. The result is sometimes grotesque, but then so are many of the gargoyles on Gothic cathedrals. Admittedly we do not know the exact speed at which Petrus de Cruce's motets (or any other mediaeval music) were performed, but because the breve was now the unit of time this did not mean that it was twice or thrice as quick as the long in the time of Pérotin. In fact there are good grounds for believing that the unit of time, no matter what its note value, has remained fairly constant right through history for what we might call standard pieces, and is roughly equal to the human heart-beat, i.e. between M.M. 70 and 80. (By standard pieces is meant those that require no pronounced subjective interpretation, such as the average hymn-tune. For further discussion on this point, see Chapter 6.) Of course, the speed of the time unit has not always remained the same because there must always be an interim period during the changeover from one time unit to another, and the introduction of shorter note values also had its effect. Thus, Pérotin's time unit, the long, would be about M.M. 80 (the breve therefore being about M.M. 240), but with Franco the changeover to the breve time unit had only just begun and the long was still an important note, with the result that the breve was neither as fast as it was in Pérotin's music nor as slow as it should have been, so to speak, i.e.M. M. 80; it was probably about M.M. 130. Petrus de Cruce's groups of semibreves, however, must have slowed the breve down considerably, and in his music it must have been about M.M. 55. We shall see in the next chapter that the breve became slower still because the semibreve became the new time unit.

The increasing animation of the motet during the thirteenth century and the growing delight in music for its own sake are perhaps most clearly shown in the curious—even bizarre—type of composition called 'hocket' (French, *hoquet*='hiccup'). In its simplest form this is a two-part piece in which each note of the tenor melody is repeated in the other part (called 'hoquetus'), with the voices singing and resting alternately (Ex. 42).

The number of actual hocket compositions are few, but it became a popular means of ornamenting part-music, particularly motets (*H.A.M.*, 35, bars 8, 9, 17, 18, etc.), and while we know that this device was used in primitive music, no European examples earlier than the thirteenth century have come down to us, although Aelred (see Chapter 2, p. 69) describes what is presumably hocketing in his *Speculum Charitatis*: "Sometimes thou may'st see a man with an open mouth, not to sing but, as it were to breathe out his last gaspe, by shutting in his breathe, and by a certaine ridiculous interception of his voyce, as it were to threaten silence, and now againe to imitate the agonies of a dying man, or the extasies of such as suffer."*

It was almost inevitable, considering the growing popularity of part-music during the thirteenth century, that some of the more educated trouvères would compose pieces in which the forms of the solo song, especially the rondeau, virelai, and ballade, are set polyphonically. This fusing of the old with the new produced an art form which reached its peak in the fourteenth century, but it had already caught on in the thirteenth, particularly with Adam de la Halle (see Chapter 3, p. 84), and Jehannot de l'Escurel [d. 1304]. Most of these pieces are based on a previously composed solo song, and in

* Prynne's translation, quoted from Davey, ibid., p. 17.

this, i.e. the use of an existing melody, they resemble the motet, but unlike the latter all the parts have the same words, and the borrowed melody is not always in the tenor, being sometimes placed in the middle part. When this happens the tenor becomes a kind of bass—in other words, its prime function is to support the upper voices. This new conception of the tenor had far-reaching results, because for the first time it was not invariably regarded as the most important part, and in writing a composition of this type a composer might first of all borrow a trouvère rondeau, say, ornament it a little perhaps, add a tenor below it, and finally write a third part above it, a method of composing quite different from that of the motet and conductus, both of which started with the tenor and added the upper parts afterwards.

Of all the types and forms of thirteenth-century music the motet is undoubtedly the most important, for, apart from being more subtle, refined, and expressive, its characteristics reflect more faithfully the artistic attitude of the times, although the conductus too shared in its impartial use on either sacred or secular occasions. It is easy enough to say this, but it is much more to the point that we should be convinced of the motet's superiority through actual performance, and in this connection a few practical tips may be useful. Sing the original words if your knowledge of mediaeval Latin or French is good enough for you to understand what you are singing; if not, then get someone to provide a translation which will fit the music and which keeps more to the spirit of the original than to the letter. Sing the parts one at a time in order to get their flavour, and then sing the two lowest parts together (tenor and motetus), and finally all three, as suggested on p. 108. In an age which takes to Debussy as our forbears took to Brahms it should not be long before this music makes its appeal. As regards actual performance, the same conditions hold as in the thirteenth century—in other words, any combination of voices or suitable instruments was permitted by the composer, but whereas the motet tenors were probably more often played by instruments only, the upper parts were performed by voices and instruments either together or separately, and this applies to all the parts of a conductus. Once again it must be remembered that the number of those taking part was small. The instruments were those already mentioned in Chapters 2 and 3.

The thirteenth century was an astonishingly rich one. The Gothic cathedral reached its highest point of development and beauty; men were becoming intellectually independent, and while the Church's authority was still regarded as absolute, individuals such as Thomas Aquinas were reconciling Greek philosophy, particularly that of Aristotle, with Christian doctrine, in spite of the fact that in 1215 the Church condemned Aristotle's works; in science the solitary voice of Roger Bacon [*c.* 1214-1292] rejected the attitude which placed tradition, popular opinion, and outside authority above experimentally verified theories, and so pointed the way toward modern scientific methods; the end of the century saw the hitherto unsurpassed lyric poetry of Dante [1265-1321]—much of it influenced by the troubadour, Arnaut Daniel [d. 1199]—which culminated in the *Divine Comedy* written during the last twelve years of his life. In the world at large Constantinople, the capital of the Eastern Roman Empire, was taken during the Fourth Crusade (1202-4), but was regained by the Greeks in 1261, largely because the Church found it increasingly difficult to raise sufficient enthusiasm for the later Crusades; the power of the Church in fact was waning, and in England Edward I was beginning to draw his country away from complete subjugation to the Pope. In no single activity, however, whether spiritual, intellectual, political, or artistic, did such enormous changes take place or was there so great a variety of expression as in music: monophony and polyphony, Gregorian chant, organum, and clausula, trouvère song and conductus, motet and secular part-song, liturgical music and music for every aristocratic occasion, the beginnings of independence from the Gregorian tenor melodies, especially in the polyphonic rondeau, virelai, and ballade (cantilenae), the increasing flexibility of rhythm and melody and with it the rapid development of notation, from Pérotin's lack of differentiated shapes to Franco's classification of note values and their extension by Petrus de Cruce, the widespread use of instruments and the epoch-making re-discovery of the keyboard. As one writer has said: "The thirteenth century is one of the greatest in music history, being comparable with the sixteenth, eighteenth, and nineteenth."*

* G. Reese, *Music in the Middle Ages*, p. 329.

PERFORMANCE

(See also pp. 108, 116-18.)

Ex. 37. This may be sung with instruments or played by instruments alone.
Ex. 38. As for Ex. 37.
Ex. 39. As for Ex. 37.
Ex. 40. As for Ex. 37, except that the lowest part is better played than sung.
Ex. 41. As for Ex. 37.

5

THE NEW ART

The pope sits on his holy chair, which stood
For rock of Peter once, but now is wood.
He looks at Fauvel there in his presence,
To whom the assembled make great reverence,
And groom him constantly from morn till night.
The pope then stretches out his hand so white,
And by the bridle through his palace rooms
He gently leads him, blaming not the grooms.
And now, while softly rubbing Fauvel's head,
He says, 'A lovely beast, he must be fed.'
The cardinals, who wish to please anew,
Reply, 'O holy Father, thou speak'st true.'*

THIS quotation comes from a very famous French poem called *Le Roman de Fauvel* ('The Fable of Fauvel') written in 1310 and 1314 by a certain Gervais de Bus. Its main purpose was a violent attack on the Church, and although the above passage may seem harmless enough at first sight, its sting will be fully appreciated when it is realized that 'wood' was symbolical of 'inconstancy' and that Fauvel was a fictitious horse or ass, the name being derived from the initial letters of the following vices: *Flatérie*, *Avarice*, *Vilanie* (depravity—'u' and 'v' were interchangeable in the Middle Ages), *Variété* (fickleness) *Envie*, and *Laschetè* (cowardice), so that when anybody groomed, caressed, or praised Fauvel they were in fact revelling in wickedness. Such a criticism would hardly have been possible in earlier centuries, and *Le Roman de Fauvel* indicates in a striking manner the disrespect with which the Church was regarded during the fourteenth century by a great many intelligent and cultured people.

The reason for this was not only due to the waxing interest in pagan philosophy and science, but also to the waning authority and saintliness of the Church herself. The trouble started near the end of the eleventh century, when a succession of popes

* Freely translated from lines 105-16.

began to claim complete supremacy in the realm of Church *and* State—in other words, to insist that emperors and kings must bow to Papal rule. To enforce their claim, armies were either hired or offered indulgences—which to the mediaeval peasants meant free tickets to Heaven—and the amount of blood that the Church shed as a result, coupled with the widespread torture and death inflicted on those she regarded as heretics (e.g. the Albigensian Crusade) and the shocking corruption of most of her clergy, caused her prestige to sink rapidly until the crowning scandal of the Great Schism (1378-1417) was reached during which two Popes, one at Avignon (France) and one in Rome, simultaneously claimed to be God's highest representative on earth and used all the religious, political, and financial means at their disposal to obtain support for their respective claims. To make matters worse, all this happened while the so-called Hundred Years' War (1339-1453) was ravaging France (the battles of Crécy, 1346, and Agincourt, 1415), and it followed shortly after the virulent plague known as the Black Death had swept over Europe from the East, killing about 25 million people, including over half the population of Britain. At the very time when the Church should have been a source of hope and inspiration, she was found lacking; small wonder, therefore, that her hitherto unassailable position began to crumble and the seeds of religious revolt and secular power began to germinate; small wonder also that composers, following the general trend of the times, found a greater incentive and satisfaction in writing for the royal courts and the aristocracy which thronged them, where new ideas and experiments were encouraged and no clerical authority hampered their creative faculty, than for a Church discredited by corruption and split by rival factions and which actively discouraged the new developments in music.

We have already quoted the criticisms on church music by Aelred and John of Salisbury, but the climax came when John XXII, an Avignon Pope from 1316-34, issued a decree in 1324–5 which contains the following sentences: "Certain disciples of the new school, much occupying themselves with the measured dividing of time, display their method in notes which are new to us, preferring to devise ways of their own rather than to continue singing in the old manner; the music, therefore, of the divine offices is now performed with semibreves and minims, and with these notes of small value every composition is pestered. Moreover, they truncate the melodies with hockets, they deprave them with discantus, sometimes even they stuff them with upper parts made out of secular song [e.g. Ex. 40] . . . . Their voices are incessantly running to and fro, intoxicating the ear, not soothing it, while the men themselves endeavour to convey by their gestures the sentiment of the music which they utter . . . . We now hasten therefore to banish these methods . . . and to put them to flight more effectually than heretofore, far from the house of God. Wherefore . . . we straitly command that no one henceforward shall think himself at liberty to attempt these methods, or methods like them, in the aforesaid offices, and especially the canonical Hours or in the celebration of the Mass.

"And if any be disobedient, let him . . . be punished by a suspension from office of eight days. . . .

"Yet for all this, it is not our intention to forbid, occasionally . . . the use of some consonances, for example, the octave, fifth, and fourth, which heighten the beauty of the melody; such intervals, therefore, may be sung above the plain cantus ecclesiasticus, yet so that the integrity of the cantus itself may remain intact, and that nothing in the authoritative music be changed. . . ."*

In other words, Pope John XXII approved of Notre Dame organum, but not the motet, especially the modern kind, which was 'pestered' with semibreves and minims. The minim (Latin, *minima*=least) takes us back to *Le Roman de Fauvel*, for, apart from reflecting contemporary criticism of the Church, the manuscript on which the poem is written also contains an important anthology of popular music of the time. The pieces comprising this anthology were added in 1316 by a musician named Chaillou de Pestain, and they range from Gregorian chants to motets. Most of the latter are written in the style of Petrus de Cruce, but some of them show significant differences which indicate a development in notation, rhythm, and construction.

The main objection to Petronian notation was that although there were in practice note values from two-thirds to one-seventh of a breve, they were all shown by the same note shape

* Adapted from H. E. Woodridge, *Oxford History of Music, I* (2nd Ed.), 1929, pp. 294–6.

—the semibreve, and in order to lessen this ambiguity an anonymous scribe later added a downward stroke or tail to some of the semibreves in *Le Roman de Fauvel* motets, thus, ⧫, which equalled two-thirds of a breve (see Fig. 2). He also began to add upward tails to the 'shorter' semibreves, ⧫, but soon realised that this was a hopeless task because the values of these semibreves varied so much. This note shape, however, became more important than any of the others that were invented round about 1300, and was called the minim. At about the same time, or, to be a little more precise, *c.* 1316–25, a Frenchman, Philippe de Vitri [1291–1361] was writing a remarkable treatise from which we have taken the title of this chapter. Indeed, it is now usually applied to the whole of the fourteenth century, but to begin with we shall limit outselves to discussing its effect on French music only.

De Vitri's 'Ars Nova', by expanding Franco's system, provided composers with a clear-cut and much more flexible notation, and one that had become an absolute necessity since the time of Petrus de Cruce. The three fundamental innovations of de Vitri's system are the placing of perfection and imperfection on an equal footing, the application of this to the semibreve (which at last could be used singly and which soon replaced the breve as tactus), and the introduction of the minim as a distinct and independent note value. Thus the dictatorship of triple time had ended and a far greater variety of rhythm was now possible (see Fig. 3).

In order to make the relationships between the notes quite clear de Vitri uses three words—*modus*, *tempus*, and *prolatio*, or 'mood' (a sixteenth-century English word which we prefer to the already overworked 'mode'), 'time', and 'prolation'. The mood is either great, when it refers to the number of longs in a double-long, or less, when it refers to the number of breves in a long. Time refers to the number of semibreves in a breve, and prolation to the number of minims in a semibreve. Each of these four relationships is either perfect or imperfect, and any combination of them was theoretically possible; in practice however, the great mood was never used owing to the length of the double-long (which roughly equalled the breve of today), and the less mood was almost invariably imperfect, so that instead of a possible sixteen combinations there were to all intents and purposes only four. In addition, de Vitri invented a number of signs, each of which stood for a particular combination, and thus showed the singer at a glance the values of the various notes; but they were hardly ever used by composers, possibly because of the fact that other musicians started inventing different ones. In order to simplify matters, those signs that were in common use in the fifteenth and sixteenth centuries and which developed out of de Vitri's are given in the following table, together with the four usual combinations and their modern time signature equivalents, with de Vitri's minim equalling our quaver (Ex. 43):

Ex. 43

Less Mood	*Time*	*Prolation*	*Sign*	*Time Signature*
Imperfect ($L=2\ B$)	Perfect ($B=3\ S$)	Perfect ($S=3\ M$)	⊙	$\frac{9}{8}$
,, ,,	Imperfect ($B=2\ S$)	,, ,,	₵	$\frac{6}{8}$
,, ,,	Perfect ($B=3\ S$)	Imperfect ($S=2\ M$)	O	$\frac{3}{4}$
,, ,,	Imperfect ($B=2\ S$)	,, ,,	C	$\frac{2}{4}$

As in Franco's system, the values of the notes also depend on their position (cf. Chapter 4, p. 113, Rule 4), this now being applied to the semibreve and minim as well. In order to make all this quite clear here is a series of note shapes with their values and grouping in modern notation in the four different combinations of time and prolation (Ex. 44):

Ex. 44

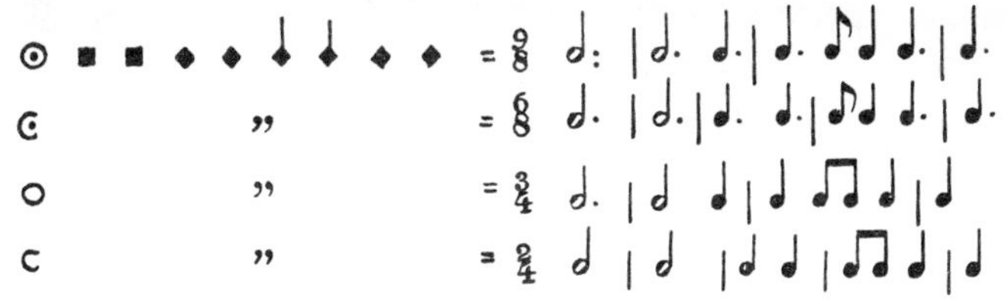

In the $\frac{9}{8}$ and $\frac{6}{8}$ examples the second minim has been 'altered', but it is quite possible for the last five notes to be sung thus: ♩ ♪ ♪ ♩ ♩., and in order to try and clarify this kind of situation composers expanded de Cruce's idea of using dots. This would have been admirable if they had all agreed on the way these dots should be used; as it is, however, the modern transcriber is often in difficulties as to the exact meaning of a dot and can sometimes only arrive at the correct solution by a process of trial and error, an unsatisfactory state of affairs which almost certainly existed for the fourteenth-century singer as well. In the succeeding centuries the number of dots was reduced, until by about 1650 only one remained—the one we use today, which adds to the note preceding it one-half of its value.

Some idea of the variety of rhythm which could be obtained from just three note shapes can clearly be seen in Ex. 44, but such was their desire for greater rhythmic freedom that composers began to use red notes as well. Apart from making the look of a musical manuscript considerably more attractive, red notes indicate certain differences in value and rhythm compared with their black brothers. They first appear in the tenor part of two motets in *Le Roman de Fauvel* (see Fig. 2), and for some time after their use was restricted to this part only.

Their value was similarly restricted at first, for redness implies the imperfecting of a note which is perfect if black, and when a number of them are grouped together they indicate a change of rhythm, as, for instance, in this example. (For reasons of economy, the original red notes are printed as white ones in Exx. 45-7) (Ex. 45):

Ex. 45

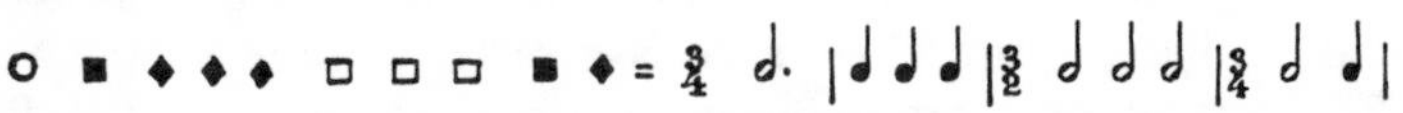

(See also Ex. 51, bb. 3–7, 13–17, and 23–7.) Later in the century red notes were used in the upper parts as well and their function became more varied, such as indicating ternary groups in binary rhythm (Ex. 46):

Ex. 46

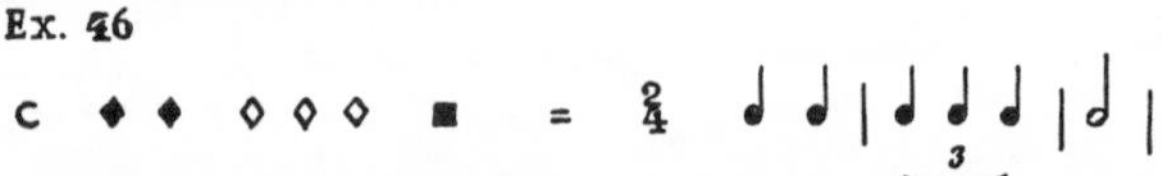

or increasing the value of a note by a half (Ex. 47):

Ex. 47

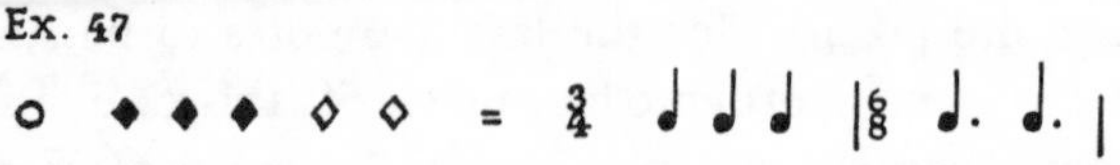

or, if written as a white note with red outlines, making it equal to half its value when black. This last use meant that in performance there was a shorter note than the minim, and near the end of the century this received a black shape, ♪, and the name 'semiminim'.

Not content with the introduction of red notes and shorter notes, nor with the new patterns which binary rhythm made possible, composers began to experiment with the more subtle technique of syncopation. To us syncopation means the upsetting in various ways of a regularly recurring number of strong beats—e.g. 4/4 ♩ 𝅗𝅥 ♩|♩ instead of 4/4 ♩♩♩♩| but regular strong beats were unknown in mediaeval music and therefore syncopation meant something quite different, and although the explanations in various theoretical works (the earliest being by an Englishman, *c.* 1326) are almost invariably abstruse, the general principle is as follows: into a normal binary or ternary group of notes is inserted another normal group—for example (in modern notation), instead of (Ex. 48)—

Ex. 48

the group enclosed in the square bracket was placed between the two notes of the first bar, thus (Ex. 49):

Ex 49

A more musical way of writing this and one which shows how the composer intended the notes to be grouped is (Ex. 50):

Ex 50

This example stands about halfway in complexity between the short, simple syncopated passages of the earlier part of the century and the long, complicated ones that can be found in some of the later pieces (see Ex. 61).

But although this development of rhythmical freedom which the composers of the fourteenth century enjoyed and exploited made a greater degree of melodic expressiveness possible, it brought with it the danger of disintegration, for the more rhythmically varied the parts become, particularly the upper parts, the more independent are they of each other, and in music as in society when the individual components have no interrelationship or are not based on some unifying principle something approaching anarchy results. In the motets of the thirteenth century, except those written in the style of Petrus de Cruce, the disintegration which the singing of different words in each part might have brought was balanced by the prevailing ternary rhythm and by the customary arrangement of the tenor in repeated rhythmic patterns that were short enough and simple enough to be heard. In the Petronian motets, however, the unifying effect of ternary rhythm in all parts is lessened by the use of semibreves of varying values, and the highest part in particular becomes more independent in every way, a state of affairs that is not adequately compensated for by the organization of the tenor, and when in the next century the scope of rhythmic variety increased rapidly, the danger of the motet falling to pieces, as it were, became real. De Vitri and many other composers seem to have been alive to this danger and they tackled it as one would expect from a rhythmic angle.

The two motet tenors in *Le Roman de Fauvel* that include red notes are arranged in repeated rhythmic patterns which only differ from those of Pérotin in being longer and more rhythmically varied; here is one of them. (The notes and rests enclosed by brackets are red in the original: see Fig. 2) (Ex. 51*):

* Transcribed from W. Apel, *The Notation of Polyphonic Music, 900-1600*, 4th Ed., p. 331.

This organization of the tenor now goes under the fearsome name of 'isorhythm' (='the same rhythm'), and the repeated rhythmic patterns—called 'taleae' (Latin, *talea*='a cutting') by fourteenth-century theorists—either fit the melody or 'color' exactly, as in the above example, in which there are three taleae, or else they overlap, in which case if the melody is repeated, which it usually is, it receives a different rhythmic interpretation, exactly as described in Chapter 2 (cf. pp. 57-8, and Exx. 24 and 25). This latter use of isorhythm became more popular than the former for the simple reason that it gives more rhythmic variety to the melody.

Isorhythm became the main structural device of the fourteenth-century motet, but so long as it was restricted to the tenor part only it hardly provided a sufficiently unifying effect on the composition as a whole with its different texts and varied rhythms in the upper parts, particularly as the longer and more complex the taleae became the less clearly audible were they to the listener—in other words, their unifying effect was felt rather than heard. In some of his motets therefore de Vitri applied the isorhythmic principle to the other parts as well, though not so strictly as in the tenor. This idea was increasingly adopted by later composers, some of whom made all the parts strictly isorhythmic, and round about 1400 this was carried a stage further when only the upper parts are isorhythmic, the tenor being free. It should be mentioned, however, that each of the upper parts, while naturally having a different melody or color from the others, always has a different rhythmic pattern; moreover, the talea of each part while sometimes of the same length as the others is often longer or shorter. Even so, the spread of the isorhythmic principle to most or all of the parts went a fair way to unifying the motet, which in fact can be regarded as a series of melodic variations on one or more rhythmic patterns. On the whole, however, it is probably true to say that the fourteenth-century motet is a less perfect art form than those written before Petrus de Cruce, because variety is not adequately balanced by unity.

Unlike most theorists, de Vitri was himself a composer of international repute, but unfortunately very few of his pieces have survived, and hence the man who most completely represents the Fench Ars Nova to us is Guillaume de Machaut [*c.* 1300 – 1377]. Though a priest, Machaut undoubtedly appreciated the things of this world, an attitude which, as we have seen, was typical of the mediaeval ecclesiastic. He certainly saw and enjoyed a good deal of Europe, for as secretary to King John of Bohemia (brother of Pope John XXII), a monarch who was fond of travel, he met many influential people and visited countries as far apart as Italy and Lithuania. When John was killed at the Battle of Crécy, Machaut was employed by his daughter and later by such high-ranking personages as King Charles of Navarre, the Dauphin of France (later Charles V), and his brother Jean, Duc de Berry. The regard in which he was held, particularly by his noble patrons, is the main reason why so much of his music has been preserved, some of it in manuscripts of great beauty. His reputation, however, was by no means confined to music, for he was the chief literary figure in fourteenth-century France, undoubtedly influenced Chaucer [*c*. 1340-1400], and was compared by his countrymen to his great contemporary, the Italian poet Petrarch.

A true child of his century, Machaut wrote almost entirely secular music, in spite of the fact that he was in Holy Orders and reached the comparatively exalted position of Canon of Rheims in 1333, and of the 140 pieces that have survived only seven are liturgical—six motets and a mass, the rest consisting mainly of ballades (forty-two), virelais (thirty-three), rondeaux (twenty-one), lais (eighteen), and secular motets (seventeen).

Nearly all the motets have isorhythmic tenors, and in many of these Machaut heightens the interest towards the end by shortening the note values when the color is repeated but keeping the taleae intact (see Ex. 52), a procedure that later composers frequently adopted. In some of the motets isorhythm is freely applied to one or more of the upper parts, and in one motet this application is strict. In Ex. 52 the isorhythmic scheme of the tenor can be shown thus:

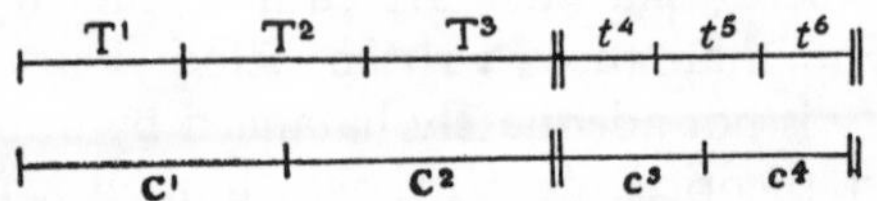

'C' stands for color and 'T' for talea; in the second section, where the note values are halved, the taleae ('t') are naturally half as long as in the first section. The two upper voices are also isorhythmic (though not strictly so), but unlike the tenor only the taleae repeat in each section, not the colores; furthermore, the talea and color in the second section are quite different from those in the first. This is a secular motet and a very lovely one, but the tenor melody is sacred, being that portion of the Gregorian chant, *Domine in tua misericordia speravi* (Introit for the First Sunday after Pentecost), which is set to the word 'speravi' ('I have hoped [for]')—an obviously deliberate choice considering the text of the triplum part (Ex. 52* pp. 132-7).

It will be noticed that the tenor has a B♭ in the signature which is lacking in the two upper voices; such a practice was very common in part-music from the thirteenth century to the fifteenth, and various explanations have been advanced of which the following is the most satisfactory.† The commonest partial signature in the thirteenth and fourteenth centuries is, from highest to lowest voice, ♮, ♭ in two-part compositions, and ♮, ♮, ♭ in three-part, as in Ex. 52. (For convenience we will restrict the discussion to three-part pieces only, though what is said below applies with equal force to two-part pieces.) The mode of Ex. 52 was called Lydian by mediaeval musicians, even though the tenor part, by which the mode of the whole piece was judged, has a B♭ in the signature and hence is really in the Ionian mode (see Chapter 1) transposed down a fifth. (As the mode with F as final but with no B♭ in the signature was also called Lydian (correctly) we shall indicate the F mode with a B♭ thus: 'Lydian'. The Ionian mode, incidentally, together with the Aeolian, was not recognized as an independent mode until the late fifteenth century.) The basic range of the two upper parts in Ex. 52 is *c′–c″*; this is the exact range of the duplum, whereas the triplum extends from the note below (*b*) to the note above (*d″*). The theoretical range of the tenor is *f–f′*, although only the notes *f–b♭* are actually used. Now, nearly all compositions that have a partial signature are in either the 'Lydian' mode—and there are comparatively few pieces in the 'Lydian' mode that do not have a partial signature —or else in the transposed Dorian mode, that is the tenor part ends on a G final, a fifth lower than the D final of the untransposed Dorian. In both cases the basic range of the upper parts is *c′–c″* when the tenor is in the 'Lydian' mode, and *d–d′* when

* Adapted from H. Gleason, *Examples of Music before 1400*, p. 88.

† Largely based on two articles by Richard H. Hoppin in the *Journal of the American Musicological Society*, Vol. VI (1953), No. 3, and Vol. IX (1956), No. 2.

Ex.52 Motet-De bon espoir - Puis que la douce - Speravi
Machaut
Triplum
Duplum
Tenor
Speravi
T.1/C.I
De Bon Es - - poir de Tres Doulz Sou - ve - nir Et de Tres
With good Hope and with such sweet Me-mo - ry And swee - test
Puis que la dou - -
Since mo - - - - - de - - sty,
Doulz Pen-ser contre De - sir Ma bon-ne A - mour
thoughts against De - sire, hast she My dear love oft
- ce rou - se - - - - e
that gen - tle dew,
mein - - tes fois se - cou - - ru, Quant il ma
helped me when all else failed, When de - sire
D'um - - bles - - se ne
Will not e'er cause
plus ai-gre-ment sus cou - - ru; Car quant De-sirs plus fort me de -
me most fu-rious-ly as - sailed; For when it more strong-ly held me
wet flo - - - - - rir Pi - - - tes,
your pi - - - - - ty To flow'r,

EX. 52 (CONTD.)

30
-strein-gnoit, Moult dou-ce-ment Es-poirs m'as-se-u-roit, Et
se - cure, Then Hope didst gent-ly come and re-as-sure, And
tant que me - u - re - - - e
un - - - til it bloom in - - - to
35
40
Sou - - ve - - nirs me mous-troit la biau-te, Le sens, l'on - -
Me - - mo - - ries showed me the beau-ty fair, The feel - - ing,
Soit mer - - - - - - cis que
That which I de - -
T.II
45
-neur, le ports et la bon-te De cel-le dont
ho-nour, worth and good-ness rare Of her on whom
tant de - - sir
-sire mer - - cy,
50
55
li a - - mou-reus pen - - ser, Mon do-lent
my lov - - ing thoughts did dwell, My sorr'w-ing
Je ne puis a - - - voir
I want not life to
C.II

EX. 52 (CONTD.)

60
cuer ve-noi-ent con - for - ter. Las! or m'as-saut De - sirs plus qu'il
heart they came to com-fort well. Now a-las more fierce-ly comes my
du - re - - - - - e, Car en
con - ti - - - - - nue, For in
65
ne suet, Mais du-re-ment en - du-rer le m'es - tuet, Car Je
de - sire, But I with firmness must endure its fire, For I am
moy s'est en - gen - - - dre - - e,
me there is born a - - new
T. III
70
75
sui pres de per-dre le con-fort De Bon Es - - poir, dont Je me
near los - ing all the com-fort dear Of good Hope, yet this doth my
Par- un- a - - - mou - - reus
By- a- great de - - sire
80
des - con - fort; Et Sou - ve - - - - -
poor heart sear, And sweet Me - - - -
de - - - - - sir,
for thee,

EX. 52 (CONTD.)

85
90
-nirs me — fait tou-dis pen-ser Pour mort las
-m'ries force me to think each day And make my
Une ar - - deur des - - me - - - - - su-
An ar - - dent pas - - sion that
95
cuer fai-re des-es-pe-rer, Car Grace, A-mour, Fran-chi-se, Loy-
wea-ry heart des-pair al-way; For her Grace, her Frank-ness, Love, and
-re - - - - - e Qu'A - - - mours
I rue, Which Love
100
-au-te, Pi-te, Doc-tri-ne et De-bon-nai-re-te Sont
Loy'l-ty, Her Pi-ty, Cour-te-sy, Gen-ti-li-ty Are
par son doulz plai - - - sir,
by its sweet fan - - - cy,
105
pour mi seul si for-ment en-dor-mi,
from me on--ly hid-den ut--ter-ly,
Et ma da - -
And my de - -
t IV/c. III

EX. 52 (CONTD.)

Car Dangiers est souvereins de Merci Et
For hard-heart-ed-ness hath conquered mer-cy And
-me desi-re-e Par sa
-sir-ed la-dy, who With grace
que ma-da-me a qui je suis ren-dus, Croit
that la-dy so fair whom I love in vain, In
biau-te cou-lou re-e,
her beau-ty doth en-due,
a Dur-te et orguil-leus Re-fus,
Cru-el-ty be-lieves and proud dis-dain;
De gra-ce y ont
Have so rous-ed
t.V
Pour ce, sans plus, que m'a-mour ne mon cuer N'en well
Hence for this a-lone my love and my heart Nei-ther
fait ve-nir. Mais puis
with in me. But since
c.IV

EX. 52 (CONTD.)

135
ne puis de par - tir a nul fuer
wishes nor can from her de - part.
Mais
But
qu'eins - si leur a - gre - e
this pain that doth en - sue
140
puis qu'e - stre ne puet o - re au - tre - ment
now, since o - ther - wise I can - not be.
Je weil hum - ble
Plea - ses them, I'll
t.VI
145
Fa - ce de moy tout son com - man - de - ment,
Let her do her will and so com - mand me,
- ment souf - frir Leur vo - loir.
bear hum - bly Their be - hests.
150
Car mal - gre li l'a - me - ray loy - au - ment.
For de - spite her, I'll serve her loy - al - ly.
jus - qu'au mo - rir.
till death claims me

the tenor is in the transposed Dorian mode, while the basic range of the tenor is a fifth lower, namely *f–f′* and *G–g* respectively. On the other hand in the great majority of compositions that have the same signature in all parts, e.g. ♮, ♮, ♮, or ♭, ♭, ♭, the range of the tenor is either within the same basic octave as the upper parts or else an octave below; in other words all the parts are in the same modal plane, whereas those pieces with partial signatures are 'bimodal', that is they are written in two modal planes. (It is important to realise that the term 'bimodal' does not mean in two *different* modes, e.g. Phrygian in the upper parts combined with Mixolydian in the tenor; it only means the combination of two forms of the *same* mode at the interval of a fifth. Furthermore the notes on which the duplum and triplum end are dictated primarily by the stock cadential figure of the period (see below), not by the mode of the voice concerned (this applies to all modal part-music), otherwise in each piece with a partial signature the upper voices would have to end on the fifth or its octave above the tenor final, and in all other pieces on the tenor final itself or its octave, thus ruling out the $^{8}_{5}$ chord and of course the later $^{5}_{3}$ chord.)

What has been stated above poses three questions. (1) Why did composers, when they wrote bimodally, nearly always use the 'Lydian' and transposed Dorian modes? (2) Why did they write on modal planes a fifth apart, and not a fourth or some other interval? (3) Why did they write bimodally at all?

Questions (1) and (2) can be taken together as they both revolve round the use of the note B♭. This was the first chromatic note to be placed on an equal footing with diatonic notes, for it is the only chromatic note to be found in Gregorian chant and, moreover, is an integral note in the Guidonian hexachord system. By far the commonest modes to employ B♭ in Gregorian chant are the Dorian and Lydian, the former because in the frequent and important melodic progression A–B–A, which hinges on the dominant of the mode, it was found that B♭ was easier to sing and sounded more graceful than B♮, and the latter because the augmented fourth or tritone F–B is avoided. By the middle of the thirteenth century it had become common practice to write a B♭ in the signature instead of in front of each B (as in Gregorian chant) for most compositions with F as final and for many with D as final, the modes still being termed Lydian and Dorian respectively, though in actual fact the former is Ionian transposed (as we have seen) and the latter Aeolian transposed. But real transposition by means of a B♭ signature, which results in the mode being transposed down a fifth, was also recognized, and although the mode with final G and a signature of B♭ was sometimes called Mixolydian because of its final, it was more often called Dorian transposed, which indeed it is. Transposition up a fifth by means of a key signature was not used by the mediaeval composer because all he wanted was the opportunity, when he desired, to write on two modal planes, and while the simplest transposition, then as now (so far as accidentals are concerned), is up or down a fifth, transposing up a fifth would have meant a new signature of F♯, whereas the means for transposing down a fifth was already to hand, namely the long-established B♭. (Not until the middle of the seventeenth century did signatures of one or more sharps become common.) The fact that the majority of bimodal pieces are in the 'Lydian' and transposed Dorian modes is almost certainly due to the traditional association of B♭ with these modes in Gregorian chant.

The reason why a composer wrote bimodally at all was undoubtedly because of his fondness for differentiating the voices of a composition; this indeed is one of the main characteristics of most of the music written in the late thirteenth and fourteenth centuries (see p. 153). Thus both the greater animation of the triplum and to a lesser extent of the duplum compared to the tenor in the latter half of the thirteenth century (see Chapter 4), and the introduction of complex cross-rhythms in the fourteenth century sprang not only from an absorbing interest in rhythm itself, but also from the realisation that rhythmic differences between parts assist greatly in differentiating the parts one from another. Similarly bimodalism, in presenting two modal planes, helps to differentiate the upper part or parts from the tenor.

An offshoot, as it were, of bimodalism is apparent in the stock cadential figure of the fourteenth century that occurs in both the untransposed and transposed Dorian, Lydian, and Mixolydian modes. It can be seen at the end of Ex. 52, and Ex. 53 overleaf is its simplest form.

The noteworthy feature of this cadence is that both the dominant and the upper final are approached by a sub-semitone or leading-note. In Chapter 1 we noted that the subsemitonal approach to the final in the Lydian mode is usually avoided in Gregorian chant; indeed, this mode occurs much less frequently in Gregorian chant than either the Dorian or Mixolydian modes. In fourteenth-century cadences however,

Ex. 53

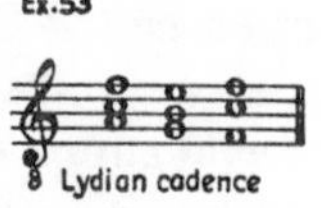

the sub-semitonal approach to the upper final in all three modes is the rule rather than the exception, and results in the progressions C♯–D in the Dorian mode and F♯–G in the Mixolydian. Moreover the sub-semitonal approach to the dominant (B–C), which occurs 'naturally' in the Lydian cadence, was also applied to the Dorian and Mixolydian cadences, i.e. G♯–A in the former and C♯–D in the latter, thus creating, in a sense, two finals a fifth apart. This type of cadence in which both the final and dominant are approached by a leading-note is a characteristic of late mediaeval and much early Renaissance music; it is sometimes called the 'Burgundian cadence', an unfortunate name, because 'Burgundian' refers to certain composers of the mid-fifteenth century, whereas the cadence was already common in the time of Machaut (e.g. Ex. 52, bb. 16–17, 24–25, 76–77, and the final cadence). A better name is 'double leading-note cadence'. In the Phrygian mode, the only mode (apart from the discarded Locrian) in which the final is approached by a semitone above (F–E), the upper final and dominant were never preceded by a sub-semitone as this results in an augmented sixth (F–D♯) and augmented third (F–A♯) respectively (Ex. 54):

Ex. 54

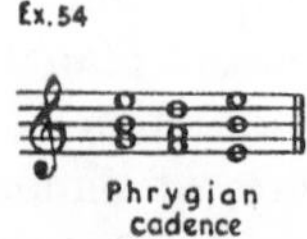

Because of its unique supra-semitonal approach to the final, this is the only mediaeval modal cadence to survive to the present day.

The fact that Ars Nova composers liked the double leading-note cadence is one indication of the waning influence of the ecclesiastical modes, another being the greater use of chromatic notes, because Gregorian chant, the largest and purest collection of modal music in Europe, is essentially diatonic, even though B♭ was admitted as a basic note quite early on, and certain other chromatic notes were in fact sung as a result of transposing a chant up a fourth or a fifth. Indeed, so far as chromaticism is concerned the fourteenth century is less modal than the fifteenth century, and it is no accident that secular music is predominant in the former period, whereas in the latter sacred music came increasingly to the fore, because sacred music, particularly that for the liturgy, was, as we noted in Chapter 1, profoundly influenced by Gregorian chant, and hence is far more modal than secular music, in which composers were less tied by tradition and hence freer to experiment, especially in the fourteenth century, when ecclesiastical authority, notably Pope John XXII, was so severe on new ideas. This distinction between sacred and secular music applies also to the thirteenth and sixteenth centuries; in the former the songs of the troubadours and their offshoots and the dance music of the period are quite frequently written in the Ionian and Aeolian modes (which, as we have seen, were not then part of the modal system), while contemporary liturgical music uses them much less often, proving that these two modes—the only two to survive to the present day—must have been popular in the folk-music of earlier times. In the sixteenth century it was the madrigal and chanson, not the mass and motet, that destroyed most of the already crumbling walls of the modal fortress.

But there is another reason for the double leading-note cadence and the increased chromaticism—namely, that fourteenth-century composers were more concerned with the 'vertical' aspect, i.e. the sonority of their music, than were earlier composers. We observed in Chapter 2 that thirds and sixths are richer sounds than the fourth, fifth, or octave, and that this increased richness is due to a greater degree of dissonance. We also observed that the ear has progressively accepted as concordant or relatively concordant what was previously heard as discordant. In the fourteenth century composers were gradually beginning to accept thirds and sixths as concords in their own right, and this new sense of sonority, together with the preference for the leading-note, led to such rules as (*a*) a third and sixth expanding stepwise to a fifth and octave respectively should be major; (*b*) a third contracting to a unison should be minor; (*c*) a fifth and octave must be perfect; if the above intervals are not naturally major, minor, or perfect, they must be rendered so by chromatic alteration. The double leading-note cadence falls under (*a*), and its popularity was probably due to the bimodal flavour it imparted as well as to a liking for the sub-semitonal approach to a final and dominant and to a natural preference for the major third and sixth, which are less dissonant than the minor forms. Rule (*b*) was most likely dictated by the leading-note tendency, because, of the three 'natural' major thirds, C–E, F–A, and G–B, the first two usually, and the third often, had the lower note sharpened rather than the upper flattened when contracting to a unison. Rule (*c*) is really an outcome of rule (*a*), which underlines the restful, poised quality of the perfect fifth and octave following the expansion (always more emotionally intense than contraction) of a more dissonant interval.

The above rules do not apply to intervals of short duration, but only to those that have some significance, i.e. those that are approached by and consist of long notes or that are cadential; even so it is certain that composers did not regard the rules as inflexible, and it seems likely that performers took the same line (see 'musica ficta', pp. 167, 171). Moreover, it is perfectly clear that notes were quite often chromatically altered, not from any 'vertical' considerations, but simply in order to enhance the melody.

Machaut's motets display the composer's rhythmic technique and melodic sophistication at their height, but the lais, all but two of which are monodic, and the virelais, of which twenty-five are monodic, seem to be an attempt by the composer to recapture something of the spirit of the trouvères, of an age of chivalry long past; apart from the forms, however, and the fact that they are mostly monodic, there is little connexion between the two, except for the echoes of courtly love that can be heard in the poems. To this extent Machaut is akin to Brahms, for, like the latter, part of his output is in a style that reflects his sympathy with a tradition that was no longer the natural expression of the times in which he lived; chivalry had little place in the disillusioned atmosphere of the fourteenth century.

The same nostalgia, though to a lesser degree, can be sensed in Machaut's rondeaux and ballades. All of them, except one

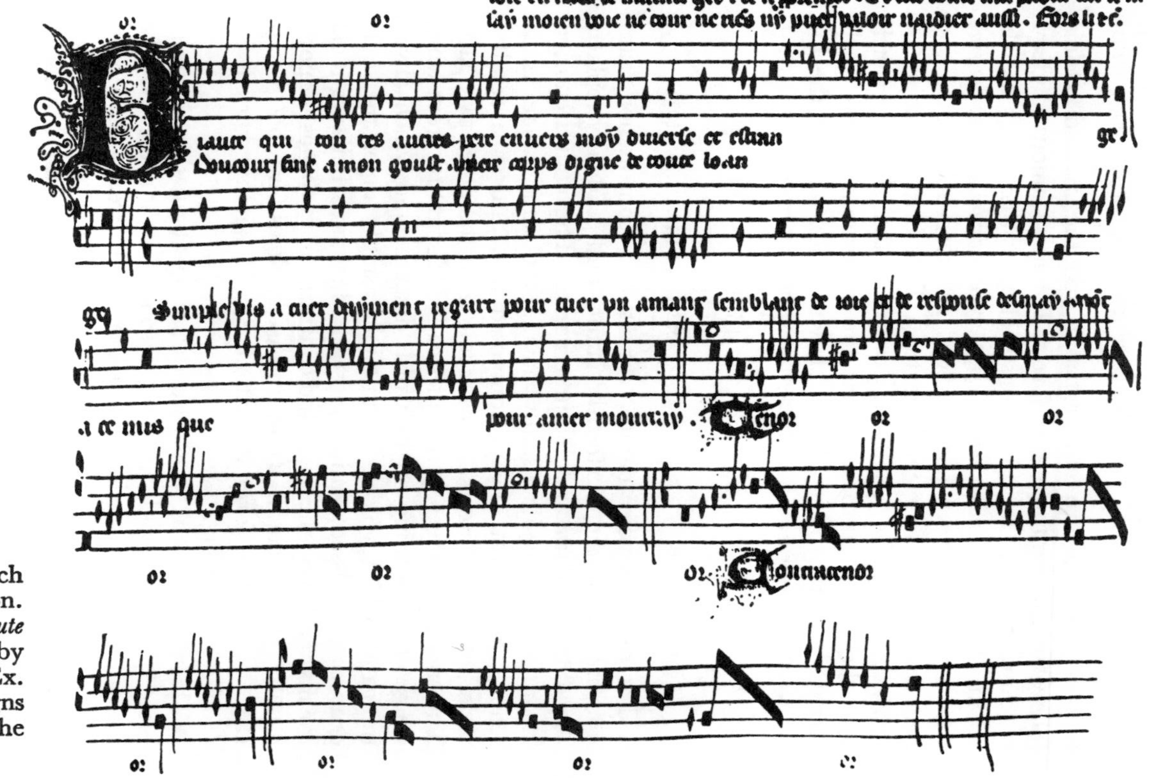

FIG. 3 French Ars Nova notation. The ballade *Biaute qui toutes autres* by Machaut. (See Ex. 55. Note the signs 'O' and 'C' in the tenor).

ballade, are in two to four parts and, like the lais and virelais, follow the thirteenth-century forms. The most famous rondeau, because of the subtlety of its construction, is that which has the refrain "*Ma fin est mon commencement, et mon commencement ma fin*" where the composer has indulged in word-painting, a rare occurence in the fourteenth century. Thus if the numbers 1–4 represent the tenor melody (the only part that sings the words) and the letters A, B represent the contratenor melody, the structure of the piece can be shown as follows and the link between the refrain and the actual music becomes obvious:

Cantus	4321 (instrumental)
Tenor	1234 (vocal)
Contratenor . . .	ABBA (instrumental)

The two new voice names, 'cantus' and 'contratenor', came into use during the fourteenth century and gradually replaced the older duplum and triplum names. The contratenor, or 'countertenor', while usually having the same range as the tenor, was almost always composed last, and as a result is melodically less interesting as a rule than the other two parts. The cantus, however (sometimes called 'discantus', from which we get one meaning of the word 'descant' and which always indicates a high voice), became increasingly important as the century progressed, and in most of Machaut's ballades it has the main melody, the tenor and contratenor serving as supports, usually instrumental, as in the example shown on p. 145 (Ex. 55*). (The form is that of Ex. 29 slightly varied, i.e. *ab ab cde F*: see Fig. 3.)

There are several things worth noting about this charming piece. To begin with, it is more sonorous than the motet of Ex. 52—in other words, there is a markedly greater percentage of triads, particularly at the beginning of each breve (=bar in the transcription). This is generally true of all Machaut's polyphonic ballades, rondeaux, and virelais compared to his motets, and represents a new unifying device that is first apparent in some of de Vitri's compositions. It also represents the beginning on the Continent of what is now known as 'tertiary harmony', i.e. harmony that is primarily based on the

* Transcribed from MS. Paris, Bibliothèque Nationale frç 9221 (fols. 152vo, 153). Facsimile in W. Apel, *The Notation of Polyphonic Music, 900–1600*, 4th Ed., p. 359.

IX Angels playing cornetts, psaltery, horn, vièle. From the 'Coronation of the Virgin' by Taddeo Gaddi (*c.* 1300–66), a pupil of Giotto.

X Positive organ. Illumination in the Belvoir Psalter. *c.* 1270.

XI Portative organ with button and pin operation. Peterborough Psalter, early fourteenth century

XII Portative organ with keyboard. English MS., fourteenth century.

Ex. 55 Ballade - Biaute qui toutes autres pere
(♦ = ♩ = MM.c.80)
Machaut
(Cantus)
Contratenor
Tenor
A
B
C
5
10
1. Biau-te qui tou - tes au-tres pe-re
3. Dou-ceur fi - ne a mon goust a-me-re,
1. Beau-ty who doth all o-ther things bless,
3. To my bit - ter - ness, gen-tle sweet-ness,
2. En-vers moy di-ver-se et es - tran
4. Corps di - gne de tou-te lo - an
2. Is to me true and con-stant ne
4. Form wor - thy of high prai-ses e

EX. 55 (CONTD.)

15
1.
2.
- ge,
- ver;
- ge,
- ver;
c
20
d
5. Sim-ple vis a cu - er d'ay - ment,
6. Re - gart pour tu - er un a -
5. Pure of face with en - tranc - ing heart,
6. Glan-ces that kill with sweet Love's
C
25
e
- mant,
7. Sem - blant de joi - e et re-pon - se d'es - may,
dart,
7. Joy - ous seem - ing but with a harsh re - ply;

† C♯ & B♮ should only be sung in the repeat.

EX. 55 (CONTD.)

third rather than on the fourth or fifth. In Britain, as we saw in Chapter 4, the acceptance of the third as a basic interval began a good deal earlier than in the rest of Europe, but the dominating influence of French music, with its stress on individualizing each part of a polyphonic composition, prevented the British conception of sonority from spreading for the richer or more sonorous the sound the more dissonant it is, and the harder it becomes for the ear to pick out the individual components. Thus the frequent use of thirds and sixths fuses the parts together more than if the less dissonant fourths and fifths are the main intervals.

Another point worth noting in Ex. 55 is the cross-rhythm in bars 9-14 and 30-35 between the tenor's syncopated breves (=minims in the transcription) in duple time and the ternary rhythm of the other parts. The change to duple time is indicated in the manuscript by the sign 'c' (cf. p. 125), one of the earliest instances of its use. These two closing passages of the two main sections are in fact rhythmically identical in the tenor and cantus parts, and the latter is almost identical melodically as well; this is known, for obvious reasons, as 'melodic rhyme' (see also Ex. 60, bb. 13–16 and 32–35, and Ex. 62). Note also the way the two motives A and B permeate the whole piece and thus give it unity, A occurring in bars 1-2, 10, 12, 14, 20, 26, 31, 33, and 35, and B in bars 4, 5, 7, 15, 16, 25, 36, and 37. This is a common feature of Machaut's music, although the delightful sequential use of motive A in the closing bars of each section is comparatively rare.

The melodic superiority of the cantus is very apparent in the above ballade, and this style of writing is usually called 'ballade style' today; a better name, however, is 'treble-dominated style', for this is a clearer definition and can be applied to other types of composition than the ballade without confusion. This style almost completely reversed the order of composition in the motet, for now the cantus was written first, the tenor next, and the contratenor last. It became enormously popular, lasting well into the fifteenth century (see Chapter 6), and when in the latter part of the fourteenth century composers began setting parts of the liturgy they often wrote in this style, thus flouting the authority of Pope John XXII. John's decree, in fact, had made things worse than before, because it encouraged composers to cultivate secular music, and when they returned to sacred composition they used a style which was, from the strict ecclesiastical point of view, far less suitable, not only in its complexity, but also in the fact that the main melody is in the top voice instead of the traditional tenor and, worse still, frequently has no connexion whatever with a Gregorian chant.

Machaut's church music, however, with one exception, is markedly more conservative in style than his secular pieces, all six of the motets being based on a Gregorian tenor and only Latin being used in the upper parts. The exception is the Mass, possibly the first complete setting of the Ordinary by one composer and the only one for nearly another 100 years, apart from the so-called 'Mass of Toulouse' and the so-called incomplete 'Mass of the Sorbonne' (sometimes mis-termed the 'Mass of Besançon'). Whether Machaut invented the idea or whether he knew either of the above two masses or the so-called Mass of Tournai (*c.* 1300), which is a collection of separate items in different styles and by different composers, will probably never be known, but in any case nothing can detract from the vigour, imagination, and technical ingenuity of the work. This Mass is sometimes and erroneously called 'Notre Dame' or 'Nostre Dame', and is often claimed to have been composed for the Coronation of Charles V (1364). It may have been, particularly as Charles had been a patron of Machaut, and the somewhat conservative style compared to his ballades, which might otherwise tend to date it as an early work, may have been deliberate for so solemn an occasion, but there is no proof.

The Mass is divided up into the usual five main sections, Kyrie, Gloria, Credo, Sanctus, and Agnus Dei, with a setting of Ite Missa Est at the end. The Kyrie, the 'Amen' at the end of the Credo and Gloria, most of the Sanctus, the Agnus Dei, and the Ite Missa Est are all in motet style with isorhythm in one or more of the parts, and all are based on a Gregorian chant in the tenor, except the two 'Amens'. The rest of the Mass is in conductus style, an obvious choice with regard to the Gloria and Credo because of the greater number of words, but the Credo is also based on a chant melody, not in the tenor however but in the motetus part, where it is highly ornamented. (The Credo of the Tournai Mass is similarly constructed.)

In order to give some idea of the way Machaut handles the motet and conductus style in his Mass, here are two short extracts, the first from the Christe Eleison and the second from the Credo (Exx. 56, 57* p. 150-2). (Translation for Ex. 57: 'And [I believe] in the Holy Ghost, the Lord and giver of life, who proceedeth from the Father and the Son, who with the Father and the Son together is worshipped and glorified, who spake by the prophets.')

This Mass anticipated that of the mid-fifteenth century and later in several ways, which it will be simplest to tabulate as follows:

1. In the Gloria and Credo movements the initial words 'Gloria in excelsis Deo' ('Glory be to God on high') and 'Credo in unum Deum' ('I believe in one God') are sung to Gregorian chant, the polyphonic setting beginning with the words 'Et in terra pax' ('And on earth peace'), and 'Patrem omnipotentem' ('The Father Almighty') respectively.

* Both examples are adapted from the edition of the Mass by J. Chailley.

2. The phrases 'Jesu Christe' in the Gloria and 'Maria Virgine' in the Credo are set to long notes, thus making them stand out from their context.
3. The Gloria and Credo are syllabically underlaid while the other movements are melismatic.
4. All the movements are linked together by a short motive, shown in the first two bars of the Triplum part in Ex. 56 (see also Triplum, b. 6, Motetus, b. 3, and in Ex. 57, Triplum, b. 13, Motetus, bb. 5–6, Tenor, b. 12); sometimes the motive is altered rhythmically.
5. Word-painting in the Credo on 'crucifixus', which is set to some unusually sharp discords. Later composers with a more refined sense of discord chose less emotional words or phrases to paint, such as 'descendit de coelis' ('came down from Heaven') and 'ascendit in coelum' ('ascended into Heaven'), making the voices fall and rise respectively.

Ex. 56 The beginning of *Christe eleison* from the Mass · Machaut

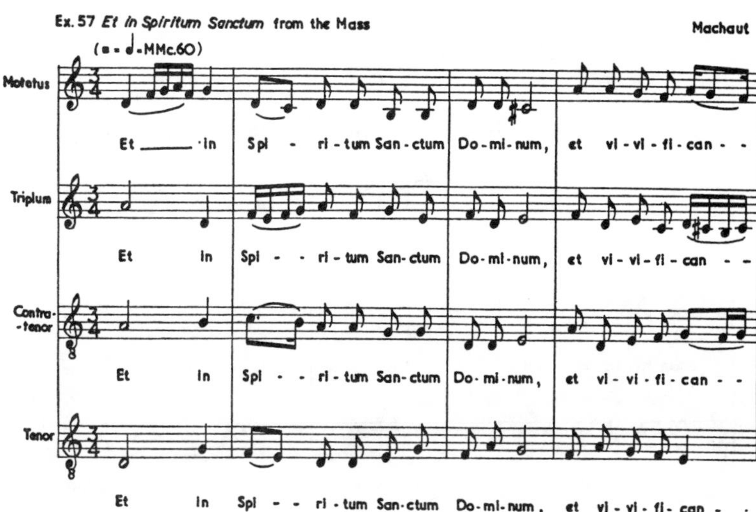
Ex. 57 *Et in Spiritum Sanctum* from the Mass
Machaut
(♩ = ♩. = MMc.60)
Motetus
Triplum
Contra-tenor
Tenor
Et in Spi - ri - tum San - ctum Do - mi - num, et vi - vi - fi - can - -

5
- tem: qui ex Pa - tre, Fi - li - o - que pro - ce - - dit. Qui

EX. 57 (CONTD.)

[10]
cum Pa - tre et Fi - li - - o si-mul a - do - - ra - tur, et con-glo-ri - fi - ca - -
cum Pa - tre et Fi - li - - o si-mul a - do - - ra - tur, et con-glo-ri - fi - ca - -
cum Pa - tre et Fi - li - - o si-mul a - do - - ra - tur, et con-glo-ri - fi - ca - -
cum Pa - tre et Fi - li - - o si-mul a - do - ra - tur, et con-glo-ri - fi - - ca - -

- tur; qui lo - cu - tus est per pro - - phe - tas.
(etc.)
- tur; qui lo - cu - tus est per___ pro - - phe - - tas.
(etc.)
- tur; qui lo - cu - tus est per pro - - - phe - - tas.
(etc.)
- tur; qui lo - cu - tus est per pro - - phe - - tas.
(etc.)

Machaut's Mass can be regarded as a summary of the French Ars Nova, for it contains nearly all the devices and styles practised by him and his compatriots—syncopation, hocket, florid melody, syllabic settings, both Gregorian and freely composed tenors, the elaboration of a chant in an upper part, the use of instruments to accompany one or more of the voices, and the four unifying devices—isorhythm, identical texts, imitation, and sonority. With reference to the last of these, there is the same distinction between the conductus style and the isorhythmic movements in the Mass that we noted between the ballades and the motets—in other words, there is a greater percentage of triads, especially on the first part of the breve, in the Gloria and Credo than in the other movements of the Mass.

As for imitation it is hardly used at all, because mediaeval composers were more interested in the differentiation of individual voices than in their integration, and imitation is the most powerful unifying device that music possesses. This desire to make each part independent of the others was natural enough if we consider that part-music was still in its infancy compared to monophony, and that, like a child with a new toy, composers wanted to, one could almost say were bound to, exploit the possibilities of this kind of music in which the more the parts are dissociated from each other the less like monophony they become.

The widespread use of instruments to contrast with the voice is another pointer in the same direction, for the similarity of range of the voices, which as a result frequently cross each other, would tend to obscure their melodic and rhythmic differences if unaccompanied, but when supported or doubled by instruments of different timbres each part stands out sharply from the others. Thus a purely vocal rendering of almost any French part-music written between *c.* 1200 and *c.* 1425 completely misrepresents the composer's intentions.

The Italian Ars Nova has usually been regarded as less important than the French, because for one thing its system of notation was less subtle and more cumbersome than the French and eventually became obsolete, and for another the school of composers that flourished from *c.* 1325 to *c.* 1425 left no followers, most of the fifteenth century being a blank so far as Italian composition is concerned. The music itself, however, which is quite different in many respects, surpassed that of France during the latter part of the century.

The 'New Art' in Italy began at about the same time as in France, and again it was a theorist, Marchettus of Padua [fl. first half of the fourteenth century], who, in his *Pomerium musicae mensuratae* ('The Fruits of Measured Music'), provided composers with a neatly classified system of notation which enabled them to exploit the new rhythmic freedom. The basis of this system is the breve, which never alters its value once this has been fixed, just as in Petronian notation, whereas in the French system the breve can be shortened or lengthened at any time by imperfection or alteration respectively (see p. 125). Like Petronian notation also, the groups of notes which make up the value of a breve are marked off by a long, a breve, a long or breve rest, a ligature, or, more frequently, a dot. Marchettus, however, expands the earlier system in two ways. He first of all divides both the ternary (perfect) and binary (imperfect) breve into four groups of smaller notes, the perfect breve consisting of three, six, nine, or twelve equal parts, and the imperfect of two, four, six, or eight equal parts. Each of these divisions is called by the number of parts it contains, e.g. 'ternaria' (three), 'senaria perfecta' (six arranged in three (i.e. 'perfect') groups of two), 'novenaria' (nine), and 'duodenaria' (twelve); 'binaria' (two), 'quaternaria' (four), 'senaria imperfecta' (six arranged in two (i.e. 'imperfect') groups of three), and 'octonaria' (eight), and in order to tell the performer which of these divisions was in operation composers sometimes, but alas by no means always, wrote the initial letters in the stave. Four of these divisions are exactly the same as de Vitri's four common arrangements of time and prolation given on p. 125, for in modern terms novenaria ('n') $= \frac{9}{8} = \odot$, senaria imperfecta ('si' or 'i') $= \frac{6}{8} =$ ${\mathsf{C}}$ with dot, senaria perfecta ('sp' or 'p') $= \frac{3}{4} =$ O, and quaternaria ('q') $= \frac{2}{4} =$ C.

Marchettus's second expansion lay in the number of note shapes, and in this he went far beyond de Vitri, who was quite content with the addition of the minim, for some of the more complex Italian pieces bristle with shapes such as these all of which have different values, depending on which 'division' they occur in, but in any one division their value is fixed; two notes, however, the semibrevis and the semibrevis major ♦ (which also occurs in *Le Roman de Fauvel*, see p. 124), have no fixed value, like the Petronian semibreve.

It may seem from the above that Italian Ars Nova notation is needlessly complex and obscure, but in actual fact it is much less ambiguous than the French system and presents far fewer difficulties to the modern transcriber once the values of the notes in any particular 'division' are known, largely because of the inevitable grouping in breves. In fact, the music of the earlier part of the century is really nothing more than an ornamented conductus-style, for instead of the parts moving together at the same time as in the older conducti, the basic notes are broken up into notes of smaller value and so produce contrasting rhythms; thus syncopation can occur *within* the breve, but not *between* one breve and the next, and it is this limitation of the system that caused it to be severely modified from about 1350 onwards, when Italian composers came into contact with French music and saw how superior the French system was as regards rhythmical expression.

The notation which evolved in Italy during the latter half of the fourteenth century is best described as 'mixed notation', for while it adopted de Vitri's basic principles and scrapped the rigid division into breve groups, it still retained the multiplicity of note shapes—in fact, it even added to these as the century progressed, despite the frequent protests of French and English theorists. To make matters even more complex, not only do red notes occur in all the parts (in France they were still largely restricted to the tenor and contratenor), but white notes as well. Yet this notation was the one used by most of the Italian Ars Nova composers (see Fig. 4, p. 156).

The influence of France on Italy was not confined only to notation or even to music as a whole, for in society, learning, and literature French customs, ideas, and forms of expression played a considerable part in Italian life and culture. On the other hand, although Paris was still the intellectual and artistic centre of Europe, some Italian cities, particularly those in the north, were beginning to be independent of outside influence, and so far as music at any rate was concerned, Florence, Bologna, Padua, Rimini, Genoa, and, in central Italy, Caserta and Perugia all had flourishing schools of composers whose output, while still clearly influenced

Fig. 4 Italian Ars Nova 'mixed' notation. The ballata *Nessun ponga speranza* by Landini. Squarcialupi Codex (see p. 167). The tenor part starts at the beginning of the 5th stave and the contratenor at the beginning of the 8th stave. Note the multiplicity of note shapes and the white breves and semibreves. Facsimile in Apel, ibid. p. 393.

by the French Ars Nova, stressed a side of part-music that had till now been of only secondary importance—namely, *melody*.

Speaking generally, we can say that the development of music up to the end of the fourteenth century took place in France and that it was almost exclusively concerned with rhythm, both in the individual parts and as a means of providing some degree of unity (isorhythm). It is possible that this preoccupation with the most fundamental characteristic of music (for rhythm exists in nature without melody, but not vice versa) was inevitable, and that the melodic aspect of part-music could not be developed until the rhythmic aspect had been more or less fully worked out. Again speaking generally, it is true to say that the French have always been more interested in the intellectual side of artistic creation (rhythm and design) than in the emotional (melody and colour), whether in music, poetry, architecture, or painting, whereas with the Italians it has always been the other way round. (Could Gregorian chant, with its almost complete lack of interest in organized rhythm, have arisen in France rather than Italy?) This generalization is not contradicted by the fact that the first great flowering of secular melody arose in Provence, for this region of France was associated most closely, both geographically and culturally, with Italy, and the songs of the troubadours were in general more purely melodic than those of the northern French trouvères in the sense that they were less concerned with overall structure and hence with melodic repetition.

But the Italian genius, although it eclipsed the French during the latter half of the fourteenth century, was too much under the influence of the latter to show its natural melodic bent as consistently as it might have done, but the one purely Italian type of composition, the madrigal, does rely almost entirely on melody for its appeal, for it not only rejected the immensely popular device of isorhythm, but the melodies themselves are smoother, sweeter, and more typically vocal than those of Machaut and his compatriots. One might indeed compare the two chief composers of the fourteenth century, Machaut and Landini, with Bach and Handel respectively, in that both Machaut and Bach were mainly concerned with structure and their part-writing is frequently instrumental in character even when written for voices, whereas Landini and Handel stressed the more sensuous and emotional aspect of music and their melodies are predominantly vocal even when written for instruments.

The madrigal was one of the two types of composition that appeared in the early fourteenth century—that is, before French influence became strong. The name possibly derives from the Italian *mandria*, which means 'sheepfold', and later the term 'mandriale' was applied to any pastoral poem. It may, however, have come from the Latin *matricale*, 'belonging to the womb', and hence denoted poems written in the mother tongue or vernacular. Whatever the derivation, the texts of the Ars Nova madrigals are by no means always based on pastoral subjects, but they all consist of two or three verses, each with three lines and a final verse of two lines called a 'ritornello' (refrain); thus the total number of lines was either eleven or eight. The music for each verse is the same, but that for the ritornello is different and, moreover, usually written in a contrasting metre, as in this charming eight-line madrigal by Jacopo da Bologna [fl. first half of fourteenth century] (Ex. 58* opposite).

The rhythmic simplicity and melodic smoothness of this piece, despite the occasional use of hocket (e.g. bb. 6-7, 14-16), is typical of the madrigal, as is the use of imitation (bb. 10-11, 43-4), and it is this last feature that provides another important difference between fourteenth-century French and Italian music, because for the first time it was consistently stressed and made an integral part of composition by the Italian Ars Nova composers, particularly those of the early generation such as Jacopo da Bologna and Giovanni da Firenze (=Florence), or da Cascia, as he is sometimes called [fl. first half of fourteenth century].

The second of the two early types of Italian composition is the 'caccia' (hunt), which shows imitation carried to its extreme, for it is either entirely or mainly written in strict canon. Like the madrigal, most cacce are in two sections, the second, shorter one being the ritornello, but whereas the first section is always a canon, usually for two voices with an accompanying instrumental tenor, the ritornello is much less consistent, and is even omitted at times. Italy was not the first

* Adapted from H. Gleason, op. cit., p. 99.

country to employ strict canon in composition, as the caccia almost certainly derived from the French 'chace'; the latter, however, did not become nearly so popular in France as the caccia did in Italy, because canon inevitably binds the parts together, and this as we have seen was completely opposed to the French conception of polyphony.

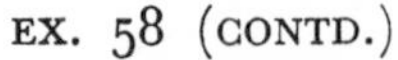
EX. 58 (CONTD.)

[20]

-ra, 3. Che vo - - lo con a - - - mor per
-to: 6. Vas - - sen la sta - - te e'l ver - - no
-dove, 3. That 'midst the beau - - teous gar - - dens
fear: 6. The sum - - mer pas - - ses hence, and

-ra, 3. Che vo - lo con a - - mor per
-to: 6. Vas - - sen la sta - - te e'l ver - - no
-dove, 3. That 'midst the beau-teous gar - - - dens
fear: 6. The sum-mer pas - ses hence, and

[25]

le bell' or - - - - - - - - - - -
vien di su - - - - - - - - - - -
e - - ver flies
soon comes win - - - - - - - - - -

le bell' or - - - - - - - - - - - - - -
vien di su - - - - - - - - - - - - -
e - - ver flies
soon comes win - - - - - - - - - - - -

[30]

- - - - - - - - - - - to ra.
- - - - - - - - - - - bi to.
with love.
- - - - - - - - - - ter drear.

- - - - - - - - - - - - - - to - ra.
- - - - - - - - - - - - - - bi - to.
with love.
- - - - - - - - - - - - ter drear.

EX. 58 (CONTD.)

Although most cacce deal with hunting in some form or other, this is often a disguise for amorous pursuit, the hunter being the lover and the hunted his mistress. In addition, animated scenes, such as a fire or market day, were sometimes used, but whatever the subject the music reflects the general excitement of the setting. In the following caccia by Giovanni da Firenze quails are the quarry, although it would seem from the end of the second verse that the hunter was himself ensnared (Ex. 59*):

* From W. T. Marrocco, *Fourteenth-century Italian Cacce.*

EX. 59 (CONTD.)

E qual di - - - ce - - - va
E qual di - - - ce - - - a
"Give to me!" one is
And one cried a - - loud:
U - - - cel - la - vam su per la ri - - -
Co - - - me fa - cea cias - cun per fug - - -
On Ad - da's shores to catch quails we
As did each one of us, the down - - -
"Da - da!" E, e qual
"Da qua, dam - - - - - mi'l man - - -
cry - ing; And, and one:
"You there, give me my
- va d'A - da E qual di - - ce - - - va
- gir l'ac - qua; E qual di - - ce - - a
were try - ing. "Give to me!" one is
- pour fly - ing. And one cried a - - loud:
"Va - cia!" "Va - rin!" "Tor - na Pic - cio - lo!" E, e,
- tel - lo!" E tal, "Dam - mi'l cap - pel - lo!" Quan - - - - - -
"Go to!" "Va - rin!" "Ti - ny, come here you!" And, and,
cloak you!" And one: "Give me my hat too!" When
"Da - da!" E, e qual
"Da qua, dam - - - - - mi'l man -
cry - ing; And, and one:
"You there, give me my

EX. 59 (CONTD.)

e,
and
"Va-cia!" "Va-rin!" "Tor-na Pic-cio-lo!" E, e,
-tel-lo!" E tal "Dam-mi'l cap-pel-lo!" Quan
"Go to!" "Va-rin!" "Ti-ny, come here you!" And, and,
cloak you!" And one: "Give me my hat too!" When
qual pren-dea le qua-glie a vo-lo a vo-lo Quan
-do lo ri-co-ve-rai co'l mio uc-cel-lo Do
one the quails caught as flight by flight they flew; When
I with my poor bird to shel-ter with-drew; There
e,
and
qual pren-dea le qua-glie a vo-lo a vo-lo
-do lo ri-co-ve-rai co'l mio uc-cel-lo
one the quails caught as flight by flight they flew;
I with my poor bird to shel-ter with-drew;

EX. 59 (CONTD.)

do con gran tem - pes - - ta un a - qua
ve u - na pas - tu - - rel - - la il cor mi
came a sud - den tem - pest, and thun - der
lay a shep - herd - ess who my poor heart
Quan - do con gran tem - pes - ta un a - qua
Do - ve u - na pas - tu - rel - la il cor mi
When came a sud - den tem - pest, and thunder
There lay a shep - herd - ess who my poor heart
ve - ne.
pun - se.
sound - ed.
wound - ed.
[Ritornello]
(𝅗𝅥 = 𝅗𝅥.)
So - la e - - ra li on - - - de fra
A - lone was I so to my - self
So - la e - ra li on - - -
A - lone was I so to

EX. 59 (CONT.)

me di - - ce - a, "Ec - - - cho la piog-gia,
I said: — "Be - hold, Here's the rain and here are

-de fra me di - - ce - a, "Ec - -
my - self I said: — "Be - hold, Here's the

ec - cho — Di - do et E - - - ne - -
Di - do — and Æ - ne - as — of —

- cho la piog-gia, ec - cho — Di - do et E - -
rain and here are Di - do — and Æ - ne - as

Besides Giovanni da Firenze, Florence boasted a number of other composers, her most brilliant—indeed, the most outstanding composer of the Italian Ars Nova—being Francesco Landini [*c.* 1325 – 1397] who, though blinded from smallpox while still a child, became not only a virtuoso organist, lutanist, and flautist, but was also widely acclaimed as a poet (like Machaut) and philosopher. It was his compositions, however, that brought him most fame, and those that have come down to us represent nearly one-third of the total number of Italian pieces of this period, a contemporary estimation of greatness that posterity for once has accepted.

Most of Landini's compositions are contained in a most beautifully written and illuminated manuscript, the Squarcialupi Codex, the largest collection of fourteenth-century Italian music that has been preserved. Twelve composers besides Landini are represented, and each is portrayed in a miniature placed at the beginning of the section devoted to his music.

Unlike Jacopo da Bologna and Giovanni da Firenze, Landini was considerably influenced by French music. This is clearly evident in his decided preference for the 'ballata' rather than the madrigal or caccia. The ballata is the exact parallel of the French virelai from which it is derived, but while the form is the same (*A bb a A*) the melodic character is quite different, being, as we should expect, smoother and more graceful. The following example has been described by one specialist of the period as "perhaps the most beautiful work of the century"; it is certainly an exquisite one (Ex. 60* overleaf).

The cadence in bars 8-9 with the inserted E between the F and the final G is very common in fourteenth-century music. It is often misleadingly called the 'Landini sixth cadence', 'sixth' because the inserted note is always a sixth—either major (as above) or minor—from the final, and 'Landini' because it was once thought (wrongly) that he was the first to use it. A better name is 'under-third cadence'. The seventh degree of the scale (F in this case) could be either sharp or flat (as in the above example), but it is possible that a contemporary singer would have sung F♯; if he did then the C in the contratenor would probably be sharpened also. This brings us to the vexed question of 'musica falsa' or 'musica ficta' (the terms are

* Adapted from H. Gleason, op. cit., p. 104.

Ex. 60 Ballata-*Gram piant' agli ochi*
(■ = 𝅗𝅥 = MM c.60)
Landini
[Cantus]
1.9. Gram pian - t'a - gli_o - chi gre - ve do - gli_a'l co - re,
7. Et ben ch'io vi - va mai non vo' se - gui - re,
1.9. Tears my eyes lad - ing, grief op - pres - sing my heart,
7. Since live I must I on - ly wish to be near thee,
Contratenor
Tenor
2.10. Ab - bon - da sem - pre l'a - ni - ma si mo -
8. Se non vo', chia - ra stel - la et dol - c'a - mo -
2.10. E - ver a - bound, my spi - rit now doth de -
8. And fol - low thee, my bright star and dear sweet -

EX. 60 (CONTD.)

15
[Fine]
re.
re.
part.
heart.
20
3. Per que-st'a ma - ra et a - - spra di - spar - ti
5. Con - - - tra mie vo - gli - a du - ra que-sta vi
3. Be - - - cause of this harsh and bit - - ter se - pa - ra
5. My life con - ti - nues a - gainst my in - cli - na

EX. 60 (CONTD.)

25
- ta. 4. Chia - - - - mo la
- ta. 6. Che mil - - - le
- tion. 4. I call on
- tion. 6. So must I
30
mor - te et non mi vuol' u - - - - di - - - -
mor - ti mi con - vien sen - - - - ti - - -
death, but a - las he doth not hear
bear a thou - - sand deaths I fear
1
2
re.
re.
me.
me.
D.C. al fine

synonymous). To the mediaeval musician this simply meant those notes that are not included in the enlarged scale of Guido (see Chapter 1, pp. 36 and 37), so that any note below *G* or above *e''*, or any chromatic note except B♭ (which is in the Guidonian system) was regarded theoretically as 'false' or 'fictitious'. Today, however, the term is limited to the chromatic alteration of certain notes (including B) which a modern editor thinks would have been made by a contemporary performer. All we know for certain is that the music as written down does not indicate all the accidentals, and that performers altered certain notes as they went along. Admittedly the theorists give us some help by stating, for example, that B is flattened in the melodic progression F–B–A or A–B–A, and F sharpened in the progression B–F–G or G–F–G, that the harmonic interval of a diminished fifth must be made perfect by altering one of the notes, and that a third expanding to a fifth or a sixth to an octave should both be perfect. This last rule ties up with the 'double leading-note' cadence mentioned on p. 140. Even so, none of the theorists provides a complete explanation of the practice, and even if some of them had done we could not apply their rules to all compositions, because it is quite clear that the practice varied according to the period, the nationality of the composer and performer, and even between one composer and another. Moreover, different manuscripts of the same period sometimes present the same composition with varying accidentals; thus it is unlikely that there ever was only one completely authentic way of performing a piece, a view which agrees with the lack of precise instructions as to which instruments should accompany or double the voice. The problems of musica ficta apply to most Renaissance music also, and in modern editions of early music the added accidentals are placed either in brackets before the notes or, better, above the stave.

The Italian Ars Nova composers are usually grouped into three generations, the more important ones in the first generation being Jacopo da Bologna and Giovanni da Firenze, in the second Landini, Niccolo da Perugia, Ghirardello da Firenze, and Paolo tenorista da Firenze, and in the third Matteo da Perugia, Antonello and Filippo da Caserta, Bartolomeo da Bologna, and the Belgian, Johannes Ciconia. The last group flourished during the end of the fourteenth and the beginning of the fifteenth century and represents, together with a number of French composers, the summit of mediaeval technique as well as some features typical of the Renaissance.

The main characteristic of mediaeval polyphony is, as we have seen, independence of parts, largely achieved by contrasting rhythms in the different voices. It was essentially a French idea and is more clearly shown in Machaut's music than in Landini's. But even Machaut provides some means of unification, either through isorhythm, the development of a rhythmic and melodic motive (see pp. 148, 150), or sonority. The climax came at the turn of the century, when a group of composers, most of them French, but including some Italians, created an art which for rhythmical and notational complexity has never been surpassed or even equalled, and which employs dissonances more freely than in any period before the twentieth century; the result is a texture composed of virtually unconnected strands of melody which at times all but disintegrates.

The leading composers of this group—often called the Mannered School—whose output was almost entirely secular, were the Frenchmen, Solage, Jacques de Selesses (Senleches), Jean Trebor, and Jean Vaillant, and the Italians, Matteo da Perugia and Antonello and Filippo da Caserta. It seems likely that the last-named initiated this new style of composition, for he was a theorist as well as a composer, and his treatise deals at length with the complicated system of notation needed to express the rhythmic subtleties of the music, and just as in the case of de Vitri, whose Ars Nova satisfied the existing desire to enlarge the rhythmical horizon, so Filippo provided the means by which composers could pursue to the utmost their obsession with rhythm.

Space forbids detailed discussion or even a complete example of this ultra-refined art; suffice it to say that cross-rhythms far more extravagant than that shown in Ex. 55 and syncopations more complex than that of Ex. 49 abound. Example 61* (opposite) will give some idea of this extraordinary art.

Such music obviously requires not only first-rate musicians, but also the appreciation of a highly cultured circle intensely interested in secular art. Both existed in a few aristocratic establishments in the south of France, particularly at Avignon, the headquarters of the French Pope during the Great Schism.

* Adapted from W. Apel, *French Secular Music of the Late Fourteenth Century*, p. 36. The words in the top part have been omitted.

To this brilliant and distinguished court men came from all over Europe, and it became famous as an international meeting-place. This explains the presence of the Italian contingent and also the fact that most of the compositions have French texts and are either ballades, virelais, or rondeaux, the first of these forms predominating.

The logical outcome of the mediaeval ideal had been reached, but alongside it there was developing a movement in the opposite direction, a movement which had already begun with the first generation of Italian composers and which aimed at a greater simplicity of rhythm, a smoother melodic line, and a more unified texture. The chief figures in this movement were Matteo da Perugia and Ciconia, most of whose works point towards the style of the mid-fifteenth century discussed in Chapter 6.

Apart from France, Italy, and Britain (see below), the rest of Europe contributed little to the development of part-music. There was tremendous musical activity in Spain, particularly in Aragon and Catalonia, the provinces bordering on to France, which reached its peak during the reign of John I of Aragon [1350-1396], but even though the cultural and political ties with France and Italy were strong and some French composers, including Selesses, visited John's court, actual composition, as in the thirteenth century (see Chapter 3, p. 90), was largely confined to solo songs in virelai-form rather than part-songs. Similarly in Germany, where Minnesang continued to flourish, but part-music was almost totally neglected, being much farther behind France and even Spain in both quality and quantity. Britain, however, whose main centre of composition seems to have been at Worcester, though stylistically out of date in that her composers preferred the conductus to the motet and rarely attempted the rhythmic complexities of Continental music, persisted in stressing the two features already referred to in Chapter 4 and which became all-important in the Renaissance—namely, sonority and imitation. The first is evident in the greater number of compositions in four or even five parts than on the Continent, and by the frequent use of $^{6}_{3}$ chords. This style is usually called 'English discant' today, and not only was it immensely popular in Britain from *c.* 1300 to *c.* 1450, but greatly influenced Continental music during the following century (*H.A.M.*, 57B). Imitation was almost entirely limited to voice-exchange, and it is rather surprising that canon was hardly used at all. Admittedly, the total number of British pieces that have survived is much smaller compared to France or Italy, but this does not fully explain the dearth of canonic writing, particularly after the *tour de force* of the Reading Rota (see Chapter 4, p. 112). Perhaps the explanation lies in the fact that it is harder to compose a canon using full triads than it is to write a sonorous piece in conductus style in which the parts exchange phrases.

Britain was also the probable home of the first harpsichord, the 'echiquier', and although we have no contemporary description or illustration it most likely consisted of a triangular-shaped sounding board with a number of strings of varying lengths stretched over it and plucked by 'jacks', which in turn were operated by pressing down a key. The appearance of these jacks ranged across the base of the triangle might very well have suggested a row of chessmen, for 'echiquier' means 'chess-board'.

The importance of instruments in the performance of fourteenth-century vocal music has already been stressed, and is further borne out by the frequent references in contemporary literature, the number of times they are portrayed in paintings and sculpture, and the great variety that existed. The almost complete lack of part-compositions intended solely for instrumental ensembles is certainly due to the widespread use of instruments in vocal music, much of which was undoubtedly performed without voices if so desired. Most of the remaining pieces that are definitely instrumental consist of dance and keyboard pieces; in the former the estampie is still the most common, and a special type called the 'saltarello' makes its first appearance. We know nothing about the actual dance steps of the saltarello, but the examples that have survived are (in modern terms) in $\frac{2}{4}$, $\frac{3}{4}$, or $\frac{6}{8}$, each having a number of 'puncti' with the usual ouvert and clos endings, and each employing melodic rhyme, as in the following delightful example (Ex. 62*):

* From A. Schering, *Geschichte der Musik in Beispielen*, p. 21.

The fourteenth century is usually regarded as the period when dancing in the modern (i.e. fashionable) sense began as opposed to folk-dancing, which of course is as old as man. Unfortunately, very little dance music has survived, and what there is is nearly all monophonic, but we are better off as regards other instrumental music, most of which consists of arrangements for keyboard of vocal pieces. These are important because they show for the first time a clear distinction between vocal and keyboard styles, and the latter, by ornamenting the long notes and filling in the leaps of the original song, and by the use of rapid repeated notes and broken-chord patterns prepared the way for the keyboard variations of the sixteenth century. In Ex. 63, (i)* is the second part of a solo song with its keyboard transcription placed below, and (ii)† is an excerpt from a transcription of a hitherto untraced song. Only one example of variation-form from the fourteenth century has come down to us, and this is entitled *Di molen van pariis* ('The Windmills of Paris'; alternatively, the title may simply mean that the composition is by a certain Mr. Windmill of Paris).

None of the manuscripts of keyboard music gives any indication as to whether the contents are intended for the clavichord, harpsichord, or positive organ, or all three. (The great organ was obviously too clumsy, and the portative, as we have observed, was incapable of playing part-music.) Probably the occasion or the performer's personal preference for one or other of the instruments was the deciding factor.

Dance and instrumental music as well as singing played an important part in the fourteenth-century Mystery and Miracle Plays that developed from the earlier church operas. In Chapter 1 we saw how the popularity of these operas led to the increasing use of the vernacular instead of Latin, to the intrusion of secular music alongside Gregorian chant, and to performances in the market-place rather than the church, with professional and amateur actors replacing the clergy. Having ransacked the Bible for suitable material, and having created a unified series of playlets which dramatized the main events from the Creation to the Resurrection—the Mystery Plays—men began to find more outlet for their dramatic talent in the miracles and lives

* Adapted from O. Plamenac, 'Keyboard Music of the Fourteenth Century in Codex Faenza 117' (*Journal of the American Musiological Society*, IV, 3, pp. 191–2).

† Adapted from O. Plamenac, ibid., p. 193.

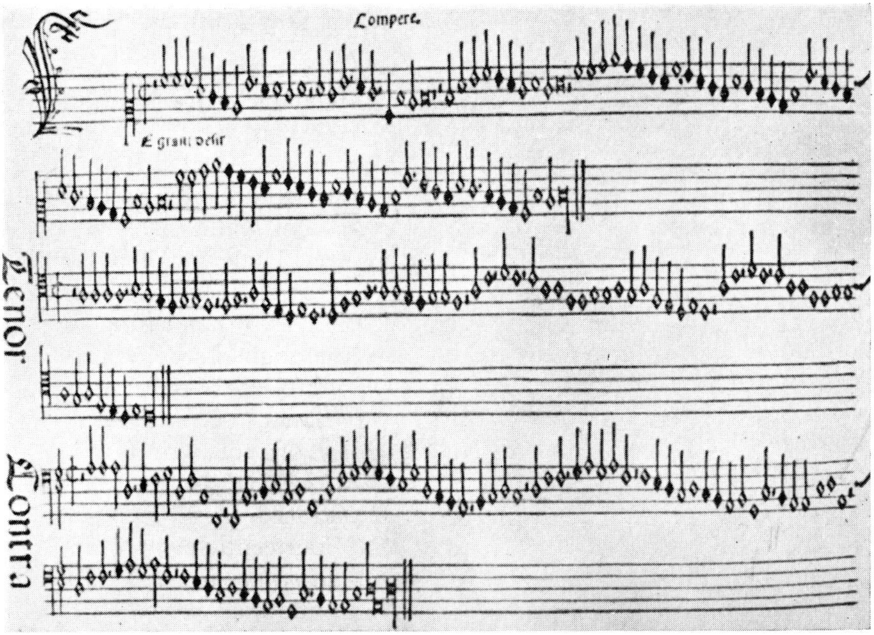

XIII The chanson *Le grant desir* by Compère as printed by Petrucci in his *Canti B. numero Cinquanta*, 2nd ed. 1503.

XIV The superius (soprano) part of the chanson *Ma fille ma mère* by Janequin (see Part II) as printed by Attaignant in 1530. Compare the uneven broken lines of the stave—caused by joining separate pieces of type—with those of the Petrucci print.

XV Dufay and Binchois. From the MS. containing the poem *Le Champion des dames* by Martin le Franc in which the quotation on p. 186 occurs.

XVI Josquin des Prez.

XVII Ockeghem (extreme right foreground) with members of Charles VII's Royal Chapel choir. Note the size of music MS. on the lectern. There would in fact be more staves on the MS. than the artist has shown. The rest of the choir sang from a MS. placed on the other side of the lectern.

Ex 63(i) (a) Part II of the song *Jour a jour la vie* and (b) a transcription for keyboard. Anon

† A in MS.

of the saints. These Miracle Plays were performed singly, not in cycles, and whereas each Mystery Play became associated with a certain locality and was performed virtually unaltered every year for generation after generation, the Miracle Play, with its wider choice of subject matter, greater freedom of treatment, and lack of sacred tradition, provided an opportunity for dramatic experiments. During the fifteenth and sixteenth centuries the Miracle Plays changed in character and content, and by portraying contemporary society to a far greater extent than formerly reflected the realistic approach to life so typical of the Renaissance. Thus, instead of depicting the conversion of a sinner by a saint, together with other holy deeds by the latter, they presented everyday scenes and people with the saint replaced by personifications of the moralities—the Morality Plays. The experience gained through these Morality Plays in having to devise both theme and plot instead of relying on historical or legendary events and figures, and their greater dramatic scope in having actual characters representing 'Good', 'Evil', etc., had a profound influence on later drama which can be traced from Marlowe's *Doctor Faustus* (*c.* 1588) to T. S. Eliot's *Murder in the Cathedral* (1935).

Mystery, Miracle, and Morality Plays were acted and produced with tremendous gusto and often considerable elaboration. Processions, tableaux, dances, choral and solo songs, buffoonery, and pathos combined to form an entertainment so popular that the purely secular drama of the late Renaissance had some difficulty in ousting it. Only in Italy did the Morality Play not catch on, a fact which largely explains the comparative failure of Italian drama during the seventeenth and to a lesser extent eighteenth centuries.

Judged as a whole, the music of the fourteenth century lacks both variety and balance when compared to the century that preceded it, even though many compositions by men such as Machaut and Landini are as good as or better than anything produced in the thirteenth century. The lack of variety is due, in the first place, to the fact that secular music completely overshadows sacred, whereas in the thirteenth century the two fields are roughly on a par, and, secondly, because the absence of lyrical solo song, which resulted when the various national minstrel movements died out, is by no means adequately compensated for by the French treble-dominated style or even by the melodiousness of Italian part-music.

The lack of balance is due to the obsession with rhythm and voice-differentiation; and while admittedly these are also the main characteristics of thirteenth-century music, their application in this century is not so extreme, and is nearly always balanced by the structural devices of isorhythm or repetition (e.g. rondeau form). In the fourteenth century, however, preoccupation with rhythm increased, and in general is not adequately balanced by structural devices, nor by the new sonority, nor by the rare use (outside Italy and Britain) of imitation, and eventually reached a pitch where the texture all but disintegrates.

This lack of balance is much less true of Italian Ars Nova music than French, but France was the dominating influence in Europe for most of the century. Even so, the quality of Italian music and its differences compared to that of France make the fourteenth century similar in one respect to the eighteenth century. Thus the latter period saw both the end of the baroque movement (Bach and Handel) and the rise—indeed, fulfilment—of the Viennese classical style (Haydn and Mozart). Similarly in the fourteenth century, where Machaut and the Mannered School on the one hand represent the culmination of mediaeval ideals, i.e. the stress on rhythm and differentiation of parts, of which the treble-dominated style was one result and varied instrumentation another, while on the other hand many of the compositions of the Italian Ars Nova show traits characteristic of the music that flourished during most of the Renaissance, i.e. the melodic and rhythmic simplicity of individual parts, and a unified texture achieved to some extent through equality of part-writing in which no voice dominates the others, but more particularly through the consistent use of imitation.

The beginnings and endings of artistic movements have always caused a good deal of dissension and none more so than those of the Renaissance. The problem becomes simpler if we realize that there never can be a hard and fast line between one movement and another, that the later develops from the earlier, and that therefore the distinction of a particular movement from other movements lies in the importance attached to certain features, most or all of which will be found in the preceding period. Thus naturalism—or the portrayal of Nature as she appears to the artist after close observation—is one of the main characteristics of Renaissance art, yet as we saw in the last chapter this had already become significant in Gothic sculpture and, moreover, continued to play a vital part in movements following the Renaissance, the difference being that Renaissance naturalism is more realistic than Gothic, and that in those later movements in which naturalism is an important feature it is either even more detailed or else treated more emotionally. Again, the chief feature of mediaeval music—the differentiation of parts—continued through most of the early Renaissance, albeit considerably modified, virtually dying out during the late Renaissance, but reappearing as one of the most notable traits of the early baroque.

We should also remember that new movements affect different countries at different times and in varying degrees—indeed, some movements may hardly affect a particular country at all, as, for instance, the Gothic style in Italy (see Chapter 2, p. 70). Similarly, the Renaissance began in Italy earlier and affected Italian society more completely than in any other country. Moreover, the various arts are not necessarily influenced at the same time nor to the same extent by a change in outlook. Architecture, for example, was affected by the Renaissance much later and less strongly than was painting.

In what ways then did fourteenth-century music reflect the Renaissance? Before we can attempt an answer to this question we must clearly understand what the main features of this movement are.

Renaissance means 'rebirth', and what was reborn was the awareness that man as an individual was extremely important, that the present was very real, and that life should be investigated and enjoyed to the full. All this was largely opposed to the mediaeval conception in which the world was renounced, the future being the focus of all man's activities. It is dangerous to crystallize the ideals of any movement into a few words, but it may help to provide a rough distinction between one movement and another. Thus the mediaeval approach to life was essentially mystical or abstract, while that of the Renaissance was realistic or concrete. This latter approach had, of course, existed before (hence it was reborn), particularly in the civilizations of Greece and Rome, and the study of classical literature, philosophy, and art, largely made possible by the labours of the mediaeval scholar-monks (see Chapter 1, p. 11), played an ever-increasing part in fertilizing the seeds that had begun to germinate in the late Middle Ages.

The corruption and division of the Church, the growing independence of temporal power that sprang from the consciousness of man's importance, and the stress laid on earthly life inevitably resulted in a pronounced swing towards the secular in art. If the style of architecture was not affected at first, its uses certainly were, and as much attention was given to the designing and construction of palaces and public buildings as to cathedrals and churches. Similarly with music; indeed, from this aspect at any rate music reflected the Renaissance more faithfully in the fourteenth century than in either the fifteenth or sixteenth centuries, and more completely than any other art, with the possible exception of literature, for as we have seen very little was composed for the Church during the Ars Nova period, especially in Italy.

In literature the great figures of the century were Dante [1265-1321], Petrarch [1304-1374], and Boccaccio [1313-1375]. In his *Divine Comedy* Dante represents in a wonderfully penetrating and poetic manner the highest flights of mediaeval thought based on the ideals of Aristotle and Aquinas. But his outlook is essentially mystical and mediaeval in that his great poem traces the journey of a soul through Hell, Purgatory, and Heaven rather than portrays purely human experiences on earth. The *Divine Comedy* was enormously popular—so much so that the Tuscan dialect in which it was written ousted all other dialects and ultimately became the basis of modern Italian. But partly because it was such an unapproachable masterpiece and partly because it did not sufficiently represent the changing atmosphere of the times, it had far less influence than the lyric poems of Petrarch, especially those inspired by his love for a certain Laura, which are usually referred to as his *Rime* (literally 'rhymes'). Although these were considered trifles by their author, who regarded his Latin treatises and verse of more importance, they were imitated and translated all over Europe. The reason for this was not only the quality of the poems themselves, but also the prestige of the poet in the field of learning, for Petrarch's passion for antiquity, which led him to value highly and accept as true much of Greek and Roman moral philosophy, went far beyond that of Aquinas. In this he gave a lead to most thoughtful men of his time who could no longer find in the Church their only guide to personal conduct. Petrarch, in fact, was the first humanist, for by humanism we mean the desire to understand the Greek and Roman civilizations and the differences between them and mediaeval Christianity and heathenism, and the attempt to fuse classical with Christian doctrines without subordinating either of them to the other. It is this last which distinguishes the humanist of the Renaissance from the mediaeval classical scholar.

Petrarch's enthusiasm for classical culture was shared by his compatriot, Boccaccio, but whereas the former was a poet whose *Rime* show the influence of troubadour verse in their refined and sensitive expression of unrequited love, the latter excelled in prose, and in his most outstanding work, the collection of 100 short stories called the *Decameron*, he describes vividly, if somewhat crudely at times, and with penetrating psychological insight the men and women of his day. His characters live because they are based on acute observation, as are those of his great contemporary Chaucer, and in this Boccaccio can be likened to the first great Renaissance painter, Giotto [1276-1336]. In Giotto's works the portrayal of the subject is no longer largely dictated by the design of the whole as in Gothic architecture, for he achieves unity and form through the realistic grouping of comparatively lifelike figures and objects, based on a close observance of Nature (Plate IX), just as the Greeks had done in their incomparable statues.

Dante, Petrarch, Boccaccio, and Giotto were all born in Tuscany, the capital of which was Florence. This 'flower of cities', as it has been called, was the heart of the Renaissance. It was also the most important musical centre of the Italian Ars Nova, not only because Landini was born on its outskirts and spent most of his life there, but also because it had a larger and more brilliant group of composers than any other city. It is no surprise, therefore, to find Renaissance traits in the purely Italian madrigal and caccia, or even in the French-influenced ballata. Thus the greater melodiousness of Italian music compared to French can be likened to the lyricism of Petrarch's verse, one of which indeed was set as a madrigal by Jacopo da Bologna, the first of countless others by later composers, for Petrarch was easily the most popular poet of Renaissance music. Again, the true-to-life stories of Boccaccio and the naturalistic paintings of Giotto are paralleled partly in the lively realism of the caccia, but more importantly in the increasing use of imitation as a means of achieving unity, for the mediaeval device of isorhythm, which the Italians virtually rejected, is abstract in that it is felt rather than heard, whereas imitation is concrete, actual, its binding effect being clearly audible.

But imitation was too powerful a means of unification to

become general for composers whose chief concern was to differentiate one part from another, and even though this was less true of Italy than France, fourteenth-century music as a whole is undoubtedly more mediaeval than Renaissance-like in its aims and outlook.

PERFORMANCE

(See also p. 153.)

All the vocal examples, except 56 and 57, may be performed on instruments alone, provided they are of contrasting timbres, but when one or more voices participate the following arrangements are recommended.

Ex. 52. The triplum and duplum parts should be sung by solo voices with instruments doubling one or both. The tenor part should be purely instrumental.

Ex. 55. The top part should be sung by a solo voice with or without instruments while the two lower parts are played.

Ex. 56. The triplum should be sung, the motetus may be sung provided that it is doubled by an instrument, and the tenor and contratenor should both be played by instruments of contrasting timbre.

Ex. 57. This may be sung by unaccompanied voices, though it sounds better if the tenor and contratenor are doubled by contrasting instruments.

Ex. 58. This may be sung by unaccompanied solo voices, or with the voices doubled.

Ex. 59. The tenor part should be played by an instrument, but the two upper parts in canon may be sung by solo voices with or without instruments.

Ex. 60. The top part should be sung by a solo voice, although instrumental doubling for the refrain is effective. The middle part should be instrumental, and the lowest part may be sung or played.

Ex. 62. This may be played on a violin or viola, as written, or doubled at the octave by other instruments. The piece is much enhanced by playing the puncti on different solo instruments with the others joining in the repeat, and with the addition, in the repeats, of a triangle and /or small drum when the ending common to all the puncti begins (i.e. bar 3 to the end in the first punctum).

6

MUSIC IN THE EARLY RENAISSANCE

THE leadership in European music during the latter half of the fourteenth century passed from France to Italy, but during the early years of the fifteenth century English influence became predominant, and mainly through the genius of John Dunstable [d. 1453] profoundly affected later composers.

English music of this period, except for that of Dunstable, is mostly represented in a large collection known as the Old Hall MS., compiled *c.* 1420, containing nearly 150 pieces, most of which are mass settings. The styles of composition are conductus, treble-dominated, isorhythmic, and caccia-influenced—that is, two upper voices, either in canon or much more animated than the lower voice or voices. The first two styles are the most common, the conductus settings being either simple, as in the thirteenth-century type, or ornamental, as in the Italian Ars Nova madrigal, and the treble-dominated pieces occasionally indulge in the kind of rhythmic complexity discussed in the previous chapter. This latter, together with the use of isorhythm and canon, shows that England was less insular than is usually made out. The prevalence of conductus style, however, indicates a conservatism which the example of Dunstable did nothing to alter; indeed, he can hardly have been known in Britain, as practically all his work is contained in manuscripts scattered about the Continent, notably those at Aosta, Modena, and Trent (all in Italy), only one piece, the very beautiful motet, *Veni Sancte Spiritus—Veni Creator*, being in the Old Hall MS., where it is given as anonymous.

Of the composers mentioned in the MS. the chief are Leonel Power [d. 1445], Thomas Damett [d. *c.* 1436], John Cooke [d. 1419?], Byttering, Pycard, Nicholas Sturgeon [d. 1454], W. Typp, Oliver, and Robert Chirbury. The pieces by Power, Damett, Byttering, Chirbury, and the anonymous *Credo* are all in conductus style, Byttering's motet* and Power's *Sanctus* showing the ornamental type. A good example of treble-dominated style is Power's *Gloria* (*The Old Hall Manuscript*, Vol. I, p. 65, ed. A. Ramsbotham), while Pycard's

* Strictly speaking, this is an antiphon, but for convenience we shall include all settings of sacred words in Latin under the term 'motet', except for the hymn and, of course, the mass and Magnificat.

Gloria (ibid., p. 92)—one of the most attractive pieces in the entire MS.—is both canonic and isorhythmic. The MS. also contains the earliest surviving part-music by an English monarch—Henry V [1387-1422].

Several of the composers in the MS., including Damett, Cooke, Sturgeon, and Chirbury, were clerks or 'singing men' of the Chapel Royal. This institution dates back to the twelfth century, when it was clearly an imitation of the Papal Chapel with its picked singers and composers. It was not confined to any one place, but accompanied the King wherever he went, and during the 200 years or so from Henry V to Charles II it included most of the leading English composers.

Although all the styles mentioned above had been and were being practised abroad, they show in general an important difference, a difference that was characteristically British—namely, a greater sonority based on the 'English discant' technique (see Chapter 5, p. 174) and evident also in the number of pieces *a*4 and even *a*5. It was this sonority which attracted Continental composers so much and inaugurated what the first great theorist of the century, Tinctoris, called a "new art". The third, and to a lesser extent the sixth, which had been gradually gaining acceptance in French and Italian compositions of the previous century, now became standard, but they did not yet seriously affect the supremacy of the fifth and octave, and in final chords especially the third was virtually excluded for many years to come, undoubtedly because it was less pleasing than the clear, open sound of the octave or octave and fifth combined (the $^{8}_{5}$ chord).

The impact of British sonority abroad was largely affected by Dunstable, who was in France for a number of years as musician to John, Duke of Bedford—Henry V's brother and Regent of France from 1422 to 1435. It seems likely that the composer visited Italy also, judging from the number of his works that exist in Italian manuscripts. At any rate he was sufficiently renowned in France to be acclaimed by a contemporary French poet, Martin le Franc, who in 1441-2 wrote:

> The English guise they wear with grace
> They follow Dunstable aright,
> And thereby have they learned apace
> To make their music gay and bright.*

* Translated by G. Reese, *Music in the Renaissance*, p. 13 (see Plate XV).

'They' refers to the two leading composers on the Continent at that time, Dufay and Binchois (see Plate XV), of whom more anon.

The 'English guise' as presented by Dunstable was not only an increased sonority, but a more pronounced feeling for chords and chord progressions, a more refined treatment of discord, a fresher, more lyrical vocal line, and a greater equality of part-writing than had existed before, the chordal sense and equality of part-writing being a natural outcome of English discant and conductus style combined.

Although Dunstable might well be called the first great composer in the early Renaissance period, mediaeval features persist in much of his music—for instance, isorhythm (which, like most of the examples in the Old Hall MS., usually occurs in all the voices), polytextuality, and distinction between the parts, both through rhythmic differences and (more especially) through the use of voices and instruments, particularly in secular pieces, the most common layout being a vocal top part with two lower instrumental parts.

Apart from general style, Dunstable's music exhibits four noteworthy features. The first is his fondness for melodic figures—particularly at the beginnings of phrases in the top part and usually ascending—which are based on the notes of a chord, e.g. *O rosa bella* (voice entry) and *Sancta Maria*, such figures clearly deriving from the increased chordal sense mentioned earlier. This feature hardly occurs in the Old Hall MS., but is fairly typical of the early fifteenth-century English carol (see p. 214), and this fact, together with the lyrical freshness of much of Dunstable's music and found in most of the carols also, makes it likely that the composer's art, or at any rate his melodic line, stemmed more from the semi-popular, non-liturgical English tradition than from the masses and motets of the professional composers of the Chapel Royal.

The second feature, which is characteristic of the English school as a whole, is the free treatment of the borrowed chant melody. In the thirteenth and fourteenth centuries this was almost always in the tenor, and although it was mercilessly chopped up into rhythmic patterns the original pitch and notes were nearly always kept. In fifteenth-century England, however, the chant was sometimes altered in pitch (transposed), either bodily or in bits, and frequently tampered with both by inserting new notes and by omitting some of the original. Furthermore, it was placed in either the highest or middle voice, especially the latter, more often than in the traditional tenor, as in the three pieces by Power and the anonymous *Credo*, the chant being transposed up a fifth in the last-named and up a tone in Power's *Sanctus*. Sometimes the chant even wandered from voice to voice, as in Byttering's *Nesciens Mater*, a practice made easy and probably suggested by the rhythmic similarity of the parts in conductus style. In the following extract from a *Gloria* by Dunstable the beginning of the top part is compared with the corresponding portion of the chant melody on which it is based; it will be noticed that the composer has transposed the chant up a fourth (Ex. 64*):

This way of ornamenting the chant is now known as 'paraphrasing'; it had already occurred, very exceptionally, in Machaut's Mass (see Chapter 5, p. 149), and although it was not peculiar to English composers (as the idea of a 'wandering' chant seems to have been), they used it more frequently than any other nation, and Dunstable was undoubtedly responsible for its increasing adoption on the Continent.

The third feature of Dunstable's music, and of some other English composers also, concerns the mass and the motet. The latter, as we have seen, had become almost entirely secular, but it gained a new lease of life in England, where for the first time liturgical motets were written in which all the parts were newly

* (*a*) *Liber Usualis*, p. 40. (*b*) Adapted from M. Bukofzer, *John Dunstable: Complete Works*, No. 9, pp. 16-17.

composed, e.g. Damett's *Beata Dei genitrix*, and all Dunstable's motets except *Ave Regina* and *Veni Sancte Spiritus*. This technique had been occasionally applied to mass movements abroad (see Chapter 5, p. 148), but nothing like to the same extent as in England, and the majority of those in the Old Hall MS., e.g. Chirbury's *Sanctus* and *Agnus Dei*, half of Dunstable's mass movements, and nearly half of his motets are not based on a chant, another indication of the creative urge which flowed from this island to rejuvenate European music.

The predominance of liturgical music in the Old Hall MS. is apparent also in the output of Dunstable, and in that of his slightly older contemporary, Leonel Power, whose works are distributed more equally between English and Continental sources. An important and influential composer, Power was one of the first (with Dunstable) to link two mass movements together by using the same chant in each. Moreover, he may have been the originator of the cantus-firmus mass—that is, a mass in which all the movements are based on the same borrowed 'fixed melody'. In one Italian MS. two such masses, *Alma redemptoris Mater* and *Rex seculorum*, are credited to Power, but in another possibly more reliable source part of one of the latter has Dunstable's name attached. In any case the original idea and its expansion was undoubtedly English, and it is the fourth of the important features mentioned earlier.

Both the above masses omit the Kyrie, a characteristic of fifteenth-century British works of this kind, probably because the majority of the Kyrie chants in the Sarum Use (see Chapter 1, p. 34) were troped, the inserted texts referring to special feast days. Thus the use of such melodies as the basis of a polyphonic Kyrie would have limited the number of occasions on which it could have been sung, so composers very sensibly set the Gloria, Credo, Sanctus, and Agnus Dei only.

Complete settings of the mass (that is, including the Kyrie) began to be common on the Continent round about the 1420s, though not until later did the practice of linking all the movements together with the same melody become general. This reawakening of interest in liturgical music reflected the wave of religious feeling that occurred when the Great Schism ended in 1417. This wave grew during the century, but the Church never recaptured its old supremacy over mind and spirit; the humanism of the Renaissance had made that impossible.

The return to liturgical music is clearly shown in the works of the next great composer, Guillaume Dufay [*c.* 1400-1474], who wrote at least eight masses, well over thirty separate mass movements, two *Magnificats* (the earliest polyphonic settings of which are English), and a number of motets, hymns, etc. But the secular influence was still strong, and Dufay's chansons (nearly seventy of them) and a considerable proportion of his motets faithfully reflect this aspect of the times as well.

Dufay was a Frenchman, or, to be more precise, a Burgundian, Burgundy being a province comprising most of central and the whole of southern France (the rest belonging to the Crown) and, during the reign of Philip the Good [1419-1467], the countries of Friesland, North and South Holland, Zeeland, and what is now Belgium. Politically Philip was, on occasion, an unscrupulous and even an unpatriotic opportunist. Some of his possessions he acquired by purchase or inheritance, but some by force. In the year after he came to power he sided with the English in the Hundred Years' War, signing a treaty with them which disinherited the Dauphin (later Charles VII). Ten years later, in 1430, his army captured Joan of Arc [*c.* 1412-1431], and his commander, John of Luxembourg, sold her to the English for 10,000 gold crowns (about £50,000 today). In the previous year Joan had insisted that the Dauphin be crowned King of France, and in 1435 Philip executed a *volte-face* by recognizing Charles VII and helping him to drive the English from French soil in return for substantial concessions. But, despite his acquisitiveness, Philip was a tolerant and imaginative ruler of considerable culture, and at Dijon, the capital of Burgundy, he maintained a court which for magnificence was unequalled in Europe and which, like so many royal and aristocratic courts of the fourteenth and fifteenth centuries, emulated the Papal Chapel at Rome with its picked band of singers and composers. A keen musician himself, he employed a number of the best men of his time, including Dufay, and if the Prince re-established much of France's former power and prestige, Dufay regained for her her old dominant position in European music by fusing English, Italian and French elements into a style that eventually became international.

Dufay and his contemporary Binchois, are usually called the leaders of the 'Burgundian School' of composers, while the next two generations are sometimes referred to as the 'Flemish' and 'Franco-Flemish' schools respectively. There have been other suggested titles, but we shall simply use the name 'Burgundian' to include all three schools, remembering that Burgundy was more a cultural than a national unit. The greatest composers of the fifteenth century were born in this province, most of them spent the greater part of their lives in it and, most important of all, they belonged to the same musical tradition—a tradition which continued long after Burgundy had been split up, when the territories north of France passed to the Hapsburgs through the marriage in 1477 of the daughter of Charles the Bold (Philip the Good's son) to the Austrian Archduke who later became the Emperor Maximilian I [reigned 1493-1519], and when the Duchy itself became reunited with the French Crown in 1482.

Of the foreign elements which influenced Dufay's style, those from Britain have already been discussed. The Italian ones are best seen in the work of Matteo da Perugia and Johannes Ciconia [*c.* 1340 – 1411], particularly the latter. Matteo, while occasionally indulging in the rhythmic complexities of his generation, favoured a style in which the two lower voices, contratenor and tenor, act more as a support for an animated top part that is less virtuosic and more graceful, approaching the treble-dominated style of Dufay more nearly than do Machaut's ballades. Matteo also shows a greater chordal sense, and his use of discord is less arbitrary.

Ciconia, although born at Liége and spending most of his life there, stayed in Italy from 1404 to 1411, and most of his quite considerable output is found in Italian manuscripts. His style is similar to Matteo's, except that he employs imitation more frequently, this being restricted to the two upper voices and hence undoubtedly arising from the earlier canonic caccia. His setting of *O rosa bella* by the Italian poet Giustiniani (see p. 225) is one of the most exquisite compositions of the early Renaissance, superior even to the fine setting usually attributed to Dunstable.

The fact that canon was common some 200 years before the general acceptance of imitation is another instance of the way in which a technique once discovered is rigidly applied at first and then modified and developed; thus isorhythm, strict in the tenor part of the mid-fourteenth-century motet, was later freely applied to all parts; again, Pérotin kept the notes of a borrowed chant intact, but Dunstable omitted some and inserted others; similarly (to skip several centuries), Schoenberg's twelve-note system was less flexible when he first used it than at the end of his life. In the fifteenth century the strict canon of the Italian Ars Nova continued in use, but it was also treated more freely and new forms were invented. Imitation, however, is still comparatively rare in Dufay's generation, and when it does occur is almost always found in the upper parts only.

Literally, 'canon' means a 'law' or 'rule', and applies to any piece of music in which two or more parts in performance are derived from only one written part. In the caccia, for example, it was unnecessary to write both upper parts out completely, for only the endings differed in order that both should finish together, and a sign indicated where the following part began. This is easy enough, but fifteenth-century composers delighted in devising much more difficult ways, using obscure sentences (usually in Latin) which were intended to help(?) the singers, as in the Agnus Dei III of Dufay's *L'Homme Armé* Mass (*H.A.M.*, 66c). Another method which became very popular later on was to place two, three, or four mensuration signs before a part, the note values of the two, three, or four parts varying according to the sign which governed each one (see *H.A.M.*, 89). This is called a 'mensuration canon'.

Dufay not only adapted and expanded the strict canon of the Italian caccia, but also the smooth sonority of English discant, which in his hands became more expressive through having the main melody in the top part instead of the middle, and in not sticking so rigidly to chains of $^6_3$ chords. This was called 'fauxbourdon' ('false bass') because the lowest voice was no longer 'true' to tradition in being the most important one. This style became very popular in the fifteenth century, particularly as a means of improvising a third inner part to two written parts moving mainly in sixths, the improvised part, while not slavishly following the contours of the top part, being sung or played a fourth below it, as, for example, in Dufay's fauxbourdon setting of the hymn, *Vexilla regis*. In his later works Dufay's treatment of fauxbourdon became much freer, but its sonority influenced all his music and was the main cause of his greater feeling for tonality—that is, the stressing of one chord (the tonic) which is regarded as the central and most important one. The most emphatic way of doing this is to cadence on this chord more often than any other, and this is what Dufay increasingly tended to do. Moreover, the cadences themselves were altering, and in addition to that given in Ex. 53, which was still very common, the following (given in its simplest form) became more frequent (Ex. 65):

and later (Ex. 66):

Both these are what we now call 'perfect' or, more strictly, 'authentic perfect' cadences, i.e. a tonic chord preceded by its dominant, but Ex. 65 is a transitional type showing the influence of the fourteenth century, in that the lowest note of the last chord is approached from the note above (the supertonic). The probable reason why the perfect cadence gained in popularity and finally ousted the mediaeval ones is that composers realized that if the lowest note or root of the final chord was approached by a leap it would stand out more clearly, and hence the whole chord would be more sharply defined, and the dominant note was the only one that would sound well with the other two, i.e. the leading-note and supertonic, both well established in the history of the cadence.

Another cadence that began to be more widely used round about 1450 was the 'plagal perfect' cadence (Ex. 67):

Dufay's tonal feeling, however, must not be overemphasized, for he continued to use the fourteenth-century 'double-leading-note' cadence with its bimodal implications.

The chordal approach affected not only cadences, but harmony as a whole, and Dufay in his more mature work shows a slight but definite preference for chords in root position, a preference which was to remain in music for centuries to come. Furthermore, the relationships between chords became less arbitrary—in other words, it began to be realized that certain chord progressions sounded more satisfactory than others because they are more closely related to a central chord. These two facts, plus the English habit of frequently placing the chant in the middle or highest part, almost certainly explains why Dufay (and all later composers) preferred to place the borrowed melody in an upper part, because this obviously enabled the lowest part to move with much greater freedom and widened the choice of chords. For instance, if we take a note—say, C—and make it the lowest one, the only concordant chords we can build on it are C-E-G and C-E-A; but if there is a lower part then we can get the same two chords (by writing a C either an octave below or in unison) plus the chords E-C-G, F-C-A, A-C-E, and A-C-F.

To move the borrowed melody up a voice would have been pointless in earlier centuries, because the range of each voice was usually much the same. In the fifteenth century, however, the range expanded first upwards and then downwards, with the result that differentiation between the voices was naturally achieved by pitch and timbre, not artificially by rhythm and the singing of different words. The equality of part-writing thus suited the new trend admirably, and the use of only one text for all voices (when more than one voice is meant to sing that is) became increasingly common.

The English cantus-firmus mass and paraphrase technique were also developed by Dufay. Of the eight masses that are definitely his, two are in three parts (*a*3) and six are *a*4. Five of the latter use a cantus firmus, which in two (possibly three) of the masses is a secular melody, an innovation that may have been his, and one that represents another and more profound break with tradition than the displacing of the melody from the bottom part. One of these masses uses the tenor part of the ballade *Se la face ay pale* by Dufay himself, and the other is based on a tune that was to become more popular than any other as a basis for fifteenth- and sixteenth-century masses—*L'Homme Armé*.

That only one of Dufay's masses uses paraphrase may be explained by the fact that he was nurtured in the French tradition and therefore attached great importance to the overall structure of the mass and the means of binding it together, and it is obvious that a melody ornamented in different ways in different movements, even if it is in the top part, is less likely to be heard as a unifying device than if it is simply and uniformly presented, even though its position in the next to lowest voice tends to obscure it. Dufay and others seem to have been aware of this latter difficulty and partially overcame it by choosing a melody that was well known, making it the last voice to enter, and anticipating its opening notes in the top voice or voices. It is certain also that the melody was played on a suitable instrument, either solo or doubling the voice.

But Dufay was not content with the degree of unity achieved through the use of a cantus firmus alone, and in most of his masses, e.g. *Missa Caput* and *Missa se la face ay pale*, he introduced (but did not invent) a device now known as a 'head motive'. This is simply a melodic fragment ('motive') which occurs at the beginning ('head') of each movement, and at various important places *en route*, so to speak, and almost always in the highest voice where it is most clearly heard. It is usually varied each time it enters, but is always recognizable, and like imitation it is an external unifying device compared to the tenor cantus firmus which, like isorhythm, is an internal one, being more felt than heard. The head-motive device became standard in mass composition until *c.* 1500, when it was gradually replaced by the use of parody (see p. 204) and pervading imitation.

The use of a cantus firmus either to link together the different movements of the mass or as a structural basis for a motet was in fact a logical development of isorhythm, and, like Dunstable, Dufay used the older technique in a number of his motets together with polytextuality, usually in those written to celebrate an important event, such as a royal wedding, the election of a pope, or the signing of a treaty, the solemnity of the occasion being the probable reason why a style hallowed by tradition was employed rather than the 'modern' one (see Chapter 5, p. 149). Most of his motets and hymns, however, are composed in the new style, but this is shown most consistently in his purely secular work, his chansons. This term is a general one covering all French secular compositions, but we shall use it only in the plural, except for an individual work that cannot be classified as a ballade, virelai, or rondeau. In the fourteenth century the ballade had been the most popular form, but in the early years of the fifteenth century the rondeau gradually displaced it, and in Dufay's chansons the latter predominates. Although the fifteenth-century rondeau is similar in structure to the mediaeval type, it is usually more concise than that of the previous century as composers preferred syllabic underlay to melismatic. This meant fewer notes per line of text and indeed less composition altogether compared to the ballade or for that matter the virelai, because the ballade usually had five different units—a, b, c, d, e (see p. 80), and the virelai three—a, b, c (*A bb a A* or *AB cc ab AB*), whereas the rondeau had only two—a, b (*AB a A ab AB*). The popularity of the rondeau probably sprang from this reduction in length and content, and may be explained by the fact that composers were feeling their way towards a new style and would therefore naturally prefer to work on a small canvas, as it were. Monteverdi in the seventeenth century and Haydn in the eighteenth, to mention only two later instances, both experimented with a new musical language in the intimate and well-established fields of vocal chamber music and string quartet respectively, before applying their results to the larger forms of opera and symphony, and it is a reasonable assumption that Dufay and his generation did the same. Thus Dufay's chansons, nearly all of which are *a*3, and some of his smaller sacred compositions (e.g. the lovely motet, *Alma redemptoris Mater*) are in general more forward-looking as regards style than the masses and larger motets.

Dufay's genius enriched the entire realm of vocal music and reached its greatest heights in sacred music, but although his versatility remained unchallenged until the advent of Josquin des Prez, his chansons were equalled if not surpassed by his fellow countryman, Gilles de Binche, usually called Binchois [*c*. 1400-1460], who was also employed by Philip the Good and in whose service he remained for about thirty years. Binchois' chansons were greatly admired and reflected more clearly than Dufay's the taste of the bourgeois merchants, whose influence—in direct proportion to their wealth—in matters political, social, and cultural was increasing rapidly, an influence which counterbalanced the almost purely secular atmosphere of the aristocratic courts, and which supported the new wave of religious feeling already mentioned. The most obvious bourgeois element in Binchois' chansons is their simplicity, not only in being mainly *a*3 and in rondeau form, but also in the texture, for the top part predominates more than in Dufay and the melodies are more 'popular', as for instance in the delightful rondeau, *De plus en plus*. The same lyrical rather than learned attitude is shown in his less frequent use of canon and, in his comparatively few sacred works, the rejection of the simple cantus-firmus technique in favour of paraphrase and treble-dominated style. He seems to have been the only major composer of the fifteenth century who wrote no complete setting of the Mass.

Binchois was born in the province of Hainaut in what is now Belgium, and some twenty years later the same province produced one of the most striking musicians of the Renaissance, Johannes Ockeghem [*c.* 1410–*c.* 1497] (see Plate XVII), a composer who, from 1454 onwards, served three kings of France, Charles VII [reigned 1429-1461], Louis XI [reigned 1461-1483], and Charles VIII [reigned 1483-1498], and whose reputation was such that at his death he was mourned all over Europe, notably by Erasmus, the great humanist and scholar, and by two leading French poets, Molinet and Crétin, the lament by the former being set to music by no less a composer than Josquin des Prez.

Like Dufay, Ockeghem was more at home in sacred than secular music, but for different reasons, for it was mainly Dufay's interest in structure that found its most satisfactory expression in the mass, but it was Ockeghem's creative vitality that found the chanson too limiting a form, and although a number of these were amongst the most popular of the century (e.g. the rondeau, *Fors seulement*), he most truly reveals himself in his masses and motets, where his rich imagination had more scope, and it is these, particularly the masses, that we shall discuss.

Ockeghem has been more misrepresented than any other major composer of the early Renaissance. On the one hand he has been accused of dryness and pedantry because he happened to write a mass, the *Missa Cuiusvis toni*, that can be sung in any of the four church modes, and another, the *Missa Prolationum*, which is mostly in double canon, the canons being at all intervals from the unison to the octave, and on the other hand he has been acclaimed as the first composer to apply pervading imitation as a structural device on the evidence of a motet whose authorship is questionable. In actual fact he was no more learned than Bach, whose cycle of canons in the 'Goldberg' Variations is a distant relation of Ockeghem's Mass, and the motet, even if it is his, is so unlike the rest of his work in its consistent imitative writing that it must have been composed towards the end of his life under the influence of Josquin des Prez.

Ockeghem's greatness lies not in his technical ingenuity, which was tremendous but discreetly employed, nor in his use of imitation, which is much less frequent than in the works of his lesser contemporary, Busnois (see below), but in the sustained power and beauty of his vocal line. Melody, in fact, is all-important, not only in the top part but in all the parts, and the resultant multi-strand texture is frequently maintained with hardly a break throughout an entire movement or piece. This continuous polyphony is achieved by replacing the clear-cut phrases of Dufay and Binchois with 'overlapping' cadences—in other words, a voice begins a new phrase before the previous one has ended, a technique that became standard in later polyphonic as opposed to contrapuntal writing.

Ockeghem also differed from his predecessors (and his successors for that matter) in the ornateness and sweep of his melodies, and his soaring melismas contrast sharply with the simpler, more syllabically underlaid lines of Dufay and Binchois. The application of such melody to all parts could only be effective if the parts did not cross, otherwise a positive tangle of sound would result, and it is not surprising therefore to find Ockeghem keeping his voices intact as it were, and as an inevitable result spreading them over a wider range, especially downwards, for the upper regions had already been partially explored by Dufay's generation. But the greater distance between top and bottom would have meant a decrease in sonority if only three voices were used, and it is from Ockeghem onwards that four-part writing becomes normal in both sacred and secular compositions.

The fact that Ockeghem paraphrases his borrowed material far more often than does Dufay provides a further proof of his strong melodic bent, as does the number of his pieces which are newly composed throughout—for example, the fine *Missa Mi-mi*. In addition, he shows distinct originality in his treatment of traditional techniques, such as paraphrasing the highest part instead of the usual tenor of a previously composed chanson, or borrowing two parts and sharing them between all the voices, or changing the rhythm of the original melody from ternary to binary. This apparent delight in doing the unusual comes precious near to leg-pulling at times, as when he writes an original tenor part in long notes but places the borrowed chant, freely ornamented, in the top voice, thus kidding the listener into believing that the tenor is the chant and the top voice original.

While Ockeghem, like Dufay, enriched both sacred and secular music, he had, like the latter, a contemporary who excelled in chanson composition, and who in fact definitely surpassed him in this field. This was Antoine Busnois [d. 1492], the most important composer in the service of Charles the Bold [reigned 1467-1477], the son of Philip the Good. In his comparatively infrequent use of imitation, Ockeghem stands somewhat apart from the general line of development from Dufay to Josquin des Prez, but it is the greater application of just this feature that is so characteristic of Busnois. Most of his chansons are in rondeau form and *a*3, and, like Ockeghem, he explored the lower ranges of the voice, but his melodies are clearly in the Dufay-Binchois tradition in their simplicity and clear-cut phrasing. However, his feeling for tonality, while perhaps not stronger than Ockeghem's, is more obvious because of the greater number of times at which all the voices cadence together, whereas Ockeghem, as we have seen, prefers to overlap. This increased tonal sense is shown in the works of both men by the more frequent occurrence of perfect cadences, particularly the normal one (i.e. Ex. 66), which now definitely began to oust the 'double leading-note' cadence with its ambiguous tonality.

Another feature of Busnois's compositions (and indeed of Ockeghem's too) which became common later on is the rhythmical interplay between the voices. For instance, one voice may begin a phrase in ternary rhythm on the first beat, and another voice imitate this phrase beginning on the third beat, but this beat receives the same accent as the first beat of the original phrase; hence there arises a conflict of 'micro-rhythms', i.e. of the rhythms of individual voices. In most modern editions of mediaeval and Renaissance music bar-lines are used to help the singer, but it must always be remembered that the originals are unbarred (with a few exceptions), and that although beating time was essential in order to keep everyone together, this simply indicated the duration of a breve or semibreve and did not imply a regular and recurring strong accent. Accent in fact is determined in two ways—melodically and harmonically. Any note in a melody becomes relatively accented if the word or syllable to which it is set is a strong one, or if its position in a phrase is higher or its value substantially longer than the surrounding notes. In mediaeval and most of early Renaissance music, composers were largely unconcerned about the way syllables fitted the music, but from the latter part of the fifteenth century on much greater care was taken and the natural stresses of the text are more faithfully reflected in the melody. Harmonic accent can hardly be said to have existed before the fifteenth century, because it depends entirely on a refined use of discord and concord. A discord in a series of concords gives rise to a feeling of tension owing to its greater sonority (see Chapter 2, p. 43), and this tension demands the relief given by a succeeding concord. Now greater sonority produces an impression of greater accentuation; thus, for example, in a succession of thirds and fifths played absolutely evenly and of equal duration, the thirds will sound more accentuated than the fifths, and the same applies with even more force to a series of concords and discords. If the discord is of short duration compared to the surrounding concords, it has little influence on the harmonic accent, but if it is of comparable length, then it will produce a definite feeling of stress which will affect the 'macrorhythm', i.e. the rhythm of the piece as a whole. That this was increasingly realized from *c.* 1400 on is proved by the growing practice of placing the longest discords at intervals of two beats or multiples of two in binary rhythm, and of three or multiples of three in ternary rhythm, thus producing a macrothythmic framework in which the harmonic stress, when it does occur, always comes on what we would call 'the first beat of a duple- or triple-time bar'. The usual length of these discords is a minim, and their treatment becomes more and more circumspect during the early Renaissance, until by the latter half of the fifteenth century by far the majority of discordant minims are approached and quitted in a very definite manner now known as 'suspension'. For example (Ex. 68):

The details varied, of course, but the three basic steps are always the same: (1) 'preparation', in which the note to be suspended is concordant with the other parts and occurs on a 'weak' beat; (2) 'suspension', in which the note is discordant with the other parts, thus producing a feeling of accent; and (3) 'resolution', in which the suspended note almost invariably falls a step on to a concord, falling rather than rising because lower notes are less tense than higher ones.

In the top part of Ex. 68 the accent most naturally falls on the F, the microrhythm of this part thus conflicting with the macrorhythm as determined by the harmonic accent, i.e. the suspension, and it is this subtle contrast between the fluid rhythm of the individual voices, with their irregularly placed stresses depending on the accentuation of the text or the shape of the melody, and the comparatively regular accents produced by suspensions which underline the prevailing binary or ternary rhythm of all the parts that is one of the chief characteristics and delights of later Renaissance music.

Other important composers of the latter half of the fifteenth century are Jacob Obrecht [*c.* 1450 – 1505], Alexander Agricola [? 1446 – 1506], Antoine de Févin [*c.* 1470 – *c.* 1512], Gaspar van Weerbecke [*c.* 1445 – after 1517], Heinrich Isaac [*c.* 1450-1517], Johannes Martini [d. 1497/8], Loyset Compère [d. 1518], Pierre de la Rue [d. 1518], Antoine Brumel [*c.* 1460 – *c.* 1515], and Jean Mouton [d. 1522], but head and shoulders above these was Josquin des Prez (see Plate XVI) [*c.* 1440 – 1521], who has been mentioned several times already in this chapter, and with good reason, for he was the greatest composer in the early Renaissance and one of the greatest of all time. His masses, motets, and chansons are as a whole superior to those of any other composer both of his time and before it, but despite a number of fine masses and chansons—

for example, the *Missa Pange lingua* (a superb work) and the chansons *Allegez moy* and *Mille regretz*—it is in his motets that his genius is most fully shown. The reason for this is probably that only the motet provided both a wide variety of texts suitable for expressive treatment together with a form large enough to contain his tremendous creative vitality and sense of structure. Previously, expressive treatment had been mainly restricted to the chanson, and structural devices and melodic expansion to the mass; now, however, in Josquin's hands, the motet not only represented more richly than any other type a synthesis of what had gone before, but introduced a style of composing that became 'classic' for the rest of the Renaissance.

To discuss in detail the variety of elements which constitute Josquin's style would take up far too much space, and a summary of the most important features must suffice. Like Ockeghem, the ease with which Josquin wrote in canon has caused some writers to over emphasize this side of his technique, but, as one scholar has aptly said, canon was as natural a form of expression to him as fugue was to Bach. To take only one instance (and one hard to equal, let alone surpass, in its combination of skill and beauty), the section beginning 'Ave vera Virginitas' from the motet, *Ave Maria*—perhaps the most exquisite motet he wrote. This section is a canon at the fifth below between soprano and tenor, the latter following after only one minim beat, with alto and bass being free. The charming simplicity of the main melody and the clear tonality and full harmony of the whole quite overshadow the technical feat involved, while the accents in the tenor part, falling as they do one beat later than in the soprano, produce an effect of indescribable poignancy.

Much more important than canon, however, is Josquin's use of pervading imitation as a unifying device, governing most or all of an extended piece. The 'point' of imitation is often double—that is, two voices introduce it and two other voices later imitate it, sometimes inverting it so that what was the top part at first becomes the bottom part when repeated ('double counterpoint'). Occasionally imitation is 'tonal', not 'real'—in other words, if the first point begins by leaping a fifth up from, say, C to G, a later entry will underline the 'key' octave (in this case C-C) by answering with the complementary fourth, G-C, not another fifth, G-D. Josquin's feeling for tonality is also shown in the greater frequency of perfect cadences and in his purely chordal writing. This latter sometimes persists throughout an entire motet, but is more often contrasted with polyphonic sections, a technique that became standard in the sixteenth century and later. Contrast is obtained also by vocal scoring (see p. 214) which, as we shall see, was a typically English feature throughout the century, but which had been largely neglected on the Continent owing to the prevalence of three-part writing, for it can only be really effective in compositions for four or more parts. Writing *a4* had become common with Ockeghem, but Josquin went further in not only composing for five and even eight voices, but in helping to establish a standard combination of four voices—namely, soprano (C clef on the bottom line of the stave, i.e. line 1), alto (C clef on line 3), tenor (C clef on line 4), and bass (F clef on line 4). Towards the middle of the sixteenth century the soprano clef was often replaced by the treble or violin G clef that we use today. Other clefs that occasionally replaced or were added to the standard combination were the mezzo-soprano (C clef on line 2), baritone (C clef on line 5 or F clef on line 3), and sub-bass (F clef on line 5).

Josquin's melodic line owes more to Busnois than to Ockeghem, although he clearly learnt the art of overlapping cadences from the latter. Also his melodies tend to reflect the text ('word painting') to a greater extent than earlier composers, and while this is normally restricted to such devices as ascending or descending passages when the text mentions 'rising' or 'falling', etc., an extreme example can be found in his chanson, *Nymphes des bois*, a deeply felt lament on Ockeghem's death (see p. 197), which is written entirely in black notes.

Apart from pervading imitation, Josquin employs all the structural devices in current use—paraphrase, cantus firmus, and isorhythm. In the first two the borrowed melody is either sacred or secular and placed either in one part or shared between them all. A fair proportion of his compositions are free, but in some of these he repeats a short melodic fragment achieving an ostinato effect, and in others he derives the main theme from the text, as in his *Missa Hercules Dux Ferrariae*, where the vowels 'e', 'u', 'e', 'u', 'e', 'a', 'i', 'e' (='ae') are regarded as solmisation syllables—namely, *re*, *ut*, *re*, *ut*, *re*, *fa*, *mi*, *re*, and these, in the initial statement of the theme, become the notes D, C, D, C, D, F, E, D. The use of borrowed material is not restricted, as it had largely been before, to the mass and motet, for a number of Josquin's chansons are based on previously composed melodies. Furthermore, canon now invades the secular domain almost as often as the sacred, and, in keeping with Josquin's freer treatment of traditional techniques and forms, strict canonic writing is sometimes replaced by free, as in the tenor and bass parts of the chanson, *Plus nulz regretz*; the chanson, in fact, has become a far richer and more expressive medium of composition than ever before, and represents not only a more complete cross-section of the composer's style than it had earlier, but also reflects the general tendency, already apparent in the mass and motet, of treating traditional structural devices more freely. Thus Josquin was possibly the first to break away from the strict rondeau, ballade, and virelai types and to create forms which, although using repetition also, are far more varied—for example, *Cueurs desolez*.

In addition to the structural devices used in Josquin's motets, there is one that occurs in his masses only. It consists of borrowing not one but usually all the voice parts of a previously composed sacred or secular work, either by the composer himself or someone else. Sometimes the entire model is quoted verbatim, but more often it is divided up into sections which are distributed throughout the mass, with the voice parts slightly altered and one or more voices added. This type of mass was later called a 'parody' mass, and it became one of the most popular types of mass composition in the sixteenth century. Although Josquin was not the first to apply the parody technique to several movements of a mass, his four-part *Missa Mater Patris* (printed in 1514) is almost certainly the earliest example of a true parody mass, in that the parodying of Brumel's three-part motet, *Mater Patris*, provides the basic means of uniting all the movements.

But important as Josquin is in the development of composition technique, his brilliance in this sphere is hardly if any greater than Ockeghem's, and his early works, like those of Palestrina (and indeed many other composers), while amply demonstrating his mastery over his material, give little indication of his real stature. Between *c.* 1474 and some time after 1503 Josquin was almost continuously in Italy, first of all at Milan in the service of Cardinal Ascanio Sforza, later as a singer in the Papal Chapel at Rome, and finally as composer to Duke Hercules I at Ferarra, to whom the mass mentioned above is dedicated. The impact of Italian culture in general and the taste of his noble patrons in particular had a profound effect on the composer. It was as if the southern sun had warmed and stirred the closed bud of his genius, causing it to unfurl until the full flower was revealed. From now on, not only did he excel in all branches of vocal composition, but surpassed all other composers before the late sixteenth century in the range and quality of his feeling and imagination; from the exquisite tenderness of *Ave verum* to the sombre depths of *Miserere* (commissioned by Hercules I); from the dramatic power of the five-part *Cueurs desolez* to the light-hearted gaiety of *El grillo*. This emotional range, expressed through sensuous harmony and melodic lines that are often of great beauty and always perfectly moulded to suit the texture, together with a profound technical skill, particularly in the use of sequence and canon, make him, as we said earlier, one of the greatest composers of all time.

Josquin's supremacy was recognized both in his own day and later, and while Martin Luther's statement that "other composers do what they can with the notes; Josquin alone does what he wishes" is somewhat exaggerated, it does in fact indicate the general estimation in which he was held, as does the high opinion of the sixteenth-century theorist, Glareanus (see Part II), who included more examples by Josquin than by any other composer in his *Dodecachordon* (1547).

Both Luther and Glareanus were well acquainted with the galaxy (for galaxy it certainly was) of composers who were roughly contemporary with Josquin, and this lends added weight to their judgements. The brightest stars—but not all of the same magnitude—have already been given on p. 201, and some of them must be singled out for individual mention.

We stated earlier that Josquin was not the first to apply parody technique to several movements of a mass; indeed the technique was known in the fourteenth century as the Gloria and Sanctus of the so-called 'Mass of the Sorbonne' and the Ite Missa Est of the so-called 'Mass of Toulouse' demonstrate (see p. 148). So far as we know, however, these are isolated instances, and it seems likely that the first composer to use parody at all frequently was Obrecht, for in a number of his masses he introduces at various places all the voice parts of his model. Indeed, in his very fine *Missa Rosa playsant* each movement contains a reworking of the original chanson, but because the chief means of unifying all the movements is through the paraphrasing of the chanson tenor—in other words, through a cantus firmus—it is not a genuine parody mass.

More important than Obrecht's use of parody, however, is the very high quality of the actual music, particularly in his masses and motets, the imaginative treatment of the stereotyped secular forms, even though secular composition occupies but a small part of his total output, and his strong sense of tonality, notably at cadences where he often places the subdominant chord before the dominant, thus defining the tonic chord with greater precision. In all these ways Obrecht was progressive, and may well have influenced Josquin, who probably met him shortly before his death at Ferrara and who was almost certainly acquainted with his music. In other ways Obrecht was rather conservative, as in his infrequent use of imitation, and in the number of times he uses strict rather than paraphrased cantus firmi, and polytextuality, but all in all he is a very fine composer, surpassed by none of his contemporaries except Josquin.

Agricola, too, was both progressive and conservative, and to a greater extent than Obrecht, for on the one hand his chansons (of which he wrote more than did any of his contemporaries, including Josquin) are often based on previously composed material, this being considerably varied, and his melodic lines in general show marked originality, even a degree of restlessness, in rhythm and contour. On the other hand, the ornateness of his melody and the complexity of his texture hark back to Ockeghem, and his occasional use of $^{6}_{3}$ progressions and hocket to the early years of the century. The restlessness of Agricola's melodies is reflected in his life, for he was in Italy twice, working in Milan, Florence, and Mantua on his first visit, and later made two trips to Spain in the service of Philip the Handsome, son of Maximilian I. Philip had married Joanna, daughter of Ferdinand and Isabella (see p. 223), in 1496, and in 1504 he became Philip I, King of Castile.

Also in Philip's retinue, from the date of his marriage till his death in 1506, was La Rue, who wrote more masses than any of his contemporaries. This fact underlines the essentially serious quality of his music, and it is not surprising that his Requiem, apart from being the high-water mark of his own output, is one of the finest compositions of the period. Another fine work, the *Missa Ave sanctissima Maria*, is probably the first six-part setting of the Ordinary and definitely the first mass to use canon *a*6, in this case the canon being 6 in 3 at the fourth above—in other words, three parts are written, each producing another part which is sung a fourth higher. The astonishing thing is that this technical *tour de force* in no way impairs La Rue's melodic suppleness or harmonic variety. Both this mass and the Requiem show the composer's fondness for contrasting groups of voices, especially for passages *a*2.

La Rue does not appear to have ranked very high with his contemporaries, yet without doubt he is the equal of Obrecht and superior to Mouton, who was widely acclaimed, both at the courts of Louis XII and his successor, Francis I, and abroad. Like La Rue, Mouton wrote little secular music, and like him too he was a master in the use of canon. Two of his motets, *Nesciens Mater virum* and *Ave Maria, gemma virginum*, both fine works, are canons 8 in 4, and another exquisite motet, *Ave Maria, gratia plena*, has a 'mirror' canon between alto and bass —that is, the 'comes' (the part that 'follows') moves in contrary motion to the 'dux' (the part that 'leads'). Although the quality of Mouton's work entitles him to special mention, he is also important as the teacher of the most influential musician of the sixteenth century, Adrian Willaert, and was thus a significant link between the early and late Renaissance.

The impact on Italy of composers from the north did not produce any really marked effect until the period after Josquin, but during his lifetime the tide had already begun to flow southwards, and in addition to Josquin himself, all the leading composers mentioned on p. 201, except Févin, La Rue, and Mouton, crossed the Alps.

Perhaps the most striking of Josquin's contemporaries was Isaac, who for the last twenty years of his life was court composer to Maximilian I. While less brilliant and profound than Josquin, and not quite the equal of Obrecht and La Rue, he was the most versatile composer of the period, writing a number of secular songs with German and Italian as well as French texts, and also a fair amount (for those days) of instrumental music. The setting of texts in different languages does not of itself, of course, denote any remarkable versatility, and it is in the musical contrasts between his French chansons, German Lieder, and Italian frottole* that the range of Isaac's gifts is revealed. Thus while both chansons and Lieder are frequently based on a borrowed melody and are generally imitative in style, the former are more sectional and freely repetitive than the latter, in which a continuous polyphonic flow is usually maintained, with the borrowed melody nearly always in the tenor part, and in which canon occurs more frequently. The differences between chanson and Lied, however, are not nearly so marked as between them and the frottola, for in this the style in general is non-imitative, less polyphonic, and simpler in texture, with the main melody, which is hardly ever borrowed, lying in the top part, though like the chanson it is sectional and employs repetition.

During the middle fifty years or so of the fifteenth century, Italy produced practically no music, although there were plenty of vocal and instrumental performers. Of the latter the most famous was Antonio Squarcialupi [1416 – 1480], owner of the important collection which is our main source of Italian Ars Nova music—the Squarcialupi Codex (see Chapter 5, p. 167)—and organist of the renowned Santa Maria del Fiore at Florence. Round about 1484 Isaac obtained this post and remained in Florence under the patronage of Lorenzo de Medici [1449-1492]—nicknamed 'the Magnificent'—and his son, until the overthrow of the latter by the ardent reformer Savonarola in 1494. This Dominican monk vigorously criticized the corruption and worldliness of the Medicean rulers of Florence and advocated government on more democratic lines. The masses acclaimed him for a time, but soon tired of his high ideals, and eventually the fury of the aristocracy and the displeasure of the Pope, whom he had also censured, led to his execution in 1498. The Medicis returned in 1512, but the old magnificence and *joie de vivre* did not, for the country had since been invaded by foreign troops and the city's future was uncertain.

The highlights of the Florentine year were the carnivals before and after Lent, and under Lorenzo these reached a degree of extravagance and ingenuity unmatched before or since. Legends, classical figures, the city guilds, etc., were all symbolized in great torchlight processions of decorated cars and

* See below.

fantastic masks. Music naturally contributed to the festivities and the 'canti carnascialeschi', or carnival songs, extolled mythical heroes or the greatness of the Medicis, and described the various trades of the city or sections of the populace, usually by means of innuendo (*H.A.M.*, 96) or even on occasion frank obscenities.

Isaac is known to have composed carnival songs, none of which, however, have survived complete, but, judging by his other pieces with Italian texts, they were almost certainly typical of the current secular style in Italy. This style, as we have seen, is less complex and 'learned' than that of the typical Burgundian chanson or German Lied, and the main melody in the top part is not only simpler than in the chanson and Lied but more clear-cut than the lower, usually instrumental, parts.

The chief type of secular music was the frottola, which strictly speaking refers to only one class of composition, but which we shall use to cover all the various types which arose from the widespread practice of reciting poetry to an improvised instrumental accompaniment. The main centre of frottola composition was Mantua, where one of the most gifted and influential women of the Renaissance, Isabella d'Este [1474-1539], resided. An ardent and accomplished musician herself, she was more than a mere patron, and in literature and poetry as well as in music she was respected by many of the great artists of her day. To her court, round about the year 1495, came Bartolomeo Tromboncino [d. *c.* 1535] and Marco Cara [d. ?1525], the first notable Italian composers of the Renaissance. The frottole of these two men, particularly of the former, were greatly admired by Isabella, to whom the musical setting of a poem in which the melody did not obscure the words was completely satisfying. The texts of most frottole, especially the earlier ones, are trivial, but the improvement in taste in the early years of the sixteenth century probably owed much to Isabella's influence.

Although the frottole are simpler in style and texture than Burgundian and German part-songs, the fact that they are mostly written *a4* ,with the lowest three parts still being quasi-polyphonic, tends to produce a heaviness which ill suits the syllabically underlaid vocal line with its clear-cut phrases. Cara seems to have realized this to some extent, for he composed a frottola in which the accompaniment is restricted to a few simple chords. This experiment, so much more typical of the Italian genius than the madrigal, mass, or motet, would almost certainly have led to the creation of monody long before the 'New Music' of the early seventeenth century (see Part II), but Burgundian polyphony intervened, and for nearly 100 years Italy adapted her natural talent to the art from the north.

The rise of the frottola occurred at the same time as the invention of music printing, some thirty years after the first printed books had been issued. At first either the lines of the stave were engraved in a wooden block and printed in black or red ink, the notes, clef, etc., being added by hand, or else the other way round, the notes being cut and the lines added. In the latter method the notes were sometimes engraved in separate pieces of wood and stamped on to the page. Later the lines were printed and the notes stamped on to them. These three methods involved difficulties in aligning the notes on the stave correctly, and this was overcome by engraving all the music on to wooden blocks and eventually metal plates. Although this method ensured the exact placing of the notes on the stave, it was lengthy and wasteful, for every page of new music necessitated a new block, and it was soon replaced by double-impression printing. In this method the lines of the stave were scratched (engraved) on a metal plate (usually copper), the number of staves depending on the size of the page; the plate was then inked and wiped, but the ink remained in the lines and was transferred to a sheet of paper when this was firmly pressed on to the plate. This was the first impression and easily performed. The second was considerably more difficult, for each note, rest, etc., was cut from small pieces of lead (type) so that the raised parts represented the shape of the note. These were then placed in a 'bed' and very carefully arranged so that when the staved paper was impressed each type would be printed in the position required. It was this exact arranging of the type that was so laborious and finicky a job and which made the method so costly, but when perfectly done it was artistically far superior to the single-impression technique which replaced it (see Plate XIII). This technique, which was invented by a Frenchman, Pierre Haultin, in 1525, dispensed with the engraved plates for the stave, using only type, each piece of which contained a note or rest, etc., placed in a small portion of the stave, these being joined together to form any length of stave required (see Plate XIV). The speed with which a page of music could now be set up was comparable to that for an ordinary book, and whereas Petrucci (see below), who used the double-impression method, issued only about fifty music-books in twenty years, Attaignant (see Part II), employing the single-impression technique, published nearly twice this number in twenty-two years.

Ottaviano de Petrucci [1466–1539] was the first important printer of music, and his publications set a standard in accuracy and artistry which have never been surpassed and rarely equalled. He issued his first book in 1501 and his last in 1520, both in Venice, where he lived from *c.* 1490 to 1511 and from 1536 to his death, the intervening years being spent at Fossombrone. Fifty-two different collections of music from Petrucci's publishing house have survived, and while most of these represent the best of Burgundian music from Ockeghem and Busnois onwards, he issued as many as twelve books of frottole, three of them being reprinted.

The general reduction in length of fifteenth-century secular music, together with the melodic equality of all the parts, led to different arrangements on the page, and in a chanson *a*3 or *a*4, the parts follow each other down the page, one underneath the other, as in Plate XIII. In long pieces *a*4, however, two pages were used divided thus:

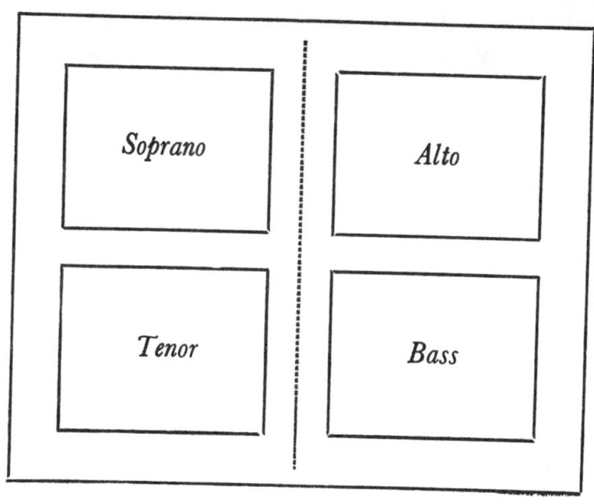

These arrangements are still basically the same as that used for the thirteenth-century motet (see Chapter 4, p. 111)—in other words, choir-book arrangement or cantus collateralis—and Petrucci used both in his early publications, but whereas a real choir-book was large enough for a small group to stand round and see tolerably clearly, Petrucci's books measure only about 8 inches long by 6¼ inches high with a stave of about the same size as that used for piano music today. It would thus have been very difficult if not impossible for four people to stand round a single Petrucci print and sing from it, and buying two or more copies was out of the question for the average music-lover because of the expense. This brings up an extremely interesting point that concerns manuscripts as well. Most of the mediaeval and Renaissance manuscripts and sixteenth-century printed music that have come down to us do not show the wear and tear of frequent use. Performers then, as now, must have made corrections or additions, or left finger-marks, etc., but these are hardly ever to be found on the copies that have survived. This leads one to suspect that these were either presentation copies or made for reference only, the ones actually used in performance always being in manuscript, which were then thrown away when they became too dirty or tattered, and fresh copies made. Furthermore, it is likely that the practice of copying each part on to separate pieces of parchment or paper was fairly common, for this would make it unnecessary for the whole choir to cluster round a single copy on which all the parts were written (see Plate XVII). Even the huge choir-books with their outsize notes and placed on massive lecterns were probably not sung from, because apart from their remarkably clean condition, the treble part (where there is one) is written at the top of the page, where it must have been very difficult for boy choristers to read, especially in the semi-darkness of the churches. On the other hand, placing the parts one after the other on a page or pages is the most obvious method if you want to present or preserve a piece intact.

The copying of each part on to separate pieces of parchment or paper naturally led to binding the pieces of the same part together, as in modern performing editions of string quartets. This is known as 'part-book' arrangement, and was used by all sixteenth-century printers, beginning with Petrucci, most of whose publications are in this form. The earliest manuscript part-books that have survived date from the last quarter of the fifteenth century, but for the reasons given above concerning wear and tear this does not contradict the argument that the idea originated very much earlier.

Although a great many manuscripts have come down to us from before 1600, hardly one of them is an autograph. This unfortunate state of affairs is explained by the fact that composers used blank sheets of parchment or paper called 'cartelles' on which the staves were indented, the notes, clef, etc., being written in ink or pencil. When the piece was completed it was copied by a scribe (often a pupil) and then wiped off, leaving the cartelle clean and ready for future use. The indented stave of the cartelle, and later the actual printing of music, explain why ledger lines occur so rarely, and as a result why there were so many different clef positions, for as the range of any individual part rarely exceeded an eleventh (the range of a five-line stave), it was obviously simpler to choose a clef which enabled the melody to be contained within the bounds of the stave than be constantly adding ledger lines.

The only example of music printing from the sixteenth century which rivals that of Petrucci is a collection of twenty three- and four-part songs published in London in 1530. Most unfortunately, it is incomplete and the printer's name is missing, but until recently it was thought (incorrectly) to have come from the press of Wynkyn de Worde, who came to London from Alsace *c.* 1477 as assistant to the famous printer William Caxton [*c.* 1422–*c.* 1491]. Nevertheless, it seems likely that the man responsible was also a foreigner, an increasing number of whom visited Britain from *c.* 1500 on. This foreign influx which, from the sixteenth to the nineteenth centuries, became such a marked feature of British culture and society, naturally affected her music to some extent, but not until the end of the sixteenth century did a body of native composers arise whose work, while it imitated, also rivalled that of the Continent.

Dunstable's influence seems to have been restricted to the Continent, as very few of his compositions are found in early Renaissance British sources, a surprising fact in view of his reputation abroad. The most important MS of late fifteenth-century British music is the Eton Choirbook (1490 – 1502); unfortunately over half the original contents are missing (including the only motet by Dunstable) or incomplete (including a setting of the Passion choruses from St. Matthew's Gospel by R. Davy. The earliest polyphonic Passion settings are British and date from before 1440). Among the twenty-five composers listed are John Browne [fl. *c.* 1490], Richard Davy [1465 – 1507], William Cornysh [d. 1523] (a poet and playwright, and a great favourite of Henry VIII), and Robert Fayrfax [1464 – 1521], who, as head of the Chapel Royal, organized the musical festivities at the famous Field of the Cloth of Gold in 1520. Apart from its seamless polyphony (reminiscent of Ockeghem) the music is typically British in its sonority (i.e. use of thirds—see Chapters 4, 5—and predominance of writing *a*5 and *a*6—see p. 186), and in its 'vocal scoring' (i.e. use of groups differing in size and timbre; also found in the Old Hall MS). But these two 'progressive' features do not always compensate for the near-monotony and lack of unity produced by a dearth of homophony, suspensions, and imitation—also true of the mature style of Fayrfax, the most notable composer between Dunstable and Taverner (see Vol. II), except that he uses homophony and imitation more often and parody once (his *Missa O bone Jesu* is possibly the first British parody-mass). Elsewhere he, like the Eton Choirbook composers, is old-fashioned in his preference for un-paraphrased cantus firmi; indeed as an exact contemporary of Josquin he is less 'up to date' than Browne, and this underlines the slow development of British vocal music compared to Burgundian. But being up to date has little to do with value, and at its best the richness and tonal variety of Fayrfax's music and that in the Eton MS redeem its weaknesses.

Although Fayrfax wrote a number of secular songs (all *a*3 or *a*2), this side of music was largely neglected by his compatriots, and the only considerable body of music that can be called secular, in that it was not an integral part of the liturgy, is the 'carol', a form peculiar to England. Nowadays the carol is usually associated with Christmas, but while this is still generally true of the fifteenth-century type, it also included other subjects, such as hymns to the Virgin, a petition to a saint, a prayer for a king, or a thanksgiving for victory, e.g. the famous 'Agincourt Song'. The common factor of all these carols is not their subject-matter, but their structure, for all consist of a 'burden' (B), which is sung at the beginning and after each 'verse' (V), the burden being clearly separated from the verses, each of which may have the same 'refrain' (R), this being part of the verse. Thus the following scheme is typical B : V_1 R : B : V_2 R : B : V_3 R : B. The carols are almost all written in English discant-conductus style, and while comparing unfavourably with Continental chansons as regards technique and expressiveness, many of them are little gems that deserve wider recognition and more frequent performance.

Among Fayrfax's contemporaries was Hugh Aston [*c.* 1485–1558], who must be the only man in the history of any art to be ranked as important on the basis of a single work. This is a 'Hornpype' for virginal (a small harpsichord), and it shows a far more remarkable keyboard technique than anything on the Continent. Here is an extract (Ex. 69*):

It is unlikely that Aston's piece was as unique in its day as it appears to be now, for there must have been an earlier tradition, now unfortunately lost, showing a similar, though perhaps not so striking use of keyboard figuration. That very few British examples of fifteenth-century instrumental music have survived—a state of affairs that applies to every European

* From J. Wolf, *Music of Earlier Times*, p. 60.

country except one—must not blind us to the fact, made abundantly clear in contemporary writing, pictures, and sculpture, that the use of instruments on every conceivable occasion was even more widespread than in the fourteenth century.

The exception is Germany, whose makers, especially of wind instruments, and performers became internationally famous, and where instrumental music, particularly for the organ, seems to have been more intensely cultivated and practised than elsewhere. The earliest collection of importance is the *Buxheimer Orgelbuch* (*c.* 1460), a manuscript containing well over 200 pieces, including two by the first notable organist, Conrad Paumann [*c.* 1410 – 1473], a contemporary of Squarcialupi. Though blind from birth, Paumann was acclaimed all over Europe, but unfortunately most of the twenty or so pieces by him that have come down to us are elementary exercises for would-be organ composers. In the latter half of the century Arnolt Schlick [*c.* 1460 – after 1521], Paul Hofhaimer [1459 – 1537], and Hans Buchner [1483 – 1538], a pupil of Hofhaimer's, also achieved international fame. Schlick was a theorist as well, and his treatise on the organ (1511), the first to be published in German, gives valuable information on construction, tuning, etc., and embodies principles and suggestions, some of which hold good to this day. He also published in 1512 the first printed collection of keyboard music, including, in addition to fourteen organ pieces, some music for lute solo. We have less than half this number of organ pieces by Hofhaimer, although his reputation and influence were greater, judging by the number of his pupils. Many of these are represented in four great manuscript collections of the early sixteenth century, totalling nearly 400 pieces, and made by Buchner, Hans Kotter [*c.* 1485–1541], Fridolin Sicher [1490–1546], and Leonhard Kleber [*c.* 1495 – 1556].

The vast majority of German organ music is either based on a cantus firmus (usually sacred) around which the other parts weave more or less elaborate counter-melodies, or else consists of ornamental arrangements of masses, motets, and chansons. The style is essentially vocal, the only main exceptions being rapidly executed ornaments which occur most frequently at cadences.

More characteristically instrumental writing is found in the lute music of the period, for while the organ and (less successfully) the harpsichord and clavichord can imitate the flow of vocal polyphony, a plucked instrument obviously cannot.

The lute was far and away the most popular of all the instruments in the fifteenth century, especially in Germany, Italy, and Spain, but as it was almost always used either in extemporizing an accompaniment to a song or, as in the case of many frottole, in playing as much of the lower parts as it could manage, very few solo pieces were written down, and inevitably even fewer have survived. The advent of music printing, however, and an increasing realization of the instrument's possibilities, led to a growing number of lute solos throughout the next century. Petrucci set the ball rolling by issuing four books in 1507-8 and another two in 1509 and 1511. Nearly all the pieces are transcriptions of vocal music, sacred and secular, but a few original pieces, such as dances and preludes, are included. The only other lute music printed during the same period was that contained in Schlick's 1512 collection.

All lute and much organ music of this period was written in 'tablature'—that is, a system of letters, figures, or signs sometimes placed on four or six lines (like a stave), sometimes above. These letters, etc., either represent the alphabetical names of the notes to be played (organ tablature only), or else indicate the frets on which the lute player must put his fingers. Organ tablature was only used in Germany and Spain, particularly the former country, where it was even used on the rare occasion by as late a composer as Bach. Lute tablature, on the other hand, was universal, and though three systems were in use, the Italian-Spanish, German, and French, the last of these eventually ousted the others towards the end of the sixteenth century. In this system five horizontal lines represent the five highest strings, the sixth (lowest) string being shown by short ledger lines underneath. The letters 'a', 'b'. 'c', 'd', etc., are placed on the lines, 'a' meaning an open string, 'b' that a finger should be placed on the first fret, etc., the frets being roughly a semitone apart. The strings, the three lowest of which were in unison pairs, were tuned either *G*, *c*, *f*, *a*, *d'*, *g'* or *A*, *d*, *g*, *b*, *e'*, *a'*, and were originally plucked by a small piece of wood, metal, or other substance (plectrum); by the end of the century, however, finger plucking was standard and remained so. The shape of the lute is the same as that described on p. 93, and the frets on the fingerboard not only serve as a rough guide to intonation, but, more important, provide a sharp edge on which to stop the string, thus making possible a clearer, more ringing tone with less difference between it and the open string than on, say, the violin, where the fleshy finger-tip presses the string on to a flat finger board and results in a markedly less brilliant timbre than that of an unstopped string.

The note values in tablature are indicated by short, vertical lines with or without one or more hooks, or else actual notes, and are placed above the 'stave'; only the shortest value is shown at any given point and this remains in force until replaced by another, so that, for example, a succession of eight minim 'chords' followed by a semibreve has only two signs, one over the first minim and one over the semibreve. This all sounds very complicated, but once the general principle has been mastered it is very easy, as any ukelele player will tell you, for he too uses a kind of tablature. The reason why lute tablature caught on so was that it not only instructed the player where to put his finger, but was also more economical of paper and far less expensive to print because it used standard type (letters or numbers) instead of complicated symbols like clefs, accidentals, and the different note shapes.

In the same year that Schlick published his organ treatise came the first printed book on instruments in general, by Sebastian Virdung. This describes and portrays through woodcuts the clavichord, virginal, lute, viol, dulcimer, harp, oboe, flute, cornett, bagpipe, trombone, trumpet, organs (positive, portative, and regal), and various percussion instruments, as well as a few other types.

The fifteenth-century clavichord is rectangular in shape, and smaller than the virginal, and the strings, which vary little in length, are hit by small pieces of brass called 'tangents' fixed to one end of a pivoted lever, the other end being the key. The impact of these tangents is regulated by the finger pressure on the key, just as on the piano, and this not only makes possible abrupt dynamic changes, crescendos, and diminuendos, but also the prominence of an inner part. Moreover, by moving the finger to and fro on the key a discreet undulation of the note (vibrato) can be obtained. The action makes the clavichord more expressive than the virginal, but, owing to its small size (which in effect means a small sound-board), the volume is much less. The strings are tuned in unison pairs stretched parallel to the keyboard, and there are fewer pairs than keys, because each pair is assigned two, three, or even four tangents, the position of which determine the pitch of the note. Thus a tangent which hits a pair of strings in their middle and causes half their length to vibrate sounds a note an octave lower than that caused by a tangent which makes the pair vibrate only a quarter of their length. If the two tangents hit the pair of strings at the same time, only the higher note would sound and playing in octaves would be impossible, and in order to get round this the makers so arranged the tangents that only notes that were not normally played together (remembering the limited chords of the time) such as G♯ and C were obtained from the same pair of strings.

The virginal of this period was the same as a small harpsichord; it is single strung, each string corresponding to a different note. The body is usually harp-shaped, like a small grand piano, and the strings vary in length as well as in thickness, material, and tension. Each string is plucked by a 'plectrum' of quill or leather, which sticks out sideways from a hinged strip of wood—the 'tongue'—fitted into the 'jack', an upright piece of wood resting on one end of a pivoted lever. When the other end of this lever is depressed by the finger the jack rises and the plectrum plucks the string; when the finger is removed the jack falls, the tongue tilts back, thus preventing the plectrum from plucking the string a second time, and a piece of felt at the top of the jack stops the string vibrating. The distance between the plectrum and the string is much smaller than that between the tangent and its pair of strings on the clavichord, and hence it is only possible to get a very slight increase in volume by striking the key harder with the finger; the increase is sufficient, however, to enable the performer to distinguish between accented and unaccented notes. The greater volume of sound compared to the clavichord is due to the larger sound-board, which gives a bigger 'boost' to the sound actually produced from plucking, the sharper edge of the plectrum compared to the tangent, and the greater tension of the strings. These last two factors result in the characteristically brilliant timbre of the instrument, compared to which piano tone sounds dull and lifeless. During the early years of the sixteenth century a larger virginal was developed in Italy, the more usual name for which is 'harpsichord'. It has a second set of strings tuned in unison with the original set, thus gaining in brilliance and volume.

The four commonest viols were the treble, alto, tenor, and bass, each of which had six strings tuned in the same manner as the lute—namely (reckoning upwards), fourth, fourth, major third, fourth, fourth. The lowest strings were treble viol-*d*, alto-*c* (in England and France, but *A* in Italy), tenor-*G* (*A* in Italy), and bass-*D*. In addition, the violone or double-bass viol (tuned an octave lower than the bass viol) was occasionally used in consort. With the exception of this last, the viols were played sitting down, the instrument being placed on or between the knees, hence the Italian term, viola da gamba, or 'viol of the leg', a term which eventually implied the bass viol only, for this member of the family was easily the favourite, owing to the beauty of its tone and the ease of execution over a wider range than the others, extending from *D* to two octaves above its top string, i.e. *d'''*. The viol bow is held in exactly the opposite way to the violin, being above the hand, which faces palm upwards, and the stick, unlike the Tourte violin bow of today, is outcurved, not incurved. This method of bowing produces even less bite or accent than with violin bowing, and, together with the natural timbre of the instrument, which is edgier but less resonant and brilliant than that of the violin, determines the character of the music written for it, a character less virtuosic but more intimate and polyphonic than keyboard or lute music, the edgy tone making the individual strands of a polyphonic texture stand out clearly. The comparative lack of resonance and brilliance is due to the thinness of the wood and strings, and the lack of tension in the latter, and the edginess is accentuated by the frets on the finger-board placed at intervals of roughly a semitone, which, as on the lute, make a clear decisive tone, with less distinction between the sound of stopped and open strings than on the violin. During the latter part of the fifteenth century a number of pieces were written for viols only, thus underlining the general trend away from the mediaeval delight in variegated sound towards a more homogeneous one.

The regal, a small domestic organ invented *c.* 1460 that became very popular in the late Renaissance, was originally an all-reed pipe instrument—that is, every pipe was conical in shape and had a small strip or tongue of metal or wood attached to the lower end which vibrated in the wind from the bellows, as in the modern reed pipe. This strengthened the upper partials of the fundamental note and resulted in a characteristic 'reedy' timbre, like that of the bassoon or oboe. The other organs originally had only 'flue' pipes, which were cylindrical in shape and which gave a rounder, more open tone, like that of the flute; by the beginning of the sixteenth century, however, reed pipes were incorporated in the great and positive organs, while many regals had a few flue pipes.

Although Germany was pre-eminent in the production of instrumental music during the early Renaissance, the quantity and quality of her vocal polyphony, particularly sacred, continued to lag behind that of Burgundy, England, and Spain during most of this period, even though her musicians were fully aware of what was going on, as is clearly shown by the contents of the three important late fifteenth-century manuscript collections, the *Glogauer Liederbuch* (='Song Book'), the earliest surviving example of part-book arrangement (see p. 212), the *Schedelesches Liederbuch*, and the *Lochamer Liederbuch*; these contain over 450 pieces, mostly copies or arrangements of secular works by Burgundian composers.

The only men who could in any way compare with the Burgundians were Heinrich Finck [*c.* 1445 – 1527] and Thomas Stoltzer [*c.* 1480 – 1526]. Finck's output is predominantly secular, and is 'up-to-date' in its use of pervading imitation, but his German songs (Lieder) show a feature that remained typical of this type during most of the sixteenth century, and which is old-fashioned compared to Italian or French secular music—namely, the placing of the main melody (nearly always a borrowed one) in the tenor rather than the treble. Stoltzer was German-born, but spent most of his life in Hungary. His output is greater than Finck's in both quantity and quality, and consists almost entirely of sacred music, the style of which shows a marked development in his later years, the seamless web of polyphony reminiscent of Ockeghem giving way to the regular imitation, careful word-setting, and harmonic feeling of Josquin. In his later years Stoltzer, like some other German composers, was considerably affected by the rise of Lutheranism, but more of this in the next volume.

The finest Lieder of the period were written by the Burgundian

Isaac, who, while adopting the feature mentioned above of making the tenor the main voice, treats the borrowed melody much more freely than his German contemporaries, preferring to paraphrase it rather than present it in long notes, and sometimes treating it canonically.

Isaac's masterpiece, however, is the *Choralis Constantinus*, written while he was at the court of Maximilian I at Innsbruck. This, the first polyphonic setting of the complete Propers of the Mass, was commissioned by the Cathedral at Constance (Switzerland) in 1508 and not quite completed before the composer's death. It is a tremendous if uneven work, containing the Propers for all the Sundays of the year, as well as for a number of feast and saints' days, and including at the end five settings of the Ordinary. The three books into which the work is divided, apart from demonstrating most of the mass and motet techniques that were current (parody does not occur and chordal passages are rare), also reveal the development in what we can conveniently call Isaac's 'Burgundian' style. Thus the voice parts (particularly the highest voice) are more florid in Books II and III than in Book I, but at the same time are more refined, and the same applies to his use of dissonance. Again, in Book III final chords include the third more frequently than in Books I and II. The first point shows an increasing mastery in writing individual lines of complex structure without their becoming angular or bizarre; the second point shows that Isaac was able to combine a number of these lines so that they offset each other rhythmically and melodically without clashing harmonically; and the last point underlines what we said earlier in this chapter about the slow acceptance of the third in final chords—on the Continent that is, for, as we have seen, contemporary British compositions end on a full triad far more frequently.

Part-music was not the only kind of vocal composition in Germany, nor indeed in other countries either, but the songs of the Meistersinger provide a larger body of monophonic song than existed anywhere else. The Meistersinger flourished from *c.* 1425 to *c.* 1600, establishing guilds in every important German town, and though they regarded themselves as the musical and poetic heirs of the Minnesinger, their art is quite different and inferior to the earlier poet-musicians. The main reason for this is that while the Minnesinger were wandering professionals mostly of noble birth and bound by no social ties, the Meistersinger were tradespeople who met together in their spare time and sang, and who as a result became highly organized. This naturally led to a system of rules, and with the spreading of the movement these rules grew in complexity and importance, thus impairing melodic spontaneity. To be a 'mastersinger' you had to compose both words and music of at least one song, but on no account had the melody to be reminiscent of any other 'master song', with the result that many of the songs are forced and artificial in their deliberate striving for originality. Most of the other rules are concerned with textual faults, such as bad rhymes or incorrect scansion. The scene in Act II of Wagner's opera, *Die Meistersinger*, gives a very good idea of what a prospective 'mastersinger' had to put up with. The chief character in the opera, Hans Sachs [1494 – 1576], was the most famous of all 'mastersingers', composing over 6,000 songs, two-thirds of which are 'master songs'!

Despite the overall inferiority of their art, the Meistersinger performed a valuable and unique service, for only in Germany was music actually cultivated by the middle classes, and the organizing of amateur musical groups all over the country established a tradition of music-making and appreciation that bore rich fruit in later centuries.

In Spain, French and—later—Burgundian influence was all-powerful, so far as music was concerned at any rate, but during the first half of the century this did not produce much in the way of polyphony, as most of the comparatively few compositions actually written down are solo songs (Spanish music, like Italian, was more often improvised than in northern Europe). In the second half, however, a number of composers were active, chief of whom were Juan de Anchieta [1462 – 1523] and, more particularly, Francisco de Peñalosa [*c.* 1470 – 1528]. The works of both these men show complete familiarity with the Burgundian style, and Peñalosa in particular reaped the benefits of a lengthy visit to Rome, *c.* 1517, where, as a member of the Papal Chapel, he met many highly trained musicians, mostly Burgundians. Both Anchieta and Peñalosa held positions at the court of Ferdinand V of Aragon [1452-1516] and his Queen, Isabella of Castile [1451-1504]. The reign of Ferdinand and Isabella has been called "the golden age of Spanish history", for they drove the last of the Moors from the Peninsula in 1492, sponsored the expedition of Columbus in the same year, and brought a period of economic and political stability unknown before. This, together with visits by a number of Burgundians, including Ockeghem and Agricola, and the fact that both Ferdinand and Isabella were keen music-lovers who laid particular stress on sacred music, may well account for the rejuvenation of native composition.

Despite the royal preference, however, a considerable body of secular music was written, the bulk being contained in four manuscript collections comprising nearly 700 pieces. The most important of these collections is the *Cancionero de Palacio* ('Songs of the Palace'), and most of the pieces (for two or more voices) are villancicos—that is, songs in virelai-form, like the mediaeval cantigas (see Chapter 3, p. 90), with secular, i.e. non-liturgical, texts. Among the villancico composers represented in the *Cancionero de Palacio* are Johannes Cornago, Francisco de la Torre, and Escobar (probably Pedro de [*c.* 1465 – after 1535]), but the most important was Juan del Encina [1468 – *c.* 1529], a notable figure in the history of Spanish drama, even though he spent most of his life in Italy, whose songs are typical in that the main melody is in the treble and the style is that of Dufay and Binchois, with occasional use of imitation; the texts are mainly concerned with love, though, like the English carol, the subject-matter covers a fairly wide range.

That Burgundy was the dominating musical influence in fifteenth-century Spain, despite the latter's long and close association with Italy, is less surprising when we realize that of all the arts in the early Renaissance music was the only one in which Italy was not predominant, for in painting, sculpture, and literature she far outstripped the rest of Europe. One has only to compile a list of Italian artists and writers and then compare it with those of other countries to see how rich was the Italian genius in these fields. Florence was still the main centre, and her leading painters were Masaccio [1401-?1428], Fra Angelico [1387-1455], Uccello [1397-1475], Piero della Francesca [1416-1492], Botticelli [1445-1510], Leonardo da Vinci [1452-1519], and Raphael [1483-1520]; her sculptors Ghiberti [1378-1455], Donatello [1386-1466], and Lucca del Robbia [1400-1482], while the greatest architect of the fifteenth century, Brunelleschi [1379-1446], was also a Florentine. So also was the poet Politian [1454-1494], the scholar Pico della Mirandola [d. 1494], and the greatest prose writer of the Renaissance, Machiavelli [1469-1527]. But if Florence was still the main cultural centre, Venice bid fair to usurp her prestige through her popular lyric poet, Giustiniani [1388-1446] (the author of *O rosa bella*), and more especially her painters, the chief of whom were Giovanni Bellini [1428-1516], Montegna [1431-1506], Giorgione [*c.* 1478-1510], and Carpaccio [1460-1522]. These men, by using rich, glowing colours with a freedom only possible in the new medium of oil, stressed the naturalism of their subjects to an even greater extent than did the Florentines, who, mixing their pigments with white of egg (tempera), or painting on plaster walls and ceilings (frescoes), relied mainly on detailed drawings governed mainly by the mathematical principles of perspective which they, in their pursuit of realism, had discovered, with colour as a largely inessential addition. But the Venetians were not only concerned with realism, for the harmony of their colours produces a unity of design which is not solely dependent on a geometrical pattern achieved through the careful placing of objects, and it was this use of colour, which conveys a more purely emotional appeal than any other European school of the time, that became intensified during the sixteenth century and was the springboard of baroque art.

Compared to the Italian galaxy, the rest of Europe produced only two important writers, the Englishman, Sir Thomas More [1478-1535], and the Dutch humanist, philosopher, and scholar, Erasmus [1466/7-1536], who through his breadth of mind, clarity of thought, and sanity of judgment exerted a greater influence on his generation (Catholics and Protestants alike) than any other man of letters has ever done. As for artists, the only ones of comparable stature were the Flemish (Burgundian) painters, Hubert van Eyck [d. 1426] and his brother Jan [d. 1441], who served Philip the Good, van der Weyden [1399-1464], who painted Charles the Bold, and Memlinc [1440-1494], and the Germans, Dürer [1471-1528] and Grünewald [b. before 1480-1528].

Dürer, who executed some fine oil paintings and exquisite watercolours, is chiefly famous for his engravings and woodcuts. In these his vivid detail, particularly of the human body, is typical of the Renaissance, and was undoubtedly influenced by

Italian art, notably that of Leonardo da Vinci; Leonardo, in fact, made tremendous strides in the science of anatomy, and by dissecting human and animal bodies and carefully drawing his findings discovered an astonishing amount, none of which however became generally known, because nearly all his notebooks, which were written backwards and partly in code, remained unpublished until the nineteenth century. These notebooks contain a mass of original and penetrating observations on art, music, warfare, philosophy, and almost every aspect of the enormous realm of natural science, and show a thoroughly modern scientific approach in their clear realization that experiment is essential and must precede conclusions.

But Leonardo was a unique individual, perhaps the most unique in the whole history of western civilization, and not until the latter half of the sixteenth century did men really begin to throw off the double yoke of mediaeval speculation and reliance on ancient authority, especially that of Aristotle and Ptolemy. Even so a few daring spirits arose, including the Germans, Regiomontanus [1436-1476], who asserted, quite correctly, that Ptolemy was frequently inaccurate, and Nicolaus of Cusa [1401-1464], who maintained on purely philosophical grounds that the earth was not the centre of the universe and in fact revolved round the sun, a view that did not, in the tolerant atmosphere of the fifteenth century, prevent his being raised to the rank of cardinal, but which 150 years later, in the heat of the Counter-Reformation, was denounced as heretical.

The striking difference between the predominance of music in northern Europe and the predominance of the fine arts, literature, and science (such as it was) in Italy is explained by the fact (already mentioned) that the Renaissance, which grew more quickly and blossomed more richly in Italian soil than anywhere else, was primarily concerned with a reality based on the close observance of man and his world, the forms, colours, and details of which are readily and naturally transmitted to canvas or stone, or described in words. But realism is fundamentally foreign to music which, in its essence, is abstract and incapable of conveying exact images, ideas, or feelings. To rejoice the ear by sheer sonority, or by weaving melody with melody into a simple or complex web of sound, yes; to express a general mood or feeling, yes; to satisfy the intellect through simple forms or delight it with structural subtlety, yes; but to portray precisely physical objects, mental concepts, or emotional states, no. The abstract mysticism and universality of outlook of the Middle Ages found music a perfect means of expression, but only in certain limited respects, some of them naïve, was the primary attitude of the Renaissance reflected in the works of her composers.

Basically the period from Dunstable to Josquin is still mediaeval (hence the title of this chapter as distinct from Early Renaissance Music), the cantus firmus, paraphrase, and parody techniques are simply developments of the borrowed Gregorian chant in the tenor of the thirteenth- and fourteenth-century motet; the predominantly linear polyphonic texture of sacred and secular music alike is only different from the earlier styles in its greater refinement of harmony, smoothness of line, and equality of rhythm, the last two being the natural application of conductus style to polyphony, while the first, being part and parcel of an increased feeling for tonality, shows the same development in part-music as that which took place in Christian chant, where the earlier semi-rhapsodic melodies were later pruned and became part of a clearly defined modal system; the optional or obligatory use of instruments, with their contrasting timbres to double or accompany the voice, is a direct continuation of mediaeval practice. Music is still the be-all and end-all, not yet the handmaiden of poetry nor the vehicle of passion; only through pervading imitation did she become in any fundamental sense Renaissance-like, for imitation is, as we observed in Chapter 5, a more realistic means of binding the parts together, but its use as the sole means of unification had still to be generally accepted. The increase in sonority achieved through the recognition of the third as a fundamental interval (though even at the end of the period final chords still frequently omitted it, except in British compositions), together with the expansion of the number and range of voices, were natural developments, the former for reasons already given (see Chapter 2, p. 43), and the latter because, as composers become more assured in any one tradition, they tend to enlarge their forces.

The most obvious realistic element in fifteenth-century music is the least important and naïve—word-painting. This can occasionally be found in mediaeval music (see Ex. 38 and the ritornello of *H.A.M.*, 52, where the voices imitate the sound of a horn), but from Josquin onwards it became conventional to set words like 'ascending', 'descending', 'flying', etc., to rising, falling, or florid passages respectively. Another less frequent device which was very popular with some later composers consisted in writing black notes when 'death', or 'night' or some such word occurred in the text (see p. 203). This is known as 'eye music', for the effect of such notation is obviously limited to the performers. Black notes were not only used for descriptive purposes, however, but more often indicate changes of rhythm and note value; they were in fact the equivalent of red or white notes in the earlier part of the fifteenth century, but whereas the normal notes of this period and earlier are usually black, those of the latter part of the century and later are usually white, or rather the minim and larger values are, just as in our notation today. Although the actual change-over can be conveniently put at *c.* 1450, white notation was occasionally used before and black notation after this date, the latter almost always being written on parchment, and this provides the reason for the change. During the fourteenth and fifteenth centuries parchment was increasingly replaced by paper, which was cheaper and less cumbersome, but paper is less resilient than parchment, and it was soon found that the solid blobs of ink representing minims, semibreves, and breves (the most frequent values of that time) not only showed through on the other side, but in time eventually ate the paper away, leaving little holes; by simply outlining these notes in ink and leaving the centres white, devastation was avoided, although the actual labour of writing was increased.

The change from black to white notation was not accompanied by any change in the actual speed of the notes, at least not from Machaut onwards, for from *c.* 1350 to *c.* 1550 the semibreve was the tactus and was equal to M.M. 60-80, though admittedly the only concrete evidence we have is the statement by the theorist Gafori (see p. 230), who equates the speed of the semibreve with the "pulse of a quietly breathing man", i.e. about M.M. 70. In the compositions of the Mannered School, however, the speed of the tactus probably slowed down somewhat, owing to the rhythmical complexity of the music and the very short notes employed.

The whole question of tempi in the music of any period is a difficult one, and with the exception of those compositions of the nineteenth century and later that have metronome markings, it is impossible to be dogmatic about the exact speed of any particular piece. This is especially true of mediaeval and Renaissance music in which not even the approximate speed indications (allegro, andante, etc.) of later periods occur, although a few sixteenth-century composers did in fact provide some hints as to tempi (see Part II). The following suggestions, therefore, while based on Gafori's statement, are simply what the present writer thinks was the practice of the time:

> The speed of the tactus, within the limits M.M. 60-80, should be governed by the nature of the words and/or the texture of the music. Thus a sad chanson should be slower than a gay one, and an 'Alleluia' refrain or ending should be quicker than the rest of the motet in which it occurs. In the mass the Kyrie, Sanctus (but see below), and Agnus Dei, because they need more time to display their flowing melismatic lines and rich polyphonic texture, should be slower than the Gloria and Credo, in which the number of words is far greater and hence the melodies are more syllabic and the texture less complex. There should, however, be slight differences in speed within the Gloria (e.g. 'Qui tollis'—either the first or second statement, depending on how the composer has sectionalized the music—to 'suscipe deprecationem nostram' inclusive should be slower), the Credo (e.g. 'Crucifixus' to 'sepultus est' should be slower), and the Sanctus (e.g. 'Pleni sunt coeli et terra gloria tua' should be quicker and the 'Osanna' quicker still, i.e. 'Sanctus . . .' could be M.M. 60, 'Pleni sunt coeli . . .' M.M. 70, and 'Osanna . . .' M.M. 80).

The foregoing instances from the Gloria, Credo, and Sanctus of the mass are not necessarily the only ones that may deviate from the normal speed of the movement in question, but once the speed of the tactus has been settled for a complete work or a section it should remain unchanged. Nothing does greater violence to mediaeval and Renaissance music than constantly fluctuating tempi and excessive accelerandos and rallentandos; accelerandos in fact should never occur and rallentandos very seldom and very discreetly; indeed, the latter are often taken care of by the composer, who will lengthen the note values and/or sustain one or more notes as he approaches a sectional or final cadence.

Composers could also quicken the speed of the tactus (they very rarely wished to slow it down) by means of 'proportional' signs, of which ¢ was the most common. This was known as 'tactus alla breve' whereas C was 'tactus alla semibreve'. When ¢ occurs in a part previously governed by C, or is contrasted with other parts in C, then the breve tactus of the former is equal to the semibreve tactus of the latter and hence the semibreve in ¢ is performed twice as fast as in C. On the other hand, from about Josquin's time on, ¢ more often means exactly the same as C! (In the late Renaissance C stood for a different kind of notation: see Part II.) This lack of precise definition concerning proportional signs is typical of sixteenth-century music, and is further demonstrated by the number 3, which sometimes stands for $\frac{3}{1}$, when three semibreves occupy the time of one semibreve in C (tripla), and sometimes for $\frac{3}{2}$ or ¢3, when three semibreves occupy the time of two semibreves in C (sesquialtera='one and a half').

The above discussion only touches on the fringe of fifteenth-century notation, and we cannot here deal more fully with the intricate proportional system which made possible all kinds of subtle cross-rhythms. The subject is obviously important when it comes to actually performing the music, and far too many modern editions give no clue as to the original notes or signs and frequently misinterpret their meaning.

A great deal of information concerning proportional signs and their effect on note values can be found in the works of contemporary theorists. The chief of these were the Spaniard, Bartolomé Ramos de Pareja [*c.* 1440-after 1491], the Burgundian, Johannes Tinctoris [*c.* 1435-1511], and the Italian, Franchino Gafori [1451-1522]. The most influential of these was Gafori, who wrote five major theoretical treatises, the most important of which from our point of view is the *Practica musicae* (1496), where the rules of composition are clearly laid down, and which includes a large section on proportions. Of greater interest, however, are Tinctoris's twelve treatises (*c.* 1476-*c.* 1484), for they contain more information about the earlier fifteenth-century composers, and compare the 'new art', as Tinctoris calls it, of Dunstable and Dufay with that of the fourteenth century. In the ninth treatise, apart from stating roundly that only music of the last forty years is worth listening to, Tinctoris scorns the mediaeval idea of 'music of the spheres' (see Chapter 1, p. 12), discusses the rules of composition (one of which bans the major and minor third from two-part writing!), and spends some time in describing the various ways of improvising, thus providing proof positive that what has survived on music-paper does not tell the whole story of fifteenth-century musical practice. Indeed, it is likely that new ideas of melodic figuration and treatment of discord may have been tried out or discovered through improvisation, particularly on a keyboard instrument or lute.

While Gafori and Tinctoris were primarily encyclopaedists without whose works we should be immeasurably the poorer, Ramos was a revolutionary, and his *Musica practica* (1482) provoked a storm of controversy. Not only did he throw overboard Guido's hexachord, hallowed by age and tradition, replacing it with other solmisation syllables based on the octave (like our present-day tonic sol-fa), but he constructed a scale which is very nearly that of equal temperament, i.e. with all the semitones the same, although he clearly did not realize its possibilities. Nor does he seem to have been aware of the full implications of another scale he devised, in which Pythagoras's rather complex method of scale-building from the monochord is replaced by a much simpler one based solely on division and multiplication by two or three, and which results in ratios for the major and minor thirds which are identical with those of just intonation (see Part II), and different from those of Pythagoras, for Ramos's sole aim was not to invent new scales, but to make the finding of intervals easier for the singer.

Ramos's innovations were severely criticized, and his eminent pupil, Giovanni Spataro [*c.* 1458 – 1541], defended his master and was in turn violently attacked by Gafori. It was not long, however, before just intonation was accepted and even equal temperament regarded as one of several possibilities of tuning keyboard instruments.

The early Renaissance has, perhaps naturally, but certainly undeservedly, lain too long in the shadow of the succeeding period, for Dunstable, Dufay, Ockeghem, and Josquin are composers of comparable stature with the greatest names of the sixteenth century. As a craftsman Josquin is the equal of Palestrina, and although he lacks the later man's utter perfection of style because his musical language is less refined, he is certainly as expressive and as profound. In other spheres, too, the early Renaissance can compare with the late—painting and architecture, for example, and while the scientific investigation of man and his universe was still in its infancy, the desire to explore the unknown parts of the world was as strong as in the period following. The journeys of the Polos to the Far East in the thirteenth century and Marco's account of them were the fifteenth-century explorers' chief stimuli, and the Portuguese Prince Henry the Navigator [1394-1460] planned a number of expeditions during which most of the north-western coast of Africa was discovered, including Rio de Oro (1436), Cape Verde (1445), Sierra Leone (1450), and the Gulf of Guinea (1460), together with the Madeira Islands (1419-20) and the Azores (1432-60). In 1487 the Cape of Good Hope was rounded, and in the same year India was reached by sea from Egypt, both by Portuguese sailors. The latter achievement fired the King of Portugal's ambition, and in 1497 he despatched one of the greatest navigators in history, Vasco da Gama [*c.* 1469-1525], to the Indian Peninsula, where a landing was effected ten months later and was followed by Portuguese settlements. The traditional route to India was open, and not long after parts of Malaya and the East Indies were conquered and even China reached (1516). In the meantime the southern Atlantic route had been blazed by the Spaniard, Christopher Columbus [1451-1506], who on his first two voyages of 1492 and 1493-6 conquered most of the West Indies, and in his third (1498) discovered Trinidad and the South American mainland. On his last voyage (1502-4) he searched in vain along the coast of Central America for a passage westwards; so did the Italians, Sebastian Cabot [*c.* 1483-1557] and Amerigo Vespucci [1451-1512]. The former, with his father, John [*c.* 1455-*c.*1498], both in the service of Henry VII of England, discovered the North American coast in 1487 and later entered Hudson Bay, and the latter, whose reputation far exceeded his achievements, even eclipsing that of Columbus, and whose Christian name as a result was given to South America, may have discovered Brazil (1499-1500), but certainly explored much of the South American coast. The passage through to the west was eventually found by the Portuguese, Magellan [*c.* 1470-1521], who, in the service of Spain, discovered the Straits that bear his name (1519), sailed across the Pacific Ocean (which he christened), and reached the Philippine Islands, where he was killed by the natives. His ship, however, continued the journey and returned to Spain in 1522, the first vessel to sail round the world. In the same year that Magellan found a way through to the Pacific Ocean, Mexico, with its ancient Inca civilization and enormous wealth, was conquered by the Spaniard, Cortez [1485-1547], and imperial expansion began in earnest.

The weeks, sometimes months, spent at sea with no or only uncharted land in sight resulted in a more scientific approach to navigation, in the improvement of the astrolabe and quadrant for measuring the angle of the sun and stars, and in the greater accuracy of maps, the first world map being published in 1507.

That Italy took comparatively little part in all this world expansion was probably due to her geographical position, for her only exit to the east or west was through the narrow and treacherous (in those days) Straits of Gibraltar. But whatever the explanation, it in no way affected the brilliance of her culture, a brilliance that shone over all Europe and drew men in all walks of life to study within her boundaries. Music was no exception, and although, as we have seen, there was little native composition during most of the period, the wealth of opportunities, compared to other countries, that were open to musicians, especially singers, in churches and aristocratic establishments attracted a host of foreigners, and, despite the lack of any Italian genius or school of composition, most of the leading composers from the north visited Italy at least once, although few stayed any length of time. In the sixteenth century, however, when the Renaissance reached its full flowering many of the outstanding Continental musicians from across the Alps settled in the peninsula for several years, some of them holding positions of considerable importance. Their effect on Italian music and vice versa takes us into the late Renaissance and Part II of this history.

PERFORMANCE

(See also pp. 195, 209, 215, 228-30.)

The expanding vocal range during the century, and the resultant natural distinction between voices through their timbres, and, in the latter half of the period, the achieving of a more homogeneous texture by means of pervading imitation make performance by voices alone less objectionable than in the Middle Ages. Nevertheless, it is quite certain that instrumental doubling or accompaniment was the rule, especially in those works that are based on an unparaphrased borrowed melody, for this should be clearly heard, and hence should be played on an instrument with or without vocal doubling. Many motets and most if not all of the movements in the mass should be varied at suitable places by altering both the number and combination of voices and instruments. In motets and masses the number of voices per part should not exceed four unless the top part is sung by boys' voices, when the number should be six or seven; instruments may be doubled or even trebled, depending on the timbre and the importance of the part played. Secular pieces should in the main be performed by soloists, whether vocal or instrumental, although where there is a refrain or burden and the texture is very simple, as in some frottole and many carols, the number of voices and instruments may be increased. In any case, considerable variety should be aimed at in all pieces employing repetition, the verses being shared by each soloist—who should sing his or her normal part, whether it be top, inner, or bottom—and the refrain being sung by all the voices, but with the instrumentation varied each time. The instruments used have already been listed in this and previous chapters, and there seems to have been less distinction than in earlier centuries as to which were suitable in church and which were not

Underlaying continues to be rather haphazard, and in melismatic passages it is usually impossible to discover the composer's exact intentions as to how the words should fit the notes, if indeed he had any such intentions. Musica ficta also is still very much of a problem, and in compositions with partial signatures too many editors and conductors remove the false relations that occur between the parts by adding an unnecessary number of accidentals. Successive false relations (e.g. when a B♭ in one part is immediately followed or preceded by a B♮ in another) are typical of the period, and even simultaneous false relations should not be removed if of short duration. In general, editorial accidentals are only permissible in order (*a*) to avoid the melodic intervals of the augmented fourth and diminished fifth (though at times even these seem to have been desired by the composer), and also to remove simultaneous false relations of a minim's length or more provided this does not result in awkward vocal line; and (*b*) to ensure that the leading note is sharpened, but only if it is the last leading note of the melodic phrase in which it occurs, is the resolution of a suspension, and does not result in a false relation of the augmented sixth with one of the other parts.

The subject of tempo has already been dealt with, but that of dynamics remains to be discussed. Violent changes in loudness and softness should never occur; crescendos should be gentle and infrequent, but a diminuendo is often effective at a sectional or final cadence where the words permit. There should of course be both dynamic contrasts and emotional warmth in performance, but in general the approach should be one of restraint.

PART II

LATE RENAISSANCE AND BAROQUE MUSIC

(*c.* 1525—*c.* 1750)

by ALEC HARMAN *and* ANTHONY MILNER

I

THE LATE RENAISSANCE: SECULAR MUSIC

THE most important type of composition in the late Renaissance was undoubtedly the madrigal, for not only did it exert a greater influence than any other type, but it eventually foreshadowed more clearly the advent of baroque music. Despite its name, there is no connexion whatever with the fourteenth-century type (which was probably completely unknown in the Renaissance, anyway), except, of course, that both were written in the 'mother tongue', not in Latin.

The sixteenth-century madrigal sprang from a fusion of the Italian frottola, the French chanson, and the polyphonic imitative style of the north European composers, who were mostly Netherlanders or Flemings.

From about 1510 onwards the frottola texts grew more serious in content and the music more 'learned' in style, but the lighter side was kept alive and eventually developed into the less sophisticated, racy villanesca (see p. 245). The most important of the serious frottola types was the canzona, in which the poetic text varies considerably in structure (a feature of the later madrigal), the music is mildly polyphonic, and the beginnings and ends of phrases are clear-cut.

The brilliance of the late Renaissance in Italy not only attracted men from all over the Continent, but exerted a powerful influence on aristocratic society, arts, and letters everywhere, particularly in France, Spain, and, towards the end of the century, England. Of all the European countries France had had the longest and most distinctive and distinguished musical tradition, and while she absorbed some of the characteristics of the early frottola—the only kind of music that was purely Italian—she produced a type of composition, the chanson, that was different in many respects and which had little connexion with the fifteenth-century Burgundian type. Its main features are a lightness, simplicity, and beauty achieved through the frequent use of rapid repeated notes, dance-like rhythms, and a predominantly chordal texture; these, together with clear-cut phrases and melodic and sectional repetitions, provide a sharp contrast with the Burgundian chanson, and while the chordal texture and phrasing show Italian influence, the frottola on the whole had never placed such a premium on melody (how could it, coming from Italy?), nor had it been so rhythmically precise. This does not mean that the chansons are tuneless, but that in most cases their appeal depends to a greater extent on their harmonic and rhythmic qualities and on the words to which they are set than on the attractiveness or expressiveness of their melodies.

The first two leading masters of the French chanson were Clément Janequin [d. 1558] and Claudin de Sermisy [*c.* 1490–1562]. The former was by far the more popular, and not only was he the first 'Composer in Ordinary' to any French king, but he also set the fashion for the 'programme-chanson', which became all the rage. These pieces carried the Renaissance delight in realistic word-painting a stage further than hitherto, and titles such as *Les chants des oiseaux* and *Le caquet des femmes* ('Women's chatter') are typical. By far his most celebrated piece, a positive smash-hit, in fact, was *La Guerre*, written to celebrate the French victory at the Battle of Marignano (1515). This was imitated more widely and arranged for instruments more frequently than any of his other songs, and its vivid word-painting in which trumpet fanfares, drum-beats, war-cries, and other battle noises are imitated in the music represents an extreme example of the programme-chanson. (Ex. 1,* see p. 241. Notice the cross-accents which, in bars 2–5, result in a stress on each crochet in one part or another, and so add to the general confusion.)

By far the greater number of chansons, however, both by Janequin himself and others, are characterized by a text, usually expressive of unrequited love, that is set more conventionally but with a greater regard for purely musical qualities. It was this type that Claudin favoured, and among his examples are some that tell a story—the 'narrative-chanson'. Most of these begin with three repeated notes in the rhythm 𝅗𝅥 ♩ ♩, a feature of some frottole, but why it became

* From *Clément Janequin: Chansons* (*Attaignant, 1529*) (*Les Maîtres musiciens de la Renaissance française*), ed. H. Expert, Vol. VII, p. 31.

XVIII A scene from *Circe, ou le ballet comique de la Royne* [1581].

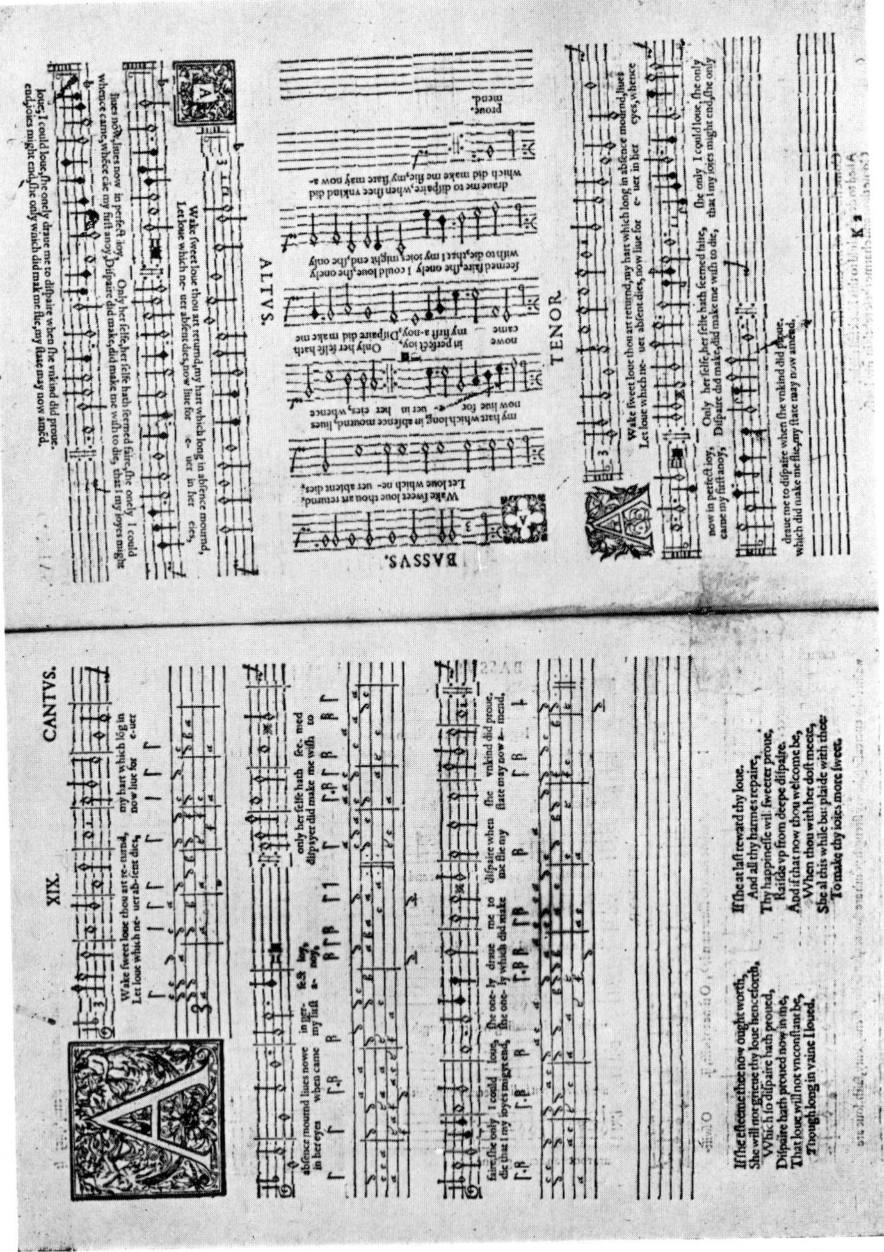

XIX *Awake, sweet love*, from Dowland's *First Booke of Songes* [1597].

(as it did) a hall-mark of all narrative-chansons is not clear. Despite Janequin's fame, his work is no better than Claudin's, though the lively if naïve realism of his descriptive pieces will probably always be more immediately attractive than the delicate charm of those of his contemporary (Ex. 2*, p. 242).

The Janequin-Claudin chanson, like the frottola, did not last against the invincible tide of polyphony that continued to sweep from the north, and imitation and through-composition rather than counterpoint and repetition were favoured by the next generation of composers, especially, as we would expect, those born in the Netherlands or of Flemish stock. Even the leading French chanson writers, Jean Richafort [*c.*1480-*c.* 1547] and Thomas Crecquillon [d. *c.* 1557], were affected, but not so

* Adapted from *Chansons au luth* . . ., ed. Laurencie, Mairy, and Thibaut, p. 14. Accompaniment omitted.

Ex.2 Chanson - Vivray-je tousjours en soucy?
Claudin
(repeat)
Vi - vray - je tous-jours en sou - - cy Pour vous ma tres
Si vous n'a - ves de moy mer - cy Je lan - gui - - ray
Be-cause of thee, sweet, my love — dear Shall I in sor - -
If pi - ty thou show'st not, I — fear That I shall lan -
loy al - le a - - my - - - - e. Vos-tre Beaul - té
tou te ma — vi - - - e
- row ex - ist — al - - - - - ways? Thy beau - ty rare
- guish for all — my — days
M'a ar res - té Por son ser - - vant; Du bon du cueur
Hast held me e'er Thy slave in thrall; As thou art kind
Son ser-vi - teur — My voys — nom - - - mant
It's ser-vant I — My - self — do — call

markedly as the northerners, Clemens non Papa [*c.* 1510 – *c.* 1555/6], Nicolas Gombert [d. after 1556], Adrian Willaert [*c.* 1490 – 1562], and Jacques Arcadelt [?1505 – 1568].

The popularity of the French chanson throughout the sixteenth century is attested by the number that were printed by the leading music publishers, particularly those outside Italy. The chief of these were Pierre Attaignant [d. 1551/2], who issued nearly seventy collections, Adrian le Roy [d. 1598] and Robert Ballard [d. 1588], Jacques Moderne [*c.* 1500 – *c.* 1562], and Nicolas du Chemin [*c.* 1515 – 1576] in France, and Tielman Susato [d. *c.* 1561], and Pierre Phalèse [*c.* 1510 – *c.* 1573] in the Low Countries. All used the single impression method (see Part I, pp. 210-11), and Moderne seems to have been the first to arrange the parts on opposite pages so that they can be read by people sitting on opposite sides of a table (Ex. 3, see p. 243).

Arcadelt and Willaert were not only important chanson composers, but also played a considerable part in the development of the early madrigal, though preceded by the Frenchman Phillippe Verdelot [d. before 1552] and the Italian Constanzo Festa [d. 1545]. The works of these last show the

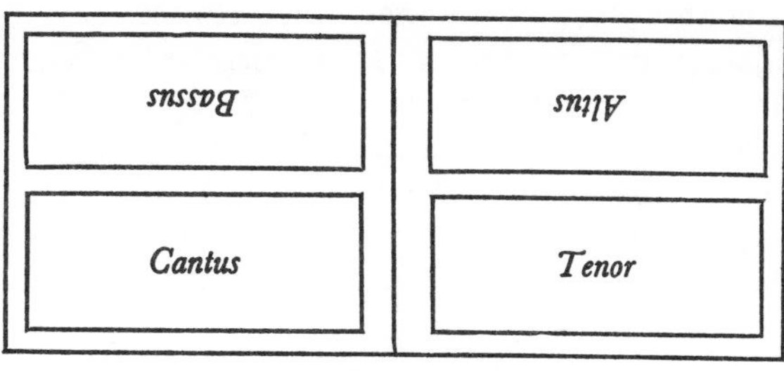

Ex 3.

opposing styles of imitative polyphony and counterpoint which in some of their madrigals are fused into an essentially chordal texture, but with the parts enlivened by short snatches of imitation or rhythmic independence. The main difference between the two men is that while Verdelot, being a northerner, preferred the richness of five or six parts, Festa favoured the greater simplicity and clarity of writing *a*3. The latter was also more 'modern' in sometimes employing a kind of notation called 'note nere' in which the mensuration sign is 'c' and in which the semiminim (our crotchet) is the harmonic unit (the tactus therefore being the minim); hence most of the notes are 'black'. In Part I we stated that from Josquin onwards most compositions were written in ¢, with the minim as the harmonic unit, the semibreve being the tactus ('note bianche', because most of the notes are 'white'), but from *c.* 1540 on note nere was increasingly used in madrigals and other secular pieces, while masses and motets continued to use note bianche. Now although the minim in ¢ ranged from M.M. 120–160, the crotchet therefore ranging from M.M. 240–320, there is some doubt as to the speed of the crotchet in c; occasionally it might be as fast as M.M. 240, as in some of the more frivolous French chansons, but in general it probably fluctuated between M.M. 120 and 160, thus equalling the range of the minim in ¢. From 1550 onwards many vocal pieces were written, in effect, in both c and ¢, in the sense that either the crotchet or the minim was the harmonic unit of a particular section, the choice usually depending on the text. Thus, for example, if the words 'joy' or 'quickly' occur in a line, the harmonic movement is usually in crotchets at, say, M.M. 180, but if 'grief' or 'slowly' occur this would change to minims, the speed of which would now be M.M. 90 (see pp. 292f.).

Of the chanson composers mentioned earlier, only Arcadelt and Willaert are important as madrigalists. The former achieved fame from the very start, and his first book of madrigals (1538?) was reprinted no less than thirty-three times by 1654. Most of his madrigals are *a4* and are characterized by clear, diatonic harmony, smooth lyrical melody, and a classical approach that rejects undue expressiveness or emotion. (Ex. 4*):

Ex. 4 Beginning and ending of the madrigal - *Il bianco e dolce cigno* (1539)
Arcadelt
(a)
Il bian - - co e dol-ce ci - - gno can-tan-do mo - - re Et
can - - tan - - do mo - re Et
io pian-gen - - do giong' al fin del vi - ver mio
mi - - o
(etc.)
(The sweet white swan dies singing, and I weeping reach the end of my life)
(b)
di mil - - le mort' il di, sa - rei con-ten - - - - - - to
di mil - - - le mort' il di, di mil - le mort' il
di mil - - - le mort' il di, sa - rei con - ten - - to, di
mil - le mort' il di, sa - - rei con - ten - to, di mil - le
di, sa - - rei con - ten - - to.
mil - le mort' il di, sa - rei con - ten - - to.
mort' il di, sa - rei con - ten - - to.
(I would gladly die a thousand deaths a day.)

* From *Trésor musical: Musique profane*, ed. Maldeghem, Vol. XXV, p. 9.

This is, deservedly, his most famous madrigal. Note the simple but most expressive slip to the flat side of the key on '*piangendo*' ('weeping'), and the ending with its held note in the top part. We call this an 'inverted pedal'; if the held note is in a middle part it is called an 'inner pedal', and if in the lowest part (the usual place) it is called simply a 'pedal', from the held tonic or dominant pedal note so common in the final bars of organ extemporisations and compositions. It was a favourite ending in both instrumental and vocal music during the late Renaissance. The last point of imitation ('*di mille mort' il dì*'), with its initial upward leap followed by a stepwise descent, became the most hackneyed of all such points during the same period. Most of Arcadelt's madrigals were written in Rome, but in 1553 he settled in France and adopted the chanson instead.

Rome was also the scene of Festa's activity, while Verdelot spent most of his life in Florence and Venice. These three cities were the main centres of madrigal writing, especially the last, owing to the pre-eminence of Willaert, one of the greatest composers, and certainly the most influential, of the sixteenth century. In 1527 he was appointed *maestro di capella* ('chapel master') of the famous Romanesque basilica of St. Mark, and apart from occasional short visits abroad he remained there till his death. Willaert's genius is equalled by his versatility, and his enormous output includes masses, motets, madrigals, chansons, and frivolous pieces, such as villanescas. These last (sometimes called 'villanelle') originated in Naples and developed from the lighter kind of frottola, becoming popular mainly through the attractive, simple, and often humorous examples of one Giovane Domenico da Nola [*c.* 1520–1592] who, while not the earliest, was certainly the first important master of this type. The main characteristics are animated rhythm, chordal texture (usually *a*3), $\frac{4}{4}$ time (note nere), and a fair sprinkling of consecutive fifths in the part writing, this last being deliberate. The texts range from the plaints of lovesick swains through caricatures of famous madrigals to scurrilous and obscene verse. The opinion commonly held that sixteenth-century music is 'proper' is due to the 'quaintness' of its style and to the shadow of sanctity cast by its most famous representative, Palestrina, but many of the madrigals, chansons, and other secular types reflect more or less bluntly the full-bloodedness of the period. This is especially true of the 'mascherata' sung during 'masked' balls and processions, and the 'moresca', in which the singers represent 'Moorish' girls of doubtful reputation.

Willaert's early madrigals, like those of Arcadelt and Festa, show the influence of the chanson and frottola in their simple polyphony, clear-cut phrases, and melodic importance of the highest voice, but his later ones reveal his northern origin in their greater complexity, use of imitation, equality of voices, and overlapping cadences. Although chromaticism is a far less significant feature of his work than is often made out, it seems likely that he was in fact more than usually interested in this aspect of composition, judging by his pupils at any rate, especially the Italian Nicola Vicentino [1511 – *c.* 1576].

Vicentino attempted to present in modern notation the ancient Greek diatonic, chromatic, and enharmonic divisions of the scale (see Part I, p. 17), and by placing dots over notes and laying down certain rules as to the meaning of sharps, flats, and naturals in conjunction with the dots, he composed pieces in which the whole-tone was divided into five parts. Such music is impossible to sing—though Vicentino is supposed to have trained a choir for this express purpose—and of more practical value are his 'normal' madrigals, which are chromatically very advanced for their time in their use of such rare notes as are included in the major chords of D♯ and D♭, and in intervals such as the augmented third, e.g. E♭–G♯. The most important aspect of these pieces is that they show a desire for a melodic and harmonic expressiveness which the modal system could not possibly give, even though the latter had expanded during the fifteenth century and now included four other modes in addition to the eight discussed in Part I. These were the Aeolian (A–A, our descending melodic minor scale), Hypoaeolian (E–E, final A), Ionian (C–C, our major scale), and Hypoionian (G–G, final C), and the first theorist to give these new modes an independent status was the Swiss Heinrich Loris or, as he is generally known, Henricus Glareanus [1488–1563], in his famous *Dodecachordon* (1547) (literally 'twelve strings'). In this treatise Glareanus demonstrates from examples by Josquin and others that a melody ending in F with a B♭ in the signature had a quite different flavour and character if there was no flat. Formerly, both had been regarded as Lydian (see Part I, Chapter 5, p. 131), but Glareanus called only the second Lydian, the first being Ionian transposed, which of course it is. In actual fact, by Glareanus's day the genuine Lydian was hardly ever used, and the Phrygian too became less common as the century progressed, leaving the Dorian, Mixolydian, Aeolian, and Ionian modes, and of these only the last two have survived to the present day.

Vicentino's experiments were strongly attacked by a number of theorists, including one of the greatest, his fellow pupil and countryman, Gioseffe Zarlino [1517–1590]. Zarlino spent most of his life in Venice, and his three main treatises, which were published in one volume in 1589, contain a great deal of valuable information, such as the statement that the two beats of the tactus are equal to the rate of a human pulse (this averages about M.M. 70, hence our calculations earlier). More important is his realization and convincing demonstration of just intonation, a system of intervals that had already been discovered to all intents and purposes by the Spaniard Ramos (see Part I, Chapter 6, p. 231) and also by the Italian theorists Pietro Aron [*c.* 1480 – *c.* 1550] and more especially by Ludovico Fogliano [d. *c.* 1539].

Just intonation is a scale made up of certain intervals that occur naturally. If, for instance, a flexible string of uniform diameter, weight, and tension (e.g. a piano or violin string) is hit, plucked, or bowed it not only vibrates as a whole but in fractions of its length as well. The vibrations of the complete string give the fundamental note or first partial, and those of the various fractions of the string give the upper partials, the total sound of the string consisting of some or all of these partials, the number audible depending on the way the string is excited, the pitch of the fundamental, its loudness, and the sensitivity of the ear. Thus if we take the bottom string of the 'cello as our fundamental note or first partial the next fifteen partials are (Ex. 5):

(The black semibreves indicate notes that cannot be correctly represented on the stave, e.g. the eleventh partial (*f''*) is not a perfect fourth above *c''*; they are therefore omitted from the discussion that follows. This succession of notes is called 'the harmonic series'.) The interval between any one note in the harmonic series and any other can be expressed by a ratio consisting of the partial 'number' of the notes. Thus (reckoning downwards) the ratio of *c–C* (octave) is $\frac{2}{1}$; of *g–c* (fifth) $\frac{3}{2}$; of *c''–g'* (fourth) $\frac{4}{3}$, and so on. Furthermore, the ratio of any interval can be found by either multiplying the ratios of its constituent intervals or else dividing the ratio of a larger interval by the ratio of the remaining smaller interval. For instance, a major sixth is made up of a fourth and major third (ratio $\frac{5}{4}$, e.g. *e'–c'*), so that $\frac{4}{3} \cdot \frac{5}{4} = \frac{5}{3}$ (e.g. *e'–g*); again, an octave minus a minor third (ratio $\frac{6}{5}$, e.g. *g'–e'*) also leaves a major sixth $\frac{2}{1} \div \frac{6}{5}$ or $\frac{2}{1} \cdot \frac{5}{6} = \frac{5}{3}$.

All the first six partial notes are, and were to sixteenth-century ears, concordant with each other, and they can be used to construct a complete major scale. The most important notes are, and were, the tonic, dominant, and subdominant, and the first step is obviously to build major triads on each of these three notes. Taking C as our 'keynote' the tonic triad, C, E, G, already exists; the dominant chord consists of G, B (ratio $\frac{5}{4}$ to G) and D (ratio $\frac{3}{2}$ to G), and the subdominant chord F, A (ratio $\frac{5}{4}$ to F), and C. But before we can play or sing this scale we must place each note in relation to C; we already know the ratio of C–E, C–F, C–G, and C–C, and the others can be found; thus the major seventh C–B = C–G plus G–B, or $\frac{3}{2} \cdot \frac{5}{4} = \frac{15}{8}$; the major sixth C–A must be $\frac{5}{3}$ (C–F plus F–A, or $\frac{4}{3} \cdot \frac{5}{4} = \frac{5}{3}$); C–D = C–G minus D–G, or $\frac{3}{2} \cdot \frac{3}{4} = \frac{9}{8}$. We can now draw a diagram of the just intonation scale showing the ratios between each note and the lower tonic (Ex. 6):

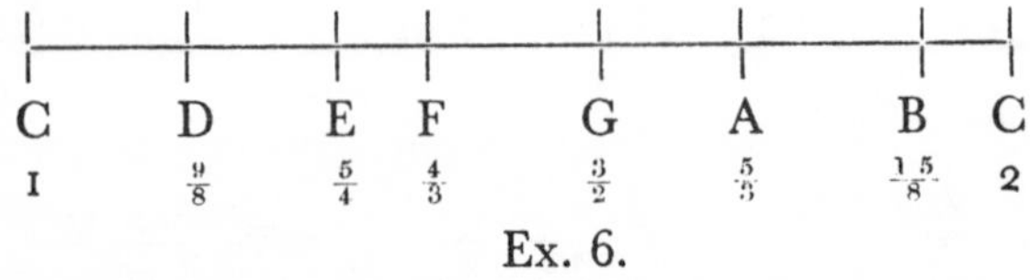

Ex. 6.

In this diagram the semitones look the same size, but the whole tones do not, and this is indeed the case, because whereas C–D, F–G, and A–B are all of ratio $\frac{9}{8}$, D–E and G–A are both $\frac{10}{9}$ (i.e. $\frac{5}{4} \cdot \frac{8}{9}$ and $\frac{5}{3} \cdot \frac{2}{3}$ respectively). Moreover, while the fifths

C–G, E–B, F–C, and G–D are all of ratio $\frac{3}{2}$, D–A is $\frac{40}{27}$ (i.e. $\frac{5}{3} \cdot \frac{8}{9}$.) Similarly, there are two kinds of fourth and minor seventh. The whole trouble arises from the fact that there are two different whole tones, the greater tone, $\frac{9}{8}$, and the lesser tone, $\frac{10}{9}$; this severely limits the possibilities of this particular scale, especially if harmony is involved, in that not only does the super-tonic chord (D minor in the key of C) sound false, but the scale of the relative minor has two notes out of tune. The chief merit of just intonation is the purity of the three main chords, tonic, dominant, and subdominant, with their true thirds and fifths, and although this scale was not recognized theoretically until the sixteenth century it is most probable that in practice competent singers and string players of part-music had always rendered sustained fifths and complete triads in just intonation, as, indeed, they should do today, the false fifth being made true by flattening the super-tonic note when necessary.

Voices and stringed instruments are capable of flexible intonation, but keyboard instruments are not, and up to *c.* 1500 organs and harpsichords must either have sounded vilely out of tune sometimes, or else some of the notes must have been slightly and inoffensively mistuned. Mistuning, in fact, is inevitable in normal keyboard instruments, and the first person to tackle this problem seriously was the German organist mentioned in Part I, p. 216, Arnolt Schlick, who advocated making most of the fifths a little flatter than the true fifth. Not until Zarlino, however, and more especially the great Spanish theorist, Francisco de Salinas [1513–1590], was a system of tuning called 'mean-tone' temperament fully worked out.

The difference between a greater tone and a lesser tone is known as the 'comma of Didymus' [b. 63 B.C.], a Greek theorist who had realized that the Pythagorean major third was not the 'natural' one, being too sharp by a small interval of ratio, $\frac{81}{80}$, which is the same as that between the lesser tone and the greater tone, i.e. $\frac{9}{8} \cdot \frac{9}{10} = \frac{81}{80}$. In mean-tone temperament half of this 'comma' is added to the lesser tone and the other half is subtracted from the greater tone, the result being two equal 'mean' tones. This tampering with or 'tempering' the notes leads to a true octave and major third (with its complement, the minor sixth), all the other intervals being slightly out of tune compared to just intonation; but the important thing is that although the fifths are half a comma flatter than the true fifth, the 'wrong 'un', D–A, has disappeared, for they are all equally mistuned and therefore all sound the same.

Chromatic notes in the upper octaves had been introduced on some organs as early as the late fourteenth century, and by the middle of the fifteenth century the keyboard was completely chromatic, except for the lowest octave. In mean-tone tuning the five 'black' keys represented those notes most commonly used—namely, C♯, F♯, G♯, B♭, and E♭, the first three being tuned a true major third above A, D, and E respectively, and the last two a true major third below D and G. On the harpsichord G♯ was sometimes retuned as A♭, a major third below C, and in the latter half of the sixteenth century E♭ was occasionally retuned as D♯, a major third above B. On our modern pianos G♯ and A♭ are the same, but in mean-tone temperament G♯ is appreciably flatter than A♭, and a true G♯ would sound horrible in an A♭ major or F minor chord. Similarly with E♭ and D♯. There were thus two kinds of semitone, the greater, e.g. G♯–A, and the lesser, e.g. G-G♯.

To overcome this difficulty, some organs were built during the early sixteenth century and later with separate pipes for A♭ and D♯ and therefore with two extra keys in each octave. Zarlino went further and in 1548 had a harpsichord built containing the greater and lesser semitone between each whole tone, which meant seventeen keys to the octave, seven 'white' and ten 'black', but Vicentino capped this in 1555 with a harpsichord in which the octave was divided into thirty intervals spread over six manuals, each manual being tuned to one of the six Greek scales (see Part I, p. 17). It was, of course, too cumbersome to be of much practical value, unlike Zarlino's, but both showed dissatisfaction with the limited harmonic range of the modal system, a dissatisfaction that rapidly increased during the latter part of the century and which resulted in a greater degree of chromaticism and modulation.

Neither Vicentino nor Zarlino were composers of the first rank, and it was left to yet another pupil of Willaert to embody the new chromaticism in madrigals that are among the greatest ever written. The pupil was the northerner, Cipriano de Rore [1515/16 – 1565], who succeeded his master as *maestro di cappella* at St. Mark's for a few years and who, after his resignation, was in turn succeeded by Zarlino. Rore was a man of serious even austere outlook, who set no frivolous texts, and whose preoccupation with mood-expression marks the beginning of a fundamental change in madrigal writing. Word-painting, both in sacred and secular pieces, had been common for some time, but this was usually a naïve and often flippant procedure; mood-expression, on the other hand, is concerned with the predominant emotion of a particular line or lines of a poem or even of a complete verse, and is thus more truly musical, for, as we observed in Part I (p. 226), music is essentially ill-suited to realism but can portray a general mood with complete success. In his striving for this kind of expression Rore employs not only chromaticism, but all the standard procedures of his time as well, e.g. imitation, polyphonic and contrapuntal textures, note nere, chains of $^{6}_{3}$ chords, etc., but everything is subject to the emotions suggested by the text, and it is these that now govern the unity of the music, not the poetic structure or rhyme endings of the verse, nor purely musical devices such as the repetition of a phrase to different words at the end of a piece, as commonly occurs in the French chanson. This treatment of the madrigal, which is chiefly to be found in Rore's mature work, set the fashion for nearly all later madrigalists, though few of them matched the intensity of his personal expression; it also sowed the seeds of destruction, for by stressing the fact that music can greatly enhance the emotional content of the written word Rore unwittingly initiated the movement which placed this ideal above all others and which, as a result, rejected polyphony in pursuit of its goal (Ex. 7)*.

The skill, sensitivity, and originality with which Rore wedded music to text, as in the superb example quoted above, makes him one of the outstanding composers of the sixteenth century, an estimation shared by his contemporaries, for not only were his madrigals reprinted many times, but an edition of all those he wrote for four voices was published in score in 1577; this, apart from being one of the earliest printed scores in existence, can only have been used for study purposes—a rare tribute to any composer.

Despite Rore's popularity and influence, two leading composers remained virtually untouched by the prevailing trend in madrigal writing—Giovanni Pierluigi [1525/6 – 1594], who later added the name of his native town, Palestrina, and

* Adapted from A. Einstein, *The Italian Madrigal*, Vol. III, p. 114.

Ex.7 Madrigal - Crudele acerba inesorabil morte (1557) (Petrarch)
de Rore
(𝅗𝅥 = 𝅘𝅥 = MM.c.72)
Cru - de - - - - le a - - - cer - ba i - ne - so - ra - - - bil mor - -
Cru - el death, bit - ter, un - re - lent - - - ing art
Cru - - de - - - le a - - cer - - - ba i - ne - so - - ra - - - bil
Cru - - el death, bit - - - ter, un - re - - lent - - - ing
Cru - - - de - - - - -
Cru - - - el
Cru - - de - - -
Cru - - el
- - te, i - - ne - so - - ra - bil mor - - - te Ca -
thou, yea, un - re - - lent - ing art thou; Ye
mor - - - te, I - ne - so - - ra - bil mor - - te Ca -
art thou, yea, un - re - lent - ing art thou; Ye
- le a - - cer - - ba i - ne - so - - ra - - - bil mor - - - te Ca -
death, bit - - - ter, un - re - - lent - - ing art thou; Ye
- - - le a - - cer - - ba i - - ne - so - ra - bil mor - - - - - - te Ca -
death, bit - - - ter, un - re - lent - ing art thou; Ye
- gion mi dai di mai non es - - ser lie - - - to Ma di me -
rea - son give me ne'er to live con - tent - - ed, But bid me
- gion mi dai, ca - gion mi dai di mai non es - ser lie - - - to
rea - son give, ye rea - son give me ne'er to live con - tent - - ed,
gion mi dai di mai non es - - - - - ser lie - - - to Ma di me -
rea son give me ne'er to live con - tent - - ed, But bid me
- gion mi dai di mai non es - - - ser lie - - - to
rea - son give me ne'er to live con - tent - - ed,

Ex.7 (contd.)

-nar tut-ta mia vi-ta in pian - - - to
pass my wretched life in weep - - - - ing,
Ma di me-nar tut - - ta mia vi-ta in pian - - - - to
But bid me pass my wretch-ed life in weep - - - - ing,
-nar, ma di me-nar tut-ta mia vi-ta in pian - - - - to
pass, but bid me pass my wretch-ed life in weep - - - - ing,
Ma di me-nar tut - - - ta mia vi - - - - ta in pian - - - - - - to
But bid me pass my wretch - - ed life in weep - - - - - - ing,
E i gior-ni o-scu - - ri e le do-glio - - se not - - - - - - - -
My days in dark - - ness, and all my nights in tra - - - - - - - - -
Ei gior-ni o-scu - - - - - ri, ei gior-ni o-scu - - ri e le do-
My days in dark - - - - ness, my days in dark - - ness, and my
Ei gior-ni o-scu - - ri e le do-glio - - se not - - - - - - -
My days in dark - - ness, and all my nights in tra - - - - - -
Ei gior-ni o - - scu - - - - - - - - ri e le do-
My days in dark - - - - - - ness, and all my
- - ti. I miei gra-vi so - - spir non van-no in
- vail. My deep sighs of des - pair rhyme not I
-glio - - se not - - - - - - - ti. I miei gra-vi so - - spir non van-no in
nights in tra - - - - - - - vail. My deep sighs of des - pair rhyme not I
- ti. I miei gra - vi so - - spir non van-no in
- vail. My deep sighs of des - - pair rhyme not I
- glio - se not - - - ti. I miei gra - vi so - - spir non
nights in tra - - - vail. My deep sighs of des - pair rhyme

Ex. 7 (contd.)

ri – – – me E'l mio du – – ro mar – tir, e'l
fear me, And my mer – – ci – less fate, and
ri – – – – me E'l mio du – – – ro mar-tir,
fear me, And my mer – – – ci – less fate,
ri – – – – – me E'l mio du – – ro mar –
fear me, And my mer – – ci – less
van-no in ri – – – – – – me E'l mio du – –
not I fear me, And my mer –
mio du – – – ro mar – tir vin – ce o-gni sti – – – – – – le, e'l
my mer – – ci – – less fate all styles doth con – – – – – – quer, and
e'l mio du – – – ro mar – tir vin-ce o-gni sti – – le,
and my mer – – – ci – less fate all styles doth con – – quer,
-tir, e'l mio du – – ro mar – tir vin – – ce o – gni sti – – – –
fate, and my mer – – ci – less fate all styles doth con – – – –
– ro mar – tir vin – – – ce o – gni sti – –
– ci – less fate all styles doth con – –
mio du – – – ro mar – tir, e'l mio du – – – ro mar – tir
my mer – – ci – less fate, and my mer – – – ci – less fate
e'l mio du – – ro mar-tir, e'l mio du – – ro mar-
and my mer – – ci – – less fate, and my mer – – ci – less
– le, e'l mio du – – – ro mar – tir, e'l mio du – ro mar –
– quer, and my mer – – – ci – less fate, and my mer – ci – less
– le, e'l mio du – ro mar – tir
– quer, and my mer – ci – less fate

Ex. 7 (concln.)

Roland de Lassus [1532–1594]. The former, who spent most of his life in Rome, found the natural outlet for his genius in liturgical music (see pp. 307f.), and his undramatic, emotionally balanced approach, in which word-painting is very discreetly used and chromaticism practically non-existent, harks back to the classically poised madrigals of Festa and Arcadelt, both of whom were working in Rome during the composer's early manhood; indeed, Arcadelt may have been his teacher for a time. While many of Palestrina's madrigals are fine compositions showing impeccable style and sensitive, if limited treatment of the text, they contributed nothing to the general development of the type, with one exception, *Vestiva i colli* (1566), a narrative madrigal which borrows the traditional opening formula of the French chanson (see p. 240) and which was so popular that literally hundreds of similar pieces were composed during the next fifty years or so.

Lassus shows Rore's influence far more than does Palestrina, and he was more versatile than the earlier master; in fact, he was the greatest international composer of the Renaissance, writing French chansons and German Lieder with as much ease and brilliance as madrigals and villanelle. Towards the end of his life he was profoundly affected by the Counter-Reformation (see Chapter 2, p. 310), and his 'spiritual madrigals' are based on texts with a strong religious and moral flavour; the musical treatment, however, only differs from his earlier style in the less frequent use of chromaticism. Although Lassus contributed little to the development of the madrigal, his superb craftsmanship, inventive genius, and powerful personality created works that are, on the whole, superior to Palestrina's, and that have stood the test of time more successfully than many more progressive pieces of his day.

Rore wrote nearly 100 madrigals, Palestrina about 150, and Lassus over 270, but these numbers pale before the astonishing output of Philippe de Monte [1521–1603], another northerner, who produced over 1,100. More important, however, is the fact that their quality is equal to their quantity, this being achieved through a completely assured technique which handles word-painting, chromaticism, voice-grouping, rhythmic interplay, and contrasts in texture (polyphony *versus* counterpoint) in a masterly fashion, together with an extraordinarily high standard of sheer musical beauty. Like Rore, he had a serious cast of mind, writing no villanelle, etc., and only a few chansons, and this partly explains why his treatment of the text, while less conservative than Lassus's, is not so progressive as his compatriot, Giaches de Wert [1535–1596], a composer greatly esteemed by his contemporaries and successors. If Monte is Rore's emotional successor, Wert is his stylistic one, and his later madrigals are typical of the late sixteenth-century trend in their detailed and vivid word-painting (e.g. Ex. 8b, at the words "*E i giorni oscuri*", where all the voices are in their 'darkest' register), striking chromaticism (e.g. Ex. 8b), increased voice range, greater tonal feeling, declamation (i.e. rapid notes syllabically underlaid, e.g. Ex. 8a), and—of particular importance, as we shall see—the tendency to make the lower voices accompany the upper. (Ex. 8,* p. 257. For a translation of (b) see Ex. 7, pp. 252-5.)

Monte and Wert were the last of the great madrigal composers who invaded Italy from the north; from now on the leading men are all Italian, and it is no coincidence that in their hands the madrigal finally merged into the accompanied monody of the early baroque, for the Italian genius naturally favours sensuous melody, clear-cut harmony and rhythm, and colourful

* (a) Adapted from A. Einstein, *The Italian Madrigal*, Vol. III, p. 221,
(b) Adapted from ibid., p. 208.

Ex. 8(a) From the madrigal - *Giunto a la tomba ove al suo spirto vivo* (1581)
(Tasso: *La Gerusalemme liberata*) Wert

(Of colour, of heat, of move ment deprived, yea marble in appearance to the marble [tomb] the face gazes)

Ex. 8(b) From the madrigal - *Crudele acerba inesorabil morte* (1588) (Petrarch) Wert

expression. Thus polyphonic texture in general and imitation in particular were increasingly superseded by a marked melodic superiority of the upper part or parts, predominantly chordal writing, dramatic contrasts between groups of voices, and a treatment of the text which for detailed realism is unsurpassed in any vocal music before or since.

The earliest Italian composer who shows the new approach is Andrea Gabrieli [*c.* 1510–1586], who, like his teacher Willaert and his co-pupils Rore and Zarlino, was associated with the Chapel of St. Mark, becoming second organist in 1564 and first organist in 1585. Like Willaert also, but not Rore, he was one of the most versatile composers of the century, excelling in all branches of his art and being particularly important and influential in the instrumental field (see Chapter 2, p. 354).

The fact that there were two organs and two organists at St. Mark's obviously encouraged the idea of polychoral writing, i.e. writing for two or more choral groups, and Willaert, though not the inventor of this technique, as is so often claimed, certainly played a leading part in its development. For some reason or other, he restricted its use to his motets, and it was left to Andrea Gabrieli to introduce it into the madrigal. This he did with great brilliance, and the resultant dramatic contrasts together with the sonorous climaxes when both choirs unite, the expressive chromaticism, and hammering rhythm achieved through declamation, give both power and colour to his music. In contrast to the splendour of these pieces he also composed madrigals which show the increasing pre-occupation already noted with detailed word-painting, and it is this aspect that is carried to its extreme by the greatest madrigal composer of the late Renaissance, Luca Marenzio [1553/4–1599].

Marenzio is the summation of practically all the previous trends in the madrigal, polychoral writing being the only exception. He can be as vivacious as Nola, as classically restrained and limpid in texture as Arcadelt, as serious and complex as Rore and almost as passionate, as declamatory as Monte, and as sonorous and colourful as Andrea Gabrieli. Moreover, he developed that feature of Wert's style which made the upper part or parts melodically superior to the lower and thus advanced a stage nearer to baroque monody; but his most outstanding characteristic, in which he outstrips all his predecessors and contemporaries, is his word-painting, and the care with which practically every word is treated that represents a sound or an object, an idea or a mood is matched only by an inventiveness that turns a technique that had been largely trivial before and, in the hands of less gifted composers, became mechanical during his time and later into something live and fascinating, and by a sensitive feeling for the whole that prevented this detailed realism from disintegrating the entire composition.

In order to give some idea of the variety of means used by Marenzio and others, here are some typical examples of word-painting; 'sea'—a wavy melodic line; 'sigh'—short rest like a catch of the breath, either after the first syllable of the word ('*so-spiro*') or else separating the word from the previous one; 'arch'—an ascending and descending 'curved' melody; 'night' —black notation; 'day'—long 'white' note values; 'suffering'— chromatic changes or major chords in which the roots usually lie a third apart, or have at least one note in common, e.g. C major to E major or G major to E♭ major. These examples, while only constituting a fraction of those that can be found, were inevitably duplicated; thus black notes are also used when the Devil or Hell is mentioned, slowness or length of time is also indicated by long notes, and undulating lines represent 'flying' as well. (Ex. 9,* p. 260. Note the ravishing effects—in their essentially diatonic contexts—of the C major–E major progression on '*sospira*', and of the held B♭ major chord on '*dolcemente*'. Note too the rising scales of anger ('*adira*') and the broken rhythm of the phrase for '*romper*').

The important thing about nearly all these devices used by Marenzio and others is that they are not only seen on paper but are actually heard. The chief exception is the use of black notation, for whereas the shape of a melody or the switch from quick to slow movement, or an abrupt chord change are all perfectly intelligible aurally, the insertion of, say, a group of black semibreves at the word 'darkness' only makes sense to the eye, in other words to the performer (eye-music). This, together with remarks by contemporary theorists, makes it quite clear that the normal madrigal was largely concerned with providing entertainment (in its widest sense) for the singers,

* From A. Einstein, *A Short History of Music* (1948), p. 232.

Ex. 9 From the madrigal - Io piango (1581) (Petrarch)
Marenzio
(o = d = MM.c.60)
So - spi - ra Dol-ce - men - - te et s'a-di - ra Con pa-ro - - le ch'i
She sigh - eth Oh so gent - - ly, then fli-eth In a ra - - ging with
et s'a - di - ra ...
and then fli-eth...
sas - - - - si rom - - per pon-no, rom - per pon - - no, ch'i
words that shat - - ter my ears, shat - ter my ears, with
sas - - - - - si rom - - per pon-no, rom - per pon - no.
words that shat - - ter my ears, shat - ter my ears.
(etc.)

and that it was sung with *one voice to each part*, as indeed we might expect, judging from the size of the printed editions. The madrigal is essentially chamber music, intimate, subtle, refined, and performances, alas only too common today, in which each part is sung by six or more voices are as indefensible as playing a Mozart quartet on the strings of a symphony orchestra, for in doubling a vocal or instrumental part purity of intonation is lost, tone becomes rougher, and the gradations of nuance and expression coarsen. There was, however, a class of madrigal in which part-doubling did occur—namely, those written for a particular ceremony, such as a wedding or a birthday. On such occasions, of course, there was an audience, either in a largish room or else out of doors; in any case, a greater volume of sound would be preferred or even required than one singer per part could give. These madrigals, which fulfilled the same function as the 'occasional' secular motets of earlier times, are invariably much simpler in texture and less detailed in expression than the normal type, a fact which supports what we have already said concerning the performance of the latter. In addition to such pieces, it is likely that many of Andrea Gabrieli's polychoral madrigals, in which sheer sonority plays an important part, were intended for a larger choral body than usual. This applies particularly to his nephew and pupil, Giovanni Gabrieli [*c.* 1553 – 1612], who represents the peak of the Venetian School, and who is, moreover, a most important link between the Renaissance and baroque eras, as we shall see in later chapters.

Giovanni, while naturally owing much to his uncle's style and teaching, surpassed him in the brilliance of his voice groupings and dramatic choral contrasts, in the rich colour of his harmony with its greater use of chromaticism, and in the power of his rhythmic drive. Colour and sonority meant far more to him than to any other composer of his generation or earlier, and by relegating imitation and, indeed, polyphony as a whole, to a very subordinate position, and revelling in the sheer delight of chord progressions as such, particularly those whose roots lie a fourth or fifth apart, he anticipated the basically harmonic approach of baroque music.

Both Gabrielis, of course, wrote normal polyphonic madrigals in which word-painting is a marked feature, and it was this aspect, not dramatic brilliance, that dominated the late sixteenth-century Italian madrigal, and while the general trend, represented to perfection by Marenzio, can be described as a balance between graphic and emotional word-painting, the latter became the main objective of one of the most extraordinary composers in the history of music, Carlo Gesualdo, Prince of Venosa [*c.* 1560–1613]. This nobleman, whose private life reads like a nineteenth-century melodrama, concentrated on the expression of mood and feeling of a line or phrase of the text rather than on the detailed description of individual words. In this respect he is Rore's and Monte's successor, but in his obsession with the emotional he went far beyond them, and by a quite astonishing use of chromaticism and violent changes in movement he all but destroyed the musical fabric of the madrigal. Indeed, the boldness and originality of his chromaticism, in which chords totally unconnected with each other are juxtaposed, e.g. A minor–F♯ major, or C minor–E major, remained unequalled until Wagner. Never before had music so depended on the words to give it meaning and unity, for without them the sudden alterations in harmony, melody, and rhythm would be largely incomprehensible. (Ex. 10,* p. 263). (Note in (d) not only the unprepared seventh in bar 2, but more especially the way the chord B♭–D–F–A♭ is resolved in bar 3; it is in fact what we now call an augmented sixth chord (the so-called 'German sixth'), because the augmented sixth (A♭—which should strictly be written as G♯) rises a semitone to A, while the root (B♭) falls a semitone to A. This is the commonest form of the German sixth, i.e. in root position, but it is found very rarely in the music of the period. A much rarer form occurs in bars 5–6, where the German sixth on F is given in its last inversion, i.e. the augmented sixth (E♭—really D♯) is the bass note. With regard to (c) it might be mentioned that the haunting effect of the minor-major ending of the first movement of Walton's Viola Concerto is here anticipated by Gesualdo nearly 350 years earlier.)

The importance of the text had been growing steadily from the end of the fifteenth century on. Before Josquin vocal compositions are largely abstract in conception, for most of them would sound just as well to other words. From Josquin on, however, not only are the syllables set with increasing regard for their

* (a), (b) From *Gesualdo: Madrigale*, ed. Weismann, p. 30. (c) From ibid., p. 6. (d) From *H.A.M.*, 161.

Ex.10(a) From the madrigal - Moro lasso al mio duolo (1611)
Gesualdo
(♩= MM.c.72)
Mo - - ro las - - so al mio duo - lo
I die from grief so wretch-ed
(etc.)
Ex.10(b) (ibid.)
O... O dolorosa sorte,
O... do-lo - ro - - sa sor - te,
O..
O...
O...
O...
O...
(etc.)
O...
(O grievous fate)
Ex.10(c) The end of the madrigal - Luci serene e chiare (1596)
Gesualdo
(♩= MM.c.72)
mor' e non lan - - - - - - gue.
e...
mor'...
mor'...
e...
mor'...
e...
(You die and languish not)
Ex.10(d) From the madrigal - Io pur respiro (1613)
Gesualdo
(♩= MM.c.72)
Deh mor - - - - te
Deh...
deh...
Deh...
deh...
Deh...
deh...
(etc.)
Deh...
(Then death)

natural accents, but the words begin to be more closely linked with the music, and in Janequin's programme-chansons they form an integral part of the whole. These latter profoundly influenced the Italian madrigal and eventually led, as we have seen, to a style in which the text is the *raison d'être* of the music. This being so, it is clearly important for us to see in what ways poetry influenced the madrigal and vice versa.

In Part I, Chapter 6 (p. 209), we stated that the practice of reciting poems to simple improvised melodies and accompaniments was widespread. Most of the melodies were simple variations on standard types which fitted all verses with identical structure, and the most common poetic form was 'ottava rime', that is verses of 'eight' lines with the 'rhyme' scheme *ab ab ab cc*. It was in this form that Ludovico Ariosto [1474–1533], one of the greatest of all Italian poets, wrote his epic masterpiece, *Orlando furioso* (1516), which has been described as "the noblest literary glorification of the Renaissance", and which swept the length and breadth of Italy. Several standard melodies were used in reciting this poem, but the most popular was called 'ruggiero', the name of one of the characters in the epic, which deals with the fight between Christian and Saracen in the days of Charlemagne. This melody was used in part-music also, but was more important in instrumental compositions.

The popularity of *Orlando furioso* among all classes of society shows that a change in literary standards had occurred during the early sixteenth century. While the early frottola texts are mostly trivial, the later ones include an increasing number of first-rate poems; this reflects the general trend of the times, and the man most responsible for the improvement was Cardinal Pietro Bembo [1470–1547], whose scholarly ideals, prestige, and, to a lesser extent, published work restored the dignity and expressiveness of the Italian language, which had sadly lapsed after Dante and Petrarch. The latter poet was in fact Bembo's model, and partly as a result of this Petrarch's collection of lyric poems, the *Canzoniere*, not only went through nearly 130 editions during the century, but were set so frequently (some of the poems exist in as many as twenty different musical versions) that no other poet, not even Shakespeare or Goethe, has inspired so much music.

But no man's reputation and influence in the literary sphere, no matter how great, can dictate which poet is best suited to a particular musical type, and although Bembo clearly prepared the way for the greater seriousness of the early madrigal compared to the early frottola, it was the character of Petrarch's verse which was the decisive factor, for it provided well-nigh perfect madrigalian texts. Each verse is short enough to permit imitative interplay between the voices without making the piece too long, the clarity and conciseness with which each mood is expressed almost dictates the musical treatment, and the emotional contrasts give the composer full scope for varying his rhythm, melody, and harmony.

Petrarch's popularity led inevitably to shoals of imitations which, as usually happens, are distinctly inferior to their model. Apart from Bembo, the earliest imitator of any importance was an otherwise obscure poet, Luigi Cassola, most of whose output was clearly intended to be set to music, not to be read as poetry. This is an important distinction and one that applies to a tremendous number of sixteenth-century poems all over Europe, and it is as unfair and as unscholarly to judge madrigal texts from a purely poetical standpoint as it is to compare opera libretti with contemporary drama.

Cassola's poems are typical of a great many madrigal texts in their freedom of rhyme and metre, their sentimentality, their contrasts of mood, and the provision of a neat conclusion. Two examples from English madrigals will make this clearer than any description. The first contrasts the opening four lines with the last two, which provide a neat conclusion; the second shows the structural freedom possible.

> So light is love in matchless beauty shining,
> When she revisits Cypris' hallowed bowers,
> Two feeble doves, harnessed in silken twining,
> Can draw her chariot midst the Paphian flowers.
> Lightness to Love, how ill it fitteth,
> So heavy on my heart she sitteth!*

> Come life, come death, I care not,
> If I may only see my lovely fere [=companion]
> But further, ah, I dare not!
> When she but spies me,
> She flies me,
> She fools me,
> She cools my desire!†

* *English Madrigal Verse*, ed. Fellowes, p. 239. † Ibid., p. 82.

The two main poetic types, epic and lyric, represented by Ariosto and Petrarch respectively, were cultivated throughout the century with the lyric in the ascendant. From *c.* 1550 on this became increasingly pastoral in character, and idealized and sentimentalized shepherds and shepherdesses, the Amaryllises, Floras, Clorises, and Phyllises vied with Petrarch's Laura. The first important pastoral poet was Jacopo Sannazaro [1455/6–1530], whose *Arcadia*, published in 1502, eventually became so popular that it gave rise to a spate of pastoral poems and madrigals that outnumbered all other types. In this it truly reflected one aspect of the Renaissance—the romantic longing for the past—and in the hands of Torquato Tasso [1544–95] and Giovanni Battista Guarini [1538–1612] it reached its peak; Guarini's *Pastor Fido* ('The Faithful Shepherd') (1581–90), though inferior poetically to Tasso's *Aminta* (1573), was more frequently set to music because its use of words and contrasting emotions is more virtuosic than in the simpler earlier poem. Tasso, however, was both a lyric and an epic poet and his *Gerusalemme liberata* ('Jerusalem liberated') (1581) virtually replaced Ariosto's great work because its more obvious darker emotional qualities suited the age of the Counter-Reformation better than the rather detached, ironic, even capricious treatment of Christianity *versus* Mohammedanism in *Orlando furioso*.

The delight in Arcadia and in the amours of the rustic characters who populated it spread to the stage, and many pastoral poems, or 'pastorales' as they were called, were intended to be either read or acted; indeed, the pastorale was the most important dramatic form in Italy during the late Renaissance, and because the lyricism of its verse was so well suited to and frequently received musical treatment it was one of the forerunners of opera, as we shall see in Chapter 3.

Music played an important part too in the only other significant drama of the Italian Renaissance, the classical tragedy and its imitations. The sixteenth-century author and producer knew that the Greeks and Romans included musical performance of some kind in their dramatic presentations, and this prompted them to insert between the acts of the plot, and often as prologue and epilogue as well, short scenes called 'intermedii', which consisted of songs, instrumental pieces, and sometimes dances. On especially festive occasions these intermedii were staged with great splendour, foreshadowing the elaborate scenic settings of seventeenth-century opera, but on all occasions they were greatly enjoyed and eventually became far more popular than the serious drama of which they were originally only appendages. Like the pastorale, the intermedio is also a forerunner of opera.

Both Tasso and Guarini spent most of their lives at Ferrara, the home of one of the oldest and most brilliant Italian families. From Hercules I [reigned 1472–1505], an outstanding patron of the arts, especially music, and the father of Isabella (see Part I, Chapter 6, p. 209) and her almost equally famous sister, Beatrice, to Alfonso II [1558–1597], the Ferrarese Court was one of the main cultural centres of Italy. Alfonso employed both Tasso and Guarini, as well as one of the leading composers of the time, Luzzasco Luzzaschi [d. 1607], who had been a pupil of Rore's. This man, who certainly knew and probably influenced Gesualdo, published in 1601 a remarkable collection of madrigals for one, two, and three sopranos, with a written-out keyboard part (the first of its kind), and with the vocal lines highly ornamented (Ex. 11,* p. 268).

We know from contemporary theorists that both instrumental accompaniment and vocal embellishment were common, and that therefore once again the music printed or in manuscript does not completely represent actual practice. Unaccompanied or 'a capella' performance, as it is often called, was certainly more widespread in the sixteenth century than in preceding centuries, but the use of instruments and the improvised ornamentation of the vocal line were typical features in certain circumstances. Thus at courtly festivities, when, as we have seen, the number of voices per part was increased, an 'orchestra' would accompany which might include a positive organ, harpsichord, viols, recorders, trombones, lutes, and cornets. On more intimate and less auspicious occasions a positive, harpsichord, lute, or viols might be used, and sometimes the lower or even all the parts were performed instrumentally. A keyboard player or lutanist (who was not, of course, restricted to pieces in tablature) would improvise chords from the lowest part, according to certain rules which were fairly simple, owing to the restricted harmony of the period. The violists would each play a separate part and, if the singer was absent

* Adapted from *Geschichte de Musik in Beispielen*, ed. Schering, p. 176.

Ex. 11 The end of the madrigal *O primavera* (1601) (Guarini *Pastor Fido*) Luzzaschi

or unskilled, very likely embellish it. This was called playing 'divisions', as the original notes were 'divided' into smaller ornamental ones.

As regards vocal embellishment, this too was mostly improvised and only occurred, ideally at any rate, when there was one singer per part, otherwise confusion would have reigned. The same applies, but less strictly, to written-out ornamentation. Taken as a whole, it is unlikely that improvised vocal embellishment was applied indiscriminately, and those madrigals or sections of madrigals in which the rhythmic movement is quick, or the music is wedded to the words, or the polyphony is complex, were almost certainly sung as they stand. In the more straightforward pieces and simpler passages, the choice of normal or elaborate rendering was doubtless dictated by the vocal dexterity and musicianship of the singer. Much the same considerations probably applied to instrumental accompaniment also.

The fact that the voices in Luzzaschi's print are sopranos illustrates the tendency already noted (pp. 256, 258)—namely, the increasing domination of the lower parts by the upper. This tendency was undoubtedly stimulated at Ferrara by the presence at various times of three highly talented ladies, Lucrezia Bendidio, Laura Peperara, and Tarquinia Molza. Tasso worshipped the first two, and Wert's passion for the third, which was returned, ended disastrously in her banishment from court. The fame of these three spread far beyond Ferrara and even beyond Italy, and Alfonso, fully aware of this and knowing that attempts had been made to find out what kind of music they sang and how they sang it, forbade the publication of their repertoire. Thus many, if not all, of Luzzaschi's madrigals of 1601 were written several years earlier.

Among the numerous composers who paid homage to the three ladies was Claudio Monteverdi [1567–1643], who spent the last thirty years of his life as 'master of the chapel' at St. Mark's, Venice. Although he is definitely more a man of the early baroque than the late Renaissance, much of his finest music stems from the older tradition. His first madrigal book (1587) already shows his dramatic feeling, and this increases in his later publications, together with an expressive use of dissonance unmatched by any contemporary. Rapid repeated notes and contrapuntal texture result in a choral recitative style that clearly aims at making the text fully intelligible (see Ex. 12b), and shows that the pieces were intended for an audience and not just for performers as in the classical madrigal. (Ex. 12.* This madrigal is an arrangement of the famous lament from the composer's opera, *Arianna* (see Chapter 3, p. 376). The opening (a) was as remarkable and memorable in its day as that of Wagner's *Tristan und Isolde* some 250 years later):

Ex.12(a) The beginning of the madrigal - *Lamento d'Arianna* Pt. I: *Lasciatemi morire* (1614)
(𝅗𝅥 = ♩ = MM.c.60) Monteverdi

Ex.12(b) From the same madrigal Pt. IV: *Ahi ch'ei non pur risponde*

(And with foul limbs fill the deep pit)

* From *Claudio Monteverdi: Tutte le Opere*, ed. Malipiero, Vol. VI, p. 3.

Monteverdi's madrigal books of 1605 and 1614 contain a separate instrumental bass part which in some cases is essential to the harmonic structure of the whole, and which thus departs from earlier practice (see p. 318).

The dramatic element in Monteverdi's madrigals was not new, for once again musical dialogues anticipated future development, but whereas the tenth- and eleventh-century Easter and Christmas tropes led directly to the mediaeval church opera and ultimately to European drama, the polyphonic 'dialogue madrigal' of the latter half of the sixteenth century, in which the 'actors' were frequently shepherds and shepherdesses and the scene 'Arcadia', only indicated a general trend and did not of itself give birth to baroque opera. This type of madrigal became immensely popular, and eventually gave rise to the so-called 'madrigal comedies', an unfortunate name, for 'comedy' smacks of the theatre and these works were neither intended nor are they suitable for stage performance. Moreover, they are more than just comic, and many of the items are not madrigals at all! However, as the name distinguishes works of this kind from the madrigal proper and also intimates that plot is an important constituent, we shall continue to use it. The greatest composer of this quasi-dramatic choral music was Orazio Vecchi [1550–1605], and his most outstanding work is *L'Amfiparnasso* (1594), in which are combined tragedy and comedy representing the twin peaks of the sacred mountain of the ancient Greeks, Parnassus. The 'cast' includes shepherds and shepherdesses as well as the traditional characters, Harlequin, Columbine, Pantaloon, Pierrot, etc., of the immensely popular, satirical, sentimental, and largely improvised type of drama known as the *Commedia dell' Arte* ('comedy of the arts'). Although *L'Amfiparnasso* is grouped into a prologue and three acts and there is some sort of a plot, it was definitely *not* meant to be acted, for in the Preface Vecchi expressly states that the work should be "seen through the mind, into which it enters through the ears, not through the eyes".

This madrigal comedy and the three others by Vecchi, together with similar works by Alessandro Striggio [*c.* 1540–1592], Giovanni Croce [*c.* 1557–1609], an important composer of church music, and Adriano Banchieri [1568–1634], who also wrote in the new style of the early baroque, give a fascinating cross-section of secular vocal music at the end of the century. Serious, sentimental, and lighthearted madrigals mix with comic, satirical, and nonsensical villanelle, mascherate, moresche, villote, and balletti. The villota usually includes one or more well-known street cries with a certain amount of gibberish and, like the balletto, is dance-like. The latter, in the hands of its most famous composer, Giovanni Giacomo Gastoldi [*c.* 1550–1622?], vied with and possibly surpassed the madrigal in popularity, not only in Italy, but all over Europe, and in its chordal texture, strong rhythm, and regular phrase construction it shows the strong influence of dance music, particularly that of France, where the ballet was first cultivated (*H.A.M.*, 158).

Banchieri, in his madrigal comedies, directs that the outline of the plot be told before the work is sung; they were thus clearly intended for an audience, and the same is probably also true of other madrigal comedies. The audience before which such compositions were given might well have been one of the many 'academies' which sprang up all over Italy during the latter part of the century and at which professionals and amateurs alike met to discuss literature, philosophy, archaeology, and even mathematics. The earliest important musical academy was founded in Verona in 1543 and included painters and poets as well as musicians, one of whom was actually employed by the academy and who, among other duties, was obliged to set to music anything a member requested! The atmosphere of these academies, in which compositions were not only performed and listened to but also criticized, and where the arts as a whole were discussed, was quite different from either the intimate music-making of a few friends or the festive performance at court, for in the first the singers and instrumentalists were their own audience, and in the second most of those who listened were there for reasons other than musical.

There is no doubt that the number and artistic standard of the academies in Italy contributed greatly to the development of the madrigal, for whether they sang and played at their meetings or in smaller groups at home, their members provided nuclei of intelligence and culture which were receptive to both the conventional and the experimental; indeed, some of these nuclei contributed directly through discussion and criticism to new ways of expression (see p. 366). Such a state of affairs was only possible in Italy, where the light of learning and artistic activity burnt more brightly than anywhere else; this

XX A design by Inigo Jones for a scene in a masque.

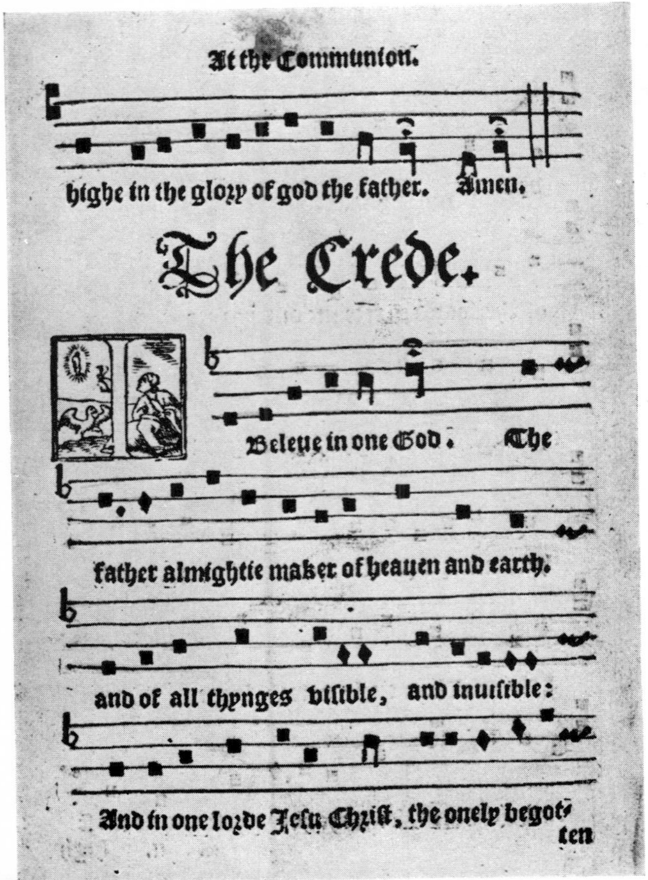

At the Communion.

highe in the glory of god the father. Amen.

The Crede.

I Beleue in one God. The

father almightie maker of heauen and earth.

and of all thynges visible, and inuisible:

And in one lorde Jesu Christ, the onely begotten

XXI (*left*) The beginning of the 'Creed' in Marbeck's *Booke of Common Praier noted* [1550].

Psalme. LXXXI. 201

Exultate deo, Psalme.lxxxi. I.H.

An exhortation to prayse God bothe in harte and voyce for his benefytes, and to worship him only: God condemneth the ingratitude, and sheweth what greate benefites they haue loste thorowe theyr owne malyce.

Be lyghte and glad in God reioyce

which is our strength & staie be ioyfull and

lyfte vp your voyce, to Jacobs God I say, prepare your instrumentes most mete some ioyfull psalme to synge, stryke vp with harp and lute so swete on euery pleasant stryng.

Blow

XXII (*right*) Psalm LXXXI from *The Whole Booke of Psalmes* [1562].

at a time when she was politically defeated and economically exhausted, for although the French invasion of 1494 failed, it was followed by Spanish and German troops who succeeded, particularly the former. Ferdinand of Spain saw his opportunity, and from 1503, when he captured Naples, to 1700 almost the whole of Italy was under Spanish rule, the only notable exception being, significantly enough, Venice. But although she was subjugated territorially and poverty-stricken through constant war and heavy taxation, the power and richness of her civilization conquered the rest of Europe.

The improved literary standards and greater importance of the text in the late sixteenth-century Italian madrigal is also found in the secular music of France, but the French, who have always tended to place literary considerations above purely musical ones, went much further than the Italians in this respect, and a group of poets who called themselves 'Le Pléiade' aimed at restoring the greatness of French poetry through the imitation of Greek and Roman dramatic and lyric verse, which, unlike the epic, were invariably associated with music. The most famous member of this group was Pierre de Ronsard [1524–1585], the greatest French poet of the Renaissance, who stressed the desirability, not only of emulating the nobleness and expressiveness of the greatest classical authors, such as Homer, Virgil, Horace, Pindar, and indeed later writers, such as Petrarch, but also of fashioning poetry so as to make it suitable for polyphonic composition. He and most other members of Le Pléiade realized that classical verse, unlike French verse, consisted of long and short syllables, and made no attempt to imitate this; but one member did, Jean Antoine de Baïf [1532–1589], who in his enthusiasm founded in 1570 the 'Académie de poésie et musique'. One of the aims of the Academy was to provide instruction, not only in music and poetry, but in such subjects as languages, geography, mathematics, military history, and even gardening and gastronomy. The breadth of the curriculum was fully in keeping with the Renaissance ideal of the 'complete man', but it seems that it did not in fact materialize. At any rate, the only definite information we have is solely concerned with the musical settings of French verse similar to that of Le Pléiade, except that it is written in classical metres of long and short syllables. This was called 'vers mesurés' by Baïf, and although he claimed to have invented it similar attempts had been made in the late fifteenth century in France and Germany, and, more successfully, towards the middle of the sixteenth century in Italy, and it is from Italy, which he visited *c.* 1563, that Baïf probably received the idea of 'measured verse', and possibly the idea of an academy also.

Unlike Ronsard, who desired his poems to be set polyphonically, Baïf insisted that all the voices should sing the words at the same time, and this, together with the shackling of the music to poetic form and metre, resulted in a largely sterile art. In Claude le Jeune [*c.* 1528/30 – 1600], however, Baïf found a composer whose melodic and harmonic gifts were sufficient to overcome the rigidity of the rules and who produced some wholly delightful songs in what was called 'musique mesurée'. Admittedly, the strict application of long (= 𝅗𝅥 or 𝅝) and short (= 𝅗𝅥 or ♩) is relieved by breaking the basic notes into shorter ones, but the essential metre is kept, and its irregularity provides one of the main attractions of these pieces (Ex. 13*):

Ex. 13 From the chanson ('musique mesurée') *O rôze reyne des fleurs* (1603)(Ronsard)
(𝅗𝅥 = ♩ = MM.c.144)

* Adapted from *Geschichte de Musik in Beispielen,* ed. Schering, p. 142.

Le Jeune, who achieved a considerable reputation in Paris and who, *c.* 1598, was appointed 'compositeur de la musique de la chambre' to Henry IV [reigned 1589–1610], also wrote 'normal' polyphonic chansons which show the influence of the Italian madrigal in their word-painting and use of chromaticism, and these differ markedly from Arcadelt's, which parallel the harmonic and textural simplicity of the early madrigal. Other composers who wrote both musique mesurée and ordinary chansons include Claude Goudimel [d. 1572], Guillaume Costeley [*c.* 1530 – 1606], and Jacques Mauduit [1557–1627], the last-named being an important member of Baïf's Academy towards the end of its existence (*c.* 1585). But, taken as a whole, the finest chansons were composed by Lassus, whose catholicity in general is reflected in the choice and treatment of his texts, and he is equally at home in the light-hearted contrapuntal type as in the serious or sentimental polyphonic one. His chansons became so popular that some were reprinted with new, even religious texts ('contrafacta'), a procedure that was much more common in the sixteenth than in earlier centuries (see Part I, p. 83), especially in Germany.

De Baïf's Academy also aimed at creating a unified spectacle in which music, poetry, dancing, and scenic display all played an equal part, an aim that was realized in *Circe, ou le ballet comique de le Royne* [=Reine], performed with sumptuous splendour at Paris by the lords and ladies of the court during the wedding festivities of Margaret of Lorraine and the Duke of Joyeuse in 1581 (see Plate XVIII).

Entertainments in which dancing occupied a prominent place had been popular with the French aristocracy from the late fifteenth century and remained so until the Revolution. With but few exceptions, of which *Circe* is the most outstanding, all the ballets produced before *c.* 1650 lacked dramatic unity, being composed of a more or less haphazard succession of scenes; moreover, the actual dances themselves were, until the latter part of the sixteenth century, less varied and less skilfully executed than in Italy. During the third quarter of the century, however, there arrived at the courts of Henry II [reigned 1547–1559], Francis II [reigned 1559–1560] (husband of Mary Stuart), and Charles IX [reigned 1560–1574], a number of Milanese dancing masters, who came as a direct or indirect result of the delight in this kind of entertainment of Catherine de' Medici [1519–1589], wife of Henry and mother of Francis and Charles. In 1573 Catherine presented *Le Ballet des Polonais* in honour of the Polish Ambassadors, who had that year elected her third son, who later became Henry III of France [reigned 1574–1589], as King of Poland. The choreography of this ballet, to music by Lassus, was more complex than that of any previous dance spectacle either in France or abroad, and if we take as true Arnold Haskell's statement that "Ballet as we know it was born when the acrobatics of the professional and the aristocratic grace of the courtier were united"* then the year of birth was 1573. But Haskell's definition is incomplete, for ballet as we know it is also a unified dramatic spectacle, and this *Le Ballet des Polonais* was not.

The first real ballet, or 'ballet de cour', as this kind of entertainment came to be called, and the first also of which the music has been preserved intact, was *Circe*, because it combined unity of plot—in this instance based on the legend of the mythological witch-goddess—with dances that exemplified Haskell's definition. These dances can be classified into two groups, the 'ballet à entrées', which were 'character' dances expressive of the principal characters in the story and often very dramatic, being the forerunners of the modern dramatic ballet, e.g. Stravinsky's *Petrouchka*, and the final 'grand ballet', which consisted of stylized dances, i.e. those fashionable at the time, such as the gaillarde and courante, and in which ladies of the court always and royalty frequently took part; from this stemmed the classical ballet of later times. The dances were accompanied by a string band of violins, violas, and 'cellos to which lutes were sometimes added, or choruses, sometimes a cappella, or solo songs with lute ('airs de cour'); the air de cour, indeed, became the most popular musical item of the late sixteenth- and early seventeenth-century ballet, and a great number were published separately in collections by Le Roy and Ballard. Its popularity extended abroad and it undoubtedly influenced the English ayre (see p. 48), though its essential lightness of subject (often pastoral), its invariable strophic verse, and almost invariable lute accompaniment compares unfavourably with the range of mood, subtlety of construction, and variety of performance of the ayre.

* A. Haskell, *Ballet*, Pelican Special, 1938, p. 20.

As we mentioned above, the character dancers in *Circe* were courtiers, the principals as usual being male, while the *corps de ballet* included, for the first time, some of the ladies of the court, and this innovation created a fashion for most of the ballets performed at court before the Revolution. Elsewhere in the ballet female characters were impersonated by suitably masked male dancers. The action of the story was unfolded by means of verses or 'récits', which were usually spoken and which contained much fulsome flattery of the king.

So far as the general purpose (i.e. a social entertainment which glorified king and country), overall plan, and function and layout of the music are concerned, all ballets during the next twenty-five years or so were modelled on *Circe*, but this ballet remained unique in its dramatic unity and the careful integration of the various components. The man who was responsible for all this and who, doubtless influenced by de Baïf's aims, supervised the writing of the verse, the composition of the music, the *décor*, and the choreography, was an eminent Italian violinist named Baldasar da Belgioioso, who later changed his name to Balthasar de Beaujoyeulx [d. *c.* 1587]. Balthasar arrived at the French court *c.* 1555 as leader of an Italian string band sent to Catherine by one of Henry II's marshals. Thus while ballet can be said to have originated in France, the seeds were sown by Italians—namely, Catherine, the Milanese dancing masters, and Balthasar.

If French taste and French talent had been so inclined, *Circe* could have led to the birth of French opera, but it was not to be. Nevertheless, this ballet, like the pastorale and intermedio, is one of the forerunners of opera in that it too consists of singing, dancing, scenic display, and unity of plot.

German secular songs, or Lieder, during the first half of the century are, on the whole, written in the same tradition as those by Isaac; in other words, they are predominantly imitative in style and are based on borrowed melodies. They reached their peak in the compositions of Ludwig Senfl [*c.* 1486 – *c.* 1542/3], a pupil of Isaac, who shows a complete mastery of polyphonic technique combined with a new melodic gracefulness. The bulk of these songs appeared in a number of collections, the most important of which are Johann Ott's *121 neue Lieder* (1534), which includes twenty of his own songs and over eighty by Senfl, and his *115 guter neuer Liedlein* (1544), which is more cosmopolitan than the first set, including pieces by Verdelot, Richafort, Gombert, and Crecquillon, as well as by Senfl, Isaac, Stoltzer, etc. The largest collection is the *Frische teutsche Liedlein*, by Georg Forster [*c.* 1510–1568], which appeared in five parts between 1539 and 1556, and contains 380 songs, mostly by Germanic writers, including Kaspar Othmayr [1515–1553], the composer of probably the first song-cycle.

In the latter half of the century Italian influence is increasingly apparent, beginning with *Il primo delle Canzone Napoletane* (1566) by Antonio Scandello [1517–1580], an Italian at the Dresden court, which was the first exclusively Italian collection of vocal music to be published in Germany. In 1567 appeared *Newe Teutsche Liedlein mit fünff Stimmen* (including a fine five-part setting, based on the traditional tune, of Luther's hymn *Vater unser*), the first of a large number of Lieder by Lassus in which, as we should expect, the influence of the madrigal and villanella is unmistakable, although they are not so varied in expression or technique as his Italian and French compositions. (All his published Lieder, incidentally, were intended for vocal and/or instrumental performance.) The success of Lassus's and Scandello's collections (the latter also brought out some Lieder in 1568) prompted a number of German and Netherlandish composers to follow suit, notably Leonhard Lechner [*c.* 1553–1606], Jakob Regnart [d. 1599], and Hans Leo Hassler [1562–1612], a pupil of Andrea Gabrieli. Lechner's Lieder show him to be thoroughly conversant with Italian vocal styles and equally successful in both gay and sombre moods. His songs are superior to Regnart's, though the latter's were the most popular of all Leider during the last third of the century (e.g. *Venus du und dein kind* that later became the well-known chorale *Auf neinen lieben Gott*) and were only superseded by Hassler's, especially those in his *Lustgarten neuer teutscher Gesäng, Balletti, Galliarden und Intraden* (1601). Hassler had already published a set of Italian canzonettes in 1590 and, in 1596, a book of madrigals that are among the finest of the century. His Lieder of 1601 are superbly written and cover a wide range of expressions, from the delightfully gay balletto, *Tantzen und springen*, to the very moving *Ach weh des Leiden*.

Taken as a whole, German secular compositions of the late Renaissance, even those written after the middle of the century, cannot compare with their Italian counterparts. The same is true of England, except that when, in the 1580s, Italian influence finally broke through the innate conservatism of English composers there resulted a spate of secular music superior to that produced in any other country save Italy. Indeed a few, a very few, English madrigals can hold their own with the best of the Italian, while many balletti surpass their models. But for sheer quantity of excellence as well as for range of expression and technique, both within the madrigal itself and in secular music as a whole, Italy holds the palm, which is not surprising when one considers the wealth of composers who worked within her boundaries and the fact that she had been actively cultivating secular music for nearly a century before England. What is surprising is the enormous difference in quality, quantity, technique, and variety between English secular compositions before and after *c.* 1590.

For most of the sixteenth century, as in the previous one, English secular song lagged far behind that on the Continent, and the comparatively few pieces that have come down to us are written in an out-of-date style and show inferior technique. This state of affairs cannot be explained by the forces of time and destruction, for this applies to every country, nor was it due to lack of competent composers, as we shall see when we deal with the Church music of the period. The reason probably lies in the widespread and ancient practice of adding parts extempore to a popular song (discanting) rather than composing them, together with the almost complete lack of lyric poets, for, apart from the satiric verses of John Skelton [*c.* 1460–1529], a few of which were in fact set to music, hardly a poet worthy of the name lived between Chaucer and Sir Thomas Wyatt [1503–1542]. Wyatt and Henry Howard, Earl of Surrey [1517–1547], introduced the sonnet into English poetry, but were at their best in the freer forms. Their poetry was very popular in court circles, but was not published until 1557. Both men were primarily experimenters and breakers of new ground, and they were the first to show the influence of Italian poetry to any marked extent, but their talent was small compared to the genius of Edmund Spenser [*c.* 1552–1599], whose work set a new standard, especially the *Shepheardes Calendar* (1579), which perhaps reveals the influence of Sannazaro and Guarini, and *The Faerie Queene* (1590–6), which has distinct affinities with Ariosto, whom, with Tasso, Spenser much admired. Spenser had many followers, both during his lifetime and in the succeeding century, the most notable of the former being Sir Walter Raleigh [*c.* 1552–1618] and Sir Philip Sydney [1554–1586].

The extent of English lyricism in the late Renaissance cannot be judged by the number of known writers, for the considerable body of verse that exists only in the secular music of the period and which has been disregarded by almost every literary historian is, unlike that of Italy, largely anonymous, but, as in Italy, much of it was undoubtedly written with a musical setting in mind. In view of the fact that secular vocal music must always be more dependent on the state of contemporary poetry than liturgical music, in which the majority of the texts have changed but little, being excerpts, translations, or adaptations from the Bible, and considering especially the close links between the words and music in the sixteenth century, it is no coincidence that the flowering of the lyric art in England occurred at the same time as that of the madrigal.

The only secular music printed between 1530 (see Part I, Chapter 6, p. 213) and 1588 was a collection of seventy-six songs for from three to five voices by Thomas Whythorne 'Gentleman' [1528–1596], published in 1571. Although he states that he had visited Italy, one would not have guessed as much from the music, for while some of the songs have a certain charm, they reveal hardly any of the madrigalian characteristics discussed earlier and are often technically clumsy. The texts are mostly moralistic in tone, and this feature is the only link between him and the first great English composer of secular music in the late Renaissance—indeed, one of the greatest composers of all time—William Byrd [1543–1623].

In 1588 Byrd issued his *Psalmes, Sonets & songs of sadness and pietie*, and initiated a spate of secular composition that lasted for a brief but glorious period of forty years. None of the pieces in the above collection are madrigals, for they were "originally made for instruments [viols] to expresse the harmonie, and one voice to pronounce the dittie", and have, as a result, an abstract quality quite different from the realistic or emotional approach of the normal late sixteenth-century madrigal. The religious or moralistic tone which permeates the book (many of the items are in fact anthems) can be likened to the spiritual madrigals of Lassus, but the musical treatment of these is not greatly different from Lassus's purely secular examples, i.e. is thoroughly modern, whereas in Byrd's pieces the main madrigalian features of word-painting and strong rhythmic contrasts are rare, and the harmonic idiom is of the simplest. His two later books of 1589 ("fit for all companies and voyces") and 1611, especially the latter, in which the music is significantly enough "framed to the life of the words", show Italian influence to a greater extent; more of the texts are secular than in the 1588 set, and their treatment is more up-to-date, but if one had only these three collections to judge from one would unhesitatingly say that Byrd was more inspired by words of a serious than a flippant nature; in fact, it is largely true that the most moving and most brilliant songs are those that either petition or praise God, and, paradoxically, he is more madrigalesque in his Catholic Church music than in his secular output.

In addition to his published work, nearly forty songs with sacred or secular words remained in manuscript. These are for the same ensemble as the original settings of the 1588 book—namely, solo voice accompanied by a consort (group) of viols—and this fact, together with a similarity in style, makes it probable that they are early pieces. Nevertheless, they show, as do those in the 1588 set, a mastery of smooth-flowing, imitative polyphony combined with a subtle rhythmic sense that produces on occasion a perfect gem, as, for example, *My little sweet darling*, and the well-known *Lullaby*.

Byrd's resistance to Italian influence was partly due to the native conservatism in general of English composers, but mainly to the view he took of his art; this is clearly expressed in his 1588 publication, where he states that "The better the voyce is, the meeter it is to honour and serve God there-with: and the voyce of man is chiefely to be imployed to that ende". At the time when this was written, Byrd was acknowledged as the foremost English composer, but his rather severe conception of the purpose of music, while plainly influencing some of his contemporaries, fortunately did not affect the most gifted of them, with the possible exception of Orlando Gibbons and Thomas Tomkins.

The youngest of Byrd's gifted contemporaries and the first genuine madrigalist was Thomas Morley [1557/8 – 1602], who more than anyone else laid the foundations of what is now called the English Madrigal School. But Morley was no lone torch-bearer who single-handed brought the light of Italian secular music to this country, for from the time of Henry VIII [reigned 1509–1547] onwards an increasing number of foreign musicians, particularly from the Netherlands and Italy, visited or settled in England. The most important of these was the Italian, Alfonso Ferrabosco (i) [1543–1588], who lived in London *c.* 1560–78 and who was so admired by Elizabeth I [reigned 1558–1603] that when he was only twenty-six years old she granted him a pension of £100 a year (the equivalent of about £1,500 today), provided he bound himself to her service for life. This he promised to do, but broke his word, spending the last years of his life in the employ of an Italian duke. Elizabeth was not alone in her admiration, for Morley calls him "a great musician famous and admired for his works amongst the best", and he was a personal friend of Byrd. Ferrabosco's reputation undoubtedly did much to stimulate interest in the secular music of his own country, for it is from *c.* 1560 on that a growing number of Italian madrigals, chiefly in manuscript, began to circulate in English musical society, and the popularity of these eventually induced a certain Nicholas Yonge to publish a selection of them under the title *Musica Transalpina* (1588). This was patently a success, and two years later Thomas Watson, a minor poet, brought out a similar book, *Italian Madrigals Englished*. The increase in home production in the 1590s probably accounts for the fact that not until 1597 did a second volume of *Musica Transalpina* appear, together with selections of Italian madrigals edited by Morley himself in 1597 and 1598. Morley had clearly steeped himself in this art, but he was no slavish imitator, and the bulk of his secular output—the canzonets *a*3 (really madrigals) (1593), the madrigals *a*4 (1594), the two-part canzonets, and five-part balletts (both 1595)—all of which appeared before any other English madrigal print, show that although he had fully grasped the technique of madrigal writing he selected, on the whole, only the pastoral and narrative types, but infused them with a greater tunefulness and sense of tonality. The former had been a characteristic of English composers for centuries, but Morley's melodies have a consistent freshness that not only mark them off from Continental pieces, but from those of his countrymen also, though to a lesser extent. This and his harmonic clarity, his tendency to stress a tonal centre by well-planned modulations to the dominant and subdominant, and his strong feeling for dance rhythms, introduced a more frankly popular element into the madrigal and set the fashion for most of his compatriots. The dance-like features of his music are most marked in his balletts, and he surpasses his models, Gastoldi's balletti, in the length and polyphonic brilliance of his 'fa la' refrains (*H.A.M.*, 139).

In 1601 Morley edited a collection of English madrigals by English composers entitled *The Triumphes of Oriana*, which was modelled on an earlier Italian collection, *Il Trionfo di Dori* (1592). It has always been assumed that Oriana was Elizabeth I, but this has recently been queried owing to the apparent fact that (a) the Collection was not sold until 1603, i.e. after Elizabeth's death, and (b) she objected to the name Oriana. However, it has now been convincingly shewn that the evidence for the latter is wholly inconclusive and misleading, and, moreover, that copies of the work were on sale by at least December 1601. (See R. C. Strong, *Studies in the Renaissance*, Vol. VI.) All the leading composers contributed to *The Triumphs of Oriana* except Byrd and Giles Farnaby [*c.* 1563–1640]. It is often assumed that Byrd, because he had published no book of madrigals and was out of sympathy with the type, was not asked, but this is unlikely, considering his prestige and that he was Morley's teacher, and it is more probable that he declined the invitation. Actually, Farnaby's omission is more curious because he had already produced an excellent book of canzonets in 1598.

As Vesta was from Latmos hill descending, by Thomas Weelkes [*c.* 1576–1623] is usually regarded as the finest of the *Oriana* collection, and is typical of much of the composer's work in its detailed and vivid word-painting. In this as in other respects he is more Italianate than Morley, and while the latter is essentially an exquisite miniaturist with a somewhat limited range of feeling, Weelkes is at his best when he is portraying a dramatic or passionate subject on a large canvas—for example, the wonderful five-part madrigal, *O Care, thou wilt despatch me*, with its equally fine second part, *Hence Care; thou art too cruel*; even so, he was more successful in shorter, fewer-voiced pieces than most of his contemporaries (his *Cease sorrows now* is the most outstanding three-part madrigal ever written). His versatility is shown by delightful settings of nonsense verse, balletts that are sometimes even more brilliant than Morley's, and madrigals that range from the conventionally amorous to the profoundly emotional and highly dramatic. In these last he was undoubtedly influenced by Marenzio (who is represented more often than any other composer in the second book of *Musica Transalpina*), and in his use of chromaticism and dissonance he is the boldest and most experimental of the English madrigalists.

The high spot of Weelkes's secular output is reached in his *Madrigals of 5. and 6. parts, apt for the viols and voices* (1600), which contains pieces unsurpassed in emotional intensity and unequalled in brilliance by any other English madrigalist. The expression "apt for the viols and voices", or something similar, was included in nearly every later madrigal print, but Weelkes was not the first Englishman to suggest that instruments should accompany or replace voices in the performance of vocal music, for not only does Byrd mention this possibility in 'The Epistle to the Reader' of his 1588 book, but a psalter of 1563 specifically states in its title that the contents "may be song to al musicall instrumentes", and another (1599) not only specifies which instruments, but actually includes in tablature a reduction of the three lowest vocal parts (see Chapter 2, p. 329).

It is a fact greatly to be regretted that Weelkes wrote no full-scale madrigals after his set of 1600, apart from the six-part elegy on Morley's death included in his *Ayeres or Phantasticke Spirites for three voices* (1608); had he done so he would almost certainly have reached a more refined style without detracting from his vivid imagination, and laid claim to be regarded as the greatest native madrigalist. As it is, however, the palm falls to John Wilbye [1574–1638], whose two sets, printed in 1597 and 1609, represent the high-water mark of the English madrigal. In the quality of his inspiration, his sensitivity to the rhythm of the text, his realistic but always musical approach to word-painting, his poetic taste, and his well-nigh impeccable technique he might well be called the English Marenzio, although he lacked the latter's versatility both in his harmonic variety and his expressive range. His *Draw on, sweet night* is not only the finest of all English madrigals, but one of the most beautiful short vocal pieces of all time.

Among the many other lesser madrigalists, Orlando Gibbons [1583–1625], John Ward [1571–1638], and Thomas Tomkins [1572–1656] must be mentioned. Each published only one set of madrigals, in 1613, 1614, and 1622 respectively. Ward rarely chose flippant texts and is at his best when writing for six voices, where his bold dissonances (he was unusually fond of double suspensions), breadth of phrase, and detailed word-painting have full scope.

Gibbons, like Byrd, produced his greatest music for the Church and is, together with the older man, the least affected by Italian influence of all his fellow madrigalists. Like Byrd, too, he took a serious view of his art, and it is perhaps no coincidence that the words of the second madrigal of the set run as follows:

> O that the learned poets of this time,
> Who in a Love-sick line so well can speak,
> Would not consume good wit in hateful rhyme,
> But with deep care some better subject find.
> For if their music please in earthly things
> How would it sound if strung with heavenly strings?

At any rate, the moralistic tone of his deservedly famous *The Silver Swan* is typical of most of the others. This piece has distinct affinities with Byrd's secular work in the clear, melodic superiority of the top voice, and even in the more purely madrigalian examples there is an abstract, almost instrumental quality about the music—which a discreet use of word-painting does not lessen—that is reminiscent of Byrd's style.

Tomkins, too, has certain affinities with Byrd (who was his teacher) in that the greater part of his vocal music was composed for the Church. Even his one 'secular' publication, which, significantly enough, is entitled *Songs*, not 'Madrigals', includes some anthems, just as Byrd's three sets had done. But Tomkins is much more madrigalian in his technique and choice of texts than either Byrd or Gibbons, and is equally at home when writing a ballett or setting a short conventional lyric, as in *Sure there is no God of love*, as when he is clothing a longer and more complex text with almost the entire range of madrigalian devices, as in *Weep no more thou sorry Boy*.

Although, as we have seen, instruments could and undoubtedly did on occasion take part in the performance of secular music on the Continent, their participation seems to have been much more frequent in England, doubtless owing to a tradition of which Byrd's unpublished secular pieces and those in his 1588 set (in their original layout) were the first notable examples. This traditional fondness for accompanied song is strikingly shown in the ayre, which, from *c.* 1600 on, gradually displaced the madrigal in popularity. The ayre was often so arranged that it could be performed in three different ways: by unaccompanied voices, by accompanied voices, and by a solo voice supported (usually) by a lute with a bass viol playing the lowest voice part. The solo part and the lute tablature are placed on one page, the other voices on the opposite page; hence all can perform from one book (see Plate XIX). Sometimes the lute accompaniment clashes with the inner vocal parts, so that presumably in these ayres the voices are not meant to be accompanied, only the solo voice. This provision of alternative methods of performance in the same volume is a distinctive feature of the ayre, as is the fact that it is almost without exception an original composition, whereas a tremendous number of Continental songs are simply transcriptions of vocal part-songs and were published separately from the latter.

Two other noteworthy features of the ayre in general are a much stronger sense of key and, through the use of a few pervading motifs, a more closely knit melodic line than existed abroad. The former is very apparent in the work of John Dowland [1563–1626], a fine singer, a lute virtuoso of international repute, and the greatest of the ayre composers. His fame, both as a lutanist and as a composer, led to several appointments abroad, where he spent much of his life, and where he met and was admired by many distinguished musicians, including Marenzio, but all his printed music was first issued in England, and his *First Booke of Songes or Ayres . . . with Tableture for the Lute* (1597) was the earliest and most popular of its kind (it was the only music-book by any composer that went through four editions during the composer's lifetime). The esteem in which his music was held on the Continent can be gauged from the fact that, as he himself says in his Preface to his last published work, *A Pilgrimes Solace* (1612), "some part of my poore labours have found favour in the greatest part of Europe, and been printed in eight most famous Cities beyond the seas, viz.: Paris, Antwerpe, Collein [Cologne], Nurenberge,

Franckfort, Leipsig, Amsterdam, and Hamburge". No other English composer and few foreign ones could claim as much.

Dowland's *First Booke of Songes* has the voice and lute parts arranged in the manner described above, and it set the fashion for most succeeding ayre prints. Indeed, its extraordinary popularity may be partly accounted for by the fact that it provided, for the first time, three alternative methods of performance, but the chief reason was undoubtedly the quality of the songs themselves. In his wide range of expressiveness, Dowland resembles Weelkes, and, like the latter, he is at his best when dealing with an emotional subject, as, for example, *Flow, my teares* from his *Second Booke of Songes or Ayres* (1600), which he had previously arranged for the lute under the title *Lachrimae* (1596). This song became enormously popular—a household word, in fact; references to it occur in many poems and plays of the early seventeenth century, and it was the basis of numerous instrumental pieces, including 'Seaven Passionate Pavans', by Dowland himself.

Although Dowland's emotionalism is akin to Weelkes's, he is more intense that the madrigalist, and a number of his songs show a passion and a sense of the dramatic which are unsurpassed by any other contemporary composer, with the possible exception of Gesualdo and Monteverdi. The fluctuating rhythms and wonderful expressiveness of his melody, the sensitive appreciation of the accentual and emotional qualities of the words, the daring use of chromaticism and dissonance, the utter perfection and variety of his lute accompaniments make him one of the finest song-writers of all time. Compared to him, most of the other ayre-composers are emotionally restricted and harmonically and melodically conventional, but this did not prevent them from producing a considerable number of charming and occasionally exquisite pieces. The chief exceptions are Thomas Campian [1567–1620] and John Danyel [1564 – *c.* 1626]. Campian, apart from being a poet of some repute, possessed a lyric gift of a high order, and his ayres, most of which are settings of his own verse, frequently show the second feature mentioned earlier—a closely knit melodic line. Danyel's ayres are uneven in quality, but the best of the twenty he published in 1606 come very near to Dowland's in their passionate intensity, and his rhythmic changes and use of dissonance are often most telling. Other notable ayre-composers are Robert Jones [fl. 1600], Philip Rosseter [1567/8 – 1623], and Michael Cavendish [*c.* 1565 – 1628], of whom the first and last also published madrigals.

Campian is also an important figure in the history of the masque, his two most notable essays in this sphere being the *Masque in honour of Lord Hayes* (1607) and *The Lord's Masque* (1613), for both of which, as for his other masques, he wrote the text and some of the music.

The masque was an offshoot of the late fifteenth-century 'mascherate', or masquerades, that formed part of the carnivals held before and after Lent in many Italian cities, notably Florence (see Part I, Chapter 6, p. 208), but in England it eventually developed into a musico-dramatic entertainment far more artistic and complex than its parent. So far as we know, the first masque took place in 1513, for a contemporary writer tells us that on Twelfth Night of that year Henry VIII and eleven others disguised themselves "after the maner of Italie, called a maske, a thyng not seen afore in Englande . . .". The masquers, wearing voluminous garments embroidered in gold, as well as gold masks and capes, appeared after the banquet and requested some of the ladies to dance. Information as to how the masque developed during the next ninety years or so is scanty, but from the end of the sixteenth century to the Civil War (1642) it was considerably influenced by the French ballet de cour, although in general it was more dramatically unified than its model.

The leading light of the Jacobean masque—that is, up to the death of James I [reigned 1603–1625]—was the famous dramatist and Poet Laureate, Ben Jonson, who, apart from writing a number of brilliantly satirical plays, of which *Volpone, or the Fox* (1606), *The Alchemist* (1610), and *Bartholomew Fair* (1614) are the best, and still performed, also produced a series of 'entertainments' from 1603 on which were commissioned by James and his successor, Charles I. In 1605 Jonson wrote the *Masque of Blackness*, and the man appointed by James to design the settings and devise the scenic effects was Inigo Jones [1573–1652], who became Royal Surveyor in 1615, and was the first great English architect. Jones probably visited Italy in 1601 and 1609, was certainly in Paris in the latter year, and in Italy and Germany in 1613–14. His study of Renaissance architecture in both France and Italy bore fruit in the classical designs of his buildings, notably the west portico of St. Paul's, the banqueting house of Whitehall Palace (now the United Services Museum), and the Queen's house at Greenwich, and also in the planning of certain small areas, such as Lincoln's Inn Fields and Covent Garden—the first instance of regulated planning in England. His studies abroad bore fruit too in his stage designs and use of stage machinery (see Plate XX), and he clearly learnt much from the Italian and French theatre. But Jones did not make his reputation as an architect, a reputation that eventually extended to the Continent, until some ten years after his successful début as a designer of masques, and in this capacity he was almost continuously employed by the Crown until the outbreak of the Civil War; indeed, he became so popular that when, in 1631, after much friction, the Jones-Jonson collaboration finally broke down, Jones was able to prevent Jonson from receiving any more commissions.

But we anticipate, for we shall here only deal with the Jacobean masque, leaving the Caroline masques, i.e. those written in Charles I's reign, to Chapter 3.

The best of Jonson's Jacobean masques are the *Masque of Queens* (1609), *Oberon* (1611), and *The Vision of Delight* (1617), which last we shall return to in Chapter 3, as the music reflects the vocal style of the Italian early baroque. While none of his masques can compare as a whole with the best of his plays, all of them contain passages that reveal the quality of his skill, learning, and wit.

Jonson and Campian were not the only writers of masques, and even if we omit Shakespeare's *The Tempest* (1611), which can be regarded as the finest masque ever written, there exist a number of excellent examples by other men, notably the *Inner Temple Masque* (1615), by the poet William Browne [*c.* 1591–*c.* 1645], and the *Masque of the Inner Temple and Gray's Inn* (1613), by the popular dramatist Francis Beaumont [1584/5–1616], whose collaboration with John Fletcher [1579–1625] provides one of the landmarks in the history of English drama.

The typical masque was very similar to the ballet de cour in that (1) its general layout consisted of dances accompanied instrumentally, or vocally, or both, and interspersed with prose and poetry, the latter spoken or set for one or more voices with or without instruments; (2) the presentation relied to a great extent on spectacular stage settings, devices, and costumes, including, of course, masks; (3) it was essentially an aristocratic entertainment containing much adulation of royalty and realm. This similarity became even more marked after 1609, when Jonson, in direct imitation of the ballet à entrées, introduced antimasques into his *Masque of Queens*. These, with their stress on characterization and dramatic expressiveness, which ranged from slap-stick to the macabre, were inserted between the 'scenes' of the masque proper and were usually so striking in their effect that they became, like the intermezzi of Italian opera (see Chapter 4), more popular than the main work. From 1609 on there were thus three groups of dances, those for the semi-professional masquers and antimasquers, and those in which the ladies of the audience joined—the final 'revels', equivalent to the French 'grand ballet', these last being the only occasions on which ladies danced on the stage, for in the remainder of the entertainment female characters were impersonated by male dancers wearing appropriate masks, as in the ballet de cour.

Apart from Campian, the chief composers of the Jacobean masque were John Coperario [d. after 1626], Alfonso Ferrabosco (ii) [*c.* 1575 – 1628], whose father we mentioned earlier in this chapter, and Robert Johnson [*c.* 1583 – 1633]. Coperario and Ferrabosco were also important composers of consort music (see p. 345), while Johnson established a considerable and well-deserved reputation in the spheres of instrumental music and songs with lute accompaniment; most of the best of these he wrote for Jonson's masques, and in general his masque music is superior, both melodically and in its sense of the dramatic, to that by Coperario or Ferrabosco, though the latter was ranked first by Jonson, an estimation that did not prevent the playwright's violent temper ending their association after 1610.

Although few of these early masques have survived with their music complete, some of it can be found scattered throughout various manuscripts or in published collections of instrumental and vocal pieces. Thus, apart from such obvious titles as *A Maske*, a number of dances which are linked with a high-ranking name, e.g. *Corranto Lady Riche* from the *Fitzwilliam Virginal Book* (see Chapter 2, p. 336), may have originally been part of a masque in honour of or presented by the individual concerned. Again, a piece such as Johnson's *The Pretty Wanton* very likely comes from a masque of that title (which in this case has been lost), or else is descriptive of the character that danced to it in (most probably) an antimasque. Similarly with vocal music; for example, *See, O see, who comes here a-maying?*, a four-part piece for two voices and two stringed instruments by Martin Peerson [*c.* 1572–1651], which was composed for Jonson's *Entertainment of the King and Queen* (1604) and published sixteen years later in the composer's *Private Musicke*. Jonson's favourite composer, Ferrabosco, also published some of his masque music several years after its first performance, and his *Ayres* (1609) include one for voice and lute from Jonson's *Masque of Blackness*.

The madrigal and its allied types, together with the ayre and masque-songs, did not cover the whole field of English secular vocal music, for all these demanded a fair degree of musical skill, and the stock melodies to which Italian poetry was sung (e.g. *ruggiero*) were paralleled by the ballads—that is, traditional tunes such as *Greensleeves*, to which a varying number of texts were adapted. In addition, Weelkes and Gibbons each wrote a piece for voices and instruments based on street cries, an idea similar to the villota, but more learnedly executed, particularly that by Gibbons, which is in fact an In nomine (see Chapter 2, p. 335), though one would never guess as much from the delightful way in which the cries are shared between the voices. More important are the three collections of Thomas Ravenscroft [*c.* 1582–1635], *Pammelia* (1609), *Deuteromelia* (1609), and *Melismata* (1611), the first of their kind printed in England. They are definitely popular in appeal and consist in the main of simple part-songs, canons, and rounds—for example, *Three Blind Mice*, printed for the first time in *Deuteromelia*. This round and some of the other pieces may well go back to the early years of the sixteenth century.

Ravenscroft's three publications fall into line with the general trend of the English madrigal and ayre, for in general these last are, with their melodic freshness and harmonic clarity, more frankly popular than Italian madrigals and allied types. That the technical and expressive range of secular music in England fell below that of Italy was partly due to the inferior quality of the texts chosen, but mainly to the fact that, unlike Italy, with her teeming generations of composers, native and foreign, and her great musical centres at Venice, Florence, Rome, Bologna, Ferrara, Mantua, Milan, Naples, and Verona, each with their discerning patrons, knowledgeable amateurs, highly trained professional performers, and academies, English musical culture was largely amateur and, apart from a few aristocratic establishments, such as Hengrave Hall, the seat of the Kytson family, where Wilbye was employed, was centred in London. Moreover, there were no academies, and a composer was therefore denied both the stimulus of composing for and the benefits of criticism by a keen intelligent group.

But if English secular music is surpassed by Italian, it can certainly compare with French and is undoubtedly superior to German and Spanish, especially the latter, and it is a curious coincidence that its late flowering occurred immediately after the defeat of the Spanish Armada in 1588, when the period of tension and uncertainty was ended. Some people think that this naval victory, by ushering in an era of peace and prosperity, was the main cause for the sudden surge of creation, but it should be remembered that Italy produced one of the most brilliant chapters in the history of civilization while suffering far more and for a longer period than England.

Spanish domination in Italy did not make her immune from cultural invasion, and the Italian madrigal was cultivated by a number of native composers together with the purely national villancico. But the difference in quantity and quality between sacred and secular music in Spain was far greater than in any other country, and all the leading composers of vocal polyphony concentrated almost entirely on the mass and motet. The reason for this takes us into the realm of sacred music and the next chapter.

PERFORMANCE

(*See also pp.* 243, 249, 261, 267 269, 284, 286)

The most notable trend in late Renaissance music—particularly evident in the madrigal and chanson—is the change from the classical poise and restraint of the early part of the period, when music and text were of roughly equal importance, to the vivid word-painting and franker emotionalism of the late sixteenth and early seventeenth centuries, when the music was dictated by and in extreme cases depended on the nature of the text. The remarkable difference in approach between, say, the madrigals of Arcadelt and Gesualdo, or (though to a lesser extent) the chansons of Claudin and Lassus should therefore be reflected in performance. Details of speed, expression, the number of voices per part, and the use of instruments will depend to some extent on personal taste, but more especially on one or other of the following considerations: the period in which the piece was written, the nature of the words, the texture of the music, and, in certain instances, the personality of the composer, but, broadly speaking, the ensuing remarks hold good.

1. *Madrigals*

(*a*) In those written before Rore's first book *a*4 (1550) the tactus (semibreve in ¢, minim in C) should be between M.M. 60–80, the choice depending on the texture and the poem; thus a mainly contrapuntal and rhythmically simple piece should be sung faster than a polyphonic and rhythmically complex one, unless the character of the poem as a whole contradicts this and/or there is a significant amount of syllabic underlay in minims (in ¢) or crotchets (in C), especially if this is allied to extended harmonic movement in minims or crotchets respectively. It should be noted in this connexion that, although in ¢ and C the harmonic units are almost invariably the minim and crotchet respectively, in that they represent the longest dissonance and the shortest rate of harmonic change, the normal harmonic change occurs on the tactus; hence a piece in which changes of chord at twice the normal rate are at all frequent should be sung at or near the speed of tactus=M.M. 60. Once the speed has been decided on it should remain invariable. Dynamic contrasts should be abrupt (i.e. only occur between phrases) and gentle (e.g. *p* to *mf*, not *pp* to *ff*); in other words, while rising and falling lines within an individual vocal phrase will naturally increase and decrease in sound to a greater or lesser degree, there should be no overall crescendos, and only cadential diminuendos. Ornaments should not be extemporized, as this involves specialized knowledge.

(*b*) In those by Rore or written between 1550 and Marenzio's first book *a*5 (1580) the expressive range widens, though one mood is generally dominant throughout a single composition. Hence while dynamic contrasts, which should still be abrupt, may cover a bigger range, the tempo decided on should remain invariable, otherwise the unity of mood will tend to be disrupted. When a piece fluctuates between semibreve and minim tacti (see p. 243) then the choice of speed should lie between minim = M.M. 60–90, the exact speed depending on the same factors as in (*a*). The individual vocal lines should be sung with a keen sense of the text, and especially of the more emotional words.

(*c*) In those written after 1580 in which detailed word-painting and mood-change are the dominant factors, abrupt changes not only of dynamics (which may cover an even wider range than before), but also of speed may occur, as may restrained diminuendos (other than cadential) and even crescendos. The exact speed will depend on the same factors as in (*a*), and if there are changes in speed within a piece these must be abrupt, except as in (*a*), and should lie between minim = M.M. 60–90. Where the text demands it, the voices may range from staccato to legato in manner and from lightness to sombreness in timbre. In general, the more varied the musical treatment of the text, the more varied the performance. (*N.B.*—Clearly not all madrigals written between 1550 and 1580 are like Rore's, nor were all Marenzio's contemporaries so concerned with word-painting as he was; 'classical' madrigals continued to be written long after Arcadelt. The deciding factor is the nature of the piece, and it is seldom difficult to decide which period it belongs to stylistically and hence how it should be performed. For example, all English madrigals were written after 1580, but some (e.g. Morley's) are often more reminiscent of Arcadelt than Rore or Marenzio. The main difference between English and contemporary Italian madrigals in performance is that the former may be partially or wholly rendered on instruments with less ill-effect than the latter because the association between text and music is not nearly so close.)

2. *Chansons*

The importance attached to intelligibility of text, the simpler part-writing that resulted, the lightness and clarity of the language, and the natural refinement of feeling made the chanson less emotionally expressive than the madrigal, but the same dynamic changes should occur during roughly the same periods and, where the words warrant it, an even greater variety of speed (depending on the same factors as for the madrigal), the minim ranging from M.M. 60 to as much as 120. As in the madrigal, the later chansons (e.g. by Lassus) may demand much more varied performance than the earlier (e.g. by Claudin), though the programme- and narrative-chansons by Janequin and others should be more freely treated.

3. *Lieder*

Instrumental participation in vocal music was much commoner in Germany than in France or Italy because of a strong instrumental tradition (see Part I, p. 216). Thus while the practice of doubling or replacing some of the voices undoubtedly occurred in both France and Italy, the French stress on intelligibility of text and the close links between word, mood, and music in most late Renaissance Italian madrigals discouraged wholly instrumental performance. Apart from this, and the fact that the language is less sonorous than Italian and heavier than French, and the range of speed should therefore not exceed tactus = M.M. 60–90, the relevant remarks concerning the chanson apply also to the Lied. The most suitable instruments for taking part in Lieder (and madrigals and chansons for that matter) are strings and woodwind, including recorders.

4. *Balletti, Villanelle, etc.*

The clear texture, dance-like rhythms, and light character of the balletti call for a quick tempo of tactus = M.M. 80–100. The range of expression is limited. They are almost as effective when played on instruments. Villanelle and the other frivolous kinds mentioned in the chapter may range in speed from tactus = M.M. 60–100, the choice depending on factors already discussed under the madrigal. The expressive range, particularly in the villanelle, is wider than in the balletti. Instruments may double the voices.

5. *Lute Songs*

Ideally, of course, the lute should provide the accompaniment or, failing this, the guitar, but as competent players of either instrument are comparatively rare, the piano may be substituted, provided that the sustaining pedal is very discreetly used. In any case, a 'cello should play the bass of the accompaniment when the original demands a gamba. The range of expression is considerable and so speeds may lie between tactus = M.M. 60–100. As variations in tone and timbre are much more telling when sung by a solo voice than by a group of voices, they should occur more often, particularly in those songs (e.g. by Dowland) that are deeply expressive; in these slight changes of speed are often effective.

2

THE LATE RENAISSANCE: SACRED MUSIC—INSTRUMENTAL MUSIC

THE fact that Spanish composers in the late Renaissance were far more concerned with sacred than with secular music was undoubtedly due to the powerful combination of passion and mysticism that is such a marked characteristic of the Spanish people, and it was this characteristic that made Spain the spearhead of the movement known as the Counter-Reformation. We have already used this term several times, but before we can define it and describe its effects on art in general and music in particular, we must find out what Reformation it countered or opposed.

In Part I we saw how the Church during the fourteenth and fifteenth centuries had become disrupted within and discredited without, and how she later attempted to put her house in order. She was not on the whole averse to reform, for she had on several occasions in the past adapted herself to new ideas—the Franciscan movement for one, and Thomism for another—but the Great Schism had seriously weakened her authority, and in order to recover at least a part of this she withdrew within herself, becoming more rigid in her orthodoxy, fearful lest change should bring chaos. This explains but does not altogether condone the often violent persecution of those sects which disagreed with her, but neither the swords of her hired soldiers nor the torture chambers and burning stakes of her zealots could annihilate the growing belief that the soul of man can establish a direct relationship with God without the mediation of a priest.

On 31st October 1517, Martin Luther [1483–1546] nailed his famous ninety-five indictments on the sale of indulgences to the door of the castle church at Wittenberg, and it is usual and convenient to date the beginning of the Reformation from this act. The practice of receiving pardon for sins by paying certain sums of money had become an outrageous scandal during the early years of the century, when funds were needed to rebuild

St. Peter's Church in Rome, and Luther's condemnation of it was the result of a growing dissatisfaction with the Church of which he was an ordained priest, for he maintained that ecclesiastical penalties and pardons can never remove guilt or divine punishment, a view which the Church herself eventually adopted. In 1520 he published three treatises which represent the kernel of the Lutheran movement, and make it clear that he did not want separation from the Church, but simply that it should be reformed. In his belief, however, of "the priesthood of all believers", in his rejection of the Pope's supremacy, and in several other respects he cut right across some of the fundamentals of Catholicism, and his defiance of the Papal Bull of excommunication, which he burnt in public, caused a tremendous stir all over Europe.

Lutheranism swept through Germany like wild-fire, finding adherents among the common folk and aristocracy alike, for Luther, by showing an indifference to secular government, had been careful not to tread on the toes of traditional authority. In 1521 Charles V [1500–1558], at the famous Diet of Worms, banned the movement from his Empire, but five years later the German princes decreed that Lutherans should be allowed to preach and worship unhindered. In 1529, however, under intense pressure from Rome, this decree was revoked, and as a result a number of princes 'protested'—the origin of the term 'Protestant', the one now used to cover all reformed Churches. Finally, in 1555 Charles was forced to grant full religious equality to the reformed Church, and in the same year abdicated in favour of his brother, Ferdinand I [1501–1564].

Luther's stress on reformation rather than separation is clearly shown in his regulations concerning the place and practice of music in the service, for the early Lutheran mass differed little from that of the Catholic Church, and even his later German mass, which, in general, conformed to his aim of making the words intelligible to the ordinary man (hence his translation of the Bible), permitted the use of Latin if so desired, though some of the traditional mass movements were omitted altogether or replaced by German songs, and the Credo was sung in German. The Lutheran mass was thus a very fluid affair, but through its predominant use of the vernacular it did encourage the congregation to take part, though to what exact extent we do not know.

As for the music itself, most of it was adapted from Gregorian chants or, more especially, from pre-Reformation religious songs, mainly of German origin. In the first group the chant was either taken over intact or else altered, the texts in any case being translated. In the second group the sources range from Geisserlieder and Minnesäng to Latin and German part-songs. In addition, a number of new songs were written expressly for the Lutheran service; some of these were composed by Luther himself, who was a competent musician and a great admirer of Josquin, but the first notable Lutheran composer was his friend and musical adviser, Johann Walter [1496–1570]. Although Walter's publications include settings of both German and Latin texts, his most popular and important work is the *Geystliche Gesangk Buchleyn* ('Little Book of Spiritual Songs'), first printed in 1524 and almost entirely made up of German Lieder for three, four, and five voices. Almost half of these are written in much the same polyphonic style as Isaac's, with the principal melody in long notes, sometimes broken, in the tenor part, the other parts being free, with occasional imitation. The rest of the pieces anticipate the later chorale in their contrapuntal 'hymn tune' texture, but the tenor still carries the main melody. As the contents of the book are all part-songs, they could only have been performed by musically educated people, and to ensure that there were sufficient of these, choral societies for both children and adults were started at which the rudiments of music were taught and the repertoire practised. Thus uneducated members of the congregation presumably sang the tunes (borrowed or newly composed) that were not treated polyphonically or contrapuntally, and possibly also sang the tenor melodies in the chorale-like settings, the choir adding the other parts. In any case, the choir and congregation were unaccompanied, as the organ did not act as a support until the following century.

Walter's 1524 publication—the first Protestant hymnbook, in fact—was followed by many others and, towards the end of the century, by numerous simple settings of the psalms. But the tradition of northern polyphony was not only too powerful to be overthrown all at once, but also gave composers far greater scope for their talents than the simple congregational hymn or psalm. Even the use of Latin, which Luther after all had permitted, died hard, and Bach's Mass in B minor is simply the greatest among a host of others composed during the sixteenth, seventeenth, and eighteenth centuries. The Protestant motet, too, is very little different in style from its Catholic counterpart, except that, unlike the Protestant mass, the text is invariably in German. Moreover, several Protestant composers wrote Latin motets and a number of Catholic composers, including Stoltzer, Senfl, and Lassus, contributed to Protestant hymn-books or set Lutheran texts independently. But their contributions, together with a number of fine hymns, motets, and masses by the leading Lutheran composers, Walter, Hassler, and Johann Eccard [1553–1611], simply cannot match in quantity or quality the output of the numerous Catholic composers who mostly centred round the Hapsburg court at Vienna, and of whom the chief were Senfl, Lassus, Kerle, and Monte, but we shall leave discussion of their works until we deal with the whole field of Latin liturgical music (see below).

The rapid spread of Lutheranism in Germany, and similar movements in Switzerland, France, England, and the Netherlands, caused great and growing concern in the Catholic Church, and resulted in the revival known as the Counter-Reformation. The first important outcome of this was the Council of Trent, at which leading Catholics met for a total period of about seven years between 1545 and 1563 and reconsidered and where necessary revised the Church's doctrine. On the whole the Council was a success, for while certain thorny theological problems were left unsolved, its deliberations undeniably strengthened the Church's position by restating more clearly her fundamental beliefs, advocating more strongly her responsibilities towards society, and cleaning up the abuses that were staining her reputation. Some of these abuses concerned music, and the Council spent over a year in deciding what reforms to adopt. The result can be summarized under two headings: the music itself and its performers. As regards the first, it was laid down that the prime aim of liturgical music is to promote a greater sense of worship in the congregation, and from this it naturally followed that no secular material may be introduced and the style of composition should allow the words to be clearly heard, this last being undoubtedly inspired by Luther. As to performance, it was decided, though largely by implication, that only the organ was to be used either in accompanying voices or playing solos, and that virtuoso or theatrical vocal and instrumental displays were to be prohibited.

These reforms give us some idea of the state of Catholic music in the 1560s, but to get a clearer picture we must trace its development after Josquin, and in so doing we shall not take each nation separately, but cover the entire field, for, unlike secular composition, which varied in language and to some extent in style from country to country, music for the Roman rite, no matter where it was written, continued to use a common language, and its style was virtually international.

Ockeghem wrote twelve masses, including a Requiem, and about ten motets; Josquin nineteen masses and about 100 motets. The difference is striking and important, as it reflects the general tendency throughout the sixteenth century whereby composers (with notable exceptions) increasingly favoured the motet rather than the mass. The reason for this was partly the composer's growing consciousness of his individuality—one of the main characteristics of the Renaissance outlook—and partly his purely artistic desire to give full rein to his talents, and, because the motet, unlike the mass, could be based on any sacred text written in Latin, it gave the composer not only freedom to choose those texts that especially appealed to his temperament, but also greater opportunities for technical experiments and expressive treatment. This tendency was not arrested by the Counter-Reformation, for the Council of Trent had been primarily concerned with the mass, the words of which, being the largely unchanging core of the service, were of far greater spiritual importance than any motet text. In a sense, then, the Council's reforms underlined and widened the distinction that already existed between mass and motet composition. Even in the second half of the fifteenth century, and especially with Josquin, the mass was more dependent than the motet on purely musical devices, such as canon and cantus firmi; in the vast majority of cases canon was introduced as a *tour de force* or for climactic purposes, and the cantus firmi, which rarely have any connexion with the text of the mass, although they may connect it with a particular feast, were generally employed as a means of providing unity or as a compliment to a patron (see Part I, p. 203). This use of canon and cantus firmus thus differs on the one hand from the earlier Italian caccie, in which canon was originally and usually a natural outcome of the subject, as in Ex. 59, Part I, p. 162, and on the other from the fourteenth- and fifteenth-century motet, where the word or words of the borrowed chant frequently have a connexion with those of the upper parts, as in Ex. 52, Part I, p. 132.

The various types of sixteenth-century mass are much the same as in Josquin's day, but it will be as well to describe the most important ones again, beginning with the 'parody mass'. In this all the parts of a previously composed piece (motet, chanson, madrigal), either by the composer himself or someone else, are used as a basis; sometimes only the opening bars are selected and placed at the beginning of each movement of the mass, but more often the original is divided into sections and these, often altered, are spread throughout the mass, each being separated by passages of free composition. About three-quarters of the masses by Lassus and nearly half of those by Palestrina are parody masses, and this preponderance is typical of the century.

Almost as common as the parody technique is that which uses a single borrowed melody or cantus firmus. This is frequently paraphrased and usually placed in the tenor, but is sometimes shared by all the voices; the paraphrase is often so elaborate that the original melody is unrecognizable in performance. Another type has the cantus firmus in long notes in one voice in each movement, the other voices being quite independent; if the borrowed melody is a chant, the voice that sings it sometimes has the original words, which naturally results in bi-textualism, as in Palestrina's *Ecce sacerdos magnus* ('Behold the High Priest'), where, for example, in Kyrie I the treble sings the entire melody and words of the antiphon on which the mass is based, while at the same time the alto, tenor, and bass sing 'Kyrie eleison'. A number of masses of this simple cantus-firmus type are based on invented melodies, such as the notes of the hexachord (e.g. C, D, E, F, G, A), ascending and descending in various rhythmic guises, or solmisation syllables derived from a laudatory address to a patron, as in Josquin's *Missa Hercules Dux Ferrariae* (see Part I, Chapter 6, p. 203). Yet another type of cantus-firmus mass, where the melody may be paraphrased or simple, is that in which each movement is based on a different chant. Except for the type of mass in which the cantus firmus is invented, all the main melodies are either chants or secular songs, but the use of the latter became much less frequent in the latter part of the sixteenth century than in the fifteenth century, due mainly to the influence of the Counter-Reformation.

Thirdly, there are the comparatively small number of masses that are, as far as we can tell, freely invented, but it is likely that some of these are in fact based on secular pieces or tunes which composers, especially after the Council of Trent, did not want to divulge. For example, Palestrina's *Missa Quarta*, published in 1582, actually paraphrases the famous old secular song, *L'Homme armé*.

Lastly, there is the 'missa brevis' or 'short mass', which, as its name implies, takes less time to perform than the normal mass owing to its simpler, more contrapuntal style and predominantly syllabic underlay. In the cathedrals and larger churches it was sung on those days that were not feast days, the elaborate polyphonic mass being reserved for the latter occasions, but in the more modest establishments it was performed much more frequently. The missa brevis, in fact, increasingly tended to replace Gregorian chant, which in earlier centuries had always been sung on 'ordinary' days, and thus reflected the general decline of the traditional chant throughout the entire Catholic Church. Because of its simplicity, the missa brevis was greatly favoured during the Counter-Reformation.

All the above types of mass composition, except the parody, can be found in the motets of the period, but they play a far less important part. The reason is not so much that composers felt that the motet, being shorter and sung all of a piece, needed a unifying device less than the mass, in which all but the Kyrie and Gloria are separated by other sung or spoken items during the service, but that the latter with its greater length and division into five separate movements gave more scope for their skill in ornamenting or varying pre-existent material. The practice of basing a composition on a borrowed melody or a complete piece has sometimes been criticized on the grounds that it shows lack of melodic originality and inventive power, but as we observed in Part I (p. 38), this attitude is comparatively modern, and in any case cannot be used to distinguish, for example, the symphonies of Mozart or the fugues of Bach from those of their contemporaries, for both are largely composed of the melodic and harmonic clichés of their time, and what makes them superior is the way these clichés are placed in their context and developed. In fact, the history of music shows that, as a rule, it is not the distinctiveness of basic material, but the way it is handled that provides the yard-stick by which a composer is measured.

Another reason why the various cantus-firmus techniques were seldom used in the motet is that its length and the comparatively free choice of texts made it more susceptible to the influence of secular music, in which the expression of the words provide both variety and unity. Thus not only was there a growing tendency to choose texts of an emotional and dramatic nature, but word-painting, chromaticism, and other elements from the madrigal and chanson became increasingly used and, during the last quarter of the century, produced a class of composition, the 'spiritual madrigal', which in its religious sentiments, vernacular texts, and musical treatment is halfway between the purely sacred and the wholly secular.

The infiltration of secular elements into the motet naturally affected its style, and the distinction between mass and motet, in this respect already present to some extent with Josquin, grew more marked as the century progressed; thus the stylistic differences between masses and motets by any one composer who died before or shortly after the Council of Trent are less than in the case of most later composers.

Although Italy, through the brilliant development of the madrigal, was undeniably the greatest centre of secular music, despite the long tradition and excellent quality of the chanson in France, she was by no means so pre-eminent in the field of Catholic composition except, as we would expect, in sheer quantity. This sharing of the honours, so to speak, by Europe as a whole was a direct result of the international character of Catholicism, which enabled a composer of masses and motets to receive fame within his own country and outside it, whereas his reputation as a composer of secular music was, in most cases, a purely national one.

Of the first six leading composers of Catholic music after Josquin only one, Willaert, spent most of his life in Italy. The others were the Netherlanders Gombert and Clemens non Papa, both of whom worked mainly in France; the Spaniard Cristobal de Morales [*c.* 1500–1553], who lived in the land of his birth, apart from ten or eleven years at Rome; Senfl, a Swiss who, from the time he became a pupil of Isaac to his death, never moved outside Germany (though biographical details are sketchy); and, finally, the Englishman John Taverner [*c.* 1490 – 1545], who remained in his native country all his life.

Taverner's music, like that of his predecessors since Dunstable, is fifty years or so behind his Continental contemporaries in its infrequent use of imitation, long florid melismas, and strong modal flavour, but it is up-to-date in the predeliction for writing *a*5 and *a*6. Although he wrote some charming motets for smaller groups and in a simpler contrapuntal style, he is essentially a master of flowing line and complex texture, and the richness of his five- and six-part polyphony, admirably set off by contrasting sections for fewer voices, represents the culmination of a tradition stretching back to the Old Hall MS. Like most English composers before him, his masses include no Kyrie (for probably the same reason as that given in Part I, Chapter 6, p. 189) and omit certain passages in the Credo.

Compared to Taverner, all the other five composers mentioned above are 'progressive', but not all of them are superior in craftsmanship or musicianship. Gombert, for instance, who used pervading imitation as a structural principle far more consistently than did Josquin, and most of whose masses are based on the parody technique, which Taverner uses only once, is reminiscent of Ockeghem in his dislike of clear-cut phrases and contrasting groups of voices, but, like the latter, he avoids monotony by the wonderful variety of his rhythms. Artistically, however, he is no greater than Taverner, and the same applies to Clemens, whose style is much less interesting rhythmically than Gombert's, though it is more varied in its texture and expressive of the text; in fact, Clemens is one of the earliest composers in whose motets we can see the beginnings of secular influence, which is not surprising when we remember that he, together with Gombert, was one of the chief composers of French chansons. In this respect these two men differ markedly from Morales, who, like Taverner, wrote almost entirely sacred music, but the Spaniard is even more old-fashioned than the Englishman in his liking for bi-textualism, especially in his motets, and in the rigid way in which he usually treats his Gregorian cantus firmi. He is more 'modern', however, in that he does not restrict the cantus firmus to one voice at a time, as Taverner does, but shares it between all the voices. He also uses parody and pervading imitation. There is a somewhat austere flavour to much of Morales' music, and also a strength and power which give it a character quite distinct from and on the whole superior to the liturgical compositions of Taverner, Gombert, and Clemens. In complete contrast are the motets and masses of Senfl, in which the technical mastery imparted by his great teacher, Isaac, is frequently allied to a lyricism reminiscent of the south, a lyricism that may, indeed, have stemmed from Isaac's Italian pieces.

The greatest composer of this early group is Willaert, whose fame both as a creative artist and as a teacher enabled him to exert an influence far more potent than any of his contemporaries or indeed any other Renaissance composer. By grafting the imitative polyphony of northern Europe on to the chordal texture of Italy, and by stressing the importance of accurate word-setting, Willaert laid the stylistic foundations of almost the entire Catholic repertoire of the late Renaissance. As with the other composers discussed above, except Taverner, pervading imitation is the essential feature of Willaert's style, but he shows Italian influence in his greater harmonic clarity. This is particularly noticeable in his polychoral writing, a technique that, we repeat, he did not invent, for it was practised in Italy, where it may have originated, during the latter part of the fifteenth century, and in France during the early years of the sixteenth; but Willaert undoubtedly gave it a new lease of life and was thus largely responsible for its magnificent development by the Gabrielis, the elder of whom, it will be remembered, was his pupil.

The colour and brilliance achieved through the dramatic contrasts inherent in polychoral writing and the fact that a predominantly chordal texture is the most effective one in this style of composition, admirably suited the Italian genius, and at the same time satisfied the Council of Trent's demands for intelligibility of text. It also suited the emotional fervour of the Counter-Reformation, and all the leading composers of the Catholic revival favoured it to a greater or lesser extent, notably the man whose liturgical music is officially regarded by Catholics as second to none—Palestrina.

On Good Friday, 1555, Pope Marcellus II, who only reigned for three weeks, summoned the musicians of the Papal Choir; after criticizing the casual and even flippant way in which they sang the service, he instructed them to perform in future "with properly modulated voices, and so that everything could be both heard and understood properly".* This sentence implies what we already know from other sources, that the singers indulged in a certain amount of vocal improvisation, and also that the complexity of the music itself made the words unintelligible. Among the members of the Choir was the newly-elected Palestrina, who was so impressed by the Pope's earnestness and ideals that he composed a Mass which expressed these ideals, some time between 1555 and 1560 (i.e., before the Council of Trent's recommendations in 1562); this is the now famous *Missa Papae Marcelli*. The style of this fine work, in which counterpoint and syllabic underlay predominate more than was usual for the period, matched Marcellus' objective, but it was not composed in order to prevent the Council of Trent from banning all music but Gregorian chant in the performance of the mass, though Palestrina, along with Lassus, Kerle, and others, did in fact write 'demonstration' masses for the Council. If anyone deserves to be called the 'saviour of Catholic Church music' (a title once given to Palestrina owing to the erroneous belief mentioned above) it is the Fleming, Jacobus de Kerle [*c.* 1532–1591], who dedicated a collection of 'preces' or 'prayers' to the Council which were probably sung at the opening of each session during the last year the Council met, and undoubtedly influenced its decisions on liturgical music. In these pieces the style, while predominantly imitative and employing discreet chromaticism and word-painting, is essentially simple, and the words come through clearly. It is indeed typical of most of Kerle's output, whether composed in Italy or (later) in Germany and Prague, and he did much to spread its influence in the two latter places.

In many respects Kerle's style is similar to Palestrina's, but as the latter was regarded by most people of his own time and since as the greatest writer of Church music, whether Catholic or Protestant, the main features of his mature style must be mentioned. Virtually all these features are the result of the composer's attempts to achieve a perfect poise, to let nothing

* Quoted from H. Coates, *Palestrina*, p. 41.

obtrude or be given undue importance, whether in rhythm, melody, or harmony. Thus a run of crotchets is balanced by a succession of longer notes; the usual range of a melody is restricted to a tenth and is often no more than an octave; a movement upwards or downwards, whether by one or two leaps or by a series of steps, is followed by a movement in the opposite direction; a weak crotchet, i.e. the second one in a minim, is rarely approached or quitted by more than a step above its neighbours, for this would make too prominent a note that rhythmically is very unimportant; leaps of augmented or diminished intervals are avoided, as are major sixths, all sevenths, and ninths; no dissonance is longer than a minim, and this is nearly always prepared, suspended, and resolved, the resolution being a step down; the most common passing dissonance is an unaccented crotchet approached and quitted by a step; remote modulations or chromatic changes of chord are avoided. These details of Palestrina's technique, while not invariable, are typical of his mature style, and, compared to that of Josquin, they represent the culmination of a refining process that had been going on in the intervening years, and one that can be seen, for instance, in the style of Gombert and Clemens. No one, however, carried this process quite so far as Palestrina, and it must always be remembered that in this he was not typical of his generation, for although he could not fully escape the influence of the madrigal, he did so to a greater extent than any of his contemporaries. Neither is he typical in the numerical relationship between his masses on the one hand and his motets and other allied works on the other, and the fact that he is at his greatest in the former is not surprising, because, as we have already seen, the mass by its very nature—and particularly after the Council of Trent—was a much more suitable mould in which to pour music so restricted in style and emotion. But this does not mean that his music lacks emotion; Palestrina was no ascetic who shut himself off from his fellow-men and composed in an aura of holiness, for he combined a warm heart and affectionate nature with a shrewd business head. Furthermore, he composed a sizeable number of madrigals which differ little in style from his liturgical pieces, and he was quite capable of a little hypocrisy if it suited his book, as when, in dedicating some masses to a Pope, he bewails the popularity of secular music, but produces another book of madrigals shortly afterwards. He even flouted the Council by using secular models for several of his masses, one of the last being based on his own famous madrigal, *Vestiva i colli.*

Whether or not he was and still is, as many people think, the greatest composer of Church music depends on what you demand from such music; if you believe that the composer should become as impersonal in this particular branch of his art as the priest at the altar, then Palestrina takes the palm, but if you believe that, given the same sincerity and a comparable technical mastery, individuality, however striking, has a place in worship, then other composers will appeal more. But whatever your view, it must be admitted that his style, while occasionally resulting in a monotony due to the limitations that were an integral part of his artistic outlook, at its best produced music which, because of these very limitations, is unique in the flawlessness of its execution, the perfect poise of its rhythmic and melodic elements, and the delicate sensuousness of its harmony. In rhythm, melody, and harmony Palestrina was conservative, but in his feeling for and delight in pure sound (abundantly evident in his part-writing, which is frequently adjusted so as to produce full triads), in his vocal orchestration, and in the number of his polychoral pieces with their predominantly chordal texture, he was a 'modern'.

In placing purely musical considerations before those of the words he was setting, Palestrina, even in his motets, is much closer to the north European tradition than is his Netherlandish contemporary, Lassus, who spent the last thirty-eight years of his life at Munich and who, to complete the paradox, was the more Italianate of the two. This being so, we should expect the latter to favour and excel in motet composition, which is indeed the case, and although his masses do not compare with Palestrina's, his motets are quite definitely superior. The versatility that he shows in general is also evident in the treatment and selection of his motet texts. Detailed word-painting, abrupt changes of rhythm, declamatory passages, and chromaticism all show the influence of the madrigal and to a lesser extent the chanson. But these by themselves are merely means to an end, and it is in the superb quality and richness of his imagination that Lassus' greatness lies, an imagination that constantly needed new texts, preferably of an emotional or dramatic nature, to set it fully alight, and although he ranged successfully over the entire field of sacred and secular vocal music, it is in the motet and its allied type, the spiritual madrigal, that we find him at his greatest. This is particularly true of his later works, for the missionary zeal of the Counter-Reformation appealed to the introspective side of his personality and affected him more profoundly perhaps than any of his contemporaries. The result was a series of works of a predominantly penitent character of which the best, in their superb technique, emotional depth, and rich expressiveness, are among the greatest contributions to our musical treasure house, notably the 'Penitential Psalms' (1563–70), the 'Lamentations' (1585), and the two books of 'Spiritual Madrigals' (1585 and 1587).

Comparing the merits of two composers is often a profitless occupation, but when one has received less than his due share, both in literature and performance, it becomes necessary, and although this is clearly not the place to give a detailed critical assessment of Palestrina and Lassus, it must be pointed out that the centuries-old veneration accorded to the former, especially and quite rightly in view of his masses, by the Catholic Church, should not blind us to the greatness of the latter. The flawless execution of worthwhile ideas will always rank high in any art, but the ideas themselves, man being what he is, will always be somewhat limited in their extent and depth. Conversely, a wide and profound emotional range will never be presented with the same utter perfection, for although practice may indeed make perfect, that which is practised must be restricted in scope. Of the perfection of Palestrina's music there is no question, and the mere versatility and increased range of expression of Lassus's output cannot of itself equal this, but when to this versatility and expressive range is added Lassus's superb technique, then there can be little, if any, doubt that he is at least equal in stature to his great Italian contemporary.

Byrd has sometimes been called 'the English Palestrina', but this is a complete misnomer, for he is much more akin to Lassus in his style, in his preference for the motet rather than the mass, and in his versatility, and while he cannot compete with the Netherlander in the variety of his secular music, he far outstrips him in the instrumental field. But Byrd's versatile artistic temperament was almost certainly not the only reason why he wrote only three masses and over 230 motets (a higher ratio than any other major Catholic composer) for he could hardly help being profoundly affected by the Reformation in England (see p. 312). This can be conveniently dated as beginning in 1529, when Henry VIII summoned the so-called 'Reformation Parliament' which five years later dutifully passed the Act of Supremacy establishing Henry as the supreme head of the English Church and putting the final seal on his break with Rome. But the Church itself remained much the same as before because Henry was suspicious of the democratic character of Lutheranism and, being a dictator, disliked its deliberate dissociation from politics, but he could not prevent the infiltration of Lutheran ideas which, during the reign of Edward VI [1547–1553], became clearly evident in the first Book of Common Prayer (1549), but much more so in the second (1552). The changes in the service, notably the replacing of Latin by English, which these Prayer Books introduced did not reflect the temper of the country as a whole, and when Catholicism reasserted itself under Mary [reigned 1553–1558] there was no violent protest. Mary, however, went too far, and by condemning to the stake some of the leading reformers she fanned the embers of a reaction against Catholicism—embers that were already aglow as a result of her unpopular marriage to the fanatical papist Philip II of Spain [reigned 1556–1598]. This reaction increased sharply on the accession of Elizabeth I, mainly owing to the return of those who, in order to escape 'Bloody Mary', had fled to the Continent and had there come under the influence of Calvinism. This, a much stricter and simpler form of Protestantism than Lutheranism, was founded at Geneva by a Frenchman, Jean Calvin [1509–1564], who viewed liturgical ceremony with suspicion, banned elaborate ritual, and replaced, as did Luther, the infallibility of the Pope by the infallibility of the Bible. To the returning English exiles from Geneva the Prayer Book (which was and still is largely a translated adaptation of the Catholic service) reeked of popery, and anti-Catholic feeling, gathering force throughout the succeeding eighty years and aggravated by the tactlessness and arrogance of James I and the stubborness and incompetence of Charles I, eventually burst into the flames of civil war.

But, despite the Puritans, as they were called, not only was the Prayer Book accepted by the majority of Englishmen during Elizabeth's reign, but even Catholics suffered little persecution;

indeed, Byrd, who remained a Catholic all his life, spent the whole of his adulthood in the service of the Anglican Church, being appointed organist at Lincoln Cathedral when he was only twenty and remaining there until, in 1572, he left to share a similar post at the Chapel Royal with his renowned teacher, Thomas Tallis [*c.* 1505–1585]. In 1575 Tallis and Byrd were granted a virtual monopoly of all music-printing for twenty-one years; later, after a gap of two years, the monopoly transferred to Morley for a similar period. In the same year the two men jointly published a collection of motets, other collections by Byrd alone following in 1589, 1591, 1605, and 1607. All these have the printer's name and date on the title-page, but the three masses, *a*3, *a*4, and *a*5, have not, and we can only guess their dates of composition (*c.* 1600) from stylistic features and one or two other clues. They are all similar in style, are freely composed, contain the normal five movements, and use the old 'head motive' technique as a means of binding together some of the movements. That Byrd wrote and published no more than three masses, that the printer's name is omitted from these, that he composed and published no Latin music at all during the last sixteen years of his life (the forty-four motets that remained in manuscript were all written before *c.* 1590), may well be explained by the growing influence of Puritanism, for while the motets were probably composed for those who still privately practised their old faith, though necessarily in a much restricted manner, and could only have been objected to on the grounds that their texts are in Latin, and that some of them are addressed to the Virgin Mary or the saints, the mass, apart from needing full ceremonial for its performance, also represents the very core of the Catholic liturgy, and would therefore have been much more offensive to the authorities and hence riskier to publish.

In his motets, and indeed in his vocal output as a whole, Byrd is the exact opposite of Lassus in one rather interesting respect, for while the latter increasingly favoured texts of a penitential, meditative nature in his sacred music, and of a serious, even religious bias in his secular, Byrd became progressively more cheerful in both. Furthermore, his later works, i.e. those issued in 1605, 1607, and 1611, reveal some important differences compared to his earlier ones. Between 1591 and 1605 Byrd published nothing, but during this period over half the total output of the English Madrigal School was published. Byrd could hardly have escaped being influenced by this rush of native secular composition; at any rate, the important differences mentioned above can most satisfactorily be explained as being due to secular influence. Thus, compared to his earlier works, his later are scored for higher voices, with the soprano part usually doubled instead of the alto or tenor in five- and six-part pieces, reflecting the trend in Italian music noted earlier. Similarly, the phrases are shorter, words are repeated less often, and word-painting is more frequent, and it is worth noting in this connexion the similarity in approach between the quotation from the title-page of his 1611 book (see p. 281) and the following excerpt from his Latin dedication of 1605: "there is a certain hidden power, as I learnt by experience, in the thoughts underlying the words themselves; so that, as one meditates upon the sacred words, the right notes, in some inexplicable manner, suggest themselves quite spontaneously".* Another distinction between his earlier and later works is the fact that nearly all the motets constructed on the old plan of a cantus firmus in long notes in one of the parts were written before 1591. In all these respects Byrd was a 'modern', but in his tonal feeling he was not, and in his treatment of discord he was often unorthodox. As regards the first, a point of imitation, say in the 'key' of F, which begins with a leap up from the tonic to the dominant (F–C), is more likely to be answered with another fifth (C–G) than with the fourth (C–F). The former is called a 'real' answer because it imitates exactly, and the latter is called a 'tonal' answer because it helps to define the tonality of the piece.

Byrd's treatment of discord is more difficult to place in perspective because in the latter half of the sixteenth century there were two opposing trends, especially in Italy, one contracting, the other expanding, as it were. The first, more typical of sacred than secular music, shows an increasing refinement in the use of discord and reached perfection in Palestrina's mature work; it also reached a dead-end, for perfection cannot be developed. The second, starting from the same point as the first—namely, the careful approach to and departure from a discord—shows a growing freedom of treatment for expressive purposes and reached its peak in the

* E. H. Fellowes, *William Byrd*, 1936, p. 83.

madrigals of Gesualdo and Monteverdi and the motets of Giovanni Gabrieli. Now, Byrd's use of discord, while much freer than Palestrina's, is not in the main employed as a means of greater expression, but is usually the result of either exuberant part-writing, where the individual lines matter more than their combination, or else of a definite liking for the actual sound of the discords.

That Byrd was fully aware of the unusual sound of some of the passages he wrote we can be sure, for in 'The Epistle to the Reader' of his 1588 book he particularly draws attention to the fact that "if ther happen to be any jarre or dissonance, blame not the Printer, who (I doe assure thee) through his great paines and diligence doth heere deliver to thee a perfect and true Coppie". If his unorthodox use of dissonance was deliberate in 1588, it was obviously intentional in his later works. Thus in Ex. 14 the exposed weak quaver (crotchet in the original) of the point of imitation, e.g. the second quaver in bar 1—which in itself is very untypical of Palestrina style—is sometimes concordant, but sometimes, owing to the melodic line of the other parts and also to chordal considerations, is treated as a freely quitted discord (bars 2, 3, 4; this treatment of a discord is now called 'échappée'). In the tenor part in bar 3 and, more strikingly because the point is augmented, in bar 6 the discord is the dominant seventh; Byrd, in fact, was very fond of the unprepared (usually dominant) seventh, and at cadences often leaps up to it from the fifth of the dominant chord. In the penultimate bar is one form of the so-called 'English cadence' in which the essential feature is a normal suspension coupled with false-relation; in this case F♮ in one part followed immediately by F♯ in another. Byrd clearly liked false-relations, and they occur in his work more frequently than in any of his compatriots, not only successively, as in the above cadence, but simultaneously, e.g. *g″–f*♯*″–g″* in the soprano against *e′–f*♮*′–e′* in the alto. It must be remembered, however, that such clashes sound more dissonant when played on the piano than when sung, for not only are voices non-percussive instruments, but the actual interval is different, being larger and less harsh owing to the fact that, in the instance given above, the *f*♯*″* is, or should be much nearer to *g″* and the *f*♮*′* much nearer to *e′* than on the equally tempered piano (Ex. 14,* opposite).

* From *The Collected Vocal Works of William Byrd*, ed. Fellowes, Vol. V, p. 18.

Ex. 14 The end of the motet—*Sacerdotes Domini* (*Gradualia*, 1605) Byrd

It may well be that Byrd's treatment of discord was the result of his fondness for instrumental composition, because not only was he much more versatile and prolific in this field than any other major composer of vocal music, either of his time or before it, but by far the greater proportion of his pieces are for the virginal or spinet, a name originally given to a small harpsichord but, which by Byrd's day often included the normal-sized instrument as well. Now, it is a fact that every composer of keyboard music (excluding that for the organ, but including the piano repertoire) uses discords with greater freedom than when he is writing for voices, and while Byrd's virginal pieces, compared to those by other composers of his day, are not exceptional in their freer use of discord, it is more than likely that, because they occupy such a comparatively large place in his total output, this particular feature affected his vocal music to a greater extent than with other composers. This is truer of his Catholic than of his Anglican works as many of the latter are chordal in texture and this is less naturally suited to discord than polyphony (see pp. 314, 331).

The expressive range and technical mastery of Byrd's Latin Church music reveal him as an outstanding creative artist, and the quality and variety of his inspiration is as apparent in his Mass for Three Voices and his three-part motets as it is in his Mass *a*5 and his motets for five and six voices. Indeed, if he had written nothing else, his compositions for the Catholic liturgy would place him high in the ranks of late Renaissance composers.

There was in fact one great composer of the late Renaissance who wrote nothing else but liturgical music, the Spaniard Tomás Luis de Victoria [1548–1611]. That he was an ordained priest of the Catholic Church does not explain his exclusive preoccupation with sacred music, for a number of clerics (like Cardinal Bembo) wrote madrigal texts, or (like Gastoldi) composed secular music. The explanation lies partly in the man's make-up and partly in the religious atmosphere of Spain, the country least affected by the secular humanistic influence of the Renaissance or the heresies of the Reformation. Moreover, as we mentioned earlier, it was Spanish fervour rather than the decisions of the Council of Trent that gave to the Counter-Reformation something of the old Crusading spirit, and in the missionary zeal, high intelligence, and devotion to duty of the Jesuits, a religious society founded in 1534 by the Spaniard Ignatius Loyola [1495?–1536] and predominantly Spanish in its early years, the Church found a powerful weapon with which to combat her enemies.

It was Spanish fervour too that revived the ecclesiastical court known as the Inquisition during the reign of Ferdinand and Isabella in order to put a check on the number of Jews and Moors who were adopting Christianity for purely social and political reasons. This institution was first organized in 1231 as a means of converting or, failing this, punishing heretics, but by the early fifteenth century it had almost entirely ceased to function, and while Ferdinand and Isabella's use of it was perfectly orthodox and correct, it was disgracefully abused later on, particularly under the fanatical Philip II, who married Mary Tudor, and whose 'crusade' against Protestant England in 1588 failed so completely and ignominiously. Philip's religious fanaticism, the largely Spanish Jesuit movement, and the new monastic flowering initiated by Teresa of Avila [1515–1582]—one of the most remarkable women in history—and her younger disciple, John of the Cross [1542–1591]—one of the greatest of Christian mystics—all contributed to make Spain the spiritual centre of the Counter-Reformation. Small wonder that Protestantism could gain no foothold nor secular music flourish in such an atmosphere; small wonder also that Victoria more than any of his countrymen reflected this in his output, for while his devotion to Catholicism was a national characteristic, it was more strongly developed in him than usual because, firstly, he was, like St. Teresa, a Castilian, a race whose pride, tenacity, and passion made them the most powerful in the Peninsula, and, secondly, he was not only probably influenced by Teresa's monastic order (the first convent of which was founded at Avila in 1562), but certainly affected by the Jesuit movement, for during most of the period he spent in Rome between 1565 and 1584 (where he may well have studied under Palestrina) he was a member and later chapel master of the Collegium Germanicum, an institution founded by Loyola to combat Lutheranism.

Whether or no Victoria was taught by Palestrina, he could hardly have helped being influenced by so famous a master, but while the high proportion of masses to motets is common to both men, this was also typical of Spanish but not of Italian Church composers in general, and reflects the different religious outlook of the two countries; so does the fact that not one of Victoria's masses is based on secular material. Moreover, his style, while lying closer to that of the great Italian than does Byrd's, is distinctive in its emotional and dramatic, even ecstatic, qualities, his melodic line is freer, the contrasts of rhythm and texture more pronounced, and there is a greater preoccupation with the purely chordal side. This last feature, indeed, may well have influenced the older man, whose later works show an increasing delight in homophony as opposed to polyphony; if this is true, then Palestrina was like Haydn, for both gave to and received from their younger and more emotionally profound contemporary.

Despite the fact that Victoria composed no secular or instrumental music and to this extent was not of his time, he is completely 'modern' in both his style and in his fondness for polychoral writing, and of his comparatively small output nearly a sixth (excluding the masses) are for two or three choirs. A few of these, published in 1600, have a written-out organ accompaniment which is simply a reduction of the music for Chorus I, and when that chorus rests so does the instrument. This feature was not essentially new, for although the provision of a complete accompaniment was rare at the time the practice of extemporizing on the organ from a bass part was fairly common. This bass part, called 'basso seguente' ('following bass'), was not necessarily the same as the vocal bass, but consisted of the lowest note at any given point, which in fact might be sung by a tenor or even an alto. A new step, and one which provides a link with baroque practice, was taken by an Italian, Ludovico Grossi da Viadana [*c.* 1560–1627], who, in 1602, published a collection of motets with an organ bass (later called 'basso continuo') that is frequently different from the lowest given part and is hence, unlike the basso seguente, essential from the harmonic point of view.

Independent instrumental accompaniments in fact were coming increasingly to the fore. We have already mentioned, in the previous chapter, the elaborate keyboard parts of Luzzaschi's madrigals for the three ladies of Mantua, but these pale before Giovanni Gabrieli's sumptuous polychoral motets, some of which have an orchestral accompaniment. Giovanni learnt much from his uncle Andrea, but he surpassed the older man, and indeed all others of his time or before it, in the brilliance of his tonal colours achieved through the blending of many voices and instruments, and in his dramatic handling of vocal groups, with or without instrumental accompaniment. It was natural that the full splendour of Giovanni's style should be revealed in his motets rather than his madrigals, because most of the latter, with their word-painting, intimate character, and basically polyphonic texture, did not favour the broad, clearly defined washes of sound and the essentially contrapuntal texture which are so typical of his mature work. Moreover, such music, especially when the voices are divided into two, three, or even four separate choirs, is only fully effective in a large hall, which in those days generally meant a church.

It is in his later motets, probably composed after 1600, that Giovanni's genius is shown at its height. Polychoral compositions abound, ranging from two choirs *a*4 to four choirs *a*4, as well as 'normal' pieces written for anything up to twenty voices. In some of these, contrary to general practice, the accompanying instruments are specifically mentioned, and include violini piccolo (violins), violini (violas), bass viols, cornetts (see Part I, p. 68), bassoons, and trombones. In one piece, *Suscipe clementissime*, a six-part chorus is contrasted with an ensemble of six trombones; another, *In Ecclesiis*, his most brilliant work, calls for two four-part choirs, a quartet of soloists, an organ, and an orchestra scored for violas, three cornetts, and two trombones. Only the bass of the organ part is given, and most of the time it is accompanying one or more solo voices, thus providing the harmonic foundation (basso continuo); the other instrumental parts are either quite different from the vocal solos or choruses they support, or else double the voices at the octave, a completely new idea and one doubtless suggested by those organ stops which combine the principal note with its octave or double octave, above or below. Particularly noteworthy is the distinction in style between orchestral and vocal writing, and also that between soloists and chorus.

With Giovanni Gabrieli, as with Viadana, we are on the threshold of baroque style, and although the greater of the two, Gabrieli, considerably enriched the expressive technique of his age, what he expressed in his sacred works does not rank him much, if at all, above some of his more orthodox contemporaries, for it must be remembered that almost every composer of any consequence, whether Protestant or Catholic, wrote fine music for his Church. Apart from those already mentioned, the chief figures in Catholic music were Monte, whose motets rank near to those of Lassus; Felice Anerio [*c.* 1564–1614], who most closely approaches Palestrina in purity of style; Andrea Gabrieli; the Spaniard, Francisco Guerrero [1528–1599], whose gentle lyricism found its natural inspiration in texts praising or supplicating the Virgin Mary; the Englishman, Thomas Tallis, who, despite a formidable technique that enabled him to write a fine motet for eight five-part choirs (*Spem in alium*) and a number of other pieces which are magnificent in their rich sonority and rhythmic interplay, is old-fashioned stylistically, but who could on occasion compose in a charmingly simple vein; Giovanni Animuccia [d. 1571], chiefly famous for his spiritual songs written for the Congregation of the Oratory, an organization founded by a priest, Filippo Neri [1515–1595], in 1544, who, in his desire to make religion attractive to the young, combined sermons and Bible readings with suitable musical and theatrical entertainments, an idea that eventually developed into the oratorio; Jan Pieterzoon Sweelinck [1562–1621], the last of the Netherlanders, who set in motet style the complete French Psalter in addition to writing Latin motets and chansons, but whose keyboard music, which we shall discuss later, is of greater importance; and, lastly, the Frenchman, Claude Goudimel, whose works are typically French in their simplicity, melodic brevity, clear-cut phrases, and predominantly syllabic underlay.

Goudimel is more famous, however, for his settings of the psalm-tunes in the Genevan Psalter. The tunes themselves were so popular that they were sung not only by Protestants, but by Catholics as well, until forbidden by Papal decree, and Goudimel's settings were written both before and after his conversion to Protestantism, *c.* 1560. The texts of the Psalter are in French metrical verse, selected and, in a few cases, translated by Calvin, the majority being translated by the most fashionable poet of the time, Clément Marot [1497–1544]. In accord with his strict religious outlook, already mentioned, Calvin, unlike Luther, insisted on the psalms being sung to simple, unharmonized tunes of a devout character, and it is ironical therefore to find that far more of these are based on secular models than is the case with Lutheran melodies. The man most responsible for these unadorned settings was Louis Bourgeois [*c.* 1510–*c.* 1561], who, although dying before the complete Psalter was published in 1562, composed or adapted two-thirds of the total of 125 psalm-tunes.

But even Calvin could not prevent the widespread popularity of part-music from invading psalm-singing, and while Bourgeois himself set some of the tunes for four voices, and a number of other composers, including Janequin, le Jeune, and Mauduit, did likewise, it was Goudimel who really established the practice, for he not only published, between 1551 and 1566, a number of fairly elaborate polyphonic settings of the psalm-tunes, but in 1564 and 1565 issued two harmonizations of the complete Genevan Psalter. The 1564 book is in simple motet style, while that of 1565 is in hymn-tune style; in the former most of the tunes are, for the first time in any psalter, placed in the soprano rather than in the usual tenor voice, but in the 1565 edition the traditional role of the tenor is re-established. This latter edition, which Goudimel specifically intended for home use, became so popular that it was reissued many times during the next 200 years; moreover, practically every psalter during this period, no matter what the language, included a generous selection of his settings.

Although the Reformation quickly found a foothold in France, it was far more bitterly contested than in Germany, and persecution under Francis I [reigned 1515–1547] and Henry II was severe, the latter monarch ordaining in the year he died that heretics should be executed. This was revoked three years later, but was followed almost immediately by the massacre of Vassy in 1562, and from this date until the accession of Henry IV in 1589 religious war was more or less continuous, the worst incident occurring on St. Bartholomew's Day (24th August) 1572, when about 3,000 French Protestants, or Huguenots, as they were called, were murdered. But persecution, as usually happens, only served to increase the ardour and influence of the persecuted, and Henry IV, who had reverted to Catholicism in order to be crowned, was obliged in 1598 to sign the Edict of Nantes, which gave his former co-religionists freedom to worship as they pleased and admission to all employment.

In the Netherlands the Reformation had an even longer and bloodier struggle to establish itself than in France, for while they, like Germany, were affected by the imperial ban of Charles V, they alone had to suffer the domination of Spanish fanaticism, particularly during the reign of Charles' son, Philip II, to whom his father left this part of his Empire, the rest going to his brother Ferdinand. For nearly 100 years from Philip's accession the Netherlands were torn by civil war between Catholics and Protestants or by bitter strife against Spanish imperialism. These terrible years probably explain the dearth of native psalters, for, apart from the monophonic *Souterliedekens* ('Little Psalter Songs'), published at Antwerp in 1540, which Clemens later set for three voices, virtually no Protestant music was produced. The 1540 print, however, became so popular that over thirty editions appeared during the next seventy years. It differs from the Genevan Psalter in that the Dutch texts are anonymous verse translations, probably by an amateur or amateurs, which were more or less forced to fit popular tunes and folk songs, and, moreover, was intended for use in the home, not in church. Clemens' settings, like Goudimel's 1565 edition, place the main melody in the tenor far more often than in the soprano.

Compared with Germany, France, and the Netherlands, England had an almost bloodless religious revolution, partly because her two most influential rulers, Henry VIII and Elizabeth

I, pursued a course somewhere between Lutheranism and Catholicism, Henry veering more closely to the latter than his daughter, and partly because of the geographical position and natural conservatism to new ideas of the English, who have always been less extremist on the whole than other nations. So far as the Reformation is concerned, the English genius for compromise resulted in a way of worship that retained the general structure of the Catholic liturgy on the one hand (which that of the Calvinists and Huguenots did not) and on the other expressly forbade, from 1549 on, the use of Latin (optional in the Lutheran Church). Thus the English Church, in replacing the mass by the Anglican service and the motet by the anthem, encouraged Protestant musical composition more than anywhere else except Germany, but the restriction to the English language, while it led to a more unified and, possibly because of this, a finer body of music than in the latter country, also presented composers with a problem of style.

The chief distinction in sound, and therefore the one that most affects music, between Latin and English is that in the former vowels are more frequent and more important than consonants. In other words, Latin is the more sonorous language and, as a result, is more suitable for melismatic writing, and it is tempting to speculate how Catholic music, from chant to polyphony, would have been affected if it had been based on a less sonorous language. Admittedly, French and German also stress consonants more than vowels, and this is reflected in the greater degree of syllabic underlay in the Protestant music of these two countries, but in neither country were composers urged to set "as near as may be for every syllable a note", as were their English brethren. The quotation comes from a letter to Henry VIII by the Archbishop of Canterbury, Thomas Cranmer [1489–1556], and was written in 1545, the year after the first English Litany appeared. It does not, as is sometimes claimed, refer to the Litany (although this too was Cranmer's work), but to the translations of certain special chants sung in procession on Sundays and feast days. In these, and in the Litany, the traditional Gregorian chant is so adapted that there is only one note to each syllable, and though in the letter there is no suggestion of enforcing this on all compositions for the Church, there most certainly is in the Royal Injunctions of Edward VI to Lincoln Cathedral issued three years later which, among other things, order that the service must be sung in English and that settings must be to a "plain and distinct note, for every syllable one". The same document also forbids the singing of anthems to the Virgin Mary or to the saints, and recommends that the best Latin motets be adapted to English use with their texts translated or, if unsuitable, replaced. A number of such adaptations dating from the 1540s or earlier, some by the composers themselves, have fortunately survived; these include masses as well as motets and make it clear that several years before the first Prayer Book of 1549—indeed, probably before 1536, when each church had to have a copy of the 'Great Bible', as this particular translation was called—the service was being said and sung in the vernacular, though the precise details of its performance must have varied from place to place, as those who opposed the Reformation would continue to use Latin. This lack of uniformity ended with the publication of the first Prayer Book, for which Cranmer was responsible; with it the Anglican Church became Protestant and a new order of service was laid down which has remained essentially unaltered to this day.

The Anglican service is divided into three main parts, Morning Prayer, Evening Prayer, and Communion. The first two parts are condensed from the Catholic offices or Canonical Hours and the third from the Catholic mass, the Latin titles of the various sections within each part being retained. (In the following discussion only those portions of the service which may properly be set to music are mentioned.) In 1549 Morning Prayer consisted of 'Venite exultemus Domino' ('O come, let us sing unto the Lord'), 'Te Deum laudamus' ('We praise Thee, O God'), and 'Benedictus es Dominus Deus Israel' ('Blessed be the Lord God of Israel'); Evening Prayer of 'Magnificat anima mea Dominus' ('My soul doth magnify the Lord') and 'Nunc dimittis servum tuum Domine . . . in pace' ('Lord, now lettest Thou thy servant depart in peace'); Communion of 'Kyrie eleison, Christe eleison, Kyrie eleison', 'Gloria', 'Credo', 'Sanctus', 'Benedictus qui venit in nomine Domini' ('Blessed is he that cometh in the name of the Lord'), 'Agnus Dei', and various passages from the Bible called 'post-Communions'. Apart from these last, the Communion service was identical in structure with that of the mass, as can be seen by comparing the above with Part I, p. 9. (Note that the Benedictus in the mass is not a separate movement, but is the second part of the Sanctus.) In the following year (1550) the parts of the Prayer Book given above were adapted by John Marbeck [*c.* 1510–*c.* 1585] to various chants drawn from the Gregorian repertoire, pruned so that there is only one note to a syllable, and published under the title, *The Booke of Common Praier noted*—the first musical setting of the English liturgy (see Plate XXI). Apart from the chants to the versicles and responses in Morning and Evening Prayer, which were used in most later harmonized versions from Tallis's famous set onwards, the music was soon forgotten because this version of the Prayer Book became obsolete with the introduction of the second Prayer Book in 1552, and in any case there was a growing demand for part-music. The 1552 Prayer Book reflects the growing influence of Continental Protestantism on the Anglican leaders, especially Cranmer, and the chief alterations occur, as we should expect, in the Communion service, for in the 1549 book this part of the liturgy most closely resembles its Catholic counterpart, the mass. Thus the three-fold Kyrie is replaced by the response, 'Lord have mercy upon us . . . ., to each of the Ten Commandments, the Gloria, Credo, and Sanctus are kept intact, but the first is placed much later in the service, while the Benedictus, Agnus Dei, and 'post-Communions' disappear entirely. In Morning and Evening Prayer no changes were made, except to add alternatives to the Te Deum, Benedictus, Magnificat, and Nunc Dimittis—namely, 'Benedicite omnia opera Domini Domino' ('O all ye works of the Lord, bless ye the Lord'), 'Jubilate Deo' ('O be joyful in the Lord'), 'Cantate Domino' ('O sing unto the Lord'), and 'Deus misereatur nostri' ('God be merciful unto us') respectively.

From the musical point of view the arrangement of the 1552 Prayer Book is retained in the later versions of 1559 and 1662, but the treatment of individual items varied considerably. For example, up to the Restoration (1660) the Venite was usually set, but the alternatives in Morning and Evening Prayer and the Sanctus and Gloria in the Communion service were almost invariably chanted, while from the Restoration on the Venite was usually chanted and all or some of the Morning and Evening Prayer, together with the Sanctus, was composed.

The effect of all these changes on mid-sixteenth-century composers was naturally very disturbing, for they had to contend not only with the switch from the Catholic mass to the Anglican Service,* but also with the differences between the first two Prayer Books. Moreover, the recommendation, which later became law, that only English be used, and that the flowing melismas and pervading imitation typical of the motet and mass be replaced by predominantly syllabic underlay and chordal texture, necessitated a far more abrupt change of style than that required by either the Counter-Reformation or Luther. It is not surprising, therefore, to find that most of the music composed for the new Church during its early years is distinctly inferior to previous or contemporary Latin compositions, nor that the anthem was preferred to the Service, for although the latter had a much greater chance of frequent performance than the former because the words were sung daily, its strong Catholic flavour probably proved embarrassing to those who still had leanings towards the older faith and objectionable to the Protestant-minded, whereas the anthem was more specifically Anglican in that its text rejected all references to the Virgin Mary and the saints and, moreover, like the motet, reflected the general tendency already noted by providing a greater freedom of choice in the words to be set compared to the invariable texts of the Service. The anthem in fact was, and is, the most characteristic musical feature of the Anglican Service, for nothing like it developed on the Continent.

Of the leading composers before Byrd who are represented either by original contributions or adaptations, the earliest is Taverner, two of whose masses, rather unskilfully adapted to English words, are found in the so-called 'Wanley MS.' This manuscript contains eight other masses in addition to Taverner's two, a few items for Morning and Evening Prayer, and almost 100 anthems, all to English words; the masses could, therefore, have been used for the full Communion service of 1549, and were almost certainly used after 1552, pruned of the altered or rejected items. Two of the anthems in this MS. are original pieces by Tallis, whose output for the Anglican Church includes fifteen similar compositions, together with nine adapted from his motets, several psalms, an isolated Te Deum (*c.* 1547), and two Services, of which the only one to survive complete, entitled 'short', follows the order of the

* Service with a capital 'S' denotes the setting to part-music of all or some of the appropriate items from Morning and Evening Prayer and the Communion Service.

second Prayer Book, but the fact that it includes settings of the Sanctus and Gloria makes it fairly certain that it, like the Te Deum, was composed before 1552. The term 'short' was frequently used by composers up to the early seventeenth century to indicate a mainly syllabic setting of the text as opposed to 'great' or occasionally 'high', in which the music is more elaborate, as in Tallis's Te Deum, for the mere preference of authority (Cranmer) for a syllable per note was clearly not sufficient cause for composers to abandon entirely the riches of polyphony—the subtle interplay of contrasting rhythms, the complex imitative web, the flowing melodic lines—and during the latter half of the century not only Services but anthems too became increasingly more elaborate, though because of the nature of the language they never became as florid as their Catholic counterparts.

Three of Tallis's anthems were included in the first printed collection of part-music for the Anglican service, i.e. *Certaine notes set forthe in foure and three partes, to be sung at the Mornyng Communion and Evenyng Praier*, by John Day [1522–1584], one of the earliest and most important printers of music in England. The first edition appeared in 1560 and contains twenty anthems and two Services, both the latter including settings of the Sanctus and Gloria. This, together with the fact that a number of the anthems were certainly written prior to Mary's reign, makes it likely that the remainder of the pieces were also. The book was evidently popular enough to warrant a second edition in 1565, and this remained the only printed collection intended specifically for the Anglican service for nearly eighty years. Even if we include Byrd's publications of 1588 and 1589 and a few other similar works, the number of printed anthems (which, like motets, are, strictly speaking, non-liturgical) was extremely small. We shall give the probable reason for this when we discuss the English Psalter.

To the ordinary church-goer Tallis is best known through his Preces and Responses, and the two tunes associated with the hymns 'Glory to Thee, my God, this night' and 'O Holy Spirit, Lord of Grace'. The Responses, like those of later composers, are based on the melodies to which they are set in *The Booke of Common Praier noted*, while the 'hymn-tunes' are two of nine originally written for *The whole Psalter translated into English metre* (1567), by Matthew Parker [1504–1575],

Elizabeth's first Archbishop of Canterbury. This was not the first metrical psalter in English nor even the first complete one; indeed, the fact that it never came into general use is probably explained by the enormous popularity of an earlier publication, *The Whole Booke of Psalmes* (1562), based mainly on the metrical translations of Thomas Sternhold [*c.* 1500–1549] and John Hopkins [d. 1570] and printed, as was Parker's version, by John Day. Even before this a complete metrical translation by the printer Robert Crowley entitled *The Psalter of David* had appeared in 1549. This contains a simple four-part setting to which all the psalms were to be sung, and is not only the first complete metrical psalter in English, but also the first of its kind in England that includes part-music, for all the earlier examples are simply selections from the psalms, and only one of these, the *Goostly psalmes and spirituall songes* (1539–1540) of Miles Coverdale [*c.* 1488–1568], the translator of the Great Bible, has any music, and this consists only of melodies.

It was probably in the year of Crowley's publication and Sternhold's death that the latter's Psalter first appeared. This contains nineteen psalms, but in the second edition published later in the year eighteen more by Sternhold were added, together with seven by Hopkins, and from this time on all psalters that use these forty-four metrical psalms as a nucleus are called 'Sternhold and Hopkins'. Both the first two editions are without music, but this did not prevent the second from becoming a best-seller, and during the next four years it was reprinted three times. In 1556, during Mary's reign, it was slightly enlarged and published in Geneva for the English Protestant refugees there; this edition is particularly important in that it was the first Sternhold and Hopkins's Psalter to contain music, this consisting of fifty-one tunes, one for each of the fifty-one selected psalms—a unique feature because in all later editions many of the tunes serve two or more psalms. In 1558 a larger collection was issued, also at Geneva, in which over half the original tunes are replaced by new ones. In the same year Elizabeth became Queen, and the tunes of the 1558 Psalter, introduced into England by the returning refugees, became so popular that in 1559 congregational psalm-singing was officially permitted in church. There followed a spate of psalters, most of them expanded editions of Sternhold and Hopkins, the number of translations and tunes growing until

The Whole Booke of [*150*] *Psalmes*, together with sixty-five tunes, was published in 1562 (see Plate XXII). This went through innumerable editions and, despite several attempts to replace it, continued to be printed until the early nineteenth century; during the latter part of this period a new translation by Nahum Tate [1652–1715] and Nicholas Brady [1659–1726], published in 1696, gradually ousted but did not long survive the earlier version.

The enormous popularity of Sternhold and Hopkins's Psalter cannot be explained by the quality of the verse nor the faithfulness of the translation, as the former is often crude and the latter misleading, though a number of the more offensive lines and words were improved in the eighteenth century. In these respects Parker's version is much better, but at the same time it is less straightforward, and this, together with the general high quality of the tunes in the earlier Psalter and in its later editions—so admirably suited to congregational use, which the artistically superior four-part settings by Tallis are not—probably provides the explanation.

The psalm-tunes themselves were either adapted from Continental models, especially those of Bourgeois, or else newly composed in imitation of these models, and, as on the Continent, their popularity resulted in their being sung at home as well as in church. This led to a demand for harmonized versions, for in middle- and upper-class families singing in parts had received a new impetus from the influx into secular society of the monk musicians, who, owing to the dissolution of the monasteries by Henry VIII, had had to find employment elsewhere, and some of whom found permanent posts as secretaries or music tutors in the wealthier aristocratic and merchant households. It was clearly to meet this demand that John Day, only one year after he had published *The Whole Booke of Psalmes*, issued a companion volume entitled *The Whole Psalmes in four partes*, for not only does he state that instruments may be used if desired (the earliest printed indication of such alternative performance), but also that the purpose of the book is to supplant "other vain and trifling ballads". This publication contains over 140 compositions based on the sixty-five tunes of *The Whole Booke* with thirty new ones, and though the music does not equal Tallis's in artistic merit, it set the fashion for a spate of similar works, all based on Sternhold and Hopkins's Psalter. The three best of these are by the printer-composer Thomas East [d. 1608], Richard Alison, and William Leighton [d. *c.* 1616]. East's Psalter (1592) consists of harmonizations by ten of his contemporaries (including John Dowland and Giles Farnaby) of most of the tunes in *The Whole Booke*, plus a few that were either completely new or had become current since 1562. Of these last, three (now known as 'Canterbury', 'Cambridge', and 'Oxford') were clearly great favourites, as over half of the psalms are directed to be sung to one or other of them. The Psalter of Alison (who also contributed to East's collection), published in 1599, is unique in that the four-part settings (and very fine ones they are too) are all his own, important in that the tune is always placed in the soprano part instead of the customary tenor, and interesting in that it contains an arrangement of the three lowest parts, for lute, orpharion, and cittern (both of the guitar family), either separately or all together, with or without a bass viol, when the tune is sung by a solo soprano or tenor. Leighton's Psalter (1614) is a collection of fifty-four psalm-settings, some with lute accompaniment, by most of the leading composers of his day, with the affecting title of *The Teares or Lamentacions of a Sorrowfull Soule.*

A number of the psalm-tunes in these early psalters are sung as hymns today, among them the Old Hundredth, Old 124th (both French melodies originally), and Winchester Old, in addition to the three mentioned above.

Most of the pieces in Leighton's collection are anthems, the distinction between these and psalm-settings being that the former are through-composed and select only certain verses of the psalm, while the latter, like present-day versions, are simpler and shorter, with every verse repeated to the same music.

As we pointed out earlier, very few anthems compared to the number of psalm-settings and not a single Service after Day's *Certaine notes* were printed before the middle of the seventeenth century; as regards the Service, the probable reason is that it, like the mass, is liturgical, and hence its proper place is the church, but the number of churches in which part-settings of the Service were sung every day or even on most days was very small compared to the number of Catholic churches abroad that performed polyphonic masses, and whereas it was worth an Italian printer's trouble and expense to issue masses that would be bought and performed in the greater part of Europe, it was simply uneconomic for an English printer to do likewise with Anglican Services. The case of the anthem is somewhat similar, for while it too was primarily associated with the Church and so the same line of reasoning can be applied as to the Service, the fact that it was not part of the actual liturgy, was shorter, and, most important of all, was usually based on that mainstay of Protestant and particularly Calvinist music—the psalms—made it more acceptable to the average Englishman and resulted in a certain number being printed. Furthermore, not only was the tradition of copying music still powerful and, of course, much cheaper than printing, but also every organist and choirmaster was expected to compose music for his own church, and hence relied less on the work of others than is the case today.

The most important composers of Anglican music were Christopher Tye [*c.* 1505–?1572], Tallis, Byrd, Weelkes, Gibbons, and Thomas Tomkins. The differences between the simplicity of Tye's Services and anthems and the complexity of his masses and motets is typical of Anglican and Catholic music as a whole, for while imitation is still used in the former, the points are shorter and syllabic underlay has replaced melismatic. The result in Tye's case is a deliberately popular hymn-like style, most clearly shown in his *The Actes of the Apostles translated into Englyshe Metre* (1553), dedicated to Edward VI, in which the verse is appalling, but the music often charming in its simple melodiousness. This work was clearly meant for home consumption, as the author states that the music could be either sung or played on the lute, although the part-book arrangements makes the latter impossible. Tye only completed fourteen chapters of *The Actes*, but the music proved a veritable mine for later adaptors, who replaced the original words with new texts and published them as anthems (e.g. 'O come, ye servants of the Lord'), or hymns (e.g. Winchester Old). Tallis's services and anthems are more numerous than and superior to Tye's, his greater technical mastery being revealed in his preference for composing *a*5 as opposed to the almost invariable four-part writing of the older man. But the output of both these composers pales before that of Byrd, who contributed some of the finest examples in the entire Anglican repertoire. Byrd's English Church music reflects more markedly than Tallis's the tendency in the latter half of the century towards greater elaboration, for, as we have remarked elsewhere (Part I, p. 191), a new style or idea is usually applied more strictly at first than later, and Byrd was writing when the severity of "for every syllable a note" was largely a thing of the past, and composers were beginning to enrich the simple counterpoint typical of mid-century settings. This enrichment and elaboration applies particularly to Byrd's anthems that remained in manuscript, and which include some of the most brilliant and expressive music he ever wrote. These were probably composed after 1600, for they are far more polyphonic in style and madrigalian in treatment than almost all those in the 1588 and 1589 books; indeed, apart from the language, some of them are no different from his motets.

The majority of Byrd's anthems are 'full' anthems—that is, the vocal parts are complete in themselves—but he also wrote a number of 'verse' anthems in which one or two solo voices are accompanied by an organ or a consort of viols, while a chorus, usually echoing a previous solo phrase, interrupts at various points. Byrd was certainly among the earliest to compose such pieces and may well have been the first, considering his fondness for instrumentally accompanied solo song. Although he introduced the verse idea into one of his Services, these are, on the whole, more restrained than his anthems in their predominantly contrapuntal texture and discreet use of imitation. This is undoubtedly due to the fact that the Service, unlike the anthem, is an essential part of the liturgy, and hence the words are of prime importance, but in Byrd's hands the simplicity of texture is offset by a remarkable rhythmic power and flexibility derived from a vivid appreciation of the verbal accents, together with a most effective use of tonal contrasts achieved through the customary division of the choir into decani and cantoris, the former being placed on the same side as the 'dean', the latter on that of the 'cantor' or 'precentor'. Earlier composers—for example, Tallis—had used this polychoral technique to some extent, but with nothing like the skill and variety shown in Byrd's 'Great' Service.

Weelkes's contributions to the Anglican repertoire were almost certainly written after his appointments to the post of organist at Winchester College (*c.* 1598) and Chichester Cathedral (1602), and the majority are therefore later than his madrigals, in comparison with which they are more conservative. While he was more prolific than Byrd in this field, his anthems, some of which are extremely fine, cannot compare as a whole to those of the older man. It is a major misfortune that none of his ten Services (six of which are verse) has survived complete, because the four that have been reconstructed, together with the skeletons of the others, show that he was second only to Byrd in his liturgical compositions.

The verse Service and anthem became increasingly popular from the turn of the century on, as is revealed not only by Weelkes's output, but also by that of Gibbons and Tomkins, whose best work, however, lies in their full anthems, despite some very fine examples of the other type. Unlike most of their compatriots, neither Gibbons nor Tomkins composed any music to Latin words, and while the latter wrote more for the Anglican Church than any previous composer, his work is uneven in quality and below that of Gibbons. Although both were major pioneers in the verse anthem, both were rooted in the older polyphonic tradition, but Tomkins, who was composing twenty-five years after Gibbons's death, was naturally more affected by the 'New Music' from Italy that slowly found its way into England, and hence his style is less pure. With these two composers the anthem was even more favoured than before, not only because, like the motet, it allowed greater freedom in the choice of texts, but also because it could and did reflect the new surge of Puritanism that swept the country when the stabilizing influence of Elizabeth's policy of religious compromise ended with her death.

In comparing English music with that of the Continent during the latter part of the sixteenth and early seventeenth centuries, two things stand out: the fondness for independent and therefore essential instrumental accompaniment, and the greater versatility of most of her leading composers. The former is clearly shown in the secular and sacred chamber songs for voice and viols (particularly Byrd's), the verse Services and anthems, and the ayres. The first of these types was practically non-existent abroad, and the second, with its combination of vocal solos, chorus, and instruments, was only used by a few foreign musicians, such as G. Gabrieli. Gabrieli, however, with his predominantly chordal style, was primarily interested in the dramatic colour contrasts that could be obtained by combining voices and instruments, and hence preferred the louder and more brilliant cornetts and trombones to the softer, even-toned viols favoured by English composers, whose polyphonic, imitative style was best served by such instruments. As for the ayres, they too were more prominent in England than anywhere else, not only because the ayre is almost without exception an original composition, whereas most of the lute songs abroad are transcriptions, but also because it occupied a larger place in the total output of English music than did the lute song in any other country.

That the majority of leading English composers of the period were more versatile than their Continental brethren is apparent in the fact that they not only contributed to most of the various vocal types and styles which were common all over Europe, e.g. mass, motet, madrigal, ballett, lute song, but also to those that were the result of the Reformation, e.g. the Service (great, short, and verse), the anthem (full and verse), and the hymn-like settings of psalm-tunes; moreover the Service and anthem were peculiar to England, as was the solo song with string ensemble accompaniment. Admittedly the full anthem can be likened to the motet, and the great and short Services to the normal mass and missa brevis respectively, but Catholic composers elsewhere were not faced with the problem of switching from Latin to another language, let alone one so markedly different as English. English versatility is also shown in the fact that instrumental music occupied a far more prominent position in England than in any other country. This is not surprising when we consider the part played by instruments in vocal music, and it underlines an attitude that seems to have persisted longer in England than elsewhere, and provides, in addition to inborn English conservatism, an explanation not only of the continued use in most compositions written in Latin, *c.* 1475–*c.* 1575, of a style long abandoned abroad, which with its long, flowing melismas and 'abstract' quality virtually treats voices as instruments, but also of the fondness for instrumental accompaniment itself, and indeed of the comparative lack of realism in the English madrigal, for it is the abstract quality of instrumental music that is one of the main distinctions between it and vocal music in that the use of words, quite apart from their treatment (e.g. word-painting), inevitably introduces an element of realism.

The most versatile of the leading English composers were Tallis, Byrd, Morley, Weelkes, Gibbons, and Tomkins, all of whom wrote successfully and often with distinction a great variety of both vocal and instrumental pieces. Of these six composers Byrd is the most outstanding in the range and quality of his work, for he not only excelled in the mass and motet, great, short, and verse service, full and verse anthem, and accompanied song, but also in music for keyboard and for viols. Tallis is less versatile, but he made notable contributions to the mass, motet, great and short service, full anthem, and the keyboard repertoire. The other four are well represented in the above types and styles, excluding the accompanied song, except that Morley and Weelkes wrote no masses, and Gibbons and Tomkins no motets either, but they were, unlike Byrd, fine madrigalists. The achievements of these men over such a wide field was not matched by any Continental musician, except possibly G. Gabrieli; indeed, if greatness is measured by versatility allied to excellence, then Byrd was the greatest composer of his time or before it.

Instrumental music in the late Renaissance can be divided into three main classes, keyboard, lute, and ensemble, and it is in the first of these that English composers were pre-eminent. From Aston to John Bull [?1562/3 – 1628], the greatest virtuoso of them all, they show a far clearer and more imaginative grasp of keyboard technique and style than any of their contemporaries abroad, and a greater feeling for the distinctive characteristics of stringed keyboard as opposed to organ music. Thus while most keyboard music of the sixteenth and seventeenth centuries was played indiscriminately on either organ, harpsichord, or clavichord, those pieces, far commoner in England than elsewhere, in which very rapid scale passages and, more especially, broken chord figures, arpeggios, and brilliant ornamentation occur, are much more effective and were clearly intended for the latter two instruments, while pieces containing a melody in long notes with elaborate figuration above or below, or in which the style is basically vocal, are more suitable for the organ. These last predominate in the earlier sources of English keyboard music, not only because most of the composers represented were organists, but also because it is simpler and usually wiser to proceed from the known (in this case vocal techniques) to the unknown (characteristic keyboard style). The vocal technique that occurs most frequently in the early keyboard sources stems from the cantus-firmus mass and motet; in other words, a Gregorian chant is either written in long notes with a florid accompaniment or else paraphrased and shared between three or four equally important parts. For example, in the *Mulliner Book*, compiled by an organist, Thomas Mulliner, between *c.* 1545 and *c.* 1585 and the most important of the earlier collections of keyboard music, over half of the 121 pieces are based on chants, and nearly all the remaining ones are vocal in style, even when they are not simple transcriptions of actual part-songs and anthems. Nearly one quarter are by John Redford [d. 1547]; Tallis and William Blitheman [d. 1591] have considerably fewer, while Taverner and Tye have only one each.

The chant most widely used in the *Mulliner Book* is 'Gloria tibi Trinitas', an antiphon for second vespers on Trinity Sunday. This melody became more popular than any other as the cantus firmus of a whole class of compositions, unique to England, written for lute and strings as well as keyboard, and called 'In nomines'. The explanation of this title has only recently been discovered, and is as follows: one of Taverner's masses is based on the above chant, and in the Benedictus section, at the words 'in nomine Domini', it is presented complete and unelaborated in notes of equal value in the alto part, while the other voices weave points of imitation above and below. This is a particularly beautiful passage, and doubtless Taverner was as anxious to make the most of it as many later composers have been with pieces they have regarded as more than usually attractive, and so he arranged it for the organ. But Taverner was not alone in thinking highly of this passage, for not only is his organ arrangement included in the *Mulliner Book*, but it was also transcribed for both lute and string ensemble and, moreover, twice adapted to English words and sung as an anthem, one of these adaptations being printed in Day's *Certaine notes*. The enormous popularity of the piece itself led other composers to set the same cantus firmus, and during the succeeding 150 years or so literally hundreds of In nomines were written, the last and among the finest examples being Purcell's two settings in six and seven parts. It is worth noting, in view of the claim made earlier concerning the exceptionally prominent position of instrumental music in

England, that the In nomine for strings was the only type of composition in Europe in which a beginner could participate with experts, for the vast majority of these, by presenting the chant melody in long notes and placing it in one part throughout, make this part extremely easy to play.

About a fifth of the *Mulliner Book* consists of arrangements of secular vocal pieces, but this does not mean that they were not played on the organ, for while this was probably the case with the great organ (used exclusively in churches and chapels) it was certainly not true of the positive or the regal, as both these instruments were used as much outside the church as in. (The portative had fallen into disuse during the fifteenth century because it was virtually impossible to play part-music on it.)

The most striking thing about the *Mulliner Book* is that there are only two dances and no variations—the two most popular types of keyboard composition with later composers, as is shown by the contents of the *Fitzwilliam Virginal Book*, the most important source of English keyboard music in the late Renaissance. This was compiled by a Catholic Cornishman, Francis Tregian, during a term of imprisonment between 1609 and his death in 1619, and of its nigh on 300 pieces, which include every type of English keyboard composition of the time, nearly half are dances and almost an eighth are variations. This latter fraction, however, does not take into account the widespread application of variation technique, for almost all the dances are made up of several sections, each of which is followed by a varied and often elaborate repeat.

The sixteenth century has well been called the 'century of the dance', for just as society in the fourteenth century rebelled against the suppression of dancing by the Church in the previous century, so did that of the late Renaissance after ecclesiastical authority had reinforced its ban during the fifteenth century. The result was a whole host of new dances, of which the most important were the 'pavane' (the first printed example appearing in 1508), a slow dance in duple time almost certainly of Spanish origin, which virtually replaced the earlier French basse danse in European esteem; the 'gaillarde' (English 'galliard'), a fairly quick dance in triple time first printed in 1530; and the 'passamezzo' or 'step and a half', an Italian dance in duple time and slightly quicker than the pavane, which it replaced in Italy during the second half of the century. The passamezzo, like the basse danse, is constructed on a simple series of notes that are repeated a number of times and placed in the lowest part (in England this was called a 'ground'); unlike the earlier dance, however, which is based on one of several grounds, the passamezzo had only a choice of two (see p. 353). The use of a ground as the basis for a set of variations was later applied to many pavanes and galliards after *c.* 1560, and represents the earliest and one of the most popular types of variation writing in the late Renaissance. In addition there was the Italian saltarello, a quicker dance than in the fourteenth century, but not so quick as the modern type, as exemplified, for instance, in the last movement of Mendelssohn's 'Italian' Symphony; it is in triple time, and in Italy was sometimes used as an alternative for the galliard. The allemande, of German origin, was a moderately slow dance in duple time that became popular after *c.* 1550, as did the French courante—a quick dance in triple time.

Examples of all the above dances except the saltarello are in the *Fitzwilliam Virginal Book*, and nearly two-thirds of these are pavanes and galliards, many of them based on the passamezzo technique of variations on a ground. In addition, there are a handful of dances not mentioned above, including the English jig.

As already stated, the earliest type of keyboard variation is that constructed on a ground bass, and the oldest example we have is a piece entitled *My Lady Carey's Dompe*, contained in the same manuscript as Aston's *Hornpype* (see Part I, p. 215). 'Dompe' or 'dump' most likely means a composition written in memory of someone—at any rate, most of the dumps that have survived are associated with some usually high-ranking personage, as in the example mentioned, where the lady in question is probably the sister of Anne Boleyn and wife of Henry Carey; she died in 1543. The bass 'themes' of the dumps, like most other grounds, are extremely simple and sometimes consist of two notes only—tonic and dominant.

Other types of variation are those in which the tune is kept in the top part all through, often being considerably elaborated, while the accompaniment changes, or in which the tune wanders from part to part rather like the old cantus-firmus mass technique, or in which the figuration, which may elaborate the tune itself or provide an ornamental accompaniment, is placed, usually alternately, in either bass or treble.

The rest of the *Fitzwilliam Virginal Book* is made up, in order of frequency, of fantasias, cantus-firmus pieces, pieces with descriptive titles, and transcriptions of vocal part-music. The fantasias, with their successive points of imitation and essentially strict part-writing, are the most closely allied to vocal style of all the keyboard types of composition, and are as effective, if not more so, on the organ as on the virginal. This also applies to most of those pieces based on a cantus firmus, among which are two by Tallis based on the chant *Felix namque* and dated 1562 and 1564 respectively. In both the cantus firmus is repeated a number of times, switched from part to part, and accompanied by figuration which becomes increasingly complex; indeed, some of the figuration is not only unique among contemporary English pieces, but quite astonishing in its complexity and sense of keyboard style, and may, in part at any rate, have been inspired by the Spanish composer Cabezón (see p. 348). The cantus-firmus pieces also include a number of In nomines, and several which use part or whole of the hexachord scale. Byrd, for example, constructed an entire composition on *ut*, *mi*, *re*, which, in terms of actual notes, becomes G B A, or C E D, or F A G, but he does not keep strictly to these three note groups, as he starts the motif and its inversion on various degrees of the scale. Byrd also wrote a piece using all six notes of the hexachord in which *ut* is not only G, C, and F, as in Guido's system, but also D, A, and B♭, and in which the notes G♯ and A♭, D♯ and E♭ occur, thus requiring a virginal with separate keys for each of these notes (see Chapter 1, p. 250). Bull went much further than this in a now famous piece in the *Fitzwilliam Virginal Book* also based on the hexachord, for the *ut* is placed on each step of the complete chromatic scale arranged in this order, G, A, B, D♭, E♭, F, A♭, B♭, C, D, E, and F♯, and includes the additional chromatic notes of C♭, C♯, D♯, G♭, G♯, and A♯. Such a piece could only have been played on a keyboard tuned to something like our present system of equal temperament, in which the octave is divided into twelve equal semitones, and all the intervals except the octave are slightly mistuned compared to the natural scale. Most of the chromatic notes in the above pieces had been recognized theoretically since the beginning of the fifteenth century, but only a limited number were used in practice, and even by Bull's time no other keyboard work contained such a wide range, although a few sixteenth-century lute and viol pieces employed even more out-of-the-way notes (see page 345).

The widespread practice of word-painting in vocal music was reflected in keyboard compositions with descriptive and fanciful titles. These were particularly popular in England and range from delightfully whimsical little pieces, such as Giles Farnaby's *Dreame*, *His Rest*, and *His Humour* [Farnaby, d. 1640], to more elaborate and frankly programmatic works, such as the fantasia by John Mundy [d. 1630], which describes a succession of thunderstorms ending with 'A Cleare Day', Byrd's charming and most skilfully written *The Bells*, and the same composer's suite, *The Battell.* This last may well have been inspired by Janequin's famous chanson, *La Guerre* (see Chapter 1, p. 240). Such arrangements of vocal music, however, were comparatively rare in England, and most of these are by the Catholic Peter Philips [d. 1628], a fine composer of motets and to a lesser extent madrigals, who left England *c.* 1590 and spent the rest of his life abroad, mostly in the Netherlands, and who, as a result, was considerably more influenced by Continental practices than his compatriots.

Another Englishman who spent much of his creative life abroad was Bull, and such was the reputation he made as a keyboard player and composer during his visits to the Netherlands, France, and Germany in 1601 that he was recalled by Elizabeth, who feared he might accept a position at one of the foreign courts. Twelve years later, however, he left England for good, and in 1617 was appointed organist of Antwerp Cathedral, a post he held till his death. Bull was the most virtuosic of all the Renaissance writers for the keyboard, and played the leading part in transmitting English keyboard style to Continental musicians. In fact, there is a direct line of succession from him to Bach, as we shall see later. Much of his music, while fascinating to the student of keyboard technique, is rather dry, even downright dull, but occasionally, as in the well-known *The King's Hunt*, usually ascribed to him, or in the *Walsingham* variations, the music is both brilliant and attractive, and some of his simpler pieces are perfectly exquisite in their strangely delicate harmony and melody.

That Bull's reputation as a keyboard composer exceeded Byrd's was undoubtedly due to his virtuosity as a performer and the technical difficulty of much of his music (he has, indeed, been called the Liszt of his age), for neither in quantity nor quality does it equal that of the older man. Admittedly, there are many pieces by Byrd which are tedious or commonplace harmonically, or in which stock rhythmic and melodic figures are used mechanically, but in most of these there are movements of beauty, and a greater number than in Bull's output show a high level of inspiration. Other important writers for the keyboard were Giles Farnaby, Orlando Gibbons, Tomkins, Morley, and Peter Philips; all of them, while composing far fewer works than either Byrd or Bull, contributed many fine pieces, some of which are perfect gems.

The two most outstanding features of English keyboard music, apart from its advanced technique, are melodic freshness and harmonic clarity. Both have already been mentioned in connexion with the madrigal and ayre, but, compared to Continental examples, they are much more distinctive in compositions for the virginal than in any other sphere. Another feature (and one that applies to other countries as well) is the inevitable intrusion of imitative part-writing, even though the instrument does not take kindly to polyphony, and the vast majority of keyboard pieces are shot through with brief and often telling rhythmic or melodic motives which are passed from part to part. As we should expect, this feature is particularly evident in Byrd's output, much less so in Bull's, and as a result, when inspiration flags, Byrd's polyphonic skill keeps our interest alive, whereas with Bull we tend to tire of mere brilliance. The combination of this imitative by-play with the melodic, harmonic, and technical characteristics mentioned above result at its best in music that is ravishing to the ear and fascinating to the mind, and which in general ranks higher than any other instrumental music of the time, either English or Continental.

Most of this music was played on the virginal rather than the clavichord, for the latter was never as popular as the former either in England or abroad, and only in Germany during the seventeenth and eighteenth centuries did it in any way rival the virginal; while the delicate, sensuous beauty of clavichord tone and its expressive subtlety is superior to that of the harpsichord, its lack of volume is probably the main reason why it was overshadowed by the latter instrument. Another reason may well have been the impossibility of re-tuning easily certain notes, e.g. A♭ for G♯, because to alter the position of the tangent would be a major operation; moreover, if the pair of strings was tightened in order to sound, say, A♭, then the other note or notes produced from the same pair would be thrown out of tune.

During the latter part of the sixteenth century another set of strings tuned an octave higher than the original unison sets was added to Italian harpsichords, and slightly later another row of jacks was so placed that the plectra plucked one of the unison sets near the end, producing a hard but brilliant tone (lute stop). There were thus four rows of jacks, two for the unison strings and one each for the octave set and lute stop, and as these could be operated either alone or with any of the others a number of variations of both timbre and volume were possible.

This large harpsichord does not seem to have been made in England, but it is certain that the English definition of virginal included it as well as the simple type with only two unison sets of strings, because many of the pieces by the later virginalists were undoubtedly written for the larger instrument, this being imported from abroad, especially from Antwerp, where the most famous family of harpsichord-makers, the Ruckers, whose instruments have never been surpassed in purity and beauty of tone, flourished from *c.* 1550 to *c.* 1670 (see Plate XXIII).

Almost the entire corpus of English keyboard composition remained in manuscript, the only exceptions being *Parthenia, or the Maydenhead of the First Musicke that ever was printed for the Virginalles* (1611) (see Plate XXIV), containing twenty-one pieces by Byrd, Bull, and Gibbons, and its sequel, *Parthenia In-violata or Mayden-Musicke for the Virginalls and Bass-Viol* (*c.* 1614), containing twenty anonymous pieces. The chief reason why so little was published was almost certainly the difficulty of setting up movable type so that clusters of short notes, particularly semiquavers and demisemiquavers, were accurately aligned with the longer ones, and although this difficulty could be partially overcome by engraving, as in the two prints mentioned above (though even here the notes are very badly spaced), this was a much more costly process. Contributory reasons, already referred to in connexion with Anglican music, were the widespread habit of copying and the likelihood of a small sale, the number of people who could afford or play a virginal being small.

The difficulty of aligning the notes on two staves did not arise with lute or ensemble music, the former being set in tablature and the latter being printed in part-books, as in vocal music. We should therefore expect more publications in these two fields, and so indeed there are, and during the thirty years or so from Whythorne's *Duos, or Songs for two voices* (1590)—the first print of English instrumental music, as all the items were intended to be either played or sung—a number of pieces for ensemble were published, some of them in madrigal books, like Morley's nine two-part fantasias contained in his *Canzonets for Two Voyces*, and some of them as separate collections, like Gibbons' nine three-part fantasias (*c.* 1610), his first published work and the earliest example in England of music engraved on copper.

The instrumental ensembles of the late sixteenth and early seventeenth centuries were called 'consorts', a misspelling of 'concert' which, like 'concerto', probably comes from the Latin verb *conserere* with its past participle *consertus*, meaning 'to combine together'. Consorts were either 'whole' or 'broken', the former and by far the most popular consisting of members of the same family, as 'consort of viols' or 'consort of recorders', and the latter of various instruments, as in Morley's *Booke of Consort Lessons* (1599), which is 'scored' for treble and bass viols, flute (=recorder), lute, cittern, and pandora (for descriptions of the last two, see below). In Part I, Chapter 6, p. 220, we stated that the practice of playing in 'whole consort' began in the latter part of the fifteenth century, but this did not become widespread until the following century. Most consort music is for treble, alto, tenor, and bass viols, and the two main types of composition are the fantasia, and that based on a cantus firmus. Of the latter the In nomines easily exceed not only other cantus firmus pieces, but also the number of In nomines written for the keyboard or lute, the reason being that this type of composition is a fundamentally polyphonic one, and hence lends itself more naturally to, and indeed sounds better on, a group of strings than on a single instrument, even an organ. Polyphony, in fact, is a far more essential constituent of extended string writing (as Haydn discovered after he had written a number of string quartets) than any other class of vocal or instrumental composition, because, being completely abstract (i.e. no words) and with only a limited range of timbre, the ear requires more than just accompanied melody, although this is perfectly satisfactory in short pieces, such as dance movements. This fact also explains the greater number of fantasias for strings than for keyboard or lute, because the fantasia consists, in the main, of imitative polyphony and, like the cantus-firmus type, usually differs little in technique and style from the contemporary motet or madrigal. In some of the later fantasias, however, especially those of Gibbons—the greatest master of this type of composition—the writing is decidedly instrumental in character, with rapid, repeated notes and wide leaps, and with more complex cross-rhythms and frequent use of sequence than in any vocal music of the time (Ex. 15*):

* From *Nine Fantasies* . . ., ed. Fellowes.

Several of Gibbons's fantasias are divided into two or more contrasting sections; for instance, an imitative first section in duple time will be followed by a simple, minuet-like second section in triple time, and a final imitative section in duple time, sometimes thematically related to the first section. Thematic relationship between different parts of an instrumental work, which occurs in fantasias by composers other than Gibbons, may well have developed from the practice of pairing pavanes and galliards, many of which are linked by similarity of melody and harmony. Another much rarer, but very important, feature of the fantasia, and one almost certainly derived from Italy, is the use of only one theme throughout a piece instead of a succession of imitative points, the theme being inverted, augmented, diminished, and rhythmically varied, a type that, in the hands of Sweelinck (see below, p. 352), led eventually to the fugue.

Dance pieces for consorts are few compared either to the number of fantasia and cantus-firmus compositions or to the number written for the virginal (the organ can be counted out for this kind of music), probably because viols lack the rhythmic 'bite' which the plucking action of the virginal gives, even though it is less capable of producing strong and weak accents. Admittedly, much of the dance music from the late sixteenth century onwards, because of its melodic, rhythmic, and polyphonic complexity, was not meant to be danced to, just as in the suites of Bach or the symphonic minuets of Haydn and Mozart, but its fundamentally rhythmic nature was still felt, and rightly so, to be more effective on a plucked or hit stringed instrument than on one that was bowed, hence the enormous number of dance suites for the harpsichord in the seventeenth and eighteenth centuries.

The leading composers of consort music, apart from Gibbons, were Byrd, Morley, Coperario, Thomas Lupo [d. 1628], an Italian who settled in England, and Alfonso Ferrabosco (ii). Coperario, the most prolific writer of fantasias, visited Italy *c.* 1604 and acquired a lyricism and lightness that influenced his compatriots on his return home, and it is noteworthy and typical of Continental influence that, compared to their output, a far higher proportion of his pieces are arrangements of vocal compositions. Ferrabosco, a better composer than Coperario, has left us some exquisite dances and extremely fine fantasias, two being of exceptional interest, one for four and the other for five viols. The one *a*4 has the notes of the hexachord in ascending order placed in the top part and repeated eight times, starting on C, C♯, D, E♭, E, F, F♯, and G respectively, and employing all the chromatic notes of Bull's hexachord piece plus E♯ and F♭. In the fantasia *a*5 the hexachord notes, placed in the next to highest part, are in descending order, starting on E (i.e. E, D, C, B, A, G), and also repeated eight times, each repeat being a semitone lower than the previous one, i.e. D♯, D, C♯, C, B, B♭, and A. All the chromatic notes of the fantasia *a*4 are used except F♭, but in addition there occur the extremely rare notes of F double-sharp and C double-sharp. In both pieces Ferrabosco manages his modulations more smoothly than does Bull.

The intimate polyphonic nature of music for viol consort gives much greater pleasure to the performers for whom, as in the normal madrigal, it was primarily intended than to the listener, for although the viol is, within a limited range, a most expressive instrument, the lack of brilliance and resonance and the fact that the beauty and structure of the music are only fully revealed to those who commune together in performing it make it less acceptable to the 'outsider' than the less sensitive but more brilliant virginal.

In addition to the four viols mentioned earlier and the violone (see Part I, Chapter 6, p. 220), there were two solo instruments, a small bass called the 'division viol' because it was chiefly used to play divisions (i.e. variations) on a ground, and the 'lyra viol', an even smaller bass which, with its flatter bridge that decreases the difference in level between the strings and its slacker bow, is capable of playing several strings simultaneously, and hence can perform part-music more effectively than can the other viols.

Despite the fact that more lute than keyboard pieces were published, several of them in song-books, there seems little doubt that the instrument was not so popular in England as abroad, even though in Dowland she possessed one of the leading lute virtuosi of the time. Thus the first four books of instruction, published between 1563 and 1596, are all translations of the whole or a part of a well-known work by the Frenchman, Adrian le Roy, and not until 1603 was an original work produced with similar aims—Thomas Robinson's *Schoole of Musicke*.

Apart from Dowland, who, surprisingly enough, issued no collections of lute solos and the bulk of whose output remained in manuscript, apart from a few pieces in other men's publications, the chief lutanist-composers were his son Robert [*c.* 1586–1641], Anthony Holborne [d. 1602], John Johnson [fl. 1579–1594], Francis Cutting, Daniel Batchelar, Richard Alison, Philip Rosseter [1568–1623], and Francis Pilkington [d. 1638]. Dowland's output consists mainly of dances and is typical of the English lutanist school as a whole, contrasting markedly with Continental production, which, as already pointed out, preferred arrangements of vocal pieces. A strong sense of rhythm and a flair for fresh-sounding melodies—the latter a general characteristic of English music of the time—are abundantly apparent in his lute music and in that of his compatriots, but his melancholic nature is revealed in a number of fine compositions that employ chromaticism to a greater degree than do other English lutanists. Apart from dances, the lute repertoire consists of In nomines, fantasias, and transcriptions of both sacred and secular vocal music, including some of complete masses. In this last category Byrd is drawn upon more frequently than any other composer, a further indication of the esteem in which he was held.

English music for the lute or for its near relations, the theorbo, guitar, cittern, and pandora, like keyboard and secular vocal music, but not like music for consort, enjoyed but a brief flowering compared to the Continent, where during the whole of the sixteenth century and much of the seventeenth these instruments, especially the lute, were enormously popular. The theorbo, which emerged *c.* 1560 in Italy, can be described as a bass lute; it had single strings at first, but by the middle of the seventeenth century was double-strung, the number of strings being either fourteen or sixteen, the lowest eight or ten tuned to the diatonic notes lying immediately below one or other of the lute tunings given in Part I, Chapter 6, p. 217. These bass strings necessitated not only a larger body than the lute, but also frets spaced at wider intervals, thus making it more difficult to play normal lute music, with the result that the theorbo became more of an accompanying instrument, and as such found a place in ensembles and even the opera orchestra as late as the eighteenth century (see p. 382).

The cittern, which has been aptly called 'the poor man's guitar', was very popular with amateurs of all classes. It has the guitar's flat back, but the lute's rounded sides. It is double-strung and ranges in size from a small one with four pairs of strings (courses) to one with twelve courses. The pandora was the popular substitute for the theorbo.

In point of time, Spain was the first European country to adopt the lute from the Moors, but during the sixteenth century and later she virtually rejected the instrument in favour of the vihuela, a name which denoted both the viol and (more especially) the guitar family. The vihuela has a flat back and slightly incurved sides, and is double-strung with either six courses tuned like the lute, or four, the lowest and highest strings of the six-course vihuela being omitted; this last was very popular with amateurs, while the six-course vihuelas were played by professionals. Why the Spaniards forsook the lute for the vihuela is not clear, but it may have been because it is easier to play and is a more resonant instrument, thus suiting the more rhapsodic, emotional nature of Spanish music. (The Renaissance guitar is very similar to the vihuela, except that it has five courses.)

The leading Spanish vihuelists were Luis Milán, Luis de Narváez, Alonso de Mudarra, Enriquez de Valderabano, and Miguel de Fuenllana, the first four living in the earlier part of the sixteenth century, the last during the middle of the century. Whilst most of Milán's pieces are fantasias, he also wrote dances, arrangements of vocal compositions, and variations, many of the latter taking the form of a varied accompaniment to a popular song with the original melody and words placed above the tablature, a unique feature of the Spanish School. The other vihuelists also wrote mostly fantasias; those by Narváez are more purely instrumental than those of his compatriots, and his variations are remarkable for their subtlety, artistry, and the way they exploit the technical resources of the instrument. Fuenllana's fantasias show a more vocal approach in their essentially polyphonic texture, and it is amazing how he manages to achieve such 'correct' and full part-writing on an instrument anything but suited to such a style.

Compared to the amount of English and Italian lute music actually written down, there is very little for the vihuela, possibly because extemporization played a bigger part than elsewhere. This dearth is even more acute as regards ensemble music, the chief composer of which was Diego Ortiz [fl. mid-century], though literary references are common. It even applies to keyboard composition, most of what there is being written for the organ. The outstanding composer for this instrument was Antonio de Cabezón [1510–1566], whose fantasias, 'diferencias' (=variations), vocal transcriptions, and settings of psalms and hymns surpass all other Spanish instrumental composers in the richness of their texture, the quality of their themes, and the exquisiteness of their craftsmanship. Furthermore, the ornateness and variety of his figuration exceeds those of his compatriots, and in some of his diferencias he achieves a greater degree of unity by dove-tailing the variations together instead of making a distinct break between each. In 1554 he accompanied Philip II to England for his marriage to Mary, and it is a moot point whether or no his keyboard technique and variation-writing opened the eyes of English composers. The latter may have developed their keyboard style from a purely native tradition stemming from Aston, but the astonishing advance in figuration shown by Tallis in his two settings of *Felix namque*, which were written only a few years after Cabezón's arrival, i.e. 1562 and 1564 respectively, make it likely that the English learned something at any rate from the Spaniard. As regards the variation, it is much more likely that Cabezón's diferencias did indeed have a marked effect on English keyboard composition, for in both style and structure they were greatly in advance of anything written outside Spain, and only after his visit did this type of composition become popular in England. Indeed, the variation was favoured far more in those two countries than anywhere else. Cabezón is undoubtedly one of the greatest instrumental composers of the Renaissance, ranking with the best that England or Italy could produce and superior to those of France and Germany.

Germany, after her notable composer-performers of the fifteenth century, rather tailed off in the sixteenth, much of her keyboard music (and there is a great deal compared to Spain) consisting of grossly ornate arrangements of vocal works. Her lute music, while roughly equal in quantity to her keyboard music, is superior in quality, using ornamentation more discreetly and being fresher and more melodious, the outcome possibly of the enormous popularity of the instrument with amateurs. The leading lute composers were Hans Judenkünig [d. 1526], Hans Gerle [d. 1570], Wolf Heckel [fl. mid-sixteenth century], Melchior Neusiedler [1531–1590], and his brother Hans [*c.* 1509–1563], Matthaeus Waisselius, and Sixtus Kangel, the two last living in the second half of the century. Although the majority of their compositions, like those for keyboard, are vocal transcriptions, they also wrote a number of dances, the most interesting of which was a specifically German type, the 'Tanz', usually in duple time, which was followed by a 'Nachtanz' or 'after dance', usually a variation in triple time of the Tanz. We shall be returning to these two dances when we deal with the dance suite in Chapter 6. Of ensemble music very little remains, but there are numerous pictorial and literary references to wind bands, of which the Germans were specially fond, and which resulted in an international reputation in the making and playing of wind instruments, a reputation that lasted until well into the nineteenth century.

France produced more ensemble music than Germany, the bulk of it consisting of dances which, unlike the mainly elaborate ones in other countries, are melodically and rhythmically simple and, in keeping with the French love of this kind of entertainment, were clearly meant to be danced to. Apart from these, a number of fantasias exist, mostly by Eustache du Caurroy [1549–1609], many of which are based on secular or sacred tunes. As in other countries, French lute and keyboard music outstrips that for ensemble, a host of pieces for both types of instrument being published and a great many more remaining in manuscript. As we might expect from the nation that gave birth to the ballet, dances occupy a more prominent position in music for the lute than in any other country. Sometimes two or three contrasting dances were grouped together, such as pavane–salterello–piva, the last being in triple time, like the salterello, but quicker, both dances occasionally being variations of the pavane. By the middle of the century the salterello and piva were replaced by the gaillarde. Most of these dances, like those for ensemble, are simple and could easily have been danced to at some intimate gathering, but hardly at a court ball, where the sound of th instrument would have been drowned by rustling skirts and chattering voices. The chief lute composers were Antoine Francisque [*c.* 1575 – 1605], Adrian le Roy, author of the text-book already mentioned (p. 346) on how to compose for and play on the lute, Guillaume Morlaye, and the Mantuan Albert de Rippe, the last two living in the middle years of the century.

French keyboard music was more 'learned' than that for lute and ensemble, as much of it consists of transcriptions of both sacred and secular vocal works which demand a fairly high degree of technical competence. As elsewhere, except England, there is little or no distinction between organ and stringed-keyboard styles, and most of the pieces are taken up with rather mechanical repetitions of ornamental figures, scale passages, and broken chords that are effective on both types of keyboard. Only one man deserves special mention, Jean Titelouze [1562/3 – 1633], an organist who was not only a gifted composer, but who knew a good deal about organ construction, and who advocated the use of two manuals and a pedal key-board, the latter being virtually unknown outside Germany.

Sweelinck, the last of the great line of composers from the Netherlands, was also important in the development of the organ as an instrument, for while he was greatly indebted to the keyboard figuration and variations of the English virginalists (largely through Bull, with whom he was probably on intimate terms), and was thoroughly acquainted with the Italian fantasia and toccata (see below, p. 355), his variations on psalm- and hymn-tunes (chorales) call for sharply differentiated registration that permits the chorale to stand out, because, unlike the borrowed melodies in English virginal variations which are usually absorbed into the general figuration, Sweelinck keeps the chorale cantus firmus virtually intact and aloof, as it were, from the lively other parts. (The same characteristic is found, though to a lesser extent, in his harpsichord variations on secular themes.)

The instrument that Sweelinck's chorale variations demand we now call the baroque organ, although its main features had been incorporated into the German Renaissance organ. The Renaissance organ outside the Germanic countries had a soft tonal structure, its mixture stops (i.e. those which reinforce two or more upper partials of the fundamental note) lacked brilliance and penetration, solo stops were rare, the flute being the most popular, and the pedal keyboard, on the few organs that possessed one, was merely a very short lower extension of the manual. (Two-manual organs were also exceptional.) This type of organ remained popular, especially in England and Italy, until the eighteenth century. In contrast to this, the German organ of the late Renaissance and baroque had not only an increased range of solo stops, particularly reeds, together with mixture stops that were more brilliant and penetrating, but not excessively so owing to light wind pressure, but also a large number of mutation stops (which strengthen a particular upper partial), and a pedal keyboard that was a more extensive continuation of the (usually) two manuals and which, moreover, was capable of carrying both a supporting bass and, by means of two-foot and four-foot stops, an independent melody on equal terms with the manuals. Such an organ provided both a clear, ringing ensemble and a number of delightfully varied solo stops, on one of which the chorale theme would be played.

Sweelinck's chorale variations were the first of a whole series of distinguished and sometimes profound examples that reached its highest point, but not its end, in those by J. S. Bach. They are essentially organ pieces, which his fantasias are not, but many of them sound just as effective on the harpsichord. In his fantasias Sweelinck laid the foundation of the fugue by reducing the succession of imitative points to one, unlike the typical polythematic fantasia of England and elsewhere. More important, however, and again unlike the few English and Italian monothematic examples, it is not the theme that is altered, but its accompanying counterpoints.

Sweelinck enjoyed considerable fame as a keyboard composer, and manuscript copies of his organ and harpsichord pieces were widely circulated all over Europe. He was also an outstanding teacher, and his pupils included Scheidt and Scheidemann, the latter of whom taught Reinken, who in turn considerably influenced Bach. In view of all this, it is astonishing that none of Sweelinck's keyboard works was printed during his lifetime, and in this respect his Italian contemporaries were very much better served.

Compared to the rest of Europe, excluding England, Italian instrumental music of the late Renaissance is, on the whole, superior in both quantity and quality, and a far higher proportion of it was printed than anywhere else. Indeed, from the lute books issued by Petrucci, the first of which appeared in 1507, until the latter half of the eighteenth century more instrumental music was published in Italy than in any other country.

Petrucci's 1507 book contains a high proportion of vocal transcriptions, and as the century progressed this proportion increased, most of the originals being madrigals and other secular types. This trend, which differs from English and even French practice, was the result of the tremendous popularity of vocal music in Italy, a popularity which, despite the close association between words and music, did not prevent the latter from being enjoyed in the abstract, as it were, i.e. in a purely instrumental form, although this would be partially compensated by various embellishments not possible in the original. Despite the preponderance of such transcriptions, the most important and, indeed, the most attractive class of lute compositions are the dances. The idea of joining two or more dances together has already been mentioned, but the pavane–salterello–piva arrangement, in which the last two are variations of the first, stemmed from Italy and was first introduced by one of the leading lutanists of the first half of the century,

Joan Ambrosio Dalza [fl. *c.* 1500]. Dalza and his contemporary, Francesco Spinaccino [fl. *c.* 1500], both wrote short pieces consisting of chords and scale passages called 'ricercari' (Italian, *ricerca*='research', hence 'study'—in this case of a technical nature). Although the term appears in their works for the first time, its character soon changed, and in the hands of Francesco Canova da Milano [1497–1543] it became for the first time the instrumental counterpart of the motet, i.e. basically a succession of points or themes each of which is treated imitatively—in other words, a polyphonic 'study'. So far as the lute is concerned, Francesco's ricercari are the finest ever written and exerted a considerable influence on other lute composers, both native and foreign, the latter usually employing the term 'fantasia', as indeed did many Italians during the latter part of the century. Apart from the ricercari and dance movements, Francesco also wrote pieces which are much freer in design, alternating between imitative, chordal, and florid passages, and in some respects anticipating the later toccata (see below, p. 355).

The idea of joining dances together remained popular right through the century and formed the starting-point of what was later to become one of the most popular classes of instrumental composition, the suite. If anyone invented the suite it was Pietro P. Borrono [fl. first half of sixteenth century], who wrote a number of them consisting of a pavana followed by three saltarelli, all in the same key, and who clearly considered this arrangement as an entity. However, the most popular dance grouping during the first half of the century was pavana–gagliarda, and in the latter half the passamezzo–gagliarda, which was sometimes expanded by the addition at the end of a padovana, a dance in quick six-eight time. Many of the dances were constructed on one of five ground basses; the two passamezzo ones were 'passamezzo antico' and 'passamezzo moderno', the other three being 'romanesca', 'folia', and 'ruggiero' (see Chapter 1, p. 264); all of these played an important part in baroque instrumental music.

The number of lute composers was legion, and included some of the leading writers of vocal music, such as Vecchi and Gastoldi, but the most important were, in addition to those already mentioned, Antonio Rotta [d. 1549], Giacomo Gorzanis [fl. second half of sixteenth century], Vincenzo

Galilei [d. 1591], father of the great astronomer, Galileo Galilei, Fabritio Caroso [fl. latter half of sixteenth century], Giovanni Antonio Terzi [sixteenth–seventeenth centuries], and Simone Molinaro [d. 1615]. Terzi and Molinaro brought the lute variation dance suite to its highest peak, and in their passamezzo–gagliarda grouping both dances are divided into sections (usually three, but sometimes as many as ten), each of which are variations on the same basic succession of chords, with the first section of the gagliarda melodically linked to the similar section of the passamezzo. A feeling for climax is shown by the use of progressively shorter note values, and the style is either polyphonic or contrapuntal.

Like instrumental music in general, again excluding that of England, Italian keyboard pieces are mainly vocal transcriptions, but original pieces for stringed keyboard or organ became more common as the century progressed and are, from our point of view, far more interesting and important. The chief of these are the ricercare and the canzona. The first we have already met, and although those by the first significant keyboard composer, Marc Antonio Cavazzoni [*c.* 1490 – *c.* 1560], are the earlier improvisational type, they became in the hands of his more important son, Girolamo [b. *c.* 1525], the standard type already described, but expanding this by increasing the number of repeats of each point of imitation. Later composers, of whom the chief were Jacques Buus [d. 1565], Annibale Padovano [1527–1575], Claudio Merulo [1533–1604], and the two Gabrielis (all of them organists at St. Mark's, Venice), displayed greater virtuosity and increased ornamentation compared to G. Cavazzoni, and Andrea Gabrieli introduced a far-reaching innovation by writing a few ricercari based on a single theme instead of several, this theme being varied and the repeats separated by florid interludes. This monothematic type of ricercare was not favoured nearly so much as the standard polythematic type.

The term 'canzona' first occurs in M. A. Cavazonni's book of keyboard pieces published in 1523, where it is applied to transcriptions of French chansons. One of the characteristics of these is some kind of sectional repetition, e.g. *a b a* or *a a b* (see Chapter 1, p. 240), and in the later purely instrumental canzona repetition schemes became one of the main features compared to the ricercare, the other being a generally lighter, less 'learned' style, cleaner, livelier rhythm, and the frequent occurrence of 𝅗𝅥 ♩ ♩ as an opening motif.

The above-mentioned composers of ricercare also wrote canzone, and the vast majority of their examples are transcriptions of chansons. There were, however, two further types of composition which were nearly always original—the fantasia and the toccata. The keyboard fantasia should not be confused with the lute ricercare-fantasia mentioned on p. 353, for it developed from the practice of testing prospective candidates for the two organists' posts at St. Mark's, Venice, by giving them a theme on which to improvise, and when composers (e.g. A. Gabrieli) actually started writing such pieces, these mostly show their origin by being monothematic (like some of Gabrieli's ricercari), but with little polyphony and much ornamentation. Almost entirely ornamental was the toccata, a term first used in a keyboard piece published in 1536. It comes from the Italian *toccare* (='to touch', i.e. the keys, in contrast to 'sounding' strings and 'singing' voices), and its essentially florid style was retained right up to Bach's day; it is not surprising, therefore, that the first great exponent of this, the most characteristic of all keyboard compositions, was the greatest organ virtuoso of the century, Merulo.

Voluminous and important as Italian lute and keyboard music is, it is less purely instrumental and indeed less attractive than that of English composers, but in the sphere of ensemble music Italy, especially through the genius of Giovanni Gabrieli, produced compositions whose rich colours and spacious designs not only compare favourably with English consort music, but also marked both the end of the Renaissance and the beginning of the baroque. While men like Willaert, Rore, and Andrea Gabrieli all wrote concerted pieces, the actual quantity produced compares unfavourably with that of England, and although Giovanni Gabrieli was the most prolific writer of such music his output is small compared to Byrd's. In his canzone, however, which, like his compatriots, he preferred to all other types of instrumental music when writing for ensembles, Giovanni treads the virtually unexplored territory of pure instrumental colour. Thus in his famous *Sonata pian' e forte* (1597) he combines two 'choruses', one consisting of a cornett and three trombones and the other of a violino (viola) and three more trombones. In general, when only one chorus is playing the music is soft (piano), but when both combine then it is loud (forte). Although Giovanni was the first to include dynamic terms in an ensemble composition, such terms had been used in lute music as early as *c.* 1520. The term 'sonata' too dates back to 1561 at least, and in literary references to 1486.

We do not know who made the first violin, or its near relations the viola and 'cello; all we do know is that it developed from the mediaeval vièle, which, unlike the viol, was placed against the shoulder and bowed in the same way as we now bow the violin, that the strings were tuned in fifths by the early sixteenth century at least, and that the first important violin-makers were the Italians Gasparo Bertolotti [1540–1609]—usually called 'da Salò' from his birthplace—Giovanni Paolo Maggini [*c.* 1581-*c.* 1632] who, like da Salò, worked in Brescia, and the brothers Amati, Antonio [b. *c.* 1540] and Hieronymus [*c.* 1561 – 1630], both of whom worked in Cremona. It was Hieronymus's son Nicola and his pupil, Antonio Stradivarius, who built the most famous violins, but their achievements take us outside this chapter.

Apart from artistic presentations (paintings, etc.), our knowledge of later Renaissance instruments is chiefly obtained, typically enough, from two German works, *Musica instrumentalis deudsch* (1529) by Martin Agricola [1486–1556] and the second volume of *Syntagma musicae* (1618) by Michael Praetorius (see Chapter 5). Other notable books of the period are the *Tratado de glosas* (1553) by Ortiz, which deals with instrumental improvisation and ornamentation, mostly for the viol, *Il Transilvano* (1597 and 1609) by Girolamo Diruta (b. 1561) which is concerned with organ playing and composition, the standard treatise on the Renaissance dance by, again typically, the Frenchman Thoinot Arbeau [1519–1595], the *Orchésographie* (1588), and a number on musical theory and composition in general, including, in addition to Glareanus's *Dodecachordon* (see p. 246), Zarlino's *Institutioni armoniche* (1558), *Dimostrationi armoniche* (1571), and *Sopplimenti musicali* (1588), the *Prattica di musica* (1592 and 1619) by Lodovico Zacconi [1555–1627], and Morley's *A Plaine and Easie Introduction to Practicall Musicke* (1597).

The feeling for colour and richness of sound shown in Giovanni Gabrieli's concerted music and in much of his choral music with instrumental accompaniment is paralleled by the school of painting which flourished in the same city and which is one of the glories of the Renaissance. In Part I, Chapter 6, p. 225, we described the main differences between Florentine and Venetian art, and mentioned the first great painters of the latter school—Giovanni Bellini, Mantegna, Giorgione, and Carpaccio. These were followed by Titian [1485?–1576], Veronese [1528–1588], Tintoretto [1518–1594], and Michelangelo Caravaggio [1573–1610]. The sumptuous, glowing colours of Titian, particularly his reds, the cooler but still rich pigments of Veronese, and the vivid contrasts of light and dark in the works of Tintoretto represent, as does much of Giovanni Gabrieli's work, the full flowering of one aspect of Renaissance art and, in their emotionalism, the advent of the baroque spirit. This is particularly true of Tintoretto and Caravaggio, for the former, an impetuous and passionate man frequently embroiled in bloodshed and violence, is often startlingly dramatic in his choice and treatment of subject-matter, while the latter, rebelling against the superficial imitation of Michelangelo, Raphael, and Titian which flooded Italy during the latter part of the century, depicted individuals and scenes from the lower classes rather than from the aristocracy, and depicted them with a realism unknown before. Caravaggio, in fact, not only carried the realistic element of the Renaissance to its farthest extent, but, through the bold emotionalism of his subjects and his striking use of colour and light, rejuvenated Italian painting and exerted a tremendous influence on foreign artists, especially those of the early baroque.

As in the fifteenth, so in the sixteenth century Italy dominated the artistic sphere, for in addition to her painters she boasted the finest architect and sculptor in Europe, Michelangelo [1475–1564], and the most exquisite craftsman in Benvenuto Cellini [1500–1571], whose statuettes, cups, vases, etc., in bronze or gold have perhaps never been surpassed in technical finish. Elsewhere in Europe the only men of comparable artistic stature were the French sculptor, Pilon [1537–1590], the German, Holbein the younger [1497/8–1543], who spent the last twelve years of his life as court painter to Henry VIII and who was one of the few sixteenth-century artists who took an interest in the rising bourgeois element in society, the Flemish painter, Bruegel the elder [*c.* 1520–1569], and lastly, and most strikingly original of them all, including the Italians, the Spaniard El Greco [1541–1614], who, though born in Crete and studying in Italy, is typically Spanish in his intense mysticism and emotionalism, the latter frequently being achieved by distorted forms, violent gestures, and exaggerated expressions. He more than any other artist of his time reflected the new spirit of the baroque; indeed, he was more baroque-like than many of his successors, and the powerful, often startling impact of his pictures is yet another salutary reminder that artistic periods are more conveniences than realities.

In the realm of literature Italy was both more influential and superior to all other countries. Her chief contribution was poetic, and men such as Tasso, Michelangelo, Ariosto, and Tansillo [1510–1568] were only partially matched by Ronsard and the Englishman, Donne [1573–1631], and to a lesser extent by Sidney and Raleigh. In the dramatic sphere, however, she was completely overshadowed by the Spaniards, Lope de Rueda [1510–1560] and Lope de Vega [1562–1635], and, more especially, by the Englishmen, Marlowe [1564–1593], Shakespeare [1564–1616], and Jonson, Marlowe and Shakespeare being the greatest European playwrights of their respective generations.

In Shakespeare's non-historical plays the basic plots and characters are borrowed from the writings of others to a far greater extent than with later dramatists, and so reflect contemporary musical practice, which, particularly in large-scale works, such as the mass, but also to a lesser extent in the motet, madrigal, etc., incorporates previously composed material as a melodic or structural foundation. More important, however, is the sometimes terrifying but always fascinating way in which Shakespeare draws his characters, describing in greater detail and with more accuracy and deeper understanding a larger aspect of human personality than any dramatist before or since. His range and penetration are astonishing and remind one of Leonardo, for while his realm was not man's environment, but the character of man himself, he shows, like Leonardo, the typical enquiring mind of the Renaissance.

In addition to the poets mentioned above, Italy could also boast of such writers as Cellini, whose autobiography gives a vivid and valuable insight into contemporary life, Vasari [1511–1574], who has left us a series of sketches on Italian painters, and the historian, Guicciardini [1483–1540]. Their contemporaries abroad include the great French writer,

Montaigne [1553–1592] and his compatriot, Rabelais [1494?–1553], whose accounts of the adventures of two mythological giants, Gargantua and Pantagruel, have remained classics to this day. Spain also produced a classic, the still popular *Don Quixote*, by Cervantes [1547–1616], and in England the writings of Francis Bacon, Lord Verulam [1561–1626], and the historian, Holinshed [*c.* 1520–1580], contain much of value and interest.

Bacon's chief preoccupation was with the philosophy of science rather than its practice, and while as a result he performed very few experiments himself, he advocated strongly the importance of making detailed investigations of nature and of forming general principles which would explain the facts discovered, an approach that cut right across the traditional one in which the authority of men such as Aristotle and Ptolemy were regarded as infallible, or in which philosophers erected a purely abstract world-system that bore little relation to the world as it is. Bacon's influence was mainly felt in the seventeenth century and hence does not concern us here, but his criticism of the general scientific attitude of his day and the originality of his thought were undoubtedly affected by the experiments and theories of a number of late Renaissance scientists and philosophers, the chief of whom were the Pole, Copernicus [1473–1543], the Italian, Bruno [1548–1600], the Dane, Brahe [1546–1601], and the German, Kepler [1571–1630]. These four men proved or believed that the earth, far from being the centre of the universe, was merely one of many planets revolving round the sun. Copernicus's book, published in the year of his death, aroused no controversy because a Preface by a friend assured the reader that the central idea was purely theoretical, but when thirty years or so later, with the Counter-Reformation in full swing, Bruno constructed a philosophy in which the Copernican system is an integral part, he was not only branded as a heretic by the Catholics, but also by the Calvinists, and from 1579 on he was constantly moving about Europe in order to avoid imprisonment and death, finally and inadvisedly returning to Italy, where he was eventually burnt at the stake.

While Bruno philosophized about the solar system, Brahe observed it systematically, the first astronomer to do so. His instruments and calculations were far more accurate than those of his predecessors, and while he rejected the Copernican system because he could not detect any change in the relative positions of the stars, he evolved one which, although the earth is the centre, is mathematically equivalent to that of Copernicus. In 1600 Kepler became his assistant, and his three famous laws of planetary motion, which still describe accurately the movements and speeds of the planets and which later provided the basis of Newton's laws of gravitation, were largely founded on his master's work, and represent an astonishing feat when one remembers that all observations were made with the naked eye, as the telescope was not invented until 1609, the year Kepler published the first two of his laws.

Copernicus's 'heliocentric' system was the great scientific and philosophic bone of contention in the sixteenth and seventeenth centuries, and was not only officially branded as heresy by the Roman Church in 1616, but rejected by many Protestants, particularly the Calvinists. The Church as a whole, however, was not opposed to science as a study, but only when scientific ideas conflicted with traditional philosophic and Christian beliefs, one of which was that the earth was the most important celestial body. In other departments, therefore, men experimented and theorized with no fear of being burnt alive, and while these men did not then and have not since achieved such fame as the four mentioned above, they contributed much to the advancement of scientific knowledge.

In England, for example, Gilbert [1540–1603] supported Bacon in his insistence on experiments, but, unlike his greater countryman, he practised what he preached and made some remarkable discoveries in electricity and magnetism.

In medicine the German, Paracelsus [1493–1541], although propounding a lot of nonsense, advocated the use of mineral drugs—compounds of mercury, lead, copper, etc.—as well as opium. More important were the painter-sculptor, Michelangelo, his compatriot, Fallopius [1523–1562], and the Belgian, Vesalius [1515–1564], all of whom made detailed dissections of the human body; in fact, Vesalius's description of the structure of the body is remarkably correct considering that he had no microscope (invented *c.* 1610). The advance in anatomical knowledge prompted greater skill in surgery, and the most outstanding surgeon of the century, the Frenchman, Paré [1510–1596], discarded the customary treatment of gun-shot wounds (i.e. the application of boiling oil) and of severe bleeding from amputations (i.e. the use of a hot iron to coagulate the blood), employing ointments for the first and stemming the flow of blood by tying up the blood vessels, a method that had not been practised since the first century A.D. The widespread ravages of syphilis, which frequently disfigured noses, prompted a number of surgeons, some of whom were apparently successful, to repair the damage by skin grafts—in other words, to practise plastic surgery.

Herbs played a large part in mediaeval and Renaissance medicine, but the descriptions and drawings of the plants themselves were merely copies from old manuscripts until the sixteenth century, when three Germans, Brunfels [d. 1534], Bock [1498–1554], and Fuchs [1501–1566], described as accurately as was possible without microscopes, and employed artists to draw in detail, both herbal and other plants. Bock even attempted a general classification. If botany before 1500 was rudimentary, zoology was practically non-existent, as the reliance on ancient authority had largely degenerated into imaginary and improbable stories about beasts. With the Swiss, Gesner [1516–1565], however, a great advance was made, and while he shows a natural uncertainty about animals in distant lands, the bulk of his illustrations and descriptions are taken at first hand.

The enquiring spirit which made some men observe and speculate upon the Universe and the position of our world in it made others venture into the unknown places of the world itself and the voyages of Columbus, Vasco da Gama, Magellan, the Cabots, Cortez, and others were succeeded by Pizarro, who conquered Peru (1532–6), Sir Francis Drake, the second man to circumnavigate the globe (1577–80), and the beginnings of English colonization in Newfoundland (1583), Virginia (1607), and New England (1620), the last founded by the Pilgrim Fathers after their historic voyage in the *Mayflower*. In 1542 the Portuguese landed in Japan, the Spaniards discovered the Solomon Islands (1567) and the New Hebrides (1606), and by the latter part of the century most European countries, especially Spain, Portugal, England, and Holland were regularly sending out expeditions westwards to the Americas or eastwards round the Cape of Good Hope to India (the East India Company was founded in 1600 and its Dutch equivalent two years later). By 1600 the main outlines of South America were known, the north-western shores of North America visited several times, notably by the Frenchman, Cartier [*c.* 1491–1557], and in the early years of the seventeenth century the Spaniards had settled in many parts of the American continent south of Mexico, and the French and English had done likewise further north.

The mass of knowledge acquired by these explorations and those of the fifteenth century showed the world maps of mediaeval geographers, who had relied mainly on Ptolemy, to be hopelessly inaccurate, and great strides were made by a number of cartographers, the most important and influential being the Fleming, Mercator [1512–1594], who produced a map of the world based on a projection which still bears his name and which has been used for nearly all nautical charts from the eighteenth century to the present day. Navigational instruments, too, improved in accuracy, and were supported by the revival of mathematics, particularly algebra and trigonometry, and, in the early seventeenth century, by the increasing use of decimals and the invention of logarithms by the Scotsman, Napier [1550–1617]. These developments naturally affected surveying, and as early as 1533 the principle of triangulation had been described; thirty years later plane tables were in general use, and in 1597 the first national atlas of any country was published in England.

Expeditions to distant lands, then as now, are expensive, and these, but more particularly the political and religious wars of the fifteenth and sixteenth centuries, with their resultant bribes either to obtain support or buy off opposition, together with the widespread havoc caused by outbreaks of plague in both centuries, rendered most of Europe very short of money, the chief exception being Spain, where the conquests of the West Indies, Mexico, and Peru brought the Spanish Treasury enormous wealth. Elsewhere the demand for silver was acute, and as a result mining and metallurgy became more important than ever before. Great advances were made in the construction of pumps that could remove water from deep mines, the smelting of ore, the ventilation of shafts, etc. The man who investigated this aspect of science more thoroughly than any other was the German, Georgius Agricola [1494–1555], who has been called "the father of metallurgy"; some of his processes for extracting metal from ore have remained virtually unchanged to this day.

The intense interest in science during the late Renaissance led to the formation of several academies which were very similar in function and constitution to the artistic ones already mentioned, and, like them, the earliest were founded in Italy—Naples (1560), Florence (1567), and Rome (1600). Although she produced few scientists of eminence, Italy was almost as much the main centre of scientific discussion as she was of musical activity, for many foreign scientists studied at her universities, and just as the galaxy of northern composers who at first dominated the Italian musical scene were followed by men such as Palestrina, Marenzio, and the Gabrielis, so Italy eventually produced one of the most famous scientists of all time, Galileo, but he belongs outside this chapter.

The Renaissance has long been regarded as one of the greatest epochs in the history of man, and rightly so, but whereas later historians have paid glowing tribute to the achievements in the fine arts, literature, and philosophy, and have fully recognized the upsurge of creative ability and desire for knowledge which lay behind these achievements, and behind the exploration of distant lands, and the new scientific attitude of experiment and deduction, they have without exception either merely fleetingly touched on the contribution music made to this period or else omitted mention of it altogether. It must be said in their defence, however, that until comparatively recently very little music of the fifteenth and sixteenth centuries was available in modern editions, and as most historians are neither competent nor have the time to undertake the lengthy and often difficult task of editing early prints and manuscripts, nor the faculty for assessing their aesthetic value, the blame rests largely on their musical contemporaries. Today there is no such excuse, and one who writes a social history of England, for example, and devotes a totally inadequate dozen lines or so to the music that flourished under the Tudors and who, while including Holbein's name, makes no mention of Byrd, is guilty of presenting a picture that is neither accurate nor complete.

Music permeated the whole of Renaissance society to an extent unknown before. Folk-singing and dancing were more widespread than in earlier centuries and art music more intensely cultivated. Although the poorer classes were allowed no opportunity to listen to madrigals or chansons and can only have appreciated to a very slight degree the masses, motets, services, and anthems that they heard in church—so complex compared to their own folk-music—the growing wealth of the bourgeois, the middle merchant class, enabled them to imitate and eventually acquire the tastes of the aristocracy; but while they could afford to pay the piper and hence call the tune, they did not at first demand an art more in keeping with their simple, homely background. Not until the seventeenth century in fact did a 'popular' art music arise, and even then it was largely restricted to one country, Italy, and one type, opera.

PERFORMANCE

The general trend described at the end of Chapter 1 is less strikingly evident in the sacred than in the secular music of the late Renaissance; nevertheless, there is a marked difference in approach between the beginning and end of the period, particularly in the motet, and the same considerations with regard to the performance of secular music in general and of madrigals in particular apply to compositions for both the Catholic and Protestant Churches. It should be noted, however, that throughout the period the Gloria, Credo, and Sanctus of the mass, and their Protestant counterparts, should include variations in speed, as in the fifteenth century (see Part I, Chapter 6, p. 229), but masses in general should be performed in a more restrained manner than motets. This restraint should also apply to the motets of Palestrina compared to those of Lassus, Victoria, or Byrd, or, indeed, most other composers of his generation and later.

Instrumental music too reflects the trend towards greater expressiveness. This is clearly shown by the development of the harpsichord (see p. 341), and most compositions for this instrument, especially those in variation-form or with repeated sections (e.g. dance movements), should make use of the timbres and dynamic contrasts that were possible at the time when the piece was written. Changes of speed may also occur between variations within the limits of tactus=M.M. 60–100. The choice of timbre will largely depend on personal taste, and of speed on the nature of the music, or the descriptive title (if there is one), or both. Many instrumental compositions include signs that indicate some kind of ornament; we do not know which ornaments were meant, and it may well be that the composer only added the signs as a general indication as to which notes should be embellished, leaving the exact choice of ornament to the player. In any case, perfectly satisfactory results can be obtained by simply using upper or lower mordants (depending on the context) and the occasional trill on long notes, particularly at cadences. With regard to speed, dynamics, and timbre, the same considerations apply to the clavichord, lute, and organ as to the harpsichord, except that contrasts in tone-colour are impossible on the clavichord and very limited on the lute. It should be realized, however, that modern harpsichords, clavichords, and lutes approximate much more closely, both in sound and construction, to the Renaissance types than do modern organs; indeed, most organ music composed before the nineteenth century, particularly that of Germany, sounds quite different and distinctly superior when played on the original instruments (or copies) than on the vast majority of modern organs.

3

THE BAROQUE:
MUSIC FOR THE STAGE—I

LOOKING back over the previous 1,600 years or so, it is clear that up to this point the history of music is predominantly the history of vocal music, and for two obvious reasons; the first is that the voice is the most natural of all instruments, and the second that during most of this period the church was the main centre of artistic activity and sacred music must obviously be vocal. Even if we leave out sacred music, the predominance of vocal over instrumental music is still overwhelming, as the strong bias towards secular composition which began in the fourteenth century was very much in evidence during the late Renaissance, the madrigal and chanson being more popular and progressive than but not necessarily thereby superior to instrumental and liturgical music, whether Catholic or Protestant. The greater popularity of secular vocal music compared to sacred that has existed ever since received a new impetus in the last two decades of the sixteenth century through the creation of a new kind of music that eventually blossomed into opera, and which continued the supremacy of vocal music during most of the baroque period. Like the madrigal and chanson, opera was not only more popular and progressive than sacred and instrumental music but also exerted a considerable influence on them.

This 'New Music', as Giulio Caccini [*c.* 1545–1618], one of its creators, called it, is a rare instance in the history of any art of theory preceding practice, for it was deliberately modelled on ancient Greek tragedy, which, so Caccini and the group to which he belonged thought, was sung in its entirety. They were wrong in this, as only the choruses were actually sung, but they were right in that Greek tragedy is essentially a lyrical art which, at moments of great emotional stress, cries out for and almost certainly received some kind of instrumental accompaniment.

The men most actively concerned in this 'revival' of classical drama were members of one of the many academies that, as we have seen, sprang up all over Italy during the late Renaissance. This particular one, which began meeting *c.* 1580, is usually known as the Florentine Camerata ('Society'), and included, in addition to the virtuoso singer Caccini, the noblemen Count Bardi [1534–1612], at whose palace the meetings were first held, and Jacopo Corsi [1561 – 1602], the poet Rinuccini [1562 – 1621], the singer-composer Jacopo Peri [1561–1633], the composer Emilio de' Cavalieri [*c.* 1550–1602], the theorist Girolamo Mei [1519 – 1594], who considerably influenced the leading spirit of the Camerata Vincenzo Galilei who was not only a lutanist (see pp. 353–4) but also a composer and theorist of no mean order.

It was Galilei who set the ball rolling with a treatise published in 1581 in which he attacks the elaborate polyphonic imitative style of the Renaissance—a style in which he himself had composed—because it can neither render words clearly nor express with sufficient subtlety or force the emotions of the text. In place of this 'old music' he advocates a style which consists fundamentally of a single vocal line that follows closely the natural accents and inflexions of the text, and which is supported by a series of simple instrumental chords. Moreover, the singer is expected to deliver the vocal line with great feeling and, if they are not actually written down, to improvise ornaments on the more important words. Such pieces are called 'monodies', and although some of Galilei's examples (all of them lost) seem to have consisted of a vocal line and a written-out accompaniment for four viols, the earliest surviving monodies have only a voice part and a bass. This last was eventually called 'basso continuo' or, in English, 'thorough-bass' from 'through' or 'continuous', and at first was played on the lute, theorbo, or a keyboard instrument; during the first decades of the seventeenth century it became standard practice for the bass line to be doubled by a viola da gamba or 'cello, as in many of the English ayres (see Chapter 1, p. 286). The bass line is sometimes figured—that is, a number or numbers are added above or (more usually) below a note which indicate the chords to be played above that note. For example '$^{6}_{3}$' means that the third and sixth (or their octaves) are to be played, i.e. a first inversion, the intervals being major or minor according to the key signature. As the method of figuring became more generally accepted the insertion of numbers was reduced, '6' implying '$^6_3$' and no number implying '$^5_3$', or root position. In some of the earlier examples the bass is entirely unfigured, the composer leaving the choice of chord to the player; but even when figures are given the player was expected to add suspensions, runs, trills, interesting or relevant melodic or rhythmic fragments, etc., at suitable places. Thus in both accompaniment and vocal line improvisation played a larger part than at any time previously. (Unless otherwise qualified, the word 'continuo', here and in the next chapters, will mean a figured or unfigured bass line supporting a series of harmonies either specified by figures or implied, and played on the harpsichord, the bass line being doubled by a gamba or 'cello in recitatives, and elsewhere by two or more of these instruments, sometimes with double basses, the latter usually playing only when the full string band (i.e., violins I and II, violas, and 'cellos) is added to the harpsichord.)

Caccini, in his treatise, *Nuove Musiche* ('New Music'), published in 1602, claims that the embellishment of the vocal line is a new departure and that the ornaments he gives are mostly his own invention. Neither is true, for, as we saw in Chapter 1, the madrigal was sometimes embellished, and many of his ornaments are in fact taken from earlier treatises. Nor is it true, as some later writers have stated, that monody was a complete break with Renaissance composition, for the solo song with lute accompaniment was extremely popular and vocal improvisation well-known in the sixteenth century, and the basso continuo was a natural development from the basso seguente (see pp. 317-18). Moreover, the importance of the text and the stress on a dominant vocal line with a subservient accompaniment were also continuations of Renaissance practice, the latter being apparent in the late sixteenth-century madrigal (see Chapter 1, p. 269), and the former in the care with which Rore, Monte, and Gesualdo matched the moods suggested by the poem, or with which Wert and Marenzio set individual words. The pendulum had swung back again, for from Gregorian chant, where the liturgy was, and is, all-important, music became more and more the dominant partner, reaching its zenith in the fourteenth century; from then on the setting of words became not only more circumspect but, in the late Renaissance, an integral part of composition, reaching its peak in the early baroque monody.

It is important to realize that the Camerata were not anti-Renaissance, but only anti-polyphony; indeed, the very fact that they tried to imitate Greek tragedy is proof of this, as the study and interpretation of classical culture was one of the main pursuits and characteristics of the Renaissance. But polyphony was too firmly established to be overthrown in a day; in fact, it never was overthrown, and while the kind of monody described above began to be written in increasing numbers, hardly any are by composers of the first rank, for the lack of melodic interest and poverty of texture was hardly likely to attract first-rate musical talent (Ex. 16*):

(*Sad shores, shady ghastly fields, that have not seen stars or suns, nor ever a flash of lightning.*)

The monody, in fact, appeals primarily to the singer, who can show off his skill in expressiveness, diction, and the improvising of embellishments, and it is noteworthy that of the first three leading monodists, Galilei, Peri, and Caccini, the last two were professional singers.

* Adapted from R. Haas, *Musik des Baroks*, p. 36.

But the melodic bent of the Italian genius was too powerful to be satisfied for long with such a limited vocal line, and the madrigals and arias in Caccini's *Nuove Musiche* reveal a more lyrical vocal part and a more interesting bass. The distinction between madrigals and arias is that the former are through-composed (as in Ex. 17: see also *H.A.M.*, 184—miscalled 'aria'), while most of the latter are strophic (see Chapter 5) and although both contain florid passages the arias are, on the whole, simpler, more clear-cut, and frankly tuneful (Ex. 17*):

(*Be moved to pity my torment, and where weeping and sighing do not reach you...*)

* Melody and bass from *I Classici della Musica Italiana: No. 4, Giulio Caccini*, ed. Perinello.

The three kinds of monody so far mentioned, i.e. the simple type (Ex. 16) and the Caccini madrigal and aria, eventually developed into the operatic 'secco recitative' (see p. 382), 'arioso', and 'aria' respectively. The first two are always through-composed with the emphasis on affective declamation of the words, the arioso being the more lyrical or impassioned of the two, while in the aria the melodic element is the most important.

Before we go any further, it will be as well to define baroque opera as a dramatic spectacle unified in style in which the entire text (libretto) is set to music, and which consists mainly of solos, but which may also include instrumental items (dances, preludes, etc.), and vocal ensembles (choruses, duets, etc.), the voice or voices being accompanied by instruments. Furthermore, by 'opera' we mean the most important and popular type—later called *opera seria*—which is based on a serious, sometimes tragic, and always emotional subject, but which may contain comic episodes, and which almost invariably ends happily. The other types of opera will always be qualified, e.g. ballad opera, *opera buffà*, etc. The word 'opera', incidentally, which literally means '[a] work', was not commonly used in the modern sense until the end of the seventeenth century, and composers and librettists employed a bewildering assortment of labels to describe the new art form, those that occur most often being *Tragedia* [or *Dramma*, or *Opera*] *rappresentata in musica*, *Dramma* [or *Commedia*, or *Opera*] *musicale*, and *Dramma per* [or *in*] *musica*.

Just as monody had its roots in earlier practice, so had opera, these being the French ballets and the Italian 'intermedii' and pastoral plays of the previous century. As we saw in Chapter 1, a few ballets in the late sixteenth century comprised a continuous series of dances based on a definite story and accompanied by instruments. The intermedii consisted of vocal solos, duets, etc., with orchestral accompaniment, together with purely instrumental pieces, and were performed before and after each act of a serious drama, the words of the songs generally being relevant to the action of the play. The pastoral play, because it was essentially lyrical in style and content, lent itself very easily to musical treatment, and from Poliziano's *Orfeo*—the earliest pastoral play and first produced in the 1470s—to Tasso's *Aminta* and Guarini's *Pastor Fido* at the end of the sixteenth century, this type of drama was frequently enhanced by musical settings of parts of the text, these settings being for one or more voices with instrumental accompaniment. Moreover, the structure and subject-matter provided the model for most early opera libretti.

Thus all the main ingredients of opera were already in existence except for a style of composition capable of conveying a story expressively and reasonably quickly. Renaissance polyphony and solo song were unsuitable because they were too complex or too concerned with pure melody, but the monodic style fitted the bill admirably.

It is most unfortunate that the music of the first opera, *Dafne*, composed in 1597 by Peri, with a few numbers by Corsi, to a libretto by Rinuccini, has been lost, apart from two fragments by Corsi. The earliest opera that has survived intact is *La rappresentazione di anima e di corpo*, by Cavalieri, produced in February 1600. This has frequently, but erroneously, been described as the first oratorio because it was first performed in one of Neri's oratories (see Chapter 2), and because it was meant to be morally edifying, being concerned with 'representations' of the 'soul' and 'body' of man, together with other allegorical figures, such as Pleasure, Intellect, Time, the World, etc. In fact, it is a genuine opera, for apart from a spoken Prologue it consists entirely of solos—mostly written in the new monodic style—choruses, dances, and instrumental interludes, and is accompanied by an orchestra. Moreover, in the Preface, as well as explaining how to 'realize' the harmonies from his figured bass and what vocal ornaments should be used, Cavalieri explicitly states that the work should be acted in a hall or theatre and that the actors' costumes should be both attractive and varied. Indeed, the opera is more forward-looking than and artistically superior to those by Peri and Caccini, because although the recitatives are more monotonous than in either Peri's or Caccini's operas, some of the solos are more frankly tuneful and thus, apart from anticipating the later aria, provide a greater degree of contrast, as do the choruses, of which there are an unusually large number for an Italian opera of any period. Furthermore, the work is divided into three acts, four being the normal number until *c.* 1640 on, and Cavalieri suggests that four intermedii be performed before and after each act, an idea that became very popular in the second half of the century (*H.A.M.*, 183).

Most history books state that the first opera to have survived in its entirety is Peri's *Euridice* (libretto by Rinuccini), presumably because, although it was performed after Cavalieri's opera—namely, October 1600—it is based on a secular subject, the famous legend of Orpheus and Euridice. But the subject of an opera is entirely irrelevant to it as an artistic type, and hence Cavalieri's work should take pride of place. *Euridice* was published in 1601, as was Caccini's setting of the same libretto, but this was not performed until 1602. Caccini, who had managed by devious means to insert some of his own music into Peri's opera, clearly took the latter as a model, for both versions are very similar, the chief distinctions being Peri's greater forcefulness in tragic expression, and Caccini's less rigid monotony of the vocal line. There is hardly any purely instrumental music in either opera, and the few choruses, which occur mainly at the ends of scenes, even when not in unison, reveal very elementary part-writing. Occasionally a solo song in regular metre occurs, but the bulk of both operas consists of long stretches of monody which, even allowing for affective declamation and ornamentation by the singer, soon tire the ear by their lack of variety and by the irritatingly frequent perfect cadences (*H.A.M.*, 182, one of the opera's more expressive passages).

None of the composers of opera or monody so far mentioned were of the first rank, and although the monodic style attracted scores of musicians, none possessed the musical and dramatic genius of the first great operatic composer, Monteverdi. He it was who clothed the bare bones of the early opera with the living flesh of strikingly forceful recitative, sensuous melody, boldly dissonant harmony, and a sense of the dramatic rarely if ever surpassed by later baroque composers. He came to monody via the madrigal, and in his fifth book (1605) the last six madrigals have an obligatory as opposed to an optional continuo part. These six and many of the 'normal' madrigals in both the fourth (1603) and fifth books contain dissonances far exceeding anything by his contemporaries, although his use of chromaticism is not quite so daring as Gesualdo's. Having experimented in continuo writing and choral recitatives (see pp. 269-70) Monteverdi produced his first opera, *Orfeo*, in 1607. This, though based on the same legend, is superior in every way to the *Euridice* of Peri or Caccini. To begin with, the story is made more poignant, because whereas in Rinuccini's libretto no conditions are imposed on Orpheus during the journey from Hades, so that he can look back as much as he likes and the pair are happily reunited (as they are in most later operas on this subject), the poem of Alessandro Striggio (the son of the composer mentioned in Chapter 1, p. 271) keeps to the original ending, even though Monteverdi transports Orpheus to Heaven on the wings of Apollo's compassion. To this famous legend the composer set music that not only enhances its dramatic and emotional possibilities, but which is also a virtually complete cross-section of contemporary styles wedded into a completely satisfying art form. Thus, instead of the almost unbroken monodic line of Peri and Caccini, Monteverdi contrasts his recitatives with choruses in two, three, and five parts, both polyphonic (madrigals) and contrapuntal (balletts), duets for solo voices, instrumental interludes and dances, and even two short lyrical songs in A, B, A form, the form that was to become standard for secular and sacred vocal solos during the seventeenth and eighteenth centuries. The recitative passages, which still predominate, are far more expressive than those of Peri, Caccini, or Cavalieri, both in the actual vocal line and in the accompaniment, and the harmonic audacities of the composer's madrigals are turned to vivid dramatic effect—for example, in the scene where a messenger tells Orpheus of Euridice's fate to the accompaniment of sudden chord changes, such as E major to G minor and C minor to E major or A major (see *H.A.M.*, 187). The choruses and solo duets rarely carry on the action, for, as in Greek tragedy, they stand aside, as it were, and comment on what is happening, and so provide the audience with moments of relaxation and the composer with opportunities to show his musical as well as his dramatic skill; these vocal ensembles, while not so strikingly original as his recitatives, do reveal Monteverdi's all-round mastery of composition.

Perhaps the most remarkable thing about *Orfeo* is the way it is constructed. Here is no haphazard succession of unconnected solos, choruses, etc., but a carefully planned series with a far greater degree of unity than any earlier and many later operas. For example, the Prologue, a monody sung by a symbolical character 'Music', consists of five variations on a ground bass, each variation being separated by a ritornello or instrumental refrain, which is also played at the beginning and end of the Prologue. Act I, which is pastoral and gay, is constructed thus:

Monody (Shepherd)
Chorus A (contrapuntal *a*5)
Monody (Nymph)
Chorus B (polyphonic *a*5) and ritornello I
Monody (Shepherd, Orpheus, Euridice)
Chorus B and ritornello I
Chorus A
Monody (Shepherd)

Ritornello II and Chorus (*a*2)
" " " (*a*3)
" " " (*a*2)

Chorus C (contrapuntal-polyphonic *a*5)
Sinfonia

(N.B.—The choruses *a*2 and *a*3 have different vocal parts, but are supported by the same bass. 'Sinfonia' can be defined as an independent instrumental piece, i.e. not connected with a vocal number, which usually occurs at the beginning and /or end of an act or scene.)

Again, in Act II the messenger's first poignant phrases are later repeated by a shepherd, and finally twice taken up by the chorus in a five-part version.

The above are only some of the ways by which Monteverdi welds what might easily have become a hotchpotch into a homogeneous whole, and this factor, together with the quality of the music itself and the, at times, deliberate choice of instruments to underline a particular dramatic episode, make the work the most outstanding first essay in any musical genre by any composer.

Monteverdi's orchestra in *Orfeo* was larger than in any previous dramatic or semi-dramatic work, and was typical of the Renaissance in the high proportion of chord-playing or 'fundamental' instruments compared to the purely melodic kinds. Thus fifteen of the former are required, including two harpsichords, two wood organs (i.e. positives with flute pipes), one regal, and three viole da gamba. The latter class comprises fourteen stringed and thirteen wind instruments, including four violins, four violas, two 'cellos, two contrabass viols (violins), two small violins, five trombones, cornetts, trumpets, and a flute. Not all these instruments played at the same time, and mostly it was left to the musical director to decide which should play when; at certain places, however, Monteverdi specifies the instrumentation exactly, as in the choruses of Act III, when the spirits of Hades sing to the accompaniment of a regal, positive, five trombones, two bass gambas, and a violone, the regal's reedy, bitter timbre and the bass strings providing a sombre background, to which a solemn note is added by the trombones; trombones, indeed, later became traditionally associated with anything 'infernal', as, for example, in Mozart's *Don Giovanni*. In Act III also occurs 'Possente spirito', in which Orpheus pleads with Charon to let him pass; most of the vocal line exists in two forms, one plain and the other highly ornamented, the latter not only showing how elaborate such embellishments could be, but also serving a dramatic function in that Orpheus is here pouring out all the resources of his art in order to soften Charon's heart. The emotional intensity of the arioso is also increased by dividing the vocal part into short phrases and inserting between each florid passages for two violins, then two cornetts, then harp, and finally two violins and gamba. In the last section Orpheus, up till now supported by the continuo only, is accompanied by an orchestra *a*4, probably the first instance of what was later called *recitativo accompagnato* (see p. 45) ; it makes a most moving climax to his song.

Considering Monteverdi's output in general and the greatness of *Orfeo* in particular, the fact that of his twenty-one dramatic compositions only six—two ballets, a dramatic cantata, and three operas—have survived complete is undoubtedly the most shattering loss in the whole history of music. The single surviving fragment from his next opera, *Arianna* (1608), gives further proof of his outstanding genius, for 'Arianna's Lament' ('Lasciatemi morire') moved the entire audience to tears at the first performance, and not only became the most famous monody of the first half of the century, but set such a fashion that hardly any serious opera of the next 150 years omitted a similar lament. ('When I am laid in earth' from Purcell's *Dido and Aeneas* is perhaps the best-known example outside the Continent.) Its fame prompted Monteverdi to include a five-part arrangement of it in his sixth book of madrigals (1614) (see Ex. 12, p. 270) and a setting to sacred words in his *Selva Morale e Spirituale* ('Collection of Moral and Spiritual Songs') (1641) (Ex. 18*, p. 378).

Both *Orfeo* and *Arianna* were produced in Mantua, where Monteverdi was court composer to the Gonzaga family from 1590 to 1612. In the latter year he was inexplicably dismissed, but after a year of unemployment spent at his native city of Cremona he obtained the post of choirmaster at St. Mark's, Venice, a post he retained until his death, and during which he composed the bulk of his dramatic music. Nothing of this remains except a dramatic cantata and two late operas, but before we discuss these we must see what progress had been made elsewhere by other composers.

After Peri and Caccini had each produced their own versions of *Euridice*, Florence declined as an operatic centre, although a few later operas were staged by these two composers and by Marco da Gagliano [1582 – 1643], whose *Dafne*, to the same libretto as Peri's lost work, was produced in 1610, two years after its first performance in Mantua. Rome and Venice—especially the latter—now became the focal points of operatic development. In Rome Cavalieri's *Rappresentazione* was followed by *Eumelio* (1606), by Agostino Agazzari [1578 – 1640], also aimed at moral edification, and, in 1620, by the first purely secular opera to be performed in the Holy City, *Aretusa*, by Filippo Vitali [d. after 1653]. Neither of these works advanced much on Florentine ideals, but in *La Catena d'Adone* ('The Chain of Adonis') (1626), by Domenico Mazzochi [1592–1665], Roman opera received a new lease of life. In this work the unending recitative of the Florentines is deliberately broken up by the insertion of arias, the characters become almost frivolous instead of statuesque, and the complexity of the plot is accompanied by all kinds of stage trickery—disguises, abrupt transformation scenes, ascents and descents of gods, etc. In plot and fantastic presentation, as in the number of arias and the rapid patter of much of the recitative as opposed to the

* Melody and bass from *Tutte le Opere di Claudio Monteverdi*, XI, ed. Malipiero. The realization is based to some extent on the five-part madrigalian version.

(Let me die; who do you think can comfort me in such sad misfortune, in so great a martyrdom? Let me die.)

expressive declamation of monody, Mazzochi's work anticipates the general trend of later baroque opera, but in the large number of its choruses it differs from subsequent developments and shows its link with the past—namely, Cavalieri's *Rappresentazione.*

A word must be said here about stage settings and machinery, as they played such an important part in baroque opera; our discussion will be limited to public theatres and those privately owned by certain of the nobility, not to the simple platforms with their roughly painted canvas or wood scenery used in market-squares and fair-grounds by wandering bands of actors.

In the Middle Ages and during most of the Renaissance, stage settings were static, the usual plan consisting of a series of 'flats' (wooden frames covered with canvas) placed at the sides or 'wings' of the stage, and so arranged as to form two solid walls on both sides (Ex. 19, *d*) from the front ('proscenium arch'—*a*) to the back ('cyclorama'—*b*), and painted so as to represent the different scenes simultaneously, the only indications of a scene-change being a series of differently designed flats that partially or wholly screened the cyclorama and which were withdrawn, either into the wings or hoisted ('flown') above the stage, or replaced, revealing or obscuring the one behind (*c*):

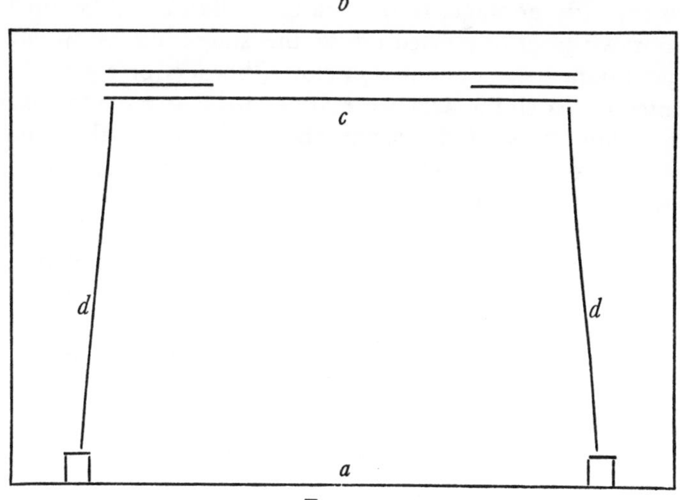

Ex. 19

The combination of the different scenes in the one setting was unrealistic and demanded the imaginative co-operation of the audience, but the realism that, as we have seen, was one of the main characteristics of the Renaissance brought about a change, and in the early years of the sixteenth century an Italian architect, Sebastiano Serlio [1475–1554], applied the then new technique of perspective. Serlio kept the two walls of flats, but painted them so as to represent a single scene, e.g. buildings flanking a street, increasing the natural perspective of the stage as seen from the auditorium by painting the buildings at the cyclorama end smaller than those near the proscenium, thus giving an illusion of greater depth.

The desire for realism brought yet another change, for while Serlio provided designs for three different types of drama—tragedy, comedy, and satire—the static set is less likely to be as realistic as when the scenery changes with the sphere of action. There had been experiments with movable scenery as early as 1530, but it did not become common until the seventeenth century, when public theatres and opera houses found that it was both cheaper and more spectacular than the elaborately painted and constructed static sets. In order to effect scene changes as quickly as possible, the flats were placed parallel to the proscenium and several feet apart, and were either fitted into grooves or else placed on wheeled carriages that ran on rails beneath the stage. In both cases the flats could be quickly withdrawn from or pushed on to the stage (Ex. 20, p. 381). In addition, strips of canvas or cloth ('borders' or 'sky cloths'), painted to match the flats, were suspended across the top of the stage, thus masking the space above the stage (the 'flies'). During the seventeenth and eighteenth centuries the flies housed a number of ropes and pulleys to which were attached not only the borders, which were thus easily raised and lowered to conform to the flats, but also various more or less elaborate 'machines', such as chariots, clouds, bowers, etc. On these one or more characters, usually gods and goddesses, could descend on to or ascend from the stage, or be suspended in mid-air.

Although the spectacular element played such an important part in Mazzochi's *La Catena d'Adone*, this aspect of operatic production was less marked in Rome than elsewhere, probably because it tended to distract the audience's attention from the plot, and the plots of later Roman operas, because of the strong

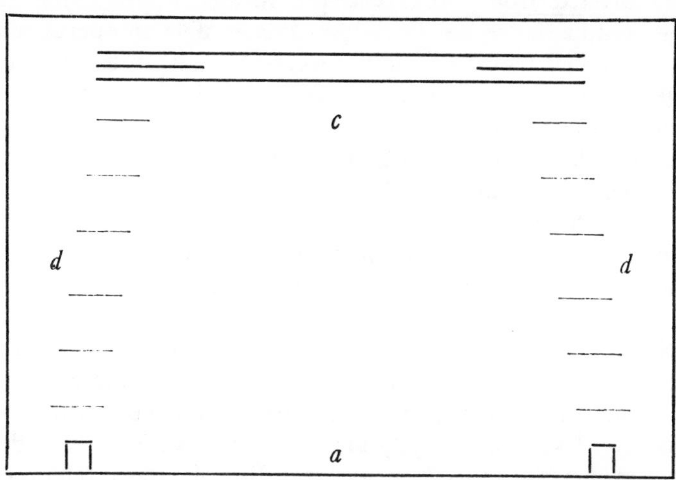

Ex. 20

religious atmosphere and despite the success of Mazzochi's secular opera, were almost invariably moral or religious in tone.

The chief patron of early Roman opera was the Barberini family, particularly Maffeo, who later became Pope Urban VIII [pontificate 1623–1644]. In 1632 the Barberinis built a theatre with a seating capacity of over 3,000, and celebrated its completion with a performance of one of the most important operas of the Roman School, *Sant' Alessio*, by Stefano Landi [1586/7 – 1639]. The libretto, based on the life of St. Alexis [fifth century], is the first to deal with a real flesh and blood individual, and it marked another step along the path of subjective expression, a path that began with Rore, was widened by some of the later madrigalists, notably Gesualdo, and deepened by the Florentine monodists; but whereas the earlier opera composers had been concerned with emotions in general, or had expressed particular ones through legendary or symbolical and therefore universal characters (Orpheus, the Soul of Man, etc.), *Sant' Alessio* is concerned with the emotions of a central figure who actually lived. The other characters, too, are clearly drawn, not from the fifth century, but the seventeenth, and in this and in the inclusion of comic scenes the opera follows the example of *La Catena d'Adone* (*H.A.M.*, 209).

From a purely musical point of view also, *Sant' Alessio* is something of a landmark in that the recitatives are clearly differentiated from the arias, the former approaching the rapid patter or 'secco' ('dry') recitative of later operas, and the latter being more obviously song-like, with occasional use of sequential phrases, and showing at times a definite feeling for form and modern tonality and a striking use of text repetition. This last had been largely rejected by the monodists, but it is a common feature of Renaissance polyphony, where it is employed for musical rather than dramatic ends. Form and tonality from now on become increasingly inseparable, for unity and variety, the twin pillars upon which all musical structures are built, depend more on the relationship and distinction of keys compared to a central key than on anything else. Thus the form A, B, A is not so much a melodic sandwich as a tonal one, because in the middle section the modulations to different keys are usually more striking than are the differences in melody: indeed, melodically B is often a development of A, containing little or no new material; hence variety is achieved largely through the temporary establishment of keys which, while providing a contrast with, also promote a desire to return to the tonic, a desire that is satisfied in the repeat of A, and which also brings a feeling of unity.

Other noteworthy features of Landi's opera are the number of vocal ensembles and choruses, the replacement of viols by violins, and the reduction in numbers and importance of woodwind and brass instruments; the string band is beginning to assume its later function as the backbone of the orchestra, although the harpsichord, lute, theorbo, and harp still play a large part. The theorbo in fact was frequently employed in baroque opera, even as late as Handel, while the harpsichord became the essential instrument of any orchestra, inside or outside the opera house, until after Haydn began to write symphonies.

Some of the instrumental pieces in *Sant' Alessio* are of more than usual interest, particularly the sinfonie that precede the three acts. The sinfonia to Act I consists of a slow chordal section followed by a quicker polyphonic one, an arrangement that became standard in the so-called 'French overture' of Lully and others (see p. 420). The other two sinfonie are in three sections, quick-slow-quick, and anticipate the so-called 'Italian overture' of Alessandro Scarlatti (see Chapter 4, p. 451) (*H.A.M.*, 208).

For over fifty years after *La Catena d'Adone* hardly any serious secular operas, and none of any significance, were produced in Rome. Of the remainder the best is the pastoral opera, *La Galatea* (1639), by the famous castrato, Loreto Vittori [1600–1670], which continues the trend towards clear-cut form through organization of keys in the aria and the rapid patter of secco recitative. (A castrato was a man who, as a boy, had had an exceptionally beautiful treble voice and who was castrated before it broke. This prevented any change in the larynx and resulted in the combination of a voice of great purity and range with the lungs of an adult. Although castrati first appeared in opera in Monteverdi's *Orfeo*, the practice had been common in the sixteenth century, but the importance in opera of the solo singer brought the castrati to the fore, and from *c.* 1650 to *c.* 1750 the more famous of them were sought after by opera-houses as keenly and acclaimed by opera-goers as vociferously as the top-ranking stars of today are by film companies and audiences.) There is, however, one serious secular Roman opera, but it was produced in Paris. In 1644, when Pope Urban VIII died, the Barberinis were forced to emigrate by his successor, Innocent X [pontificate 1644–1655]. They settled in Paris, where Cardinal Mazarin [1602–1661], who had succeeded Cardinal Richelieu [1585–1642] as 'prime minister' of France, made it possible for them to bring many of their musicians. Among these was Luigi Rossi [*c.* 1597–1653], and his *Orfeo* (1647), while not the first Italian opera to be performed in Paris, was the first to be commissioned and expressly written for the French capital. Dramatically it is a hotchpotch of comedy, tragedy, ballets, and spectacles, but the musical numbers, although as varied as the plot, show more clearly than any other opera hitherto the refinement and sensuousness of melody and harmony which is the hall-mark of Italian music from *c.* 1650 onwards.

In 1653 the Barberinis, having become reconciled to Innocent X, returned to Rome, and to mark the occasion a comic opera with the appropriate title *Dal male il bene* ('Good from Evil') was performed. The music is by Antonio Maria Abbatini [1609/10-1677/9] and Marco Marazzoli [d. 1662], and the libretto was by a friend of the Barberinis, Giulio Respigliosi [1600–1669], who for the last two years of his life was Pope

Clement IX. This man was virtually the creator of Italian comic opera, for, apart from writing the libretti of several serious operas, including *Sant' Alessio* with its comic scenes, he was the author of the first comic opera text, *Chi soffre, speri*, produced in the Barberini theatre in 1639, with music by Marazzoli and Vergilio Mazzochi [1597–1646], brother of Domenico, and witnessed by a distinguished gathering, including Mazarin and John Milton. The plot is romantic, the comedy being provided by stock characters taken over from the *Commedia dell' Arte* (see Chapter 1, p. 271). Musically it is interesting in that its recitatives follow the rapid patter or secco type already noted in *La Galatea*, but it is less important than *Dal male il bene*, for this work, while continuing the marked distinction between recitative and aria, includes a feature which later became one of the main characteristics of *opera buffa*—namely, the ensembles (i.e. pieces for two or more soloists—duets, trios, etc.—as opposed to the chorus) which occur at the end of each act (see p. 483).

The year 1639 not only saw the birth of comic opera in Rome, but also the production, in December, of Monteverdi's opera, *Adone*, his first to be produced in the first public opera-house in Europe. This had been opened in 1637 through the private enterprise of the famous theorbo-player, Benedetto Ferrari [*c.* 1603 – 1681], and the composer, Francesco Manelli [1594 – 1667], under the name of Teatro di San Cassiano. All operas up to this year and many of them after it were performed in the private theatres of the aristocracy, such as that in the Barberini Palace, and it is an indication of the popularity and importance of Venetian opera that it was in this city, where, as we saw in Chapter 1, the seeds of baroque art found their richest soil, that the most characteristic type of Italian music from the seventeenth century to the present day was first made accessible to the man in the street. But the man in the street has never the same taste and understanding as the aristocratic connoisseur, and as he who pays the piper calls the tune, the tunes and their harmonizations, the libretti, and the productions as a whole underwent a remarkable transformation. Melodies became simpler and eminently singable, except for those virtuosic passages in which the composer gave the singer scope to show off his vocal acrobatics, rhythms became more obvious, and harmonies tended increasingly to crystallize round a firm major or minor centre. This last affected form, which became more clear-cut, because the stronger the tonal centre the greater the effect of modulation away from and back to this centre, unity being achieved through the repetition, often sequential, of melodic-rhythmic motives. The libretti, using the legends of classical antiquity simply as pegs on which to hang some kind of plot, are so constructed as to present a series of rapidly changing scenes in which the characters are either mere symbols of emotions or else provide comic relief.

Naturally, the man in the street was not entirely responsible for this transformation, for we have already seen that developments in Roman opera included more tuneful arias, a clearer sense of tonality and form, and abrupt, often fantastic, changes in scene, but he was unquestionably responsible for the speed at which it took place. Moreover, Venetian opera only reflected, albeit more strikingly than elsewhere, the changing literary and musical tastes of the times. Italian literature, already in decline during the Counter-Reformation, reached its lowest ebb during the seventeenth century. In poetry, prose, and drama there was hardly a writer with a spark of originality or genuine feeling, and, as so often happens, for this lack was substituted an extravagancy and insincerity of expression that but thinly disguises the underlying poverty of invention. The most suitable sphere for such an art was the theatre, where exaggeration, whether of plot, gesture, look, or speech, in order to communicate, is more often both necessary and natural than in either poetry or prose. And here we must make a distinction between 'dramatic' and 'theatrical'; the former, in its colloquial sense, means the occurrence, in any sphere of life, of an unusual, often striking, and always emotionally heightened event or succession of events, either actual in the present or the past, or fictitious, or an idea or succession of ideas (including the products of artistic imagination). Theatrical, also in its colloquial sense, means 'presented in an exaggerated manner', but, in view of what we have said above, it is not, neither should it be, used as a derogatory adjective when applied to the stage. Thus a symphony or a century at Lord's may be dramatic but should never be theatrical, whereas an opera or play should be both.

Theatricality permeated the whole of seventeenth-century Italian culture; it even invaded the Church, where not only the Jesuits (and after them other monastic orders) used the theatre as a means of propagating their religion, but the priest in the pulpit and even the liturgy itself, much of which is inherently dramatic, became affected; so much so that some foreign visitors were scandalized, finding little to choose in atmosphere and presentation between church and stage.

The change in musical taste was the result of the growing desire for greater emotional expression, a desire that, as we noted earlier, began with Rore. So long as polyphony held sway, however, the degree of expressiveness was checked, for polyphony is essentially classical in function in the sense that it tends to promote a balance between the various musical elements (melody, harmony, rhythm), as well as between the individual parts themselves. The declamatory madrigals of the Gabrielis and the chromaticism of Gesualdo stretched polyphony almost to breaking-point, but the desire for greater expression which they represented found complete freedom in the Florentine monody, and the way was open once again for Italian genius to express itself most naturally—that is, through the supremacy of melody. Ever since she had created, virtually single-handed, the magnificent repertoire of Christian chant, Italy had had to contend, so to speak, with part-music, and it is no coincidence that on the three occasions during the reign of polyphony, i.e. from the twelfth to the sixteenth centuries, on which she produced something distinctive her natural bent asserted itself. Thus, compared to the music of other countries, the upper voice or voices of the Ars Nova madrigal and caccia are more prominent and singable, the top part of the late fifteenth- and early sixteenth-century frottola is more clear-cut and 'popular', or else recitative-like with the accompaniment, on at least one occasion, reduced to a few simple chords (see Part I, Chapter 6, p. 210), and lastly the vocal part-music of the late sixteenth century, especially the madrigal, is more sensuous and colourful, with a distinct bias towards high voices. In this connexion, it should be remembered that Italian composers only came to the fore at the very end of the Renaissance; in fact, apart from Palestrina, who, as we have seen, was not fully representative of his time or country, the leading men —Marenzio, the Gabrielis, and Gesualdo—produced most of their work contemporaneously with the monodies of the Florentine Camerata. Furthermore, the amount of frankly popular music, such as carnival songs and balletti, was far greater than elsewhere in Europe, and the madrigal in which the soprano voice predominates was essentially the creation of an Italian—Luzzaschi.

But to return to Venice and Monteverdi. *Adone* was not only his first opera for the first public opera-house, but the first opera by a great composer that the public ever witnessed, and as we know it was a resounding success, it is doubly unfortunate that the music has been lost. However, its popularity prompted Monteverdi to compose three more operas, *Il Ritorno d'Ulisse*, *Le nozze d'Eneo con Lavinia* (music lost), and *L'incoronazione di Poppea*. The first of these was produced at the same theatre as *Adone*—the San Cassiano—in 1641, while the other two appeared in 1641 and 1642 respectively at the Santi Giovanni e Paolo, the second public opera-house in Venice, opened in 1639. This creative activity when the composer was between seventy-two and seventy-five years old inevitably brings to mind his great nineteenth-century compatriot, Verdi, who wrote his last two operas, *Otello* and *Falstaff*, when he was aged seventy-four and eighty.

The two operas that have survived of Monteverdi's last four show a profound difference in style and approach when compared to *Orfeo*, a difference that is more marked in *Ulisse* than in *Poppea*, for the earlier work is more typically Venetian in the rapid succession of scenes—comic, serious, or spectacular—the quick patter of its recitative, which is frequently broken up by short, song-like passages, the infrequency of instrumental numbers, and the way in which every opportunity for emotional expression is seized; as one writer has well said, "one senses the effort to be immediately understood, along with an almost nervous dread of monotony . . .".* Despite some fine musical and dramatic moments, the opera is inferior to *Poppea*, Monteverdi's last essay in this genre. Here the composer's musical taste and dramatic insight largely reject the purely spectacular and the restless succession of scenic contrasts, relying more on the vivid and subtle characterization of the leading figures in the drama, and it was surely no accident that Monteverdi chose an historical plot concerned with the ambitions and emotions of real people. *Poppea*, in fact, is the first great historical opera, foreshadowed by Landi's *Sant' Alessio* and succeeded by a large number on similar themes,

* D. Grout, *A Short History of Opera*, I, p. 87.

but although it was much admired for the brilliance of its characterization, its genuine passion, and the quality of its music, operatic taste, whetted by typical Venetian fare, preferred the sensuousness of pure melody, the excitement of coloratura (virtuoso) singing, and the fascination of gorgeous and variegated spectacles to the more profound, subtle, and hence less easily appreciated (or created) art, wherein music and drama achieve some kind of balance. In most baroque operas, indeed, the characters are treated as symbolical types, not as living flesh-and-blood individuals, the composer being far less concerned with the dramatic situations and characterization than with the purely musical side, and provided that the latter satisfied both its own artistic laws and the audience's love of melody and vocal display, it was quite on the cards that he would write a work that was both excellent of its kind and a 'smash-hit'. Moreover, a second- or third-rate composer with little sense of overall structure or of dramatic situation, but who could write catchy tunes and cater for virtuosity, found it easier to make his mark in serious music than in any other period of history, for at no other time was melody exalted to so high a position.

But we anticipate, because both Monteverdi and his contemporaries maintained some kind of balance between rhythm, melody, and harmony, and between music and drama. In *Poppea* the balance is well-nigh perfect, the music springing directly from the personalities of the characters and their interaction with each other, and revealing a marvellous variety in treatment—secco recitative, arioso, songs in *da capo* aria form (A, B, A), strophic and through-composed songs, songs with ritornelli, and songs supported by a ground bass (see Ex. 21: we shall define a ground, or ground bass, or 'basso ostinato' as a continuous set of variations built on a short recurring motive which is restricted to the lowest part). In order to give some idea of the passion and beauty of the music in this opera, here is the last section of the duet (in A, B, A form) between Poppea and Nero with which the opera ends. In the original the part of Nero was sung by a castrato (soprano), but no violence is done by the substitution of a natural male voice (Ex. 21*, pp. 389, 390).

So long as the music to *Adone* is lost, we cannot tell whether

* Melody, bass, and translation from *Songs and Duets from the Works of Claudio Monteverdi*, No. 3, ed. J. A. Westrup.

Ex.21 The end of the duet *Pur ti miro (L'incoronazione di Poppea)* (1642) Monteverdi

Ex.21 (contd.)

* The small notes are editorial and are necessary owing to Nero's part being an octave lower than the original.

Monteverdi's style in this opera owed more to public taste than to the work of his gifted pupil, Pietro Francesco Calletti-Bruni [1602–1676], who, as often happened, adopted the name of his patron, Cavalli, and who was the first great popular operatic composer. January 1639, the same year that *Adone* was produced, saw the performance of Cavalli's first opera, *Le nozze di Teti e di Peleo* at the San Cassiano Theatre. This, the first of forty-two operas, two-thirds of which have survived in score, and the first Venetian opera of which the music has been preserved, shows a greater preference, compared with Monteverdi's late operas, for simple, graceful melodies in which the whole consists of well-balanced sections; Cavalli, in fact, ushered in the style known later as *bel canto*, which reached its peak in the late baroque and in which, in marked contrast to recitative patter and monodic affective declamation, melody is all-important—melody typified by smooth-flowing, sensuous lines, sequential patterns, a slowish tempo, and a simplicity of movement that is not destroyed by occasional florid passages. As a result, the character of the bass tends to that of the melody, even to the point of actual imitation, harmony is unobtrusive, with occasional flashes of chromaticism, and rhythm is simple and usually in triple metre, because the melodic flow is naturally smoother in this than in duple metre as the strong accent occurs less frequently. (Quadruple metre is really an extension of duple, for there is a strong secondary accent on the third beat.) Most of these features can be seen in Ex. 22c.

With Cavalli *bel canto* style is not yet an end in itself, but only a means, and although he favoured the aria more than his master, the drama, not the music, is still the backbone, as it were, of his operas, the most famous of which was *Giasone* (1649). Thus, as with Monteverdi, Cavalli selects his musical type—secco recitative, arioso, or aria—according to its dramatic fitness, and not as a result of purely musical considerations (Ex. 22,* pp. 392-4. See also *H.A.M.*, 206).

Like Monteverdi also—indeed, like Venetian opera-composers in general—Cavalli wrote few instrumental numbers and fewer choruses: in fact, none of his operas written between 1644 and 1661, representing the bulk of his total output, contain any choruses at all. The reason for this was the public's preference

* Melody and bass from R. Haas, *Musik des Baroks*, pp. 136–8.

Ex.22(a) Secco recitative *Alle ruine (La Didone I.7)* (1641)
Cavalli
Hecuba
Al - le ru - - i - - ne del mio Re - - - - gno a - dun - que so - pra -
Thus, by the ru - ins of my king - - - dom, I, an old weak
- vi - vo de-cre - pi - ta, e son giun - ta a ri - pu - tar il pian - to,
wo - man, sur vive, a - las, And I now do be - lieve that tears and weep-ing
te - sti - mon tri - vi - - al de miei do - - lo - - ri.
low - ly wit - - nes-ses are of my deep sor - - row
(etc.)

Ex.22(b) From the arioso - *L'alma fiacca svanì (La Didone I A)*

(♩ = MM.c.54)
L'al - - ma fi - - ac - ca sva-nì, la vi-ta, ohi - mè, spi-rò,
Spi - - rit so wea-ry thou'rt gone, life al-so, a - - las ex-pir'd,
Co - re - bo, oh Dio, mo-rì, e so - la mi la-sciò!
Co - re - bo, O God, is dead, and hath left me all a - lone!
Per spo-sa ei mi vo - - le - va, ed io qui pian - go, e pria che
As a bride did he de - - sire me, and here I weep so, for ere a
spo - sa ve - do - va ri - man - - go.
bride a wi - dow'd maid re - - main I.
(etc.)

Ex.22 (c) Aria – Padre, ferma i passi (La Didone I.1)
(𝅗𝅥.=𝅗𝅥 – MM.c.84)
Ascanio
Pa-dre, fer-ma_i pas - si_e l'ar - mi, non la -
Fa-ther, halt thy steps and wea - - pons, This fair
- sciar que-sta ma-gio - ne, non sò dir - - ti
house leave not I pray thee, I've no rea - - son
al-tra ra - - gio - - - - ne, non do - - ve - - vi ge - ne -
else to gain - say thee, Thou should'st ne - - ver have con -
- rar - - mi, se vo - - le - - vi ab - ban- do - - nar - - mi.
- ceiv'd me If thou e'er de - - sir - ed to leave me.
(4 more verses)

for solo singing, and as this meant that the management had to spend a great deal in engaging 'star' performers, and as most of what was left went on scenery in order to satisfy the demand for the spectacular, there was precious little left for the chorus. The orchestra too was much less important than in the earlier part of the century, and its size and constitution had undergone a marked transformation. This had been heralded as early as 1624 in Monteverdi's dramatic cantata, *Il Combattimento di Tancredi e Clorinda* ('The Combat of Tancred and Clorinda'), in which the heterogeneous assortment of instruments called for in *Orfeo* is replaced by a harpsichord and string band. *Il Combattimento* is important not only because it marks the beginning of the modern orchestra in the sense that the strings are the fundamental unit, but also because it increased the dramatic rôle of instrumental accompaniment through the use of, for example, reiterated rhythmic figures to denote a galloping horse, and rapid, repeated notes (tremolo) and plucked strings (pizzicato) to depict the clash and fury of the fight (see *H.A.M.*, 189). The idea of pizzicato seems to have been invented by Monteverdi himself, and he was also the first to use tremolo for dramatic purposes, although the device itself occurs in a few earlier violin pieces. This participation by the orchestra in the drama did not catch on in Venetian opera until later in the century, and during Cavalli's time instruments were entirely subservient to the voice. Even the introductory sinfonia was reduced to a few bars of slow, solemn chords, usually in duple time, that can have done little more than call the audience's attention to the fact that the opera was about to commence. Actually, Cavalli's *Giasone* is something of an exception in that the slow section is followed by a quick one in triple time in which the opening theme is derived from that of the preceding movement.

In the same year and month, but not in the same theatre, that *Giasone* was produced, the first opera, *Orontea*, by Pietro Cesti [1623–1669] was performed at the opening of the fifth public opera-house in Venice. Most writers from the eighteenth century to the present day have replaced 'Pietro' by 'Marc Antonio', this presumably being a corruption of 'Frate Antonio', a title he adopted on his admission to Minor Orders in 1637. Cesti is usually and rightly regarded as a Venetian composer, because although he spent very little of his life in Venice, oscillating between Rome, Innsbruck, and Vienna, and although only a small proportion of his operas were first performed in Venice, his style is typically Venetian. Of the 100 or so operas that Cesti is supposed to have written, only fifteen have survived, including his three most famous, *Orontea*, *La Dori* (Florence, 1661), and *Il pomo d'oro* (Vienna, 1667). In general his operas owe much to those of Cavalli, but in particular he widens the distinction between recitative and aria and carries the *bel canto* style a stage further, applying it to his ensembles (duets, trios, etc.); with Monteverdi and Cavalli these last are still somewhat madrigalian in their use of imitation, but Cesti favours the sensuousness of parallel thirds and sixths.

We have stated earlier in this history that when composers stress any one aspect of music the other aspects tend to be neglected or simplified. This is true of *bel canto* style, and one result is the lack of harmonic variety, compared to Monteverdi or Cavalli, of Cesti's and later Venetian composers' accompaniments; Cesti, indeed, relies to an almost irritating extent at times on tonic, dominant, and subdominant chords, and rarely moves away from closely related keys. With him *bel canto* style became the first real instance of homophony in the history of music, for by homophony we mean a texture in which an all-important melody (sometimes doubled in thirds and sixths) is provided with an essentially chordal accompaniment. Admittedly a number of Renaissance lute songs tend towards homophony, but in the great majority of cases the lute accompaniment is basically contrapuntal or polyphonic, even if it is not in fact an arrangement of the lower voices of a part-song. In real homophony, however, the harmony is conceived as a progression of chords, not as a combination of melodic lines, and hence the movement of the lower parts is quite unimportant, provided, of course, that in ensembles (but by no means necessarily on the harpsichord) consecutive fifths and octaves are avoided (compare the definitions of counterpoint and polyphony in Part I, p. 48). This explains why *bel canto* accompaniments for continuo only were preferred to full orchestra until well into the late baroque, as the former allows the melody greater prominence.

The harmonic restriction of Cesti's *bel canto* style was not only an outcome of letting melody predominate, but also the result of a greater concern for a central tonality. Cesti, in fact, belonged to the generation of composers who marked the watershed, so to speak, between the period when the idea of a central tonality was not yet established and when chromaticism was used for purely emotional ends (as in Monteverdi and Cavalli, e.g. Ex. 22b and c) and the period when the idea had become firmly rooted and chromaticism was used both emotionally and to contrast with or offset the main key without disturbing its central position. The most notable feature of Cesti's chromaticism is his use of the so-called 'Neapolitan sixth' chord, which nearly always occurs in minor keys and which can be described as the first inversion of the flattened supertonic. Thus in Ex. 23b, bar 5, the key is D minor, but the first inversion of B♭ major is treated as the flattened supertonic (Neapolitan sixth) in A minor, for it is followed by the last inversion of the dominant seventh in A (bar 6), and later by a perfect cadence in A (bars 7–8). The same progression occurs in bars 9–12, but a fourth higher, i.e. in D minor. (N.B.—The lowest note of the Neapolitan sixth usually moves up a step to the dominant of the key, e.g. D–E in A minor or G–A in D minor.) (Ex. 23*, pp. 398-9).

The growing concern for a central tonality shown by all composers during the latter half of the seventeenth century is also apparent in the number of pieces (much greater in this period than in the eighteenth century) which are either wholly or mainly built round an ostinato motive. These motives invariably consist of a progression from tonic to dominant and so back to the next statement (Exx. 21 and 23a), or else from tonic to tonic, and were either restricted to the bass (basso ostinato), as in Exx. 21 and 23a, or else occasionally invaded the upper parts (passacaglia). By reiterating the tonic to dominant or tonic to tonic progression, these motives helped to underline the main key, even though the separate notes of the motive were not always harmonized in exactly the same way.

In rhythm and melody, as well as harmony, Cesti shows less variety than Monteverdi or Cavalli, favouring smoother contours and regular, often sequential, patterns. His cadences, too, occur more frequently, and almost invariably comprise the progression subdominant (or supertonic first inversion)–dominant–tonic (IV (or IIA)–V–I) of whatever key he happens

* Melody and bass from *Alte Meister des Bel canto*, ed. Landshoff.

Ex. 23 From the aria - Vieni, vieni Alidoro (Orontea) (1649)
Cesti
(♩ = MM.c.54)
(a)
Silandra
Vie - ni, vie - ni
A - li - do - ro, vie - ni, vie - - - - - ni,
Con - so - la, con -
- so - la, chi si mo - - - - - re!
(etc.)

(Come, Alidoro, come, comfort one who is dying!)

(b)
vie - - - - ni, vie - - - - - ni, vie - - ni mia
vi - ta, — vie - - - - ni, vie - - - ni mia vi - ta, —
vie - - - - - - ni!
(Come, my life, come!)
(etc.)

to be in. Some of his melodies are long-breathed, but most of them are constructed of short phrases; these last are, in fact, no shorter than those of most individual voice parts in late Renaissance polyphony, but the latter, by overlapping the phrases of the different voices, avoids the frequent 'full stops' of the early *bel canto* style. Harmonic restriction, rhythmic simplicity, and melodic short-windedness are also characteristic of the style that formed the bridge between Bach and Haydn, and when in the works of some late baroque composers and in the Viennese School, polyphony reasserted itself, harmony became more varied, rhythm more subtle and flexible, and melody more sustained. Polyphony, in fact, is and always has been a richer vehicle of expression than homophony, for it not only maintains a balance between the various musical elements, but it also reveals more completely what is perhaps the most unique and wonderful aspect of music—the ability to present distinct and individual ideas (i.e. strands of sound) within an integrated and satisfying whole.

Cesti was probably the most popular operatic composer before Alessandro Scarlatti (see Chapter 4), and the seal was set on his fame by *Il pomo d'oro*, written for the wedding of the Emperor Leopold I of Austria [reigned 1658–1705] with the Infanta Margherita of Spain, and performed in Vienna in 1667. The occasion made this opera something of an exception to the normal Venetian type, and, apart from costing a small fortune to produce with its sixty-seven scenes, forty-eight characters and twenty-four different stage settings (some of them requiring the most elaborate machinery—see Plates XXVII and XXVIII), there are a number of ballets and choruses (one in eight parts) and an unusually large orchestra, including trumpets, trombones, cornetts, bassoons, lutes, and a regal, in addition to the customary string band and harpsichord (see Plate XXVI).

Cesti's operas represent one point at which the swing of the pendulum away from polyphony started to move back (N.B. the part-writing in *H.A.M.*, 221), for his Venetian successors, while cultivating the *bel canto* style as ardently as ever, began to enrich their vocal ensembles and instrumental accompaniments with real part-writing, and hand in hand with this came an expansion of melody, harmony, and form. This development is clearly seen in the works of the three most outstanding opera composers between Cesti and A. Scarlatti, Giovanni Legrenzi [1626–1690], Alessandro Stradella [1642–1682], and Carlo Pallavicino [*c.* 1630–1688]; with them the aria becomes more spacious, with frequent sequential passages (in Pallavicino's operas especially), the orchestra plays a larger part, accompanying the voice more often than in Cavalli's or Cesti's arias (in most of which the harmonic support is provided by the continuo), forms are more varied and include, besides the *da capo*, such types as A, B (binary form) $A_1\ B_2\ B_1$, $A_1\ B_2\ B_1\ C_2\ C_1$, etc. (1 =tonic key, 2 =different key(s)), there is a greater variety of harmonic resource and modulation, now set within a firm tonal framework, and the instrumental writing, especially the bass, is more interesting, often anticipating in a short ritornello the main theme of an aria before the voice takes it up. (*H.A.M.*, 241). This last feature, indeed, was sometimes applied to the introductory sinfonia, as, for example, in *Il pomo d'oro*, where the second main theme of the overture reappears later as a chorus. This brings to mind Monteverdi's *Orfeo* (see p. 375), and in some ways, e.g. the greater importance of the orchestra and the less haphazard structure of the whole, mid-baroque opera partially returns to the ideals of the first great operatic composer. In addition, a number of arias begin with a short vocal phrase or 'motto' expressive of the main mood, a feature typical of many of Cesti's arias. (For the full significance of the 'motto' beginning, see Chapter 4, p. 440.)

Side by side with and yet in opposition to this trend towards expansion and enrichment came a pronounced preference for rhythmically simple and melodically catchy songs. Occasionally the two tendencies can be found in a single aria, as when a simple vocal line is supported by a bass that is either florid or else provides scope for a wide range of chords.

The tremendous impact of Italian Renaissance culture overflowed into the baroque era, and the rest of Europe would have followed Italy's lead, for a time at any rate, no matter what kind of music she had produced. Thus the transalpine countries adopted opera, but only with varying degrees of success, and the enthusiasm for this particular art form was and still is more completely natural and spontaneous in the country that gave it birth than any other art form has been in any other country.

That Austria, the southern German states, and Bohemia imported Italian opera before the rest of Europe was only to be expected when one considers their geographical position and remembers the interchange of musicians between the two regions during the Renaissance. Cesti's *Il pomo d'oro* was by no means the first Italian opera to cross the Alps, this distinction, so far as we know, being held by *Andromeda*, by Giralomo Giacobbi [1567 – 1629], performed in Salzburg in 1618. Other cities followed suit, and performances are recorded at Prague from 1627, Innsbruck from 1655 (where Cesti was employed, though frequently absent, from 1652 to 1666), Regensberg from 1653, and Munich, where the first opera-house was opened in 1657.

The opera produced in Regensberg in 1653 was *L'inganno d'amore*, by Antonio Bertali [1605–1669], who lived in Vienna from *c.* 1623 to his death, was appointed court conductor in 1649, and who first introduced regular performances of Italian opera into the Austrian capital (the first recorded performance took place in 1626). Vienna, for obvious reasons, soon became the main centre of Italian opera outside Italy, and in Antonio Draghi [*c.* 1635 – 1700], who resided in the city from *c.* 1658 to his death, she found the most prolific operatic composer of the seventeenth century, whose mature style is similar to that of Legrenzi, Stradella, and Pallavicino.

During the latter half of the century Italian opera spread to most of the other large German cities, among them Dresden, the capital of Saxony, where the Elector held court. Here in 1687 Pallavicino was appointed director of the first permanent opera house, although the first operatic performance dates from 1662. But Dresden is associated with a far greater name than Pallavicino, for Heinrich Schütz [1585–1672], the greatest German composer before Bach and, with Monteverdi, Lully and Purcell, the most outstanding musician of the century, was director of the electoral chapel from 1617 to his death. Although Schütz greatly admired and was considerably influenced by Giovanni Gabrieli, whose pupil he was from 1609 to 1612, and although his enthusiasm for the new Italian music, especially that of Monteverdi, prompted him to cross the Alps a second time in 1628, he never became completely Italianate, as did many of his contemporaries and successors. Thus the delight in expressive polyphony, chromatic harmony, and colourful sonority which he imbibed from Gabrieli, and the dramatic recitative, lyrical melody, and sensuous use of thirds and sixths which he learnt from later Italian composers, were restrained by that meditative, philosophic outlook on life that has always been one of the chief characteristics of his countrymen and which he possessed to a marked degree.

In 1627 Sophia Eleonora, Princess of Saxony, was married in the Saxon town of Torgau, and to mark the occasion Schütz wrote an opera, *Dafne*. The libretto is largely a translation of Rinuccini's text for Peri's opera of 1597, and, like the earlier work, the music is lost. This is doubly unfortunate, because it was Schütz's only opera and the first by a German composer.

The earliest German opera that has survived intact is *Seelewig*, by Sigmund Theophil Staden [1607–1655], produced in Nuremberg in 1644. This is more in the Roman than Venetian tradition, as it is described as a 'spiritual pastorale', and is concerned with the attempts of the 'false deceiver' Trügewalt, aided and abetted by allegorical figures representing Art and the Senses, to capture the 'soul' (Seelewig), but she, with the help of Wisdom and Conscience, evades their evil designs, and virtue ends triumphant. The setting is pastoral, the characters being nymphs, shepherds, and satyrs, while the music consists almost entirely of short, lyrical strophic songs, the through-composed dramatic or impassioned recitatives being conspicuous by their absence, and there are a number of instrumental pieces. The orchestra is remarkable in that there is no part for a harpsichord, theorbo and lute being the only chord-playing instruments, the others consisting of violins, a viola, recorders, flutes, shawms, bassoons, and a horn. Each character or group is associated with a definite instrumental ensemble, e.g. strings and recorders accompany the nymphs, flutes and shawms the shepherds, while the horn is reserved for Trügewalt.

Although the few German operas that are known to have been written during the first seventy-five years of the seventeenth century almost certainly do not constitute the total number actually produced, it is clear that in the south, where Italian influence was strongest, native opera simply could not compete against the constant flow from across the Alps. But even in the north native opera found difficulty in taking root owing to the political and cultural divisions characteristic of the whole country, divisions that were more pronounced than anywhere else in Europe, and which were aggravated by the so-called Thirty Years' War (1618–48). Initially this was an outcome of the Reformation and Counter-Reformation, but it soon developed into a purely political affair. The chief contestants were France and the Habsburg Dynasty, and before it ended two Holy Roman Emperors, Ferdinand II [reigned 1619–1637], and Ferdinand III [reigned 1637–1657], and the Spanish King Philip IV [reigned 1621–1665], three of the most powerful Catholic rulers of their time, were opposed by the Catholic King of France, Louis XIII [reigned 1610–1643], his astute adviser, Cardinal Richelieu, and by the Pope himself, Urban VIII; Richelieu, while he had bitterly persecuted the Huguenots, had no scruples in forming alliances with the Protestant countries of Sweden, Denmark, Holland, and England.

While the Treaty of Westphalia (1648) marked the end of the war and settled the religious frontiers of central Europe, it brought even greater political disunity to the German States, because the homage, however slight, that each State had formerly paid to the Emperor had now gone, as the Treaty recognized the absolute sovereignty of each ruler within his own territory. The war did not affect the States so acutely as is sometimes supposed, for the devastation only visited certain strategic areas and economic stability actually increased during the latter part of the struggle, due in no small part to the founding, in 1619, of the 'Hamburger Bank', which, despite the huge inflation of 1620–3, improved the value of German currency. Hamburg, a flourishing port whose history and tradition of independent government had much in common with Venice, was of all the large German towns the most northerly. She was thus less influenced by Italian music, and it is no coincidence that not only did she build, in 1678, the first public opera house in Europe, apart from those in Venice, but she also became the home of German opera.

The Hamburg opera-house was inaugurated by a performance of *Adam und Eva*, by Johann Theile [1646–1724], a pupil of Schütz; while the music is unfortunately lost, the libretto tells us what we might have guessed anyway, that this is a moral opera. But although a number of similar operas were written during the succeeding years, indicative of the characteristic German seriousness noted earlier, and partially placating that body of Lutheran opinion that inveighed against the worldliness and immorality of the stage, the secular element proved too strong, and plots and translated libretti from the Italian and French theatres soon predominated. In addition, a number of Italian operas were produced in their original language, and sometimes a compromise was reached in which the arias were sung in Italian and the recitatives in the vernacular, a practice that was adopted elsewhere and which has been adversely criticized by some historians, but which is not as absurd as it seems, as we hope to show in the next chapter.

Despite the strength of foreign influence, particularly from

Italy, the actual music of the Hamburg German opera school reveals several independent features, and the leading composers, Johann Georg Conradi [d. 1699], Johann Wolfgang Franck [*c.* 1641–after 1695], and Johann Sigismund Kusser [1660–1727], all show a less virtuosic vocal line, a preference for long-phrased melodies in contrast to the shorter, snappier tunes of the Italians, and a recitative style that is more akin to the arioso than to the Venetian recitativo secco. In addition, Conradi and Franck wrote most of their arias in simple binary form (i.e. A, B), whereas Kusser, who was the most cosmopolitan of the group, preferred the Italian *da capo* form. Kusser, in fact, is the most important composer of the three, as not only did he probably teach and certainly influence the greatest composer of German operas in the entire baroque period, Reinhard Keiser (see Chapter 4, p. 462), but also profoundly affected the course of German instrumental music during the early years of the eighteenth century. The source of his influence on Keiser was Italy, and on instrumental music France, and it is to the operatic developments in the latter country that we now turn.

Earlier in this chapter we stated that Rossi's *Orfeo*, produced in Paris in 1647, was not the first Italian opera to be performed in the capital; it was in fact preceded by at least three others during the previous two years, all of them under the patronage of Mazarin, who, knowing the French nobility's love of entertainment, used them as means of distracting his opponents from the powerful position he was building up for himself. That he was temporarily unsuccessful and was one of the main causes of the civil war that lasted from 1648 to 1653 is reflected in the fact that the next performance of an Italian opera did not take place until 1654. Only two more performances followed during the ensuing eighteen years, not because Mazarin had lost interest in the art of his native land, or power in the country of his adoption, but because Frenchmen, while admiring the skill and invention that could clothe an entire play with music, were not enthusiastic over the way in which it was done, although naturally enough they enjoyed the ballets which were specially introduced in order to satisfy French taste, and were enthralled by the stage machinery invented by Giacomo Torelli that raised the spectacular element to a pitch never before seen in France.

Although France, unlike Germany and, as we shall see, England, repelled the first invasion of Italian opera, she was sufficiently attracted to try to create her own. The two earliest attempts (the music of both is lost) were *Akebar, roi de Mogol*, by a certain Abbé Mailly, performed at Carpentras (near Avignon) in 1646, and *Le Triomphe de l'Amour sur des bergers et bergères*, by Michel de La Guerre [*c.* 1605–1679], performed at the Louvre, Paris, in 1655, and again before Louis XIV [reigned 1643–1715] in 1657. In a dedicatory letter to the King, La Guerre calls his piece "une Comédie française en Musique", and claims that it is the first of its kind in France ('comédie' meant 'drama', not 'comedy'; see p. 410). Two years later an almost exactly similar claim was made by Robert Cambert [*c.* 1628–1677] for his comédie, *Pastorale* (music lost), produced at Issy (near Paris) in April 1659 and then, at Mazarin's suggestion, at Vincennes before the King. His Majesty was delighted, and, thus encouraged, Cambert and his librettist, Pierre Perrin [*c.* 1620–1675], continued in their collaboration, the next fruits of which were *Ariane, ou le Mariage de Bachus* and *Pomone*. It is almost certain that *Ariane* was completed by 1661, but in that year Mazarin died and performance was indefinitely postponed. Thirteen years later an opera with the same title and with Perrin's libretto was produced in London, but, according to the title-page, with music by Cambert's pupil, Louis Grabu [d. after 1694]. Cambert himself was in London at the time and in charge of the performance, but whether the music is essentially his—Grabu's rôle being restricted to arranging it and possibly supplying additional items—or whether Grabu composed an entirely new setting will never be known until the original score is found.

Mazarin's death caused a temporary hiatus in French opera because no influential person possessed his enthusiasm for this particular form of entertainment, and it was not until 1671 that *Pomone* was staged publicly. It was an immediate success and ran for eight months to packed houses. *Pomone* is the first extant French opera, as it is sung throughout; the same may have been true of *Ariane*, but *Akebar*, *Le Triomphe*, and Cambert's first opera were probably pastorals—that is, plays with songs—for these, modelled on the pastorales of Tasso and Guarini (see p. 266), were much in vogue during the earlier part of the century. Two years before *Pomone* Perrin had obtained a royal privilege that gave him a monopoly of all performances of French opera. In 1670 he and Cambert converted a large building into a theatre, and in the following year founded the 'Académie Royale des Opéra' (the original home of the Paris Opéra), marking the occasion by the performance of *Pomone* mentioned above—the first public presentation of any French opera. Only the libretto and the music to the Prologue, Act I, and parts of Act II have survived (*H.A.M.*, 223), and the same applies to *Les peines et les plaisirs de l'amour*, produced in 1672 with music by Cambert and libretto by Gabriel Gilbert.

The success of these two operas, especially of *Pomone*, was immense, but disaster for Cambert and Perrin was at hand. The latter, a gifted but unstable man, was imprisoned in 1672, and there he was visited by no less a person than Molière [1622–1673], the brilliant actor-dramatist whose comédies are performed as frequently and enjoyed with as much relish today as in his own time. Molière, who had included a certain amount of music and dancing in his comédies from *La Fâcheux* (1661) on, and who clearly saw the possibilities of such entertainments, can have had little difficulty in persuading Perrin to sell the royal privilege. It availed him little, however, for within a few weeks the privilege had become worthless owing to the machinations at court of one of the most outstanding musicians, and certainly the most unscrupulous, in the whole history of French music, Jean-Baptiste Lully [1632–1687].

Lully, an Italian by birth, was brought to France when only a lad of about ten years old. At twenty he so captivated the Dauphin, later Louis XIV, by his violin playing that not only was he appointed to the royal band, the famous Vingt-Quatre Violons du Roi, but in 1656 was permitted by Louis to train sixteen specially selected fiddlers—Les Petits-Violons. This smaller band (which later expanded to twenty-one players) surpassed the larger in both volume and expressiveness, and soon led to Lully's appointment as conductor of the 'King's violins', a body that became internationally famous under his direction. Like other conductors of his time, Lully was expected to provide most of the music for his orchestra, but some years before this, probably in his late 'teens, he had realized that without the ability to play the harpsichord and compose he would never get very far. He accordingly took lessons, and such was his talent for composition that in 1653 he was commissioned to write some music for a ballet de cour.

In Chapter 1 we traced the development of the ballet de cour up to the early years of the seventeenth century. The first notable change occurred *c.* 1605, when the récits, which had formerly been spoken rather than sung, began tentatively, but with increasing sureness, to be set in the Italian monodic style. This change was undoubtedly due to the presence of Caccini at the court of Henry IV in 1604–5, for his dramatic manner of singing made a great impression on the musicians at court, especially Pierre Guédron [d. 1619/20], who succeeded Claude le Jeune as chief court composer, becoming Maître de la Musique du Roi to Louis XIII, and who, in his numerous ballets written between 1608 and 1620, did much to further the adoption of monody at the expense of part-music. The monodic style also affected the popular air de cour, though indirectly, in that the stress on declamation and the affective rendering of the text soon became all-important, the regular rhythms and simple melodies of the Renaissance type being replaced by the irregular patterns of musique mesurée and by numerous improvised embellishments of the vocal line and accompaniment. Italian influence waxed during the succeeding years, and by 1620 the literary element in the ballet was completely overshadowed by the musical. This resulted in an even greater disregard for dramatic unity than before, and the dances, particularly the ballets à entrées, became a series of virtually unconnected if spectacular tableaux.

This state of affairs persisted until *c.* 1650, when a new lease of life was infused into the ballet de cour by the poet Isaac de Benserade [1612–1691], who reintroduced the feature that had made *Circe* so outstanding—namely, a unified dramatic plot, an example that was followed by the greatest writer of ballets de cour, Molière.

Of the composers who wrote ballet music between *c.* 1608 and *c.* 1650 the two most notable were Guédron and his son-in-law and successor at court, Antoine Boesset [*c.* 1586 – 1643], who also became Surintendant de la Musique de Roi in 1623. In the next and last important period of the ballet de cour (it had a late brief flowering under Louis XV), when Benserade and Molière raised it to a literary and dramatic level unknown before, the chief composers were Jean-Baptiste Boesset [*c.* 1614–1685], who succeeded his father as Maître and Surintendant to the King, now Louis XIV, and his successors to these titles, Jean de Cambefort [*c.* 1605–1661] and Lully.

The ballet music Lully wrote in 1653, his first so far as we know, was for Benserade's *La Nuit*, in which the part of 'Le Roi soleil' was so superbly danced by Louis that the title stuck to him for the rest of his life. Other composers also contributed to *La Nuit*, for it had long been the custom to share out the music of a ballet between two or more composers. (This, indeed, applies also to Jacobean and most Caroline masques.) During the next four years Lully contributed music to nine ballets, one of these being inserted into an Italian opera, and all but two by Benserade. In 1658, however, he composed the entire score for Benserade's *Alcidiane*, and its success, together with his dislike for sharing royal or public acclamation, resulted in his never again collaborating with another composer. Between 1658 and 1671 Lully wrote the ballet music for thirty stage works, over half of them by Benserade, the best of which is *Les Muses* (1667); most of the remainder were comédies and comédie-ballets by Molière, beginning with *L'impromptu de Versailles* (1663) and reaching their peak in *Le bourgeois gentilhomme* (1670).

The two chief dancing masters during this period were Beauchamp and Lully himself, and they were the first to advocate a strict professional training for the ballet, which, as we have seen, had been previously performed by men and women who were courtiers first and dancers second. As a result, the Académie Royale de la Danse was founded by Louis in 1661, and in 1672 this was enlarged to the Académie Royale de Musique et de Danse, which still exists, with its headquarters at the Paris Opéra, and which marked the beginning of State ballet with its professional dancers and public performances. Actually the public had first witnessed ballet in the preceding year (1671), when *Pomone* was staged, for in this opera, as in practically all later French operas to the end of the nineteenth century, ballet was a large and important constituent. Only male dancers performed in public at first, but in 1681 the first woman professional solo dancer (ballerina) appeared on the public stage in Lully's *Le Triomphe de l'Amour*, perhaps the most sumptuously staged ballet he ever wrote.

Among the ballets by Benserade for which Lully composed the music were two for the operas, *Serse* (1660) and *Ercole amante* (1662), by Cavalli, whose compositions Lully studied and from them derived his own musico-dramatic style, a style that was fully formed by the time he wrote his first real opera in 1673.

By this date the ballet had become much more than a display of dancing, though naturally dancing was the main attraction, and Lully, apart from writing numerous pieces for the dramatic ballets à entrées and the conventional ballroom types, such as the gaillarde and courante, also made famous a number of newer dances, all of French origin. These were the 'menuet' in stately $\frac{3}{4}$ time, which is said to have been first danced, to Lully's music, by Louis as 'Le Roi soleil' in *La Nuit*; the more animated but still dignified 'gavotte' in $\frac{2}{2}$ or $\frac{4}{4}$; the 'rigaudon' and 'bourée' in quick duple time, the latter appearing for the first time in composition in Lully's ballets and operas, though mentioned considerably earlier in literary sources; the lively, spirited, and very popular 'passepied' in $\frac{3}{8}$ or $\frac{6}{8}$; and finally the 'loure', with its dotted rhythm in $\frac{6}{4}$ time.

But the attention which Lully was bound to pay to the dances in his ballets, because of their popularity with King and court, did not prevent him from extending and developing the part played by both vocal and purely instrumental music. Thus he increased the number of solos and choruses, and adapted the Italian *bel canto* and recitativo secco styles, both of which he had learned from Cavalli. The latter he employed to connect the separate scenes in Molière's comédie-ballets, while the influence of the former is clearly apparent in his récits and airs in both the comédie-ballets and ballets de cour, although the ornamental turns, grace notes, etc., are still very much in the French tradition. When we add to this the fact that he stressed the importance of the orchestra to a far greater extent than any other composer, whether French or foreign, then we can begin to appreciate how richly varied had become the musical element in his ballets, especially the comédie-ballets of Molière, with their dramatic recitatives, affective airs that include both low comedy and tender sentiment, sonorous choruses, striking instrumental pieces, sometimes in five real parts, and dance music that ranges from the vivid characterization of the ballets à entrées to the noble grace of the menuet. It was but a short step from this to opera, and it is to Lully's operas, or 'tragédies-lyriques' as he called them, that we now turn.

Up to 1671 Lully had been contemptuous of Perrin and Cambert's essays in French opera, but the granting of the royal privilege to Perrin, the founding of the Académie Royale des Opéra, and, finally, the enormous success of *Pomone* aroused his jealousy. He executed a rapid *volte-face*, exercised all his influence with the King, and within two months of the production of *Les peines et les plaisirs de l'amour* obtained the privilege for himself. Molière was robbed of his rights, Perrin died in misery three years later, and Cambert, embittered by Lully's deceit, repaired to England, where he became court composer to Charles II until he was mysteriously assassinated. Not content with his ill-gotten power, Lully repeatedly petitioned the King to extend the scope of his privilege; thus in 1673 no theatre was allowed to employ more than two voices and six violins, and in 1684 no opera could be performed without his permission. While his unscrupulousness in achieving his ends irregardless of others can only be condemned, Lully's musical genius matched his lust for power and his dictatorial methods, and he created a type of opera and a style of operatic composition unique to France, and one that lasted for over 100 years; indeed, his third opera, *Thésée* (1675), remained in the repertoire until 1779.

The chief characteristics of Lully's operas and a comparison with those typical of Italy at the time can best be shown as follows:

Lully	*Italian*
1. The libretto is more important than the music.	1. The music is more important than the libretto.
2. As a first result, the recitatives are models of correct declamation, which at times become lyrical, are frequently accompanied by the orchestra, and are of major importance.	2. As a first result, most recitatives are taken at great speed (recitativo secco), are accompanied by a few simple continuo chords and are of minor importance.
3. As a second result, the airs are few, short, melodically simple, and of minor importance.	3. As a second result, the arias are many, extended in form, often very ornate melodically, and of major importance.

Lully	*Italian*
4. The *raison d'être* of the whole is to glorify the king—his person, his realm, his deeds.	4. The *raison d'être* of the whole is to entertain the aristocracy or the populace or both.
5. As a first result (French taste being what it was), the action and music are conventional, never seeking to express violence or passion, and introducing wit rather than broad comedy as light relief.	5. As a first result, composers, in order to satisfy their public, always played on the emotions, and violence and passion are the rule rather than the exception, with broad comedy rather than wit introduced as light relief.
6. As a second result, allegorical scenes abound in which the spectacular element is chiefly used to glorify king and country, which include numerous ballets, and in which the chorus and orchestra play an important part.	6. As a second result, elaborate spectacles involving some of the most complex stage machinery ever devised are common, but there are few ballets. The chorus is hardly ever used and the number of purely orchestral items small.

The importance of the libretto and Lully's insistence that it should make dramatic sense and have some literary distinction falls into line with the traditional French attitude to music mentioned earlier (see p. 273), for whereas composers of opera in the Italian manner did not bother about the quality of the text nor about the probability of the plot, and thus, apart from scenic effects, relied wholly on the impact of their music, Lully made sure that the dramatic and literary sensibilities of his audience were not insulted. It must be remembered in this connexion that in the sphere of literature (including the theatre) France stood head and shoulders above the rest of Europe, and that the so-called 'Classic Age' (*c.* 1660–90), one of the major peaks in her literary history, coincided with the period of Lully's operatic activity. As we saw earlier, Italian literature and drama were at their lowest ebb in the seventeenth century, and this, apart from the Italian temperament, fostered the kind of opera already discussed; similarly in France, where the distinction of such men as Molière, La Fontaine [1621–1695], whose *Contes* and *Fables* reveal him as one of the greatest of French poets, the outstanding playwright, Racine [1639–1699], whose tragedies, particularly his two finest, *Phèdre* (1677) and *Athalie* (1691), display a violence of passion that stepped right outside the aristocratic conventions of his time, and Pierre Corneille [1606–1684], whose *Le Cid* virtually created French classical tragedy, not to mention a number of lesser lights, created a literary standard among the intelligentsia which French opera was bound to reflect to some extent if it was to succeed; that it reflected it to such a large extent was due to Lully, and it is not surprising that he called his operas tragédies-lyriques, for this places the stress on the drama rather than on the music.

Although Lully had provided the music for several of Molière's comédies, he preferred as his regular librettists, both for ballet and opera, men of lesser talent and more docile disposition, the reason undoubtedly being that writers of the calibre of Molière, Racine, and Corneille (the last two also collaborated on occasion) were less likely to abide by his dictates and, moreover, were too distinguished in their own right to permit Lully's star to shine as brightly as he desired, for he wanted no reflected glory. Thus of the nineteen ballets composed between 1658 and 1670 of which he wrote all the music, six are based on texts by anonymous authors, and of the remainder all but one are by the comparatively obscure writer, Benserade.

In November 1672, only eight months after he had obtained the royal privilege, Lully produced *Les Festes de l'Amour et de Bacchus*, a work that stands halfway between his ballets and his operas. His librettists were Benserade, Molière, and Philippe Quinault [1635–1688], and it was the last-named, a dramatist of little significance, who supplied Lully with the libretti of all but two of the thirteen complete operas composed between 1673 and 1686, beginning with *Cadmus et Hermione*, Lully's first opera, and ending with *Armide et Renaud*, his masterpiece, and the first French opera to be performed in Italy (Rome, 1690).

In some ways Lully's operas revive the principles of the early Florentines: in the importance of the text and the insistence on correct and affective declamation, and hence in the preference for the arioso as opposed to the secco recitative so common in contemporary Italian opera. This arioso style—which differs from the Italian in that the voice is often accompanied by violins, and even, at times, the full string band, in addition to the invariable continuo—is clearly shown in Ex. 24, as is the close alliance between the stress and value of notes and syllables which result in fluctuating time-signatures.

(Notice the animated bass line and rapid changes of harmony in the middle of the recitative where the poetic imagery is most intense.) The majority of Lully's airs fall into one of two types, in both of which the underlay is predominantly syllabic, as one would expect from a composer who laid such stress on the importance of the words. The first type stems from the air de cour, and includes most of his serious or sentimental airs, particularly those of a pastoral nature (e.g. the well-known 'Bois épais' from *Amadis de Gaule*, 1684, Lully's most popular opera after *Thésée*.) The second type, characterized by clear-cut rhythms and melodies, is the dance-song, and it is hardly surprising that this occurs more frequently than the first type. The air in Ex. 24 is a typical dance-song, being in fact a gavotte; typical also is the trochaic rhythm of the melismas on '-phez' and '-chai', which so captivated English composers, notably Purcell, and which, via the French overture especially, spread to other European countries north of the Alps (it was too jerky for the Italian *bel canto* style). (Ex. 24,* pp. 415-91. The cross in front of some of the notes indicates an ornament, probably a mordant. See also *H.A.M.*, 225.)

In order to improve his settings of French words and the declamation and acting of his singers, Lully spent much time studying the movements and speech of the greatest actors of his day at the Théâtre Française, but before long the position was reversed, the actors attending the Académie Royale, for Lully's ability to train and discipline, already noted in connexion with the King's orchestra, produced a standard of acting and declamation that was second to none in France, or, indeed, anywhere else, and musicians from all over Europe came to study with him. Even so, it was not the vocal element in Lully's operas that caught on abroad—Italian influence was far too powerful—but the instrumental, a constituent of opera that the Italians treated with comparative neglect.

The importance of the orchestra in Lully's operas was due not only to the enormous quantity of dance music it was called on to play as a result of the numerous ballets, but also to the quality of the music itself. Instead of the rather perfunctory instrumental items of contemporary Italian opera in which only the top and bottom lines mattered, Lully composed pieces of distinction, some of them of considerable length, a number

* Solo and violin parts and bass from the 2nd ed., Paris, 1709, p. 59.

Ex.24 Recitative - Au généraux Roland and Air - Triomphez charmante Reine (Roland I.6) (1688) Lully
(♩= MM.c.96)
Ziliante (carrying a bracelet to Angelique)
Au gé-né-raux Ro-land Je dois ma dé-li - - vran - ce, D'un char-me at-
My blest de-li - ve - rance to Ro - land do I owe it, From charms so
- treux Sa va-leur m'a sau - - vé; Il n'a vou - - lu de ma re - con - nois -
dire me he no-bly did save; My gra - ti - - tude he bid me not be - -
- san - - ce, Que ce pré - - - sent qu'il vous a ré - ser - - vé. Je viens pour vous l'ot-
stow it, But that this gift thou'd ac-cept he did crave. I bring it from the

Ex. 24 CONTD.

-trir du Ri-va-ge où l'Au-ro-re ou-vre la Ba-riè-re du Jour.
East where the sun e'er hath fla-med T'ope the gate of morn-ing with fire.
Vous em-bra-sez Ro--land d'un feu qui le dé-vo-re: Mais qui peut
With burn-ing pas-sion Ro-land is by you en-fla-med: But who the
voir la beau-té qu'il a--do-re Voit sans é-ton-ne-ment l'ex-cès de son a-
beau-ty sees that him hath clai-med Is not a-sto-nish--ed at his in-tense de--

Ex. 24 CONTD.

(𝅗𝅥 = MM.c.60)(Violins)
-mour.
-sire.
Tri-om - phez, char-man - -te Rei - ne, tri - om - - phez des plus grands
Tri-umph thou, O queen al - - lur - ing, Tri - umph, all great hearts en -
(Ziliante & continuo)
coeurs, tri - om - phez, tri - om - - phez,
flame, tri-umph thou, tri-umph thou,
char-man - te Rei - ne, tri - om - - phez, tri - om - - phez des plus grands
O queen al - - lur - - ing, tri-umph thou, tri-umph, all great hearts en - -

Ex. 24 CONTD.

(Fine)
coeurs. Ce n'est qu'aux plus fa - meux Vain - - queurs qu'il est per - -
flame. 'Tis on - ly he of great - est fame May wear your
- mis de por - - ter vô - tre chai
fet - ters of pas - - sion en - - dur
- ne, ce n'est qu'aux plus fa-meux vain - - queurs qu'il est per - - mis de por -
- ing, 'tis on-ly he of great-est fame may wear your fet - - ters of

Ex. 24 CONTD.

-ter vô-tre chai
pas-sion en-dur
4 ♯ 6

–ne, ce n'est qu'aux plus fa-meux vain- -queurs qu'il est per- -mis de por-
–ing, 'tis on-ly he of great-est fame may wear your fet--ters of

–ter, de por- -ter vô-tre chai- -ne. Tri-om-
pas--sion, of pas--sion en--dur- -ing. Tri-umph
(Dal 𝄋)

of them in five parts, and all of them showing a greater care in the writing of the inner parts; these last were, in fact, often added by his pupils, but only at Lully's command. Here, for example, is part of the fine chaconne (153 bars in length) from Act II of *Phaëton* (1683), an opera so successful that it was nicknamed 'l'opera du peuple'. (We shall define a chaconne as a continuous set of variations on a recurring succession of basic chords which almost invariably lead from tonic to dominant and so back to the tonic again. Thus a chord may not only change its position (e.g. a root may become a first inversion, as in variation (*a*), bar 2, of Ex. 25) and its mode (i.e. major may become minor, as in variation (*b*), bar 2), but it may also be preceded, succeeded, and even replaced by a different chord or chords (as in variation (*a*), bar 3, and (*c*), bar 2), always provided that the route, as it were, from tonic to dominant is recognizably the same: Ex. 25,* p. 421).

Lully's orchestral style, particularly as revealed in his overtures, swept the length and breadth of Europe, penetrating even Italy. The operatic overture in Italy is usually, as we have seen, a rather casual affair, but Lully the violinist and conductor saw in it an opportunity to show off the King's string band as well as to satisfy his royal master's delight in instrumental music. The first distinct example of a Lullian or French overture occurs in the ballet *Alcidiane* (1658); this consists of two movements, a slow, pompous one in a predominantly dotted rhythm, followed by a quick one in duple time which begins in imitative style and is based on a short motive. Lully's ballet music to Cavalli's *Serse* (1660) contains an overture on similar lines, except that the second movement is in triple time; this became standard practice. Some French overtures are concluded by an adagio coda which has been classed as a separate movement by some writers, who, as a result, give the overall plan as slow-quick-slow. This is wrong, so far as Lully's overtures are concerned at any rate, because the final section is not a regular feature, and when it does occur it is simply a broadening out of the concluding bars of the second movement (e.g. *Alceste*, *H.A.M.*, 224). This two-movement plan, slow-quick, was not invented by Lully, as it can be found in a sinfonia in Landi's *Sant' Alessio* (see p. 382), and in a few Venetian operas, such as Cavalli's *Giasone* (see p. 395), as well

* From 3rd ed., Amsterdam [1711], p. 160.

as in the 'ouvertures', as they were called, of a few earlier ballets dating back to at least 1640; indeed, the first movement of some of these ouvertures display the dotted rhythm typical of the Lullian type. That Lully was acquainted with some of these early sinfonie and ouvertures can scarcely be doubted, but he was the first to adopt the slow-quick plan as a standard procedure, and its success, due partly to the admirably contrasted movements, partly to the quality of the actual music, was such that it became the first significant example of orchestral music to achieve independence—in other words, to be composed and played for its own sake without being attached to a stage work.

The country that was most influenced by Lully was England, largely through the enthusiasm of Charles II [reigned 1660–1685], who, after the execution of his father, Charles I, and during the Commonwealth, spent most of his exile in France and became thoroughly enamoured of French music, especially Lully's ballet music. But Charles did not introduce opera into England, for while he may have seen La Guerre's *Le Triomphe* and Cambert's *Pastorale* while in exile, the first English opera, *The Siege of Rhodes*, had already been produced, with great success, four years before he was crowned. This opera is subtitled "A Representation by the Art of Prospective [=perspective] in Scenes, And the Story sung in Recitative Musick". There is no mention of it being a dramatic entertainment, because the Puritans, under their leader, Oliver Cromwell [1599–1658], were strongly opposed to anything that smacked of the traditional theatre; they did not, however, object to music, and so Sir William Davenant or D'Avenant [1606–1668], who, besides being a dramatist and Ben Jonson's successor as Poet Laureate, was also an astute theatrical manager, wrote a play and commissioned a number of composers to set the words in recitative style and to provide songs and instrumental music, none of which unfortunately has survived. (It is worth noting that the performance of this opera marked the first occasion when a woman appeared on the English public stage, i.e. the first professional actress; she was Mrs. Coleman, wife of Edward Coleman [d. 1669], one of the composers engaged by Davenant.)

The Siege of Rhodes was not Davenant's first essay in the musico-dramatic sphere, as he had already written a number of masques for the court of Charles I; nor was the use of recitative the first instance of this style in an English stage work, for as early as 1617 Ben Jonson's masque, *The Vision of Delight*, was partly and his *Lovers make Men* wholly (according to him) "sung after the Italian manner, *stylo recitativo*, by Master Nicholas Lanier . . .". Lanier [1588–1666], of French descent, was Master of the King's Musick to both Charles I and II, and one of a group of composers who sought to adapt Italian monody to English use. This group included Henry Lawes [1596–1662], another contributor to *The Siege of Rhodes*, his brother William [1602–1645], and Simon Ives [1600-1662]. It was William Lawes and Ives who wrote the music for the most elaborate, fantastic, and costly masque ever produced in England, *The Triumph of Peace* (1633), by the popular and prolific dramatist, James Shirley [1596–1666]. This extravaganza was organized in protest against the violent attack on masques and plays contained in *Histriomastic: The Players Scourge*, by William Prynne [1600–1669], and published earlier in the same year. The masque included a procession on horseback from Holborn to Whitechapel of all the characters, and cost the Inns of Court, who commissioned the work, over £21,000 (at least £200,000 in modern money), of which about £1,000 was spent on the music, Lawes and Ives receiving £100 each.

The Triumph of Peace represents, albeit in an extreme form, the general decadence of the Caroline masque, in which realism rather than fantasy was the aim and which, as a result of increasing French influence, relied to a greater extent than did the Jacobean masque on the purely spectacular. It was French influence also, rather than Italian, that was reflected in the English recitative style, a style in which the rhythm of the words is more or less faithfully transmitted to the vocal line, but which lacks the affective nature and harmonic variety of the French and Italian arioso. It was this projection of verbal metre into musical rhythm that prompted Milton, in 1646, to write of Henry Lawes:

> Harry, whose tuneful and well-measured song
> First taught our English music how to span
> Words with just note and accent, not to scan
> With Midas' ears, committing short and long ;
> Thy worth and skill exempt thee from the throng,
> With praise enough for Envy to look wan;
> To after age thou shalt be writ the man,
> That with smooth air couldst humour best our tongue.

Milton was not alone in praising Lawes, but he in particular should have known better, for not only was his father a distinguished enough composer to contribute to *The Triumphs of Oriana*, but he himself had heard Italian opera in Rome (see p. 384). In actual fact Henry's songs are hardly "tuneful" or "smooth"; neither was he the first to set English words "justly", nor are the results superior to those by Lanier, his brother William, and others. Even his fairly well-known setting of Milton's fine masque, *Comus* (1634), owes its distinction to the beauty of the poem, for the music's melodic and harmonic monotony is only occasionally relieved by the comparative tunefulness of such songs as 'Sweet Echo' (*H.A.M.*, 204).

Five years after *Comus* came the last of the court masques, Davenant's *Salmacida Spolia*, but masques for private entertainment continued to be written during the Commonwealth, the most outstanding being Shirley's *Cupid and Death*, presented before the Portuguese Ambassador in 1653, with music presumably by Matthew Locke [*c.* 1621 – 1677], another contributor to *The Siege of Rhodes*, and Christopher Gibbons [1615–1676], second son of Orlando. We say 'presumably' because the only music to this masque that has come down to us is that for the later performance of 1659 which is unquestionably by Locke and Gibbons. Locke's contributions, which exceed in both quantity and quality those by Gibbons, show a keener sense of drama and a bolder imagination than any previous English composer for the stage. Unlike Henry Lawes and his generation, he is more concerned with the dramatic impact of the whole than with the accurate rendering of speech rhythm, and as a result his vocal lines are more tuneful and flexible, his harmonies more varied, and his part-writing freer. (Ex. 26,* p. 425. Notice the shiver on "cold" the abrupt change of chord on "Bright", and the melismas on the unaccented "a" and "-to" of "into", a breach of verbal rhythm that must have made Henry Lawes shudder, but which arouse a feeling of expectancy for the word following.)

The affective treatment of the words in Ex. 26 shows that Italian influence was beginning to make itself felt in England, an influence that grew as the century progressed. But while Locke's melodies are, in the main, smoother than those of the previous generation of composers, their wayward rhythm and frequent wide leaps still contrast sharply with the simple, often sequential, pattern and melodic curves of the *bel canto*. More important is the comparative lack of feeling for a central tonality, for although there are signs of overall key-planning

* Melody and bass from *Musica Britannica*, II, ed. E. J. Dent, p. 38.

Ex. 26 Beginning of recitative - *What will it, Death,* from the 'Fourth Song'
(♩= MM.c.60) (*Cupid and Death*) (1659) Locke
Voice
What will it, Death, ad - - vance thy name Up - - on cold — rocks to
waste a ——— flame, Or by mis - - take to throw Bright
tor - - - ches in - - to ——— pits of snow?
(etc.)

(i.e. within a group of movements) in Locke's music to *Cupid and Death* (and even in that of William Lawes to *The Triumph of Peace*), the chord progressions within a movement, which often lead to a wide variety of keys, lack the single tonal direction that alone can give both greater meaning to such excursions and at the same time a feeling of unity.

Locke never developed a strong tonal sense, even in his later works for the stage. Of these the most important are the incidental music to, and the masque, *Orpheus and Euridice*, that formed part of *The Empress of Morocco* (1673)—a tragedy by the minor playwright, Elkanah Settle [1648–1724], the so-called opera, *Psyche* (1673)—an imitation of Molière's and Lully's comédie-ballet of the same name by the Poet Laureate and successful dramatist, Thomas Shadwell [1642–1692], and incidental music to Shadwell's version of Shakespeare's *The Tempest* (1674). (Adulterated versions of Shakespeare's plays, in which original passages and sometimes whole scenes were omitted and new material and even new characters added, together with songs and dances, became very popular during the Restoration period and later.)

In *Psyche* Locke's vocal line is less angular than in *Cupid and Death*, and his harmony more orthodox, but his instrumental pieces for *The Tempest* contain a number of what the English historian, Charles Burney, called "crudities". Burney's pronouncements are usually sound, but he was prone, like many other critics since his time, to judge an earlier work by later standards, in this case the smooth chord progressions and unerring sense of tonal direction of the late eighteenth century. Locke's harmonic language is undoubtedly sometimes rough and occasionally startling, compared to that of his contemporaries abroad, but to label unorthodoxy as crude is to imply that the composer was incompetent and his ear imperfect. Locke knew perfectly well what he was doing because not only is his harmonic style consistent within a work, but his free use of dissonance nearly always 'comes off'. Indeed, he was but part of that English tradition which stretched back to the Middle Ages, when the comparatively dissonant thirds and sixths were much more favoured than on the Continent. Byrd's use of dissonance is in the same tradition, and so too is Purcell's, as we shall see. In Ex. 27 the dissonant entry in bar 2, the unusual dominant seventh in bar 5, and the false relation in bars 3 and 5 all 'come off' (Ex. 27,* p. 427).

The movement from which Ex. 27 is taken contains the directions "soft" and "lowd", and in the 'Curtain Tune', which is frankly programmatic in that it portrays a 'tempest', occur the expressions "soft", "lowder by degrees", "violent", "lowd", and "soft and slow by degrees", of which the second and last are the most remarkable for the time at which they

* From '*The Tempest*' *Music*, Suite I, ed. W. G. Whittaker.

Ex.27 From 'The First Musick' (*The Tempest*) (1674)

were written, because while abrupt expression marks, e.g. 'lowd' or 'forte', were uncommon enough before *c.* 1750, graduated ones, such as 'soft and slow by degrees' or 'diminuendo e ritardando', were extremely rare.

Locke's masque, *Orpheus and Euridice*, has been described as "the first surviving example of true operatic writing in England" (Anthony Lewis), for, apart from the fact that, unlike all earlier masques, it contains no spoken passages, the vocal line is very reminiscent of early Italian opera in its occasional use of sequence, its oscillation between arioso and aria styles, and its general smoothness, despite the fondness for iambic rhythm, i.e. ♪ ♩ or ♬, which can be regarded as a fingerprint of late seventeenth-century English vocal writing. It is the first surviving example, because the music to *The Siege of Rhodes* has been lost, as has that to Davenant's two later operas, *The Cruelty of the Spaniards in Peru* (1658) and *The History of Sir Francis Drake* (1659). The notable feature common to all three operas is that they are concerned with what was then recent history. This is obvious enough in the third opera, but the first is based on an actual siege of the city in 1522 by the Turks under Solyman the Magnificent, while the second summarizes the history of Peru from pre-Inca times to the Spanish conquest in 1532, ending with a scene, admitted by the author to be entirely fictitious, in which the Spaniards are expelled by a combined Peruvian-English army. This opera was intended as a kind of lecture-recital, with music, dancing, and scenery to gild the pill, so to speak; in this it was poles removed from the Italian and French conception of opera, which was solely concerned with entertaining, not informing. In complete contrast too are the subjects of Davenant's operas, for, as we have seen, Continental librettists delved mostly into ancient history and classical mythology, even though the characters behaved like seventeenth-century men and women.

Whether Davenant had any intention of founding a school or tradition of English opera we do not know. He was an ambitious man and an opportunist who managed both to evade Puritanical objections and to capture popular appeal with his operas. As early as 1639 he obtained a patent from Charles I which gave him permission to build his own theatre, and to perform in it or other theatres "musical presentments, scenes, dancing, or any others the like . . .". If this meant opera, then he was ahead of the French, but it is more likely that he only had masques in mind, for he could not have seen any opera before his visits to France in the 1640s. Even after the public theatres were reopened in 1660 Davenant produced no new opera, despite the success of his first three. He seems to have clearly understood the nature and purpose of recitative, judging by the speech he puts into the mouth of the Musician, one of the characters in his medley of plays entitled *The Playhouse to Let* (1663):

> Recitative Musick is not compos'd
> Of matter so familiar, as may serve
> For every low occasion of discourse.
> In Tragedy, the language of the Stage
> Is rais'd above the common dialect;
> Our passion rising with the height of Verse;
> And Vocal Musick adds new wings to all
> The flights of Poetry.

By "Recitative Musick" Davenant almost certainly meant something akin to arioso, not the rapid patter of secco recitative, which, in fact, was hardly ever used by English composers before Handel. Perhaps he sensed that opera, while satisfying the lack of public dramatic entertainment during the Commonwealth, could not compete in normal times either with straight drama or with the masque, in which music serves only to heighten, at certain points, the emotional impact or the spectacular element, but which is not used for narrative or conversational purposes; in other words, that a play interspersed with vocal and instrumental numbers was acceptable, but one sung throughout was not. This was certainly Locke's view, for in the Preface to *The English Opera* (1675), which contains his music to *Psyche* and *The Tempest*, he says that the former work "may fitly bear the title of Opera though all the tragedy be not in Musick; for the author prudently consider'd that though Italy is the great Academy of the World for that Science and way of entertainment, England is not: and therefore mix'd it with interlocutions as more proper to our genius".

It seems from the above quotation that Locke would have liked to write a full-scale opera if conditions had been favourable; as it is, however, the first surviving English opera, although it is sub-titled 'A Masque for the Entertainment of the King', is *Venus and Adonis*, by John Blow [1649–1708], composed *c.* 1682. This work has closer affinities to Continental models than Davenant's operas (so far as we can judge the latter from the libretto and contemporary accounts), being a mixture of Italian but more especially French styles and ideas, with a few features peculiar to England added. Thus the overall plan is Lullian in that, unlike Davenant's operas, which were divided into a number of scenes, *Venus and Adonis* consists of a French overture leading straight into a pastoral Prologue and succeeded by three acts. Both French and Italian influence is shown in the fact that the plot is taken from classical mythology, that the libretto is sung throughout, and that the recitatives combine Lully's careful word-setting with the affective line of the Italian arioso; indeed, Venus's outburst of grief when the dying Adonis lies before her reaches a degree of passion unknown before in England and rarely equalled abroad (Ex. 28,* p. 430).

* Melody and bass from *Venus and Adonis*, ed. A. Lewis, p. 89.

Italian rather than French influence is shown by the preponderance of airs over recitatives, the former being, in the main, not only clearly set off from the latter, but more tuneful and regular in their construction than in any previous English vocal music for the stage. The English features are a certain angularity of line in the recitatives, an uncertainty in tonal direction, and the importance of the chorus, solo ensembles, and instrumental music. This last, to be sure, is also true of Lullian opera, but it undoubtedly stemmed from the masque tradition, as did the inclusion of a large number of choruses (they comprise nearly a quarter of the vocal music) compared to foreign operas. The greater use of the chorus was also due to the amateur and private nature of the performance, in which there were no 'stars' whose talents and temperaments had to be considered (*H.A.M.*, 243).

In its tunefulness, range of mood, and general structure, *Venus and Adonis* represents a considerable advance on what had gone before, even though Blow's grasp of tonality is only slightly superior to Locke's, and it is a pity that he never wrote another work for the stage, particularly as his association with the greatest English composer of the baroque era, Henry Purcell [1659 – 1695], led to a new clarity and simplicity in his melodic and harmonic styles.

Purcell was in fact a pupil of Blow, and the musical relationship between the two was very similar to that between Haydn and Mozart, for both Purcell and Mozart were influenced by and in their turn influenced their older contemporary, and both were the more profound artists. This last is clearly revealed in Purcell's only opera, *Dido and Aeneas* (1689?), for whereas there are sufficient similarities to *Venus and Adonis* to show that Purcell had studied his master's work, the differences are much more striking and significant. The first and most important difference is simply that Purcell's music reveals a far greater skill and imagination. Thus while both Dido's famous lament (*H.A.M.*, 255) and Venus's passionate outburst mentioned above represent the climax of their respective operas (as did 'Arianna's Lament' in Monteverdi's opera), Purcell's air conveys a deeper sense of tragedy which is sustained by a well-nigh perfect fusion of a highly expressive vocal line and poignant harmony supported by a chromatic ground-bass. Again, although Purcell's opera, like Blow's, reveals Italian influence in the number and character of its airs, and French-Italian influence in its arioso-like recitatives, the former are far more 'catchy' and the latter more expressive than in Blow's work. His tonality too is much more assured than the older man's, for although the key structures in *Dido*, both within each Act and as a whole, are only slightly better planned than in *Venus* (but not nearly so well thought out as in the masque from *The Prophetess, or the History of Dioclesian*), his tonal sense within a key is firmer and his modulations smoother. *Dido* also includes, and for the same reasons as *Venus*, a greater number of choruses, ensembles, and instrumental pieces than was common abroad.

Despite the superiority of the music, Purcell's opera is less perfectly constructed than Blow's, the major flaw being the totally inadequate treatment of Aeneas. This is all the more marked because, whereas Venus and Adonis, despite the former's outburst of grief, are presented as dramatic figures roughly equal in stature, though neither are profoundly drawn,

Dido is revealed through two wonderfully expressive airs as a mature and deeply passionate woman, while Aeneas's character is never given a chance to establish itself, as he is only allowed a few recitatives, including an almost perfunctory lover's quarrel with Dido; indeed, Belinda, Dido's sister, is a far more vivid personality. Admittedly the librettist, Nahum Tate [1652–1715], is also to blame, and as the opera was written for a boarding-school for gentlewomen run by a well-known dancing master, Josias Priest, it was natural that the part of Aeneas, which was obviously sung by an imported tenor, should be limited, but not to the extent that it is. Even so, if Purcell had had more operatic experience he would doubtless have insisted that Aeneas be given a larger share in the drama. Actually, however, his experience before *Dido* was limited to providing songs and instrumental music for seven plays, including *Theodosius* (1680), by the minor dramatist, Nathaniel Lee [1649–1692], the composer's first and most popular contribution to the stage, and *Circe* (1685?), by Charles Davenant, son of Sir William, which contains one of Purcell's finest ariosos, 'Pluto arise'. In addition, he almost certainly studied Locke's stage music, and may have seen *Psyche* performed. He may also have been present at the London productions of Perrin and Grabu's (?) *Ariane* in 1674 (see p. 406), and of Cambert's *Pomone* (adapted by Grabu) in the same year, and must have seen *Albion and Albanius* (1685), by John Dryden [1631–1700], the greatest English poet and playwright of his generation, with music by Grabu, and, in the following year, Lully's *Cadmus et Hermione*, given by a visiting French company.

Purcell was probably as impressed by Lully's music as he was appalled by Grabu's, whose songs in *Albion* show an almost laughable unacquaintance with the English language, and the whole revealing a woeful poverty of invention. Why Dryden ever collaborated with him is a mystery, even if we admit that at the time he regarded both Purcell and Blow with disfavour (largely because of their low opinion of Grabu), for he was fully aware of the difficulties in setting English words to music; as he states so admirably in his Preface to the opera, "'Tis no easie Matter in our Language to make Words so smooth, and Numbers so harmonious, that they shall almost set themselves. ... The chief Secret is in the choice of Words; and by this

XXIII (*above* Virginal) by Andreas Ruckers [1610].

XXIV Pavane and Galliard, *The Earle of Salisbury*, by Byrd, from *Parthenia* [1611].

XXV 'Trio des Parques' from Rameau's *Hippolyte* (II.5) (*from the first edition*).

Choice I do not here mean Elegancy of Expression; but Propriety of Sound, to be varied according to the Nature of the Subject." Any English musician could have made a better job than Grabu of setting Dryden's libretto, but the complete failure of the opera cannot be laid entirely at the composer's door, as Dryden was also to blame by turning what was originally intended to be only a prologue to a "Tragedy" into a full-blown three-act opera. Dryden's conception of opera was admirable: "An Opera is a Poetical Tale, or Fiction, represented by Vocal and Instrumental Musick, adorn'd with Scenes, Machines and Dancing. The suppos'd Persons of this Musical Drama, are generally Supernatural." He is clear on the distinction between recitative and aria, or what he so delightfully calls "the Songish part", but in the projected tragedy, mentioned above, he shies away from the genuinely operatic, for he says that it would have been "a Tragedy mix'd with Opera; or a Drama written in blank verse, adorn'd with Machines, songs and dances: So that the Fable of it is all spoken and acted . . . the other parts of the Entertainment to be perform'd by . . . Singers and Dancers. . . . It cannot properly be called a Play, because the Action of it is supposed to be conducted sometimes by supernatural Means, or Magick; nor an Opera because the Story of it is not sung."

Even if Dryden's tragedy had materialized and Purcell had written the music it would only have been another semi-opera, like the five that Purcell did in fact write after *Dido*. Of these, two are adaptations from Shakespeare, *The Fairy Queen* (1692) and *The Tempest* (1695?), one an adaptation from Beaumont and Fletcher, *The Prophetess* (1690), and two by Dryden, *King Arthur* (1691) and *The Indian Queen* (1695), the latter being adapted from the play by Dryden and Robert Howard. All these works are characterized by the great importance of the chorus, and abundance of instrumental numbers (ritornelli, dances, preludes, and descriptive pieces), spoken dialogue, very few recitatives (all of the arioso type), elaborate sets and stage machinery, and the fact that none of the principal characters in the drama sing.

The Masque from *Dioclesian* so impressed Dryden (and it has impressed everyone ever since) that, despite the failure of *Albion* and his slight of Purcell, he asked the composer to collaborate in a new play specially designed for musical treatment—*King Arthur*. This, the only semi-opera by Purcell that is not an adaptation of an earlier play, contains the remarkable 'Frost Scene', with its vocal and instrumental 'shivering' tremolandos and its weird harmony, and a host of fine solos, ensembles, and choruses, e.g. 'Fairest Isle' and the superbly extended 'passacaglia'—really a ground—that comprises most of Act IV.

King Arthur loses far more by being presented in a concert version than do any of the other semi-operas, particularly *The Fairy Queen*, which is really a succession of highly spectacular masques with the original text of *A Midsummer Night's Dream* grossly mutilated and used merely as a series of connecting episodes. It is the longest of Purcell's dramatic works, but it is remarkable how very few items there are that strike one as commonplace; indeed, the quality of inspiration is consistently higher than in either of the two earlier works, as, for instance, in such fine songs as 'If love's a sweet passion', 'Hark how all things in one sound rejoice', 'Hark the echoing air', and some delightful fairy music. It also shows more clearly the influence of Italy in the use of coloratura and of the *da capo* aria. (In *Dido*, *Dioclesian*, and *King Arthur* there is only one air in this form—Belinda's 'Pursue thy conquest love'; in *The Fairy Queen* there are four.)

In the three years that elapsed before Purcell's last two semi-operas, he composed incidental music to well over twenty plays, some of them by such well-known authors as Dryden, William Congreve [1670–1729], Thomas D'Urfey [1653–1723], and Thomas Southerne [1660–1746]. Several of the songs from these and earlier plays are among the best he ever wrote—'Nymphs and Shepherds' (*The Libertine*, 1692?), 'Music for a while shall all your cares beguile' (*Oedipus*, 1692), 'Man is for the woman made' (*The Mock Marriage*, 1695)—and reveal an astonishing versatility, ranging as they do from lighthearted amorousness and rustic comedy to passionate declamation and 'mad songs' in which rapid changes of speed and style represent passing fits of insanity. The overtures, dances, and other instrumental pieces, like the songs, are a veritable mine of first-rate music, from hornpipes and jigs to poignantly chromatic adagios.

The experience Purcell gained from all this incidental music bore rich fruit in *The Indian Queen* and *The Tempest*, which are not only the greatest of his works for the stage, but also represent the peak of his entire output. To enumerate the gems they contain would be simply to compile a list of most of the vocal and instrumental numbers; indeed, both works display a technique that accomplishes with ease the dictates of a rich, versatile, and mature imagination, a melodic gift that is universally recognized as being one of the most remarkable in history, a firm sense of tonality that is undisturbed by certain features typical of earlier English compositions, and a style which absorbed but did not submit to French and Italian influences.

The typically English harmonic features mentioned above are essentially a free and (for the time) unorthodox use of dissonance, including false relation, which sprang from a mode of thinking that we can call 'horizontal'. Such a mode of thought had practically ceased in Italy, where melody and bass were all-important and where inner parts, even when written down, were primarily 'fillers-up' of the harmony; the same is largely true of France, for while Lully paid more attention to part-writing than the Italians, the parts themselves have less independence than in English compositions. In England, however, the tradition of polyphonic writing had been maintained right through the seventeenth century in both vocal and instrumental music, and most of Purcell's harmonic quirks, like Byrd's dissonances (see Chapter 2) are the result of this, e.g. his use of false relation, either in passing—often for descriptive reasons, as in the chorus, 'Full fathom five' (*The Tempest*)—or in the so-called 'English cadence' (see Chapter 2), as in 'What ho! thou Genius of the Clime' (*King Arthur*).

Roughly speaking, one can say that in Purcell's music for the stage, particularly that written during the last five years or so of his life, Italian influence is most apparent in the vocal numbers and French influence in the instrumental pieces, although there are examples of the Italian canzona and sinfonia on the one hand and of French dance-songs on the other. Thus the overtures, in the main, follow Lully's pattern, and most of the dances are those popular at the court of Louis XIV, while the songs reveal their author's study of Italian models in their greater regularity of structure, their lyricism, and the range of mood within a single number, apart from an increasing but still comparatively infrequent use of *da capo* form and coloratura. In addition a number of features occur so often in his melodies as to be characteristic, e.g. the rhythm ♩ 𝅗𝅥 | 𝅗𝅥 ♩ in $\frac{3}{4}$ time, successions of trochees, (♩. ♪ ♩. ♪) and the expressive use of iambs (♪♩.), in which the short accented note is usually an appogiatura (i.e. a dissonance) that is often followed by a falling fourth or fifth (see Ex. 28). This last feature was more common in England than in France or Italy, probably because of the more marked accentual nature of the language, but the other two features are typical of Lully's style. Purcell's fondness for repeated motives (ground bass and passacaglia) was also typical of French, and indeed Italian, composition, and it is interesting to note that he used this technique less as his tonal sense developed (see p. 397). What distinguishes Purcell's stage music from that of the Continent is the combination of French-Italian sequential structure with a greater freshness, breadth, and irregularity of phrase, supported by harmonic progressions that are basically orthodox but which include 'odd' dissonances.

Purcell never travelled abroad, and while he almost certainly saw one of Lully's operas (see p. 432) he never saw one by an Italian. His knowledge, therefore, of operatic performances in Italy was acquired at second hand, either from Englishmen, like his teacher, Pelham Humfrey [1647–1674], who had been sent there at the King's expense, and Dryden, or from Italians who, from the Restoration on, visited or settled in England in increasing numbers. These last brought with them a fair quantity of vocal and instrumental music, chiefly cantatas and trio sonatas (see Chapters 5 and 6), and it must have been from these manuscript copies that Purcell's enthusiasm for and knowledge of the Italian style chiefly derived.

In the Preface to *The Fairy Queen*, after defining opera as "a Story sung with proper Action", and praising *The Siege of Rhodes* as "a perfect Opera", except that it lacked "the Ornament of Machines, which they Value themselves so much upon in Italy", the anonymous writer says: "That a few private Persons should venture on so expensive a Work as an Opera [i.e. *The Fairy Queen*] when none but Princes, or States exhibit 'em abroad, I hope is no dishonour to our Nation: And I dare affirm if we had half the Encouragement in England, that they have in other Countries, you might in a short time have as good Dancers in England as they have in France, though I despair of ever having as good Voices among us, as they have in Italy." From this it may be deduced that there would have been some support for full-scale operas in the Italian manner to English libretti, and, judging by the tremendous success of Arne's *Artaxerxes* (1762), it is possible that had Purcell lived another twenty years or so he might well have established a national operatic tradition.

4

THE BAROQUE: MUSIC FOR THE STAGE—II

"*. . . no Music can support an opera without great and favourite singers.*" (CHARLES BURNEY, *A General History of Music*, 1776, Vol. IV, p. 457.)

ITALIAN opera, or, more precisely, the opera that stemmed from Naples, during the late baroque, (i.e. *c.* 1680–*c.* 1750) has been adversely criticized more widely, consistently, and violently than the music of any other period, country, or type. From the eighteenth century to the twentieth, Englishmen, Frenchmen, Germans, and even Italians have poured contumely if not ridicule on an operatic type that inspired men of the calibre of Alessandro Scarlatti, Handel, and Hasse to write some of their finest music. In recent years, however, a more imaginative approach has been made, and as a result the virtues as well as the vices of Neapolitan opera have been shown in a truer perspective.

Up to *c.* 1680 Venice was the main operatic centre, and even in second-rate Venetian operas, not to mention those by Cavalli, Cesti, and the later generation of Legrenzi, Stradella, and Pallavicino, dramatic integrity and, though to a much lesser degree, musical characterization were important, but not to the same extent as with Monteverdi. As a result, the nature of an individual aria depended on the composer's reaction to the story or the poetic quality of the libretto at that particular point. In Neapolitan opera, musical characterization is almost totally lacking, and dramatic integrity is entirely subservient to musical variety. This last was achieved partly through the alternation of secco recitative and aria (as in late Venetian opera), in which the former is primarily concerned with action (i.e. the unfolding of the drama by means of dialogue), but is musically negligible, while in the latter action is non-existent, the stress being entirely on the music which reveals the emotional response of one character to the preceding events in the drama. Variety was also achieved by ensuring that successive arias were of different types and, less important, that they were sung by different characters.

The chief types of aria were the 'aria cantabile', the most popular type, in slow tempo, sentimental, and providing more opportunities than the other types for displaying the singer's all-round technical mastery; the 'aria di portamento', dignified, and containing many long notes on which the singer could reveal his sustaining powers and beauty of tone; the 'aria parlante' or 'agitata', the most highly emotional type, characterized by syllabic underlay, and sung at a quicker speed and with great intensity of feeling; and lastly the 'aria di bravura' or 'agilita', the singer's show-piece, in which the rapidity, agility, and sometimes the extreme compass of the voice (see p. 461) were abundantly displayed. In addition to being classified as a certain type, each aria was governed by a single mood or 'affection', and this feature, while it was typical of all music during the late baroque, represented the culmination of an aesthetic approach to music known as the 'doctrine of temperaments and affections', and was first fully revealed in the opera aria, particularly of the Neapolitan School.

In the seventeenth and eighteenth centuries the word 'affections' (Italian *affetti*, German *Affekte*) had a far wider meaning than it has today, because it stood for a considerable number of what we may call mental activities. Thus affections included not only general emotions, such as 'pleasure', 'sadness', 'joy', 'anger', but also feelings of association, e.g. 'pastoral', 'warlike', and, especially in instrumental music, abstract mental states impossible to describe accurately in words, but which, nevertheless, were (and are today) clearly recognized and understood. In other words, baroque composers were primarily concerned with "rendering and translating into music the temper, disposition or frame of mind, passions, and mental reactions characteristic of man" (Lang). While this approach bears some resemblance to Plato's equating certain emotions with scales and instruments (see Part I, p. 13)—the latter, in fact, were also classified 'affectively' by some late baroque theorists, the horn being 'pompous', the flute 'modest', the kettledrum 'heroic', etc.—and is a natural development of the Renaissance technique of word-painting, it has much more in common, and indeed can be said to have originated with Rore's mood-expression (see p. 251). Not until the advent of monody, however, did the affections become of paramount importance, although monody, unlike its offspring, the fully-fledged opera aria, was not necessarily governed by a single affection.

The development and fulfilment of the doctrine took place in vocal music because the clearest way of establishing it was through the use of words which alone can impart a precise affection. Moreover, instrumental music, while it certainly added on occasion to the emotions conveyed by the singer, both in the aria and, often with great power, in the *recitativo accompagnato* or *stromentato* (i.e. recitative accompanied by the orchestra), could not by itself express either the intensity or the range of feeling of a well-trained voice. The doctrine reached fulfilment in opera, rather than in the cantata or oratorio, because firstly, from Monteverdi and Cavalli on, opera, to the Italians, was so vital, all-absorbing, and popular that it both reflected more clearly the artistic aims of its time, and also provided a more natural medium for experiment and innovation than any other kind of music. Secondly, only the opera aria was theatrical; in other words, the basic affection was much more easily and naturally 'put across' by the actor whose facial expressions and bodily movements would all contribute.

The basic affection, which, by the late baroque, dominated each independent musical movement, whether of an overture or concerto, or an aria, is always expressed as clearly as possible by means of a distinctive musical idea or motto. Each motto thus represents the quintessence of a basic affection, and while most of them naturally consist of a combination of melody, rhythm, and harmony, the distinctiveness of a motto nearly always lies in the greater importance of one of these elements, quite apart from whether it is in the major or minor mode. Mottoes that are primarily harmonic or rhythmic are first presented, as one would expect, in the opening ritornello, because the solo voice cannot express harmony and is an unsuitable vehicle for pure rhythm, but when melody is the prime feature of a motto it was natural that, with the affection clarified by words, it should be delivered by the voice at the very beginning of an aria. This 'motto beginning', which, as we have seen, became common with Cesti and later

Venetian composers (p. 401), is usually succeeded by a short instrumental ritornello which either imitates the voice (see Ex. 30, p. 450), or else introduces a related or new but always subsidiary and never strongly contrasted figure (for this would disrupt the affective unity) which is used in the course of the aria (see Ex. 34, p. 473).

Motto beginnings are musically artistic and emotionally significant when used with skill and imagination, but they became an empty mannerism in the hands of inferior composers who accepted mechanically the pseudo-scientific classification that took place during the early years of the eighteenth century. This linked affections with mottoes, usually in general terms, but the German theorists Scheibe, Heinichen, and Mattheson (see p. 488) went so far as to equate a particular motto with a specific affection, an absurd belief, for music cannot be so specific; thus in Ex. 31 (p. 453), for instance, the most distinctive falling fifth (the germ of the aria) might imply a number of affections, resignation or sadness, and not until the voice enters do we know it to be 'faithfulness unto death'. Obviously, if the mode becomes major, with or without a quickening of tempo, different affections will be implied. Even before this classification it was taken for granted that performers would recognize and their interpretation be dictated by the basic affection; hence the dearth of expression marks in baroque music. But the reliance placed on performers would have been unthinkable if the doctrine of affections had not been generally accepted and if the performers themselves, especially soloists, had not received a much more all-round musical education than is customary to-day. The performer, moreover, was much more than an interpreter in the modern sense; he was also a co-creator, and both composer and audience expected him to embellish in performance what was written down on paper. This applied with particular force to opera singers, especially the castrati, who were the first real virtuosi in the history of music, and in Neapolitan opera virtuosity was ranked higher than in any other art form before or since.

Operatic embellishments were of two kinds, ornaments and cadenzas. The former decorated the written notes with trills, grace-notes, scales, arpeggios, etc., particularly in the repeat of the first part of a *da capo* aria (the reprise); in the words of Pier Francesco Tosi [*c.* 1653 – 1732], one of the greatest singing masters of his time, the first part of an aria needs "nothing but the simplest Ornaments, of a good Taste and few, that the Composition may remain simple, plain, and pure; in the second they [i.e. the audience] expect, that to this Purity some artful Graces be added, by which the Judicious may hear, that the Ability of the Singer is greater; and, in repeating the *Air* [i.e. the reprise], he that does not vary it for the better, is no great Master".* Cadenzas very often occurred on the final vocal cadence in both the first and second sections of the aria, and always in the reprise; they varied from short flourishes to extended passages of considerable virtuosity, and, like the ornamentation, the cadenza in the reprise was the most elaborate. The degree of virtuosity depended on the singer's technical mastery, the affection of the aria, and the aria type—ideally at any rate, though by no means all singers exercised such taste and discretion. The cadenza nearly always occurred on the ante-penultimate tonic $^6_4$ chord, and in the classical concerto as established by Mozart, not only the actual idea of a cadenza for the soloist, but also its position in the movement and its announcement by means of a cadential tonic $^6_4$ chord were taken over directly from the Neapolitan opera aria.

The most famous castrati were Nicola Grimaldi or Nicolini [1673–1732], Antonio Bernacchi [1685–1756], Francesco Bernardi or Senesino [d. *c.* 1759], Gaetano Maiorano or Caffarelli [1710–1783], Giovanni Carestini [*c.* 1705–*c.* 1760], and, the greatest of them all, Carlo Broschi or Farinelli [1705–1782]. Bernacchi was taught at Bologna, where he later founded a famous singing-school of his own; he placed execution before expression, unlike his fellow Bolognese, Senesino, whose voice, in the opinion of many, was purer even than Farinelli's, and whose clarity of diction and sensitive delivery in recitatives was unequalled. The other castrati named above were all trained in one of the Neapolitan conservatories that became world-renowned during the eighteenth century. Caffarelli and Farinelli were pupils of the most outstanding singing-master and one of the most influential teachers of composition of his time, Nicola Porpora [1686–1768], who travelled extensively, was sufficiently esteemed as an opera composer to be invited to rival Handel in London, and who, towards the end of his life,

* *Opionioni de' cantori antiche e moderni*, 1723. Translated by J. E. Galliard as *Observations on the Florid Song*, 1742.

taught young Haydn the fundamentals of composition. As a singing-master, Porpora's aims were those of Bernacchi, and his most famous pupil, Farinelli, after he had received some further instruction from Bernacchi, who defeated him in a contest of vocal virtuosity in 1727, was acknowledged as the most brilliant singer in Europe. Four years later, however, he changed to a much simpler and more expressive style of singing, and such was his art that when, in 1737, he visited Spain, he was able, like David before Saul, to banish the prolonged fits of melancholy suffered by Philip V [1683–1746] which had caused the King to neglect his realm. The Queen, by offering a most handsome salary, persuaded Farinelli to stay, and every night for the next ten years he sang the same four songs to Philip. Naturally, he became a great favourite (but never, as is sometimes stated, Prime Minister), and under Ferdinand VI [1713–1759] enjoyed a position of greater confidence and power than any official of the Crown. When Ferdinand died, Farinelli returned to Italy a very rich man, and spent his remaining years entertaining his many friends, among them noblemen from all over Europe, at his palatial mansion near Bologna. According to Giambattista Mancini [1716–1800], a pupil of Bernacchi and one of the leading singing-masters of his generation, Farinelli's voice "was thought a marvel, because it was so perfect, so powerful, so sonorous and so rich in the extent, both in the high and the low parts of the register, that its equal has never been heard in our times. He was, moreover, endowed with a creative genius which inspired him with embellishments so new and so astonishing that no one was able to imitate him."*

We have dwelt on Farinelli at some length not only because he was the most brilliant singer of his time, but also because his position at the Spanish court reflects, albeit in an extreme form, the enormous popularity, power, and prestige accorded to the castrati in every European country except France. But the vocal accomplishments of these men were not lightly achieved, and from the age of nine or ten until their late 'teens or early twenties they underwent a rigorous education that included acting, elocution, musical theory, and composition in addition to exercises that aimed at producing voices of extraordinary beauty, control, flexibility, and power. These four qualities

* Quoted from *Grove's Dictionary*, III, p. 25.

were not always regarded as of equal importance, and in the Neapolitan conservatories the last three took pride of place, as they are the most natural means whereby virtuosity and embellishment can be displayed.

The exceptional popularity and power of the castrati affected Neapolitan opera in a number of ways. Firstly, the lower male voices were virtually restricted to minor parts, because the chief 'male' characters were always castrati. Secondly, even women found it difficult at times to gain a principal rôle unless they were extremely gifted. The three most famous 'cantatrices' (i.e. virtuoso women singers) were the sopranos Francesca Cuzzoni [*c.* 1698–1770], noted for purity of tone and intonation, and whose trills were so ravishing that on one occasion an enthusiast from the gallery of a London opera house shouted, "Damn her ! she has a nest of nightingales in her belly!", and Faustina Bordoni [1700–1781], wife of Hasse (see p. 460), and who, apart from a charming face, figure, and personality (unlike Cuzzoni) was a most gifted actress, and possessed an unsurpassed agility of voice. The third cantatrice was Vittoria Tesi [1700–1775], whose compass was larger than Cuzzoni's or Bordoni's, but who excelled as a contralto of great power, so much so, in fact, that she became renowned in masculine rôles, an unnatural state of affairs that many less-gifted women singers were forced into by the supremacy of the castrati. Thirdly, the ordinary opera-goer was perfectly prepared to accept the spectacle of a castrato (most of whom, because of their operation, were taller and broader than the normal man) looking magnificently masculine as, say, Hercules draped in a leopard skin, but singing in a soprano voice. Lastly, most composers and librettists, apart from being more concerned with the placing of arias according to the conventions noted on p. 439 than with wedding music to drama or the natural development of the latter, were obliged to alter, replace, or add to what they had originally written if a 'star' singer so required.

Nevertheless, there were a few composers and librettists whose reputations were such that they were not bound to comply with the largely egotistical demands of the virtuoso singer. The two most important librettists were Apostolo Zeno [1668–1750] and Pietro Trapassi or Metastasio [1698–1782]. Zeno, whose first libretto, *Gl'Inganni Felici* (1695), achieved considerable popularity, was a Venetian. From 1718–29 he was court poet and historian to the Emperor Charles VI [reigned 1711–1740] at Vienna, and he effected a notable reform in opera libretti. Influenced by the French dramatists, notably Racine, he introduced a greater degree of unity into his plots (most of which are historical in theme) by largely rejecting comedy, the purely spectacular, and the arbitrary intervention of supernatural beings (except for the final *deus ex machina* which, because all his dramas end happily, was often used to resolve the complicated situation in the last act), and limiting the number of subsidiary plots that had formerly been introduced for spectacular or comic reasons. Each drama is generally divided into three acts, each act being divided into a number of scenes, and each scene into (usually) two parts, the first and by far the larger part unfolding the story by means of dialogue (secco recitative), and the second consisting (usually) of two four-line verses written in a highly polished and unimpassioned style, the first of which was meant to be repeated (A, B, A-aria); the verses express either the reactions of one of the characters to the situation of the moment, or else some more general sentiment, and in any case represent a unity of mood or basic affection.

Zeno's reforms, because they eschewed comedy and the irrelevantly spectacular, resulted in a type of opera known as *opera seria*. These reached their peak, so far as the libretti are concerned, in the hands of Metastasio, who wrote his first full-length libretto, *Didone abbandonata*, in 1723. This Roman poet quickly established a reputation, and in 1730 Zeno recommended him as his successor at Vienna. Metastasio was not only a better poet than Zeno, and a more imaginative dramatist (one of his plots even dared to end tragically), he was also a trained musician, having studied under Porpora at Naples, where he met and began a lifelong friendship with Farinelli. As a result, his verse, while it follows the same pattern as, and is no more impassioned than Zeno's, is more lyrical, its imagery is more alive, its language more conducive to a musical setting. This explains why his libretti were more popular than any other, for not only were they the basis of over a thousand operas in the eighteenth century (some of them, indeed, being set as many as seventy times), but, unlike Zeno's, were published in his lifetime.

Neither Zeno nor Metastasio were Neapolitans, but they restored to Neapolitan opera something of the literary distinction, dramatic integrity, and sincerity of expression of the early Venetian opera, the libretti of which, by Rinuccini and his imitators, were frequently, and sometimes luxuriously, printed, and were taken seriously by opera-goers, many of whom read them during performances. But the libretti of late Venetian opera began to deteriorate, and in Neapolitan opera, excluding those by Zeno, Metastasio, and a few others, the libretti are little more than loosely constructed patchworks of threadbare clichés and stereotyped situations. But it was the music and, more particularly, the way it was sung that mattered most.

The first opera produced in Naples was Monteverdi's *Poppea* in 1651. Three years later came *L'Orontea regina di Egitto*, by Francesco Cirillo [1623 – after 1667] who, while a Neapolitan composer, spent most of his life in Rome. The first real Neapolitan composer was Francesco Provenzale [1627?–1704], of whose eight operas only two have survived complete —*Il Schiavo di sua moglie* (1671) and *Difendere l'Offensore* (1678). These display not only a remarkable melodic gift heightened by a most expressive use of chromaticism, but also an intimate connexion between music and drama and considerable variety of form (*H.A.M.*, 222); the era when the *da capo* aria and the castrati dominated opera had yet to come.

In 1684 Provenzale, who was highly esteemed in Naples, both as a teacher and composer, resigned from his position as second chapel-master to the Spanish Viceroy because the senior post, which he naturally expected to get, had been offered to a young musician from Rome, Alessandro Scarlatti [1660–1725]. Scarlatti's work was not unknown in Naples, as his first opera, *Gli equivoci nel sembiante* (Rome, 1679), had been presented in 1680, and three years later a new opera, *Psiche*, was performed for the first time in the city, followed by a revival of *Il Pompeo* (Rome, 1683) only a few weeks before his appointment. During each of the ensuing eighteen years Scarlatti composed at least one opera and sometimes as many as four. The demand for his work and the taste of his public caused him increasing irritation, as he was forced to write in a 'popular' style that offended his artistic standards. Matters came to a head in 1702, when his salary was in arrears and the city was politically disturbed. He asked for and was granted four months' leave, and went to Florence, where he enjoyed the patronage of an ardent music-lover, Prince Ferdinand de' Medici, for whom he composed some operas. The Prince, however, offered him no permanent position, and rather than return to Naples, Scarlatti accepted an inferior post as assistant chapel-master at the Santa Maria Maggiore in Rome. Here he suffered another disappointment, because opera was disapproved of by the Pope on the grounds of morality. To compensate for this, he composed a few operas for Venice and a considerable number for Prince Ferdinand.

In 1709 Scarlatti returned to his former post at Naples. His fame was now at its height and he could compose more or less as he liked; the result was a series of operas that are a considerable improvement on those he had written earlier for Naples, notably *Tigrane* (1715), his 106th opera. But Rome, the scene of his first successes and later disappointments, was undoubtedly his favourite city, and in 1717, realizing that Papal disapproval had waned and that he had a considerable following there, he left Naples and did not return until 1722 or 1723. In Rome he composed his only comic opera, the delightful *Il Trionfo dell' Onore* (1718), and also his finest work for the stage, *Griselda* (1721), on a libretto by Zeno. This was his 114th opera, and the last of the thirty-six that have survived complete from a total of 115.

Scarlatti's operas reveal not only his development as a composer, but also, up to 1709 at any rate, the influence of the audiences for whom he composed. His earliest attempts display Venetian influence—then all-powerful in Rome—via the works of Stradella and Legrenzi. In these the dramatic situation dictates the musical treatment, aria forms are varied (see p. 400), recitatives are carefully composed, coloratura writing is restrained, ensembles are common, but crowd choruses are rare, though often highly effective in their realistic cries of praise, anger, etc. The music itself is short-phrased, rhythmically clear-cut, and sometimes dance-like, harmonically limited with rather angular and often ostinato basses, the texture is frequently polyphonic or contrapuntal, and is most strikingly revealed in orchestral accompaniments in four real parts none of which double the vocal line (Ex. 29*).

* A. Lorenz, *Alessandro Scarlatti's Jugendoper*, II, p. 28.

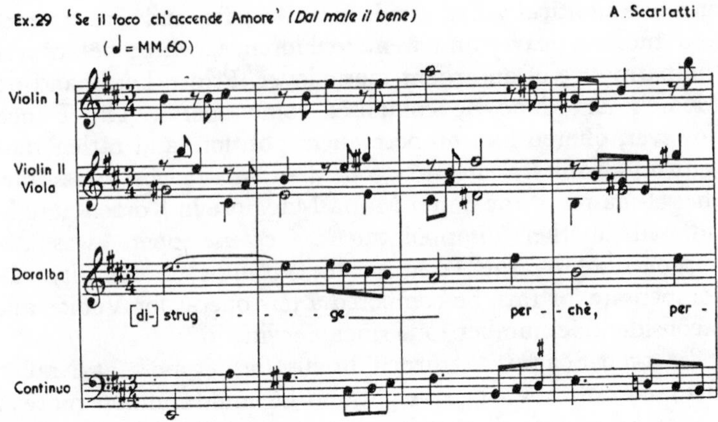

(destroys so that he should not escape)

These early operas, of which the only ones to survive are, apart from *Gli equivoci*, *L'honesta ne gli amori* (1680), and *Dal male il bene* (1681), show Scarlatti's fundamentally serious approach to music; they also show his immaturity in melodies that are haphazardly phrased and extended by exact repetition rather than by free or sequential development, and in the curious and occasionally harsh sounds that result from polyphony being unmatched by a sufficiently sure harmonic sense.

In Naples, during what we shall call his first Neapolitan period (1684–96), his technique and style became more polished, as he increasingly tended to work within a narrower field. This tendency may well have been partly self-imposed for artistic reasons, but it was also due to the necessity of satisfying the taste of his viceregal master and his audiences. As a result, the characters and dramatic situations of the libretti that he chose or was asked to set become more and more conventional, with the *da capo* aria prevailing, the importance of the orchestra gradually wanes to the point where most arias are accompanied by the continuo, sometimes with a single violin line added, the full orchestra being restricted to the ritornelli; polyphony and imitation seldom occur, and ensembles decrease in number, being mostly dialogue love-duets—the most popular type of ensemble in all Neapolitan opera. These somewhat negative features are more than balanced by others of a more positive kind. Thus partly because he was working within narrower limits, both formal and dramatic, and partly as a result of his natural musical development, his melodies become more regularly phrased, grateful, and sensuous, their construction less fragmentary, and their extensions less purely repetitive, with sequential passages more prominent. Moreover, the dramatic situations, although more conventional, cover a fairly wide emotional range, but any emotional intensity depended entirely on the composer and the singers, and Scarlatti demonstrates his exceptional gifts by producing an impressive array of arias that vary from grief to skittishness, from tenderness to bellicosity, with accompaniments ranging from continuo to full string band, sometimes with wind instruments added. Particularly striking are the arias in which a solo trumpet concertizes with the voice, a very popular feature in Neapolitan opera, as it enabled the singers, especially the castrati, to display their superior agility. The trumpet was chosen because in the seventeenth century its technique was more advanced than that of any other melodic instrument, and when, in the early eighteenth century, the violin surpassed it in this respect, it was still preferred as it alone could vie with the castrati in power and brilliance (Ex. 30,* p. 450).

Four features from the operas of this first Neapolitan period deserve special mention. First, the scene in which one or two characters express conflicting or changing emotions. For instance, in *La Rosaura* (1690) a lady laments her lover's fickleness in a largo aria, but her maid interrupts in an attempt

* Adapted from A. Lorenz, ibid., II, p. 46.

Ex. 30 'Sù, sù fieri guerrieri' (*Anacreonte tiranno*, Naples 1689) A. Scarlatti

(Arise, brave warriors, rouse yourselves to arms !)

to cheer her up with a popular allegro tune. This is an extreme example, and the more usual treatment is to present different shades of the same emotion through a mixture of secco recitative, arioso, and aria. In at least one of his later operas—*Attilio Regolo* (1719) (III, 9)—Scarlatti developed the mixed scene into something approaching the strikingly dramatic 'grand scena' of Handel (see p. 478) and Gluck.

The second feature, accompanied recitative, combines the lack of form (i.e. of sectional repetition) and verbal clarity of the secco recitative with the semi-lyricism of the arioso, the resultant vocal line being set within an expressive orchestral framework (otherwise exclusively reserved for the aria) that might consist of sustained notes, rushing scales, tremolos, agitated rhythms, sweeping arpeggios, loud punctuating chords, etc. Admittedly this feature can be found in earlier works, e.g. Monteverdi's *Orfeo* (see p. 376) and Schutz's oratorios (see Chapter 5, p. 522), but Scarlatti was the first to make it operatically significant, beginning with *Olimpia Vendicata* (1685). In his last Roman and Neapolitan operas, accompanied recitatives occur regularly, usually preceding the more important arias, a position that became standard for late baroque vocal compositions, and largely through his example they became one of the emotional highlights of Neapolitan opera.

The third feature is the presence of comic characters (usually two) who enliven the proceedings in often broadly humorous episodes and who frequently round off the first two acts on a note of hilarity with a comic duet distinguished by a rapidity of patter and a vivacity of repartee impossible in the serious sentimental love-duets of the principal characters. It was this vivacity and its position that made the comic duet the starting-point of one of the most distinctive features of *opera buffa*—the end-of-act ensembles (see p. 483).

In 1696 Scarlatti revived *Dal male il bene*, composing new introductory music which established the form and texture of the 'Italian' overture or 'sinfonia', as it was called. This, our last feature, is in three movements, quick-slow-quick, its most significant characteristic being its essentially homophonic texture as compared to the contrapuntal-polyphonic French overture. Scarlatti's opera sinfonia, like his *da capo* aria, was shorter, simpler, and less expressive than the overtures of Lully and his successors. Its popularity, which caused the demise of the latter, *c.* 1750, and its expansion and structural development by later composers led to an entirely independent composition (see Chapter 6, p. 553) and ultimately to the classical symphony (see Part III).

In his second Neapolitan period (1697–1702) Scarlatti was forced to adopt a much more popular style. Polyphony gives way to virtually unrelieved homophony, coloratura passages occur in greater profusion, but are usually not excessive, recitatives are scamped, with the cadential falling fourth, axiomatic in later Neapolitan opera, becoming common, accompaniments are thin, the rôle of the orchestra being much diminished, and melodies grow increasingly facile, repetitive, and limited in expressive range, but more highly polished. Most of these last are either square-cut and strongly rhythmic, following the latest successful fashion in arias set by his younger contemporary, Giovanni Bononcini [1670–1747], or else impart, sometimes to the point of cloyingness, a sense of pathos that is one of the composer's most enduring traits. This is particularly true of his sicilianos, admired and imitated wherever Italian opera held sway, and characterized by a lilting $\frac{12}{8}$ rhythm, minor mode, and the prominence of the Neapolitan-sixth chord (Ex. 31,* p. 453).

This was Scarlatti's worst period, only slightly redeemed by some attractive arias (including Ex. 31, p. 453) and the comic episodes, now usually sung by a soprano and tenor or bass. In the Roman operas, because women were not allowed on the stage, the comic characters were generally an old woman (sung by a tenor—the forebear of the pantomime 'dame') and an old man (bass), and such was the popularity of this incongruous pair that they were not replaced by the more realistic young couple (the ancestors of Papageno and Papagena) until *c.* 1700.

We can only assess the operas Scarlatti wrote for Prince Ferdinand if we assume (and it is a reasonable assumption) that the two surviving ones written for Venice during the same period are similar in style. The better of the two, *Mitridate* (1707), is not only remarkable for its political plot and the fact that hero and heroine are brother and sister, but also for the dignity, sincerity, and at times passion of the music, particularly the accompanied recitative 'O Mitridate mio' and aria 'Cara tomba' sung by Mitridate's sister. For the first time since his early Roman days Scarlatti gave rein to his inherent seriousness. In *Mitridate* polyphony and counterpoint again become significant, incisive and fascinating rhythms abound, melodies are more varied and expressive, and are extended by sequence and motivic development (i.e. the use

* Adapted from A. Lorenz, ibid., II, p. 160. Words omitted.

Ex. 31 Opening ritornello from 'Non mi tradir mai più' (*La donna ancora è fidele*, Naples 1698)
(♩. = MM. 36) A. Scarlatti

of short distinctive figures, usually taken from the main affective motto, which permeate and unify the texture and provide the chief means of modulating (see Ex. 34, p. 473), coloratura passages are frequent and sometimes reveal unmistakable instrumental influence in typical violin figurations, but seldom pander to mere virtuosity and are often very effective, the orchestra regains its earlier importance, even at the expense of the harpsichord, the string writing in particular being far more interesting and vivid as a result of the general improvement begun by Corelli (see Chapter 6, p. 551), and aria and even recitative accompaniments are enriched by a wider harmonic vocabulary (including the chords of the diminished seventh and augmented fifth in addition to the Neapolitan sixth) directed by a firmer feeling for tonality. Moreover, a number of arias are more extended than usual through the introduction of mildly contrasting ideas in both sections. Ensembles, while they occur in each opera, are infrequent, and so are solo choruses, i.e. choruses sung by all or most of the soloists; crowd choruses, as in the second Neapolitan period, are non-existent.

The most distinctive features of the operas that Scarlatti composed during the last sixteen years of his life, taken as a whole and compared to those immediately preceding them, are the greater number of accompanied recitatives, the more highly organized internal structure of each section of the aria, the occasional ensemble in which the characters express slightly different emotions or states of mind, and especially the more imaginative handling of the orchestra. Thus, horns, used rather tentatively for the first time in *Tigrane*, are employed more extensively and effectively in *Telemaco* (1718) and in every later opera; string parts show a considerable advance in technique, and the tendency, noted earlier, to treat the strings as a self-contained body, i.e. without the harpsichord, frequently results in a complete reversal of the usual procedure by accompanying the voice with strings alone, the harpsichord being restricted to the ritornelli. In this last period, too, recorders (always called 'flutes' in the baroque period), flutes (always designated as 'flauti traversa' or just 'traversa'), oboes, and bassoons occur more often than in the earlier operas, but, despite a few arias in which they have characteristic solos, their chief function is to sustain notes or double string parts, as in the symphonics of the early classical period. Scarlatti, in fact, in his operas written after 1702, laid the foundation of the Viennese classical style in the polish, sensuousness, expressive range, rhythmic precision, and impeccable phrasing of his melodies, in the motivic development of his arias, in his clear but colourful chromatic harmony, and in the variety of his texture, although his harmonic and textural richness was not imitated by most of his immediate successors.

It has been said that Scarlatti inaugurated the decadent Neapolitan operatic style; even if we admit the adjective, this statement is untrue, because his only 'decadent' operas were those written in his second Neapolitan period, in order to please a taste already formed. That he fostered this taste and, through his outstanding melodic gifts, did more to popularize the 'aria opera' than anyone else, is undeniable, and while we may regret the fact that he lowered his standards for a time, we must also recognize their essential seriousness, and also that they are manifest in a considerable number of operas, none of which can be called decadent and some of which are outstanding; indeed, his last operas contain a wealth of fine music, hardly any of which has been published, e.g. the arias 'Come presto nel porto' (*Griselda*, I, 6) and 'Ho in seno due fiamelle' (ibid., III, 7), and the 'mixed' scene in *Attilio Regolo* already mentioned, where the heroine, suffering nightmare visions of Hades, goes mad (see p. 450). As has been well said, Scarlatti, like J. S. Bach, was "a great man . . . forgotten by his own generation" (E. J. Dent).

But was Neapolitan opera decadent? The answer depends on two things. First, that we judge it not on its libretti, either as drama or as literature, but on its arias, which, as we have seen, were so arranged as to provide an admirable series of musical contrasts. (Such a judgement, incidentally, was, and is, applied to many late eighteenth and nineteenth-century operas, some of which are still popular, e.g. Mozart's *Magic Flute* and Bellini's *Norma*.) Secondly, that we are able, to some extent at any rate, to imagine the effect of these arias in performance, remembering that both composer and audience expected them to be embellished, and that hence what appears undistinguished in cold print would on the stage, even if we discount the atmosphere of the theatre with its lights, costumes, and elaborate scenery, be transformed, in the hands of a skilled singer, into something fascinating and even moving. It is this that is the main difficulty in assessing Neapolitan opera, because it is very doubtful whether sheer vocal virtuosity will ever again rank as high or achieve such brilliance as it did in the late baroque, it is even more doubtful whether the practice of extemporized embellishment will ever again become as important, and it is certain that the peculiar beauty and remarkable power of castrati tone will never again be heard.

If we judge a Neapolitan opera as it was meant to be judged by those who created, sang, and listened to it, and if we can imagine it as it was or might have been performed by the star singers of the day, then even if the libretto is a hotch-potch and the music commonplace, the work, far from being decadent, was vital in that it was partially and spontaneously created through the art of the singers. But if a singer fell below the best that was possible in beauty of tone or technique, and, relying on the tasteless ornamentation of some hack singing-master, failed to impart an air of naturalness and spontaneity to the embellishments, then his or her arias failed dismally, unless (and this happened but rarely, considering the enormous amount that was written) the music was so outstanding that it compensated for the singer's deficiency. This was the price Neapolitan opera had to pay for relying so heavily on the performer, and it explains the seemingly incredible behaviour of Italian opera audiences, who talked, played cards, and generally treated a visit to the opera as a social occasion. Such behaviour usually occurred after the first two or three performances, when those who attended had either been before and so knew which were the best arias and singers, or else had acquired this knowledge from those who had already seen the opera, but even on a first night the audience would soon realize whether an aria or singer was good or not, and, if the latter, would prefer to talk and eat, for Italian opera audiences were, and are, much less tolerant of incompetent singers than the audiences of other countries. The recitatives were seldom listened to because the story was usually well-known or followed conventional lines. To sum up, Neapolitan opera at its best was a brilliantly executed, emotionally varied, and vital work of art; at its worst it was musically and dramatically sterile, a vehicle for vulgar display. Before we condemn what we see in the score we should remember the quotation at the head of this chapter, for Burney was an ardent and serious student of opera, and, moreover, was writing when the supremacy of the castrati was on the wane.

By the early years of the eighteenth century Neapolitan opera dominated, to a greater or lesser extent, the stages of all the principal Italian cities and those of every European country in which opera was important, except France. In Russia, for example, the Empress Anne [1693–1740] founded, in 1734, a permanent opera at the Imperial Court at St. Petersburg (now Leningrad), importing an Italian company under the Neapolitan Francesco Araja [b. 1709]. Araja resigned in 1759 and was succeeded by a long line of Italian composers, including such distinguished men as Galuppi (see p. 484), Traetta, Paisiello, and Cimarosa (see Part III, p. 709). While Russia had no native opera until the late eighteenth century, Spain had a flourishing tradition of comic opera, the 'zarzuela' (see p. 485), and this, plus the powerful religious atmosphere that persisted in circles of authority for most of the seventeenth century, explains why, in spite of the close ties with Italy, the first Italian opera house was not opened until 1738 (Madrid), the inaugural work being Hasse's *Il Demetrio* (see p. 460), although a few Italian operas had been produced earlier in both Madrid and Barcelona.

Every composer of Italian opera, no matter what his nationality, derived his style from that of Scarlatti, and unfortunately most of them took as their models the works of the second Neapolitan period, which, as we have seen, were the worst and least characteristic. Of Scarlatti's contemporaries and successors at Naples the most noteworthy were Leonardo Vinci [*c.* 1690 – 1730], Francesco Mancini [1672 – 1737], Francesco Feo [1691 – 1761], Leonardo Leo [1694 – 1744], Francesco Durante [1684 – 1755], Porpora, Niccolò Jomelli [1714 – 1774] (see Part III, p. 712), and the Spaniard Davide Perez [1711 – 1778]. Vinci expanded the Scarlattian aria, often by more strongly contrasting motives within each section, and favoured rhythmically arresting melodies and highly dramatic accompanied recitatives. Feo, Leo and Durante (the last the most outstanding teacher of opera composers of the century) were also notable church composers, and hence employed polyphony more than Vinci. Porpora was the virtuoso singer's composer *par excellence* (as one would expect), and his arias, while often excessively florid, are always extremely well written for the voice.

The most important centre of opera after Naples was Venice, and the leading composers were Carlo Francesco Pollarolo [*c.* 1653 – 1723], Francesco Gasparini [1668 – 1727], Antonio Caldara [*c.* 1670 – 1736], Tommaso Albinoni [1671 – 1751], Antonio Vivaldi [1678 – 1741], Antonio Lotti [*c.* 1667 – 1740], Giovanni Porta [*c.* 1690–1755], and Giovanna Battista Pescetti [*c.* 1704-1766]. Apart from the more important rôle of the orchestra and the greater stress on the spectacular, Venetian opera was similar to Neapolitan, and the same is roughly true of opera elsewhere in Italy, except that in Rome, always the most conservative of Italian cities from early Christian times, sheer virtuosity was less favoured. Elsewhere in Italy the leading men were Francesco Pistocchi [1659–1726], a well-known castrato and the founder of a famous singing school in Bologna, G. Bononcini and his brother, Antonio Maria [1677 – 1726], Attilio Ariosti [1666–*c.* 1740], and Francesco Conti [1681–1732]. (Most of the composers mentioned above visited other European countries at least once, and some of them stayed for several years.)

Before we discuss the development of Neapolitan opera in Europe, we must make a distinction between what we shall call southern and northern Neapolitan opera. The former was predominant in Italy and relies entirely or very largely on pure melody and the art of the singer; as a result, the texture is basically homophonic, both in the arias, even when accompanied orchestrally, and in the instrumental numbers, notably the sinfonia. The northern type derived from the late works of Scarlatti, but was first actively cultivated in Germany by both Italian and German composers; compared to the southern type, it reveals Germanic traits in the frequency of contrapuntal textures and in the greater significance of the orchestra. Thus although the arias are still the most important items, they are more frequently accompanied by an orchestra in which the lower parts are more interesting, especially the bass, or by solo 'obbligato' instruments, particularly woodwind and brass, beloved by the Germans for centuries, which concertize with the voice; in addition, ensembles and solo choruses occur more often, and the French overture is preferred.

The main centres of Italian opera outside Italy were Munich, Hanover, Vienna, Dresden, and London. At Munich the chief figure was Agostino Steffani [1654–1728], an extraordinarily gifted and versatile man, and one of the most outstanding composers of the late baroque. Ably supported at first by Johann Kaspar Kerll [1627–1693], one of his teachers and a very accomplished musician, Steffani accentuated the difference between southern and northern Neapolitan opera by combining the German penchant for polyphony and instrumental music, imbibed from Kerll, with his native Italian lyricism and sensuousness. His melodies flow effortlessly, avoiding virtuosic excesses, his basses are interesting in themselves, not merely harmonic supports, ensembles, especially duets (see Chapter 5), are commoner than in the south, and his orchestral accompaniments are imaginative, with 'obbligato' arias particularly prominent, though the majority are accompanied by continuo only. During the last forty years of his life he was mostly at Hanover, first as the Elector's chapel-master and later as his chief diplomatist. His most successful operas were *Servio Tullio* (Munich, 1685), *Henrico Leone* (written for the opening, in 1689, of the Italian opera house at Hanover), *La Superbia d'Alessandro* (Hanover, 1690), and *I Trionfi del Fato* (Hanover, 1695).

Polyphonic texture, orchestral writing, and ensembles are also very apparent in the works of the Viennese composer, Johann Joseph Fux [1660–1741], and, though to a lesser extent, in those of his colleagues, Caldara, the Bononcini brothers, and Conti. Fux, a very learned but very dry and pedantic theorist, was the author of a famous text-book, *Gradus ad Parnassum* (1725), which classified Renaissance polyphony in general and Palestrina's in particular into five 'species', and remained the standard authority on strict modal composition until well into the nineteenth century. The best of his operas, however, while they display his academic skill, are by no means as dull and dry as they are sometimes made out to be, for although they lack the sheer lyricism of the Italian style they are full of noble arias, many of them 'obbligato', and some of them presented as fugues and even canons. He also achieves considerable variety by the frequent insertion of solo ensembles and crowd choruses. The least satisfactory items are the overtures, which in form hark back to the early baroque canzona or church sonata (see Chapter 6, p. 532) and are written in a very muddy, semipolyphonic style. His most famous opera was *Constanza e Fortezza* (1723), written to celebrate the Coronation of Emperor Charles VI as King of Bohemia, and produced on an even more lavish scale than was usual in Vienna.

Although Germany and Austria teemed with Italian composers, the greatest and most famous exponent of the southern Neapolitan type was a German—Johann Adolf Hasse [1699–

1783]. Hasse's first Italian teacher was Porpora, but he quickly changed to Scarlatti, for whom he subsequently entertained a lifelong admiration; later he married Faustina Bordoni, and became the favourite composer of Metastasio (all of whose libretti he set at least once) and the leading figure at Dresden. His operas were performed all over Europe, the best of them being *Il Sesostrate* (Naples, 1726), *Artaserse* (Venice, 1730), *Cleofide* (Dresden, 1731), *Il Demetrio* (Venice, 1732, a revival of which Mozart heard in 1770), *Tito Vespasiano* (Pesaro, 1735, which Mozart also heard in 1770 and which was performed in Moscow in 1742), *Demofoonte* (Dresden, 1748), and *Solimano* (Dresden, 1753); they reveal such an astonishing gift of elegant, exquisitely shaped, and effortless melody supported by smooth, limpid harmonies that the Italians called him *il caro Sassone* ('the beloved Saxon'). His aria style represents the quintessence of what we shall call *stile galante*, which stemmed from Scarlatti and which Burney called 'modern'; it was indeed one of the foundations of the Viennese classical style, lacking only the variety of texture and harmony found in the later operas of Scarlatti.

The Italian *stile galante* should not be confused with the French *style galant* (hence the distinction in language), for although both are completely homophonic in texture and the former derived from the latter, *stile galante* developed typically Italian characteristics (compare the following with p. 486), these are a type of melody that is clear-cut, mildly ornamented, rhythmically simple, constructed of short motives that are often repeated exactly, and are largely an extension, so to speak, of the chords which accompany it, and which is, above all, lyrical and sensuous; the rate of chord change is slower than in baroque style, the same chord often being repeated for several bars, with tonic and dominant pedals common, the chords themselves are less varied, the clarity of root position being much preferred to first inversion, and the individuality of the bass line is supremely unimportant. Compare Ex. 34—mature baroque style—with Ex. 35—early *stile galante*—and the aria on p. 497—fully developed *stile galante*. In Ex. 35, notice the waltz-like bass, the amount of repetition, and the way the three motives, *a*, *b*, *c*, are stuck together rather than joined. On p. 497 notice the purely functional bass line, the simplicity of the chord progressions and their slow rate of change, and the basically chordal nature of the melody when stripped of its *fioritura* (i.e. 'flowering' embellishments). Notice also the similarity to many slow movements in Haydn's and Mozart's piano sonatas.

We use the adjective 'gallant' in describing this style because it reflected the same attitude to life as the eighteenth-century courtier, particularly at the Court of Louis XV (see p. 487), when woman was the centre of a hot-house society in which man existed but to please, to charm, to captivate. Apart from *lèse-majesté*, almost anything was permitted, provided that it did not depart from an accepted code of behaviour that placed control of feeling and polished manners before everything, and provided also that it was expressed in elegant, refined language in which the exquisitely turned phrase, the *bon mot*, was more to be desired and commended than originality or sincerity of thought.

Hasse was more than just a melodist, and although the continuo aria predominates in his earlier operas, his later ones contain very few; indeed, he was superior to all his Italian contemporaries, except possibly Steffani, in his handling of the orchestra, in the greater care with which his secco recitatives are set and the music matched to the dramatic situation (hence his popularity with Metastasio), in the expressiveness of his accompanied recitatives that at times achieve real power and depth of feeling, and in his ability to extend a passage and increase its effect by motivic development instead of mere repetition (compare p. 497 with Ex. 35). To compare the best of Scarlatti with the best of Hasse (e.g. *Griselda* with *Demofoonte*) is most instructive, but we can here only mention a few general points. Apart from the features of *stile galante* mentioned, the arias in *Demofoonte* are longer, with secondary motives more clearly marked, and coloratura passages are more frequent and extended, most of them containing an implied vocal cadenza over a held tonic $^6_4$ chord near the end of the first section, and some of them demanding a truly instrumental agility (e.g. II, 2), and an astonishing range (e.g. *e–g″* in I, 13; both arias, incidentally, were composed for Carestini). The harmony, on the other hand, is simpler, with diminished sevenths and Neapolitan sixths (both very common in *Griselda*) rarely used, and the texture, even when strings plus woodwind and brass are employed, is more transparent, owing to the greater amount of doubling. In a number of arias section B is in a different tempo, and/or time signature, and/or key from section A (e.g. I, 5, where A=G major, $\frac{2}{4}$, Allegro di molto, and B=G minor, $\frac{3}{8}$, Un poco lento); this feature was probably copied from Handel, many of whose operas were performed under Hasse in Dresden after their début in London.

Hasse was so enamoured of Italian music that he remained quite unaffected by the music of his own country, though late in life he 'discovered' Keiser's excellence, much to his own astonishment (see below). In this respect he differed from his compatriot George Frederic Handel [1685–1759], the greatest opera composer of the late baroque, for Handel assimilated Italian, German, and French elements into a truly culminatory style. The Italian element we have already discussed; the French can be found in Lully's operas; so it is to the German that we now turn.

The chief centres of German opera were the courts of Brunswick (formerly called Wolfenbüttel) and Weissenfels, and, more especially, the city of Hamburg, where the mantle of Kusser fell on the most gifted composer of late baroque German opera, Reinhard Keiser [1674–1739]. Keiser, a man of flamboyant personality and luxurious tastes, and a musician whose talents aroused the admiration of Steffani, Handel, and (later) Hasse, composed well over a 100 operas (most of which have perished) and inaugurated the last and most brilliant period of Hamburg opera. His works, in the immediate appeal and often frankly popular flavour of the music, reflect the fact that he was writing for the public, not for nobility, and they reveal an extraordinary facility of invention and assimilation of diverse styles. From Italy he borrowed the recitative (secco and accompanied), arioso, and *da capo* aria, which last he often modifies slightly by altering the reprise and in which he ranges from lyrical and emotional *bel canto* to bravura passages of extreme difficulty; indeed, the voice is sometimes treated as a solo instrument with typically violinistic figurations and, in concerto grosso style, pitted against an orchestra that may consist of brass and woodwind. In *Croesus* (1711) he introduced the clarinet, which had recently been developed from the chalumeau (a single-reed, recorder-shaped instrument) by Johann Christoph Denner [1655–1707]. Denner added two finger-operated keys and discovered the speaker hole, which enabled a new series of notes to be obtained whose fundamental is a twelfth above the natural fundamental—the distinctive feature of the clarinet. Its tone was more like a deep oboe and reminiscent of a distant trumpet, hence its name (from 'clarion'). French influence, which is apparent in the work of all German composers of German opera in the late baroque, is shown in the dance rhythms of some of his songs, in the number of dances, choruses, and ballets, and in the overtures, while native traits appear in catchy or comical Lieder often, like those of his predecessors (see p. 405), in simple binary form, in the comparatively complex texture of his orchestral accompaniments, and in the unusual depth of expression that he occasionally reveals. His best operas, apart from *Croesus*, are *Die Macht der Tugend* (1700), *Octavia* (1705), *Der Carneval von Venedig* (1707), *Fredegunda* (1715), and the comic opera *Der lächerliche Printz Jodelet* (1726).

But Hamburg opera, brilliant and successful as it was under Kusser and Keiser, was not approved of by all sections of the community (see p. 404), and in that branch of Protestantism known as Pietism, which became powerful *c.* 1700, opera found its bitterest opponent. Like the Calvinists, the Pietists believed in simplicity of worship, which meant the avoidance of both elaborate ceremonial and music that smacked of the concert hall or opera house, this last in particular being quite definitely of the devil; to them the congregational hymn (chorale) was the only acceptable kind of church music. The orthodox Protestant, however, believed that the styles and forms of secular music were not evil in themselves and that they became hallowed when set to sacred words, a view that, in Hamburg at any rate, eventually won the day after much controversy. Nevertheless, the split in the ranks undoubtedly weakened the position of German opera in the city and hastened the deterioration that began in the late 1720s and ended with the closing of the opera-house in 1738 and the extinction of German opera for over fifty years. This deterioration, which even Keiser, let alone his less-gifted successors, Georg Philipp Telemann [1681–1767] and Johann Mattheson [1681–1764], could not stem, was due to two factors, one internal, the other external. The former was the essentially popular nature of the operas in which, because castrati were forbidden to appear, the soprano and alto parts were taken by women, some of whom had doubtful reputations well known to the public. The element of vulgarity they introduced was held in check by Keiser's genius and the excellent libretti of a number of poets, of whom the best and last was Barthold Feind [1678–1721]. Feind was a serious writer with a first-rate dramatic sense, but his successors were not, and, pandering to the lowest taste of their audiences, they produced patchworks of inconsequential scenes which, if not obscene, were vulgar or trivial. This internal deterioration was accelerated by the invasion of Neapolitan opera from southern Germany. At first only a few arias in Italian were introduced, but these, owing to the liquidness of the language compared to German and to the enormously superior tone and technique of the Italian singers (castrati were eventually allowed *c.* 1730), increased in number. The result was bilingual opera, which was not so absurd as might appear because, as the recitatives were in German, the audience had a very good idea what each Italian aria was about, and in any case it was the music and the singing that really mattered. (Keiser's *Circe* (1734) is a good example, with twenty-one German and twenty-three Italian arias, the latter mostly by Vinci, Hasse, and Handel.) By 1739 Italian opera reigned supreme, and in 1741 the opera-house reopened under an all-Italian management.

The failure of German opera at Hamburg was paralleled in other German cities and courts. At Weissenfels not even the total ban on the Italian language prevented the eclipse of native opera in 1736. At Brunswick Italian opera was all the rage by the early 1730s despite the presence of Georg Kaspar Schürmann [*c.* 1672–1751], the most gifted composer of German opera after Keiser, and the only one capable of writing arias in the best Italian manner. By 1740 German opera had capitulated everywhere, and Italian *opera seria* reigned supreme until well into the nineteenth century.

The enormous influence of Italian opera is most clearly demonstrated in the works of Handel, for if anyone could have fought the Italians on their own ground and kept German opera alive it was he. As it was, however, after writing a few works for the Hamburg stage in his native tongue, and even after the success of *Almira* (1705), which made Keiser look to his laurels, he decided that a visit to Italy was imperative. Undoubtedly he learnt much from Keiser, but the sweetness of the

XXVI The interior of the wooden theatre specially constructed in Vienna for the performance of Cesti's *Il pomo d'oro* by the greatest theatrical architect and designer of his day, Lodovico Burnacini [1636–1707].

(*a*)

(*b*)

XXVII and XXVIII Two scenes from Cesti's *Il pomo d'oro* designed by L. Burnacini. (*a*) Hades. Pluto and Proserpine (left, centre), demons, and ghosts of the damned. Note the Fury on the flying dragon. (*b*) Last scene: Jove holding thunderbolts and seated on his eagle, with Juno near him (top, centre), destroying Mars's tower. Chorus of Gods and Goddesses in the clouds, Venus in her chariot. (The eagle later descends and returns to Jove with the apple.)

Italian style that he had as yet only half tasted, largely through the music of Steffani, whom he had met and impressed in 1703, was too captivating, and, from 1707–10, he visited Rome, Florence, Venice, and Naples, meeting and being acclaimed by some of the leading men and musicians of the day, including Scarlatti, Corelli, Lotti, and, once again, Steffani, and hearing, studying, and assimilating everything. At first his reputation rested on his keyboard playing, and as a harpsichordist he rivalled Italy's most brilliant virtuoso, Domenico Scarlatti, son of Alessandro (see Chapter 6, p. 554); but it was not long before his creative genius manifested itself, and only six months after his arrival his first Italian opera, *Rodrigo*, was performed in Florence. The following year (1708) he went to Naples, where he composed *Agrippina*, first performed, amidst scenes of wildest enthusiasm, at Venice in 1709. His rising reputation, the great success of *Agrippina*, and the recommendation of Steffani (who was vacating the post) led to the appointment of chapel-master to the Elector of Hanover, whose younger brother met Handel in Venice during the performance of the opera. The English Ambassador also suggested a London visit, an idea that was clearly so full of possibilities, in that London had no resident composer of any standing whatsoever, that Handel accepted his Hanoverian post on condition that he was allowed to visit England almost immediately.

In January 1710 Handel was in Hanover; six months later he was in London, where he found native opera moribund and Italian opera growing in popularity, but lacking a significant composer to really establish it. With his inherent shrewdness and flair for opportunism, he was soon convinced that richer rewards, both financial and artistic, lay in London than in Hanover, a conviction that was supported by the success of *Rinaldo* (1711), even though much of this was filched from earlier compositions and hastily put together. But he was not yet sufficiently sure of his own reputation to neglect his duties at Hanover for too long, and he left London soon after. When he returned in 1712 he knew the esteem in which he was held by the Elector and the extent of his own powers, and hence had no qualms about overstaying his leave.

Before we discuss Handel's operas, we must describe the operatic scene in London from Purcell's death to 1712. It is a dismal one; nothing new appeared until 1705, when Thomas Clayton (*c.* 1670–*c.* 1730] arranged a number of arias that he had brought back from a recent visit to Italy, added some music of his own, chiefly recitatives, adapted this miscellany to an English libretto by a naturalized Frenchman, P. A. Motteaux, and produced the result as *Arsinoë, Queen of Cyprus*. It was a fair success, and was described by Joseph Addison [1672–1719], poet, essayist, and Editor of the *Spectator*, as "the first Opera that gave us a Taste of Italian Musick", for the purpose of making this sweeping and stinging indictment of Italian opera: "That nothing is capable of being well set to Musick that is not nonsense." But while Italian opera was anathema to Addison, he seems to have had visions of founding a national school; unfortunately, he thought Clayton had talent and asked him to set a libretto of his, *Rosamond*. Clayton must have exhausted his stock of Italian arias on *Arsinoë*, and so composed all the music himself, with the result that the opera, produced in 1707, was such a failure that neither librettist nor composer ventured into the operatic field again.

Only two English operas followed: *Prunella* (1708), which directs that some of the tunes be borrowed from *Arsinoë*, *Thomyris*, and A. M. Bononcini's *Il Trionfo di Camilla* (for these last, see below); worthless as an opera *Prunella* is interesting as the earliest example of English intermezzi (see p. 482) and the first operatic satire on Italian opera. The second opera was *Calypso and Telemachus* (1712), by John Ernest Galliard [*c.* 1680–1749] (the translator of Tosi's treatise mentioned on p. 442), a work that Handel admired, and the last English opera until Thomas Augustus Arne [1710–1778] set Addison's *Rosamond* in 1733.

The "Taste of Italian Musick" afforded by *Arsinoë* was sufficiently sweet to encourage the Swiss librettist J. J. Heidegger [1659?–1749], Manager of the newly built Queen's Theatre, Haymarket (later King's Theatre, now Her Majesty's Theatre), to inaugurate, in the same year, a season of Italian opera, beginning with *Gli Amori piacevoli d'Ergasto* ('The Loves of Ergasto' as he called it), specially composed by Jakob Greber [d. 1731], the first opera in London that was sung in Italian throughout. (The Queen's Theatre, designed by the well-known architect Sir John Vanbrugh [1664–1726], and, after its destruction by fire in 1789, its successor, remained the principal centre of Italian opera in London until after 1847, when the Royal Italian Opera House (now the Covent Garden Theatre was formed.)

From 1705 to 1712 at least one new Italian opera, either adapted or composed specially, was given at the Queen's Theatre, the most notable being by Gasparini, Scarlatti, Mancini, Conti, and the Bononcini brothers. Gasparini's *Ambleto* (Venice, 1705; London, 1712) is the earliest *Hamlet* opera on record, but is not based on Shakespeare's play; Scarlatti's *Pirro e Demetrio* (1708) was arranged by a resident Italian, Nicola Haym [1678–1729] (who later wrote several of Handel's libretti), with additions from *La Rosaura*, libretto being translated into English by O. MacSwiney, though some arias were sung in Italian, as the famous castrati Nicolini made his London début in this opera. Nicolini also sang in Mancini's *L'Idaspe fidele* (Naples, 1705; London, 1710), a very successful work sung entirely in Italian. This became customary from 1705 on, owing to the increasing number of Italian singers who visited England; indeed, most of those connected with opera were of foreign extraction and included, in addition to Heidegger, Motteaux, and Haym, the German composers Greber, Galliard, John Christopher Pepusch [1667–1752], and John Frederick Lampe [*c.* 1703–1751], and a host of Italians who, from 1700 on, quickly replaced the French musicians, favourites during the Restoration period. The chief of these were the castrati mentioned on p. 442, together with Angelo Maria Monticelli [*c.* 1710–1764], Gioacchino Conti or Gizziello [1714–1761], and Valentino Urbani or Valentini (London, 1707–15), the women Cuzzoni, Bordoni, Anna Strada del Pò (London, 1729–38), Francesca Margherita de L'Épine [d. 1746], who married Pepusch, and Margherita Durastanti [fl. 1700–1734]; and the basses Antonio Montagnana (London, 1731–after 1738) and Giuseppe Boschi (London, 1720–28), the most celebrated bass of his time. In addition there was the French-born but Italian-trained Elizabeth Duparc ('La Francesina') [d. *c.* 1778]. Instrumentalists included the violinists Geminiani, Veracini, Pietro Castrucci [1679–1752] and his brother Prospero [d. 1760], Giacomo Cervetto [*c.* 1682–1783], the Frenchman Charles Dieupart [d. *c.* 1740], and the Fleming W. Defesch [1687–?1757]; 'cellists included Filippo Amadei [b. *c.* 1683] (usually and wrongly called

Mattei), A. Caporale [fl. mid cent.], and J. M. C. Dall' Abaco [1710 – 1805], while the woodwind players, as we might expect, were mostly Germans, e.g. the flautist Karl F. Weidemann [d. 1782], the oboists Kytsch and Galliard, and the bassoonist Lampe, the only notable exception being the Flemish flautist J. B. Loeillet [1680 – 1730]. The only English performers who could compare with this galaxy, none of whom could compete with the best, except the two trumpeters mentioned below, and possibly Beard, were the sopranos Catherine Tofts [d. 1756], Cecilia Young [1711 – 1789], who married Arne, and Anastasia Robinson [*c.* 1692 – 1755], the basses Richard Leveridge [*c.* 1670 – 1758], Lewis Ramondon [d. *c.* 1770] and William Savage [1720 – 1789], the tenor John Beard [*c.* 1717 – 1791], the violinists John Banister [d. 1735], John Clegg [1714 – *c.* 1750], and Matthew Dubourg [1703 – 1767], the flautist Jack Festing [d. 1772], and the trumpeters John Shore [d. 1752] and Valentine Snow [d. 1770].

The most successful operas before Handel appeared on the scene were, apart from *L'Idaspe fidele*, *Thomyris* (1707), one of the many pasticcios (literally 'pie', i.e. 'medley') so popular in the late baroque, and arranged in this case by Pepusch (who composed the recitatives) from arias by Scarlatti, Steffani, Gasparini, Albinoni, and G. Bononcini to an English libretto by Motteaux, the anonymous *Almahide* (1710) and, finally, A. M. Bononcini's *Il Trionfo di Camilla* (Naples, 1696 ; London, 1706), arranged by Haym to an all-English libretto; later, for reasons already given (see p. 467), many of the arias were sung in Italian, but it was never performed wholly in this language, a fact that largely explains why it was the most successful opera in London during the entire eighteenth century.

When Handel returned to London in 1712 he lost no time in establishing both himself and Italian opera with *Il Pastor Fido*, based on Guarini's pastoral play (see p. 266), and *Teseo* (1713). In 1714 Queen Anne died and Handel's master became George I [d. 1727]. The strained relations between Handel and the King have been exaggerated by many writers, and the Water Music story, charming as it is, has no foundation in fact. What is certain is that George I attended a performance of *Amadigi* in 1715, and shortly afterwards doubled the pension of £200 a year settled on Handel by Queen Anne. In 1719, with the King's support, Handel founded the Royal Academy of Music at the King's Theatre and left England in search of singers, returning with Senesino, Boschi, and Durastanti. As the Academy's Director, Handel invited G. Bonocini and later Ariosti and Heidegger to assist him. Bononcini arrived in 1720 and stayed until 1732; Ariosti arrived in 1722, but was not a success.

The Academy got off to a flying start, both artistically and financially, with performances of Porta's *Numitore* (1720), followed by Handel's *Radamisto*, but almost from the beginning friction began to creep in. Bononcini allowed himself to be set up as a rival by an anti-monarchy group, led by the Prince of Wales, who were jealous of the German's prestige at Court. In 1722 Cuzzoni was engaged, and while she was artistically a great asset, her enormous fee, added to that of Senesino, financially weakened the Academy. It managed to keep going, however, largely through a succession of superb operas by Handel, but the end was hastened by the incredibly tactless engagement of Bordoni in 1725. The strife between the two cantatrices spread to their supporters in the audience and eventually developed into free fights, the culmination being a stage brawl in Bononcini's *Astianatte* (1727). In 1728 the disruption within and the tremendous success of *The Beggar's Opera* without (see p. 479), caused the Academy to collapse bankrupt. Handel, undismayed and hardly affected financially, entered into a contract with Heidegger, visited Italy to obtain new singers, and on his return composed *Lotario* (1729). This was a failure, the public's taste, always tickled by something new, being temporarily but completely captivated by the realism and natural freshness of *The Beggar's Opera* and its successors, the so-called 'ballad operas'. But Handel persisted despite repeated financial failures, recouping some of his losses with revivals of his cantata *Acis and Galatea* (1719) and *Rinaldo*, and the first performance of his first oratorio, *Esther* (1732). Handel's quarrel with Senesino in 1733 and, in the same year, the establishment of a rival Italian opera company (the 'Opera of the Nobility') brought Handel's second operatic venture to a disastrous close in 1734. Heidegger gave up the King's Theatre, and the Opera of the Nobility moved in, with first of all Porpora, later Hasse, as chief composer and the star singers

Farinelli, Senesino, Cuzzoni, and Boschi. Again Handel refused to admit defeat and continued to compose operas, which he presented at Covent Garden until 1737. Exhausted by his creative effort and depressed by his financial failures, he spent some months abroad refreshing both mind and body. On his return Heidegger, who was once more Manager of the King's Theatre, after the Opera of the Nobility had also failed in 1737, commissioned two operas, neither of which were successful, nor was his last opera, *Deidamia* (1741).

Handel was unquestionably the greatest composer of operas in the late baroque, but inevitably, in view of the difficulties in justly appraising them (see p. 455), they have been almost completely overshadowed by his oratorios, particularly in England, where, apart from the question of language, opera has never, until recently, taken root. This is both unfortunate and unfair, because we cannot fully appreciate his genius unless we take into account that considerable part of his creative output which was, after all, his first love, and into which he poured so much of his finest music.

When Handel first went to Italy he already had a fair grasp of the Neapolitan style, and on his visit he undoubtedly acquired the final polish. In *Agrippina* he is already revealed, not only as a melodist of the first water, but also as a complete master of his craft, with an expressive range and harmonic vocabulary as wide as Scarlatti's, and an equal if not superior skill in handling the orchestra. His melody and harmony did not develop greatly from *Agrippina* on, for, like Mozart, he reached maturity at a time when musical style was stabilized, i.e. when there was a common stock of melodic and harmonic 'formulae' from which everyone drew, and one of the things that distinguishes his work from that of his contemporaries is the extraordinary consistency with which he unerringly selects and combines some of these formulae to form melodies that make a direct appeal, are seemingly inevitable, often memorable, and remarkably varied, and which are supported by chord progressions, actual or implied, that, while they sometimes surprise, are always apt. None of his contemporaries possessed this melodic gift, not even Bach, who in any case was less concerned with immediate melodic appeal, for while composers like Hasse and Scarlatti, who most nearly approach him in this respect, wrote a great many flawlessly constructed melodies, the proportion of these to their total output is considerably smaller than in Handel's case.

It is impossible to give here even an adequate summary of the riches to be found in Handel's operas, but we can give some idea of the variety that they contain by analysing *Agrippina* (*A*) and *Rinaldo* (*R*) and mentioning in addition the most notable features of later operas that are not included in these two.

All Handel's overtures are based on the French model, and in that to *Agrippina* the Adagio coda to the second movement, common in both Lully and Handel, takes the form of a most effective oboe cadenza. This is a fine overture scored for strings plus third violins, oboe, and continuo. (By strings we mean first and second violins and violas.) In many of the overtures the second movement is in $\frac{4}{4}$, as opposed to Lully's almost invariable $\frac{3}{4}$ (see p. 420), and most of them have one and sometimes two extra movements (often dances), e.g. *Rinaldo*, where the overture is really an orchestral Corellian sonata (see Chapter 6, p. 551) in that the fugal second movement is followed by a short Adagio passage ending on the dominant of the relative minor by means of a typically Corellian Phrygian cadence (Ex. 32*):

Ex.32 Phrygian cadence from the overture to *Rinaldo*

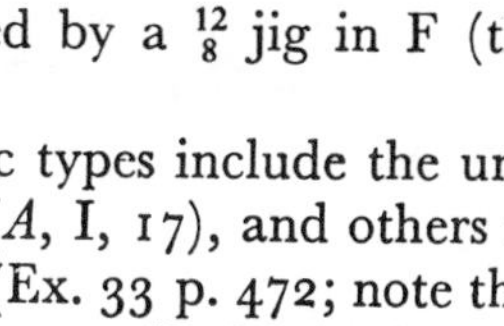

and is followed by a $\frac{12}{8}$ jig in F (the key of the overture) in A, B form.

The melodic types include the undulating pathetic siciliano *à la* Scarlatti (*A*, I, 17), and others in gently lilting $\frac{6}{8}$ or $\frac{12}{8}$, the popular song (Ex. 33 p. 472; note the superbly placed top A in bar 8): the *bel canto* (*R*, I, 7), the strongly rhythmic, undoubtedly learnt from G. Bonocini (*A*, II, 1), the florid 'bravura' (*A*, III, 11—all the aria types mentioned on p. 439 can be found in every Handel opera), and the spacious, boldly-arched type. (Ex. 34, p. 473. The ritornello that follows the vocal motto beginning shows one of the commonest of all Handel's

*Exx. 32–35 are taken from the Complete Edition, ed. Chrysander.

Ex.33 From 'Ho un non sò che nel cor' (Agrippina)
Handel
(♩ = MM.96) (Violins in unison; no continuo)
Agrippina
ho un non sò che nel cor, ch'in ve-ce di do - - lor ch'in ve-ce di do-
-lor gio-ja mi chie - - de, ho un non sò che nel cor, ho un non sò che nel
cor, ch'in ve - - ce di do - - lor gio-ja mi chie - - - de.
(etc.)
(I have a strange feeling in my heart which bids me rejoice rather than grieve)

motives, and is a typical example of late baroque expansion through melodic and harmonic sequence.) In addition there are arias based on the popular dances of the day (see Chapter 3, p. 410), such as the bourée (*R*, 'Il Tricerbero'), corrente (*A*, II, 21; see also Ex. 35, p. 278), sarabande (*R*, the well-known 'Lascia ch'io pianga'), and, most common of all, the minuet (*A*, III, 14. There is no gavotte-aria in *A* or *R*, but several occur in his later operas, e.g. *Ottone* (1723), II, 9.) We must also mention the very unusual Ländler-like $\frac{3}{8}$ aria (*A*, III, 10) with its opening rhythmic phrase and its later. It was clearly popular enough for Handel to include in *Rinaldo*, and is typical of his greater rhythmic freedom compared to his contemporaries.

As well as *da capo* arias, which, as we would expect, predominate, there are ariosos (*A*, I, 7) and ariettas, i.e. songs, in one section (*A*, I, 21). The *da capo* arias themselves are remarkably varied in texture, character, accompaniment, and key relationship between the two sections. As regards the last, in arias in the major mode section B ends usually in the mediant minor (e.g. if section A is in C, section B ends in E minor), and in arias in the minor mode B nearly always ends in the dominant minor.

The accompaniments can be divided into three main categories, those for continuo alone or in which strings play only in the ritornelli (*A*, I, 7), those for orchestra and continuo throughout section A (the accompaniment for B frequently differs from A and sometimes is just continuo), and the much

(Today my happy fate comes down upon me from the stars)

rarer class where the continuo plays only in the ritornelli (e.g. Ex. 33, p. 234). In the first category the distinctive feature is usually the character of the bass line, which may consist of an incisive ostinato motive (*A*, III, 2), a persistent dotted rhythm (*A*, II, 16), or running semiquavers (*A*, I, 19), etc.

It is in the second category that Handel's resource in varying his arias is most fully shown. Strings and continuo are the basic group, and these are permuted in all sorts of ways. (Unless otherwise stated, the voice is doubled by an instrument for most or all of the time.) Thus the texture may be homophonic with violins I and II mostly in thirds (*A*, I, 14), contrapuntal (*A*, II, 12), or polyphonic (*A*, I, 13). In this last there are some sudden and, because of their context, most dramatic unison and octave passages with the voice, a technique that Handel used with extraordinary effectiveness, even for a whole aria (e.g. *A*, II, 14). Violins in unison plus continuo were, in fact, a very popular accompaniment in the late baroque, owing to the clear, brilliant, and sometimes striking effect they produce (e.g. *A*, III, 20, where the jagged violin motive that leaps to *e'''* three times punctuates and accompanies a vocal line that is almost as restless. It is worth noting here that unison violin passages occur much more often in the works (vocal and instrumental) of the Italianate Mozart than in those of the more Germanic Haydn). At the other extreme is the contrapuntal texture in five real parts (*A*, III, 8), and imitative polyphony *a*5 and even *a*6 (*A*, II, 5). (In these last two instances the vocal part is quite independent.)

The oboe was the favoured wind instrument, and remained so through most of the century, because, unlike the bassoon, it is a high-melody instrument whose tone, then, could approach both the softness of the recorder and the brilliance of the trumpet; it was thus capable of blending with, but at the same time giving an edge to violin tone, and also of maintaining an independent line more successfully than the recorder or flute. Trumpets and horns could only play successive notes of the diatonic scale in their top register and were usually reserved for hunting, martial, and suchlike arias and choruses, e.g. the magnificent bass aria (*R*, I, 3) scored for two trumpets, tympani (kettledrums), oboe, etc. (i.e. strings and continuo), the 'Battle' music for four trumpets, tympani, two oboes, etc. (*R*, III, 10), and the triumphal opening and closing solo choruses in *Giulio Cesare* (1724) for four horns, two oboes, etc.

Many of the more spacious of Handel's arias are written in the concerto style ('stile concertante'), when one or more solo ('concertino') instruments are set off against an orchestral ('ripieno') body that normally comprises strings and continuo. For example, the concertino group may be violin and bassoon (*R*, I, 9), two trumpets (*R*, III, 9), two trumpets and oboe (*R*, I, 3), or two oboes, two violins, and two 'cellos (*A*, III, 11). Allied to this type of aria are those in which the orchestra is divided into two (*R*, II, 8, where one group consists of violins I and II, oboe, and continuo, the other of violins III, violas, and 'cellos doubled by bassoon; each part is separate and no part doubles the voice; see also pp. 476–7). In this last example, which opens with a poignant, imitative duet between bassoon and oboe, the grief of Armida is underlined by the two groups exchanging the short rhythmic fragment 𝄾♪♩ that later intensifies to 𝄾♬♩—a simple but extraordinarily telling accompaniment. This is an example of mood-painting, which, together with the much rarer word-painting, occurs more frequently and is more imaginatively expressed in Handel's operas than in those by any other late baroque composer, except possibly Rameau. In 'Cade il mondo' ('Let the world fall') (*A*, II, 4), the opening bass phrase in $\frac{6}{8}$ quavers plunges through two octaves (*d′-f-e-d-A-D*), and the whole aria demands the remarkable range of *D-f′*. In 'Vaghe fonti, che mormorando' (*A*, II, 7) the 'murmuring fountain' is delightfully portrayed by two recorders that double muted violins in slow quaver chords in $\frac{3}{4}$ time with a little rippling turn on the third beat, and accompanied by muted violas, pizzicato 'cellos and basses, and no harpsichord. Garden and country scenes never failed to call forth some picturesque music from late baroque composers, and Handel was no exception, the 'Pastoral Symphony' from *Messiah* being the famous but by no means the best example. Instances abound, but we must only give one further reference, the arietta 'Augelletti che cantate' (*R*, I, 6), where 'the birds that sing' are delightfully imitated in a long introductory ritornello, most of it played by a sopranino and two treble recorders accompanied solely by violas, the aria ending with an entrancing five-bar unaccompanied cadenza for the sopranino. The fact that Handel uses the violas (the Cinderellas of the string family) as a support is typical of his imaginative use of instruments and keen ear, for viola tone gives just the right amount of 'weight' to the light-toned recorders and sopranino.

Handel's superior dramatic sense compared to other composers of Italian opera is demonstrated in his accompanied recitatives (e.g. *A*, II, 5, where tremolo strings and shoals of diminished sevenths underline Ottone's shock at being called a traitor), in mixed scenes (*A*, II, 13), and in arias where section B is in marked contrast to A. For example, the aria in the mixed scene referred to begins in $\frac{3}{4}$ Andante, the voice, after a ritornello of broken, restless unison fragments, entering with

'Pensieri voi mi tormentate' ('Thoughts, you torment me') set to a falling phrase echoed by a solo oboe, which later concertizes with the voice on two long melismas to the penultimate syllable of 'tormentate'. (Notice the 'modern' use of the oboe, i.e. as an emotional instrument.) Section B, on the other hand, is in $\frac{4}{4}$ Allegro, and the forcefully syllabic vocal line, accompanied by strings and continuo (but not, be it noted, oboe), impassionately declaims 'Ciel, soccorre a miei disegni' ('Heaven, aid my schemes'). To be sure, most composers would have made some distinction between the two sections, for musical if not dramatic reasons, but none of them at the age of twenty-four created what is in effect a dual-affection aria of such power. Dual-affection arias can, indeed, be found in many of Handel's operas, and also in some ensembles (e.g. *R*, II, 6, and *R*, III, 7); a more striking instance occurs in *Orlando Furioso* (1733) (III, 8), where Angelica sings 'questo pianto e sangue ancor' to a chain of 'sobbing' suspensions, while Orlando sings 'ma non placa il mio giusto rigor' in quick but firm dactyllic rhythm.

If, to the above brief analysis of *Agrippina* and *Rinaldo*, we add two-, three-, and four-part recitatives, trios, quartets, and solo choruses, and purely instrumental pieces, we get some idea of the amazing variety contained in a single opera, a variety typical of all Handel's later operas. Few of these exceed *Agrippina* or *Rinaldo* in this respect, but some of them display individual items that, musically or dramatically, are an advance on or cannot be found in the two earlier operas. A few examples must suffice: in *Orlando* (III, 8) the voice is accompanied by two 'violette marine' (that is, two viole d'amore) played originally by the Castrucci brothers, of whom Pietro was the leader of Handel's opera orchestra; in addition to strings and continuo, we find two horns and two oboes (*Radamisto*, III, 6), two trumpets, two horns, and two oboes (ibid., final solo chorus), two recorders and two oboes (but alternatively, as the same performers played these two instruments, but rarely the flute) (*Alcina* (1735), II, 5), and, finally, the most sumptuously colourful music in Handel's entire output, the seventeen-bar Sinfonia for double orchestra that accompanies the vision of Parnassus, where Virtue, attended by the nine Muses, sits enthroned (*Giulio Cesare*, II, 2); the first orchestra, which plays the first nine bars, consists of strings, 'cellos, oboes (doubling violins I), bassoons (doubling 'cellos), theorbo, viola da gamba (playing two- to four-part chords), and harp (bass doubling 'cellos, treble mostly doubling violins I); in the last eight bars the harp indulges in semiquaver broken-chord figures, and the second orchestra, consisting of strings, oboes (doubling violins I and II), and basses, joins in. There is no harpsichord part.

The importance of the orchestral accompaniment in Handel's operas can be readily appreciated from a casual perusal of the scores. Sometimes the term 'orchestral accompaniment' is positively misleading, because the quality and character of the instrumental parts is as essential to the whole as the vocal part, and it is both amusing and instructive to read that some of Handel's singers objected to the unusual richness and interest of his scoring on the grounds that their thunder was being stolen; nearly 150 years later much the same objections were made against Wagner's music dramas. Nevertheless, it is not so much his skill as an orchestrator as his development in dramatic expression and characterization that distinguishes many of his later operas from *Agrippina* and *Rinaldo*. Again only a few instances must suffice: at the end of the very moving aria 'Stille amare' (*Tolomeo* (1728), III, 4) the dying hero sings 'la morte a chiamar' ('death calls'), and in the final repetition of this phrase Handel, in a stroke of sheer genius, omits the last word as Tolomeo falls lifeless to the ground, ending the vocal line unaccompanied on an implied dominant seventh which the orchestra softly resolves, and, incidentally, anticipating by over a century the final bars of Schumann's *Mondnacht* (see Part IV, pp. 823, 824). Occasionally emotion is intensified by an exceptionally chromatic passage or by unusual chord progressions (e.g. *Rodelinda* (1725), III, 3). In complete contrast to the above are the *stile galante* arias (Ex. 35, p. 478) and those in the racy *buffo* style (see p. 483) that Handel learnt from the operas of Pergolesi and others during his 1733 visit (*Serse* (1738) I, 15). In some of the last operas the solo chorus is replaced by the potentially much more dramatic crowd chorus, especially in *Alcina* which in this respect and in its numerous ballets, was probably influenced by the enormous success of Rameau's *Hippolyte* (1733; see pp. 492-3). Finally, there are the mixed scenes which developed considerably from those in *Agrippina* and *Rinaldo*, and two of these (*Tamerlano*

(1724), III, 10, and *Orlando*, II, 11), because of their length and dramatic impact, are veritable 'grand scenas'; the latter, in fact, is the most powerful scene in Handel's entire output, its most striking aspect being the vivid portrayal of Orlando, here no symbolical type, but a living being in the last stages of mental collapse. In the vast majority of baroque operas neither librettist nor composer was concerned to present the characters as flesh-and-blood figures, and while there are a few exceptions, e.g. Ottone and Ottavia in Monteverdi's *Poppea*, the brother and sister in Scarlatti's *Mitridate*, and Purcell's *Dido*, Handel surpassed all other baroque composers in the extent of his characterization and in the number of occasions in which one feels that he identified himself with the emotions of a particular character. One must not exaggerate this aspect of Handel's operas, for most of his principal figures are treated conventionally enough, but it is possible that his distinction in this respect was influenced by the individualism of English society, so much more marked than on the Continent, and reflected in the detailed observations of ordinary men and women and their affairs portrayed in the largely satirical art of William Hogarth [1697–1764], and more especially in the novels of Samuel Richardson [1689–1761], the founder of the modern novel.

To sum up: Handel, in his operas, drew together a number of different threads, as it were, and wove a musical fabric that is more skilfully constructed, varied, and consistently excellent than the operatic output of any of his contemporaries. Italy gave him the foundations of his style—the supremacy of sensuous melody supported by clear, diatonic, though sometimes richly spiced harmony, and the homophonic *galante* and *buffo* styles, as well as the *da capo* aria and the secco and accompanied recitatives. French influence is revealed in his dance-arias, in his overtures, and his German origin in the frequency with which contrapuntal and polyphonic textures occur. The frankly popular element, the use of non-*da capo* forms, the greater contrast of vocal timbres through the use of natural male voices (favoured by Handel more than any of his contemporaries except the French), and, above all, the delight in instrumental sonority and colour also stem from his native country.

The waning fortunes of Handel's operatic ventures after 1728 were due to a number of causes, of which *The Beggar's Opera* and its successors were but one. This work is another example of a pasticcio, for the poet and dramatist John Gay [1685–1732] selected a number of popular pieces, asked Pepusch to add a bass to those that had none and compose an overture, and strung them on to a story about London's thieves and vagabonds. The result is by no means a ballad opera, because only a few of the tunes are folk-songs, the majority being well-known items by Handel, Lully, Purcell, etc. It was very successful because it was a completely new kind of entertainment in which the Government, particularly the Prime Minister, Walpole, was satirized (always good box-office this) and Italian opera caricatured (but not violently). Moreover, it was performed in English throughout, with spoken dialogue instead of recitative, the story was up-to-date and down-to-earth, and the tunes were both popular and of a high standard. It was neither intended as nor did it become the death-blow of Italian opera (Gay and Pepusch, in fact, were both personal friends of Handel), and the period immediately after its production witnessed not only a host of similar ballad operas, but also the most intensive activity in the field of Italian opera.

Most of the ballad operas were performed at the Lincoln's Inn Fields Theatre, where the actor-dramatist John Rich [1682?–1761] was Manager from 1714 to his death. He is important as the founder of English pantomime (originally, as the word implies, a mime or dumb show), which he developed from the Italian *Commedia dell' Arte* characters, and presented annually from 1716 to 1760. In 1728 he accepted *The Beggar's Opera* (refused by his rival, Colley Cibber [1671–1757], then Manager of the Drury Lane Theatre), and its success, in the words of a contemporary wit, "made Gay rich and Rich gay". In 1730 he opened a subscription list for building the Covent Garden Theatre, which was completed in 1732. The next year, at Lincoln's Inn, he switched from ballad opera to Italian opera (the 'Opera of the Nobility'), a significant fact that helps to place in its right perspective the sometimes exaggerated effect of the former on the latter. Ballad opera, indeed, was only really popular for seven years, during which nearly fifty were produced (further evidence of the passion for novelty), and not until Arne's *Love in a Village* (1762) was there a brief revival. Arne was the only English composer of any distinction during the late baroque and early classical periods, and while he shows the influence of *stile galante* much more than does Handel, he imbued it with a freshness, simplicity, and charm that one can only describe as 'English', and which is best displayed in the numerous songs he wrote for the stage, e.g. 'Blow, blow, thou winter wind' and 'Where the bee sucks'. In 1733 he successfully re-set Addison's *Rosamond*; other operas followed, including *Artaxerxes* (1762), on a translated libretto by Metastasio, in which the music is completely Italianate, but, unlike most native operas of the time, is sung in English throughout (i.e. recitatives, not spoken dialogue). It was a great success, but instead of following it up with another similar one, Arne, like the vast majority of opera composers of his time, must needs emulate the Italians on their own ground; the result, *L'Olimpiade* (1764), on an original Metastasian libretto, was a complete failure.

Apart from Gay, the chief ballad-opera composers were Fielding, Cibber, and the playwright Charles Coffey [d. 1745]. Any success they or other writers had depended primarily on their wit and satire, which, as in *The Beggar's Opera*, was directed mainly at political and social targets, not at Italian opera. Musically they are inferior to their model, and contain, as do all the later ballad operas, a greater number of specially composed pieces mostly by the popular song-and comedy-writer Henry Carey [*c.* 1687–1743], Pepusch, and an obscure musician named Seedo. These satirical operas, once their novelty had worn off, proved much less satisfying to the musical élite than Italian opera, and during the last two seasons of the ballad opera craze, i.e. 1733–5, there were, as we have seen, actually two Italian opera companies, both of which managed to keep going until 1737. Even after this date at least one new Italian opera (not to mention revivals) was produced at the King's Theatre every year, including works by Hasse, Pescetti (both of whom had several successes), Leo, Galuppi, Pergolesi, Jomelli (for these last three, see below), and Gluck, who composed two operas for the Theatre in 1746 (see Part III, p. 715.)

The collapse of 1737 was due partly to the effect of the ballad operas on public taste, partly to the rivalry between the two companies, which naturally reduced the audience potential of each one (far smaller then than now) and which exhausted the supporters of both, and partly to two deliberately aimed satires, Fielding's play *Pasquin* (1736) and Carey's enormously successful *The Dragon of Wantley* (1737), with music by Lampe that burlesques superbly the Italian style. Like *The Beggar's Opera*, it contains a brawl between the two principal female characters (*à la* Cuzzoni-Bordoni), and was inspired by and directly tilts at Handel's *Giustino*, produced earlier in the same year, in which a sea-monster figures prominently.

The failure of Handel's company was also due to his lack of sufficient first-rate singers and to the uneven quality of the music, for the operas composed after his second Italian visit (1733), although they contain much fine music, including some delightful *stile galante* and *buffo* arias, do not, in general, reveal the same consistent quality of inspiration, nor the vigour, spontaneity, and, because of the mixed styles, the unity of the operas from *Agrippina* to *Admeto* (1727). It may be that consciously or unconsciously he was beginning to lose heart, but went on writing operas because he had been writing them all his life and because opera was the only vehicle he knew at the time through which he could express his exceptional dramatic gifts. These two reasons together account for his slowness in exploring the dramatic possibilities of oratorio, even after his ventures into this field had brought him a small fortune.

Although the ballad opera phase was both short and artistically undistinguished, its scheme of set musical numbers interspersed with spoken dialogue became a characteristic of most later English operas. This is also true of the German *Singspiel*, which, in the hands of its first important composer, Johann Adam Hiller [1728–1804], became very popular during the later part of the century. (In the late seventeenth and early eighteenth centuries *Singspiel* meant any opera in German, but after *c.* 1750 it was used in the restricted sense described below.)

The *Singspiel* sprang directly from the English ballad opera, in particular Coffey's *The Devil to Pay* (1731), which, as *Der Teufel ist los*, was frequently performed and imitated from 1743 on, first of all in north Germany, as a reaction against Italian opera, and later in the south. Hiller's entirely new setting of Coffey's text (Leipzig, 1766) established *Singspiel* as a significant art form which, unlike ballad opera, *opéra comique*, and *opera buffa*, was not limited to comic plots. This is particularly evident in the works of Georg Benda [1722–1795] whose two melodramas, *Ariadne auf Naxos* and *Medea* (both 1775), profoundly impressed Mozart. (A melodrama contains, in addition to set musical numbers (arias, etc.), spoken dialogue much or all of which is accompanied orchestrally.)

The roots of *opera buffa* go back to the Renaissance intermedii (see pp. 266–7) which, during the latter part of the seventeenth century, developed into the intermezzi. These were scenes (usually two) of a light and often humorous nature placed 'in between' the normal three acts of a serious opera, partly in order to give the audience their money's worth (people expected far longer entertainments in the seventeenth and eighteenth centuries than they do now), and partly to satisfy that craving for variety already noted. By 1700 the two scenes formed a continuous plot, by 1725 what we call '*buffo* style' was fully fashioned, and by 1740 *opera buffa* was a completely independent art form.

We must make a distinction here between *opera buffa* and comic opera; the latter can be traced back to *Chi soffre speri* (see p. 384), and most opera composers of the early and late

Baroque wrote at least one, the main difference between it and *opera seria* being the nature of the story. In *opera buffa*, however, like ballad opera, the plot is not only humorous and often satirical, but is also concerned with contemporary life. Another distinction is the small number of characters, sometimes only two, as in the comic scenes of Neapolitan *opera seria* (see p. 451). More important is the naturalness of the characters and their doings reflected in arias often vivacious, sometimes sentimental, and always expressing the text in a life-like manner (coloratura passages are rare), in recitatives that are little more than musically inflected conversations, in a completely homophonic style, often in only two real parts, and in the fact that all the voices are natural (i.e. no castrati). The conversational character of the recitatives is also found in the ensembles at the end of each act, these being a direct offshoot from the comic episodes of many Neapolitan operas (see p. 452), and, undoubtedly stimulated by the range of timbre of natural voices, they eventually developed into the most dramatically distinctive feature of *opera buffa*.

Opera buffa was essentially a Neapolitan creation—many of the early libretti, in fact, are in Neapolitan dialect—and, like ballad opera, it represented a partial reaction against the largely stereotyped characters and situations, and the often excessive coloratura of *opera seria*. But, like ballad opera also, it did not oust *opera seria*, for although it was musically more unified and skilfully written than ballad opera, it satisfied neither the love of virtuosity nor the delight in contrasting emotions, occasionally profound, that were possible in *opera seria*; indeed, all composers of *opera buffa* from Pergolesi to Mozart also wrote *opera seria*, and most of them were successful in both fields.

The earliest surviving example of the fully-fledged *buffo* style is Vinci's three-act comic opera in Neapolitan dialect, *Li Zite'n Galera* (1722), but the first genuine, original, and successful *opera buffa* was by Giovanni Battista Pergolesi [1710–1736], a pupil of Durante and Feo. In 1733 he composed two intermezzi entitled *La Serva Padrona*, which he placed between the acts of his *opera seria*, *Il Prigionier Superba*, and while the former, like his next intermezzi, *La Contadina astuta* (1734—sometimes known as *Livietta e Tracollo*) was much more favourably received than the main work, it did not become famous until after 1738; indeed after 1752, mainly owing to the violent controversy caused by its production in Paris (see p. 495), it became an international smash-hit. In most of the later performances the work was given as a whole, i.e. not as two separated intermezzi, and while a few earlier intermezzi had been similarly presented and hence, to this extent, qualify for the title *opera buffa*, none possesses the vivid characterization, the racy vivacity allied to sincere but never profound sentiment, and the delicate vein of tender pathos that distinguish both *La Serva Padrona* and *La Contadina astuta*.

The success of Pergolesi's *opera buffa* stimulated other composers to follow suit, and it was not long before *buffo* style and even *buffa* characters invaded *opera seria*, as in Handel's *Serse*. Conversely, *opera buffa* itself began to change, and in the late 1740s a much greater degree of sentiment was introduced, the original two acts were expanded to three, and the cast became larger, often consisting of two clearly defined groups, the comedians (usually three men and two women) and a pair of young lovers; in other words *opera buffa* became more conventional, but never to the same extent as *opera seria*.

The leading composers of comic opera, intermezzi, and *opera buffa* were, apart from Pergolesi, the Neapolitans Leo, Nicola Logroscino [1698–after 1765], Niccolò Jomelli [1714–1774], Rinaldo di Capua [*c.* 1705 – *c.* 1780], and Tommaso Traetta [1727 – 1779], and the Venetian Baldassare Galuppi [1706 – 1785]. Leo, who taught Jomelli and Piccini (see pp. 711 – 12), achieved fame with *Amor vuol Sofferenza* (1739); Logroscino was so successful that he was called '*il dio dell' opera buffa*'; Jomelli, one of the first to break away from the rigidity of the *da capo* aria, had an exceptional flair for popular melody; Rinaldo stressed the emotional possibilities of the orchestra, particularly in accompanied recitatives; Traetta was very highly regarded in his time, notably by Burney, and, in his *opera seria*, anticipated Gluck in the importance he attached to the drama; Galuppi, the greatest of them all, wrote *Il filosofo di compagna* (1754), the most popular *opera buffa* after *La Serva Padrona*. Galuppi is important also because he was the first to extend the rather limited finales that then existed, constructing them of five or six linked movements, during which the plot developed. Thus the finale of Act I of *Il mondo alla roversa* (1750) is constructed as follows: (1) C major, $\frac{4}{4}$, Allegro non molto, 56 bars ending in G major; (2) G minor, $\frac{3}{8}$, Allegro, 34 bars ending on the dominant of A minor; (3) C major, $\frac{4}{4}$, Tempo primo, 50 bars partially based on (1) ending in G major; (4) C major, $\frac{6}{8}$, Larghetto, 19 bars ending on the dominant of C; (5) C major, $\frac{4}{4}$, Tempo primo, 19 bars. There is no musical climax in this finale, and the three characters that sing at various times are on the stage all through; there is thus no dramatic climax either, as there is, for example, in the finales of Mozart's *Figaro*.

Galuppi wrote nearly 100 operas, the majority being *opera seria*; of his comic ones most are on libretti by Carlo Goldoni [1707–1793], the most popular Italian playwright of the eighteenth century, whose comedies paralleled *opera buffa* in their delightfully vivid portrayal of lower- and middle-class life, and their satire of the aristocracy. Much the same is true of the Spanish 'tonadilla' which flourished during the last half of the eighteenth century. The tonadilla was preceded by the 'zarzuela', which was very popular during the latter half of the previous century, and which consisted of two acts of spoken dialogue interspersed with solos, ensembles, and choruses (a few were, in fact, sung throughout), and which relied to a considerable extent on scenic effects; it was thus somewhat similar to the Lullian comédie-ballet and the English masque. A tremendous number of zarzuelas were written by the host of fine dramatists whose achievements represent the peak of what is usually called 'the Golden Age of Spanish Literature', and of whom the most outstanding was Pedro Calderón de la Barca [1600–1681], the successor to Lope de Vega (see p. 358). Nevertheless, the popularity and excellence of this native art crumbled during the early eighteenth century before the invasion of Italian opera, although a flicker of the national culture remained in the 'entremés' (intermezzo) performed between the acts of a play. The entremés often concluded with a song or tonadilla, and *c.* 1750 this expanded into a number of separate items linked by a simple plot, eventually, in the hands of Luis Misón [d. 1766], Pablo Esteve y Grimau, and Blas Laserna [1751–1816], becoming sufficiently highly organized and popular to achieve an independent existence.

We turn finally to France, the one country that did not capitulate to Italian opera, though she could hardly escape being influenced to some extent, despite the widespread admiration for Lully's works. Lully's operatic aims, indeed, were partially continued by his pupil, Pascal Colasse [1649–1709], whose *Thétis et Pelée* (1689) remained in the repertory for sixty-five years, but his successors, to a greater or lesser degree, tended towards a conception of opera that, while it maintained the importance of dancing and scenic display, placed charm and elegance of melody and harmony before literary distinction and dramatic integrity. This can be seen in the operas of André Cardinal Destouches [1672 – 1749], and more particularly in those of André Campra [1660–1744]. Both composers produced a smash-hit in 1697, the former with the opera *Issé*, which remained popular for nearly eighty years, and the latter with a new kind of entertainment, the 'opera-ballet' *L'Europe galante*. In *Issé* the recitatives are Lullian, but the airs are mostly written in *style galant*—that is, a style similar to the Italian *stile galante* (see p. 460) but more profusely ornamented with grace notes, turns, etc. These had been rigorously controlled by Lully, as they would have interfered with the clear enunciation of the text and marred the clarity of his vocal line, but they became an integral part of *style galant*, reflecting the taste of contemporary society which abhorred simplicity and tedium. This delight in ornamentation is also apparent in the painting, architecture, and sculpture of the period and is known as 'rococo art' (from the French *rocaille*, which implied artificially and elaborately decorated rockwork). Thus while both *style galant* and *stile galante* can be defined as a homophonic texture with melody governed by harmony, rococo refers to melody that is highly embellished and, in order to avoid being tedious, short-phrased, and it is the rococo element that chiefly distinguishes the French from the Italian gallant style.

The mood of *Issé* is predominantly pastoral and frivolous, in contrast to the classically statuesque nobility of Lully's tragédies-lyriques. This contrast is even more marked in *L'Europe galante*, the airs being more *galant* and Italianate in their lyricism (Campra, incidentally, was of Italian descent), with coloratura passages commoner and modulations, chromaticism, and discord more freely used; recitatives are less declamatory and more perfunctory, and the orchestra is sometimes most strikingly employed to heighten the drama by means of tremolos, rapid scale passages, etc., as in the Italian *recitativo accompagnato,* all these features serving to adorn a series of loosely connected scenes of great splendour, but of little dramatic or literary merit.

Issé is a finer work than *L'Europe galant,* but the influence of the latter was far greater and led to a host of similar opera-ballets in which the pastoral gaiety and charm of the music, together with an abundance of dances and frequent changes of scene, with the orchestra often providing a highly effective background, satisfied that craving for variety already mentioned more than once in this chapter, a craving that explains the enormous vogue of the *spectacles coupés,* where favourite airs, scenes, and even acts from operas of one or more composers were torn from their contexts and performed as concert pieces. This craving was more intense in France than elsewhere because in the unparalleled sophistication, elegance, superficiality, and sinfulness of the French aristocracy during the Regency [1715–1723], and for most of Louis XV's reign [1723–1774], boredom was the most intolerable of all states, and amusement the only goal worth pursuing. Morally, we can but condemn such a society, but artistically we must recognize its exquisite refinement and, considering the narrow emotional limits that were *de rigeur,* its variety.

Perhaps the most remarkable feature of the entire baroque period is its duality—the way in which strongly contrasted and even opposing trends existed side by side. Thus the period covering the reigns of Louis XIV and XV is commonly called both the 'Age of Absolutism', when the life of every individual was more completely subject to the King than in any other country, and also 'the Enlightenment', when the freedom of thought that originated in the Renaissance received a new impetus through the scientific discoveries of the sixteenth and more particularly the seventeenth century. These discoveries encouraged men to regard as true only what could be tested by direct observation or proved by logical deduction, and to accept the premise of the first great modern philosopher, Descartes, that doubt is the starting-point of philosophy. This attitude struck right at the roots of absolute authority, and it was almost inevitable therefore that, fanned by the *Lettres philosophiques* (1634) of Voltaire [1684–1778], which caused an uproar by implicitly criticizing French society through extolling the personal and political freedom that he experienced in England, the bitterest struggles between absolutism and enlightenment should have taken place in France.

The achievements in science, mathematics, and philosophy in the eighteenth century elevated the power of reason to a position never held before or since, and was strikingly exemplified in France by the group known as the Encyclopaedists. This was formed in 1749 when Denis Diderot [1713–1784], the most original French thinker of the eighteenth century, became Editor of what has been called "the great literary monument of the age of enlightenment"—the *Encyclopédie*, published between 1751 and 1772 in twenty-eight volumes. Diderot gathered about him some of the most distinguished men in France, including the German writer Melchior Grimm [1723–1807], who arrived in Paris in 1749, the mathematician Jean Le Rond d'Alembert [1717–1778], who became co-Editor, and the Swiss Jean Jacques Rousseau [1712–1778], of whom more anon. These men aimed at creating a society entirely governed by reason, and which permitted freedom of thought and speech (hence their rejection of the Church's authority), and so reflected the spirit of their times in which men attempted to classify everything, and in which a subject's status was raised immeasurably if it could be treated in a scientific and philosophic manner. Of all the arts, music was most affected by this rationalist approach, because its raw material (sound) is most readily expressed in mathematical terms (ratios and logarithms), and its affect on man had been recognized ever since Plato. The first type of classification we can call scientific and the second philosophic; the latter has already been partly covered in our discussion of the doctrine of the affections (see pp. 439-41); it reached its peak theoretically in *Der critische Musicus* (1737–40) by Johann Adolf Scheibe [1708–1776], *Der General-Bass* (1738) by Johann David Heinichen [1683-1729], and *Der vollkommene Kapellmeister* by Johann Mattheson [1681-1764] but practically in the operas of the great French composer of the late baroque, Jean-Philippe Rameau [1683–1764].

It is typical of both the man and his period that Rameau first achieved notoriety through his theoretical work, the *Traité de l'harmonie* (1722), which was received with scorn by professional musicians, and which attempts, with some success, to classify music both scientifically and philosophically. As regards the first, Rameau believed that music "depends on reason, nature, and geometry", and that it is "a physico-mathematical science"; he also believed that "melody is born of harmony"—in other words, that every melody implies its own harmonization, which is certainly true of late baroque, especially *galant*, melody. In his *Traité* and later works (see below) Rameau 'proved' that the major triad was the basis of all harmony because it is the only triad in the harmonic series (see pp. 247–8), that $^{6}_{3}$ and $^{6}_{4}$ chords are inversions of a triad, and that the tonic, dominant, and subdominant are the three fundamental chords in any key, these two last propositions being his most important discoveries. The three fundamental chords had, of course, been recognized in practice for some time, but Rameau was the first to classify them and point out their tonal significance. Unfortunately, his desire for a neatly classified system led him into a number of errors, including the assertion that all chords are derived from the three fundamental ones (discords being obtained by adding thirds), and that each chord has what he called a *basse fondamentale*, for the discovery of which he gives quite arbitrary rules; this bass is supposed to link all chords together, but in fact it often makes nonsense of tonality.

Some of the assertions in the *Traité* were corrected or modified in later publications, notably the *Nouveau système de musique théorique* (1726), *Génération harmonique* (1737), *Démonstration du principe de l'harmonie* (1750), and 'new thoughts' on the last in 1752. The errors in the *Traité* were not, however, the cause of its hostile reception, as no musician was sufficiently well versed in the science of music to point them out; the probable reasons were the pedantic and turgid style and the fact that the author was virtually unknown as a composer (apart from a few claveçin (harpsichord) pieces which everyone was turning out, anyway), and in the baroque, especially the late baroque, musical theory and practice were more inseparable than in any previous period. At any rate, the work was not accepted until after Rameau had fully established himself as a creative artist in the late 1730s.

In the philosophic treatment of his art, Rameau was as convinced about the power of music as was Plato. "It is certain", he says in his *Traité*, "that harmony can arouse in us different passions, depending on the particular harmonies that are employed." He then lists in detail the various emotional effects of concords, discords, keys, modulations, chromaticism, and cadences; melody he does not classify, for although he states that it is just as expressive as harmony, it depends more on good taste than anything else; nevertheless, his use of intervals and figures follows conventional practices, some of which go back to the Renaissance.

The importance that Rameau attached to nature was more than scientific-acoustic, for one of the most characteristic features of the Regency-Louis XV period was the way in which all art sought to imitate or portray Nature. But it was Nature idealized, not "red in tooth and claw", Nature limited to superbly ornamental gardens and sunny landscapes with well-trimmed hedges and pleasant, sheep-filled meadows in which elegantly-dressed courtiers wandered, conversed, and flirted in the shade, attended by charming shepherdesses and servile shepherds. The 'back to Nature' movement affected France more than any other country because it was more akin to French taste, which had never subscribed so completely to the emotional full-bloodedness of the early baroque as had other countries, and which, always avid for variety, revelled in a pastoral paradise where courtly manners and morals still obtained, but where the environment provided both the illusion of a new life and fresh scope for the delicately sensual and superficially refined attitude to living.

Although Rameau's treatises are important and alone entitle him to a distinguished place in the history of music, it seems strange to us, who regard him primarily as a creative artist, that all his life he was more sensitive to criticism of his theories than of his compositions, though he fully realized that he could only demonstrate the validity of the former through the latter, which meant in effect composing successfully for the theatre. Three *opéra comiques* appeared in 1723 and 1726, none of them of much merit, but in 1733, at the advanced age of fifty, he wrote his first important dramatic piece, the tragedie, *Hippolyte et Aricie*. At first audiences were stunned, because they never expected a learned theorist to compose such emotional stuff, nor were they prepared for some of the startling dissonances, modulations, and orchestral effects. It was not long, however, before most of the musical élite, headed by Campra, became enthusiastic, while the more reactionary musicians, plus a strong bourgeois element, remained antagonistic, faithful to the glories of the past—Lully's operas. The two rival parties, the Ramistes and the Lullistes, waged a bitter pamphlet war which was aggravated by having to share the only opera-house in Paris, but Rameau himself was much less partisan than his followers, and, as he plainly stated in the Preface to his ballet héroique *Les Indes galantes* (1735), had the greatest respect for his predecessor. The merits of *Les Indes galantes*, the ballet *Les Fêtes d'Hébé* (1739), and, more particularly, the tragédies *Castor et Pollux* (1737, revised 1754) and *Dardanus* (1739) did not convert the Lullistes, but as time went on their numbers waned as Rameau's popularity increased, especially after his appointment at Court in 1745, until by 1750 there was virtually no opposition; he was at the height of his fame.

At sixteen Rameau's father sent him to Italy for three years to study music, and although he was apparently unimpressed by what he saw and heard, Italian influence is clearly apparent in all his stage works; indeed, this was one of the chief criticisms of the Lullistes. Nevertheless, his conception of dramatic entertainment is much more in the Lullian than in the Italian tradition, for his airs, while more Italianate than Lully's, i.e. more sensuous, graceful, and sequential in structure, particularly the ariette type (e.g. 'Venus, que ta gloire réponde', *Castor* (1754), Prologue), are less purely melodic and important than in Italian opera. His recitatives are thoroughly Lullian in their overall importance, rhythmic freedom, careful underlay, and arioso-like style, although on occasion they contain bolder leaps (sevenths and ninths), richer harmony, and more vivid accompaniments. Lullian, too, are the spectacular but usually irrelevant scenes and elaborate ballets, both of which occur in greater profusion, and in the position to which he raised the orchestra Rameau was but accentuating one of Lully's outstanding traits.

The big flaw in Rameau's stage works is the lack of literary distinction and dramatic unity insisted on by Lully. Contemporary Italian opera is superior in this respect, for many libretti, especially those by Zeno and Metastasio, have some literary merit, are dramatically consistent, and avoid superfluous spectacle. Even if the story that he boasted he could set

La Gazette de Holland to music is untrue, it indicates his attitude, for he clearly did not bother about the quality of the language, nor did he care how many absurdities the plot contained, nor how many irrelevant scenes and dances were incorporated. In this he was truly the child of his time and nation, faithfully reflecting the excessive appetite for variety of the French aristocracy, but he was ahead of his time in his use of the orchestra, for, apart from the rarity of solo continuo accompaniments (true also of contemporary Italian opera), the orchestra is considerably more 'affective' than the voice, and even on occasion paints an introductory vignette of a character, e.g. the ritornello before Iphise's first appearance (*Les Fêtes d'Hébé*, II, 1). Compared with Italian opera, the great similarity between recitative and air is underlined by the frequency with which the orchestra accompanied the former and in the more varied orchestration of both, in which woodwind and brass instruments are added to strings and continuo more often. In most of the airs the nature of the accompaniment is orthodox, i.e. it is homophonic, contrapuntal, or polyphonic ('Brillez, astres nouveaux', *Castor* (1754), V, 7; 'Hâtez-vous', *Dardanus*, II, 3; 'Cruelle mère des amours', *Hippolyte*, III, 1, respectively), but in what Rameau called 'récitatif accompagné pathétique' the orchestra becomes sensational, portraying a violent emotion, such as suicidal grief ('Grands Dieux', *Hippolyte*, V, 1), the appearance of a monster (*Dardanus*, IV, 3), an earthquake (*Les Indes galantes*, II, 5), thunder (*Hippolyte*, I, 4), etc., by means of all the devices used in the Italian *recitativo accompagnato* but in a more vivid manner. Moreover, such recitatives occur far more often than their equivalents in Scarlatti, Hasse, or even Handel, and were, in fact, enormously popular, particularly those depicting storms—a direct result of the aim to imitate Nature.

The importance that Rameau attached to the orchestra was not only a reflection of the 'back to Nature' movement, nor merely the continuation of a tradition begun by Lully and continued by Campra; it was also an expression of his belief that harmony is the basis of music, for orchestral harmony can obviously be fuller, richer, and more affective than continuo harmony. This same belief also explains his fondness for ensembles and choruses, and here, as in the vocal line of his recitatives, which are further removed from speech and hence are less 'natural' than secco recitative, the scientific approach overruled the philosophic, for in nature people do not normally speak at the same time, except when they are part of an enthusiastic or angry crowd. Ensembles, in fact, occur far more frequently in Rameau's stage works than in Italian opera, and choruses, virtually non-existent in the latter, are even more common, and contain some of his best music, e.g. the extraordinarily dramatic 'Trio des Parques' (*Hippolyte*, II, 5; see Plate XXV), with its violent orchestral accompaniment, the almost as fine demons' chorus, 'Que l'Averne' (ibid., II, 3), the delicate gaiety of 'Volez, Zephirs' (*Les Indes galantes*, I, 6), the pastoral languor of the musette 'Suivez les lois' (*Les Fêtes d'Hébé*, III, 7), and the unusually long, imitative, almost Handelian 'Que ce rivage retentisse' (*Hippolyte*, III, 8).

The choruses and, more especially, the spectacular scenes and ballets provided the contrast which would otherwise have been lacking owing to the similarity between recitative and air. Indeed, it is generally true that the choruses cover a wider dramatic range more effectively, and the incidental music is on a consistently higher level than the solo vocal numbers. In the choruses, which are mostly contrapuntal with occasional snatches of imitation and even canon, melody is less exposed than in an air or recitative, less ornamental because of the number of voices singing each part, and the short phrases typical of Rameau are made less objectionable by the ejaculatory nature of the text or by the overlapping of one voice with another.

In the purely orchestral pieces, the dance and incidental music, Rameau, unfettered by the lack of accent and prevalence of feminine endings of the French language, produced a wealth of attractive, rhythmically clear-cut melodies in which rococo phrasing is more natural (for all dance music must be sectionalized) and ornamentation more effective (because fingers are nimbler than vocal chords) than in recitative or air. This mass of instrumental music, from which several excellent ballet suites could be culled, includes marches (*Hippolyte*, V, 8), rigaudons (ibid., III, 8), minuets (*Dardanus*, Prologue, 2), tambourins (*Les Fêtes d'Hébé*, III, 7—the well-known one from the 1724 book of claveçin pieces), gavottes (ibid., I, 8), musettes (ibid., III, 7—also adapted from the 1724 book), passepieds (ibid., III, 7), loures (ibid., III, 7—delightfully scored for piccolo and strings), chaconnes (*Les Indes galantes*, IV, 6), etc. Most of these dances were strongly pastoral in character and mood, particularly the tambourin (in duple time) and the musette (in triple time), both of which have a bagpipe-cum-drum flavour by being wholly or largely constructed on a tonic and/or dominant pedal.

In Rameau's later works the pastoral and spectacular elements become even more important, and the tone, with a few exceptions, more frivolous. Thus of the eight stage pieces composed between 1733 and 1740 five are 'tragédies' or 'opéras', but of the twenty-six composed from 1744 to his death only three are so designated, the majority being ballets. Admittedly in Louis de Cahusac, who contributed to at least seven of the later pieces, Rameau found a librettist who to some extent anticipated Gluck's collaborator, Calzabigi (see Part III, pp. 718, 719), by making the ballets and spectacles more an integral part of the story, but in general dramatic and literary considerations mattered even less than formerly.

The best of the later works are the tragédie *Zoroastre* (1749), the tragédie-lyrique *Abaris, ou les Boréades* (1763)—both with libretto by Cahusac—the ballet bouffon *Platée* (1745), and the acte de ballet *Pygmalion* (1748). The overture to *Zoroastre* is interesting because, apart from typifying the breakaway from the Lullian model, its three movements portray (according to the composer's own descriptive notes) a general picture of the whole opera, and it underlines a feature of Rameau's overtures that was exceptional for the time, but was fully in keeping with his views on the expressive powers of music—namely, an association either of mood- or word-painting or of actual music with part or the whole of the rest of the work. For example, the overture to *Zaïs* (1748) paints the chaos of the opening scene, that of *Pygmalion* imitates the chipping of the sculptor's chisel, the first section of the overture to *Hippolyte* is thematically linked with the opening chorus of nymphs, and so is the same section in *Castor* with the 'Entrée des Astres' (V, 7). But remarkable as this feature is, it is not Rameau's overtures to the later works that show him most consistently at his best, though that to *Pygmalion* is delightful; nor is it his airs, though there are a number of fine ones; it is, as in his earlier stage pieces, the choruses and dances that contain the highest proportion of first-rate music, e.g. the battle chorus in *Zoroastre* (V, 4), the choruses 'Douce paix' (ibid., V, 4) and 'Hymen l'Amour t'appelle' (*Platée*, II, 5), the two gavottes in *Abaris* (IV, 4), the two minuets in *Platée* (III), the musette in G (*Zaïs*, IV), the 'gavotte en rondeau' in *Naïs* (1749; IV, 6), and the sarabande in *Pygmalion* (Sc. 4).

Platée was the first and almost the only avowedly comic stage work by Rameau. The plot is appalling, but the music not only contains many excellent numbers, but is also more Italianate in the sense that much of it is melodically and rhythmically simpler than anything written previously. It was performed once as part of the wedding festivities of the Dauphin Louis and Maria-Theresa of Spain, when it aroused no comment, and again in 1749 at the Opéra, when it was favourably received. In 1754 it was revived during the famous battle against Italian *opera buffa* known as the 'Querrelle (or 'Guerre') des Bouffons'. This had been sparked off in 1752 by performances of a visiting Italian troupe of Pergolesi's *La Serva Padrona*, and Paris was divided immediately into two camps. The Lullistes, forgetting their earlier strictures on Rameau's Italianisms, joined forces with the Ramistes and, backed by Louis XV, engaged in a most acrimonious war of words with the pro-Italian group headed by the Encyclopaedists and encouraged by the Queen. *La Serva Padrona* was followed by a number of *buffo* operas by Leo and others which were opposed by revivals of *Platée*, *Pygmalion*, *Les Indes Galantes*, *Les Fêtes d'Hébé*, and *Castor* during the years 1752–4, the performance of *Castor* in the latter year deciding the issue (but only temporarily) in favour of French opera.

Why did the Parisians, who had consistently withstood the invasion of Italian opera and who were completely indifferent to an earlier performance of *La Serva Padrona* in 1746, suddenly become so violently partisan in 1752? There are three reasons. Firstly, the successful public performances of *Platée*, which took place only three years before, prepared the way for *opera buffa* via the ballet's comic character and Italianate style. Indeed, Grimm, who was self-confessedly pro-Italian and prejudiced against French opera, called it "a sublime work", and *Pygmalion* "a ravishing ballet", though he later became one of Rameau's most violent detractors. Rousseau, also pro-Italian and more consistently antagonistic than Grimm, described it as "divine", "Rameau's masterpiece", and "the most excellent piece of music that has been heard as yet upon our stage", while in 1753 d'Alembert wondered "whether *La Serva Padrona* would have pleased so greatly if *Platée* had not accustomed us to that kind of music?" Secondly, many Frenchmen, because of their craving for variety, seized on *La Serva Padrona* which, with its limpid texture, simple harmony, conversational recitative, and catchy tunes, its few characters and straightforward plot, could hardly have contrasted more strongly with Rameau's rich harmonies, complex scoring, and the spectacular irrelevance and unreality of most of his libretti. Thirdly, *La Serva Padrona* was more 'natural' because its arias were less artificial (in the original sense of that much-abused word), its recitatives nearer to speech, and, above all, its situations more lifelike.

The last reason brings us back once more to the 'imitation of Nature', the influence of which, in what we may call its philosophical aspect, became considerable *c.* 1750, partly as a reaction to scientific Rationalism, partly as a result of the Rationalists' rejection of Christianity but acceptance of God as revealed in Nature. This aspect was ardently advocated by Rousseau, the most versatile and inconsistent of the Encyclopaedists. In 1762 he published his *Contrat social*, the main theme of which is that the individual must be completely subservient to the community, and which thus repudiates freedom of thought and speech, but in his *Discours* (1755), *La Nouvelle Heloïse* (written 1756–9, published 1761), *Émile* (1762), and his last works he stresses the individuality of man, whom he regards as essentially good, but corrupted by civilization, and who can only be 'saved' by communion with Nature.

Rousseau expressed his 'back to Nature' philosophy not only in books, but also in music. He had studied the art in Switzerland, and later invented a new system of notation, but his few compositions, which include an opera, *Les Muses galantes* (1747), reveal a poor harmonic sense, for which Rameau duly castigated him. In 1752 he produced, in support of *opera buffa*, his comic opera *Devin du Village*, and followed it up with the now famous *Lettre sur la Musique Française* (1753), the most important musical manifesto of the period. The *Lettre*, apart from its vituperous attacks on Rameau, is sensible and constructive, but the opera reveals the paucity of his talent. Its enormous success was due to its *opera buffa*-like simplicity, its completely rustic setting, and the greater 'naturalness' of spoken dialogue compared to recitative. This last was an essential feature of the French equivalent of ballad opera—the vaudevilles of the *théâtre de la foire* which, almost entirely due to the brilliant playwright Charles-Simon Favart [1710–1792], had developed from rather primitive and often vulgar comedies interspersed with songs mostly to popular tunes, to polished, witty satires with newly composed vocal solos and ensembles. The success of *Devin* and of Favart's translation of *La Serva Padrona* gave a new lease of life to the *théâtre de la foire*, and with the merging, in the 1760s, of vaudeville and *opera buffa*, *opéra comique* was born.

The beginning of the aria 'Di gli ch'io son fedele' from *Cleofide* (1731), by Hasse, as sung at the first performance by the castrato Porporino (Antonio Uberti) [1697–1783], a pupil of Porpora ; it is in Frederick the Great's own hand.

5

THE BAROQUE: MUSIC IN CHURCH, HALL AND HOME

By Anthony Milner

At the beginning of the seventeenth century in Italy the interaction of the developing monodic technique and the declining madrigal proved a fertile source of new forms. The success of the early monodies was not due merely to their simplicity, but also to the presence of features deriving from popular music. Their melodic style continued that of the frottola (see Part I, p. 209) which had, so to speak, survived 'underground' in popular music, occasionally reappearing in the upper parts of the polyphonic villanella and balletto (see Chapter 1, pp. 245 and 272). This similarity between the frottole and the monodies is especially noticeable in the use of straight forward rhythms and sectional repetitions: Ex. 36 provides a simple comparison:

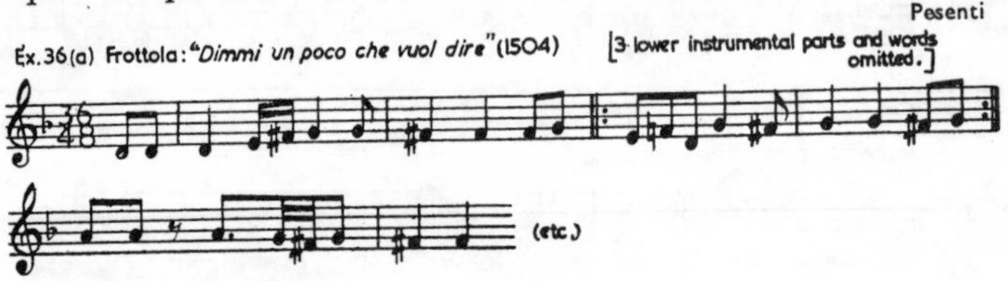

Repetition offered an easy solution of the chief problem facing the monodists—namely, how to provide a formal organization that would not impede the free expansion of the melody while avoiding the formlessness of the primitive operatic monody which quickly became intolerable apart from the drama. Here the monodists were influenced by the new 'continuo madrigals' (see Chapter 1, p. 271), whose instrumental basses frequently used repetition in the form of sequential patterns, or the ostinato melodies traditionally employed in accompanying poetry (see Chapter 1, p. 264, and Part I, p. 209), or strophic variation. The last of these became a favourite device of the later monodists: each stanza of the poem had the same bass, but the melody of the opening was elaborated in subsequent stanzas. Such basses did not possess sufficient individuality to make them ostinati, but the mere fact of repetition provided a simple method of sectional structure. Sometimes the strophes were separated by instrumental ritornelli. The monody *Tempo la cetra* from Monteverdi's 'Seventh Book of Madrigals' (1620) has four strophic variations separated by repeats of a ritornello whose material is taken from an introductory sinfonia. Alessandro Grandi [d. 1630] was apparently the first to describe an aria of this sort as a cantata in his *Cantade et arie a voce sola*, published in the same year as Monteverdi's collection.

The appearance of the *bel canto* style marks the beginning of the typical baroque solo cantata. Consisting of a dramatic or pastoral narrative poem set to a mixture of aria, arioso, and recitative, it offered the music-lover a means of enjoying in his home the kind of music he heard in the opera-house, and thus had much the same place in Italian social life of the seventeenth century that the madrigal had in the sixteenth. Moreover, it served as a training-ground for opera composers, who frequently experimented with new harmonic, melodic and formal features in the cantata before proceeding to their employment in opera. Its popularity may be assessed from the fact that thousands of examples survive, many in still uncatalogued manuscripts.

Luigi Rossi, the first great master of the cantata, composed over 250 works in this form. Some, the simplest, merely repeat an aria for every stanza of the text; others change the middle section while preserving the first as a refrain. The majority, however, and the most interesting, are 'rondo' cantatas, in which a succession of sections in arioso and recitative is interspersed with repetitions of an aria. Strophic variation and ostinato basses are found in these rondo cantatas as also instrumental ritornelli (generally for continuo, but occasionally for violins) which mark the separation of secco recitative and aria.

Some thirty cantatas for two and three voices preserve features of the continuo madrigal, ensemble sections alternating with solo arias. Rossi preferred the AB_1B_2 aria form to the ABA (see *H.A.M.*, 203 for an example of the latter), a preference shared by his contemporary, Giacomo Carissimi [1605–1674].

Compared with Rossi, Carissimi reveals a capacity for longer melodic lines, a closer organization of internal details of form by means of contrapuntal sharing of thematic material between melody and continuo bass, and an increasing tendency to abandon strophic variation for sequential passages in the bass. Cesti, Carissimi's pupil, continued and developed these features of his master's style, bringing to cantata composition all the characteristic technique of his operas (see Chapter 3, pp. 395–400). From Cesti onwards the formal devèlopment of the cantata closely parallels that of the opera. Legrenzi and Stradella (who composed 190 cantatas) increased the average overall length of the form by employing a sequence of two contrasted arias, each preceded by a recitative.* They regularly preceded their arias with instumental ritornelli. Although they used the *da capo* aria form more frequently than their predecessors, they by no means neglected the ABB forms, which are to be found even in the cantatas of such late baroque composers as Scarlatti and Handel. A noteworthy feature of many of the later cantatas is the elaborate quasi-virtuoso writing for the continuo bass instrument, which thus becomes the equal partner of the voice.

Rossi and Carissimi designed their solo cantatas in the first instance to please the sophisticated élite of the Roman aristocracy and clergy. The same public also fostered the development of the oratorio, which may be defined as a religious drama presented without stage action. From the beginning of the seventeenth century the Oratorian Church of S. Marcello was a fashionable centre for experimental combinations of quasi-dramatic music, religious services and sermons, especially in Lent, when the opera-houses were closed. Much of the music consisted of 'dialogues': descriptions or narrations by a *testo* (narrator), with comments by a chorus. When Carissimi in 1650 took over the direction of these musical activities, he embarked on a series of Latin oratorios (only sixteen survive) that established the form as a musical entity independent of a

* Cf. *H.A.M.*, 258, for an example of this form by Scarlatti.

liturgical setting. The libretti, composed by an unknown Jesuit, are mostly based on Old Testament subjects, such as the Flood, the judgement of Solomon, and the history of Jonah (see *H.A.M.*, 207). Although the *testo* is retained, its importance is considerably reduced; for example, in Carissimi's masterpiece, *Jepthe*, the narration is confined to the minimum necessary to ensure the continuity of the story: the chorus no longer merely comments, but sometimes takes over the narration, frequently participating in the drama first as the Israelite army and later as the attendants of Jepthah's daughter. Both stylistically and formally, Carissimi's oratorios present a striking contrast to his cantatas. All have features characteristic of the early baroque: the simple triadic harmonies of the choruses, the rapid succession of brief recitative and *arioso* sections, the absence of the ternary aria (though *bel canto* style occasionally appears in the arioso). The instrumental accompaniment consists only of two violin parts and continuo. This deliberate restriction of musical means was probably due to the need to keep each work short (since it was heard in the context of a religious service) and to the desire to emphasize the sacred narrative as strongly as possible, thus fulfilling the original moral and didactic purpose of the oratorio form. Carissimi's importance in the history of oratorio lies chiefly in his choruses, whose massive strength deeply impressed his contemporaries and successors: Handel occasionally 'borrowed' from his works when pressed for time. But generally his oratorio style had few imitators: faced with the competition of the all-dominant opera, composers turned to its religious counterpart, the *oratorio volgare* with Italian text.

Like the Latin type, the Italian oratorio flourished only under princely or prelatical patronage: it never shared the popularity of the opera. It was performed not in theatres, but in large halls or churches before an aristocratic audience, for whom it served either as a Lenten substitute for opera or as a musical garnish on important liturgical feasts. Since it was virtually opera without the stage, the same sort of music that in opera portrayed the anguish and transports of lovers accompanied the penitence of a sinner and the ecstasy of a saint. Thus it is scarcely surprising that some examples were dubbed *oratorii erotici*. In most of the mid-century oratorios the chorus was confined to exclamations and moralizing finales, but later composers restored the chorus to its previous importance and, availing themselves of the growing resources of tonality, wrote for it more and more in contrapuntal style. The chief opera composers of the period were also the leaders in oratorio. Legrenzi's *La Morte del Cor Penitente* is noteworthy for its elaborate fugal choruses that look forward to the Handelian type: Stradella's *S. Giovanni Battista* for the richness of its harmony and the use of obbligato instruments in the arias. Both show the same developments in harmony, tonality and formal expansion to be found in operas by these men (see Chapter 3, p. 400).

Eighteenth-century Italian oratorios are generally not as interesting as the operas: in most of them the chorus is again relegated to a subordinate rôle so that the oratorios, like the operas, become strings of arias and recitatives. Alessandro Scarlatti's works in this form, though full of charming music, are often hampered by utterly undramatic libretti: *La Santissima Trinità* (1715), for example, consists of theological discussions between Faith, Divine Love, Theology, etc. Two are unusual in presenting the lives of post-Reformation saints: *S. Casimir Re di Polonia* and *S. Filippo Neri*. But they are insufficiently represented in modern publications, and it is very possible that closer acquaintance might perhaps entail reassessment. A new type of subject, the so-called 'secular oratorio' is found in such works as A. Marcello's [1684 – 1750] *Il pianto e il riso delle quattro stagioni dell'anno* (1731), i.e. "The weeping and the laughter of the four seasons of the year", whose inscription "for the Death, Exaltation, and Coronation of Mary ever Virgin, assumed into Heaven" is perhaps due to an attempt to make the best of two worlds, for the Feast of the Assumption in mid-August was traditionally an occasion for holiday-making and carnival. The secular oratorio is related to the numerous cantatas and serenatas commissioned for occasions of public importance, consisting usually of a mixture of arias and instrumental movements: thus Scarlatti's *Nato è già l'Austriaco sole* (1716), written to celebrate the birth of an Imperial heir (who died in infancy) has the four seasons for *dramatis personae* and thus has close parallels in subject matter with Marcello's work.

Composers of liturgical music in the first decades of the seventeenth century had two methods of composition: the *stile antico* and *stile moderno*. The *stile antico* resulted from the attempts of conservative Roman composers to maintain the tradition of Palestrina (already revered as the supreme master of Catholic church music) on the grounds that it was the most suitable for worship. In fact, under the influence of the new continuo harmony the older technique was misunderstood: it is significant that arrangements of Palestrina's works were published which provided a continuo bass. But the distinction between the two styles endured throughout the baroque period and its influence may still be seen to-day: firstly, in the division of a composer's training into 'strict' and 'free' work,* which begins in the treatises of Berardi, who classified the older contrapuntal techniques in five 'species' a century before the publication of Fux's famous *Gradus ad Parnassum*; and, secondly, in the mistaken notion that certain styles are inherently more suitable than others for church music. All the leading composers of the seventeenth and eighteenth centuries from Monteverdi to Lotti wrote works in *stile antico*.

In 1610, while still in the service of the Duke of Mantua, Monteverdi published a collection of liturgical music which provides a representative cross-section of the changing forms in this field. Its chief work, a parody mass in *stile antico* based on a motet by Gombert, shows the effect of the new vertically-conceived continuo harmony on the melodic movement of ostensibly individual parts: its rhythms are more square-cut than those of late Renaissance polyphony and the harmonies tend to emphasize metrical accents. The remainder of the collection, consisting of Vespers of the Blessed Virgin (responsory, five psalms, hymn and Magnificat) with some other pieces, is designated on the title-page "for use in princely rooms and chapels"; unfortunately, several editors in the present century, ignoring this direction, have attempted to group all together as a vast choral work, despite the facts that the texts of the additional pieces cannot be fitted into the Office of Vespers and that the music is obviously intended for performance by small forces. The several parts of the Vespers are written in the *stile concertato* developed by Giovanni Gabrieli, which blends and contrasts solo, choral, and instrumental

* Which would have been inconceivable in previous centuries. One has only to try to imagine Josquin giving his pupils exercises in the style of Machaut to realize the enormous revolution in musical attitudes involved in this method of study.

groups (see Chapter 2, p. 318). In the psalms Monteverdi changes the manner of musical treatment for each verse and frequently separates the verses by ritornelli. For the most part he retains the psalm-tones as canti firmi, accompanying them with vocal and instrumental counterpoints which in spite of their frequently ornamental style and agitated rhythms are built on very simple harmonies with strongly marked cadences, but he also sets them in *falso-bordone* (derived from fauxbourdon: see Part I, p. 192) reiterated chords under the melody in the rhythm of the words. Passages for two and three voices alternate with sections in six and eight parts; *Nisi Dominus* employs two five-part choirs. The hymn 'Ave Maris Stella' (whose plainsong is heard in a decorated form in the top part throughout) has two four-part choirs for its first and last stanzas, using solo voices and single choir for the remainder; each verse except the last is followed by a ritornello.

Monodic writing appears in the extra-liturgical pieces, either throughout a movement or in sections alternating with choir or solo trio. *Audi coelum*, which begins as an alto monody and concludes with a six-part chorus, shows how the affective ornamentation of the secular music was transferred bodily to religious works: the triumphant scales on 'aurora' in Ex. 37.* closely resembles those in *Orfeo* where the hero overcomes Charon's opposition. The *Sonata sopra Sancta Maria* testifies to the growing importance of instrumental music for church use in the new style. Although not a liturgical work, the elevenfold repetition (at long intervals) of a plainsong intonation by a solo soprano gives it a quasi-liturgical air which is almost completely belied by the independent music for two violins, viola, cornetti, trombones, and organ.

Monteverdi's contemporaries and successors mostly abandoned the use of a cantus firmus in their preoccupation with the affections of the text. In their hands the *concertato* style split into two: the first used only solo voices with or without instruments and came more and more to resemble the secular cantata in its forms and in the use of ritornelli; the second, the 'grand' *concertato*, employed one or more choirs and groups of instruments, but minimized the importance of soloists. Some Roman composers attempted to blend the contrasts implicit in the *concertato* style with the 'imitation' renaissance polyphony

* *Tutti le Opere de Claudio Monteverdi*, ed Malipiero, Vol. XIV.

(Who is she arising that shines like the dawn, that I may bless her?)

of the *stile antico* in polychoral works. These were mainly intended for the newer baroque churches and can be appreciated properly only when heard in this kind of architectural setting. A French viol-player, Andre Maugars [fl. 1600–1640], who visited Rome in 1624, described the manner of performance: "This fairly long and spacious church had two great organs erected on both sides of the main altar with room for choirs around them. Along the nave there were eight more choir lofts, four on each side, elevated on scaffolding eight or nine feet high, and separated by the same distance, but facing each other. In every one of these choir lofts there was a portable organ. . . . The master composer beat the principal measure at the head of the first choir accompanied by the most beautiful voices. In every one of the other choirs there was a man whose only duty was to keep his eyes on the original beat given by the chief *maestro* in order to conform the measure of his choir to it. Thus all choirs sang in the same measure without dragging the movement."* Despite their apparent complexity, the continuo parts by which such compositions were held together reveal a very simple, even banal, harmonic organization. The zenith of this musical gigantism was reached by Orazio Benevoli [1605–1672] whose fifty-three-part Mass for the consecration of Salzburg Cathedral has two eight-part choirs (each supported by continuo, two string ensembles, two of wind instruments, and three of brass).

As the seventeenth century proceeded the operatic forms increasingly influenced those of liturgical music. While in the early baroque solo singing was generally a subordinate part of mass and motet, the rise of the Neapolitan opera saw the introduction of solo arias in full operatic style, commencing in the motet, which by this date could mean any piece of music set to a Latin text (other than those of the mass Ordinary) and often denoted forms which were in fact cantatas of several movements. Eight of Scarlatti's ten masses are in *stile antico*, but his *Concerti Sacri* (*c.* 1710), subtitled 'motets', for one to four solo voices (some with alternating choral sections) accompanied by two violins and continuo, consist mostly of recitatives and *da capo* arias with instrumental ritornelli. In the hands of Leo, Durante, Feo, and other eighteenth-century composers, the mass was expanded into a huge cantata in which independent choruses and arias were combined with instrumental movements. The employment of double choirs and of the contrast between soloists and chorus in individual movement was paralleled by the adoption of the concertino and ripieno structure of the concerto grosso (see Chapter 6, p. 551) for instrumental sections. An overture in French or Italian style frequently served as an introduction to the mass. The liturgical consequences of such music were disastrous: "the liturgy was not only submerged under this ever-growing art but actually suppressed, so that there were festive occasions which might best be described as 'church concerts with liturgical accompaniment'. Even the connexion with a text was taken very ill by music such as this. Texts which could be chosen at random—as was permitted after the elevation—were transferred to other places in the mass. On the other side, the celebrant often tried to continue with the offertory even while the choir was still

* Quoted in Lang, *Music in Western Civilization*, p. 362.

singing the Credo, or to restrict the singing of the Preface and *Pater noster* to the initial words so as to leave the rest for the music and the organ."*

In France the development of church music was largely determined by the requirements of the court, the artistic and cultural centre of the nation. Louis XIV preferred to attend a low mass, i.e., a mass in which the priest, officiating without deacon and subdeacon and thus with greatly reduced ceremonial, recites the text throughout without any admixture of chant. An elaborate setting of the Ordinary could not be used for a low mass, since there was insufficient time: yet music was considered an essential part of a ritual performed in the King's presence. The result was the so-called *messe basse solenelle*, the performance of motets for voices and instruments during certain parts of the service. The development of the baroque French motet commences with the works of Nicolas Formé [1567–1638] and Thomas Gobert [d. 1672], which frequently employ double choirs in the Venetian manner, though their style is rooted in the polyphonic methods of the previous century. Henri Dumont [1610–1684], Superintendent of the Chapelle Royale from 1663 to 1683, reveals the growing influence of the Italian baroque by the inclusion of an organ continuo in his *Cantica Sacra* (1652); his later motets employ the contrast of solo voices with chorus and the typical instrumentation of the contemporary Italian motet. From the middle of the seventeenth century onwards, Italian style and forms dominate French vocal music. In the works of Marc-Antoine Charpentier [d. 1704], a pupil of Carissimi, all the characteristic traits of the *bel canto* are to be found: his numerous church compositions for the Dauphin's private chapel exhibit greater variety than those of his predecessors and also, since the ritual of the chapel was not restricted by Louis XIV's impatience of solemn liturgical functions, a wider range of forms, including masses, motets and *Leçons des Tenèbres*. The latter provided a remarkable example of musical interference in liturgical ceremonial: the Lamentations of Jeremiah which provide the initial group of lessons for Matins ('Tenebrae') in the final days of Holy Week are traditionally chanted by an unaccompanied soloist, but Charpentier and later composers set them as independent cantatas with instrumental accom-

* J. A. Jungmann, *The Mass of the Roman Rite*, p. 149.

paniment, drawing out their length to five or six times that of the chant version, and destroying textual unity by constant repetition of words. In motets intended for festive or other occasions of importance, Charpentier employed a much larger instrumental band than any previous French composer of church music.

Lully brought to the motet the pomp and brilliance of the *tragèdie-lyrique*. His *Miserere* (1664) and *Te Deum* (1687) are scored for full operatic orchestra, including trumpets and drums. Operatic overture, double choirs, solo aria and recitative are blended with instrumental 'symphonies' (i.e. interludes and ritornelli) to produce some of the most elaborately brilliant church music ever written. Michel de la Lande [1657–1726], Dumont's successor at the Chapelle Royale, continued the style of Lully's motets, extending it to the mass Ordinary, of which he wrote twelve settings, but despite an almost Handelian grandeur his music has a seriousness, an occasional tinge of melancholy, not to be found in Lully. This perhaps is partly due to the fact that his chief works were composed in the last melancholy years of Louis XIV's reign, when *la gloire* of the *Grand Siècle* was out of favour, whereas Lully's appeared at its zenith, but even more to a perception of the religious meaning of his texts and their relevance to the liturgy that is entirely lacking in the older man's approach.

Rococo style is evident in the sprightly dance rhythms of Campra's motets for one to three voices (cf. *H.A.M.*, 257) and in the sensuous ornamentation of the church music of François Couperin Le Grand [1668–1733]. Much of Campra's music is purely decorative, but Couperin's, even when most ornate, always maintains a vital connexion with the text, a feature particularly evident in the subtle, deeply-felt chromatic harmonies of his *Leçons des Tenèbres* (1713–15). Neither Campra nor Couperin wrote for the Church in the massive style of Lully and De la Lande (which became unfashionable simultaneously with the change from *tragèdie-lyrique* to opéra-ballet), confining themselves almost entirely to solo voices accompanied by small instrumental forces.

Charpentier was the first to establish oratorio in France. His libretti, whether French or Latin, are often based on the same subject as those of Carissimi, whose works he made his models. Compared with the older man, Charpentier shows a greater concern for flowing melodic lines and longer sections: moreover, he employs the full harmonic resources of his time combined with a more contrapuntal approach, which reveals itself in the important parts allotted to instruments and concerted numbers for the soloists. Thus, in *Le Reniement de St. Pierre*, the meeting between Mary Magdalen and the risen Christ begins as a dialogue, but develops into a duet with close imitation between the voices (*H.A.M.*, 226). Like his oratorios, Charpentier's cantatas are heavily indebted to Italian models, though he achieved a stylistic compromise by blending *bel canto* melody with French ornamentation. This Italian influence continued throughout the development of the French cantata, reaching its height in the works of Louis-Nicolas Clerambault [d. 1749], which contrast French-style recitatives with Italian-style arias and instrumental 'symphonies'.

English church music was slow to follow the lead of the masque in incorporating the new vocal styles of the Continent. Compared with those of the opening years of the seventeenth century, compositions written for the Anglican liturgy in Charles I's reign have little musical, as distinct from historical interest: that the majority of church musicians preferred the older music may be seen in *The First Book of Selected Music* [1641] of John Barnard [?1591 – *c.* 1641], Canon of St. Paul's, which contains works by all the chief composers of the Elizabethan and Jacobean periods from Tallis to Orlando Gibbons, but none by the younger men. The first experiments occur in verse anthems by William Child [1606/7–1697], Henry and William Lawes, and Walter Porter [d. 1659], forming the chief contents of a Chapel Royal choirbook of 1635: these show the beginning of a trend towards a more declamatory and 'affective' vocal line, a trend continued in Child's *First Set of Psalmes* (1639) for three solo voices and continuo "newly composed after the Italian way". The Civil War and the establishment of the Cromwellian Protectorate interrupted further development for nearly twenty years, for, while approving in principle of music as an art and pastime (the destruction of organs and music libraries by some extremists were no part of official policy), the Puritans forbade choral services in churches and cathedrals and disbanded the choirs. At the Restoration a fresh start was made: Charles II appointed Henry Cooke [d. 1672], whom the diarist Evelyn [1620–1706] described as "the best singer in the Italian manner", Master of the Chapel Royal, and gave directions about the type of music to be used. Thomas Tudway [d. 1726], who, like all the famous English composers of the next generation (including Pelham Humfrey [1647–1674] and John Blow, both Purcell's teachers), was one of 'Captain Cooke's boys', has left an account of the royal interest in the newer music: "His Majesty, who was a brisk, and Airy Prince comeing to the Crown in the Flow'r, and vigour of his Age was soon if I may say so tyr'd with the grave and solemn wayes And Ordered the Composers of his Chappell to add Symphonys etc. with Instruments to their Anthems; and ther upon Establis'd a Select number of his private Music to play the Symphonys and Ritornellos which he had appointed."* Charles was partial to the French style (his string band was formed in imitation of the famous *Vingt-quatre violons du roi* of Louis XIV's court), and as soon as he observed that Humfrey showed exceptional promise he sent him to study in France and Italy. Humfrey's early death, two years after he succeeded Cooke at the Chapel Royal, robbed English music of a fine composer: his verse anthems show a sensitive and deeply-felt approach to the problems of English word-setting which he imparted to Purcell.

Though both Blow and Purcell wrote magnificent music in the older quasi-polyphonic style (chiefly 'full' anthems and services, but also Latin motets), their most original and striking contributions to church music is found in their verse-anthems with string accompaniment. There were two chief types of such anthems: the first, composed for occasions of great importance, is well exemplified by Purcell's *My heart is inditing* (1685) for the Coronation of James II [reigned 1685–1688]. This commences with a 'symphony' for strings and organ continuo in the slow-quick French overture form; the eight-part choral sections are accompanied by the strings, but the verses for eight soloists only by continuo. Ritornelli appear in the verse-sections, and the symphony is repeated entire in the middle of the work. The shorter type has a single-section symphony, a solo group consisting of counter-tenor, tenor and two basses, and fewer choruses. Blow's *The Lord is my Shepherd* has arias for three of the soloists, reserving the entry of the chorus for the last verse of the psalm; Purcell's *My Beloved Spake*

* Quoted in E. H. Fellowes, *English Cathedral Music*, p. 134.

has two choruses, but only one arioso section. Blow mingles the strings with the solo voices: Purcell alternates them, save in the previously mentioned arioso, where the solo tenor is accompanied by a single violin. The solo writing of both men has all the 'affective' power of their operas, Purcell's in particular having some astonishing pieces for bass designed for the extraordinary compass and agility of the Chapel Royal singer, John Gostling [*c.* 1650 – 1733]. Though the contrapuntal writing for large chorus retains much that is reminiscent of the older style, notably in close imitative entries and frequent 'false relations', the secular element dominates the solo writing. Dotted rhythms and lively sections in triple time characteristic of the French style are found equally in the homophonic choruses (e.g. the choral entry, "And the time of the singing of birds", in *My Beloved Spake*) and solos: if Ex. 38 be compared with such well-known tunes of Purcell's dramatic music as 'Let monarchs fight' the vital connexion between sacred and secular is immediately obvious:

Ex. 38 Tenor Solo from Anthem: *Blessed is he whose unrighteousness is forgiven* (♩=MM.84) Purcell
Thou art a place to hide — me in, Thou art a place to
Continuo
hide — me in, Thou shalt pre - serve me from trou-ble,
(etc.)

Purcell's and Blow's duties as court composers required them to celebrate royal birthdays, marriages, and the monarch's return to the capital from holiday with ceremonial 'odes', i.e. cantatas for solo voices and chorus with four-part strings and continuo, sometimes with added wind instruments and trumpets. Blow's compositions of this sort are uneven and at times downright dull; it may well have been that he disliked the fulsome flattery and habitual doggerel of the texts provided by the court poetasters. Purcell, on the other hand, seems not to have minded, for though there are occasional dull patches in a few of his seventeen 'Welcome' and 'Birthday' odes, they are far fewer than anyone first reading the poems would expect, and each work contrives to transfigure the wretched verse by some excellent music. The last of the six odes that he wrote for Queen Mary's birthdays, *Come, ye sons of Art* (1694) shows Purcell at his most brilliant. It commences with an overture in three sections (previously used in *The Indian Queen*) for oboes, trumpets, and strings, leading to a counter-tenor* solo which is repeated with full harmony by the chorus. A duet for counter-tenors, the well-known 'Sound the trumpet', is followed by another counter-tenor solo, accompanied by two flutes and continuo and concluded with a 'symphony' that is in effect an instrumental repetition of the solo. Next come a bass solo with string accompaniment, repeated by the chorus; a soprano solo with an oboe part that imitates and echoes the vocal line; another bass solo, and finally a duet for soprano and bass which the chorus repeats with the orchestra strengthened by timpani. All the solos are in binary form with repeats; the counter-tenor duet, the first soprano and second bass solos are built on ground basses which modulate.

Purcell's other odes were written for the wider audience of the public concerts that since the Restoration had become an important part of London's musical life. The first series of such concerts was organized in 1672 by a former violinist of the Royal band, John Banister (i) [d. 1679] at a public house in Whitefriars: concerts "by excellent masters" took place every afternoon at four o'clock, and the price of admission was 1*s*. In 1678 Thomas Britton [1644–1714], a coal-merchant, began a series of weekly concerts at his house in Clerkenwell which continued till his death, becoming very famous for their presentation of well-known artists; admission was at first free, but later an annual subscription of 10*s*. was imposed. Numerous small bodies of amateurs also sponsored concerts, among them

* Counter-Tenor (or Male Alto) Voice : a falsetto development of a normal tenor or bass voice.

the Musical Society which in 1683 commenced annual celebrations of St. Cecilia's Day (22nd November), whose main item consisted of a commissioned work to a poem specially written for the occasion. Purcell wrote four odes for the Society and a *Te Deum and Jubilate* (1694). *Welcome to all the Pleasures* (1683) for three soloists, chorus, and strings has the same basic design as a Birthday Ode; *Hail, Bright Cecilia* (1692) for four soloists, chorus and orchestra is a much larger work which may well be considered Purcell's masterpiece. The instrumental and vocal writing is of exceptional brilliance and variety; the choruses, with their occasional quasi-fugal texture, reveal a more highly developed choral style than is to be found elsewhere in his works, and one which anticipates very strikingly some features of Handel's 'English' style in anthem and oratorio. The opening symphony, scored for oboes, trumpets, drums, and strings, has four movements: a slow introduction in dotted rhythms; a canzona, really a double fugue; an adagio in slow triple time with antiphonal writing for the oboes and violins; an allegro built on a trumpet fanfare followed by a slow section without trumpets which in turn leads to a repeat of the allegro. Nowhere in Purcell's work is the 'affective' power of his word-setting more strikingly and movingly evinced: whether it be in the alto solo, ''Tis Nature's voice' (sung by Purcell himself at the first performance "with incredible graces"), with its descriptive ornamentation and passionate chromaticisms, or in the duets with obbligato instruments (especially that for alto and tenor with two recorders, 'In vain the am'rous flute' (which is perhaps the most sensuous and erotic music that Purcell ever wrote), or in the chorus, 'Soul of the world', with its pictorial matching of texture and rhythm to the various images of the text. Over two centuries passed before any English composer wrote a work that combined masterly composition with the same "genius to express the Energy of English Words whereby he mov'd the Passions as well as caus'd Admiration in all his Auditors".* According to the *Gentleman's Journal and Monthly Miscellany* of November 1692, the Ode was performed twice in that month "with universal applause"; it was repeated with similar success in January 1694. Fifteen contemporary manuscript scores, an unusually

* Henry Playford's Preface to the 2nd edition of *Orpheus Britannicus* (1706), a collection of Purcell's songs.

large number for a work of this period, testify to the esteem in which it was held.

Purcell and his contemporaries provided much vocal music for domestic performance by the music-lovers and amateurs of which the new audiences of concert-goers consisted. In his nine chamber cantatas for two or three voices with continuo (several with additional violins and flutes), twenty sacred songs for one or two voices with continuo, forty-two duets, and over a hundred solo songs Purcell displayed an inexhaustible variety of form and content. His works in this field form a body of song second to none in English musical history and one which is still too little known and appreciated by modern audiences.

Handel's first settings of English texts show that he had studied Purcell's music closely. Before the *Birthday Ode* for Queen Anne and the *Utrecht Te Deum and Jubilate* (both written in 1713), his choral music, apart from the early *St. John Passion* (1704), had consisted of Latin psalms and motets for the Catholic liturgy in the choral cantata forms of Scarlatti and other contemporary Italian composers. (The *oratorio volgare*, *La Resurrezione* (1708) only employs the chorus at the end of each of the two acts; otherwise it consists entirely of operatic-style arias which do not reveal Handel at his best, though their accompaniments contain some remarkable orchestration.) Between 1717 and 1720, Handel was resident at Cannons, the seat of the Duke of Chandos, for whose private chapel he wrote the twelve *Chandos Anthems*. These represent a synthesis of the form and style of the late baroque Italian motet and the more massive choral writing of the English tradition: each anthem, like a motet, consists of a succession of choruses, recitatives, arias, and orchestral movements. In the *Chandos Anthems* Handel laid the foundations of his 'English' style and learnt, as far as he ever did learn, how to set English words correctly; he returned to them over and over again as a source from whence he drew material for his oratorios.

Life at Cannons brought Handel into close contact with the leaders of English literary and artistic circles. The poets Gay, Alexander Pope [1688–1744], and John Arbuthnot [1667–1735] were frequent visitors under whose influence Handel turned his thoughts to English music drama. Although the masque as a musical entity had tended to merge with the late seventeenth-century 'semi-opera' (see pp. 432-4), it still had importance as a literary and dramatic form. Gay's libretto for Handel's *Acis and Galatea* (1719), while following closely the structure of its model, *The Judgement of Paris*, by Congreve, has two important changes from the traditional masque: descriptive choruses replace the older scenery and 'machines', and spoken dialogue is absent. The result is one of Handel's happiest creations: the contrast between the idyllic pastoral world of the lovers and the "monster Polypheme" inspired some of his most original choral writing, while the development of the individual characters in successive arias looks forward to the masterly portrayal of dramatic personalities in the last oratorios. *Acis and Galatea* was the first of several works which mingle elements from cantata, masque, ode, opera, and oratorio. *Alexander's Feast* (1736), a setting of Dryden's poem, is noteworthy for the manner in which the solo arias are taken up and expanded in choruses; the *Ode for St. Cecilia's Day* (1739), also to words by Dryden, is full of original and striking illustrations of the words; and *L'Allegro ed Il Pensiero* (1740), partly based on Milton's poems to which a third section (*Il Moderato*), by Charles Jennens [1700 – 1773] was added (and later omitted), contains some of Handel's most 'Purcellian' music.

Sir John Hawkins relates in his *General History of the Science and Practice of Music* (1776) that Handel "was used to say, that, to an English audience, music joined to poetry was not an entertainment for an evening and that something that had the appearance of a plot or fable was necessary to keep their attention awake".* Another masque, *Haman and Mordecai* (1720), with libretto by Pope, produced at Cannons with costumes and scenery, is a comparatively slight work, but of historical importance, for in 1732 Handel reconstructed it (with an amended libretto) as *Esther*, his first English oratorio, in an attempt to recoup from the financial losses he had sustained in opera. The advertisement in which he announced its forthcoming performance refers to his *Coronation Anthems* for George II [reigned 1727–1760] of five years before, which had proved immensely popular, being the first example of his massive choral style blended with ceremonial brilliance of orchestration to be heard by the general public: "There will be no acting on the stage, but the house will be fitted up in decent manner for the audience. The Musick to be disposed after the

* P. 890 in Novello's edition of 1853.

manner of the Coronation Service." *Esther* is really a pasticcio designed to catch the public ear by the inclusion of sections from two of the *Coronation Anthems* (*Zadok the Priest* and *My heart is inditing*) and the employment of castrati; the remainder of its music is a blend of *Haman* (considerably rewritten) and selections from the *Chandos Anthems*, *La Resurrezione*, and a Latin motet. Its success prompted Handel to try again: *Deborah* (1733), another pasticcio of his own works, made a great impression by reason of its choruses.

Esther and *Deborah* would never have been written but for Handel's pressing need for money; his haste betrays itself in the perfunctory treatment of the characters. *Athaliah*, composed a few months after *Deborah* for performance at Oxford, is a much better work: for the first time in his oratorios, Handel keeps the drama moving, and depicts a convincing protagonist. After *Athaliah* he became absorbed again in his operatic struggles, and it was not till 1738 that he resolved to concentrate mainly on oratorio composition, though he did not abandon opera entirely for another three years. *Saul* and *Israel in Egypt*, both composed in 1739, show him still hesitating over the best way to construct an oratorio, for whereas *Saul* is a true drama (and could be staged today with very little difficulty), *Israel* is a series of choral frescoes in which the solo arias are merely contrasting interludes. *Messiah* (1741), commenced within a fortnight of the failure of his last opera, *Deidamia*, is not a drama at all, but a lyrical narration and meditation; its popularity is probably the greatest single obstacle to the revival of Handel's oratorios today. The typical Handelian oratorio, a heroic drama, appears for the first time in *Samson* (1743). *Joseph and His Brethren* (1744), *Judas Maccabaeus* (1747), *Alexander Balus* (1748), *Joshua* (1748), *Susanna* (1749), *Theodora* (1750), and *Jeptha* (1751) are all cast in this form; *Solomon* (1748) is a choral pageant resembling *Alexander's Feast* more than oratorio; *Semele* (1743) and *Hercules* (1744), 'secular' oratorios in name, are really operas with large parts for chorus, the former having a remarkable dramatic continuity which makes stage presentation not only easy but imperative.

The chief differences between Handel's operas and his oratorios and choral odes lie in the importance, use and style of the choruses. Otherwise all the characteristics of his operatic technique are to be found in the oratorios. Most of the overtures begin with a slow French-style introduction, but the following quick movement is often a fugato in Italian style; *Saul* commences with a complete three-movement sinfonia (or Italian overture: see Chapter 6, p. 552) followed by a minuet, while *Theodora's* overture follows a French opening and Italian allegro with a sarabande and courante. For those who know only *Messiah* the orchestration of the arias in Handel's other oratorios is full of surprises, e.g. 'Breathe soft ye gales' (*Esther*) has flute, two oboes, violins in five parts, bassoons and theorbo; 'Hark, he strikes the golden air' (*Alexander Balus*) has two flutes playing antiphonally with two 'cellos, harp, and mandoline; the appearance of Samuel's ghost in *Saul* is accompanied by counterpoints for two bassoons playing in their lowest register; trombones and flutes alternate antiphonally for the 'Dead March' in *Saul*. Dance rhythms occur equally in arias and choruses, such as the sarabande for 'Mourn, Israel' (*Saul*), minuet in the aria 'From virtue springs' (*Theodora*) and 'alla hornpipe' for the chorus 'Now Love, that everlasting boy' (*Semele*).

Although Handel occasionally used the counter-tenor voice for his young heroes (e.g. David and Joseph) he ceased to write for castrati in oratorios after *Deborah*. "While in Italian opera the tenor and bass voices were still used to portray villians and comic characters, in oratorio Handel made them heroes and patriarchs. His Hebrew leaders thus attained a virility unknown to the more effeminately cultured emperors and princes of the operatic stage."* Nevertheless, he could still write the leading male role for a soprano (but female) voice in as late a work as *Solomon*.

Handel's choral writing forms his most personal and influential contribution to the development of music. Those choruses which maintain complete 'affective' unity (e.g. the fugue 'And with His stripes' in *Messiah*) are a very small proportion of the total number; often a fugue† with a single subject has a subordinate counterpoint of contrasting character to different words (e.g. 'They loathed to drink of the river' in *Israel* has a counterpoint for 'He turned their waters into blood', which, while it never becomes exact enough in its repetitions

* Julian Herbage, 'Handel's Oratorios' (from *Handel: A Symposium*, ed. G. Abraham, p. 104).

† For an explanation of fugal terms, see Chapter 6, p. 533–4.

to constitute a second subject, provides 'affective' variety throughout). Fugal writing occurs most often as part of a larger movement, particularly those in concerto style, where the chorus (single or double) has the same relation to the orchestral tutti as the solo instruments have in a concerto grosso; generally such movements begin with an orchestral ritornello (e.g. 'For unto us a Child is born', *Messiah*), but occasionally the chorus gives out the main theme, as in 'Your harps and cymbals sound' (*Solomon*). Massed chordal harmony used for choral recitatives (e.g. 'And Israel saw that great work', *Israel*) also occurs in the course of 'concerto style' movements, both as a contrast to figuration, and to mark beginnings and ends of sections. The movements that present an unfolding 'narrative' without formal repetitions are unlike anything else in baroque music. In 'The people shall hear and be afraid' (*Israel*) there are four sections, each with its own thematic patterns; the first three are bound together by a continuous dotted rhythm in the orchestra which ceases just before the chorus begins the fourth section: 'They shall be as still as a stone'; the orchestral bass from this point provides a series of pedal points, representing the 'stone', over which the chorus develops its new theme (rising scales) to the words 'till Thy people pass over, O Lord'. Formal variety is matched by widely-ranging contrasts of mood and colour; one has only to think of the splendid evocations of barbaric magnificence in the 'pagan' choruses of *Deborah*, *Belshazzar*, and *Samson* (Handel generally adds horns, trumpets, and drums to the orchestra for such choruses), the oracular power of the Plague Choruses in *Israel*, or the nature-painting of the double choirs in the third act of *Solomon*. No matter how complicated his counterpoint may seem on paper, Handel's basically homophonic and harmonic approach to all techniques of composition produce a feeling of fundamental simplicity; the listener never complains, as he may when listening to Bach, that Handel's music is 'too complicated'. In this Handel showed his understanding of eighteenth-century Englishmen; "what the English like", he told Gluck, "is something they can beat time to, something that hits them straight on the drum of the ear". Sometimes he deliberately played down to their level: the hero of *Judas Maccabaeus* (written after the rebellion of the Young Pretender (1745)) was obviously chosen to represent 'Butcher'

Cumberland, the bombastic character of the music reflecting the triumphant militarism of the London public.

Not all Handel's oratorios were box-office successes in his lifetime: he wrote quickly and consequently sometimes unevenly. Also, he succumbed far too frequently to the temptation to use movements, sections and themes from earlier works. The late Donald Tovey used to remark that "All Handel's works live by taking in one another's washing"; unfortunately, they sometimes take in the washing of other composer's works as well: *Israel in Egypt* uses material from compositions of Stradella and other composers in sixteen out of a total of thirty-five numbers. Such 'borrowings' do not involve stylistic inconsistency but their presence generally indicates a decrease in musical intensity. For example, the chorus 'Egypt was glad when they departed' (*Israel*), which is a note-for-note transcription of an instrumental canzona by Johann Kaspar Kerll, sounds very lame after such magnificent numbers as 'The people of Israel sighed'. Nobody in the early eighteenth century would have objected strongly to the practice of pasticcio-making, but it is impossible not to feel that a great deal of Handel's work would have been better without it.

The development of German Protestant music was profoundly influenced by the Lutheran congregational hymn or 'chorale' (see p. 299). Although new texts and tunes continued to be published throughout the seventeenth century, not all of these found a permanent place in the service hymnbooks. The melodies of Johann Crüger [1598–1662] and the poems of Paul Gerhardt [1607–1676] represent the highest achievements of this second period of chorale composition. Side by side with the new tunes the practice of adapting secular and older religious melodies continued: thus the tune of Gerhardt's famous *O Haupt voll Blut undwunden* (a paraphrase of the Catholic hymn, *Salve caput cruentatum*) is that of Hassler's love-song *Mein G'mut ist mir verwirret* (1601). The growth of Pietism (see p. 463) in the latter half of the century produced a great many devotional songbooks (not only by Pietists, but also, in rivalry, by orthodox Lutherans) the style of whose tunes resembled that of the aria and secular Lied (see p. 525) and whose texts were almost invariably sentimental; while very few of these songs became liturgical chorales, their exaggerated emotionalism ultimately permeated all branches of church music and was thus one of the chief causes of the decline of Lutheran church music in the later eighteenth century.

The practice of accompanying congregational chorale singing on the organ began around the turn of the sixteenth century: the first printed example of organ accompaniment is a Hamburg *Songbook* of 1604. Johann Hermann Schein [1586–1630] published the first chorales with figured continuo in his *Cantional* (1627), while Samuel Scheidt [1587–1654] in his *Tabulaturbuch* (1650) provided elaborate accompaniments with quasi-contrapuntal patterns and occasional chromatic harmonies that are second only to Bach's in originality and beauty. The growth of tonality gradually brought about a change in chorale-rhythm from the free unbarred metre of the sixteenth century to the regular one-syllable-to-a-beat style found in works by late baroque composers.

From the beginning of Lutheranism the choir was allotted an important part in the liturgy. Every town regarded its church music as a matter of civic concern, and thus all church musicians were appointed, not by the church elders, but by the town council. Though the larger churches were staffed by paid professional musicians, the small churches were frequently served by enthusiastic amateurs drawn from the numerous *Kantoreien* (singing societies) and *collegia musica* (music clubs) that sprang up all over Germany in the seventeenth century. Apart from the fortunate few who were able to attend the court chapels of those German princes that had weathered the upheavals of the Thirty Years' War, the average music-lover could hear elaborate music only in church and thus supported the expenditure of money and time required to achieve it. Choral music for the Lutheran service included both Gregorian chant (either in Latin or German translation) and motets in *stile antico* (two large collections of such motets by Italian and German composers, published in 1603 and 1613, were reprinted many times), but both of these were of secondary importance compared with compositions based on the chorales. "Consistent with the Lutheran idea of exegesis as the foundation of the liturgy, Protestant church music had the function of interpreting the 'word' of the Gospel. This goal could be achieved in two ways: the word could either be objectively 'presented' by a chorale, the quintessence of the dogma, or subjectively 'interpreted' by a free concertato composition."*

In 1601 Michael Praetorius [d. 1621] commenced the publication of *Musae Sioniae*, a collection in nine volumes of over 1,200 of his compositions based on chorales. These represent the first German experiments in the new baroque styles, including unaccompanied duets, four-part motets with continuo, simple homophonic harmonizations, and works for two, three, and four choirs. In a Preface to the ninth volume, Praetorius described three main methods of treatment: (i) the 'chorale motet', each phrase of the melody being used as a point of imitation in the older polyphonic style; (ii) 'madrigal-fashion', in which the chorale is split into small motifs that are employed in dialogue between groups of voices; (iii) the chorale in long notes forms a canto fermo over which the other parts develop either independent or derived contrapuntal patterns. A later collection, *Polyhymnia caduceatrix* (1619), adopts the Venetian techniques of Gabrieli, setting alternate phrases of a chorale for solo and choral groups, sometimes separating them with short instrumental passages. Though many of them are of uneven quality, Praetorius' works are of importance as the commencement of a development that led ultimately to the Lutheran church cantata.

Schein's *Opella nova* or *Geistliche Konzert* ('Spiritual Concertos') in two books [1618 and 1626] consist of chorale-settings for small groups of voices and instruments that apply the full virtuoso style of solo-singing to be found in the works of Gabrieli and Monteverdi for the purposes of emphasizing and illustrating the meaning and mood of the text; the melody may appear in single phrases accompanied by elaborate ornamental writing in the other voices, or it may be broken down into tiny groups of notes that are passed from one voice to another. Some of the pieces are monodies in which the chorale is transformed into a flexible solo part in the Italian manner, but accompanied by a bass moving in regular rhythms. Scheidt, Mathias Weckmann [d. 1674], Franz Tunder [1614–1667], Andreas Hammerschmidt [1639–1675], and many others continued to develop the treatment of chorales in large compositions along the lines of Schein's works. Scheidt combined the various methods, choral, ensemble, and monodic,

* M. Bukofzer, *Music in the Baroque Era*, p. 79.

in a continuous form, giving each stanza of the text its own distinctive character. Some of Scheidt's works are really a series of variations over a chorale canto fermo which show the influence of organ methods of chorale elaboration (see p. 483). Tunder and Hammerschmidt sometimes abandoned the chorale melody completely while retaining the text.

Schütz seldom employed either chorale melodies or text in his works. This may have been due partly to his Italian training and partly to an inherently dramatic approach to composition (his chief work using chorales, the *Musikalische Exequien* (1636), a polychoral setting of Biblical texts from the Burial Service, is mainly elegiac and meditative). As director of the Elector of Dresden's Court Chapel, one of the largest musical establishments at that time in Central Germany, Schütz had plenty of opportunities for introducing choral works on the very largest scale. The polychoral 'Psalms of David' (1619) achieved a perfect marriage of the rhythms of the German language and the techniques of Gabrieli, being the first settings of the German Bible that rank as supremely great music. In the *Symphoniae Sacrae*, written after his second visit to Italy, Schütz paid homage to Monteverdi without in any way relinquishing his personal style. For example, the concertato motet for bass and four trombones, *Fili mi Absalom*, published in the first volume of the *Symphoniae* (1628), shows a far more elaborate method of accompaniment than is usual with Gabrieli and Monteverdi: the interweaving trombone parts produce a rich harmonic background to the vocal line. The second part of the *Symphoniae* (1647) includes several striking psalm settings for solo voice, two violins, and continuo in which this style of accompaniment is developed further. Ex. 39 is a passage which no Italian composer of Schütz's generation would have written, preferring to hear the elaborate instrumentation in separate ritornelli rather than combined with the voice, yet for all its 'thick' harmonic texture, it remains faithful to baroque principles of word-painting, the doubling by the violins of the soprano line in sixths and thirds evoking the 'crowding multitude' of stars while solemn chords emphasize the contrast of 'what is man'. Though this contrapuntal elaboration of harmony is to be found in all later baroque music, it is more marked in German than in either French or Italian compositions, reaching its

Ex.39 Excerpt from German Concerto No.3 Symphoniae Sacrae Pars Secunda
Schütz
(b) (♩= MM.80)
2 Violins
Soprano
Basso Continuo
den Monden und die Ster - - - -
nen, die du be-rei - - test.
Was ist, was ist, was ist der Mensch, das du sein ge - - den - - kest?
etc.
([When I behold] the moon and the stars which Thou hast made, what is man, that Thou art mindful of him?)

height in the works of Bach. In the final volume of the *Symphoniae* (1671) Schütz returned tc the polychoral forms of his youth in works of profoundly dramatic intensity; *Saul, Saul was verfolgst Du mich?* (*H.A.M.*, 202), scored for six soloists, two four-part choirs, two violins, and organ continuo, is perhaps the crown of his achievement in the concertato style.

The development of German Passion music in the earlier part of the seventeenth century had at first little connection with that of concertato and chorale compositions. The Lutheran church continued the older method of reciting the Passion narrative to a special chant while punctuating it by settings of the 'crowd' portions of the text in polyphony (see Part I, p. 214). In the sixteenth century this was called a 'dramatic' Passion to distinguish it from the less usual 'motet' Passion in which the whole text was rendered by the choir. Later composers developed the 'dramatic' Passion into what may be called the oratorio-Passion by introducing orchestral and organ accompaniment and inserted sections with non-liturgical texts. The *St. John Passion* (1643) of Thomas Selle [1599–1663] alters the orchestration for each character, though a quasi-liturgical recitative is maintained, and divides the text into three parts introduced and separated by large choral and orchestral movements. Christian Flor [1626–1697], in his *St. Matthew Passion* (1667), breaks up the narrative by frequent arias and orchestral symphonies, while Johann Theile (a pupil of Schütz) introduced chorales in alternation with arias.

Schütz's Passions according to Matthew, Luke, and John [1666] stand apart from those of his contemporaries by reason of their austere, unaccompanied style. His earlier *Seven Words from the Cross* (1645) is a mixture of recitatives, ensembles, and arioso sections introduced and concluded by instrumental and choral movements in the style of the smaller pieces from the *Symphoniae Sacrae*, the words of Christ being emphasized by additional instrumental parts imitating the vocal line in two-part counterpoint. The *Christmas Oratorio* (1664), while continuing the sectional organization of the *Seven Words*, breaks new ground in the recitatives (as Schütz pointed out in his Preface) by abandoning the 'affective' style of the monody. In the Passions he returned to a quasi-Gregorian type of melody whose rhythmic notation indicates only the points of repose, so that the singer is free to vary the rhythm of the reciting tone according to the verbal pronunciation. It seems likely that Schütz adopted this method of recitative in his concern to establish a truly native musical style for German word-setting. Towards the end of his life he warned young composers not to imitate Italian continuo and concertato music until they had a thorough grounding in the old methods of polyphony and experience in native forms. His warning seems justified when the Latin church music of Catholic Southern Germany and Austria is considered; dominated by the compositions of resident and visiting Italians, it never developed any specifically German character. Not until the beginning of the classical period did German Catholic composers produce liturgical works of major importance (see Part III, pp. 607-11).

In the field of secular song German composers concentrated on the new continuo Lied, a strophic form deriving from the various adaptations and imitations of monody and continuo-madrigal by Schein, Scheidt, and others which frequently incorporated ritornelli for one or more instruments. The *Arien* of Heinrich Albert [1604 – 1651], a cousin and pupil of Schütz, range in style from simple tunes obviously influenced by the chorale to elaborate arias in the Italian manner (*H.A.M.*, 206). Albert's songs were sung all over Germany and inspired a vast body of similar songs which became the chief fare for domestic music-making. Nearly every important city in Northern and Central Germany had its group of song composers whose productions included not only original works, but also parodies of French, English, and Italian songs (Dowland's 'Can she excuse' appears in one collection). The continuo Lied reached its height in the works of Adam Krieger [1634–1666] whose *Arien* for solo or small vocal ensemble with ritornelli for five stringed instruments combine the melodiousness of the *bel canto* with the sturdy rhythms characteristic of German dance-tunes (*H.A.M.*, 228). Some of Krieger's compositions resemble the Italian solo cantata in their contrasts of aria and orioso sections, and thus foreshadow the later decline of the Lied under the growing popularity of Italian opera in Germany.

By the turn of the seventeenth century the styles of the later Italian opera were already exerting a strong influence on German church music. The blending of the various choral forms based on a chorale with the concertato style of Schütz and his pupils had produced a large composite type of composition later described as a church cantata. The cantatas of Dietrich Buxtehude [*c.* 1637 – 1707], which the young Sebastian Bach found so impressive, employ arioso, strophic variation, ground basses and canto-fermo treatment of the chorale, while those of Georg Böhm [1661–1733] and Johann Pachelbel [1653–1706] consist of a series of extended variations on the chorale melody. Many composers of the younger generation, deeming these methods antiquated, welcomed the 'reform' of the cantata advocated by Erdmann Neumeister [1671 – 1756], a Hamburg pastor who in 1700 published the first of three cycles of cantata texts for the liturgical year on avowedly operatic lines. Regarding the cantata as "a fragment of an opera", he discarded all Biblical passages and hymn texts in favour of poetical paraphrases that could be set as secco recitatives and *da capo* arias. In the face of criticism he modified his scheme to include choruses in his second cycle (1708) and some Biblical verses and chorales in his third (1711). One of the first to set Neumeister's texts was the opera composer Philipp Krieger [1649–1725]. Other poets altered Neumeister's layout still further, producing a compromise which enclosed the solo arias and recitatives setting the poem between two stanzas of a chorale. Friedrich Wilhelm Zachau [1663–1712], Handel's teacher, and Johann Kuhnau [1660–1722] preferred to make the setting of the opening chorale stanza a large choral and orchestral movement while treating the second as a simple harmonization. This became the commonest type of cantata employed by later composers.

A similar development took place in Passion music. Keiser's *The bloody and dying Jesus* [1704] was the first of a series of 'opera-Passions' that abandoned the Gospel narrative for a lyrical poem which did not so much present the story as comment on it with a wealth of blood-curdling detail and exaggerated expressions of emotion. The music, apart from a few choruses, consisted entirely of recitatives and *da capo* arias. Handel's *St. John Passion*, written in the same year as Keiser's work to a text by Christian Postel (Keiser's opera librettist), was in much the same style, save that some portions of Scripture were retained. The most famous of Keiser's later Passions, *Jesus, martyred and dying for the sins of the world* (1712), set a libretto by Neumeister's friend, Heinrich Brockes [1680–1747], a Hamburg City Councillor. Brockes' poem became a 'best-seller' within a year of publication and was translated into several languages. All the leading north German composers set it, including Telemann, Mattheson and Handel (1716). The 'opera-Passion' form enjoyed great popularity, not only during the heyday of the Hamburg opera, but for the rest of the century throughout Germany: Telemann, as prolific in church music as he was in opera, wrote forty-four Passions. Another 'best-seller', *Der Tod Jesu* (1755), by Carl Graun [1703/4 – 1759], has features derived from the earlier oratorio, such as choral fugues, but is even more sentimental and tearful in style than Keiser's works.

The *Passions* according to St. John (1723) and St. Matthew (1729) by Johann Sebastian Bach [1685–1750] represent a compromise between the earlier 'dramatic' and the new 'opera' forms of Passion composition. Bach retained the complete relevant Gospel portions in both works, adding chorales of his own selection. For the solo arias and accompanied recitatives of *St. John* he drew on Brockes' previously-mentioned text, while for *St. Matthew* he had a libretto written for him by a Leipzig poet, Christian Henrici [1700–1764], better known by his pseudonym of Picander. *St. John* is more obviously dramatic by reason of the fewer lyrical interruptions to the narrative and the extended 'crowd' sections (the largest, 'Let us not divide', has fifty-five bars); *St. Matthew*, though it has dramatic moments, is more meditative and leisurely in its progress. The relative proportions of the constituent movements (apart from the narrative recitative and 'crowd' choruses) is shown in the following table:

	St. John	*St. Matthew*
Solo arias . .	4 (none *da capo*)	10 (7 *da capo*)
Orchestrally-accompanied recitatives	2	11 (one punctuated by a chorale)
Arias with chorus .	2	5 (including one duet)
Chorales . . .	11	13
Chorus movements .	2	5

Bach's characteristic expansion of musical forms appears particularly in the choral and orchestral movements. The opening and concluding choruses of *St. John* are built in *da capo* form; the vast opening of *St. Matthew* has a chorale sung by boys over a double choir and double orchestra developing the thematic material of one of the largest ritornelli that Bach ever wrote. Bach's treatment of the Gospel narrative is peculiarly his own: he abandoned every trace of the old chant 'intonations', substituting a vocal line ostensibly based on the secco recitative, but with a lyrical turn of phrase not to be found there that conformed entirely to the requirements of the German language and to the expressiveness required by the subject. To those of his contemporaries more obviously influenced by the later opera (especially that in *style galant*) Bach's works seemed old-fashioned. The rich accompaniments of his arias, the elaborate quasi-instrumental writing for voice contrapuntally combined with instrumental parts in which he indulged to the full the traditional German love of 'contrapuntalized harmony' (see p., 567) bewildered or bored many musicians. If, like Handel, he had depended on popular approval for his livelihood, he might have imitated more of the newer styles, but since he remained all his life a paid servant of either prince or town council (as nearly all the long line of his musical ancestors had been before him), he was under no urgent compulsion to tickle the public ear. Whereas Handel's music looks outward, every note being designed to make an immediate impression on its audience, Bach's is introspective, full of detail that can only be perceived through careful listening and sympathetic understanding. It was not always appreciated by his employers: when Bach applied for the post of Cantor at St. Thomas's, Leipzig, he obtained it only because Telemann, the Town Council's first choice, had refused it; "since we cannot secure the best", as one councillor put it, "we must take what we can get".

Bach's attitude to composition sprang directly from orthodox Lutheran notions of the value of music and particularly of its importance in church music: he was a church composer for most of his life and his largest single group of works consists of cantatas for the Lutheran liturgy. Like his predecessors, he believed that the greater the art and craftsmanship that went to the making of a work, the better it praised God, and, as he wrote in a student's notebook, "the aim and final reason of all music is none else but the Glory of God and the recreation of the mind. Where this is not observed, there will be no real music but only a devilish hubbub." Consequently, while he used all that his contemporaries had achieved, combined with the best elements of the Italian and French music of his day, he developed it in his own intensely personal manner to a point where he revolutionized it far beyond the understanding of most of his contemporaries and juniors.

To study Bach's cantatas profitably, it is important to remember their intimate connexion with the liturgy: their texts frequently contain quotations from, or reference to, the Epistle and Gospel of the day. The music is full of symbolism, allusion, and word-painting which only become clear when the works are viewed in their liturgical context. There is but one example of the variation cantata (see p. 522) in the 200 odd surviving works in cantata form: *Christ lag in Todesbanden* (no. 4); most of the cantatas commence with a large-scale movement of the type favoured by Kuhnau (see p. 526). Bach frequently gave this opening movement vast size by blending it with the Italian concerto style, but where Handel would have a largely homophonic texture (see p. 518), Bach develops the chorus in elaborate counterpoint, e.g. the Ascension cantata (no. 11). Sometimes this is combined with a chorale canto fermo in the top voice of the chorus (*Wachet auf*, no. 140). The first movement may also be built on a French overture (no. 61) or preceded by it (no. 119); the opening chorus of *Jesu der du meine Seele* (no. 78) has a chaconne bass. Several cantatas use a chorale melody as a thematic basis for all movements, but treated very freely: Ex. 40 shows this principle applied in Cantata 93, where it extends even into the (unquoted) recitatives. Most of those cantatas employing chorale melodies have them only in the first movement (as a canto fermo) and the last (a simple harmonization), though many cantatas use the entire *text* of a chorale. Cantatas having two or more chorales are generally narrative cantatas, e.g. the six constituting the so-called 'Christmas Oratorio'.

A similar variety of style and form is to be found in the solo arias, duets, and trios which form the middle sections of cantatas: ground basses, concerto movements, dances (the arias of Cantata 194 form a dance suite), and even fugue. In Cantata 54 (for solo alto) the second aria is a three-part fugue for voice, violins and violas over a continuo bass in which, inevitably, the voice is treated exactly like an instrument. The movements in which obbligato instruments figure are often those of mystical intensity, such as the two duets in *Wachet auf* for soprano and bass with violin obbligato which portray the love of the Redeemer for mankind in an ecstasy of ornamentation.

The solo items in the Mass in B minor are similar in style to those of the cantatas, some of them actually being adapted from earlier works. The massive choruses of the Kyrie and Gloria reveal Bach at his most magnificent: here both Passion and cantata are eclipsed. In the five-part orchestral and choral fugue of the initial Kyrie eleison, Bach produced both his longest single movement and his richest contrapuntal texture. Neither the Mass (written to gain the title of Court Composer from the Catholic Elector of Saxony) nor the *Magnificat* (1723) were intended for the Catholic liturgy: the first two movements of the Mass were heard at a service welcoming the Elector to Leipzig in 1733, and the *Magnificat* formed part of Christmas Vespers in Bach's first year of office at St. Thomas's.

6

THE BAROQUE: INSTRUMENTAL MUSIC

BY ANTHONY MILNER

WHEREAS in the fifteenth and sixteenth centuries the forms of instrumental music were for the most part derived from those of vocal music, in the baroque era instrumental music gained its complete independence. The works of the Roman organist Girolomo Frescobaldi [1583 – 1643] represent the final stages of the transition from renaissance to baroque styles. In place of the steady tempo and stylistic homogeneity of the former, Frescobaldi's music is characterized by sudden changes of mood, unprepared dissonances, and rhythmic restlessness, typical of which is the constant succession of short, jerky motifs combined in syncopations and cross-rhythms that are found in his toccatas. The prefatory instructions to his *Fiori Musicali* (1635) bid the performer "find out the affection of the passage before he plays it", vary the tempo, and slow down at cadences. In his keyboard variations (significantly termed 'partite') on traditional melodies with ground basses (*H.A.M.*, 192) he accentuates the differences between them by sharp contrasts of figuration and changes of metre. The same technique occurs in his canzonas, though in some he obtains a fundamental unity by building the sections on modified versions of the same theme. This type of variation-form appears in many of his ricercars: either the theme is altered for each fugal exposition,* or the unaltered theme is combined successively with new counterpoints. The latter form, which he sometimes describes as 'Fuga sopra un soggetto', approximates closely to the later baroque fugue (see p. 534).

The short sections and strong contrasts of Frescobaldi's keyboard works are also typical of the ensemble compositions of his contemporaries, which initiate a new type of ensemble

* FUGAL EXPOSITION: the presentation of a theme ('subject') by a number of 'voices' entering in turn at prescribed intervals: thus if the first begins on the tonic, the second voice ('answer') starts on the dominant, the third on the tonic again, and so forth.

NOTE. "Portions of chapter 6 are based on material from a Ferens Fine Arts lecture *The musical æsthetic of the Baroque* given in the University of Hull, and subsequently published by the University in 1960."

writing by adopting the continuo and hence the emphasis on top part and bass characteristic of the monody. Many ensemble pieces of this sort were dances, often paired and with variations (see p. 354), or ground bass variations for one or more violins, or canzonas with numerous sections. This later form of canzona allied to the continuo was soon known as 'sonata' (which at the beginning of the baroque referred not to the form of the work, but to its style), of which there were two chief kinds: the 'solo' sonata for one violin, continuo instrument (harpsichord or organ), and bass stringed instrument, and the 'trio' sonata for two violins and similar accompaniment. While both maintained the multisectional form of the canzona, the solo sonata tended to concentrate on exploiting the virtuoso possibilities of the violin; double stopping, pizzicato, large leaps, elaborate scale and arpeggio passages, and the use of harmonics are all to be found in the works of Biagio Marini [*c.* 1587 – 1663], Giovanni Battista Fontana [d. *c.* 1630] and many others. The trio sonata, on the other hand, avoided virtuoso writing and preserved the contrast between chordal and imitative sections of the older canzona far more than did the solo sonata. Salomone Rossi [d. 1633?] in his first set of works for trio ensemble, *Sinfonie e Galiarde* (1607) showed a preference for an initial imitative or 'fugal' section, and for a slow dance-rhythm in a subsequent section.

The next generation of composers gradually abandoned the mixture of dance and contrapuntal sections to establish two different types of trio sonata: 'the sonata da camera' (chamber sonata), which was really a dance suite (see below, pp. 535, 538), and the 'sonata da chiesa' (church sonata), consisting of four or five slow and fast movements in alternation, generally commencing with a slow movement, and whose first quick movement was always in fugal style. The opera composers of northern Italy took the first steps towards this formal differentiation by reducing the number of sections in their canzonas to five (or less), expanding each section till it became a virtually independent movement. Legrenzi's sonata *La Cornara* (published 1655) affords an example of the intermediate stages between the multisectional canzona and the trio sonata.* It begins with an extended fugal allegro movement, but continues with three much shorter sections of which the second is a transitional Adagio leading to a recapitulation of the allegro's first bars.

* Recorded in *History of Music in Sound*, 6.

Larger sections necessitated more highly organized music, and here Legrenzi excelled in inventing themes whose sturdy up-beat patterns and sequences provided plenty of material for subsequent development. The Church of S. Petronio in Bologna, already famous for the instrumental music of its services, became under Maurizio Cazzati [*c.* 1620 – 1677], Music Director from 1657, the centre of a notable group of composers known as the 'Bologna school'. Cazzati's pupil, Giovanni Battista Vitali [1632 – 1692] was the first to distinguish clearly between church and chamber sonatas in his publications. His church sonatas of 1667 have the normal four-movement plan (slow-quick-slow-quick) of the late baroque,* but later publications, such as the *Sonate a due, tre, quattro e cinque stromenti* of 1669, exhibit traces of the older canzona structure. *La Graziani*,† after an imitative Vivace, has a largo preceded by a seven-bar link and followed by a longer movement expanding the material of this link. Vitali's works are important for the habitual contrapuntal style of their quick movements which became an accepted feature of the trio sonata henceforward. Many of his sonatas are built on the variation principle of the later canzona whereby all movements employ transformations of the same basic material. All forms of ensemble music were cultivated at Bologna, including the first solo sonatas for 'cello and sonatas for large instrumental groups. The latter became the foundation of the concerto grosso.

The main development of German keyboard music in the opening decades of the seventeenth century was carried out chiefly by Sweelinck's pupils. Sweelinck, as we have seen (Chapter 2, pp. 351-2), blended the figuration technique of the English virginalists with the earlier Italian style of Andrea Gabrieli and Merulo, and, like Frescobaldi, laid the foundation of the fugue. Scheidt's *Tabulatura nova* (1624–6), so called because it was written in the new Italian 'open score' notation instead of the older German tablature, contains fugal pieces, chorale harmonizations, and a large group of variations and fantasias on popular songs and chorales that apply figuration patterns with logical severity, each pattern being used over and over again till its possibilities are exhausted. Although Scheidt's exhaustive elaborations are occasionally a little dull, they are of

* No. 3 is recorded in *History of Music in Sound*, 6

† *H.A.M.*, 245.

great importance in that they showed German composers an economical method of preserving the unity of a piece in the smallest details, and which proved very useful in later fugues for the sections called 'episodes' in which the subject is absent. Scheidt's choral fantasias have the same structure as the chorale motet (p. 521): each phrase of the melody is treated in fugal exposition. Heinrich Scheidemann [*c.* 1595–1663], Matthias Weckmann [1619–1674], and Tunder relaxed Scheidt's rather rigid contrapuntal treatment of chorales: their chorale fantasias share features in common with the toccata, such as rhapsodic virtuoso passages, and absorb the melody into the general fabric by decorating it with copious ornamentation. In Tunder's hands the fugue received the general shape that has characterised it ever since (e.g. *H.A.M.*, 215): a piece built on a subject presented in contrapuntal exposition which, together with its accompanying counterpoints, forms the material for subsequent expansion in episodes, the episodes being punctuated by statements of the subject in various keys.*

Up to the middle of the century German composers made very little distinction between organ and harpsichord music: the organ was by far the more important of the two instruments and, since the pedals were little used (when they were necessary the composer always indicated the fact in the title), most of its music could be played quite adequately on the harpsichord. The beginning of idiomatic German harpsichord music is closely linked with that of France, which thus requires prior consideration.

In France the lute remained the fashionable solo instrument well into the seventeenth century. Though its repertoire still consisted mainly of dance pieces, the influence of the English Jacobean lutenists brought about important changes of style. The compositions of Jacques Gaultier (Court lutenist in England, 1617–47) and his famous cousin, Denis Gaultier [1603–1672], are far more 'polyphonic' in the implications of their broken-chord patterns than those of previous French lutenists; moreover, they exhibit a great increase in the use of ornamentation (e.g. *H.A.M.*, 211). Denis Gaultier's music was composed for the sophisticated circle of the French Court: it is

* While this definition is quite adequate as far as it goes, it should always be remembered that fugue is not so much a form (in the sense that the classical sonata first movement is) as a technique, a method of musical thinking; one can therefore speak of passages being written 'in fugue'.

essentially intimate music for a favoured minority. Most of it consists of stylized dances (in forms which had nearly all ceased to be danced to), the chief being the allemande, the courante (see p. 538) and the sarabande (a slow triple-time dance with feminine cadences and an accent on the second beat), which Gaultier combined with earlier dances like the pavane and more modern ones like the gigue (see below, p. 538) and canaries in a suite. Sometimes these suites were built on the variation principle, but more usually the only principle of unification was the fact that all its constituent pieces were in the same key. The suite was generally introduced by a prelude written in notes without fixed values which the player strung together in a freely improvised texture of arpeggios and broken chords. Gaultier continued the English practice of giving suggestive titles to his pieces, such as *La Majestueuse* or *La Voluptueuse*; some of his allemandes were called 'tombeaux', i.e. a piece in memory of some dead patron or friend. Many of his courantes were followed by 'doubles': ornamentalized repeats in which the original notes were replaced by broken patterns of notes of half value, thus 'doubling' the number.

When the lute began to yield in popularity to the more sonorous harpsichord (or clavecin) the keyboard composers transferred all the chief aspects of lute style, such as broken chord patterns and continuous ornamentation, to the latter instrument. The works of the chief clavecinists of the seventeenth century, Jacques de Chambonnières [1601/2-1672], and his two pupils, Louis Couperin [d. 1661] and Jean Henri d'Anglebert [1635–1691], contain many movements marked 'a la luthe' which require the use of the 'lute stop' (p. 341) invented in France at this time. These composers increased the number of keyboard ornaments so much that an elaborate system of signs had to be designed to indicate their positions in the texture. Chambonnières in his *Pièces de Clavecin* (printed 1670, but composed nearly thirty years earlier) provided ornament tables and explanations in notation. These signs were adopted by composers of other countries and still survive (though with altered implications) today. Some of the best pieces of Chambonnières and L. Couperin are pavanes in the older lute tradition, often elaborately polyphonic, with spacious lines and a fundamental grandeur not to be found in their dance suites. These are very similar to Gaultier's lute suites, the individual movements having titles and the customary bipartite dance structure, but the basic order of the movements is more usually fixed as allemande-courante-sarabande, with optional doubles after the courante and any number of other dances after the sarabande. Both composers favoured the lower part of the harpsichord's range, which corresponds to the compass of the lute. This is particularly noticeable in their chaconnes and passecailles (e.g. *H.A.M.*, 212) which, as in nearly all such pieces by French clavecinists, employ rondeau form* instead of the traditional variations. D'Anglebert exploited the full range of the instrument: his style is more clavieristic and his textures richer. Though L. Couperin developed the Gaultier type of prelude into a toccata-like form consisting of two rhapsodic sections flanking a central fugue, D'Anglebert preferred the older form (e.g. *H.A.M.*, 232) since a simple introductory movement provided a stronger contrast to the closely-patterned style of his allemandes. His numerous transcriptions of airs and overtures from Lulli's operas are the first important examples of such arrangements in baroque keyboard music.

Johann Jacob Froberger [1616–1667], a pupil of Frescobaldi and Court organist in Vienna, combines both Italian and French traits in his keyboard works. In his organ compositions he surpasses his master in tonal, melodic, and structural organization, but seldom matches his bold and arresting harmonies. His toccatas are generally divided into three sections of which the second and often the third are in fugal style; each section has distinctive material, though there may be one motif which appears in more than one section, thus unifying the piece (e.g. *H.A.M.*, 217), which has a six-note chromatic-scale motif dominating its second and third sections. His canzonas and ricercars apply the patterned rhythmic figuration of Scheidt and Sweelinck to melodic lines influenced by the operatic *bel canto*. The French influence is to be seen in his most important compositions, the harpsichord suites. Froberger adopted the dance suite's order of movements as he found it in Chambonnières' works, but restricted the number of dances to three or four, the optional movements being the gigue, which he inserted between the courante and sarabande (though, when his suites were published posthumously, the gigues were placed

* RONDEAU FORM: a 'refrain' section alternating with 'couplets': ABACAD . . . A.

after the sarabandes). Frequently his courantes are variations of the preceding allemande, a 'pairing' of dances similar to that of the Tanz and Nachtanz of the preceding century (see p. 349). Froberger's capacity for blending French and Italian stylistic elements (characteristic of nearly all German composers of the later baroque) is demonstrated in the remarkable variations (*partite*) on the popular song, *Mayerin.* The first presents the theme accompanied by the broken chords typical of the French lutenists (Ex. 41a), but the second employs figuration in the North German style (Ex. 41b); similar figuration is applied to an Italian gigue for variation 3 (Ex. 41c). Variations 4 and 5 dissolve first the melody and then the bass in continuous semiquavers reminiscent of the chorale fantasia, while the sixth is chromatic and intermittently polyphonic in the style of Frescobaldi's ricercar sections. The last three variations are French dances, a courante (Ex. 41d) followed by a double and a sarabande (Ex. 41e), all of which have a 'figured' German texture of scale-patterns:

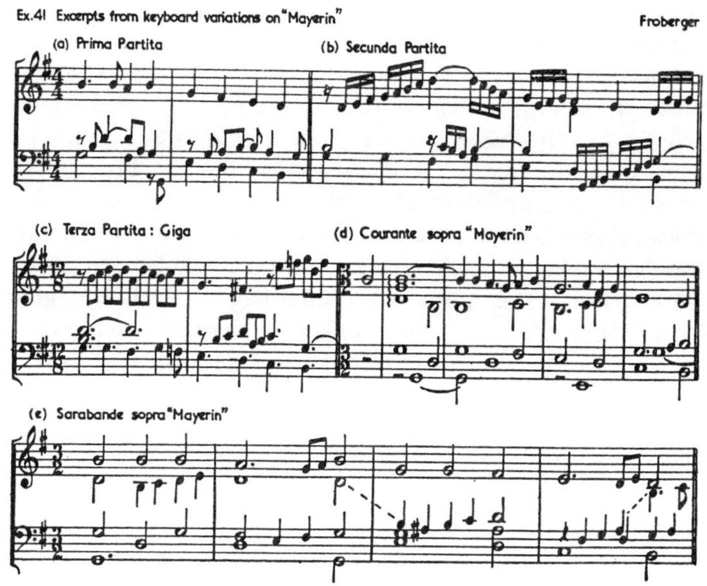

Some of Froberger's allemandes are *tombeaux*. The beautiful *Lamento* on the death of the Emperor Ferdinand III contains features that are 'programmatic', such as the ascent of the Emperor's soul to Heaven depicted at the close. Froberger was unusual among his contemporaries in that, as Matheson relates, "he could depict whole histories on the clavier, giving a representation of the persons present and taking part in it, with all their natural characters". Matheson mentions a suite (which is now lost) "in which the passage across the Rhine of the Count von Thurn, and the danger he was exposed to from the river, is most clearly set before our eyes and ears in twenty-six little pieces".* The ancestry of such musical narratives can be traced back to the numerous instrumental arrangements of Jannequin's *La Guerre* (p. 240) through imitations, such as Byrd's *Battell* in *My Ladye Nevell's Book*. Froberger started a vogue for them in Germany which continued into the eighteenth century.

The establishment of the suite as a stereotyped form was the work of Froberger's successors; keeping his order for the four main dances† (the gigue being last), they inserted optional dances between the gigue and sarabande which were the newer 'modern' dances of the contemporary French ballet (minuet, bourree, gavotte, etc.) and hence simpler in texture than the older forms. When the Italians adopted the dance-suite in the sonata da camera they varied the order and number fairly frequently; moreover, the Italian courante (*corrente*) and gigue (*giga*) differed markedly in style from the French. The 'corrente' (actually the older form, being found in the *Fitzwilliam Virginal Book*) was in quick $\frac{3}{4}$ or $\frac{3}{8}$ time with quick running figures; the 'courante' was in moderate $\frac{3}{2}$ or $\frac{6}{4}$ with a frequent shift from one to another. Similarly the 'giga', generally in rapid compound duple time, had running rhythms over a straightforward harmonic foundations whereas the 'gigue', in compound triple time, was a little slower (often in fugal style) and had dotted rhythms. Some German composers wrote 'Ouvertures': suites commencing with a French (operatic-style) slow-quick overture followed by several French ballet dances.

German ensemble music at the beginning of the seventeenth century was chiefly influenced by Italian older-type dances

* Quoted in Spitta, *Bach*, I, p. 236.

† Originally each represented a different 'national' style: German (allemande), Italian (courante), Spanish (sarabande) and English (gigue).

and English consort music. Schein's *Banchetto musicale* [1617] shows both coupled with the favourite German scoring for mixed wind and string instruments (*H.A.M.*, 217). The trio sonata was developed by Paul Peuerl [b. 1570], Johann Vierdanck [*c.* 1605 – 1646], and Johann Rosenmüller [*c.* 1619 – 1684], the last of whom amplified the form by adding a slow introduction or 'sinfonia'. All these men composed sonatas for four, five and six instruments which maintained the slow-quick alternation of their Italian models while writing in a considerably more contrapuntal style. The long quasi-fugal themes of Rosenmüller's movements strongly resemble those of contemporary German organ canzonas, but without the strict 'patterning' to be found in Scheidt's contrapuntal writing. In central and southern Germany a school of violinist-composers explored the virtuoso technique of their instrument to the utmost: at a time when Italian violinists had virtually abandoned the earlier baroque experiments in multiple stopping of strings, the Germans had perfected a polyphonic technique of great subtlety by the use of 'scordatura' (i.e. altering the tuning of the strings). The greatest of the group, Heinrich Biber [1644–1704] wrote a cycle of fifteen *Mystery Sonatas* (*c.* 1675), each a meditation on a 'mystery' of the Catholic devotion known as the Rosary, in which every sonata has a different tuning. Biber mingles church and chamber sonata movements with 'arias', ground-bass variations and elaborately rhapsodic preludes in a stylistic synthesis typical of many later German composers. In the MS. the titles are indicated by small pictures placed before each sonata, a device copied from the French lutenists. Some of the sonatas are strongly programmatic: for example, the sixth, *Christ's Agony in the Garden of Gethsemane*, for which the violin is tuned a♭-e♭′-g′-d′, begins with a slow lamento followed by a presto filled with repeated double-stops and rapid semiquavers as the agony increases. The third movement, an andante in triple time, depicts Christ's prayer by a leaping figure for the violin which is filled in with rapid scales as the agony redoubles. A passionate recitativo adagio follows which clearly portrays the petition, "Father, if it be possible, let this chalice pass from me; nevertheless, not as I will, but as Thou wilt". (Ex. 42). The quiet finale suggests Christ's acceptance of His passion.

The use of musical symbols in these and other works is

EX. 42 From Mystery Sonata No. 6 H. I. F. BIBER

closely bound up with the instrumental application of the 'doctrine of the affections' (pp. 439-41) and the monothematic conception of musical composition it involved. Instrumental music approached monothematic form in a different way from vocal. As we have seen, the earliest baroque instrumental pieces were sectional; thematic unity, or figural consistency, within each section was mainly the result of the north German organists' contact with the patterned variation of the English virginalists as applied by Sweelinck to the elaboration of chorales. When joined to the Italian ground bass technique with its repetition of a fixed order of harmonies (p. 562) the variation-cycle provided the first instrumental solution of the problem of overall musical consistency. The development of the fugue from the ricercar is fundamentally the replacement of a sectional form elaborating successive affections by a unified form based on one affection. But whereas in vocal music the affections expressed a mood or notion, specified in the text, their meaning in instrumental composition was not defined: hence a purely abstract art that relied on musical consistency alone. Hence also a tendency to regard instrumental music as inferior to vocal. "An instrumental player or composer must observe the rules which lead to good melody and harmony much more clearly and assiduously than a singer or choral composer, because when singing, the singer is aided by the great clarity of the words, which are always missing in instrumental music" (Mattheson). Biber's sonatas and the French lute and clavecin pieces previously mentioned are examples of the frequent employment of titles, pictures, and emblems to elucidate the affections in instrumental works. Some of the apparently 'abstract' use of figures in instrumental music disappears if it is remembered that many of them held 'affective' values from their use in vocal and dramatic music. When Purcell used a descending chromatic counterpoint in the Allegro of his 7th Trio Sonata he did so well aware of the associations it would have in his hearers' minds: a storehouse of allusive memory would thus be awakened, heightening its poignancy.

By the end of the seventeenth century "the specific formal principle is the statement of the 'basic affection' and its subsequent exploitation by continuous expansion".* This 'basic affection' may be a ground bass with its harmonies, a fugue subject, an aria or concerto ritornello, or a tiny figure that pervades the texture of a dance movement or contrapuntal study. Bach's well-known two-part invention in C major affords a compact illustration. The 'exploitation' of the affection was not, of course, necessarily as strict and exhaustive as this. Handel's Allemande from his first harpsichord suite shows a somewhat similar figure receiving broader treatment in the context of a dance movement. Sometimes it is possible to compare two composers' treatment of the same theme. Johann

* Lang, *Music in Western Civilization*, p. 443.

Caspar Ferdinand Fischer's E major fugue in his *Ariadne Musica** (1715) has the same subject as Bach's 9th fugue in the second book of *The Well-tempered Klavier*. The comparison recalls Tovey's remark: "A theme belongs to the man who knows how to use it."

The selection of the musical formula which is the basic affection of a piece may often have been determined by extra-musical considerations; the theorist Chabanon justified this when he wrote that "music cannot reproduce images for the ear but must always fall back on metaphors contrived by the intelligence". Originality in the invention of themes was not expected: the interest lay in the unfolding and elaboration of the basic material and the composer's individual method of treatment. The figures were regarded as already existing. Composers had fundamentally the same attitude to the notion of 'artistic inspiration' as Locke had to the sources of human knowledge: "All those sublime thoughts which tower above the clouds and reach as high as heaven itself, take their rise and footing here; in all that great extent wherein the mind wanders in those remote speculations it may seem to be elevated with, it stirs not one jot beyond those ideas which sense and reflection have offered for its contemplation."†

During the first quarter of the seventeenth century English instrumental music was second to none. Its excellence was recognized in northern Europe: Roger North [1653–1734] wrote that "the foreigners themselves use to owne that the English in the instrumentall and the Italian in the vocal musick excelled". The influence of English keyboardists on German organ music has already been mentioned; composers such as William Brade [1560–1630] and Thomas Simpson [fl. 1600], most of whose lives were spent in north Germany and Scandinavia, where all their chief works were published, were no less influential in the development of ensemble music. But this supremacy was short-lived: the golden age of keyboard music did not long outlast that of the madrigal. Tomkins was the last great master in both fields. Only in ensemble music did a strong native tradition survive. Composers continued to write polyphonic fantasias and In Nomines up to the Restoration period, the last being those of the twenty-one-year-old Purcell.

* *H.A.M.*, 247.

† Locke, *Essay concerning Human Understanding*, II, i, 24.

The newer instrumental styles of France and Italy made little headway except in Court circles; even in Charles II's time, to quote North again, "the French manner of Instrumental musick did not gather so fast as to make a revolution all at once, but during the greatest part of the King's reign, the old musick was used in the countrys and in many meetings and societys in London".

Whereas Elizabethan chamber music usually employed a consort of viols (the 'broken' consort of viols, wind, and plucked-string instruments being restricted to theatrical or outdoor performances), Jacobean composers preferred to mix violins and viols and to support them with a continuo instrument. Dowland's *Lachrimae* pavans (1604) are written for this new type of 'broken' consort. The continuo instrument could be a lute (as in *Lachrimae*) or harp, but the later Jacobeans and most of the mid-century ensemble composers preferred the chamber organ, except in dances for which the organ was inherently unsuitable. As far as England was concerned, the harpsichord did not become a normal continuo instrument for chamber ensembles before 1680. Some of the Jacobean and Caroline fantasias have the continuo fully written: others merely provide a bass line.

William Lawes, John Jenkins [1592–1678], and Matthew Locke were the most important ensemble composers of the mid-century. Lawes's compositions fall into three main groups: (i) fantasias, pavanes, and In Nomines for five and six parts, designed to cater for the conservative tastes of music-lovers outside the immediate influence of Court society; (ii) fantasias for various combinations from three to seven parts, all with elaborate harp or organ continuo, to please the more 'up-to date' chamber players; (iii) *The Royal Consort*, a collection of sixty-six dances grouped in six suites, which were originally used for Court dancing, first scored for two violins, two bass viols, and two theorboes, but later arranged for the trio sonata ensemble of two violins, bass viol, and continuo. With the exception of the dances, Lawes's works are characterized by frequent large melodic leaps and the typically English use of 'free' dissonance in false relations and abrupt chord changes (cf. Chapter 3, p. 426).

Jenkins, the most prolific English instrumental composer of the century and, as North, his pupil, confirms, regarded as 'the mirrour and wonder of his age', exhibits even greater stylistic variety in his works than does Lawes, reflecting the many changes in taste and society that occurred during his long life. From his first youth he was encouraged by powerful patrons, who probably recommended him to Charles I (himself a proficient viol-player and a pupil of Coperario), whom he served as Court musician from 1625 to 1640. During the Puritan interregnum he had the good fortune to find refuge and employment in country houses far from the capital. Shortly after the Restoration he joined the Court musicians of Charles II. His last years were spent at Kimberley, Norfolk, in the house of the music-loving Wodehouse family. Over a hundred of his fantasias survive, of which those for four parts were nearly all written during the earlier years of Charles I's reign. Their polyphony is as intricate as Lawes's and seems even more complicated by reason of their longer melodic lines. A group of three-part fantasias in the same style written over twenty years later suggests that there was still much demand for this sort of music, though several five- and six-part fantasias and pavanes dating from the same period show the partial influence of newer styles in more homophonic textures and shorter simpler themes. One of these, *The Bell Pavin* for six parts, depicting the mingled evening chimes of Oxford, was perhaps his most famous piece. The largest section of his output consists of several hundred dance suites, the majority dating from the Restoration period; designed for various combinations of two, three, and four instruments (the favourite being the trio sonata ensemble), they contain anything from two to fifteen movements, such as ayres (bipartite pieces in French style), pavanes, allemandes, courantes, sarabandes, and gigues. Pavanes are used as introductory movements (they had long ceased to be danced to), sometimes being replaced by fantasias. Another group of fantasias for trio sonata ensemble composed when Jenkins was over seventy employs forms of short sections reminiscent of the Italian canzona and early sonata. Also dating from the same period are works for one or two bass viols with continuo which demand the utmost skill and dexterity. The bass viol had become a popular solo instrument towards the middle of the century: the *Division-Violist* (1659) of Christopher Simpson [d. 1669] not only provides instruction for beginners, but includes several sets of 'divisions upon a ground' using techniques for improvisation described a century earlier by the Spaniard Ortiz (p. 348) and kept alive in England long after their virtual disappearance elsewhere.

Matthew Locke's 'fantasias' are really four-movement works based on the plan of some of Jenkins's suites. Each consists of a fantasia in polyphonic style, followed by a courante, ayre, and sarabande. The influence of the trio sonatas is evident in the fantasia motifs (up-beat patterns often closely resembling the fugal themes of Vitali) and in the attempt to unify several works by following the sarabande with a short section (often only six to eight bars) which recalls the style of the opening contrapuntal movement. On the other hand, the imitative counterpoint of the fantasia style appears in many of the dance movements. Some works having the same basic plan are named 'consorts': *The Broken Consort*, like Lawes's *Royal Consort*, is a collection of six suites. All Locke's instrumental works exhibit the same harmonic freedom and daring found in his dramatic music.

Purcell wrote nearly all his chamber music during his early twenties. Though the harmonic writing of his fantasias, pavanes, and In Nomines is influenced by that of Locke, all preserve the older contrapuntal style without admixture of dance elements. Their characteristic intensity of expression is combined with complete mastery of the most varied devices of counterpoint. Though he described the first of his two sets of trio sonatas (published in 1683 and 1697) as "a just imitation of the most famed Italian masters" intended "to bring the seriousness and gravity of that sort of Musick into vogue, and reputation among our countrymen", their instrumental style retains considerable traces of the older fantasia polyphony. He studied Vitali's sonatas closely, yet in neither set is he content merely to 'imitate': while he often followed Vitali in the order of the movements, he frequently has five or six instead of the usual Italian four. Some sonatas have their movements arranged in an order utterly unlike the Italian: the fifth of the first set has three slow movements flanked by two quick ones. The sixth sonata of the second set is a chaconne with variations. In the title-page of the first set Purcell designates the continuo instrument as organ or harpsichord.

Thurston Dart has recently demonstrated that the organ is the ideal continuo for the apparently very insufficient figured-bass provided: "simple and slow-moving organ chords form a perfect background for the elaborate harmonies and intricate counterpoints of the strings. It allows the bass viol to take leave of the thorough-bass from time to time, in order to play an independent inner part above it."* Thus Purcell links the older organ continuo style of the later Jacobean fantasia to the newer style of the Italian 'sonata da chiesa'.

Purcell, like Locke, whom he succeeded in 1677 as Court Composer in Ordinary for the Violin, was required to produce dance music for the King's entertainments; all that survives are three Overtures and a suite for strings and continuo which mingle French rhythms with typically Purcellian harmonic and contrapuntal treatment. Large-scale instrumental music in seventeenth-century England existed only in connection with drama or choral music: some of Purcell's best instrumental writing is to be found in the dances and interludes of *The Fairy Queen* and *King Arthur* and in the introductory symphonies to his anthems.

The increasing number of public concerts, the success of the semi-operas, and the Royal patronage of the newer types of instrumental music brought about the gradual eclipse of the older instruments and the chamber music in which they were employed. Thomas Mace deplored their loss and the changing taste in his *Musick's Monument* (1676): "Very little of This so eminent Musick (for viols) do we hear of in These Times, the Lesz the Greater Pity. Then again, we had all Those Choice Consorts, to Equally-Seized Instruments (Rare Chests of Viols) and as Equally Performed: For we would never allow Any Performer to Over-top, or Out-cry another by loud play; but our Great Care was, to have all the Parts Equally Heard; by which means, though we had but sometimes indifferent, or mean Hands to Perform with; yet This Caution made the Musick Lovely, and Very Contentive. But now the Modes and Fashions have cry'd These Things down, and set up a Great Idol in Their Room; observe with what a Wonderful Swiftnesz They now run over Their Brave New Ayres; and with what High-Prized Noise; viz. 10, or 20 violins, etc. to a Some-Single Soul'd Ayre; it may be of two or three Parts, or some Coranto . . . and such like Stuff; seldom any other; which is rather fit to make a Man's Ear Glow, and Fill his Brain full of Frisks, than to Season, and

* Thurston Dart, 'Purcell's Chamber Music'. *Proceedings of the Royal Musical Association*, Session 85.

Sober his Mind, or Elevate his Affection to Goodness." Such complaints are always made when the new supplants the old. The abandonment of the viol consort music would not have mattered at all if Purcell's lead had been followed, tempering the fashion for all things Italian by the continuation of a strong native tradition. The tragedy in the state of affairs described by Mace lay in the virtual cessation after Purcell of anything characteristically English in the instrumental music written by English composers.* Keyboard music had languished after the great Jacobeans: Blow and Purcell produced some attractive trifles, Arne in the following century a few sonatas in the manner of *style galant.* Thomas Roseingrave [1688 – 1766] was the only Englishman who tried to maintain a 'national' approach; his keyboard works, while showing the influence of his friend Domenico Scarlatti, still preserved the typical freedom in dissonance treatment that had marked English music for over a century. His contemporaries' lack of appreciation is summed up in Burney's judgement: "harsh ungrateful harmony, and extravagant and licentious modulations". Most English composers in the eighteenth century adopted an Italianate style: "rightly recognizing the greatness of Handel's work, they mistakenly set themselves to use it as their model and to imitate its style and character. Thus they fell between two stools, for they failed to achieve success in the Handelian manner, and they warped their own natural gifts."† Even the best works of the period, such as the symphonies of William Boyce [1711 – 1799] and the violin sonatas of Joseph Gibbs [1699–1788], though competent, polished, and charming, provided nothing of importance for the future development of English music. By the middle of the century, music for the average educated Englishman had become, as Burney defined it, "an innocent luxury, unnecessary, indeed to our existence, but a great improvement and gratification of the sense of hearing . . . a manufacture in Italy, that feeds and enriches a large portion of the people; and it is no more disgraceful to a mercantile country to import it than wine, tea, or any other production of remote parts of the globe".‡

* The corresponding situation in English vocal music did not develop so quickly by reason of the strongly conservative trend in Anglican church music, and thus lies outside the scope of this volume.

† E. E. Fellowes, *English Cathedral Music*, p. 179.

‡ *A General History of Music* (1776), Preface to Vol. I.

The contrast between French and Italian styles of instrumental music (which reflects that between *tragèdie-lyrique* and opera) is of fundamental importance for later baroque music. Each style had its own tradition of performance (not indicated in the written appearance of the music) concerning methods of string bowing, phasing, details of tempi, ornamentation, and alterations or departures from the notated rhythm, the last being especially important in French music. These matters are far too complicated to be discussed here:* suffice to say generally that the French style was more 'mannered' and had a stylized system of ornamentation, whereas the Italian was less sophisticated and added freely extemporized ornamentation to slow movements. A few quotations will serve to show how marked from the listener's standpoint were the general differences between the two.

The Abbé François Raguenet [1660–1722], in his *Parallèle des Italiens et des Français* (1702), compared French music unfavourably with Italian: "As the Italians are naturally much more brisk than the French, so are they more sensible of the passions and consequently express them more lively in all their productions. If a storm or rage is to be described in a symphony, their notes give us so natural an idea of it that our souls can hardly receive a stronger impression from the reality than they do from the description; everything is so brisk and piercing, so impetuous and affecting, that the imagination, the senses, the soul, and the body itself are all betrayed into a general transport; it is impossible not to be borne down with the rapidity of these movements. A symphony of furies shakes the soul; it undermines and overthrows it in spite of all its care; the artist himself, whilst he is performing it, is seized with an unavoidable agony; he tortures his violin; he racks his body; he is no longer master of himself, but is agitated like one possessed with an irresistible motion.

"If, on the other side, the symphony is to express a calm and tranquillity, which requires a quite different style, they however execute it with an equal success. Here the notes descend so low that the soul is swallowed with them in the profound abyss. Every string of the bow is of an infinite length, lingering on a dying sound which decays gradually till at last it absolutely expires. Their symphonies of sleep insensibly steal the soul from

* Cf. Thurston Dart, *The Interpretation of Music* (Hutchinson's University Library), for an admirable summary of the chief points involved.

the body and so suspend its faculties and operations that, being bound up, as it were, in the harmony that entirely possesses and enchants it, it's as dead to everything else as if all its powers were captivated by a real sleep. . . . Their violins are mounted with strings much larger than ours; their bows are longer, and they can make their instruments sound as loud again as we do ours. The first time I heard our band in the Opéra after my return out of Italy, my ears had been so used to the loudness of the Italian violins that I thought ours had all been bridled. . . . Their bass viols are as large again as the French, and all ours put together don't sound so loud in our operas as two or three of those basses do in Italy."*

Raguenet was answered three years later by Jean Laurent le Cerf de la Viéville, Lord of Freueuse, in his *Comparison de la musique italienne et de la musique française* (1705), written in the form of dialogues. The following observations occur in the sixth dialogue in the section entitled "Treatise on good taste":

"I reduce the merit of a player upon an instrument to three things: exactness (*netteté*), delicacy, getting the most out of his instrument . . . exactness is the principal quality, especially for the players of instruments which are played directly by the fingers, without a bow. Count that of five hundred players of the lute, the harpsichord, etc., there will not be one who succeeds in playing as exactly (*nettement*) as one has the right to ask. And without exactness, what is a piece for the lute or the harpsichord? A noise, a jangling of harmonies in which one understands nothing. I would sooner listen to a hurdy-gurdy. After this precious exactness comes delicacy. It is in instruments what neatness (*propreté*) is in singing. . . . Last, to get the most out of the instrument. It is certainly necessary that an instrument should sound (*parle*), and it is true that to make it sound well is an art and a most important talent, but let us not lose sight of the capital maxim, the golden mean. In truth, your Italians carry too far a certain desire to elicit sound from their instruments. My intelligence, my heart, my ears tell me, all at once, that they produce a sound excessively shrill and violent. I am always afraid that the first stroke of the bow will make the violin fly into splinters, they use so much pressure. Besides, you comprehend that the sovereign perfection of an instrumentalist

* From the eighteenth-century translation in Strunk, *Source Readings in Music History*, pp. 478, 486.

would be to ally the three qualities and . . . to combine them in equal proportions. But I think I have observed that they never have all three in equal measure."*

The most important feature of instrumental music of the later baroque, a fully-organized system of tonality, which first appeared in the Neapolitan opera and the instrumental works of the later Bologna composers (p. 533), has already been surveyed in Chapters 3 and 4; we need only consider now its consequences in instrumental composition, which were:

(i) increased range of modulation, because since all the harmonies used (including discords and so-called chromatic chords) were now fully related to a tonic triad and key, so too the degrees of relation of all neighbouring keys were established according to the number of notes each related key had in common with the main key;
(ii) longer movements, because the interior structure of a movement could be organized on a modulatory plan far wider than that of earlier compositions;
(iii) far more elaborate counterpoint by reason of the firm harmonic basis now provided;
(iv) an increasing tendency to unify a movement by employing the same themes, patterns and figuration throughout.

A cadence was now more than ever before a central point in the musical organization, and therefore it had to be approached in a manner that made it sound important and inevitable. A favourite way of achieving this was the sequence: a harmonic,

* Strunk, op. cit., pp. 502-3.

melodic, and rhythmic formula repeated over and over again (generally on a descending bass) till the cadence was reached. Passages like Ex. 43 (p. 550) are typical of late baroque music.

The implications of fully systematized tonality were first realized in the concerto compositions of Archangelo Corelli [1653–1713] and his contemporaries. His concerti grossi (heard in Rome as early as 1682, but not published till 1714) exploit the contrast of smaller and larger instrumental groups within a movement that had been used previously by Gabrieli and the later Venetian composers, particularly Legrenzi. Corelli's treatment differs fundamentally from that of his predecessors, for whereas they had merely detached small groups from a main orchestral body from time to time to vary the texture, he opposes a fixed 'concertino' string trio of two violins and 'cello to a 'ripieno' string band, each group having its own continuo. He makes little or no difference between the two groups either of material or treatment: the soli tutti contrast is his chief concern. He was not an innovator in formal organization, usually following the patterns of the earlier Bolognese church and chamber sonatas in the number and order of the movements: thus the *Concerti da chiesa*, nos. 1–8, have normally five movements (occasionally supplemented by brief linking movements) alternating slow and quick tempi; the *Concerti da camera*, nos. 9–12, consist of a prelude in contrapuntal style and three dances, with either brief links or contrapuntal movements between the dances. In matters of style, however, his works were of fundamental importance for the subsequent development of Italian baroque music. His allegros are characterized by rapid changes of harmony underlining the metrical structure, repeated notes, widely ranging themes, more idiomatic violin writing than any previous composer had used, and above all a mechanically progressive rhythm which, in conjunction with the sequential progressions and strictly organized harmonies mentioned above, gives an impression of inevitable development and relentless progress. In contrapuntal adagios he produces an effect of diversity of parts without thickening the texture by continually crossing the lines of the two violin parts, the apparent polyphonic complexity being heightened by chains of suspensions and seventh chords. His fugues achieve a similar effect by frequent entries of the subject in a texture which shifts rapidly from two- to three- or four-part counterpoint.

Giuseppe Torelli [1658 – 1709], Corelli's fellow-student at Bologna, distinguished three types of concerto composition: (i) concertos for string orchestra without the concertino-ripieno division, the title referring to the instrumental style; (ii) concerti grossi; (iii) concertos for one or two solo violins and string orchestra. After his first essays in the new style, he dropped the initial slow movement of the Bolognese sonata forms and established the typical three-movement form of quick-slow-quick (very like that of the opera sinfonia) used by all later Italian composers. He distinguished between concertino and ripieno by giving the former virtuoso figuration. In the first movements (and occasionally in the finales) he repeated the opening orchestral tutti in rondo-fashion, though in different keys and with slight variations. This ritornello form* (so named because the return of the tutti was called a ritornello) closely resembles the basic ABA shape of the *da capo* aria in its broad aspects, though each 'section' may contain more repeats (whether partial or complete) of the ritornello than occur in the normal aria. Antonio Vivaldi [1676–1741], the greatest Italian master of the concerto, gave the ritornello an even greater importance in the formal design (especially in his solo concertos), often breaking into the solo sections with a partial repetition of its material. Moreover, he made an important innovation by frequently giving the solo new material which had not appeared in the ritornello. Many of his concertos have titles and programmes: the best-known is the group entitled *Le Stagione* ("The Seasons"), in which each of the four concertos is preceded by a sonnet describing the events and setting depicted. The imitations of birds and other onomatopoeic effects are confined to the solo passages, the formal structure of the concerto being strictly maintained. Vivaldi's themes were much admired by his contemporaries for their simplicity and vigour: their strong rhythmic patterns commencing on an upbeat were imitated by all the leading composers of the day, including Bach and Handel.

Alessandro Scarlatti's concertos closely resemble those of Torelli in their general style while looking back to the earlier Bolognese sonatas in form and number of movements. In his later opera sinfonias, Scarlatti incorporated many elements of the concerto style:† the brilliant violin figuration, the up-beat

* Cf. *H.A.M.*, 246, for an example.

† Cf. *H.A.M.*, 259 and 260, for a comparison of a concerto and *Sinfonia avanti l'opera* by Scarlatti.

rhythmic patterns, and occasional if brief opposition of contrasted instrumental groups. Public performances of concertos encouraged concert repeats of opera sinfonias. About 1730 Pietro Locatelli [1693–1764] and Gian Battista Sammartini [1700/1 – 1775] began composing sinfonias intended purely for concert performance: these had the usual allegro-adagio-allegro form, but the individual movements tended to be longer than those of the operatic sinfonia. Such movements contained much important subsidiary material which contrasted strongly with the themes of the ritornello. This type of sinfonia in the hands of later composers led ultimately to the classical symphony (Part III).

In his trio sonatas, Corelli established the four-movement structure used by all Italian composers of the late baroque. His works in this form are noteworthy not only for their rich 'harmonic' counterpoint, but also for the fact that in them the bass instrument participates fully in the contrapuntal texture. While preserving the main differences between the church and chamber sonata, he blended elements of both. Apart from the few that employ the techniques of the variation canzona or the five short movements characteristic of his predecessors, his church sonatas begin with a contrapuntal slow movement that has two imitative parts over a bass moving regularly in quavers; this is followed by an allegro in fugal style and two dance movements, an adagio in stylized sarabande rhythm, and a gigue. The chamber sonatas have a closely knit contrapuntal prelude and two or three largely homophonic dances. In his twelve solo sonatas, six church and six chamber sonatas, the same characteristics are evident,* but the violin is treated in a far more virtuoso style. Many of the adagios in the solo sonatas provide only a simple melodic line for the violin, the player being expected to embellish this according to the Italian conventions of 'gracing' (e.g. *H.A.M.*, 252, for a contemporary written version of such ornamentation). These observations apply equally to the sonatas of Corelli's contemporaries, of whom the chief were Felice Evaristo dall'Abaco [1675–1742], whose trios are far more varied in manner and whose counterpoint is often much more interesting than Corelli's,† Tommaso Vitali [1663 – 1745], son of G. B. Vitali and the last member of the Bologna school, F. Geminiani [1687-1762], and P. Locatelli [1695-1764].

* E.g. *H.A.M.*, 253.
† E.g. *H.A.M.*, 269.

The solo sonatas of Francesco Veracini [1690-1768] represent the end of the true baroque form: they not only virtually abolish the distinction between church and chamber sonata, but include movements in *da capo* aria, ritornello, and French overture forms. Veracini's occasional use of *style galant* bears witness to the continuing influence of the opera on the development of instrumental music. In the trio sonatas of Pergolesi and the solo sonatas of Giuseppe Tartini [1692–1770] this influence appears even more strongly, for the instrumental adaptation of *da capo* aria led to a new type of opening movement which repeats the opening section in the original key. The resulting structure is one of many that led to the classical sonata form at the end of the century.

Italian keyboard music has little of interest or importance after Frescobaldi (save in the works of Bernardo Pasquini [1637-1710], who composed harpsichord sonatas modelled on the forms of the violin sonata) till Domenico Scarlatti [1685–1757], son of Alessandro. Most of his 544 sonatas (really single movements) were written for his employer, Princess Maria Barbara of Portugal, whose service he entered in 1729 when she was betrothed to the Spanish Infante Ferdinand (later Ferdinand VI [1746-1759]) and in which he remained, living in Spain for the rest of his life. Consequently, apart from the thirty published in 1738 under the title *Esercizi per Gravicembalo*, the majority of these pieces were virtually unknown (save for a few MS. collections made by wealthy admirers) till they were published in a complete edition* at the beginning of the present century. The majority have a basic bipartite form whose first section modulates from tonic to dominant with the reverse modulation in the second part, but within this general structure the organization of the material varies considerably. Often the modulation is marked by new material which sometimes contrasts dramatically with the main theme. The second section may begin with a repeat of the main theme in the dominant, or introduce entirely new material in another key which may displace repeats of previous material, or may 'develop' the material of the first section, ending with a condensed reprise of the opening. This bipartite structure and its interior variants derive from the new

* By Alessandro Longo. This, still the only complete edition, contains many editorial additions and inaccuracies, some of which are listed in *Domenico Scarlatti*, by Ralph Kirkpatrick.

aria forms of the Neapolitan *opera buffa*.* Recent research has demonstrated that many of Scarlatti's 'sonatas' were originally paired together to make a two-movement composition, such as occur in the keyboard works of the opera composers, Giuseppe Paganelli [1710–1765], Giovanni Rutini [1730–1797], and Galuppi. These men followed Scarlatti's lead in adopting the simple harmonic basis of the *buffa* aria and *stile galante*, which relied mainly on the primary triads of tonic, dominant, and subdominant, but whereas their harmonic treatment sounds often perfunctory and conventional, Scarlatti's is marked by a highly individual approach, seen in the contraction of conventional cadence formulas, the use of multiple acciaccaturas (which often obscure the fundamental chord completely), unorthodox resolutions of sevenths, and unexpected modulations. His brilliant keyboard writing is unparalleled in its frequent crossing of the hands, the wide skips from one end of the keyboard to the other, the elaborate figuration (often derived from the violin concerto style), and the dazzling use of staccato, as also in its occasional imitations or suggestions of the sounds of guitar, bells, trumpet, and bagpipes. His textures are correspondingly varied: melodies with Alberti bass or other figuration accompaniments, melody and bass in octaves, polyphony more often implied than actually present, and frequent use of broken-chord patterns involving rapid large leaps that require hand and finger movements unknown to previous players.

Although French composers acknowledged the importance of Italian music in the late baroque and yielded in some measure to its influence, their strong native tradition preserved them from being dominated by it. Since the musical stage in both France and Italy provided the chief source of new developments, the considerable differences between *tragèdie-lyrique* and opera of vocal style, conceptions of the dance, and performance had their counterpart in instrumental music. Only two important composers, Jean Aubert [d. 1753] and Jean-Marie Leclair [1697-1764], wrote concertos, and, while they modelled their allegros on those of Vivaldi, their slow movements have much in common with the form and style of the instrumental adaptations of the *air tendre*. The term 'concert' in French music of this period was never used as the equivalent of 'concerto', but always as implying

* A typical example is the duet 'Lo conosco' from Pergolesi's *La serva padrona*, *H.A.M.*, 287.

chamber music: Aubert's *Concerts de symphonie* (1630) are trio sonatas. Moreover, the adoption of *style galant* involved abandoning the broad, formal conceptions of Lully and his followers for shorter phrases and profuse ornamentation, characteristics inimical to any fundamental adoption of Italian forms. The main effects of French interest in Italian music appear in the general adoption of fully-organized tonality and in the works of a small but distinguished group of Parisian composers who wrote in both styles, sometimes in contrasted movements within a work, or, less often, blending elements of both in a single movement.

Marin Marais [1656-1728], a pupil of Lully, is a typically ambivalent composer of this group. His chief works, the accompanied suites for viola da gamba (which continued to be a popular solo instrument in France for longer than elsewhere), are generally conservative save for their sprightly melodies and delicate ornaments, yet he was one of the first French composers to publish works for the trio sonata ensemble. Though the medium of his *Pièces en trio* (1692) is Italian, their style has little in common with that of the sonata; the descriptive titles and programmes reveal their fundamentally national cast. The first composer to attempt to meet the Italians on their own ground was François Couperin [1668–1733]. His seven sonatas written in 1692 and 1695 adopt the basic four-movement plan of the sonata da chiesa and imitate Corelli's contrapuntal style for the first and second movements. But neither form nor style are slavishly followed: No. 3, *La Visionnaire*, follows the two opening movements with a canzona, gigue, and double fugue; No. 7, *La Sultane*, exceptional in requiring two violas da gamba in addition to the normal violins and continuo, has six movements, of which the third is an *air tendre*. In all sonatas the passages and sections employing chromatic harmony are far richer than anything to be found in Corelli, since they preserve something of the English freedom of dissonance as inherited by the French lutenists and developed anew by the clavecinists and organists. When Couperin published these works in 1726, he renamed four, added to each of these a set of dances, and entitled the group *Les Nations*: thus each work consists of a sonata da camera plus a French suite. The general stylistic contrast implied by this division is not strictly followed, however; both French and Italian types of courante and gigue occur and he distinguishes between two kinds of sarabande, *tendre* and *grave*, the second related to the $\frac{3}{2}$ sarabande of the Italian sonata da camera. While Couperin follows the Italians in making the allemande the most extended of the four main dances and in treating it polyphonically, his 'suites' are truly French in their final chaconnes (both in ground-bass and rondeau forms) and ornamentation. The stylistic blending of *Les Nations* is continued in the programme sonatas *Le Parnasse ou L'Apothéose de Corelli* and *L'Apothéose de Lulli* (both published in 1725). In the Lully *Apothéose* (whose Preface enumerates alternative methods of performance, such as two harpsichords or with flutes replacing the violins) forms from the tragèdie lyrique are mingled with the church sonata. It begins with an *Ouverture*, 'Lully in the Elysian fields', followed by theatrical pieces entitled 'The singing shades', 'The Flight of Mercury', 'The descent of Apollo', 'The subterranean noise' of Lully's rivals and 'the tender complaints' of his contemporaries. The Italian style first appears in a canzona, 'Lully taken up to Parnassus' and continued in a largo in which Corelli and the muses welcome Lully, who thanks Apollo in an Italian aria with French ornaments. At Apollo's suggestion of a united French-Italian style, the muses have an *Essai, en forme d'ouverture*, consisting of a section in dotted rhythms followed by a triple-time tune in quaver rhythm. Two *airs légers* follow for the violins unaccompanied (Lully has the tune in the first and Corelli the accompaniment, reversing rôles for the second), leading to a complete sonata da chiesa in the mingled styles. Couperin's two sets of *Concerts royaux* (1722 and 1724) are extended dance suites introduced by a prelude in slow tempo. The mixture of French and Italian styles is emphasized in the title of the second set, *Les Goûts Réünis*, and in its Preface, wherein Couperin observes: "I have always valued works which deserve it without making exceptions of composers or nations." Alternative media of performance are again indicated: either harpsichord, or an ensemble of violin, oboe, viola, and bassoon.

Leclair's trio sonatas represent the complete union of Italian and French chamber-music styles. He keeps the four-movement scheme of the Italian sonata, generally avoids programmes and uses Italian tempo indications, yet his ornamentation and violin-writing are always French. His solo sonatas exhibit a very advanced violin technique (*H.A.M.*, 278) in which multiple stoppings and difficult bowings are combined with highly elaborate ornamentation in some of the most personal and beautiful music of the period. Occasionally he links the movements by common thematic material, thus looking back to the earlier canzona, but the form of his second movements (i.e. of the contrapuntal allegros) has the brief reprise of the main theme that characterizes the later Italian sonata.

Rameau's *Pièces de clavecin en concert* (published 1741, but composed from ten to twenty years earlier) are not trio sonatas: the harpsichord is treated as a virtuoso solo instrument and the other instruments (violin or flute and viola or second violin) are regarded as 'accompanying' the harpsichord. Keyboard works 'with accompaniment' were increasingly common in France from 1730 onwards. The 'accompaniment' was not by any means always subordinate: apart from unison and octave passages, and sections where the harpsichord is supported by harmonic figuration, there are frequent examples of true 'concerted music' where the material is shared equally by all the instruments, as also of the harpsichord accompanying melodic lines in the flute and violin with arpeggios. Rameau afterwards arranged some of these pieces for harpsichord solo, and he orchestrated others as instrumental movements for his operas. *La Livri*, a *tombeau* for Rameau's patron, the Comte de Livri, exists in three versions: concerted, solo harpsichord, and orchestrated as a gavotte in the third act of *Zoroastre*. 'Accompanied' keyboard music of this kind was taken up by the German composers of the mid-eighteenth century. Some of Haydn's 'violin and piano sonatas' are really works of this type, while several of his early piano sonatas exist in an alternative form, with optional violin accompaniments.

French keyboard music, whether for organ or harpsichord, remained a stronghold of the native musical tradition. Couperin's two organ masses,* composed at the age of twenty-one, look back to the older polyphonic tradition in their close, imitative technique and in the frequent use of shifting chromatic progressions only loosely bound to the home key, though these are combined with sections inspired by the style of the ballet dances. Most of the organ music of Couperin's contemporaries, chief of

* Compositions in which solo verses (or, in French parlance, *couplets*) replace alternate sections of the plainsong. The first complete examples were printed in Cavazzoni's *Intravolatura* of 1542 (e.g. *H.A.M.*, 117).

whom were André Raison [*c.* 1650–1719], Louis Marchand [1669–1732], one of the great virtuosi of the period, Jean Dandrieu [*c.* 1682-1738], and Claude Daquin [1694-1772], is similarly liturgical in form, but increasingly coloured by elements of style deriving from opera, by harpsichord ornamentation, and by broken chord patterns. In their publications they give detailed indications of registration (unusual elsewhere in Europe), professing, as Nicolas-Antoine Lebègue [*c.* 1630–1702] wrote in the Preface to his *Premier livre d'orgue* (1676), to give instruction in "the manner of playing the organ on all stops and particularly on those in little use in the provinces . . . to distant organists who are unable to come to hear the diversities that have been discovered on quantities of stops during the last few years". French baroque organs, while conforming generally to the previous description in p. 351, had generally a higher proportion of mixture and mutation stops than the German or Italian organs.*

Couperin's four books of clavecin pieces, grouped into twenty-seven *ordres*, form the culmination of French harpsichord music. An *ordre* is not a strict formal structure, such as the German suite of four basic dances or the sonata da chiesa, but a loose collection of as many as twenty movements in the same key or closely-related keys. Although Couperin used the conventional dance forms, he did not preserve any fixed order of succession, omitting them and adding other forms as he wished. Each movement has a title, and sometimes directions for performance: he was the first composer to write pieces expressly designated for performance on two manuals. In his tutor, *L'Art de toucher le clavecin* (1716), he prescribes a reformed system of fingering, gives detailed instruction on phrasing and style, provides a table of ornaments with explanations (following the custom of all clavecinist-composers from Chambonnières onwards), and concludes with a group of preludes to illustrate the technical and interpretative matters discussed. The range of style, form, and mood in these works is very wide, being surpassed only by that found in Bach's keyboard compositions. While in the shorter pieces† he avoids the long lines of the earlier clavecinists, substituting the short phrases typical of French rococo style and embroidering them with exceedingly intricate and delicate ornamentation (Fig. 2), in the longer dance pieces his quasi-polyphonic

* Cf. Wilfrid Mellers, *François Couperin*, pp. 326-8, for a detailed description of Couperin's organ at St. Gervais and the effects of the various stops.

† E.g. *H.A.M.*, 265.

textures move in broad paragraphs that are obviously influenced by his intimate understanding of Italian music. Allemandes like *La Raphaele* and sarabandes like *L'Unique* (both

'La Garnier', from *Pièces de Clavecin*, Book I, '2nd Ordre' (1713), by François Couperin Le Grand.

from the 8th Ordre) were closely imitated by Bach in his French suites. Many picces employ rondeau form, such as the gigantic *Passecaille* in B minor (8th Ordre) and *Les bergeries* (6th Ordre) which Bach included in Anna Magdalena's *Clavierbüchlein*. Dance forms from the French opera ballet appear frequently (including the *air tendre*), but the *ouverture* only once, in the opening movement, *La Visionnaire*, of the 25th Ordre. The chaconne variations *Les Folies françaises* (13th Ordre) and the group of movements, *Les Fastes de la Grande et Ancienne Ménestrandise* (11th Ordre), are both 'programmes' of satirical character sketches.

Rameau's clavecin music is closely related in style and harmonic orientation to the instrumental movements of his operas. Though most of it was written before he began opera composition, the essential connection between the two is shown by the number afterwards orchestrated and included in the operas. After his first book, he abandoned many of the conventional aspects of clavecin procedure, especially the imitation of lute chords and the profuse ornamentation of Couperin. He employed arpeggio figuration and wide skips much more frequently than previous French composers. Certain movements, such as *Les Cyclopes*, demand a virtuoso technique in advance of anything hitherto written in France, approaching in difficulty the most elaborate of Scarlatti's sonatas.

French and Italian styles and forms bulk large in German instrumental music of the late baroque. Many composers deliberately tried to combine them to produce a characteristic 'German' style; thus Johann Quantz [1697–1773], writing in 1752, could say: "When we know how to select with due discrimination from the musical tastes of various peoples what is best in each, there arises a mixed taste which, without overstepping the bounds of modesty, may very well be called the German taste, not only because the Germans were the first to hit on it, but also because, introduced many years ago in various parts of Germany, it still flourishes there."* The chief ingredients combined by the Germans were the orchestral technique of Lully, Couperin's keyboard style and technique, and the forms and styles of the Italian concerto. Lully's pupil, Georg Muffat [1653–1704], issued two books of orchestral pieces in the French style entitled *Florilegium* (1695 and 1698), with detailed instructions for correct performance. Later, having studied with Corelli in Rome, he issued a third collection of "instrumental concertos, blending the serious and the gay, entitled 'of a more select harmony' because they contain (in the ballet airs) not only the liveliness and grace drawn intact from the Lullian well, but also certain profound and unusual affects of the Italian manner,† various capricious and artful conceits, and alternations of many sorts. . . . These concertos, suited neither to the church (because of the ballet airs and airs of other sorts which they include) nor for dancing (because of other interwoven conceits, now slow and serious, now gay and nimble, and composed only for the express refreshment of the ear), may be performed most appropriately in connection with entertainments . . . and

* Strunk, op. cit., p. 596.

† Cf. *H.A.M.*, 240, for a passacaglia by Muffat amalgamating French and Italian methods.

assemblies of musical amateurs and virtuosi."* Many composers preferred to devote themselves mainly to one style: the Austrians, among whom Fux was the chief, normally followed the Italian closely, while some North Germans, particularly Johann Kaspar Ferdinand Fischer [1670 – 1746] devoted their efforts to the thorough assimilation of the French.† The blending of the two styles and their (sometimes profound) modification by the fundamentally polyphonic German approach to composition can be most easily seen in keyboard works because the keyboard was for the Germans the natural medium of polyphonic expression.

The German treatment of ground-basses affords many illuminating examples of stylistic incorporation and adaptation. Ex. 44a shows three common basses whose implied harmonies were normally used by the Italians as a foundation for variations built on arpeggio and scale patterns (Handel's two G major chaconnes are typical of this style). Ex. 44a is the opening of an organ chaconne by Johann Pachelbel [1633–1706] on the first bass: the basic harmonies implied serve as an accompaniment to a graceful melody which is not heard again till the end; the twenty-two intervening variations add to and embellish the harmonic structure, clothing it in many different textures (mostly polyphonic), each variation being but a link in a continuous expansion that is only equalled in the chaconnes of Dietrich Buxtehude [1637–1707] and J. S. Bach. Fischer's treatment of the second bass is characteristically decorated in the French manner (Ex. 44c) and modifies the bass (a device found in Couperin's chaconnes) by diminution in the later variations, yet the patterned motifs of the contrapuntal variations and the chromatic progressions in variations 6 and 8 are nearer to Froberger's adaptations of French technique than to the rococo style of the later clavecinists. Pachelbel's D major chaconne on a modified version of the third bass (Ex. 44d)‡ uses the melody, harmony, and bass of its opening as material for variations, some of which are typically Italian in their harmonic figuration, while others resemble the German chorale variations of the mid-seventeenth century.

* Strunk, op. cit., p. 449.

† Cf. *H.A.M.*, 248, a suite by Fischer.

‡ The complete works are readily available in modern editions: both Pachelbel's chaconnes in the edition of his organ works, published by Bährenreiter, and Fischer's in *Alte Meister des Clavier*, published by Peter.

EX.44

(a) Chaconne Ground basses:

(b) Organ chaconne in F minor J. PACHELBEL

(c) Harpsichord chaconne in G J.K.F. FISCHER

(d) Organ chaconne in D J. PACHELBEL

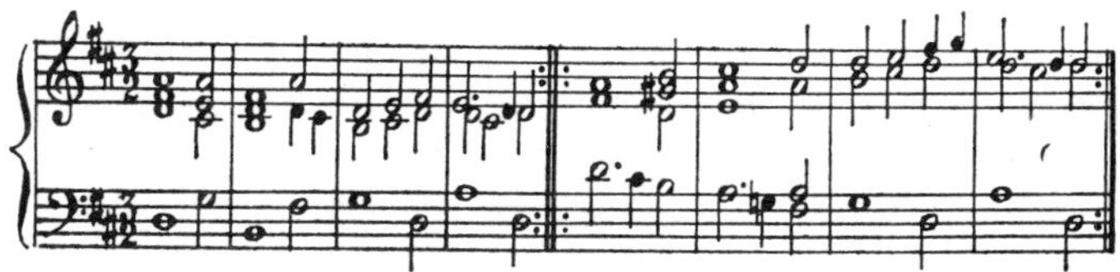

Similar partial adoption of foreign styles appear in the works of Johann Kuhnau [1660–1722], whose harpsichord sonatas employ the forms of the sonata da chiesa, but whose programme sonatas, based on Biblical incidents (e.g. *H.A.M.*, 261), have very little in them that is French, apart from the use of titles and a few French dances. Buxtehude's harpsichord suites follow Froberger's order of movements and also his combination of dance rhythms with 'patterned' variations, while using French ornamentation and lute-style broken chords. Telemann's *Three Dozen Fantasias* include twelve each in Italian and French style, and another twelve in 'mixed' German style. Telemann's chamber music is nearly all written in *style galant*, though the German conception of this was rather more affected and sentimental than the French. Fux, Christoph Graupner [1683–1760], whose music was much admired by Bach, and the Hamburg organist, Jan Reinken [1623–1722], all wrote trio sonatas in the forms of Corelli, but their strict fugal (often canonic) counterpoint was alien to a truly Italian style.

Buxtehude, Pachebel, and Georg Böhm were the three chief organ composers of the generation immediately preceding Bach. Buxtehude's treatment of the instrument displays originality of a very high order. He was one of the first composers to demand virtuoso technique on the pedals, as may be seen in his toccatas (e.g. *H.A.M.*, 234). In compositions based on chorale melodies, he combined the older variation form with the dance suite, and treated the chorale fantasia very rhapsodically. Pachelbel continued to write counterpoints against a chorale canto fermo while experimenting with patterned variations. Böhm introduced French ornaments and lute-style broken chords. Both he and Buxtehude developed the new chorale prelude in which the melody was heard complete in the treble, often profusely ornamented, accompanied by harmonic patterns or quasi-contrapuntal writing.

Handel's instrumental music is basically Italian, though it includes movements written in French style. His twelve concerti grossi for strings (op. 6) have few movements in the Vivaldi form: at least one movement in each employs Torelli's 'orchestra concerto' form, while those that have the Corelli trio concertino are decidedly conservative in manner. The astonishing variety of forms (including French overture, hornpipe, and *da capa* aria) and outstanding melodic appeal make these works some of the greatest in this genre. The six concertos for woodwind and strings (op. 3) exhibit the same general characteristics (several show marked resemblance to some of his trio sonatas, even sharing common material) as do the organ concertos, though these are marked by an improvisatory character which even extends to leaving entire movements to be extemporized by the soloist. On the other hand, the *al fresco* style of the *Water Music* and *Royal Fireworks Music* shows Handel responding to the English musical situation in a strong individual style analogous to that of the choral writing in his oratorios.

Most of his trios have a basic church-sonata structure, but vary greatly in the number of movements and in additional dances: a few (e.g. op. 5, no. 2) consist of a French overture and suite. His keyboard music (which is unjustly neglected today) includes six 'grand fugues' which are masterpieces of the Italian fugal style, eight suites, chaconnes, and sonatas in concerto forms. The suites are as formally varied as the concertos of op. 12 no. 7, for example, opens with a French overture, continues with the four dances of the sonata da camera, and concludes with a passacaglia; no. 6 has a French prelude and Italian largo, a double fugue, and gigue. Handel assumes that the player knows the different style and the correct methods of ornamentation: the full transcription of ornamental signs into musical notation for the aria of the third suite (Ex. 45a) is exceptional and highly personal in its improvisatory style. Bach's transcription for keyboard of the slow movement from Marcello's oboe concerto shows a more systematic approach to the

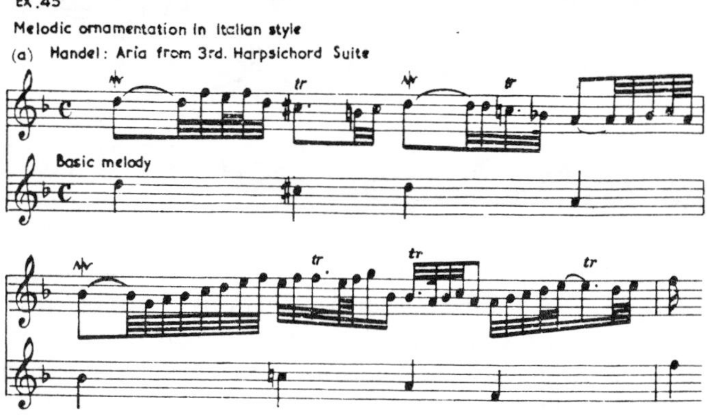

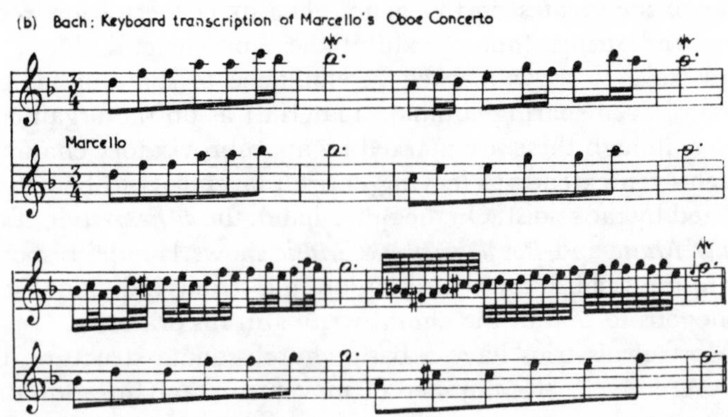

technique of gracing an Italian adagio. The cumulative use of rhythmic division suggested by these bars (Ex. 45b) appears at its height in the second movement of Bach's Italian Concerto, where the subtle thrust and balance of the ornamentation strengthens the long lines of the melody in a manner that, while superficially Italian, is more the result of German habits of melodic decoration learnt in the organ treatment of chorales. The free method of varying a chorale by altering the entire metrical structure of the original tune (as in Ex. 46) permits a greater scope and a broader design than the superimposition of ornaments on a metrically fixed melodic skeleton.

EX. 46
Melodic ornamentation in Bach's chorale prelude: Nun komm', der Heiden Heiland.

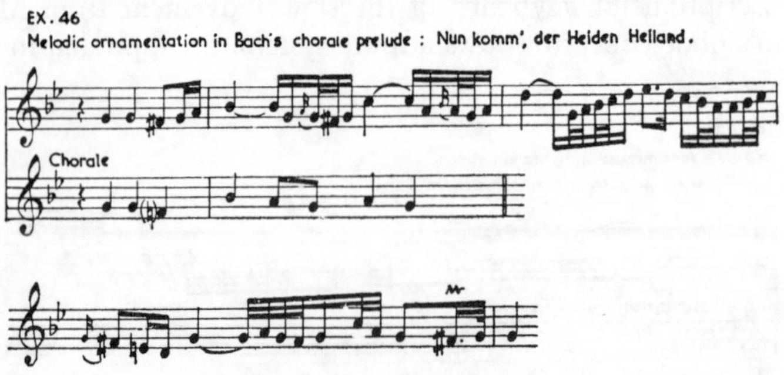

Bach's chorale preludes afford examples of all the forms previously mentioned. He transformed them by choosing the style and texture best suited to the poem to which the chorale melody was originally set. There are many places in his chorale forms (particularly in the preludes) where the harmony or counterpoint cannot be fully understood without reference to the poetical text. In the broad canto fermo pieces, such as *Come, Holy Ghost* from the *Eighteen Chorale Preludes*, he obtains large forms partly by enriching the counterpoint by elements from the concerto style, but mainly by harmonic and contrapuntal textures far richer than those of his contemporaries. This is partly due to the way in which he adds notes which are not part of the fundamental harmony of each beat, but nevertheless blend rather than clash with it, but still more it is due to the nature of his melodic (and therefore contrapuntal) lines, which often imply a two-part or three-part framework. Ex. 47 (a comparatively simple example) shows how a melody can be resolved into two components. When such melodic writing occurs in the individual lines of a fugue the effect is overwhelming in its complexity and yet always immediately compelling. In writing of this sort Bach is unequalled anywhere. "His melodies have the maximum of linear energy, but are at the same time saturated with harmonic implications. His harmonies have the vertical energy of logical chord progressions, but are at the same time linear in all their voices. Hence, whenever Bach writes harmonically the parts also move independently, and whenever he writes polyphonically the parts move also in tonal harmony."*

As a young man Bach acquired his knowledge of French and Italian styles by making copies of other men's compositions and then imitating them. Examples of the first are the early keyboard arrangements of Reinken's trio sonatas and the transcriptions of Vivaldi's and Marcello's concertos for harpsichord; the experience thus gained bore fruit first in such works as the organ fugues on themes by Corelli and Legrenzi, leading later to the better-known orchestra and keyboard suites in French style, the keyboard partitas, containing both French and Italian forms, and the *Concerto in the Italian manner* for harpsichord. The *Brandenburg Concertos* employ the forms of Vivaldi, but are transformed by the German penchant for wind instruments and the fundamentally German contrapuntal approach. In the harpsichord and violin concertos, the sonatas for flute and violin with harpsichord, and the solo sonatas and suites for violin and 'cello, Bach carried the polyphonic instrumental tradition to its conclusion, enriching it always with stylistic elements drawn from French and Italian sources. In organ music he drew little on

* Manfred Bukofzer, *Music in the Baroque Era*, p. 303.

foreign styles, mingling the best of the three 'schools' of German organists (north, central, and southern) into a personal synthesis.

It is still frequently said that Bach wrote *The Well-tempered Clavier* (two books each of twenty-four preludes and fugues in all the major and minor keys) to urge the abandonment of the mean-tone system of tuning (see p. 247) for the method known today as 'equal temperament', which is the accepted basis of modern music. (In this all intervals except the octave are slightly 'out of tune' by the measure of 'just intonation': since all semitones are equal, the fifth is a little flatter, and the fourth a little sharper than they ought to be, and similarly for the other intervals, but as the error in tuning is small and evenly distributed it forms an acceptable compromise.) It is quite true that Bach's

pieces in extreme keys would need to be performed on an instrument tuned in 'equal temperament', and that in his time there was much discussion on methods of tuning and their problems. But similar collections were written by other composers, not so much because of the question of tuning as to satisfy a desire for abstract order in the arrangements of a musical composition. Bach never intended a complete performance of one book of *The Well-tempered Clavier* at a sitting any more than he did of *The Art of Fugue* or *The Musical Offering* (canons, fugues, and a sonata on a theme given to him by Frederick the Great of Prussia). He, like many Germans of his time, found such systematic arrangements logical and intellectually satisfying. This attitude was partly the result of the scientific trend of his age; music was regarded both as an art and a science, and therefore demonstrations of its techniques (as the above-mentioned works are) demanded a 'scientific' presentation. This did not (and does not) mean that such music was 'dry' or 'unemotional'—quite the contrary; the 'intellectual' order of the music was felt to be a reflection of the Divine order of the Universe, "an Hieroglyphical and shadowed lesson of the whole world", and greater pleasure was accordingly derived from it.

PREFACE TO PARTS III AND IV

To WRITE about the past, which we call history, is difficult, for the obvious reason that we cannot experience it at first hand. To write about music is also difficult, because although we may experience it at first hand we are forced, in the act of writing, to translate our experience into another language. To write about history and music simultaneously is therefore a task which one ought to approach with both circumspection and humility. It is not enough to write a bit of potted European history and then to cite musical parallels; nor is it adequate to write about music as though it could exist apart from the context of human life. One has to experience music 'from within'; and in so doing to see it as historical evidence of a more inward kind than the documents with which historians usually have to deal.

One can hardly begin to experience music as historical evidence until one has faced up to a more fundamental question: if music 'conveys' experience as a language does, what kind of a language is it? The language of poetry is basically the same as the normal means of communication between human beings. The poet may use words with a precision, a cogency, and a range of emotional reference which we do not normally find in conversation. Yet though the order he achieves from his counters may be more significant than the desultory patterns achieved in talk by Tom, Dick, and Harry, at least the counters (words) are the same in both cases. Even with the visual arts there is usually some relationship between the order of forms and colours which the artist achieves and the shapes and colours of the external world. The relationship between the formal and representational elements is extremely complex and not easily susceptible to analysis; but it is at least usually clear that some such relationship exists.

With music, the relationship between the forms of art and the phenomena of the external world is much less readily apprehensible. It is true that composers have always made attempts to imitate the sounds of nature—from the bird-calls and clattering water-mills of Ars Nova down to Strauss's bleating sheep. But no one would claim that the imitative aspects of

Rameau's hen or Beethoven's cuckoo were the essential experience with which the music was concerned; the 'Pastoral' Symphony was not composed to do what cuckoos and quails can do much better. Yet if music is not imitation, there would seem to be uniform agreement that it does express, or at any rate mean, something. Charles Avison could find plenty of support, down the centuries, for his contention in his *Essay of Musical Expression* (1751) that 'the force of Sound in Alarming the Passions is Prodigious'. When he goes on to speak of the 'pleasing sorrows' and 'grateful terrors' we experience in listening to music he implicitly suggests that music is not synonymous with self-expression. It is neither the whoop of joy nor the yell of pain or fright: though it may include such manifestations. This is equally true of *King Lear*: for we are in a profound sense 'pleased' and 'gratified' by a sorrow and terror that in life the humanity of Lear, let alone our puny selves, can scarcely bear. So music as a language is perhaps, after all, not radically distinct from poetry and painting. All the arts are an order made out of reality. Music differs from the other arts only because it embodies its reality not in words, nor in shapes and colours, but in sound. It can do this because certain properties of sound are correlatable with some aspects of our physical and mental lives.

Thus we all live in time; and music essentially involves movement. Any sequence of two notes implies a progression in time: a sense of direction either up or down or, if the two notes are the same, in a straight line. The intervals of octave and fifth—whether sounded in sequence (melodically) or simultaneously (harmonically)—suggest stability because the vibration rates of the two tones bear to one another a simple arithmetical relationship. The intervals of major seventh, minor ninth and tritone* suggest unrest and tension because the two wave motions are in complex vibration ratio to one another; they therefore agitate the diaphragm of the ear and, in turn, the nervous system. All melody consists of alternations of tension and relaxation existing in time. Big leaps, jagged rhythms, tend to imply agitated movement; stepwise progressions, in even rhythm, suggest repose. Pentatonic† melodies come as close as is possible to a tensionless state, because their formulae are

* The augmented fourth or diminished fifth, i.e. F♭ to B♭ or B♭ to F♭.

† For an account of the pentatonic scale see Part 1.

most directly derived from the prime members of the harmonic series. Chromatic melodies tend to be most emotionally disturbing because they disrupt the melodic formulae which, for scientific reasons, the human voice most naturally sings.

The tenser a melodic progression, the more it is apt to carry harmonic implications. The major sixth (for instance, C to A) may suggest the harmonic centrality of the triad, or it may be absorbed into floating, pentatonic-like arabesques, as it is in the opening of Dvořák's 'Nigger' Quartet. The minor sixth (C to A♭), however, always seems to be seeking 'resolution' in the fifth. It tends to feel like a suspension, which is essentially a harmonic concept. Such harmonic concepts too have a precise relationship to physiological and psychological facts. Thus the suspension—the tense or dissonant note which resolves by a stepwise droop on to the relaxed or consonant interval—is a literal musical equation for the sigh. The major triad (C, E, G) is a musical symbol of natural order because its relationship to the fundaments of the harmonic series is simple: while the tritone has always been a symbol of disorder because its relationship is ambiguous and complex. The minor triad (C, E♭, G) is less final, less resolved, than the major triad because the vibration ratio of the minor third is complicated by the presence of lower partials or combination tones.

Sometimes the presence of words in a vocal composition makes clear the relationship between these—and many other—sound symbols and our physical and mental experience. Consider, for instance, the conventional stepwise movement of the classical operatic *scène de sommeil*; Bach's scalewise floating angels; his chromatic crucifixions; his weeping appoggiaturas.* Yet whether or no words offer a verbal gloss, the language of music always speaks in the same basic terms. Bach's last chorale prelude and the D sharp minor fugue from Book I of the *Forty-eight* are 'about' the same experience, as we can demonstrate from an analysis of their technique, though we have an implicit verbal commentary on this experience in the first case, none in the second.

Whether or no a musical composition has verbal associations, our comments on it will be valid only in so far as they have reference to the fundamental symbols of sound, as outlined

* APPOGGIATURA: a dissonant 'ornamental' note on the strong beat which resolves on the weak. See *Ornamentation* Part II.

above. In the course of this book I refer, for instance, to a melodic phrase as 'caressing'. Of course, the adjective is a metaphor; but is it valid and relevant? When I looked at the score I decided that just possibly it was valid; for the contour of the phrase describes a curve that looks like the curve of a caressing hand; it is a physical gesture in time. None the less, the word 'caress' is not purely descriptive; it introduces an emotional overtone that may or may not be pertinent. We can decide whether or not it is pertinent only when we see this phrase in relation to the composition of which it is a part. For although our comments about music are invalid unless they are based on the facts of sound rather than on those of another medium, we are not concerned with those facts in themselves. For us, such facts exist only within the context of particular pieces of music; and this context is at once personal experience and an aspect of history.

For instance, the acoustical distinction between the major and minor triad is of crucial significance in Schubert's music. But that the minor triad is, scientifically speaking, less resolved than the major triad does not take us far in understanding the extraordinary, and highly personal, poignancy of Schubert's use of alternating major and minor. We need to know not only that the alternation happens, but why it happens when it does. In the slow movement of Schubert's last piano sonata in B flat the ultimate appearance of the theme in the major is heart-breaking. But why this major transformation proves, in apparent paradox, to be so much sadder than the minor version is something we can understand only in reference to the complete movement and, indeed, sonata—or even to the context of Schubert's work as a whole. Though we have started from a fact of musical technique, we have found that the facts become significant only in relation to the whole of which they are a part. In the long run, this whole involves the strange, fascinating phenomenon of Schubert's psychology—his human experience, which becomes part of our experience while being at the same time unlike that of any other human being.

If this seems a matter of 'personality' rather than of 'history,' another example will reveal how inseparable the two concepts are. The chord of the dominant seventh* has certain specific acoustical properties which depend on the fact that it involves

* See Part I.

both a stable major triad and a tense tritone that seeks resolution. Yet the effect of the chord when it appears in the Agnus Dei of Byrd's five-part Mass is utterly different from its effect in the sequential modulations* of Chopin's C major Etude (opus 10, no. 1, bar 24, et seq.). There is a historical reason for this: Byrd and Chopin lived in different worlds both temporally and geographically. Byrd's 'suspended' seventh is a harmonic catch-in-the-breath, a sob, approached as a movement of independent vocal lines; Chopin's dissolving sevenths are an effect of harmonic 'colour' in part suggested by the movement of his hands on the keyboard. But this technical distinction is not merely a difference between two epochs: it rather comes to us as a distinction between two human beings who were, inevitably, representatives of the worlds in which they lived. Nor is the emotional and intellectual life of a single personality ever absolute and constant. Chopin's treatment of the dominant seventh is different from Byrd's because the nineteenth century is not the sixteenth, and because Chopin is not Byrd. But his treatment of the chord also varies, within the basic assumptions of his age, according to the context. Whenever we talk about music we are discussing two things simultaneously. We are concerned with the fundamental assumptions of an age about the way in which (say) a dominant seventh ought to behave; this is the technical complement to some part of the values by which a society lives, or thinks it lives. We are also concerned with the way in which this dominant seventh does in fact behave at a given moment in a given context; this is the experience of the individual artist.

No work of art can be 'explained' by reference to its historical connotations. Every artist self-evidently 'reflects' the values and beliefs of his time; he has no choice in the matter, even though he may, like Swift, express them largely in negative terms. At the same time, any truly creative artist is also making those beliefs. It is true that we cannot fully understand Beethoven without understanding the impulses behind the French Revolution. It is equally true that we cannot fully understand the French Revolution without some insight into Beethoven's music. We can see in his music those elements which are conditioned by his time (for they could not be otherwise) and yet are beyond the topical and local. Beethoven is a point at

* A SEQUENCE is the repetition of a passage at a different pitch.

which the growth of the mind shows itself. He is a part of history: and also the human spirit making history.

This is fairly obvious in the case of an artist who, like Beethoven, deliberately wanted to be an 'epoch-making' force. It is hardly less true of a relatively small, marginal figure such as César Franck. There can be no distinction between Franck's curious psychological make-up and the equivocal quality of his music—the contradiction between the fluidity of his tonality and the disintegration of his harmony on the one hand, and on the other hand the nagging reiteration of his metrical patterns and thematic contours, oscillating obsessively around the mediant.* Yet this element of frustration in both technique and personality is also what makes him historically representative. Even with composers living in more stable and homogeneous societies it is impossible to separate personal from historical significance. In the sixteenth century there was a common European idiom which we now know as Palestrina style. This was music's common denominator for certain assumptions of the Catholic Church and of Renaissance society. Yet it matters to us because it was the framework within which men such as Byrd, Lassus, Victoria, and Palestrina himself expressed very different attitudes to those assumptions. Handel's basic idiom was so universally accepted that he could lift into his own work large sections of other people's music without anyone noticing, or caring if they did notice. Yet what we remember of eighteenth-century baroque music is the revivifying experience of creative minds. We respond to the profound equilibrium between acceptance and protest, tradition and revolution, lyricism and tonal drama in the music of Haydn and Mozart; while we have forgotten the innumerable symphonic hacks who exploited the small change of rococo style as an easy way of passing the time—and making money. Most of all, perhaps, we see Bach's crucial position in European history in relation to his independence of time. Firmly rooted in what was then present, he philosophically and even technically harked back to a medieval past, while looking forward not merely to nineteenth-century romanticism, but still more to the twentieth century.

So in talking of Music and Society we should not think we are saying anything worth saying in pointing out that there are

* The third degree of the scale.

connexions between what has happened in music and what has happened in the external world. That is, or should be, a truism. We should, however, in listening to the music which great and less than great men have created at different times in the past, learn to experience that music as the deepest kind of evidence as to the ways men have thought, felt, and acted. In order to do this we need a historical sense: but only because—or in so far as—the past is relevant to the present. Before the nineteenth century any musician would have thought it odd to listen to music of the past rather than of the present. We take it for granted that we listen to more music of past ages than of our own. But if we are all historically minded, we are learning to understand that the historian's task is both to apprehend the significance which past music had when it was still present: and to differentiate between those elements of the past which have lost, and those which retain, a meaning.

The delicacy and complexity of the historian's task is thus only too pointed. Nothing he says is valid unless it is based on concepts related to the nature of sound, and on the particular ways in which a composer has used these sound-symbols at a given moment. Yet the historian has also to see these given moments in relation to the composer's personal experience, in the context of his life and in the wider context of history. Above all, he has to be able to distinguish between those elements of history and biography which are relevant to the musical experience and those which are not; and to do this no amount of accumulated learning will help him. Indeed, learning may hinder as much as help him; for the amount of music which one man can know—in the real sense of experiencing it from within—is restricted both by the limitations of human understanding and by time. This historian, at least, would claim no more than that he has approached his task with humility, and that he has tried not to lose sight of the living reality of history: which is the point of intersection between the private and the public life.

Thirty years have elapsed since this book was first published. During that time it has been consistently in print, and still seems to serve a purpose. Rereading my volumes, I find that I hold by most of what I then said, though inevitably I would now do some things differently and, I hope, more wisely. In an age when musicology has become something of an obsession much work has been done in all the areas under discussion. Although this mass of knowledge and even information would naturally affect any rethinking or rewriting one embarked on, only one book, Charles Rosen's great study of *The Classical Style,* has profoundly modified the way we think and feel about a phase of music history. In a more general sense, Robert Donington's Jungian writings about Wagner have led us, or at least me, to a deeper understanding, as have Donald Mitchell's monumental work on Mahler and Ian Kemp's book on Tippett. It is perhaps not surprising that these writings, which seem to me to reopen the mind and the ears, should accord with, rather than contradict, my approach of thirty years back. For me, the most valuable writing about music must inevitably start from the fact that music, being made by human beings, cannot but be a psychological and social activity.

The years from 1957 to 1987 have been in several senses momentous; both mind and imagination boggle at the multifarious and seemingly contradictory music activities thrown up by an electronic revolution. I have been allotted a little space to catch up on these tumultuous years: a task best served not by an approach by way of national or regional 'schools' of composers, as in the core of this book, but by an attempt globally to trace the metamorphosis of old, and the infiltration of new, techniques and forces. That suits our 'pluralistic' world; though it should be unnecessary to add that I have had to be rigorously selective, and that no two persons' decision as to what 'really' matters could hope to be identical. In dealing with the present and the incipient future one chances one's arm; even one's mistakes may be interesting, because they must be symptomatic. It will be observed that the Afterword mells the musical genres – art-music, folk, jazz and pop – more freely than does the main book. This is in part a consequence of our culturally amorphous times, though it's worth saying that, had I written *Man and his Music* ten years later, I would have thought it essential to include some account of these demotic musics – some manifestations of which have lasted longer and worn better than much socially more respectable music – even at the expense of still more stringent coverage of conventional areas. This too is a sign – in my view a welcome sign – of the times.

York, 1988 WILFRID MELLERS

PART III

THE SONATA PRINCIPLE

(from c. 1750)

I TRADITION AND REVOLUTION

II OPERA, RITUAL, AND MYTH

by WILFRID MELLERS

I TRADITION AND REVOLUTION

I

THE BIRTH OF SONATA

THE second half of the eighteenth century is a crucial turning-point in the history of European music. During this period a revolutionary principle of composition was created. We call it Sonata Form, though the term is misleading because it suggests that 'form' can exist independent of the musical 'content'. Sonata, like fugue, is not so much a form as a principle, an approach to composition. The sonata movements of Haydn, let alone Beethoven, resemble one another in their approach, but not in the details of the pattern. One might even say that there is no such thing as sonata form; there are only sonatas. Sonata is a way of composing which grew out of a particular set of circumstances: which is apposite to those circumstances and not necessarily to others. A new approach to composition grew out of new human needs and desires. Certain conventions were, of course, gradually deduced from this new approach and hardened into cliché and dogma: social small talk which could be used by composers who had nothing to say as an agreeable way of passing the time and making money. But for the masters style never becomes dogma; form remains principle which perpetually renews itself under the pressure of experience.

At the outset, therefore, we have to enquire what were the social and philosophical circumstances that created a new musical style; and how did this new music differ from previous kinds of composition. Let us first look at two pieces of music which were composed before this great new epoch. The first is J. S. Bach's last chorale prelude, *Vor deinen Thron tret'ich allhier* (the 'Eighteen' Chorale Preludes).* This piece is founded on a chorale or hymn which was not Bach's own creation, but was the property of his Church; the tune enters intermittently in comparatively long note values. When we examine the music more closely we find that the other parts, which might seem to

* For a detailed analysis of this piece see Hermann Scherchen, *The Nature of Music.*

be accompanying the melody, are in fact thematic. Each phrase of the chorale is treated in diminution as a fugue subject, the answer usually being in inversion. The concluding phrase appears in its original hymn-tune time values, in diminution and in double diminution simultaneously, and both ways up. It is almost true to say that there is not a single note in the piece which is not derived from the liturgical melody.

Moreover, the progression of the parts is mainly by step or by small, smooth intervals, moving at about the speed of the human pulse. The persistent answer by inversion creates an equilibrium of emotion, each rise being balanced by a fall; and though the harmony which the parts create is often tensely dissonant, this pathos dissolves away in the measured flow of the lines. Bach's personal feeling is powerful (he knew he was dying as he dictated this piece); but it is absorbed into something greater than himself. All this we can deduce from the technique of the music itself. In this case it also happens that the implicit words of the chorale corroborate what the music is telling us in its own terms. Into Thy hands I commend my spirit; in the fragmentary disintegration of the theme during the extended plagal cadence* of the concluding bars man is united with the infinite.

Bach [1685–1750] was in many ways an archaistic composer, and the thematic and fugal unity of this last chorale prelude is more typical of earlier creative periods than of his own. At least we may say that there is some connexion between fugal unity as a principle of composition and an age dominated by religious faith—by belief in something more than human potentiality. Now let us look at another piece of music, this time by Handel [1685–1759], a contemporary of Bach, but a man who, unlike Bach, was progressive in his time. The well-known air from *Messiah*, 'How beautiful are the feet', is again an expression of unity; but it is not fugal. The unity this music achieves is architectural. There is again only one theme which falls, however, into a number of clearly defined segments. The first half modulates from tonic minor to relative major; the second half returns to the tonic by way of related keys. The purpose of these modulations is to emphasize the grouping of the clauses, not to provide a dramatic contrast. Bach's chorale

* The cadence formed by the progression from the subdominant chord (that on the fourth degree of the scale) to the tonic. See *Cadences*, Part I.

prelude is an instrumental piece constructed on principles which are inherently vocal. Handel's aria is a vocal piece which is constructed on principles derived from the architecture of the dance.

Perhaps one might say that a general principle is involved: Bach tends to think fugally even when he writes dances; Handel thinks in terms of the dance even when he writes fugues. Bach's unity is the growth of the single melody in all the parts; Handel's unity is imposed on his tunes by periodic dance metre and by the definition of tonality. And Handel is the representative musician of the baroque era; for whereas Bach reveals the order inherent in melody, Handel creates order by a balance of clauses and keys—just as the architects and gardeners of his age established order through the symmetry of shapes and contours. Bach still expresses a theocratic —a God-centred—view of the universe, while Handel's attitude is humanistic. Bach wrote for the Church, even in his instrumental music. Handel writes for the opera-house, even in his church music: and the opera-house was the symbol of King and State, of the man-made autocracy in which the King became God. The importance of the chaconne form in baroque music is not fortuitous; for the chaconne is a longish piece constructed over the regular repetition of a dance rhythm and of a harmonic bass. This periodic pattern disciplines the music's passion in much the same way as the conventions of aristocratic society aimed to control personal feeling in the interests of the community. Couperin's terrific *Passacaille* in B minor is an extreme example of this. The chromatically violent harmony reaches its climax in the penultimate couplet; but the emotion is dammed up by the relentless repetitions of the rondeau (Ex. 1). The vehement passions of the individual seem to be

desperately struggling against the conventions that make civilization possible. In so well ordered a world there is never any doubt that civilization will triumph.

We have commented on two kinds of unity in music previous to the sonata epoch: that of Bach, which is at once melodic and harmonic, and religious in impetus; and that of Handel, which is primarily rhythmic and tonal, and based on a ritual of the State. Both kinds of unity imply reference to a central authority outside the self; and it is not surprising that the relationship between social ritual and art which we find in Handel, and still more in the composers of Louis XIV's France, should have been precarious. It depended on the existence of a public small and unified enough for a system of values to be universally intelligible. The decline of the aristocracy meant its end; and we can observe the beginnings of a change even in the work of Rameau [1683–1764], who regarded himself as an heir to the classical baroque tradition. Although many of Rameau's later operas were presented at the court of Louis XV, we may say that he, unlike his predecessor, Lully [1632–1687], wrote with the Parisian public in mind. It is significant that his patron was Le Riche de la Pouplinière, a financier and one of the wealthiest members of the new bourgeoisie.

Rameau starts from the old heroic operatic conventions, yet repeatedly he recreates them for new ends. In place of ceremonial grandeur, he offers a still more voluptuous harmony and a richer orchestral colour. Whereas the style of Lully and Couperin [1668–1733] had depended on melodic continuity and harmonic order, there are many passages in Rameau which depend solely on instrumental figuration and on rhythm to make a sensational effect. Consider, for instance, the earthquake in *Les Indes Galantes*, or the *bruit de mer* in *Hvppolyte* with its shooting scales, percussive rhythms, and picturesque orchestration (Ex. 2). This is a deliberate attempt to make an im-

Ex. 2. Rameau: *Hyppolyte et Aricie*

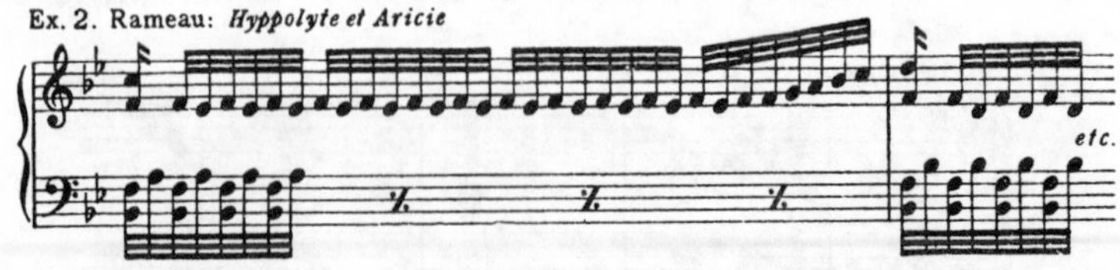

mediate impact on a relatively large and untrained public. It was a new style of composing; but its implications were not yet to be explored in France, where the aristocratic central authority was strong enough to suppress internal dissension. The more sensitive spirits of the classical age—such as Fénélon and La Bruyère—had been painfully aware that their autocracy occasioned misery among those less fortunately placed. None the less they believed in their world with an almost religious intensity. It was not until many years after Louis XIV's heyday that the undercurrent of revolutionary fervour came to the surface.

In Austria and Germany, however, the Thirty Years' War had left in its wake a legacy of chaos and disintegration, and had established the dominance of a foreign power. In these conditions the petty princelings attempted to maintain an oppressive feudal serfdom, while they themselves emulated the fashionable French and Italian models in their palaces, their art, their music, their codes of etiquette. Austrian culture became cosmopolitan; the Catholicism and Italianate elegance of the Habsburgs could not provide a unifying force comparable with that of the *Roi Soleil* in France. By the middle of the eighteenth century the conflict latent in society had become patent. The split was noticeable even within the nobility itself, for the Emperor Joseph II, who opposed the Papacy, attempted to abolish serfdom, and established an Edict of Toleration, came into bitter conflict with the patriarchal feudal landlords, such as Haydn's patrons, the Esterházys. The fantastic dream-world of the Esterházy palace in the marshes was a conscious attempt to transplant Louis XIV's glory into Austria—an oasis, even a mirage, in a desert of misery, for it depended on serfdom for its existence. The reformist's zeal was defeated; Joseph had to withdraw his Edict. Revolutionary aspirations broke out again, and were again defeated, innumerable times down to the twentieth century.

Yet the victory of the feudal landlords was more apparent than real. Their sun was setting, and a new aristocracy was arising in their midst. This aristocracy was bourgeois and middle-class, and rational rather than Catholic. Its power is exemplified in the rise of Freemasonry; for although the Masons were an elect, they did not come from the landlord or the military classes. While many Masons were formally Catholics, the Church (and with it the State) was suspicious of the movement in so far as it encouraged equalitarian ideas. The Church traditionally distrusted Reason; the Masons believed that society could be regenerated through the exercise of Reason, which would bring Enlightenment—without, presumably, the intervention of Grace. Haydn, ostensibly a pious Catholic, got into hot water with the Church because of the Masonic implications of his oratorio, *The Creation*. Mozart's Masonic opera, *The Magic Flute*, was regarded with suspicion by the Church as a subversive manifestation. These facts alone indicate how powerfully democratic ideas permeated the work even of artists who had been aristocratically nurtured. The growth of eighteenth-century sonata style is the musical expression of this new democracy. Indeed, the symphony orchestra itself reflected a democratic ideal; Joseph von Holzmeister, in a speech delivered on the occasion of Haydn's admission to the Masonic Order, pointed out that Haydn had created a new order in the orchestra, 'for if every instrument did not consider the rights and properties of the other instruments, in addition to its own rights, if it did not often diminish its own volume in order not to do damage to the utterance of its companions, the end—which is beauty—would not be attained'.

When the Austrian composers began to feel around for a style that would be appropriate to a changing view of the world, they were able to profit from the Italian domination in Vienna. For the rage of the moment was the *opera buffa*, which while taking over many conventions from the degenerating *opera seria*, was in part a reaction against the heroic view of life. The *opera seria* dealt with figures larger than life: humans swollen to gods or monsters, as were the monarchs of the great autocracies. The *opera buffa* debunked the sublime and dealt with the low life of Tom, Dick, and Harry—and, of course, that of their young women. The musical style of the *opera buffa* was related to urban popular music; and the instrumental sections, especially the overtures, most significantly modify the techniques of classical baroque music.

The basic formal conventions of the baroque had been the binary dance movement and the *aria da capo*. In the former, as we saw from our example from Handel's *Messiah*, a single melody is divided into two sections, the first of which modulates from tonic major to dominant or from tonic minor to relative, the second moving back to the tonic by way of related keys. In the *aria da capo*, there is an extended melody in dance rhythm, which may itself be in binary form; then a middle section based on a different aspect of the same theme, and often in the tonic minor; then a repeat of the first section, with elaborate ornamentation. Except for the intensifying ornamentation the theme is not *changed* by what happens in the middle section, for the *da capo* aria, like binary dance form, is architectural, not dramatic. It is obvious, however, that the modulatory sections in both binary and ternary aria *could* be exploited as an effect of dramatic contrast. This begins to happen in some of the later examples of the concerto grosso.

This form was a reduction into instrumental terms of the conventions of heroic opera: the soloistic group took the place of the singers, the *tutti* that of the operatic orchestra. The alternation of *soli* and *tutti* suggests the use of different, even contrasting material in association with the two keys—tonic and dominant, or tonic and relative—which are the orthodox props of binary structure. When once the idea of contrast is admitted, modulation may be used as a shock tactic, rather than for architectural reasons. In the concertos of Vivaldi [1675–1741], for instance, the slow movements are always based on continuous melodic growth, in the heroic manner of Handel or Bach. But the quick movements, especially the finales, already suggest a dualistic rather than a monistic principle of construction. They exploit the exciting effect of tonal and rhythmic contrast; and that they do so is inseparable from the fact that their themes are no longer heroic, but popular in style.

If this is true of Vivaldi's concerto movements, which grew out of the baroque heritage, still more is it true of the stock operatic overture, which was in part a reaction against that heritage. Here, if the modulatory sections are not dramatic, or at least momently surprising, they are nothing: for there is no melody, as Bach or Handel conceived it, to extend. In Paisiello's overture *Nina*, for instance, there is no lyrical theme. There are little tootling arpeggio phrases and prancing scales in perkily periodic rhythms. The props of tonic and dominant are established only in order to be contradicted, so that the music moves in short, contrasted sections punctuated by cadences, rather than with the continuity and unity which Bach and Handel, in their different ways, sought after. The music is heterogeneous in effect and, as a noise, superficially exciting: consider Paisiello's use of a new instrument, the clarinet. But although the surprises—in modulation, dynamic contrast and tone-colour—arouse expectation, expectation remains unfulfilled. The composer shows no capacity to organize his multifarious material, nor was he much concerned to do so. His overture was to be chattered to rather than listened to. If it created a general feeling of ebullience, it sufficed.

There is no real difference in principle between many of Vivaldi's finales to his concertos, an Italian operatic overture, and the quick movements of the innumerable works which, after about 1740, appeared in Austria under the designation of symphony. Sometimes the link with the concerto grosso is direct, since the symphonies are in four movements, slow, quick, slow, quick. Only the rapid movements are in the new popular manner, though the slow movements are becoming pretty rather than heroic. Sometimes the symphonies have three movements, quick, slow, quick, in the fashion favoured by the Italian theatre; again, the two allegros are in *buffo* style, with a prettified aria in the middle. At other times symphonies may have five or even six movements, since reminiscences of the suite suggest the inclusion of more than one dance movement, either in binary form or in ternary style, like the minuet and trio.

The four movements into which the symphony finally settled down involved a medley of all these elements. First movement allegro came from the *buffo* overture, though it might still be prefaced by a slow introduction derived from the concerto grosso and from French heroic opera: this introduction was habitually preserved by Haydn, exceptionally by Mozart and Beethoven. Slow movements were always derived from the operatic aria. The third movement, the survival from the dance suite, became traditionally a minuet, though its aristocratic elegance gave way to a rustic vigour. The finale might again be in the *buffo* binary style which we have come to call 'sonata', though it too might betray a dance origin by being in rondo—a symmetrical tune intermittently repeated, with varying episodes between each repetition. Whatever form their symphonies assumed, the Austrian composers had found in the Italian *buffo* overture and the popular elements of the concerto grosso just the materials they needed to create a 'democratic' instrumental style. These Italianate features could easily be reconciled with the urban and rustic popular music of their own country.

If one listens to the music of Johann Stamitz [1717–1757], who was an Austrian by birth, but worked for Rameau's patron, Le Riche de la Pouplinière, and for the Elector Palatine at Mannheim, one can observe how he is using theatrical elements to create an easily intelligible dramatic style in purely instrumental terms; one contemporary chronicler significantly remarked that Stamitz makes the instruments sing '*so that one forgets that such things as voices exist*'. In addition to the new type of melody and rhythmic accompaniment, Stamitz introduces many devices intended to excite and astonish his audience. In his orchestration he concentrates all his attention on getting the tune across. The harpsichord continuo, which in baroque music supplied the harmonic background to the interweaving melodies, disappears; ostinato string figures and sustained notes on the horns now fill in the middle parts since melodic definition in any part except the top is unimportant. The crescendo and diminuendo, tremolos, sudden changes of dynamics, marks of expression and nuance—all the effects which in Rameau's operas had grown from theatrical exigencies (such as earthquakes), become an end in themselves. The bouncing upward arpeggio figures 'across the strings' (known as the Mannheim sky-rocket), the twiddling figurations (the Mannheim birdies), the long crescendo over a reiterated bass, to which the audience rose to its feet as one man (the Mannheim steam-roller) became famous or notorious all over Europe. Stamitz vigorously expressed the feelings of a growing public which had been unrepresented in the aristocratic art of the previous generation. The bourgeois forces in the Age of Enlightenment knew that the future was with them. Their self-confidence is reflected in the jaunty vitality of Stamitz's music.

Stamitz's recipe for excitement may seem to us, as it would have seemed to Bach or Couperin, a little crude; yet, since he was a composer of personality and talent, the recipe worked. It was, however, fatally easy to imitate; and the thousands of rococo symphonies that appeared in the second half of the eighteenth century are a phenomenon comparable with commercial dance music to-day, except that, being less mechanized, they were less synthetic. If the formulae were mass-produced, they were at least in no particular, rather than in offensive, taste. The contemplation of these countless symphonic corpses is the more depressing because depressing is the last thing they were meant to be; nothing is more dismal than jokes that have lost their savour, or thrills that have become routine. Even in the eighteenth century, however, truly creative spirits began to feel that this eupeptic middle-class style could not be permanently satisfying. Their sympathies were with Feeling and the Enlightenment; but they wanted to express themselves at a deeper level than would be likely to appeal to a mass audience. The new aristocracy will depend neither on birth nor on acquired riches, but on innate ability and sensitivity; Tom, Dick or Harry might be the architect of a new world. So there grew up, alongside the popular manner, a style of Sensibility which finds its most distinguished expression in the work of J. S. Bach's most talented son, Carl Philipp Emanuel [1714–1788]. To his music there are two aspects which are at once independent and complementary.

Consider the first movement of the F minor Sonata from the series which he composed in 1763, not for *hoi polloi*, but 'for Connoisseurs and Amateurs' (amateurs in the strict sense, of course). This is in orthodox binary form, like most of his father's dance pieces, and has no contrasting second subject. The initial figure is a bounding Mannheim sky-rocket (Ex. 3); and the

interest of the music lies not in the themes, which as melody do not exist, but in the tonal conflict which is generated from them. The point of the movement is the dramatic crisis which occurs in the middle section—we can now legitimately call it a development—on the surprising chord of F flat major: a 'Neapolitan' relationship to the minor of the relative (A flat) (Ex. 4).* Here the popular manner of Stamitz has not lost its

* The 'Neapolitan' cadence substitutes a minor for a major sixth over the subdominant root, in the conventional progression from subdominant to dominant to tonic. The 'minorish' feeling of a cadence in the minor key is thus greatly intensified. Neapolitan opera composers were especially partial to this harmonic piquancy in moments of dramatic pathos. See Part II.

vitality; but it has gained a personal urgency. C. P. E. Bach reveals that the surprises and explosive contrasts of the new style become significant only when they achieve a new kind of order; and this order, depending on oppositions of tonality and harmony, is inherently dramatic. The drama is no longer projected on to a stage; it is embodied in self-contained instrumental form.

C. P. E. Bach's creation of dramatic order within the popular manner can thus be reconciled with the mode of Sensibility which he explores in his slow movements. The remarkable E flat largo from the second sonata of the fifth book (1784) achieves by way of its broken, limply ornamented melody, its chromatic harmony and enharmonic transitions a brooding, introspective pathos (Ex. 5); it could be adequately realized

Ex. 5. C.P.E. Bach: Adagio from Sonata in B♭

only on an instrument, such as the new piano, capable of nuance and tonal gradation. One can see a similar quality in his church music, as compared with that of his father. J. S. Bach uses operatic techniques in his cantatas without ceasing to be liturgical in spirit: acutely dissonant harmony and elaborately expressive ornamentation are absorbed into the flow of the lines. In the church music of Carl Philipp harmonic and decorative pathos take—to use an appropriate metaphor—the centre of the stage, disrupting continuity of line. The effect of the music is powerful, but more subjective, less devotional, than J. S. Bach's. This is especially evident in the intimate solo songs or *Geistliche Lieder*, like the beautiful *Tag und Nacht, du Heil der Frommen*. There is no melodic or harmonic element in the song which could not, considered by itself, be found in the music of J. S. Bach; but whereas in J. S. Bach the weeping appoggiaturas and stabbing Neapolitan chords would intensify a continuously evolving line, in C. P. E. Bach they are the essence of the music. There is a comparable distinction between the texts set by J. S. and C. P. E. Bach respectively. J. S. Bach's texts tend to deal dramatically but impersonally with liturgical dogma or biblical history. The poems of Carl Philipp's *Geistliche Lieder* deal with the relationship between God and Myself.

The music of another of Bach's sons, Wilhelm Friedmann [1710–1784], suggests a similar comparison. Consider, for instance, J. S. Bach's E flat minor Prelude from Book I of *The Well-tempered Clavier* alongside W. F. Bach's Polonaise in the same key. Both pieces are in binary form, and intensely passionate. But in J. S. Bach's Prelude the dissonant harmony reinforces the wide soaring and declension of the melodic line: while in W. F. Bach's Polonaise the melody is broken, fragmentary, subservient to details of harmony, ornamentation, and sequential modulation. J. S. Bach's piece sounds like a Passion aria: the suffering is Christ's, which happens also to be Bach's and ours because Christ died for us. W. F. Bach's piece is a passion aria, which is about his own suffering, because he was an eccentric and a misfit who became, before his time, the typical artist of romanticism.

The creation of a Popular style and a style of Sensibility means the beginning of a split between artists' music and 'people's' music. We can observe an interesting example of this in the career of another of Bach's sons, Johann Christian [1735–1782]. He started his musical life as a composer of Italian opera; after he settled in London as a composer of instrumental music for the drawing-room, he was normally content to exploit rococo elegance in a manner that was superficially entertaining. His tunes are pretty if short-winded, his texture pleasing, his harmonies and modulations mildly titillating to the senses without being disturbing. But he also wrote a few works, notably a piano sonata in C minor, which hint at a different and a deeper world. The first movement opens with dissonant suspensions, accompanied by a surging arpeggio bass, which suggest the liturgical grandeur of Johann Sebastian; while the second movement begins as a fugue which has something of the power of J. S. Bach and of the dramatic energy of Carl Philipp. The surging arpeggios of the prelude degenerate, at the appearance of the second subject, into an

XXIX The Mozart Family. From a painting by della Croce.

PROSPECT DER FÜRSTLICHEN RESIDENZ ESZTERHAZ VON DEN
HAUPT THOR GEGEN NORDEN.

XXX The Castle at Eszterháza. An engraving from *Beschreibung des Hochfürstlichen Schlosses Esterhasz im Königreiche Ungern*, 1784.

Alberti figuration* as footling as it is inconsistent; and the fugue soon relapses into comically automatic sequences. But though Johann Christian was no longer able to realize the potentialities of the baroque idiom, he still respected it. Such is the way Bach would write—he once said, speaking of this sonata—if he did not have to address himself to the children.

This must be the first instance of a composer admitting that the style which he adopted for commercial reasons was distinct from that in which he would naturally express himself. This 'split personality' was to have far-reaching consequences later on, and we shall have much to say about it. For the moment, we are concerned with the way in which the Popular style and the style of Sensibility interacted on one another to produce the mature sonata idiom of the Age of Enlightenment. We have already indicated how in the sonatas of C. P. E. Bach the dualism between the two modes came to exist within the works themselves; we may even see a hint of it in W. F. Bach's E minor Polonaise, which begins with a lyrical, J. S. Bach-like cantilena and then introduces an abruptly contrasted arpeggio motive that fulfils, within the space of a few bars, the function of a second subject, with a miniature 'development' after the double bar. This conflict grows increasingly intense throughout the sonata forms of the eighteenth and nineteenth centuries, for it is related to a conflict in society itself. In tracing its course through the work of Haydn, Mozart, Beethoven, Schubert to Bruckner, Brahms, and Mahler, we shall observe that although Tradition and Revolution are variously interrelated in their music, the thread of a creative principle links both their art and their lives.

* A keyboard device whereby the player's left hand spreads out chords into rhythmic arpeggio figures, usually rotating on the bass note of the harmony.

2

HAYDN

JOSEPH HAYDN [1732–1809] was a revolutionary composer without conscious volition, perhaps even without conscious awareness. His crucial position in European music is related not only to the nature of his genius, but also to his mere longevity. When he was born in 1732, J. S. Bach had still to write many of his greatest works; when he died, in 1809, Beethoven had already begun to create some of the music which marked the end of the classical sonata as Haydn and Mozart had conceived it. He was writing music himself as early as 1750; he was still vigorously creative in the first decade of the nineteenth century.

We think of Haydn as a representative of an urbane civilization, and rightly so. Yet we misunderstand his society if we fail to see how closely it was interlinked with the countryside. His parents were musical in that they were country people who spontaneously made music, singing to the harp. Haydn's early consciousness was permeated with folk· music, as one aspect of the everyday activities of an Austrian village. His tranquillity of soul was based partly on the peasant's simple acceptance of nature, rather than on the romantic cult of Nature as a refuge from humanity.

When, as a boy, he moved to Vienna to the choir school at St. Stephen's Cathedral, he did not lose this awareness of country life, for Vienna was a small city by our standards. If it was small, however, it was highly sophisticated and cosmopolitan. Traders of all nations and constellations of Italian singers and composers abounded in this stimulating, glittering world. If it was already corrupt, the young Haydn was emotionally too direct to be aware of its corruption, as Beethoven and Schubert were later to be.

At St. Stephen's, Haydn would have become familiar with a certain amount of counterpoint, in the old-fashioned manner of Fux [1660–1741]; his brother Michael [1737–1806], who was primarily an ecclesiastical composer, never lost touch with this style throughout his career. But most of the music Joseph sang and played would have been 'modern', in spirit as well as in date: and most contemporary church music was operatic in style, since Italian opera was the central expression of rococo sensibility. The difference between baroque art and rococo art may perhaps be summed up by saying that in baroque art the ornamentation is an integral part of the 'expression', closely related to structure: whereas in rococo art—whether visual or aural—ornamentation tends to be an end in itself, a delight in profusion and sensory adventure, related loosely, if at all, to structure. Yet the Viennese, in Haydn's day, were right to worship God according to their own lights, which were brilliant, if unstable: for they had no others. They were not mystical or devotional; it was well that they did not pretend to be so. Their very frivolity helped Haydn to discover his own profundity. Even after he left St. Stephen's, his training remained Italianate. He became accompanist for singing lessons given by an Italian opera composer and singer, Niccola Porpora [1686–1766]; receiving in return a modest stipend and lessons in vocal composition.

But the greater part of Haydn's working life was spent outside Vienna as household musician to the Esterházy family. Living in seclusion in this dream-palace in the marshes, Haydn was a feudal dependant to several generations of Esterházys. He wore livery, dined with the servants, produced quantities of music for the entertainment of the court, and directed the band and singers in the performance of it. He was a servant of autocracy, as the baroque musicians had been; unlike Mozart, he never consciously resented his position. Such troubles as he had were personal—his marriage was unhappy, and his belated love-affair with one of the singers could not offer the secure serenity he needed. In his professional existence, he was comfortable and uncomplaining. He was able to compose music as a full-time occupation, and to hear it performed; even his remoteness from the centre of civilization had compensations, for, as he said: "My Prince was always satisfied with my works; I not only had the encouragement of constant approval, but as conductor of an orchestra I could make experiments. I was cut off from the world, there was no one to confuse me, and so I was forced to become original."

No doubt, in this 'originality', there was an undercurrent of revolutionary resentment, of which Haydn was no more aware than his master. Certainly, after he had become an international celebrity, Haydn relinquished his post as household musician and became a free-lance. Lully, court composer to Louis XIV, also came of artisan stock, but he would never have said with Haydn: "I have had converse with emperors, kings, and great princes and have heard many flattering praises from them; but I do not wish to live on a familiar footing with such persons, and I prefer people of my own class." It is significant that Haydn formally entered the Masonic Order only after he had left the Esterházys' service; and that when, at the instigation of the impresario Salomon, he made his triumphant visits to London, he took with him his greatest symphonies and brought back, from a study of Handel and English oratorio, a new conception of religious music. Henceforth he was able in his church music to express, not liturgical dogma, but his deepest ethical convictions.

Indeed, Haydn's long development may as a whole be described as a gradual discovery of his own nature. In his earliest works he is preoccupied with formal problems: how convincingly to integrate his heterogeneous material—the Mannheim quirks and quiddities—by means of a developed sense of tonality. He is not at first greatly concerned about the significance of his structures as human experience: so that the music is Entertainment in no discreditable sense. One can see this in his approach to both string quartet and symphony, which to begin with were for him interchangeable.

The most important form in baroque chamber music had been the trio sonata, as the concerto grosso had been in music for a band. The trio sonata was again a distillation of operatic conventions into instrumental terms. The two sustained singing voices of the solo violins were poised over the string bass and the harmonic filling in of the continuo instrument; this might be organ or harpsichord, according to whether the sonatas were to be played in church or at home.

Whatever its subsequent development, the birth of the string quartet was once more a democratic process; music moved not merely from church and court to the chamber or living-room, but even into the streets. Vienna was a-jingle with serenading parties playing in the open air. If this music was to be effective, its style had to be even simpler than that of *opera buffa*. It called for perky tunes at the top, easily recognizable rhythms, and a rudimentary accompaniment filling in the harmony with repeated notes and arpeggios, since it was hardly practical to carry around a continuo instrument such as harpsichord or piano. These *quadri*—pieces in four parts of which only one had melodic significance—could be played either on a quartet of solo instruments, or by small bands with the parts doubled. Even in the solo quartet medium Haydn often writes in only two parts, each doubled at the octave—a primitive technique which can sound delightfully fresh in open-air performance.

Haydn himself composed a large number of trio sonatas, usually involving the baritone, an obsolete stringed instrument favoured by Prince Esterházy. These charming, trivial pieces were a *galant* simplification of baroque style; Haydn's first quartets differ from them mainly in discarding all traces of the heroic. These divertimenti, cassations, and serenades, the earliest of which were composed around 1750, still show the influence of the suite. They are always in the major key, with five dance-like movements, including two minuets. The trios of the minuets, which are peasant Ländler* rather than courtly dances, are sometimes in the tonic minor; dominant, sub-dominant, or relative are occasionally employed for the slow movements. While almost all the sonata movements are different, and diversified in their material, Haydn makes no more attempt at thematic development than did the stock composer of *buffo* overtures. The slow movements are usually operatic arias sung by the first violin to an accompaniment of pizzicato chords or the like. They are not convincing, for Haydn seems to have relinquished the grand manner without knowing what to put in its place. The unequivocally 'low' movements are the best, and much more stimulating in performance than they look on paper. Haydn was a practical musician, who wrote music to be heard, in given conditions. The crudities of his first works in part reflect the change in music's social status.

Haydn was composing these works—whether one regards them as rudimentary quartets or rudimentary symphonies—between 1750 and 1760. It cannot be said that he approaches Stamitz in fire or precision of effect: nor that he adds anything

* An Austrian country dance in slow waltz time, usually in regular two-bar periods and with simple (mainly tonic and dominant) harmony.

substantial to his other models—the Austrians Monn [?1717–1750], Wagenseil [1715–1777] and Richter [1709–1789], and the Italian Sammartini [1701–1775]. But it is not long before he begins to acquire character as a symphonist. The twenty-second Symphony, known as 'The Philosopher', is especially interesting in that its transitional position—half-way between baroque and rococo—is clearly evident. Its four-movement structure—slow-quick-moderate-quick—follows that of the baroque concerto grosso, with a peasant Ländler minuet substituted for the aristocratic sarabande. Moreover, Haydn's method of handling the orchestra recalls the chamber style of the baroque rather than the modern symphonic manner of Stamitz; the wind instruments, in particular, are given solo parts to play.

The first movement is grave and austere, an archaic *canto fermo* which seems to look backwards to Bach and forwards to Mozart's Masonic works—a significant re-creation of outmoded techniques. The second movement, on the other hand, is rococo and symphonic, briskly popular, but without Stamitz's energy in key contrasts, since Haydn allows himself no contrasting subject matter and almost no time for development. The minuet is a rustic Ländler, which introduces a vestigial counterpoint in the trio. Counterpoint, we have seen, was rigorously avoided by the early symphonists, who wished to make the easiest possible appeal. Haydn reintroduces it, not as a basic principle of construction, as did Bach, but to avoid empty passage-work and thus to assist his search for symphonic coherence. We shall note a much more important development of this in his and Mozart's mature music. The last movement returns to *buffo* style, with an episode in the minor which is at once witty and dramatic.

This is by no means the only one of Haydn's early symphonies in which he attempts to enrich the musical significance of the *quadri* by a compromise with old-fashioned techniques. In Symphony No. 31 ('*Auf dem Anstand mit dem Hornsignal*') he treats the wind instruments in the concertante manner of the solo group of the concerto grosso: though he emulates Vivaldi in creating by means of them sound pictures of everyday life, rather than a refined, relatively abstract music for the court. The quick movements, replete with shooting scales and repeated notes, and even a faint suggestion of a contrasting 'lyrical' idea, are much more dramatic than the comparable movements in 'The Philosopher'. The slow movement has difficult concertante parts for violin and 'cello, with four obbligato horns. The seductive melody sounds like an Italian operatic duet, its sophistication modified by a popular Viennese lilt; Italian elegance has come within the reach of ordinary rustic folk. The presto conclusion to the final variations has a Stamitz-like ferocity, and is full of surprises both in figuration and in scoring.

These two symphonies, and the triptych describing country life at Esterházy called *Le Matin*, *Le Midi*, and *Le Soir*, were composed during the 1760s. Despite their originality and their musical substance, they still come into the category of the 'entertainment' symphony: they are half-way between symphony and serenade. With the approach to the 1770s a remarkable change comes over Haydn's music. There are a number of external reasons that help to account for this. He may have become familiar with the anticipatory romanticism of the poets and prose writers who were known collectively as the *Sturm und Drang* group; he had certainly embarked on his love-affair with Luigia Polzelli; and he had certainly made a renewed study of the music of C. P. E. Bach. But these are only superficial causes. The real reason was the complex of impulses which had given rise to the fashion for 'Storm and Stress' in the first place: that had prompted C. P. E. Bach to create a a music based on conflict between Sensibility and popular feeling. In any case, in his music written during the '70s Haydn exploits the dramatic potentialities inherent in rococo style. In the G minor Symphony, No. 39, for instance, all the stock rococo features—shooting scales, repeated notes on the horns, sudden breaks, contrasting dynamics, dissonant appoggiaturas—are used not as a pleasing titillation of the senses, but for their dramatic intensity (Ex. 6). The panting, repeated

Ex. 6. Haydn: Symphony No. 39 in G minor

quavers of the opening are almost hysterical, while the whirling scales of the last movement (also in sonata form) have a frightening energy. The music is fiercer, if less melancholy, than Mozart's G minor mood; indeed, there is little lyricism in the whole work. The modulations jump to extravagant keys; though Haydn still likes to derive his second subjects from his first. In opposition to rococo variety, he feels a need to give his music cohesion. Seeking unity in diversity, he relates his subject groups ever more intimately, without sacrificing the dramatic tension which we have seen to be the essence of sonata style. The majority of these stormful symphonies are in minor keys or, if in the major, in outlandish keys, such as B. Many of them have descriptive titles, '*La Lamentazione*', '*La Passione*', 'The Farewell'; all the slow movements show the influence of the *affetuoso* manner of C. P. E. Bach.

The tempestuous features in these works strike one's attention immediately; one should not overlook the fact that they also represent a significant development in Haydn's humour. The funny elements in his earlier work were in the main a simple *buffo* frivolity. Such comic movements as occur in the *Sturm und Drang* works tend—in an abrupt contrast of key, a melodic ellipsis, a sudden pause or contraction of rhythm—to startle as much as to amuse. Procedures that may in some contexts be drama are in other contexts wit: an intense levity that entails a recognition of 'other modes of experience that are possible', and therefore an awareness of instability. Consider the approach to the coda of the presto in his Symphony No. 52 in C minor (Ex. 7). All through Haydn's mature music—and in a more

Ex. 7. Haydn: Symphony No. 52 (Presto)

poignant way in Mozart's also—one finds this precariousness: the sudden defeat of expectation, the interruption of a norm of behaviour, whether of tonality or of melodic, harmonic, or rhythmic formula. One does not usually find this quality in composers who lived before the Age of Reason, in an age of Faith, whether in God or the State. Bach and Handel are sometimes comic, seldom if ever witty.

At about the same time as he was composing these first 'Storm and Stress' works, Haydn was also achieving a genuine quartet style. His opus 9 and opus 17 appeared in 1769 and 1771 respectively. Both collections—especially the quartets in minor keys—show signs of the conflagration of *Sturm und Drang*; while for the first time Haydn writes for each instrument as an independent entity. It would be impossible to play these works as band pieces, for they are already, in Goethe's words, a dialogue of 'four sensible people conversing with one another'. The key contrasts are much more enterprising than in the earlier quartets, and the developments, instead of being perfunctory, tend to be longer than the expositions. The D minor quartet of opus 9 and the C minor of opus 17, with their chromaticisms, sforzandi, syncopations, and passionate declamatory passages in particular suggest the influence of C. P. E. Bach, while attaining a more convincing continuity of line and of dramatic evolution.

The 'Sun' quartets, opus 20, dating from the following year, 1772, intensify all these features and add another, which we have already referred to in the symphonies. Many of them have fugal finales; and in all of them counterpoint is used in a manner remote from the conventionalities of *style galant*. The F minor quartet ends with a fierce fugue on a theme that was almost a stage-property of the baroque—the two most famous examples are 'And with his stripes' from Handel's *Messiah* and the A minor fugue from Book II of Bach's *Forty-eight*. The re-creation of the baroque fugue was not, however, the solution Haydn was seeking. He wanted to give the quartet dignity and coherence, and counterpoint was a means to that end; but the counterpoint he wanted to evolve was not baroque, but symphonic, and therefore reconcilable with the pathos of a movement such as this quartet's opening allegro. Here the second theme, though related to the first, is unmistakably also a lyrical contrast, and the development, with its remote modulations, is as long as it is dramatic. The recapitulation is itself modified and extended; and a final consummatory development occurs in the strange coda, with its remote transitions (Ex. 8).

Haydn's phase of overt passion and protest did not, however, last long. In his music of the 1780s, passion is absorbed into acceptance; and while his own creative development was the fundamental reason for this, the example of Mozart had

something to do with it. The mature Mozart taught Haydn how both counterpoint and themes of lyrical contour could be adapted to the dramatic purposes of the symphony. The D minor Symphony, No. 80, shows Haydn in the process of discovery. Apart from the wittily syncopated finale, all the movements have melodies which are more Italianate, lyrical and Mozartian than those of Haydn's previous works. But Haydn has not yet learned to create a lyricism appropriate to his own kind of symphonic thought. Here the contrasts of mood between the lyrical phrases are queerly abrupt, in the operatic adagio even more than in the allegro: so that the music reminds one of Mozart's slightly revered D minor mood without the resolving power of his cantabile melody. The work is enigmatic and disturbing: and a critical stage in Haydn's career.

When, in the sequence of symphonies he wrote for his first visit to England, Haydn finally achieved his synthesis of protest with acceptance, he had solved the problem of writing themes which have lyrical amplitude; which are at the same time susceptible of treatment in sonata style; and which no longer sound in the least like Mozart. The search for unity in diversity, which must be attained without impairing dramatic tension, here reaches its apotheosis. This remains true though Haydn's treatment of sonata form in his mature works is unpredictable, no two movements being quite alike in structure.

If one compares Symphony No. 104 in D with the earlier

symphonies the most immediately striking difference is the power and serenity of the opening theme, which is a singing melody, moving mainly by step, rather than a rhythmic 'motive' (Ex. 9). The second subject is a modified version of the

first; out of it grows a little rhythmic figure in the codetta* of the exposition (Ex. 10). The development is based mainly on this little motive, combined with fragments of the main themes.

A tremendous dramatic intensity is generated without disturbing the continuity of the texture. In the recapitulation the material is creatively modified; it has been born afresh in the course of the development. Indeed, one might say that Haydn's mature movements are all development, which starts in the exposition, since the second subject is a development of the first. Whereas Bach and Handel—in their different ways—are concerned with states of Being, Haydn's sonata movements already deal with growth and change—with Becoming.

The andante is based on one of those measured, spacious melodies which are the unique creation of Haydn's later years (Ex. 11). Their lyricism is utterly different from Mozart's:

non-chromatic, less operatic; more homely, one might say, if the tunes were not also sublime. Yet this movement, which opens with a theme so tranquil of soul, turns out to be a dramatic sonata movement, with weird modulations in the development, proceeding from G to D flat, and home by way of C sharp minor and F sharp minor and major. Here Haydn has

* A coda in a classical sonata movement is a peroration which rounds off, and gives finality to, the recapitulation. A codetta is a 'little coda' which occurs, not at the end of a movement, but at the end of a section of a movement—usually the exposition.

indeed attained a new resolution of the conflict between the artist and his world; and it is not extravagant to say that Haydn's true religion is enshrined in this prophetic music. He celebrates the Enlightenment's Discovery of Man. Democratic man had to find himself in order to rebuild civilization in the light of Reason: thus his passions were important, but were not the be-all and end-all of existence. They were a means towards the Apollonian equilibrium which became the classical ideal: which is epitomized in Haydn's late symphonic allegros and hymn-like andantes, as it is in Mozart's Masonic style. It is present too in the apparently slighter scherzo and finale of this Symphony No. 104; for the minuet, with its sudden breaks and trills, attains an almost Beethovenian power, and the rustic joviality of the finale, with folk-like theme and bagpipe drone, grows through its symphonically developing counterpoint into a paean of praise. It is at once comic and majestic.

If Mozart's example helped Haydn to reach maturity as a symphonist, Mozart admitted that the appearance of Haydn's opus 33 was a turning-point in his own development. Haydn said that in these quartets he was composing in 'an entirely new and special manner'. This was not strictly true, for we have seen that there was already plenty of 'thematic development' in the quartets of the 'Storm and Stress' period. It is true, however, that by his opus 33 Haydn has learned how to achieve concentration in sonata style, using counterpoint as a means to an end, without returning to baroque techniques. The quartets written in the '80s, like the symphonies of the same period, show a Mozartian leaning towards a more lyrical type of melody: in slow movements, for instance, Haydn tends to abandon sonata form in favour of variations, or a simple song tune in ternary form, with a minor episode in the middle. Even the most melancholy of the quartets comprising opus 54 or 64, such as the F sharp minor or the B minor, have not the feverishness of the 'Storm and Stress' years; they are mellowed by their lyricism. On the other hand, the wit of the comic pieces is enriched by touches of Mozartian chromaticism in the harmony.

Haydn attains his Apollonian equilibrium in the last series of quartets, opus 71, 74, 76, and 77. If one compares his last completed quartet, the F major of opus 77, with one of the early *quadri* or even the well-known 'Serenade' quartet from opus

3, it seems as though the composer has not so much developed a technique as created a new world of thought and feeling. As in Symphony No. 104, the finale is a superb piece of symphonic counterpoint; and the first movement opens with a theme rich, ample, cantabile. The second subject is a creative development from the first, but in consolatory inversion. The development, again like that of the allegro of the symphony, is based not on the cantabile melody, but on a rhythmic figure which appears in the codetta of the exposition. The repeated quavers of rococo convention are no longer cheerfully footling; nor are they frenzied, as they were in the stormy and stressful works. They become, as the music modulates flatwards through remote keys and with an ever acuter dissonance, pregnant with wonder and mystery (Ex. 12): so that the movement can be succeeded

Ex. 12. Haydn: Quartet opus 77 No. 2.

inevitably by the hymn-like andante with variations. The melody remains almost unaltered, being an entity complete in itself; the variations are arabesques embroidered around it. The same is true of the treatment of the most celebrated of all these great andante tunes—that from the C major quartet of opus 76. In this case the tune is in fact a hymn, for it is the most noble national anthem ever written.

The development of Haydn's piano sonatas follows a pattern almost identical with his symphonies and quartets. A little work like the A major of 1762 is in the orthodox binary structure of Bach's or Handel's dances. It is quite different in spirit, however, because it has almost no melody. Its appeal depends on its superfices—its twirls and twiddles. Then Haydn discovers how to extract drama from these frolics. For instance, in the F major Sonata of 1776 the first movement has nothing worth calling a melody. There is a rhythmic figure (tum-ti-tum): a percussive series of repeated notes in the bass: and some pathetic sighing appoggiaturas: all these being presented in the tonic key and its relative minor (Ex. 13). After a modulation to the dominant we have two other little figures, one based on a rapid arpeggio, the other on a scale (Ex. 14). Thus instead of baroque unity and continuity we have contrasting and heterogeneous material associated with two different key centres. The

structure of the piece is no longer the unfolding of melody, but the conflict between two groups of material and between different keys. The development begins with some sensationally rapid modulations; all the material is presented in startling oppositions of key, often with false starts and changes of direction (is there a faintly comic undertone to the equivocal use of the natural or flat second?). When the recapitulation happens we can at last appreciate the dramatic significance of the apparently innocuous fragments of tune and rhythm from which we had started. This dramatic purpose is still more marked in those sonatas which, like the fierce B minor, are directly influenced by the mood of 'Storm and Stress'.

In the late sonatas, particularly those written after the first English visit, both the themes and the keyboard writing acquire a new ripeness; again the themes tend to be closely interrelated. The great sonata in E flat, with its lyrical adagio in E major (approached as a kind of Neapolitan F flat) is a worthy pianistic counterpart of the London symphonies and the opus 76 and 77 quartets. In sonatas, symphonies, and quartets equally the dramatic urgency is increased rather than diminished, as compared with earlier works; only the drama is now resolved in a structure radiant with light. Apollonian order implies a new kind of belief. Haydn's God was not the mystical divinity of Bach, nor the Lord of earthly glory of Handel; but all his later music is religious in the sense that it reflects the beliefs that had meaning for him—an ethical humanism based on reason and the love of created nature. The development of his own ostensibly religious music shows him gradually discovering, in ecclesiastical terms, the religion that is implicit in his later instrumental music.

In his youth, Haydn composed a great deal of church music on commission, in the accepted rococo style. To object to the frivolity of this style is irrelevant; as we have seen, it was appropriate to the garishly decorated churches, and to the spirit of the people who worshipped with its help. In the sixteenth century, church motet and secular madrigal were basically the same in idiom, and the liturgical manner dominated the secular. In Haydn's day it was the other way round; the opera-house dominated the church to such a degree that even ecclesiastical buildings began to look like opera-houses. The style of Haydn's early masses is related to the secular operatic cantata and to the concerto grosso, with solo voices and choir fulfilling much the same functions as the concertino and ripieno instruments. One of his first pieces, a *Salve Regina* for soprano, contralto, two violins, and bass, is treated like a baroque trio sonata. It was written while he was a pupil of Porpora, and pays Italianate homage to his master.

Haydn felt no qualms about the frivolity of the masses he composed in the 1750s. On the contrary, he revived the first mass of all quite late in his life, considering that it merited the addition of wind parts: "What I particularly like about this little work", he said, "is its tunefulness and a certain youthful fire." But Haydn regarded these early masses in much the same way as he regarded his cassations and serenades for instruments. His carelessness in setting the text is significant: hardly ever does he attempt to interpret the words; sometimes he makes nonsense of them. Although late in life he was profoundly shocked at the imputation that he was not a pious Catholic, he never had any interest in the mysticism of Catholic dogma. In his youth he was content to say: "Since God has given me a cheerful heart, He will forgive me for serving Him cheerfully. Whenever I think of the dear Lord, I have to laugh. My heart jumps for joy in my breast." When in his mature years he discovered the nature of his own faith, it was profound enough, but it had nothing to do with mysticism or dogma.

During the 1770s the passions of 'Storm and Stress' effect a change in Haydn's church music comparable with that in his instrumental works. Two pieces contain the essence of this transformation: the *Stabat Mater*, in which C. P. E. Bach-like chromaticisms, sighs, syncopations, and sforzandi are obviously appropriate to the text; and *Tobias*, ostensibly a return to the baroque oratorio which resembles the more symphonic style of Rameau's or Gluck's operas, rather than the monumental grandeur of Handel. Both choruses and orchestral writing are impressively dramatic.

During the early 1780s Haydn composed a number of large-scale festival masses. Though these hardly suggest the direct influence of Mozart, they are Mozartian in that their theatrical manner is no longer a cheerful noise existing in its own right, like a symphony or a serenade: the music now underlines the meaning of the words. At least this is true of movements such as the Crucifixus of the 'Mariazell' Mass, in which Haydn can regard Christ not as a superhuman divinity, but as a man, suffering. In 1783, however, the progressive Emperor Joseph banned complicated church music; and Haydn wrote no more officially liturgical music for fourteen years. The only exception to this is the wonderful *Seven Last Words from the Cross*, a series of orchestral meditations on Christ's words which Haydn composed, at the instigation of Boccherini, for performance on Good Friday at Cadiz Cathedral. These seven adagios all, like the andante of Symphony No. 104, combine a sublime lyrical serenity with intense tonal drama. The themes are, however, more Italianate than the Masonic hymns of Haydn's last years. Perhaps for this reason the music has a meditative ecstasy which makes it seem more Catholic in spirit than any music Haydn wrote.

However this may be, when he turned to church music again his approach had been transformed—partly by his experience as a symphonist, partly by what he had learned, on his visits to England, of Handel and English oratorio. He had no moral objection to the theatrical manner; he merely felt that it was no longer capable of expressing his deepest thoughts and feelings. Handel himself had re-created heroic baroque conventions in a more middle-classical manner; Haydn, in *The Creation*, fuses Handelian oratorio with the dramatic thrust of his own symphonic style. Rococo affectations disappear; instead, Haydn celebrates ethical humanism and the glory of God in Nature.

Baron von Swieten's text was a re-hash of a re-hash by Linley of Milton; it is utterly un-Miltonic in that it divests God of spirituality and man of the sense of sin. "An object must be found", said von Swieten, "for music which, by its fervour, its universal sufficiency and perspicuity, may take the place of the pious emotions of former days"; and he turned God into a working mechanic, the story of the Creation into a Masonic parable. 'Now vanish before thy holy beams The spirits of the ancient Night.' Light triumphs through Reason, darkness is vanquished; but what makes the victory significant is precisely mankind's 'fervour, sufficiency and perspicuity'. Haydn's genius, in this case, stands for mankind.

The Creation falls into three parts. The first describes the birth of Order from Chaos; the second deals with Created Nature; and the third with human love (the Adam and Eve story). From this account it is clear that the story of *The Creation* is simply an explicit statement of the experience we have seen to be implicit in all Haydn's mature symphonies, sonatas, and quartets. The creation of Order from Chaos—Unity from Diversity—is the impulse behind the marvellous prologue to *The Creation*, in which the lucidity of C major emerges from the mysteriously veiled tonality and the chains of dissonant suspensions, with their romantic orchestration. It is also, we have seen, the motive force behind Haydn's greatest symphonic music. The famous blaze of C major at the words 'Let there be light' implies a large-scale symphonic architecture, for such an assertion of tonality has point only in reference to the ambiguities that have preceded it; one cannot recognize order unless one has first seen chaos. Similarly, the realistic portrayal of Nature in the second part is an extension of the simple acceptance of Nature as a background to human life which we have commented on in the symphonies: Nature is to be valued for its relation to human conduct, not romantically for its non-humanity. Similarly, again, in instrumental music no less than in the third part of *The Creation*, it is through the agency of human love that life is redeemed. So *The Creation*, like creation itself, forms a circle and ends at the point where it began. Life is perpetual renewal; the alternation of Light and Darkness, Order and Chaos, is perennial—as Beethoven was to discover in a more deeply subjective sense. Thus Haydn and the Enlightenment inherited the Christian doctrine of redemption, while believing that the agent of redemption was man become God, not God become man.

After returning from his first trip to England, Haydn composed several more masses for the Catholic Church. The spirit of them is distinct from that of the early masses. The rococo perkiness has gone. Instead, we have the dramatic power of Haydn the symphonist, reconciled with the monumental counterpart of the baroque: and thus translated into the relative impersonality of liturgical style. The *Missa in Tempore Belli* was composed while Napoleon's armies were pressing across the Styrian border. The trumpet-calls and kettledrums of the slow introduction to the Kyrie have the dramatic solemnity of one of Haydn's, or even Beethoven's, symphonic openings; and the Kyrie theme is a symphonic rather than operatic motive. The orchestra is handled with powerful independence throughout, in the same style as the last symphonies; the choruses, on the other hand, have a contrapuntal grandeur which suggests Bach even more than Handel. A movement such as the Miserere Nobis is a liturgical act which is also a personal utterance. Haydn's true religion has burst through the façade of dogma.

This is still more evident in the masses that post-date *The Creation*. The 'Nelson' Mass of 1798 is a humanistic mass with a tremendous Kyrie in full sonata form, combined with magnificent counterpoint, especially in the Credo. The 'Theresa' Mass of the following year is remarkable for the way in which elements of sonata and of opera are absorbed into a *dramatic* fugue to the words '*Et vitam venturi*'. The last of the masses, the *Harmoniemesse* of 1802, is perhaps the greatest of all. The large-scale sonata of the Kyrie and the majestic use of the wind band almost suggest the Beethoven of the *Missa Solemnis*: on the other hand, the counterpoint of the Qui tollis comes closer to the spiritual essence of Bach than did any other composer of a later generation. Mozart only once attempted anything comparable with this in church music; and the work remained unfinished. He was no longer a man of faith. Haydn's faith was changing in ways of which he was but obscurely conscious; yet he came just in time to make the best of two worlds.

In a work such as the *Harmoniemesse* he rebuilds the Church in the spirit of the Enlightenment which he celebrates in his greatest instrumental works. The serenity he attains may not be mystical; it certainly entails what one can only call Belief.

"Often", he once said, "when I was wrestling with obstacles of every kind, when my physical and mental strength alike were running low and it was hard for me to persevere on the path on which I had set my feet, a secret feeling within me whispered: 'There are so few happy and contented people here below, sorrow and anxiety pursue them everywhere; perhaps your work may one day become a spring from which the careworn may draw a few moments' rest and refreshment.' And that was a powerful motive for pressing onwards". His prophecy has been fulfilled; and we find his music increasingly valuable to-day, when belief in life, and in man's potentialities, is subject to much discouragement.

3

MOZART: MUSIC FOR HOME AND CHURCH

HAYDN'S CAREER covers a long tract of time and a still wider range of experience. He was twenty-four when Mozart [1756–1791] was born, and had written none of the music by which he is remembered. When Mozart died Haydn was nearly sixty. He had another eighteen creative years before him, in the course of which he learned from Mozart while becoming more deeply himself. Mozart had less than half as long as Haydn to live. By the time he was twenty-four he had advanced about as far in his creative development as Haydn had at the age of forty. It is as though he knew he had but little time, whilst Haydn knew that he need not hurry. This temperamental difference is a deeper matter than a distinction between personalities; it has reference too to the sense in which Mozart is the more 'modern' composer. Like Haydn, he was aristocratically nurtured; but the elements of protest in his temperament were more strongly marked, if not less strongly disciplined.

Haydn was a countryman who could move easily among the great in centres of sophistication, while being content to spend most of his life in seclusion; his character, like his music, is a mingling of peasant horse-sense, feudal gallantry, and middle-class Masonic morality, all reborn in his creative fire. Mozart was born in 1756 in rococo Salzburg, a smaller town than Vienna, but perhaps for that reason more exquisite, more precious. Haydn remained in some ways a countryman all his days; Mozart was from early youth a townsman and cosmopolitan. At the instigation of an ambitious father, who was a professional whereas Haydn's father had been an amateur musician, the young Mozart was launched on a musical career at an age when Haydn had scarcely become aware that he was a sentient being. Mozart's career as virtuoso and child composer carried him all over Europe; whereas Haydn for sixty years did not move further than a few miles from Vienna. As a result, Mozart never acquired a settled position, either as a household musician like Haydn, or as director of an opera-house or church. Such jobs as came his way he found increasingly irksome. A turning-point in his career came when, in 1781, he quarrelled finally with Colloredo and was kicked out by the Archbishop's secretary. This incident used to be recounted in the history books as evidence of the composer's noble nature rebelling against the odious tyranny of service. But there is nothing intrinsically wicked about patronage, so long as one believes in the system that supports it. From a material point of view, Mozart's action was silly; it was his own fault that he was buried in a pauper's grave. None the less, from another point of view, the history books are right. Mozart's action was inevitable, given the kind of man he was, the kind of music he was writing, and the conditions under which he worked. At that particular moment it was what he had to do: a symbolical gesture against a world in which he was ceasing to believe. No more than Haydn was he a conscious revolutionary. Indeed, unlike Haydn, he believed passionately in aristocracy, though in an aristocracy of the spirit. He was painfully aware that the reality was remote from his ideal; and he was seeking for that ideal in his subjective interpretation of Freemasonry during his last fevered years. Though he never found it in the outside world, he left it, for us, in his music.

The one fundamental quality which Mozart has in common with Haydn is his humanity. Belief in human nature excludes all other interests except music; and for Mozart the two can hardly be separated. Haydn saw human beings against their environment and in relation to Nature and a humanistically inclined God. But we know from Mozart's extraordinarily vivid letters that even as a young man—one might almost say as a child—people and music absorbed his whole being. Travelling through Italy, he makes scarcely a reference in his letters to art, architecture, or the beauties of scenery. His pen-pictures of people—celebrities, intimate friends, and chance acquaintances—and his comments on the music he heard are, on the other hand, astonishingly acute—and neither bitter nor sentimental. We should not therefore be surprised that Mozart was fundamentally an opera composer, whereas Haydn was fundamentally a symphonic and instrumental composer. Haydn wrote operas, but himself said that in this field he was a nonentity compared with Mozart. Mozart's operas are the core of his work, though his notion of what opera was differed from that of any previous composer. His changed conception of opera is associated with the fact that he was a composer of the sonata epoch; it is also true that his conception of sonata was modified by the fact that throughout his life he thought in vocal and operatic terms.

In a superficial sense this is evident even in Mozart's boyhood training. Any composer brought up in eighteenth-century Austria would have been nurtured on Italian opera; but we saw that the music which first fired the young Haydn's imagination was rather the instrumental vitality of Stamitz, and the northern passion of C. P. E. Bach. The first music Mozart knew well was naturally that of his father. Leopold was a typical Salzburg composer; his music was in the popular middle-class manner, but prettily elegant, without the Mannheimers' power. As soon as Mozart was old enough to know what he felt, he liked the prettiness in his father's music, but despised the popular element: just as he came to hate the bourgeois Salzburgers in whose bovine pranks he had played his part. Unlike Haydn, he could never accept the middle-class style without transforming it into the spiritually aristocratic. As for rural folk-song, for him that was something to be parodied.

Most of the music which Mozart heard on his Continental travels was operatic and Italian. As a boy composer he willingly acceded to his father's ambition that he should become a successful creator of Italian operas, both serious and comic. His childhood operas did, indeed, achieve a considerable measure of acclaim, by no means entirely due to the fact that they were written by a child. They show evidence of a command of vocal technique and of lyrical melody which conditioned his approach to all kinds of music-making. One would not expect them to be distinguished by originality or depth.

Among sonata composers Mozart would, as a youth, have studied the music of C. P. E. Bach, who was accepted as one of the great masters. He admired but did not love Carl Philipp's music. Nordic introspection did not spontaneously appeal to a composer who, thinking operatically, preferred to objectify his passion. This is one reason for the apparent lack of connexion between Mozart's music and his biography.

There were, however, two sonata composers who made a deep impression on the young Mozart. One was Johann

Schobert [1720–1767], a composer from the Polish border who had settled in Paris, where Mozart met him while on tour. Schobert's music is emotional and instinct with Sensibility; but, unlike C. P. E. Bach's, it is also elegantly urbane. Mozart probably relished its rococo charm rather than its nervous intensity. That the intensity was there, however, must have been a subconscious reason for the appeal; for as he grew only a little older Mozart was to discover his own passion beneath the rococo façade.

There was another composer whom the boy Mozart met on his travels: that was J. S. Bach's youngest son, Johann Christian [1735–1782]. In him Mozart found a kindred spirit; for J. C. Bach was a German composer who had turned from the Protestant north and settled in Milan, where, having become a Catholic, he composed innumerable operas and cantatas in a prettified version of Italian baroque. He also composed much instrumental music in the new *style galant*, especially after he moved to London and became a leader of musical fashion. His music in sonata style was always modified by his early love of and training in Italian lyricism; this suited a public that liked their music to be superficially enlivening so long as it did not ruffle complacency. Only very occasionally, and in spite of himself, did he allow the dualistic energy of sonata style or the gravity of the Bachs' Protestant heritage to disrupt the rounded pleasantries of his art—as in the C minor Piano Sonata we referred to earlier. Like his brother Carl Philipp, he wrote for the new public of 'connoisseurs and amateurs'; but whereas Carl Philipp regarded this public as an intellectual élite, for Johann Christian it was a source of revenue—and no doubt of pleasant social intercourse. "My brother lives to compose," remarked Johann Christian. "I compose to live."

The appeal of Johann Christian's music to the young Mozart is easy to understand. It was 'modern', and in that sense superficially youthful in spirit; it was also instinct with a cantabile lyricism which seemed antipathetic to sonata style. Again, Mozart's inclinations were prophetic in a way deeper than conscious understanding. For if Stamitz—and Haydn in his early days—achieved symphonic drama by sacrificing lyricism, and J. C. Bach preserved lyricism only by refusing to realize the dramatic implications of sonata, in Mozart's mature music lyrical melody and tonal drama are to be accorded equal rights. The equilibrium between lyricism and drama which Haydn so gloriously achieves in the music of his last years is evident in Mozart's music almost from the moment he becomes a person. In his instrumental works the parts sing, as do the voices in his operas; and both create an interplay of character and motive. One might almost say that the two elements of vocal lyricism and instrumental drama in Mozart's sonata movements are synonymous with acceptance and protest.

It is mistaken piety to maintain that Mozart's boyhood compositions are intrinsically very valuable; though by adolescence he must have attained a stage of emotional development that few reach by the age of thirty. Certainly, he had a greater technical assurance at fourteen than Haydn had at twenty-four. Haydn's earliest works are, in their popular virility, sometimes wilfully uncouth. Mozart's early works—whether he writes serenades for weddings of the local bourgeoisie or symphonies which are not radically distinct from them—have always an Italianate sweetness and polish. Even street tunes acquire a courtly grace. At about the age of puberty—an important experience for everyone, though not many are at that age blessed with the faculty of creative expression—Mozart begins to adapt the clichés of *opera buffa* and of J. C. Bach to his own modest purposes. The little symphony, K.22, contains a chromatic andante which is more than an evocation of fashion; and even Mozart's accompanying figurations become cantabile.

It is interesting too that almost the first group of works to betray a Mozartian personality is a set of violin sonatas, K.55–60. Now whereas in the baroque violin sonata string melody had been the music's life-blood, which the keyboard succours and supports, in the rococo period the functions of the two instruments had been reversed. The early violin and piano sonatas of Haydn make sense if played as piano solos—a violin part is provided should a fiddle and sociable fiddler be handy; for the idiom of the classical sonata, being at first harmonic and rhythmic rather than melodic in approach, was in some ways radically opposed to the genius of the violin. This is why Haydn favoured the piano sonata and more or less ignored the violin as solo instrument. But with Mozart, even in early youth, the violin comes once more into its own as an instrument allied to the singing voice. His piano sonatas are relatively insignificant. His mature violin and piano sonatas are neither accompanied song-without-words, like the baroque sonata: nor dance action with a few perfunctory tunes thrown in, like rococo sonatas for piano 'with violin accompaniment': but real *duos* that achieve an equilibrium between symphonic drama and song.

In the 1770's Mozart, like Haydn, went through a phase of 'Storm and Stress'. Haydn was in his forties at the time; Mozart was adolescent. A symphony such as K.133 is still wittily poetic in its lyricism; but its grace becomes imperceptibly dramatic, especially in the subtly modified recapitulation and coda to the first movement. The influence of the genius of Haydn—and of growing up—is beginning to deepen the rococo charm he learned from J. C. Bach. The next year brings a still more remarkable development. The little G minor Symphony, K.183, is fascinating both for its resemblances to and differences from Haydn's minor moods in his *Sturm und Drang* compositions. It has the same passionate repeated notes and brusque changes of dynamics which we noticed in Haydn's G minor Symphony (No. 39). But whereas Haydn is fierce, Mozart is melancholy; and the difference consists in the sweetly singing quality of Mozart's themes as compared with Haydn's explosiveness, and in the persistently sighing appoggiaturas (Ex. 15). This does

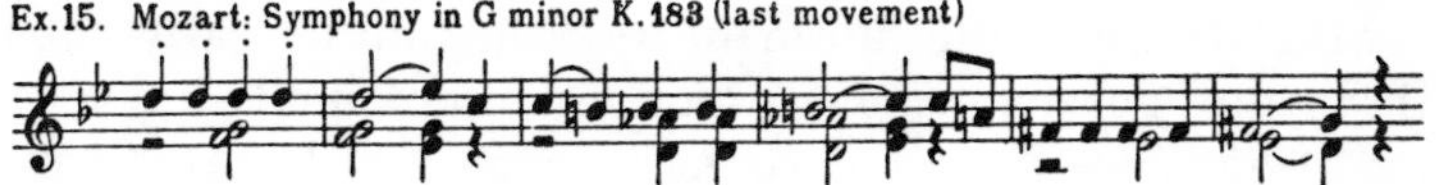
Ex.15. Mozart: Symphony in G minor K.183 (last movement)

not mean that Mozart's melancholy is limp. It is acute, because it is already inherently dramatic. It is worth noting that whereas Haydn and C. P. E. Bach and Beethoven—who were not *primarily* lyrical composers—prefer to unify their material as closely as is consistent with their dramatic intentions, Mozart and J. C. Bach, who naturally think lyrically, can afford to introduce more obvious contrasts between their themes. Even Mozart's A major Symphony, K.201, which is a radiant piece, places sinuously chromatic melodies alongside airily dancing *buffo* tunes: and contains the longest and most exciting development that Mozart had yet created.

'Storm and Stress' was, however, an element inherent in Mozart's temperament, rather than absorbed from without.

His equilibrium between lyricism and drama involves too a balance between joy and sorrow; nor are we ever quite sure whether his music is happy or sad. This characteristic of mature Mozart is already evident in the E minor Violin Sonata of 1778. The first of the two movements is passionate in its soaring themes, tense in its chromaticism and modulations: the excitingly re-harmonized recapitulation is itself a further development. It is followed by a little minuet with a trio in the major which ought to be consolatory, but is in effect more heart-breaking than the minor allegro (Ex. 16). This is partly

Ex. 16. Mozart: Violin and piano sonata K. 304 (second movement)

because the exquisite singing melody is harmonized with an unexpectedly seductive richness; partly because each phrase dissolves away in a sigh—a falling dissonant appoggiatura. The sigh and the chromatics imbue the theme with a sense of yearning. The bliss of such a melody seems seraphic: and so unattainable in this world.

Mozart's growth to full maturity occurs in the early 1780s. If Haydn's development was soon to be profoundly influenced by Mozart, we have the younger man's word that his own development was decisively affected by Haydn's opus 33. Mozart's first quartets, modelled on the Milanese style of Sammartini and J. C. Bach, were simply three-movement Italian symphonies without wind. The quartets composed between K.155 and K.172 approach the *galant* quartet style of Schobert; they manifest some of the emotionalism typical of the early violin sonatas, along with a half-hearted attempt to emulate the fugal discipline with which Haydn had experimented in his opus 9 and 17. After that, Mozart wrote no more quartets for ten years—a long time in so short and crowded a career.

In 1783 Mozart composed—after long and wearisome toil, he tells us—a set of six quartets which he dedicated to Haydn. The older man had shown him how to compose for four stringed instruments in dramatic dialogue. Yet although these quartets contain movements which were obviously intended to be modelled on movements by Haydn, they at the same time attest Mozart's independence. The opening theme of the E flat Quartet, K.428, with its tritone and sinuous chromaticism, is as personal and un-Haydnesque an utterance as the hauntingly seductive andante. Even the last movement, which opens with a Haydn-like wit, develops elements of chromatic pathos. Haydn's great lyrical melodies are never chromatic; when he does use melodic chromaticism it is usually for a parodistic effect. Mozart's melodies are always liable to acquire chromaticism, even if they are not chromatic to begin with. Again, his irregular phrase lengths and his emotional use of contrasting dynamics are almost always, as here, associated with the articulation of melody. Haydn's tend to be associated with rhythmic and harmonic surprises.

Perhaps the most profoundly representative quartet of the group is the D minor K.421. All four movements have the slightly fevered intensity which seems typical of Mozart's D minor utterances. The last movement, a variation-set in siciliano rhythm, is an instance of Mozart's ability to invest an apparently innocent pastoral with the force of tragedy: partly by means of violent syncopations, of a subtle ambiguity between major and minor, and of a cadential use of the Neapolitan sixth which introduces an uncannily strange perspective into the tonality (Ex. 17). In the coda the repeated Ds high up on the first violin send a chill down the spine; and the frightening

Ex. 17 Mozart: Quartet in D minor K. 421 (last movement)

quality of this music is inseparable from its restraint. It is devoid of rhetoric, yet more dramatic music has never been created.

In the first movement of this quartet, all the themes sing, and much of the figuration is chromatic. The melodies seem to be complete in themselves, like the vocal themes of opera. Yet the modulations of the development are powerfully dramatic, and the continuity of the texture is assured by masterly counterpoint: fragments of the themes are bandied about between the four instruments as they might be in an operatic ensemble. The slow movement is another of Mozart's idylls in the major key, which appear to be relief from the stress of the minor, but are in fact still more melancholy. Here the pathos springs from the way in which the caressing curves of the melody and the warm harmony are intermittently broken by abrupt sequential modulations. Again, the movement suggests an operatic situation: the love scene in which a transitory bliss hides heaven or hell knows what perturbations of spirit. The overlapping asymmetry of the phrases emphasizes this hint of dramatic dialogue; the speakers interrupt one another in the urgency of their passion (Ex. 18):

Ex. 18. Mozart: Quartet in D minor K 421 (slow movement)

The C major Quartet, K.465, is a still more remarkable instance of this quasi-operatic instrumental technique. The notorious slow introduction which so alarmed Mozart's contemporaries is a subjective rather than ceremonial re-creation of the old baroque overture: its chromaticisms and dissonant suspensions possibly suggested to Haydn the mysterious

Prologue to *The Creation*. In the development of the first movement, Mozart treats quartet style in a manner comparable with his handling of an operatic ensemble. It is worth noting that although all these quartets contain magnificent contrapuntal writing, the counterpoint is always symphonic and dramatic. Even the fully-fledged fugue at the conclusion of K.387 is an immensely invigorated *buffo* finale.

Naturally enough, this approach which Mozart brought to quartet-writing invaded too his symphonic style. K.425 (the 'Linz') is the first of his symphonies to acquire something of the urgent grandeur, as well as the wit, of Haydn's mature works. More surprisingly, we find this new approach also in the 'occasional' music which Mozart still composed in the manner of the divertimento. The C minor Serenade for wind instruments of 1781 is one of the darkest and most serious of his works: so much so that Mozart later arranged it for string quintet, a medium which he normally reserved for his most personal utterances. It sounds magnificent in its original form—as worthy a companion to the solemnity and power of *Idomeneo* as the string quintets are to the later, less heroic operas. Mozart was probably justified in thinking that it would disturb rather than satisfy the folk at whose commission it had been written.

It was some time before Mozart followed the 'Haydn' set with further quartets. He rather turned to experiment in the combination of strings, and sometimes wind instruments, with piano, producing in the G minor piano Quartet one of his most passionate instrumental works, and in the Trio for clarinet, viola, and piano one of his most enigmatically profound. For this kind of dialogue between melody instruments and piano Mozart had virtually no models: even C. P. E. Bach had attempted in this manner only works of rococo charm. Mozart did not consider these hybrid combinations entirely satisfactory, because the contestants were not equally balanced. But it is easy to see why he devoted such care to these works. They were studies towards his great cycle of piano concertos; and in this medium Mozart was to discover the consummate form of his fusion of operatic techniques with sonata. It is significant that the cycle of piano concertos was composed during Mozart's greatest period of operatic creation; and that in these years he wrote only one symphony.

It is hardly extravagant to say that Mozart created the classical concerto—created and fulfilled it, for his concertos have no successors. Before him, the rococo concerto had been even less pretentious than the rococo symphony. It was a not very taxing display piece for a soloist with instrumental accompaniment. It whiled away idle moments with a pleasing euphony, but its wayward and improvisatory nature hardly lent itself to the dramatic urgency of sonata style. Mozart's own Flute and Harp Concerto, written on his visit to Paris, is a more than normally distinguished example of such rococo entertainment; it exploits the sonorities of the instruments to woo the senses, and highly effective is its courtship. Even Mozart's early violin concertos, written (at Leopold's instigation) to show off his virtuosity, are unambitious; and the beautiful Sinfonia Concertante for violin and viola, which directly emulates operatic aria in instrumental terms, remained an isolated experiment.

Mozart did not enjoy composing his violin concertos, and found the Flute and Harp Concerto a sore trial. When he took up concerto form in earnest he ignored melody instruments and turned to the piano. We have seen that as an instrument for solo sonatas Mozart preferred the cantabile violin to the piano. As a concerto instrument, he preferred the piano to the violin, because in its power and contrasting timbre it could be a worthy opposite number to the orchestra. He sees the piano concerto as a duality in unity: was subconsciously fascinated by it because it offered an allegorical expression of the separation of the individual (the soloist) from society (the orchestra). But this separation is made in order that the soloist and orchestra can, in the course of the music, evolve a new relationship. The Mozartian concerto threatens, only in order to vindicate, civilization. So Mozart remains a classical artist, even though his preoccupation with this new medium is indicative of a romantic strain more developed in him than in Haydn. The older master composed no concertos of significance in comparison with his greatest symphonies and quartets.

Composers before Mozart had written piano concertos, some of which—notably those of C. P. E. Bach and Schobert—contain fine music. But the impressive passages are intermittent, for these composers were content to accept the origins of the style in improvisation. The boy Mozart wrote many concertos on the model of C. P. E. Bach and Schobert—and of Wagenseil and J. C. Bach—for himself to play on his Continental tours.

But in 1776 (significantly during the 'Storm and Stress' phase) he produced a concerto which gave intimation of the importance which the form would later have for him. It has been said that this concerto, K.271, was a step forward in Mozart's development comparable with that which Beethoven took in proceeding from the Second Symphony to the 'Eroica'. The claim is hardly too extravagant.

The most immediately striking point about this concerto is that Mozart is clearly trying to give the form a stature comparable with the most serious kind of symphony he knew of. Compared with rococo concertos, it is long, and very difficult; and although in the orthodox three movements of the concerto, the last telescopes the symphonic rondo and minuet. While this rondo tune is itself comic, the interjections of the minuet as episodes are deeply disturbing: as is the passionately operatic slow movement in the relative minor, in which the pianist emulates the operatic singer by breaking into recitative. All the cadenzas reveal their operatic origin; and they were all carefully written out by Mozart. The concerto was too much for Mozart's public, who considered it noisy and overburdened with notes.

The cycle of mature concertos begins in 1782, alongside the cycle of operas. If his violin concertos are based on the principle of operatic aria, the piano concertos are founded on the principle of operatic ensemble; his first-movement form in concerto is almost always more complicated than it is in symphony. Soloist and orchestra always have equality of status. The orchestra makes its statement with independent matter in a long prelude. The soloist enters, often with different material. There are thus two complimentary expositions with four, five, or even six subjects, which can be interlinked in constantly changing sequence. All these themes may be developed simultaneously in ensemble, creating a new clarity out of complexity. This technique implies a new conception of orchestration. Mozart's scoring is not purely linear, like the baroque, nor purely harmonic, like the rococo: it is a mixture of both, in which all the parts are volatile, whether they be themes or melodic figurations that support the harmony. There is nothing in music to which this technique may be compared, except Mozart's own mature operatic ensembles in which a number of characters sing together phrases different in mood and psychology: yet the result is not chaos, but understanding.

Mozart's slow movements in his concertos are varied in form. They may be simple A-B-A song forms (which he often calls *romanza*),* serving as a relief from the first movement's clear complexity. They may be in adagio sonata form, with the evolution of aria-like melody more important than dramatic development: as in the wonderful F sharp minor *napolitana*† from K.488. Or they may be in variation style with or without coda. His finales are usually rondos crossed with elements of sonata, in that the episodes may introduce dramatic modulations which carry the rondo tune with them. When the rondo theme returns to the original key it has the effect of a recapitulation: though rondo style remains more easy-going and improvisatory than first-movement form. For Mozart, and still more for Beethoven later, sonata has become the dynamic principle, variation the static; while rondo is a hybrid between the two.

The great Mozartian cycle begins with two lightweight concertos, K.413 and K.414. Perhaps Mozart felt that in presenting his new kind of ensemble-concerto, he should let his public down gently. These amiably pastoral works reveal unsuspected depths which the listener may bypass if he wishes. But K.449 he can only take or leave. It is grand, powerfully melancholy, and full of intimate associations with *Figaro*. So is K.459, with its nocturnal slow movement which reconciles the popular and the learned in fusing symphonic homophony with fugato and operatic ensemble. K.482 has a comparable relationship to *Così fan tutte*, and the 'demoniacal' D minor to *Don Giovanni*, whose tragedy is likewise rounded off in *buffo* merriment.

The peak point of the Mozartian concerto is, however, the C minor, K.491, which has all the D minor's passion, ennobled with a classical grandeur. The long orchestral prelude is based on material most of which is creatively modified in the concertante sections; the effect of the soloist's entry, with a new (and pianistic) theme, is extraordinarily telling. The final variations are again grand and sombre in their resilience, endlessly resourceful in their handling of dialogue between soloist and tutti. The last concerto of all, the B flat K.595, is as different in

* For Mozart's generation the *romanza* was a short movement in song style, in single binary or ternary form, moderate in tempo, intimate and sentimental (in the strict sense) in mood.

† Originally a popular song [for several voices, in lilting 6–8 time, allied to the sixteenth-century Villanella, and much cultivated in Naples.

XXXI Symphony No. 94 by Haydn. From the MS. possibly written by Joseph Elssler Jr. Formerly in the Archives of Prince Eszterházy.

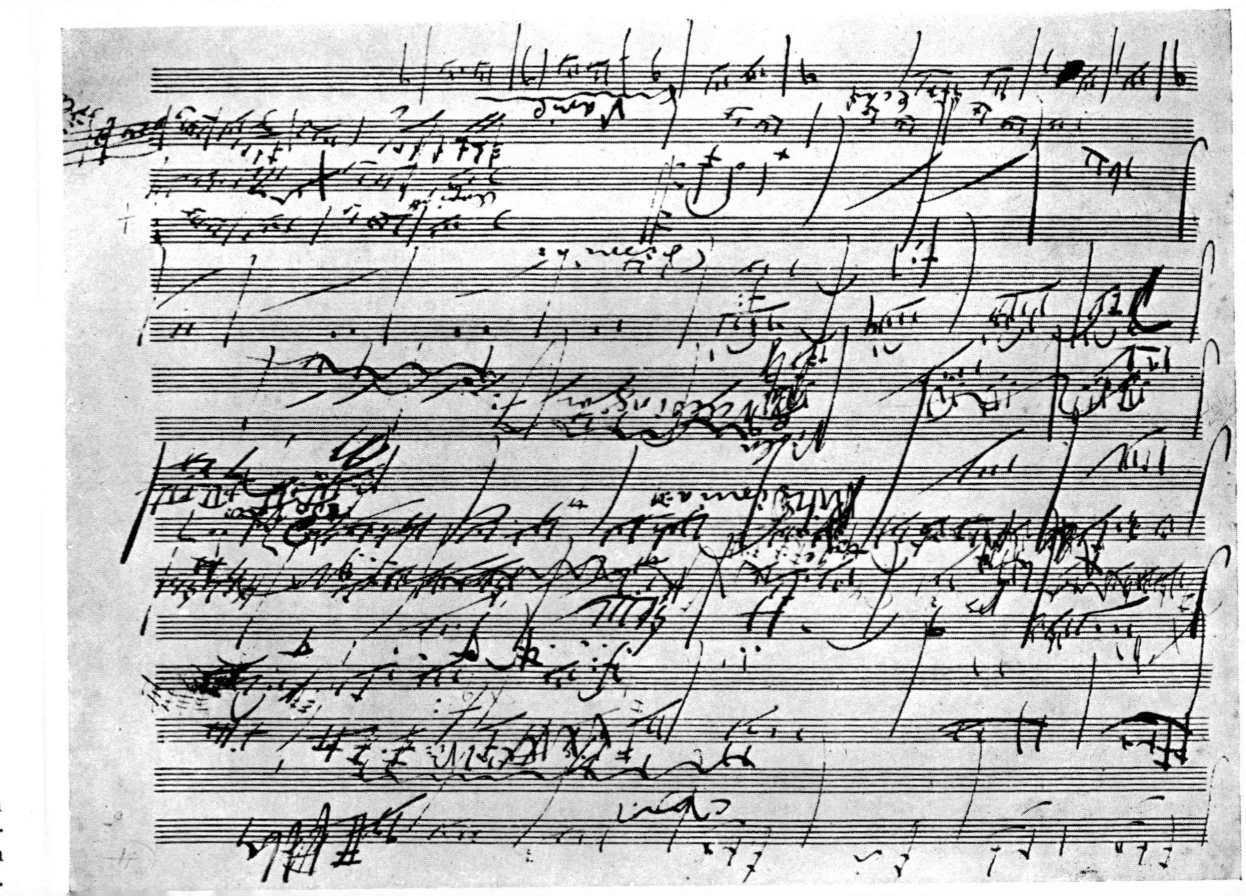

XXXII Page from a Beethoven sketch-book: sketch from Pastoral Symphony.

mood from the severity of K.491 as could be imagined. It sounds childlike only because its subtleties are so lucent. Yet this exquisite music was composed in conditions of appalling mental and physical suffering; and when we have heard it we find ourselves wondering whether this concerto or the C minor is the sadder.

The rondo finale of this B flat Concerto is based on an early song of Mozart which sounds like a nursery tune. Its significant title was 'Longing for spring'. Spring is still present in the transformed version it assumes in the concerto; in the modulatory episodes longing wellnigh breaks the heart. Yet the work as a whole seems to glitter with light. It is never self-regarding music; the melancholy inherent in its chromatic figurations and poetic felicities of scoring is absorbed into the precision of the music's structure. So the sadness within its gaiety seems to be not Mozart's, but the mutability in life itself.

This concerto seems to be gay; the G minor Quintet, written a few years earlier, is the most melancholy piece Mozart ever wrote. But the percussive repeated note accompaniment, the dissonant suspensions, the yearning lift to the sixth and the minor ninth in the second subject, have none of the feverishness of the youthful G minor Symphony, or the violent passion of the G minor Piano Quartet. In both concerto and quintet, whether gay or melancholy, the passion is purged: realized so consummately in musical terms that it is beyond either our laughter or our tears.

We have observed that counterpoint, half operatic, half symphonic in character, plays a conspicuous part in Mozart's mature music. There is a further aspect of this: for in his last years Mozart made a detailed study of the music of Bach, remarking that here at last was something from which he could learn. Some of the works which Mozart deliberately wrote in a Bachian manner—notably the Adagio and Fugue for string quartet, K.546—are very odd in their emotional effect. Mozart so crams in his contrapuntal devices of inversion, augmentation, diminution, and stretto, and thereby so coruscates the harmony that the music produces an impression of a driving energy strained almost to breaking-point. These 'monistic' pieces of Mozart are thus more agonized than his most dualistic sonata movements: exactly contrary to Bach in spirit, however they may follow the letter of his technique.

But the Bachian exercises are interesting not only because they helped Mozart to perfect the kind of counterpoint that was valuable for him; they were also one of the elements that went to create the Masonic style of his last years. We can see this in the great trio of symphonies which were Mozart's last word in this form. The only symphony he had composed during the period of his piano concertos was the 'Prague', which is full of 'operatic' polyphony and is, like the D minor Concerto, related to *Don Giovanni*. But the last three symphonies he wrote to please himself; and he made in them the affirmations about life and death which he had embodied in his emotional reinterpretation of Freemasonry. He has transformed the symphony from rococo entertainment into a personal testament.

The key of the first of the group is E flat; and this key has a symbolical significance in all the works Mozart wrote for Masonic ceremonies. Woodwind instruments were also associated with Masonic rites; and they play an important part in this symphony, especially in the *passionately* ceremonial introduction. The G minor Symphony,* like the Quintet in the same key, is a distillation of suffering: all the 'properties' of 'Storm and Stress' are divested of rhetoric, so that the drama is pure music and the music drama, and the suffering is neither Mozart's nor ours, but mankind's. The C major is an assertion of order. In the last movement Mozart's masterly fusion of sonata conflict with operatic-ensemble counterpoint triumphs over pain and darkness. The last three symphonies are not 'better' than the great concertos, but they mark a new development. The concertos are the instrumental epitome of the operatic Mozart; in the last symphonies he offers a purely musical expression of what he had discovered to be his religion.

His spiritual career thus follows a path in many ways parallel to that of Haydn, though the point at which he arrived is different. Neither man could have put into words what he had come to believe, and as much of Mozart's beliefs as found its way into the libretto of *The Magic Flute* distorts by oversimplification. Since Haydn and Mozart were musicians, not poets, this is of little consequence: from their music itself we can see that there is a distinction between their attitudes both to the orthodox creed of their time, and to the religion which they had discovered in the course of their creative lives. Haydn

* For a detailed analysis see Rudolf Reti, *The Thematic Process in Music.*

modified traditional Catholicism in the light of his and his age's rational humanism; the qualities distinguishing his last ethical works such as *The Creation* also make an imprint on his last masses. But he never wilfully broke with Catholic dogma, nor had any conscious desire to substitute for it a new ideal.

In his youth, both at Salzburg and during his Italian travels, Mozart composed a considerable amount of church music because it paid him to do so. Like all rococo church music, it is completely theatrical in style, except for a few archaic, undigested survivals of baroque counterpoint. As music, it is best when unashamedly simple and sensuous, as in the tender Lorettine Litanies and the *De Profundis*, K.93: exquisite music which has no more connexion with mysticism than the ludicrously lilting setting of the words 'Miserere Nobis' in the *Litaniae de venerabili altaris sacramento* of 1772.

It is significant that Mozart gave up composing church music as soon as his official duties no longer called for it. The only exceptions to this are the Mass in C, K.337, and the *Kyrie*, K.341, written while he was working on *Idomeneo*: very beautiful works which, like the opera, manage to reconcile some of the ceremonial majesty of the baroque with symphonic drama; and then the big C minor Mass, K.427, and the *Requiem*, both of which he left unfinished.

These two supreme climaxes of Mozart's church music were both composed for personal rather than for dogmatic reasons. The Mass he wrote at the time of his marriage, as an avowal of praise and gratitude. Its models are the great baroque masters, Handel, Caldara, Alessandro Scarlatti, and above all the polyphony of Bach, in whose music Mozart found so much to fascinate him. It interprets its baroque models symphonically and dramatically, however, as Haydn had done in his last masses; and relates the Italianate vocal style of the baroque to Mozart's own type of operatic lyricism. The Qui Tollis, like that of Haydn's *Harmoniemesse*, is especially Bachian, the Et Incarnatus especially operatic; but there is no longer any confusion of genres.

We do not know why Mozart left this superbly powerful work unfinished. Perhaps the reality of his marriage proved less inspiring than his ideal conception of it; very probably he had to put the Mass aside to meet commitments which brought in more immediate financial return. In any case, this was not the kind of music in which he was most interested. The *Requiem* is a different matter. The Mass, written for Constanze, is still ostensibly Catholic in spirit. The *Requiem* he wrote for himself, and its spirit is personal and Masonic. The story of the Dark Stranger who came to commission the work is well known. There was a rational explanation of his presence; he was the emissary of a Count who wished to preserve anonymity in order to pass off the work as his own composition. To Mozart's sick imagination he seemed an emissary from another world. He wrote the Mass feverishly, conscious that death was overtaking him.

The elements of Mozart's Masonic style are all present in the *Requiem*. One of them is still Bachian counterpoint; but although this may sometimes be thrillingly monumental, as in the Rex Tremendae, its habitual manner is more intimate and restrained than in the Catholic Mass. It has a tense serenity such as we can observe too in the profoundly lovely fugal movements that Mozart included in his Masonic works for mechanical organ. In the *Requiem*, especially the Introit, the suspensions, tied notes, and syncopations create a suppressed agitation beneath the solemnity. This is enhanced by the dark Masonic orchestration, with pairs of clarinets, basset horns, and bassoons (Ex. 19):

Ex. 19. Mozart: *Requiem*. opening of Introit

There is another style in the *Requiem*, however, which is as purely homophonic as the Bachian movements are contrapuntal. The Hostias is a hymn-like melody—in the 'Masonic' key of E flat—harmonized with the utmost simplicity (Ex. 20):

Ex. 20. Mozart: *Requiem*. Theme of Hostias

Melodies such as this occur in instrumental works (for instance the slow movement of the clarinet concerto) as well as in Masonic motets like the *Ave Verum* and in *The Magic Flute*, where they are associated with the triumph of Light. They are quite different in effect from the grander melodies of Handel and Gluck that may have been their prototype; though we may consider them alongside the hymn-like themes of Haydn's last years, and regard them as anticipatory of a type of theme to be developed by Beethoven (for instance, the slow movement of the Violin Sonata, opus 96). In any case, the significance of these melodies in relation to Mozart's 'religion' is unmistakable. He associated them with the triumph of Light: but only in the negative sense that their consolatory gravity robs death of its power. This is why Mozart's Masonic music is so different in effect from Haydn's. Haydn celebrates life; in the orthodox religion on which he had been brought up death was accounted for, and it is unlikely that he often thought about it. Mozart lives so intensely that the consciousness of death can never be far off; he increasingly sees death, not as a mystical release from the sufferings of his and our life, but simply—or profoundly—as the context in which we exist. On this theme he wrote a most remarkable letter to his father:

"I need not tell you with what anxiety I await better news from yourself. I count upon that with certainty, though I am wont in all things to anticipate the worst. Since death (take my words literally) is the true goal of our lives, I have made myself so well acquainted during the last two years with this true and best friend of mankind that the idea of it no longer has any terrors for me, but rather much that is tranquil and comforting. And I thank God that he has granted me the good fortune to obtain the opportunity (you understand my meaning) of regarding death as the key to our true happiness. I never lie down in bed without considering that, young as I am, perhaps I may on the morrow be no more. Yet not one of those who know me could say that I am morose or melancholy, and for this I thank my Creator daily and wish heartily that the same happiness may be given to my fellow men."

Mozart never lost his belief in the potentialities of the human heart; but he came to accept man's natural limitations.

Can we see something of this acceptance of life and death as complementary even in the smallest works of Mozart's last years? Although his life was so short and so intense, the completeness and perfection of his music leave nothing to be said. Had he lived longer, he would presumably have added something to a musical experience that seems already all-inclusive, but it is impossible to imagine what. Even Mozart's slightest works appear, in his last years, to exist independent of time or place. The little works for glass harmonica, not to mention the great E flat Divertimento for string trio, are poles apart from the serenades and cassations of his youth. They diverted Mozart himself, no doubt, and they would divert a company of angels; but they are no longer music to eat or to chatter to. It almost seems as though Mozart has given up the attempt to write music for a society in which he only half believed. He now writes in a celestial drawing-room, where the only audience is himself and silence (and he does not need to listen): just as Bach in his last years, composing *The Art of Fugue* in an outmoded fashion, played to himself in an empty church.

4

BEETHOVEN

IT IS the essence of the personality of Beethoven [1770–1827], both as man and as artist, that he should invite discussion in other than musical terms. We cannot begin to understand him unless we recognize that for him music was not merely a pattern of sounds nor even merely an aural means of self-expression; it was also a moral and ethical power. On the other hand, if we do recognize this we may be tempted to talk about what we imagine to be Beethoven's message rather than about his music; and Tovey properly deplored this tendency in pointing out that remarks about the French Revolution do not help us to listen to Beethoven's music more sensitively or more intelligently.

Yet the case is not as simple as Tovey makes it seem. There *is* a connexion between Beethoven's music and the French Revolution, since even in so strikingly personal a work as the Fifth Symphony he was directly influenced by French revolutionary music. This—and the related fact that one of his first works was a cantata dedicated to the progressive Emperor Joseph—may not be very important. But the general relationship between Beethoven's music and the *idea* of revolution certainly is: for if Haydn and Mozart were incipiently revolutionary composers, Beethoven is overtly so. The Fifth Symphony revolutionizes the then accepted notion of symphonic form, and its technical revolution is inseparable from the fact that it conveys in musical terms a message—a new approach to human experience. If we ignore that message we cannot claim to understand Beethoven; but we must be sure that the message we discover is Beethoven's, and not our own or someone else's. It must be a deduction from the nature of the musical technique, not something tacked on to the music fortuitously.

We have seen that both Haydn and Mozart achieved a classical equilibrium between acceptance and protest; in Mozart's case one can almost equate the two sides of the balance with lyrical melody and tonal drama. His equilibrium, we said, is at once a threat to and a vindication of civilization: so that we do not, in listening to his music, consciously think of change. But from the start Beethoven desired change. He wanted to build a new world; and he thought of his music as a means to that end. Mozart's art, as we can see most readily from his operas, is based on acceptance, tolerance, and understanding. This does not preclude stringent criticism; but he has no ethical intentions. Beethoven was probably the first composer consciously animated by a desire to do good. Religious composers of the past presumably wrote for the good of man's souls, but they did not consciously aim to promote good actions. Beethoven disapproved of Mozart's *Don Giovanni* because he thought it promoted bad actions; even as early as 1792 we find him writing in a friend's album:

> To help wherever one can.
> Love liberty above all things.
> Never deny the truth
> Even at the foot of the throne.

If change is necessary—and it is—it will come only through individual effort. In the fight for truth one will always be opposed to convention; one must rely on oneself because there is nothing else to rely on.

Haydn, Mozart, and Beethoven were all men of middle-class provincial origin. Haydn was content to remain socially, though not spiritually subordinate; Mozart became himself cosmopolitan and sophisticated; Beethoven insisted that fashionable society should remake itself in his image. We saw that the very perfection of Mozart's last works entails a kind of spiritual isolation; and though he was so interested in people, he was hopelessly incompetent in dealing with practical affairs. But he was never a wilful misfit, like Beethoven, who as a schoolboy had been "shy and taciturn, observing more and pondering more than he spoke"; who as a young man was clumsy and gauche in his movements, "an unlicked bear;" and who in mature years "found the world despicable, but did not thereby render it any the pleasanter either for himself or for other people". At school, Beethoven had learned to read and write easily and was, of course, musically precocious. That, however, was the extent of his intellectual attainments; he never learned to accomplish the simplest arithmetical calculation. Though the sordid conditions of his childhood had something to do with this, they were not the main reason. From earliest youth Beethoven was a dedicated spirit. He was alone, and he had a purpose. Anything which distracted him from that purpose—including arithmetic—he rejected. In Vienna, his rudeness to members of the aristocracy and to any persons in authority was a calculated gesture. "*My* nobility," said Beethoven, "is *here* and *here*"; and he pointed to his head and heart.

Beethoven's attitude to life is inevitably reflected in his approach to his art. As he was the first composer to wish to change the world, so he was the first composer to believe that originality in a creative artist was an asset. He once said that he did not often listen to other people's music, for fear it might impair his individuality. Although the remark was a gruffly characteristic joke, it was a significant joke for Beethoven to make. Another story is relevant enough to recount. A reverential friend, examining a new score of Beethoven's, ventured to point out to the master that in one passage hidden fifths had crept in.* Beethoven truculently demanded what was wrong about that. The timid answer was that 'the rules' do not permit them: to which Beethoven retorted, "Then *I* permit them." In musical technique, as in life, the ultimate authority is the self.

But though Beethoven believed that change was essential, he also still believed in civilization. He was born into a great musical tradition which he respected; for with all his disrespect towards people and things he considered unworthy, he had the true humility of the great. So the subversive tendencies of his music are not immediately evident. He accepts the conventions which he inherited from Haydn and Mozart: but emphasizes the revolutionary at the expense of the traditional features in them. It is interesting that when, having moved from provincial Bonn to Vienna, Beethoven took a course of composition lessons with Haydn, they were a failure. From a great master of the previous generation he could learn nothing. The Viennese tradition he absorbed, as it were, with the air he breathed; the only lessons he ever found profitable were

* Parallel fifths are forbidden in the orthodox grammar of the harmonic period of European music (roughly the sixteenth to the twentieth centuries) because they weaken independent part-writing. Hidden fifths are parallel fifths which are less apparent to the *eye* in that they are disguised by passing notes in one or more of the parts.

studies in strict counterpoint with Johann Albrechtsberger [1736–1809]. These taught him facility in his craft, while having no reference to problems of creation. Such problems were his own concern, exclusively.

If one considers the piano trios that comprise Beethoven's opus 1—and still more the string trios of opus 3—it is clear that although they establish a strong personality and contain remarkable audacities, they are music which Haydn would have recognized as having a kinship with his own. But the piano sonatas of opus 2 are already a new world of feeling. The dimensions of the first sonata, in F minor, are those of a normal classical sonata; indeed it is shorter than Haydn's later sonatas. Nor is there anything unorthodox about the treatment of sonata form; indeed, the first movement is more orthodox than most of Haydn's mature works, with a Mannheim sky-rocket for first theme, a free inversion of it for second subject, and a not extravagant modulatory scheme in the development. It differs from Haydn, and still more from Mozart, in the almost complete subservience of the melodic element to a dynamic treatment of piano technique. This is even more strongly marked in the last movement, also in sonata form. This ferociously whirling toccata is an assault on the listener's nerves. When a relatively lyrical theme occurs at the opening of the development, it is of so primitive a nature that it has, intentionally or not, an effect of parody. One can imagine the explosive violence of the young Beethoven's performance of this movement: the truculence of its abrupt conclusion. If the piece seems crude both melodically and rhythmically in comparison with Haydn and Mozart, it already shows complete self-assurance. Beethoven knows what effect he is after, and is willing to sacrifice much in its interests.

Though apparently a cheerful work, compared with the F minor's vehemence, the second sonata of the group (in A major) is subversive in an altogether subtler way. According to rococo convention, the exposition of a sonata was supposed to establish the basic tonalities of tonic and dominant, associated with the first and second subject groups respectively. Beethoven here opens his second subject in the minor of the dominant—a slight but not extreme abnormality often found in Haydn and Mozart. Then, in the space of twenty bars, the theme develops sequentially through no less than eight keys, touching on tonalities as remote from home (A major) as G major and B flat major (Ex. 21). Such extreme modulations, if permitted at all, were normally reserved for the climax of the

Ex. 21 Beethoven: Piano Sonata in A opus 2 No. 2 (first movement)

development. Here they occur in the exposition, the point of which is conventionally to establish tonality before development begins. Yet the effect, though startling, is not anarchic, because the whole of this passage has a bass line which rises by step from E up an octave; and then finally establishes the dominant in which the exposition concludes. The passage is a boldly expanded but logically convincing dominant preparation. Beethoven then attains his climax in the development by building his modulations not on step-wise progressions, but on a series of descending thirds.* Such passages are an exact counterpart in musical terms to the young Beethoven's flouting of social etiquette—his rudeness to duchesses and his unceremonious hurling around of crockery. Although these latter examples may seem frivolous, it is not too much to say that the same motives prompted both Beethoven's musical and his social bad manners.

At first, Beethoven's fashionable audience enjoyed his truculence. Up to a point, they liked being shocked by his boorish behaviour; and they found his music exciting, while at the same time it was based on premises they could understand. It is significant that the most representative music of Beethoven's youth is in his piano sonatas. His early fame was as pianist and improviser; and we have seen that the piano was becoming, for him, a dynamic rather than a melodic instrument. His early violin sonatas are much less aggressive than the piano

* For a detailed analysis, see Tovey's commentary on this sonata.

sonatas of the same date. The subversive qualities of his opus 12 sonatas for violin and piano consist in their ironic modulations, and the pawky wit of their rhythmic surprises. Yet they preserve an almost aristocratic elegance in the spare keyboard texture which Beethoven considers a fitting complement to violin tone; and they include no real slow movement, no outburst of rhetorical passion. His opus 12 remains domestic entertainment music of a personal distinction; his opus 13—the C minor Piano Sonata—is a call to arms.

One can appreciate the force of this if one compares Beethoven's C minor mood in this 'pathetic' sonata with the C minor of Mozart's late Fantasia and Sonata, K.475 and 457, Mozart is fiery, but classically disciplined, even in the improvisatory Fantasia. Beethoven cracks sonata form with a passion that is almost melodrama. The sonata allegro is prefaced by a slow introduction deriving from the French operatic overture, even to the detail of the dotted rhythm. But this introduction is no longer ceremonial, but even more passionately subjective than C. P. E. Bach in its accented appoggiaturas, enharmonic modulations, and sequences: indeed, it forcibly suggests Wagner's *Tristan* (Ex. 22). Moreover, it is not merely an introduction; it reappears in different keys at crucial points in the

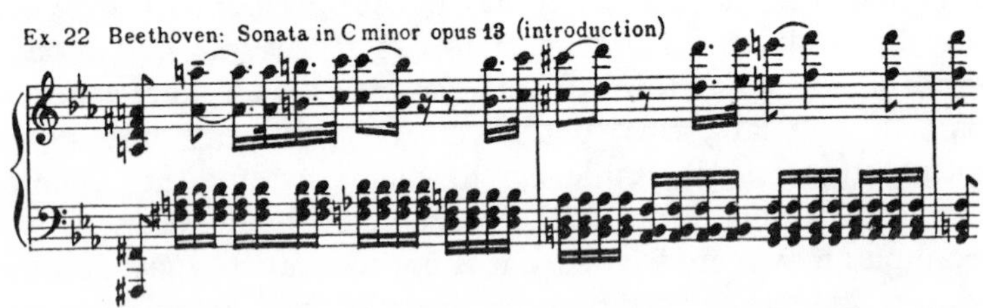

development, preceded and followed by dramatic silences. No composer before Beethoven had exploited silence in this way, so that it becomes a part of the musical argument. And although the structure of the sonata allegro does not itself depart from classical precedent, except for the tremendous stroke in the recapitulation when the syncopated minims are screwed up from C to D flat, it is true that the music demands a new technique of performance. It is not merely facetious to say that this is the first music to be composed for ten fingers and a lock of hair. Physical gyrations of the limbs, tossings of the head, are unavoidable if one is to play the piece as though one believed in it. While it may be melodrama to Mozart's tragedy, its implications were prodigious.

We do not have to wait long to see the shape the prodigy will assume. In opus 13 the classical mould is still evident, though the way in which the introduction is used threatens to break it. By the time we get to opus 27—the two sonatas which Beethoven described as being *quasi una fantasia*—subjective experience has completely remoulded the mould. The so-called 'Moonlight' Sonata no longer even looks like a sonata. Indeed, the only sonata movement is the last; we might term its three sections Prelude, Interlude, and Sonata. The slow prelude appears to be calm because its movement is smooth; but beneath the surface hides a tremendous intensity. Its binary structure is like a miniature sonata movement without a second subject. We get a hint of its subterranean conflict when, in the third bar, the Neapolitan chord of D major (in C sharp minor) strangely disturbs the harmonic perspective. Then follows a mysterious modulation from the minor of the relative (E) to the flat submediant (C major)—all this in a piece in C sharp minor! But this C major proves to be only a kind of 'Neapolitan' preparation for B minor: which leads to the subdominant (F sharp minor), followed by a long dominant pedal which takes us back to the tonic and a recapitulation. The tension is expressed melodically as well as harmonically, in the interval of the diminished third (a 'Neapolitan' C natural to A sharp): this produces acute dissonances of minor ninth and major seventh with the accompanying figuration (Ex. 23). In the pseudo-recapitulation this passage is screwed up a tone.

Ex. 23. Beethoven: Sonata in C♯ minor opus 27 No. 2. (first movement)

The interlude that forms the second movement is in the major, D flat standing for C sharp. The theme is a transformed version of the prelude's motive; but whereas the prelude is, in its modulations, all suppressed tension, in the interlude there is virtually no modulation and no tension at all. It is a dream-minuet, wherein the illusory nature of the tranquillity is suggested by the persistent syncopations that disguise the simple harmony. The dream is abruptly shattered by the tornado of the last movement, a full-scale sonata presto which in ferocity of modulatory conflict and in dynamic keyboard technique far outstrips anything Beethoven had attempted previously. Here the anguish that was deceptively hidden beneath the rocking movement of the prelude, to be dreamfully soothed away in the illusory minuet, breaks loose; and the relation to the flat supertonic which had been the root of the prelude's tension becomes the rhetorical climax of the storm. When this syncopated outburst on the flat supertonic reappears in D major during the recapitulation, its violence is so extreme that the movement explodes in a rhetorical coda of seething scales and arpeggios. Thus in the relationship between the three movements of the sonata, form is reborn in the light of Beethoven's spiritual autobiography; and the end of the sonata is like a bursting of dykes, a drowning of consciousness.

This remark is specifically apt, for the work was composed during the first of the two spiritual crises of Beethoven's life. He was experiencing what we would now call a nervous breakdown, the causes of which were complex. They had something to do with his relations with women, or a woman; more to do with his maladjustment to people and the world in general; most to do with the threat of approaching deafness, of which he first became aware about this time. All these causes were so subtly interlinked as to be in essence one; indeed, one might say not perhaps that Beethoven's deafness was self-willed, but at least that it was metaphorical as well as physical. It was a symbol of his separation from the world; his physical deafness complements the spiritual isolation to which he had committed himself, even before his deafness was manifest.

However this may be, it is certain that in 1802 he retired to the country, shut himself up in solitude, and went through a period of terrifying mental suffering. While in the country he wrote an extraordinary, not entirely sane document which is now known as the Heilingenstadt Testament. It is not in fact a will, though it makes a few bequests to his brother; it is, however, a document in which, in lamenting his condition, Beethoven appears voluntarily to relinquish all hold on life. Some say—on rather inadequate evidence—that Beethoven's sanity was preserved only by the love of the Countess Giulietta Guicciardi, to whom he had dedicated the 'Moonlight' Sonata. But in any case he did not die. He came to admit that henceforth he would be cut off from the world physically as well as spiritually; but that in becoming a law unto himself he would find salvation. "For you, poor Beethoven," he said, "there is no happiness to be found outside. I have no friends, must live with myself alone." But his isolation is a challenge. "Even with the frailties of my body, my spirit shall dominate. . . . I shall seize Fate by the throat; it shall never wholly subdue me." If he despises the world, it is because 'it never divines that music is a greater revelation than the whole of philosophy". If he has no friends in the flesh, he has them in the spirit. If the world is beastly, malignant, and chaotic, he can create order in his art. The more ferocious are the blows of Fate, the more energetically must Beethoven's will subdue them. His art becomes the imposition of order on chaos. The Mozartian equilibrium between the artist and his world has gone. Now the artist's will must shape the world anew.

This process starts in the work which Beethoven began to conceive at Heilingenstadt, though he did not complete it until some years later. His first two symphonies contain anticipations of his later technique, while being based on classical principles. They are insignificant compared with the greatest works of Haydn and Mozart, though fascinating as the creation of a young man of revolutionary genius working within an established tradition. But the Third Symphony is a new kind of music; and we can learn something about the nature of its newness from the sketch-books in which Beethoven recorded the gradual shaping of his works.

Of no composition did he leave more copious annotations than of the 'Eroica' Symphony,* which he was well aware was a key-point in his development—and in that of European music. From these sketch-books it becomes apparent that Beethoven did not, at this period of his career, begin to conceive his symphonic allegros with themes in what one accepts as the 'normal' way. He began by notating brief figures and rhythms, planning the whole movement as a conflict and resolution of motives and tonalities. The precise form of the opening theme of the 'Eroica' emerged only at an advanced stage of the creative process. For Beethoven, at this period of his development, music is conflict, a battle with forces outside the self, before it is self-contained song.

* For a detailed analysis, see the appendix to Riezler's *Beethoven*.

The first movement opens with two hammer-blows of Fate, on the whole orchestra. Then the first theme enters, in the bass. It is not a melody, but an arpeggio of challenge; and it ends, not in triumph, but in conflict, for the bass line lands up on an ambiguous C sharp which might be D flat (Ex. 24). Out of

Ex. 24. Beethoven: Symphony No. 8 (first movement)

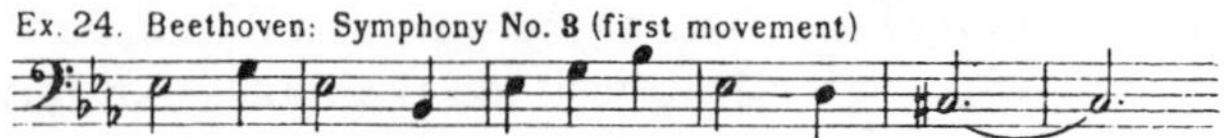

this equivocation two new motives emerge—a figure rotating around a fixed point, and a rhythmic pattern; these lead into a long dominant preparation in hemiola rhythm (a cross rhythm of 3–2 against the basic 3–4). Then there is a transitional theme built on leaping ninths, another version of the arpeggio motive, inverted and filled in with bouncing semiquavers, more dominant preparation, and then the second subject group: this is partially derived from the rhythmic motive and from the turning figure. This multiplicity of contrasted material goes to create the longest sonata exposition yet written.

The development is on a vast scale, modulating through two cycles of fifths: an upward followed by a downward cycle. Fugato —contrapuntal writing which is freely fugal in character— adds to the excitement; and the climax comes in a tremendous expansion of the hemiola rhythm in which the whole orchestra builds up a progressingly accumulating dissonance (Ex. 25):

Ex. 25. Beethoven: Symphony No. 8 (first movement)

Here the orchestra is used like a gigantic percussion instrument; one sees why the piano and the symphony orchestra, rather than the string quartet or violin sonata, were Beethoven's favoured media during the middle years of his life. The screeching, percussive minor seconds of this climax also introduce the most remote possible modulation—to E minor, which stands for F flat minor, the flat supertonic. And then, in this already enormous movement, Beethoven gives us a new theme, which is contrasted in mood, though derived from the turning figure and the motive in triple rhythm. (The sketch-books tell us that Beethoven decided very early on that there should at this point be a new theme, and a modulation to the remoteness of E minor.) The music slips down to the tonic minor, varied scraps of the initial themes reappear, until softly and tentatively the horns re-enter with the arpeggio motive: only too soon, so that they clash with the harmony of the strings! (Even as progressive a musician as the young Wagner used to 'correct' this passage in performance.) In the recapitulation the ambiguous C sharp of the exposition behaves this time as though it were D flat; but apart from the altered modulations produced by this stroke the recapitulation is orthodox. No straight recapitulation could, however, be an adequate resolution of this cataclysmic upheaval; so Beethoven expands the recapitulation into a coda which is itself nearly as long as the exposition. Here the arpeggio theme is transformed so that the tension in its chromatic tail disappears (Ex. 26). It becomes jubilant major

Ex. 26. Beethoven: Symphony No. 8 (first movement)

arpeggio; and the excitement is enhanced because the themes are combined in double counterpoint. Conflict becomes triumphant apotheosis.

Both the slow movement and the scherzo are built on themes which have hidden affinities with the challenging arpeggio motive. In the *Marcia Funebre* Beethoven deals, in the relatively static form of rondo, with the Hero's death; in the dynamic scherzo with his resurgence. He was not thinking of a literal birth and death; he meant that for him life was the process of Becoming, so that being alive was a series of spiritual deaths and rebirths. The goal of the work thus proves to be the last movement, which is built on the 'monistic' principle of the chaconne: variations on a bass which remains constant. The chaconne theme is the simplest and boldest possible version of the E flat arpeggio with which the symphony had opened; the battle won, the theme can now exult in its strength. It is significant that this theme had first been used by Beethoven in his ballet, *Prometheus*, and again in the 'Eroica' Variations, opus 35.

Now Prometheus challenged the gods and, with the gift of fire, offered man the potentiality to control his own destiny. The Hero about whom Beethoven wrote his symphony is not, of course, the God-King of eighteenth-century autocracy, but the man of strife who is the architect of a new world. Napoleon seemed such a man; though Beethoven contemptuously tore up his dedication when Napoleon proved to be only the architect of a new tyranny. In any case, the real Hero of the symphony is Beethoven himself, as Prometheus; and the battle he fought is not Napoleon's, but the more terrible one he fought alone at Heilingenstadt. He was right in thinking that the battles for his and Europe's salvation were closely related. Haydn and the Enlightenment had seen the alternation of Light and Darkness, Order and Chaos, as primarily a social evolution in which the individual played his part. For Beethoven the alternation of Life and Death has become primarily subjective: because social regeneration can spring only from what used to be called 'a change of heart'.

Immediately after he had finished the 'Eroica', Beethoven started work on a Symphony in C minor, now known as No. 5. He put it aside in order to write the Fourth; but in the Beethovenian cycle the Fifth is the natural successor to the Third, for it develops still further the technique of thematic transformation. The Fifth is the state of Becoming in music, as Bach's last chorale prelude is the state of Being. The movements are not four more or less closely related pieces. They are evolving facets of experience which grow, or are willed, to an inevitable end. The 'form' is the process of evolution, like life itself.

The assertion of the Will in the 'Eroica' had called for a gigantic expansion in the dimensions of the classical symphony. In the Fifth, Beethoven concentrates, and thereby intensifies, his power.* In its aggressive metrical patterns and contrasts of tonality the first movement is the most vehement conflict piece that had ever been written. But Beethoven's intention was not merely to fight a hostile world and an obdurate destiny, but also to subdue them. And in fact each movement is dominated by the same thematic contour, which is transformed during the course of the symphony. In the first movement it takes this

* For a detailed analysis, see Rudolf Reti, *The Thematic Process in Music.*

shape—the rising minor sixth and seventh, with their expression of yearning: followed by the falling and rising third: followed by the minor triad (Ex. 27). The music continually seeks the stability of this arpeggio phrase, with its implied tonic and dominant; and is repeatedly frustrated by the interjections of the rhythmic Fate motive.

In the slow movement each of these three elements reappears, slightly modified, in the passive key of the flat submediant. This

more lyrical version of the theme is a dream of serenity, which is destroyed by the Fate rhythm (associated with a tonally disruptive diminished seventh), and then transformed into a battle-cry in C *major*. Rondo form is here used to express unresolved fluctuations between submission to dream and challenge to reality. In the scherzo the 'basic' theme is even more clearly evident; until, through the strange melodic wanderings over the dissonant timpani note in the coda, the latent theme emerges in the last movement, born afresh. Now the last phase of the theme appears first, translated into jubilant major arpeggio; the rising *major* sixth and seventh follow (Ex. 28). The fateful rhythm which pervades the figuration is

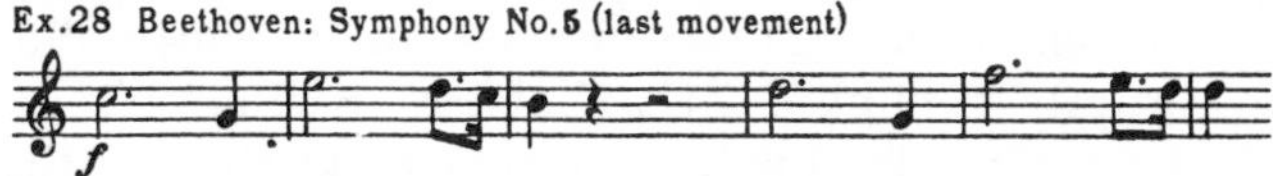

no longer threatening, but an expression of power; even the direct reminiscence of the scherzo's battle resolves tension into arpeggio. One might almost say that the form of the symphony is the search for the shape which the implicit theme takes in the last movement. At the end even themes are unnecessary; the blaze of C major is enough, for we hear it as though for the first time. A new world and a new sound are born. This is literally true, for Beethoven's orchestra has no precedent: no one before had used trombones in the way Beethoven exploits them at their first entry in the major apotheosis, while piccolo and double bassoon are added purely as noise, to extend the sonorous resources.

In the Fifth Symphony Beethoven has imposed unity on chaos, integrating highly disparate modes of experience. This is reflected both within the single movements, and in the relationship between the movements. The first three movements are not fully intelligible except in relation to the last; and in all his mature music Beethoven seeks, under the pressure of experience, for new relationships between his basic principles of sonata, variation, and rondo—to which he later added fugue. This interrelation exists too between groups of works; we may regard the Third and Fourth, and the Fifth and Sixth Symphonies as complementary.

Beethoven is a composer of strife, and strife between wildly contrasting kinds of experience may sometimes be not tragic, but comic. We are apt to forget that Beethoven's music is often funny; and we have some excuse for forgetting, since his humour is a disruptive force, like his passion. Both his humour and his self-assertion are dramatic, a threat to complacency. We are told that after Beethoven had held his audience spellbound with the rhetoric or pathos of his improvisation he was liable to round on them with a burst of raucous, scarifying laughter, calling them dolts or blockheads. The humour in his music is often similar in effect. Perhaps humour is not the word, and we may rather find in Beethoven's music an exaggerated form of the intense levity which we discovered in Haydn and Mozart, but which disappears in the age of romanticism.

Intense levity we may certainly find in the Fourth Symphony. It opens in archaistic fashion with a slow introduction, solemn, veiled in tonality and orchestration. This heroic sublimity is then abruptly debunked by a burst of Beethoven's raucous mirth—a tootling, footling allegro theme like those of the *buffo* overture or the early rococo symphony. During the development, however, the most weird things happen to this frivolous tune; and the recapitulation is approached by a mysterious passage of enharmonic modulation,* in which a pianissimo pedal note on the timpani gradually changes its significance from A sharp to the tonic B flat. This is a musical pun, and puns are supposed to be funny. But the effect of the passage as a whole is far from comic; it is dramatic and, still more, strange. And its strangeness was already implicit in the mysterious equivocations of the slow introduction: so that, as things turn

* ENHARMONIC MODULATION depends on the fact that, in the equal tempered scale, two notes with different names and functions may have the same pitch. Thus the tonic note in B flat is identical in pitch with A sharp, which might be the leading note in B major or minor, or the major third of the tonic chord of F sharp.

out, it is not the sublime but the debunker who is debunked. Things are not what they seem. There are no clear-cut barriers between the varieties of human experience. The solemn may be absurd, the absurd sinister; the simple mysterious, the mystery an illumination.

Before he had finished the Fifth, Beethoven had already started work on a sixth symphony; in this case he deliberately planned it as a companion-piece. The Fifth is a work about Experience: suffering, frustration, conflict lead to rebirth. The Sixth is its polar opposite, dealing with the state of Innocence. It is 'pastoral' not because it depicts the external sights and sounds of Nature (though it does that to some extent), but because it expresses a peasant simplicity which is the opposite of Beethoven's tormented self-consciousness. Haydn accepted Nature as the background to human life, and—in *The Seasons*—indicated that the 'laws' of Nature were to some extent a guide to human conduct. Mozart rejected Nature in favour of human beings. Beethoven, more romantically Rousseau-like, used Nature as a refuge from people, saying that only when alone with meadows, woods, and hills did his spirit feel entirely free. As his deafness increased, he became more and more devoted to solitary country walks.

We shall note later than an ambivalence between a peasant-like innocence and the artist's self-consciousness is the impulse behind Schubert's most representative music; and in Beethoven's own last works we shall see him attaining, in a reborn technique, an innocence which is the ripest fruit of experience. The innocence of the 'Pastoral' Symphony is distinct from either of these. One might almost say that it is a deliberate study in innocence by a sophisticated consciousness: Beethoven depicts the state in which he is not, because he cannot understand Experience unless he also knows what Innocence is. So the work is in essence a paradox: a sonata with the minimum of conflict! Tonic and dominant are musical symbols of stability and simplicity, and all the main subjects of the Sixth are pervaded by tonic and dominant arpeggios. An extraordinary proportion of the work is based harmonically on static tonic or dominant chords as a pedal; in the last movement the 'bagpipe' chord of the open ninth compresses tonic and dominant into one chord (Ex. 29). The only section of the symphony to be more richly harmonized is the 'Storm': and this is an objective presentation of conflict, in the archaic fashion of the operatic storm (scurrying scales and diminished sevenths), instead of the subjective drama of sonata style. The peasant

consciousness has its storms in the outside world, without being racked by inner conflict; the only characteristically Beethovenian feature here is the transformation of the theme when the storm is over.

The treatment of the development section in the first movement is especially interesting. Here, of course, the conflict and drama ought to occur. In fact, there is no conflict. Beethoven avoids it by making his modulations simply an effect of colour. One rhythmic motive and one major triad are repeated innumerable times in a cycle of descending thirds, with changing instrumental colours. The effect is significantly like many of Schubert's submissive modulations to the submediant; modulation is made to express not strife, but a relapse into sensuous enjoyment; Beethoven suns himself, like a cat, in these warmly floating triads. As a whole, the symphony contains many anticipations in scoring and harmony of Schubert and even Wagner: consider the romantic use of horn and woodwind in the telescoping of tonic and dominant seventh in the last movement (bars 57–64); or the climacteric use of the chord of the ninth (bar 227).

Though its simplification of technique was a part of Beethoven's evolution, the Sixth Symphony is in some ways a 'sport' in his creative career. In the Seventh he carries on from the point where the Fifth left off. Conflicts are seething beneath the surface—Beethoven's modulations have never been more ruthlessly abrupt, and the whole work is obsessed by the same contrast between tonic and flat submediant as occurs in the Sixth, only it is no longer submissive, but a dramatic event. These conflicts are now, however, obliterated by the fierce assertion of metre; the wilder the passion, the more vehement is Beethoven's desire to control it, come what may. Thus the first movement has only one basic rhythm and one theme; at least if there is a second subject it serves no function as contrast. Even the frenzy of the last movement is strictly controlled. The coda owes its shattering power to the fact that the whirling scales in which it explodes reveal themselves—if only to our subconscious minds—as the fulfilment of the solemn rising scales of the introduction to the first movement. There is still law and order in Beethoven's wild music, though he has become a law unto himself. "Power," he said, "is the morality of those who stand out from the rest, and it is *mine*." That demoniacally obsessive rhythm, those savage transitions, pauses, and silences, the sheer physical impact of the orchestration with its fanatically barking horns—have we perhaps heard these things so often that we have ceased to hear them at all? If we listen afresh, we shall surely find this one of the most terrifying pieces of music ever written, far more scarifying, after a hundred and forty years, than Stravinsky's *Rite of Spring* after forty. If it is 'joyful', it can only be the bloodcurdling joy of battle. No wonder that Weber, on first hearing the extraordinary revolving ostinato that introduces the coda to the first movement, said that Beethoven was now ripe for the madhouse. Weber was no old fogy. He was a younger man than Beethoven, clever, sensitive, one of the most progressive musicians of his day.

The Seventh Symphony relies for its impact largely on metre, tonality, and scoring; melody is comparatively unimportant in all the movements. Indeed, almost the only works in Beethoven's middle period in which cantabile melody is the essence of the music are the Violin Concerto and the slow movements of the third and fourth piano concertos, which preserve the classical relationship between concerto style and opera. In the 'Emperor' Concerto, however, Beethoven associates the exhibitionism of the display-concerto with the emotional exhibitionism of his middle years. It seems that in a sense Weber was right: Beethoven could have done nothing further along the lines of the 'Emperor' Concerto and the Seventh Symphony without going mad. In any case, he wrote no more concertos; and the Seventh Symphony and its comic but scarcely less volcanic complement the Eighth are followed by a significant gap in his creative output. For about five years he composed very little music. When creative fecundity returned, he was already producing music radically different from his previous works.

How are these differences manifested in terms of musical technique? What do they signify in philosophical terms?

Before we attempt to answer these questions we must look at two works which Beethoven composed during his fallow years. The E minor Piano Sonata, opus 90, resembles the middle-period piano sonatas in being highly dramatic; it differs from them in being concentrated rather than expansive, and in using themes which combine trenchancy with a *song-like lyricism.* This sonata movement is followed by one other movement—a rondo in the major, on one of the loveliest song-tunes ever written. Conflict still exists in the modulatory episodes; but dissolves away in the lyricism. Now Beethoven himself said that the first movement of this sonata dealt with the conflicts and passions of human love—love between man and woman: and that the second and last movement dealt with their consummation and resolution. Into this rondo Beethoven introduced streams of trills, written out as semiquavers; and we shall see in a moment that trills came to have a peculiar significance for Beethoven in his last years.

Shortly after writing this sonata, Beethoven returned to the violin and piano duo. During his 'middle' period his opus 47 had been his only attempt to apply the shock tactics of his piano and orchestral music to the relatively inapposite medium of the violin sonata. Now, in these transitional years, he creates in his opus 96 a first movement in which the mysterious drama of the modulations is absorbed into the radiant lyricism of violin melody; a slow movement which is a hymn-like aria typical of Beethoven's final years; and a rondo which is a subtly dramatic metamorphosis of the innocence of popular song. In all the movements trills play a significant part. Both opus 90 and opus 96 seem to attain the peace of earthly love; and perhaps their trills suggest that, for Beethoven at least, earthly love was a necessary step towards heavenly.

With the 'Hammerklavier' Sonata, opus 106, we cross the threshold into Beethoven reborn world. The first movement in many ways carries on from the Seventh and Eighth Symphonies. It is one of the most titanic of Beethoven's conflict pieces, based on assertive metre and modulation. These qualities are, however, modified by several features. The second subject is extremely cantabile in character, and is accompanied by extended trills; there is a considerable amount of fugato writing in the development; and these passages tend to employ a hollow, wide-spaced texture very different from the massive, percussive keyboard style which Beethoven exploits in the opening of this sonata, and consistently throughout a middle-period work such as the F minor opus 57. The Scherzo is also a development from dynamic, middle-aged Beethoven, differing from earlier works mainly in being more elliptical; not even in the Eighth Symphony does Beethoven indulge in punning as terse as the conclusion of this movement.

With the slow movement, however, we approach a new conception. Here we have a sublime song movement in Italian aria style, even with quasi-vocal coloratura. Although the piece is in sonata form, it does not sound like a sonata movement. The second subject does not serve as a dramatic contrast, but is an unbroken lyrical evolution from the first; and the subtle modulations that occur (for instance, the Neapolitan G major within F sharp—really G flat—minor) are harmonic 'colourings' rather than incidents in a tonal argument (Ex. 30). The

Ex.30 Beethoven: Piano Sonata opus 106 (slow movement)

brief development section is also a climax to the expanding lyricism; and the recapitulation is so long and so floridly decorated that it sounds like, and is, a further lyrical growth of the themes. Rhetorical passion dissolves into melody.

Then follows a strange interlude like a recitative, out of which the last movement strives to emerge. Gradually it gathers momentum until it burst into a stupendous fugue: the lyrical evolution of the adagio leads into the principle of Unity itself. But it is a fugue such as never was before or since—a titanic assertion of power. Unity is attained, but after how wild and terrible a struggle. If in the Fifth Symphony Beethoven is in conflict with the forces that threaten the fulfilment of personality, with Fate or Providence or a hostile society, here he is in conflict with himself. He strains to make the ultimate assertion: I will *not* be divided; I *will* be whole. The screaming trills which dominate the theme and therefore the contrapuntal texture would seem to express the anguished determination to achieve unity of being; and in the serene D major episode which succeeds the most prodigious of all the climaxes he is afforded a brief visionary glimpse of the peace which this grinding movement is seeking (Ex. 31). Here the parts move mainly by step,

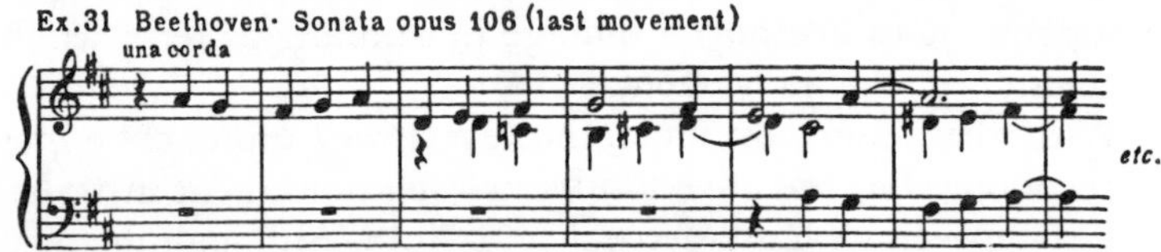

and the texture is as luminous as in the main fugue it is opaque. The grinding quality of the music is expressed in the struggle with the medium itself: which is why attempts to orchestrate this work—or the comparable *Grosse Fuge* for string quartet—are misguided. The fugue is almost unplayable because it is an experience that is almost unattainable. Even Beethoven does not fully attain it here. The vocal-seeming D major episode is soon routed by the trills of the first fugue-subject; the movement ends in wild disintegration, only partially redeemed by a final assertion of the will. So the sonata ends at the point where it started; and the cycle begins afresh.

What Beethoven strives after in opus 106 he achieves in his last three sonatas, especially the last of all, opus 111. Here the first movement is a profound fusion of the contradictory principles of sonata and fugue. There is one theme, tense in its harmonic implications, which acquires a more relaxed and cantabile quality when freely transformed in inversion for the second subject (in the flat submediant again). This theme is treated now in fugato, now in sonata style. The two principles are resolved in the coda that provides a transition into the second and last movement. The reconciliation of sonata conflict and fugal unity flows into the oneness of the arietta with variations. The adagio of opus 106, though it no longer sounds like a dramatic conflict, is still a sonata movement; in this arietta the tonal conflict of the first movement is stilled in heaven. The texture is almost purely diatonic—it even suggests a Palestrina-like modality; and the theme, having been conceived during the turmoil of the first movement, with the introduction's fierce descending diminished seventh translated into a serene fourth, is not again transformed (Ex. 32). Rather are the variations the continuous flowering of melody, resembling not so much the eighteenth-century notion of variation as

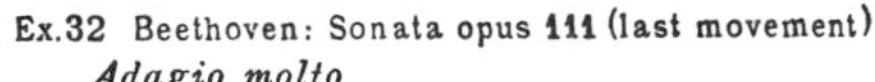
Ex.32 Beethoven: Sonata opus 111 (last movement)

the sixteenth-century principle of divisions on a ground—a technique whereby a melody is progressively decorated by being divided into smaller note values. Finally, the divisions become so rapid and so ecstatic that there is nothing left except dissolving trills. The searing trills of opus 106 have found their rest in the unity of being which is sometimes called Paradise. Something similar happens at the end of the greatest of all works in variation form—the Diabelli Variations, opus 120.

Now just as Haydn and Mozart had used symphonic techniques within their liturgical counterpoint, so they—and Beethoven himself—had all used fugal techniques in their sonata movements long before this. But Haydn's counterpoint is symphonic and Mozart's (even in the last movement of the 'Jupiter') is operatic; while Beethoven's fugato in the coda to the finale of the Fifth Symphony is simply a rhetorical means of increasing the excitement. None of them had attempted the identity of opposites which Beethoven seeks in his final works. For here he combines the dualistic idea of key conflict with the apparently irreconcilable idea of melodic growth and fugal unity: principles which we have seen to be apposite to earlier, more unified societies. In so doing, Beethoven has once more recreated form itself. It is worth noting that during his unproductive period preparatory to the last phase, Beethoven made a detailed study of the music of Bach, especially of the *Art of Fugue*; and that he devoted a good deal of attention to Palestrina also.

Similarly, Beethoven had used the technique of division-variation in earlier works. The variations that form the slow movement of the 'Appassionata' Sonata, for instance, are a set of divisions which are completely static: the theme is not transformed and the movement is entirely without modulation or conflict of any kind. The difference between this movement and the late variation movements lies in the fact that in the late works song melody has become the core of the music. The tune of the slow movement of opus 57 is not significant in itself, and is not intended to be; the point of the movement is to serve as a static contrast to the dynamism of the two allegros. Indeed, it is a dream, like the interlude in the 'Moonlight' Sonata: an illusion of peace which is brutally shattered by the ferociously metrical assertion of the finale's diminished sevenths (Ex. 33):

Ex. 33 Beethoven: Sonata opus 57 (transition from slow movement to finale)

But the song melodies that are the basis of the variations in the 'Archduke' Trio, or still more in the piano sonatas, opus 109 and 111, are all Beethoven knows in earth or heaven, and all he needs to know. The divisions into which they flower are not a dream, but a vision. And—particularly in opus 111—the rebirth of Song is also an escape from metre: a liberation from the shackles of Time.

In orchestral music Beethoven never reached this point. The Ninth Symphony* occupies a transitional position similar to the 'Hammerklavier' Sonata. It is a vast expansion of the technique of thematic transformation which Beethoven explored in the Fifth, in that all the themes of the work are interrelated and coalesce in the song theme of the finale: the point of the 'retrospective' introduction to the last movement is precisely to reveal these interrelations before song melody suggests the physical introduction of the human voice. The technique of division appears in the adagio; the finale is a gigantic fusion of variation and rondo.

But it is in the *Missa Solemnis* that 'late' Beethoven attains his most monumental expression. The work is symphonic in that, like the Ninth Symphony, it is thematically generative; but this style is now fused with a contrapuntal technique that is, like Bach's, basically vocal and, in the Incarnatus and Sanctus, almost as strictly modal as Palestrina. The Benedictus is pure

* For a detailed analysis, see Rudolf Reti, *The Thematic Process in Music.*

song melody, soaring into ecstatic trills, like the Arietta of opus 111. So there is no real distinction between the God Beethoven worships in his Mass and the God he discovers in his last instrumental works; indeed he once said: "The relationship of men towards art is religion." In the Credo, dogma is reduced to a minimum; Christ for him is spirit incarnate, and therefore himself in the moments of *raptus* for which he lived and (spiritually) died. He would not, of course, have said blasphemously that he lived and died (several times) to save mankind; but when he called the Agnus Dei "a prayer for inner and outward peace" he had certainly come to feel that the peace he had himself created in the Benedictus was the only resolution of conflict within the soul or without. He seems to regard the trumpery hurly-burly of the world, which so oddly surges up in the Agnus, from an immense, almost godlike height.

Yet monumentality—godlike or human—is not the most representative quality of Beethoven's music in his last years. The string quartet is the quintessential medium of his 'late' phase, as the piano was of his youth, and the symphony orchestra of his middle period. Previously, he had devoted comparatively little attention to the quartet, which, as a concourse of equal-voiced instruments, did not naturally lend itself to his dynamic style. When, in the opus 18 series, he composes a Quartet in C minor to some extent inspired by Mozart's G minor Quintet, he does all he can to imbue Mozart's taut tragedy with rhetorical melodrama; while in the only quartets of his middle period, the three of opus 59 and opus 74, he inflates the quartet into a pseudo-symphonic style. The linear nature of quartet writing prompts him to create themes rather more lyrical than his symphonic motives; but the first movement of opus 59, no. 1, is not only symphonic in its dimensions; even the texture acquires a symphonic richness and solidity. Though superbly written for the instruments, in that all the effects come off, this is hardly a true quartet style.

An authentic string quartet idiom appears for the first time in the F minor Quartet, opus 95. The first movement is symphonic in that, as Tovey said, an immense drama is packed into a few minutes; but its extreme concentration relates it to a movement such as the scherzo of the 'Hammerklavier' Sonata. The second movement is a cross between lyrical song and fugue. The flow of the lines purges the chromatic harmony of subjective emotion, much as it does in the polyphony of Bach (Ex. 34). This is probably the earliest instance of Beethoven's creative 're-thinking' of Bach's style. Already the texture has acquired that luminosity typical of the slow movements of Beethoven's last years.

Ex.34 Beethoven: Quartet opus 95 (slow movement)

The cycle of 'late' quartets begins with opus 127 and ends with opus 135. Perhaps the most comprehensive, and certainly the most complicated, of the works of Beethoven's last period is the C sharp minor Quartet, opus 131, which Beethoven himself believed to be his greatest work. The first movement is pure monism, pure fugue, completely thematic to its smallest detail. The texture of the music is as smoothly vocal as a fugue of Bach or even a Renaissance polyphonist; yet the augmented second in the theme imbues the harmony with an acute inner tension (Ex. 35). Only in the last movement shall we become fully aware of the fierce spiritual turmoil which has gone to create this painful serenity.

Ex.35 Beethoven: Quartet opus 131 (first movement)

Then there is an abrupt transition to a scherzo in sonata form, but with only one subject. This is in the apparently remote key of D major. Again, the significance of this modulation, in relation to the fugue, will be revealed to us in the final allegro. Only then shall we understand why the scherzo theme, for all its contrasting emotional temperature, should have a hidden affinity with the theme of the fugue. After the scherzo, an odd recitative passage leads into the great central piece, an aria with variations in A major (again the flat sub-mediant, the key of relaxation which Beethoven favours for so many of his late slow movements). Like the Arietta of opus 111, this is the flowering of melody: lyrical generation creates divisions, fugato, and finally 'a halo of trills', to use Tovey's profoundly appropriate metaphor.

Then follows a strict scherzo, the theme of which is again obscurely related to the Fugue subject. If this is a dance movement, with a Ländler-like trio, it never suggests the earthiness of Beethoven's middle years, nor even Schubert's nostalgia for a sensuous beauty that has passed. The texture is now ethereal, other-worldly. The last movement is prefaced by an arioso passage balancing that between the D major Scherzo-sonata and the variations. Here the original fugue theme stirs as it were, in its chrysalis, striving to emerge as aria. When, however, the last movement finally bursts upon us we find that we face directly the passions that had been resolved into fugue and lyrical variation. For this is a dramatic sonata movement on a theme which is a freely inverted version of the fugue subject. The harmonic tension of the augmented second has, in this transformed version, become much more obtrusive (Ex. 36); while the development involves a modulation first

to the relative minor of the flat supertonic, then to the flat supertonic itself—the key of the sonata-scherzo that had followed the fugue. In the recapitulation and coda occurs a fight between unifying, stabilizing fugato and sudden eruptions of flat supertonic scales. Fugal unity achieves its victory, though in a singularly melancholy, drooping inversion of the theme, rounded off by a desperate assertion of the tonic major. After this the work can, by implication, start again. Next time we hear the opening fugue we are not surprised that its vocal-seeming calm, its unified diminutions, augmentations, and stretti, should be none the less instinct with suffering.

Just as the quartet forms a cycle of human experience, so it is a kind of microcosm of European musical history. The drama of the sonata principle is resolved back into its elements: first into operatic aria and recitative—with no longer any direct suggestion of the theatre—out of which the interior drama of sonata had grown; then into the rediscovered unity of song variation and fugue. A similar process is evident in other works, such as the A flat Piano Sonata, opus 110. Most subtly of all, perhaps, we find it in the last quartet, opus 135—a work which seems superficially not only shorter, but also more conventional in structure than the other late quartets.

The first movement is a terse example of Beethoven's technique of thematic generation: the basic material of the quartet germinates as we listen. The scherzo is Beethoven's middle-period rhetoric restated in epigrams; its tonal shocks are rarefied in the tenuous texture—as is a long passage built on an obsessive revolving 'cam' comparable with the notorious ostinato in the Seventh Symphony. To the slow movement, which is a cross between aria and variation, in the flat submediant once more, Beethoven appended the significant direction '*cantante e tranquillo*'. There is virtually no modulation. Melody dissolves into figuration. In the introduction to the finale the theme 'created' in the first movement is stated in unison, and then in a reversion to operatic recitative. The allegro finale itself is halfway between sonata and fugue; and the texture grows increasingly rarefied until the theme has shed both sonata and operatic drama and become as simple as a folk-song. But this is not, like the 'Pastoral' Symphony, a study in innocence: it is the innocence that is born of experience. Beethoven has gone back beyond sonata to opera; beyond opera to religious polyphony; beyond polyphony to song melody which is an end in itself; beyond song to the source of melody in the undivided human consciousness.

In his last works Beethoven has given up the struggle with the external world so typical of the middle-period symphonies, because he has fought and won a more important battle in his own spirit. He had wished to conquer himself in order to conquer life: "even with the frailties of my body my spirit shall dominate". But now he says: "O God, give me strength to conquer myself, for nothing must bind me to this life." This is the profoundest sense in which his deafness is both a physical fact and a spiritual allegory. While Beethoven lay dying a thunderstorm was raging. Just before the end, he raised himself from the pillows and shook his fist defiantly at the heavens. Then he fell back; on his face there was an expression of infinite beatitude. His death, like his life, is a parable which complements his music.

Against the theme which is stated in unison at the beginning of the finale to his last quartet, Beethoven wrote the words: "Muss es sein? Es Muss sein." (Must it be? It must be.) This musical motive has been derived from the thematic discovery of the first movement. The first half of it—the question—is tense, with a diminished fourth (Ex. 37); the second half—the answer—is relaxed, with a perfect fourth (Ex. 38). From this, the angelically childlike song of the coda is evolved. Now Beethoven said that the words he wrote against the theme had

Ex 37 Beethoven: Quartet opus 135 (last movement)

Ex.38 Beethoven: Quartet opus 135 (last movement)

reference to a request by his housekeeper for more money. Possibly they did: the explanation is typical of the Beethoven who would rend his audience's awe-struck silence with harsh mirth. But the words are also metaphysical. The question summarizes Beethoven's years of revolt against destiny; the answer summarizes his new-found humility. In his last work question and answer have become one. Like Blake, Beethoven knew that 'without contraries there is no progression'.

With the exception of Bruckner, Beethoven was the only composer born after Bach who had, or, rather, came to have, a profoundly religious mind. A movement like the 'Song of Thanksgiving on Recovery from Sickness' (from the A minor Quartet) is an altogether new kind of religious music, however much its modality may link it with techniques that were obsolete in Beethoven's day. Haydn's religion was ethical humanism, and Mozart's was love of life balanced by an acceptance of death. But Beethoven in his last works found, like Kant, that "we live in an invisible church, God's kingdom is in ourselves". Unlike Palestrina or Bach, he had no accepted creed to help him. He had to win his joy and his peace—his unified being, his glimpse of Paradise—out of "air which is now thoroughly small and dry, smaller and drier than the will. . . . Consequently I rejoice, having to construct something Upon which to rejoice."

And that we have paraphrased T. S. Eliot's *Ash Wednesday* is no accident. It is well known that Mr. Eliot wrote his cycle of poems, *Four Quartets*, with the impact of Beethoven's late quartets in mind. He would not claim to be a Beethoven; but in his smaller and more self-conscious way he has been trying—and in circumstances that seem now even more 'unpropitious' than they were in Beethoven's day—to deal with precisely the kind of experience with which Beethoven was preoccupied. We should perhaps leave a great poet with the last word; for the conclusion of *Little Gidding* comes about as close to describing in words what Beethoven's last quartets are about as is humanly possible:

> We shall not cease from exploration
> And the end of all our exploring
> Will be to arrive where we started
> And know the place for the first time.
> Through the unknown, remembered gate
> When the last of earth left to discover
> Is that which was the beginning;
> At the source of the longest river
> The voice of the hidden waterfall
> And the children in the apple-tree
> Not known, because not looked for
> But heard, half-heard, in the stillness
> Between two waves of the sea.
> Quick now, here now, always—
> A condition of complete simplicity
> (Costing not less than everything)
> And all shall be well and
> All manner of thing shall be well
> When the tongues of flame are in-folded
> Into the crowned knot of fire
> And the fire and the rose are one.

5

SCHUBERT

We have seen that Haydn, Mozart, and Beethoven were all revolutionary composers in the sense that they reacted against certain elements in the society in which they lived. Mozart's reaction was more conscious than Haydn's, and Beethoven's was more conscious than Mozart's. Yet Beethoven no less than his predecessors still believed in civilization; at least until the last years of his life he thought that although change was necessary it was feasible, and that the future was worth living for. Not all his calculated will to be misunderstood can alter the fact that he achieved as great a material success as any composer has a right to expect. He was an international celebrity who, on his own admission, had seven or eight publishers—blackguards though they might be one and all—vying with one another for permission to publish his works. He was able proudly to follow through his destiny.

With Schubert [1797–1828] one approaches the typically romantic view of the world. When he was born, in 1797, Mozart had been dead six years, and Beethoven was approaching the first crisis of his career. By Schubert's time, the corruption within Viennese society could be disguised neither by the tawdry frivolity of a degenerating aristocracy, nor by the industry, piety, and cosy sentimentality of the middle class, to which Schubert's parents belonged. Both aristocratic triviality and the bourgeois mentality represented by the newspaper cartoon Biedermeier—an anticipatory 'little man' or 'man in the street'—were an escape from fear. Schubert had no use for either, except in so far as he absorbed Italian opera from the the one and urban popular music from the other. He rather sought his salvation in a communion of kindred spirits. Popular legend used to interpret the 'bohemian' behaviour of the Schubert circle as the irresponsible gaiety of the artist's life. In fact, it grew from a deepening despair. The members of the Schubertiad were poets, dramatists, painters, all university men and mostly brilliant, cultivated, worldly-wise. Schubert would not have been their companion had he been no more than the unthinking song-bird of romantic myth. So far from being irresponsible, Schubert and his friends were acutely conscious of political oppression in Austria, even to the point of revolutionary fervour. At the same time, they felt powerless to change their own and their country's destiny. Corruption had gone too far. All they could hope to do was to find in friendship a society which, being based not on autocratic power, but on human feeling, kept alive, instead of stifling, the spirit. They were an intellectual minority, awaiting their doom, if not calmly, at least with their eyes wide open.

One might almost say that Schubert is a composer of Friendship as Bach had been a composer of the Church and Handel a composer of the State. We shall see later that although Schubert wrote music for the Church, he no longer believed in an institution which he equated with political oppression: so that his music is never liturgical in spirit. He also wrote operas, though he no longer believed in the State which heroic opera had been designed to celebrate: so that his operas remained unperformed or were unsuccessful. All his greatest music he wrote for himself and his friends; yet by writing this music he was no longer able to keep himself alive. Beethoven may have felt bitter that his greatest material success was *The Battle of Vittoria*, while his last quartets left the public bemused, if not hostile; none the less, he made a substantial income by composing, by and large, the kind of music he wanted to compose. Schubert, on the other hand, as a freelance musician, had to produce entertainment music for a degenerate aristocracy and a sentimental bourgeoisie whose tastes he could no longer fully share. While he enjoyed writing his innumerable waltzes, marches, and polkas, he would have preferred to spend some of the time composing symphonies and sonatas; and while it would be going too far to say that there is a split between Schubert's 'occasional' and his 'serious' music, it is not extravagant to say that they are beginning to differ in kind as well as, like Mozart's, in degree.

So there is throughout Schubert's personality and music a strange equivocation. As a man he was, like Beethoven, conscious of political oppression in Austria; unlike Beethoven, he did not think it was possible or perhaps even desirable to do anything about it. As a musician, he revered Beethoven with self-obliterating fanaticism; yet he deplored what he called Beethoven's "eccentricity, which drives a man to distraction, instead of resolving him in love". And so his own quintessential music seems to be created simultaneously out of conflict with the world as it was (the Beethovenian aspect of his work) and out of a utopian yearning for Viennese civilization as he imagines it had once been (the early Mozartian, lyrical, and vocal aspect of his work). Hence his music's combination of strength with melancholy. From one point of view, like Beethoven, he heroically protests; from another he seeks in his music to resolve his frustration in love, to create a world in which ideals are not corrupted by people's malice or stupidity. "Often I feel I do not belong to this world at all," he once said. He becomes his own Wanderer. Communing with solitude, he discovers a world of the imagination which can soothe and satisfy as real life cannot.

We have observed that the essential characteristic of Mozart's mature music is its equilibrium between lyrical melody and tonal drama: which is the musical epitome of a precariously balanced civilization. We have seen too that through the course of his life Beethoven achieved out of tonal drama a rebirth of the lyrical and contrapuntal principle: which is also a re-creation of a religious view of life. Schubert, with his romantic sense of separation, has not the Mozartian equilibrium; lyricism and tonal drama are not miraculously at one, but have to win through to a reconcilation. On the other hand, there is nothing in Schubert's work comparable with Beethoven's conquest of serenity. The innocence that Beethoven attained was the fruit of experience; the innocence that Schubert seeks is, like that of the 'Pastoral' Symphony, the expression of a pre-self-conscious state. We shall see that his most representative music springs from an ambivalence between the anguish of the conscious mind and a nostalgic reversion to the simple acceptance of childhood.

It is significant that whereas Beethoven discovered song melody through the course of a spiritually tormented life, Schubert was, as the saying is, 'born' with a gift of unpremeditated song. He is essentially a lyrical composer; and of the classical masters only Mozart seems to have had no problems in accommodating song melody to sonata drama. We must say 'seems' because we have Mozart's own admission that the critical works in his career, the 'Haydn' quartets, cost him a great deal of trouble. Certainly, Schubert's first efforts as a sonata composer were not convincing; and he achieved maturity as a song composer at an age when his symphonies and sonatas had not advanced beyond prettiness and pastiche.

The importance of solo song in Schubert's day was not fortuitous; for the Lied was domestic and intimate, an art of friendship. History books used to refer to Schubert as 'The Father of Song'. Although the description is nonsensical—in so far as great solo songs have been created from the troubadours to Dowland, from Dowland to Mozart himself—it is not as silly as it seems: for Schubert's *kind* of song is a creation of his age. A song of Dowland is passionate, but never dramatic; the passion is absorbed into the flow of line. A song of Bach or Handel is dramatic, but never subjective. Even Mozart, who was still essentially an opera composer though his notion of opera differs from Handel's, in his songs objectifies his experience in 'characters'. Thus his little song, '*Als Luise die Briefe ihres ungetreuen Liebhabers verbrannte*', summarizes an operatic situation in a couple of pages; we experience Luise's feelings through the glass of Mozart's creativity. Even the lovely setting of Goethe's *Das Veilchen* incorporates into its tender lyricism something of operatic rhetoric and of the interior drama of sonata style: consider the development-like minor opening of the middle section, and the diminished sevenths of the recitative climax. *Abendempfindung* is perhaps the only song of Mozart which approaches the introspective lyricism of the Lied; and it is still partially Italianate in line.

Now, Schubert was brought up on Italianate opera: on reminiscences of the high baroque; on Gluck; on his beloved Mozart; on Rossini [1792–1868], whose fashionably glittering re-creation of bel canto was all the rage in Vienna. The earliest works of his adolescence were operatic scenas in recitative and arioso. Like their prototypes, the ballads of Zumsteeg [1760–1802], they deal, in the German language, with subjects usually taken from German folk-myth, rather than from the myths of classical antiquity. Musically, however, they simply transfer Italian opera to the drawing-room, with the piano taking the place of the orchestra. The young Schubert even set a scene from Goethe's *Faust* in this style; the music is interesting in both its strength and its weaknesses. The vocal line is powerful and the setting of the words sensitive; the harmony and modulations are bold. But the young composer shows no capacity to organize his audacities; and in the drawing-room he cannot rely on the adventitious support of dramatic action. After his youth, he composed no more of these scenas. To the model of the Rossinian aria, however, he returned intermittently throughout his life. *Der Hirt auf dem Felsen*—in which sophisticated Rossinian coloratura merges into the Austrian rusticity of the yodelling song—is a composition of Schubert's maturity. One of his last compositions was a series of settings of poems by the old-style Italian opera liberettist, Metastasio.

While the operatic element remained potent in south German song, there was another tradition in the north. The prototype of this we can examine in the beautiful religious songs of C. P. E. Bach. These were meant to be sung in the home rather than in church, to the accompaniment of a chamber organ. They may be grouped into three main types: songs based on the style of the Lutheran chorale; songs in cantata aria style; and songs in the rococo manner, with tunes of a more popular flavour. Of these types the two former were developed from the techniques of his father, though Carl Philipp emphasizes the 'pathetic' effect of chromaticism and of appoggiaturas so strongly that the music seems more subjective than liturgical. The third type, in being related to folk-song, forged a link between Sensibility and the Bourgeois.

Such domesticated religious songs provided a model which was finally secularized by composers such as Reichart and Zelter; in whose songs, of course, the piano takes the place of the chamber organ. Musically, their work seems pallid compared with C. P. E. Bach's pathos; but their historical interest is considerable, for they rendered Sensibility homely. Their declamation is supple; their harmony and piano writing gently illustrative of the text. J. S. Bach had developed illustrative figurations in his instrumental parts for symbolical as well as for musical reasons. The early composers of Lieder used them for their naturalistic appeal; for their music is a portrayal of everyday life.

The intimate character of these Lieder is thus inseparable from their relation to their texts; the growth of a new school of song parallels the growth of a school of lyric poetry. All the members of Schubert's circle wrote verse; Mahyrofer was a poet of romantic melancholy who may claim a modest distinction in his own right. The supreme figure of Goethe dominated the literary scene, and most song composers set his lyrical poems. A collection of folk poems published under the title of *Das Knaben Wunderhorn* also made a deep appeal to romantic sensibility, as an escape from introspective perplexities; so did the philosophical abstraction of Schiller, and the 'gothick' medievalism of Sir Walter Scott. The lyric poets were all romantically subjective: Novalis dealing with frustrated love, consumption, and heavenly aspirations, Rückert, Rellstab, and Heine with the ego in love and torment.

All this ruminative poetry found an ideal partner in the early nineteenth-century piano. For Schubert the piano, as opposed to the harpsichord, was an evocative instrument. It could be warmly cantabile, while at the same time it could efface itself to create a poetically 'orchestral' background. Song for him is a union between lyric poetry, the human voice, and the piano. Each element is equally important. The words must be heard, but the voice must sing, not speak; the piano must both support the singer and underline the meaning of the text. Schubert once said that when Vogl and he performed his songs, singer and pianist were as one. Such a performance is essentially intimate; Schubert gave only one public concert in his life. He wrote his songs for himself and his friends to sing and play. If they were published, they could be performed by other people in their homes also; but they were not addressed to the outside world.

In his adolescence, Schubert composed two kinds of song: domesticated operatic scenas of the type we have already discussed; and simple strophic songs in folk style, on the model of Zelter [1758–1832]. His first songs of genius fuse these two manners. Two of the most justly celebrated songs—*Gretchen am Spinnrade* and *Erlkönig*—were written in his teens. Both have lyrical melodies of great beauty; both use figuration in the piano part suggested by the poem (the spinning wheel and the galloping horse); both develop this figuration as a purely musical means of organization, as J. S. Bach had done; both extract a tremendous dramatic urgency from the interplay of vocal line and piano figuration.

One cannot imagine these songs being improved if Schubert had composed them at a more mature age. None the less, his art deepens and develops; during the next decade he learns to imbue his song writing with the melodic flexibility, harmonic richness, and symphonic breadth of his later instrumental works. Thus his setting of Goethe's *Prometheus* is a through composed song* which derives from the quasi-operatic scenas of his youth; only whereas they were diffuse, this is concentrated. The declamatory line now has lyrical power; and the audacious modulations—the sequence of diminished sevenths and the extraordinary chromatic climax—become progressive stages in a structure related to both melody and tonality, rather than unco-ordinated, if fascinating, incidents. The association of this massively potent song with the Promethean legend is significant; the Beethovenian aspect of Schubert here finds its apex in song writing.

Prometheus is a declamatory song which has become lyrical and symphonic. *Die Junge Nonne* is a lyrical and meditative song which has become dramatic. It tells a story and paints a scene: but does so by means of a self-contained melody and a piano figuration suggested by the poem. The girl who is singing has retired to a convent as a consequence—it is implied, if not stated—of frustrated love. Outside, a storm is raging. She welcomes her heavenly bridegroom, instead of an earthly lover; and the tolling of the convent bell gradually transforms the storm's conflict into ecstasy. The melody has the girl's simplicity; while the storm figuration of the piano part—oscillating enharmonically between the tonic minor and the minor of the flat supertonic—suggests the suppressed agitation of her soul. The change from agitation to ecstasy is effected through the alternation of minor and major—a relationship of peculiar significance in all Schubert's mature music.

This song is thus lyrical in character. Yet its lyricism includes passionate drama; and this drama is a projection of Schubert's own situation. It is not a religious song. The nun, like Schubert, is voluntarily separated from a pain-inflicting world. Having lost her real lover, she idealizes him into a dream-lover who is free of the imperfections of mortality. She seeks a new Eden. The contrast with Mozart is interesting. His Luise is a being other than Mozart, though we experience her sufferings through

* Through Composed Song: a song in which the words are set to music continuously, as compared with a Strophic Song, in which the same music is used for each verse.

Mozart's personality; Schubert's young nun is one of many masks for Schubert himself. Mozart's song is operatic and objective; Schubert's is domestic and self-revelatory.

Schubert's use of the mask reaches its culmination in the two Müller cycles which are his supreme achievement as a song-writer. Müller was born in the same year as Schubert, and died a few months earlier. He was an intellectual and a soldier, and in both capacities a misfit. His cycle of poems about the miller tell a story, set in the Austrian countryside, of a young man's disappointed love. The girl is stolen from him by a mysterious Green Huntsman; left alone, he contemplates suicide. As poetry, Müller's verses are undistinguished. He expresses a stock romantic myth in conventional romantic gestures. Yet this myth has deep roots in the human mind. Whether or no Schubert had a soul-destroying love affair of the kind described here, there is no doubt that this is how he—as well as Müller—saw himself as a lover. He cannot compete with the Huntsman's buoyant vitality. It has even been suggested that there may be another strand to the allegory: the Huntsman is Beethoven, the puny hero Schubert, and the girl Recognition and Success.

The *Winterreise* songs form a sequel. The girl has gone before the cycle opens. Winter has followed spring, and the pilgrim trudges down a solitary road. He lulls himself with a dream of spring renewed, but has to awaken to a cold and hostile world. A signpost points the way he must go; at the end of the path is the setting sun. His life's sun sinks, following the suns of love and hope. As he walks on his lonely road the only human figure to be seen is the hurdy-gurdy man who grinds out a wheezy tune to which no one listens. The brook, the trees, the raven, the weather-vane, the hurdy-gurdy man to whose one tune the pilgrim sings his story become projections of the unconscious. If in the Miller songs Schubert wrote out of his own frustrated life and love, in the *Winterreise* songs he was thinking of his illness and death. He called the cycle "a bunch of terrifying songs", and said that he thought more highly of them than of anything he had created. Almost immediately after their completion, his health broke down finally. Terrifying is the right word: not because they are grisly, but because of their complete absence of emotional indulgence. "Human-kind cannot bear Very much reality": but this Wanderer can, to the point of madness or death. The two cycles are the apotheosis of the personal life in lyrical song, as is Wagner's *Tristan* in a new kind of opera.

Musically, for the Miller songs Schubert returns to the lyric types of his youth, as befits the simplicity of the miller, and the rustic setting which appealed to him with so deep a nostalgia. But the folk-song-like tune is subtly enriched, partly through the intrusion within the strophic pattern of arioso elements (or lyrical declamation); partly through the symphonic treatment of the piano part and the structure of the cycle as a whole. Thus the cycle opens with the miller singing at his work, in unaffected innocence, unseared by experience. The brook is murmuring in the background, and in the next song rambles at its own sweet will. As the miller's story unfolds, the sounds of brook and birds become an emotional commentary in the piano part. At the end, only the brook is left, oblivious of human suffering. The songs that deal with the brook itself and with the miller in his Eden are in the simple strophic form, unmodified. When the vocal line becomes more distressed and declamatory, the piano parts tend to become more symphonic: consider the use of the ostinato figure in *Pause*.

This tendency is developed much further in the *Winterreise* songs, in which the vocal lines are relatively tortuous. Lyricism acquires elements of arioso and recitative in order to express the intensest feeling. The falling leaves of *Letze Hoffnung* suggest a distraught rhythm that disrupts the bar-line; *Der Greise Kopf* is built on an immense ascent up a thirteenth which falls like a breaking wave, to express the anguish that destroys the body as well as the soul (Ex. 39). The wandering line of *Die Krähe*,

with voice and piano in unison, accompanied by inexorably flowing triplets, marvellously evokes a mental and spiritual desolation; and all the introspective lamenting is finally projected into the figure of the solitary beggar, in the whine of whose hurdy-gurdy rest the sorrows of the world. This is the conclusion not only of a song cycle, but of a cycle of experience. Schubert has passed beyond the romantic individualism which was his original impetus, and has reached the tragic apotheosis. The Pilgrim is himself; but the beggar with whom he becomes identified, who sings his song and whose song he sings, is other than himself. His suffering is absorbed into that of humanity.

The same is true of Schubert's 'swan-songs', the Heine settings. In *Die Stadt*, that strange anticipation of the static harmonic technique of impressionism, the traveller's sorrow merges into the desolation of the silent town; in *Am Meer* personal grief is swallowed in the eternal lament and consolation of the sea. Finally, in *Der Doppelgänger*, the *alter ego* meets the Self and "mocks those torments I went through years ago". Schubert stands apart from his suffering; the intense declamation of his new lyric style is controlled by a passacaglia-like austerity of form. Even the piercing enharmonic modulation at the climax does not break the remorseless repetition of the Dies Irae motive in the bare, skeletonic piano texture (Ex. 40):

There is one song in the *Winterreise* cycle which epitomizes the Schubertian paradox. In *Frühlingstraum* the sensuously harmonized, folk-like melody, yearning up to the major sixth and drooping down to the fourth, is his dream of spring, his nostalgia for a lost innocence (Ex. 41). The Raven of experience shatters

the dream in acute dissonances and in rapid sequential modulations ending in the minor (Ex. 42). The slow section that follows hovers ambiguously between major and minor, questioning whether the dream be revelation or deceit (Ex. 43). The final answer is the stark minor triad; innocence once lost is lost for ever. Perhaps this is why the major melody in this song is even more melancholy than the minor section: the heart remembers spring, but cannot reawaken it.

Ex.42 Schubert: 'Fruhlingstraum'
Quick
da war es kalt und finst - er es schrieen die Rab-en vom Dach
etc.
Ex.43 Schubert: 'Fruhlingstraum'
Wer mal - te die Blät-ter da? Ihr lacht wohl ü - ber den Träumer

If this equivocation between innocence and experience is the core of Schubert's music, we can understand why he should have taken longer to attain maturity in instrumental terms than in song. As an instinctive song-writer, he created melodies which were self-contained, rather than material for development. Similarly, his romantic harmonic and modulatory sense lent itself to rhapsodic effects that were convincing in a song but disruptive in a symphony. Yet he could ignore his melodic and harmonic gifts only by denying his creativity. So at first, in instrumental music, he had to be content with pastiche of the masters he revered and feared. Playing down the tense equilibrium of Haydn and Mozart and the subversive violence of Beethoven, he accepted the hedonistic style that was so popular in Vienna. Gradually he learned how to make his own kind of melody and harmony symphonic.

Many movements in Schubert's early symphonies and quartets, being modelled upon particular movements of Haydn, Mozart, and Beethoven, are inspired by art rather than by life. Their fundamental weakness is not, however, the parasitic nature of the material, but the tug-of-war between the dramatic, classical nature of this material and the lyrical, romantic nature of Schubert's temperament. His second subjects tend to be too long and cantabile; in enjoying them, Schubert forgets the dramatic structure of his symphony. Even when the themes are short, they are usually self-contained tunes, so that there is nothing to be done with them except to repeat them in sequences. Schubert's expositions then anticipate the only technique he can use to extend the music during the development section. Even when—as in the approach to the recapitulation of the first movement of the First Symphony—he lights on an impressive idea, the effect is no more than a romantic incident. To repeat the material of the slow introduction in the tempo of the allegro leads one to expect a grand apotheosis. In fact, nothing happens except a literal repeat, bathetic after so exciting a preparation.

Schubert's passive luxuriance in flatwards-tending modulations is another source of trouble to him. Frequently he will introduce his second subjects not in the dominant, but in the flatter subdominant; to compensate for this he has to append a long codetta insisting on the dominant. These threefold expositions are partially responsible for the inconclusive nature of his developments: and for his reliance on mechanical sequences to effect a recovery.

In the Fourth Symphony, which he himself termed 'Tragic', Schubert courageously attempts to advance beyond rococo pastiche and to measure up to the Beethovenian ideal. The slow introduction suggests not only Beethoven, but the Mozart of the 'Dissonance' Quartet and Cherubini. Its sweeping phrases, romantic modulations, and acute dissonances are powerful, as is the opening theme of the allegro. If this boldly leaping arpeggiated theme reminds us of Beethoven's opus 18 Quartet in the same key and to a lesser degree of Mozart's G minor Symphony and Quintet, it also has character of its own. It grows into a contrasting, consoling theme in the flat submediant —a key-relationship which is to play so important a part in Schubert's later music. This theme is abruptly cut short by a descent to E major, standing for F flat—a further descent to the flat submediant at once sensuous and dramatic. This is a magnificent opening which Schubert is unable to sustain. Drama is frittered away in sequential modulations; and none of the other movements even attempts a Beethovenian grandeur.

Having failed to create a Beethovenian symphony, Schubert

seems, in his Fifth and Sixth, to take a contrary path. The Fifth is as unpretentious as early Mozart; and though he calls the Sixth a 'Grand' symphony, the heroic manner survives for no more than a few bars of the introduction. The first allegro theme is song-like and unsymphonic. It lasts eight bars; but is spun out by sequences and appendices to seventy-four, before we arrive at the dominant. The second subject is also Rossinian. On such material the development can be no more than a charming amble; and without any dramatic argument there is no way of bringing the music to a stop except a *più mosso* coda to work up the excitement in a synthetic theatricality. The movement is not unsuccessful since it is without pretension. But it did rather seem that, as a composer of symphonies and quartets, Schubert had lost heart.

A way out was perhaps suggested by the E major Quartet of 1816; for this work shows how Rossinian vivacity can be imbued with the dramatic urgency of the Viennese sonata. When, after a period of four years, Schubert composed another work for string quartet he had entered a world that was neither Rossinian nor Beethovenian, but his own. In the Quartettsatz in C minor the melodies are no longer Italianate; their yearning lyricism marks the emergence of the solitary Schubert of the last years. The fluttering ostinato accompaniment suggests some demoniacal night-ride such as he depicts in the piano parts of his songs; and the contrast between this feverish C minor and the sweetly submissive flat submediant in which the second subject appears is the impetus behind the music's structure.

In the two succeeding years Schubert achieved a comparable maturity as a symphonist. In the E major and the 'Unfinished' B minor he is no longer writing classical pastiche nor emulating Beethoven; he has created his own type of autobiographical symphony, for "my compositions are the product of my mind and spring from my sorrow; only those that were born of grief give the greatest delight to the outside world". Songs such as *Die liebe Farbe*, *Suleika*, and *Der Doppelgänger* suggest that B minor had a peculiar evocative significance for Schubert. Not only the poetic theme, but also many of the musical motives of the songs appear in the symphony. The unharmonized opening theme, with its rising third and falling fourth, is a melodic seed from which song generates. The strings hum as the theme slowly comes to life on oboe and clarinet—an effect which

Bruckner was later gigantically to expand. The music comes to rest on a sustained D which changes its meaning from a third to a fifth: so that the second subject appears in the flat submediant again, without preparatory modulation. It is a song tune with a folk-like simplicity, though its persistently drooping fourths are full of regret. It flows to silence: which is savagely sundered by a C minor arpeggio.

The development creates a tremendous battle out of the lyrical material of the opening eight bars. The first-group song themes try to re-establish their identity, but are repeatedly shattered by the surging arpeggio. The consolatory second subject does not reappear until, after a terrific martial climax on the Neapolitan chord to B minor, the music dies back to its source. Song melody has achieved its victory: so the andante that follows can be lyricism unperturbed. It is in rondo form, but unlike Schubert's earlier, cheerfully fragmentary rondos in that all the richly exquisite lyricism grows out of the rising third of the opening. The movement is in E major—the key of the nostalgic heaven of the Wanderer in *Der Lindenbaum*, *Des Baches Wiegenlied*, and many other songs; and in its unity and its unfettered songfulness is a vision of bliss. But the heaven of Schubert's Pilgrim is not the mystical state of pure Being for which Beethoven sought in his last works. It is the recovery of Eden, of the innocence of direct response to Nature. For this reason it is in essence sensuous: as is the mellifluous woodwind scoring in this most poetic of all symphonic movements.

These three crucial works in Schubert's development—the Quartettsatz in C minor, the E major and B minor Symphonies—were all left unfinished. Various explanations have been offered. May not the basic reason be very simple? Schubert had finally solved his most difficult technical and imaginative problem. He had resolved drama into song; and in the andante of the B minor had followed this resolution with the bliss of Eden. He could not rest permanently in a recovered Eden; but at this stage in his career he could not see how he could continue without descent to bathos. He found an answer only in the last three quartets and the C major Quintet, composed during the last four years of his life.

In some ways, the A minor Quartet is the most representative of all Schubert's instrumental works. It opens with one of his most nostalgic song themes, oscillating around the mediant: a relationship very common in Schubert's tunes and partially responsible, no doubt, for his fondness for mediant modulations. This song melody is surrounded by a pianissimo haze of floating quavers: a romantic, orchestral sonority which suggests the withdrawal of the lonely singer from the hurly-burly of life (Ex. 44). The world of dream appears in the andante, which is

Ex.44 Schubert: Quartet in A minor (first movement)

based on a song from *Rosamunde*; but its pastoral innocence is threatened by upsurgings of feverish energy. The minuet adapts Schubert's earlier setting of Schiller's *Schöne Welt, wo bist du*: 'O lovely world, where are you? Return once more, O fair and flowered age of Nature.' The key is minor, the mood as desolate as that of the *Winterreise*. Innocent happiness appears in the major interlude of the trio; but the theme is again dreamily nostalgic, the happiness retrospective. Throughout, yearning for the 'fair and flowered age of Nature' alternates with despair of ever attaining it. Even the last movement, though it seems to be gay, is mysterious beneath its exuberance; continual alternations of major and minor recall the *Frühlingstraum* rondo.

The A minor Quartet is pervaded by the consciousness of death, but soothes in its lyricism. In the posthumous D minor, the poetic idea is contained in the andante, a series of variations on Schubert's early song, *Der Tod und das Mädchen* ('Death and the Maiden'). Although the maiden's song flowers from its elegiac opening into a blissful major conclusion, the mood of the quartet is more fevered than that of the A minor. Perhaps because he is more death-haunted, Schubert organizes his material more tautly. All the movements are dominated by a grim rhythmic motive which, in the final sonata-rondo, gathers itself into a Dance of Death in tarantella style. The music is fiercer than anything in the *Winterreise* cycle: but equally unflinching.*

The last quartet, in G, is the biggest and most powerful of all.

* It is worth noting that Vienna, in the decade following Schubert's death, produced perhaps the first two distinguished composers to devote all their energies to the creation of 'functional' music for entertainment—the waltz kings Lanner [1801–1843] and the elder Strauss [1804–1849].

Schubert's first quartets had been domestic music for amateurs. This quartet is extremely difficult to play, and extracts from the four instruments an almost orchestral sonority. The alternation of major and minor, which we have seen to be both a poetic idea and a sensuous effect in Schubert's music, here becomes dramatic and structural. It is stated at the massive opening (Ex. 45), is the source of the development's conflict, and is stated in inverse order at the beginning of the recapitulation. The

Ex.45 Schubert: Quartet in G (first movement)

andante expresses the alternation of innocence and experience in one of Schubert's typical modifications of rondo form. A sweetly lyrical melody, with nostalgically yearning sixths, is repeatedly interrupted by a feverish agitato figure. This both disrupts the flow of melody with its frantic tremolandos and splinters the music's tonal stability with its weird enharmonic modulations. An obsessively reiterated figure strives to preserve a tonal centre against these destructive forces (Ex. 46); in the

Ex.46 Schubert: Quartet in G (slow movement)

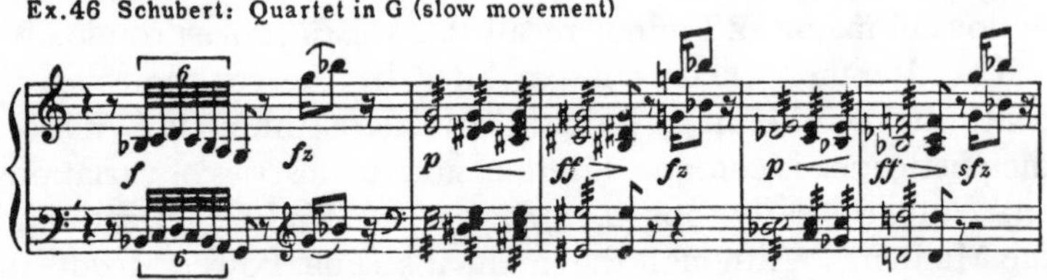

coda the terrifying Reality is resolved in a major apotheosis of the Dream. The innocence attained, if attained it is, is retrospective, and therefore melancholy. In music such as this one might almost say that Schubert has become a 'modern' composer: not merely because his technique is advanced, but also because the experience which the technique serves is centred in moral isolation, rather than in the solidarities of belief.

The last movement of the G major Quartet is again a wild tarantella, with kaleidoscopic modulations and abrupt oppositions of major and minor. Though it is less frenzied than the finale of the D minor Quartet, there is something obsessional in its driving vitality; and in that respect it points the way to the C major Symphony—the Grand Symphony which Schubert had aspired to create throughout his working life. Aiming at epic grandeur in the manner of Beethoven's Ninth, this symphony turns out to be as unlike Beethoven as it is unlike the lyrical 'Unfinished'.

The slow introduction with which it opens is a classical precedent reborn in the spirit of romanticism. The solo horn theme is one of the earliest horn-calls through the forest of German romanticism. But the tune itself is in a sombre march rhythm, like a chorale or a pilgrim's song; and the marching pilgrim is the solitary Wanderer of the *Winterreise*, for the symphony is an epic statement of what the *Winterreise* songs say in intimate terms. Despite its classic grandeur, the theme is romantically irregular in rhythm, and wavers in tonality between C major and A minor. It leads by way of a gigantic crescendo into the first allegro theme, in an energetic motor rhythm. The second subject opens in the minor of the mediant—not the flat submediant in this powerfully assertive work. It is derived from the rising third of the introduction, as is much of the material of the whole symphony. The development is short, after so vast an exposition; but there is an enormous coda in which the chorale returns accompanied by a multiplicity of subsidiary marching and stamping rhythms. Song melody proves triumphant after metrical violence and tonal drama have done their worst; but the song is not itself transformed, so this glorious conclusion has no resemblance to Beethoven's symphonic finales.

The slow movement is a Schubertian rondo which alternates a wry oboe theme in the Wanderer's march rhythm with a cantabile melody is Schubert's passive flat submediant. This march rhythm may have derived from Schubert's obsession with the allegretto of Beethoven's Seventh Symphony; the significance it came to have for him is certainly un-Beethovenian. The Wanderer in *Der Wegweiser* trudges on because he cannot escape his destiny; even in the symphony the appeasing hymn melody, with its sensuous scoring, is a dream of peace which the march obliterates. In both song and symphonic movement the music peters out through sheer inanition. In the scherzo, which is a combination of scherzo and trio with conflict sonata, Schubert attempts to emulate Beethoven and to "seize Fate by the throat". Yet we rather feel that Fate seizes him—in this cataclysmic eruption as much as in the implacable monotony of the Wanderer rhythm; and that the nostalgic trio reflects once more his desire to escape.

The motor rhythm of the last movement again recalls the last movement of Beethoven's Seventh, and the paean of triumph at the end of the Ninth, from which Schubert quotes the 'joy' theme. But Beethoven's finale to the Seventh is a battle-piece in which the Morality of Power subdues all opposition; and the finale of the Ninth is a song theme created from chaos during the growth of a vast symphonic structure. Beethoven is a man in possession; Schubert, in the last movement of the C major, is a man possessed. Although Schubert increasingly seeks for interrelations between his themes and employs a motivic technique throughout a large-scale work, he does not create themes through metamorphosis, as Beethoven does. For all its romantic trappings—for instance, the 'impressionistic' scoring and harmony of the approach to the recapitulation—this finale is closer to the classical tradition than the mature works of Beethoven.

And so even after he has evolved his own kind of lyrical-romantic or epic symphony, Schubert retains something of the reverence with which, in his youth, he had regarded his classical heritage. As a piano composer, he had always been less awed by tradition. The piano was his own instrument: domestic, intimate, improvisatory. His first piano sonatas reveal the fluency of the improviser's melodic gift and the luxuriance of his harmony more spontaneously than do the early symphonies and quartets. The E major Sonata of 1816 is not a successful solution of the problem of the lyrical sonata; but the typical features of Schubert's later work are all present—the song tunes that proliferate in motives capable of development; the keyboard figurations derived from song accompaniments; the sonorous spacing of the keyboard texture; the sensuously wandering modulations, usually tending flatwards.

The youthful phase of Schubert's piano sonatas concludes with his first entirely successful song sonata—the exquisite A major of 1819: a work on a modestly Mozartian scale which is essentially Schubertian in spirit. The first song melody is smilingly innocent; the presence of the Wanderer rhythm in the second subject suggests, however, that the possession of such innocence is precarious. In the little coda the chromatic alteration and the warm spacing of the piano writing emphasize the retrospective quality of the happiness (Ex. 47). Already this is a young man's dream of youth.

Ex. 47 Schubert: Piano Sonata in A opus 120 (1st movement)

Schubert did not compose another sonata for four years; he then produced three works utterly different in character from the A major. This work epitomizes Schubert the lyrical song-writer in terms of the piano sonata. The two tragic A minor sonatas (opus 42 and 143) and the unfinished C major are the apotheosis of Schubert the dramatic song-writer. They have one quality—their economy—in common with the A major. But it is now an economy of tension, observable as much in the elliptical ambiguities between major and minor tonality as in the stark, austere keyboard writing, as compared with the earlier luxuriance. In all these qualities—and in the quasi-orchestral use of pianistic tone-colour—the sonatas might be studies for the *Winterreise* cycle.

The next sonata, the D major, opus 53, is again different in mood. Unique among Schubert's sonatas in being written for a professional virtuoso, it is appropriately opulent in lyricism, harmony, and keyboard technique. The bareness of the A minor sonatas and the richness of opus 53 meet in the style of the last four sonatas, which are the culmination of Schubert's work as a piano composer. The radiant G major, opus 78, resolves tragedy in love; the posthumous A major at last exorcises the daemon of Beethoven by reconciling his grandeur with Schubertian lyricism. But Schubert's most profound (and un-Beethovenian) fusion of song melody with drama is the first movement of the posthumous B flat Sonata. The serenely singing first theme oscillates between the tonic and Schubert's submissive flat submediant. It appears to soothe: no Beethovenian aggression here, but rather regression to childhood's single-minded simplicity. Yet the most mysterious drama is attained in the modulatory equivocations of the long, quiet approach to the recapitulation. The movement's 'heavenly length' is inherent both in the nature of the themes and in Schubert's conception of the dramatic.

Much the same is true of the slow movement. We are lulled to bliss by the seductive melody's barcarolle rhythm, until the softest enharmonic modulations seem to open the ground beneath our feet (Ex. 48). We are unsure whether the dream comforts, or breaks the heart. Even more poignant than this sudden enharmonic transition is the final appearance of the

bararcolle melody in the major. The effect is visionary: yet profoundly sad, because the happiness is subject to mutability. In a letter to his father, written in 1825, Schubert said, speaking of a mutual acquaintance: "He probably still keeps crawling to the Cross; and he will certainly have imagined himself to be ill another seventy-seven times and to have been on the point of death nine times, as if death were the worst thing that could happen to us mortals. If he could only take a look at these divine mountains and lakes, whose aspect threatens to stifle and devour us, he would not be so attached to this petty existence as not to think it a piece of great good fortune to be confided once more to the incomprehensible power of the earth to make new life." Haydn, we saw, regarded man and Nature as partners in a humanitarian scheme; Mozart considered Nature as insignificant in comparison with man; Beethoven used Nature as a means towards his own salvation. But Schubert has no humanitarian morality, no mystical salvation; he has only the moments of ecstasy given him by his exquisitely tuned senses, which are pitifully subject to Time. For this reason he is scared of death, as he is awed by mountains and lakes because they are impervious to human feeling. He can but conquer fear in his pantheistic acceptance of his pettiness.

The letter quoted above is an extraordinary document to come from an ostensible Catholic. In fact, Schubert merely paid lip-service to his Church. He wrote masses in his youth, because they were a legitimate source of income. But he cut out the words, "I believe in one Catholic and apostolic Church"; and his was never a religious nature, either in the doctrinal or the Beethovenian sense. His early masses sound like the operas of Pergolesi [1710–1736] or, occasionally, Mozart; they even have *buffo* finales. This is the traditional, Austrian, theatrical side of Schubert's Catholicism. The other side is fervent, ecstatic, Marianic, and has nothing to do with the Church. It becomes personal—indeed, sensuous—experience; and finds its expression in songs—notably the Novalis settings, the Scott *Ave Maria*, and the four-part setting of *Psalm 23* for two sopranos and two altos—and in the unfinished oratorio, *Lazarus*, which Schubert composed partly as a palliative for his operatic failures.

When in the last years of his life Schubert turned to the Church again, he no longer pretended to make his masses liturgical. They become choral and symphonic poems of a subjectively romantic nature. The A flat Mass contains some of Schubert's boldest harmonic and modulatory flights. The tonality is the 'romantic' key of A flat. But the Gloria is in E (the flat submediant again), the Gratias in A, the Credo in C, the Sanctus and Hosanna in F: the main key does not return until the Benedictus. The only compromise with tradition is the big fugal Gloria; even this Schubert shortened in a later version. He makes little attempt to emulate convention and none to approach the new contrapuntal spirituality of Beethoven's *Missa Solemnis*. He is content to be a romantic harmonist; and in being himself becomes almost a mystic of the senses, as he is in the barcarolle of the B flat Piano Sonata, and as Wagner was to be in *Parsifal*.

The E flat Mass of the last year of Schubert's life is more stable in tonality and stronger in line: less subject to the sensory flux. But it has no more in common with traditional church music: or at least the liturgical elements in it play much the same part in relation to secular Experience as folk-simplicity does in his songs and instrumental works. For instance, in the Domine Deus the Gregorian-like melody with its solemn trombones symbolizes a Faith which is shattered by the agitated figurations of the strings and the weird modulations of the chorus. There is a similar equivocation in the Agnus Dei—a chromatic, harmonically founded contrapuntal movement with a double theme, one part identical with the subject of Bach's C sharp minor Fugue from Book I of the *Forty-eight*, the other with Schubert's own *Doppelgänger*. The marriage of Schubert's *alter ego* with religious assurance seems unlikely: perhaps we may say that it is not consummated.

Powerful as is this equivocal music, one would not expect to find Schubert's most representative achievements in his liturgical works. The single work which most comprehensively embraces every facet of his genius is probably his last chamber work, the String Quintet in C. We see at once how the second 'cello gives Schubert the sonority his harmony demands. The first subject group combines lyricism with the dynamic manner of the big C major Symphony, with bounding dotted rhythms; the second subject is one of the most acutely nostalgic of his song-tunes. The wild conflict between these two moods has already been anticipated in the dissonant cadential harmony of the opening phrase.

In the slow movement we are in the E major bliss of Schubert's Eden, harmonized at first in warmly sustained diatonicism, then in melting, regretful sevenths and ninths. This song melody is followed by a 'middle section' which jumps abruptly from the blissful E major to the 'Neapolitan' flat supertonic, F minor. In panting, almost hysterical rhythms, accompanied by sinister triplet figures, a more operatic theme flows through a range of enharmonic modulations that sunder tonality no less than the mature work of Wagner. When the E major song returns, the triplets have become delicate demisemiquavers. At the end, the threat of F minor again obtrudes; but this time leads not to the fever of Experience, but to a simple cadence to the tonic. The effect is psychologically very odd. The childlike coda is warmly secure, though we know that terror is but a little way beneath the surface.

The mysterious, if not the terrible, crops up again in the enharmony of the scherzo's trio. The scherzo itself returns to the dynamic exuberance of the C major Symphony, with startling modulations. With the rondo finale Schubert seems to forget the tempests of his joys and sorrows in recalling the café music of his early days. Yet the movement begins oddly in C minor, and goes through several keys before establishing the major; and the more jaunty the figurations grow, the more enigmatic grow the adventures of harmony and tonality. The strangest things of all happen when Schubert adopts the conventional Rossini device of concluding a movement by whipping up the tempo. As the music becomes ostensibly more frivolous, it grows also more hectic; and the final section of the coda takes us back to the enharmonic dissonance of the first movement. The last thing we hear is the cryptic 'Neapolitan' relationship of D flat to C.

This strange metamorphosis of café music occurs in what is perhaps Schubert's greatest, and certainly his most personal work. To the end of his life he continued, for commercial reasons, to compose occasional music alongside works of subjective experience; and the nature of this music gradually changed. On the comparatively rare occasions when Schubert had composed display music for the platform, he had usually been content with the decorative techniques of fashion; such music always involved the piano, and adapted its pianistic style from Hummel [1778–1837]. Now, in the two piano trios and in the 'Trout' Quintet, Schubert imbues even café music with personal feeling; while in the G major Duo for violin and piano he creates a virtuoso piece which is great (and characteristically mysterious) music. The big virtuoso Fantasy for piano on the Wanderer theme is not only serious music, but also one of Schubert's most progressive experiments: for in attempting to evolve all the material of a four-movement work from a single theme he anticipates Liszt's romantic re-creation of monothematic principles.

These display pieces were all written on commission. There is a comparable change in the small works intended for domestic performance. The medium of the piano duet (symbol of friendship) prompts Schubert to some of his most tragic utterances, which might have been symphonies if orchestras had been available to play them. Even the salon pieces themselves became personal confessions. The early dances were occasional music that both technically and imaginatively measured up to the occasion. The last dances, the C sharp minor *Moment Musical*, and the *Klavierstücke* of 1828 are testaments as romantically lonely as the dances and nocturnes of Chopin. Probably Schubert himself was not conscious of the change. Publishers and public probably felt that they, rather than Schubert's music, had been sold.

Schubert died at the age of thirty-one—four years younger

than Mozart. He is closer to Mozart than is any other composer, but the lyrical and dramatic bases of his art are more widely separated; from the struggle to reconcile them sprang the mingling of passion and nostalgia which is his music. From this point of view, we may compare Mozart's 'Longing for Spring' in the last movement of his last concerto with any of Schubert's *Frühlingstraum*-like movements. Mozart, we saw, is graceful and apparently impersonal in his perfection: the dancing interplay of parts seems the Essence of mutability itself. Schubert's singing melodies and harmonic ambiguities are his own consciousness of mutability, romantic in spirit: so that, despite his respect for the past, his late music is inexhaustibly prophetic—especially of the sensuous individualism of Wagner. With him we therefore feel, as with Mozart we do not, a tragic sense of potentialities unfulfilled.

On the other hand, the anticipations of romanticism in all his mature music are perhaps inseparable from the sense of doom which hung over his world and himself. He composed much superficially merry music; yet from the moment he attained personality, the merriment is tinged with melancholy; and the spine-tingling beauty of his last works is related to their consciousness of death. Again, the essential Schubertian experience is sensuous. We feel this beauty with our melodic and harmonic senses; and in knowing from his music (not from the books we have read) that he himself had so little time in which to experience it, we become aware that for us too beauty is as transient as a dream. The music is still almost before we have heard it; the dream is past that was more real than the waking life.

6

BRUCKNER, BRAHMS, AND MAHLER

THE MUSIC of the Viennese classics depends, we have seen, on a balance between Tradition and Revolution: between an Age of Faith and an Age of Anxiety. Haydn was born into a faith against which he did not consciously rebel, though he unwittingly transformed it from mystical dogma to ethical humanism. Mozart reinterpreted the faith in personally emotional terms, so that it was no longer a faith that the Church could recognize. Beethoven rejected the past, but created new belief out of conflict. Schubert turned still more violently from orthodox Catholicism; but discovered nothing to take its place except a vague pantheism. Beethoven said he could have 'no friends'; Schubert used friendship, as he used music, as a bulwark against a hostile world. Yet Beethoven created a faith through his music, whereas Schubert found only moments of illumination. This is why Schubert's late music is, in its loneliness, inexpressibly sad: while Beethoven's late music is, in its profundity, inexpressibly joyful. There is no deeper experience than the joy Beethoven discovered; though conventional romanticism came to believe that only unhappiness could be profound.

The change in the attitude to belief which develops between Haydn and Schubert runs parallel to the slow deterioration of Austrian Catholicism. Schubert's dismissal of the Church was echoed by his successors as Catholicism in Austria grew increasingly remote from the realities of the nineteenth century. By the time of Francis I, the identification of the Church with oppression was unmistakable; and the Jesuitical spirit pervaded every aspect of life. The revolutionary stirrings of 1848 were soon suppressed; conditions returned to an even more reactionary conservatism. The Concordat of 1855 handed over the entire educational system to the Church.

Yet the fact that Austria preserved through the nineteenth century a fossilized feudalism alone made possible the strange phenomenon of Anton Bruckner [1824–1896]. For in Bruckner one finds again the innocence that the self-conscious mind of Schubert yearned for; he is a medieval survival in a country cut off from the creative development of Europe. He believed in his Church as unequivocally as a medieval peasant; the evils consequent upon it in nineteenth-century Austria he either failed to see, or considered as an entirely secular matter. He must be unique among nineteenth-century artists in being completely without self-consciousness: anecdotes about his *naïveté* are innumerable. A penchant for counting stars is a fixation that has a touching, cosmically medieval flavour; and his grave acceptance of the waggish intelligence that he was to be elected Emperor of Austria is more beautiful than ludicrous. He knew—maybe at a pre-conscious level of understanding—that he had the heart of the matter within him. He was kingly and saintly by nature: which was more than could be said of those officially in power.

Born in 1824, the son of a schoolmaster, Bruckner spent his boyhood remotely in the country, where village life had not substantially changed for hundreds of years. When Anton was thirteen, his father died, and the family moved to Ebelsberg, near Linz. Anton became a pupil and chorister at the neighbouring monastery of St. Florian, thereby acquiring his first taste of the musical riches of Europe and his first experience of Catholic domination, both of which he accepted with enthusiasm. Grown to manhood, he became, as professional musician, a servant of his Church, working at St. Florian and later at Linz for more than twenty years. When eventually he settled in Vienna he was a mature composer of forty-two, with several large-scale works behind him. He had to wait another twenty years for recognition; for the cultural backwater of Vienna had no more use for him than it had had, thirty years earlier, for Schubert. He felt no bitterness at this lack of recognition; it did not occur to him that he might be getting less than his due. Provincially self-taught, he knew that his technique was defective. All his life he was learning to compose better: for he wrote music to praise his God, and for God nothing less than his best could suffice. Believing in musical, as in religious, dogma, he had no ambition but to follow his revered masters. If he was not aware of the revolutionary elements in most of his predecessors, still less was he aware of the originality within himself.

Yet in matters that deeply concerned him Bruckner was hardly naïve; he had an intuitive insight that amounted to clairvoyance. At St. Florian he had acquired a firm basis in traditional harmony and counterpoint; but his acquaintance with the European classics was certainly not wide and probably not deep. When he first visited Vienna to acquire a more adequate technique he found in Simon Sechter a truly great teacher. Now, Sechter was the man from whom Schubert, in his last years, had hoped to take counterpoint lessons. From the strangely sensuous Bachian texture of the C sharp minor *Moment Musical* we can but vaguely hazard what profound technical and spiritual changes might have developed in Schubert's music, had he lived to put this scheme into effect. In Bruckner's case, the meeting with Sechter in 1855 was the first decisive event in his career. What he gained from Sechter was knowledge and love of the music of Bach, and of the late works of Beethoven. Whether Bruckner divined that Sechter would give him what he wanted, or Sechter had the insight to see what Bruckner needed, is immaterial. Bach was a religious composer who employed techniques based on contrapuntal unity. Beethoven was a *modern* religious composer who in his last works fused the dualism of sonata with the monism of fugue. Bruckner was a man of faith, like Bach; yet he lived in a world which, since Beethoven had recreated it, would never be the same. To find them, and to reconcile elements in them that seemed discordant, was to find himself. They were perhaps the only two composers from whom he could have learned.

We think of Bruckner as primarily a symphonist. Yet the symphony depends on conflict; and to Bruckner's quasi-medieval mind conflict might seem to be extraneous. We shall see later that there was a real and deep reason why Bruckner wished to write symphonies as well as liturgical music. It is none the less true that Bruckner is a symphonist of unusual character; and that some of the apparent weaknesses in his symphonic method seem more convincing when we consider them in relation to his own church music, rather than in relation to the nineteenth-century sonata. With Haydn, Mozart, Beethoven, and Schubert, church music is an appendix to their instrumental work; they recreate traditional liturgical techniques in the light of their experience in sonata and symphony. For Bruckner the opposite is true. He starts from the liturgy of the

Church; and transforms the symphony into a confession of faith.

As a natural conservative, Bruckner, beginning his career at St. Florian, accepted the liturgical styles that were handed down to him by his predecessors. His models were Haydn, of whose 'Nelson' Mass he possessed a score, and from whom he learned to conceive the liturgy symphonically: and Schubert, from whom he derived the roots of his lyricism and his harmonic sensuousness. It never occurred to him, any more than it had occurred to his masters, to wonder if his style were too theatrical. Yet the spirit of his church music is not Haydnesque, and is remote from Schubert. We saw that Schubert began in his church music by being prettily frivolous, and ended by expressing that search for a lost innocence which is the impulse behind his instrumental work. Bruckner had never lost his innocence; so he can turn rococo theatricality into a paean of praise. He achieves this not by throwing over the rococo, but by absorbing it once more into the baroque. The tarnished splendour of the monumental baroque lives again in Bruckner's church music, for he was born, as most of his contemporaries were not, with an instinctive sense of glory. Baroque grandeur involves baroque counterpoint—of the type that was handed down from the seventeenth century to Fux, and from Fux to Sechter: so that in a sense Bruckner had rediscovered Bach before Sechter revealed to him the depths of Bach's art.

The mature E minor Mass returns, beyond Bach, to the vocal principles of Palestrinian counterpoint, and even revives the traditional baroque scoring for double chorus, brass, and woodwind. The melodic lines, despite the Schubertian sensuousness of the harmony, are frequently tinged with Gregorian modality, with which Bruckner became familiar during his association with the Cecilian movement. Yet despite this archaism, there are other features in this resplendently noble music which are neither baroque nor rococo. We may associate them with the obsessive influence exerted on Bruckner by Beethoven's Ninth Symphony and by the mature music of Wagner—especially *Tristan*, the production of which at Munich in 1865 marked the second spiritual crisis of Bruckner's life.

The tremendous impact made by the Ninth Symphony on Bruckner is significant. It is an evolutionary piece, dealing with the experience of Becoming. Yet it is a monumental work, and in that sense related to the baroque; and the slow movement attains the serenity of a reborn belief typical of Beethoven's last years. The obsession with *Tristan* is superfically more difficult to understand, though not quite so difficult if one sees *Tristan* as complementary to the sensuous abnegation of *Parsifal.* For Bruckner, Wagnerian harmony, on the Wagnerian orchestra, was simply the most beautiful sound he had ever heard. To refuse to use this sound to praise God with would have been blasphemous. It is interesting that Bruckner used to sit through Wagner's operas with his eyes shut. To the end of his days he had not the faintest idea what it was all about; had he known, he would have been revolted. Almost the most remarkable evidence of the original force of Bruckner's genius is the fact that he transforms Wagnerian harmony and orchestration into radiant spirituality—into the liturgical and baroque.

Yet these subterranean hints of the Ninth Symphony's cosmic strife and of *Tristan's* heroic egomania must surely imply some oddity in Bruckner's religious experience. Do they suggest, perhaps, a pre-conscious uncertainty—some intuitive awareness that after all the world was no longer medieval? His 'innocent' fixations were at times not far removed from pathological neurosis. His faith saved him from the dementia that destroyed Wolf's spirit; but faith had to win its victory over the obscure terrors of the subconscious mind, and victory is not won without a fight. In Schubert's mature work the Beethovenian features and the anticipations of Wagner testify to a split in sensibility of which he was certainly aware emotionally, and possibly intellectually. Bruckner, Schubert's successor, was not so aware. He achieved sublimity; but he moves us so much because we know, as he knew in the depths of his heart, that his sublimity soared over an abyss.

It is interesting that Bruckner unconsciously carries Schubert's modulatory experiments to still more extravagant lengths. With a Schubertian fondness for Neapolitan relationships, Bruckner will write not single chords, or even progressions, but extended sections in the flat supertonic. The E flat trio to the D minor scherzo of the String Quintet, the G flat slow movement to the F minor finale, extend this Neapolitan complex to the relationship between two movements. Bruckner's fondness for mediant relationships derives partly from Schubert, partly perhaps from his knowledge of sixteenth-century polyphony, with its 'melodically' related triads. It is worth noting that Bruckner had an especial fondness for the work of Jacopus Gallus [1550–1591] among early seventeenth-century polyphonists; for Gallus's work is often enigmatic, chromatically unstable, and even, perhaps, secretly revolutionary.

The essential Brucknerian experience is contained in the symphonies, which were naturally more personal than his liturgical music. But it is impossible sharply to differentiate the religious and the symphonic elements in Bruckner's work. Both masses and symphonies are constructed on broadly the same principles, except that the former involve voices and a literary text, and so can afford to be relatively episodic. Now, we have seen that all the Viennese symphonists before Bruckner dealt in varying degrees with the experience known to philosophers as Becoming. It is therefore understandable that Haydn, Mozart, Schubert, and above all Beethoven should manifest a prodigious spiritual and technical development during the course of their lives: that the first and last quartets of Haydn or Beethoven should seem to belong to distinct imaginative worlds. Bruckner significantly differs from his predecessors in this respect. His last three symphonies reveal his genius more richly than his previous symphonies; but they add little new to his experience. Nor did he intend them to. There was for Bruckner only one experience worth writing about; and though one's comprehension of God's love and glory may deepen, love and glory are themselves unchanging and unchangeable.

So the pattern of all Bruckner's symphonies is basically the same. The first movement never opens directly with a theme, but with an ostinato bass or tremolando that serves as a neutral background. Here Bruckner's model was the opening of the Ninth Symphony, and possibly the tremolando which Wagner used to arouse expectation. Yet the effect, in Bruckner's music, is quite different. In both Beethoven and Wagner expectation leads to drama; whereas from the neutrality of Bruckner's openings emerges the creative life of melody. The enormous asymmetrical melody that swells from the void at the beginning of Bruckner's Seventh Symphony has a kind of divine inevitability: and nothing in common with the assertiveness of Beethoven's middle years. Even when Bruckner's first themes have a heroic quality (expressed in a prevalence of trumpet-like fifths) or a dynamic quality (expressed in gigantic Beethovenian upward leaps in dotted rhythm, like a vastly expanded Mannheim skyrocket), they temper their energy with a Schubertian lyricism and with a prose rhythm resembling the 'endless melody' of late Wagner. The first theme of the Ninth Symphony embraces all these elements in its soaring splendour (Ex. 49):

Ex. 49 Bruckner: Symphony No. 9 (first movement)

Bruckner's second-group themes are very lyrical and Schubertian. He usually introduces two, sometimes three, such themes, treating them in double counterpoint. They thus acquire a winging ecstasy which counteracts the nostalgia inherent in their chromatic harmony (Ex. 50). We have seen

Ex. 50 Bruckner: Symphony No. 6 (first movement)

that Schubert is often seduced from dramatic argument by the lyricism of his second subjects. All Bruckner's secondary themes are in the classical sense unsymphonic. Though they are usually built on four-bar phrases sequentially repeated, they are characterized by their enormous span and by a sense of flow reinforced by Bruckner's partiality for quintuplet rhythms (a bar of four crochets divided into two crochets plus a triplet).

The themes do not need development except in so far as they are, as melody, growing all the time.

Now Bruckner's first-subject group tends to be firmly diatonic, while the second group is usually chromatic in harmonization and sometimes in linear contour. The codetta themes of his exposition usually re-establish diatonicism, and a more clearly defined metre. His two main groups of themes thus bear some relation to the classical notion of dualistic contrast; but with themes of such vast scope it is no use expecting from his development sections anything approaching the operatic cohesion of Mozart, let alone the rhetorical argument of middle-period Beethoven. Bruckner allows his themes to expand of their own volition, and builds up his climaxes over relatively static ostinatos and pedal points. Then the music breaks off and starts again, with another theme. These recurrent climaxes, being spaced over a considerable period of time, do not attempt to build up a progressive drama. None the less, the sequence of keys in which they appear gradually changes the tonal perspective, so that the succession of climaxes becomes cumulative. By the time we reach the ultimate climax we have usually arrived at the most remote tonality. Though his modulatory effects are never Beethovenian, Bruckner's command of tonality was masterly. If we listen to his symphonies without preconceived notions as to what a symphony ought to be like, we shall sense how inevitably the climax of the subsidiary climaxes becomes the goal of the movement. It is interesting to note how often Bruckner's ultimate climaxes resemble his vivid, almost visual treatment of the Et Resurrexit in his masses, especially the symphonic F minor. In these passages harmonic oppositions disappear and the music blazes for several pages on a single major triad. Climax becomes not conflict, but the glory that renders conflict superfluous.

The constructive principles of Bruckner's slow movements are not radically different from those of his opening allegros. The adagio to the Seventh, for instance, opens in C sharp minor, has important structural modulations to F sharp and A flat (the major of the sub-dominant and dominant), attains its final climax on the remote triad of C major, and ends in the major of the tonic. But whereas the first movements are in essence preludial, the adagios are self-contained song. If they are in sonata form, they recall the slow movement of the

'Hammerklavier' in that they purge sonata of interior conflict. More commonly they are modelled on the adagio of Beethoven's Ninth or the 'Song of Thanksgiving' from the A minor Quartet in being in a compromise between sonata and rondo: a solemn, hymn-like first theme alternates with a celestially floating melody, often treated in double counterpoint. The harmony is richly chromatic and the modulations often enharmonic, emulating *Parsifal*; the orchestration too appears to follow Wagner, even to the point of introducing Wagner tubas. Yet out of this humility towards his masters grows one of the most original manners in musical history. Even the Brucknerian orchestra, influenced by his experience as an organist, sounds more baroque than Wagnerian in its use of distinct groups of strings, woodwind, and brass. The incandescent blaze of brass in the adagio of the Ninth, followed abruptly by pianissimo woodwind, produces an effect of almost Byzantine splendour, instinct with the awe of God as well as with His peace. Again we may observe that Bruckner's symphonic adagios are similar in treatment to the Benedictus and Sanctus in his mature masses, for which his prototype was the comparable movements in Beethoven's *Missa Solemnis*. Bruckner was an 'orthodox' Catholic, unlike Beethoven; but both of them, having profoundly religious minds, were aware of the terror within God's majesty—as most artists of the nineteenth century were not.

Bruckner's scherzos are usually in Ländler style, following the Schubertian type. Their trios might even be said to intensify Schubert's nostalgia in their chromatic part-writing and modulations. The scherzo of the Seventh, however, employs one of Bruckner's metrical trumpet themes, perhaps to compensate for the lack of such a theme in the first movement; while the scherzo of the Ninth is a weird movement in which the abyss beneath Bruckner's sublimity gapes wide open. Its chromaticism becomes spectral, its tonality being always slightly out of perspective (Ex. 51). Intermittently, the sensuous dream is battered by the stark metrical assertion of percussion and

Ex. 51 Bruckner: Symphony No. 9 (Scherzo)

brass, hammering out a peasant dance rhythm with Beethovenian ferocity.

In his finales Bruckner attempts to synthesize the previous movements, in the manner of the finale to Beethoven's Ninth. He does not, like Beethoven, re-create his themes; but their interrelation leads to an epilogic statement of a kind of Catholic 'chorale' on the brass—the Hymn which has been implicit in the whole symphony finally takes explicit form. The most impressive of Bruckner's finales is probably that to the Fifth, which has an introduction recalling the themes of the previous movements, on the analogy of Beethoven's Ninth; and then coalesces the material into a double fugue which also embraces elements of sonata style, rounded off with a chorale. The contradictory elements of fugue and sonata remain much more loosely co-ordinated than they are in Beethoven's ultimate synthesis of opposites. None the less, this is one of the very few movements by later composers which can strictly be compared with Beethoven; and again there is a parallel in Bruckner's church music—the Agnus Dei that concludes the F minor Mass.

In later symphonies Bruckner discarded the retrospective introduction to the finale, feeling perhaps that it was justified only by Beethoven's thematically 'generative' technique. His instinct, as usual, was right. Yet noble and satisfying though his chorale epilogues may be, one cannot altogether regret that he left his last symphony unfinished. What could possibly succeed the meditation of this adagio? And in this case we cannot regard such a confession of faith as divinely anachronistic: for this symphony is at once profoundly religious and profoundly modern. It is revealing to compare it, from this point of view, with the Seventh. The rhythmic energy of the Seventh's scherzo is, on the whole, rural and positive, the seductiveness of its trio is a visionary Golden Age. In the sublime song melodies of the adagio the slowly rising sextuplets of the accompanying figure can surge inevitably upwards into resurrection. But the scherzo of the Ninth, with its neutral tritonal chords and melodic figurations, its fiercely destructive rhythm, its harsh scoring, is a vision of Hell. In the following adagio there is thus a sense of strain in the vast leaps of the melodies: while the panting, broken demisemiquavers of the figuration *strive towards* resurrection. Both the enormous leaps of the themes, and the sharp, acid edge which Bruckner gives to his rich scoring, reappear in Mahler's bitter-sweet anguish; and Schoenberg [b.1874] inherited them from Mahler [1860-1911], so that they have become part of our own tormented century. In no later composer, however, does one find anything approaching the bliss of the final pages of Bruckner's adagio, when his yearning achieves resurrection in the serenity of the major triad. (The key—E major—is the same as that of Schubert's heaven.)

Many of the apparent weaknesses in Bruckner's music—his long-windedness, his inconsequentiality, his naïve literalism—prove to be motes in our eye rather than in his ear. We listen with irrelevant preconceptions; and this is not entirely our fault because it is not easy to hear Bruckner's scores as he wrote them. So great was his humility that he allowed well-meaning friends to rewrite and rescore his works in order to make them more acceptable to conventional notions of symphonic style. His themes—except perhaps in the scherzos—are spacious and not time-obsessed; and although the first movement of his Fifth is undeniably shorter without its recapitulation, it does not make better sense. Even if one never comes to recognize the logic in Bruckner's vast structures, there are still moments when one wonders, listening to these last three adagios, whether since the last works of Beethoven music has reached this point again. The climax of the adagio to the Seventh—and therefore of the whole work—is a conflictless paean of bells on a C major triad, which grows out of softly upsurging scales on the violins. It is naïve, if you like. Yet it is also an incarnation of Glory, and only a man who had seen this vision could have written the elegy with which the movement then concludes: funereal music, inspired by the death of Wagner, in which there is regret, but no shadow of fear. In his very innocence, Bruckner seems in such moments to belong to a nobler race than our own. It is no more than a sober statement of fact to say that we shall not look upon his like again.

In their lifetime, Bruckner and Brahms [1833–1897] were the unwilling leaders of rival factions: the acrimony among their disciples at times amounted to hysteria. Nowadays, we find this difficult to understand, for both composers seem to us late romantics who worked within the same tradition. Yet there is a sense in which the disputants were right. They argued about the wrong things, or at least about differences that now seem superficial; yet they must have felt, if they did not know, that beneath these superfices Bruckner and Brahms represented opposite poles of the human spirit. In Bruckner's personality such contradictions as there may be are buried as deep underground as they are in his music. Brahms's personality is in essence a contradiction; his is as much a dualistic temperament as Bruckner's was single-minded and simple-hearted.

Bruckner's early background was that of a Catholic Austrian peasant; he preserved a peasant-like innocence throughout his life. Brahms's family came from the north, of bourgeois Protestant stock; he had both the stolidity and the tenacity of his kind. When, having settled in Vienna, he came to move in exalted circles he was as arrogant and offensive as Beethoven, but for the opposite reason. Beethoven exulted in the pride of his spirit; Brahms was afraid of the passion that burned within him. The stolidity, the caution, the gruff exterior hid another Brahms whose soul was all that the northern bourgeois and Protestant was not. We can see this in his approach to his art. Like Bruckner, he reverenced the Masters. But Bruckner reverenced them in humility: feeling himself 'a pygmy' beside Beethoven, he could not think of himself as a rival. Brahms was not conspicuous for humility. He paid homage to the past because this was one means of controlling the turbulence of his spirit. His use of the past—and to some extent his interest in folk-song—was a conscious intellectual activity, rather than an instinctive gesture.

From this point of view Brahms's opus 1, the C major Piano Sonata, is a fascinating document. It begins with an act of homage to his master, Beethoven—an almost literal quotation from the heroic opening of the 'Hammerklavier' Sonata; and then builds a fierce conflict on the same tonal opposition that Beethoven exploits in the first movement of the 'Waldstein' Sonata. This is both a tribute to the past and an assertion of the combativeness of his own temperament. The effect is quite different from the opening of the 'Hammerklavier'. Beethoven's opening bars are an epic challenge: Brahms's suggest a vigorous bourgeois stolidity, partly because the pace of his harmonic movement confines him to the earth (he has at least two, sometimes four chords a bar to Beethoven's one). Similarly, Brahms's modulations suggest physical energy, whereas Beethoven's hint at mystery—at the new tonal perspectives which are to be explored in the later movements. Brahms's second movement is folk-like in spirit: Schubertian in its lyricism, Schumann-like in its poetic treatment of the piano. The scherzo also has a Schubertian, nostalgic trio; but is in the main aggressive and exuberant, with a typical use of thick thirds and sixths. This technique Brahms probably picked up from the 'Hammerklavier', though he creates from it a quite different effect—sturdier, earthier, if not less fierce. The final rondo again has a lyrical, rather folk-song-like theme: which is developed in Beethovenian sonata style.

Though aggression and nostalgia—the two contrasting elements of Schubert's temperament—are already present in the work of the young Brahms, their relationship is different. Instead of being in conflict, they become allies: the conflict in his music is between lyricism and drama as symbols of romantic individuality, on the one hand; and, on the other hand, his innate caution and Teutonic stolidity. In order to become allies, the two elements have to change their natures. One can see this if one compares Brahms's lyricism with that of Bruckner or Schubert. The cantabile symphonic melodies of Bruckner, and to a lesser degree Schubert, tend to be long and supple; direct references to a folk-like style are usually restricted to the scherzo. Though Brahms's lyrical melodies are frequently asymmetrical, their component phrases tend to be relatively brief; he has nothing comparable with the enormous winding melodies at the beginning of Bruckner's last three symphonies. Moreover, his lyrical themes frequently introduce arpeggio formations. In Bruckner's long themes arpeggio figures tend to be absorbed into step-wise progressions planned on a vast scale: consider the opening theme of the Seventh Symphony, in which the arpeggio 'opens up' the slow growth of the melody, sending it winging to the heavens. Brahms's arpeggio formations divide the melody into harmonic segments, and so tend to root it to the earth. This we can see most immediately in his songs.

Schubert, in his mature songs, is always at once musical and psychological; his variety of song forms is apparently inexhaustible. Brahms is much less interested in the poems he sets; he regards them not as psychological experience, but as the impulse to a tune. These melodies are often of extraordinary beauty and richness; yet in their clearly defined and subtly balanced phrases

—as well as in the firm harmonic basis to even the folk-like tunes—they are often melodies that would be amenable to development in sonata. Indeed, some of the greatest songs, such as the *Sapphische Ode*, seem to demand symphonic scope for their adequate realization; certainly the grand arpeggiated contours of the phrases call for instrumental powers of sostenuto from the singer. Brahms actually used two of his loveliest songs as basic material for sonata movements in his G major and A major violin sonatas. When Schubert uses themes from his songs in instrumental works, it is almost always in movements in the more static technique of variation or rondo.

So it is that Brahms's lyricism and his dynamism temper one another. In Schubert's bitter-sweet idiom there is a tug-of-war between the two impulses: but Brahms's lyricism, with its relatively harmonic bias, curbs his exuberance, while his ferocity protects his lyricism from too painful a nostalgia. This is why the works that sum up the achievement of his youth are the piano quartets, especially the F minor. Strings are cantabile instruments; the piano, for Brahms as for middle-period Beethoven, is a percussive instrument. When Brahms brings them together he expresses all the dynamic power and lyrical passion of his romantic youth and of his love for Clara Schumann. Already, however, their interrelation creates a controlled sobriety in the realization of passion which became his ideal. We can see this again in his first large-scale work, the D minor Piano Concerto. This began life as a symphony closely modelled on Beethoven's Ninth; it turned into an extremely difficult virtuoso concerto in which there is the minimum of ostentation. The piano writing has Brahms's singular massiveness and richness, the orchestration is darkly sensuous; yet the heroic proportions of the work are never endangered by the incidental seductions of chromatic figuration or scoring.

The D minor Concerto is the climax of the romanticism of Brahms's youth. A new phase begins as his instinct towards self-discipline prompts him to renewed contrapuntal studies. Unlike most sonata composers, Brahms had always been contrapuntally minded; his opus 1 is full of polyphonic ingenuities which help to give coherence to its figuration. This was partly due to his Protestant and northern background: for even Schumann, the most romantic of his masters, was trained in the Bachian tradition. Some of the works Brahms composed at this time hardly claimed to be more than exercises in outmoded techniques; others, like the choral motets, revived archaic styles while achieving through their harmony a personal flavour. This series of works culminates in a number of piano compositions built on the static principle of variation.

The biggest and finest of these variation-sets is the 'Handel Variations' of 1861. These conclude with a fugue which, like that of Beethoven's 'Hammerklavier' Sonata, is an assertion of power. It is, however, in every sense an easier and earthier work. The fugue subject itself is harmonically conceived; except perhaps in the magnificent A flat minor Organ Fugue and a few of the late chorale preludes, Brahms's counterpoint—despite his veneration for Bach—is less Bachian, more Handelian, than that of late Beethoven. He has little of Bach's tension between line and harmony, and none of Beethoven's recalcitrance between a stable diatonicism and the direction in which the counterpoints want to move. So although in this assertion of fugal unity Brahms, like Beethoven, wins a victory over himself, he has less to conquer; the struggle has been less wild because the opposing forces have always been ready for compromise. Beethoven's triumph over the self is a prelude to a vision of Paradise. Brahms cannot take this further step. When he achieves his own resolution, it takes the form of a stoic resignation, rather than a winged joy. This we can see in the course of his development as a symphonist.

The first of the symphonies, the C minor, was conceived about the same time as the D minor Piano Concerto, though Brahms did not complete it until he was over forty. In it, his Beethovenian ambitions are so obvious that it was known, either waggishly or reverentially, as 'the Tenth'. It is a dynamic work which begins in conflict and ends in triumph with a tune comparable with the Joy theme in Beethoven's Ninth. Brahms himself deprecated any attempt to relate this tune to the Ninth Symphony: not merely because 'any jackass' could see that the tunes were similar, but because he knew, as many of his disciples did not, that in spiritual essence the tunes were not related at all. Beethoven's theme has not the Paradisal joy which flowers in his last slow movements in variation style; but it is a gateway to Paradise. Brahms's theme may be hymn-like; but it is a hymn to earthy contentment, stocky, burgomaster-like, a bourgeois modification of the folk spirit. It resolves the turbulence of Brahms's youth, as expressed in the first movement of the symphony, into sanity and power. It neither achieves nor attempts Beethoven's apochryphal resolution.

Though it seems slighter, the Second Symphony, in D, is more subtly Beethovenian. It is the most lyrical, and therefore Schubertian, of all Brahms's large-scale works; yet it also employs a technique of thematic transformation as complex as Beethoven's. The singing opening theme characteristically weaves arpeggio figures into its contour, so that it is easily susceptible of both harmonic and contrapuntal treatment. A second, transitional theme is a more fluid expansion of the first theme: and the second subject group derives from this transitional melody. Brahms's contrapuntal skill becomes the means whereby the disintegrating and reintegrating themes preserve continuity during the modulations of the development. The complex organisms that are his themes can be split into their components, without resorting to mechanical sequences to keep the music moving.

As in Beethoven's mature works, all the transformations of Brahms's symphonic themes tend towards the last movement, which is their resolution. We have seen that the last movement of the First Symphony emulates the superfices of the finale of Beethoven's Ninth without touching its essence. The last movement of the Second, however, attempts and achieves something different. Here the metamorphosis of the themes leads to a march-tune that one might possibly call jubilant. But if it is jubilant, it is also strenuous: certainly more so than the spring-like melodies of the first movement. Whereas Beethoven—even in his First Symphony, and still more from the 'Eroica' onwards—tends to free his themes of harmonic tension in the last movement, here Brahms increases their tension. Not only in the modulatory passages of the development, but even in the exuberant coda there is an undercurrent of unease; so that the exuberance becomes fierce. This fundamental change is much more obvious in the Third Symphony, in which the first movement is built on a Beethovenian arpeggio of challenge (in the major), while the last movement transforms the themes into minor conflict and turmoil. The work ends with a quiet coda in the major, wherein the arpeggio motive becomes not Beethovenian triumph, but Brahmsian resignation.

This prepares us for the elegiac power of the Fourth—and last—Symphony. The initial theme leaps aspiringly up a sixth, but then falls in descending thirds, broken by rests. The Beethovenian arpeggio of challenge now droops in fragmentary valediction; and its harmonic components lend themselves as readily to contrapuntal ingenuities as to dramatic opposition. The slow movement's phrygian opening—E minor with flat second—hints at a distant, modal world of religious consolation; but the implacable rhythm makes it seem very remote. The scherzo returns to bourgeois earthiness: which for all its ebullience cannot answer the melancholy of the first two movements. The resolution which Brahms finally achieves is monistic, but it is neither song melody nor fugue. Beethoven attains unity in song variation and in polyphony. Brahms establishes unity by the rigid repetition of a rhythmic ground and a harmonic pattern which remorselessly controls the tempests of tonal drama. Passion and suffering are subjected to the archaic formality of a passacaglia; and the contrapuntal extensions of the passacaglia theme reveal that its stern monumentality was incipient even in the sighful theme of the first allegro (Ex. 52):

Ex. 52 Brahms: Symphony No. 4 (first movement theme)

This movement is truly noble because Brahms accepts suffering without rhetoric or emotional excess. But it is not joyful. It ends unflinchingly in the tonic minor; its spirit is stoical, not religious.

The harmonic and metrical unity of the passacaglia is perhaps the supreme expression of Brahms's abnegation and agnosticism. He had earlier given us a more explicit though less intense statement of it in the *German Requiem*: which he deliberately set not in hieratic Latin, but in the German language, and from which he excluded all metaphysical elements. There is no emphasis here on Christ the redeemer; since the dead are beyond hope or help, our care must be for those left living. And so the music of Brahms's last years becomes at once elegiac and consolatory. He writes a few works like the magnificent C minor Trio, opus 101, which revive his urgently Protestant and protesting fire. But in general his music is quieter, gentler, more mellow: and at the same time more melancholy. The fiery scherzos of his youth give way to the retrospective allegretto; the words *non troppo* appear with ever greater frequency in his tempo directions.

The series of small piano pieces, many of them under the unassuming title of 'Intermezzo', are an old man's distillation of the romantic Schumanesque piano writing of his youth. They are almost all in lyrical ABA song forms, rather than in sonata style; and though the texture is lucid compared with the massiveness of his early days, the sensuousness of the sound—in pieces such as the autumnally rich A major Intermezzo—is enhanced rather than diminished. Brahms's preoccupation with the tone-colour of the clarinet is also revealing. The Clarinet Quintet is perhaps his most beautiful chamber work. Although it preserves the externalities of sonata conflict, it has many features in common with baroque variation technique.* One elegiac theme dominates all the movements—even the rhapsodic coloratura of the slow movement, which is a twilit reminiscence of the gipsy ardours of his youth. The work reveals but does not transform this theme in the course of a key-scheme of classical sobriety: so that formally the quintet is much more retrospective than, say, Brahms's Second or Third Symphony. The final sighing of the theme by the clarinet, followed by the strings' repeated minor triads, are both a farewell to earthly beauty and a recognition that there is nothing else. Yet the lucidity of texture and structure safeguards the music from self-pity.

Several of the piano pieces of Brahms's last years invert classical precedent by beginning in the major and ending in the minor. Yet although their temper is so consistently elegiac, one finds nowhere else in Brahms's music so many features anticipatory of the future. The irregularity of the phrases, the cross rhythms, the counterpoints within the figuration have never been more supple; they frequently combine to create a harmonic texture which, in its linear and tonal relationships,

* For Bach and Handel variation was not so much permutations of a 'tune' as lyrical evolution over a constant harmonic basis, i.e. a free version of the chaconne principle.

is as audacious as the mature music of Wagner. (The extraordinary, indrawn E flat minor Intermezzo is especially interesting from this point of view.) It is not altogether surprising that Brahms's pessimism should have been paradoxically fertile; for artists of the twentieth century were nurtured in a climate of disillusion comparable with that of Brahms; and his search for salvation in discipline anticipates the twentieth century's turning from sonata to a somewhat negative use of baroque forms. Certainly Brahms's last considerable work speaks to us, as it spoke to him, with peculiar poignancy.

In the *Four Serious Songs* of 1896, Brahms choses texts from Ecclesiastes which reflect his own death-consciousness; and effects a compromise between the style of the Lied and that of the baroque cantata. The third song is a miraculously wrought structure based on the same descending third motive that appears in the Passacaglia of the E minor Symphony (Ex. 53):

Ex. 53 Brahms: O Tod, O Tod, wie bitter

Brahms's obsession with falling thirds would seem to be unmistakably associated with his obsession with death: and from this point of view we may contrast him with Bruckner. For Bruckner, death is a liberating force; the contemplation of death promotes long, soaring melodies that float in stepwise movement, with intermittent, ecstatic leaps. For Brahms, death suggests the sequence of falling thirds which roots the music harmonically, in the earth: dust returns to dust. This idea recurs throughout Brahms's music whenever he is most deeply moved. In the little B minor Intermezzo the falling thirds form suspended triads which create an effect of polytonality (Ex. 54):

Ex. 54 Brahms: Intermezzo in B minor

If in the E minor Symphony and the third of the *Four Serious Songs* the body returns to the earth, in the B minor Intermezzo it is as though the human dust were dissolving away into air and rain.

The contrast between Brahms and Bruckner suggests a similar comparison between Brahms and Bach. The vocal line and piano texture of the third of the *Serious Songs* are so permeated with progressions of thirds and their inversion into sixths that the music is almost as completely thematic as the Chorale Prelude of Bach, from an examination of which this book began. The complex lucidity of Bach's counterpoint seems, however, as inevitable as the softly breathing pulse which, in the protracted plagal cadence, stills itself to silence. Life flows into death, almost without Bach's conscious volition. The lucid complexity of Brahms's more harmonic texture has not this inevitability; it is the ultimate act of self-discipline whereby he subdues death's terrors.

We may also compare this 'cantata' of Brahms's old age with a cantata of Bach's youth, the *Actus Tragicus*, no. 106. There is plenty of evidence—in the tenor aria '*Ach Herr, lehre uns bedenken*' and still more in the strained fugato on '*Es ist der alte Bund*'—that the terrors of death were vivid to Bach. Yet for him, in youth as on his death-bed, the grave could become, through Christ the Redeemer, the promise of bliss, as the music unfolds to the seraphic obbligato of flutes and gambas. In Brahms's songs there is no attempt to justify death; there is only a reminder, in the last song, that human love justifies life, if it cannot redeem it. When the text refers to 'faith, hope and love', which are what remains when Death has done his worst, Brahms's vocal line swells and soars in this stupendous phrase (Ex. 55):

Ex. 55 Brahms: Wenn ich mit Menschen
Nun - aber blei - bet Glau-be, Hoff-nung, Lie - be, die-se drei.

It is almost as though human love had itself become winged and angelic. And so although Brahms never learned to transcend death, as did Beethoven, or to accept it, as did Schubert and Mozart, or not to care about it, as did Haydn, one can say that at the end he arrived at a point not so far distant from Haydn.

Both found that human love was the ultimate reality, but with this difference: for Haydn, human love could regenerate a world; for Brahms, it was a dying man's solace for the ineradicable follies of the past.

Yet that is not quite all. If we look again at that 'winged and angelic' vocal phrase we shall see that its huge leaps suggest the more bitter ecstasy of Mahler and the early Schoenberg, as does the theme of the adagio to Bruckner's Ninth. So, after all, Brahms comes to terms with his polar opposite. Perhaps this reminds us that if love is the only seed of creation, in the long run it does not greatly matter whether we think of it as human or divine.

We have said that when Brahms and Bruckner finally meet, both suggest Mahler [1860–1911]: whose work is an epilogue to the Viennese symphonic tradition. Like Beethoven, Mahler is a composer of strife; like Bruckner, he is a composer of exaltation; like Brahms, he is a composer of elegiac disillusion; like Schubert, he equivocates between reality and dream. But he was born later than Schubert, later even than Bruckner or Brahms; for him the dream is more elusive, his nostalgia the more deep.

The sense of separation which we have commented on in Beethoven, Schubert, and Brahms becomes, in Mahler, racial as well as spiritual. Though he worked in a rich musical tradition, he had himself no spiritual home; and his isolation was reinforced by his family's poverty. For he was not only a Jew; he was also a poor boy who made good. His life was a battle—not only, or indeed mainly, for his own music, but for other people's. His fearsome autocracy, his tyranny as opera conductor and as a director of Vienna's musical life, were entirely disinterested; he worked himself to death through a selfless devotion to his art. The ferocious hostility he aroused only exacerbated the anguish in his spirit. Beethoven could devote all his energies to his own salvation; even Schubert could spend all his time writing music, though not always the kind of music in which he was most interested. But for Mahler composition had to be a spare-time activity: though this activity was in the deepest sense the meaning of his life.

Apart from his songs and an early cantata, all Mahler's music is symphonic; and he regarded his nine symphonies as experiments in spiritual autobiography. The technique of symphonic growth and metamorphosis which Beethoven had explored in the Fifth Symphony, and vastly expanded in the Ninth, is the basis of Mahler's approach to symphony. He said that a symphony should embrace all aspects of human experience—banal and trivial as well as tragic and profound—and that it should be a complete spiritual world, with its inherent laws of birth, growth, and decay. Beethoven, however, had the classical tradition in his blood and bones. The revolutionary elements in his music affect us so powerfully because we are clearly aware of what he is revolting against; his contradictions of tonality are not fully intelligible except in reference to a norm. In Mahler this is no longer so. His harmonic thought was far more diatonic than Wagner's; yet he treats the relationship between keys with more freedom. The early *Songs of a Wayfarer* begin innocently in D minor, modulate through F sharp minor, B major, and E minor, to end distantly in F minor. The climax of the third song, prompted by the words, is an abrupt modulation to the flat supertonic; instead of drooping back to the tonic, the music stays in the new key until the end. In such tonal vagueness it is not so much Mahler's personality as a world itself that seems to be in flux. He was aware of this, as Bruckner was not; and his awareness intensifies his music's poignancy.

A certain contradictoriness—an inextricable medley of positive and negative responses—is thus the essence of Mahler's musical temperament. Consider his relation to popular music. His genius—like that of Schubert and Bruckner, but unlike that of the symphonic Beethoven—was essentially lyrical and vocal. He did not 'belong' to an Austrian peasant community; he lived and worked in the country only during the summer months, when free of his duties as conductor and opera director. But the contours of his melodies are permeated with the inflexions of Austrian song; and the childlike simplicity of some of these melodies represented an ideal of innocence to which Mahler, like Schubert, repeatedly turned. With him, however, the sense of estrangement is stronger, as his personality was the more tormented. Schubert oscillates so sensitively between reality and dream that he is sometimes doubtful which is which. Mahler often wishes he were a child, free of adult perversities and perturbations; but his nostalgia expands the folk-like phrases into periods that become yearnfully emotive, while he subjects them to enharmonic treatment even more extreme than that favoured by Bruckner.

Urban popular music, as well as rural folk-song, is involved in this relationship to his environment. Sometimes café songs are presented nostalgically, as they are in Schubert; more often they are rhythmically distorted or tonally dislocated, as though Mahler were trying to express both his yearning for such simple-minded vulgarity and also an insidious corruption within popular music itself (Ex. 56). There is a similar ambiguity

in the military music which haunts his work as it haunted Schubert's. The fanfares and march rhythms convey a genuine delight in imperial splendour, coupled with a sinister atmosphere of nightmare (Ex. 57). The military rhythm is always

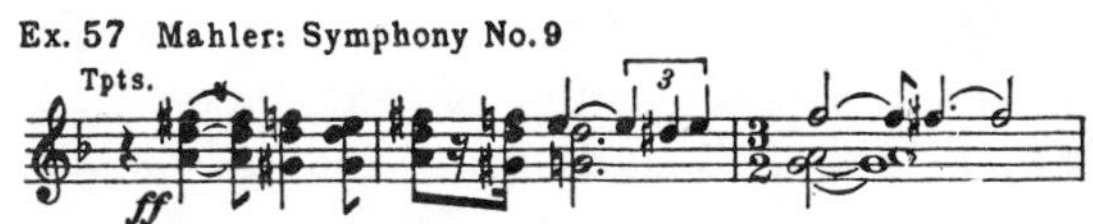

liable to be transformed into one of Mahler's phantasmagoric funeral marches, in which the trumpets' tattoo becomes a mortuary tolling of bells. Nostalgia for past splendour may at any moment become at once an elegy, and a dark prophecy of chaos. The dissolution of the Austrian Empire was indeed to release horrors dreamt of only in the imaginations of artists of Mahler's neurotic sensitivity. Even his horn-call themes—which derive from the heroic aspects of Beethoven, Brahms, Schubert, and Bruckner—become tonally precarious, fateful in their singularity.

Hardly less equivocal is the liturgical element in Mahler's music. Bruckner was a Catholic by birth and instinct. Mahler was a Jew who embraced Catholicism as a part of his lifelong struggle for peace. Only at moments did he achieve Bruckner's singlemindedness; never did he experience the serenity of revealed faith. But the faith implicit in Catholic dogma became a symbol of the Grail he was seeking: and led him consciously to relate his music to certain aspects of Catholic polyphony. As a Viennese, he would naturally turn to the monumental baroque which Bruckner had absorbed intuitively. How he related this to his Beethovenian conception of the symphony is revealed in his two choral symphonies, the Second and the Eighth.

The first movement of the Second Symphony is a conflict piece on a vast scale, with a first theme that surges up like a strifeful Mannheim skyrocket, straining to break the bands of the harmony's solemn processional rhythm. In the fourth movement a solo voice enters: lyrical song symbolizes a vision of innocence and light, as in Schubert and Bruckner; only such simplicity of being can lead into the resurrection of the last, choral movement. The death and resurrection of the work are subjective, as they are in Beethoven's 'Eroica'; yet they are also presented with all the naïve realism of Bruckner. Mahler did not, like Bruckner, believe in a literal resurrection; but in his search for a faith he relates his symphonic struggles to the techniques of baroque polyphony. This is still more obvious in the Eighth Symphony, the first part of which is a tremendous symphonic-choral setting of the Catholic hymn, *Veni Creator*; while the second part is a setting of the final scenes of Goethe's *Faust*. Catholic dogma is transformed into a Goethean spiritual quest; while a personal testament becomes dogmatic. Bruckner makes a Catholic hymn out of a symphony: Mahler makes a symphonic battle out of Catholic polyphony.

The polyphonic element in Mahler's music reminds us that he is after all a composer with a classical heritage, even though tradition disintegrates in his work. Vienna is not what it was and the Church cannot mean for him what it meant for Bruckner; but in the midst of decay and corruption an ideal 'essence' of the Church and of the Viennese tradition were absolutes to which Mahler yearned back, or towards which he aspired.

As a starting-point, let us look at the simplest and shortest of his symphonies, the Fourth, in G. In the first movement he begins with the classical, symmetrical phrase: at once Haydnesque and folk-like (Ex. 58). This is an evocation of a vanished world. Gradually he injects into the phrase something of his

Ex. 58 Mahler: Symphony No. 4

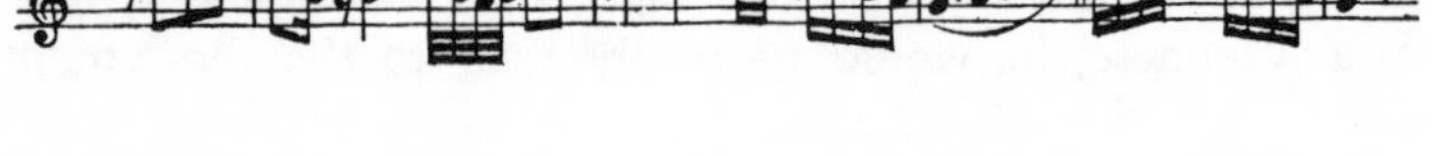

personal quality of rhapsodic exaltation, with wide leaps and drooping suspensions (Ex. 59). He does not exactly transform the theme into an entity of different emotional significance, as

Beethoven would; but he increasingly sees it from the standpoint of his own self-consciousness. As the intervals and rhythms are expanded the phrase loses its polished urbanity: becomes so free in tonality and rhythm that it implies a trend away from stable diatonicism. Mahler naturally thought polyphonically; his spare texture is habitually based on two-part writing, and frequently on fourths and fifths rather than on the triad. In that respect, as in many others, he anticipates some of the early music of Schoenberg.

With this polyphonic bias, Mahler orchestrates in a manner quite different from the classical composers. His scoring becomes almost a chamber music technique, delineating the orchestral voices with the maximum precision. The Italian element evident in Mahler—as in Mozart and Schubert and most Viennese art—is here explicit; and the wheel comes full circle. For Haydn's glowing periods had clipped the free vocal phrase of seventeenth-century Italian madrigal and opera into the symmetrical, diatonic, instrumental phrase. Starting from Haydn, Mahler stretches out the phrase, loosens it, until he arrives once more at principles analogous to the baroque rhetoric of early Italian opera, and to the supple line-drawing of the Italian polyphonists. This means that his conception of symphonic form must change even more radically than does Schubert's or Bruckner's in their attempt to create a symphony based on lyricism. The full implications of this are not apparent in the Fourth; for this is deliberately a revocation of the past which ends, with the appearance of the human voice, in the dream-world of a child's heaven. A traditional folk-poem inspires a folk-like directness of melodic speech; even the exquisite lucidity of Mahler's orchestration, though in fact sophisticated, produces an effect of naïve candour.

The implications of the Mahlerian symphony are most consummately realized in his last completed work, the Ninth. The immense first movement opens with a dreamfully singing melody in D major, in which each rising phrase nostalgically droops in an appoggiatura. (Against this theme Mahler wrote, in the original score, "O vanished days of youth, O scattered loves.") Opposed to it is a ferocious, upward-surging theme in the minor; a sinister rhythmic figure that had originally been the bass of the song melody: and one of Mahler's mysterious trumpet calls in march rhythm. The impact of these wild and striving elements on the nostalgic vision of 'Viennese' serenity changes its significance each time it reappears. Its component intervals and rhythms become increasingly attenuated; it splinters up into fragments divided between the first and second violins; it proliferates in acutely dissonant counterpoints. The 'conflict' themes themselves mate in wildly contrarious polyphony: until finally they carry the song melody far from the stable props of diatonic tonality into a spare, widely spaced, glassily scored linear counterpoint. Yet the whole of this vast movement is enclosed within a dominant-tonic progression. The symbol of the stability of the classical world is strained to breaking-point; it hangs on the single thread of the final high D on piccolo and 'cello harmonic.

The second movement is a gigantic Ländler which is now not merely nostalgic, but also spectral. It is a ghost of the past, frightening as well as endearing: which again disintegrates into linear fragments. The third movement, called 'Rondo Burleske', is a wild parody or inversion of both positives of Mahler's art—folk-song and monumental polyphony. The simplicity of folk-melody and the solemnity of monumental counterpoint become savagely grotesque; though just before the end there is a visionary, serio-comic anticipation of the final adagio. This seems to suggest that for Mahler neither folk-song nor dogmatic polyphony could offer salvation; such peace as he can find must be in the meditations of his own spirit. So the last movement is a passionately subjective adagio, carrying the vast leaps of Bruckner's exaltation and the fluidity of his (and *Parsifal's*) enharmonic transitions to so extreme a point that the music literally breaks with its world-weariness. First harmony disintegrates into linear counterpoint, in the chamber-music scoring which anticipates so many developments in twentieth-century music (Ex. 60, plate XXXIV). Then melody itself disintegrates in piteous chromatic fragmentariness; with the fading of the melodic strands there vanishes too a world and a mode of belief. Even the basic tonality has sunk from the first movement's D to D flat.

In the passages of linear polyphony in the Ninth Symphony, and still more in the last movement of his symphonic song-cycle, *Das Lied von der Erde*, Mahler attains a translucent texture that seems in some ways more Eastern than European. The cycle sets Chinese poems without superficial Orientalisms. But in the 'Farewell' appear strange linear arabesques—sometimes pentatonic, sometimes in chromatically inflected modes, sometimes almost as non-tonal and inhuman as bird-calls: while in the ineffably protracted suspensions on the word '*ewig*' music strains to release itself from harmony and metre. Beethoven, we saw, had to free himself from Time and the Will if he was to preserve his sanity. He found his salvation, if Europe did not. In the dying fall of Mahler's last music the madness of a world burns itself out. The obsession with Time, which has dominated Europe since the Renaissance, begins to dissolve into Asiatic immobility; and the process is a laceration of the spirit. Mahler lingers on those suspended dissonances, his last hold on the life he loved with all his richly attuned senses; while the hollow reverberations of percussion sound like falling masonry, thudding through an eternity of years. The chord on which the 'Farewell' finally fades to nothingness is a 'verticalization' of the pentatonic scale; and of all melodic formulae the pentatonic is most void of harmonic implications. Yet out of harmonic disintegration grows a new seed. The linear principle of twelve-note music already is inherent in the texture of the music of Mahler's last years.

II OPERA, RITUAL, AND MYTH

I

THE BIRTH OF A NEW KIND OF OPERA

We have seen that during the second half of the eighteenth century the seminal force in music was sonata; and we have touched on some of the reasons why its development was associated with Austria. None the less, its impact was felt all over Europe. France of the Revolutionary era had in Gossec [1734–1829] a symphonist whose energy and audacity rivals the early Beethoven; while Italy produced in Boccherini [1743–1805] a composer of symphonies and chamber music who achieves a highly personal fusion of Italian lyricism with instrumentally dramatic fire—more sensuous and popular, less bitter-sweet than Mozart. Both Gossec and Boccherini are, at their best, great composers; yet it is none the less true that in Italy and France the central stream of music remained operatic rather than symphonic. Nor was this surprising, for these countries had seen the rise of the great autocracies of the seventeenth and eighteenth centuries; and we have already noted that baroque opera was a projection into visual and aural symbols of the rituals by which the heroic age lived. In Austria, perhaps, the revolutionary force of sonata could come into the open; in Italy the conventions of aristocracy, in art as in life, were so deeply entrenched that they were more likely to be undermined from within. And so the comic interludes that used to provide light relief between the acts of heroic operas gradually encroached on the main performance. The *opera buffa* became a 'low' parody of the heights of heroism, which now seemed stilted rather than tall by nature.

We have already commented on this popular operatic style, in relation to the development of the Austrian sonata. It is perhaps worth adding that the three leading composers of *opera buffa* all spent part of their lives in prison for political reasons. Piccinni [1728–1800] was a man of the old world who, brought up on *opera seria*, still composed fine music in the baroque tradition. He made a fortune by composing operas in the new style, was embroiled in politics vicariously through his relatives, and died in misery, bemused to the last. Paisiello [1740–1816], who also made a vast fortune out of the new opera, was an opportunist of a modern type. He wrote for whichever party happened to be in power, often using the same music, with different words, for either side; he found himself in trouble only because he was not agile enough to keep in step. Cimarosa [1749–1801] represents the third stage. Though in his art his aim was the same as Paisiello's—to entertain and to make money—he was a sincere revolutionary, martyred for the cause.

In France, the change in operatic style ran parallel to that in Italy. The grandeur of Lully was superseded by the more sensational heroics of Rameau [1683–1764]: which in turn gave way not to a deliberate cult of the Low, but to a Rousseauistic cult of Nature, simplicity, and moralistic rationality.* In his own amateurish compositions Rousseau opposed the naturalness of Italian *buffo* style to the archaic splendours of Rameau. Italian *opera buffa* had reduced recitative—always an important element in classical French opera—to a patter that was almost speech. Rousseau, in *Le Devin du Village*, took the further step and employed spoken dialogue, interspersed with descriptive musical interludes and songs: this 'musical comedy' being presented in a setting of idealized rusticity, rather than of mythological magnificence. The composers who followed his lead—Duni [1709–1775], Philidor [1726–1795], and Monsigny [1729-1817]—soon realized that partisanship between the French and Italian cause in what came to be called the *Guerre des Bouffons* was a waste of time. The sprightly symmetries of Italian *buffo* melody could be employed by French composers to good effect; but that was no reason for excluding tunes founded on French popular music, or even on simplifications of the old-fashioned aristocratic *air de cour*.

So it came about that *opera buffa* and *opéra comique* met in the Opera of Sentiment that flourished in both countries. Whereas *opera buffa* based its characters on the stock types of Italian Comedy, but transformed mythological beings into ordinary folk, *opéra comique* started with ordinary people and romanticized them. Both represented a democratic 'levelling'. In

* Jean-Jacques Rousseau [1712–1778] was, as writer and philosopher, a premonition of romanticism in that he believed in the significance of the intimate inner life, as opposed to the public life of Church or State. He was also an amateur composer and musical theorist.

opera buffa the heroic becomes commonplace, in *opéra comique* the commonplace becomes extraordinary; the new sentimental operas might deal with a low subject glamorized, or with a high subject domesticated. One of the greatest European successes of the time was Piccinni's *La Buona Figliuona* (1767), based on a permutation of Richardson's *Pamela*. This heroine of English middle-class sensibility might be you or I, for we all relish a self-righteous assumption of virtue. Perhaps we also like to think of ourselves as the rakish seducer, or as the girl whom an aristocrat might want to seduce; certainly we take pleasure in a nice cry over our misfortunes. The popular opera audiences of the later eighteenth century were not so different from the cinema audiences of to-day; their partiality for variations on the Cinderella story—the poor girl who is the potential princess—is especially interesting. But Piccinni's music must have given a richer satisfaction than the average product of Hollywood, for it manages to combine the virtues of Italian and French opera without the impoverishment of either.

This is equally true of the most representative opera composer of the French school in the second half of the century. Grétry [1742–1813]—a Belgian, born at Liège—spent his adolescence in Rome. He then went to Geneva as a fully-fledged Italianate composer; heard the operas of Monsigny and Philidor; and moved to Paris, determined to emulate their success. His triumph was not long delayed; for to offset a restricted harmonic range and a rudimentary contrapuntal technique, he had a spontaneous melodic gift and a sure instinct for theatrical effect. Most of his operas were in the fashionable vain of the *comédie larmoyante*. When he attempted a heroic theme, as in *Richard Cœur de Lion*, he simultaneously domesticated and romanticized it by concentrating on the Blondel story. When he attempted a mythological theme, as in *Zémire et Azor*, he and his librettist, Marmontel, adapted a fairy tale of the classical age in a way that became unconscious allegory. For the Beast in this version of the Beauty and the Beast legend becomes a Common Man (or animal) who—in a romantically exotic setting—proves himself worthy of the glory that was Versailles. The glory is tarnished, of course. Artistically there is little to justify the claim of Grétry's disciples that he was 'the Molière of music'; the moral intensity beneath the wit has gone, nor has the music the linear power and harmonic subtlety of Couperin and Rameau. On the other hand, his admirers' description of him as 'the French Pergolesi' was valid, for he certainly recreates the easy delights of *opera buffa* in French terms. Though it was considered impolitic to present *Zémire et Azor* at the Dauphin's marriage in 1772 (and perhaps would have been so, for reasons deeper than the obvious one), the music the Dauphin missed owes its charm partly to the fact that its fresh lucidity, heralding the dawn of a new world, is reconciled with an aristocratic past.

The overture and most of the allegro arias are Italian *buffo* music of no very distinctive character. But the duo in Act I, '*Le temps est bel*', testifies to Grétry's dictum that "La parole est un bruit où le chant est renfermé". Although he dispenses with recitative in favour of speech, his melodies recall Rameau's, and even Lully's, in their intimate relationship to the French language. Even Azor's touching air in Act III, '*Du moment qu'on aime*" is no more Italianate than the comparable if richer airs of Rameau; and takes its place beside a chanson-like ariette such as Zémire's tender '*Rose chérie*'. Orchestrally and theatrically, the loveliest moments in the opera are simplified, popularized versions of classical convention. For instance, the orchestral texture of the duo mentioned above, with its softly floating quavers on the strings, and sustained notes on the bassoon, derives from the Lullian *scène de sommeil*, while the trio in the magic mirror episode has its prototype in the supernatural scenes in Rameau.

It is irrelevant to complain that the music lacks Rameau's grandeur and intensity. Grétry dramatized a fairy tale which was not, as it seems, mere make-believe; and inserted into it sequences of songs and dances with little attempt at formal cohesion. He did this not because he was irresponsible, but because, as an ardent Encyclopaedist, he wanted his art to be immediately intelligible to as large a number of people as possible; so concerned was he about intelligibility that he even maintained that it would be a good idea to add explanatory words to Haydn's symphonies! We may doubt whether he appreciated the undercurrent of tragic power in Haydn's music. Yet there had been theatrical composers who did appreciate it, and who had created a new grand opera which combined the musical power and subtlety of the baroque with the psychological interest appropriate to a more democratic order.

Even by the time of Grétry's relaxed, popular manner the old conventions had not been entirely forgotten. In the operas of Jomelli [1714–1774] and Traetta [1727–1779] they preserved their grandeur, while absorbing the more flexible techniques of *opera buffa*, *opéra comique*, and the Italo-Austrian sonata. Significantly, the consummation of this recreated tragic opera came through one of the international figures dear to an age of rationality and enlightenment.

Christoph Willibald Gluck [1714–1798] was born in Bohemia, of peasant ancestry. His cultural heritage was thus German; but since in 1736 he went to Italy to study with Sammartini, his training was entirely Italian. In 1745 he visited London, where he was much impressed by the music of Handel; on his way through France he became familiar with the operas of Rameau and the new *opéra comique*. During the next sixteen years he divided his time between Vienna and Paris, with intermittent excursions to other European cities, producing operas in both Italian and French.

In the early part of his career Gluck wrote a stream of Italian operas, all in the heroic manner. It is unreasonable to suppose that these works contain no evidence of his later genius: but certain that they can lay no claim to the lyrical power and harmonic imaginativeness of Handel or Alessandro Scarlatti. Nor is there much to be said for Gluck's direct attempts to emulate the *opéra comique*, for his talents tended no more to a homely charm than to the *buffo* humour which he cannily avoided. His instinct in turning to France was, however, sound, since in Rousseauistic philosophy he found not so much a moral principle as an emotional attitude which could regenerate old forms. It is significant that his first creation of genius should have been not an Italian opera, nor even a French opera, but a French ballet; and the ancestry of the ballet in France went back beyond the heroic opera and tragedy to the court ritual of the Renaissance.

In Gluck's day there was a movement for reform in the ballet comparable with that which he was to initiate in opera. In heroic French opera, ballet had been as intrinsic a part of the ritual as poetry and music. With the decline of the heroic, ballet had degenerated into the *divertissement de danses*—pretty, but unrelated to the action, as rococo ornament is unrelated to structure. The protagonists of the new ballet, notably Noverre and Angiolini, found their impetus in the operas of Rameau, wherein ballet became not decorative, nor even purely formal, but dramatic action in pantomime. When Noverre decided to create a ballet-pantomime based on the Don Juan legend, he had lighted on a theme which, as an expression of a clash between the individual and social convention, went home to his society with peculiar force. He had also found a subject which had to be treated with dramatic immediacy, or not at all.

That Gluck, in composing a ballet, did not have to think about the human voice was a tremendous asset. Unburdened with operatic convention, Gluck creates a symphonic score which in dramatic urgency can stand beside the music which Haydn and Mozart were to compose twenty years later. Certainly no symphonic music written in the 1760s approaches Gluck's prelude or the fight scene in concentrated ferocity: or the awesome graveyard scene in imaginative orchestration. The exigencies of dance gesture prompt Gluck's vigorous instrumental style, with its wide leaps and prancing rhythms; here the ceremonial dancing of heroic opera becomes dramatic action (Ex. 61). It is obvious that Mozart was familiar with

Gluck's score when he wrote his own *Don Giovanni*, which also centres around the key of D minor. Though Mozart's musical-dramatic sense is subtler and more highly organized, he nowhere displays a more vivid awareness of theatrical effect than does Gluck in the terrifying single note crescendo at the appearance of the Commandant.

Gluck found himself in creating dramatic-symphonic music for the dance. In the following year (1762) he produced the first of his so-called 'reform' operas, *Orfeo*. Superficially, this differs but little from the many other Italian operas he had produced in Vienna. It is based on a classical myth; it is a singers' opera rooted in Italian *bel canto*. True, it combines its Italian aria and arioso with dance pantomime from the French ballet, and with big homophonic choruses of the type so magnificently developed by Rameau; but there was nothing new about that, since both Rameau as a Frenchman and Traetta as an Italian had effected a fusion of French and Italian techniques. The only technical innovations which Gluck makes are negative: he avoids vocal ostentation, and dispenses with the *da capo* aria and with the harpsichord continuo. He is thus able to achieve greater dramatic continuity; the music stops less frequently to accommodate the reflective aria, while the recitative, being accompanied by strings, can be absorbed more readily into the symphonic texture.

Although *Orfeo* appears to be an Italian opera, this amounts to a victory for the French cause. From the time of Lully onwards the French had regarded opera as a tragedy in music. Monteverdi's notion of opera had been much the same; but by the eighteenth century opera had become, for the Italians, a theatrical concert. There was no reason why opera should not be virtuoso music for star singers; indeed, the baroque essentially involves display. But with the decline of autocratic culture, the display ceased to serve an imaginative purpose; opera began to lose its moral and ritualistic significance when display became an end in itself. In *Orfeo* Gluck re-created the heroic ideal. He did not—indeed, he could not—merely revive it, for the moral values he was trying to portray could not be the same as those of the baroque age. The way in which they differed from the past is expressed precisely in his more symphonic conception of the heroic. He looks back to Rameau and Traetta; he looks forward not so much to Mozart as to Beethoven.

In purely musical inventiveness Gluck is inferior to a great master such as Rameau, or even to a minor composer of genius such as Traetta. But it is erroneous to accuse him of defective technique. He had the kind of technique he needed: more counterpoint (even as much as Handel's cook), more opulent lyricism, would have been not only superfluous, but wrong. In *Orfeo* his vocal writing is very simple, compared with that of Rameau or of Alessandro Scarlatti; but it is wonderfully sensitive to dramatic propriety, and where necessary is content to be subservient to the drama of the choral and orchestral writing. In the scene of the Furies both the orchestral music—with its scurrying scales and hectic repeated notes—and the choral invocations have their precedent in Rameau and even in Lully.

In Gluck, however, the spirit is quite new; the music acquires—largely through its remorseless rhythmic impetus—an urgent terror and awful simplicity which suggests Beethoven in his revolutionary mood (Ex. 62). Again, the scene in the Elysian

Fields derives from the pastoral convention of heroic opera; yet its melodic directness, its simple homophonic texture and lucent scoring create a new world of feeling—the vision of order and light which the eighteenth century associated with Hellenism. Even Gluck's preservation of the castrato* is given dramatic relevance. In baroque opera the male soprano voice was considered god-like and super- rather than sub-human, natural male voices being employed only for low characters; Gluck associates the silvery tones of the male contralto with Orpheus in *his* non-human aspect—not as god-king, but as the spirit of music.

Throughout, the conventions of heroism are becoming themselves the symbols of change; and that change is inseparable from Gluck's insight into the human heart. It is significant that, as compared with the extravagant intrigue of baroque opera, there is virtually no action in *Orfeo*: the drama takes place in the minds of the two chief characters. Gluck prefaced his second 'reform' opera, *Alceste*, with a manifesto in which he explained that he had resolved to divest opera of "all those abuses introduced into it whether by the mistaken vanity of singers or by the too great complaisance of composers. . . . I have striven to restrict music to its true office of serving poetry by means of expression and by following the situations of the story without interrupting the action or stifling it in a superfluity of ornaments." He goes on to point out, quite justly, that he was aided in his endeavours by a librettist, Calzabigi, who had substituted for "florid descriptions, unnatural paragons, and sententious cold morality, heartfelt language, strong passions, interesting situations, and endlessly varied spectacles". Between them, they have proved that "simplicity, truth, and naturalness are the great principles of beauty".

* CASTRATO: the artificial male soprano or alto. See *Castrati* Part II.

The last of these remarks is a valid comment on this wonderful opera; but Gluck did not really mean, any more than did Wagner, that he wanted music to be subservient to poetry. He meant that he wanted the music to evolve as a coherent dramatic structure related to the text: so we find that musically *Alceste* does not depart radically from the style of *Orfeo*, but carries further Gluck's symphonic orientation of the heroic. Thus Gluck accepts from Rameau the conventional association of key-relationships with human emotions: modulations sharpwards imply an increase of animation, flatwards modulations a depressive influence, and so on. But these relationships now become part of a symphonic argument; the classical equilibrium which we commented on in the mature work of Haydn and Mozart is already evident in the moving scene between Alceste, the High Priest, and the chorus, with its pathetic, symphonically developed motive on the oboe. Greek myth is no longer a vehicle for the rituals of autocracy, usually based on a fight between personal passion and duty to the State: it is a means of exploring the passions of men and women who, while not being themselves heroic, were becoming increasingly conscious of their humanity.

Gluck deliberately set himself a different human situation to deal with in each opera. In *Paride ed Elena* Calzabigi makes Helen an honest woman and Paris the wicked seducer, so that the legend becomes an ennobled version of the Pamela story that appealed so deeply to eighteenth-century moralistic piety. Gluck significantly says that he has not scrupled to make the music banal and trivial where the dramatic sense demanded it. "He who is concerned with truthfulness must model himself to his subject, and the noblest beauties of harmony and melody become serious faults if they are misplaced." He gives the Greeks a rather bare, uncouth music, the Trojans a more Latin and sensual style, and symphonically objectifies the tension between his two principal characters in this racial differentiation. Again there is almost no action outside the minds of the lovers.

Although these two operas were extremely successful when produced in Vienna, Gluck seems to have felt that this centre of *buffo* frivolity was no suitable place for the fruition of his talents. Despite its Italianate elements, *Alceste* had already indicated that Gluck's art was in some ways the fulfilment of

French philosophical and theatrical ideals. He sought for 'truthfulness and simplicity', and in that sense was a Rousseau-like Child of Nature as well as a '*Paysan du Danube*'. It is not therefore surprising that, having obtained an opera commission from Paris, he should have experienced a triumph with *Iphigénie en Aulide*. This was followed immediately by French versions of *Orfeo* and *Alceste*; then he paid the French tradition the compliment of resetting one of the opera-books that Quinault had written for Lully. The comparison of the two *Armides* is interesting, if by no means always to Gluck's advantage. The change in stress is significant. For Lully, the central character is Renaud, a man torn between passion and duty. For Gluck, the central character is Armide, a woman conscious of her power. He even adds a scene at the end in which Armide, left alone, frustrated in her love, determines to destroy the world she has created, and herself with it. In this subtly psychological conclusion, the heroic conventions become subjective experience. Armide's monologue is woven into a little wailing orchestral figure sequentially repeated, with almost romantic melancholy; the final cataclysm attains, within its apparently limited convention, a Wagnerian violence. The sudden change from the tempestuous D minor scales and arpeggios to the unison Fs, and the re-establishment of a solemn D major when the dust of ruin has blown away, is a stroke of the highest imaginative genius (Ex. 63):

Ex. 63 Gluck: *Armide*

For his next opera Gluck turned from the sensuality of *Armide* to the wild passion of Euripides. Guillard's admirable libretto on *Iphigénie en Tauride* chooses a subject which Goethe himself had adapted, and the highest praise one can give to

XXXIII The Schubertiad: Jenger, Anselm Hüttenbrenner and Schubert.
From a drawing by Joseph Teltscher.

XXXIV From Symphony No. 9 (Ex. 60) by Mahler: last movement.

Gluck's opera is to say that it stands with Goethe's poem as the climax of the eighteenth-century re-creation of the Greek ideal: the Apollonian discipline which enables man to bear the most appalling suffering; the cult of friendship as an act of faith. *Armide* harks back to Lully, while being prophetic of romanticism. *Iphigénie en Tauride* looks back to Rameau—even the famous 'pathological' recitative of Orestes in Act III, with its simple yet extraordinary orchestral interjections, has antecedents in Rameau's *récitative accompagnée*.* At the same time it looks forward to Beethoven's *Fidelio* (the dungeon music in Act II), to Berlioz (the gruesome dance of the Eumenides, with its weird scoring for trombones), and even to Wagner (it opens with a storm which is both operatic and subjective, and a human situation parallel to that at the beginning of *Die Walküre*). Heroism has died to be reborn. Man is no longer a king pretending to be a god; but he becomes godlike in challenging the gods, in resisting whatever Fate has in store for him. This is a Beethovenian step towards Wagner's attempt at self-metamorphosis into God Himself.

Iphigénie en Tauride was not Gluck's last opera. In *Echo et Narcisse* he returns to the tradition of pastoral mythology, now imbued with his own interest in the workings of the human mind. There is nothing odd about this, for we have noted that Gluck never wished to destroy the classical ideal—only to render it once more morally valid. The notorious contest between Gluck as composer of 'reform' operas and Piccinni as upholder of the Italian cause proved only that the opposition was unreal: Gluck could not but respect Piccinni's melodic gifts, while Piccinni knew that he would have been a more effective and a better composer had he had a modicum of Gluck's dramatic integrity. Throughout his career Gluck interspersed his reformatory operas with returns to the old-fashioned *opera seria*, complete with display arias. Though the new elements in Gluck's operas were those which most powerfully expressed his genius, we should guard against thinking that because his operas were different from the baroque ideal they were necessarily better. They were better for him, and perhaps better for us, since we can never again enter into the ritual of the heroic

* Récitative accompagnée : recitative in lyrical or arioso style, accompanied by the orchestra instead of by continuo instruments. Such arioso was reserved for dramatic highlights or supernatural occurrences.

age; yet *opera seria* remained for many years the highest ambition even of as progressive a musician as Mozart. His very last, unfinished work was an *opera seria*, *La Clemenza di Tito*, commissioned to celebrate the Coronation of Leopold II—in the old monarch-glorifying style, modified only by a prevalence of Mozartian ensemble numbers. It may be true that by that date (1791) the commission went against the grain; yet Mozart undertook it, and incorporated into it some extraordinarily beautiful music.

As a boy, Mozart—a no less international figure than Gluck—tried himself out in all the current operatic manners. His training was Italian, not only because he learned his technique from such men as J. C. Bach and Martini, but because he had singing lessons from Manzuoli and the castrato Ceccarelli. His first opera, *La Finta Semplice*, written at the age of twelve, was a stock *buffo* piece on a text of Goldoni, with the conventional *commedia* characters and a musical style modelled directly on Piccinni and Pergolesi. In the same year he composed *Bastien et Bastienne*, which although in the German language was a French opera based on Rousseau's *Devin du Village*. But these exercises in the fashionable *opera buffa* and *opéra comique* were literally mere child's play. The ventures to which Mozart devoted his youthful energies were all heroic; and *Mitridate* and *Lucio Silla* fail not because of inadequate integrity and devotion on Mozart's part, but simply because he was not old enough to attempt grandeur without seeming pretentious. Yet *Lucio Silla* is an important step in his development, significantly associated with the passionate *Sturm und Drang* violin sonatas which he composed in the 1770s.

Certainly he was not pleased to have to return, in *La Finta Giardinera* (commissioned by Munich) and in *Il Re Pastore*, to the stock *buffo* and *galant* types; he complained that "some people think one remains twelve all one's life". When at the (for him) mature age of twenty-five he received a commission to compose a big *opera seria* for Munich, he considered it the most important event of his career. To the end of his days he regarded *Idomeneo* as one of his supreme achievements, and strove repeatedly to get it performed. Only our inherited mistrust of baroque ideals can prevent us from seeing that he was right.

Idomeneo is the only opera in which Mozart was directly

influenced by Gluck. Like Gluck, he combines Italianate aria and recitative with choruses and orchestral interludes derived from French sources; while the orchestrally accompanied recitative he models directly on Gluck's *Alceste*. He too tends to replace the static *da capo* aria with arias in elliptical sonata style; his symphonic treatment of operatic techniques gives to the grand manner a psychological intensity. Events, for Mozart as for Gluck, are less important than their effects on the characters. Though its old-fashioned libretto makes *Idomeneo* less stageworthy than Gluck's masterpieces, it is the only opera by Mozart to achieve the note of classical tragedy. The tremendous outbursts of Electra have Gluck's dramatic perspicuity, with superb lyrical panache; the overture has Gluck's nobility, with Mozart's symphonic control, in a richly contrapuntal texture, over the boldest modulatory excursions. In the great quartet in the last act Mozart achieves something which Gluck never attempted. Here the two lovers, resigned in their mutual confidence, the furious Electra and the despairing *Idomeneo*, sing together, expressing the emotions which are peculiar to each of them, yet related because provoked by a single situation. This is the first great Mozartian ensemble number, in which the sonata composer's search for unity in diversity is projected into operatic terms: the psychological tension is paralleled in the modulatory drama, controlled by the classical symmetry of the form and the cantabile power of the contrasted voices. Mozart had virtually no precedent for this musical-psychological organization. Heroic opera dealt with absolutes rather than with the interplay of character, and Alessandro Scarlatti and Rameau are the only baroque composers who even attempted to exploit the musical and dramatic significance of the ensemble.*

Mozart's justifiable pride in *Idomeneo* did not, however, carry him far with the progressive Emperor Joseph II, who opposed

* There are, however, a few impressive examples of the 'psychological' ensemble in Handel's later oratorios, which are operas without stage action, wherein the heroic theme has become national and humanitarian rather than aristocratic. The quartet in *Jephtha* presents Isis's sacrifice simultaneously from her own and her lover's point of view, from her father's, and from the official or public point of view. Neither a composer of the old aristocratic world nor a composer of profound religious conviction, like Bach, would have allowed himself to suggest such a dubiety of intention as is contained in Iphis's and Hamor's unaccompanied cadenzas. Church, State, and Father may be willing to resign Iphis, in the general interest, to God's will; but the lovers' acceptance of the inevitable is rueful, to say the least.

the *opera seria* in much the same spirit as he opposed the Papacy. The forces of reaction, in any field, were to be discouraged; a local operatic art should be developed as a complement to the Italian *opera buffa* and the French *opéra comique*. The first national *Singspiel* theatre was opened in Vienna in 1778; it turned out to be rather different from what the Emperor had intended. *Singspiel* was supposed to be a popular art distinct from international Italian opera. Yet in a city as impregnated with Italian culture as was Vienna, it was inevitable that elements both of *opera seria* and of *opera buffa* should crop up, if in a cruder form; and that the German *Jezter* should be closely related to the *Commedia* characters.* The simple dance-songs of *opéra comique* also crept in; and all these international features acquired, in the decaying world of Vienna, a dream-like fantasticality. The fairy poetry of Wieland—the main literary impulse—was submerged in knockabout farce and music-hall numbers. Joseph II had intended that *Singspiel* should be a national gesture, and in that sense implicitly if not explicitly political and revolutionary. It became what we would call an escape art: and of a more obvious type than the sentimental opera as practised in Italy and France.

It was for this theatre that Mozart wrote his next opera, *Die Entführung aus dem Serail*. Coming to it fresh from the musical riches of *Idomeneo*, Mozart could hardly be content to produce a gallimaufry of music-hall turns. Parts of *Die Entführung* are in full-flown Italianate style, performable only by great virtuoso singers. Other parts—notably the character of Osmin—are pathological studies of deep insight. Other parts again are unaffectedly popular in manner. This confusion of genres weakens the opera's theatrical effect; while each element is in itself brilliant, the relationship between them is ill-defined. When Mozart turned to opera again he had discovered that all the conventional modes of his time—even the *Singspiel*—could be converted to his imaginative ends.

Although *Die Entführung* is not a successful opera, it was for Mozart a step in the right direction. *Idomeneo* may be Mozart's

* The essence of the Italian comedy was improvisation on a number of mythological characters and situations. Its origins were medieval; its heyday, in Italy and France, was the seventeenth and early eighteenth centuries. Many of Watteau's paintings and Couperin's pieces '*dans le goût burlesque*', give some notion of the beauty, pathos, and wit that the improvisation of the greatest of the *Commedia* actors must have given to the conventional framework.

supreme tragic work; but as a man of the Enlightenment, seeking on ever greater humanity, Mozart was not to find his deepest utterance in heroic tragedy. Increasingly he found himself drawn towards an inextricable mingling of tragic and comic. In this, his art is Shakespearean; and when he said in a letter, "I deem nothing human alien to me", he expressed an attitude similar to Prospero's "This thing of darkness I acknowledge mine". He was thus able to take over the fashionable conventions of his day, for the reasons that made them fashionable: and at the same time to reveal the human impulses behind fashion, which only genius could interpret. He could do this partly, of course, because of the fruition of his talents; but also because he found in Da Ponte a librettist who had, if not genius to match his, at least genius enough to see what he wanted.

Superficially, *Figaro* is a direct descendant from *opera buffa.* The characters are founded on the *Commedia* types: Susanna is Pergolesi's Servina and also Columbine, Figaro is Harlequin, Bartolo is Pantalone, and Cherubino is Lelio and also an adolescent Don Juan. (The convention of soprano playing boy is itself a survival from the castrato soprano, and Cherubino's descendant is the principal boy of pantomime.) But Beaumarchais's play, before Da Ponte adapted it, was already a far cry from the *Commedia.* In so far as it dealt with a conflict between a 'common man' and a decaying aristocracy, it was of revolutionary significance, and Mozart was well aware of this. At the same time, *Figaro* is not anti-aristocratic. It implies an ideal aristocracy in which all classes of people—both socially and psychologically speaking—are given their due. Figaro and Susanna are commonplace common people: yet sympathetic, lovable, important (because like you and I). The Count is a villain; yet he is also a profound pathological study: his arias of rage are no longer an operatic convention, but a revelation of the heart, in which we feel for as much as against him. And the countess, though an aristocrat, is not a villainess at all, but, in the solitude of her introspection, a tragic figure.

The stock types have become real people; and the musical-dramatic structure is the interplay of their personalities. We find therefore—even in comparison with *Die Entführung*—that the set arias are fewer, and more closely wedded to the dramatic action. Opera becomes, for Mozart, dramatic conversation in music; and the ensemble numbers, especially the act finales, become the core of the work. Here Mozart attains a complexity of organization, both musical and psychological, which is approached by no other composer. We have seen how deeply this conception influenced his most representative, and perhaps his greatest instrumental works, the piano concertos.

Profoundly as it enriches convention, *Figaro* is still an opera in the *buffo* tradition. In *Don Giovanni* the Don himself is a stock figure from popular mythology, Leporello is the conventional comic servant, and Zerlina the serving-maid soubrette; yet in all the characters Mozart develops further the revolutionary elements inherent in his work. The basic theme of heroic opera and tragedy had been the conflict between Love and Duty (to the State). To minds nurtured in the early eighteenth century, the Don Juan legend was thus the story of a villain-rogue who destroyed civilization in championing an individualistic, self-justificatory love. For the romantics, on the other hand, the Don became a hero who died tragically because his passions flared beyond the limits imposed by social and religious convention. Mozart's attitude—as we would expect from our knowledge of his instrumental music—is balanced almost equally between these two extremes. His Don is at once villain and hero: a villain because if everyone behaved as he does, civilization would be impossible; a hero because if civilization has grown moribund, it is in need of assault and renovation. For Mozart, Don Juan is thus a Faust-figure; and his attitude to him is somewhere between Marlowe's and Goethe's attitudes to their Fausts. Goethe's Faust is himself, and his challenge to the gods is man's highest endeavour; Marlowe's Faust is himself, yet for the sin of pride he is justly tugged to Hell. But for Mozart the descent to Hell is tragic and comic at the same time. He could urbanely approve of Don Giovanni's fate in so far as he passionately believed in civilization; yet he could not suppress a lurking suspicion that this civilization was not worth saving. To omit the *buffo* epilogue after the descent to Hell is romantically to falsify Mozart. Its so-called 'cynicism' is both subtle and profound: for it tells us that though the Don's fate has been frightening and in a sense tragic, none the less civilization is saved (hurray): while managing to suggest that its bustling gaiety must in the nature of things be ephemeral.

This abrupt transition to *buffo* merriment from one of the most solemnly terrifying moments in music—the appearance of the Commendatore (with sepulchra trombones) and the demoniacal ride to Hell—is typical of Mozart's interfusion of contradictory realms of experience. Similarly lifelike in its apparent paradox is the through-composed duel scene: which passes from Leporello's peevish commentary on Don Giovanni's escapades to the reality of the Don's struggle with Donna Anna, while Leporello's asides become not only comic, but scared; from there to the appearance of the Commendatore, with dramatic tremolandos that almost suggest *The Flying Dutchman*; and from there to the old man's death in the duel, when the shooting-upward scales dissolve in pathetically drooping chromaticism (Ex. 64). The varieties of human experience

Ex. 64 Mozart: ***Don Giovanni***

which we observed in *Figaro*—ranging from the extrovert charm of Figaro to the adolescent troubles of Cherubino, from the Countess's tragic loneliness to the grim lunacy of the Count—are still more sharply delineated in *Don Giovanni*; even at the most awesome penultimate moment—the appearance of the statue—Leporello is still cracking his sad, jittery jokes. These imply a "recognition of other modes of experience which are possible" such as we commented on in the distinctive poise of Mozart's instrumental music.

It is interesting that until the catastrophe Mozart's attention is concentrated not so much on the Don as on the women he seeks to seduce, and on Leporello as the eternal underdog. The Don has no theme, and no real arias—only set numbers like the Champagne song or the Serenade. He is protean, like experience itself. For Mozart (but not for Beethoven) the assertion of the ego is less significant than its infinitely varied effects. He lives in a changing world: but is fascinated more by the people who are changed than by the force which is changing them. Again, this is why he was essentially an opera composer, as Beethoven was not.

The *buffo* conclusion to *Don Giovanni* is a reassertion of the artifices of convention which has been (wrongly) accused of cynicism. The libretto of *Così fan tutte*—possibly da Ponte's masterpiece—is also usually described as both artificial and cynical. Yet its main point is to contrast the artifices of convention with life as it is: while it is the essence of Mozart's genius to admit that human creatures are frail and yet, in their fallibility, worthy of love. The aristocratic modes of behaviour which these young people would like to respect may be charming, elegant, even noble: only they do not square with human nature. Mozart does not suggest that in a better—more 'democratic'—world, social conventions would necessarily be more adequate. Indeed, the explicitly revolutionary *Figaro* and *Don Giovanni* had implied that some fundamental human values belonged more to the old world than to the new; and in *Così fan tutte* he seems to admit that a society ideally compassionate and civilized could never be more than a creation of the human imagination. It is significant that the style of *Così fan tutte* tends to dispense with realistic *buffo* elements in favour of a golden, Italianate limpidity comparable with that of Mozart's last instrumental works, such as the B flat Piano Concerto. Its simplicity, tenderness, strength, and grace are not 'unreal', for they are a distillation of Mozart's knowledge of himself and of other people. But such compassion, and such disinterested detachment, presuppose genius of Mozartian or Shakespearean stature.

It was therefore logical enough that Mozart should have created his next—and last completed—opera in allegorical terms. In making his most comprehensive imaginative statement he no longer even attempted to 'imitate' reality. At the height of his powers he returned—at the invitation of Schikaneder, an actor-impresario who was, like Mozart, a Freemason—to the local tradition of *Singspiel*. In *Die Zauberflöte* he produced a work that can, if the audience wishes, be taken as the usual medley of music-hall turns and fairy-tale whimsey—an 'escapist' musical comedy. At another level, it can be taken as a Masonic allegory about universal brotherhood, ethical humanism, and the triumph of Light. Though Schikaneder took care to avoid overt offence to the Church, his text is anti-Catholic; and it appealed to the interests which most deeply engaged Mozart during the last years of his life. He even managed to instil into it his own death-consciousness, which was no accredited part of Masonic creed.

There are three main strands to Schikaneder's allegory. First there are the Masonic beings who represent Progress and Enlightenment. Tamino is the Emperor Joseph II, Pamina the Austrian people, and Sarastro Ignaz von Born, a Masonic prophet, half rational, half mystical. Then there is the realm of the Queen of Night—what seemed to Masonic enlightenment the effete Catholic world of sorcery, superstition, and seduction. The Queen is Maria Theresa, Monostatos (semi-comic creature of lust and vengeance) is the clergy, and in particular the Jesuits. Finally, there is the world inhabited by those incapable of the heights of humanism: Papageno being, in his innocence, a kind of comic Parsifal.

This, however, is only the external allegory, which is less important than the internal or psychological allegory. The fight between light and darkness goes on inside as well as outside the mind; and this is expressed not only in incidents such as the encounter with the Snake, but in a strange intermingling of good and bad forces which parallels Mozart's attitude to his characters in his more realistic operas. The sinister Queen of Night has three ladies-in-waiting eager to perform charitable acts; on the other hand, the High Priest of Light entrusts Pamina to the lustful slave of the temple. The Prince and the Bird Catcher depart together on their search for the ideal: the peasant simplicity for which Schubert yearned is the first step in the quest for serenity.

This medley of fantasticality and pseudo-philosophy prompts a heterogeneous assortment of musical styles, which miraculously become one. We have sophisticated Italian arioso, which sometimes, as in Pamina's G minor aria, achieves a withdrawn intensity almost reminiscent of Bach. We have dazzling coloratura pieces like the Queen of Night's scalp-prickling D minor aria. We have doggerel rhymes and street tunes like Papageno's songs. Alongside all these there is music like the trio for Pamina, Tamino, and Sarastro in Act III, or the Men in Armour episode in the Trial Scene. Here we find a Bachian austerity of counterpoint, and a new type of chorale-like melody, usually in the Masonic key of E flat, and with Masonic scoring for woodwind and trombones (Ex. 65). This music is at once innocently simple and mysteriously solemn; and although Mozart may have found hints for this in Bach, Handel, and Gluck, it suggests more readily and more profoundly the hymn-like melodies that first appear in Beethoven's music about the time of the Fifth Symphony. In this respect it is significant that the opera deals, in its allegorical terms, with the *growth* of character. Pamina and

Ex. 65 Mozart: *Die Zauberflöte*

Tamino are real people as well as symbols; and at the end of the opera they are not the same people as they were at the beginning. Mozart does not seek Beethoven's mystical salvation; he creates a humanistic serenity that almost becomes divine.

Die Zauberflöte was the only Mozart opera of which Beethoven approved; and interestingly enough it was Schikaneder who first offered Beethoven a commission to compose an opera. Beethoven was to produce an opera in competition with Cherubini, who was working for a rival impresario, Baron Braun. He did not fulfil this commission, but deserted to Braun's camp, partly for financial reasons, partly because he was offered a libretto that appealed to him. Bouilly's *Leonora* was a pain-and-torment and rescue libretto: a typically realistic, revolutionary modification of heroic convention. The brave girl disguised as a boy enters the dungeon as gaoler's assistant to help her wrongfully imprisoned husband. After sundry improbable adventures provoked by the infatuation of the gaoler's daughter for the new assistant, the old-style *deus ex machina* of baroque opera* is replaced by a realistic Minister of State who brings a last-minute reprieve, with a phalanx of trumpets symbolizing an earthly Day of Judgement.

Beethoven took this task very seriously. He studied the operas of Cherubini with care, finding in the Italian's fusion of classical form, symphonic grandeur, and traditional vocal technique a basis for an idiom appropriate to his own designs. He even took lessons in vocal composition from Salieri. Yet though he reworked the opera several times, he remained dissatisfied. The reason is not far to seek: even if the libretto

* There is no resolution of conflict, no 'Becoming', in baroque operas. At the end the god-king descends from the heavens to put to rights the chaos created by human perversity. Unruly passions must be liquidated in the best ordered of all possible worlds.

had shown a subtler insight into human nature, Beethoven was not the man to be inspired by vocal characterization through lyricism, let alone by the complex interaction of character such as we find in Mozart. Unlike Mozart, he had next to no interest in other human beings; but abstract moral qualities, black and white and all the various shades of grey, interested him profoundly, because they were what he had experienced within his own mind and senses, and expressed in his instrumental music. The subjective nature of Beethoven's music was against opera composition; for opera—notwithstanding Wagner, as we shall see—of its nature implies objectification.

Nevertheless, *Fidelio* contains some magnificent music: which all occurs when abstract human qualities fire Beethoven's imagination. The love affair of Marcellina is conventional Italianate grand opera, not especially well composed; but Leonora's music, which grows from nobility of nature, fidelity, hope, justice—all the Beethovenian virtues—is tremendously impressive. With the scene in the dungeon, Beethoven reaches tragic heights. Here is no longer an episode in a stagey story: imprisonment and freedom becomes one of Beethoven's universal themes, most of all when the prisoners themselves are actively involved. The prisoners become humanity, and their music not operatic, but a choral symphony. Their hymns anticipate both the Joy theme of the Ninth Symphony and the impractical, because superhuman, vocal writing of that work and of the *Missa Solemnis*. The story has it that Cherubini, as a tactful hint, sent Beethoven a text-book of Italian vocal technique. This choral music is Beethoven's answer, which came from the depths of his being: for he certainly would not have wished consciously to rebuff the man whom he considered the greatest living composer—at least until his own maturity.

It is unlikely that Beethoven's interest in *Die Zauberflöte* went as far as conscious imitation; but it has been pointed out that Beethoven conceived his story as a realistic counterpart to Mozart's allegory. In both operas, a pair of lovers win through an ordeal, in Mozart symbolically, realistically in Beethoven. Human fortitude brings the victory of Light: which Beethoven expresses in the F major duet when the lovers are at last freed from the dungeon's gloom. In so far as it leads on to *Fidelio*, *Die Zauberflöte* was the end of the eighteenth century, and of the Mozartian 'equilibrium'. The odd thing is that Beethoven should have wished to follow up *Fidelio* himself; he even angled for a post as opera-house composer on a yearly salary, producing one big opera a year, plus several divertimenti. The management of the opera house was, in this case, wiser than he. They fobbed him off with a commission for a mass.

In fact, one has no need to look further than the *Leonora* overtures to see how inessential opera was for Beethoven. Between Mozart's operas and his instrumental works there was always an intimate relationship; but all the drama Beethoven deeply feels is embodied in these instrumental sonata movements. Moreover, the third *Leonora* overture is more dramatic than the second because it is more symphonic; the Day of Judgement trumpet-call now merely initiates the development, instead of being the piece's 'theatrical' climax. The *Leonora* overtures are sonata movements about the triumph of the individual spirit, as the *Coriolan* overture is about self-will and the *Egmont* overture about revolution. All this was expressed at one level in the stock revolutionary operas which became the nineteenth century's restatement of the heroic. But at a deeper level this revolution had already been effected in the instrumental music of Beethoven's middle years: and from there he had gone on to a point where no external revolution could follow him.

Though the moralistic opera *Fidelio* may have been in one sense a descendant from *Die Zauberflöte*, it is not musically in the Mozartian tradition. Perhaps no one after Mozart achieved the ideal balance between music and drama; but at least one can say that the elements that were in his operas inextricably mated became, in the work of Rossini and Weber, the source of creative operatic development during the nineteenth century.

We have seen that in the 1820s Rossini was the most popular composer not only in his own country, but also in Italianate Vienna. This is easy to understand; for he was a direct successor to the *buffo* composers of the eighteenth century, while possessing incomparably more wit, vivacity, and fire than the average. One must not expect from Rossini the disturbing undercurrents of passion and melancholy that occur in Mozart's ostensibly similar operas. He does not attempt Mozart's close interplay of character-drawing and music; his art is at a further remove from life. Writing for a larger theatre and a more superficial audience, he expatiates on his jokes, theatrically 'presenting' his characters instead of allowing them to create themselves: it is significant that Rossini's characters habitually, Mozart's only exceptionally, address the audience rather than one another. This fundamental difference in approach is indicated in Rossini's abandonment of the psychologically dramatic sonata aria and his partiality for the non-evolutionary rondo aria—in which a symmetrical tune is stated twice, followed by a somewhat perfunctory 'middle' phrase and a third repetition of the original clause, usually embellished: the whole being rounded off by a rhythmic coda to work up the applause. The notorious 'Rossini crescendo' is another instance of this desire to achieve the maximum effect with the minimum effot.

Yet Rossini is not superficial in a derogatory sense. Indeed, the accusation of rococo affectation levelled at him by critics from Wagner onwards is singularly inappropriate: for, being no longer willing to trust to the taste of his singers, he merely wrote out in his scores virtuoso arabesques that in earlier operas —even Mozart's and Gluck's—would have been improvised. Nor can an eye or ear for effect be considered a liability in an opera composer. The thin orchestral and harmonic texture which (except perhaps in his two French operas) he habitually adopted was a legitimate convention which concentrated attention on the singers: only Mozart could write music which is theatrically lucid while being both vocally and orchestrally elaborate. Even in Rossini's stock *buffo* operas, such as *La Cenerentola* (again the poor girl who makes good), the virtuosity of the vocal writing, the bubbling zest of the rhythms, the lucent simplicity of the scoring are enough to express a personal view of life. In *The Barber of Seville*, where for once he has a convincing libretto based, like *Figaro*, on Beaumarchais, the *buffo* figures again become flesh and blood. Admittedly, *The Barber* is farce to *Figaro's* tragi-comedy. But it is not mere make-believe. The 'human comedy' does not always hide a Mozartian poignancy beneath the absurd façade. The slip on the banana skin—the affront to human dignity—is a joke rooted deep in our tangled natures; and Rossini's buffoonery sometimes strikes home more disturbingly, more dangerously, than we like to think. The Rossini crescendo in the slander song from *The Barber* is frightening as well as funny; we cannot always dispel the suspicion that our hearts may be as hard as Rossini suggests.

Rossini was not only a survival from the eighteenth century.

His fame was international; and while the operas he composed for Italy and Vienna adhered to tradition, the two operas he composed for Paris were startlingly prophetic. His last funny opera, *Le Comte Ory*, is a descendant from eighteenth-century *opéra comique*, revivified with Italian musicality; it is also the ancestor of nineteenth-century French light opera. The effervescence of Offenbach and the elegance of Messager are here combined with a harmonic subtlety that suggests Bizet, and a loveliness of line-drawing and of orchestral sonority that reminds us of the lighter works of Berlioz. According to Berlioz, the trio '*A la faveur de cette nuit obscure*' was the composer's masterpiece, and worthy of Mozart.

If *Le Comte Ory* is the progenitor of French light opera, Rossini's next work, *Guillaume Tell*, contains the seed of the new grand manner in France and indirectly in Germany also. He had composed, earlier in his career, a few serious operas, if not *opera seria*, some of which (notably *Otello*) contain impressive music. But *Guillaume Tell* was a new kind of music: a heroic opera which found its epic theme not in a mythological glorification of monarchy nor in a conflict between love and duty, but in historical events and national aspiration. Musically, it reconciled Rossini's Italian vocal training with the massive, homophonic choral style which Spontini and Méhul had evolved from Gluck: with the character-drawing more typical of *opera buffa*: and with an expressive use of orchestral harmony and colour. Many of the revolutionary features in the early work of Wagner are already evident in *Guillaume Tell*, along with a supple beauty of vocal line which Wagner could never emulate. An aria such as '*Sombres Forêts*' from Act II is not, as Stendhal said, "the art so popular in Germany of expressing the sentiments of the characters by oboes, 'cellos, and clarinets; it is the far rarer art of expressing by means of instruments that portion of their sentiments which the characters themselves could not convey to us". In the face of music such as this, one can understand why so many composers—even such unlikely men as Beethoven and Wagner himself in his early days—should have had so high a regard for Rossini's musicianship.

Rossini was probably right in thinking that the second act of *Guillaume Tell* was his finest work. Yet he had to force himself to create such music, which was opposed to his eupeptic temperament; and the opera as a whole is unequal. That did not affect its prodigious success; though perhaps it influenced Rossini's decision to retire immediately from the theatre, at the height of his fame, and at the early age of thirty-seven. The reasons for this renunciation are complex. The familiar charge that Rossini was congenitally lazy can hardly be substantiated of a man who had been in the habit of producing half a dozen or so operas a year. That he had made enough money to live on in comfort for the rest of his days was a relevant factor, though it could not of itself have stifled so spontaneous a creativity. The most probable explanation is that Rossini knew that the future development of opera would be opposed to his own temperament and to the traditions which he respected. In *Guillaume Tell*, indeed, he had himself anticipatorily experienced these new impulses; he could not bear to see them eventually destroy the music he held most dear.

So although he lived for another forty years, he composed henceforth only works—mostly little piano pieces and songs—designed to amuse his friends at his celebrated evening parties. To these 'sins of my old age' he adopted a somewhat ironically condescending attitude. Yet though the songs and duets of the *Soirées Musicales* are often witty, they are also often of a melting lyrical beauty which, in the 1860s, seemed to belong to a forgotten art. Nor do they ignore the chromatic and enharmonic developments associated with Wagner: only the audacities of the exquisitely lucid piano parts are a background to the emotion concentrated in the vocal lines.

Rossini himself said that he composed his last large-scale work in order that the true art of vocal writing should not be finally lost. The whimsically titled *Petite Messe Solennelle* is a full-length operatic mass for soloists and chorus, with an elaborate piano part in the style of the *Soirées Musicales*, and harmonium to support the voices. The superbly vivacious fugal movements are an extension of the *buffo* finale, with only a slight infusion of ecclesiastical learning. The solo arias and ensembles are operatic music, not merely of charm and elegance, but of unexpected profundity. This reaches its climax in the final Agnus Dei, a passionate contralto solo with suavely homophonic choral interludes. When soloist and chorus ultimately sing together—in the strangest enharmonic modulations—Rossini achieves a pathos and even a tragic power which are paralleled only in the greatest moments of Verdi (Ex. 66). At the end of the mass Rossini appends a little address to *le bon Dieu*: "La voilà terminée cette pauvre petite messe. Est-ce bien de la musique sacrée que je viens de faire ou bien de la sacrée musique?*

Ex. 66 Rossini: *Petite Messe Solennelle* (Agnus Dei)

J'étais né pour l'opéra buffa, tu le sais bein. Un peu de science, un peu de cœur, tout est là. Sois donc béni, et accorde moi le Paradis." It would be a hard deity indeed who could resist so winning an appeal, let alone such moving music. Rossini's use of the familiar *tu* in addressing his god suggests, perhaps, how eighteenth-century self-confidence is changing into nineteenth-century independence: just as this music effects a transition from *buffo* jauntiness to the romantic pathos of the Agnus Dei.

So Rossini, trained in the eighteenth century, contemplates ironically the premonitions of the future that flicker beneath his urbane art. His younger contemporary Weber [1786–1826] resembles him in being essentially an opera composer; and both followed Mozart who, as Rossini pointed out, was "lucky enough

* Rossini's pun is untranslatable. *La musique sacrée* means sacred music; *la sacrée musique* means damned (i.e. shocking, awful) music.

to go to Italy at a time when they still knew how to sing". But Weber started not only from Italian opera, but also from the German *Singspiel.* His romanticism became a part of his awareness of nationality—a force which ultimately destroyed the classical tradition.

Being German, Weber (unlike Rossini) wrote a certain amount of instrumental music in sonata style. He was, however, justified in claiming that there was no kinship between his music and Beethoven's. Subjective conflict is extraneous to his temperament. When he composes concerted chamber music he adopts a coloured, theatrical version of the style of the salon, with virtuoso keyboard writing suggested by rococo vocal ornament, and with 'picturesque' alternations of instrumental sonority. This rococo manner is used by Beethoven very rarely, and then with a slightly parodistic flavour, as in the slow movement of the G major Sonata from opus 31. Weber's biggest instrumental work, the *Konzertstück* for piano and orchestra, is a brilliant piece of melodrama which seems to imply visual illustration on a stage—quite unlike the subtly 'interior' operatic drama of Mozart's piano concertos.

Even when Weber actually writes in sonata form, the conventional exposition and development are not much more than a gesture. In the A flat Piano Sonata, for instance, the resonant spacing of the protracted tonic chord at the beginning is an orchestral effect; while the second subject is rococo virtuosity. The development is sensational, with marvellously pianistic aplomb; but it is not a dramatic argument in Beethoven's sense; and the movement has to be wound up by a Rossini-like curtain-coda that plays the applause. Similarly, in the last movement Mozartian chromaticism is no longer pathetic, but an effect of colour. The first movement of the D minor Sonata opens 'allegro feroce' in operatic melodrama. The second subject is again operatic aria, and no attempt is made to relate the two. Indeed, the effect of the music depends upon its arbitrary succession of moods: which can thus be rounded off by the brilliantly extrovert virtuosity of the rondo finale. Only in the last, E minor Sonata does Weber attempt dramatic continuity, using a single rhetorically operatic theme, and basing the development on a non-melodic figuration that appears in the codetta.

All the themes in Weber's sonatas are Italianate and operatic;

yet they could never be confused with Mozart's. Rossini's melodies are still in the Mozartian tradition, though they are normally less chromatic, and have more rhythmic vigour, if less rhythmic finesse. Weber's melodies use the same vocal formulae as do Mozart's and Rossini's, but render these formulae more obvious in their emotional appeal—as did Beethoven in his youth. One reason for this is that they introduce a greater proportion of wide leaps, especially upward leaps of sixth, seventh, and even ninth. Another reason is that their rhythmic structure is almost always regularly periodic. If this divests them of Mozartian subtlety, it gives them a powerful drive. Chromaticism in Weber is usually decorative: perhaps this is another way of saying that his pathos tends to be a theatrical gesture. The big leaps in his melodies are again often associated with his rhetorical approach to harmony; the leaping gesture produces, or is accompanied by, the emotive dissonance. A theme such as this from the D minor Piano Sonata—with its leaping sixths from strong to weak beat—is exactly comparable, both in its contour and in its four-bar periodicity, with one of the most famous of all Weber's operatic tunes (Ex. 67):

Ex 67 Weber· Piano Sonata in D minor (first movement)

as is the harmonic texture of this passage from the E minor Sonata with this operatic use of the chord of the ninth (Ex.68):

Ex.68. Weber: *Sonata in E minor* (first movement)

We can see already how Weber's musical style entails the exaggerated gestures of nineteenth-century operatic acting: gestures which would be utterly inappropriate to Mozart.

As an opera composer, Weber aimed to make his Italianate rhetoric serve a national purpose. *Der Freischütz* starts from the *Singspiel*, even preserving spoken dialogue; but the escape art of musical comedy now becomes the central experience of romanticism. Characteristically, the romantic sensibility seeks to 'get it both ways'. German folk-myth suggests German folk-song. This modifies the Italianism of the melodies and creates a style of rustic simplicity that serves as a refuge from introspection. On the other hand, folk-myth provokes the horrors of the Wolf's Glen, offering the thrills which everyday life denies us. Both complementary kinds of escape find expression in Weber's theatrical sense, his rhetorical harmony, and above all in his feeling for orchestral colour—which as we have seen pervades even his chamber works and piano music. Schubert had hinted at a dream-world of rustic tranquillity; in the *Freischütz* overture this becomes vividly immediate, and one of the creative forces in nineteenth-century music. Weber's extroversion—he was a magnificent virtuoso pianist and conductor—is one reason for the forcefulness of his impact. At a time when music was turning increasingly 'inward', he developed techniques which later composers were to use for a radically different purpose. The *Freischütz* overture is a typical modification of the sonata principle. The slow introduction 'poeticizes' the ceremonial grandeur of the old operatic overture; the sonata allegro is an exciting tussle between Bad forces (the Zamiel theme and the agitato rhythm) and Good (the Agathe theme, which begins in the relative major). The working-out excites expectation, rather than resolving this opposition. When the piece ends with a grandiose coda in which the Agathe theme is stated in the tonic major, instead of the agitato section's tonic minor, we know that virtue will triumph over evil; but the overture itself has not told us how this will happen. That is as it should be: for Weber's sonata-overture is not psychological drama in Beethoven's sense. It is designed, with theatrical acumen, to lead into the externalized presentation of conflict on the stage.

Weber's choice of subject for his next opera is no less historically significant; for *Euryanthe* deals with medieval chivalry from a romantic standpoint, and undoubtedly influenced Wagner's early choice of theme. In *Euryanthe* Weber attempts to elevate the *Singspiel* to nobility: to create a German opera worthy to be placed beside the Grand Manner of France. The grander the music gets, the more Italianate, and the less German, is the style. With *Oberon*, which resembles a *Singspiel* in so far as it is based on a poem of Wieland, the fairy-tale opera becomes an expression of romantic faith. Gluckian music drama comes to terms with the new Teutonic, rustic manner and with the new orchestral technique. There are aspects of *Oberon* which derive from Cherubini and Méhul, from Spontini and Rossini; yet Weber remains a composer of extraordinary originality in that he invests the theatrical 'property' with poetic evocativeness, almost always by orchestral rather than vocal means. The solo horn and the muted strings of the opening to the overture to *Oberon* are an exhibition of orchestral genius which is to be valued for itself. None the less, it is testimony to the potency of Weber's magic that his outward-turning theatricality should contain in embryo the dream-life of the romantic spirit.

Formally, Weber is sometimes credited with an anticipation of Wagner's continuous symphonic texture. It is true that, although he does not use leitmotives, he sometimes associates particular characters with specific key-centres: and that even when he adheres most obviously to the old-fashioned division into aria and arioso, he plans the structural sequences of his scenes with care. That his operas are no longer theatrically tenable is due not so much to his dangerous instinct for the immediate 'effect' as to his intractable libretti. Schubert's operatic ventures failed for a similar reason; and one might say that Beethoven's *Fidelio* suffers from a disparity between the conventionally operatic elements in the libretto and those which inspired Beethoven's moralistic-symphonic imagination.

This trouble over libretti is not fortuitous. Baroque opera books may seem to us idiotic, yet the philosophical bases of Metastasian convention were intelligible to both composer and audience; the glorification of the god-king and the fight between love and duty was a consistent theme which entailed consistent stylizations. Mozart found the themes which were precisely relevant to what he wanted to say in musical terms and, with the help of Da Ponte, effected a perfect balance between the world of operatic artifice and real life. This was never possible again—not even in Italy, where opera remained the central tradition. In France, the supreme opera composer, Berlioz, did not even establish a valid relationship to the public; in Germany Wagner achieved such a relationship only after herculean labours and by a prodigious exhibition of will-power. The fashionable operatic traditions in France and Germany became essentially escape-art. On the comic side, Rossinian frivolity turned into the effervescent 'musical comedy' of Offenbach [1819–1880]; while the simple, domestic aspect of Weber's German fairyland blossomed into the charming light operas of Lortzing [1801–1851] and Nicolai [1810–1849]: works which displayed a quiet musicianship without resorting to Italianate glamour. On the tragic side, the romantic horrors of Weber's Germany were taken up in the operas of Marschner [1795–1861] and Spohr [1784–1859]: works which preserved Italian lyricism in a harmonically and orchestrally more sensational setting; while the cult of the sensational as an end in itself reached a climax in French grand opera after Rossini. Opera composers had relinquished the heroic view of life because they had ceased to believe in it; but having lost their awareness of purpose, they found it difficult to establish a convincing relation between reality and convention. Both Marschner and Lortzing express only a partial truth, for life is neither as nasty as the one nor as nice as the other. The hedonistic Rossini evades less, and has a harder reality at the core of his art.

'Unprincipled' is the adjective habitually applied to Giacomo Meyerbeer [1791–1864] who—after the retirement of Rossini and the early death of Weber—became perhaps the most prodigiously successful composer in history. A cosmopolitan rather than international figure, he was a wealthy and cultivated German Jew who settled in Paris, determined to exploit the craving for a forsaken grandeur that seethed beneath the complacence of the revolutionized bourgeoisie. In the absence of an aristocracy of spirit such as could be recovered only by a mind as rare as Berlioz's, this grandeur was bound to be flashy: a rhetorical attitudinizing which found complementary expression in the plays of Hugo. Yet Meyerbeer was not artistically insincere. His command of Italianate vocal line was as powerful as Weber's and more supple: perhaps more impressive, musically, than the attempts of the young Verdi or Wagner to emulate him. His monumental use of the French choral 'tableau' was aesthetically thrilling and dramatically justified, if without the nationalistic fervour of its model—the magnificent final scene of *Guillaume Tell.* His exploitation of German orchestral technique was dramatically vivid, never merely noisy or an end in itself; and his powers of musical construction were far above those of the average operatic hack in any of the three countries to which he vicariously belonged.

It is therefore unjust that his name should have become synonymous with the meretricious, in so far as his musical technique was not only brilliant, but honestly devoted to his dramatic intentions. The trouble lies, of course, in the dubiety of those intentions—or rather of those of his librettist, the efficient Scribe. For the high solemnity of Scribe's politico-historical manner is an attitude, not a belief. Meyerbeer brings to Scribe's grandiosity his excellent musicianship and a sense of theatrical effect for which only a fool would reproach him. But like Scribe he lacked two qualities: a sense of purpose, and a sense of humour. With the former, like Wagner, he could have dispensed with the latter. With the latter, like Rossini (except in *Guillaume Tell*), he could have managed without the former. To have possessed both, like Mozart, would have been asking too much of the age of romanticism. Berlioz, who alone relived the heroic world, was alone in preserving the 'intense levity' of the classical equilibrium—at least until Verdi, in extreme old age, rediscovered it when the fire of romanticism was spent.

So the problem of the valid musical convention in opera is again inseparable from the creation, not necessarily of the good, but of the morally and socially valid libretto. As we consider the careers of the three greatest operatic composers of the nineteenth century, we shall see that Verdi paid ever-increasing attention to the nature of his libretti until he found his ideal partner in Boito; and that Berlioz and Wagner themselves created the only feasible literary foundations for their musical forms.

2

WAGNER

BEHIND the sonata epoch there are two great creative impulses: the idea of Revolution, and the escape to Dream. We have observed the former in Beethoven, and both impulses in Schubert. With him, the tendency to substitute a world of the imagination for reality is no more than tentative, for he was trained in the classical tradition. It grows stronger, however, as commercialized industry produces a world to which sensitive spirits feel increasingly inimical; and the situation is epitomized in the career of Richard Wagner, who called himself 'an outlaw for life'.

Unlike his predecessors of the classical age, Wagner [1813–1883] was born to sophistication and self-consciousness. His parents, though not affluent, belonged to cultivated society; he received a university education, read widely and—in his egocentric, emotional way—thought much. But his intellectual awareness was from the start an awareness of self. He was an outlaw because he was right, and the world wrong. Beethoven too wanted to change the world, but gave up the attempt when he discovered a deeper truth. Wagner—like Carlyle, a middle-class prophet haranguing a materialistic world—never gave up, even in the face of obstacles that would have cowed a lesser man. His courage really was—like the creatures of his imagination—superhuman, and his ultimate triumph one of the supreme achievements of the human mind. That we have to admit, however obnoxious we may find some aspects of his personality: and even if we think his victory hollow compared with Beethoven's.

Although in his youth Wagner was engaged in political activity, there is a significant difference between his interest in revolutionary movements and Beethoven's. The latter was interested in revolution as a means towards a better world. Wagner was interested in it in a purely negative sense, in so far as the corruptions of society hampered the free expression of his own desires and the fulfilment of his artistic ambitions. He was the Way and the Life; and if contemporary society refused to see that, it could only be because of the machinations of evil-doers and anti-Wagnerians, for whom the Jews could serve as a scapegoat. (Meyerbeer was a Jew, and internationally famous, as Wagner at this time was not.) If Jews are wicked, the Aryan Folk must be good; but Wagner extolled them not for themselves, but as a kind of allegorical representative of himself as Aryan Hero. "A nation of high-souled dreamers and deep-brained thinkers", he called the German people; and that is exactly how he would have described himself.

Now Weber, we saw, in his brilliantly externalized music, created many of the techniques whereby Wagner was to evoke the world of his inner life; yet he never discovered the theme implicit in his technique. It is testimony to the powerful 'inwardness' of Wagner's genius—as compared with Weber's outwardness—that he should have discovered his quintessential theme long before he had evolved a personal technique. When he was nineteen, he started an opera called *Die Hochsteit*, which is about a woman who kills a man who threatens her honour; knowing that she passionately loves him, she then dies of grief by his grave. This myth, in which the love-murderer becomes the self-murderer, lies at the heart of the Wagnerian experience. It was not until many years later that this was to be revealed in the consummatory achievements of his art. But after he had written *Rienzi*, which is a stock Franco-German-Italian opera inferior to, but in the pompous and circumstantial manner of, Meyerbeer, Wagner began to use opera as a medium for spiritual autobiography. He himself wrote libretti which present his basic theme as seen by his conscious mind. *The Flying Dutchman*, *Tannhäuser*, and *Lohengrin* are mainly about Wagner as he liked to think of himself: only in his later work, and especially in *Tristan* and *Parsifal*, do we see him as quintessentially he was.

The legend of the Flying Dutchman seemed to him to parallel his own history during the years 1839–41. He too had been driven from place to place, had been harried by indefinable longings, and was always on the point of being redeemed by a woman prepared to sacrifice all for him. Other young men have had similar experiences, without feeling the need to elevate them into a programme of universal regeneration. But Wagner is quite explicit: "My course was new", he says; "it was bidden me by my inner mood, and forced upon me by the pressing need to impart this mood to others. In order to enfranchise myself from within outwards . . . I was driven to strike out for myself, as artist, a path not yet pointed me by any outward experience."

The Dutchman suffers, is alone, and is redeemed (and implicitly deified) by Senta's love and death. Tannhäuser is also alone, fleeing from a base, materialistic, and sensual world. Again the "longed-for, dreamt-of, utterly womanly woman, the Woman of the Future" leads him from the passions of Venusberg to heaven. Even at this early date we have a relatively crude statement of the inescapable link between eroticism and renunciation; it crops up still more obviously in *Lohengrin*, in whose person Wagner becomes not only the lonely hero in an alien world, but also the god-like figure who, because he is superhuman, is bound to be misunderstood. Superficially, *Lohengrin* seems a silly story of a pompous young man who refuses to tell his name to a girl only too anxious to love him. To Wagner, "it was the type of the only absolute tragedy, of the tragic element in modern life; and that of just as great significance for the Present, as was the *Antigone* for the life of the Hellenic state. . . . Elsa is the Unconscious, the Undeliberate, into which Lohengrin's conscious, deliberate being yearns to be redeemed; but this yearning again is itself the unconscious, undeliberate necessity in Lohengrin's being, whereby he feels himself akin to Elsa. Through the capability of this 'unconscious consciousness', such as I myself now felt alike with Lohengrin, the nature of Woman also came to even clearer understanding in my mind. . . . This woman, who with clear foreknowledge rushes to her doom, for the sake of love's imperative behest—who amid the ecstasy of adoration, wills yet to lose her all, if so be she cannot all-embrace her loved one; this woman, who in contact with this Lohengrin, of all men, must founder, and in so doing must shipwreck her beloved too . . . this Elsa, the most positive expression of the purest instinct of the senses—made me a revolutionary at one blow. She was the Spirit of the Folk, for whose redeeming hand I too, as artist-man, was longing." Who would have thought it: and who, having been told, can believe it? We cannot take Wagner's interminable verbal rhapsodies seriously, any more than we can stomach his prose; but they have a kind of unholy fascination, as evidence of the completeness with which Wagner identified his own emotional turmoils with the destiny of mankind.

To turn to the music of Wagner's first two autobiographical operas, after reading his verbal expatiations on them, is a blessed relief which reveals the gulf, at this stage in his career, between his practice and his intentions. Eventually he was to fulfil his ambitions at a level deeper than consciousness; but no one would suspect this from a glance at these scores. The vocal lines in *The Flying Dutchman* are still basically Italian, and move even more squarely in four-bar periods than do those of Weber. Diminished sevenths, tremolandos, and other operatic 'properties' of Meyerbeer and Spontini reappear in much the same context; and although chromaticisms and enharmonic transitions intensify moments of emotional crises, they are no bolder than those which appear in the operas of Spohr or Marschner. The sensuous colours of the orchestra comment on the characters' passions with rather less than Weber's sensitivity. The singers no longer carry the whole burden, as they do in Rossini, but they are still the centre of the action.

Even in *The Flying Dutchman*, however, there is a sense in which Wagner was justified in claiming that he owed nothing essential to the tradition of Gluck and Weber. He always maintained that he was the heir to Beethoven, and his first works had in fact been instrumental symphonies modelled with vigour and confidence on the Beethovenian symphony of power. In *The Flying Dutchman* the structure seems to be based on the conventional division into aria and arioso, even including a direct survival from French sentimental opera like the *Romance*. Even so, the work is much more symphonic, in Beethoven's sense, than any previous opera; and this is especially true of one of the set pieces—the *Ballade*—which contains the creative essence of the opera. Here Senta's motive itself is an arpeggio challenge-theme which Wagner handles in much the same way as Beethoven handles his similar motive in the development section of a symphony. Already Wagner is beginning to project symphonic conflict into operatic terms.

The full implications of this are not evident in *The Flying Dutchman*; nor in *Tannhäuser*, though the fight between Elizabeth and Venus for the soul of the hero creates a symphonic drama which overrides the episodic effect of the set pieces. In *Lohengrin*, however, the interfusion of aria and accompanied recitative produces an almost continuous orchestral texture, and the technique of the leitmotive—the association of particular characters or places or ideas with specific musical figures—becomes an application of Beethoven's symphonic methods to opera. This aspect of the leitmotive as a principle of musical organization is much more important than its function as an aural guide-book to the action. Henceforth, Wagner's works will have 'the unity of a symphonic movement . . . that consists in a tissue of root themes pervading all the drama, themes which contrast, complete, divorce, reshape and intertwine with one another as in a symphonic movement'. It is no accident that whereas Wagner's earlier operas had been composed in the hurly-burly of a tempestuous professional life, *Lohengrin* was the result of long meditation; he wrote it (appropriately enough) in exile, after he had been hounded out of Germany for his political activities. Nor is it an accident that with *Lohengrin* Wagner discovered the first consummate form of the myth round which his life's work centred. The descent of the Grail and the ascent to Heaven in the miraculous opening may be said to symbolize the aspiration to godhead which became the essence of Wagner's life and of nineteenth-century romanticism (Ex. 69). Perhaps it is not altogether an accident either that this

Ex. 69. Wagner: *Lohengrin* (Prelude to Act I)

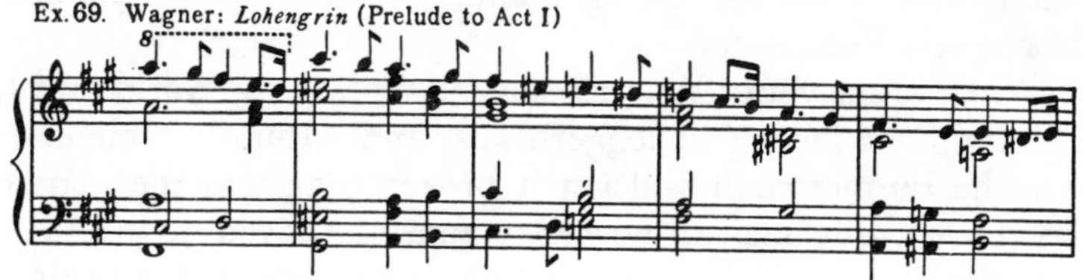

passage should be Wagner's first transcendental moment of orchestral virtuosity. The aria-like passages, pilgrims' choruses, and other 'operatic' survivals in *Lohengrin* are often very impressive, but this orchestral prelude is more than that: it is a new sound, which tells us already that Wagner's dream will be realized not on the stage, but in the orchestra pit.

Wagner was aware that *Lohengrin* marked at once the end of a phase of his career and the beginning of something new. The precise nature of this new art was not yet revealed to him, however. After the completion of *Lohengrin*, awaiting the revelation, he wrote no music for six years. During this period, he began to plan the vast undertaking of *The Ring of the Nibelung*; and attempted to explain his attitude to art, man, Nature, and God in pamphlets that grew into tracts, tracts that grew into books, books that were swollen into elephantine tomes. It is doubtful if all the great composers of history together have written as many self-justificatory words as Wagner. We may regret that he wasted so many years writing so much nonsense. Yet the nonsense, being a pseudo-rationalization of his most irrational emotional life, was necessary to him, if not to us. Before he could create his masterpieces he had to believe in himself to the exclusion of all other positives, including the eighteenth-century values of Reason, Truth, and Nature. It was unreasonable to suppose that his own emotional life was 'the *only* modern tragedy'. It was untrue that his 'sacrifice' (like Christ's!) could provide the theme for a ritualistic union of music, poetry, and visual spectacle precisely analogous to Greek drama. It was not only unnatural, but wellnigh lunatic, to believe that because Wagner suffered from digestive troubles as a result of sensuous indulgence, the 'nobler nations' of Europe could be induced to adopt vegetarianism as a philosophic creed; and might even be willing to consider mass-migration to warmer parts of the world, where meat-eating would be less of a temptation! Yet even the lunacy is sublime. Compared with Wagner's egomania, Beethoven seems a model of respectable sobriety.

When in his youth Wagner said, "We two, the world and I, are stubborn fellows at loggerheads, and naturally whichever has the thinner skull will get it broken", he was the heir to Beethoven. But one can never imagine Beethoven saying, with the late Wagner: "I'm not made like other people. I have finer nerves. I must have brilliance and beauty and light. The world owes me what I need. I can't live on a miserable organist's post, like your master, Bach. . . . Mine is a highly susceptible, intense, voracious sensuality which must somehow or other be flattered if my mind is to accomplish the agonizing labour of calling a non-existent world into being." Wagner meant this quite literally. The world owed him what he needed because he was the world's future. It was only proper that men should give him their money and women their love (and preferably their money too) in order that Germany and Europe could fulfil their destiny. The main function of society was to help him to realize his dream. The one-time revolutionary ended by stating not only that art was a dream-image, lifting us above actuality: but that his dream was the only true reality. It is Wagner's stupendous achievement that he brought it off; the myth became fact, even if only through the agency of a young, mad king.

In *The Ring* Wagner based his poems on German folk-myth, but his identification of himself with the German race soon becomes explicit. Siegfried is Wagner as the child of Nature and the instinctive artist; the Ring itself symbolizes the prostitution of Art to Gold, or commerce. *The Ring* is thus a gigantically expanded version of the Lohengrin story; and the tendency (initiated in the earlier opera) to conceive the characters as symbols of moral and metaphysical qualities is developed to its furthest extreme. Wagner now makes no attempt to imitate human behaviour. The autobiographical element in his earlier themes is frankly accepted, so that the characters become projections of different aspects of his own mind: thus Siegfried, symbol of the instinctive life and Strength-through-Joy, is balanced by Wotan, who represents the complementary quality of sacrifice and renunciation. The other supreme opera composers—Monteverdi, Mozart, Berlioz, and Verdi—deal with men and women who are other than themselves: with dramatic action experienced through their personalities. As we have seen, Mozart's opera is essentially conversation in music. Wagner's characters never converse. They merely explain themselves; and in the deepest sense, as we shall see, their explanations are unnecessary.

Now Wagner always maintained that his music-drama was the natural successor to Beethoven's Ninth Symphony. He even suggested that this supreme work of spiritual autobiography in music anticipated his own techniques, in that in the last movement Beethoven called upon words (and ought to have used the stage) to 'illustrate' his meaning. We may think that it would be truer to say that Beethoven employed words for a fundamentally musical reason, in that the whole symphony had been the creation of a vocal melody, and if voices are introduced they may as well have words to sing. Yet Wagner's account makes sense in the light of his own experience, which was all he was interested in. For him, as for Beethoven, drama was essentially subjective, and inherent in the working out of the motives. These motives are symphonic ideas which undergo musical permutations which are mirrored in the permutations of the action: *because* the musical technique is, like Beethoven's, inherently dramatic, it must imply dramatic presentation. The literary text which the singers pronounce and the visual action which happens on the stage are thus merely one among many possible illustrations of the subjective myth which evolves in the orchestra. This is why it is possible, if undesirable, to perform extracts from Wagner's mature operas with the voice parts left out. We lose one strand of the complex symphonic texture, though often the least significant one. We lose the verbal 'illustration' of what is happening, but that may even be an asset, since what the voices say is often philosophically banal. We do not lose the rich imaginative life which is the growth of the music; and this—though Wagner was wrong in thinking that his emotional life was an explanation of the universe—is very far from being banal.

Wagner's peculiar approach to the voice, however, lands him in a fundamental inconsistency. If the voice parts are there to explain what is happening, in a style based on declamation, one would expect them to move at a pace not much slower than speech. But symphonic drama, which is the core of Wagner's music, proceeds at a pace immeasurably slower than verbal language. As a result, the singers have either to stand about doing nothing for long periods, or to repeat their phrases in a manner dramatically no less absurd than the lyrical repetitions of the conventional opera Wagner despised, or to stretch out their non-lyrical phrases into inordinately long note-values. Wagner—whose dramatic sense was so much weaker than his musical—was probably not conscious of this difficulty; and his genius sometimes managed to turn it to advantage, since all three compromises (especially the last) imbue his creatures with a certain ponderous grandeur. Their superhuman stature is thus emphasized; they remain true to Wagner's imaginative world, if not to life.

There was another and deeper problem that Wagner had to face in constructing a subjective symphony on so vast a scale: this was what he himself called 'the beautiful and convincing necessity of transition'. He could have no more set arias and recitatives; nor could he allow the stage business to prop up the musical structure, since the dramatic action illustrated the music, rather than the other way round. In fact, although he has many more themes or thematic motives than Beethoven employs in a symphony, they behave in broadly the same way. In a tonal drama planned on so gargantuan a scale, Wagner has to be content to forgo—to a more extreme degree than Beethoven—the melody of self-contained song. Melody becomes 'unending *melos*'; and Wagner used the Greek term because the word 'melody' might, to contemporary minds, have suggested Rossini. But themes built on arpeggio formations still imply stability and diatonicism; more chromatic step-wise figurations still imply instability and a sundering of tonality. The alternations between consonance and dissonance, between simple and complex modulations, extend but do not contradict established precedents. An incident that may seem to be a clumsy dramatic device—for instance, Siegfried's narration of his early life in *Götterdämmerung*—may in fact be a musical recapitulation of gigantic proportions; and in *Tristan*—Wagner's most extreme departure from tradition—the *Liebestod* begins as a recapitulation of the Love duet in Act II. Indeed, it has been demonstrated that Wagner's disposition of material and of tonal relationships was deliberately analogous to certain medieval poetical forms known as the *Bar* and *Stollen*: and is thus architecturally, if not dramatically, more formalized than the classical symphony.

One would not expect a work on so vast a scale as *The Ring*, created over a period of more than twenty years, to be consistent in style throughout; Wagner's ability to create at least an illusion of consistency is testimony to his tenacity of purpose. The first two parts of *The Ring* are certainly closer both to the Beethovenian symphony and to orthodox operatic tradition than the two later parts. In *Die Walküre*, the voice parts are still of equal importance with the orchestra, and even some of the stage business—for instance, Brunnhilde's dive into the lake of fire—adapts conventional operatic properties to Wagner's 'metaphysical' purposes. But *Götterdämmerung* and the latter part of *Siegfried* are quintessentially Wagnerian: the change can be understood in the light of the fact that, half-way through *Siegfried*, Wagner turned aside to create *Tristan und Isolde*. We have seen that *The Ring* is in a general and indirect sense spiritual autobiography projected on to a stage. *Tristan* is quite explicitly autobiography, for it is a dramatization of the situation existing at the time between Wagner and Otto and

Mathilde Wesendonck. Wagner was driven to create it by the overwhelming intensity of his experience; and the force of his egoism now begins to destroy most of the vestiges of tradition which survived in his earlier work.

To concentrate thus directly upon himself, without symbolical or metaphysical apparatus, was for Wagner an immense advantage. The love story is legendary, but both simple and—as Wagner was reliving it—true. The text he produces may be inferior poetry, but is admirably designed as a complement to the music. Its short lines and flexible rhythms allow Wagner the freedom he needs; and his passion is so fierce that he no longer feels any diffidence about allowing the music to speak for itself. The voice parts may be dispensable (the *Liebestod* is often performed without them); but they, in common with every thematic strand in the score, certainly sing. The music glows with desire, and neither we nor Wagner care that there is little external action—or at least little that can decently be represented on a stage. We are only relieved at the absence of any attempt to symbolize the inner drama by stage dragons: which anyone with a modicum of humour, let alone theatrical sense, would have avoided like the plague.

In the music of *Tristan*, the extreme chromaticism of the lines and harmony, the continuity of the rhythms, the enharmony of the modulations are themselves a freeing of the individual spirit. The succession of harmonic tensions, reinforced by the physical impact of the orchestra, becomes an emotional orgy; and almost all overt trace of the structural principles which had characterized the classical sonata up to Beethoven's last works has disappeared. The effect of this subjective approach on the eighteenth-century key system is the same as that of the chromatic madrigal of the early years of the seventeenth century on the modal techniques of the previous period.* *Tristan* bears about the same relationship to a classical symphony as a madrigal of Gesualdo [1560–1615] bears to a motet of Palestrina. We may note that Gesualdo too was a romantic individualist and exhibitionist: though since he lived in a strong religious tradition, his egoism seemed to his contemporaries a melancholic aberration, rather than a world-shaking force. If we think of him alongside Hamlet, we shall see that the revolution he represents was in fact no less crucial than Wagner's.

* See Part II.

XXXV A scene from Act I of Wagner's *Flying Dutchman*, performed at Covent Garden, July 16th, 1877.

XXXVI ‘Un Concert à Mitraille’—a caricature of Berlioz by Grandville (1846).

Although Wagner in his individualism departs far from classical tradition, this does not mean that *Tristan* has not its own principle of order. But normally Wagner no longer thinks of himself in Beethovenian terms, as a man in conflict with a hostile world. His passions have become so intense that they are themselves the universe; everything outside himself is engulfed in the surge of sound. Isolde and Mark are Mathilde and Otto Wesendonck. They are also aspects of love-hate within Tristan-Wagner himself; so the whole of the vast symphonic texture is unified by the dominance of a single psyche. We can see this in the musical unity which underlines the dramatic-symbolical unity of the leitmotives. The three 'Tristan' chords, built on overlapping fourths, with which the work opens, reappear in transmuted forms at every climacteric point in the opera. Ultimately they become the melodic basis of the *Liebestod* itself, and the harmonic basis of the final, consummatory resolution into B major (Ex. 70):

Now, the opening pages of the *Tristan* prelude, in which these chords occur, have been analysed in innumerable ways according to orthodox harmonic principles: the variety is itself evidence of the music's disintegration of traditional techniques. But what anyone can agree on is that the music's overwhelming intensity derives from the fact that Wagner concentrates on the dissonant harmony at the expense of its resolution; it is always the dissonant chord that falls on the strong beat. Moreover, the effect of the passage as a whole depends on the way in which the brief, upward-yearning, chromatically falling phrase, underlined by its dissonance, is repeated several times at progressively rising intervals. This mounting excitement leads one to expect a big climax when the discord will finally be resolved on to the tonic. Instead, we get an unexpected chord (the submediant) (Ex. 71):

Ex. 71. Wagner: *Tristan and Isolde* Prelude to Act I

So we have a building up of harmonic tension, which is partially frustrated: and a tendency towards rhythmic fluidity, which is counteracted by the continuous repetition of the phrases in sequence. Wagner strains both to resolve harmonic stress and to dissolve Beethoven's metrical obsession with Time; and neither resolution nor dissolution is, in life, achieved.

Just some such combination of passionate yearning with frustration is the essential feature of Wagner's adaptation ol the Tristan story; and between this and his own psychologicas make-up—and as we have seen the actual events of his life—there is a more than usually direct connexion. Wagner haf expressed at once the ultimate triumph, and the fallacy, of humanism. He believes only in himself; his own feelings are the universe. That being so, his feelings can lead to nothing but their extinction. A yearning so fierce can be appeased only in its cessation: so the fulfilment of love is death.

This is why in Wagner's mature work passion and renunciation are inseparable; one might even say that for him renunciation is as much a sensuous experience as eroticism. In his last opera, *Parsifal*, he returns to the Grail legend which had obsessed him in his youth, and sees in it an allegory of his own quest for fulfilment. Though written several years later, it is *Tristan's* imaginative complement; nor is this at all odd, since the Grail myth, with its symbols of Sword and Chalice, is as much sexual as mystical. Nietzsche, who had welcomed the younger Wagner as a Dionysiac superman who would regenerate a decaying world, held that *Parsifal* was a denial of the hero's birthright: that its religiosity was both spurious and offensive from a man who had insisted, throughout his life, on the satisfaction of every desire. Yet if Wagner had not lived in and for his senses, renunciation would have been less important. He did not advocate renunciation in a momentary disgust with sensuality, but simply because the man who lives for his senses has to submit to the irremediable renunciation of death. *Parsifal* is certainly not mystical in Beethoven's sense; but for all its metaphysical mystifications it is as profoundly felt an experience as *Tristan*. Indeed, it is the same experience seen, as it were, mirror-wise. Of all Wagner's works it is closest to *Tristan* in technique.

Both operas are incantatory, hypnotic; both effect a curious inversion of the ritualistic or religious approach to music. In a Palestrina mass the personal element—the expressive harmony—grows out of the singing together of a number of vocal lines that are in themselves 'religiously' impersonal, devoid of harmonic stress. Wagner, in *Tristan* and *Parsifal*, starts from the tensions of harmony, which are the passions of his nerves and senses, and then 'spreads out' the chords into a complex of linear motives which he called a new polyphony. The 'religion' which this polyphony celebrates is a fanatical belief not in God, nor in Civilization, but in Richard Wagner. In the *Liebestod* of *Tristan und Isolde* this new harmonically derived polyphony attains an orgiastic ecstasy; in the melting enharmony of interlacing lines in the prelude to Act III of *Parsifal*, it attains a mysterious sweetness (Ex. 72). At bottom, these

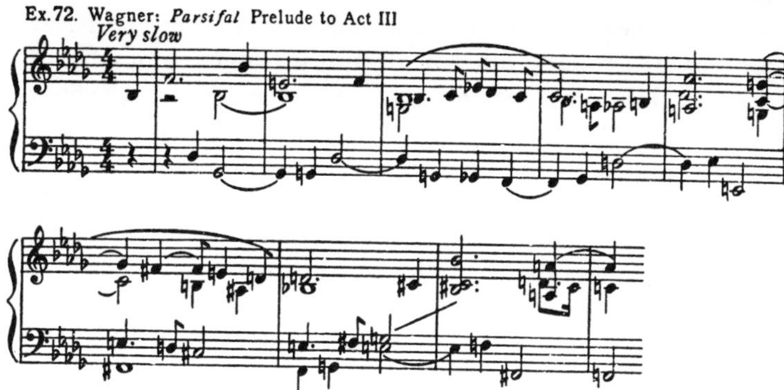

Ex.72. Wagner: *Parsifal* Prelude to Act III

experiences are identical. Tristan and Isolde find that the excruciating agony of their passion can lead only to oblivion;

Parsifal, the pure fool, redeemed in this music by the carnality of Kundry's kiss, finds that renunciation in death leads to an ecstasy synonymous with love.

Wagner's life's work thus culminates in a deification of the ego which is also an admission of the ego's insufficiency. Opera becomes a substitute for religion: for the deification of the ego could hardly go further than the Wagner cult at Bayreuth, where a temple is built for the performance of the Artist's creations—instead of the music being composed to fulfil the needs of the temple, as was Palestrina's to serve God, or Handel's to serve the State. Wagner himself said that Bayreuth was the fulfilment of the destiny which he had planned for himself and humanity. And the deepest if most obvious truth, as well as the deepest irony, is that that destiny was death.

Tristan is consistently chromatic in texture. *Parsifal* is sometimes chromatic, at other times diatonic and—especially in the Grail music—even modal. Yet even when the component lines are diatonic or vocal in contour, the enharmony suggests a sensuous dissolution. The glowing orchestral polyphony is still harmonically conceived; its voluptuousness is retrospectively savoured, if not orgiastically enjoyed. None the less, there are passages in *Parsifal* which have more in common with Bach than anything in the music of such conscious Bach-addicts as Brahms and Mendelssohn. This helps us to understand why Wagner should have been able to create, alongside *Parsifal*, another opera which seems to be the polar opposite not only of *Parsifal*, but of the development of Wagner's work as a whole.

Wagner began to sketch the poem of *The Mastersingers* as early as 1845, intending it to be a comic complement to *Lohengrin.* He composed the music between 1861 and 1867, two years after he had finished *Tristan. The Mastersingers* is the only one of Wagner's mature operas to deal with real people in action. It thus bears some relation to the traditional notion of opera, and its technique manifests in some ways a return to traditional methods. It employs Wagner's symphonic leit-motive technique in its most developed form; but it also finds room for (dramatically justified) set pieces like the *Preislied*, and uses chromaticism mainly as an intensification of a clearly defined diatonicism. Moreover, the harmonic-polyphonic texture of Wagner's late work assumes a form more closely related to traditional counterpoint; chorale, fugue, passacaglia and other Bachian techniques are obviously appropriate to the subject and setting.

Yet this apparently objective presentation of a sturdy world far removed from the subjective orgy of *Tristan* or the confessional intimacy of *Parsifal* is not as remote from the main tenor of Wagner's work as it seems. For Wagner himself said that while the story unfolds before the audience in something that looks like medieval Nuremberg, it really takes place in the minds of Walther and Sachs: and Walther is the Artist-Hero or Wagner-Siegfried, while Sachs is Wagner-Wotan, the man who loves but renounces a woman (significantly called Eve). We can see from the beautiful monologues of Sachs, in which Wagner adopts a mellower form of Tristan's chromaticism, that *The Mastersingers* too is a part of Wagner's religion of art. "All poetry", says Sachs, "is but the truth of dreams made manifest."

Though Wagner called *The Mastersingers* a comedy, it has become, as an expression of the German Soul, a national institution, almost a rite. It bears more resemblance to external reality than the dream-world of Wagner's subconscious which, in the orgiastic ritual of *Tristan* or the incantatory ritual of *Parsifal*, takes the place of God and Civilization. But it may be that this Nuremberg existed in fact no more than the visionary Vienna which haunted the imagination of the dying Schubert. Those who are repelled by Wagner's egomania are apt to consider *The Mastersingers* a uniquely 'healthy' and therefore acceptable work. Those who find *Tristan* and *Parsifal* among the most profoundly (as well as violently) moving experiences in art, are apt to dismiss the healthiness of *The Mastersingers* as synthetic. The distinction may well be invalid: as dubiously defined as are most boundaries between the conscious and the subconscious mind.

Whatever our opinion as to the merits of *Tristan* and *Parsifal* on the one hand and *The Mastersingers* on the other, it is indisputable that the two former music-dramas sum up his contribution to European history. One thinks of him as a historical, rather than as a merely musical force: for with these two operas Europe reaches the end of a cycle that began with the Renaissance. So although no composer has ever had a more powerful influence on the music that immediately followed him, Wagner was wrong in thinking that he had created the art-form of the future. It was because his music was an end that

Schoenberg, who inherited his chromaticism, had to start afresh. His only direct successors are consistently elegiac. From this point of view we shall see that the music of Delius is both technically and philosophically an epilogue to Wagner's peroration.

3

BERLIOZ

If Berlioz [1803–1869] is still a problematical composer, he is so largely for the simple reason that he was French. He lived and worked at a time when the dominant tradition in Europe was German; and his music has been misunderstood because it has been judged by irrelevantly Teutonic criteria. It is true that even in his lifetime he was appreciated in Germany rather than in his own country; but that was because the general level of musical cultivation in France was so low. The Germans, admiring his orchestral virtuosity, could respect him for the wrong reasons: which was at least preferable to not respecting him at all. A hundred years later, we can begin to see Berlioz in perspective; and the more we do so, the clearer it becomes that he has nothing in common with German romanticism, while belonging in a profound sense to the culture of France.

We have noted that in France the revolution of sonata style was less obtrusive than in Germany: and that the conventions of French music remained basically operatic. This was partly because the aristocratic order had been, in France, so deeply entrenched; partly, perhaps, because the French, having accomplished their revolution in fact, had less need to resolve their frustrations in their art. In any case, Berlioz was born in 1893, early enough to inherit the artistic traditions of a long-established order. In Germany, most of the great artists of the Enlightenment and of romanticism came from the lower middle class, or even from the peasantry. In France, they tended still to belong to the ruling class, and to preserve aristocratic pretensions to honour and riches, as a just reward for their talents' service to the nation. Such aspirations were, in a revolutionary era, opposed to the materialistic spirit of a commercial society; and so—in the absence of an aristocracy—the artists tended to support the common people against the bourgeoisie. The people were to be the new aristocrats, who ran society in the interests of humanity and art, not for private aggrandizement. Thus the artists were *grands seigneurs* by instinct, members of the bourgeoisie by circumstance, and by sympathy something that we would call Tory Democrats.

Like the men of 1830, Berlioz intended to revolutionize; but to do so in the interests of order. His first opera, *Benvenuto Cellini*, has for theme the Artist as Hero. As a social being, the artist-hero is the opponent of all that is philistine and base. Yet while as a social being he must destroy, as an artist he must, by the nature of his calling, order and create. If he is a bandit, his banditry is purposeful. Wagner's *Tannhäuser* and *Lohengrin* had the same theme, and we saw that his banditry was purposeful in the ultimate sense that the strength of his sensations annihilated everything outside himself. But Berlioz wished to renovate a decaying world both in his own interests and in those of civilization. Like Beethoven, he had a social conscience. So we find in his music a balance between his individualism and his respect for tradition. The inward-turning aspects of his art are complemented by outward-turning elements; he creates music which expresses his inner life, and also music designed to fulfil a ceremonial and social purpose. And the one kind of music is conditioned by the other. His respect for tradition tends to objectify the expression of his inner life; his romantic individualism tends to give subtlety to his music of social purpose. This is what one might expect; for the New World depends on the strength and sensitivity of the individual spirits who live in it.

In his youth, Berlioz had two musical idols: Beethoven and Gluck. "I took over where Beethoven left off," he once said, using words similar to those frequently uttered by Wagner. In some ways, Berlioz and Wagner revered Beethoven for basically the same reason: because he embodied drama entirely in musical terms, recreating form in the interests of autobiographical expression. The aristocratic opera house was to be reborn in the democratic concert-hall; drama was to be implicit in the instrument which represented the triumph of nineteenth-century industrialism—the symphony orchestra. In his dramatic symphonies, Berlioz wished to make the drama inherent in the musical form, as it is in Beethoven's Ninth. Even when he composed for the theatre, he tried to preserve the music formally independent of, if related to, the literary and visual elements. But though Berlioz followed Beethoven thus far, he did not emulate Wagner in seeking to equate music—and life and death—with his own sensations. The fundamental difference in his approach is suggested by the manner in which he associated Beethoven with Gluck, whom Wagner dismissed as a survival of a moribund tradition.

From one point of view, Gluck might be said to have anticipated Beethoven in that he 'dramatized with the orchestra', crystallizing a dramatic situation in instrumental terms. But from another and perhaps more radical point of view, he was the heir to the vocal and operatic tradition that went back to Lully and Rameau as much as to the Italians. The line is unbroken from Lully to Rameau, from Rameau to Gluck, from Gluck to Spontini, Cherubini, Méhul, and Lesueur: and from these men to Berlioz. It is improbable that Berlioz had any intimate knowledge of Lully's operas, and his acquaintance with Rameau's scores was less than the evidence of his own later music would lead one to expect. But—apart from his fanatical devotion to Gluck—he knew the music of Cherubini [1760-1842] well; and discovered in his church music as much as in his classical operas such as the superb *Medeae*, a style which appealed to his deepest instincts. Its vocal lyricism and declamation were as gravely proportioned, and as passionate, as French heroic tragedy; its command of tonality was spacious and grand, yet instinct with a Beethovenian fire. In Spontini [1774-1851] and Méhul [1763–1817] he found a similar compromise, especially in their explicitly revolutionary operas which were the 'modern' complement to classical heroism. Here, perhaps, something of Cherubini's nobility was sacrificed in favour of a more melodramatic instrumental vehemence; in Lesueur [1760–1837], on the other hand, Berlioz found less power, but a more rarefied sensuousness, partly derived from the composer's fondness for modal melody and for exotic orchestration.

For a time Berlioz was a pupil of Lesueur at the Conservatoire. We know that he greatly admired his teacher's music. None the less, Lesueur's interest in what was then an unusual kind of melody and scoring merely confirmed Berlioz in an innate habit of mind. Paradoxically, his vehemently expressed hatred of the past—except for a few of his immediate predecessors—was an aspect of his traditionalism. He had none of the romantic reverence for Antiquity because he was conscious of being, not an imitator of, but a natural successor to, the great masters of the French tradition. We can approach Berlioz's music with understanding only when we see that he is not, as is often supposed, a completely isolated figure. His Beethovenian forcefulness is modified by his relation to the French operatic tradition; complementarily, his formal inventions all derive from the melodic rather than harmonic nature of that tradition—and of his own genius.

We can already observe this in one of Berlioz's earliest representative works, the *Symphonie Fantastique*, which was first performed in 1830—three years after the death of Beethoven. Berlioz appended to this work a literary programme purporting to describe the relationship of the music to his own (or the Artist's) biography. In so doing he was conforming to fashion and perhaps flattering his literary ability; but nothing could be further than this music from the subjectivism of Wagner. Though the musical structure may differ from that of a classical symphony, it is no less cohesive. In harmony and in key-relationships it is less advanced than Beethoven; its originality consists in the way in which a long-breathed melodic line, harking back to Gluck and classical opera, is subjected to Beethoven's technique of thematic generation and transformation. Berlioz himself pointed out that the *idée fixe* functioned on two levels: the programmatic motive itself, which recurrently obsesses the Artist's imagination: and the gradual, musical metamorphoses of the motive which are his spiritual history.

The theme of the first Allegro runs to forty odd bars (Ex. 73):

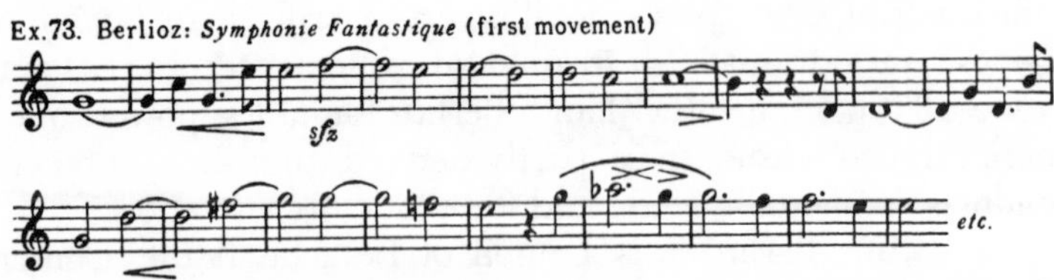

The initial arpeggiated phrase, with its rising sixth, suggests a Beethovenian challenge; but it is asymmetrically extended in declamatory style, always aspiring upwards but straining back to the F which droops to E natural. This aspiring phrase is balanced by a clause falling through a seventh, followed by the original sixth inverted, with a chromatic intrusion creating a change to a triplet rhythm. The cadence finally returns to the

F and E: the musical embodiment of the 'fixation' that will not allow the flexible phrases to soar. In the subsidiary themes and the development Berlioz's dramatic climaxes are attained by large-scale thematic evolution of this type, rather than by tonal contrast. In the scherzo-valse melody seems to be breaking loose from its fixation in the compulsive grace of dance movement. In the adagio *Scène aux Champs* melody learns to accept its limitations (even at the original pitch but in a different key); and from acceptance wins a luminous serenity: a Claude-like classical landscape only remotely disturbed by premonitions of storm. With the *Marche au Supplice*, however, the F–E fixation is back in a remorselessly frustrating form, reinforced by the implacably rigid rhythm; and in the last movement the complete shape of the first-movement allegro theme is parodied into a witches' sabbath; even the elaborations of the Dies Irae motive become a contrapuntal development of the work's melodic seed. Far from being romantic rhapsodizing held together only by an outmoded literary commentary, the *Symphonie Fantastique* is one of the most tautly disciplined works in early nineteenth-century music. This is only what we might expect from our knowledge of Berlioz as a man. For all the immense mane of red hair, the transports of rage, and the *grands amours*, Berlioz was, even as a young man, remarkable for an intellectual acumen rare among musicians. In this, again, he was characteristically French. He chased his beautiful Countess around Europe, equipped with phials of poison for use if she refused to love him. But he did not forget to pack the stomach-pump.

From this ostensibly autobiographical, yet fundamentally classical work of Berlioz's youth, let us turn to another earlyish work, this time composed for a ceremonial occasion. In the *Symphonie Fantastique* Berlioz was thinking of himself, but objectified his feeling in a stringently linear structure. The *Symphonie Funèbre et Triomphale* was composed in 1840, to be performed by massed military bands in the Place de la Bastille, in memory of those who lost their lives in the July Revolution of 1830. Berlioz envisaged himself conducting his vast forces with a drawn sword, and then collapsing in tears over the kettledrums. The music is not intended to be personal expression, but a vision of Napoleonic grandeur, not perhaps as it was, but as it might be. The military motive that dominates early nineteenth-century music here becomes sublimely idealistic; martial discipline becomes synonymous with the suppression of the inflated ego.

Yet although march rhythms pervade this music far more than in the restless, fluid rhythms of the allegro of the *Symphonie Fantastique*, one need look no further than the magnificent theme of the first movement to see that martial glory is recreated in the light of Berlioz's sensitivity (Ex. 74):

Ex. 74. Berlioz: *Symphonie Funèbre et Triomphale* (first movement)

The march rhythm does not prevent the melody from soaring in proud arches which recall the declamatory phrases of classical opera rather than the symphonic themes of the Viennese tradition; and the asymmetry of the clauses is complemented by a tonal precariousness created by chromatic intrusions in the melody, and by the dialogue between the melody and the cantabile bass. Berlioz's chromaticism, unlike Wagner's, is almost always melodic, not harmonic; it extends, rather than disrupts, the span of the theme. Even the sequences which sometimes appear in his melodies are seldom strictly reflected in the harmony. Wagner's grandeur is the apotheosis of the personal. Berlioz thinks melodically in vast phrases that acquire a more than personal grandeur. This is as true of Berlioz's ostensibly miniature works as of his most monumental: consider the longdrawn melodies of the songs *Le Spectre de la Rose*, *L'Absence*, and *Sur les Lagunes*.

Berlioz's approach to the *Symphonie Fantastique* and to the *Symphonie Funèbre* is thus, though the works seem to be diametrically opposed, basically the same. In all his mature music it is impossible to separate the inward- from the outward-tending elements. His two 'dramatic symphonies', *Roméo et Juliette* (1838) and *Harold en Italie* (1834), objectify his own experience in persons and situations outside himself. In *Roméo* he presents Shakespeare's drama in instrumental microcosm. Especially in the love scene, the soloistically treated instruments take the place of operatic voices; and the structure of the work as a whole is a curious, not entirely convincing compromise between symphonic and operatic techniques. In *Harold en Italie* Berlioz objectifies symphonic drama by writing a *concertante* part for solo viola which operatically represents himself, as symbol of the Byronic legend. Except in the last movement, the lyrical germination of the viola's song is the impetus behind the growth of the music. Even in the last movement, which is closest to orthodox sonata style, the bandit's ferocity, like Berlioz's own, is ordered and purposeful, as well as an electrically exciting noise (consider the use of the screaming, trill-like figure on the violins).

In general, however, Berlioz is least successful when he tries to emulate the sonata principle, most convincing when he allows his lyrical impulse to generate form. For all his reverence for Beethoven, his melodies are never motivic; and he was correct in maintaining that his music was misunderstood because nineteenth-century musicians had lost the feeling for sustained lyrical line:

"Generally speaking, my style is very bold, but it has not the slightest tendency to subvert any of the constituent elements of art. On the contrary, it is my endeavour to add to their number. I have never dreamt of making music 'without melody', as so many in France are stupid enough to say. Such a school now exists in Germany, and I hold it in detestation. It is easy to see that, without confining myself to a short air for the theme of a piece, as the great masters often do, I have always taken care that my compositions shall be rich in melody. The value of the melodies, their distinction, novelty and charm, may of course be disputed. It is not for me to estimate them; but to deny their existence is absurd and unfair. But as they are often on a large scale, an immature or unappreciative mind cannot properly distinguish their forms; or they may be joined to other secondary themes which may be invisible to that class of mind; and lastly, such melodies are so unlike the little absurdities to which the term is applied by the lower stratum of the musical world that it finds it impossible to give the same name to both."

It is certainly difficult to think of any later music in the nineteenth century which can approach the love scene from *Roméo* in lyrical sensitivity. Berlioz's expressiveness, like Bach's, is always in the theme; and he disapproved of Wagner's attempt to 'dethrone music and to reduce it to expressive accents'. While he may have been wrong about Wagner himself, Berlioz's instinct was right: in the hands of lesser men Wagner's leitmotivic technique could and did become a literary and philosophical substitute for musical coherence.

Since melody—and a rhythm that is melodically rather than metrically conceived—is the essence of Berlioz's music, we shall not be surprised to find that his approach to harmony is un-Wagnerian. It is hardly extravagant to say that his basic harmonic material is closer to Gluck than to Wagner: and that what appear to be oddities and crudities in his harmony, when considered in vocal score, are often the result of his thinking directly in orchestral terms—instead of, like most romantic composers, at the piano. When his harmony is more complex, the complexity is never a matter of Wagnerian 'added' notes or appoggiaturas; it is rather the consequence of the rhythmic flexibility and tonal ambiguity of the melodies themselves. Sometimes there is a conflict between classical harmonic convention and the direction in which the lines want to move: so that the result is odd rather than satisfying. But whenever Berlioz's imagination is working at pressure, the individuality of his melody creates the harmony: for instance, in the wonderful Sanctus of the *Requiem* a single chromatic alteration in the tenor solo transforms the radiant D flat melody into the remoteness of D major; and the music finds its way home by way of another enharmonic change and a dissolving sequence of neutral diminished sevenths (Ex. 75):

The mysterious harmonic transitions created by chromatic alteration in melody and bass in the first movement of the *Symphonie Funèbre* are another example (see p. 764). Often, again, the modal features in Berlioz's melodies leave their imprint on his harmony: consider the phrygian cadence—with flattened leading note and flattened second—at the end of the Kyrie of the *Requiem*, or Marguerite's famous *Romance*, which is one of the characteristically Berliozian moments in the unequal *Damnation de Faust*.*

The freedom of Berlioz's part-writing is the fundamental reason for the originality of his harmony. The succession of apparently unrelated triads at the opening of the Agnus Dei in the *Requiem* is an harmonic effect produced by melodic

* It is significant that the romantic interpretation of the Faust legend made little appeal to Berlioz. His *Faust* contains better music than Schumann's, but is decidedly less Goethean in spirit.

means—as are most of the comparable passages in sixteenth-century music. This reference to the sixteenth century reminds us that, since Berlioz is essentially a melodist, he is also a polyphonic rather than homophonic composer. It is true that he is unconvincing when he attempts to write an orthodox fugue in the eighteenth-century tradition; but the opening of *Harold en Italie*, no less than the more recognizably polyphonic sections of the *Requiem* and *Te Deum*, is evidence that Berlioz is a master of free fugato. The Quaerens Me of the *Requiem* achieves a tender radiance almost suggestive of the vocal texture of sixteenth-century polyphony, while the fugato passage in *Harold en Italie* is chromatically taut and sinuous. In neither is the harmony 'correct' according to eighteenth-century convention; in both it is correct in so far as it is inevitable, given the nature and distinction of the component themes.

The basically polyphonic nature of Berlioz's music finds expression in the fact that he is mainly a composer for orchestra, or for voices with orchestra. Just as the root of his structures is melodic generation rather than tonal architecture, so he thought polyphonically in the orchestra, rather than harmonically at the piano: an instrument which, almost alone among nineteenth-century composers, he could not play. For all his ill-deserved reputation as a noisy composer, Berlioz's style of orchestration is a chamber-music technique. His scoring is thin, limpid, translucent, compared with Wagner's rich blurring of timbres. Again, the polyphonic texture of his scores implies objectification, as against Wagner's engulfing surge of sound. Wagner drowns you in sensation; Berlioz involves you in an imaginative act. This becomes especially noticeable in Berlioz's last works, where for the first time his music betrays some kinship with Mozart's. Until the last decade of life, Mozart had meant little to him compared with Gluck. But in his second opera, *Béatrice et Bénédict* (based on Shakespeare's *Much Ado*), the ensemble number becomes much more important than in *Benvenuto Cellini*, compared nearly thirty years earlier; and the highly personal idiom acquires an almost Mozartian lyrical lucidity. Like Mozart, too, the opera has a Mediterranean warmth in its acceptance of human frailty: and an implicit melancholy, because real life so seldom attains this union of creative understanding with critical wit.

In this connexion we may recall a most significant remark

which Berlioz made when speaking of his difficulties in composing *Les Troyens*: "Another hurdle in my path," he said, "is that the feeling to be evoked moves me too much. . . . This is bad. *One must try to do coolly the things that are most fiery.*" At the opposite pole to Wagner, he seeks always to externalize his feeling. This is why his supreme achievements were in opera and in his own kind of church music: for opera normally involves other people in action, and church music involves the absorption of the ego into something greater than itself. Berlioz displayed considerable literary skill in writing his own libretti, and it is interesting that after *Benvenuto Cellini* he chose themes which bore no relation to his immediate personal problems. His great Virgilian opera *Les Troyens*, finished in 1864, is the culmination of his career. It is an idealized vision of a new heroic civilization: or rather of the old world, and the old technique born anew. This was no puerile revolutionary utopia. Dido is a heroic figure, but also a woman, with human passions and frailties. In Berlioz's imaginary aristocracy, people, like Dido, would still love, suffer, and die, as they have always done; but human life would acquire once more the dignity and sanctity of the heroic age.

Nothing could be more remote from Wagner's sublime egomania than this nobly lyrical music, which preserves even the externalities of the French classical opera in its pastoral interludes, heroic marches, choruses, and danced pantomimes. The relationship between Berlioz's aria and in particular his accompanied arioso and that of Rameau, is here as intimate as it is subtle. Since Berlioz did not betray much conscious enthusiasm for Rameau's operas, one can only assume that this spiritual and technical kinship was intuitive. Certainly it does not affect the profound originality of Berlioz's music. The Royal Hunt and Storm is a traditional ballet-pantomime in classical style, with Gluck's dramatic intensity and Rameau's lyrical range; but only Berlioz could have created that strange opening theme—gravely proportioned, yet at the same time acridly melancholy in its chromaticism. Similarly, in Cassandra's tremendous aria at the end of Act I of *La Prise de Troye* or the septet in *Les Troyens à Carthage*, the grandeur comes from the splendour of Berlioz's reborn civilization: the melancholy from his growing sense of disparity between the ideal and the real.

Berlioz's operas, being imitations of human beings in action, imply belief in something outside himself, and an awareness of human potentialities. But no more that Schubert or Wagner had he any specific religious faith; one might almost say that he found his bible in Shakespeare and Virgil, whose tragi-comic vitality justified life, while being reconcilable with intellectual scepticism. He could find an emotional identity with the heyday of Christian and of pagan humanism; while having nothing but contempt for those vulgarized nineteenth-century 'spirits' who had nothing better to do than to levitate tables. To the romantic sensibility, Beethoven's last works seemed to offer freedom from restrictions. Berlioz, with his linear approach to his art and his understanding of the technique of thematic transformation, was perhaps the only composer intuitively to appreciate their formal and spiritual logic. None the less, their mysticism could not be for him. He had to seek a world of spiritual aristocracy, projected into classical operatic mythology; and when he composed church music that too became an objectified vision of majesty. From this point of view we may note that the relationship between his 'liturgical' and operatic manners is exactly comparable with the relationship between the ecclesiastical and secular styles of Cherubini.

The earliest of Berlioz's three great liturgical works, if they can be so called, is the *Grande Messe des Morts* of 1837. Berlioz once said that if he were threatened with the destruction of all his works save one, he would crave exemption for this requiem. One can understand his choice, for no single work more powerfully fuses the personal and the ceremonial aspects of his genius. It embraces every facet of his complex sensibility, from the tenuous, vocal texture of the Quid Sum Miser or the luminous polyphony of the Quarens Me to the volcanic eruption of the Lachrymosa, with its operatically declamatory line and spasmodically surging rhythm: from the chromaticized modality of the Offertorium to the weird serenity of the Agnus Dei, with its grotesque orchestral interjections for three flutes and bass tuba. As a whole, the work is the supreme example of the apocalyptic side of Berlioz's imagination—not because it (very occasionally) employs four brass bands which Berlioz intended to be placed at each corner of the main orchestra and chorus: but because of the incandescence of the music, as much in the piteous, fragmentary desolation of the Quid Sum Miser as in the blaze of the Rex Tremendae. Though this is not religious music it has, like Berlioz's operas, the visionary gleam. Wagner's operas deal with the redemption (which means for him the fulfilment) of the self. Berlioz's requiem evokes a world redeemed; and the process is as terrible as it is beautiful, as impersonal as it is unique.

Berlioz's *Te Deum*, composed in 1849, complements the requiem. The latter transmutes intense personal feeling into impersonal ceremonial; the *Te Deum* recreates ritual ceremony into personal feeling. Even its moments of tragic terror (such as the Judex Crederis) have a classical monumentality that relate them to the splendour of *Les Troyens*. The Napoleonic legend becomes an ideal revocation of vanished glory: a vision, as opposed to Meyerbeer's delusions, of grandeur. *L'Enfance du Christ*, Berlioz's Christmas oratorio, written in 1854, achieves grandeur out of intimacy. The exquisitely strong vocal writing and linear scoring of *Le Repos de la Sainte Famille* hark back beyond Gluck and classical opera to the seventeenth-century cantata. The frequent modality of the themes (especially in the section dealing with Herod's dream) generates some of Berlioz's most piquant harmonic subtleties. He approaches the story not as a Catholic, nor as a Protestant, nor even as a Christian: but as a man whose heart warms to one of the great human myths, as it warms to Shakespeare or to Virgil. Thus it is again not religious music; and though it is often serene, it remains characteristically mysterious and, in such moments as the *Marche Nocturne*, even sinister. Its loveliness is a tribute to the strength as well as the sensitivity of Berlioz's humanistic imagination. He was justified when he reprimanded those who affected to see in *L'Enfance du Christ* a complete *volte-face* in his style:

"The prevailing characteristics of my music are passionate expression, intense ardour, rhythmical animation, and unexpected turns. When I say passionate expression I mean an expression determined on enforcing the inner meaning of its subject, even when that subject is the contrary of passion, and when the feeling to be expressed is gentle and tender, or even profoundly calm. . . . Many people imagined that (in *L'Enfance du Christ*) they could detect a radical change in my style and manner. This opinion is entirely without foundation. The subject naturally lent itself to a simple and gentle style of music, and for this reason alone was more in accordance with their taste and intelligence. Time has no doubt developed these qualities, but I should have written *L'Enfance du Christ* in the same style twenty years earlier."

Though *L'Enfance du Christ* is an oratorio, it is, like all Berlioz's large-scale works, classically operatic in approach. There can be little doubt that he would have been a full-time opera composer had conditions in France made that possible. Even in Germany, only Wagner's colossal force of personality enabled him to realize his operatic dream. Berlioz's strength was not thus egocentric, and he had to accept the fact that the French would ignore, without even bothering to reject, his evocation of a civilization that, whether tragically or comically, once more attained the heroic. Berlioz died a broken and fatally misunderstood man. His revivified aristocracy was to renew society in the interests of the downtrodden; the search for Splendour was to be the people's instinctive protest against the spiritual tawdriness of an age dominated by trade. But the tragedy was that, having attained Power and Glory, the people, not being artists, were incapable of dealing with them. Berlioz lived to see that the rule of the people meant, not the rebirth of heroism, but the establishment of lack of thought, absence of discipline, and want of skill—the very reverse of the artistic virtues. The world which he had hoped would symbolize the Artist's triumph destroyed all that he held most dear; and he was denied even the consolation of seeing his imaginative vision adequately projected on to a stage.

Yet if Wagner triumphed and Berlioz failed, there is room, perhaps, for discrimination about the nature of failure and success. In fulfilling his dream Wagner became a part of European history. At the same time he was an end of a phase of consciousness. His art could be, and was, debased; but of itself it could lead to nothing further. About Berlioz's career, as compared with Wagner's, there is a melancholy sense of non-fulfilment. He was himself disillusioned in every creative ideal; and whereas composers all over Europe strove—both hopelessly and irrelevantly—to emulate Wagner, Berlioz did not even have any direct successors who could carry on the work he left incomplete. None the less, in the long run Berlioz has become the creative force who, as Busoni said, "pointed the way to untold generations"; the influence of his melodic approach to formal problems and of his polyphonic approach to orchestration has grown during the twentieth century, and is still increasing. Wagner is a climacteric point in the growth of 'the mind'—or perhaps one should say the senses—'of Europe'; now Wagner's music has happened we shall never be the same again. But it is possible that Berlioz—a romantic who was rooted deep in classical tradition while anticipating our fumbling attempts to rescue civilization from chaos—may express the nineteenth century more comprehensively and more deeply.

It is not a question of the relative stature of the two men, about which argument must be as profitless as it is inconclusive. We must take what they offer, not what they might have offered if they, or 'things', had been different. We shall return to Wagner because we are all preoccupied with our (significant or insignificant) selves and, whether we like it or not, inescapably wedded to love and death. We shall return to Berlioz because we are all fascinated by human nature and, if we had his imagination, would envisage the contexts in which, were we nobler and more humane, we might hope to exist. So Wagner's fulfilment instils into us regret for the life we ourselves have not time enough, or capacity enough, to live: Berlioz's disillusion fills us with hope for the unborn lives that make our passion seem petty. The woof of hope and regret is the essence of our being; so although Berlioz and Wagner are opposites, they are necessary the one to the other.

The anti-Wagnerian nature of Berlioz's art is, in an indirect sense, a key to the subsequent history of his country's music. In his day the arbiters of taste were the complacent bourgeoisie who had made fortunes out of the new social order. Their cultural standards were not very different from those of their twentieth-century successors. Aristocratic hauteur and visionary splendours and sorrows were not for them. They wanted an art that would flatter their opulence and promote daydreams, as a relief from the cares involved in getting richer; the 'tired business-man' was not a twentieth-century innovation. Two opera composers pre-eminently fulfilled this demand: Gounod and, later, Massenet.

Born in 1818, Gounod [1818–1893] was close enough to the eighteenth century to inherit—instead of Berlioz's or Cherubini's classic nobility—a certain rococo charm. As long as he is content to compose *opéras comiques* or little songs, his music has a delicious frothy elegance. Eighteenth-century wit becomes rounded and prettified in the languid symmetries of his chanson-like tunes, and in the chromaticisms that cling like rouge to his basically simple homophony. It is remarkable how frequently his tunes are grouped in two-bar periods, each beginning in crochet values, quickening to quavers, and then slowing to minims in the 'feminine ending' that accompanies the harmonic cadence: the melodies attempt to flow, but soon subside in cosily relaxed sentiment (Ex. 76):

So while one does not need to be a tired business-man to be titillated by the love-delights of *Philémon et Baucis*, one has to admit that even Gounod's most pleasurable successes depend on an element of deceit. This becomes still more obvious in the work of Massenet [1842–1912], for while his operas have very varied settings, they revolve around a single theme. Massenet, with a sure instinct for box-office appeal, mastered the modern equivocation and 'got it both ways': the theme of the Repentant Whore can stimulate erotic feeling under cover of self-righteousness. But we, unlike Massenet's public, cannot afford to be smug: if it is true that there is a little of Massenet at the heart of every Frenchman, we can perhaps dispense with the national qualification. In *Manon*, at least, Massenet's eroticism is so tenderly felt in the short-breathed, caressing phrases and the softly lilting rhythms that we are even prepared to accept his outmoded notion of Woman as a kind of sensual seismograph. So apparently mild an aphrodisiac that preserves its effectiveness after more than a hundred years may be assumed to have something which the cruder aphrodisiacs of Hollywood miss.

The moral duplicity of Massenet's music is part of its insidious appeal. As the century advanced, however, moral duplicity began to assume nastier forms: especially when it became associated musically with the impact of Wagner.

Gounod himself, having fallen a victim to religious mania, concentrated no longer on the aspect of his talent represented by the delightful love-music in his *Faust*, but on the bland beatitudes prompted by his comically pathetic attempt to measure up to Goethe. In his innumerable oratorios, *Parsifal*-like harmony interjects a dose of 'mysticism' into the pretty, lethargic two-bar periods, and into the stolid homophony which he picked up in England from the Mendelssohnic oratorio. A genuine, if eccentric, Wagnerian force came into French music with César Franck [1822–1890]; but his influence became decisive only towards the end of the century. Around the 1850s, the spurious Wagnerism of Gounod's later operas and oratorios carried all before it: and while it was bad enough that the French should ignore their greatest genius, Berlioz, it was worse that they should worship in his stead a god intrinsically false. The falsity was not, of course, Gounod's personal responsibility. He was one reflection of the Bourgeois Dream.

Berlioz was born early enough, and had original genius strong enough, to remain creatively unaffected by the spiritually torpid conditions in which he had to work. This was not the case with the most brilliantly endowed composer whom France produced between Berlioz and Debussy: for Bizet's short career [1838–1875] is a series of false starts; and even when he ultimately solved his artistic problems, he died before he could reap the fruits of success. In 1855, when he was seventeen, he composed a symphony which expressed, with uncanny precocity, the essence of his personality. The themes have something of the lyrical suavity of Gounod in his most amiable mood: but remind one still more of the Italianate culture of Mozart and Rossini, whom Bizet admired above all other composers. The capriciousness of the modulations suggests Schubert rather than the enharmonic side-steppings of Gounod; for whereas Gounod's mildly sensual chromatics tend to oscillate around a fixed point, producing a self-regarding, narcissistic effect, Bizet's part-writing and basses have resilience and momentum. The liveliness of his texture is reinforced by his seductively individual scoring, especially for the woodwind; and although the symphony, like Schubert's boyhood efforts, is too long for its non-dramatic material, it remains an astonishing exhibition both of technique and of personality. Ironically enough, Bizet spent the next few years trying to deny the nature he had revealed in this adolescent masterpiece: sometimes in grandiose pseudo-Germanic symphonic music like *Roma*, sometimes in monumental operas that hovered disastrously between Gounod and Meyerbeer.

His rediscovery of his real self came by way of two commissions that forced him to self-discipline. Pretension was obviously inappropriate to children's pieces for piano duet: so in writing *Jeux d'Enfants* Bizet could concentrate on the intimacy of his melodic gift, which was as sensuous as Gounod's but so much more sensitive; while the chromatic and enharmonic subtleties of his harmony could gain in effect through concentration. The delicately asymmetrical melody of *La Poupée* is a lovely example of Bizet's lyrical flavour (Ex. 77):

and the kaleidoscopic polyphonic texture of *Saute Mouton* illustrates his harmonic piquancy which leads on to Chabrier, and ultimately to Ravel (Ex.78):

The relationship to these later composers suggests too how in writing of childhood, Bizet recovered the Mozartian objectivity of his vision. Like a child he is, even in his subtleties, simple and single-minded; his attitude is distinct from the romantic nostalgia of Schumann's pieces about childhood.

The other crucial commission which Bizet received was to compose incidental music to Daudet's play, *L'Arlésienne*. Composers are apt to regard incidental music for the theatre as an unrewarding task; it is certainly difficult to think of another composer who created his first masterpiece in this hybrid medium. But Bizet's success was not fortuitous: for in writing for a chamber orchestra, without voices, he was not even momentarily tempted to emulate the sentimentalities of Gounod or the monumentalities of Meyerbeer. He could be himself: or rather could find himself in losing himself in a play which dealt with real people in a contemporary setting. The music he creates is in fact much more dramatic than any of his earlier operas; of which the first had been an exercise in Italian *buffo* style, while the others were hampered by imbecile, inadequately motivated libretti—the inevitable product of a society that demanded no more than the easiest emotional appeal.

Each of Bizet's twenty-seven musical intrusions into *L'Arlésienne* is etched with the precision of the *Jeux d'Enfants*, though his emotional range is here incomparably wider. It is no longer a matter of entering into the self-contained hearts of children; Bizet's objectivity enables him to recreate even the love of the ageing couple who meet after fifty years' separation. The radiant tenderness of their *Adagietto* is an instance of the dependence of Bizet's harmonic originality on flexible movement in the inner parts: which again explains why his music has so much more delicate a vitality than Gounod's. The chords in both are frequently the same; the contexts in which the chords appear are very different. Gounod's melodies have charm but little character. Bizet's melodies have so personal a distinction that they communicate their vitality to the accompanying parts: and therefore to the harmony also, whether in the pathos of the suavely flowing texture of the *Adagietto*, or in the wit of the unexpected relationships created by the moving parts in *Saute Mouton*.

L'Arlésienne dealt with peasant life in Provence. Bizet incorporated a number of folk-tunes into his score, and in his orchestration achieved a translucency that, for all its sophistication, often suggests the bold colours of Provençal village bands. The earthiness of the subject, and the sunniness of the setting, aided Bizet's instinct for 'externalization'. It is significant that in his abortive operatic ventures the exotic elements had always been at once the most original and the most convincing: not because they were an escape from reality, but because they offered an alternative to Gounodesque complacence. Djamileh moves us not because she is exotic but because her exoticism expresses—through her sinuous melodic lines and ostinato rhythms, and her vivid orchestral colouring—a flesh-and-blood woman. In *Carmen* the exotic, Spanish element is likewise an approach to reality. This time Bizet knew that he had found in Merimée's story the theme which could call forth the Latin intensity of his nature.

Carmen herself provoked at the time a reaction bordering on hysteria not because she was Spanish, nor because she was a prostitute, but because she was a real woman. For Bizet's public, the operatic heroine was expected to be either virtuous and sinned against, or (better) vicious but redeemed. Carmen did not fit into either of these categories; she might be (and later was) glamourized, but sentimentalized she could never be. You cannot pretend she is a figure in a fairy tale; indeed the subject of the opera is not so much her powerfully delineated personality as its devastating effect on Don José. His tragedy was, and is, common. The initial hostility to Bizet's opera arose largely from its truth.

Musically, *Carmen* is in many ways an extension of the styles explored in *L'Arlésienne*. It is a genuine *opéra comique* with spoken dialogue which spills over into music. It is thus a play in music, the dramatic immediacy of which is weakened if sung recitative is substituted for speech. The music that flowers out of speech has all the psychological precision of *L'Arlésienne*, with a vibrant ardour appropriate to the theme of love and jealousy. The orchestral music does not in Wagnerian fashion embody subjective drama; it creates in vivid immediacy the world and atmosphere in which the characters live and move: consider the raucous, piercing passage for piccolos, cornet, and pizzicato strings at the entrance of the gamins behind the soldiers; the fatefully cumulative use of the brass in the fortune-telling scene; as compared with the magical use of low flute with horns at the of the duet '*Là-bas dans la montagne*'. In aria and arioso Bizets' style has now extraordinary plasticity. Only Micaela, a Gounodesque character, sings in conventional French lyricism; and even her music has considerably more vitality than its model. The melodies of the other characters have acquired a fervency that suggests that Verdi's example has helped Bizet to 'realize' himself in the understanding of other people. Like Verdi, he refines the banalities as well as the subtleties of human nature into 'something rich and strange'. The Toreador's Song is to be sung '*avec fatuité*'; but if the music that a fatuous man sings were really fatuous it would hardly have exerted so hypnotic a spell over so many people for so long. Even in his trivialities, Bizet has the art that hides art.

The formal lucidity of *Carmen,* despite the ferocity of its passion and the apparently episodic technique of the *mélodrame,* is typical of the French classical spirit rather than of the pretty formalities of Gounod: or perhaps it would be truer to say that that it is classical *because* of the ferocity, for the essence of classical order is that there should be something to control. *Carmen's* musical concision is thus inseparable from its dramatic force; it stands with Berlioz's operas at the furthest extreme from the symphonic operas of Wagner. We can see this in the way Bizet uses motives in association with the different characters. Wagner's leitmotives are a means of symphonic organization; Bizet uses his motives for essentially dramatic reasons. They are not subjected to symphonic development; they merely reappear, in varied harmonizations and orchestration, with uncannily powerful effect, often with ironic implications. The prevalent irony is another instance of Bizet's Latin classicality; no great artist has ever been more impervious to irony than Wagner.

Dramatic irony in *Carmen* is a counterpart of the wit which we have seen to be implicit in Bizet's harmonic texture. It distinguishes him not only from Wagner, but also from Verdi, who, though he ended his career with one supreme manifestation of wit, seldom if ever allowed irony to obtrude in his tragic operas. This is partly a difference of temperament, partly of cultural tradition: which does not alter the fact that Bizet and Verdi have one profound quality in common, beneath the superficial affinities. *Otello,* the culmination both of Verdi's work and of Italian grand opera, appeared in 1876, the year after *Carmen.* Musically and psychologically it is much richer than Bizet's masterpiece; but *Carmen* at least approaches it in the force of its impact, because it shares with *Otello* a terrifying honesty. If *Otello* is, in a sense, the end of Italian grand opera, in *Carmen* French grand opera and *opéra comique* become one. Bizet no longer thinks of the high and heroic on the one hand, the low and popular on the other: life as it is—abrupt, brutish, and short—becomes a tragic theme. The lover who kills the beloved is the eternal, and perhaps the most fundamental, human tragedy; and although Bizet at thirty-six did not see as deeply into it as did Verdi in his seventies, he too faced it without flinching.

It was this acceptance of reality that appealed to Nietszche when he reacted against his clay-footed, one-time idol, Wagner. For him, *Parsifal* was subjective mumbo-jumbo, whereas *Carmen* was Life—not in the raw, but as realized without evasion, in the lucidity of art. His dismissal of *Parsifal* now seems as superficial as his earlier idolatry of Wagner had been fanatical. Yet he was on the right lines in his appreciation of *Carmen*; for we are involved in that drama and at the same time detached from it, whereas to Wagner we must submit body and soul, if the music is to mean anything at all. Berlioz's remark that one must do coolly the things that are most fiery would apply as much to *Carmen* as to *Les Troyens*: for Bizet, even more than Verdi, has in common with Berlioz not only the wiry virility of his orchestration, but also the objectivity of his approach. At the same time, *Carmen* deflates the sublime; and it may be because it preserves the virtues of the old world while freeing them of hypocrisy that it makes so powerful an appeal to sophisticated and unsophisticated alike. In any case, no later composer revealed the tragedy of instinctive human nature with Bizet's honest precision. His natural successor was Chabrier [1841–1894], whose significant music displays a comic genius more vigorous than Bizet's in its chanson-like lyricisms, its harmonic and rhythmic ambiguities and ironies, its sharp or tender orchestral colours. But despite Chabrier's flirtings with Wagnerism, *Le Roi Malgré Lui* is essentially a brilliant extension of the French comic tradition. Ironically enough, the tragic honesty which is the core of *Carmen* led only to an operatic style as remote from Bizet's lucidity as it is from the visionary tragedy of Berlioz.

At the beginning of the twentieth century—on 5th February 1900—Debussy wrote in a letter these words, which sound a funeral knell on an epoch, apropos of Charpentier's *verismo* opera, *Louise*:

"I have been to the show of the Charpentier family. . . . It seems to me that this work had to be. It supplies only too well the need for that cheap beauty and idiotic art that has such an appeal. You see what this Charpentier has done. He has taken the cries of Paris which are so delightfully human and picturesque and, like a rotten Prix de Rome, he has turned them into sickly cantilenas with harmonies underneath that, to be polite, we will call parasitic. The sly dog! It's a thousand times more conventional than *Les Huguenots*, of which the technique, though it may not appear so, is the same. And they call this Life! Good God, I'd sooner die straight away. What you have here is something of the feeling after the twentieth half-pint, and the sloppiness of the chap who comes back at four in the morning, falling over the baker and the rag-and-bone man. And this man imagines that he can express the soul of the poor! It's so silly that it's pitiful. . . . But then people don't very much like things that are beautiful—they are so far from their nasty little minds. With many more works like *Louise* any attempt to drag them out of the mud will completely fail."

We may find this hard, and think Debussy's conclusion a bit priggish. Yet fundamentally he was right. Bizet had discovered a truth within common human nature; Charpentier [1860–1956] and the *verismo* composers journalistically exploited the commonplace to inculcate lies. Debussy's letter was intuitively prophetic; he could not have known that the musical-theatrical technique on which he comments was to become one of the bases of Hollywood's mechanized assault on our emotions. Bizet's fight against the Bourgeois Dream of Gounod would indeed seem to have been in vain: for all we are left with is on the one hand Charpentier's journalistic prostitution of truth, and on the other hand the more mechanized offspring of Offenbach's deliberate (if delightful) separation of 'entertainment' from reality. Offenbach at least never pretended that life was *really* an eternal can-can; and the music-hall turn, indulged in zestfully, may be a welcome relief from tedium. The 'decadence' lies, perhaps, in the tedium: in the fact that either deceit or escape should be necessary.

4

VERDI
AND NINETEENTH-CENTURY ITALIAN OPERA

We have seen that Berlioz's approach to composition was in part conditioned by the fact that the main stream of music in France remained operatic, at a time when the German instrumental sonata dominated Europe. In Italy, conditions were in some ways similar to those in France. If the survival of the operatic tradition in France was attributable to the power of the old autocracy and of classical drama, in Italy it was due to the vigorous multiplicity of petty autocracies, and to the 'vocal' nature of the Italian language: to which we may add, perhaps, the amiability of the Italian climate.

None the less there was in Italy no lack of revolutionary fervour. Austrian tyranny encouraged patriotic feeling and a burning enthusiasm for liberty: and made national heroes out of artists such as Manzoni and Verdi, as much as out of political leaders like Cavour. It is not therefore surprising that Italian opera in the nineteenth century should have departed further from classical precedent than French opera. The nobility of *Les Troyens* is the culmination of the line that begins with the operas of Lully and Rameau; but except in so far as both are good to sing, there is little connexion between Verdi's operas and those of Handel and Alessandro Scarlatti. Only in his last works is there a (not very specific) link with the style of Monteverdi.

At first, the Italian's operatic reaction to revolutionary feeling was largely negative. Rossini dealt directly with nationalistic aspiration in *William Tell*; but that was his last opera, and was not intended for an Italian public. His native operas are mostly in the *buffo* tradition. Though they deal with real, mostly 'ordinary', people and with themes (such as the Cinderella story) which appealed to his middle-class audience, they cultivated a deliberate, and delightful, social irresponsibility; even the premonitions of romanticism in his serious Italian operas can hardly be accused of political intentions. At the further extreme from Rossini's hedonism stands the elegiac melancholy of Bellini [1801–1834]. He alone among Italian composers of his time indulges neither in *buffo* irresponsibility nor in popular patriotism. With him, a national and communal distress is submerged in personal sorrow. This sorrow is partly his own, for he possessed the consumptive's hypersensitized nerves, and died pathetically in his early thirties. But he none the less belongs to the classical world in that he expresses himself mainly through vocal melody, and objectifies his feeling in people other than himself. In *La Somnabula* the girl who sleep-walks herself into such awkward predicaments is a young girl exquisitely 'realized' in melody; she is also Bellini himself, in the very virginal quality of her sensitivity. In *Norma*, again, we have a deeply characteristic conflict between the life of passion and the seclusion of the cloisters; from this personal theme the music derives its poignancy, rather than from the fortuitous political motive that was perhaps responsible for the opera's success.

All the music of Bellini which still lives deals with potentially tragic themes; and although he borrowed certain external features—for instance, the choral episodes—from French grand opera, his music is essentially intimate. The subject of *La Somnambula* may seem to us suitable for the debunking technique of Rossini; yet the whole point lies in the fact that Bellini takes the girl's troubles seriously. He feels them in personal terms; and he can do so because Romani's poetry is simple, sensitive, and direct, and because his response to poetry is subtler than that of any of his contemporaries. His emotional sincerity and his literary sensitivity are related; both are inseparable from the flexible nature of his melodies, the sustained pliancy of which was admired by Verdi and even—in comparatively early life—by Wagner. Alone among his contemporaries, Bellini preserves the expressive intimacy of classical *bel canto* as it had been developed by Gluck and Mozart: making the curves more rounded, the leaps more expansive, without having recourse to rhythmically crude rhetoric such as we have commented on in Spontini, Meyerbeer, and Weber. Even when his melodies are grouped in two-bar periods, the phrases manage to preserve continuity and flow. In his greatest moments, like the famous 'Casta Diva', he achieves, in his withdrawn, valedictory manner, a lyrical span which seemed to have vanished with the heroic world: and which is recovered by no later composer except Berlioz and the Verdi of *Otello*.

The range of feeling which Bellini expresses through his lyricism is much wider than one might expect; and although his potency derives largely from his sensitive response to the text, it is not true that the harmonic and orchestral elements in his music are insignificant. There are passages in his work—such as the chains of dominant sevenths in the duet in Act II of *I Puritani*—which suggest that he was not impervious to the influence of his friend Chopin, who had in his turn learned so so much from Bellini's vocal style; and in general we may say that Bellini's technique, like Gluck's, was precisely appropriate to his intentions. He wished to express the subtlest refinements of feeling through the setting of poetry in vocal melody. If he was to concentrate attention on the vocal line, other elements must be sacrificed. The (normally) conventionalized harmony, the guitar-strumming accompaniments, the absence of polyphony are means to an end. Simplicity need not preclude subtlety; the most modest change of harmony or of accompanying figuration may, in association with a melodic phrase of peculiar poignancy, have an emotional effect disproportionate to the means employed. For instance, this transition from major to minor, followed by the modulation to the supertonic minor on the climacteric note of the phrase, harmonically complements the melody's ascending tritonal tension, answered by the declining chromaticism (Ex. 79):

The structure of the melody as a whole is a series of such arch-like ascents and descents, each of which culminates a tone higher than the last: until the highest note (A flat) introduces a brief vocal cadenza which also creates the resolution of a harmonic cadence. All Bellini's melodies follow this arch-shaped contour, proceeding basically by scale-wise steps, however much vocal leaps may intensify the conjunct movement. This is why his music seems both sighfully romantic and classically poised; at once melancholy and serene.

Bellini's melody is the purest form of Italian *bel canto* in the nineteenth century. Later composers, such as Verdi and Puccini, adhered to the fundaments of this melody, though they neither achieved nor desired its refinement. Even in his own day, Bellini was an isolated figure. The most representative composer of the time was Donizetti [1751–1848], who produced sequences of comic and tragic operas designed to fulfil an insatiable demand. A comic masterpiece like *Don Pasquale* continues the tradition of *buffo* frivolity, with less vivacity than Rossini, but more grace. His tragic operas continue the romantic evasion in the cult of the extraordinary. If life seems too difficult, one can always go mad. One of the ways in which the romantics used Shakespeare was as an excuse for the Mad Scene: the difference being that whereas in Shakespeare madness is the consequence of the overwrought mind, in romantic drama and opera it becomes an end in itself—or at least its motivation is either perfunctory or synthetic. The cult of madness—like the cult of Gothick horrors and the phenomenal vogue for the novels of Scott as material for opera libretti—may have been a romantic escape, but it is not therefore contemptible. We most of us spend a considerable part of our lives trying to evade the consequences of our actions, thoughts, and feelings; Donizetti's mad scenes, especially the celebrated one in *Lucia di Lammermoor*, admit our evasiveness, and create beauty from the admission. Certainly they discover a new dramatic justification for operatic coloratura. To say that it is new is not, perhaps, entirely accurate, for there had been magnificent mad scenes in the operas of Handel. But in baroque opera madness is never the centre of the action; rather is it an aberration from man's heroic potentialities. Donizetti's vocal gymnastics, on the other hand, lead inevitably to the point where coherent melody cascades in extravagant mirth or frenzy.

There is something madly fortuitous even in his successes. He wrote so fast that he had no time to develop a lyrical gift as fecund as Bellini's, if less sensitive: or to explore a harmonic sense that might have approached the vivid immediacy of the Rossini of *Guillaume Tell.* The superb sextet from *Lucia* testifies not merely to the lyrical power of which he was capable, but also to the technical assurance of his harmonic polyphony. He owed this assurance partly to the tradition of professional craftsmanship within which he worked; yet this tradition prevented the romantic elements in his temperament from attaining comprehensive expression. So there is a melancholy appropriateness in the fact that his finest music should consist of delusions of passion, as Meyerbeer's consists of delusions of grandeur: and that, being nervously exhausted by the rigours of professional life, he should have rounded off the parable by going mad himself.

A tougher spirit than Donizetti, let alone Bellini, was needed to weather the cultural conditions of Italy in the early nineteenth century. He appeared in the figure of Giuseppe Verdi [1813–1901], who came of peasant stock and spoke soberly enough when, later in life, he said: "My youth was hard." While Verdi was growing to manhood, political affairs could hardly have been worse. With Rossini in retirement, Donizetti in the madhouse, and Bellini dead, the musical outlook was equally dismal. As a boy, Verdi exhibited some precocity and much pertinacity in acquiring a musical education in the face of odds; when he took up a professional musical career, he did so without extravagant ambitions. He wanted to compose music for the local military band, and to produce operas on the stock, saleable models. Like any other craftsman, he expected to learn his technique the hard way, partly by study, more by practical experience. The melodic clichés, the horror-struck diminished sevenths, the tremolandos—all the survivals from eighteenth-century theatrical convention which the early nineteenth century had reduced to their lowest and commonest denominator—were basic material which Verdi accepted without the faintest glimmer of shame. No more than Bellini or Donizetti did he seem to be aware that a great Austrian instrumental literature had but recently come to fruition; and as a young man he had neither Bellini's nervous refinement nor Donizetti's instinctive expertise.

Yet the exclusiveness of the tradition in which he worked had its compensations. If he was not tempted to experiment, neither was he lured from his course by extraneous distractions. Even the incompetence of the opera-house orchestras meant that in restricting the orchestra to a few theatrically effective gestures he could concentrate—as for that matter Bellini had done—on the elements that most interested him. Moreover, he had, as part of his unself-consciousness, one quality which Bellini and Donizetti had not. This was an ardent sense of a more than personal purpose. *Buffo* frivolity was not for him; nor was the luxury of personal lament. His opera was to be as serious as he knew how to make it: only its seriousness was to be inseparably linked to its popular appeal. Directly or indirectly, he had to express the passion for freedom which was to unite Italy under Cavour. He chose the historical-political theme not, with Meyerbeer, to encourage day-dreams of grandiosity, but to stimulate real people, in a real situation: perhaps even to excite them to action. Grandeur his opera hardly aimed at; power and energy it achieved—largely because its primitive technique was the servant of a passionate integrity.

Nabucco, the opera which in 1842 made Verdi famous overnight, had a historical theme to which the audience saw a contemporary parallel; they identified themselves with the enslaved Jews labouring under oppression. Yet its success, if to some extent extra-musical, could never have been so overwhelming but for the power of Verdi's music: to which the most effective testimony is that it still thrills us to-day, more than a hundred years after the event. Nor is it an accident that the greatest moments in the opera are choral. The solo vocal writing was at the time much more original than it now seems, and has great power if we accept its rhetoric and do not look to it for the languid subtleties of Bellini or the lyrical-dramatic complexity of Mozart; but it is not in itself evidence of genius, as the choral music is. It is significant that the next opera, *Ernani*—a version of the notorious Hugo play—is less impressive because Verdi has attempted more. Although in *Nabucco* the main characters are sharply delineated, it is the vehemence of the *turba* that gives the opera such momentum. In *Ernani* the fantastic embroilments of the principal characters are the centre of the action; and Verdi has not yet learnt to create, rather than reflect, the inner life of human beings in music.

As he matures, he begins to 'relive' his historical-political themes through his understanding of specific human creatures; this development coincides with the growth of his passion for Shakespeare, and with the appearance within his operatic style of dramatic techniques suggested by Beethoven. Both Wagner and Berlioz had started from an obsession, partly musical, partly philosophical, with Beethoven. As a peasant, trained in a professional tradition, Verdi did not encourage obsessions; one could not say that at any point in his career he experienced a conscious desire to modify his natural growth as an operatic composer. But if his admiration for Beethoven did not directly influence his development, it provides evidence as to the nature of that development. Nor is there anything odd in this, if we remember that from the start Verdi had been a composer of revolutionary operas.

The two operas that mark the beginning of this evolution in Verdi's work are *Macbeth* and *Luisa Miller*. He wrote *Macbeth* to please himself, knowing that its box-office appeal was dubious as compared with that of his historical-political operas. He took considerable pains over it, and preserved such an affection for the work that he revised it, nearly twenty years later, for performance in Paris. English people inevitably find it difficult to accommodate their knowledge of Shakespeare to the melodramatic clichés of nineteenth-century Italian opera; yet even as we recall Shakespeare, we cannot but be stirred by Verdi's sleep-walking scene, with its hypnotic, chromatic wail which pervades both the voice parts and the orchestra. Verdi here directed his performers to speak rather than sing their melodies —a procedure that must have seemed almost as abhorrent to his public as to his singers! One can see, however, what he had in mind; he has created an arioso style which, although it depends for its effect on being sung in time, aims at realistic immediacy. This urgency in the vocal lines is emphasized by the scoring, which, though never complex, is highly atmospheric: consider the sepulchral use of the low registers of the clarinet. Shakespeare has evoked in Verdi a power to 'realize' characters such as he had not previously possessed; and as a corollary of this his music begins to acquire a Beethovenian trenchancy. The first act in particular reminds us of the more rhetorical aspects of early Beethoven—both in the contour of the phrases and in the persistent syncopated *sforzandos*.

Verdi had dealt imaginatively with the burning political issues of his day; Shakespeare had revealed to him some of the darker depths of the human heart. Now, in *Luisa Miller*, Verdi's political consciousness and his interest in the human psyche meet in a story of immediate contemporary relevance. For Luisa is an ordinary middle-class girl sacrificed to bourgeois convention. Her tragedy is gloomy indeed, but never—like earlier bourgeois opera—sentimental. Verdi's passion is here not heroic, like Gluck's or Berlioz's; but it is no less powerful for being intimate. If the melodies lose something of the earlier Verdi's brutal force, they take a further step towards the sinewy flexibility of the creations of his maturity.

Maturity certainly arrived in *Rigoletto*, which, first produced in 1851, was to remain one of the peak points of Verdi's career. The story, based on Hugo's *Le Roi s'amuse*, is as complicated as it is melodramatic, but being admirably constructed, is continuously gripping. In so far as it deals with human relationships warped by environment and circumstance, it was again close to Verdi's heart; it is worth noting that the theatre management wanted to transform Rigoletto into a handsome young man, and that Verdi had to fight strenuously to preserve him as a physical, as well as spiritual, cripple. One would not immediately think of the vital energy of middle-period Verdi in association with the subtle humanity of Mozart; and it is true that Verdi has none of Mozart's civilized irony. Yet *Rigoletto* is in conception a Mozartian opera, and not merely for the superficial reason that the famous minuet is modelled on the minuet from *Don Giovanni*. It is significant that Verdi refused to compose an additional aria for a vainglorious singer on the grounds that *Rigoletto* was an opera not of arias, but of duets. Like Mozart's operas, it is conversation in music. The conversation may be rhetorical, flamboyant, even crude compared with Mozart's wit and tragic pathos; but its sincerity and dramatic impact carry all before them. The thrilling quartet is, again, closer to Mozart than to the quintet in *The Mastersingers*. Wagner's ensemble is a static set-piece. Verdi's is dramatic movement, in which the interlocking passions of the characters create unity from tension, the Duke's nonchalant tune and Maddalena's chatter being counterpointed against Gilda's sustained, lamenting phrase and Rigoletto's gloomy ostinato (Ex. 80).

Verdi's intensifying imagination has learned, too, how to make even the 'hit-number' dramatically relevant. It would never have occurred to him to call '*La Donna è mobile*' or any other of his tunes vulgar; but he knew that it had every quality essential

for popular appeal without being, in its rhythmic blatancy, a tune of profound subtlety or beauty. He also knew that it expressed to perfection the Duke's cynicism; and most of all he knew that its effect when sung off-stage to a Rigoletto who has murdered his own daughter in mistake for the Duke would be shattering. A 'better' tune would not have served. Only a tune such as this could have expressed the appalling indifference of life to the sufferings of its blind, deluded creatures.

The Elizabethan, if not Shakespearean, immediacy of Verdi's imagination in *Rigoletto* fulfils the promise of *Macbeth*. Similarly, *La Traviata* raises the more intimate manner of *Luisa Miller* to a higher plane. The theme is neither heroic nor rhetorical. It deals with the conflict between the real life of human emotion and the life of Society. Violetta is the outcast who yearns to 'belong' to the glittering world to which she is pretty butterfly and parasitic gadfly, and is thereby denied the love which alone would give her life meaning. All the characters—in Dumas' play as in Verdi's opera—dramatize themselves and are, in their very theatricality, true to human nature; indeed, the characters seemed so faithful to some aspects of French provincial life as to provoke offence—especially since Piave presented them in a more or less contemporary setting. Donizetti had used operatic coloratura to express madness; Verdi here gives it a much subtler dramatic propriety, for Violetta's *fioriture** express the feverishness both of the *demi-mondaine* and of the consumptive; her gaiety is melancholy as much because she is spiritually rootless as because she is soon to die. Again, Verdi merges personal feeling into a being remote from himself; and the growing depth of his insight is reflected in the music's 'psychological' fusion of aria and recitative. Moreover, the orchestra no longer, as in the earliest operas, reinforces the excitement with theatrically effective cliché, nor provides, as in *Macbeth*, an atmospheric background. Although it never, in Wagnerian fashion, subverts the pre-eminence of the voices, it becomes an intrinsic part of the psychological drama. The tender preludes and interludes extend our understanding of character and situation, apart from serving the baser theatrical function of providing time for scene-shifting.

Rigoletto and *Traviata* are the culminating points of what we have come to think of as Verdi's 'middle' period. The operas that follow—notably *Simone Boccanegra*, *Un Ballo in Maschera*, and *Don Carlo*—are a transition between the middle period and the last. Verdi here returns to the historical-political theme: the setting of *Un Ballo* had to be transferred from contemporary Sweden to a highly improbable Boston in order to avoid trouble with the censor. The theatrical vehemence of early Verdi now comes to terms with the psychological intimacy of *La Traviata*; and if these operas have not the terrific impact of *Rigoletto*, they manifest a distinct advance in symphonic organization. Verdi has mastered the art of building whole scenes on the evolution of instrumental figurations prompted by the action. One no longer thinks of the music as a setting of the drama (as with Monteverdi), or of the drama as an illustration of the music (as with Wagner); instead, music and drama become synonymous (as with Mozart). *Un Ballo* is especially interesting in that it introduces in Oscar a character whose glinting, fragilely

* FIORITURE: literally flowerings, flourishes. Ornamental figurations decorating a melodic line, in the vocal style usually referred to as coloratura.

scored music suggests a rebirth of the *buffo* spirit. This is the first appearance of any quality that could be called wit in the gloomy violence of Verdi's world. It provides evidence of a widening emotional range, from which alone the glories of Verdi's old age could have sprung. In this opera too Verdi employs extended passages of fugato—dramatically justified, since they symbolize the machinations of the conspirators.

The greater orchestral and scenic richness of these transitional operas was in part prompted by emulation of the Grand Manner of Meyerbeer: which Verdi can recreate with none of Meyerbeer's self-consciousness. Certainly Meyerbeer never composed a 'grander' opera than *Aïda*, which Verdi produced in 1871 for festival performance at Cairo. The Amneris story is the peak point thus far of Verdian passion, the Aïda story of his lyrical amplitude: a comparison of the duet in the last scene with any of the duet scenas in *Norma* will reveal how Verdi preserves the arching contours and stepwise evolution of Bellinian *bel canto*, even while incorporating into the phrases ecstatic leaps of seventh and ninth. The grandiose choral elements now grow cumulatively, along with the unfolding of the personal drama. Even the dances—and Verdi had seldom advanced beyond the conventional except when stimulated by voices and a human situation—acquire poetic richness: Verdi's orchestration now has a translucence, especially in its handling of woodwind, which is a no less personal achievement than Wagner's massive horn-pervaded sonority. In the last scene the ethereal scoring for divided strings, flute, harp, and clarinets surrounds the ever more tenously cantabile melodies like a halo: the music is the more deeply moving because it follows the cataclysm of Amneris's altercation with the priests. Passion disintegrates as the lovers' physical bodies die, until nothing remains but the low monotone of Amneris's repeated D flats, praying for peace. The rest is silence. The Hamlet-like melancholy that hides beneath Verdi's flamboyance has made *Aïda* a 'grand' opera to end grand opera. He was to write one grander still: but not in external magnificence, only in the terrifying honesty of its response to the perversities of the heart.

At the height of his fame Verdi had bought a farm, retired to the country, and adopted the life of a squire. During the years in which he was, as a composer, a national hero, he was also on a modest scale a man of affairs, engaged in local government and politics. Wagner, who talked so much about the divinity of the Folk, really meant the divinity of himself; Verdi refused even to write his memoirs, on the grounds that the public which had put up with so many of his notes deserved to be excused the perusal of his prose. Verdi's nationalism was expressed practically in his love of the countryside and of the peasant community; in his work as landlord and parliamentarian; in the fact that many of the tunes he created became part of popular tradition; in his reverence for the musical traditions of his country.

This last point is evidence of the sense in which, like Berlioz, he stands at the opposite pole to Wagner. His human interests were centred in the multifarious variety of people other than himself. His musical interests embraced most creative aspects of contemporary music; his immediate predecessors, especially Rossini, whom he greatly admired; and—increasingly as he grew older—the Italian masters of the sixteenth and seventeenth centuries. "Everybody should preserve the characteristics of his own nation," he said. "You are fortunate in that you are still the sons of Bach. And we? We too once had a great school of our own, but it has become bastard and looks like perishing utterly." He once gave Boito a list of composers whom he thought it profitable to study. They included Palestrina, Carissimi, Marcello, Scarlatti, Pergolesi, and Piccinni—but, significantly, not Gluck. All these composers thought primarily in terms of vocal melody; and when Verdi advised students to return to the old if they wanted to progress, he meant what he said. He did not mean that archaic models should be imitated passively; he meant that respect for traditional principles would lead to the only true creative development. He proved it himself: for no composer thought less about problems of technical and spiritual evolution, or showed a more continuously stimulating growth from the first creative years of a long life to the last.

This becomes clear in the church music which Verdi composed during a pause in his operatic activity between *Aïda* and the two final Shakespearean operas. His *Requiem Mass* was prompted by a particular occasion—the death of a great artist and patron, Manzoni. It is an act of homage to human greatness, not fundamentally a religious work: for although Verdi lived in a Catholic country, he was, like Wagner and Berlioz — and to the deep distress of his wife—an agnostic. He expressed his humanist creed when he said: "Music needs youthfulness of the senses, impetuousness of the blood, fulness of life"; and it was inevitable that one who believed so vehemently in life as self-justificatory, should have been subject to recurrent pessimism. "Life is suffering," he said; "when we are young, the exuberance of living, activity, and amusement torment and fascinate us. We shoulder our portions of good and ill as they come and do not notice life at all. As we grow old we may be tormented less, we may even achieve our ambitions; then we wonder what our ambitions are worth." Verdi's own life, after the tragic death of his first wife and children, was outwardly sane, happy, uneventful; yet in his music he expressed through the personalities of other human beings the wildest extremities of passion, desire, and despair. The turmoil is perhaps more real than the placidity. Hamlet-like, he oscillates between violent activity and spiritual torpor; and though he fears death no more than he fears suffering, he hates it because for him death is the end of strife, and therefore of hope.

We would, therefore, hardly expect that Verdi, in composing a requiem, would attempt to emulate, however much he admired, the devotional serenity of Palestrina. The only occasion on which Verdi directly approached the manner of Palestrina was in the little *Ave Maria* included in the *Pezzi Sacri* of 1898. Even here Verdi employs not an ecclesiastical mode, but an invented 'enigmatic scale' which offers to the part-writing strange harmonic potentialities; and Verdi regarded the piece as an experiment outside the main line of his music. In the *Requiem* there is a slight flavour of modality in the Agnus Dei and Offertorium, and occasionally a use of harmonically unrelated concords which may have been prompted by sixteenth-century practice: consider the moving intrusion of the G major chord into the B flat amens of the Dies Irae (Ex. 81):

In general, however, any recollections of sixteenth-century technique—or of the monumental choral style of Carissimi and Marcello, or the nobly operatic church music of Cherubini—are absorbed into the operatic style that was Verdi's spontaneous language. The *Requiem* deals with living and dying—with the same immediacy and splendour as does *Aïda*. The passion of its soaring cantabile themes, of its violent harmonic and tonal oppositions, of its glowing, even garish orchestration is so intense as to seem sublime: though the music has none of the enigmatic, visionary singularity of Berlioz's *Requiem* (which Verdi knew and admired). The sobs of the Lachrymosa are grander, but identical in spirit and technique with the sobs of Violetta in *Traviata*, for this requiem is of the earth, earthy. Perhaps it is also of the sun, sunny; the fury of the Dies Irae terrifies us because, when death shuts out the sun, we become 'a kneaded clod'. The opposition between being alive and the suspension of movement which is death, is the core of the Requiem, as it is of Verdi's greatest work, *Otello*.

It seems probable that Verdi's response, in his church music, to the scope of the Italian tradition had something to do with the final maturing of his operatic style. A more richly civilized musical technique came to meet the texts not of a hack librettist, however theatrically astute, but of a poet who had the literary talent, and the musicianship, to release the Shakespearean range of Verdi's genius. The Othello story, as a fight between instinctive passion and destructive intellect, between over-exuberant life and irremediable death, was quintessentially Verdian; and Boito's poetry, often closely modelled on Shakespeare, is beautiful enough to prompt Verdi to seek the 'justest delineation' of the words in his power. In *Otello* there is no single element that is new. There are passages in *Simone Boccanegra* which effect as powerful a fusion of recitative and aria, of vocal lyricism and orchestral drama, of melodic and symphonic organization; certainly there is no justification for maintaining that the enhanced cogency and continuity of *Otello* had anything to do with the example of Wagner. What has happened is that the aged Verdi's dramatic imagination now functions on so consistently intense a level that even the survivals of melodramatic convention—like Iago's inverted Credo—become moments of revelation which forward, rather than disrupt, the action. Only in Mozart can we find a fusion of music and drama as complex, and seemingly as inevitable, as this; and we could pay Verdi no greater compliment than to say that whereas in *Macbeth* our acquaintance with Shakespeare is an embarrassment, in *Otello* we accept Verdi's drama as different from, but parallel to, Shakespeare's.

Perhaps the most remarkable, and Shakespearean, quality about *Otello* is its restraint. Verdi never wrote wilder music than the physical and psychological storm scene, or Othello's arioso of hysteria. Yet the ultimate climax comes in the eternal quietude of the Willow Song and Ave Maria: and in Othello's unaccompanied, almost Monteverdi-like sob: '*Come sei pallida, e muta e bella*' (Ex. 82):

That which was quick and glowing is motionless, silent. It is not so much that Othello (like Verdi himself in the *Requiem*) cannot accept this, as that he cannot believe it. Nothing could be more remote from the end of *Tristan und Isolde*. The mutual self-destruction of those lovers is a merging into oneness; the fulfilment of love offers them no choice but death. But Verdi's Othello and Desdemona had no choice but life; and Othello can but gaze dumbly at the being who was living and is now dead: and in death eternally other than himself, separated. He does not fulfil himself in dying; he atones for what was for Verdi the only cardinal sin. His tragedy moves us so deeply because we have all—Verdi among us—at some time destroyed what we love through blindness, perversity, or masochistic malice. In so doing we—or the Iago within us—kill a part of ourselves. The greatest of Italian grand operas owes its grandeur to the fact that it offers, not romantic evasion, but a fearless admission of our stupidity and our guilt.

Otello is the culminating point of Verdi's career, but it was not his last word; its Mozartian and Shakespearean restraint leads on to a development as logical as it is unexpected. Having expressed the essential Verdian tragic situation with unflinching honesty, the octogenarian composer can at last contemplate life ironically. In extreme old age, he writes his first comic opera: in which the relationship to Mozart—and to Rossini, Cimarosa, and the minor *buffo* composers—becomes for the first time explicit in musical technique. Of course, the man who had created *Otello*, not to mention the lurid sequence of operas from *Rigoletto* onwards, could not merely revive *buffo* gaiety; once more, to return to the past is for Verdi a step forward. So although he insisted that *Falstaff* was unambiguously comic, that is not how it affects us. Ford's jealousy recalls the madness of Othello; the music of the young lovers relives with virginal grace the first magical love scene between Othello and Desdemona; even Falstaff himself is a figure of fun who is fundamentally tragic, in so far as his 'youthfulness of the senses, impetuousness of the blood' are all too obviously subject to age and decay.

But the passions of mortal life, as Verdi had experienced them with so acute an immediacy, are now viewed from a distance. The ultimate objectification of experience occurs in this exquisitely wrought score into which is distilled the quintessence of Verdian lyricism, while the linear orchestral texture becomes as kaleidoscopic as life itself. Apart from Fenton's tender love song, there are no arias; and the sequence of moods is so continuously flexible that although most of the music moves rapidly, the opera seems suspended in time. The unreality and artifice of the old *Commedia* here reaches its consummation; for the opera is a dancing dream which is not a substitute for reality, but a microcosm of the passions of a long life. The plot against Falstaff is not a crude parody of, but a deliciously ironic counterpart to, the many conspiratorial scenes in the earlier operas; even the fairy music is a distillation of human wit, not an evocation of a world of fancy like the fairy music of Weber or Mendelssohn. Perhaps it is no accident that, whereas Verdi's middle-period works had suggested some relationship to the rhetorical aspects of Beethoven, in the complex interrelations of the through-composed score of *Falstaff* we can detect some kinship with the cryptic linear organization of Beethoven's last quartets. (Consider especially the first movement of opus 135.) Though the 'philosophical' significance of Verdi's music may be far removed from that of late Beethoven, both have in common a release from the domination of Time.

From this point of view it is worth noting that *Falstaff* ends with a fugue. In some ways one can think of this as the last breath of the *buffo* spirit, comparable with the sextet that ironically concludes *Don Giovanni.* But it is not just a *buffo* ensemble; it is a fully-fledged fugue with a witty, rhythmically complex theme (Ex. 83):

which in polyphonic development creates a subtly fluctuating harmony. In this agile counterpoint all the contradictions and perversities of life become one. The fugue does not deny Verdi's belief that life is suffering: only suffering itself becomes a kind of joy; or suffering and joy together make sense. They coalesce in this great fugal laugh, which is the reverse of *buffo* irresponsibility, because it is an affirmation of life.

Verdi once said: "I admit the past and the present, and I would admit the future too, if I knew it and found it good." If it were not for his music, that might seem an odd remark from a man who held that life was suffering. Knowing his music—and in particular the fugal epilogue to *Falstaff*—we can see what he meant: in the profound subtleties of his old age, no less than in the powerful banalities of his youth, his strength lay in his self-sufficiency. In 1875 he wrote in a letter:

"I am unable to say what will emerge from the present musical ferment. Some want to specialize in melody, like Bellini; others in harmony, like Meyerbeer. I am not in favour of either. I should like a young man, when he begins to write, never to think about being a melodist or a futurist or any other of the devils created by this kind of pedantry. Melody and harmony should be only means to make music in the hands of the artist. If ever the day comes when we cease to talk of melody and harmony; of Italian and German schools; of past and future, etc., etc.—then perhaps the kingdom of art will be established.

"Another calamity of the present time is that all the works of these young men are the products of *fear*. Everybody is excessively self-conscious in his writing and, when these young men sit down to compose, their predominant idea is to avoid antagonizing the public and to enter into the good graces of the critics.

"You tell me that my success is due to a fusion of the two schools. I never gave either of them a thought."

One could not wish for a more moving tribute to the advantages of being born into a living tradition. But when tradition is in decay, it takes uncommon genius so unquestioningly to assume one's ability to renew the past. Verdi was justified in pitting his intuitive self-sufficiency against our self-conscious fears. Perhaps the measure of his greatness, however, is that he understood our fears while being himself as unafraid as any man who ever lived.

Otello and *Falstaff* would seem to round off the Italian tradition of tragic and comic opera, leaving no more to be said. The relation of Verdi's successors to *Otello* is, indeed, comparable with the relation of Bizet's successors to *Carmen*: both prostituted the truth which their master had discovered. Mascagni [1863–1945] and Leoncavallo [1858–1919] and the Italian *verismo* school degraded Verdi's immediacy to cinematic sensation, making journalistic fiction out of the appearance of truth. But Verdi at least had one successor who, though he may have prostituted truth, did so with insidiously fascinating genius.

At first, Puccini's ambition was unambiguously to follow his idol, Verdi. Even in his earliest operas, however, we find that he combined Verdian lyricism with harmonic and orchestral techniques suggested by the 'expiatory' operas of Wagner and by the sentimental lyric dramas of Massenet. This is significant, because it soon became clear that, Italian though he was, Puccini [1858–1924] had none of Verdi's dramatic objectivity—his ability to understand and to create people utterly different from himself. Though he had not Wagner's sublime egomania, his music comes to life only when he can, even if momentarily, identify himself with his characters. Since the range of experience which genuinely moved him is extremely narrow, his plots and operatic conventions tend to be stereotyped: he went to great pains to persuade his librettists to produce—if necessary, to contrive—the kind of situation which interested him.

If we compare his *Manon Lescaut*—his first really representative opera—with Massenet's *Manon*, we can see at once that there is a core of personal feeling in Puccini's work which Massenet's lacks. Massenet is like his Manon, easy-going, sensually wanton, emotionally coquettish; sincere enough, but not deeply engaged. Puccini becomes his Manon, whose eroticism is not merely a surface titillation like Massenet's fragmentary phrases and tripping rhythms, but a melancholy obsession that flows into lyricism. The characteristic Puccini melody has already emerged. Italian *bel canto* still soars in scale-wise moving arches, but with little of Verdi's virility: for the phrases now tend to droop further than they rise. Moreover, Puccini's themes, lyrical though they may be, have in common with Massenet's a partiality for feminine endings; they tend to split up into clauses rounded off by falling appoggiaturas, or even fifths—an interval which, since it usually implies cadential finality, slows down the lines' momentum (Ex. 84):

In order to counteract this drooping tendency, Puccini frequently groups the clauses in sequences which rise: so that the melodies produce an effect at once limp and hysterically wrought. The more sophisticated harmony—as compared with Verdi—emphasizes the subjective emotionalism of the melodies: especially since Puccini's fondness for the neutral 'Tristan' chords tends to deprive his harmony of the sense of movement. When in later years he picked up from Impressionism the devices of parallel fifths, sevenths, and ninths, and whole-tone progressions,* they all tended to reinforce this harmonic neutrality, creating a more potent form of the narcissistic quality we commented on in Gounod. This harmonic aspect of his work is thus associated with his fondness for pentatonic figurations which deprive melody of the sense of progression, for long sustained pedal points, and for ostinato rhythms. All tend either to induce hypnosis or to provoke hysteria.

One might almost say that Puccini did not use these techniques because he dealt with exotic subjects; he chose exotic subjects because these were the techniques through which he

* The Whole-Tone Scale : that consisting of whole-tone steps only: e.g., C, D, E, F♯, G♯, A♯, C. It contains no perfect fifth and no feeling of tonality.

could say what he had to say. In his later work his limp but nervously strained melody, his obsessional harmonies and ostinato rhythms, are associated with his preoccupation with physical suffering, whether sadistic or masochistic; and while this type of neurotic experience is the genuine element from which Puccini created a language, it is also paradoxically the source of a quality inherently synthetic. Having so narrow a range of experience, he is tempted to resort to any expedient to stimulate it; and stimulation may become simulation, as his hysteria becomes self-induced, and sentimental, because in excess of the object. We can see this even in his mastery of theatrical effect. His sense of the theatre is consummate, in that his effects usually strike home. But he is not a great musical dramatist, for his effects are seldom subservient to an artistic purpose. So long as he is excited, he can excite others. It did not occur to him that theatrical excitement, though necessary, is not an end in itself.

Madame Butterfly is probably Puccini's most successful full-scale opera because the theme of passive suffering is here unambiguously the core of the action, while the final catastrophe is executed with comparative restraint. *The Girl of the Golden West* is probably his worst opera because, having chosen a fashionable theme that did not accord with his emotional interests, he had to drag in those interests by hook or crook (for he could never produce the pot-boiler in which his feelings were unengaged). Something similar happens in his last opera, *Turandot*, in which Puccini tries to extend his range by dealing with a heroine who was neither frail nor passively suffering. But sadism is an inversion of masochism, hardly a richer experience; and although *Turandot* contains some of Puccini's most powerful and remarkable music, it is—not merely in the sense which Puccini intended—a monstrous work. It is revealing both that the scene of the torture of Liu is gratuitous, being without dramatic justification: and that Liu has the most personal and beautiful music in the score.

Artistically, Puccini's most impressive work is the sequence of three one-set operas in which he as it were segregated the melodramatic, sentimental, and comic aspects of his talent. *Il Tabarro* is the most powerful of *verismo* operas (unless one counts *Carmen* as such) because, although it tells a sordid murder tale journalistically, it presents 'the facts' with horrid authenticity.

We (and Puccini) are involved in what the newspapers call 'the tragedy' because murder is necessarily sadistic; but in this trenchantly nasty little piece Puccini offers the minimum of emotional indulgence. *Gianni Schicchi* succeeds because, being inspired by Verdi's *Falstaff*, it is funny. The comic elements in Puccini's full-length operas exist mainly to enhance the pain and pathos by contrast. But *Gianni Schicchi* is comic, even witty, in its own right: as are the satirical impressions of convent life in the third member of the triptych, *Suor Angelica*, which describes, with unexpected simplicity and reticence, a girl's attempt at repentance after an illicit love affair.

The comic and satirical music in *Il Trittico* suggests that the theatre lost a brilliant operatic comedian in Puccini's slavery to his neuroses—and to their box-office appeal. Yet it is unfair to accuse Puccini of cynicism in his self-exploitation; if the qualities on which his commercial success depends were not also the most genuine thing about him his works would have lost their kick long since. What is sad is that, while Verdi's career had proved how arduous is the process of growing up, Puccini takes us back to adolescence—and leaves us stranded. He has something to say; but what he says unmans us. He panders to our weakness, and scares himself in scaring us. At the time, we may find the experience exciting. But we have to turn again to Verdi, to rid our mouths of the ashes of fear.

Comparisons between Wagner and Hitler have been discouraged because Wagner's imagination functioned on a plane at once more profoundly human and more sublime; yet the fact that *Tristan* is one of the greatest works ever created by the mind of man does not alter the fact that resemblances between Wagner and Hitler exist. Puccini is as much above the horror comic as he is below Wagner; yet if we think of him as standing somewhere between the two we shall understand better the potency of his appeal. It is a tribute to his perverse genius that he still has the lure of danger: and that we can no more 'reject' him than we can reject our subconscious minds.

PART IV

ROMANTICISM AND THE 20th CENTURY

(from 1800)

I INTROSPECTION AND NATIONALISM

II INTROSPECTION AND ISOLATION

by WILFRID MELLERS

I INTROSPECTION AND NATIONALISM

I

CHOPIN, SCHUMANN, AND MENDELSSOHN

SONATA, we have seen, was the expression of a creative ideal. Because it involved conflict, it implied too a basic conception of order, associated with a clearly defined scheme of tonality; throughout the works of Haydn, Mozart, and Beethoven the dualism between individual passion and the accepted norm grew increasingly acute. Ultimately, the force of the personal will was to destroy the old notions of tonality and order, creating in Wagner's operas a new mythology out of subjective dream. But this colossal deification of the ego was, at the turn of the century, still far distant. The general tendency in instrumental music around 1820 was for the sonata principle to be superseded by small forms expressive of the passing whim and fancy; and this intimate approach to personal feeling was in particular associated with the development of the piano.

We have commented on some of the reasons why Schubert found the piano an ideal instrument for the poetic reveries and drama of his songs. As a solo instrument, it had the advantage that it possessed an orchestral range of sonorities while remaining under the control of the individual's hands and spirit—almost always those of the composer himself. It lent itself readily to harmonic experiment, through which—rather than through melodic growth or counterpoint—the romantic cult of personal feeling found expression (in this connexion, the fact that Wagner always composed at, whereas Berlioz could not even play, the piano is a matter of more than biographical interest). Even the virtuoso element prompted by the composer-pianist's dexterity was a form of emotional revelation. The artist who retreats into his private dream emphasizes his distinction from *hoi polloi* by an exhibition of his magical powers.

A disintegration within the sonata principle is evident as early as the sonatas of Muzio Clementi [1752–1832]. Trained in the Mozartian tradition, Clementi had a ripe command of Italian operatic lyricism, along with a feeling for tonal drama comparable with Beethoven's. The element of rhetorical drama within him was too strong for him to achieve Mozart's classical equilibrium.* On the other hand, as an Italian, he was neither (like Beethoven) willing to relinquish operatic melody in favour of a new ideal: nor (like Schubert) to evolve a more intimate, subjective lyrical style. As a result, Clementi's sonatas, while containing magnificent music, seem uncertain in aim. His late G minor Sonata admits its operatic origin in its subtitle, which projects his personal passion into the abandoned Dido. Its first theme is operatically sighful in a flowing dance rhythm, harmonized with dissonant appoggiaturas in a manner that significantly suggests Chopin (compare the first theme of the G minor Ballade). The tonal conflicts of the development are bold and grandly planned; yet they lose direction because the theme itself does not imperatively demand this kind of development. Compensatorily, Clementi tries to give the movement concentration by calling on his contrapuntal skill. As such, his counterpoint is impressive; but—unlike Mozart's counterpoint—it does not succeed in tightening up the movement's *dramatic* development. Only rarely does Clementi create a taut work like the B minor Sonata of opus 40, which, in fusing aria, recitative, and sonata, gives full vent to his operatic lyrical ardour, while achieving a Beethovenian trenchancy in tonal drama.

If in Clementi's sonatas operatic melody and instrumental drama are becoming uneasy partners, in Weber's sonatas—as we have seen—the two elements hardly attempt to come to terms: flamboyant operatic melody alternates with improvisatory harmony and virtuosity.† Dussek [1760–1812] preserves the externalities of classical convention, while allowing the wayward beauties of romantic harmony to distract attention from strenuously argued tonal conflict. In the sonatas of Hummel [1778–1837], who had studied with Mozart and with Clementi, the divorce is complete. Italian lyricism becomes elegiac, pianistic arabesque emulating the vocal decoration of opera: tonal drama becomes rhetoric. It is easy to understand why Hummel was the most fashionable composer of the salons. He does not call for the radical reorientation demanded by a Beethoven. He offers the delights of intimate feeling in the sonorous spacing of his keyboard texture and his occasional chroma-

* See Part III, pp. 612 et seq.

† See Part III, pp. 736 et seq.

ticisms and enharmonics: a hint of regret for the past in the valedictory, Bellini-like contours of his slow melodies: and an ebullient acceptance of the present in the improvisatory brilliance of his virtuosity which binds us, wizardlike, in its spell. At least, such was its effect on contemporary audiences. If it now seems less spellbinding than the finest work of Clementi or even of Dussek, that is because it came from a nature not insincere, but comparatively superficial. His themes and melodies are not strong enough to bear the complexity of his texture and ornamentation: so that his historical significance—in his treatment of the keyboard and in his intermittent concern with harmonic surprise unrelated to structure—is more considerable than the intrinsic value of his compositions.

This is clear enough in his influence on John Field [1782–1837]—one of the few composers of talent and personality to work in England, but in a cosmopolitan idiom—in the early years of the nineteenth century. His opus 1 consists of three piano sonatas dedicated to his master, Clementi, who had settled in London. Compared with Clementi's finely rounded themes, complex part-writing, and refined counterpoint, Field's sonatas seem impoverished, even rudimentary, in technique. Yet comparison with Clementi is perhaps hardly valid; for these sonatas are no longer within the classical tradition. The caprice of the modulations has become an end in itself. The emotional point of the first sonata lies in the 'false' recapitulation in the tonic minor, which surprisingly invests a conventional theme with melancholy. Even the insouciance of the salon-like rondo finales acquires, through the improvisatory modulations, a poignant frailty. The glitter suggests impermanence: and therefore an element of pathos beneath the frolics, similar to that in the *vers de société* of Field's contemporary, the consumptive Winthrop Praed.

One might almost say—discounting his clumsy technique—that the significant features of Field's sonatas and concertos are a contradiction of the sonata principle. It is not therefore surprising that the music by which he still lives is contained not in his sonatas, but in the short pieces for which he coined the term Nocturne. He found a hint for these pieces—in which his technique is as expert as in the opus 1 sonatas it is gauche—in the slow movements of Hummel which translated Bellinian *bel canto* into pianistic terms. But his shy temperament comes much closer than Hummel's to the intimacy of Bellini's style. The melodic line—in its smoothly arching contours and its irregular arabesques which emulate the nuance of the singing voice—is a stylization of Bellini's virginal grace: consider this exquisitely 'vocal' *sospirando* passage from the E minor Nocturne (Ex. 1):

Ex.1. Field: Nocturne in E minor

The widely arpeggiated accompaniments are both harmonically and decoratively less congested than Hummel's; for although Field was a virtuoso pianist who made his living by demonstrating pianos for Clementi's music warehouse, his nocturnes are never display pieces. Operatic lyricism becomes elegiac self-communing in these tenderly melancholic reveries, which are in simple ternary song form, or in a binary form devoid of any hint of sonata conflict: consider the etherially remote modulations in the Fourth Nocturne, in A. Here the quintessence of romanticism flowers—as it does in Bellini himself—from classical tradition. It is appropriate that Field should have been a kind of Irish Harlequin—a cross between Chatterton and Oliver Twist—who worked, dismally unhappy and undernourished, in a London music shop;* should have exiled himself in Russia after a concert tour; and should have had in later life a brilliant cosmopolitan career as a virtuoso, only to die, homeless, of 'dissipation and despair'.

Chopin [1810–1849], like Field, was a voluntary exile from his native land. Born into an affluent and cultivated family, he

* Spohr, in the *Autobiography*, describes Field as "a pale, melancholy youth, awkward and shy, speaking no language but his own, and in clothes which he had far outgrown".

spent his adolescence in a world of glittering gaiety and grace. At the age of twenty he left Poland, partly to gain a deeper knowledge of the culture of Europe, partly because political troubles at home threatened his aristocratic world. After a short period in Vienna, where he heard much Italian opera, he settled in Paris in 1831. Here he became the idol of an aristocratic *élite*, and was soon the friend, not merely of musicians such as Berlioz, Rossini, and Bellini, but also of the leading painters and poets congregated in Paris. Only against the background of this glamorous social and intellectual life can we understand the loneliness of his heart.* His spiritual exile had little connexion with his physical exile; for although he identified his own sufferings with those of aristocratic Poland, he was more at home in the artistic life of Paris than he would have been anywhere else. Poland became for him a mythical dreamland: a symbol of nostalgia not for a 'native land', but for the human solidarity he lacked. This subjective nostalgia he expressed entirely through the medium of the piano, for which he created both a new idiom and a new performing technique. His originality was commented on by all his contemporaries. He was fortunate in having a public intelligent and sensitive enough to see that his limitations were the essence of his romanticism, and, paradoxically, the secret of his forceful impact on his successors.

His very first works would not have led one to expect this. The C minor Sonata, which Chopin himself did not publish, is duller than Field's, if less technically inept. Chopin's attempt to measure up to the classical ideal inhibits even his sense of the keyboard. In his other apprentice works he avoids any approach to sonata style, and confines himself to the episodic forms of rondo and variation. A work such as the '*La ci darem*' Variations betrays occasional flashes of Chopinesque personality, while adding nothing substantial to its models, Hummel and Spohr.

Chopin's other early attempts at large-scale composition founded on classical principles are much more interesting, if only a little more successful. In the two piano concertos Chopin

* Cf. "You exaggerate the influence which the Parisian salons exerted on Chopin. His soul was not in the least affected by them, and his work as an artist remains transparent, marvellous, ethereal, and of an incomparable genius—quite outside the errors of a school and the silly trifling of a salon. He is akin to the angel and the fairy; more than this, he sets in motion the heroic string. . . ." Letter of Liszt to Wilhelm Leng, 1872.

is a composer of genius who has not yet discovered the forms appropriate to his experience. The rondo finales are still salon music in which the butterfly impermanence of Field's or Hummel's virtuosity acquires a more subjective, slightly feverish flush. The slow movements too have their prototype in the concertos of the two older men; but Chopin translates Bellinian *bel canto* into pianism with greater refinement than Hummel, and with a luminous warmth such as we do not find in Field. Something of Field's chastity of line has gone; the delicacy of Chopin's ornamentation and pianistic texture is charged with a languishing sensuality. But these movements are the perfectly realized expression of a sensibility. Even Chopin's reticent handling of the orchestra here emphasizes the music's seductiveness.

The sonata movements are a different matter. Unlike those of the C minor Sonata, the themes are now memorably Chopinesque; precisely because of this they are unhappy in their context. The classical notion of tonality and development meant nothing to Chopin. In the E minor Concerto his development section consists of harmonic improvisation by the soloist, into which the orchestra interjects, with hopeful perfunctoriness, fragments of the themes. It is significant that although Chopin occasionally composed in large forms later in life, he never again attempted a compromise with sonata tradition. This was also the last occasion on which he permitted himself the redundancy of an orchestra.

One hardly needs, however, to consider the inadequacies of the piano concertos in order to understand why Chopin was essentially a composer in small forms: one needs merely to examine the nature of his melody and harmony. Chopin's melodies have two main roots: Bellinian *bel canto*, which, as we have seen, came to him both direct and by way of its pianistic metamorphoses in Hummel, Spohr, and Field; and Polish folk-music, which is responsible for his preoccupation with dance movement, especially triple rhythm. Yet his themes are a highly personal sophistication of his 'sources', largely because his melodies are so intimately related to his harmony. The justly celebrated melody of the E major Etude, for instance, has the external features of Bellinian *bel canto*, while being unmistakably Chopin in that its rise and fall reflects the sensuously fluctuating tensions of the harmony. It differs from Bellini's themes in that, when once we have heard it in its harmonization, we cannot even mentally hear it apart from its harmonic implications.

Basically, Chopin's melodies are diatonic and, like Italian *bel canto*, are constructed in regular eight-bar periods. But the metrical periodicity is frequently disguised by elliptical cadences, and by modifications to the pattern arising from the improvisatory subtleties of his harmony. Moreover, his ornamentation (like Mozart's) is often chromatic, as it emulates the operatic singer's portamento and rubato; and this creates a link between the fundamentally diatonic melody and the chromaticism of the harmony. Recollections of Polish folk-music are responsible for the frequent intrusion of the lydian sharp fourth into his themes. This again is associated with one of his most obsessive harmonic mannerisms—the use of the second inversion of the neutral diminished seventh. Folk-like thematic phrases frequently proliferate into chromatic arabesques which suggest the ornamental, sophisticated idiom of the nocturnes and waltzes. Such arabesques lend subtle ambiguities to the already rich harmonic texture: consider the oscillating thirds in opus 63, no. 2 (Ex. 2):

Chopin's harmonic texture always offers the exile's nostalgic commentary on the direct vitality of folk-like tunes and rhythms.

It is perhaps already evident that although Chopin is a distinctive melodist, the essence of his art is in his harmony. This, again, is fundamentally diatonic; but the movements of his hands on the keyboard, as he writes 'through' the technique of his instrument, provoke him to continual fluctuations of harmonic stress, complementing the emotional irregularities of his melody. Pianistic figuration creates chromatic alteration: indeed, there are so many 'altered' notes that the unresolved appoggiatura may become a substitute for the 'real' note. Far from establishing classical tonality, Chopin's harmony seeks mysteriously to disguise it: the A minor of the second Prelude, for instance, is present mainly by implication. Passing chords flow so rapidly beneath his fingers that they cease to have tonal significance, and become an effect of colour. The harmonic figuration in the middle section of the E major Etude modulates so rapidly that no sense of key survives: except in so far as we hear it as a protracted, mysteriously disguised dominant pedal leading to a restatement of the serenely diatonic melody with which the piece had opened. In this passage we can see how readily the tonally neutral diminished seventh lends itself to this harmonic chiaroscuro (Ex. 3):

but chains of dominant sevenths, chromatic and enharmonic side-steppings, and mediant relationships are used in much the same way. Many of the more extravagant sequential modulations in Chopin's music do not really imply a change of key: they are as much effects of colour as his chains of diminished sevenths.

So Chopin's nervous sensations flow into the behaviour of his hands on the keyboard, which precipitates the swiftly coruscating texture of his harmony. So fluid a harmonic movement could be applicable only to forms conceived on a small scale; and in his early works the self-enclosed nature of his melodies or the regularity of a dance rhythm suffices to give unity to his pieces. It is, however, significant that the first work in which Chopin attains consummate maturity should be a set of Etudes, opus 10. His discovery of himself is here explicitly related to his discovery of the keyboard; for the unity of each piece now comes not merely from self-enclosed melody or periodic dance rhythm, but from the consistent use of piano figuration, derived from a specific technical problem. This frequently suggests a kinship with some of the Preludes from Bach's *Well-tempered Klavier*. In the E flat minor Etude from opus 10, for instance, a consistent accompanying figuration supports a strong, unbroken line; and in this sense the piece is more classical in spirit than the disintegrative slow movements of C. P. E. Bach [1714–1788] or

W. F. Bach [1710–1784], who lived so much closer to the classical tradition.* Chopin's virtuosity, like J. S. Bach's, is never a platform manner. The technical difficulties of his music are a product of his nervous intensity; his exploitation of his instrument reveals his personal style.

Chopin's generative use of piano figuration enables him to achieve extraordinarily varied transformations of his simple ternary song or dance form; the growth of the figuration disguises the basic pattern in much the same way as the subtleties of harmony and rhythm disguise the periodicity of the themes. In the 'Revolutionary' study the surge of the figuration is so consistent and so cumulatively exciting that we are hardly aware of the primitive ternary structure which underlies it. More complicated instances are those in which a coda figure usurps some of the functions of the decorated repeat of the first section: in the B major Nocturne, for instance, the 'Wagnerian' drum-beat coda introduces a new emotional dimension which grows inevitably from the previous material.

Most subtle of all, perhaps, is a case like the isolated Prelude, opus 45, which is ostensibly in C sharp minor, though only the first bars and the last touch upon this key. The main theme is a distillation of Bellinian *bel canto* that starts in a sub-dominant-flavoured E major; the accompaniment is a pianistic figuration evolved from the conventional operatic arpeggiated bass. This accompaniment becomes much more important than the melody, generating a succession of dreamfully remote modulations which seem the more hazy since no basic key has been established. These culminate in a cadenza of dissolving tritones, which does not even hint at a key. Only after this disintegration does quasi-operatic recitative lead back to song melody: and to the long-delayed resolution into a sombre minor tonality.

Maturity also enabled Chopin to create works on a larger scale which do not deny the sensory, emotive roots of his art. The G minor Ballade looks superficially like a sonata movement, while no longer attempting to imitate sonata procedure. It opens with a slow introduction, followed by two subject-groups, one in the tonic minor, the other in the flat submediant major, both lyrical and in dance rhythm. Instead of a thematic development, Chopin builds up his climax by harmonic 'improvisation' travelling through a kaleidoscopic range of

* See Part III, pp. 590 et seq.

keys—a large-scale expansion of the effect of the cadenza in the C sharp minor Prelude. This leads, in a kind of mirror structure, to a restatement of the second group modified, a curtailed repeat of the first group, and a coda to balance the introduction. Still more remarkable is Chopin's treatment of the sonata in the only two mature works to which he gave that title. The B flat minor Sonata is a big piano composition in which unity is virtually derived from keyboard figuration. The motive which is stated at the opening in long-note values is expanded into different figurations in all the movements; and this pianistic extension of a single idea supplants the conventional dualism of sonata style. One might even say that the work represents a reversal of the sonata principle (which creates unity from the diversity of tonal conflict). Chopin's first movement is closest to an orthodox sonata, preserving a balance between song melody (the second subject) and the disintegrative force of piano figuration (the *agitato* first subject). In the scherzo classical tonality is broken by a dynamic assault of harmony and figuration. This is followed by a funeral march, in which song melody appears, in the trio, only retrospectively, nostalgically. Thus the fourth and last movement, which seems so oddly brief and immaterial as the conclusion of a large-scale work, proves to be inevitable. Here line itself becomes harmonic disintegration: for the movement is in unison throughout, and in effect entirely harmonic. During a considerable proportion of the piece, tonality disappears. The music becomes a fluttering of the nerves which tells us, in an intimate whisper, what *Tristan* tells us in its grandly impassioned lament: the battle between man and God, between man and the World, has been absorbed into the inner life of a single, hypersensitive soul.

This reference to Wagner is significant; for the force of Chopin's restricted genius is attested in the fact that so many of Wagner's harmonic processes are anticipated in Chopin's keyboard style. Of course, the originality of Chopin's talent exists in its own right, not as a preparation for something else. But it is revealing that so subjective and limited a style should so strikingly complement the titanic force that was to emerge later in the century; the Chopinesque preoccupation with the ego was to have consequences far beyond his reckoning. There is even a parallel between Chopin's development and Wagner's. It is often said that, having established its identity in the Etudes of opus 10, Chopin's music never developed. In a sense this is true, for opus 10 is a perfectly realized work of art which could not be improved. But we have only to consider Chopin's ornamentation to see that, as he grew older, he revealed the intimacies of the solitary heart with an ever-increasing precision.

In his first works quasi-vocal ornamentation is mainly decorative, as it is in much of Rossini. In his earlier mature works altered notes and chromaticisms in the ornamentation become an intensification of the line, as they are in Bellini. In his late works ornamentation becomes itself melodic, almost thematic; and creates the harmonic ambiguities typical of his sensory style. This is clear in the almost polytonal* arabesques and intertwining, subsidiary polyphony in his two last and ripest essays in pianistic *bel canto*—the *Berceuse* and, still more, the glowingly sensuous Venetian evocation of the *Barcarolle*. Here the irregular *grupetti* and swaying parallel thirds of Bellini's vocal *fioriture* become a pianistic quiver of sensation: a haze of light and water suggestive of, though more powerful than, impressionistic technique. Bellini's tendency to withdraw from operatic projection into the inner dream is here consummated in instrumental terms.

This thematic ornamentation is, however, only one aspect of the more linear style of Chopin's last years. We know that towards the end of his life he studied Cherubini's treatise on counterpoint, and the creative manifestation of polyphony in the preludes and fugues of Bach—as well as in the part-writing of his beloved Mozart. Although it would be extravagant to say that the last mazurkas are contrapuntal in Bach's sense, they manifest a more economical texture than his earlier works, along with a partiality for canonic devices. These canons (see, for instance, opus 50, no. 3) may have been suggested to Chopin by a traditional feature of peasant dance—the flight of the 'danseuse' before the 'danseur'; yet they become, in their context, highly sophisticated. The tightly-wrought part-writing throughout the last mazurkas would seem to be derived from harmony in much the same way as Wagner's 'new polyphony' in *Tristan* and *Parsifal* results from a horizontalization of chords.† The mazurkas are small, reticent works compared with the searing passion of *Tristan*; but like Wagner's masterpiece they

* POLYTONAL: the use of more than one key simultaneously. Polytonality is not systematically exploited until the twentieth century.

† See Part III, pp. 755.

create, from the harmonic fluctuations of personal sensation, a whole world of thought and feeling. Wagner's elegy is passionately monumental; Chopin's is twilit and phantasmagoric. But Chopin's mazurkas already intimate a new approach to form. Though ternary song and dance forms still pervade them, their inner unity lies in the fact that the nervous oscillations of the harmony themselves generate the motives which build up the texture (Ex. 4):

From this point of view they are no longer dances, but miniature symphonic poems: so that we are not surprised when the opening pages of Chopin's last considerable work, the *Polonaise Fantaisie*, vividly suggest not merely the late work of Wagner, but also the ripe harmonic-polyphonic texture of Richard Strauss.

While the last mazurkas come closest of all Chopin's works to the spirit of Polish folk-music, they are not nationalistic. Chopin was fascinated by the modal and rhythmic ambiguities of folk-music because they both stimulated and complemented the harmonic and pianistic subtleties through which he expressed his nervous life; his deepest revelation of the self is also his most nostalgic evocation of a private dream-world. It is interesting to compare his last waltz (the A flat, opus 64, no. 3) with his last mazurka (the F minor, opus 68, no. 4). In the waltz the chromatic passing notes in the melody and the strange enharmonic modulation to E major flush the 'social' elegance with a slightly fevered wistfulness. In the mazurka the chromatic sequences and enharmonic transitions create a disintegration of the entire tonal structure; the pathos cannot be resolved, and the piece is left suspended, without even a

XXXVII An afternoon at Listz's. From a lithograph by J. Kriehuber.

XXXVIII Chopin in Marseilles, May 1839.

final cadence. One might say that the melancholy of Chopin's waltzes comes from the sense of alienation that underlies his portrayal of a gracious aristocracy. The melancholy of the mazurkas is more profound, because whereas the world of Parisian vivacity did exist, or had existed, Chopin's Poland was 'real' only in the sense that some such nostalgia haunts every man, to the measure of his nervous capacity. The 1848 Revolution destroyed the only kind of society which Chopin could breathe in; and the final rupture with George Sand broke the one human contact that gave stability to his tremulous nerves. Yet we do no honour to Chopin's memory if we romanticize his biography. His consumption, like Bellini's, was symbolic in the sense that he died because he burned up his nervous vitality; yet he had a central source of strength of which he was well aware when he referred to himself as a minor talent, but a master. No artist was ever less the unconscious rhapsodist; his power lay in the precision of his realization of his inner life. The strength of the last mazurkas—more than of the big polonaises or scherzi—is in the crystallization of subjective melancholy into the timelessness of art. This is why his highly personal idiom foreshadows so much of the evolution of nineteenth-century music; and is why his spell, having survived commercialization, is as potent to-day as ever.

It is odd that although there has never been an artist more preoccupied with personal sensation than Chopin, or one more chained to a specific environment, his music remains undated. In every bar of his work is the chivalrous aristocratic gesture, the rustling of silk in shuttered drawing-rooms; yet he is never enslaved to a time and place that are past. He becomes a mythical Pierrot-figure, symbol of our youthful yearning for the moon, and of the unappeasable cravings that remain when the years have taken their toll. He is unique in his perfection. Only the youthful Schumann may be said to parallel his achievement; and his case is more complicated, because he belonged to the German tradition.

Chopin came from a country that had lost or forgotten its musical tradition. The music he was brought up on was Italian; the language he spoke and the books he read were French. From the start there was little to distract him from his romantic individuality. Schumann [1810–1856] came of respectable middle-class stock, was brought up on the Viennese classics and on German romantic literature; and was intended for the law. As a boy he was, like Chopin, moody and hypersensitive, oscillating between exuberant gaiety and a black hypochondria. His earliest musical passion was for Schubert: a significant fact, since whereas Chopin was always content to live for his own passions, Schumann followed Schubert in cultivating friendship as a bulwark against a hostile world. His 'Davidsbund' was not merely an artistic coterie directed against philistinism: it was also an alliance of all solitary Pierrots against those who would destroy them through misunderstanding, if not through wilful malice. But there was nothing revolutionary about Schumann's circle. It was more exclusive, more private than Schubert's: indeed, as it affected his music it turned out to consist of himself, in various disguises, and of the women he loved, who—because he loved them—became at once a part of himself and a barrier between himself and other people. This is why a kind of ideal domesticity is so moving an element in Schumann's work. It is revealing that while Chopin too was a passionate lover, his music seems independent of his loves. In listening to his music we may sometimes think of Chopin himself—the pale face, the fragile fingers, the unexpectedly fierce eyes—but we do not think of George Sand. Ernestine von Fricken or Clara Wieck are never far from Schumann's most beautiful and typical music.

Schumann's opus 1 was inspired by love: or at least by a passing fancy for a pretty girl he met at a dance. The young woman's name, Abegg, happened to be a sequence of musical notes. Out of them Schumann made a waltz tune, suggestive of Schubert in its nostalgically rising and falling arpeggio, yet strangely personal in the regularity of its clauses, which seems to inhibit the music's flow. The bird would soar, were not his wings clipped (Ex. 5):

Ex.5. Schumann: Abegg Variations Op.1

The variations that follow are less interesting, with a faint suggestion of Hummel's drawing-room elegance; but they establish the importance of variation technique throughout Schumann's formative years. No more than Chopin did he have any instinctive feeling for the sonata principle; variation was the only technique whereby he could create works on a reasonably extended scale. In a sense, all his works were variations on his own sensibility; his sequences of small piano pieces in simple ternary or binary form were free variations on an often latent theme. Each passing mood was related to the others, if only because all the moods were his.

This is already evident in Schumann's opus 2, the revealingly titled *Papillons*. Schumann gave this chain of waltzes a literary programme derived from the neurotically sentimental romances of Jean Paul;* but he also said, "When I play Schubert, I feel as though I were reading a romance of Jean Paul set to music," and the real impetus behind these pieces is Schubert's waltzes and polonaises. The difference is that whereas Schubert's dances, though idealized, were in fact *musique de société*, Schumann's exist only in the dream-world of Pierrot. In the first number we have again the upward-soaring phrase which then declines, twice repeated in four-bar periods. After the double bar come four bars of rapid sequential modulations which seek to destroy both tonality and symmetry; but are prevented by a repeat of the opening phrase. Two other Schumannesque features should be mentioned: a fondness for canonic devices in aggressively regular metre—a wilful discipline, in opposition to the lilting dream (consider the second dance); and a use of chromatically intertwining inner parts which create, through dissonant passing notes, a pathos that is acute rather than languishing (consider the fifth number).

Papillons, written in Schumann's teens, may be regarded as a preliminary sketch for *Carnaval* (1834), described by Schumann as "*scènes mignonnes sur quatre notes*". The four notes in question (A-S-C-H) are also the place where Ernestine von Fricken was born; Schumann again unifies the sequence of fleeting moods by basing the movements on various permutations of these notes. Though the work is not strictly in variation form, it is another instance of Schumann's variation principle linked, once more, to autobiography. In this Carnival the characters are Schumann himself in his two contradictory personae—Florestan the extrovert, Eusebius the brooding

* Johann Paul Richter (1763-1825), German novelist of Sensibility.

melancholic; Estrella and Chiarina, who are Ernestine von Fricken and Clara Wieck—the woman he loved at the moment and the girl (then fifteen) who was to be his wife: and the traditional figures of the *Commedia*, joined significantly by Chopin and Paganini. The two latter were Pierrot-figures actually living in the early nineteenth century; and it is no accident that the mythical Pierrot who himself broods over the Carnival is portrayed in a piece which is the quintessence of early Schumann. The short, chromatically involuted phrase closes in on itself, and is obsessively repeated in regular clauses which contradict the bar-line (Ex. 6):

Again, the metaphor of the trapped butterfly, the caged bird, springs to mind; but in this exuberantly youthful work he seems to fly free. The cycle ends with the march of the Davidsbundler against the Philistines which, in routing the vulgar and academic, reveals the interrelations between the themes. Only a certain fanatical quality in the rigid rhythm hints that the powers of darkness have not said their last.

The haunted and hallucinatory are certainly present in the sliding chromatics and rhythmic elusiveness of the *Kreisleriana*. The title was suggested by an autobiographical story in which Hoffmann described his own sufferings through the mask of an imaginary Kapellmeister. Schumann told Clara that the pieces were about himself, in relation to her; and significantly said the same about the *Kinderscenen*, which one might have expected to be less directly personal. He wrote these pieces, he said, because Clara had remarked that she sometimes thought of him as a child. This child is himself, and the self-sufficiency of the child's world is a refuge from the turbulence of adolescence. Again, the revocation of passed moods is unified by a free variation principle, since all the pieces are dominated by premutations of the phrase with which the work opens—the rising sixth (sometimes changed to a fourth), followed by a descending third and a slow turn.

Schumann's keyboard texture, his harmonic reverie, his fondness for dotted-note march rhythms, may owe something to Beethoven's 'transitional' piano sonatas, such as the A major, opus 101; but the originality of his style was rightly recognized by his contemporaries as hardly less potent than Chopin's. There is nothing Italianate about his melodies, which derive from the simple symmetry of German folk-song and the Lied. The pathos of his harmony, even when it is extremely chromatic, depends less on a rapidly coruscating texture than on the clear spacing of the part-writing which rounds off the sharpest discord in its resonance. Often these inner parts are precipitated out of a texture of richly flowing arpeggios; often again they are associated with the repetition of a rhythmic figure, as in the beautiful piece describing the child asleep. The lucid sonority of Schumann's part-writing may have something to do with his early enthusiasm for Bach, though his polyphony seldom betrays Bach's tension between line and harmony. Fundamentally, Schumann, like Chopin, thinks in harmonic terms; one might even say that the canonic passages in Chopin's last mazurkas are more Bachian in spirit than anything in Schumann.

The essence of Schumann's youthful fantasy is to be found in the pieces he explicitly called *Fantasiestücke*. We are told that Schumann liked to play to his friends at twilight; certainly the first piece of the set, *Des Abends*, reveals how intimately Schumann lives in half-lights and ambiguities. The time signature is 2–8, but the figuration is in 6–16. What we hear melodically, however, is a tune in 3–8; and this rhythmic equivocation leads to harmonic ambiguities created by the figuration: consider the transition, rather than modulation, from D flat to E major (Ex. 7):

Ex. 7. Schumann: Des Abends Op. 12 No. 1

In the second piece, *Aufschwung*, the romantic spirit soars in a more than normally extended ternary form, while the cross-rhythms imbue the bird's floating ecstasy with a certain fearful precariousness. In the exquisite *Warum?* the tenderly rising and drooping phrase never flowers; its question floats pathetically from voice to voice, leading into strangely shifting harmonies and keys that are no resolution. In *Grillen* the fantasticality lies equally in the rhythmic and tonal contradictions, which are not so much witty as weird. In *In der Nacht* we have one of Schumann's favourite whirling arpeggio figures, above which a melody strives to soar, but is pulled back by the appoggiatura in the middle part. When, in the middle section, the melody manages to free itself, the harmony becomes frustrated, because the decorative appoggiaturas in the arpeggios create an ambiguity between major and minor. Even the jovial *Ende vom Lied*, in which the *amici* make merry, contains some oddly abrupt enharmonic transitions in its middle section; and concludes with a slow coda which transforms geniality into dream. This is a beautiful instance of the harmonic nature of Schumann's counterpoint.

In 1840 Schumann turned from small piano pieces to song-writing, in a mood of lyrical expansiveness appropriate to a marriage that seemed to offer all he asked of life. The stream of songs which he created in this *annus mirabilis* stands with the finest of his piano works as his supreme achievement; but they add nothing new to the experience the piano works had expressed. The physical presence of the human voice inspired Schumann to some of his most moving melodies, and perhaps he never achieved in his piano works a melody which has the inevitable drive, the cumulative, wavelike motion of *Ich grolle nicht*. But both the periodic nature of this melody, and the relation of its melodic development to the tensing and relaxing of the harmony, do not radically differ from the idiom of the piano pieces: even Schumann's partiality for the turn (see, for instance, *Er, der Herrlichste von Allen*) comes as much from pianistic habit as from unconscious reminiscence of opera. Many of his songs, indeed, double the vocal line in the piano part, so that they could be played as piano pieces and still make sense. Moreover, the psychological interest which Schumann displays in his songs is implicit in his piano pieces also, for most of them have reference to a specific emotional situation, usually autobiographical.

It is significant that the majority of Schumann's songs should be love songs. Schubert too created his greatest songs when he discovered an identity between his poets and himself; but he still preserved a measure of classical objectivity in his ability to project himself into other, and very different, people. Schumann is musically moved by poetry only when the singer is himself—whether as Florestan or Eusebius—or Clara; and this spiritual identity between composer and poet is more important than the quality of the poetry, however highly developed his literary taste may have been. His settings of Heine, or even of Chamisso, are musically superior to his settings of Goethe, because in Heine especially he found a poet whose pathology was extraordinarily close to his own. Beneath the rosy languors of romantic convention there is in Heine's verse a masochistic melancholy that frustrates passion: a schizophrenia parallel to the break in rhythmic continuity, the sudden dissonance, the abrupt enharmonic transition that in Schumann's music may threaten the bloom of a melody that would sing in heart-easing, folk-like simplicity. Only in this light can we understand the obsessive quality in Schumann's rhythms. Initially, his fondness for square rhythms may have had something to do with his susceptibility to poetic metres, and especially to the simple stanzaic forms of folk verse. Ultimately, however, he drives his metrical patterns so hard because he is terrified of what might happen in the silence, were they to stop. The implications of this become evident only later, in his orchestral and chamber music.

The *Dichterliebe* cycle is one of the richest and most comprehensive of Schumann's works because in these Heine settings the two contradictory sides of his and the poet's ego sing together. Although the songs show a profound understanding of the workings of the mind in love, they are lyrical reflections on, not dramatic presentations of, experience. The climax of the cycle is significantly the lovely piano postlude, which rounds off the passion in nostalgia. Perhaps one might say that the spirit of all Schumann's finest songs is nocturnal; in the tenderly resonant harmony of *Mondnacht* we find the bliss of sleep, in *Allnächtlich im Traume* we have night as the augury of dreams and phantoms. Schumann evokes the night, either because its darkness may lap him in warm security, or because obscurity is filled with uncertain fears, the nameless shapes that flit by owl-light. Chopin's music has no such external associations; knowing the limitations of his nerves, he has an inner strength denied to Schumann.

This becomes clear when we turn from Schumann's short piano pieces and songs to his attempts at large-scale composition. His greatest songs are all settings of short poems, especially those of Heine which have an epigrammatic, folk-like directness. His treatment of the text is often strophic; in any case, his structures in song-writing usually preserve the simple ternary or binary form of his piano pieces, and he achieves some of his most beautiful effects when the harmonic structure 'overlaps' the literary setting (consider the exquisite harmonization of the last sung note of *Mondnacht*; the dominant seventh is resolved in the postlude, when the voice is silent). But Schumann, unlike Chopin, was never completely fulfilled in his mastery of short forms. Partly, perhaps, because he lived within the German tradition, he felt impelled to tackle the sonata, even though his youthful attempts were written with a laboured anguish very different from the spontaneity with which he composed piano pieces and songs.

In 1835 he composed three piano sonatas, dedicating the first to Clara. While they are less convincing than his other big piano work, the *Etudes Symphoniques* of 1837, written in his free variation technique, they are certainly not negligible, like Chopin's C minor Sonata. The material is as vital as one would expect from Schumann at the height of his youthful powers, and all three slow movements are nocturnal songs of the richest beauty. The themes of the first movements, too, have an aphoristic quality which might have lent itself well to sonata development, had such development made any appeal to Schumann's imagination. But while enharmonic transitions and Schubertian mediant relationships fascinated him as a means to express his dreams and fancies, in tonality as a means towards dramatic argument he had no interest at all. As a result, he tends to substitute simple transposition for development; and however excitingly remote the transpositions may be, to repeat is not to develop. Indeed, the sonata principle is rendered nonsensical when Schumann repeats long passages of his 'development' in the recapitulation, as he does in the last movement of the G minor Sonata. In the first movement of this sonata Schumann evades his difficulties by way of the continuity of his figuration and rhythmic pattern, and through the use of canonic devices in the development. In remarking that the movement portrayed "the wild dance of a desperate couple, Florestan and Chiarina", Schumann admitted the autobiographical genesis of the music; and while its stormy surge is not the less impressive for having little in common with the dualism of the classical sonata, it would have been still more impressive if it had been a little shorter. In these early sonatas he does not approach Chopin's inspired rethinking of classical precedent in his B flat minor Sonata. Schumann rather attempts to accommodate his genius to the past; and while genius would have told him when to stop, he preferred to listen to the spirit of tradition.

Very gradually, he came to realize what Chopin perceived intuitively: that he had not to copy, but to renew the past. In 1841 he consciously prepared himself to tackle the symphony itself by a study of the symphonies of Beethoven. Now Schumann's free 'variation' principle involves the metamorphosis of a motive into related forms; and Beethoven's symphonies involve, as we have seen, thematic growth and transformation. The difference is that whereas Beethoven's transformations are growth—the creation of an idea—Schumann's are variations on a mood. Thus when Schumann consciously takes over a technique which in Beethoven was in part subconscious, he creates an effect radically distinct from Beethoven's. Both derive their material from a basic motive or motives, usually stated in a slow introduction; but whereas in Beethoven the seed inevitably germinates, in Schumann the interrelation of the themes serves—often in association with obsessive rhythmic patterns—as a substitute for evolution. He links his themes *because* they have no inner capacity for growth.

Though this is often held to be a deficiency in Schumann's symphonies, it is not necessarily so. Greater stamina is needed to create a symphony, rather than a set of piano pieces or a song cycle, out of interlinked, mosaic-like moments of fancy; but we cannot simply say that Schumann lacked that stamina. We may love the Eusebius of the slow movement of the C major, with its almost Brucknerian soaring sixths and drooping sevenths and its ripe chromatic texture; we may be exasperated by the Florestan of the first movement, with its fanatically square rhythms, its rigidly reiterated motto, its 'development' by transposition. Yet each movement is an integral part of Schumann's contradictory nature; and if, like Mozart or Beethoven or even Schubert, he had created a classical synthesis from dualism, he would not have been Schumann. The fascination of his symphonies consists as much in their weaknesses as in their strength. In attempting to express all he had in him—and perhaps a bit more—he reveals his soul in a manner peculiarly touching. We see that his cosy domesticity is the inverse of his hypochondria: that his compulsive energy may at any moment flare into frenzy. We cannot claim his depth of feeling nor even perhaps, his integrity; but we can understand his troubles—and even forgive his orchestral texture which was dominated by the movements of his hands at a keyboard.* We are all heirs to romantic sensibility, all variously 'maladjusted' souls.

In the latter part of his life Schumann never relinquished his attempts to create works of symphonic stature. His three string quartets, for instance, show his technique of thematic interrelation in an even more extreme form: most of all in the lovely A major, which is significantly his most complex work harmonically. The texture at times suggests Chopin's last mazurkas, or even *Tristan* (Ex. 8):

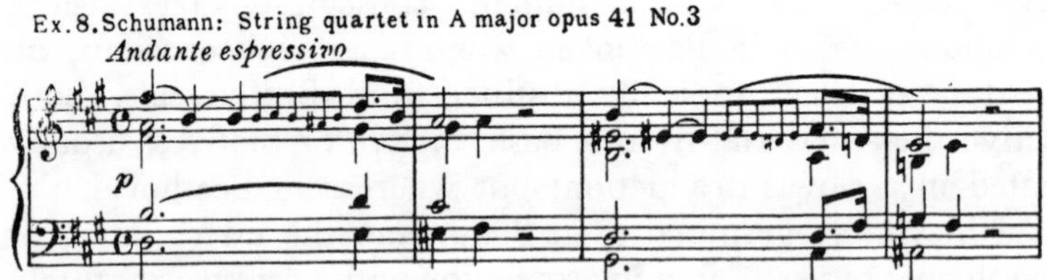

It almost seems as though in a work such as this, even more than in the D minor Symphony, Schumann was seeking a formal ideal of which he was but dimly conscious: a completely thematic unification of transitory moments of harmonic sensation, such as we find tentatively in Liszt's Sonata, consummately in the earlier work of Schoenberg.

In any case, the A major Quartet has no successor in Schumann's work. His most experimental works, though in some

* If one attempts to read one of Schumann's orchestral scores at the keyboard, the parts 'lie under the hands' with almost no modification. Berlioz's orchestral scores have to be radically rewritten before they make any sense in pianistic terms.

ways his most fascinating, are not those which wear best, if frequency of performance means anything. On the whole, his most convincing large-scale works are those which involve the piano, because the improvisatory element suggested by the keyboard usually provokes some relaxation of his fanatical search for unity. The Piano Concerto is largely a monothematic, even a monorhythmic, piece, yet its vitality flows and sings. It compels us, rather than forcibly compelling itself; even its orchestration glows, shedding inhibition as it follows and enriches the soloist's fantasy. Virtuosity for Schumann was never exhibitionism (his piano studies on Paganini's Caprices revealingly contrast with Liszt's from this point of view). Nor was it nervous excitement, as in Chopin. It was an emotional liberation; and it is no accident that both the Concerto and the *Phantasie*, opus 17—perhaps Schumann's greatest work for solo piano—should have been so closely associated with Clara.

In the face of works such as these it seems hardly valid to say that Schumann, like Chopin, was essentially a master of small forms. Yet it is true that an uninhibited outburst of passion on the grand scale, such as the *Phantasie*, is exceptional in his career; and that although the symphonies are a part of the essential Schumann, respect for tradition prevented him from creating a symphonic cosmos out of a kaleidoscope of moods. Only Wagner could feel sensations so heroically that they became a cosmos. Schumann revered Weber and sought for a suitable opera libretto all his life; yet the failure of *Genoveva* proves that he could never have been the creative link between Weber and Wagner. The twilit fancies, the ardent loves, the exuberant passions, the fireside simplicities, the nocturnal glimmerings of his youthful piano pieces and songs faded as he tried to build more from them than their nature warranted; and while the later symphonies and chamber works have many fine qualities, it is unquestionable that the later piano pieces are a decline. Only fitfully—most of all in the haunting, pitiful *Bird as Prophet*—is the old magic recaptured. Is it too fanciful to think that what this solitary bird prophesies—we recall the fluttering, pinioned birds and butterflies of Schumann's youth—is the darkness that ultimately overwhelmed him: the silent melancholy that proved too strong even for Clara's love? The terror of his last years was that he, who had lived for feeling and communion with the beloved, was caged in the silence of his solitude. Feeling was followed by inertia; the dreams of his youth became hallucinations. Schubert dictated to him sublime themes which he could not, alas, remember; the obsessive rhythms which had pounded through his youth became a single hammered note reiterated in his head—sound and fury, now signifying nothing. This German Pierrot's fate was more fearful than that of the Franco-Polish Pierrot whom consumption destroyed when his nerves were spent. For Schumann came to live in a past which he could no longer believe in; in the dream of his madness, the dreams he had lived for seemed a sham. His music, if sometimes almost unbearably poignant, is never tragic; but in contemplating the romantic myth which is his life one certainly feels both pity and terror. It is difficult to imagine anything more appalling than the letter which he wrote to Clara from the asylum, asking her to send him the little tune he had written for her, "long ago, when we were in love". He was forty-two.

Schumann was a no less original artist than Chopin. None the less, his desire to 'belong' to a tradition grew more urgent with the years; his divided and distracted soul could not, like Chopin's, be sufficient to itself. The kind of spiritual struggle which he experienced would have been equally unintelligible to Mendelssohn [1809–1847] or to Liszt, but for diametrically opposite reasons. The hints of romantic sensibility in Mendelssohn do not disturb the conservatism of his nature; in many ways he is closer to the eighteenth century than to Chopin. Liszt, on the other hand, was from the start the romantic hero-prophet, the conscious innovator whose work was a stimulus to others. Moreover, as conductor and teacher he did everything in his power to encourage other progressive artists—even when their appreciation of his efforts was as scant as Wagner's.

Mendelssohn's father was Jewish and a banker. His wealth was associated with a moralistic strain that found an only too ready outlet when his son settled in Victorian England, where material prosperity was considered the legitimate reward of virtue. During Mendelssohn's childhood, however, the family circle was cultivated and vivacious. He himself was intellectually precocious, and as socially amenable as Chopin was isolated in his nerves, or Schumann in his dreams and his personal affections. Thus although he too wrote little piano pieces, he designed them to fit comfortably into the drawing-room, rather than to express his private fancies. Chopin's short piano pieces are an exploration of piano technique, which is also a harmonic (and emotional) discovery; even Schumann's domesticities, being personal rather than social, imply a new approach to keyboard style. In Mendelssohn's *Songs without Words*, on the other hand, there is no pianistic feature that suggests the pressure of new experience. Melodically, they compromise. The tunes are habitually andante, neither fast nor slow: neither operatic nor folk-like. The gracious melody of the first piece of the first book, for instance, domesticates the step-wise contours of operatic lyricism far more thoroughly than do Schumann's Lied-like themes (Ex. 9):

The quasi-vocal turn coos; the arpeggiated accompaniment purrs on the hearth; the tune sinks in the sweet contentment of its persistent feminine endings.

In harmony and modulation, the piece attempts no breach with classical precedent. The harmonic flow of the arpeggios is sensitively spaced, and the use of mediant relationships is touching; but Mendelssohn's modulations nowhere approach the visionary unexpectedness of Schubert's, or the dream-like fantasy of Schumann's. The limpness of the melody is here justified by a mood of exquisite relaxation. Sometimes, however, it droops into sentimentality because Mendelssohn's chromaticisms, though less frequent than those in the last works of Mozart, have little of Mozart's linear vitality. Mozart's chromaticisms stimulate movement; Mendelssohn's, like

Spohr's, tend to clog the growth of the line. A tiny song piece like the E major from Book 2 seems pretentious because the harmony gives a disproportionate stress to the slight, fragmentary tune. At our fireside, dreams may be encouraged, but pretence we must avoid at all costs.

There are no dreams in Mendelssohn's *Songs without Words*, though there are often charming fancies like the B minor piece from the sixth book, or the last of the Gondoliers' songs (in A minor, from the fifth book). To compare this last piece with Chopin's rich and strange evocation of Venetian light and water in his *Barcarolle* is to see that the two belong to irreconcilable worlds. Chopin's unprecedented sonorities create a visionary Venice within his sensibility; Mendelssohn's prettily melancholic piece brings a picture postcard into our parlour. It is a tasteful, indeed a beautiful postcard; but it is not, and does not pretend to be, an imaginative revelation.

How far Mendelssohn is from Chopin and Schumann is revealed in the fact that the most successful pieces in the *Songs without Words* tend to be those which approximate to sonata form. In the B minor from Book 2, for instance, the energy of the repeated note figuration to some extent counteracts the periodicity of the clauses; the onward drive of the music even provokes abrupt, but convincing, modulations in the brief development. It is interesting too that although the piece is grateful to play, it is not pianistic; it rather suggests string technique, most of all in the coda, when the repeated notes gradually still themselves. This reminds us that in his earliest, adolescent works Mendelssohn had already used the classical symphonic convention with an authenticity unapproached by his contemporaries. The Octet for strings—written in his seventeenth year—pays homage to tradition by employing sonata form for all the movements. It recalls Mozart in its lyrical grace, the youthful Beethoven in its dramatic vigour, and Weber in its richness of sonority; yet in working within an inherited tradition Mendelssohn does not stifle his personality. Significantly, the movements in all his early works which most reveal his nature are the scherzi, in which the formalities and symmetries of classical precedent become a dancing play of fancy. Although these movements are formally strict, and tonally less adventurous than Haydn, Mozart, or Beethoven (let alone Schubert), they seem to suggest that tradition itself is dissolving into insubstantiality, so rapid is the movement, so feathery the texture. Mendelssohn's overture to *A Midsummer Night's Dream*, also composed in his seventeenth year, manifests the true classical spirit in creating an entity out of material as diverse as the fairies' gossamer-like frolics, the ceremonial theme for Theseus's wedding, and the grotesque 'translation' of Bottom. At the same time, its delicately poetic scoring eternalizes sensation in a manner comparable with that of Weber's fairy music. Mendelssohn, like Weber, still lives in the classical world, while admitting that it is now a world of exquisite artifice.

This is why his adolescent works remained in some ways his best. For a boy of sixteen, or even twenty, the sonata principle could legitimately become excitingly fanciful rather than dramatic. As he grew older, he became more aware that he had been born 'late'. Deeply though he loved Mozart's music, he could emulate only its surface elegance, not the intensity within the charm; greatly though he revered Beethoven, he could but fitfully recover the fire that had made his sonatas a revolutionary force. The *Hebrides* overture is probably Mendelssohn's finest work, because he here challenges middle-period Beethoven on his own ground, developing a pithy subject admirably adapted to sonata style, while attaining a strange immateriality in the hazily floating modulations at the opening of the development. The battle is thrilling, though the issues are no longer a matter of life and death. The Beethovenian trumpet-calls no longer summon one to action; they lure one away to a Hebridean fairyland.

Occasionally, the drama of the classical tradition lives again unambiguously in Mendelssohn's work. The first movement of the E flat Quartet, opus 44, for instance, has a powerful sonata theme incorporating a wriggling semiquaver figure which may become either a rhetorical gesture or an accompanying figuration. The subsidiary themes—especially a wailing descending figure in dotted rhythm—are also strong, and interlock with the first theme in a development at once exciting and spacious. The scherzo is even more impressive, since it combines sonata drama with the feathery, dancing texture which is the essence of Mendelssohnian fancy. The last work which Mendelssohn completed—the F minor Quartet—is even more nervously intense: so much so that Mendelssohn forgets his impeccable manners in creating a string texture that strains the medium.

He evens begins the recapitulation of the first movement anticipatorily, at what appears to be the climax of the development.

Music of such force is, however, exceptional in Mendelssohn's career. Perhaps the pent-up emotion of years was released by his sister's death and his own increasing physical frailty; certainly something more than the example of Beethoven's opus 95 in the same key is needed to explain it. More representative is the Mendelssohn of the symphonies, especially the 'Italian'. Here he handles classical convention more expertly than Schumann; yet the music fascinates less. The themes are often fetching, and if they lack the innately symphonic character of those of the *Hebrides* overture, they serve as well as the lyrical tunes of the average rococo symphony. The orchestration is as sensitive as Schumann's is gauche. Yet Schumann was striving to create a new symphonic ideal, approximating, perhaps, to the Lisztian symphonic poem; Mendelssohn was accepting a legacy from the past. Only seldom could he feel that past so powerfully that it became present. For the rest, he was content to manipulate his pseudo-classical material mechanically; and to rely on the fact that he was close enough to the classical tradition for its conventions to be still acceptable to a middle-class audience that then, as now, feared change.

It is revealing that although Mendelssohn could afford to be influenced by the dramatic rhetoric of middle-period Beethoven—most notably in the F minor Quartet—he failed whenever he attempted to imitate the lyrical or contrapuntal manner of Beethoven's last years. Both Beethoven and Mendelssohn studied Bach; and Beethoven developed in his late works a unique contrapuntal texture which yet resembled Bach's in effecting a tension between line and harmony. Mendelssohn's counterpoint is Bachian imitation, but even less than Brahms's or Schumann's is it Bachian in spirit. When successful, as in the Preludes and Fugues of opus 35, it hardly pretends to be genuine linear writing. The well-known E minor, for instance, begins with a richly arpeggiated prelude leading to a harmonically derived fugue subject; this reaches an almost Lisztian 'apotheosis' in a chorale, accompanied by a resurgence of the flowing arpeggios. The work is structurally convincing, and more romantically 'progressive' than Mendelssohn was wont to be; but it has no more to do with Bach than with late

Beethoven. This is not surprising, for Mendelssohn betrays no interest in, let alone knowledge of, religious experience.

His attempt, when he settled in England, to create a nineteenth-century version of Handelian oratorio and Bachian cantata was thus doomed to failure. The English still sang Handel; but the zest of the Chosen People in an age of mercantile expansion was by now wearing shoddy; and there had never been any organic connexion between the spiritual implications of Handelian oratorio and those of the Bach passion. There are moments of genuine and powerful dramatic feeling in Mendelssohn's *Elijah*; but one has to admit that his harmonic mannerisms—for instance, his fondness for inversions of the diminished seventh—are much more obtrusive in his religious than in his secular instrumental music: and that the weak periodicity of his phrases, with their limp feminine endings, is the more damaging in music which aims at drama and monumental grandeur.

During his visits to London, Gounod was greatly impressed by Mendelssohn's pseudo-oratorios. To us, perhaps, Gounod's sweetness seems preferable to Mendelssohn's solemnity; we can take a little Tennysonian honey, so long as we are not simultaneously bullied with a pietistic morality that seems to us irrelevant. It is significant that Mendelssohn should have reached the pinnacle of his fame in a rapidly and recently industrialized England. Our native musical tradition being moribund, we were the more prepared to accept a consciously archaistic style: and to welcome in musical convention a spurious religiosity which reflected the element of unconscious humbug in our morality and beliefs. George Bernard Shaw hit the nail on the head with characteristic trenchancy when he pointed out that Mendelssohn, "who was shocked at Auber's writing an opera in which a girl sang '*Oui, c'est demain*' (meaning 'To-morrow I shall be a bride') at her looking-glass before going to bed, was himself ready to serve up the chopping to pieces of the prophets of the grove with his richest musical spice to suit the compound of sanctimonious cruelty and base materialism which his patrons, the British Pharisees, called their religion."

We may think that Shaw was going a little far when he said: "Set all that dreary fugue manufacture, with its Sunday School sentimentalities and music school ornamentalities, against the expressive and vigorous choruses of Handel and ask yourself on your honour whether there is the slightest difference in kind between Stone him to Death and Under the Pump with a Kick and a Thump from Dorothy." He was none the less making a valid and important point. In an industrial society the values of art were becoming indistinguishable from those of commerce. It is not a question of the decline of a talent, for, as we have seen, Mendelssohn's last work, the F minor Quartet, was one of his finest, if not most characteristic. In a sense, Mendelssohn's case is sadder than slow decay, for he prostituted his gifts wilfully, and with the most high-minded intentions.

2

LISZT AND ROMANTIC VIRTUOSITY

LISZT [1811–1886] was born two years later than Mendelssohn: spiritually it might have been twenty. His acquaintance with Mendelssohn, if not extensive, was cordial; yet it is difficult to imagine a temperament more remote than Liszt's from Mendelssohn's socially 'safe', musically conservative gentility. It is interesting that for Liszt, as for Wagner, the Jews became synonymous with the triumph of the world of trade and mechanization. Wagner did not think of the Jew romantically, as the solitary outcast, like himself; the Jew was Meyerbeer, indecently successful, the degraded and degrading architect of a commercialized world. Liszt too—though it was not in his nature to hate—believed that the Jew was opposed to the Artist-Hero, whose duty was to preserve the aristocratic virtues, while striving for liberty both spiritual and political.

It is odd to think that during Liszt's childhood on the Esterházy estate many people must have been able to recall the days when Haydn was Director of Music. Much of the cosmopolitan glitter of the palace still survived; the vast grey wastes that surrounded the aristocratic oasis were certainly as unchanged as the gipsies who roamed the countryside. Years later Lizst wrote a book in which he contrasted the avaricious, factory-enslaved life of the city-dwellers, the Jews, with the 'poetical Egotism' of the gipsies. Possessed by "a mad love of Nature, the gipsy would enjoy his passions completely, fully, on every occasion and forever. He is not the passive instrument that reproduces the feeling of others and adds nothing to them"; in possessing the passions of others, he is always himself a creator, 'the natural virtuoso'.

Whether or no this is an accurate description of the gipsy—and whether or no Liszt had gipsy blood in his own veins—it certainly describes the kind of artist he himself wanted to be. But of course he was not in fact primitive. The world to which he gravitated was as aristocratic and cosmopolitan as that of the Esterházys. In the early 1830s he was living in Paris, a youthful prodigy of virtuosity who, through his talents, magnetism, and extreme physical beauty, became the intimate friend of the most brilliant group of poets, painters, and musicians in Europe: and the lover of a succession of women, all beautiful, mostly of noble birth. Unlike Chopin, he turned outwards to meet this resplendent society, becoming the prototype of the Artist as Hero. Aristocratic hauteur is fired by a primitive frenzy; unruly passion is rendered amenable by exquisitely gracious manners; the acceptance of cultural and intellectual aristocracy is reconciled with an ardent if unspecific enthusiasm for the ideals of the 1830 Revolution. The impact of Liszt on Europe is, indeed, something to which there is no musical parallel. Only in Byron do we find the same combination of aristocratic elegance with revolutionary force, of fearless sincerity with histrionic virtuosity. Even in youth, Liszt became a legend; the long mane of fair hair, the eccentric 'Bohemian' garb, became more familiar, as well as more interesting, than the private life of the most fabulous film-star. Medallions were showered on him, town bands turned out to meet him, riots accompanied his gladiatorial progress through Europe. Significantly, the only country where he was a relative failure was industrialized England. Distrusting his histrionics, we put our faith in, and money on, Mendelssohn.

But we must return to Liszt's early days in Paris, where there were three musicians Liszt knew who decisively stimulated his imagination. The greatest of them, Berlioz, affected him the least directly. Though he was impressed, even overwhelmed, by Berlioz's "Babylonian and Ninevehan imagination", his nature was much more egotistic.* Berlioz forgot himself in operatic pro-

* There is, however, another pianist-composer—Charles Henri Morhange, known as Alkan [1813–1888]—whose affinity with Berlioz is profound. His melodies, like those of Berlioz, have a poised grandeur deriving from the classical operatic tradition, while his harmonies—seldom chromatic, sometimes modal—have an enigmatic flavour arising from the fact that they are frequently prompted by an unexpected melodic progression. (Consider the Funeral March from the Symphony for piano in relation to that from Berlioz's *Symphonie Funèbre et Triomphale.*) Both composers combine their melodic, operatic approach with a deep understanding of Beethoven's dramatic architecture (consider the first movement from the Symphony for piano); and there is perhaps some similarity between Berlioz's orchestral virtuosity and the necromantic quality of Alkan's pianism. The highly original variation-set *Le Festin d'Aesope* suggests Berlioz not only in the aristocratic bearing of the theme, but also in the manner in which it "does coolly the things that are most fiery": consider the astonishing final variation and coda.

jection, whether or no he wrote for the stage. Liszt became his own actors, in life as in his art.

The impact of Chopin was more immediately significant; for he was a pianist-composer. Yet while his opus 10 studies certainly influenced Liszt's keyboard technique, the effect of Chopin's music on Liszt was neither lasting nor deep. Chopin, like Liszt and unlike Berlioz, was an egocentric artist. But whereas his egoism was introverted, Liszt's found expression in extrovert exuberance. Chopin's virtuosity became the revelation of his dreams; Liszt's was designed, exhibitionistically, for the platform. This is why the third musical personality whom he met in Paris was, for him, the most immediately important.

Paganini was not a great composer like Berlioz, nor a profoundly original minor master like Chopin. But he was one of the most phenomenal executants, on any instrument, who has ever lived; and his virtuosity—like that of Liszt's gipsies—was essentially creative. Few living violinists are capable of playing Paganini's unaccompanied Caprices—the only works he wrote down in a form approximating to what he played on the concert platform. Even from those players who can negotiate the notes, we can acquire but a shadowy idea of the effect of Paganini's performance on contemporary audiences. The music is not—in the medium it hardly could be—remarkable for harmonic experiment of the type associated with Chopin's emotional exploration. None the less, the audacities of its virtuosity translate its incisive, mordant lyricism into Hoffmanesque necromancy. The icy glitter of the music is the inverse of the hot blood of romantic harmony: just as the sinister, cadaverous figure of Paganini himself haunts the nineteenth century, transforming romantic glamour into the spectral and demoniacal.

In a keyboard-dominated nineteenth century it was no accident that this dark undercurrent to romantic afflatus should have exerted a greater influence on piano technique than on that of the violin. As a youth, Liszt had been famed not as a composer, but as a virtuoso and improviser of mythical powers. The first works to reveal his creativity are his pianistic transcriptions of Paganini's violin caprices, and his *Etudes d'Exécution Transcendante*, which were intended to be a pianistic complement to Paganini's work. In both, exhibitionism releases, rather than disguises, creative energy. Even when the youthful Liszt does not call for 'transcendental' virtuosity, his music usually implies exhibitionism. The first book of his *Années de Pèlerinage*, for instance, is a musical record of his tour of Switzerland with the first of his aristocratic loves, the Comtesse d'Angoult. The pieces—prefaced with literary quotations from Byron, Schiller, and other apostles of romanticism—express his reactions to the places they saw: the beauties of art and Nature. The most remarkable piece in the collection—*La Vallée d'Obermann*—has a long quotation from Etienne de Senacour, which indicates how Liszt's consciousness of place was, like his virtuosity, a stimulus to his egocentric imagination: "Vast consciousness of Nature everywhere overwhelming and impenetrable, universal passion, indifference, advanced wisdom, voluptuous abandon, all the profound desires and torments that a human heart can hold, I have felt them all, suffered them all, in this memorable night." In this piece keyboard technique becomes self-dramatization; the transitory moods of the chromatics and the quasi-orchestral sonorities convince because they involve us in Liszt's rhetoric. Chopin communicates his dreams to us; Liszt 'presents' himself in a given situation. He could say, with Childe Harold, "I live not in myself but I become Portion of that around me"; and he acts with such aplomb that we are swept into the play, willy-nilly.

This is still more evident in the second book of *Années de Pèlerinage*, inspired by his visit to Italy in 1838–9. These pieces are all evoked by works of art, rather than by Nature. *Il Penseroso*, for instance, was inspired by the Michelangelo statue in San Lorenzo at Florence. The tenebrous gloom of its chromaticism and viscid keyboard texture is a romantic gesture. Yet this theatrical presentation of the Artist as Melancholic is profoundly felt: to dramatize oneself is not necessarily to be insincere. Indeed, this brief but oppressively powerful piece haunted Liszt's imagination for nearly thirty years, for recollections of it crop up in later works. It both epitomizes Byronic melancholy, and anticipates *Tristan* by more than a decade. The difference is that whereas Wagner in *Tristan* had become a force that shook Europe, Liszt in this little piece is an artist acting a part: just as he acts, with equal conviction, an utterly different part in the *Eclogue* from the Swiss book, with its innocent, diatonic tune and exquisitely sensuous 'added notes' in the piano texture.

Since Liszt is a histrionic artist, it is not surprising that the basis of his idiom is operatic; he translates operatic gestures into pianistic virtuosity. Chopin's style, too, absorbed Italian *bel canto*; but his model was the most reticent, the most inward, in a sense the least characteristic of Italian dramatic composers. Bellinian lyricism could become a part of Chopin's inner life; Liszt, on the other hand, preserves, even enhances, the panache of the stage. He had no need of a theatre because, on the concert platform, he acted all the parts himself. We must remember that in his youth Liszt's creative work was centred in paraphrases and arrangements of other people's music, designed as a vehicle for his virtuosity. Sometimes—as in his masterly arrangement's of Berlioz's orchestral works—these were written in order to introduce the music of his friends to an audience that would be unlikely to hear it in its original form. Most often, however, they were potted versions of the operas that were his public's staple musical diet. These 'paraphrases' served much the same function as the gramophone record to-day, at least when they were not too difficult for the talented amateur. More exciting, and more significant, were the big *fantasies dramatiques* in which the well-loved operatic themes became no more than a stimulus to the virtuoso's improvisatory genius. As the actor needs the play to exhibit his talent, so Liszt needs the impetus of someone else's music. In the beautiful fantasy on Bellini's *Norma*, for instance, he is as though possessed by the themes; his virtuosity recreates Bellini's refined lyricism into full-blooded passion of almost Verdian directness. Chopin reveals the inwardness of Bellini's art; Liszt makes it almost more 'operatic' than Bellini's own operas. The fantasy on Mozart's *Don Giovanni* is an equally impressive, if more complex piece. Liszt chooses from the opera those aspects that appealed to his imagination—the Don's amorous abandon, the sepulchral horror of the graveyard scene—and created from them a tone-poem in which piano sonority is hardly less rich and multifarious than the sonority of the nineteenth-century orchestra. The work is not a tawdry substitute for Mozart; it is an aspect of Mozart, re-enacted by a consummate rhetorician.

The operatic nature of Liszt's talent is revealed most directly, of course, in his songs. His early setting of Goethe's *Freudvoll und Leidvoll* is highly Italianate in its persistent use of the falling sixth, of wide-spanning arpeggio phrases, and of the aspiring turn: while the emotional sixths themselves generate the sobbing alternations of major and minor, and the piquant 'Neapolitan' alterations, in the arpeggiated accompaniment (Ex. 10):

Ex. 10. Liszt: Freudvoll und Leidvoll

The song acts itself, as it is sung, as much as a narrative scena like Liszt's lovely, luxurious setting of *Kennst du das Land*, in which the softly piercing dissonances of ninth and eleventh 'point' the sobs in the melody. There is nothing here of the 'innig' quality of Schumann's songs. If we compare Liszt's setting of Heine's *Anfangs wollt ich fast verzagen* with that of Schumann, we can see that whereas Schumann's song is lyrical reflection, Liszt's is dramatic presentation. The lyrical phrases break under the stress of feeling; the poem's bitterness is summed up in the unexpected, inverted resolution from major to minor. The tremendously powerful setting of *Vergiftet sind meine Lieder* is a similar, but more extreme case. Liszt, unlike Schumann, here dispenses with lyricism altogether; the dissonant appoggiaturas of the opening and the ninths of the climax are as violent as *Tristan*, and much starker, more abrupt (Ex. 11):

Ex. 11. Liszt: Vergiftet sind meine Lieder

When Liszt sets French words his style is usually less declamatory, more lyrical. But the tender contours of *O quand je dors* are not less Italianate because they are relatively less robust.

Liszt transformed three of his songs—settings of Italian

words—into piano pieces: the set of three Petrarch sonnets which appears in the seconc' book of the *Années de Pèlerinage.* Though these ripely beautiful pieces bear a generic relationship to the style of Chopin's nocturnes, they could never be mistaken for Chopin. Chopin's melodies are often reveries which stimulate his harmonic and pianistic invention, without being in themselves significant. Liszt's *bel canto* themes are the essence of his passion: which is reinforced by the arabesques of his virtuosity and the luxuriance of his harmony. Consider, for instance, two of the finest pieces of Lizst's early maturity, from the collection *Harmonies Poétiques et Religieuses. Funérailles* is a heroic elegy, an 'oration' dedicated to the memory of friends who died in the Hungarian Revolution of 1849. It opens with a slow introduction exploiting 'orchestrally' the percussive depths of the piano, with dissonantly prepared diminished sevenths sighing frenziedly above the drums. This leads to a slow funeral march that suggests Berlioz in heroic grandeur, Verdi in robust vitality; the rising sixth, as so often in Liszt's themes, is prominent. A contrasting melody in the relative major, marked *lagrimoso*, brings Italian *bel canto* into its own: note how the chromatic alteration in the sighing, hypnotically repeated two-bar periods suggests the harmonic sob of the Neapolitan chord (Ex. 12):

Ex. 12. Liszt: *Funérailles*

Then follows a march section which builds up a terrific virtuoso climax over an ostinato bass, and leads to a 'triumphant' restatement of the funeral march. The passion explodes in recitative; the orator is so moved that his voice breaks. Then the piece concludes with a whispered reminiscence of the *bel canto* melody, *dolcissimo*, passing through sensuous mediant modulations: and a mysterious reference to the revolutionary ostinato. The *dolcissimo* recollection takes us into the realm of personal regret for our friends; the wild coda reminds us again of the epical significance of their death.

The other piece, *Bénédiction de Dieu dans la Solitude*, is even more remarkable. It is not deliberately oratorical, and therefore operatic, for it deals with God's power, through Nature, to soothe the turbulence of passion. The serene first theme is again, however, operatic *cantilena*, surrounded by a haze of 'added' notes in the piano figuration, warmly luminous in the key of F sharp major. The theme is repeated several times, ranging enharmonically through remote keys, and becoming more impassioned as the figuration grows more rich. Again, chromatic alteration in the melodic line suggests the emotional change in harmony, especially in the frequent transitions to the flat submediant. A brief diatonic middle section in this flat submediant soon leads to an enormous expansion of the first song theme, with ever more opulent figuration; the ultimate climax comes in B flat—a second remove to the flat submediant. Finally, the figuration dissolves away in tensionless, pentatonic arabesques, leading to a consolatory statement of the 'middle section' in the tonic. A short retrospective epilogue both sums up the essence of the song theme and expresses elliptically the relation between tonic and flat submediant (Ex. 13):

Ex. 13. Liszt: Bénédiction de Dieu dans la Solitude

Many of Liszt's song-like pieces have this kind of valedictory coda, in which all passion is spent; not often, however, does he achieve so deep a serenity out of his operatic lyricism, his sensuous harmony and virtuosity. Whether or no the piece is religious in the orthodox sense, it certainly represents the romantic Artist's spiritual fulfilment; and the same is true of the two *Légendes*. St. Francis of Assisi speaks to the birds in tender operatic recitative; the birds chirrup in glinting pianistic virtuosity, their song being tonally ambiguous owing to a prevalence of augmented triads. In the companion piece ('St. Francis of Paola walking on the waves') the song theme is more hymn-like than operatic; but the virtuosity of the waves again threatens tonality with its chromatic sequences and seething diminished sevenths. The piece is a superb example of the colouristic and dramatic use of the piano. The music is not 'orchestral', for only the piano could create this astonishing sonority; yet it evokes a scene and a situation as vividly as could an orchestra, combined with the scenic resources of an opera house.

Perhaps one might say that operatic lyricism was the positive pole of Liszt's self-dramatizing talent, harmonic and pianistic experiment the negative. Certainly we find that in his middle years the Paganinian, demoniacal side of his virtuosity led him to create a number of works associated with the infernal: and that harmonically and pianistically these are often of breath-taking audacity. The *Fantasia quasi una Sonata*, composed "after reading Dante", is the earliest and one of the strangest of these excursions to Hell. More tightly wrought, less rhetorical, and therefore more frightening, are the first *Mephisto* waltzes, and the *Totentanz* for piano and orchestra—a series of variations, inspired by Orcagna's frescoes at Pisa, on the Dies Irae. Alongside lyrical reminiscences of opera we find here ferocious passages of metallic dissonance which, in their simultaneous use of appoggiaturas and the resolutions, suggest Bartók and Stravinsky (Ex. 14):

Even Listzt's fantasy on the waltz from Gounod's *Faust* seems dominated by the spirit of Mephisto; for Gounod's footling tune, as redolent of the tawdry, gas-lit glamour of the Parisian theatre as it is remote from Goethe, is transformed by Liszt's harmonic ellipses and sinister virtuosity into a devil-dance. In the haunted, tritonal metamorphosis of the tune in the coda and the hectic chromatic stretto, a world shatters in ruins. The showpiece designed to amuse Society acquires an almost Berliozian, apocalyptic quality: at least we can see that this piece of ostensible frivolity came from the same mind that created the

Mephisto waltzes and the appalling vision of chaos in the first section of the symphonic poem, *Hunnenschlacht*.

Whether as romantic Hero or as Mephistopheles—though especially in his Satanic role—Liszt betrays a fondness for harmonic processes (augmented chords, mediant relationships, whole-tone progressions, chromatically altered notes) which weaken tonality. A large-scale piece like the *Bénédiction de Dieu* is formally convincing because it is mainly an elaboration of a single melody; virtuosity becomes creative expansion. In the more demonic ranges of his imagination he cannot, however, rely simply on lyrical decoration; the stranger are his harmonic progressions, the more urgent is his search for a new formal criterion. From this point of view, the key-work in his career is the Piano Sonata of 1855. Liszt had long been fascinated by Schubert's 'Wanderer' Fantasia, which is a four-movement sonata built on transformations of a single theme, the keys of the four movements standing in mediant relationship to one another. In his own sonata, Liszt telescopes the movements into one, and builds all the material on four interrelated motives stated at the beginning. He expresses a much more violent alternation of moods than does Schumann in his cycles of piano pieces; and the wilder the alternation the more important is it that the moods should preserve their inner identity. So the work is unified not by the classical disposition of key centres, but by a vestigial 'serial' technique. The motives are transmuted into widely contrasted themes: the snarling, demoniacal phrase derived from the diminished seventh becomes nostalgically lyrical; the sinister repeated note figure is metamorphosed into cantabile grandeur, or into pathetic *bel canto* (Ex. 15):

The romantic lover and the devil are synonymous, for all the actors in this drama are aspects of a single ego; as were the actors in Wagner's later music dramas. Liszt's embryonic serial technique is, indeed, an anticipation of Wagner's creative method far more significant than the superficial resemblances between the chromaticism of the two composers. We may note how frequently—especially in the quicker sections of his sonata—Liszt employs a quasi-Wagnerian 'harmonic polyphony'; the music becomes a tissue of linear motives, derived from a harmonic progression.

The sonata is Liszt's greatest virtuoso piece; yet its formal discovery no longer necessarily entails virtuosity. Henceforth, pianism was in itself less important for Liszt than composition. His celebrity had been not merely European, but international. In a specially constructed, luxuriously appointed coach, with his medallions and insignia and his three hundred and sixty-five cravats (one for each day of the year), he had performed to the barbarians among the minarets of remotest Russia and Turkey. Now he voluntarily relinquished fame and riches and retired to Weimar, to devote his energies to composition and also—with un-Wagnerian altruism—to the cause of progressive musicians everywhere. Again, Wagner *is* the prophet, who can see and feel nothing but the force of his prophecy. Liszt acts the prophet, seriously and sincerely, becoming the guide and mentor of the rising generation. Whereas Wagner accorded to Liszt no more than a grudging homage in so far as he identified himself with the Wagnerian cause, Liszt reverenced Wagner with something approaching idolatry; he was prepared to abandon his own creative work if only he could raise adequate funds to finance a production of *The Ring*. Yet though Wagner's genius is self-justificatory, he himself admitted that "since my acquaintance with Liszt's compositions my treatment of harmony has become very different from what it was formerly". He added, characteristically, that "it is, however, indiscreet to babble this secret to the whole world".

This curious blend of self-advertisement with humility in Liszt's make-up is evident when, at Weimar, he took time off from conducting other people's music to work on his own compositions. At the age of thirty-six he returned, as it were, to school. He studied orchestration, for he realized that the formal conception inherent in his sonata could achieve a more satisfactory resolution in orchestral terms. His symphonic poems all have a literary basis which is also a musical idea: they deal with the Artist as Hero, his tribulations and ultimate triumph. The basis of the musical structure is usually a quite primitive and traditional ternary or rondo form; but the works adapt the technique of Liszt's sonata to the orchestra in being monothematic. The various aspects of the Hero's ego are separate, yet the same; and the form of the music is the revelation of their identity. Liszt does not create themes through conflict, as Beethoven does; his music, like Wagner's, is self-revelation rather than evolution. But although his substitution of repetition for development sometimes creates an easy alternative to composition, Liszt is not necessarily wrong in principle because he differs from classical tradition. Indeed, the closer he approaches to Beethoven the less convincing he tends to be; his 'apotheosis' codas, for instance, are usually an intention rather than creative realization.

Yet the historical importance of Liszt's symphonic poems can hardly be overestimated. He achieved Schumann's unconscious ambition, creating a technique whereby the fluctuating passions of the personal sensibility could be organized not merely in miniature, but on an extended scale. Perhaps it is not fortuitous that both Schumann and Liszt scored in a manner dictated by the movements of their hands at a keyboard. The difference was that Liszt's piano texture was itself of 'orchestral' richness and variety. Texturally as well as formally, he had more to teach his *immediate* successors than Berlioz. Although Wagner would have found his salvation in any case, it is hardly excessive to say that Liszt showed the way to all post-classical orchestral composers, and most of all to those who, like the Russian school, were the least deeply rooted in tradition.

The ultimate revelation of Liszt's genius comes, appropriately enough, in a symphonic version of Goethe's *Faust*—a supreme masterpiece that epitomizes at once the romantic yearning to make the ego self-sufficient, and the Satanic spirit of denial. The Faust theme of the first movement and its various mutations are Liszt as the arbiter of human destiny. The theme is significantly Wagnerian in being based on a series of augmented triads—and so almost entirely harmonic in its implications; the 'new man' brings with him a new tonal world. The Marguerite theme of the second movement is Woman in relation to Liszt—and the passive side of his own nature. In the last movement, portraying Mephistopheles, the same themes are metamorphosed into snarling venom. Frequently one feels in Liszt's music that the Satanic impulse is the strongest; in the companion symphony, inspired by Liszt's other literary hero, Dante, the Inferno is much more convincing than the Paradiso. The 'Faust' Symphony, however, is so deeply felt that the Devil does not have the last word. His malformations are restored to pristine beauty in a thrilling choral epilogue, where for once the apotheosis is justified. Perhaps it is precisely because Liszt knew so much about the Devil at first hand that the religious resolution impresses us. Certainly it points the way to the last phase of his work, when this surprising virtuoso, having relinquished the concert platform for the gospel of Art, dedicated his art to the gospel of God.

We cannot say that he experienced a religious conversion, for even as a youth he had been fascinated by the glamour of Catholic ritual. If there is an element of theatricality in his final admission to the Faith, we have seen that theatricality is the essence of his temperament, not to be confused with insincerity. Apart from Bruckner, most of the great composers of the nineteenth century—Schubert, Berlioz, Brahms, Wagner, Verdi—were agnostic. Liszt was genuinely a man of faith, according to his own rather lurid lights; his attempts to reform Catholic church music was thus a profoundly serious undertaking, whether or no it was successful. If he was sincere, he had to create a church music that grew from the demands of his own nature. The Church might be unchanging, as God certainly was. But man's attitude to it and Him changed inevitably; and one did no honour to God or the Church by pretending otherwise.

St. Elizabeth—the first of the gargantuan creations of Liszt's Roman period—is thus a very operatic kind of oratorio; and *Christus* employs a polyphony which is as harmonically rooted as that of the Piano Sonata or of *Tristan*. Liszt had already experimented with a highly chromatic polyphony in piano works like the *Weinen, Klagen* Variations and in the Organ Fantasia and Fugue on B-A-C-H. In these works he often approaches atonality—a chromaticism so extreme as to be without even an implied tonal centre. The pretence of strict fugal writing is not sustained much longer than in the Piano Sonata; but even more than in that revolutionary work it is the serial interrelations of the motives that keep the music from collapse. In Liszt's very last works this disintegrative, sensuous atonality is paradoxically combined with vocal, Gregorian modality, creating—especially in *Via Crucis*, a series of meditations for soli, chorus, and organ—a brooding, involuted ecstasy to which there is no parallel in nineteenth-century music. The glowing, continuous texture of *Parsifal* seems, in comparison, supremely self-confident. *Via Crucis* has some resemblance to the most advanced chromatic writing of the early seventeenth century; only whereas a composer such as Jacopus Gallus starts from vocal modality and disintegrates it into the chromatic *frisson*, Liszt works the other way round. Chromatic disintegration and whole-tone ambiguity seem to be seeking resolution in serene modality. Liszt seeks, and does not find. The poignancy of this music is conditional on its senile fragmentariness; and something the same is true of the single symphonic poem which he composed in these final years. The last movement of *From the Cradle to the Grave* is called "To the Tomb: the Cradle of the Future Life". Again a spare linear chromaticism and ambiguous whole-tone progressions create an atmosphere of hovering expectancy. The music lives between sleeping and waking; but what we are waking to is indeterminate.

We find the same disturbing fragmentariness in the small piano pieces and songs which are the secular counterpart of the ecclesiastical works of his last years. It would be difficult to imagine music superficially more remote from the flamboyance of his youth. In the third and last book of the *Années de Pèlerinage* the water-music of *Les Jeux d'Eaux à la Villa d'Este* has acquired a lucid precision that suggests Ravel; and while the two beautiful threnodies, *Aux Cyprès de la Villa d'Este*, preserve the operatic melodies and arpeggiated accompaniments, the texture is sparse, the harmonic progressions epigrammatic (consider the Tristanesque opening of the second piece). Liszt the romantic lover here recollects in tranquillity; the mane of hair has grown white instead of golden, but it sits well on the Abbé's robes. Mephistophelian fire may still dart from his eyes, too; the virtuosity of the last *Mephisto* waltzes is sharp, brittle, more scarifying in its restraint than the romantically 'horrid' rhetoric of the 'Dante' Sonata. The very last pieces are perhaps not so much fully-fledged artistic creations as sketches towards new worlds of thought and feeling. The *Czardas Macabre* suggests

XXXIX Clara Wieck.

XL A portrait of Gilles by Watteau.

Bartók in being based largely on barbaric parallel fifths. *Nuages Gris* is a keyless study in the impressionistic use of augmented triads; *Unstern* creates nightmare from whole-tone progressions and harmonic ostinatos. In the last songs, the vocal line is mostly in fragmentary, non-tonal recitative, while the piano part is exiguous. Usually the songs peter out on an unresolved dissonance. The most remarkable of them is (significantly) a setting of Musset's 'J'ai perdu ma force et ma vie'. The barless *parlando* vocal writing, the unresolved appoggiaturas, the aphoristic enharmonic modulations remind us that though Liszt was born two years after Haydn's death, he died only two years before the birth of Alban Berg.

The suggestion of Bartók in the last piano pieces is interesting in view of the fact that in old age Liszt developed an intense, perhaps nostalgic devotion to things Hungarian. The early Hungarian Rhapsodies are Liszt playing at gipsies. But the Hungarian element in the song *Die Drei Zigeuner* or the weird piano piece *Sunt Lachrymae Rerum* uses the stark texture and irregular rhythms of folk-music to effect a dissolution of traditional tonality and form. In discovering the folk, Liszt paradoxically discovers his own loneliness and disillusion. It is significant that the last pieces are not especially pianistic, nor do they suggest any instrument except possibly a spectre of the human voice. At the end of his life Liszt the play-actor no longer addresses an audience. He talks to himself, as did Bach in *The Art of Fugue* or Mozart in his last chamber works. Nor is it an accident that his fragmentary self-communing should seem—in comparison with the profound lucidity of Bach or Mozart—an old man's mumble.

It is revealing that the most artistically successful of these last piano pieces should be not one of the Hungarian evocations, but the two versions of *La Lugubre Gondole*, a queer, spectral elegy on a passionately operatic life. The piece opens with unisonal recitative, rocking on the neutral diminished seventh; the yearning upward sixths of Liszt's youth droop in fragmentary, linear chromaticism. When the arpeggiated barcarolle accompaniment tentatively appears it oscillates dreamfully between the major and minor triad, suggesting the enigmatic harmonic style of Liszt's great virtuoso successor, Busoni. But the waves of the arpeggios cannot flow. The music clogs in chromatically descending six-three chords, over which fragments of recitative grind dissonantly. The music fades out in unison recitative, metreless, without tonality (Ex. 16):

There is no music in the nineteenth century which disrupts tonality so completely as this linearly chromatic piece: for even *Tristan* implies a long-range tonal architecture, while Chopin's harmonic chromaticism is merely a transitory disintegration. It is ironic that Liszt should have thought of *La Lugubre Gondole* as a premonition of the death of Wagner, for whose cause he had sacrificed so much. Partly through Liszt's efforts, Wagner had found complete fulfilment; Liszt ends with this pathetic whimper. Yet it is Liszt, even more than Berlioz, who looks to the future: directly in the technique of the symphonic poem, which became the basic constructional principle that succeeded the sonata; more remotely in the 'expressionism' of his final epigrams. Berlioz preserved a visionary grandeur which we cannot aspire to. Liszt's ultimate fragmentariness goes home to us acutely, for we live in the wake of the disintegration he so honestly recorded. His honesty is the more impressive because he had been an actor all his life. When the play no longer interested him, he was no longer able to create an integrated work of art. But his stammered ejaculations are profoundly touching in their incoherence. We accept them as our birthright. We would complete them if we could.

3

THE RUSSIAN NATIONALISTS

Liszt, hero of romanticism, was also a great cosmopolitan, a citizen of Europe, as Lasso had been in the sixteenth century or Handel in the eighteenth. Lasso and Handel both lived and worked in three countries, spoke and thought in at least three languages. Even Byrd in the sixteenth century or Bach in the eighteenth—composers who did not travel widely and who worked within a relatively local culture—employed a musical language which was intelligible all over Europe. Haydn, living in seclusion on the Esterházy estate, was international in approach as well as in renown; Mozart, as much Italianate as German, would have considered an aggressive nationalism in music—or in life—bad taste. With the development of the 'democratic' sonata, however, we can detect the beginnings of a change. Beethoven, trained in the same European tradition as Mozart, hints that *The Magic Flute* is Mozart's best work partly because it is the most German. We have seen to what enormities this attitude was to lead in the career of Wagner.

Gradually, the cult of the individual nation grows alongside the cult of the individual personality. National differences complement the inexhaustibly surprising differences between human beings; and the nineteenth century becomes the age of cut-throat competition in both personal and political life. Naturally, a preoccupation with 'nationhood' is most vigorously evident in small countries which were just growing to political consciousness (we may recall Liszt's mild mania for things Hungarian during his last years): or in a large country which had no deep roots in the cultural heritage of Europe. Russia became the nerve-centre of musical nationalism because she had long been an outsider from the European community. Having been untouched by that vast, complex phenomenon we call the Renaissance, she had moved straight from medieval feudalism to eighteenth-century autocracy and, incipiently, to revolution.

In so doing, she had suffered a cultural bifurcation. The ruling aristocracy spoke and thought in French, and fostered French and Italian art; the peasant community spoke and thought in Russian and lived out their passions in an indigenous folk-art. In Elizabethan England folk-art and the European conventions of 'art' music mutually enriched one another, for Elizabethan society involved a homogeneous interrelation of all classes. Even Haydn and Mozart, living in a relatively heterogenous community, did not feel that their music was in any way opposed to popular music. But the European elements in eighteenth-century Russian music were simply importations. The music was created mainly by Frenchmen and Italians for Russians who wanted to become as nearly French and Italian as possible. The European could not be absorbed into the local culture, since, apart from folk-music—which the aristocracy despised—no local culture existed.

The tradition of Russian 'art' music, like the Russian literary tradition, thus begins to appear only when revolution is incipient. Consider the career of Glinka [1803–1857], whose hypochondria was perhaps a sign of senility in a world that had had its day. He was the son of a rich landowner. After a pampered childhood, he moved to St. Petersburg, where he lived the life of a young man of good birth, fashion, and fortune. He dabbled in musical composition, as one among many mild diversions; and the music he wrote, reflecting the brittle merriment of serenades, balls, and opera parties, was inevitably amateurish in technique, Italian in manner. He then travelled briefly in Germany, where he gained some acquaintance with the music of Mozart, Cherubini, and Beethoven: and more extensively in Italy, where he revelled in the delights of Bellini and Donizetti. At the height of these frolics, however, "homesickness led me to the idea of writing in Russian". Italian opera, he felt, needed the Italian sun; he had to create a music which belonged to his moody and volatile people ("for us it is a matter either of frantic merriment or bitter tears . . . love is always linked with sadness"). Naturally, he chose to write an opera, because opera was the only form he was familiar with; naturally, with the amateur's enthusiasm, he began to compose it *ad hoc*, before he had even seen the libretto. The opera which finally emerged, on his return home, was *A Life for the Czar*; in 1836 it was produced at court with considerable pomp. Superficially, with its mingling of big choral numbers and dance scenes, it resembles a French grand opera: while the vocal writing for the soloists and most of the instrumental accompaniments are—for all their technical gaucherie—charmingly Rossinian. Yet the essence of the work lies not in its fashionable emulation of Western manners, but in its portrayal of peasant life. Somewhat to the dismay of his aristocratic audience—and possibly somewhat to his own consternation—Glinka had produced an opera about peasants rather than about Czars; for in the choruses and the orchestral dances he recalled the folk melodies and rhythms which he had heard in his country childhood. His opera had been prompted not by aesthetic ideals, still less by a desire to express himself, but by the observation and imitation of the life around him. Only he was discovering, perhaps painfully, that 'real' life was not the world of fashion to which he had been committed. It was the Russia remotely remembered from his childhood: which seemed to be as eternally unchanging as the rhythms of the folk-songs that sinuously wound themselves around a single note; which was in fact being changed in the process of becoming articulate.

Glinka's only other attempt at opera, *Russlan and Ludmilla*, is a great advance on the first, partly because the fantastical subject suits his empirical methods, partly because his technique has improved with experience. The well-known overture, for instance, shows that he could on occasion control classical form effectively, without sacrificing his incidental delight in harmonic surprise and in rhythmic or colouristic excitement: the whole-tone passage for trombones in the coda provides a genuine, if unorthodox, climax to sonata drama. On the whole, however, *Russlan* is a more subversive opera than *A Life for the Czar*, technically if not politically. The fantastic subject suggests the use of more barbaric, sometimes Oriental, kinds of folk-song, far removed from traditional diatonicism; and this in turn influences the harmony. In particular, the use of folk-scales with the sharp fifth encourages the Russian partiality for augmented triads, for false relations,* and for 'colouristic' oscillations between tonic major and relative minor (the third of the subdominant minor triad becomes enharmonically identical with the seventh of the relative minor). Many of Glinka's most

* False Relations: the simultaneous or closely adjacent sounding of two notes a semi-tone apart, usually the major and minor third. See Part II, p. 314.

astonishing harmonic passages are directly modelled on peasant-band music: for instance, the telescoping of tonic and dominant in the Caucasian *lezginka* in Act IV. This harmonic effect—like the orgiastic dances or choruses in five-four or seven-four time, and the sharp, barrel-organ acidities of the orchestration—lead on directly to the early work of Stravinsky. Glinka may have learned something from Weber in creating a music of fantasy; yet the core of this opera lies not in its unreality, but in his pungent imitation of sounds he had actually heard.

It cannot be said that the idiom Glinka creates is self-consistent, since the two main roots of his music would seem to be mutually irreconcilable. Folk-songs are melodies complete in themselves; Russian folk-songs, in particular, tend to move in short reiterated periods, and to oscillate around a fixed point. They can be repeated, incrementally, in varied orchestral colours; but they cannot be developed, either through lyrical expansion (as in operatic melody) or still less through the tonal argument of the sonata. Hence a desire to compose nationalistic music almost necessitates an episodic technique, while encouraging an interest in orchestral titillation. The episodic method of composition may be convincing, and would seem to be intimately related to the Russian approach to life as well as art. But it is bound to depend largely—and dangerously—on 'inspiration'. The composer who creates from moment to moment, from bar to bar, may lose sight of the whole in his preoccupation with the parts. We know from accounts of Balakirev's teaching that the Russian nationalists habitually criticized each other's works in this empirical fashion, commenting on a chord here, a modulation there. They wanted their music to be effective, exciting, at a given moment. They trusted to genius to see that the moments, put together, made sense; and genius sometimes, not always, obliged.

Balakirev himself [1837–1910], the senior member and perhaps the most powerful personality among the Big Five, is the most conspicuous exponent of the Russian principle of hit-or-miss. By the time he started to compose, German symphonic music, as well as Italian and French opera, had penetrated to Russia. His symphonic works have, however, little in common with the classical tradition. In his early B minor *Overture on Russian Themes*, for instance, he simply strings the tunes together in the manner of Glinka's fantasias. The themes are brilliantly treated and decorated in harmonic and orchestral terms, for Balakirev is technically much more adept than his predecessor; but they do not make a whole. In *Russia*, on the other hand, Balakirev uses virtually the same method in treating folk-songs: only genius takes possession. Though the themes do not develop, they coalesce in a structure of extraordinary power.

Much the same is true of the fantastic virtuoso piece for piano, *Islamey*. The work is modelled on the virtuoso pieces of Liszt, who made so deep an impression when he visited Russia. But Balakirev's Oriental folk-themes are much more static than Liszt's Italianate melodies; indeed, the themes are less important than the profusion of harmonic and pianistic 'colour' they provoke. Pianistic decoration—an aural titillation—becomes itself a creative act. Balakirev's two symphonies, which he tinkered at over a period of thirty years, are not radically different in approach. The motto theme of the introduction to the C major is extended in monothematic elaboration, in varying contexts of harmonic and orchestral colour. The music has a tremendous barbaric power; but it is not a dramatic argument, however logical its thematic structure may be. The technique has something in common with that of Liszt's symphonic poems; and there is a similar relationship between the method of Liszt's Piano Sonata and Balakirev's remarkable Sonata in B flat minor. Though Balakirev's work is in four separate movements, it is impregnated with thematic relationships which are varied repetitions, rather than development. The first movement is a most striking fusion of sonata and fugue, in which the subject—a long, sinuous Russian *cantilena*—is equally remote from classical notions of fugue or sonata, while being superbly devised for creative elaboration. Whether it is conceived in orchestral or pianistic terms, Balakirev's music thus owes its power to its rhythmic momentum, to its bold scoring, and to the power of the themes to proliferate in ornamental arabesque. Balakirev's obsessional partiality for side-stepping modulations (especially from D major to D flat major and from B flat minor to B minor, the four keys being interrelated) is relevant in this connexion. The modulations are an incidental intensification: an elaboration rather than a point in an argument.

The First Symphony of Borodin [1833–1887] is an even more remarkable example of this anti-traditional tendency. He too was an amateur who worked at his compositions over a number of years. In small works, such as the exquisitely written quartets or his French rather than Italianate songs, he proves that he had command of an assured, even polished European technique. Indeed, if we compare his use of unresolved seconds in the song *The Dark Forest* with that in the song *The Sleeping Princess*, it would seem that he was perhaps the first composer to reveal the subtle relationship between empirical primitivism and a sophisticated nervous impressionism* (Ex. 17):

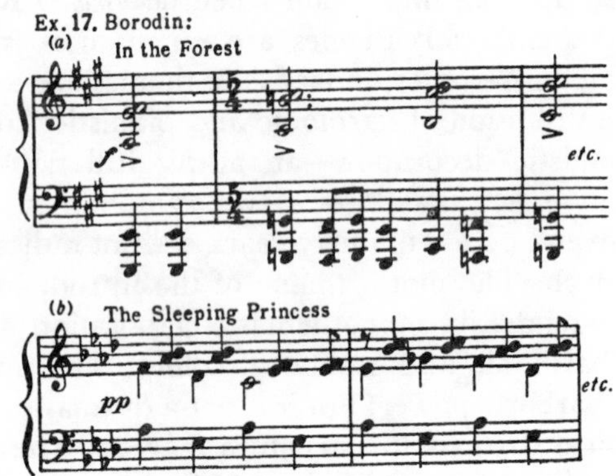

Moreover, whereas Balakirev's themes are usually derived from folk-song or are relatively undistinguished, Borodin's themes attain—within a restricted range, oscillating around the fourth, third, and augmented second—a most personal, expressive pliancy. Any apparent oddities in his symphonic technique are therefore unlikely to be due to deficient inventiveness or skill. If the first movement of his E flat Symphony looks superficially like an orthodox classical sonata, but does not in fact behave like one, we may suspect that the reason is that Borodin did not intend it to.

The terrific rhythmic impetus of this first movement of the E flat Symphony carries the music onwards; while the modulations tend to have an almost contrary effect. Sharing Balakirev's partiality for the side-stepping modulation, Borodin will make the most abstruse enharmonic transition, only to return to the chord and the ostinato rhythm form which he had started; anything approaching the Beethovenian notion of evolving tonality is avoided. When we examine the movement

* For instance, between Debussy and the Stravinsky of *The Rite of Spring.*

in detail we find that it is in fact no longer a dualistic structure. The first and second subjects are not after all contrasted; they are interrelated fragments which are varied and integrated until finally they become a theme. This is different from the technique of Liszt's symphonic poems, which thematically unify widely disparate feelings; for whereas Liszt's themes do not—any more than Balakirev's—grow, Borodin creates a theme in the course of the movement. Beethoven sometimes does this, but never stops there. More normally, the process which takes place in Borodin's movement has gone on in Beethoven's mind and sketch-books before the composition begins—and the composition is the revelation of the themes' destiny. In this sense, Borodin's technique in this movement is as original in its primitivism as is Beethoven's in its maturity.

The other movements of Borodin's E flat Symphony make no attempt to establish any organic relationship to the first; they might be part of a pleasing, more than normally competent, Russian suite. Nowhere else, perhaps, did he approach this deep discovery of Russian primitivism. The implications of the technique of incremental repetition are, however, apt to crop up in his most civilized sonata movements. Even his opera, *Prince Igor*, is not so much a drama as an epic, presented episodically in a series of tableaux; and Borodin achieves an unexpected cohesive force by using throughout the score a number of motives, derived from the contours and rhythms of folk-music. They are not leitmotives; they are an application to opera of the technique whereby motives in themselves static are varied, as they are in Balakirev and in Borodin's own instrumental works. To achieve this unity out of episodic moments is even more difficult in a large-scale work like an opera than it is in a symphonic piece, though the composer has, of course, the element of theatrical illusion to help him. In *Prince Igor* the conventional Western operatic elements are not musically integrated with the Russian and Oriental elements, masterly though the score intermittently is. Perhaps one might say that the years which Borodin spent on *Prince Igor* found their ultimate justification in his B minor Symphony, a work which expresses, with epigrammatic trenchancy, the opera's essence. The unisonal opening, with its reiterated notes and its oscillations between flat second and the major and minor third, seems to epitomize Borodin's creative personality (Ex. 18):

Borodin thought more convincingly in instrumental than in operatic terms; but the greatest—and most revolutionary—work of Russian nationalism was to be an opera of precisely the epical and episodic type which Borodin had struggled with. Moussorgsky's career [1839–1881] was also a struggle, both creatively and spiritually. In his case, however, the vindication of the amateur's empiricism is his genius. In no composer are genius and ignorance so inevitably linked.

Born in 1839, he came of a wealthy landowning family and was intended for the Army, though he resigned his commission in 1858. As a youthful dilettante he composed a little piano music in the style of the minor romantics. The realization that he was a composer came simultaneously with the realization that he had not the slightest interest in the kind of music he had been writing. He was not merely anti-academic; he was also anti-artistic in the sense that he believed, or affected to believe, that art was simply the revelation of truth. "That object is beautiful", he said, "which speaks to us of life." He sought "not beauty for itself, but truth, whatsoever it may be". And the cosmopolitan society into which he had been born was neither life nor truth. Now that he had cast off his cosmopolitan past he felt "reborn; everything Russian" was close to him. Life, as opposed to make-believe, was the life of the Russian peasants. In his fragmentary autobiography (written most significantly in the third person) he said: "Under the influence of his nurse, he became familiar with the old Russian folk-tales. It was mainly his familiarity with the very spirit of the life of the people that impelled him to extemporize music before even knowing the most elementary rules of piano-playing." This may or may not have been true. It was certainly what Moussorgsky wanted to think; and it was certainly true that he developed so deep a love for the peasants that he seemed to be identified with them, moving "in another world, in a far-away past". But in thus revealing the collective spirit of his race, he would destroy a degenerate world and, like Tolstoy, create a new, instinctive life from the ashes of the past. This was why, for him as for Tolstoy, art could never be an end in itself, but must be communication, of the most direct kind possible. He could not be content even with Balakirev's abstract racialism; after his juvenalia, all his music is inherently dramatic.

His concern with 'reality' implied too a passionate desire to free his country's music from Italian and German slavery. Nothing could better indicate the connexion between nationalism and individualism than Moussorgsky's comment that his *Night on the Bare Mountain*—an operatic scena without voices—was "Russian and original": it would never have occurred to Handel or Mozart to claim either nationality or originality for their compositions. In creating a "Russian and original" style he did not have to work entirely alone. He had the example of the popular elements in Glinka's operas, the early symphonic works of Balakirev, and Dargomyzhsky's rather pedestrian attempt, in *The Stone Guest*, to create a melodic line from the inflexions of speech. Interest in the contours of peasant speech became the most positive influence on Moussorgsky's attempt to slough off tradition; we can see the immediate result of his efforts in the short opera, *The Marriage*, based naturalistically on Gogol's brusquely comic tale. Moussorgsky said that he had here tried to note down those changes in intonation which crop up in human conversation for the most futile causes, on the most insignificant words. . . . I should like to make my characters speak on the stage exactly as people do in real life, without exaggeration or distortion, and yet write music which will be thoroughly artistic. . . . What I foretell is the melody of life, and not of classicism. . . . I call it well-thought-out, justified melody. Some day the unexpected ineffable song will arise against classical melody, intelligible to one and all."

In *The Marriage* Moussorgsky has hardly succeeded in his ambition to make speech-melody 'artistic', for the piece is not much more than a play in music, with speech sometimes intensified to chant, harmonized with a deliberately rudimentary starkness. These harmonies were arrived at empirically at the piano, usually prompted by the words or dramatic situation: consider the notorious coruscation of parallel seconds suggested by the word 'nasty'. But if Moussorgsky fails to achieve artistry in his first attempt at the complex art of opera, he soon does so in the medium of the song. His earliest songs preserve some contact with traditional lyricism; his mature songs have become dramatic scenas in miniature. In all of them his startling originality manifests itself in an un-Wagnerian forgetfulness of self; he finds himself in becoming identified with people utterly remote from his own personality. The seven Nursery Songs, for instance, use the incantatory rhythms and pentatonic formulae of folk-song and have the direct, unsentimental simplicity of the nursery jingle. Yet they are profound studies of the workings of a child's mind, which only a man of Moussorgsky's intuitive imagination could have written. One cannot say that the *parlando* vocal parts are 'accompanied' by the piano; the song-speech is involved in the drama of the piano's fragmentary ostinatos, its abruptly changing rhythm, its grammatically unrelated concords, sevenths, and ninths. Even the most abstruse dissonance is used empirically, as in the middle-period works of Debussy. The suggestion of Debussy is even more potent in the cycle called *Sunless*, where the *parlando* line reflects a Dostoevsky-like introspection instead of a childlike innocence: consider, in the second song, the weird use of the pedal D, and the unresolved six-three chord which leaves the singer's pain suspended in the void of his solitariness (Ex. 19):

Ex. 19. Moussorgsky: *Sunless*

But the greatest of Moussorgsky's songs are undoubtedly the *Songs and Dances of Death*. If we may still call these dramatic scenas, they are so starkly 'truthful' that no stage presentation could ever do justice to the honesty of Moussorgsky's imagination. The meeting of the drunkard with Death on the lonely road has the same simple, impersonal acceptance of reality as the children's songs: yet nothing could be more frightening than the gradual intrusion of the chromatic wriggle into the monotonous pedal note under the wailing folk-lamentation; or more desolate than the peace of the empty fifths at the end. The *Cradle Song* is a colloquy between a mother and Death, fighting for her sick child. The two characters are sharply differentiated in this tiny operatic conflict. Death's hypnotic lullaby to the child droops caressingly from the tonic through a tritone, then a fifth, then a sixth, on to the third of the minor triad: an unexpected, ambiguous 'resolution' after the warmly sinister chromatics. The final descent, in the last repeat, to the low tonic instead of the third conveys with uncanny simplicity Death's last, tranquil word. There is no more to be said; yet this minor triad reverberates in the memory (Ex. 20):

One finds the same impersonality in the grinding dissonances that accompany Death's appearance on the battlefield in *Field-Marshal Death*: or in the effect of the ninth chord, followed by the nagging, diminishing tonic pedal, that occurs in Death's dreamy, wooing, modal incantation in the *Serenade*. In the context, we are not sure whether that ninth is the bliss of peace or the honey of corruption; fear is inextricably twined in our welcome. Such 'moments of truth' are certainly among the most remarkable manifestations of instinctive genius in music; yet Moussorgsky's greatness, and the intensity of his imagination, are revealed still more in the fact that, from a concatenation of such moments, he was able to create an episodic yet cumulative work on a vast scale. *Boris Godunov* is both a psychological drama of guilt and conscience and an epic of destiny and race. Moussorgsky understands 'history' because he knows that history is made of the experience of individual human beings. To create *Boris* called both for Moussorgsky's imaginative insight and for his detachment.

If one looks at any particular passage in the score, the technique seems much the same as that of the songs. Yet the various episodes form a whole, without calling on the recognized methods of achieving tonal and theatrical coherence. Consider, for instance, the scene of the Clocks. Boris, grimly reflecting on his guilt, is interrupted by the wild flurry of the squabble between the nurse and his young son's parrot. Feodor, left alone with his father, offers to explain what happened. He tells the story in a simple folk-monotone, in rigid periods alternating between three-four and five-four. The phrases tend to be pentatonic, harmonized with simple diatonic concords, often without the third. When he begins to describe the hubbub itself the centre of 'modality' shifts abruptly from F sharp to F, and the droning phrases are now harmonized with instable seventh chords, with a bass rocking between a tritone. Boris then sings—in G flat, the major of his son's initial modal F sharp—of his hopes for his son. His melodic line moves largely by step rather than by pentatonic thirds, within a very restricted range; it is accompanied by smoothly flowing triplets over long pedal notes on D flat and G flat, as opposed to the harmonic unrest of the parrot episode. Boris ends by warning Feodor of Councillor Shuisky's deceit. Meanwhile, Shuisky has entered, to tell Boris of the threat of rebellion. Boris rounds on him, his *parlando* phrases now accompanied by diatonic triads enharmonically related, then by seventh chords embellished with trills; the tonal instability increases the sense of shiftiness. Shuisky's phrases are also restricted in range, close to speech inflexion, but incline to be pentatonic, like Feodor's. As melody, they look innocent; but their innocence is belied by the fluctuating sevenths of the harmony; they are sweetly lyrical, cooing in their repetitiveness.

When Shuisky at last names Dmitri as the pretender, Boris utters a yell, and orders Feodor out of the room. He leaves, to the accompaniment of skirling chromatics that recall the parrot's flurrying. Boris tries to brush aside his fears, decrying the supernatural. The flowing triplets that accompanied his vision of Feodor as Czar return, in distorted chromaticism, in frenzied contrary motion. He pleads with Shuisky to confirm that he had in fact seen the boy Dmitri, dead: while the chromatics in contrary motion have become sustained, fateful minims. The contrary motion scales lose their chromaticism and become slowing moving crochets while Shuisky describes the dead boy, "a smile most gentle" on his lips, a toy still in his hand. The tonality is a modal C sharp, pentatonic in the more tender moments.

Boris's frayed nerves can sustain it no longer. He dismisses Shuisky—with an outburst of the contrary motion triplets; and at this moment the clocks start chiming. The pendulum swings between the notes of the tritone (the domestic madness of the parrot episode has become a spiritual frenzy); the violins wriggle in snake-like chromatics; brass and woodwind interject polytonal fanfares. This ghastly whirring and clanking accompanies Boris's strangled cries until an apparition of the dead Dmitri appears before his fevered eyes. The pedal E flat returns below string tremolandos; and provides a transition to the wonderful close when the whirring is stilled in Boris's chromatically descending prayer for forgiveness. His voice finally sinks to rest on the major third, over the timpani's pianissimo A flat.

Moussorgsky was certainly conscious of some of the subtle interrelations that give cohesion to the sequential episodes of *Boris*; but in most cases one suspects he was conscious only after the event. *Boris Godunov* is a miracle of art almost fortuitously. Moussorgsky rehashed it several times, accepted the advice of Rimsky-Korsakov and of other people incompetent to give it, worked simultaneously on other opera projects, none of which came to fruition. His art has a frightening ludicity; his life is chaos: and this is perhaps related to the fact that there is nothing in his art that can be called love. The second version of *Boris*, which develops the theme of Boris's personal crisis, is deeper than the first, which considers the story mainly in national terms; but in some ways the first version is more typically Moussorgskian. In his art, he loses himself so completely in becoming other people that he has nothing left to give. The search for reality entailed a loss of identity that is almost delirium. Moussorgsky drank himself to lunacy and death in bringing a new world to birth.

The old world did not die easily. Throughout the nineteenth century the two streams that flowed from the stylistic 'bifurcation' in Glinka's music ran parallel. The Russian revolutionary stream culminated in Moussorgsky's empirical genius; at the same time the cosmopolitan cult of Italian, French, and German art found in Tchaikowsky a personality intense, if not strong, enough to recreate it in Russian terms. Nor is it an accident that Tchaikowsky's work should centre around a feverish search for love—around the attempt to mend the sundered personal relationship.

Tchaikowsky [1840–1893] came from much the same background as Glinka, but both his nervous sensitivity and his musical talent were more potent. He could not be content to forget his nervous instability in vapid distractions; nor could he accept an intermittent dilettantism in his creative work. Glinka was the passive creature of a world in decay, his talents vitiated by inertia. In Tchaikowsky, decay flares into neurosis His Chekovian anguish at times approaches insanity. Whereas Moussorgsky, who probably suffered from the same psychological perversion, preserved his impersonal art free from the contagion of his lunacy, Tchaikowsky used his art as a safety-valve. Only in his music could he escape from the prison of his pathological devotion to his family—above all, to his mother. Schumann too had sought in domesticity a refuge from a hostile world. But his domesticity was the normal, grown-up relationship of man and wife. Tchaikowsky never grew up; the desire to regress to the womb, which we all have in varying degrees, remained the strongest impulse through the years of his harried life.

His mother died when he was fourteen; this negative event coloured his whole future. Almost immediately afterwards, he began to compose; and when he said "undoubtedly I should have gone mad but for music" we may—in the light of later events—take his words as literal. For the rest of his days he sought a substitute for the maternal relationship. His strange relationship to his patroness, Mme von Meck, was the closest he came to finding it; and both he and she were aware that their weirdly passionate association could be sustained only so long as they did not meet. He was the artist-son of her neurotic imagination; she was the lover-mother he had lost—with the additional advantage that she provided a comfortable income. Debarred by his identification with mother and sister ("those angels come down from Heaven") from normal relations with women, Tchaikowsky became a homosexual: and a homosexual obsessed by feelings of guilt. He embarked on his marriage partly to stifle slander, partly to quiet his own sense of sin. The result was an almost complete mental breakdown. After having tried to commit suicide by contracting pneumonia, he was unconscious for forty-eight hours. He never saw his nominal wife again. Significantly, this second crisis in his life was associated with his supreme period of creative activity. He saved himself from madness in creating *Eugene Onegin* and the Fourth Symphony.

For, unlike Chopin and Schumann—also introverted artists —Tchaikowsky had the pronounced histrionic streak which often accompanies homosexuality. Involved in his nerves, he instinctively dramatized himself, whereas Moussorgsky shed the burden of self in identifying himself with others. Only by being, or pretending to be, proud of his oddness could Tchaikowsky save himself from the self-revulsion—and the doubts about his creative ability—which periodically overwhelmed him. The desire to be loved was inevitably involved with self-pity: and therefore with self-hatred, because of what he described as the'Thing' in him that held love at bay.

Tchaikowsky's histrionic sense found an immediate echo in the music on which he was brought up, for this was almost all theatrical. In a sense, Tchaikowsky loved most the music that was furthest from his own introversion. The more subjective of nineteenth-century composers he disliked. Wagner he considered a bore, maintaining that *Götterdämmerung* was inferior to the ballets of Delibes; even for Beethoven he had no more than a grudging respect. But Mozart was for him "the Christ of music"; and the Mozart he adored was the Italianate Mozart who, in opera, objectified passion in lyricism. Bellini, Rossini, and Verdi he admired ardently; Massenet, more understandably, moved him to tears. Among other French composers, he loved the ballets of Delibes: and considered Bizet's *Carmen* to be the greatest work of his time. *Carmen* was the kind of music he would liked to have written himself; for it was vibrant with life, colourful, passionate, dominated by a sense of fate; yet at the same time elegant, emotionally detached.

The detachment of Moussorgsky seemed to him barbarous; he set out to write music based on the very Italian, French, and German models which the nationalists had rejected. Yet because he was a Russian—and not the less because he belonged to a degenerating world—the music he created was very different from his models. Like the nationalists, Tchaikowsky had, as a child, been brought up on folk-song. For Moussorgsky folk-song had become the symbol of a new world; he loved folk-song as the expression of the 'collective soul' of his race, beyond personal feeling. For Tchaikowsky, the significance of folk-song was almost entirely personal; he loved it because it reminded him of his childhood, of his mother and sisters, of the security of home. For this reason his musical approach to folk-song is quite different from that of the nationalists. They felt the songs so inwardly that they could evolve techniques whereby folk-song became the basis of substantial works. Tchaikowsky, on the other hand, naturally thought in terms of Italian *cantilena* or the French dance tune; when he introduces folk-songs into his symphonic works they seem unhappy in their context. This is not because they are insensitively treated, but simply because they conflict with the melodic, harmonic, and orchestral language that came to him most naturally.

None the less, at a level below consciousness folk-song influenced Tchaikowsky profoundly. Folk-melody is not the essence of his thought, as it is with Balakirev or even Borodin; but his French and Italianate melody was modified by his nostalgic recollection of the folk-music of his childhood. This we can see most immediately, and most expressively, in his songs. In *Had I only known*, from opus 47, for instance, the singer is ostensibly a Russian peasant girl who has fallen in love with a dashing young man and been jilted. In the poem she recalls her love story—her tremulous desires, her joys, her despair. The song is both dramatic and lyrical. It opens with a piano introduction—a tootling little balalaika tune that seems to have no connexion with the song itself, though it is in fact thematically related, and a masterly piece of dramatic craftsmanship. For it sets the scene, providing the background of everyday trivialities, at once carefree and care-laden, against which the girl's personal experience is to be seen. Her opening phrase is broken, brief, folk-like in its continually drooping fourths. It is interspersed with a hypnotic repeated figure on the piano—a drone-like folk monotone which suggests the nagging thrust of her sorrow. The phrases rise sequentially, in cumulating despair, but always tend to droop back nervelessly to the piano figure's subdominant (this and other flatwards modulations are significantly more important in Tchaikowsky's music than modulations to the dominant and sharpwards). The drooping interval expands, the phrases grow more lyrical: until they lead into a 'middle' section in which the same phrases are transformed into a frenzied waltz. This is the familiar waltz-song of the cosmopolitan Tchaikowsky—the evocation of the glittering gaiety from which he is shut out. The phrases are still brief, obsessively repeated, but are now carried forward by the swirl of the rhythm. The climax comes in a tremendous cry of pain, in an unexpected irregular (five-bar) phrase, followed by a piano interjection based on feverish descending appoggiaturas. Thus the music returns to a retrospective, yearning repeat of the first section. The drooping phrase rests inert, on repeated Gs: until a wonderful lyrical arioso consummates the girl's passion. Then the balalaika tune sounds again, tinklingly, from afar. The world goes on, oblivious of our sufferings.

We can hardly doubt that the strange power of this song comes from Tchaikowsky's identification of the young woman with himself. Moussorgsky would have become the woman. Tchaikowsky makes the woman become himself, while at the same time his histrionic sense enables him to present his (her) suffering in quasi-operatic terms: from this point of view, the transition from folk-lamentation to operatic waltz and back is especially interesting. The larger part of Tchaikowsky's working life was spent on the creation of theatrical music. If he is not on the whole as successful as an opera composer as he is as a writer of songs, the reason is that he needed a libretto that—like this song—offered him a character and a situation close to his own. In this he is utterly distinct not only from Moussorgsky, but also from Verdi and Bizet—the two composers who, superficially, influenced him most.

When he did find such a libretto, however, he created, in *Eugene Onegin*, his masterpiece. Tatiana was a character with whom Tchaikowsky could—and on his own admission did—identify himself; and if we remember his dreadful account of the circumstances leading to his marriage, it would seem that there was more than a little of Onegin in his make-up also. It is interesting that he deprives Onegin of the sympathetic characteristics which Pushkin had given him, making him merely a negative foil to Tatiana's tender, hopeless passion; he is the hard world's dusty answer to the need for love. The setting of Pushkin's drama—the world of the small provincial landowners—took Tchaikowsky back to his childhood, and enabled him to introduce both nostalgic folk-melodies and the gay, melancholy waltzes and mazurkas of the world of fashion. The central preoccupation with Tatiana's character naturally lent itself to the intimate lyrical style which Tchaikowsky adapted from Massenet and Bizet. The letter scene—which was the starting point as well as the core of the opera—achieves the direct simplicity which Tchaikowsky admired in Bizet. Its unbroken lyricism is harmonically more heavily charged, more scented, than that of the French composer, but it nowhere impedes the growth of the drama. The harmonization of the descending phrase with the chord of the flat sixth creates a pathos which seems, in the context, as Russian—but Chekovian rather than Pushkinesque—as it is inimitable (Ex. 21):

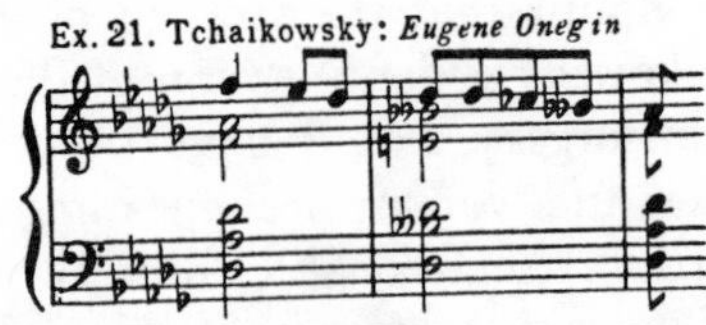

A cliché of theatrical lyricism becomes related to the nagging iterations of the folk-lament. Something the same is true of the theme of the slow movement of the Fourth Symphony, on which Tchaikowsky was working at about the same time.

Only on one other occasion did Tchaikowsky find a libretto which, avoiding the historical or fantastical, dealt with a world he knew at first hand, and with a character sufficiently like himself to stimulate his interest. Pushkin's original story, *The Queen of Spades*, was much sharper, more satirical, more eighteenth-century in spirit than the libretto which Modest Tchaikowsky made from it. Yet the adaptation provides in Hermann a dark, frustrated lover who can become Tchaikowsky, while the merely potential union of Hermann and Lisa stands as a symbol of the desire for love, which remains unfulfilled. What frustrates fulfilment is the macabre figure of the aged Countess, a projection of the nervous frenzy of a world in senile decay. Although the opera is not as a whole convincing, the scene in the bedchamber, in which Hermann and the Countess confront one another, touches a nerve of neurotic horror which came from deep in Tchaikowsky's being, yet is magnificently realized as art. The hysteria is the more pointed by contrast with the snatches of a Grétry air which the Countess croons to herself as she makes her toilet. In the Countess the eighteenth-century aristocratic world has grown corrupt and nightmarish; in the Grétry tune we have an evocation of rococo elegance as it once was. Perhaps we can understand why Tchaikowsky adored Mozart. He once wrote in a letter to Mme von Meck: "You say that my worship of Mozart is quite contrary to my musical nature. But perhaps it is just because, being a child of my time,

I feel broken and spiritually out of joint, that I find consolation and rest in Mozart's music."

As it happens—and, of course, these things do not really happen by accident—the action of *The Queen of Spades* provides an opportunity for Tchaikowsky to introduce a masque in what is usually described as Mozartian pastiche. If the term is supposed to imply that the music is patched together from the rag-bag of Mozartian cliché, it is unjustified; but the music is certainly a most exquisite and personal act of homage in which formulae of the rococo age merge into Tchaikowsky's lyricism, and into the chromatic extensions of his harmony. The eighteenth century becomes for Tchaikowsky a fairyland. Perhaps it is significant that the rococo scenes are a masque, not an opera. The voices are silent, or sing with stylized formality; the action becomes pantomime, a game. This helps us to understand why Tchaikowsky was supremely successful as a writer of ballet music: why all his ballets are based on fairy tales: and why the greatest of them, *The Sleeping Princess*, tells in dance and mime one of the fairy myths of the classical age. Nor is it an accident that Perrault's beautiful legend concerns the miraculous renewal of life by love.

Tchaikowsky's adagio melodies in *The Sleeping Princess* recall not so much Bizet and Massenet—nor even their immediate models, Delibes and Adolphe Adam—as Bellini, in whose elegiac lyricism operatic action was transmuted into an inner dream. It is almost as though, for Tchaikowsky, the fairy tale of Russian ballet seemed truer than life, because life itself was so strange. In precisely following Pepita's instructions—which were hardly less exacting than the mathematically measured schedule of the modern film score—Tchaikowsky could forget his neurosis in projecting emotion into the physical movements of the human body. There has never been music that more intimately provokes, as it is provoked by, the dance. Consider how in the famous waltz the conventional hemiola rhythm—the cross-accent of 3+3 against 2+2+2—grows from bodily movement while being the source of the superb momentum of the cantabile melody; consider still more how in the Rose Adagio physical gesture flows into such serenely balanced lines that it creates from movement a paradoxical immobility. At last, the mythical lovers of Tchaikowsky's imagination are united in a world of calm and grace. But their union is only make-believe; for Tchaikowsky's most perfect music depends on the admission of theatrical illusion. This eternal-seeming bliss is only mime, the artifice of movement which Pepita evokes from Tchaikowsky's muse; and the end of this greatest of classical ballets is musically most queer. After the penultimate, ecstatic restatement of the Rose Adagio which Beauty, awakened, dances with her Prince, everybody joins in an exuberant, fanfare-dominated mazurka. This can only be—one thinks—the end; as in all good fairy stories, everyone lives happily ever after. But it is not the end. The mazurka is followed by a coda which, though it may be majestic, is certainly not joyful. The tonality changes from resonant major to a stark minor, with a slight flavour of 'Russian' modality; the rhythms lose their extrovert flow, becoming frigidly symmetrical, austere. There is not the slightest hint, in this severely disciplined music, of the hysteria that we find in Tchaikowsky's more subjective symphonic and even operatic music. None the less, the effect is oddly—and on Tchaikowsky's part quite unconsciously—chilling. As the curtain falls the music dispels illusion. The stage lights are obliterated by the dark of reality; and what our eyes blink at, as we emerge from the theatre, is neither merry (like the mazurka) nor (like the Rose Adagio) serene.

Tchaikowsky was proud of his ballet music, and rebuked those critics who complained that his symphonic works were too reminiscent of the dance. Yet he also took himself very seriously as a symphonist: and believed that in his symphonies he was dealing with the reality which the illusory world of his ballets evaded. He could not understand that criticism of the ballet element in his symphonies did not discredit ballet music in general, let alone his own: that Taneiv was justified in pointing out that lyrical dance themes were no more suitable than folk-tunes for development in classical symphonic style; and were perhaps still less amenable to the kind of organization which Balakirev and Borodin explored in their symphonic works. Tchaikowsky hardly attempts to use folk-song symphonically, though he shares the nationalists' partiality for side-stepping modulations. He does, however, attempt to incorporate into his symphonies the big, self-contained song or dance tune; and he was only too sensitively aware that his problems as a symphonist derived from that fact. "The seams", he said, "always show, and there is no organic unity between the episodes." With careful revision, he can to some extent disguise this; but though he can superficially improve the form, he cannot fundamentally alter it, for he cannot alter the "essential qualities of my musical nature". Whether he wrote symphonies or overtures or symphonic poems, Tchaikowsky's compromise with classical tradition was almost always the same. He begins with a slow, atmospheric introduction; then follows an allegro, with a first subject, usually rather frantic, extended into sequential repetitions. Then comes a long bridge passage; and a second subject, strongly contrasted, usually slower and more lyrical (in *Romeo and Juliet* it is an operatic *cantilena*, in the Fourth Symphony a waltz). This, again, is sequentially extended. Then there is another long bridge passage, followed by a recapitulation of both themes and a coda, based on the introduction, or on a modified version of one of the allegro themes. This structure is essentially an alternation of episodes. In the classical sense there is no development at all, because the themes, though opposed, do not interact. The trouble lies, of course, in the bridge passages. Apart from the ubiquitous sequences, Tchaikowsky relies on ostinato figurations, agitato rhythmic motives, and sustained pedal points to create an illusion of continuity. Along with the sensationally modified scoring (the cantabile theme is almost always 'recapitulated' by all the strings in octaves, accompanied by skirls on the woodwind and brass chromatics), these devices certainly heighten the hysteria. But they do not make it less mechanical; they suggest, indeed, that Tchaikowsky's histrionics, divorced from theatrical projection, are partly self-induced.

Nor is there normally any relationship between the movements of Tchaikowsky's symphonies, as there is between the movements of a symphony of Mozart or Beethoven. The most completely successful movements are unadulterated ballet music, like the pizzicato movement from the Fourth (whether it was inspired by Delibes' *Sylvia* or by a balalaika orchestra), the waltz from the Fifth, or the bedraggled, slightly tipsy waltz in five-four from the Sixth. Only in this sixth and last symphony does Tchaikowsky begin to create a kind of symphony which is relevant to his nature; and this significantly proves to be closer to operatic techniques than to the classical ideal. It is not merely that the second subject resembles Don José's D flat aria from *Carmen*, nor that the excited semiquaver figuration of the first subject is strikingly similar to that in the final bedchamber scene of Verdi's *Otello*, both of which operas must have been fresh in Tchaikowsky's memory. Much deeper than this is the fact that there is now much more thematic interrelation both within the individual movements and in the work as a whole. In the first movement, for instance, the transition from the first to the second subject seems to consist of a banal sequence of descending scales; these, however, generate the declining phrase of the second subject, and its continuation proves to be a free inversion of the agitated semiquavers of the first subject. This and many similar transitions may not be very impressive as musical architecture: but as dramatic transitions, similar to those between the episodes of his *Eugene Onegin*, they would be entirely satisfying. Perhaps we may say that if Tatiana is a mask for Tchaikowsky himself, in the Sixth Symphony he dispenses with the mask and offers us self-dramatization in a strictly comparable technique. We may think that he writes better when he has the human voice and a theatrical situation to canalize his emotion. We may even think that he writes best of all when he accepts the limitations of the dance and lives in the illusion of mime, for his ballets, especially *The Sleeping Princess*, are undoubtedly his most consummately realized music. Yet not even the loveliest illusion is in the long run preferable to reality. So his richest, most rewarding music is in *Eugene Onegin*; and we can at least say that in the Sixth Symphony he was beginning to understand how the symphony might express his own strange, very partial, truth.

Moussorgsky, who intended to create a people's music which was anti-academic and even anti-artistic, proved a dead end in musical history; for he had virtually no influence on any composer except Debussy in his middle years, when he became the supreme musical representative of the cult of the Ivory Tower! Tchaikowsky, on the other hand, who was an artist of personal neurosis if ever there was one, and highly professional at that, has become the most popular of all 'classical' composers among the vast, musically illiterate public of industrialized Russia, Britain, and America; and has become so, moreover, on the strength of his most hysterically self-indulgent works. We do not need to deduce from this that industrial democracy has produced a society of psychopaths, for the potency of Tchaikowsky's melodic appeal is self-evident, and we all enjoy self-dramatization. We have none the less to admit that it is curious, if but obscurely revealing, that Tchaikowsky should thus have become equated with the Common Man. It is difficult to decide whether he or the Common Man would be the more appalled, could he see the other as he really was and is.

In some ways, at least, the plain man's partiality for Tchaikowsky is encouraging, for it is better to be alive and hysterically kicking than dead and canned. The real mechanized music of our mechanized society derives not so much from Tchaikowsky as from Rimsky-Korsakov [1844–1908], whose technical expertise is exceeded only by his spiritual nullity. He acquired a brilliant technical equipment comparatively late in life, and then spent years rewriting the works of the empirical Russian geniuses in order to "remove the crudities of the originals". We may think his labours misguided; but they were certainly as disinterested as they were strenuous. He omits 'ungrammatical' passages in Moussorgsky, adds bars where he thinks the original too elliptical, corrects the harmony and part-writing and smoothes off the sharp edge of Moussorgsky's orchestration. Some of his alterations were essential if the music was to be performable at all; most of them can be defended on the grounds that, but for Korsakov's revisions, the music would never have gained a hearing in the nineteenth century. None the less, one cannot avoid the suspicion that the revisions are evidence of their perpetrator's imaginative poverty. He quite genuinely could not see that Moussorgsky's incompetencies were never *simply* incompetent. His own mechanical competence makes a curious appendix to a musical tradition which had been nothing if not truthful or heartfelt.

Rimsky-Korsakov, though the most prolific Russian creator of operas, was not essentially an opera composer at all, for he had no interest in human beings. His most conventionally dramatic operas are the least successful. *Ivan the Terrible* is a weak imitation of *Boris*, and even the character of Krishka in *Kitesh* owes his power more to the dramatic than to the musical conception. In so far as his love-scenes are usually feeble, Rimsky-Korsakov resembles most Russian composers other than Tchaikowsky: but it is certainly not fortuitous that his invention sounds most spontaneous when he is dealing with pantheistic or inhuman experience. His *Snow Maiden* seems a prettily decorated, synthetically concocted fairy-tale compared with the poignant nostalgia of Tchaikowsky's *Sleeping Princess*. But if we are looking for decoration, Rimsky-Korsakov's is delightful; and he certainly understood a heroine who was tormented because her heart could not melt to human love. Most of his best music is associated with beings—such as Lel and Sadko—who symbolize the power of art, as opposed to life.

Throughout his long career, Rimsky-Korsakov handled expertly all the 'artistic' ingredients of Russian opera—folk-song, realistic speech inflexion, choral dances in irregular metres, quasi-medievalisms, Orientalisms, Italianate lyricism, 'colouristic' orchestral effects. He added some mannerisms of his own: melodic formulae to which he returned all through his life, harmonic and orchestral devices which he experimented with at the dictates of fashion. His music is recognizable by its mannerisms, while seldom speaking with an authentic voice. Symphonically, his operas are always sectional, however much he may have picked up from Wagner; they are most convincing when they pretend to be nothing more, as in the deliberately non-dramatic, masque-like 'tableaux' of *Sadko*, with its sonorous evocation of the sea. Rimsky-Korsakov never, like Moussorgsky or even Borodin, creates a cumulative logic from the sequence of episodes. The 'situation' which impresses him is used over and over again, from opera to opera: just as, within each work, his musical repetitions are simply repetitions—a labour-saving device rather than a constructive principle. The repetitions are, indeed, as systematically contrived as the elaborate cycles of keys; and this is most evident in the realm of the fantastic, where so much of his music pretends to live. Even in *Sadko*, which contains much wooingly lovely music, the underwater world of fantasy is expressed by way of a most unfantastic (because deliberate and excessive) exploitation of the harmonic neutrality of augmented fifths and whole-tone progressions. Rimsky-Korsakov is here a conjurer, rather than a genuine magician of music; he produces water-sprites, but it might just as well have been rabbits. He creates illusion, knowing it to be illusion: whereas the illusion of Tchaikowsky's ballets becomes, for the time being, truth.

Yasterbtsev reports that Rimsky-Korsakov once said to him: "You would scarcely find anyone in the world who believes less in everything supernatural, fantastic, or lying beyond the boundaries of death than I do—yet as an artist I love this sort of thing above all else. And religious ceremonial—what could be more intolerable? And yet with what love have I expressed such ceremonial customs in music! No, I am actually of the opinion that art is essentially the most enchanting, intoxicating lie." Nothing could be further removed from Moussorgsky's belief that art is reality: or for that matter from Tchaikowsky's belief that art is the overflowing of the full heart. A sceptical magician is a contradiction in terms—unless he be the degenerate modern type who performs on the seaside pier. Certainly there is nothing in Rimsky-Korsakov's music to disprove his statement; for while *Kitesh* contains the most sensuously beautiful, even moving, music he ever wrote, this music is all associated with the pantheistic forest creature Fevronya, and especially with her final dissolution into earth, air, and trees. To admire her vocally sustained, exquisitely scored lullaby is not to support those who would claim *Kitesh* as 'the Russian *Parsifal*'. Music can be manufactured, but not the human heart—nor the kind of experience to which *Kitesh* pretends. It is appropriate that Rimsky-Korsakov's last work should have been not *Kitesh*, but *The Golden Cockerel*: a fantastic allegory of which no one today knows the meaning, and of which one suspects Rimsky-Korsakov did not know the meaning himself. The reason is simple: there is nothing to know. Beneath the carapace of orchestral scintillation and of 'advanced' chromatic and enharmonic devices, the bird is a mechanical toy. The only dawn his crowing heralds—in a manner far more sinister than the emotional orgies of Tchaikowsky and Puccini—is the slick fatuity of Hollywood.

4

THE NATIONALISTS OF CENTRAL EUROPE

THERE is something to be said for the view that the Russians are the only true musical nationalists. Russia's geographical vastness and her remoteness from the culture of Europe meant that the nationalism of Balakirev and Moussorgsky could be largely an indigenous growth. Bohemia, on the other hand, had been for centuries an integral part of Europe: so much so that she was, in the early nineteenth century, under both the political and cultural domination of Austria. Her 'nationalism' was a rebellion against tyranny; but she was not and could not be spiritually or culturally distinct from her oppressor. Perhaps this is evident even in Czech folk-music itself. The dances have none of the irregular rhythms characteristic of Russian or Magyar dances; and while the songs are sometimes pentatonic, they never employ the chromaticized scales—with sharp fourth or fifth—typical of eastern Russia; on the whole, they tend to a straightforward diatonic major. They can thus be readily incorporated into the traditional language of Western classical music. They neither suggest any disturbing rhythmic or harmonic alterations, nor imply a different approach to form.

Living in such intimate contact with Austria and a centre of European civilization, Czech composers naturally have little of the primitivism of the Russians. Indeed, the most obvious characteristic of Smetana's music is not its national flavour, but its technical maturity. His first works, it is true, are rather characterless in their cosmopolitan style; but it was not long before he developed a masterly control of the two techniques which, in Vienna, had long been interrelated—Italian opera and Austrian sonata. At the same time, Smetana's respect for tradition was modified by his progressive independence. He sought the acquaintance of Liszt not so much because he too was a virtuoso pianist as because he admired the creative enterprise of Liszt's mind. One who fought spiritually for the future of his country could not ignore one who fought so strenuously for the future of music.

Trained in the Austro-Italian tradition, Smetana [1824–1884] began by composing in the idiom of the classical sonata. He soon came to realize, however, that "absolute music is impossible for me"; for fundamentally he was not concerned with inner strife. Living in a predominantly rural community which was, for all its yearning for freedom, in itself stable, he instinctively tended to express himself in operatic terms. Indeed, self-expression was hardly his creative intention; opera for him was a social act, rather than an excuse for autobiography. He wished to give his society an opera in every *genre*; and in these operas personal drama was to be seen against the background of communal life.

The work which made Smetana a celebrity—the comic opera known to us as *The Bartered Bride*—was an unpretentious affair. Its success was due partly to the fact that it is the most obviously nationalistic of Smetana's operas, in that it deals directly with peasant life, and includes many dance numbers of exuberant vitality. But it is not a peasant opera, like Moussorgsky's *The Marriage*. Melodically, harmonically, and formally its technique is Austrian and Italian; the popular element merely injects fresh virility into its cosmopolitanism. In conception, the opera is closer to Mozart than to Moussorgsky. Smetana may not embrace the variety and complexity of experience which Mozart crystallizes into the lucidity of *Figaro*, but he is Mozartian not merely in technique, but also in his compassionate feeling for human beings. His opera deals with the interplay of real people in action, living in his own community and also in a self-consistent world of art. It is significant that ensemble numbers are frequent in Smetana's operas, as in Mozart's. In Russian opera, the ensemble is both infrequent and unimportant. Tchaikowsky's best operatic music goes into monologue, in which the individuality of each vocal phrase is somewhat exasperatingly emphasized by being echoed by an instrument. Moussorgsky's most typical music is in the monologues and the epically elemental choruses. Neither in Moussorgsky's nor in Tchaikowsky's case is this due to defective contrapuntal skill. The Russians were not greatly interested in people in their social relationships, as were Mozart and

Smetana. Primitivistically, they were concerned with the People generically: with individual creatures who were, like Boris, in one way or another outcasts from society: or, in Tchaikowsky's case, with themselves.

In his tragic opera, *Dalibor*, Smetana finds a revolutionary theme from Bohemia's past which was capable of a contemporary interpretation. The medieval setting means, however, that he is not much concerned with the evocation of a regional environment. The only element in the style which suggests folk-music—apart possibly from the energetic rhythm of some of the quicker arias—is Smetana's partiality for passages built over a tonic or dominant pedal, or over a single chord employed like a bagpipe drone. In these passages—often associated with some ceremonial or ritualistic episode, like the first appearance of Vladislav—the unmodified tonality, the repeated phrases and rhythmic patterns, the brilliant scoring in contrasted groups of brass, woodwind, and strings, seem to suggest the simple power, the unchanging stability, of the agrarian community. But their significance is dependent on their context: for they are startlingly opposed to the complex, fluctuating linear and harmonic texture in which the interplay of the principal characters is expressed. Smetana is a man of the nineteenth century, though his sophistication lives in the context of a peasant world.

We can examine the essence of his operatic style in Dalibor's D flat aria towards the end of Act I. There is, perhaps, the slightest hint of folk inflexion in the pentatonic tail to the opening phrase; but the lyricism is Italianate, and of Verdian directness. The harmony, however, is much richer than anything Verdi had written in the 1860s: note how the augmented triads and ninth chords shift the melody slightly askew, so that the tonality rises from D flat through D major, E flat, and E, gaining in exaltation until it reaches the subdominant, G flat (standing for F sharp in the scale-wise ascent) (Ex. 22):

It is interesting to compare these step-wise modulations with those in Balakirev or Borodin. With the Russians, they are a momentary effect of colour, unrelated to tonal argument or line. With Smetana, they lead progressively to the climacteric G flat: from which point the melody descends chromatically, over a sustained tonic pedal which balances the tonal unrest of the first section. The aria concludes with a triumphant choral and orchestral assertion of tonic and dominant.

No less thrilling is the love-duet at the end of the second act. Here the enharmonic changes and mediant relationships are an ecstatic intensification of the lyricism rather than, as in Schubert, a nostalgic relaxation of tension. Even at its most chromatic the music has a melodic and rhythmic drive which preserves its positive vigour. For instance, if one compares the chromatic meandering at the opening of the prison scene with the similar passage at the beginning of Moussorgsky's *Cradle Song*, it is evident that whereas Moussorgsky's passage exists in its own right as a manifestation of desolate vacillation, Smetana's passage owes its effectiveness to its context. Moussorgsky reveals a 'moment of reality'; Smetana, portraying characters in action, makes us aware of chromaticism in relation to the tonality it disrupts. Indeed, all the elements of his technique reveal the development of emotion and of character. As Milada approaches the prison, chromaticism gives way to fluent cantabile lyricism; but if the lyricism expresses her joy, the fluctuating sevenths of the harmony, the repeated notes of the bass, the intertwining orchestral texture, suggest the excitement, the fearful expectancy, with which she approaches the lover who is also the murderer of her brother.

To Smetana's deep disappointment, *Dalibor* was not a success, partly because the chromaticism and rich orchestration provoked the charge of Wagnerism. While the music may occasionally recall the more Italianate Wagner of *Tannhäuser* and *Lohengrin*, it is closer to Verdi: and is in any case most remarkable for its independence of mind. If Smetana was directly influenced by any composer, it was by Liszt rather than by Wagner. A passage such as Ex. 23 betrays a Lisztian fusion of ripe Italian lyricism with luxuriant enharmony, and there is a deeper relation to Liszt in that the formal conception of *Dalibor* has much in common with that of the Lisztian symphonic poem. The noble, slowly rising theme which is first stated in the overture appears throughout the opera in innumerable, emotionally varied metamorphoses. Few nineteenth-century operas have a structure so closely knit: so musically self-subsistent and at the same time so intimately related to the dramatic argument. Thus at its appearance

the theme's rising aspiration is given an expectant uncertainty by the freely sequential enharmonic modulations: whereas at the end of the love-duet it is resolved into serene diatonicism. This tender transformation is not merely 'brought in' as a cunning dramatic reference; it is a genuine musical resolution of the material of the love-duet and therefore—since the duet is the climax of the act—of the structure of the act as a whole. The simplified, rarefied version of the theme sung by the women's voices as a counterpoint to Jitka's consolatory aria at the original end of the third act is the ultimate resolution of the opera's revolutionary force. It is indeed a pity that Smetana did not remain true to his instinct and his formal logic. In response to criticism, he added a further scene in which Dalibor's death is presented on the stage.

Each of Smetana's operas represented a different kind of experience and a different social function: and therefore involved a different problem of form. *The Bartered Bride*, being a simple comic opera designed to entertain, could employ the relatively episodic technique of traditional *opera buffa*. *Dalibor*, being a heroic and tragic opera concerning personal conflicts within a national theme, called for more complex and stringent organization. *Libuše* is a large-scale festival opera which deals with an episode from Bohemian history in a visionary, almost mythological way; to it the Wagnerian technique of the leitmotive therefore seems appropriate. A late comic opera, such as *The Secret*, uses elements derived from *buffo* style, from the leitmotive technique, and from the Lisztian serial principle explored in *Dalibor*; for in such an opera the relatively external vivacity of *The Bartered Bride* is deepened by something of the strength and tenderness which characterize Smetana's tragic and heroic operas.

Although Smetana was fundamentally an operatic composer, he considered it a part of his self-appointed task to create an orchestral literature for his people. This he planned—with the same intellectual probity that he manifests in his operas—as a national epic. He described the sequence of orchestral works known collectively as *Ma Vlast* as symphonic poems, and gave them a literary programme which stresses their dramatic, rather than abstract, nature. But the works are musically as self-contained as the operas, and are in some ways more traditional in approach, for they do not employ Lisztian techniques. Thus *Vyšehrad* is in a vast ternary form, *Vltava* is a rondo, *Šárka* a telescoped sonata, *Z Ceskych* a classical suite consisting of prelude, fugue, chorale, and polka, all thematically related, and *Tábor* and *Blaník* form together an enormous variation-set or chorale prelude.

In later years, after he had more or less discarded the sonata principle as irrelevant to his experience, Smetana composed few chamber works. The two string quartets are, however, impressive instances of the application of a large-scale dramatic conception to an intimate form. The well-known First is autobiographical not so much in the sense that it deals with subjective drama as that it evokes the scenes of Smetana's youth. The late Second Quartet, which is supposed to describe the struggles of the deaf composer to capture the themes that elude his fallible ears, is perhaps the only introspective work which this vigorously operatic composer ever created. Even so, it achieves objectivity in its laconically aphoristic language. No wonder that Liszt said that Smetana was harmonically in advance of Wagner; for this weird, moving piece is prophetic of the

Moravian master who, following Smetana, linked his rich sense of communal tradition to the spiritual isolation of the twentieth century.

Smetana has, indeed, more in common with Janáček than with Dvořák [1841–1904], with whom he is conventionally coupled. Smetana and Janáček both impress by the positive virility of their art; if Dvořák has Smetana's spontaneity, he has but little of his strength. A smaller personality, he is more reliant on the past; and while from one point of view he was able thus to rely on tradition only because of the vitality of the agrarian society in which he lived, from another point of view his adherence to the past stood between him and complete artistic realization. This is evident in what one might call the positive and negative poles of his relation to the Austrian classics.

The positive pole is his relationship to Schubert, whose lyrical spontaneity and harmonic instinct he inherited. But his was a simpler, less subtle nature. In Schubert, the mediant relationships and enharmonic changes may suggest a passive luxuriance in the senses; but we experience them with an acute poignancy, since we hear them in relation to Schubert's dramatic intensity. In Dvořák there is normally no such conflict; he enjoys his lyricism and his sensuous rhapsody for their own sake. Something the same is true, we saw, of Smetana's enharmony: only in his case sensuous experience is one part of a powerful intellectual and dramatic organization. Such organization is not in Dvořák's nature. He sounds most completely himself when he admits this and adopts a rhapsodic approach to composition, as in the movements based on the emotionally volatile folk-rhapsody of the dumka.

Unfortunately, he was not always content to be himself. He could not, like Smetana, free himself from the inheritance of the sonata; nor had he, like Schubert or Bruckner, the creative vitality to evolve a sonata style at once lyrical and dramatic. But he felt he had to measure up to the classical ideal; and the negative pole of his traditionalism was his admiration for Brahms, to whom he turned in later years as the progressive Smetana turned to Liszt. Dvořák's attempt to produce large-scale works in symphonic style sometimes—notably in the D minor Symphony—led to music of remarkable power; but it is undeniable that in writing such music Dvořák was forcing his nature. The grandiose peroration of the last movement of this symphony wears less well than the pastoral quietude of the slow movement: or than the more relaxed, less 'symphonic', movements of the Fourth Symphony in G, or the Third in F. Even the last movement of this symphony, however, sounds self-conscious when it attempts to provide a convincing culmination by recapitulating earlier themes: especially if one considers it alongside the transmuted codas in Smetana's *Dalibor*. Self-consciousness is disastrous in a composer as instinctive as Dvořák. It is significant that he found it so difficult to finish his symphonies. The true symphonist is always getting somewhere; the essence of Dvořák's temperament is that he is content to be and to enjoy.

Dvořák seems to have come to realize that although, as a nineteenth-century composer in the classical tradition, he ought to write symphonies, his talents did not naturally tend in that direction. After his visit to America, he turned from the symphony to the symphonic poem; yet he was hardly on happier ground here, for the monothematic Lisztian symphonic poem allows less for discursiveness than the symphony. Dvořák provided himself with a detailed literary programme and conscientiously illustrated it in music, forgetting that for Liszt the programme was no more than a general evocation of mood or atmosphere. Dvorák's symphonic poems are full of the most ravishing sensuous moments; but they do not wear well because they fall, structurally, between two stools. They relinquish classical precedent, while showing no understanding of the thematic techniques practised by Liszt and Smetana. Nor has Dvořák any grasp of the more complex structural techniques of Wagner, whose harmonic and orchestral luxuriance fascinated him no less than the economy of the anti-Wagnerian, Brahms.

It is no accident that Dvořák's most convincing large-scale instrumental work is the 'Cello Concerto. The virtuoso nature of nineteenth-century concerto style permits some relaxation of dramatic logic; and the 'cello is a singing instrument, sensuously mellow, which—unlike the piano—does not readily lend itself to rhetoric. Dvořák's own Piano Concerto is a fiasco because the soloist's rhetoric is not merely unrelated, but even opposed, to the lyrical essence of the music. In the 'Cello Concerto, on the other hand, the heart-easing warmth of the melodies is matched by the inevitability of the music's rhapsodic growth. Schubert wished, in his music, to resolve his distractions in love. Dvořák, less distracted, has less to resolve; but the love is hardly less potent. When a composer can create a theme such as this—in which the relaxed pentatonic arabesques of folk-song are absorbed into a flowing lyricism reconcilable with the richest harmony, scored with a magical instinct for the sonority of each instrument—we can but return his love in gratitude (Ex. 24):

It is sometimes said that the pentatonic inflexions of themes such as this—or the hardly less beautiful one from the slow movement of the G major Symphony—were prompted by Dvořák's experience of Negro music on his visit to the United States. It would be truer to say that acquaintance with Negro music emphasized a proclivity inherent in the folk-music of his own people (and indeed in all folk-music): and that the innocence of such melody was consistent with his own temperament, irrespective of racial considerations. In this connexion it is interesting to compare Dvořák's use of the interval of the sixth with Smetana's. For Smetana it usually implies an emotional expansion, with the higher note on the strong beat, accompanied by an increase of harmonic tension (as in Verdi); for Dvořák the sixth often becomes an inversion of the pentatonic third, floating, relaxed, with the higher note on the weak beat. The effect—consider the opening phrase of the 'Nigger' Quartet, and the use of the sixth in the approach to the recapitulation—is of softly-smiling, sensuous abandonment (Ex. 25):

and although this comes more naturally to Dvořák than the

stilted solemnity he sometimes affects in his symphonies, it has its own dangers.

Pentatonic melodies, indeed, being without a leading note, are not likely to prove convincing as the *basic* material for a sonata movement. They can serve as relaxation; but there must first be something to relax from. The charming irresponsibility of Dvořák's lighter chamber works bears only a superficial relationship to Haydn's wit. Occasionally—for instance, in the delicious E flat Quartet, opus 51, especially the last movement—he approaches the 'intense levity' which Haydn habitually achieves, because dramatic tension is implicit in his frivolity. In the average run of Dvořák's lighter works, however, vivacity has lost the edge of wit—the classical awareness of "other modes of experience that are possible". It would be curmudgeonly to complain of deficiencies in such delightful café music as the A major Quintet or the opus 96 Quartet. It would none the less be stupid not to recognize that such music represents a lower level both of human experience and of 'entertainment' than the ostensibly comparable works of Haydn.

Only rarely did Dvořák attempt 'symphonic' drama in his chamber music; the F minor Trio is unique in the manner in which Dvořák modifies his improvisatory, sonorously expansive keyboard style to create a Brahmsian trenchancy, even ferocity. It is a powerful, but hardly characteristic, work. At the end of his life, however, Dvořák at last managed to reconcile his symphonic ambitions with the instinctive sensuousness of his nature—in the two string quartets, opus 106, especially the Second, in G major. The luxuriantly lovely slow movement of this quartet is significantly a dumka. It is formally unpretentious, being a rudimentary kind of rondo. It is unambitiously reliant on the past—on the pentatonic inflexions, drone effects, and reiterated phrases of folk-music, and on such Schubertian features as an oscillation between the major and minor triad, a climacteric modulation to the flat sub-mediant, and a quasi-orchestral sonority in the string writing. Yet in being thus relaxed, Dvořák reveals his original genius most clearly; and creates not merely his most appealing, but his most poignantly imaginative music. Perhaps the major-minor alternation—which is far less habitual in Dvořák's music than in Schubert's—is mainly responsible for this pathos. It is interesting, however, that the minor is here a momentary disturbance before the radiant major: whereas in

Schubert the minor key is usually the stronger, making major seem sadder than minor, because illusory.

While Dvořák creates his most convincing music in a rhapsodic style, one can hardly say that he is incapable of handling large forms. Symphonic idiom was not congenial to him, except in an occasional lyric compromise, like the 'Cello Concerto; but both his operas and his church music are formally adequate. He is not innately an opera composer, for he has none of Smetana's objective awareness of human character. But his spontaneous flow of melody, his command of orchestral colour, and his instinct for the picturesque serve him well when he deals with peasant life, or still more with Nature, and with magical rather than human creatures. One has only to compare the music of the Nature sprites in *Rusalka* with any example of Rimsky-Korsakov's supernatural music to see the difference between the creative magician and the conjurer.

Equally beautiful are Dvořák's large-scale liturgical works; for here he has a text to discipline him, while having no need of the opera composer's response to character and situation. It is interesting that Dvořák was a sincere Catholic, whereas Smetana, like Schubert, was agnostic. His Catholicism was not an ardent, mystical exaltation, like that of Bruckner. It was rather synonymous with his easy-going temperament, which, unlike Smetana's sturdily independent or Schubert's acutely divided nature, accepted traditional dogma in religious belief, as in art. It is not therefore surprising that the *Te Deum* and the *Requiem* exhibit the same technical features as the instrumental music, though their structure is more coherent. This is particularly true of the big *Requiem*: for the sinuous unaccompanied chromatic phrase with which the work opens pervades the entire score. While it does not subtly change its identity, like Smetana's *Dalibor* theme, it provides a link between, on the one hand, the pentatonic folk-like lyricism, the simple choral homophony, and the luminous, rustic scoring (especially the parallel thirds for woodwind): and, on the other hand, the more conventionally Italianate lyricism and the caprice of the enharmonic modulations. (Consider the tremulously fluctuating 'In Memoria aeterna', or the Tristanesque opening to the 'Tuba Mirum',—Ex. 26.) Both in its pastoral and itssensuous aspects, Dvořák's attitude to his God would seem to be pantheistic rather than dogmatic; it is significant that the only weak passage in the score is the 'Quam olim', a conventional oratorio fugue of Mendelssohnic squareness. Smetana could still think and feel naturally in fugue, even

within the apparently light-hearted context of an operatic overture like that to *The Secret*, not to mention the magnificent full-scale fugue in *Z Ceskych*. Dvořák could not. He merely felt that a fugue was expected of him at this point, just as he felt that a symphony 'ought' to end with a heroic peroration. In this connexion, it is interesting to contrast the richly spontaneous pagan opening of Dvořák's oratorio, *St. Ludmilla*, with the depressing academicism that sets in with the arrival of Christian redemption!

Smetana was born in 1824, Dvořák in 1841, and Janáček—the third and last of the great Czech nationalists—only nine years later. Dvořák lived until 1904, but was not temperamentally prone to experiment. Janáček lived (and composed) until 1928, and experimented throughout a long life. Like Smetana, he was brought up in a peasant community. His father was a village schoolmaster who encouraged him—with his numerous brothers and sisters—to play in the village band, as well as introducing him to the Viennese classics. At the age of ten he went to a local monastery school, where he gained his first formal instruction in music and heard the plainchant which, along with folk-song, was the most important musical influence on his youth. When he moved to Prague Conservatory, he acquired a sound Austrian technique similar to Smetana's. Born thirty years later, however, he was more consciously artistic in his nationalism. He began to feel, as the Russians had felt earlier, that a national style implied the rejection of cosmopolitanism; to be Moravian was to be original. Eventually he founded at Brno his own conservatoire, which was deliberately opposed to the conventionally academic. It is easy to deplore the time that Janáček wasted in apparently fruitless bickering with the members of more orthodox academies; but one cannot separate the development of his attitude to his art from the art itself. It was during these years that he wandered around the countryside listening to the cries of birds and beasts, the ripple of streams and the whining of wind—above all, to the voices of the peasants, the different rhythmic and tonal traits they assumed under the stress of varying emotion. The theories which he based on his observations were also a deduction from his creative practice. If a no less powerful, he was a later, more self-conscious revolutionary than Moussorgsky; he had to understand intellectually what, in emotional terms, he was trying to do.

Later Janáček said: "The study I have made of the musical aspects of the spoken language has led me to the conviction that all the melodic and rhythmic mysteries of music can be explained by reference to the melody and rhythm of the musical motives of the spoken language." From this point of view, folk-song was a sublimation of speech; and Janáček believed, with Moussorgsky, that the speech-song of simple people, living close to the earth, was both more musical and more 'real' than that of sophisticated people. He did not, however, follow Moussorgsky in equating art with the 'moment of reality'. This was not merely because he had, like Smetana, a background of traditional technique; it was also because, like Smetana and unlike Moussorgsky, he saw life as growth. *Jenůfa*—the opera which made his name—shares with Smetana's operas the positive vitality of a folk-culture and a rich inheritance of Austro-Italian technique. But Janáček's explorations into peasant speech and into the sounds of rural life more profoundly modify his sophistication. The flexible vocal lines approach speech without ceasing to be powerfully lyrical; the orchestral texture emulates the sounds of Nature while creating an elaborate network of interrelated motives. Consider, for instance, how the figuration suggested by the sound of the mill becomes a musical motive related both to an abstract concept like fate, and also to the development of pathological obsession within a character. Janáček's music becomes more 'realistic', less formally conventional, because he aims to embrace in his opera all the complexity and perversity of life. His greatness consists largely in the fact that he preserves something like Smetana's positive strength, even in expressing the abysmal depths of guilt and conscience. *Jenůfa* and *Katia Kabanova*—though one ends happily, the other tragically—involve an awareness both of the terrors within the human mind and of the will to live. Folk-vitality merges into Christian abnegation and a Dostoevskian sense of sin: just as peasant community and monastery school had moulded Janáček's childhood, and folk-song and plainsong meet in the contours of his melodic lines.

The essence of Janáček's originality lies in his approach to rhythm, which was influenced by his study of speech and of the sounds of Nature. Most of the chords he uses are in themselves simple—he is more sparing of sevenths and ninths than Smetana. But the complex and elliptical nature of his rhythm means that he discovers unexpected relationships between the chords; exploiting the acoustical 'period of reverberation', he sometimes dispenses with the normal grammatical transition. His conception of incremental rhythm also modifies his conception of form, as we can see most convincingly in an instrumental work which, while moving within a more restricted range than an opera, employs an exactly comparable technique. The third movement of the late *Sinfonietta*, for instance, opens with a lyrical phrase comparatively richly harmonized (Ex. 27a):

this music belongs to Smetana's world. The rising semitone and falling tone with which the piece opens gradually expands until it becomes an ascending fourth and descending fifth, then a sixth: at which point a violently contrasted, syncopated rhythm on the brass, interspersed with wild squeals of flute and piccolo, destroys the melody (Ex. 27b):

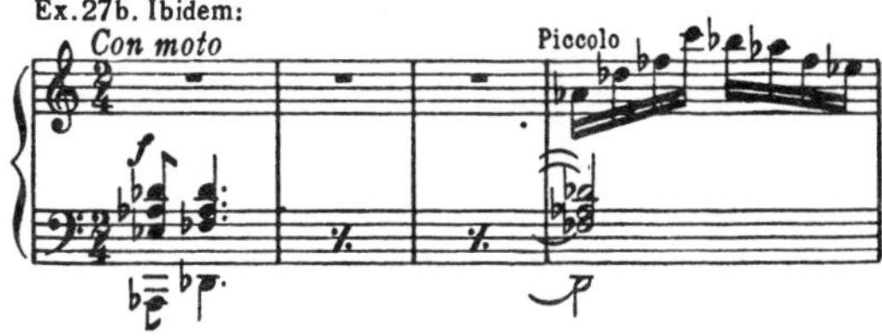

The lyrical theme then reappears, rondo-wise, but is not allowed to sing. The brass interjections and the woodwind skirls are now telescoped with it, so that it becomes a frenzied dance, growing increasingly panic-stricken until the syncopated motive barks ferociously on horns and trombones, and the music explodes in a flute and piccolo scream. In the ominous silence that follows, fragments of the melody sound forlornly. This kind of structural technique has little in common with nineteenth-century symphonic methods; we hardly need the comparable examples from Janáček's operas to see how powerfully it suggests a dramatic or psychological crisis.

The fourth piece is similar, only this time it begins, not with a lyrical song motive, but with a folk-like dance tune, hypnotically repeated. The brief phrase is decorated with chromatic skirls on the violins and telescoped into ever more elliptical rhythmic patterns: until suddenly the chromaticism, which we had thought of as an embellishment, becomes the core of the music. A wailful descending phrase, starting high on the woodwind, splinters the folk-like vivacity (Ex. 28):

The little tune tries pathetically to re-establish its identity, but fails. The movement ends with an abrupt, almost hysterical assertion of dance metre, built on reiterated fourths. In these two strange, frightening movements the simplicities of a peasant world are transformed into a 'modern' nervous frenzy. The disruptive originality does not, however, bring a loss in power. The work opens and concludes with a broad ceremonial movement, mainly pentatonic in line, scored for brass and drums. Despite the intrusion of chromatic elements and elliptical rhythms into the pentatonicism, this has the extrovert exuberance of a peasant festival. The oppositions of tonality may be violent, but Janáček's music has none of Smetana's tonal fluidity. Even in his operas, Janáček will often maintain a single key until some external event occurs to destroy it; and his association of certain keys with specific emotional states (for instance, the D flat major he habitually uses for love scenes) reminds us of the statically symbolic use of tonality in the old heroic opera.

In all Janáček's music we find this balance between the vitality of an agricultural inheritance and the introspective exploration of the Freudian bugaboo. In the series of experimental operas that followed *Katia Kabanova*, the stress tends to fall increasingly on the disruptive elements. Yet even the last of the operas—*The House of the Dead*, which has a libretto freely based on Dostoevsky—has a virility that belies the brutality of the melodies, the strange orchestration, the fantastic rhythmic complications of the trombone and percussion parts. However complex the detail, the operatic 'projection' is so vivid that the effect of the music is extraordinarily simple, and simply extraordinary. This is true not only of the operas, but of Janáček's work in any medium—the tremendous revolutionary choruses, the two string quartets (both of which have programmatic subtitles), and the *Diary of a Young Man Lost*, for tenor, soprano, women's chorus, and piano. This work, an opera in miniature, provides a microcosm of every aspect of Janáček's technique —the plastic, *parlando* line, the rhythmic complications, the lugubrious dissonance, the nervous texture. There is no more sensitive portrayal of the agonies of adolescence than this work of a sixty-three-year-old composer; and it is significant that the piece was prompted directly by life, rather than by art. The young man of the title was not imaginary, but a peasant boy who left the safety of home for the wild love of a gipsy. After his disappearance, the folk-poems in which he described his experience were found and published in a local newspaper, where Janáček saw them. His music makes the story live again; and because he wanted us to live through the experience as we hear the music, he said that the cycle should be performed, as nearly as possible, in the dark.

In his seventieth year Janáček said, speaking of his new Wind Sextet, which he called *Youth*: "I listen to the birds singing, I wonder at the manifestations of rhythm in its million different forms in the world of light, colour and shapes, and my music remains young through contact with the eternally young rhythm of Nature." No finer testimony to this could be imagined than his last, and possibly greatest, work—the Mass for soli, chorus, orchestra, and organ. Intended for performance in the open air, like the medieval Slavonic festival mass, this is at once a Catholic act of praise to God and a pagan act of homage to the earth. But again the technique resembles that of the operas; the aphoristic lyrical phrases, the pentatonic contours, the compulsive metrical rhythms erupt volcanically, so that the powerfully positive music seems to contain the cataclysmic upheavals and inner torments of the twentieth century. Yet for all Janáček's genius, and for all his modernity, this music is inconceivable except in relation to a world we shall never see again. If Janáček does not belong to the nineteenth century, we can only say that he is *sui generis*. He has had and can have little influence on the music of the twentieth century; and though he may not be the greatest of contemporary composers, there is a sense in which he makes most twentieth-century music seem impotent.

5

THE DECLINE OF NATIONALISM

JANÁČEK is the last *great* composer whose music is inspired by a folk tradition. Bartók was born in an agrarian community; but folk-music was for him not so much a positive in itself, as a stimulus to exploration. For the rest, the national composers who followed the great Russian and Czech schools are minor figures. There is no successor to Moussorgsky; and even the successors to Tchaikowsky's Europeanized Russian idiom could not recapture his neurotic energy. Medtner [1880–1951] the most musically distinguished of these composers, adopted a style Teutonically Brahmsian rather than Russian, while attaining a discreet originality by way of his pianistic invention. Rachmaninov [1873–1943], one of the great virtuoso pianists of history, was not unnaturally even more wedded to the keyboard in his technique as a composer. The original and evocative moments in his music—for instance, the development section and cadenza of the first movement of the D minor Concerto (No. 3)—are almost always expansions of harmonic devices suggested by the behaviour of his hands at the keyboard. So it is not surprising that his large-scale, Teutonically constructed works are seldom convincing as wholes.

Perhaps they do not need to be. Rachmaninov's lyrical sense, caressingly drooping like Tchaikowsky's, makes it possible for him to create songs as insidious as, if less powerful than, Tchaikowsky's; and this nostalgic lyricism, in combination with the sultry chromatic embellishments of his harmony and his mastery of pianistic ornament, even suffices to make his formally inconclusive concertos hypnotic in their appeal. Some part of Rachmaninov's fascination for the vast popular audience may come from his very insecurity, his hypochondria, his lack of self-confidence. "If ever I believed in myself, it was a very long time ago, when I was very young", he wrote in 1912 from his self-imposed American exile. There was always a fight in him between material success and creative ambition. Small wonder that this finds an echo in our hearts, living as we do in a society dedicated to material gain.

For all the Russian quality of his pessimism, nostalgia, and instability, Rachmaninov is hardly a national composer. More typical of the latter-day nationalist is Grieg [1843–1907], whose distinction is closely related to the smallness of his talent. Norway, like Russia, was cut off from Europe; but there was little in her history to promote an 'epic' operatic or symphonic music comparable with that of the Russians. A certain cosy sweetness, rather than barbaric grandeur, was typical of Norwegian society; and except for the fact that his country was not much industrialized, Grieg's position was comparable with that of a composer in nineteenth-century England. Like Delius—and most British composers of his generation—Grieg studied in Germany, for there was no local tradition in which he could have been trained.

His first attempts to write large-scale symphonic works in the German tradition were failures. Even the later Piano Concerto is not a symphonic work, but a series of charming salon pieces strung together, and his only formally convincing large-scale work is the Piano Ballade, which is in non-developing variation style. He had nothing like Smetana's powerful sweep or Dvořák's spontaneity; nor had he Moussorgsky's ability to build up, through an inner dramatic momentum, a big structure from small components. Grieg habitually thought in two-bar periods, and his tunes, like Norwegian folk-songs, moved through a narrow range. The pentatonic flavour resulting from a fall of a tone followed by a descending minor third is as characteristic as the tendency of his themes to avoid the leading note.

Though this folk-like flavour is connected with Grieg's restricted emotional range, it certainly does not mean that he felt with primitive vitality. The composers he most admired were Chopin, Schumann, and—for his chromaticism and elegance rather than for his dramatic power—Mozart; Chopin's mazurkas were the model for his treatment of folk-melodies. Since folk-songs do not develop and are relatively devoid of harmonic implications, the simple repeated phrases could be harmonized with seductive chromaticisms and enharmonic sequences which are no more than a momentary distortion of tonal perspective.

The harmonic progression moves very slowly, if at all; the Wagnerian sevenths and ninths become sensory moments, chained to the two-bar phrases, instead of a cumulating passion. This static conception of harmony has melodic consequences also; Grieg is especially fond of themes consisting of chains of thirds—horizontalized chords of the seventh or ninth.

The nostalgic flavour of Grieg's little piano pieces comes largely from the odd way in which simple folk-like tunes thus come to terms with sophisticated harmony. The effect is much more artificial than that of Chopin's mazurkas, in which there is an interpenetration of the primitive and the sophisticated. Chopin's harmonic-polyphonic epigrams are much deeper in their yearning. Yet the superficial quality of Grieg's music is inseparable from its later date. He could not become part of a folk-tradition—as Chopin did, ideally and retrospectively; he could only offer an emotional commentary on it. Chopin is a highly emotional composer who is never sentimental; the *flow* of his harmony preserves an inner vitality. Grieg's static sequences, anchored by internal pedal points, are frequently sentimental. Revolving around themselves, emphasizing their pathos, they seem in excess of the object—the simple, undeveloping tunes.

Grieg is most successful as a song-writer, partly because a vocal line prompts greater pliancy and subtlety of contour, partly because the folk-inspired poetry of the *Vinje* or *Haugtussa* songs released hidden depths in his nostalgia. It is interesting that Grieg's finest music looks not backwards to the days when nationalism was a creative force, but forwards to some of the 'disruptive' techniques from which twentieth-century music was born. Especially in some of the songs dealing with Nature, the harmony becomes almost as statically impressionistic as Debussy's; the evocation of a folk-culture has been transformed into a private world of the senses. Grieg's music was significantly fashionable in Paris during the 1890s.

On the other hand, Grieg now accepts the primitive as primitive. He sees in the unself-conscious integrity of folk-techniques potentialities that may extend the boundaries of 'art' music. The late *Slåtter* for piano, for instance, can be legitimately compared with the folk-song arrangements of Bartók. Here Grieg attempts neither to sophisticate nor to sentimentalize the bagpipe drones, the telescoped tonics and dominants, the acrid tritonal arabesques of Norwegian fiddle music. He transfers the sharp, crackling sound of the village fiddler with miraculous skill to the piano (Ex. 29):

and although the little pieces are as undeveloped and as undevelopable as the folk-tunes themselves, they suggest techniques which greater European composers were to use to revitalize convention. Grieg's approach is quite different from Janáček's. For all his urgent modernity, Janáček was still a part of the folk-tradition whose idiom he remade. Grieg in these little pieces is already, like Bartók, the folk-song collector, consciously preserving a dying art.

The decline of nationalism is most comprehensively illustrated, however, by the phenomenon of Spanish music. Like Britain, Spain had a great musical literature in the Middle Ages and the Renaissance. During the eighteenth and nineteenth centuries the Spanish tradition had withered like the British, though perhaps for the opposite cause. We were the progressive nation; too rapidly industrialized, we lost contact with our spiritual roots. Spain, on the other hand, was so backward that the past ceased to be creative; the roots themselves dried up. Both countries lost the essential balance between tradition and creativity.

The decline of both traditions is symbolized in the failure to create a national opera. There is a close parallel between, on the one hand, the music-hall opera of the English Restoration and the ballad opera of the eighteenth century and, on the other hand, the Spanish *zarzuelas** and *tonadillas*.† In Spain, however, the popular tradition, even in its urbanized forms, remained vital when 'serious' music virtually disappeared and

* ZARZUELA: a comic operetta, usually in one act, and satirical in character. Some of the dialogue is spoken and improvised. Often the *zarzuela* was a musical guying of a popular play.

† TONADILLO: a sung interlude in a spoken play.

most of the talented composers were voluntary exiles in France. Britain's John Field went to Russia, Spain's Arriaga [1806–1826] began the migration to Paris. Ever since, the cultural connexion between Paris and Spain has been intimate: consider the cases of Picasso, Debussy, Ravel.

Spanish music, like British, re-emerged at the end of the nineteenth century in association with a self-conscious folk-song revival. Though folk-music in Spain was still a living tradition, cultural decay had gone so far that composers of 'art' music were unable to use folk-music to regenerate their work. There is no Spanish complement to Janáček or Bartók; hardly even a Spanish complement to the later work of Grieg. The cult of folk-music became a kind of escape. Thus Granados [1867–1916] composed an enormous quantity of picture-postcards in sound, incorporating Spanish folk-rhythms and melodic formulae into a conventional pianistic style founded on German salon music. We remember him, however, because on two occasions he rediscovered, almost fortuitously, the real soul of Spain.

Almost, but not quite, fortuitously: for the first of these works, the *Tonadillas* for voice and piano, were based directly on the eighteenth-century popular tradition. Nineteenth-century harmony is rejected in favour of a simple, guitar-like piano texture, while the vocal line has the vivacity of eighteenth-century popular opera; it is no longer necessary artificially to graft a native idiom on to the style of the salon. In the other work, the piano suite, *Goyescas*, Granados finds himself through the stimulus of an immeasurably greater artist—the painter Goya. The piano style, founded on Liszt, is now ripely exuberant; and the liberation of technique is a liberation of feeling. These tone poems for piano are too long in their opulence: yet depend on their opulence for their emotional effect. Though their chromatic sequential writing is powerfully nostalgic, it is at least nostalgic for the real Spain, not the picture-postcard version.

Albéniz [1860–1909] is a similar but still odder case. His output of picture-postcards for piano was even more prolific than Granados's, and even less enterprising harmonically and pianistically. Then, in the last few years of his life he created the piano works, *Iberia* and *Navarra*—perhaps the most impressive Spanish music since the Italian Scarlatti. Indeed, these pieces have much more of the spirit of Goya than Granados's *Goyescas*. The haunting modal themes have the true *flamenco* spirit,* the unsentimentalized *cri de cœur*, and are no more nostalgic than Spanish folk-music itself. The pianistic arabesques suggested by *flamenco* music are likewise fierce and hard, not 'picturesque'; and although the harmonic concept was greatly influenced by Debussy (whose *L'Ile Joyeuse* was a revelation to Albéniz), the effect of the harmony is altogether un-Debussyan. Harmonic side-steppings off-key, similar to those in Debussy's misty pieces, become a background to strong melodies and violent rhythms, so that they are almost percussive in effect. Percussive unresolved appoggiaturas and acciaccaturas† relate back to guitar technique and to Scarlatti's harpsichord style. Albéniz's immediate, vibrant music thus becomes deeply traditional. Inevitably more self-conscious than the much greater art of Janáček, it may be an exercise in Spanish style. None the less, an exercise so positively felt left virtually nothing for Spanish nationalism to say.

In the music of Falla [1876–1946] Spanish nationalism is already singing its swan-song. In Albéniz's *Iberia* impressionistic techniques become percussive, embellishing strenuous lines and rhythms. In Falla's *Nights in the Gardens of Spain* (1907) regional vigour dissolves away in an impressionistic haze of harmony and orchestration. The music is poetic, and technically interesting in its guitar-like use of the piano as concertante instrument. But this is already the exile's Spain, viewed retrospectively, as in Debussy's *Ibéria*. All three movements sound much alike and are too long for their content: as is almost all Spanish national music, even Albéniz's masterpiece.

Perhaps the only exception to this emotional inflation or dissipation is a late work of Falla, the Concerto for harpsichord, oboe, clarinet, and 'cello (1923). Falla's preoccupation with traditional Spanish subjects in his operas and ballets stimulated an interest in the music of Spain's great traditions. In this masterly little work, Falla fuses folk-song, medieval liturgical music, Renaissance polyphony, eighteenth-century popular music, and the harpsichord style of Scarlatti and Soler into a twentieth-century evocation of Spain's spiritual history. The

* FLAMENCO: a version of traditional Spanish songs of lamentation, as sung by gipsies in the nineteenth century. The melodies are elaborately ornamented and often employ intervals smaller than a semitone.

† ACCIACCATURAS: a discordant ornamental note struck almost simultaneously with the principal note—like a very rapid appoggiatura.

harsh, unsentimental clatter of the street band meets the clangour of church bells in this terse score, which provokes comparison with Stravinsky's *Soldier's Tale*. But whereas Stravinsky's Russian fairy tale was a prelude to a reborn, European style, Falla's miniature incarnation of Spain's forgotten glory was a *post mortem*. It reminded us that Spain had once had a great culture; no more than Albéniz's *Iberia* did it create a new tradition. Falla had made the past present; for the later stream of Spanish nationalists the past has been no more than a period-piece. The figures in the postcards may be togged up in eighteenth-century, instead of nineteenth-century, costume; that does not make them more alive. The point about Stravinsky's Russian puppets, from *Petrouchka* onwards, is that they come to life. The Spanish puppets mimic real people, while deceiving no one—not even, perhaps, those who jerk the strings.

II INTROSPECTION AND ISOLATION

I

TWO SONG-WRITERS

THE paradoxical poignancy of Schubert's music, we saw, came from the way in which his reverence for the classical tradition—and all that it implied in terms of social stability—was undermined by nostalgia. He wished to 'belong'; yet he was aware that, isolated within his private dream, he could claim solidarity only with a few kindred spirits. Wagner inflated the private dream into a new mythology, becoming himself God and Society: in this sense he is the *ne plus ultra* of romanticism. Now Hugo Wolf [1860–1903] was Schubert's natural successor, and at the same time the idolator of Wagner. Far more completely than Schubert, he was centred in his nerves, subject to alternating bouts of exuberance and melancholia, composing in hectic fits of inspiration, or not at all. Like Wagner, he was an egoist ready to sacrifice anyone to the behests of his genius and —despite his petty irascibilities and pomposities—was personally so fascinating that people vied with one another to be sacrificed. Yet although part of him yearned to make a quasi-Wagnerian universe out of his feelings, he could never accomplish this. His obsession with Wagner involved hate as well as love: his *alter ego* held him back from self-deification. On the contrary, he rather sought, like Schubert, to find his own personality in losing it in the minds of others. The classical spirit won its most impressive victory in the man who, in the most obvious sense, was the typical romantic artist.

Wolf's future destiny was already implicit in the extraordinary String Quartet, which, started in 1878, was his first large-scale work. He was then in his nineteenth year, and had already come under Wagner's spell. Yet more significant than the Wagnerian influence in this music are its classical affiliations. The key (D minor), the expectant, tremolando opening, the epic proportions, suggest Beethoven's Ninth Symphony; while the gigantic leaps of the melodic lines and the 'orchestral' texture of the string writing resemble the Beethoven of the *Grosse Fuge*. Beethovenian, too, is the strife between the wild power of the imagination and the recalcitrant medium; though Wolf's Quartet, being a young man's music, cannot attain to Beethoven's strenuously won wisdom and serenity.

For if the Quartet is Beethovenian in intention, it is Schubertian in effect. The resonant chordal writing, the D minor tonality, and the fevered *moto perpetuo* of the last movement recall the death-haunted finale of Schubert's 'Death and the Maiden' Quartet; the wide melodic leaps and ambiguously oscillating tonalities of the slow movement remind us of the fight between lyrical dream and oppressive reality in Schubert's prophetic work in G. Listening to Wolf's Quartet, we are not surprised that it was the only composition, apart from student exercises, that he completed during adolescence. He felt that he had burned himself out in it; and it seems certain that madness would have overtaken him in early youth, but for the ability he discovered to objectify his sufferings in the passions of others. His experience was too vehement, too searing, directly to be embodied in instrumental terms. He became a song-writer because, in submission to the poet, he could find release from the burden of personality.

In Mörike Wolf found the poet who could unlock the clogged contortion of the nerves which had gone to make his Quartet; the noble, Beethovenian song which stands at the beginning of the Mörike volume—*Der Genesene an die Hoffnung*—was intended as a tribute to Mörike, through whom Wolf's creative spirit had been reborn. The extreme nervous intensity of the verse of this Protestant pastor with a Catholic imagination was controlled by ironic detachment; his religious feeling was infused (in the autobiographical Peregrina poems) with fervent eroticism. He was closer to Wolf than Müller was to Schubert; for whereas Müller was a minor poet who offered the themes which Schubert wished to transfigure, Mörike was a major poet who was Wolf's equal in range and depth. He was the first of Wolf's Masks; only in becoming Mörike could Wolf bring his creative energies to flower. Subservience to the poet certainly did not mean that the composer had to forget he was a musician.

Wolf's approach to song-writing is Wagnerian in the sense that the text generally speaks itself, while the meaning of the words creates thematic or harmonic ideas which are developed symphonically in the piano part. The parallel with Wagner must not, however, be pushed far. Wagner wrote his own words which amounted to little more than a literary illustration of his symphonic drama; if they were to be intelligible in the theatre, they called for a spacious, rather than an incidentally subtle, treatment. The words which Wolf set were usually great poetry; the vocal lines into which they flower must be the core of his songs, however minutely they reflect the nuance of the text, however complex are the motives which the words generate in the piano part. Consider, for instance, *Erstes Liebeslied eines Mädchens*, which Wolf said "would lacerate the nervous system of a block of marble". The piano opens with a fierce figure characterized by an abrupt drop at the end. The 'symphonic' structure is a continuous development of this figure, while the voice phrases its words breathlessly, "with the utmost force and passion". For all its speechlike disjointedness, the vocal part builds up into a coherent line, which coalesces with the piano line, while overlapping it rhythmically. The agitation and the suffering—the psychological insight—become the musical form; just as the girl who sings exists in herself, yet is at the same time Wolf.

Though this approach to song is common with Wolf, it is not habitual. He seeks, always, the musical corollary of the poem, so his musical structures are as varied as the poems he sets. If *Erstes Liebeslied* is a declamatory song, *Um Mitternacht* is entirely lyrical. The poem is in two stanzas, each presenting the same idea: that of the streams singing to the Night of the Day that is over, while Night broods on the oneness of Time, which is beyond diurnal change. Symphonic evolution would clearly be inappropriate here: so Wolf adopts the strophic form and allows both stanzas to be pervaded by the continuous rocking figure suggested to him by the images of the 'golden scales' and the evenly balanced yoke of the hours. Yet the two stanzas of the song are not quite identical; a climax within this quietude is created by the heavenly felicity of the expanded lyrical arch at the words "ihr klingt des Himmels". Response to verbal nuance again becomes the essence of the musical structure, even in this lyrical, rather than dramatic, song.

Another formal concept is implicit in a song like *Nixe Binsefuss*. Superficially, this is in the tradition of the fairy ballads of Loewe. Its naïve, whimsical humour becomes in Wolf's hands highly sophisticated; personal passion dissolves into the glinting tenuity of the piano part. Far from being simply strophic, the structure is characteristically subtle. The piano part works out two figures, the first associated with the descriptive introduction, the second with the words the nixy speaks. The first and third sections are in triple time, the second in duple: so that the form is an ABA structure, the speaking nixy being framed by the two descriptive pieces. The song resembles a miniature operatic scena; and perhaps the same is true of so utterly different a song as *Das verlassene Mägdlein*, at least if Wolf's setting be compared with Schumann's. Schumann becomes the desolate girl who sings through his lyricism. In Wolf's song the monotonous rhythm, the bare texture, the prevalence of neutral augmented fifths, project both character and scene; we feel the chill, wan dawn, in the house, in the heart.

Every element of Wolf's genius is present in the Mörike songs, except his command of a broad symphonic architecture. This becomes evident in the Goethe songs of the following year, 1889. In *Grenzen der Menschheit*, for instance, Wolf accepts Goethe's literary organization, in which each of five stanzas presents an idea complete in itself, though related to the central idea of the limitations imposed by God on man. But Wolf transforms this literary concept into a large-scale principle of musical order. Thus a minim pulse dominates the first and fifth sections, which deal with the gods in relation to man. The three middle sections, which describe man's vain attempts to transcend his limitations, introduce a more restless crochet pulse, and a harmony more chromatically contorted than the god-like diatonicism of the first section. But in the final stanza the agitated rhythm and harmony of man are fused into the minim pulse of the gods, since we are now concerned not with man in himself, but with man against the background of eternity. Even the directly 'pictorial' elements become, as with Bach, devices of musical organization. The repeated hammering note which portrays man's attempt to steady himself on the solid earth provides a transition from the restless harmony of the second section to renewed stability; and the symbolic wave movement carries the music forward into the final stanza, in which the vast leaps are at once illustrative and a climax to the song's growth.

The Goethe songs conclude the first phase of Wolf's career. With the Spanish song-book of 1890 the 'objectivity' which had counterbalanced his Wagnerian egoism becomes explicit in a preoccupation with Latin themes. Even the fanaticism of some of these Spanish folk-poems that fascinated him in Paul Heyse's translations acquires a Mediterranean lucidity. The Calvary songs may be related to Wolf's self-laceration; yet the implicit identification of Wolf with Christ imbues the theme of crucifixion with tragic severity. The vocal phrases have an almost plainsong-like austerity, but are splintered by chromaticism, with El Greco-like distortion. The piano parts touch an extreme of Tristanesque dissonance such as Wolf approached nowhere else and, in this spare texture, the tension is not mollified by the continuity of the harmonic flow (Ex. 30):

Ex. 30. Wolf: Herr, was trägt der Boden hier
Herr, was trägt der Bo - den hier
f
p
f
p

At the further extreme from these Calvary songs stands a group about the Holy Family: tender, limpidly diatonic, unrhetorically lyrical. In the secular love-songs the fervour of the Mörike songs is both raised to fever pitch and modified by a mordant irony. Erotic passion is now adult, no longer (however ardently) adolescent.

Irony, as opposed to the fey whimsicality of some of the earlier German songs, pervades the last phase of Wolf's work, the Italian song-books; even the tragic and lyrical songs have an epigrammatic concision. This aphoristic quality characterizes the verse forms of *rispetti* and *velote* which Wolf set in Heyse's translation. His misunderstanding of the mannered conceits of the poetry was the highest inspiration of his genius; the most impersonal poetry he ever set provoked what he himself called his most original and artistically consummate music. The Mediterranean clarity would have been little without the pressure of experience behind it; without the lucidity, however, the pressure of experience would have driven him mad before he had left, as his legacy, some of the greatest songs in European history.

The range of technique and experience in these miniature compositions seems inexhaustible. *Geselle, woll'n wir uns in Kutten hüllen*, for instance, is character-portrayal of a subtlety which an opera composer would need several scenes to establish: the hypocritical monk's *parlando* line tells us what he says, with vivid realism, while the piano part's mincing seconds and thematically evolving, pawkily insinuating motive tell us what he means. On the other hand, a song such as *Nun lass uns Frieden schliessen* is the purest lyricism; the falling sevenths that mark the emotive points in the verse are the more touching because the vocal range of the song is normally so restricted. The incidental nuances suggested by the words do not disrupt the music's flow: on the contrary, they give it momentum—consider the cross rhythm provoked by the words "ein Paar zufriedner Herzen", or the hint of pain beneath the tenderness created by the piano's chromatic appoggiaturas at the cadences (Ex. 31):

Such music is gracefully elegant, like the poem: yet it epitomizes at once the happiness and the pathos of love. There is a similar quality in that exquisite vision of the transitory bliss of love, *Wir haben beide lange Zeit geschwiegen.* After the hesitant chromaticism of the opening, the diatonicism of the piano's E flat melody seems transfigured. Only to a spirit as tortured as Wolf could this swaying lullaby mean so much: even here a chromatic intrusion in the vocal line provokes a heart-breaking return from sub-dominant to tonic by way of the flat supertonic (Ex. 32):

Ex.32. Wolf: Wir haben beide
die Lie - bes en-gel ka-men ü - ber Nacht und ha-ben
Frie - den mein-er Brust ge bracht

The momentary peace of love seems heavenly because, in loving, one suffers so much.

In other songs the playful element which is inherent in the poems disappears completely from Wolf's setting. In *Der Mond hat eine schwere Klag' erhoben*, for instance, a conventional conceit becomes a universal lament. Each vocal phrase climbs slowly upwards and then droops through a wide interval, usually a seventh. The piano preserves one figure throughout—widely spaced falling thirds in dotted rhythm, often clashing acutely with the repeated notes of the vocal line. The voice part reaches its climax at the end of the poem, in a wonderful phrase which telescopes the slowly rising third and the falling seventh which dominate the song: while the piano's tension crystallizes into a grinding dissonance which softly uncoils itself not on to the tonic chord, but on to the flat submediant. In this setting the conventional conceit associating the moon with the 'starry' eyes of the beloved seems to be obliterated, in Wolf's imagination, by the profound mythological associations of the moon with solitude. No doubt it was his awareness of his own isolation which gave to the song so tragic an intensity; yet feeling could hardly be more objectified than it is in the austere progression of this piano part, or in the voice's reticent response to the inflexions of the words.

In his greatest songs Wolf is a miniaturist who epitomizes a dramatic situation in the lyrical moment. Yet the part of him that nursed Wagnerian ambitions pursued, or was pursued by, the desire to create a large-scale opera. At the same time he was half afraid of his desire. In his heart he knew that if he was to create a big work, its basis would be different from Wagner's. He sought a comic—and Mediterranean—subject, as opposed to Teutonic gloom, because in such a theme he could find the objectivity he sought in his songs. If *Der Corregidor*, his only completed opera, is a failure the reason is that he had not the courage of his convictions. The Wagnerian treatment is appropriate neither to the subject nor to Wolf's professed intentions.

Though the libretto is confused and dramatically intractable, one suspects that Wolf came to approve of it precisely because it encouraged him to compose from point to point, using the leitmotive technique—as Wagner did not—as a substitute for musical coherence. He was capable of thinking in extended terms, as is proved by his adolescent quartet and by the superbly rich, if over-complex, symphonic poem, *Penthesilea.* Presented with a dramatic situation, however, his instinct was to crystallize it into a moment of musical and psychological illumination. Thus *Der Corregidor* contains some magnificent music, which occurs whenever isolated incidents fired the composer's imagination. The Tio Lukas and Frasquita duets have the glow of Wolf's Latin love-songs, while the continuous thematic evolution of the orchestral parts acquires, within the surge of Wagnerian harmony, an almost Bachian lucidity. Such music, however profound in its tenderness, is a part of the opera's comic world. Lukas's tragic monologue of jealousy, on the other hand, is not; and Wolf noticed no discrepancy because he was interested only in the climacteric moment which summarized a situation. In this sense *Der Corregidor* is less an opera than a Wolfian songbook with orchestra. It is interesting that Wolf showed not the slightest concern over the theatrical aspects of opera production; he never even noticed when changes were made, let alone offering any opinion about them. His operas were projected in his mind as completely as were his songs. For him, the stage was a redundancy.

Manuel Venegas, however—the opera which he had recently started when mental breakdown finally overtook him—suggests that he might ultimately have created the kind of opera he wanted and needed to write. The fifty pages of score which he completed do not reach the dramatic core of a libretto as powerful as *Der Corregidor* was ramshackle; but there is enough music to give promise of a new, impressive operatic technique. Though there are still leitmotives, the texture of the music is now quite un-Wagnerian, as simple as it is passionate. The change that has come over Wolf's operatic style exactly parallels the change that occurred between the Spanish and Italian song-books. Manuel's part is, as Wolf said, "a part to tear a cat in"; precisely because his passion is so violent, it is objectified in simple, lyric grandeur, as in the noble diatonicism of his invocation to his home town. Even the love music, though more chromatic, is strong and direct in its contour, with none of the orchestral proliferation of *Der Corregidor*; Wolf significantly said that he was going to orchestrate the opera "like Mozart". Whether he would have been able to sustain continuity throughout the whole drama we cannot tell. We can say, however, that the surviving fragment, dealing mainly with introductory matter, has a cumulative sweep that Wolf did not approach in his earlier opera.

Whether or no *Manuel Venegas* could have been an operatic complement to Wolf's mature songs, it is fitting that his last completed work should have been the most intimate songs he ever wrote. In setting Michelangelo's sonnets he identified his own bitter lot with that of the sculptor, expressing his disillusion in what he called a "truly antique simplicity". The bare, skeletonic *Alles endet, was entstehet*, with its grinding ninths and diminished sevenths, would prove unbearable in its pessimism, were not the 'Bachian' texture of motives in both voice and piano parts a paradoxical germination. The muffled wail of the single semitone swells to the stepwise rise and fall of a third, then to the arch of the third prepared by the tense diminished fourth, then to the rising sixth followed by a scale-wise descent, then to a combination of several of these metamorphoses in various rhythms (Ex. 33).

Wolf's life had been a tension between potentially overwhelming passion and the discipline of art; in the tightly wrought, monumental simplicity of this song he finds freedom in submitting to the ultimate discipline of death. He was, he said, "really scared" by the song and, contemplating it, feared for his reason. Indeed, there was nothing further he could say.

Ex. 33. Wolf: Alles endet
den die Zeit flieht und die Son ne sieht, dass Al - les
pp

He lingered for several years in the mental home, his mind and spirit destroyed. Megalomaniac delusions could at last reign unchecked.

There is a strange appendix to Wolf in the work and career of Henri Duparc [1848–1933], who composed all of his exiguous output sporadically between 1870 and 1885. He shared with Wolf a pathological nervous intensity and a devotion to Wagner. His response to verbal inflexion is hardly less sensitive than Wolf's, though his melody—deriving from Bizet's *opéra comique* and the delicately sensuous curves of Gounodesque *cantilena*—is less declamatory, more spontaneously lyrical. The intensity of his personality, however, carries his melodies far beyond the range of conventional French charm. The suave curves grow ample, the resonant spacing of the piano's Wagnerian dissonance gives to the themes a noble passion.

Formally, Duparc has a more direct relation to classical tradition than Wolf. Compare, for instance, Wolf's Calvary song, *Herr, was trägt der Boden hier* with Duparc's setting of a prose translation of Tom Moore's *Elégie* on Emmett. Both have in common a preoccupation with the Wagnerian appoggiatura; but whereas in Wolf the dissonances painfully shatter the line, in Duparc they serve rather to underline the melody's growth (Ex. 34). The 'hidden resolutions', the rising sequences, do not destroy the simple architectural tonality, which moves from tonic minor (with a suggestion of major deriving from the insistence on the dominant seventh of the subdominant) to relative major, and then back to tonic minor (with the major feeling rather more strongly defined). Even in *Phidylé*, where the tonalities range far from the home tonic, the mediant relationships are both broadly and symmetrically

planned. The effect is quite different from that of Wolf's more fevered, tonally ambiguous epigrams.

In some ways the spaciousness of Duparc's periods is—for all his architectural classicism--more Wagnerian than Wolf's intimate precision. The big dramatic songs, such as *Le Manoir de Rosamunde* or *La Vague et la Cloche*, have a compulsive sweep like that of Wagnerian opera: consider the transition, in the latter song, from the clanging bare fifths to the pulsing chromatic accompaniment to the voice's soaring phrase at the words "Pourquoi n'as-tu pas dit, O rêve". Even a song such as *Au pays où se fait la Guerre*, in which the texture is less obviously Wagnerian, depends for its effect on the fact that the beautiful modal melody develops under the stress of a dramatic situation; it gains intensity from the increasingly chromatic part-writing of the piano, until the grandly 'operatic' peroration in the final strophe. Such music seems to call for theatrical presentation as Wolf's music—even in his opera—does not. The purely lyrical songs, like the wonderful *Invitation au Voyage*, also have this Wagnerian amplitude; for although incidental chromatic and enharmonic subtleties abound, the basic progression of the harmony is extremely slow, moving over and around sustained pedal points. The piano parts are beautifully written and a delight to play; but they are all orchestral in the sense that they suggest the 'pianistic' orchestration of the nineteenth century. Floating arpeggios approximate to a haze of strings, pedal notes to sustained horns.

From the depths of his introspection, Wolf had found, through the Mediterranean lucidity of his art, a vision of the bliss of love. Similarly, the quintessence of Duparc's passion leads to his invocation to the "ordre et beauté" of art, the "luxe, calme et volupté", which is Baudelaire's heaven. And the discovery killed his mind and spirit, as it killed Wolf's. Having created thirteen compositions which are the greatest achievement of French song after Berlioz, Duparc lived on for nearly fifty years, creatively mute, imaginatively dead. The paralysis that afflicted him was perhaps more dreadful than the delirium of Wolf's last years, both because it was so prolonged and because the creative flame had produced, from him, so little. He was not mad; his spirit simply withered into inanition. His life and death are, even more than Wolf's, a parable of the terrors of moral isolation.

2

FRANCK AND HIS DISCIPLES: WITH A NOTE ON SKRYABIN

We have noted that, during the nineteenth century, French culture did not suffer the disintegration that afflicted German culture—possibly because the French had experienced their revolution in fact. Yet the preservation of a façade of orthodoxy could not suppress dissensions within the mind. Composers such as Berlioz, or even Fauré, are not less original for maintaining a classical objectivity. Minor figures such as Gounod and Saint-Saëns can remain creative while being guardians of academic respectability; though they may not be great composers, they are musical personalities, in a way that the 'academic' composers of Germany or of this country were no longer.

While French composers of the generation following Berlioz were conservative in a very different sense from that revolutionary autocrat, the French none the less had their minor masters of romantic isolation. Duparc was such a composer, in whom Wagnerian passion was controlled by classical lyricism. Only in one composer, perhaps, does this discipline break down; and it is no accident that at the end of the nineteenth century César Franck [1822–1890] became a Myth which modestly parallels the Wagnerian legend. Franck's music, according to Vincent d'Indy, was the natural successor to Beethoven's *Missa Solemnis*, which had been written in 1822, the year when Franck was born! Nowadays, we are suspicious of the halo of stained glass with which the disciples adorned Franck. We cannot see much connexion between his music and the *Missa Solemnis*; and if we can see that there is a relationship between Franck's music and *Parsifal*, we doubt whether that makes him a saint and a mystic. *Parsifal* is the inverse of *Tristan*; renunciation and eroticism are inextricable: and in Franck's chromaticism and enharmony there may be a similar equivocation. A passionate and simple nature struggles against circumstances—the oppressive influence of his father, the subtler domination of his no less monstrous wife, the bad taste of his time, the adulation of his disciples, and possibly a certain innate lack of intelligence.

Though these would seem to be formidable obstacles, we cannot merely regret them, for they called forth Franck's latent genius. The music of what d'Indy dignified as Franck's First Period was written between 1841 and 1858, while his father was trying to launch him as a piano virtuoso. It is salon music almost entirely destitute of personality. When in 1858 he was appointed organist of St. Clotilde's, he deserted the salon for the church; but his music did not radically alter. This was a bad period for French church music, for, in a materialistic world, the average liturgical work could not be spiritually committed. The music's chromaticism was in itself neither good nor bad. An eighteenth-century composer such as Couperin could write—in the Elevation settings from his organ masses—music as chromatic as anything in Gounod, or—in the "Recordata est" from the *Seconde Leçon des Ténèbres*—could compose an aria operatically ripe in its lyricism, voluptuous in its dissonant suspensions. Yet the music remains pure, strong, spiritually valid: perhaps because the seductions of harmony reinforce a nobly sustained line. Gounod's pretty pieties and sanctimonious eroticisms fall into tepidly disintegrative two-bar periods. Franck's oratorios live on a higher plane of creativity; yet the passages in which his harmonic imagination catches fire are hardly frequent enough to discount the conventionalities. Significantly, when Franck tries to portray Satan he relapses into musical comedy.

Mme Franck would have liked her husband to compose hymn-book insipidities all his life; it was not the flights of harmonic genius which she admired in *Les Béatitudes*, but the tracts in which the salon composer donned a surplice. When, in his middle fifties, Franck finally discovered the springs of his creative energy, it was not through the agency of the Church, nor from the example of his revered master. Even in the later oratorios, in which Gounod was his ostensible model, the deepest formative influence was Liszt—and indirectly through him Schumann, Beethoven, Wagner, and the German tradition. The dominance of an alien culture led to his becoming one of the Originals of the nineteenth century. Like Wagner himself, he took a long time to discover what he wanted to say; if he took even longer than other hyper-individualist composers, such as Moussorgsky and Delius, this may have been because he could not start *ab ovo*, but had first to live down a tradition that was, for him, moribund.

However this may be, the real Franck emerges when he abandons the search for the sublime and allows his sensuous imagination free play. The symphonic poem, *Les Eolides*, strives after no religious ideal and emulates no academic model. It is deliberately episodic; chromaticism breaks up the lines into fragmentary phrases which create a shimmering texture, scored for divided strings and cooing woodwinds, in a manner that already suggests Debussy's impressionism. Yet although *Les Eolides* intimates a new technique it is not in itself a decisive turning-point. This comes in the Piano Quintet of 1879, in which for the first time we have the direct expression of the Franckian ego. We are not surprised that Mme Franck loathed it ("César, I do not approve of that music you are playing"); that the respectable Saint-Saëns refused to play it in public; nor even that it brought a blush to the cheek of so experienced a sensualist as Franz Liszt. Whether or no it was composed in the heat of a (suppressed?) passion for Franck's pupil, Augusta Holmes, it sums up the essential Franckian theme: eroticism curbed, or rebellious passion that struggles to break free. Franck's most typical melody—oscillating chromatically around a single note, or see-sawing between the tonic and the mediant—embodies precisely this desire to escape from fixation: as does the extreme chromaticism of the harmony, as contrasted with the metrical rigidity of the four-bar periods (Ex. 35):

Ex. 35. Franck: Piano Quintet (first movement)

The more remote and enharmonic the modulations, the more metrically strict the prison of the sequential periods becomes; or, alternatively, the more rigid is the periodicity, the more abstruse become the tonal relationships, as compensation.

In this particular, Franck offers a more extravagant version of a technique which we saw to be characteristic of Schumann. Enharmony—the static point that changes its meaning, striving to become something else—has as crucial a significance in Franck's psychology as it has in Schumann's; and Franck's cyclic form, even more than Schumann's thematic recurrences, becomes a prison for the waywardness of harmony and melody. Beethoven transforms his themes in the course of the creative life of his compositions; Franck brings his themes 'back' as a protest against his instinctive harmonic and modulatory licence. Both Franck's and Schumann's cyclical processes are an *idée fixe* in a sense more frightening than their overt intentions. Indeed, all Franck's 'weaknesses'—his repetitive clauses, his artificial transitions, his chromatic sequences, his cluttered texture—are part of his essential experience. Beethoven was the rebel who strove to create a new world. Franck was the unwilling rebel whose only desire was to be able to accept.

This quintet—a work of genius, of however hectic a character—let loose the creative flood. For the remaining years of his life Franck poured out a series of works which seemed to his disciples *sui generis*, and a spiritual illumination. At this date, looking at his large-scale piano works, we can see that Franck derived his 'motivic' conception and his piano technique from Liszt: his harmonic polyphony from Wagner: his philosophical solemnity from Beethoven: his interest in counterpoint and to some extent his chromaticism from Bach—or at least from Liszt's mutation of Bach's chromaticism in his *Weinen Klagen* Variations. Yet Franck's contemporaries were justified in thinking him a profoundly original force. For what he learned from Liszt concerned only the superficies of his art; what he has in common with Wagner is more an innate affinity than an influence; and his relationship to Bach and Beethoven is a creative misunderstanding. Bach's counterpoint depends on tension between linear independence and the dramatic logic of harmony; Franck's counterpoint is always dominated by harmony. The fugue subject of the *Prelude, Chorale, and Fugue* has a generic resemblance to the subject of the B minor Fugue from Book I of Bach's *Forty-eight*. But whereas Bach's theme—chromatic though it is—creates a continuous line through all the vagaries of tonality, Franck's soon becomes an excuse for harmonic passage-work (Ex. 36):

Franck's method is not 'wrong'; it merely suggests that, whereas in Bach personal feeling is absorbed into a creative act, in Franck the quasi-mystical sublimity of the contrapuntal opening is absorbed into subjective passion. Franck's technique is here, as elsewhere, not so much Bachian as Wagnerian, without Wagner's heroic stature.

In his Symphony Franck thought he was emulating the evolutionary form of Beethoven's last years. Yet the Symphony's most impressive moments are purely sensuous, as in the haunting allegretto. Cyclical form is here not so much growth as imprisonment, as it had been in the first of Franck's truly representative works, the Quintet. Once more the main theme is tied to a naggingly reiterated mediant; and its Lisztian apotheosis in the last movement sounds more like neurotic obsession than a hard-won victory over the self. The only work of Franck which has any real resemblance to late Beethoven is his String Quartet, in which his melodic sense is freer and more expansive, less anchored to obsession. The harmony, being conceived in terms of four equal-voiced melodic instruments, achieves orchestral luxuriance without being crabbed or cluttered. The thematic transformations may be quite unlike Beethoven's; but here, perhaps for the first time, the senses sing and flow, so that the music's evolution becomes creative fulfilment. Much the same is true of *Psyché*, his last orchestral work, which stands as a companion piece to *Les Eolides*, the first creation of his maturity. The earlier work had been momentary impressionism; the last work is more linear, more transparently scored, more continuously generative. Inhibitions of more than usual severity had first pricked Franck's muse into activity. He triumphs over them in the opulence of his Quartet and of this symphonic poem—to which Mme Franck refused to listen.

In his very last works, the Organ Chorales, Franck tries to

epitomize his new sense of power by creating works in which the form *is* the generation of the theme—as it is in the first movement of Borodin's E flat Symphony and in some movements of Sibelius. D'Indy thought that these pieces contained the best of Bach, Beethoven, and Wagner in one! It would be more appropriate to say that they combine the improvisatory virtuosity of Franck's youth with the eroticism of his old age; but that they suffer, in comparison with the Quartet or *Psyché*, from a suggestion of keyboard rhapsody. They are freer, formally and texturally, than the Quintet, which ten years earlier had provoked the swelling tide of Franck's passion. But though the emotion screams less stridently against the barriers of inhibition, it is perhaps more febrile. When Franck no longer feels repulsion at his own desires, we find ourselves feeling it for him.

Once more we react against an element of pretence in Franck's sublimity. We can be swept away by his passion, but not by his grandiloquence; and we return with most affection to his most spiritually modest works. In the Symphonic Variations for piano and orchestra, for instance, he took as his model Schumann, a composer whom we have seen to have an even more intimate relation to Franck than has Wagner; and he found in the variation style of Schumann's *Etudes Symphoniques* an idiom that suited him to perfection, for it offered free fantasy without an oppressively dramatic purpose. He further showed intuitive insight in devising a double subject, each part of which approximated to one of the contradictory aspects of his nature—submission and rebellion. Franck could not be content that the loveliest, most sweetly sensuous music he ever wrote should be the first appearance of the Acceptance theme. Each part of the subject must have its own development, and the two must coalesce in the spiritual radiance of an apotheosis Finale. Yet perhaps the most revealing feature of Franck's art is that this does not, in fact, happen. Instead, the Finale returns to the climate of Franck's youth, being delightful salon music, better than Saint-Saëns, utterly remote from Bach, Beethoven, or for that matter Wagner. The Variations are not so consistently fine a work as the Quartet. But their deficiencies, as much as their virtues, make them perhaps Franck's most representative, and most moving, work.

For a composer's power over his auditors depends on the

authenticity of his experience, even when authenticity involves damaging limitations. This is obvious enough if we compare Franck with two of his younger contemporaries, Chausson [1855–1899] and d'Indy [1851–1931]. In ultimate achievement, Chausson is probably a finer composer than Franck. Though he learned much from both Franck and Wagner, his elegiac nobility is without Franck's hysteria, largely because his lyrical line has an almost Berliozian power and span. One can see this in a fervently nostalgic song like *Le Temps des Lilas*, in the cantabile violin writing of *Poème*, or in the broad opening theme of the symphony (Ex. 37):

and one has only to compare his Symphony with Franck's to appreciate the difference between true nobility and the grandiose intention. Chausson's Symphony, like Franck's, is cyclical: yet is at the same time genuinely Beethovenian in its thematic evolution. Even d'Indy, though melodically less distinguished than Chausson, shares with him a nobility of conception derived both from Beethoven and from the French classical tradition. The massive drama of his Symphony or Piano Sonata, the *Parsifal*-like harmonies of his operas, acquire the dignity of an inherited ideal of civilization. This is perhaps still more strikingly evident in the work of two of Franck's younger disciples, Albéric Magnard [1865–1914] and Paul Dukas [1865–1935]. Both were highly personal composers whose dramatic potency had more real affinity with Beethoven than with Franck; and both had an instinctive feeling for the serene grandeur of Rameau and the French classical age. Yet Franck's neurotic music has had a greater influence on European history than the civilized, imaginatively felt art of Chausson, d'Indy, Magnard, or Dukas. Its lure is insidious; and this may be because, in his divided sensibility, he is not only less French than his younger compatriots, but also more deeply representative of something that happened, during the nineteenth century, to 'the mind of Europe'.

From this point of view, there is an odd appendix to Franck's career in that of Skryabin [1872–1915]—a cosmopolitan Russian who settled in Paris. Skryabin's early music shows an affinity with Tchaikowsky in the drooping pathos of its lyricism: with Chopin in its fondness for enharmonic progressions and for a languishing decorative elegance: and with Liszt in its exploitation of the bravura possibilities of the piano. In the larger works, such as the early piano sonatas, the strenuous quality of the quick movements and the conception of sonata as a dramatic conflict suggest continuity with the methods of Beethoven and Brahms. By 1903, however, the date of the Fourth Sonata, the wealth of higher chromatic discords in Skryabin's music has made sonata form anachronistic. A conflict of keys is impossible unless tonality is at first clearly defined; in this music the prevalence of *Parsifal*-like augumented chords—along with the complexity of the counter-rhythms—gives the music a flushed and fevered atmosphere that leads on to the first of Skryabin's explicitly revolutionary works, the Sixth Sonata (1911).

Key signatures are here abandoned; and instead of the organizing force of tonality, Skryabin seeks to derive all his material from a basic chord formation. He is thus doing deliberately what Wagner in *Parsifal* was beginning to do without conscious awareness. Skryabin usually derives his 'mystic' chords from the harmonic series, treating sevenths, ninths, and thirteenths as concords, splitting them up to obtain linear motives that can be imbued, in his mind at least, with transcendental significance. The chord structures he chooses tend to be built on fourths rather than on thirds—the ground chord in the Sixth Sonata is G, C sharp, F, B, E, A flat, and D; and the function of the chord is in some ways comparable with that of the twelve-note row,* in that it is supposed to give coherence to every aspect of the composition. But whereas the row is an entirely linear means of organizing a composition, one could not hope to find a more complete example of the subservience of line to harmony than is represented by Skryabin's late works.

It is obvious that such a conception of harmony is essentially static, and therefore more suitable to short than to long compositions. We shall see later that Skryabin's music has much in common with the music of Debussy's middle years; both use the higher chromatic discords and the piano's overtones in a way

* See pp. 990, et seq.

that is nervous rather than structural. But Debussy's artistic maturity enabled him to know what he was about: to perceive that his 'moments of reality' implied a new—and in some ways very old—criterion of form remote from the harmonic processes of the nineteenth century. Skryabin had no such self-knowledge. He even tried to write big 'sonata' movements by basing the music on two chord formations rather than on one. The two chord formations cannot possibly have the effect of the traditional tonic-dominant opposition, for they are both so complex that the harmonically derived themes cannot be recognized as such. All the chords are so neutral in their complexity, all the lines so flaccid in their rhythmic elaboration, that the music could hardly be more remote from the dynamism of the sonata principle; it is pertinent to note how frequently Skryabin's basses alternate between the two notes of the harmonically neutral tritone. The music becomes a titillation of the aural palate. It depends on the pedal effects of the modern grand piano, which dominates all Skryabin's musical thought, even that for the orchestra.

As musical sensation, these titillations are often very beautiful. The fluttering overtones of his *céleste volupté*, the tolling bells of his *appels mystérieux*, the ecstatic shimmer of sound in the *douce ivresse* of his prestissimo dance movements—these represent a genuine minor contribution to European music, in that there is nothing quite like them, for all their affinities with Wagner, Franck, and Debussy. The danger inherent in this rhapsodic utterance—in anything other than very tiny pieces—is monotony of mood; and while to Skryabin's early disciples the Ninth Sonata (the 'Black Mass') was a hellishly gloomy piece and the Tenth Sonata (the 'White Mass') a seraphically happy, to us at this date they sound much alike. Skryabin whipping himself into ecstasy is not so different from that other cosmopolitan Russian, Tchaikowsky, whipping himself into fury or despair: except that Skryabin's melodic vitality is so much lower.

Franck fascinates us as long as he is preoccupied with a fight between his eroticism and his inhibitions: or when, as in the Quartet, his eroticism develops into something not less passionate, but less subjective. He begins to bore us when, as in the Organ Chorales, he has nothing to offer us *except* his masochism and auto-eroticism; for the fact that these experiences are genuine and common does not make them less tedious for other people.

In reducing every element of music to the momentary harmonic thrill, Skryabin in his later work has gone much further than Franck to create a music which is simply (if not purely) masochism and auto-eroticism. We can respond to Franck's turmoils because we have probably experienced something similar ourselves: whereas the heat of Skryabin's narcissism now leaves us cold. We are suspicious of a composer who *tells* us he is celestially voluptuous. He knows when he is voluptuous, no doubt; but what about the other part? We have more respect for Debussy, who wrote celestially voluptuous music if ever any man did: "Vous avez été au ciel, M. Debussy?" "Oui, mais, j'en cause jamais avec les étrangers."*

Wagner heroically made a new religion out of his senses; Franck's disciples, in a smaller way, tried to do as much for him. Skryabin, in later years, would have regenerated the world with a cosmic theosophy derived from the oscillations of his nerves. The gigantic symphony of sounds, smells, and colours which he was planning when he died was to be a rite and a sacrifice, its creator the new Messiah. The Mystery was to be performed in a hemispherical temple in India, mirrored in a lake so as to create a circle, the perfect form; and the performance would produce in the participants a "supreme final ecstasy", wherein the physical plane of consciousness would dissolve away, and "a world cataclysm" begin. The only objection was that, even in his lifetime, the Messiah was lunatic. Wagner's egomania was 'abnormal'; but he was great enough to persuade his contemporaries to believe in it, and still more to convince us, a hundred years later, that his madness was, while it lasted, truth. Skryabin, on the other hand, seems to us a man of exquisite sensibility who went crazy: by turns silly, pathetic, horrifying, a portent of Europe's sickness. In Skyrabin's music the bubble of the inflated ego bursts; and the metaphor, though grotesque, is apt if we think of the limp flaccidity of his technique. Perhaps it is not fortuitous that the only later composer who, starting from an unambiguously Wagnerian aesthetic, can still move us deeply, came to learn a new humility. Delius's humility has nothing to do with Franck's religious conscience; in the long run, however, it is difficult to know what to call it, unless it be a pagan, pre-Christian religious awareness.

* "You have been to Heaven, M. Debussy?" "Yes: but I never chatter about it to strangers."

3

DELIUS, SIBELIUS, AND NATURE

DELIUS's hyper-romanticism is in part associated with the fact that he was born, in the nineteenth century [1862–1934], in Britain—not, moreover, in the pastoral gentleness of the English countryside, but in industrial Bradford. His childhood passions were for the music of Chopin and for Byron's *Childe Harold*; and the sensitive soul and solitary pilgrim could hardly have been more completely a misfit in a materialistic world. In adolescence he was put into the family business. Mercantile visits to Norway produced few contracts for Bradford wool, much admiration of Norwegian scenery and of the non-industrial melancholy of Norwegian folk-song. Business trips to Paris were hardly more productive. Here the young Delius, romantic, athletic, handsome, affluent, became the associate of artists, poets, and (to a lesser extent) musicians in the bohemian coteries of Montmartre.

Delius's father not unnaturally regarded his son as a liability rather than an asset to the business. An opportunity occurred to acquire for Frederick a grapefruit farm in Florida; Delius accepted such a career, largely because Florida was exotic, remote from Bradford. The grapefruit did not prosper. On the other hand, Frederick's artistic proclivities developed so vigorously that they finally overcame the business-man's distrust of art. His father agreed that he should study music; so he went, of course, to Germany, for there was in Britain no indigenous school of composition. Here he developed a wild enthusiasm for Wagner and a lesser fervour for Strauss; and composed quantities of music, all undistinctive in style, passively Teutonic with a mild infusion of the chromatic nostalgia of Grieg.

Then in 1899 he produced a mammoth symphonic poem, *Paris*, a Nocturne, the Song of a Great City. The orchestral texture and to some extent the structure are modelled on Strauss; yet *Paris* is a work of unmistakably original genius. "It came to me very slowly what I wanted to do", said Delius; "and when it came, it came all at once." In *Paris*, Straussian opulence and vitality have already become retrospective. The music has the brilliance and energy of Delius's youth; yet the piercing chromatic intensity of the slow section—the first quintessential Delian moment—tells us that he is already cut off from the gay abandon of his Parisian days. 'Paris in spring' has become a cinematic cliché. Yet it can stand as a symbol of the hopeful joys of our youth. Delius's *Paris* recreates the impetuous joy, while transmuting the hope to regret.

Despite its superficial resemblance to Strauss, *Paris* is much further from the classical tradition than are Strauss's symphonic poems. The continuity of flow which Delius achieves between the sections has more affinity with Wagner; and his relationship to Wagner's last works is, like that of Franck, not so much conscious imitation as an intuitive discipleship. Like Wagner, Delius believed that the only reality is one's own passions. "The chief thing is to develop your own personality to the uttermost." Never mind if you make mistakes, nor even if you hurt other people, so long as you keep your soul intact. Like Nietzsche, he was a Dionysiac genius who held that the decline of the Greeks came with the growth of intellect; who held that all ethical judgement (and hence Christianity) was bad because it inhibited spontaneity.* The human creature's one essential duty was to have "high courage and self-reliance": which necessarily involved contempt for God and Society. "Humanity is incredible; it will believe anything to escape reality"—to avoid relying on its own resources. Yet Delius did not see that his attitude was itself an unrealistic extension of the Wagnerian Dream: for it is literally impossible to be entirely self-sufficient, and difficult to ignore the world unless, like Delius, you are economically independent of it.

This Dionysiac rejection of thought—this belief in personal feeling as the only absolute—is reflected in Delius's approach to composition. "I don't believe in learning harmony and counterpoint. Learning kills instinct. Never believe the saying that one must hear music many times in order to understand it. It is utter nonsense, the last refuge of the incompetent. . . . For me music is very simple. It is the expression of a poetical and

* Delius's biggest work—though not his best—is a setting of Nietzsche. The title of *A Mass of Life* is itself anti-Christian.

emotional nature." Just as Delius could afford to talk so grandly of courage and self-reliance because he had no material problems, so he could afford to ignore technique only because he came at the end of a great creative period whose conventions he accepted ready-made. He could compose empirically because he did not have to think about first principles.

Within his Teutonic inheritance, his extravagantly personal mannerisms grew alongside an increasing hatred of other people's music. He preserved a lifelong admiration for Wagner and a minor enthusiasm for Chopin and Grieg. He dismissed Beethoven's opus 110 Sonata as rhetorical passage-work, could see nothing in Palestrina but mathematics, and tolerated little twentieth-century music except that which was dedicated to him. In his pathetic old age he spent hours listening to recordings of his own music, which alone seemed to measure up to his ideal of Fine Feeling. And for him Fine Feeling meant the flux of sensation through the creator: the apotheosis of the personal life in chromatic harmony. Other composers have written music which is momentarily as chromatic as Delius's. But in Weelkes, Bach, or Mozart the chromatic intensification or disintegration is conceived in relation to an accepted norm of tonality. In such a passage from Delius as the wonderful entry of the wordless chorus in *A Song of the High Hills* this norm is ceasing to exist; the graded tensions and relaxations of the chords are themselves becoming the form (Ex. 38):

Now and again Delius's music hints at a classical procedure —a hypothetical recapitulation, or a section built on a dominant-tonic relationship. More normally, his criterion of consonance and dissonance has become personal and empirical, rather than the property of a tradition. Like Wagner, he feels (rather than thinks) improvisatorily at the keyboard; and this is a dangerous method of creation because the composer has to be 'inspired' to carry it off. A failure of inspiration is less obvious in a composer who can fall back on a traditional mould. Delius can rely on nothing external to himself; 'inspiration' has to create the form appropriate to each composition. We can see why the one positive comment he ever made about musical technique was that "a sense of flow" was the only thing that mattered. His strength lies in the fact that, like Wagner, he so frequently attains this flow: that whereas Skryabin's obsession with the harmonic moment disintegrates line and structure, Delius creates in very long harmonic and melodic periods. His norm of progression may be personal rather than traditional; but his music, no less than Wagner's, does imply growth and cumulation.*

In one particular, however, Delius goes beyond Wagner. In *Tristan*, Wagner reduces God and Civilization to projections of his own ego. Other people exist only as the objects of his love and hate. But this at least implies the existence of people to be loved and hated: whereas in Delius's most typical music there is no human population at all—only himself and solitude. *Paris*, the earliest of his mature works, is the only one that is about people living and loving, together; and even then the passion is partly retrospective. It is significant that Delius's early operas, which deal with real people in a more or less realistic setting, are failures dramatically and, as music, not even typical Delius. The finest of his smaller works, *In a Summer Garden*, conveys the passive reactions of his senses to the sounds, sights, and smells of a summer in which he is alone. Among his larger works, *A Song of the High Hills* embodies his own yearning in communion

* In this context we may refer to the music of another composer of romantic nostalgia, Arnold Bax [1883–1953]. His most successful works are those in which his lyricism is most ecstatic. In the wonderful *Ora Mater Filium* the sensuous choral sonorities are given vitality by the compulsive flow of the vocal lines: and to a lesser degree this is the case with the instrumental writing of the finer (more rhapsodic) symphonic poems, such as *The Garden of Fand.* The big three-movement symphonies, on the other hand, tend to be convincing only when they are rhapsodic and non-symphonic in style. Though constructed with great care, they are apt to sound illogically episodic, because the elaborately engineered correspondences and thematic transformations do not 'work'. Wagner was right to insist on "the art of transition"—which was also what Delius meant by "a sense of flow". For the relationships between the elements of a composition cannot in themselves create order; what matters is how one gets from one 'correspondence' to the next.

with the solitudes of Nature; and the human voices of the chorus are impersonally wordless.

From this there is a significant technical development. The essence of the music may be the flux of sensation—the sighing of the Wagnerian appoggiaturas with which the work opens, the fluctuating chromatic woof of the choral texture. None the less, all the component lines which make up the harmony *sing* and are, individually considered, vocal, often modal, in contour. Still more in the works involving a solo voice or instrument along with orchestra and chorus, the rhapsodic solo melody tends to be pentatonic, like folk-song or medieval monody, as though it were seeking a oneness beyond the sensory flux (Ex. 39):

Again, the celebration of life in and for itself leads to the desire to lose the self in the contemplation of Nature or in the supposedly simpler satisfactions of a lost youth; for the passion is too strong to be borne. Hatred of orthodox religiosity leads to a pantheistic view of human experience. The theme of Delius's first mature and representative opera is that, while passion is the only reality, the sham that passes for reality renders passion untenable. The ideal love of the Village Romeo and Juliet, like that of Tristan and Parsifal, can find consummation only in oblivion.

The desire for Nirvana as the only resolution of passion is common to Wagner and Delius; the pantheistic ecstasy is peculiar to Delius. Wagner never lost his belief in himself, even when he found that his passions were synonymous with death. Delius's hatred of God and Man was more radical, yet he found something positive in his very isolation. His nature-mysticism parallels that of Whitman and of Richard Jefferies. His music is a Song of Myself and the Story of My Heart; and there are obvious parallels between his empirical harmonic flow and the free verse rhythm of Whitman, the surging prose of Jefferies. His most perfect work—*Sea Drift*—is a setting of Whitman; and it is music pervaded by regret for life once vivid and vital, from which one is now separated. The technique whereby the solo baritone line is woven within the orchestral and choral texture contrasts strikingly with the technique of Debussy's *La Mer*. Debussy's piece is a seascape which is also an epic of the strife of human existence. In Delius's work the all-encompassing sea is the eternal mystery from which emerges and into which dissolves the self—symbolized in the frail, lonely bird who sings of his separation from the beloved. Both Delius, who hated the crowd, and Whitman, who loudly proclaimed his identity with it, came to see—as had Wagner—that the relationship of lover and beloved is inevitably transient. The inescapable loss of innocence entails too the loss of love; it is significant that Delius's final evocation of past happiness (in E *major*) is even more heartbreaking than the immediate recognition of death.

Most people, when they think of Delius, remember not the magnetic, Byronic figure of his youth, but the blind, paralysed old man in his garden at Grez. This is not merely a popular misunderstanding; for there is a profound allegorical significance in the fact that Delius was crippled, that he became a spectator of his own imaginative life. His nostalgia—and his compensatory Nature-mysticism—is obviously 'limited'. It is also a perennial and universal human experience, in a way that Skryabin's auto-eroticism is not. This is why, though his weaker works sound faded, those works in which his inspiration flowered should remain impervious to changing fashion. He is not a fashionable composer at present; and the peculiar experience with which he was concerned may never again seem as important as it did when he was creating. On the other hand, it is unlikely, in any foreseeable future, to lose all meaning. Not even a Welfare State—nor anything short of the Kingdom of Heaven—will appease the ambiguous cravings of man, who will remain, as Delius came to see, at once "a proud, and yet a wretched thing".

Sibelius was born in 1865, three years later than Delius and, like him, in a country without a musical tradition. He too was in youth a fascinating personality who disliked big cities and loved solitude. But whereas Delius was driven by hatred for the world in which he was born, Sibelius was brought up, not in a vast mechanized society, but against the background of Nature—more or less the same lonely landscape that had so impressed the adolescent Delius.

Since Finland had never had a musical tradition, and England had forgotten hers, both Sibelius and Delius started to compose in what was then the accepted European idiom. The first works of both composers are Teutonic in style, and devoid of personality; both were well over thirty before they produced any music we could recognize as theirs. There is, however, a fundamental difference between them, associated with Delius's desire to escape from, and Sibelius's acceptance of, his environment. Delius was anti-traditional and anti-intellectual, and his musical god was Wagner. Sibelius was also an individualist, but one who still believed in civilization; his musical god was Beethoven, whom he admired as much for his character as for his musicianship. As an artist, Sibelius at least intended to be a reintegrative force.

From this point of view we may contrast Sibelius with his Danish contemporary Carl Nielsen [1865–1931], who is perhaps the only later symphonist to have worked consistently within the Beethovenian tradition. His First Symphony is obviously Brahmsian in temper; and while his later symphonies have grown increasingly personal in manner and thematically more distinguished, they remain 'conflict' symphonies based on the interplay of themes and rhythmic motives, and on a clash—and ultimate resolution—of tonalities. The range of key relationship is wider and more complex than Beethoven's, but the similarity of approach is unmistakable. Both Beethoven and Nielsen are preoccupied with the experience of 'Becoming'; Nielsen's themes change their identity through conflict just as Beethoven's do, and the victory his symphonies achieve is a triumph of humanism won, not in the interests of the self, but of civilization.

Perhaps Nielsen was able to attain this equilibrium between the ego and society because he lived in a highly developed civilization which was basically stable while being in touch with the violent upheavals Europe experienced during the early twentieth century. Both Tradition and Revolution had meaning for him, as for Beethoven. Yet his society did not, like Beethoven's, carry with it a rich musical tradition; and it is difficult to resist a suspicion that the revolutionary drama in his later work is sometimes too independent of the music. The Second and Third Symphonies are consistent and cogent musical arguments of a type related to Beethoven's symphonic principle.

The Fourth and Fifth Symphonies are certainly more interesting, more personal in their melodic invention; yet this invention seems less purposeful in its musical growth. The famous percussion improvisation in the Fifth Symphony—wherein the side-drum player attempts to destroy the music's evolution—is an externalized presentation of conflict which is exciting once or twice, but less exciting with repeated hearings. For Beethoven, Fate was not an external force which could be thus segregated from the battle of his inner life, which was his music.

It may be that it is no longer possible for a composer to maintain a Beethovenian view of the symphony. If we think that Sibelius's symphonies are in the long run more rewarding than Nielsen's, this may well be related to the fact that Sibelius's affinity with Beethoven is not what it seems, nor even what he thought it was. True, his First Symphony (and most of the Second) is broad, heroic music in the tradition of the nineteenth-century 'conflict' symphony. But in the first movement of the Second Symphony he explores a technique which was to have increasing importance in his later work. Whether or no the technique was suggested to him by the first movement of Borodin's E flat Symphony, he too starts with fragments of line, rhythmic motives, even the tone-colour of an instrument, which slowly interact and evolve until they coalesce in the main themes of the movement at what would normally be the recapitulation. The process is similar to that exemplified in Beethoven's sketchbooks: only whereas in Beethoven's case the creation of the themes marks the beginning of the treatment of them—that is, of the composition—in Sibelius's case, as in Borodin's, the growth of the theme is the structure of the movement.

A similar technique is used, with more epigrammatic concision, in the last movement of the Third Symphony and the first movement of the Fifth. But if on the one hand Sibelius investigates the creation of themes from their constituents, on the other hand he winnows down the conventional symphonic structure to its bare bones. Both procedures are often used simultaneously: for instance, the first movement of No. 5 or the last movement of No. 3 may be regarded either as self-generative movements engaged in the creation of themes and of tonal order, or as elliptical telescopings of the customary sonata allegro and scherzo.

The climax of these complementary tendencies towards concentration is reached in the Fourth Symphony of 1911. However Germanic his origins may have been, Sibelius has by this date created an idiom as aggressively personal as that of Delius. The whole of this extraordinary work grows from various ramifications of the tritone—the interval which is most destructive of tonal stability. The first movement generates itself from a brief contorted figure involving a tritone (Ex. 40):

Ex. 40. Sibelius: Symphony No. 4 first movement

rises to a climax by way of a fluttering *moto perpetuo* on the strings; and subsides to its source. The scherzo reverses this process, beginning with a deceptively innocent pastoral theme on the oboe, which is gradually dissected and finally routed by vehement interjections of the tritone. Its stable tonality is also threatened; the tenuous whimper of a fragment of the melody at the end, in a remote key, is disturbingly jerked back to the tonic by the softest, most mysterious notes on the timpani (Ex. 41):

Ex. 41. Sibelius: Symphony No 4 Scherzo

The slow movement is a cross between thematic generation and a skeletonic sonata structure. In the last movement classical rondo style disintegrates into its components. The initial themes are fluid, even gay; but they soon split into their constituent elements of line and rhythm, and the work ends in desolation.

In his First Symphony Sibelius had used the dualistic conventions of the classical symphony in the normal way; in the slow movement of the Second Symphony he had exploited them in an exaggerated form. But it is obvious that his typical method of thematic growth is monistic: and that his winnowing down of the constituents of classical form likewise tends to destroy the dramatic implications of sonata development. So the taut concentration of his symphonies leads him to the one-movement structure of the Seventh, in which all four movements arise out of, and are telescoped into, a single rising diatonic scale and a perfect cadence. Every aspect of the music is a part of the thematic growth; in no music is it less possible to separate orchestration from line, since the tone colour is itself part of the structure—the means of imparting the appropriate stress to each strand.

In later years Sibelius has shown a considerable interest in the music of Palestrina, and it is not fanciful to see Palestrina's influence in the 'pure water' of the Sixth and Seventh Symphonies. Yet despite the hints of modality in the transparent texture of this music, Sibelius is not naturally a polyphonic composer; nor does he seek the late Beethoven's profound fusion of the contradictory principles of sonata and fugue. Indeed, the point at which he arrives in his later work turns out to be closer to Wagner and even to Delius than it is to composers—such as Palestrina and Beethoven—who may seem superficially to resemble him more; and this remains true despite his professed veneration for Beethoven and Palestrina, and his aversion to Wagner. In parts of *Tristan*, Wagner creates a continuous texture which grows from a seminal germ. It is true that the linear motives have less intrinsic importance than they have in Sibelius: that the effect of the music depends more on the flow of the harmonies which the motives generate. None the less, there is a deep affinity between Wagner's sultry and Sibelius's more Nordically austere harmony; and this affinity becomes more strongly marked in Sibelius's later work, especially the Seventh Symphony and *Tapiola*.

Wagner's 'monistic' generation of lines from harmony reduced the universe to his own passions. Sibelius was never thus egocentrically romantic. His preoccupation with formal problems testifies to an awareness of social issues which he inherited from the classical tradition; it was not for nothing that he said he regarded the Mozart allegro as the ideal symphonic movement. But neither is it surprising that Sibelius did not find the preservation of civilization as apparently simple as Mozart found it: that there should be, all through his work, another strain—a tendency towards separateness, a Delian desire to relinquish his personality in nature. Wind, light, space, solitude, all the qualities which he admits to finding in the Finnish landscape, do not concern him because he wishes to create a musical picture postcard (he has never shown the slightest interest in the nationalist approach to folk-music); they fascinate him because they suggest an experience with which, as the years have gone by, he has grown increasingly obsessed.

Delius, in *A Song of the High Hills* or *Sea Drift*, strives to lose the burden of personality in the pentatonicism of his recurrent cadential formulae; but he cannot free himself from the pull and throb of the harmonic tensions. Sibelius, as he communes with Nature, goes further in self-obliteration, perhaps because his respect for civilization implies a measure of detachment. He goes furthest of all in *Tapiola*, his last-completed, large-scale work. This piece is the ultimate consummation of the trend we have observed, growing gradually stronger throughout his music. The search for oneness could hardly be carried further, for here the entire structure is monothematic, proliferating from a single seed. *Tapiola* is the *ne plus ultra* of Sibelian technique; and in it the human personality seems to dissolve away in Nature's infinities of time and space. It is possible to contend that the Fourth and Sixth Symphonies are more central achievements of European civilization. It is impossible to deny *Tapiola's* significance as a document of our time, or at least of our spiritual legacy from the immediate past. It is surely one of the most terrifying pieces of music ever written.

Sibelius once said: "Look at the great nations of Europe and what they have endured. No savage could have stood so much. I do believe in civilization." When we hear the final assertion of the tonic triad at the end of *Tapiola* we realize what moral strength was necessary to make that assertion, at the end of such a work. And when we look back from *Tapiola* we can see that something like this dissolution of the personality is implicit even beneath the civilization of the earlier symphonies. The spine-chilling *moto perpetuo* towards the end of *Tapiola* has its smaller counterpart in the *moto perpetuos* that occur from the Third Symphony onwards. The wild, inhuman howls of the long internal pedal points in *Tapiola* prove to be an extension of one of the most typical features of Sibelius's scoring. And we see that when all four movements of the Fourth Symphony, having grown from their seminal figures, fade away into their origins, their 'humanity' returns to the earth and air: to that which is not human. Perhaps this oneness in Nature is one of the few means whereby an artist may approach religious experience, in a non-religious and materialistic society. But it is not the oneness for which Beethoven fought so strenuously, nor that which Palestrina or the medieval monodist discovered in making a positive affirmation of faith. It is an escape from humanity. In *A Song of the High Hills* ecstatic strength is not joyful, but melancholy; in *Tapiola* ecstasy can hardly be distinguished from a frigid terror.

That Sibelius was aware of this is suggested by a remarkable letter which he wrote in 1911—the year of the Fourth Symphony: "Yesterday I heard Bruckner's B♭ major Symphony, and it moved me to tears. For a long time afterwards I was completely transported. What a strangely profound spirit, formed by a religious sense. And this profound religiousness we have abolished in our country as something no longer in harmony with our time." Sibelius, like Delius, had a religious sensibility without a faith; and it is possible that his music is a dead end, technically as well as spiritually. It is significant that in the thirty years that have elapsed since he wrote *Tapiola* he seems to have created no music of consequence; what, indeed, could come 'after' the hell of *Tapiola*? He has expressed an impasse in Europe's spiritual history and has brought home to us, with terrifying integrity, a predicament both social and philosophical. Perhaps we have to 'go through' *Tapiola* in order to live again.

4

DEBUSSY AND RAVEL

DELIUS is the composer of the twilight of a world; Debussy [1862–1918] is at once an end and a beginning. He carries the isolation of the sensory moment a stage further than Wagner or Delius; yet with him the cult of the ego became also a renewal of civilization. No less than Delius he was non-political, non-philosophical, non-religious, a sensual and instinctive atheist. No less than Wagner—and with more exquisite refinement—he was a hedonist and gourmet of the senses who adored cats, women, and silk. With Delius, he believed that learning kills instinct: that "there is more to be gained by watching the sun rise than by hearing the 'Pastoral' Symphony. To some people rules are of primary importance. But my desire is only to reproduce what I hear. Music was intended to receive the mysterious accord that exists between nature and the imagination."

In response to an outraged professor who asked him, during his student days, what 'rule' he followed, Debussy replied: "Mon plaisir." He accepted only "le règle de l'ouie", for "there are no more schools of music, and the main business of the musician to-day is to avoid any kind of outside influence". Living in the ivory tower of his senses, he always preferred " a subject where action is sacrificed to feeling". His ideal of the instinctive composer was Moussorgsky, whose empirical treatment of chords in some ways anticipated his own. He loathed Tchaikowsky because he attempted to stifle his spontaneity in academic convention. He loved Franck because, even in his weaknesses, he was spiritually innocent. He abominated d'Indy and Saint-Saëns because they were intellectually knowing—and also partially 'Teutonic'. He distrusted Beethoven's moral earnestness and, indeed, everything represented by the sonata principle. In apparent paradox, he loved Bach above all composers, even Moussorgsky; on the significance of this we shall have something to say later.

Again, he resembles Delius in that his early music is insignificant and unrepresentative. Naturally, he followed the French tradition in which he had been brought up, rather than the German; and he emulated not Saint-Saëns and the hated academics, but the unpretentious Massenet, who aimed always to charm the senses. None the less, his musical awakening came from Germany, though not from the symphonic tradition. The early symphonic poems of Strauss impressed him; while in Wagner's *Tristan* and *Parsifal* he saw the mingling of all the arts for which the Symbolists yearned. The relationship to Strauss was not, in the long run, important; his affinity with Wagner's last works was profound. Wagner, however, was heroic, Debussy intimate. Wagner wanted to become God, imposing his will on others. Debussy was content simply to be, to exist in his passive reaction to external stimuli. It is interesting that after the initial impact of Wagner Debussy was influenced, during the formative years 1890–1904, far more by impressionist painting and symbolist poetry, and by Nature herself, than by any aspect of European art-music. The music that did interest him was either exotic or primitive, or both—Spanish and Russian folk-music and, most of all, the Javanese music which he heard at the Paris Exhibition. Like Van Gogh, he saw in exotic art another world, valuable because it was remote. Just as Van Gogh found a new experience in the decorative colour of Oriental painting, so Debussy savoured exotic music—the clanging gongs of the Javanese Gamelang—as a new aural sensation.

This preoccupation with 'sound in itself' takes us to the core of the revolutionary element in Debussy's technique. We saw that although the logic of Delius's harmonic progressions is becoming more a matter of personal feeling than of traditional sanction, the idea of progression is still relevant to his music: from which point of view he is still intelligible in relation to the nineteenth-century tradition. For Debussy, however, a chord became an emotional experience in itself. As Wagner and Delius translated their feelings as directly as possible into the symbols of sound, so Debussy transformed into music the reactions of his nerves to the sounds, smells, and colours of Nature. We observe a paradox similar to that which we commented on in Delius: the absolute reliance on personal sensation leads, not to domination over things, but to subservience to them.

From the beginning there was, within Debussy's egoism, a strange humility.

Debussy's desire passively to exploit the aural effect of the overtone series is itself a kind of subservience to Nature. A chord becomes for him a complex of aural vibrations which are also nervous sensation, ranging from the absolute calm of the unison and octave, and the relative tranquillity of the fourth and fifth, to the higher chromatic relations of the harmonic series. One can say, if one likes, that such a passage as the opening of *La Cathédrale Engloutie* revives the technique of medieval organum* (Ex. 42):

Yet Debussy's attitude to his material is different from that of the medieval composer. "The effect of fifths and fourths", he seems to be saying, "is very calm." The medieval composer also wanted his organum to sound calm, in so far as it was an act of praise, free from personal distress. But he did not think of it in terms of his own nervous system. He used the technique because it was an accepted convention; and it was an accepted convention because it was a natural way to write for voices. In this passage of Debussy's prelude the nerves remain relaxed, whereas they are subtly disturbed in the passages where he employs parallel ninths or elevenths (Ex. 43):

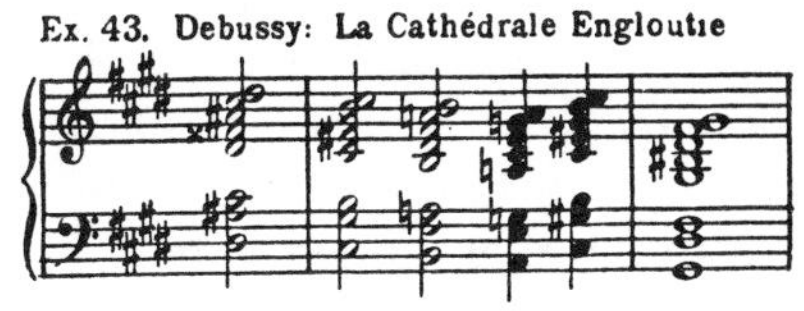

or thickens out passing notes into passing chords, or fills in two

* ORGANUM: see Part I, pp. 41 et seq.

different positions of the same chord with chords of embellishment. But the method is identical in each case: the sense of progression from one point to another is almost entirely lost. Similarly with the many passages that employ added seconds without their resolution. These may sound wistful, nostalgic, and so on *because* they are unresolved; yet to Debussy the concept of resolution is hardly appropriate. These are simply titillations of the aural palate which, in their own right, create an atmosphere of nostalgia.

The most extreme instances of Debussy's tendency to isolate chords from the development of line and structure occur in those pieces which are sometimes described as being in the whole tone scale, though it would be more accurate to refer to them as experiments in the use of augmented fifths suggested by the whole tone scale. No chord is more devoid of tonal implications. *Voiles* presents it in varied 'registrations' and figurations, and the piece depends on the impression made by this single chord on the listener's nerves (Ex. 44):

Ex. 44. Debussy· Voiles

The only passage in which any other aural concept occurs is a brief pentatonic section, in which we have melody as nearly as possible devoid of harmonic implications, to balance the cessation of harmonic movement throughout the piece. The music is thus static, has no growth and, in the conventional sense, no structure. Of such music the term 'impressionist' is almost justified. It approximates as closely as music can to painting, in that it destroys the temporal sense and, against music's nature, exists 'spatially' in the given moment.

The historical significance of this aspect of Debussy's music is immense. Because of, rather than in spite of, his preoccupation with chords in themselves, he deprived music of the sense of harmonic progression, broke down three centuries' dominance of harmonic tonality, and showed how the melodic conceptions of tonality typical of primitive folk-music and of medieval music might be relevant to the twentieth century. In a little piece like *Voiles* the musical significance lies in the delicacy of the melodic tendrils that undulate round one or two unmoving nodal points; in a comparatively large-scale piece like *La Cathédrale Engloutie* the modulations are never parts of a tonal argument, but shifts of perspective created, again, by melodic pattern. Even Debussy's most transitory 'moment of sensation' has thus a criterion of order, though it is not the harmonic criterion current during the eighteenth and nineteenth centuries. He wrote his greatest music when he was able to reconcile this profoundly revolutionary element in his work with an innate respect for classical tradition. Of this respect he was, as a young man, but dimly conscious. As he grew older he came to see that one part of his 'newness' was to experience afresh a comparatively distant past.

It is probably no accident that Debussy's relation to tradition and to the humane values of French civilization was manifest in his songs much earlier than in his piano music. The songs deal with his determination to preserve the purity of his sensuous perceptions, even in "ces lieux d'exil où il semble qu'être quelqu'un ne puisse aller sans cabotinage et où la musique manque d'infini". Only within "la vie intérieure" can the infinite still be found; and even in the Wagnerian eroticism of the Baudelaire songs of 1887 Debussy evokes a world of delicate artifice—the world of Pierrot, of the twilit balcony, of the paradisal park, of the Watteauesque dreamland which is more real than a reality seared by trade. The static, immobile harmony in the songs—even more than in the songs of Duparc, if not as completely as in the piano pieces to which we have referred—suggests precisely this withdrawal into the inner life of the senses. On the other hand, the supple vocal line safeguards the songs' humanity. For one thing, it is close to the inflexions of the speaking voice, so we cannot but be aware of the proximity of a human creature. For another thing, it already implies a relationship to the classical tradition. Lully and Rameau were later numbered among Debussy's enthusiasms. The Watteauesque world became not merely an ivory tower, but a once real world into which genius could breathe new life.

In the more mature songs, especially in the *Proses Lyriques*—settings of impressionist prose-poems by Debussy himself—the vocal line humanizes the harmony, while the harmony divests the line of drama. The songs thus combine intense human feeling with a dream-like detachment; and it was precisely this subtle ambivalence which Debussy brought to fruition in the work that sums up the first phase of his career. The songs led him to opera: to which form his attitude was characteristically equivocal. He approved of opera because it was a mingling of all the arts; he disapproved of it because it trammelled music's freedom—and perhaps because the state of the French theatre in his day was hardly encouraging to a man of delicate perceptions. In any case, his opera, *Pelléas et Mélisande*, is Wagnerian in the fact that most of the emotion is contained in the orchestra, while the characters sing in a recitative no more lyrical than Moussorgsky's; it is anti-Wagnerian in its reticence and objectivity. *Tristan* is the projection of Wagner's own life. The passions in *Pelléas* are mundane and ferocious, and are certainly emotions which Debussy, as an experienced amorist, had felt deeply; yet he stands at a distance from them. The medieval dream-setting suggests a plainsong-like declamation; plainsong suggests a link with Renaissance monodists like Claude le Jeune; and they link up with Lully, Rameau, and the classical tragedy and opera. So, however instinctive Debussy's art may have been, however intimate his early affiliation with Wagner, he is on the way towards the classical objectivity of his last years. Though his conception of tonality still has more in common with the melodic 'node' of plainsong than with Bach's compromise between counterpoint and harmonic order, his reverence for Bach already seems less odd than we might have thought.

The relationship between *Tristan* and *Pelléas* is closely paralleled by that between Delius's *Song of the High Hills* and Debussy's *Nuages* from the orchestral *Nocturnes*, begun in 1893. Delius is interested mainly in himself in relation to solitude—hence the Tristanesque fervour of his appoggiatura-laden harmony, which 'points' the melodic phrases. Debussy shows a characteristic humility before appearances. Instead of Delius's emotionally-charged aspiration, the harmony of Debussy's clouds is organum-like, without tension or sense of progression, and such melodic contours as develop towards the end are pentatonic. The human element is symbolized by a desolate, fragmentary phrase, usually on the cor anglais, which wanders in and out of the clouds' organum. There is no interaction between the man (who is not specifically Debussy) and the clouds: none of Delius's yearning to resolve his harmonic passion in an endless, floating pentatonicism. The man is man, the clouds are clouds; each is irremediably distinct from the other. Delius's scoring is lustrously Wagnerian, to reinforce the passion of his harmonies and soaring lines. Debussy's orchestration, though sensuous, is transparent; the music disintegrates, at the end, into particles of light and air—into patches of 'sound-colour' which parallel his moments of harmonic sensation. In Sibelius's *Tapiola* the impersonal forces of Nature threaten to destroy the human personality. Debussy, in *Nuages*, accepts Nature's *otherness*. This is equally true of the second Nocturne, *Fêtes*, which is supposed to be gay; for the gaiety is someone else's, heard in solitude, from the dark hill. We are alone with Nature; but our exile is accepted, without conscious regret.

Though the lines are brief, the orchestral *Nocturnes* are more linear in conception than Debussy's piano works tend to be, and in this are closely related to his songs. In the orchestral sketches, *La Mer* (1903–5), this melodic strength shows a surprising development. Whereas the themes of the *Nocturnes*, though highly expressive, are incapable of growth, those of *La Mer* are unexpectedly grand in conception, and are treated in a manner not altogether remote from the classical symphonic tradition. Thus the first movement is a symphonic allegro with three clearly defined themes in D flat, B flat, and D flat; the second movement is a scherzo in free rondo form, beginning in C sharp minor and ending in the relative major; while the third movement, though the freest in form, also betrays the most striking capacity to develop the themes from within. The final metamorphosis of the rather Franckian theme on the brass is perhaps one of the most thrilling climaxes in the orchestral repertory. Yet although the traditional notion of progression and even of dramatic argument is again relevant to this music, Debussy preserves his detachment. The symphonic drama is epic rather than personal. The battle of the sea becomes the drama of mankind. The pictorial element is also an incarnation of moral qualities. The play of the waves involves grandeur, vivacity, tenderness, malice.

Even Debussy's *pointilliste* scoring serves, in *La Mer*, a structural purpose. Perhaps one might say that whereas in his earlier works Debussy exploits sonorities in much the same way as a painter like Monet exploits effects of light, in later works Debussy seeks a relationship between sonorities and structure which broadly parallels Cézanne's balance between colour and geometrical form. In *La Mer* Debussy's classical affiliation is with the symphonic tradition. When, in the next few years, he became consciously interested in the re-creation of the past, it was rather to baroque and still more to Renaissance and medieval music that he turned. This was not surprising; for, as we have seen, his technique, concentrating everything on the 'moment of reality' rather than on time-progression or rhetorical argument, had much in common with medieval and with Oriental music. This remains true however different, philosophically, his point of departure may have been.

So Debussy, the artist of Instinct, became the master of Artifice, admiring troubadour music, medieval polyphony, the Renaissance chanson, Couperin, and Rameau as much as, in later years, he hated Wagner. In songs like the *Promenoir des Amants*—settings of the mannered, seventeenth-century poet, Tristan l'Hermite—we can see how Debussy's interest in Renaissance declamation came to terms with his harmonic nervosity. In the *Chansons de Charles d'Orléans* we can see him adapting the technique of the chanson to his more harmonic ends. In the Villon songs and the wonderful *Martyre de St. Sébastien* we find him effecting an intimate, pagan re-creation of medieval organum and of Renaissance polyphony. The swaying parallel fourths and fifths of this work, and the static oscillations of the higher chromatic discords, can all be found in the earlier piano works: only whereas in the piano pieces they are isolated moments of sensation, here they become part of a sustained, ecstatic lyricism.

There is a comparable development in the late orchestral works: compare, for instance, *Gigues* from the orchestral *Images* with the earlier *Fêtes*. The music is more acutely melancholy in its gaiety, because the linear structure is more finely drawn—the harmonic tension more a part of the line. This is especially clear in the scoring. Debussy's scoring remained 'magical'; yet the spell now depends on the revelation of nuance within the instrumental phrasing. In *Images* he makes no attempt to approximate to the symphonic ideal; none the less, short, apparently self-contained melodic periods grow into structures of astonishing power. The dance rhythm of *Rondes de Printemps* gives the fragmentary, repeated phrases a cumulative vitality; elements of Renaissance tradition merge into Debussy's sensuousness, and that into the new traditionalism of his successors. If the *Rondes* look back to the past, they also look forward to Milhaud, Roussel, and Stravinsky.

The forward-looking implications of the late work of this apparently self-contained artist is most clearly revealed in the set of three sonatas, which were all he lived to write of a projected series of six. They are not sonatas in the classical sense—though the first movement of the Violin Sonata has something that might be a recapitulation. But they are works for solo instruments; and a piece for solo violin or solo 'cello with piano, or for flute and viola with harp, cannot rely on the sensory flux of harmony. It must be thought in melodic terms, however unconventional the melody may be. Thus, though the first movement of the 'Cello Sonata is short, the string line is so sustained, so spacious in its troubadour-like arabesques, that the music achieves an expansive grandeur. More habitually, Debussy's melodies in these sonatas move in short periods which surge up, with a slightly flushed intensity, to recurrent climaxes and then subside. Yet the fragmentary phrases now build up a cumulative line. Even Debussy's old habit of repeating his phrases in pairs, over an immobile harmony, is turned to structural purpose in the last movement of the Violin Sonata, when the broken sequential repetitions in ascending thirds provoke the thrilling liberation of the coda. The earlier works seldom move, harmonically, even when the tempo is fast. In these sonatas the harmony itself tends to be relatively simple; but it has unexpected momentum because it is always related to the melodic phrase. Consider the 'modal' juxtaposition of the unrelated triads at the opening of the Violin Sonata, where the E flat minor chord so poignantly underlines the tension in the melody (Ex. 45):

Ex. 45. Debussy: Violin Sonata first movement

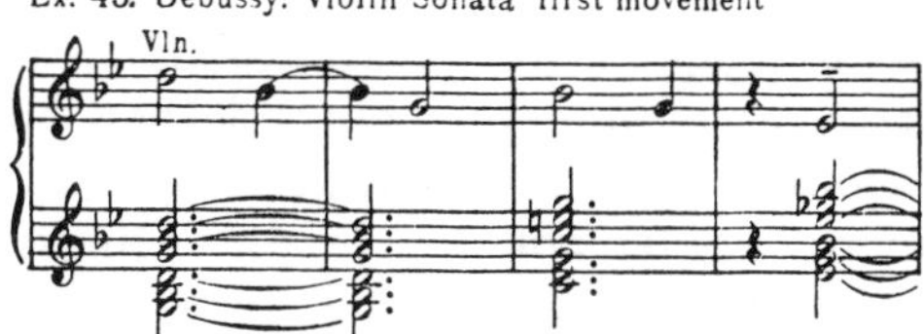

consider the way in which, in the *Intermède*, the old processions of sevenths and ninths are no longer passively indulged in, but create a decorative background to the melody's piquancy.

The element of formal stylization in the harmony, in the structural devices, and in the melody itself, is perhaps the secret of this music's original force. The contours of the melody, for instance, are often exotic, and we have observed how important a part exoticisms played in Debussy's early music. Then, the exotic evoked the private dream—except perhaps in the thrilling *L'Ile Joyeuse*, where Watteau's 'Ile de Cythère' becomes vibrantly immediate in a profusion of Oriental arabesques. In the late works the exotic elements—the pentatonic roulades, the taut augmented intervals, and the Spanish rhythms—are no longer used for their glamorous associations. They rather produce a sense of deliberate stylization—as do the mannered sevenths and ninths in the lucidly spaced harmony.

In this respect it is interesting that each of the sonatas includes, by way of slow movement, a Harlequinade. Watteau and Couperin had seen in Pierrot a mythological creature who symbolized both man's dissatisfaction and his desire. The world of the *Fête Champêtre* was not real, but it was sufficiently like real life to be potential. In Debussy's early work Pierrot has become simply a figure of dream: the yearning for another world, intrinsically good because different from this. Now, at the end of his life, worn out by disease and by the attrition of the war, he begins to see that the Mask and the Phantom cannot be permanently satisfying. He looks back on his life, and sees it in the likeness of a puppet-show, himself moon-eyed, desiring but perpetually dissatisfied, in the mask of Harlequin; so regarded, his life seems at once a tragedy and an ironic comedy. He originally gave the first of the sonatas a sub-title— 'Pierrot fâché avec la lune'. He is fed-up with the moon. His newly-won self-knowledge is revealed in the lucidity of the works' technique. The Mask and the Phantom have failed him; and the failure is a new start.

This is why, although the sonatas are disillusioned music, they none the less convey an impression not of sickness, but of health. Without religious or social sanction, they take their place in a great tradition. Contemporary malaise achieves nobility, objectivity, wit, and tragic pathos. Debussy said of the last sonata: "C'est affreusement mélancolique, et je ne sais pas si on doit en rire ou en pleurer. Peut-être les deux. Rude et belle

XLI Hugo Wolf in 1895.

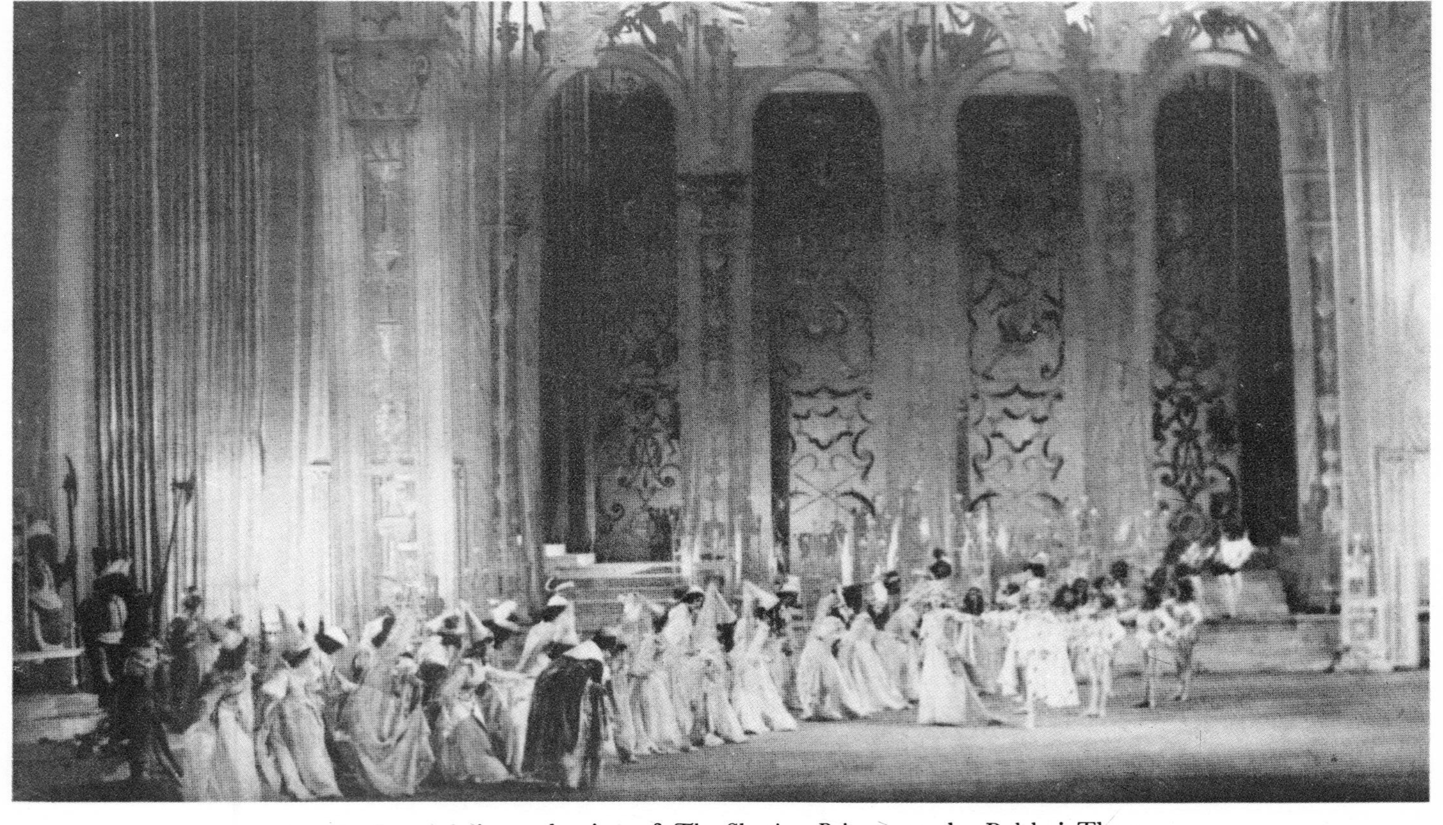

XLII Lavrosky's production of *The Sleeping Princess* at the Bolshoi Theatre,

musique, jamais fausse pourtant. . . . Combien il faut d'abord trouver, puis supprimer, pour arriver jusqu'à la chair nue de l'émotion." Debussy never wrote anything more perfectly realized than the "chair nue" of these calmly complex sonatas. So although in one sense *opera ultima*, they are also pregnant with intimations of the future—their wry lucidity has, for instance, much in common with the music Stravinsky was to write shortly after he had dedicated his beautiful Wind Symphony to Debussy's memory. It is worth noting that the Harlequin-figure plays a significant part in Stravinsky's work also, as he does in the career of Picasso. This fact alone indicates how Debussy, who began as a composer of romantic twilight, ended as the herald of however pale a dawn.

Delius remained a composer of Instinct all his days. Debussy became a composer of Artifice as he learned to contemplate his experience ironically. Irony is no more conceivable in Delius's egoistic music than it is in Wagner's; in the music of Ravel [1875–1937], on the other hand, irony was implicit from the earliest years. As a youth, like Debussy, he hated academic authority and systematically shocked his teachers. The composers he admired were Weber (for his elegantly evoked fairyland), Chopin (for the richness of his harmonic sensibility), and Schumann (for his Pierrot-like nostalgia); yet he loved Mozart perhaps above all. Among his contemporaries he revered not only Debussy, but also Satie and Chabrier—and even the *grand seigneur*, Saint-Saëns. In 1897 he became a pupil of Fauré. Henceforth his affinities with the classical tradition were no less evident than his revolutionary sensuousness.

This traditional bias may have helped him to find himself relatively early. From the first, his music differs from Debussy's in three closely related ways, Firstly, he never attempts to sunder the bases of classical tonality, as Debussy does in some of the piano preludes, notably *Voiles*. While he is fascinated by the nervous titillation of the higher chromatic discords, he hardly ever seeks to isolate their effect from line and progression. Indeed, his harmonic experimentalism probably has more in common with Chabrier than with Debussy.

Secondly, his music is, even from the beginning, melodic in impetus. The *Habanera* of 1895 is a typical Ravel *tune*: it would hardly be excessive to say that there is no such thing as a typical

Debussy tune. The early piano piece, *Jeux d'Eaux*, may have anticipated Debussy's various experiments in water music; but it has more relation to Liszt's *Jeux d'Eaux à la Villa d'Este* than to Debussy's *Reflets dans l'eau*. Unlike Debussy's impressionistic 'reflexion', it is constructed like a sonata movement, with two well-defined themes that proliferate in pianistic figuration.

Thirdly, Ravel's music is always dominated by dance movement, whether exotic and Spanish, or with the courtly elegance of the eighteenth century. This preoccupation with physical movement may have had something to do with Ravel's Basque origin; Spanish virility was innate in him, rather than an exotic dream. Again, the lilt of the dance suggests an affinity with the robust vivacity of Chabrier, and complementarily with the refined grace of Couperin and Rameau.

Ravel's conception of tonality, line, and rhythm means that his music—even during the period of the String Quartet and of *Schéhérazade*, when he came directly under Debussy's sway—never disintegrates into moments of sensation. His most impressionistic work is the piano *Miroirs*, which are "mirrors of reality", in Debussy's phrase. Yet even these are highly organized pieces, in which piano figuration acquires melodic significance, and classical tonality is preserved throughout the experiments in multiple harmony. The climax of this phase of Ravel's work comes in the piano suite, *Gaspard de la Nuit* (1908). The first piece, *Ondine*, is a developing variation-set, with the figuration growing increasingly melodic until it explodes in a cadenza. In *Le Gibet* a dissonant internal pedal note and a series of unresolved appoggiaturas create a sinister impression of vacancy, while the separate planes of tonality remain clearly defined. In *Scarbo* dance rhythm and harmonic ellipsis combine with transcendent virtuosity to create black magic. There is nothing comparable with this in Debussy's piano music, not even *L'Ile Joyeuse*, where the excitement is incremental and incantatory, rather than structural. The music's demoniacal glitter finds a parallel only in some of the pieces from Albéniz's *Iberia*, which also exploit the percussive effect of unresolved appoggiaturas.

Ravel's ironic objectivity suggests that he was by nature a theatre composer, as Debussy was not. The *Histoires Naturelles* of 1906 were an exercise in declamatory technique, linked to French prose rhythm and to the declamation of Lully and

Rameau; and were a study for Ravel's first opera, *L'Heure Espagnole*, which is almost entirely a conversation piece. The orchestra has all the tunes and the dance structure, while the singers employ a recitative more civilized, but no less close to speech, than that of Moussorgsky's *The Marriage*. The scoring is exquisitely sensuous, yet sharp; the ironic detachment of the music matches that of the cruelly comic tale. Yet being essentially a melodist, Ravel could not remain satisfied with an opera in which the singers never achieve lyrical flesh and blood. The growth of his melody is the growth of his humanity; and the decisive work in which lyricism becomes the centre of the music was a theatre piece. *Daphnis et Chloé*, usually heard nowadays in its orchestral version, was originally written for Diaghilev's Ballet, and scored for orchestra and chorus, with solo instruments personifying the characters. Ravel said that he conceived the score, and imagined the *décor*, in the spirit of eighteenth-century French painting. Greece becomes for him a world of eighteenth-century enchantment; but the classical theme and the luxuriance of the theatre lead him to envisage his theme with unwonted grandeur. In the aubade a rich, supple song tune of enormous span grows out of a shimmering void. Ravel's instinctive vitality comes to flower in his desire to repeople a vanished world.

After this climax in his career, Ravel embarked on a phase of clarification both melodic and harmonic. Two works may be associated with this purgative process: *Ma Mère l'Oye* with the melodic clarification, the *Valses Nobles et Sentimentales* with the harmonic. We have seen that Ravel had always had a distinctive melodic gift; in the virtuoso figuration of *Gaspard* or the orchestral excitement of *Daphnis*, however, melody was only one contributory element. In the simple, piano-duet scoring of *Ma Mère l'Oye* melody becomes the music's essence. The typical Ravel tune is modal, frequently Dorian or Phrygian, sometimes pentatonic. Whether or no he owed his innate modalism to his Basque ancestry, its archaic flavour is far from being a romantic evasion. The 'antique' world which it evokes is that of the eighteenth-century *conte de fées*; but it is also an ideal of spiritual simplicity which, beneath his sophistication, Ravel associates with the mind of the child. It is significant that both the modal melodies and the harmony of this work strikingly resemble certain pieces of Satie, especially his *Gymnopédies* (Ex. 46):

In the strange, simple-sophisticated art of Satie,* childhood had become a symbol of a spiritual integrity which seemed alien to the adult world.

In the *Valses Nobles* for piano Ravel said that he aimed at a concentration of the harmonic processes explored in *Gaspard* and the *Miroirs*. He wanted to "condense the harmonies and bring out the contrasts", thereby "freeing the melody", in something the same way as Debussy had done in his sonatas. Many of his melodic mannerisms are here extended into the harmonic plane: for instance, his partiality for melodic processions of thirds leads to secondary seventh and ninth chords, formed on the modal tonics of D and E (Ex. 47):

Again, Ravel develops the technique of the unresolved appog-

* In a small way Erik Leslie Satie [1866–1925] anticipated the 'cubist' re-ordering of the disintegrated materials of tradition such as we find in Stravinsky's work. In the first phase of his career he sought to organize apparently unrelated chords in reference to clear, usually modal, melodic patterns. In the second phase he related this linear pattern-making to an ironic distortion of popular music. In the third phase—notably in the *drame symphonique*, *Socrate*—he relinquished irony, but went as far as is humanly possible—perhaps a bit further—towards losing the personality in the 'pattern'. His art, like Stravinsky's, was closely associated with the formalization of ballet. *Parade*—the ballet he created in 1916, in collaboration with Cocteau and Picasso—was known as the cubist manifesto.

giatura melodically, so that he often writes bitonally, without destroying his tonal roots (Ex. 48):

The music thus acquires its characteristic bite: the slightly acrid flavour which gives an ironic undertone to its sensuousness. It is worth noting that although Ravel is as fascinated by augmented fifths as was Debussy, he never uses them with whole-tone implications.

The fruits of this phase of clarification come in the great Piano Trio of 1915. Superbly written for this most difficult medium, the work has the luxuriance of *Gaspard* with the melodic and harmonic precision of *Ma Mère l'Oye* and the *Valses Nobles*. The long-drawn modal melodies lend themselves naturally to baroque structures such as the passacaglia; but the first and last movements are by no means deficient in sonata rhetoric. The music is both elaborately sophisticated and, in essence, simple: both passionate and chaste. Then, however, there is another change of front. A note of acerbity creeps in, as the Satiean and Chabrier-like irony which had tempered the sensuousness gains the upper hand. During the war years, Ravel creates a series of experimental works. The Duo Sonata for violin and 'cello explores a new linear virtuosity. The Mallarmé songs develop a style that is colouristic but at the same time severely linear, comparable with Schoenberg's *Pierrot Lunaire* and with some of the war-time works of Stravinsky. The black magic in all these works reaches a climax of frenzy in the extraordinary coda to the choreographic poem, *La Valse*; and perhaps a belated consummation in the sinister, exotically decorated Piano Concerto for the Left Hand. Here the passion is wild but disciplined, the scoring brilliant but taut—in a manner Debussy approached only in the *Images* and the strange ballet, *Jeux*.

This desperate exoticism is not, however, Ravel's last word. There is a second clarification; the white magic of the eighteenth-century *conte de fées*, the innocent eye of childhood, bring an ultimate serenity. Perhaps the first intimation of this is the exquisite slow movement of the (two-handed) Piano Concerto, in which rococo ornament becomes disembodied and Ravel writes the kind of music that his beloved Mozart might have written, had he really been 'childlike'. The Violin Sonata of 1923–7 resembles Debussy's in lucidity of texture, and likewise has for slow movement a Harlequinade—a blues which distils the mood of a generation into 'something rich and strange'. But in the first movement especially Ravel achieves continuity of line in place of Debussy's volcanic *fioriture*. This luminous serenity is still more evident in the vocal works of Ravel's last years—for instance, the "green paradise of childish loves" of the *Chansons Madécasses*.

In such music Ravel, like Satie, miraculously becomes the child's mind: whereas Schumann—or even Delius—is the adult who yearns for his lost childhood or youth. In Ravel's last testament—the opera, *L'Enfant et les Sortilèges*—Colette's touching libretto deals specifically with the theme that was nearest Ravel's heart: the war between instinct and sophistication and the child's discovery of his humanity. So we are not surprised to find that musically the score fuses the different economies of *Ma Mère l'Oye* and the *Valses Nobles*. "Here", said Ravel, "the vocal line should dominate"; and if we remember his first opera, *L'Heure Espagnol*, we shall understand how the triumph of vocal line is also the victory of humanity. In the first opera, toys and mechanical clocks were more interesting than men; in *L'Enfant et les Sortilèges* birds, beasts, insects, even inanimate objects, teach humanity to the child, who is man regenerate. In the second act we have a parable of redemption through the renewal of innocence. Throughout, the vocal writing has been richly supple, whether in the Fire's coloratura, the tranquil modality of the fairy-tale Princess, or even the love-song of the cats, a parody of Ravel's own *La Valse*, from which hysteria is purged, leaving only tenderness. But a new dimension comes into the music in the serene modality of the choral epilogue (Ex. 49). Birds, beasts, and trees sing a hymn of gratitude because the pity they have felt has found an echo in the corrupted heart of the child. He sings with them, until his song is stifled with a sob as he awakes—on the threshold of the house of man.

If Ravel seemed cold and aloof as a man, it must have been,

not because he felt too little, but because he felt too much. He feared, not without reason, that the unimaginative harshness of the adult world would kill love. Irony shielded the innocence of

Ex. 49. Ravel: L'Enfant et les Sortilèges

a child, for the salvation of which, in a more than usually corrupt world, the artist lived.

5

TWO TRADITIONALISTS: FAURÉ AND STRAUSS

THE composers whom we have discussed in this section of the book, being individualists, are in many ways sharply distinguished from one another. Most of them, however, have one thing in common: they were misfits in the world into which they were born. Delius sought a refuge in Nature, Debussy in the creation of a private world of Art, Ravel in the evocation of an eighteenth-century fairyland which was also the spiritual integrity of the child. In our next two chapters we shall consider some composers who, though born into the mid-nineteenth century, accepted their world with dignity, even with enthusiasm. From this point of view, Fauré, Strauss, and Elgar form a natural sequence. France was the country whose cultural tradition had been least radically disturbed: so a composer of genius might still be a traditionalist and at the same time creatively original. Germany had seen the tremendous revolutionary phenomenon of Wagner, yet to counteract that had established, in the work of the Viennese classics, what had become Europe's dominant academic convention. England, at the further extreme, had forgotten her musical tradition ever since the seventeenth century and, at the height of her mercantile prosperity, was content to be musically parasitic.

For Fauré [1845–1924] academicism was an organic part of French life; he felt no urge to rebel against his masters, Gounod and Saint-Saëns, and the only hint of romantic protest in his early music is a suggestion of Schumann's poetic reverie in his treatment of the piano. The difference between his early songs and those of Debussy—or even Duparc—is striking. In Debussy the voice part tends to speech inflexion, while the piano's harmonies suggest, through their immobility, a withdrawal into the sensory inner life. The essence of Fauré's songs is in their melodies; and their form depends on a traditional balance between the tune and a freely moving bass. The poetic world of the songs is similar to that of Debussy's, for Fauré frequently set the same poets. But whereas for Debussy this world existed only in his inner dream, for Fauré it was an idealized version of a still living tradition. It would not have occurred to him that the world of his imagination was separate from the real world, except in so far as it was more lucid and more beautiful. Even his partiality for modal melodies (as in the exquisite *Lydia* or *Le Secret*) does not suggest an 'antique simplicity', as it does in Ravel. His modality is a part of his melodic thought, which merely proves the depth of his traditionalism. He did not, like Debussy or Ravel, rediscover the past. He was simply the natural successor to Gounod, Berlioz, Rameau, Couperin, Lully; and so, ultimately, to the Renaissance polyphonists and medieval monodists.

This becomes clear as soon as we turn to Fauré's instrumental music: for we see that his modality is inseparable from the fact that he is a linear composer. Fauré was born in 1845 and was composing up to 1920. It is extraordinary that, working during such a period, he could have remained apparently so impervious to the development of European music. He lived through the Wagnerian cataclysm, through Debussy's disintegration of harmony and orchestral sonority, through Stravinsky's disintegration of rhythm. Yet he showed virtually no interest in tone colour or the potentialities of the orchestra, being content to allow his pupils to orchestrate most of his larger works; while in rhythmic variety or pianistic figuration there is nothing in his music that would have alarmed Saint-Saëns or Schumann.

Yet his unhurried traditionalism is the root of his originality. Though in his chamber works he usually composes in the sonata form he inherited from Saint-Saëns, his approach is closer to Bach's than to Beethoven's. The core of his music, as of Bach's, is continuity of line and consistency of figuration; rhythmic variety is unnecessary where the form of the music is a spirally evolving melody that combines massiveness with grace. Of course, Fauré is not a Bach, and had not his social and religious advantages; he does not completely solve the problem of creating a large-scale melodically evolving movement which has the argumentative logic of a sonata. Climax, in such a structure, has to be created by the flow of melodies that move, mainly by step, through a continuous series of modulations, often enharmonic, often provoked by the modal behaviour of the lines;

Fauré, like such very different (but also modally-tending) composers as the Russian nationalists and Vaughan Williams, is especially prone to modulation between two keys a tone or semitone apart. It is true that his modulations tend to be more tightly packed in what corresponds to the development section; but he has hardly stamina enough to preserve the music's vitality over such immense melodic periods. The early chamber works are more successful than the later ones because, allowing in more conventionally romantic style for harmonic climax and repose, they show more respect for the listeners' ears and nerves. None the less, the late chamber works are a remarkable achievement. The early First Violin Sonata is as strong as it is beautiful, with sustained *élan* in its melodies, vitality in its rhythms, sensuous refinement in its Schumannesque approach to the piano. But the late Second Violin Sonata has a profoundly Bachian quality in the calm and ordered strength of its relation between evolving melody and bass; and this implies a fundamental serenity such as we can find in virtually no other music of the first twenty years of this century. We must pay homage to such serenity, even though we may find it anachronistic and, in the long run, less satisfying than the music of Debussy and Ravel, who were more in tune with what seems to us, if not to Fauré, the spiritual essence of their time.

The basis of Fauré's technique, we have said, lies in a tension between melody and bass. How close his approach is to that of classical composers, such as Bach and Couperin, we may see by comparing the dialogue between melody and bass in the Libera Me of Fauré's *Requiem* with the opening of Couperin's noble chaconne, *La Favorite* (Ex. 50):

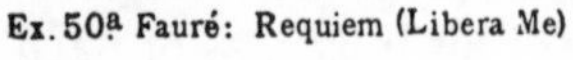
Ex. 50a Fauré: Requiem (Libera Me)

Ex. 50b Couperin: La Favorite

In Fauré's music, however, this architectural solidity is modified by two features. The first is the incidental freedom of his phrase-grouping within the conservative framework of the metre. This may have been prompted by his sensitivity to the inflexions of language and by his early interest in Gregorian music; but while it is most obvious in his vocal music, it exerted an influence over his instrumental thinking also. There is usually a subtle balance between the metrical rhythm of the harmony and the incidental rhythmic inflexions of the melodic parts.

This incidental subtlety of rhythm is complemented by an incidental harmonic complexity. The harmony may be moulded by a clear tonal scheme, expressed in the relationship between melody and bass, as in Bach or Couperin; but the modal contours will create delicate modifications to the triadic harmony, partly through their tendency to avoid leading notes, and partly through a fondness for chromatic alteration which, as in the work of some early seventeenth-century polyphonists, produces a rapidly coruscating texture. In the song *Le Parfum Impérissable*—an extreme instance—the firm progression of the bass, centred on E, controls continuous enharmonic modulations which, being melodically derived, have no connexion with the nineteenth-century notion of modulation as a dramatic event (Ex. 51):

Ex. 51. Fauré: Le Parfum Impérissable

The strength of Fauré's music may thus be equated with its Bach-like characteristics: its long, serene melodies and basses, its unperturbed rhythms, its command of canonic devices, its spacious structure which has as much in common with baroque monistic 'continuity' as with the dualistic sonata. The charm of his music may be associated with his Mediterranean culture: his modalisms, his elliptical harmonies and enharmonic transitions, whereby his harmonic originality consists not in the chords he uses, but in the contexts in which they appear. Strength and charm come together in the creations of his maturity—the *Requiem*, the Verlaine song-cycle, *La Bonne Chanson*, and the operas *Pénélope* and *Prométhée*, significantly on Greek themes. So deep are the imaginative roots of Fauré's civilization that for him the Greek ideal can approximate to an order achieved in his own, superficially more tormented world. The only intimation that so joyous an order might no longer have an objective existence in the world outside is contained in the fact that, in the music of Fauré's last years, the radiance diminishes. The technique remains basically the same; but in the last chamber works, piano pieces, and song cycles the serenity has acquired an autumnal gloss. There is a descending mournfulness in the mirror-like stillness and undulating figuration of the song, *Danseuse*; in the gravely shaped dialogue between soprano and bass in the Tenth and Eleventh Nocturnes; in the glassy four-part writing of the final Nocturne and of the String Quartet (Ex. 52):

Ex. 52. Fauré: Nocturne No. 13

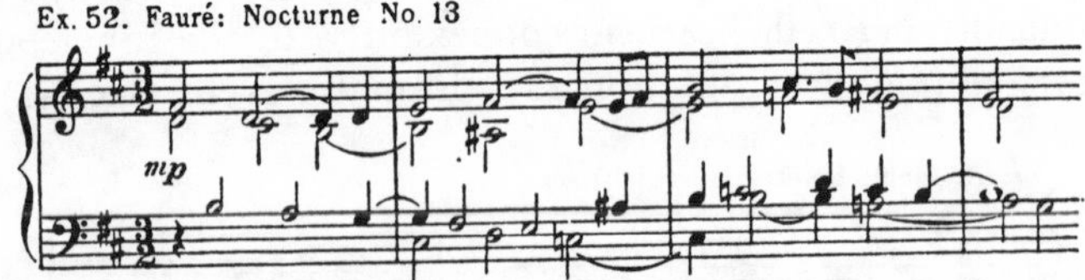

In the last Barcarolle there is even a suggestion of the phantasmagoric, for the softly fluttering harmonies suggest a scene viewed between sleeping and waking—a twilight phenomenon the more odd in a music that had habitually been as clear as day. It is as though in his last years Fauré became not only an incarnation of, but an elegy on, French civilization; and in this respect he resembles another conservative, Paul Valéry, whose poetic technique has certain features in common with Fauré's musical.

A Fauré could hardly have been born at a later date, as we can see if we consider his natural successor, Albert Roussel [1869–1937]. He was brought up under the aegis of Franck and the impressionist movement; yet as early as 1905 his *Poème de la Forêt* is not so much a Nature-impression as an evocation of the eighteenth-century *parc*; while the *Divertissement* for piano and wind instruments, written in the following year, is a bucolically sophisticated re-creation of tradition which has by-passed impressionism far more decisively than Ravel. If Fauré was still the representative of what seemed to him a living tradition, Roussel in his later work has more self-consciously to recover a tradition: which may explain the more strenuous quality of his (often polymodal)* melodic power, the more frantic quality in his rhythmic ostinatos. The fact that he composed four symphonies is evidence of the more vehement and dramatic quality of his imagination; yet his symphonies, like Fauré's chamber works, have some relationship to the melodically unified techniques of baroque music. Each movement tends to be dominated by a continuous figuration or rhythmic motive which to some extent negates the dramatic contrasts of sonata style. The symphonies are a (sometimes rather desperate) assertion of civilization, rather than a revolutionary challenge.

Fauré once said: "L'artiste doit aimer la vie et nous montrer qu'elle est belle. Sans lui, nous en douterions."† He would have wished for no greater satisfaction than to know that his best music falls not far short of his promise. Roussel, too, is one of the few twentieth-century composers whose music tells us that the artist loves life and finds it good. With him, however, we are more conscious of the ironic undertone in Fauré's last sentence.

Fauré—and perhaps even Roussel—had so deep an awareness of the traditional values of French civilization that one is hardly conscious, as one listens to their music, that they lived in

* POLYMODAL: a passage in which several melodic lines move independently in different modalities. This is a process different from, and more natural than, systematic polytonality, in which all the lines are in the same tonality while having different key centres.

† "The artist ought to love life and show us that it is good. Without him, we might have doubts about it."

a society dominated by trade. But Germany's industrial expansion in the second half of the nineteenth century was so rapid that no artist could have been indifferent to it. Thus though Strauss [1864–1949] was brought up in the wake of a great musical tradition, it never occurred to him that there was any disparity between these artistic values and the values of commerce. On the contrary, he not only accepted, but rejoiced in, his commercial world, and was by a long way the most materially successful composer of his time. He made a large fortune out of writing operas, and was a professional man of the theatre like Meyerbeer or Verdi. To have been able thus to accept the world in which he lived may have implied some deficiency in perceptiveness and spiritual refinement. It certainly involved a tremendous creative exuberance.

This is evident enough in Strauss's adolescent work. Nothing could be more striking than the contrast between his early career and that of Delius, Debussy, and even Wagner. They were all driven by hatred of the academic conventions of their day, which for them symbolized a moribund world. Strauss accepted those conventions not passively, but with enthusiasm. While Wagner and Delius were creating their own forms to replace the sonata which, in the minor works of Spohr and Mendelssohn, had become a shell rather than a living organism, Strauss breathed into the shell new life. This new life in, for instance, his Violin Sonata is quantitative rather than qualitative. Themes that in Mendelssohn are sweetly cantabile acquire in Strauss an energy that is soon exhausted; harmonies that in Mendelssohn are mildly cloying become in Strauss a chromatic orgy. At this date the music sounds no less faded than Mendelssohn's feebler works: perhaps more faded, for a period costume is more obtrusive when every flounce is exaggerated. Yet though its energy springs from a certain banality of mind, in the Century of the Common Man such energy is something to be reckoned with.

It is interesting that Strauss turned aside from academic convention and took up with the progressive composers of his youth largely at the instigation of Hans Richter.* Instinctively, he had no desire to be a revolutionary. But, living in a revolutionary era, he accepted Richter's suggestion that a fully

* Hans Richter [1843–1916], conductor closely associated with Wagner. He first conducted *The Ring* at Bayreuth in 1876.

professional composer ought to be aware of the most advanced developments of his art. So he studied the works of Liszt and Wagner and, with his superb traditional craftsmanship, soon became their acknowledged successor. Taking over the basic principle of the symphonic poem from Liszt, he combined it with techniques suggested by the late work of Wagner; but it is significant that his symphonic poems have more in common with classical tradition than have either Liszt or Wagner. *Don Juan* (1888) is a one-movement Wagnerian opera without voices, which tells a story and unfolds a dramatic situation in a flowing harmonic polyphony of more than Wagnerian opulence. But—though the Don was, of course, the kind of man Strauss admired and understood—it is operatic character-portrayal, in the traditional sense, rather than Wagnerian self-inflation. The structure sounds 'continuous' and closely related to the plot; it is also not very far from the classical rondo. *Tod und Verklärung* describes a dramatic situation in still greater detail; yet its continuous Wagnerian texture falls into three sections—a slow introduction, a middle section closely resembling sonata form, and a conclusion that recreates the introduction in the light of the sonata movement. In *Till Eulenspiegel* (1895) and *Don Quixote* (1897) Strauss unambiguously employs rondo and variation style for objective character-portrayal. Only in *Zarathustra* does he attempt Liszt's 'psychological' permutation of themes, and this work, though more ingenious, as well as more complicated, than anything of Liszt, is a triumph of craftsmanship rather than of art. Lisztian technique calls for something of the visionary temperament which Liszt developed during his later years. Strauss, with his feet firmly and prosperously on the earth, had little real sympathy for Liszt's ideals; and the excessively literal realism of his symphonic works is evidence of this.

Liszt's programme is always psychological; Strauss's realism, insignificant in itself, testifies to the dominance over him of the material world, which was all he knew and loved. He is at the opposite pole to Debussy. The latter always preferred feeling to action; Strauss is at his best when dealing with action. The tempestuous life and loves of Don Juan, Till Eulenspiegel, or Don Quixote provoke music of tremendous creative genius; even *Ein Heldenleben* is not so much a revelation of Strauss's inner life as a gigantic, externalized portrait of Strauss's ideal Man of Action. In *Tod und Verklärung* the fear of death may stimulate human activity: whereas transfiguration was for Strauss (as it was not for Liszt in the 'Faust' Symphony) an abstract idea. All his transfiguration music sounds, by now, cinematic.

Strauss began as an orchestral composer who related progressive techniques to classical precedent. The centre of his life's work, however, was in opera; and here again he re-created Wagnerian opera with a classical bias. Though he inherited Wagner's sensuousness he could not, in his worldly materialism, follow Wagner in identifying love—and the personal life—with death. *Salome* and *Elektra* sound Wagnerian in that they employ a luxuriously chromatic, massively scored harmonic polyphony, while the voices either declaim or double the instrumental melody. But the operas are immense symphonic poems constructed on broadly the same principles as Strauss's orchestral works; and the relationship between Strauss's chromaticism and Wagner's is superficial. *Tristan's* ecstatic dissolution of tonality implied a new formal technique and an experience that was an historical event. Strauss's music remains basically traditional; his dissonant techniques are applied to his diatonicism in order to build up a sensational effect. Thus side-stepping parallel seconds, sevenths and ninths obscure but do not—as they do in Debussy—destroy a traditional progression (Ex. 53):

Ex. 53. Strauss: *Elektra*

bitonal effects may be created, as in Elektra's notorious 'blood' chord, by thickening out a conventional movement of parts into triads; and the most abrupt modulations may be suggested by an extension of (say) the classical device of the Neapolitan cadence. Wagner's chromatic dissonance grows from within; Strauss's is applied from without: for *Salome* and *Elektra* are not a Wagnerian overflow of the ego, but an 'operatic' situation externalized. The brilliantly extrovert genius of Strauss deliberately presents sensation for sensation's sake; he is more interested in the effect of morbidity and hysteria on his audience than he is in the minds of his characters. This is a kind of artistic decadence, but it is not dishonesty. Strauss's melodrama would not be so devastatingly effective—and, at times, so beautiful—if it did not correspond to something dark that lurked beneath his buoyancy. Perhaps the wilfully manufactured horrors of *Salome* and *Elektra* delighted as they appalled his audience because there was an element of wilful sadism in the competitive spirit of an industrial community. The horrors of *Elektra* were to become life, instead of art, in two world wars; and modern war is likewise a prostitution of feeling, as well as of life.

Certainly though we cannot altogether believe in the manufactured horrors in these operas, we cannot ignore them: whereas the positive moral virtues of the 'good' characters seem to us, in a dismal way, funny. Strauss was aware of this, remarking that he was constitutionally unable to portray "a chaste Jesuit". The genuine positive bases of his art consisted not in moral qualities, but in physical activity and in sensual enjoyment, as was already evident in the prancing themes and elaborate texture of his symphonic poems. In *Elektra* he had first entered into collaboration with Hugo von Hofmannsthal, an artist whose poetic sensitivity was deeper than his own. As well as providing Strauss with the most poetically distinguished opera libretti that any composer has had to deal with, Hofmannsthal revealed to Strauss the true nature of his genius. Henceforth his art becomes a tribute to humanity and a celebration of a social world.

We have seen that an inherent classicality of approach had modified the Lisztian and Wagnerian elements in Strauss's orchestral works. In the same way, Italian vocal *cantilena* always played a much more significant part in his operas than it did in Wagner's; and though he may have inherited this direct from Liszt, it also suggests a link with classical opera and with Mozart in particular. In later years Strauss seems to have felt intuitively that the moments of unexpected tenderness in *Elektra* were more significant than the melodrama, for he advised orchestras to play the score as though it were 'fairy music'—something by Mendelssohn. Superficially, the advice seems both unrealistic and perverse. What is the point of composing sensational music scored for an enormous orchestra unless you intend to play it as though you meant it? Yet if we think of *Elektra* in relation to the next Strauss-Hofmannsthal opera, *Der Rosenkavalier*,

Strauss's remark seems not altogether absurd. *Der Rosenkavalier* is also a symphonic opera scored for a very large orchestra. But the chromaticism of *Salome* and *Elektra* is discarded in favour of the chromaticized diatonicism which, in the orchestral works, had seemed to be Strauss's natural language; and the lyrical writing for the voice, especially the sopranos, acquires a Mozartian fluency. Mozartian and Schubertian pastiche is even introduced, and the Viennese waltz which pervades all Strauss's music assumes a particularly voluptuous and insidious form. The pastiche occurs because the opera is intentionally a period piece; it is justified because the period is one in which Strauss's imagination naturally lived. Of course, Mozart's world no longer existed, and Strauss was wrong in thinking he had written a Mozartian opera: the quicksands of his modulations may have much the same significance, in relation to Mozart, as the quicksands of Bruckner's modulations have in relation to Bach. But something approaching Mozart's Vienna at least existed within living memory; and the world of *Der Rosenkavalier* is a periwigged, rouged reminiscence, which embodies Strauss's positive values as *Elektra* embodied the negative. In a sense, both are synthetic, and at the same time true to Strauss's experience. This is what Busoni meant by saying that Strauss was an industrialist, even in his art. He sees the delights of eighteenth-century aristocratic society through the eyes of a nineteenth-century business-man. Though aristocratic values are vulgarized, in being vulgarized they at least become relevant.

This being so, Hofmannsthal's next libretto was a no less acute perception than *Der Rosenkavalier*; he rewrites *Le Bourgeois Gentilhomme*, re-enacting a heroic opera, on the classical theme of Ariadne, in a bourgeois setting. The myth and the reality prove to be more excitingly related than the *bourgeois gentilhomme* had bargained for. Musically, the work shows its classical affiliations not so much in the fact that it includes transcription and pastiche of Lully's original music, as in the fact that it is scored for chamber orchestra and is a singers' opera. The music of the divertissement substitutes an inspired bourgeous banality for classical grace. The lyrical expertise of the vocal writing is as mellow as Mozart, without the edge of Mozartian wit; it floats over the self-indulgent suavity of the sensuously scored texture, which is a compromise between rococo lucidity and Wagnerian harmonic polyphony.

The sequence of operas that follows *Ariadne* returns to more normal operatic resources, but preserves the link with classical tradition. In writing *Capriccio*, a virtuoso opera about operas, and *Intermezzo*, a 'bourgeois comedy' based on an incident in his own domestic life and introducing his wife and himself as characters, Strauss seems to admit that, in an ever more democratic world, the classical idea of opera as a social act is no longer relevant. Yet if opera is becoming a game, this is perhaps only an extension of Strauss's habitual attitude. The 'classical' world of *Daphne* or the *Danae* remains the business-man's glamourized Vienna, in which Strauss plays the game of life with far more zestful humanity than the business-man—or than his namesake, Johann. After all, thirty years back Salome's Dance of the Seven Veils had turned out to be a bourgeois Viennese waltz which by now willy-nilly recalls the palm court. The evil of *Salome* and *Elektra* may be all the nastier for being only skin-deep. If the haunting beauty of the *cantilena* of the later operas is skin-deep also, we must none the less be grateful for so rich an expression of the delights of *l'homme moyen sensuel.* It is not fortuitous that some of Strauss's finest music should be contained in *Die Frau ohne Schatten*, a parable about man in relation to woman: nor that the last act, in which Hofmannsthal offers a mystical interpretation of fecundity, should be a relative failure.

So Strauss went on composing for thirty years, master of his craft, oblivious of changing fashion. The mirth, passion, and glamour in his music seem half-vicarious, an epitaph on a fashion that the old man would not allow to sleep, though it was long past nightfall. The liquid *cantilena* has, in the suave context of the Wagnerian harmony, a precious, manicured elegance. There is in the music an odd feeling, as of the gaiety of ghosts: "So round and round the ghosts of beauty glide And haunt the places where their honour died." The instrumental works of Strauss's old age, mostly scored for small combinations, have the same ghostly seductiveness. The Oboe Concerto, for instance, is an epitaph on rococo vivacity, with the solo oboe treated in much the same way as Strauss treats the soprano voice (Ex. 54).

One work, however—the *Metamorphosen* for twenty-three solo strings—suggests a different approach. For the first time in his long career Strauss approaches the 'inwardness' of *Tristan's* harmonic polyphony. The themes of his youth had been a development from the Beethovenian Heroic. Here he incorporates into the complex texture of the harmonic polyphony the

theme of the Funeral March from the 'Eroica' Symphony; and in the whirling virtuosity of the string writing and the extreme fluency of the enharmonic modulations a world seems to be in dissolution—as it is in some of the late music of Mahler and the early work of Schoenberg.

The Oboe Concerto is a serio-comic epilogue to Strauss's world. *Metamorphosen*—the title is accurate and significant—is Strauss's ultimate farewell, in which he came to admit that his world had literally destroyed itself. Schoenberg had admitted this thirty years ago, without needing two wars to prove it. That Strauss could have gone on living in the world of his youth, and have written this music as late as 1945, is testimony both to the strength of his convictions and to the deficiency of his imagination. The contrast with Fauré is revealing. The Frenchman never wanted to be other than conservative, yet his style grew with experience and became, in its reticent way, progressive. Strauss made his reputation as an aggressive modernist and relapsed into reaction. The composer of civilized refinement turns out to look forward, while the composer who seemed most vigorously in sympathy with an industrial, bourgeois world remains arrested in the modernity of his youth. Perhaps Strauss, who relished nineteenth-century prosperity, is not after all so remote from Delius, who hated it from the depth of his soul. The most beautiful music Strauss ever wrote is the Countess's lament, in *Der Rosenkavalier*, for her lost youth; and not even Delius's music is more nostalgic than the lyricism of the trio with which the opera concludes. At the end, the socially-minded Strauss and the most a-social composer who ever lived both wrote from the consciousness of loss. In any case, the warmth of this music suffices to prove that a 'reactionary' is not necessarily inferior to a 'progressive' art. Everything depends on the conviction behind the experience. We may find Fauré's rarefied music congenial and some aspects of Strauss's music repulsive; we can hardly deny that Strauss has the greater vitality, the more significant power.

6

ELGAR AND VAUGHAN WILLIAMS

With Fauré, an awareness of civilization proves stronger than an industrial environment; with Strauss, a great musical tradition and an industrial environment come to terms. England in the latter part of the nineteenth century was, however, more decisively dedicated to material prosperity than France, and more oblivious of her musical heritage than Germany, largely because the Industrial Revolution had here been longer entrenched, if not more violent in its effects. One result of this was that the less 'poetic' forms of art, such as the novel, tended to flourish at the expense of the more immediately creative forms. There was plenty of room for imaginative and critical commentary on the human situation; but the burgeoning of the human spirit in lyrical poetry, painting, or music was apt to be stifled. If music suffered most disastrously, the reason may be that music, by nature a relatively abstract art, needs to be nourished by a continuous tradition; if the tradition is once broken, the symbols cannot easily recover intelligibility. Our musical tradition, largely owing to the effects of the Civil War, had lapsed as long ago as the late seventeenth century. Since then our music had been dominated by foreign models. It was no longer a question of an intimate relationship between a native and a European idiom, such as had existed in the time of Dunstable, of Byrd, or of Purcell. As industrialism grew more rampant, the local tradition withered. Our composers turned out synthetic Handel, and later synthetic Mendelssohn, because they had no inner conviction to suggest an alternative.

Into this materially prosperous, spiritually non-creative world two men of tremendous creative energy were born. Speaking of the position of the artist in an uncreative epoch, W. B. Yeats once wrote:

> The rhetorician would deceive his neighbours,
> The sentimentalist himself; while art
> Is but a vision of reality.
> What portion in the world can the artist have
> Who has awakened from the common dream
> But dissipation and despair?

Perhaps we may say that, if Delius ran the risk of being the sentimentalist, Elgar [1857–1934] always felt the lure of rhetoric. At least, he is superfically as remote from Delius as is Strauss. He accepted Edwardian society as zestfully as Delius rejected it; and although both composers took over the idiom of German romanticism, Delius exploited it to express an egocentric isolation, Elgar to express a social conviction no less purposeful than that of Strauss. That Elgar could use this idiom with a technical expertise equal to Strauss's is a most remarkable achievement; he was able to assume the existence of a great symphonic tradition which, in this country, had never happened.

In order to do this he had to believe implicitly in his world, taking the bad (as we would think it) with the good. Before he discovered his genius, he wrote a quantity of second-hand, third-rate music in the Victorian oratorio convention stemming from Mendelssohn and Spohr; and throughout his life he composed 'functional' music expressly to celebrate Edwardian imperialism. He disliked, or affected to dislike, the company of artists and had bourgeois pretentions to High Society; *Swanee River* moved him (and George V) to tears. He was never ashamed to be the rhetorician, consciously addressing an audience and sharing with it tastes that may seem crude, even repulsive. In this, as in his technical mastery, he resembles Kipling.

Yet we cannot merely deplore this aspect of Elgar. We may not like his world; yet if he had not believed so powerfully in all its manifestations, he could never have revealed the soul of which it was but obscurely conscious. Elgar's jingoistic works, such as the 'Pomp and Circumstance' Marches, do not live in a different world from his symphonies and concertos. He believes in them no less: which is why they are, of their kind, so powerfully effective. Elgar's 'serious' works reveal the real nobility which was behind the strutting pomp, the *nobilmente* swagger. For all its tawdry materialism, Elgar's world had a greatness at which we can ill afford to sneer; but it took a genius to manifest in music the spirit that justified apparent banality, even brutality, of thought and feeling.

It is not surprising that Elgar, like Delius, took a long time to discover what he wanted to do. He was over forty when the 'Enigma' Variations, the first completely Elgarian work, appeared. In the Finale, we have Elgar the rhetorician, orchestrating with Straussian brilliance. But in 'Nimrod' we have the nobility that comes from within; while in 'Dorabella' and most of the quiet variations we find a sensitive melodic line, humanly intimate rather than rhetorical: a music of personal relationships, dedicated to Elgar's friends, rather than a social manifestation. Every element of the technique seems, on paper, German; yet one could not imagine a more individualistic or—we have come to think—more English style. The originality is perhaps more melodic than harmonic. Elgar's lyricism has the seething energy of Strauss's early symphonic poems, but the curves are more rounded. The surging-upward figures on the strings—usually beginning with a small interval which grows progressively larger—are balanced by a slow fall; and the persistent rise and fall of the sixth or seventh, with the upward leap often landing on an accented passing note, gives to his most exuberant phrases a relaxed amplitude (Ex. 55):

Harmonically, Elgar adds nothing to Wagner's vocabulary and is less enterprising than Strauss. None the less, the way in which he uses harmony and tonality is highly personal. Consider, for instance, his partiality for the Wagnerian sequence. With Wagner, the sequence is absorbed into the flow of the lines, so that one loses consciousness of the point at which the sequences begin and end. Elgar's sequences—which favour movement by thirds rather than by step—serve to build up climax; but we are usually aware of the cumulating planes of tonality. Wagner's sequences sweep us away on the harmonic swell. Elgar's sequences are rhetorical in no derogatory sense; our hearts uplift and our arms open. Again, the music has a spaciousness, an open quality, for all its ripeness. Possibly Elgar's familiarity with Handelian oratorio had some effect on his treatment of the sequence.

In later works this spaciousness becomes increasingly typical of Elgar's melodic and harmonic thought. While the sequences and the intermittent drooping sevenths and ninths do not disappear, the periods grow muc' larger. Most of the themes of the Introduction and Allegro for strings, the main theme of the first movement of the E flat Symphony, the first allegro theme of the 'Cello Concerto are all typical Elgarian melodies, undulating with apparent placidity, usually in step-wise movement, until they attain a peak from which they abruptly descend: only to start once more on their cumulative cycle. The length of the themes entails lengthy developments; far more than Strauss, Elgar approximates to the inward, evolutionary nature of Liszt's thematic metamorphoses—not merely in obvious instances like the translation of the A flat Symphony's scherzo theme into the theme of the slow movement. Yet Elgar manages to reconcile this with a subtle modification of the classical symphony. He starts off with tremendous dynamic impetus, and the development section seems at first to be a relaxation rather than an increase of tension. He meditates discursively on aspects of the themes, taking up now one, now another, gradually revealing the hidden affinities between them. The climax of the movement comes not in the development, but at the beginning of the recapitulation, when we discover the true identity of themes we had but partially understood. To some degree, of course, this is true of any vital sonata movement; no composer before Elgar, however, had made this feature the very core of sonata style. Regarded in this light, his symphonies are characterized not by excess, but by concision. If the rhetorician is still present in the impressive apotheosis of the A flat Symphony, the quiet conclusion of the E flat reveals the *spirit* of delight beneath the grand façade. Though it may come but rarely, it is worth waiting for.

The spiritual nobility behind Elgar's grandeur is related to his Roman Catholicism, though he is not a religious composer in the sense that Bruckner or Vaughan Williams is. It is both technically and philosophically interesting that the loveliest music Elgar ever wrote—the Prelude to Part II of *The Dream of Gerontius*—should deal with bliss attained, and should strikingly remind us of the modalism and diatonicism of Vaughan Williams. Yet on the whole Part II of *Gerontius* is less convincing than Part I, which deals with the search after faith. The work may be an implicit protest against the materialism of the age, but for Elgar—if not for Cardinal Newman—it is a drama rather than a liturgical affirmation. Elgar's fusion of the brilliant, stable operatic idiom of Handelian oratorio with the more subjective passion of Wagner's endless *melos* and enharmonic modulation, controlled by interrelated leitmotives, is beautifully appropriate to his purposes. The music becomes at once a social act and an intimate spiritual history; its ecstasy is remote from the religiosity of Victorian stained glass. Only when he tries to depict devils are we aware that Elgar's knowledge of supernatural beings was comically or pathetically subject to materialism. They are not much better than Franck's: with the difference that Elgar never really pretended to believe in them, whereas Franck would have believed in his if he could.

In his earlier works, Elgar, like most post-Handelian oratorio composers, had shown scant respect for English declamation. From the vocal writing of *Gerontius*, however, it would seem that the Englishness of Elgar's ostensibly Teutonic style may have had something to do with an intuitive, subconscious response to the language. For the sweep of the lines, even in recitative, is unmistakably Elgarian, while being related to the rhythm of speech. Certainly the Englishness of Elgar's melodies becomes more evident in his last works. He had long shown a fondness for the flat seventh in pastoral moods; the swinging tune with which the 'Cello Concerto opens even suggests the contours of English folk-song, in which Elgar betrayed no more conscious interest than he did in the revival of Tudor music, though he was acquainted with both. There may also be some connexion between his sensitivity to speech inflexion and the plastic nature of the phrasing in, say, the slow movement of the 'Cello Concerto. In music such as this the rhetorician is silenced; in the free rubato of the lyricism an intimate human voice speaks directly to you and to me, while an unexpected chord or modulation reveals the private heart beneath the public manner (Ex. 56):

Ex. 56. Elgar: Cello Concerto

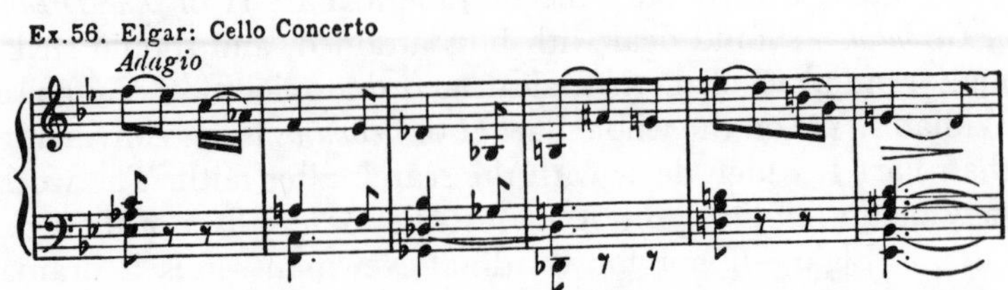

This flexibility is enhanced by Elgar's scoring, especially in the way in which he uses instrumental doubling not to make more noise, but to 'point' his phrases. Despite his debt to Wagner and Strauss, he scores much more 'melodically' than they do; in this respect his admiration for Meyerbeer is evident in all his scores, though he was going a little far when he said that he learned more about orchestration from Delibes than from Wagner! In any case, the most subtly constructed of Elgar's works is also the most subtly scored. *Falstaff* is a big symphonic poem which tells a story in Straussian terms, while being also a free sonata movement incorporating a scherzo and a slow movement. The construction is broadly and firmly planned; yet the plasticity of the melodic phrasing and harmonic detail reveals Falstaff as by turn manly, witty, malicious, robust, cowardly, tender, trivial—as was Shakespeare's Falstaff. Elgar's Falstaff is, however, not Shakespeare's, but his own: for he is in essence noble. He is Elgar's representative Englishman: perhaps even the kind of man Elgar wanted to be. Certainly he was a type of Englishman who was becoming rarer with the passing of the years.

It is interesting that although Elgar lived for twenty more years after composing *Falstaff* and the 'Cello Concerto, he wrote no more music of consequence. People no longer wanted his kind of music, he said: and he could create no other. In so far as the concert-going public was concerned, this seems manifestly untrue; yet in a deeper sense Elgar was right. He stopped composing (whereas Strauss went on), because his art belonged to a world that had had its day. Whether our day, though different, is any 'better' is extremely dubious; but better or worse we listen to his music in the same spirit as we listen to any other music of the past. In any vital art of the past there are some elements which speak to us, others which were meaningful once, but are so no longer. As we listen to *Falstaff* or the drooping chromatics of the closing pages of the E flat Symphony, we forget what seem to us pomposities, and admire a prodigious moral strength. Elgar had the power to make us believe, momentarily, that the Edwardian world was as grand as his music; while at the same time he subtly suggests that in his heart he knows, and knows that we know, that the grandeur is in his imaginative vision.

Elgar's music belonged to a past world, Delius's yearned for a vanished youth; both used a technique basically German. If there was to be a future for our music, it was likely to be associated with the recovery of a national consciousness: which was not, of course, a purely musical matter. The revival of English music during the early years of this century was connected with the rediscovery of English folk-song; but the folk-song movement in this country is not really comparable with the folk-song movement in nineteenth-century Russia. Though it implied, no doubt, a protest against an industrialized world, no one could have seriously believed that folk-song in our urban community could again be a living tradition, as it was in Russia. For our composers, the significance of the folk-song movement was more exclusively technical. After a century of German hegemony, it taught us once more what an English musical line, growing naturally out of the English language, was like. In middle life, Holst [1874–1934] referred to his early works as "good old Wagnerian bawling". To discover his real roots, the English composer had to start again from the beginning, to find himself in unaccompanied vocal monody. The essence of Holst's renewal of tradition is in his smallest works—the songs for voice and violin, in which he set medieval lyrics in lines that are vocally modal, and as free in rhythm, as closely related to the words, as folk-song or plainsong. Only a certain tonal precariousness tells us that Holst was not in fact a medieval cleric or peasant (Ex. 57):

Ex. 57. Holst: I sing of a Maiden

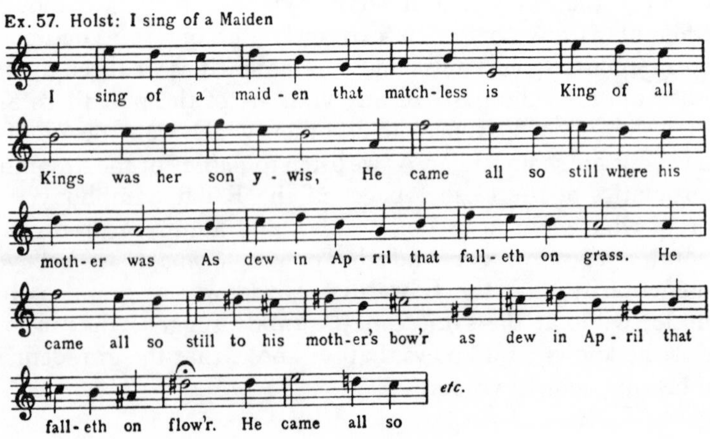

But the implications of unaccompanied monody are philosophically poles apart from a man of Holst's generation. Though he could find himself in a world irremediably remote, he could hardly be content to express himself exclusively in small lyrical songs, or through the prose declamation of a 'play in music'. In *Savitri*, for instance, the freely rhythmed, modal declamation of the early part is deeply moving. When, however, Holst feels a need to create a *musical* climax, he relapses into a Pucciniesque manner which, though admirable in itself, has no valid relationship with the modal declamation. Holst's difficulties become still greater when he tries to create choral and orchestral works on an extended scale, starting from a folk-like, medieval seeming modality. They are greatest of all in purely instrumental works, when he has neither a text nor stage action to provide continuity.

Now, all European music since the Renaissance had been based on the notion of harmony as alternating tension and relaxation, associated with a metrical time-sense. Even in his larger works, involving considerable orchestral and choral resources, Holst evades, as far as possible, this traditional conception of harmony. Thus, despite his admiration for sixteenth-century composers, there is little genuine polyphony in his music, of the kind which depends on tension between line and harmony. The texture of his music is influenced far more by the medieval organum principle; even a notorious harmonic audacity, like the clash of the triads of F sharp and G in *The Hymn of Jesus*, is created by an organum of 6:3 chords moving in contrary motion (Ex. 58):

Ex. 58. Holst: Hymn of Jesus

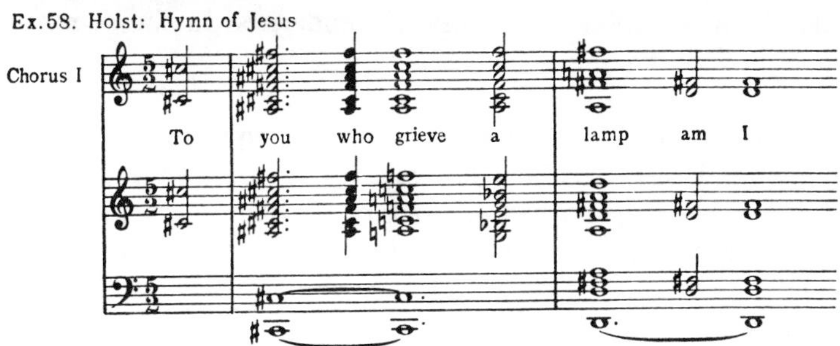

Holst's fondness for bitonal effects has a similar basis; and although he developed an almost pathological horror of sensuous seventh and ninth chords and confined himself mainly to unexpected melodic relationships of diatonic concords, his harmonic thinking is, in principle, very similar to Debussy's. His harmony, too, tends to deprive his music of the sense of progression.

The self-contained nature of Holst's modal melodies, the lack of progression in his harmony, mean that he has to rely on rhythm, or rather on metre, to keep the music going if he wishes to compose in other than small forms. The most primitive of all methods of achieving continuity is the ostinato; and the dominance of the ostinato over British music dates from Holst. His ostinato patterns are often in irregular measures of five, seven, or eleven, so that they do not conflict too strongly with the prose-like flexibility of his melodies. Paradoxically, the effect of the ostinato is again to destroy the time sense. We are conscious of time when rhythm is associated with alternations of harmonic stress; divorced from harmonic tension, a repeated metrical pattern tends to induce hypnosis. All Holst's most characteristic music deals with experience to which the time sense is irrelevant: consider 'Saturn' and 'Neptune', the two most impressive movements of *The Planets*. In his finest, most representative work, *Egdon Heath*, he is alone with the emptiness of the heath, as Delius is alone with the high hills, or Sibelius with the vast forest. Perhaps Holst achieves what Delius passionately strives for: his personality is purged away in the bare organum-like harmony and transparent scoring. Yet if *Egdon Heath* is, in a strict sense, a metaphysical work it is without the consolation of faith. Only in the late Lyric Movement for viola and chamber orchestra is there a hint of lyrical warmth in the soloist's melody, of tenderness in the sonorous spacing of the harmony.

Holst greatly admired the music of Stravinsky. When we come to discuss Stravinsky we shall see that every element which in Holst's technique assumes a somewhat abortive form, reaches fruition in the work of the Russian. Apart from any difference in natural endowment, this is largely because modal figurations, organum effects, and ostinatos had a profound relationship to the experience of a Russian and cosmopolitan *émigré*: whereas their significance in the history of English music was mainly purgative and clinical. Vaughan Williams [b.1872] from the start had a more positive relationship to the English tradition than had Holst. As a countryman, he experienced folk-song as his own inheritance, treating it dramatically, rather than with ruminative nostalgia. The 'tragedy' of Housman's 'Shropshire Lad' poems may be not so far removed from the synthetic emotionalism of the popular Press; but they made it possible for Vaughan Williams to respond to folk-song with vivid immediacy. In *Is My Team Ploughing*, from *On Wenlock Edge*, the lad's folk-tune is modally self-contained. The ghostly answers to his questions, on the other hand, employ sophisticated harmonies closely associated with opera. Similarly, the most beautiful song in the cycle—*Bredon Hill*—becomes a dramatic experience. Self-contained folk-melody is here accompanied by superimposed thirds and fourths used impressionistically and statically; a personal grief becomes universal because it is seen against the eternal joy or lamentation of the bells.

Not only folk-song, but still more Tudor polyphony was for Vaughan Williams a positive value, as it could not be for Holst. The work in which, perhaps, he first found himself—the *Tallis Fantasia*—and the later Mass for double chorus employ antiphonal choirs of strings or voices in almost exactly the same way as Tallis himself used them. But the difference from Holst's organum technique is crucial: for what most fascinates Vaughan Williams in Tudor polyphony is the device of false relation, and this is essentially an interaction of linear and harmonic thought, such as is alien to Holst's music. The *Tallis Fantasia* and the Mass may look like pastiche; but their large-scale structure convinces because Vaughan Williams's obsession with false relation is already implicitly dramatic. These works already intimate the harmonic style of later pieces, such as *Sancta Civitas* (Ex. 59):

Ex. 59. Vaughan Williams: Sancta Civitas

Vaughan Williams's preoccupation with this tonal ambiguity inherent in sixteenth-century style suggests that he was aware that even a man of religious temperament—as Vaughan Williams is and Holst was not—cannot merely go 'back' to the sixteenth century. The Renaissance may be closer to us than the Middle Ages; but the composer still has to face up to the fact that between vocal polyphony and his own time the tremendous phenomenon of the sonata had occurred. Holst evaded the problem, and never attempted to create a work which approximates to the Beethovenian symphony of 'Becoming'. The *Scherzo* which is all he completed of a projected symphony is one of his most remarkable works, but it is a denial of classical symphonic style in that the elements in conflict never attempt a reconciliation. It exists in a state of suspended animation, of deliberate irresolution.

Vaughan Williams, on the other hand, has been preoccupied with the symphony throughout his long life; one might say that the core of his work lies in his attempt to reconcile the dramatic conflict of the symphony with the vocal modality typical of his melodic language. The 'Sea' Symphony, his first effort, hardly comes to grips with the problem, for it is a cross between a German symphony and an English oratorio. Vaughan Williams gained a new insight into the English choral tradition—into Purcell as well as Handel—from the pioneer work of Germanically trained composers, such as Stanford [1852–1924] and Parry [1848–1918]. Even his earliest music has, however, a creative energy far richer than their art, which was a product as much of scholarly study as of life.

The Second, or 'London', Symphony was a more direct attempt to fuse modal thinking with the dramatic symphony; it was but partially successful. In the Third, the 'Pastoral', Symphony of 1922, Vaughan Williams seemed to be relinquishing the attempt to reconcile incompatibles; for even though one may recognize groups of themes which can be equated with the conventional first and second subjects, there is no hint of sonata conflict. The score grows melodically, from monophonic—usually pentatonic—principles, and ends with a wordless human voice, unaccompanied.

Such music seems comparable with works of Holst, like *Egdon Heath*, except that Vaughan Williams's dissolution of the personality achieves a poetic ecstasy, whereas Holst's vocal rhythm is that of prose. None the less, the 'Pastoral' Symphony is a work of symphonic scope. Though it is not an orthodox sonata conflict of keys and motives, its pentatonic lines generate tension through their very independence of one another. The

XLIII
Debussy
From a drawing
by Jean Dulac.

XLIV
Stravinsky
From a drawing
by Picasso in 1920.

XLV
Webern autograph score. A page from *Five pieces for Orchestra*, op. 10.

melodies move on several modal planes simultaneously. There are 'false' relations not only within the triadic harmony, but also between the swaying lines of organum; and Vaughan Williams employs a large orchestra in this almost consistently quiet score precisely because he wants to delineate the melodic strands with the maximum clarity. There is drama beneath the unruffled surface; and this incipiently dramatic linear style finds a more extreme expression in *Flos Campi*, which starts with 'gapped'* arabesques which are specifically bitonal. The form of the work is the slow generation, from the fight between two melodic entities in themselves rhapsodically relaxed, of a spacious, lyrically modal 'theme'.

In *Job* this technique is given direct dramatic presentation; for the story inspired by Blake's reinterpretation of the Book of Job, is objectified in a 'masque for dancing'. In the introduction, describing Job blessing his children, pentatonic arabesques and organum movement suggest a 'state of Nature', while chromatic intrusions perhaps hint at an inner instability. Broad modal lyricism ('Saraband of the Sons of God') expresses the divine attributes of Job's spirit; tritonal progressions, fierce metrical patterns, immense leaps and fourth-founded, triad-disrupting harmony express the Satanic spirit of denial. All the themes are related, because they are all aspects of a single soul. The musical structure of the work is a conflict between forces of good and evil, resolved in the rebirth of pentatonic lyricism in Elihu's 'Dance of Youth and Beauty'. In the 'Galliard of the Sons of the Morning' the pentatonic 'state of Nature' theme becomes a noble modal tune related to the divine theme of the Sons of God. The epilogue restates the work's neutral opening, except that the final cadence replaces an ambiguously modal G minor with the affirmation of B flat. The chromatic instability is still present, however; for though a battle has been won, it is a battle that must be fought again and again in the soul.

Job is not only one of Vaughan's greatest works; it is also a crucial point in his spiritual evolution. Only after this dramatic presentation of conflict could he turn again to the symphonic problem without denying the bases of his art. The Fourth is the most obviously dramatic work Vaughan Williams ever wrote and, in its metrical ferocity and fourth-founded harmony, is

* GAPPED: pentatonic and other primitive modes are sometimes described as 'gapped' because some of the steps in a scalewise progression are missing.

closely related both to Satan's music from *Job* and to Holst's fiercely unresolved *Scherzo*. It is a lesser work than *Job* because the positive elements are here in abeyance; Satan's minor ninths, tritones, assertive metres, and harsh instrumental colours are more violent than they are in *Job*, but the tension is in the long run less, for there is little effective opposition. Perhaps Vaughan Williams had to let Satan have sway symphonically, before he could achieve in symphonic terms the resolution which he had achieved dramatically in *Job*. Certainly that resolution occurs in the Fifth Symphony, a work which is, at last, both modal and genuinely symphonic.

Though the Fifth Symphony is ostensibly in D, it opens with a soft horn-call over an unresolved, modal flat seventh (Ex. 60):

and all the themes are vocal in contour, far more lyrically sustained than Holst's. Traditionally, first and second subjects are associated with the central tonalities of tonic and dominant. Vaughan Williams's modulations are not so much contrast as evolution; the modal behaviour of the themes promotes side-stepping modulations into keys a tone or a semitone apart. Beethoven's modulations to the flat supertonic are dramatic events; Vaughan Williams's are a shift of tonal perspective, occurring as one theme grows into the next. The 'second subject' is an extension of the opening horn call; and it is in E, arrived at by way of E flat (with a hint of C minor).

Such an evolutionary conception of melody and tonality may convince in the exposition; but what is to happen in the development? Vaughan Williams solves this problem—and it was, of course, an instinctive, not a conscious intellectual solution—by not developing the main themes at all. In a much more extreme form, he does what Haydn does in some of his later symphonies. In the codetta of the exposition he introduces a tiny motive—a fall to the flattened second. This chromaticism, usually in the penetrating tone-colour of oboe or cor anglais, naturally generates harmonic tension, as opposed to the lyrical modality of the main themes. The development is founded entirely on this motive, while the modalism of the themes becomes pentatonic arabesques, woven around the increasingly restless modulations. This pentatonic figuration is comparable with that which so frequently appears in the development sections of Sibelius's symphonies; its effect, however, is much more positive, since pentatonicism is a natural part of Vaughan Williams's melodic thought. The ultimate climax, in B flat, is hardly less powerful than that of a Beethoven symphony; but whereas Beethoven's drama implies a conflict between the Will and the forces that impede its fulfilment, in Vaughan Williams's symphony the drama is inherent in the process of growth. The climax of the development leads to a recapitulation, in which the themes soar in liberated lyricism. But the flat seventh on the horn is left suspended. The cycle of birth, growth, and decay is perennial.

The scherzo is a more traditional symphonic movement; and although it follows a key-sequence almost exactly parallel to that of the first movement, the dramatic effect of tonal conflict is much more in evidence. Thematically, the hollow fourths of the F minor Symphony appear again, though they have now become remote and spectral. The fight between Bunyan's Pilgrim and the foul fiends, viewed retrospectively in this diaphanously scored music, has none of the frightening immediacy of the (technically comparable) devil music in *Job*. The movement thus fits the context: for though the symphony is about a battle of the soul, the battle is recollected in tranquillity.

This becomes evident in the last two movements. On the original score of the romanza, Vaughan Williams wrote a quotation from *The Pilgrim's Progress*: "Upon that place there stood a cross and a little below a sepulchre. . . . Then he said: 'He hath given me rest by his sorrow and life by his death'." The movement opens in liturgical diatonicism similar to that of the *Tallis Fantasia*, with modally related concords of C, A, and B flat. Against the string choir the cor anglais sings an Aeolian melody, rising and falling very slowly, step by step. This melody expands, in a distinctly operatic style, into woodwind arabesques. At first pentatonic, these grow increasingly strenuous and chromaticized: until they are lulled to rest by the liturgical music of the opening. The serene close prepares the way for the final passacaglia, which resolves the whole symphony into the unity of the seventeenth-century technique of divisions on a ground. Hints of the alleluias of the Easter hymn *Lasst uns erfreun* had been heard in the Romanza; now they become increasingly obtrusive. When the first theme of the first movement finally reappears, with its unresolved horn-call, we are aware that the melodic material of the whole symphony had been leading towards these consummatory alleluias. And in the Epilogue the alleluias create, at last, a harmonic resolution also. The flat seventh is sharpened. The final resolution of the cadence is the end of what had seemed to be an eternal cycle; so the alleluias of the Epilogue can only herald another life. "When the Day that he must go hence was come, many accompanied him to the River side, into which, as he went, he said Death, where is thy Sting? And as he went down deeper, he said, Grave, where is thy Victory? So he passed over, and the Trumpets sounded for him on the other side." Slowly, almost imperceptibly, entry upon entry, the strings spread out until the vision is fulfilled: it is as though one had found, unawares, that the sky is suddenly filled with angels. Despite the beautiful prologue to Part II of *Gerontius* which so resembles Vaughan Williams, Elgar stops short at the river-bank, as Vaughan Williams does not. Whereas Delius and Holst, in their search for a metaphysical ecstasy, disintegrate cadential resolution, Vaughan Williams discovers it. His greatness consists in his positive assurance.

In the Sixth Symphony modal serenity and the turbulence of sonata conflict are much more sharply opposed, and end in a metreless no-man's-land similar to that of Holst's *Egdon Heath*. In the last movement Vaughan Williams's obsession with false relation is divorced from melodic and harmonic growth, so that the music creates a tension which is paradoxically disembodied. Of all Vaughan Williams's works this is perhaps the most powerfully representative of our time. None the less, the religious assurance of the Fifth Symphony—and to a lesser degree of *Job* and of some choral works, such as *Sancta Civitas* and the *Magnificat*—is the quality that makes his art uniquely valuable; and it is no accident that this assurance should be closely associated with the figure of Bunyan. The Fifth Symphony is intimately related to Vaughan Williams's opera on *The Pilgrim's Progress*. Since he worked on the score for more than thirty years, it is not surprising that reflexions of this great 'liturgical opera' should appear at every period of his career. Bunyan had a profoundly religious, richly traditional mind; yet he was also a product of that Puritan consciousness which, turned sour, helped both to destroy our musical tradition and to create the chaos of the modern world. In Vaughan Williams's music Bunyan is, as it were, reborn in love and charity. The religious assurance of Vaughan Williams's greatest music may place it outside the experience of most of us; yet it is not altogether an eccentric phenomenon in the twentieth century. For Vaughan Williams recovers contact with our cultural tradition at precisely the point in the seventeenth century when it disintegrated. He shows us, not perhaps what we are or can be, but what we might have been. Though we cannot follow his path, we can, with his help, recover our self-respect.

After Vaughan Williams, the English composer may again become a European. His problems are those of his neighbours: those of any society cosmopolitan, eclectic, uprooted. Schoenberg, Hindemith, Stravinsky, and Bartók are probably the greatest composers of our time, as they are certainly the most influential. In discussing them, we shall come up against most of the issues involved in twentieth-century music. It is worth noting that they have all been deracinated, one of them twice.

7

SCHOENBERG AND HINDEMITH

We may perhaps usefully approach the four central figures in modern music by way of a composer who seems marginal: yet in whose career we find an allegory of the position of the twentieth-century artist. Busoni [1866–1924] was a man of prodigious personal force and intellectual distinction; yet the impact of his creative and intellectual power was less than it might have been, because he was culturally and spiritually divided. Born in Italy, he was educated in Germany; torn between two traditions, he belonged to neither. His rootlessness was emphasized by his career as a concert pianist. He was one of the greatest—and most creative—pianists of all time; and the familiar tug-of-war between career and creative ambition assumes, with him, a peculiarly poignant form. For his career involved creative activity of a kind, while frustrating in him another and more important creativity.

If we take the E minor Violin Sonata (1899) as representative of the first phase of his work, we can see how the basis of his style was the Teutonic tradition of Beethoven and Brahms; yet the sun-baked vitality of Verdian operatic lyricism was already in conflict with this northern introspection. The first phase of his work culminates in the mammoth Piano Concerto (1908): in which work we can observe how his hero Liszt was the catalyst who showed him how the Italian and German traditions might be fused. Yet what appealed especially to Busoni was the necromantic quality in Liszt's virtuosity: his ability to 'possess' and recreate other composers and other traditions. Busoni was always seeking a spiritual home, trying to accommodate his personal experience to that of other men and other traditions; this became increasingly difficult as he grew more deeply conscious of his isolation.

The Piano Concerto is thus the last of his works which attempts a relationship with the classical tradition: with the sonata principle as the musical synonym for 'Becoming'. The piano Elegies (1908–9) inaugurate a new phase in his work which may be related to the late piano pieces of Liszt. The Elegies are richer and more developed than Liszt's disintegrative epigrams, but they have the same pathological queerness: the Italian *cantilena* that breaks into stuttering recitative; the bitonal washes of piano 'colour' in the accompanying figurations; the persistent ambiguity between major and minor third; the abrupt distortion of tonal perspective that suggests a glimpse into another world. In the *Berceuse* the multi-plane figuration may be compared with that in Liszt's *La Lugubre Gondole*: it seems to carry us, in its lulling rhythm, away from the earth into space. But space is an airy void, rather than a heaven: for there is no lyrical fruition. In *Die Nächtlichen* a similar technique draws us into a murky night of the spirit. The first, traditional phase of Busoni's work was summed up in the Piano Concerto. This second phase is consummated not in a work associated with German sonata style, but in an opera, *Die Brautwahl* (1914). Significantly, Busoni's libretto deals, not with any of the traditional operatic themes, but with the artist as visionary.

Liszt was not, however, the only composer who had fused Italian and German traditions. German polyphony and Italian *cantilena* meet in the music of Bach, whose art represented an ideal spiritual resolution towards which Busoni aspired. The Elegies had included a chorale fantasia which became a starting point for the *Fantasia Contrappuntistica*, Busoni's completion of the unfinished 'problem' of Bach's *Art of Fugue*. Henceforth, Busoni's search for order becomes basically contrapuntal: though his counterpoint cannot in fact be the same as Bach's. In Bach the ultimate order and serenity of the counterpoint is inseparable from an inner turbulence contained in the complex harmonic texture; it is because Bach's serenity involves such profound suffering, as well as joy, that it means so much. In a passage from Busoni's counterpoint such as Ex. 61 the separation of the lines on, as it were, different planes of tonality creates an effect strangely disembodied, suggesting a deliberate withdrawal from experience. This phase of Busoni's work was again consummated in a large-scale work—the opera *Dr. Faustus* (1916–24), a highly personal reinterpretation of the Faust myth which emphasizes the isolated artist's visionary significance far more than *Die Brautwahl.* The tenuous polyphony and polyphonically derived harmony and orchestration of *Dr. Faustus* are a moving and disturbing experience, in which

Ex.61. Busoni: Fantasia Contrappuntistica

the almost continuous false relations suggest the enigmatic, equivocal quality in this personal vision. Perhaps it is not surprising that this music should have had so great an influence on later composers who are likewise isolated, in quest of serenity: and that at the same time the vision should remain in essence incommunicable.

A modern composer cannot start from the same point as Bach, as though everything represented by the sonata principle had never happened. Busoni used to say that middle-period Beethoven and Wagner between them brought ruin on music, Beethoven through his rhetoric, Wagner through his lasciviousness. He hardly convinces us, however, that his purged world of the spirit could satisfy most fallible mortals as richly as the symphonic Beethoven or as Wagner; and there is no valid connexion between his visionary serenity and that of Beethoven's last quartets. Beethoven, as we saw, won through to his 'monistic' serenity through sonata conflict; Busoni—in the 'disembodied' polyphony of his late style—suggests that the visionary moment is an *alternative* to the turmoil of world, flesh, and devil.

Busoni's single-minded integrity is itself conditioned by his art's limitations; the sense of solitude and the search after the personal, visionary moment are manifest in the work and career of all the great central figures in twentieth-century music, even in those who, like Schoenberg, were born into a long musical tradition. For, like Mahler, Schoenberg [1874–1951] was a Jew, and in that sense an isolated spirit. Whatever his ultimate stature may be, it is no longer possible to doubt his crucial position in European history. He was the heir to Wagner: who was the heir to Beethoven: who inherited the traditions of the classical sonata. Now both Beethoven and Wagner, we saw in Part III, had been preoccupied with the assertion of the ego. Beethoven, however, in his last works had appeased the fury of the Will by reconciling the sonata principle with its apparent opposite—the unity of fugue and of aria variation; in so doing he had created a new kind of religious art wherein we may understand, with Kant, how we may 'live in an invisible church', since 'god's kingdom is in ourselves'. Wagner, on the other hand, came to deify the ego itself in its most fundamental impulse, that of sex; had derived a whole cosmos from the surge of erotic feeling through his nerves and senses; and had ultimately come to admit the paradox inherent in such dedication to the self—the inescapable association of life-instinct with death-instinct, of love with guilt, of passion with renunciation. This being so, we can understand why one part of Wagner's legacy should have been a search for oblivion: such as we find in the music of Delius. But we can also understand why any composer, looking to the future from the heights or depths of the Wagnerian crisis, had to seek a renewal of life within the psyche itself. We can observe the beginnings of this in one of Schoenberg's earliest works, *Verklärte Nacht*, originally for string sextet.

This piece tells a story (based on a poem of Richard Dehmel) which is closely related to the theme of *Tristan*. A woman and her lover walk, through the night, in a wood. She bears within her the child of the husband she does not love; but the beauty of the moonlit night transfigures both sensuality and guilt, so that they do not, like Tristan and Isolde, die in the flesh. Their passion is spiritualized and they can accept the husband's baby as mankind's fulfilled sensuality and in that sense as the fruit of their own love. The metamorphosis of physical into mystical experience is directly reflected in the musical technique. For although the piece is of continuous, chromatic-harmonic, Tristanesque texture, the lines attain an ever-increasing degree of independence. The further they flow from the introverted harmonic tensions—the more freely they leap and sing—the more ecstatically transfigured the night becomes. This is why the piece is in effect so different from the Straussian symphonic poem that it superficially resembles. Despite the highly charged, harmonic nature of Schoenberg's music the structure, even in this early work, involves genuine polyphonic thinking: whereas Strauss's polyphony, which is not less elaborate, could be removed without completely destroying the sense. As with Mahler, this development in texture is also a development in experience: a search for a more spiritual, even mystical, resolution of the Wagnerian crisis within the Self.*

This technical evolution is still more evident in those early works which Schoenberg scored for an orchestra even more gargantuan than that of Strauss. Strauss scores superbly, but as a harmonist; and there are passages in the music of his middle years in which the orchestral polyphony, in obscuring the harmonic structure, defeats its own ends. Mahler and Schoenberg score with impeccable lucidity; however complex the texture, the lines are aurally intelligible. Wagner and Strauss think polyphonically in the sense that their harmony is composed of a number of interdependent strands; Mahler and Schoenberg think polyphonically in the sense that polyphony becomes itself a contributory means of order. The chromatic harmony is a tonal disintegration; to compensate for this, the whirling lines seek contrapuntal organization among themselves. The enormous scores of the *Gurrelieder* and of *Pelléas*—vast symphonic operas without stage action—sound as rhapsodically sensuous as Wagner. Yet the interweaving parts are full of contrapuntal devices of a complexity and ingenuity rivalling that of the unjustly maligned and misnamed 'Netherland' polyphonists.

It was well-nigh inevitable that, as his music grew increasingly chromatic, Schoenberg should turn from the mammoth orchestra to chamber music. In the first two string quartets and the First Chamber Symphony, the chromaticism has

* A comparable 'spiritualization' of Wagnerian harmonic polyphony occurs in the music of Hans Pfitzner [1869–1949]; but with him erotic sensuality is modified by deep respect for the social and religious values of the past. It is revealing that his finest, most representative work should be an opera, *Palestrina*, concerned with the life of a Renaissance humanist who, as composer, was also a man of the Church. Perhaps one might say that the piece stands halfway between *Parsifal* and the ascetic mysticism of Busoni's *Faustus*.

become inherent in the contours of the lines. Though the works all start from a tonal basis, there are passages in which the lines modulate so rapidly that they seem not to modulate at all. We lose consciousness of a tonal centre; and to offset this instability, Schoenberg emphasizes linear means of construction. Though the lines in these works are even freer than those in the big orchestral pieces, being characterized by enormous leaps and irregular rhythmic groupings similar to those in Mahler, they are subjected to elaborate contrapuntal treatment. Counterpoint is becoming more important, as an organizing principle, than the progression of tonal roots. It is significant that in the First Chamber Symphony Schoenberg strongly stresses the interval of the fourth, at the expense of the traditional triad.

At the time, Schoenberg probably did not appreciate the full implications of his preoccupation with counterpoint; he was more concerned with linear chromaticism than with the new principle of order it might entail. His next works, at least, appear to move in a contrary direction. He strives above all to make his disintegrative chromatic lines expressive in themselves, divorced from tonal implications or from any external organization. Wagner's last works and his own early music, he argued, had expanded tonality so far that it was possible to introduce into a given key any note foreign to that key. If a key can be expressed as well by other notes as by those proper to it, can it be said to exist? To talk of any notes as being foreign to the key is nonsensical, for harmony is simply a sounding together of tones. It is therefore time to create a music which accepts the twelve equal-tempered semitones as of equal significance, without reference to tonal concepts based on the triad.

Music composed thus empirically must either be confined to pieces of very short duration, or must serve as illustration to a literary text. In the *Buch der hängenden Gärten*, Schoenberg sets Stefan George's poems to a vocal line that is as much speech as song, while the piano offers a 'nervous' commentary on the text, without reference to traditional tonality, without relation to the vocal line, and even without repetitions of phrase. The fragmentary lines and harmonies are to be quintessentially expressive: feeling in itself, unmodified by traditional usage or even by the artist's conscious volition. Similarly, the third piano piece of opus 11 and the tiny pieces of opus 19 carry Debussy's 'seismographic' technique to an even more extreme point. The second piece of opus 19, for instance, is a study in the aural effect of the interval of the third, in which the interval is even more disembodied, more remote from a tonal context, than it is in Debussy's *Les Tierces Alternées*. It is true that the pieces of opus 19 are not as surrealist in approach as the *Buch der hängenden Gärten*, for the quivering sonorities are full of discreet contrapuntal imitations. None the less, the fact that Schoenberg regarded the exquisite final piece as bell-music—a funeral bell tolling for Mahler's death—suggests that the music is apprehensible only as a moment of sensation, and is of its nature incapable of development (Ex. 62):

Debussy evaded this dilemma by a compromise with tonality and tradition. For Schoenberg, compromise was impossible. For him there were only two ways out. One was to ally music not merely with a literary text, but with the stage, so that coherence, development, climax could be provided by the dramatic element. This was only a stop-gap, for it left unsolved the problem of musical form. The other way out was to discover a new principle of order, to take the place of that which Wagner's and Schoenberg's chromaticism seemed to have discredited. At first, Schoenberg worked towards these two ends simultaneously. We can see this in his operatic monologue *Erwartung*, which deals with a story closely related both to *Tristan* and to *Verklärte Nacht*.

The libretto was written by Marie Pappenheim from the composer's own suggestions; and the piece is an operatic work that makes explicit the implications of *Tristan* and *The Ring* in that there is only one character, within whose mind the action takes place. Again a woman is wandering 'through the blind mazes of this tangled wood'. She is possessed by a sexual passion of Tristanesque violence. Waiting to meet her lover in the wood, she seems at the same time to know that he will not come: that he has deserted her for a ghostly white-armed other love (probably, psychoanalytically speaking, his mother). The climax comes when she stumbles on his murdered body. It is not clear who murdered him; she refers, confusedly, to the other woman and to an indeterminate 'they'. But it is unclear because, of course, the action has no real existence outside her mind. She enters the dark wood of the unconscious; and the first stages of her wandering are a mingling of her memories and inchoate desires. Her discovery of the body is her recognition of loss: and complementarily of guilt and renunciation. From this point the unconscious takes over completely; text and music become hallucinatory. Yet the pattern established by *Tristan* and *Verklärte Nacht* is continued: for submission to the unconscious brings release from terror; and the piece ends with a 'transfigured' vision of her lover, wherein passion is fulfilled, hatred forgotten.

This fulfilment exists, of course, only in the music. The vocal line carries Wagnerian song-speech into realms of the most intense expressiveness, as it follows the vagaries of the half-thinking, half-feeling mind. The orchestral texture—with its high degree of dissonance, its lack of traditional tonal organization, its extraordinary polyphonic density and complexity—expresses the gradual disintegration of mind and senses. At the same time, the resilience and power of the lines created out of apparent dislocation, the radiant luminosity of the orchestral fabric, convey a fundamental affirmation. Tenderness and strength are inextricable in the passage in the second scene when she thinks of her meeting with her lover in the walled garden; ineffably moving is the cry of longing she utters at the end when she imagines she sees her lover, and the sensory life of the orchestral texture dissolves away in contrary motion chromatics. It is difficult to know what to call this if it is not, as well as a moment of vision, an act of faith.

So although Schoenberg's disintegration of tonality is in one sense a breakdown within the consciousness, it is also a step towards liberation and rebirth. It is not an accident that Schoenberg was born and worked in the same city as Freud. He starts (like Wagner) from the primary human urge of sexuality; he faces up to a hiatus in the flow of creative vitality that man's dedication to Self has led him into; then he seeks a linear and polyphonic integration of the chromatically splintered fragments of mind and senses. It is not extravagant to say that there is a relationship between this search for integration and the Freudian reintegration of the dislocated facets of a personality; and both have affinities with what used to be called religious experience.

So Schoenberg's invention of the twelve-note or serial technique was at once a technical and a spiritual necessity. The technical need was simply that, since the traditional tonal basis of European music seemed, after Wagner, to be played out, a new principle of order was essential if composers were to construct works of reasonable dimensions. In the world of the equal-tempered semitone this principle cannot be harmonic. It must, therefore, be linear; so Schoenberg's early preoccupation with counterpoint answered to a deep need of his nature. In the later works of his 'expressionist' period, such as *Pierrot Lunaire*, we find that the declamation of a literary text is accompanied not by an empirical sound-commentary, but by a tenuously scored tissue of fragmentary motives, all related by the most elaborate canonic devices. The literary meaning of the poems concerns the Pierrot-figure as symbol of the sick, broken spirit of modern man; but the music—even more that that of *Erwartung*—achieves a radiant wholeness and compassion out of its apparently fragmentary complexity. The musical commentary seeks its own order in becoming a principle of perpetual variation. From his earliest years, Schoenberg had thus tended to think 'serially'; nor was the serial principle itself new. All that was new was the consistency with which the principle was to be applied. In twelve-note music every note in a composition is part of a variation, or rather a permutation, of a given series; every note is conditioned by linear, not harmonic, relationship.

The basis of a twelve-note composition is what came to be known as the 'row'—a specific arrangement of the twelve chromatic semitones. The row is not a theme, nor need it be aurally apprehensible. It is not a scale, though it serves some of the functions of a mode in that all the melodic material of the piece and to some extent the harmony is derived from the row and its permutations (the series inverted, or backwards, or backwards and inverted). Notes of the row cannot normally be repeated out of their order in the series, since concentration on one note might suggest a tonic. Consecutive members of the series can be combined to form chords. The row may be transposed to any pitch, and divided between the parts. Sometimes the row may consist of two segments of six notes, or three segments of four notes.

Schoenberg has said that the row is a linear means of organizing tones which concerns the composer rather than the listener. Far from being an arbitrary sequence of notes, it is the creative germ from which the composer derives themes and harmonies. Its relation to what is commonly called 'inspiration' is at least as intrinsic as the relation between inspiration and the seminal motives which Beethoven jotted down in his sketch-books; the composer's liberty of choice is neither more nor less limited than in tonally organized music. At first the rows selected would tend to be divorced from harmonic implications, for, in creating a purely chromatic music, it was necessary to avoid suggestions of diatonicism. Yet Berg, even after he adopted the twelve-note technique, tended to use rows which included major and minor triads, and therefore made possible some compromise with traditional tonality. In the elegiac Violin Concerto he can even introduce a Bach chorale, in Bach's original harmonization, without committing a stylistic solecism —and without entirely surrendering the row.

Schoenberg was probably right in thinking that this kind of compromise, though appropriate to Berg's relatively regressive, romantic temperament, was not intrinsically desirable; for the more the row compromises with traditional tonality the less need would there seem to be for any purely linear means of organizing the semitone. None the less, Schoenberg increasingly came to feel that even in music constructed serially the composer had, from these linear relationships, to discover his own tonal criteria. The lower members of the harmonic series may not have the importance in our tonal thinking that they once had; yet the harmonic series itself remains a scientific fact. There must still be a relationship between the 'horizontal' and the 'vertical' aspects of music; and although a purely chromatic tonality is still in process of evolution, the harmony in Schoenberg's 'purest' serial works is never fortuitous. Far less than Debussy does Schoenberg, in most of his mature works, break with traditional notions of harmonic progression. In the opening of the Fourth Quartet the music acquires richness and intensity because each harmony and accompanying figuration, being serially derived, is related to the main melody. But the passage is aurally intelligible because the main melody is immediately recognizable as such, not so much because it has a D minorish tinge as because it is sharply defined in rhythm: because the 'accompanying' parts also have a clearly defined rhythm and proceed in ways related to the traditional treatment of leading notes and appoggiaturas (Ex. 63):*

The serially derived superimposed fifths at the end of the wonderful Violin Concerto are a similar example: we do not need to listen to this music with new ears—as we do with the music of some of Schoenberg's successors—to perceive that its harmonic logic parallels its serial integrity.

It is unfortunate that, for valid historical reasons, Schoenberg has encouraged us to talk more about his system than about his music. All musical techniques are artificial, artefacts that

* For a detailed analysis of this passage see the article by Oliver Neighbour published in *The Score* for June 1956.

are man-made. If a twelve-note composer works within preconceived patterns, so does a pentatonic or a diatonic composer. It is true that the pentatonic scale is related to more fundamental acoustical facts than the chromatic, and that there is a difference between Mozart's equal-tempered chromaticism and Schoenberg's. It is true that mental vocalization is the means whereby themes become memorable, and that not all our familiarity with equal-tempered scales can alter the fact that a purely chromatic music is difficult to memorize because it is difficult to sing. Yet it is also true that Schoenberg's music becomes tonally viable when we have listened to it enough; and that—as he pointed out—singers find his music comprehensible and performable when they have acquired a consciousness of the row, which indirectly conditions the music's tonal logic in directly conditioning its linear structure.

This is why an abstract work like the Violin Concerto can move us deeply, and in the same way as a piece such as *A Survivor from Warsaw*, in which we have a speaker's verbal language and an urgently topical subject to help us. It is profoundly significant that in Schoenberg's later chamber works—such as the Third and Fourth Quartets and the String Trio—the Wagnerian resolution of his early works should come to terms with the 'religious' resolution of late Beethoven. They are the same *kind* of music as Beethoven's last quartets (which also use serial processes): though they do not enter Beethoven's paradise. They seek 'God's kingdom', which exists below the level of consciousness, along with nameless horrors and fears; and in this sense all Schoenberg's music is basically religious, and related to the unfinished opera, *Moses und Aaron*, on which he worked for so many years. In this work Schoenberg associates himself—as Freud had done also—with Moses, the spirit's deliverer, as against Aaron, the man of practical affairs. He creates music which is not only overwhelmingly dramatic, but also lyrical, and both technically and spiritually lucid. His Jewish fanaticism—which was also his 'modern' isolation—becomes the new world of the spirit at which Mahler's orchestral polyphony had hinted. And although Schoenberg could not complete the opera's vision of man regenerated, the integrity of his search remains truly heroic—from *Erwartung's* final cry of 'Ich suchte' to the tortured but undespairing polyphony of his last work: a *De Profundis*.

The new world that Schoenberg seeks, springing as it does from the decay of the past, gives him his central significance in the history of our time. We do not find this 'centrality' in the more readily accessible, but more elegiacally limited, music of his pupil, Alban Berg [1885–1935]. Romantically, Berg's music is half in love with the 'decadence' it reflects, and technically compromises between past and present as Schoenberg's music does not; none the less, Berg does renew decadence, if not with Schoenberg's religious intensity, at least with compassion. This we can see in his best-known and perhaps most representative work, the opera *Wozzeck*, which although not produced until 1925, after the appearance of Schoenberg's first twelve-note pieces, had been conceived, and partially composed, many years earlier. It is thus (significantly) an instance of the transitional phase between free atonality and the serial principle.

It is based on a play by George Büchner, a writer of precocious genius who was born in 1813 and died in his twenty-third year. Büchner lived through an era of appalling political oppression. He was typical of his time in the intensity of his response to suffering, not altogether typical in his unromantic acceptance of it. By the time of Schoenberg and Berg pessimism had become an accredited romantic attitude; but their pessimism was also a valid response to a sick world. Berg's *Wozzeck*, like Büchner's, is peopled by beings obsessed with neurotic terrors: the megalomaniac doctor who regards human beings merely as subjects for clinical dissertation and who, in Büchner's play, though not in Berg's opera, has the last word; the power-addict, the silly-sinister drum-major; and Wozzeck himself, the eternal scapegoat. The story, presented not in developing narrative but in a series of 'impressions', tells how the wretched Wozzeck is goaded by his 'superiors' into murdering his unfaithful mistress, who, slut though she may be, is his one hold on humanity. It is as gloom-crazed as any product of German expressionism; yet though Büchner's world is decadent, his play is not. Compassion, not hysteria, comes of the torment. Büchner was justified when he said: "I have always turned on suffering, downtrodden humanity more glances of compassion than I have expended bitter words on the cold hearts of those in authority."

No theme could have better suited Berg's nervously sensitive temperament. His music, like the play, is simultaneously decadent and revolutionary. In some respects his method is Wagnerian for—like Schoenberg in *Erwartung*—he gives a minute musical illustration of the drama. Each character has his motive, developed both as psychological commentary and as part of the musical structure. Some recurrent phrases—such as that which Wozzeck first sings to the words "Wir arme Leut" —have a kind of ideological significance comparable with that of Wagner's 'Ring' or 'Sword' motives. Like Wagner, Berg concentrates the psychological drama in the elaborate orchestral part. The vocal lines have their origin in Wagnerian declamation, but approximate much more closely to the speaking voice, or at least to the voices of speakers who are distraught. They range from passionate but brief lyrical outbursts to passages which, modelled on Schoenberg's 'free' atonal works with speaker and instruments, are more spoken than sung.

At the same time, however, as he pursues this psychological realism, Berg strives to impose on the drama a purely musical shape. Thus the opening scene is in the form of a classical suite (prelude, pavane, gigue, and gavotte with two 'doubles');* the scene in the doctor's study is a passacaglia; the opening of Act II is described as being in sonata form; while Act III takes the form of six inventions in different types of variation technique. Some of these forms are perhaps valid only on paper. The classical suite and sonata depend so much on a conception of tonality which Schoenberg and Berg had repudiated that it is doubtful if they can have aural meaning. They may suggest to the composer phrase-groupings, effects of balance and repetition, even—in the case of the sonata—transpositions of motives collateral to modulation; but the absence of a tonal centre and the non-metrical nature of the rhythm mean that the form, architecturally considered, is not normally perceptible to the listener. Essentially the organization is linear, not architectural; and is therefore not radically different from Berg's experiments towards a completely thematic technique by way of variation, passacaglia, and fugue. As early as this transitional work we can see how appropriate are these linear forms to Berg's conception of music drama: consider the association of the doctor's *idée fixe* with the obsessive ostinato of the passacaglia.

What strikes one most forcibly about *Wozzeck*, as one looks

* DOUBLE: a repeat with ornamental modifications. See Part II, p. 535.

back at it after thirty years, is the flexibility of the technique. There are many sections, such as the scarifying scene in the copse, which now seem to belong to the ripely autumnal world of Strauss, though the highly charged emotion is expressed with an orchestral translucence more suggestive of Mahler or, quite often, Debussy. Yet *Wozzeck* achieves consistency of style. *Elektra*-like chromaticized diatonicism exists alongside extreme atonal passages without incongruity, just as the distorted, banal military music outside Marie's window is no more an anachronism in this fear-haunted world than is the almost diatonic lullaby she croons to her child. Once again, creativity renews decay. Though we do not know what will happen to him, the child at the close remains innocent in his play, as the water engulfs his father. Similarly, Berg's 'decadent' technique hints at a world of pure chromaticism that still awaited exploration in the mature music of Schoenberg and Webern.

While we may think that Schoenberg's response to chromatic disintegration faces up most squarely to the 'humanist crisis' of our time, it does not follow that all compromise with the past is 'decadent'. One of Schoenberg's senior pupils—born in the same year as Berg—provides a link between complete chromaticism and the re-created diatonicism of a composer such as Hindemith. As a young man in Vienna, Egon Wellesz [b. 1885] was associated with both Mahler and Schoenberg, but made his mark with theatrical works—ballets and operas on classical themes—that achieved an equilibrium between Schoenbergian chromaticism and conceptions of tonality suggested by Wellesz's researches into Byzantine monody and seventeenth-century opera. Both Byzantine music and heroic opera were ritualistic forms of art, one liturgical, the other secular; and whereas Mahler and Schoenberg were Jews whose religion was part of a Faustian struggle towards self-awareness, Wellesz is a Roman Catholic with a deep respect for religious and cultural tradition. It is significant that both the church music and the five symphonies which he has created comparatively late in life resemble Bruckner's in fusing sonata style's dualistic tonal conflict and kinetic motor rhythms with 'baroque' counterpoint and types of melodic organization derived from medieval cantillation. Perhaps the contradictory elements are juxtaposed rather than fused: on which fact depends the emotional and physical strenuousness of the composer's affirmation. One finds something similar in the music of Hindemith: for although his music does not share Wellesz's Catholic mysticism and Austrian lyricism, it attempts to subdue twentieth-century tensions to a concept of unity which is not, like Schoenberg's, discovered within the psyche, but is inherited from the past.

So although Hindemith [b. 1895] started, like Schoenberg, against the background of German romanticism, he was always more in sympathy with the classical tradition than with Wagner. Both Schoenberg and Hindemith had much in common with the elegiac gravity of Brahms; but whereas Schoenberg was interested in the revolutionary potentialities of Brahms's cross-rhythms and elliptical harmonies, Hindemith saw in Brahms the romantic heir to classical tradition. In so far as Wagnerian chromaticism affected him, it was by way of the pseudo-contrapuntal chromaticism of Reger [1873–1916].

The texture of Reger's music is no less complex than that of Strauss or early Schoenberg; but his chromatic elaboration did not follow Tristan into a transfigured night. He did not even attempt to romanticize the symphonic ideal; instead, he sought to control his chromaticism by a deliberate re-creation of pre-symphonic forms, relating his chromaticism, as Liszt had sometimes done, to that of Bach. In so doing, he created intermittently some moving and powerful music, while evading the central problem of form and tonality in his day. The subject of Bach's B minor Fugue from Book I of *The Forty-eight* includes every note of the chromatic scale, and the texture of the music looks superficially like that of a fugue by Reger. But Bach preserves continuity of line and tonal direction through all the chromatic vagaries; indeed, the form of his fugue is synonymous with the tension between the tonal progression and the apparent disintegration of the lines. Reger's fugues nearly always lack both tonal direction and linear continuity: so that, for all the growing elaboration of the parts and the piling up of *stretti*, they seem to be without climax. They have neither true contrapuntal form, nor Wagner's cumulative harmonic logic. One might even suggest that Reger is most impressive when he is least in awe of Bach: in large-scale works like the lovely Mozart or Hiller Variations in which, though avoiding the symphonic problem, he has a lilting cantabile lyricism to give buoyancy to the chromatic texture; or in works like the piano sonatinas, in which the modest proportions make the texture subtly sensitive rather than extravagantly rich.

In his most Bachian works Reger was attempting to put new wine into old bottles; and Hindemith soon became aware—emotionally if not intellectually—that if the composer today is to create a music convincingly contrapuntal in the same sense as Bach's music, it can only be within a tonal scheme as relevant to our world as Bach's was to his. Wagner may lead ultimately to a purely chromatic, serial technique; Bach never can, even though in his last chorale prelude he creates a completely thematic—and in that sense a serial—composition.

The first phase of Hindemith's discovery of Bach, which was also a discovery of himself, was perhaps mainly negative and corrective. Schoenberg found a new objectivity through accepting all the implications of his romantic individualism; Hindemith began by wilfully suppressing personal feeling. If the twentieth century wanted Utility music, he would provide it. Of course, his functional music did not really serve any function; he was a craftsman making solidly constructed chairs that no one would sit on, because they were not the commercially accepted shape. Moreover, a responsible artist cannot really believe that music is *merely* utilitarian, any more than he can discard his self-consciousness to become primitive and unreasoning. Yet Hindemith's utilitarian phase was of great significance in his development, and its importance was analogous to that of the primitive phase in the careers of Stravinsky and Bartók. In each case the primitive or utilitarian diverted attention from the self-regarding ego. Music became a creative act. In becoming ritualist or craftsman the composer encouraged forgetfulness of self; and this was a prelude to a fresh creative impulse.

Hindemith's utilitarian music has a direct bearing on the 'serious' music which he composed during the 1920s, for the preoccupation with sharp, hard sonorities and with continuous motor-rhythms which he learned from jazz became absorbed into neo-baroque techniques. Such sonorities and motor-rhythms gained a fresh vivacity when they served to discipline melodic lines of a nervous compulsive energy, or of unexpected tenderness. The tingling acidity of the *Konzertmusik* for piano and brass becomes an emotional rejuvenation; so in a different way does the lyrical *cantilena* for the solo instrument in the

Chamber Concerto for viola. A deliberately sharp, 'inexpressive' tone-colour, a deliberately stylized, quasi-baroque melodic pattern, a deliberately archaic structure usually veering to an ostinato or canonic device, become stimulating, even revolutionary in impact. The lines are aggressively diatonic, the rhythms metrically rigid; yet the mechanical patterns of the counterpoint create an acutely dissonant texture. If the music is only intermittently sensitive, it preserves a high degree of vitality.

In this music Hindemith creates a counterpoint which, while resembling the surface of Bach's texture, makes no attempt to achieve Bach's tension between line and harmony. On the contrary, the disturbing quality of the music depends on the apparently fortuitous way in which the parts bump into one another. The more Hindemith came to understand the spirit of Bach's art, however, the more he attempted to create lines which, like Bach's, imply their own harmony. First, he experimented with a number of works for solo stringed instruments; the difference between these pieces and Reger's suites for unaccompanied stringed instruments is interesting. The Reger works are simply pastiche of Bach; they add nothing to his technique and have not, of course, his genius. The Hindemith works emulate Bach's method; but the harmony their line implies expands the 'tonal universe' within which Bach worked, for Bach's world was still basically diatonic, whereas Hindemith wrote in the wake of Wagnerian chromaticism. When Hindemith began to combine several such lines polyphonically, in large-scale chamber or orchestral works or in operas, he produced a texture comparable with that of Busoni's later works. Hindemith's piano sonatas and Busoni's *Sonatina in Diem Nativitatis Christi*, for instance, are neither of them sonatas in the classical sense; and their transparent, luminous texture depends on an unusual degree of independence between the lines, which sometimes implies bitonality. But whereas in Busoni the 'separateness' of the lines grew sharper in his later music, in Hindemith the separate lines increasingly seek for harmonic relationships. These relationships are flexible and complex; but a new Bachian polyphony must inevitably entail a new concept of tonality, adequate to our time.

It was this that induced Hindemith to work out a theory of tonality which, being based on the harmonic series, was derived from scientific facts, but which offered a means of evaluating all possible combinations that could occur in music, whether modal, diatonic, or chromatic. If he is right, a composer will be able to employ any harmonic or melodic combination, while being able to assess its significance in relation to a criterion of tonality. He will know that some intervals, some melodic shapes, are more stable, more convincing, than others in a given context; and he will know why. The 'meanings' which the symbols of music have will be basically the same as those understood by Bach or any other composer. But it will be possible to relate to a criterion combinations and procedures of which Bach could not have been aware.

Hindemith has attempted to provide for the twentieth century a theoretical basis to composition similar to that which Rameau offered to the eighteenth century. It is a theory of tonality, not—like Schoenberg's serial technique—a method of composition; but, like Schoenberg's method, it was deduced from the composer's creative practice, and it certainly has a direct bearing on the way a composer works. Hindemith wrote *Ludus Tonalis*—a series of fugues and interludes for piano—to demonstrate his theory of tonality in much the same spirit as Bach wrote *The Forty-eight* to demonstrate equal temperament. It is a pedagogical work which is also fine music; nor is it fortuitous that Hindemith's most representative work—the opera *Mathis der Maler*—should be that which most clearly reveals that his technique is a chromatically expanded, logically disciplined, continuation of the German tradition of Bach, Schütz, and the sixteenth-century polyphonists. The theme of the opera is that the Artist, as the representative of truly creative Tradition, is indeed the 'unacknowledged legislator' of the world.

On the other hand, it seems possible that Hindemith, having evolved his theory, has in later years sometimes been tempted to write music to fit it. The more vocal, modal quality of his lines, the smoother harmony, the more fluent polyphony are not necessarily more convincing because they obey Hindemith's 'degree-progressions'. One may certainly question whether the revised version of the *Marienlieder* is an improvement on the original; and it is interesting to note that the finest song in the cycle, the deeply impressive passacaglia-like *Pieta*, is the only song that Hindemith left virtually untouched. Hindemith would like to think that his scheme of tonality represents a cosmos as universally applicable as that within which Bach worked: perhaps more so, because it is evolved with superior scientific knowledge. There is, however, little evidence that it is being universally adopted. It probably has fewer adherents than Schoenberg's pure chromaticism, which, according to Hindemith, is tonally arbitrary and, strictly speaking, nonsensical. That does not seem to be an adequate account of Schoenberg's music, though there are good and bad composers in any system. In the long run, the system does not matter. Such music of Schoenberg and Hindemith as may survive will probably prove that they have more in common than either would wish or suspect.

8

STRAVINSKY AND BARTÓK

Schoenberg and Hindemith both worked within the German—which was the main European—tradition. Stravinsky [b.1882], as a Russian, never came directly under the sway of the symphonic principle or of Wagnerian chromaticism. In his student days he was a pupil of Rimsky-Korsakov; and such tonal disintegration as occurs in his early work is associated, like Rimsky-Korsakov's, with the evocation of a Russian fairyland. The tritonal theme of King Kastchei in *The Firebird* is one example; the elaborate, but significantly more linear, chromaticism of the later fairy opera, *The Nightingale*, is another.

Even in his earliest music, however, we can observe a tendency to reintegrate traditional materials in untraditional ways. The horizontalization of chords, producing two or more harmonic streams that proceed independently of one another, is a typical method, which we have already noted in such composers as Holst and Vaughan Williams. As with Holst again, Stravinsky's partiality for bitonal effects is basically a linear, rather than a harmonic, habit; frequently—as in the notorious clash between the triads of C and F sharp in *Petrouchka*—the effect is neither linear nor harmonic, but percussive. The 'noise' is expanded into a long piano cadenza: much as Satie will construct a whole piece out of the alternation of two chords.

The influence of Rimsky-Korsakov on Stravinsky was no more than superficial. Soon he discovered that his Russian heritage had a deep relationship to the isolated sensibility of the twentieth century. We have remarked that the most distinctive feature of Russian history was that Russia had no Renaissance; to a Russian, therefore, the preoccupation with personal feeling, characteristic of most European art between the sixteenth and twentieth centuries, seemed comparatively extraneous. He was more prone to think of his art in terms of ritual and liturgy; and

Stravinsky gradually became imaginatively aware that such a ritualistic approach might be an answer to the disrupted self-consciousness of the modern world.

The first evidence of this is in the works directly inspired by primitive ritual. Even in *Petrouchka* a modern isolation is embodied not in a human being, but in a puppet, whose tragedy is enacted against the impersonal, ritual-like background of folk-incantation. By the time of *The Rite of Spring* and *The Wedding* the patterns the composer imposes on his material are almost exclusively metrical. In opposition to the chromatic flux, he insists on the validity of metre; for the wildest metrical eccentricity is conceivable only in relation to a norm. Thus all the elements of music are adapted to reinforce rhythm. Line is reduced to a series of insistently repeated modal patterns the effect of which is dynamic and incantatory; harmony becomes percussive; instrumentation is exploited for its physical and nervous impact. The long passages of parallel seconds, thirds, fourths, fifths, sixths, sevenths, ninths, and tritones, often moving simultaneously a semitone apart, are not harmony. They are thickened line; and since the line is deliberately without melodic interest, the effect is entirely rhythmic (Ex. 64):

Ex. 64. Stravinsky: The Rite of Spring

The music is orgiastic, like the primitive ritual it recreates. Positively, it represented a search for a new source of vitality in an emotionally hypertrophied world; negatively, it was an offshoot of the sadism latent in the war years. From either point of view it meant a regression from personal sensibility to the collective Unconscious: and was, in terms of musical technique, at once a reaction against chromaticism and a part of the same disruptive process. As Debussy in some of his middle-period piano pieces, and Schoenberg in his 'free' atonal period, reduced music to the vertical effect of simultaneously sounding notes, so Stravinsky reduced melody and harmony to rhythm. Harmony without melody and rhythm,

rhythm without melody and harmony, are static. Both the pandemonium of Stravinsky's *Rite of Spring* and the whisper of Debussy's *Voiles* deprive music of the sense of motion from one point to another. Though they started from diametrically opposed points, both composers mark a radical departure from the traditions of European music since the Renaissance; both are in some ways as much oriental as occidental.

Thus in *The Wedding* tonality is far more stringently restricted than it is in the Viennese classics: only it is a melodic kind of tonality, consisting of oscillations (usually pentatonic) around a nodal point. That the accompanying figurations are often a semitone apart from the melody does not affect this at all: for the figurations are percussive unresolved appoggiaturas which 'stand for' and sadistically intensify the note to which they should resolve. This technique enhances both the primitive barbarity and the 'modern' hysteria of the music; but it is significant that Stravinsky does not attempt to resolve the hysteria except when, at the end, the percussive dissonance ceases to accompany the vocal line. The male voice finally sings his pentatonic love song unaccompanied, his phrases being interspersed by gong-strokes and by pianos imitating gongs, in an immensely slow pulse which gradually swings to rest. This is the first of many such conclusions to Stravinsky's works, in which Time stops. This one, however, though impressive, hardly seems to have much relationship to Europe or the twentieth-century; it might be by an anonymous Balinese composer.

If Stravinsky had stopped at this point he would have been an historically interesting, but not great, figure in European music. But just as Debussy went on to relate the revolutionary technique of his middle years to a renewed tradition, so Stravinsky began to explore the relationship between his interest in primitive ritual and his position as a European composer, culturally uprooted. Now *The Rite of Spring* and *The Wedding* were both ballets. Stravinsky's primitive ritual could not, after all, be 'real', for he was not in fact primitive: so that in these works the two bifurcated strands of Russian culture meet. The primitive realism of peasant ritual (which had found its greatest representative in Moussorgsky) now finds expression through the sophisticated, westernized fairy-ritual of ballet. Obviously, Stravinsky's primitivism could be no more than a starting-point in the attempt to revive a ritualistic approach.

There was, however, a twentieth-century ritual that expressed itself in physical movement, and that had a direct and 'realistic' relationship to the stresses—and perhaps the evasions—of the modern world. Basically, the vitality in jazz came from a primitive (negro) source; and its technique was founded, like that of so much Russian music, on the ostinato and on incremental repetition. Consisting almost entirely of variations on a ground, it is music with no before and after. It is unconcerned with the process of Becoming and exists, not, like plainsong or Bach's last Chorale Prelude or Beethoven's last quartets in a metaphysical state of Being (!), but in the immediate physical moment. In its more extravagant flights it tends to encourage a state of trance; and in that sense may be said, like primitive orgiastic music, to carry one outside Time.

There was and is, however, a difference between the vigour of real primitive music and that of jazz: for the music the negro sang in slavery and in urban exile was very different from that which he sang in his native village. Jazz is the music of a dispossessed race; and it was precisely because its vitality was uprooted, dislocated, that it made so potent an appeal to sophisticated, urbanized western man. Stravinsky responded both to the vitality and to the sense of dislocation; and he valued jazz the more because it suggested to him how primitive ritualistic techniques might be reconciled with the sophisticated techniques of western Europe.

For the materials of jazz were in part European. The rhythmic drive came from primitive sources, the roots of the melody, with its flat sevenths and false relations, from pentatonic and modal folk incantation: as did the rhythm and melody of Stravinsky's own early music. But the harmony and texture of jazz came from Europe: from the white military band of the Civil War days, and from the Christian hymn. These in turn derived their material from nineteenth-century Italian opera and from the English oratorio (with German choral homophony behind that). Jazz showed Stravinsky how traditional European conventions—degraded perhaps to *cliché*—could be exploited in ways which divorced them from the idea of harmonic progression: and so liberated them from the European consciousness of Time.

Stravinsky's direct experiments in jazz style—the *Piano Rag-Music* and the *Ragtime* for 11 instruments—have worn extraordinarily well because they order into art the uncompromising harshness of texture, the dislocated rhythmic energy of the New Orleans blues player and band. How closely their immediacy is related to the 'realism' of one side of the Russian tradition is revealed in a work Stravinsky composed in 1918, the year following *The Wedding*. *The Soldier's Tale* is a morality based on a Russian legend which, like the text of *The Wedding*, is half pagan, half Christian. The story, telling of a soldier who sells his soul to the devil, is spoken by a narrator, while the action is mimed and danced—again in ritualistic style—to a septet of instruments which is more or less the New Orleans jazz band. The basis of the music's technique—rhythmic dislocation over seemingly interminable ostinatos—is identical with that of *The Wedding*; the difference lies in the nature of the material. Whereas the themes of *The Wedding* are mostly pentatonic, oscillating in a very narrow range around a nodal point, the fragmentary tunes in *The Soldier's Tale* are diatonic and related to *clichés* common to European art music. Thus the thematic material of the Royal March is comprised of snippets of early nineteenth-century Italian opera and corny Spanish figurations. These are employed, however, in exactly the same way as are the pentatonic phrases in *The Wedding*. They are not developed, and there is virtually no modulation; the music depends on the exciting effect of the tug-of-war between the patterns made out of the melodic *clichés* and a tonic-dominant ostinato in 7:8 which never coincides with the bar-lines.

Still more interesting is the opening Soldier's March. Here, there is an unceasing ostinato in the bass consisting of the note G followed by D and E sounded together, a ninth apart. This seems to suggest the key of G. But the fragmentary tootling tune, nearly always out of step with the ostinato, is unambiguously in D (with a few decorative bitonal flourishes on the cornet). This suggests that the D-E in the ostinato is really the tonic and dominant of D major elided together: and that the G of the ostinato represents the subdominant. Traditional harmony revolves between the poles of tonic, dominant and subdominant. In telescoping two or even all three of these chords Stravinsky places in space, as it were, chords that would normally progress into one another. Instead of a resolved argument, we have a tension clinched, suspended in time.

Thus although Stravinsky is now thinking in terms not merely of metrical rhythm, but of rhythm in relation to line and harmony, he still tends to avoid the notion of harmonic progression; patterns of line and harmony remain for him physical gestures existing at a point in time. Before his final dance in *The Soldier's Tale* the devil hymns his triumph in a Chorale. This looks like a parody of a Bach chorale: yet it is more disturbing than comic; and is so because it is an inversion of Bach's technique. A Bach chorale is an equation between melody and harmony. Each of the four parts is a singing line; yet its apparent independence helps to create the rich interplay of tension and relaxation which makes the music seem at once human and divine. In Stravinsky's chorale there are few chords that, considered as such, could not be found in Bach; their effect is, however, utterly remote from Bach. The major sevenths and minor ninths which in Bach resolve so poignantly occur in almost every chord in Stravinsky; since they remain unresolved their effect becomes, again, almost percussive. The recurrent cadences bear no tonal relationship to one another: they leave one suspended in a void. The only cadence that has any effect of resolution is the last; and it is significant that by this time the hymn melody has virtually disappeared, or at least has turned into a ritualistic incantation rocking through the interval of a fourth, and then by step around a nodal G.

Of course, it is dramatically appropriate that a Devil's Chorale should invert the technique of Bach. None the less, this Chorale is not a special effect in Stravinsky's music; rather does it suggest the technique he habitually uses when he turns to recreate the sophisticated materials of European tradition. In depriving Bach's style of those harmonic elements which we may refer to as humanistic, Stravinsky re-discovers a pre-Bachian ritualistic style. This is what he almost always does when he seems to be imitating the conventions of the baroque. Although the *clichés* of baroque music appealed to Stravinsky because baroque music was centred in opera, which was itself a sophisticated—as opposed to a primitive—ritual, he uses these *clichés* in a way that no baroque composer would have recognized. For instance, the last movement of the *Octet* for wind instruments opens with a bassoon tune that looks, in the cut of the phrases and the implied modulations to relative and dominant, like a typical baroque instrumental theme. But the contour of the theme is increasingly disguised by octave displacements and jazzy contractions and ellipses: while the tonal basis is neutralized by the fact that the tune is accompanied by an ostinato consisting of a rising and falling scale of C major. The clashes that occur between the tune and the ostinato have no relation to the dissonances in baroque music, which always implies an equilibrium between expressive melodic accent and tonal direction. As we shall see, however, they have some relationship to certain pre-Renaissance European techniques.

In Stravinsky's first neo-classic works the melodic patterns, the ostinatos, may have become more linear than they were in his 'primitive' works, but their purpose is the same. They establish rhythmic and modal 'cells' within which the music moves very slowly. Although all Stravinsky's music implies objectification in theatrical terms, it is a theatre to which the progression of Time is no longer relevant. This is why he favours ballet rather than opera. When, in *Oedipus Rex*, he adapted conventions from heroic opera he deliberately emphasized the ritualistic at the expense of the humanistic features, using a static chorus, a narrator, and a dead language, Latin.

"Composing for me," Stravinsky said, "is putting into an order a certain number of sounds according to certain intervallic relationships." The scale, he maintains, consists of seven diatonic notes with five intensifying chromatic notes. Not only is he always—until perhaps his most recent works—a tonal composer; he is also extremely cautious in his treatment of tonality. Whereas Schoenberg's early music is perpetual modulation, Stravinsky's modulates seldom. When, after the long sustained pentatonic ostinato in the beautiful G flat major section of *Persephone* the music at last modulates, the effect is as though a dancer moved from one almost sculpturesque posture to another. Even to the *Symphony in Three Movements* the notion of development is extraneous. Though the material of the successive sections is sharply contrasted, there is no suggestion of conflict between them. The elision of tonic, dominant and subdominant harmony which we referred to in

The Soldier's Tale may in that instance, as in Glinka's music, have been suggested by Russian peasant bands, as well as by jazz. But in his later music Stravinsky gives this peculiarity of Russian harmony a much deeper significance in relation to the European tradition. In this passage from *Persephone*, for instance, gradations of tension are immensely important; but each harmony tends to be telescoped into the next, to be heard in relation to the pattern of lines and rhythms rather than in a developing harmonic context (Ex. 65):

With Stravinsky, time is what links a succession of harmonic 'postures'. He is less concerned, if at all, with the movements whereby the dancers proceed from one posture to the next. Though architecture may not be frozen music, it is not altogether inapt to describe Stravinsky's music as architecture or sculpture existing in time.

This balletistic effect is observable in Stravinsky's harmony whether he is using diatonic concords or chords, such as sevenths and ninths, which usually suggest a more romantic and personal expression. The transcendental alleluias at the end of the *Symphony of Psalms* are a supreme example of this dissociation of a chord from its normal emotional connotations. There is a similar 'dissociative' tendency in Stravinsky's linear thinking. Two or three ostinato patterns in different lines may establish independent modalities. This does not mean that the music is strictly polytonal, for, as Hindemith has proved, music cannot have two tonal roots at once. But it does mean that the parts emphasize their separateness from one another; and that Stravinsky's counterpoint has little in common with the traditional notion of polyphony as an interaction of line and harmony, involving alternations of tension and relaxation. For him, counterpoint is the link between his mosaic-like sections, his means of passing from one dance-posture to the next. The counterpoint precisely articulates the pattern of rhythmic and harmonic gestures which is his music. The pattern *is* the 'expression'.

It is obvious that while this conception of musical technique differs radically from that current in Europe during the last three centuries, it has much in common with medieval music. The harmony in an organum of Pérotin, or even a motet of Machaut, does not involve our sense of progression. Like Stravinsky's, it is centred around the fundamental consonances of octave, fourth, and fifth, while what happens in between the points of concord is dictated more by linear and rhythmic than by harmonic considerations. In medieval music, too, dance patterns become a constructive principle independent of the normal association of dance movement with time; the medieval technique of isochronous rhythm—whereby a consistent rhythmic pattern is maintained throughout a part, though the interval relationships change—is similar to Stravinsky's rhythmic and modal ostinatos. In the music of his middle years, in which Stravinsky based his music largely on baroque models, this medieval affiliation was probably unconscious. The *Symphony of Psalms* superficially resembles a baroque oratorio; the *Symphony in Three Movements* is related to the principle of the concerto grosso; *Oedipus Rex* is based directly on the seventeenth-century opera-oratorio. Yet these three great works are all liturgical in spirit. In all of them the technique is fundamentally closer to Machaut than it is to Handel or Bach. Among Stravinsky's major works the only exception to this is *The Rake's Progress*. Owing perhaps to the nature of the theme, the technique is here less ritualistic, closer to the 'humanistic' techniques of late eighteenth-century opera, though it preserves the objectivity of a parable. Classical harmony is treated in a characteristically elliptical fashion; but it is significant that the score contains relatively few ostinatos. Even in *The Rake's Progress*, however, the ritualistic, ostinato-dominated style is employed at the ultimate climax—the Dirge sung over the dead Rake. This is logical enough: for his 'progress' is at an end. The dead, at least, are outside Time; and the timeless 'Devil's Chorale' of *The Soldier's Tale* has after all become an agent of the divine.

So in Stravinsky's apparently quixotic development we can trace a coherent line. Primitive ritual gives way to the sophisticated ritual of the classical theatre; and that in turn leads into the ritual of the liturgy. This becomes explicit in words like the Mass for chorus and wind instruments and the *Cantata*, in which Stravinsky consciously adapts techniques from Machaut and fourteenth-century polyphony. In his most recent works he has carried this linear conception of order to its logical conclusion, and has adopted a serial technique. He does not employ a completely chromatic series; but he uses diatonic and modal 'rows' in a way that amounts to a compromise between the isochronous patterns of medieval music, his own earlier use of ostinatos, and the serial technique of Schoenberg's pupil, Webern. In the sense that it is based not on a twelve-note, but on a five-note row, Stravinsky's *In Memoriam Dylan Thomas* is even more rigid than Webern (Ex. 66):

Every note in this piece is derived from this series which, since it consists of only five notes, is more aurally intelligible and memorable than a twelve-note series, and can thus serve the function of a mode. Music could scarcely be more stringently disciplined nor, in the tenuous scoring for tenor voice with antiphonal strings and trombones, more stylized. Yet no music could be more strikingly individual in its ritual impersonality, more powerfully moving as it liberates us from self-regarding passion.

Stravinsky has composed music in a number of very different manners: think of the frightening grandeur of *Oedipus Rex*, the austere solemnity of the Mass, the tender limpidity of *Persephone*, the wit of *Dumbarton Oaks*. Yet all his mature works are linked by their ritualistic quality; and all have an intense seriousness, even when they are comic. In the music he wrote during the First World War there are many movements of parodistic, even cynical intention. Yet they are never merely parody. In *The Soldier's Tale*, as we have seen, Stravinsky employs techniques suggested by jazz in irreverent association with the liturgical chorale. Yet this work is also an order achieved out of new and startling sonorities; and this kind of scoring was one of the means whereby Stravinsky evolved the odd kind of counterpoint typical of his most 'serious' music.

He experiences afresh the sound stuff which is his material, inviting us to listen again to the noises instruments make. The composer's task is to integrate certain specified sounds. Every aspect of his art—tone-colour as much as melody, harmony, and rhythm—is a question of form, of the creation of an adequate 'objective correlative'. The new sound which is *The Soldier's Tale* is also a formal discovery: as is the scoring and spacing of the final chord of C major in the *Symphony of Psalms*.

One can thus draw no sharp division between Stravinsky's serious works and those which are apparently slighter and lighter. As with Mozart, the difference is one of degree, rather than of kind. The first movement of the Septet, for instance, comes close to the rococo aria form that Stravinsky had employed in many works, culminating in *The Rake's Progress.* In the coda, however, the music slows itself down like a pendulum coming to rest, by a process of rhythmic modification common throughout Stravinsky's work; and thus prepares us for the disembodied timelessness of the Passacaglia, Webern-like in its serial structure, and in the splitting up of the theme between various instrumental colours. Even the Gigue—in which each instrument has its own row, or rather an invented scale from which themes are derived—is the contemplative Essence of gaiety, rather than gay in itself. This piece—and still more a little piece like the *Tango* for piano—is entertainment music which is at the same time synonymous with ritual, and with Stravinsky's philosophy of art.

The same is true when Stravinsky borrows, in *Baiser de la Fée*, from such an apparently improbable composer as Tchaikowsky; for he sees in Tchaikowsky's ballet music the crystallization of emotion in gesture. Reference to Tchaikowsky also provides a precedent for Stravinsky's cosmopolitanism; for we saw that the Russian tradition had always been bifurcated between two cultures, one racial, the other rootlessly European. Stravinsky has merely made this rootlessness symbolic of the modern artist in general. He has salvaged what he can from Europe's past, and reintegrated it in ways that were possible, perhaps, only to a deracinated Russian. We can hardly deplore his cosmopolitanism, since all modern communities are cosmopolitan when they are not parochial.

Because he was Russian, Stravinsky's cosmopolitanism was

inherent in him. For Bartók, as a Hungarian, a national culture had a more positive significance; yet it was not long before his concern for a racial heritage began to merge into issues that were of much wider relevance. "Kodály and I", he said, "wanted to make a synthesis of East and West. Because of our race, and because of the geographical position of our country... we felt this was a task we were well fitted to undertake. But it was Debussy, whose music had just begun to reach us, who showed us the path we must follow. . . . Debussy's great service to music was to reawaken among all musicians an awareness of harmony and its possibilities. In that, he was just as important as Beethoven, who revealed to us the meaning of progressive form, or as Bach, who showed us the transcendent significance of counterpoint. . . . Now, what I am always asking myself is this: is it possible to make a synthesis of these three great masters, a living synthesis that will be valid for our time?" The problem, as Bartók [1881–1945] presents it, is not specifically musical; it is hardly excessive to say that in these words he has summarized everything that makes his contribution to our battered century of central significance.

Like Schoenberg and Hindemith, he had started with a background of German romanticism. Brahms was his model, and later Strauss, with a superficial Hungarian garnishing from Liszt. His awakening to musical independence was inseparably associated with his fervent nationalism; and that was inseparable from his courage as a human being, his passion for liberty. "That man in his misery finds precious comfort in praying to an omnipotent Being is understandable. . . . But how unspeakably feeble! We should rejoice in life and be interested in everything that goes on in the world around us. . . . Were I to make the sign of the Cross I would say, 'In the name of Nature, of Art, and of Science.' " That is a positive confession of faith. It is also anti-clerical, for Bartók believed that Authority, both ecclesiastical and secular, had in his country proved to be against life and humanity. For this reason he hated all coteries, whether political or artistic, and said that he felt truly alive only among peasants. In Hungary a folk-tradition was still a living reality, as it could not be, in industrial Britain, for Holst and Vaughan Williams. Bartók did not collect folk-songs as a matter of antiquarian research. He did so to discover his own soul.

So folk-music was for him both a spiritual and a musical

liberation. In particular, the oriental origins of Magyar song suggested to him modal types of melody and complexities of rhythm which were alien to the conventions of nineteenth-century Europe. Bartók said unambiguously that although he and Kodály [b. 1882] were interested in transcribing the songs for their own sake, in the simplest possible manner, that was only a start. In the long run, they valued the songs for their evocativeness, for their power to generate an 'imaginary folk-music'. Pentatonic and modal melodies, themes in Eastern scales with sharp fourth or sixth or oscillating in inflected scales around a nodal point, became as natural to his musical language as asymmetrical rhythms—measures of fives and sevens, and all the possible permutations of eight beats a bar. Especially interesting is Bartók's statement that folk-music was as fruitful in revealing new harmonic possibilities as it was in enriching conventional conceptions of melody and rhythm. To take a simple example, the free use of the chord of the seventh was naturally suggested by familiarity with pentatonic melodies. "We so often heard intervals of third, fifth and seventh as of equal value, that what was more natural than that we should try to make them sound of equal importance?"

But although Bartók achieved creative liberation through folk-music he was not, any more than Holst, a peasant. As a sophisticated European, he could use primitive material as a release from moribund convention; but he could not turn his back on Europe because some of it had died. This is why the music of Debussy had so crucial a significance for him. Debussy too had rebelled against academic convention. He had liberated the chord from harmonic argument; and had shown how such a static harmony could be combined with pentatonic and modal melodies that are not susceptible to classical principles of thematic growth. To Debussy, such melodies were exotic; to Kodály and Bartók they were their own racial heritage. So we find that throughout Kodály's career his music depends on an odd equilibrium between the 'communal' passion of folk-melody and the withdrawn sensibility of Debussyan harmony. Always a regional composer, he at once belonged to his community and was apart from it.

Bartók's first opera, *Bluebeard's Castle*, is a score of Debussy-like sensuous refinement, and a parable dealing with the cult of personal sensibility in opposition to a decaying world. There is a strongly Debussyan flavour about the harmony of so linear and modal a work as the Second String Quartet; and traces of Debussy's sensuousness are evident in the music of his last years. Yet Bartók's affinity with Debussy goes deeper than any incidental harmonic similarities; for we saw that the essence of Debussy's revolution lay not in its disintegrative character, but in its reconciliation of a melodic, modal tonality with the harmonic tonality of French classical music. Not being French, Bartók could not do precisely that; but he could absorb both his folk-culture and his nervous sensibility into a renewed respect for European tradition. In his early work, such as the piano *Bagatelles* of 1908, it is possible to 'explain' the dissonances as unresolved appoggiaturas, irregular passing notes, and so on; but it is not very profitable to do so. In effect, the dissonances are as static as the dissonances in Debussy's piano style and as nervously percussive as those in Stravinsky's 'primitive' works. As in Debussy and Stravinsky, the tonal order of the pieces is non-harmonic, consisting in the way in which the melodic lines oscillate around a nodal point. In his later work Bartók never entirely relinquished this folk-like, melodic criterion of tonality (cf. the slow movements of the Fourth and Fifth Quartets and of the Music for Strings, Celesta, and Percussion). But as he matured, and his powerful melodies became more complex, chromaticized, and sustained, he increasingly sought to reconcile this melodic tonality with the harmonic tonality of classical music. In so doing he established contact not only with Debussy, but also with Hindemith and Berg.

From this point of view, a key-work in his career is the Second Violin Sonata. In many passages of this work folk-like rhapsody in the violin line is organized melodically around nodal points, which the piano underlines with chords conceived statically and vertically. In other passages, however, Bartók returns to the classical conception of dissonance as harmonic *movement*, whereby the discordant passing note keeps the melodic parts flowing and adds emotional intensity. Although the resolution of the dissonance is often implicit rather than explicit, one is aware of a basic diatonic pattern; and dissonance, whether appearing vertically in the chord structures or in passing notes in the melody itself, serves to give direction—in the traditional classical manner—to this harmonic base.

This technique has interesting possibilities. For instance, an unresolved passing dissonance on D sharp may accompany a C major triad. The result is a major-minor ambiguity similar to that explored in the later work of Busoni. Further, the unresolved passing note suggests the unresolved passing chord, and that in turn suggests the unresolved neighbouring tonality. Two different tonalities may be suggested by the presence of two fundamental fifths, yet though the effect is polytonal, the relationship to a root is maintained; for the two lower notes are unresolved appoggiaturas which are taken as identical with the notes to which they should resolve. Thus Bartók can introduce long passages in (say) G during which the tonality of G flat is never relinquished, as in the piece from *Microcosmos, The Diary of a Fly* (Ex. 67):

In the quartets there are several passages in which the four instruments enter within the space of a few bars, a semitone apart. Again, he does not regard the parts as having separate tonal roots. Bartók's music is always fundamentally tonal, even when his ambiguous harmonic processes are complicated by his partiality for modally inflected, non-diatonic scales.

Bartók seems to have associated his rediscovery of classical principles of structure with the influence of Beethoven, likewise a revolutionary composer who modified established precedents under pressure of personal feeling. The core of Bartók's work is in his six string quartets. Superficially speaking, the grounds of comparison between Bartók's quartets and the late quartets of Beethoven may seem far to seek—apart from the obvious resemblance between the opening of Bartók's First and the opening of Beethoven's C sharp minor. Yet there is a profound sense in which the comparison is justified, for both composers are seeking to reconcile the dynamism of sonata conflict with the apparently contradictory, monistic principles of counterpoint. In so doing, both of them modify traditional notions of tonal organization.

Consider, for instance, Bartók's Fifth Quartet, composed in

1934. The first movement is in dynamic sonata form. The first subject is split into two groups: a reiterated percussive figure in or around B flat, and a phrase syncopated across the bar-line, involving a trill and a glissando suggestive of Magyar music. The second subject, more flowing, sinuous and chromatic, also has a Magyar flavour (Ex. 68):

The development begins in—or rather on—E, a tritone apart from the main key. As in Beethoven's quartets, the material is itself transformed as it is developed in tonal conflict. In the recapitulation all the material reappears, though not in the same order, and in linear inversion and sometimes reversion. Again there is a compromise between the tonal organization of the Beethovenian sonata and the linear organization of Bachian counterpoint. All the themes are gathered together and telescoped in a coda in close stretto which ends unambiguously on, if not in, B flat.

The second movement, adagio molto, opens with frail wisps of sound which coalesce in a modally harmonized chorale, reminiscent in mood of the Lydian adagio in Beethoven's opus 132. Over the chorale the first violin sings fragmentary lyrical phrases which, since they contain unresolved appoggiaturas, seem to be off key. These lyrical phrases are evocatively extended in a middle section. An elliptical recapitulation of the chorale fades into the whispered trills and glissandi of the opening. Both Beethoven and Bartók associate trills with the relinquishment of Time's shackles; though Bartók's paradise, if that is what it is, is certainly the more tenuous and tentative. One could hardly say that his peace brings a Beethovenian joy.

The third movement is a scherzo and trio on classical lines. It is in Bulgarian folk-rhythms, 4 plus 2 plus 3 quavers a bar in the scherzo, 3 plus 2 plus 2 plus 3 quavers a bar in the trio. The first theme, built on rising and falling thirds, has an almost Debussyan pizzicato accompaniment; the second is more jaunty and folk-like in character, with an obtrusive Lydian fourth. The trio creates a magically sensuous sound while following classical convention in being based on the bagpipe drone. Its rusticity is disembodied, however, like the comparable musette trio in the scherzo of Beethoven's opus 131. In the repeat of the scherzo both themes are treated in their original form and in inversion.

Then occurs the work's only departure from classical precedent: a second slow movement which balances, and is thematically related to, the adagio second movement. In this nocturnal music mysterious glissandi, pizzicati and swirling chromatics accompany a canonic dialogue between violin and 'cello. In the coda the themes disintegrate on viola and 'cello, while the two violins play a rarefied version of the adagio's chorale.

The last movement is a rondo which, like Beethoven's rondos, makes some compromise with sonata style and has also a good deal of contrapuntal organization. The first theme is stated twice, the second time in inversion and canon. Another theme, marked leggierissimo, fulfils some of the functions of a second subject. All the material is developed in close counterpoint, and the climax comes when a fugato passage reveals the relationship between the first movement themes and those of the last movement. After the climax there is a strange passage in which the first theme appears in augmentation, in unambiguous A major. This moment of queerly comic relaxation is swept away by the contrapuntal frenzy of the coda, which ultimately lands us on the unison B flat of the opening of the work.

This work has been discussed in some detail because it includes every aspect of Bartók's creative relationship to tradition. Of the four great, 'central' twentieth-century composers we have considered, he is the only one whose idiom derives its force from the sonata principle: which may be why he has gone further than the others towards establishing some relationship to a public. Yet even with him, as we have seen, counterpoint modifies his conception of the sonata; and the highest point his music reached—the first movement of the

Music for Strings, Celesta, and Percussion—is a 'monistic' expression of the Bachian contrapuntal principle. The theme itself, narrow in compass, winding around a nodal point, seems to adhere to the melodic tonality of folk-song; but the structure of the piece as a whole is an expansion of the basic harmonic principle of classical music, for the fugal entries take place at successive fifths, beginning on A, in alternate ascending and descending cycles. When the two cycles meet on E flat—the tonality which stands at the ultimate distance from the initial A—there is a tremendous tritonal climax; the celesta enters for the first time (a vision of the bliss to be attained?); the theme is inverted and the cycle of fifths continues until it once more reaches A. There is a short coda, in which the theme and its inversion are stated simultaneously, ending on the unison A.

This is perhaps a fugal movement which, like that in Beethoven's 'Hammerklavier' Sonata, grindingly seeks the unity of paradise, rather than one in which paradise is attained. None the less, this climacteric point of Bartók's music is certainly monistic to the core; and we may recall that his melodic and rhythmic conception is in some ways as much Eastern as European. When we look back at the other central figures we have discussed, we remember that Hindemith too has tried to recreate the Bachian notion of fugal unity, and to establish a tonal order 'cosmically' related to the medieval view of music as science and ritual. Stravinsky's conception of music is still more specifically ritualistic. Whether in his primitive or his neo-baroque phase or in the serial works of recent years, his music implies a kind of unity as much medieval as modern, as much Eastern as European. And Schoenberg's twelve-note method is a technique of perpetual variation, an entirely monistic conception of form in which every note of a composition is a permutation of a single entity.

9

EUROPE TODAY

We have seen that Debussy, Schoenberg, Stravinsky, Hindemith, and Bartók—the five central figures in twentieth-century music—have manifested, over the past fifty years, a partial but spontaneous turning-away from the humanism and time-obsession that are our European birthright. Nor is this tendency confined to these major figures, for we can observe something comparable in distinguished, but marginal, composers of the same generation, such as Karol Szymanowsky [1883–1937] and Ernest Bloch [b. 1880]. The Pole Szymanowsky began as one of the 'last romantics', creating in his opera, *King Roger*, a third act which is a single Tristanesque climax lasting some forty minutes—superbly luscious in its chromatic, polyphonic-harmonic texture and in its opulent orchestration. The nostalgic lyricism of this opera—significantly dealing with a conflict between Christianity and paganism—strikingly complements that of Delius's *A Village Romeo and Juliet*, just as the soaring cantilena of Szymanowsky's First Violin Concerto parallels that of Delius's concerto. The restless, fluctuating movement of the harmony is similar in both composers, producing an impression of inordinately slow tempo, even when the figuration is rapid. Both use the orchestra in the same way, though Szymanowsky is texturally much more sophisticated. Yet this elegiac composer of a world's twilight goes a stage further than Delius: the movement becomes so slow that it almost stops; and as this happens a new, linear element comes into Szymanowsky's music, suggested by the Eastern affiliations of Polish folk music and liturgical chant. The sensuousness is still present in his impressive *Stabat Mater*; but the music is now a ritualistic, rather than auto-erotic, experience. Ripely sonorous, harmonically conceived passages exist alongside sections that depend mainly on Asiatic-tending melodic arabesques in a sharply dissonant linear texture, with little harmonic movement.

This tendency is still more evident in the music of Ernest Bloch, the first Jewish composer whose music springs from his consciousness of alienated race. He is perhaps the most passionately ego-centred of all twentieth-century composers, and his rich scoring and thick texture have obvious affinities with Wagner and even Strauss. Yet the insidious power of a piece like his *Schelomo* for solo 'cello and orchestra depends on a dichotomy between the hysterical fervour of the orchestral climaxes and the improvisatory conception of the solo part: which assimilates into itself the age-old, basically pentatonic phrases of Jewish cantilation, and evolves by the Asiatic technique of melismatic decoration and 'division'; while the scoring often emulates the actual sounds of the Hebraic folk-band. Even when Bloch writes music closer to Western tradition, as in the first movement of his First String Quartet, the violent tonal and metrical tensions are combined with declamatory, prayer-like themes that also lend themselves to oriental melodic extension; and the anguish is not resolved in an orthodox recapitulation. Resolution—in this quartet as in the still finer Piano Quintet—ultimately comes in extended cantabile melody which is also an elegiac lament. The relationship of this singing lyricism to the liturgical manner—half Hebraic, half Renaissance European—of Bloch's *Sacred Service* indicates how Bloch's elegy—unlike Delius's—implies a tragic resignation to suffering. This quality, too, may affect us as Eastern rather than European.

While we cannot yet know what this general, cumulative trend away from the West means, it is at least feasible that we are living at the end of a cycle that began with the Renaissance: and that the values inherent in our music may come to reflect, in a vast international society, a changed conception of man's nature and destiny. Certainly there is evidence to support this in the evolution of serial music since Schoenberg: for while Schoenberg's music usually maintains a link with post-Renaissance ideas of progression, a serial technique need not necessarily do so, and some later developments of twelve-note music have attempted a far more radical departure from harmonic implications. The early music of Anton Webern [1883–1945], for instance, is sensory experience that titillates the nerves in the same way as does Debussy's music. In the tiny *Bagatelles* or the early pieces for string quartet the senses exist 'absolutely', apart from the Will: until they are so winnowed away that they dissolve into spirit. By the time this happens Webern's music has become completely serial in the organization of its pitch-relationships; and while it is possible that the dominance of a certain interval, or a relationship between a group of intervals, may sometimes serve as a nodal point which takes the place of tonality, there can be no doubt that Webern habitually selected rows which were as remote as possible from tonal implications. He especially favoured rows in which the parts were inter-related mathematically—for instance, in which the second half is a mirror reflexion of the first; often the two segments are linked by the neutral interval of the tritone. The texture is tenuous in the extreme, and the thematic line is often subdivided between a number of parts, each note having a different tone-colour.

Webern's instinct for sonority is of uncanny precision and the aural effect of his serial music is of the most exquisite sensuous beauty. Yet the effect is different from that of his early free atonal pieces, or from that of Debussy's impressionism, or from that of Schoenberg's early 'seismographic' works; and the difference lies in the fact that the 'moments of sensation' are no longer fragmentary. Each single note in the wonderful slow movement of the *Concerto for Nine Instruments* seems part of a preordained order, a revelation of cosmic mathematical law, as are the notes of a medieval 'isochronous' motet.* It is not coincidental that Webern should have been an expert scholar in the field of mediaeval music. Though his style evolved out of Viennese chromaticism, with no conscious trace of mediaeval or oriental influence, there is a quality both mediaeval and oriental in the form of the *Piano Variations*, opus 27: for the piece describes the ultimate unity, the circle, in that the theme is accompanied by itself, backwards and inverted. The serpent eats its own tail. It is not surprising that in this work time seems to stop; and that the piano's bell-like noises should suggest, however remotely, the gongs of the Balinese gamelang. Nor, perhaps, is it entirely fanciful to sense a relationship between Webern's treatment of the human voice—far more 'unvocal' than Schoenberg's—and the deliberately unnatural vocal techniques used by mediaeval and oriental singers. The voice is

* Isochronous Motet: one in which the parts are organized in metrical series which remain constant though the pitch relationships do not. The metrical series sometimes have doctrinal significance (for instance, references to the Trinity). Cf. rhythmic pattern in mediaeval motets, Part I, pp. 57, 103, etc.

deliberately dehumanized because it must become supernatural law.

Almost all the poems Webern chose to set are, significantly, mystical and esoteric; yet although his music is much more remote than Schoenberg's from traditional European procedures it is still, in its precision, quintessentially expressive. We can see from the two beautiful cantatas how, in his maturest work, Webern as vocal composer still expressively 'interprets' his texts; and even so apparently abstract a work as the *Piano Variations* depends for its effect on the sensitive nuance of its melodic contours, as we know from the testimony of Peter Stadlen, who studied the work with Webern before giving the first performance. Thus we may suspect that while Webern would have appreciated the manner in which Stravinsky has used certain aspects of his technique as a ritualistic discipline (the latest of his many masks), he would be chary of acknowledging those who claim that he has inaugurated a new order in European music, above and beyond the concepts of 'expression' and 'communication'. Across the Austrian border, in Germany, Karlheinz Stockhausen [b. 1928], taking Webern as his point of departure, has developed a music that is serial not only in pitch relationships, but also in rhythmic pattern and dynamics. Sometimes it is so complicated that it can be performed only by electronic means. Such a revelation of mathematical law dispenses with the human intermediary of the performer and possibly with the audience as well. The composer is alone in his laboratory; recent experiments by Stockhausen in the direction of 'disciplined improvisation' would perhaps suggest that he is aware that the laboratory may be a new kind of plastic Ivory Tower.

But it is not only in the work of Webern and his disciples that a radical change of approach—and of philosophical implication—can be observed. Webern rarefies the senses into an exquisitely tense, hyper-subtle heaven-beyond-becoming: a hermetic paradise. Carl Orff [b. 1895], in Germany, seeks a comparable end by an opposite route: by reducing music to a lowest common denominator, divesting it of virtually all harmony and expressive melody, leaving only rhythm and the contrast of sonorities. During the years of the Second World War he has done again what Stravinsky did, in the *Rite of Spring* and *The Wedding*, during the years of the First World War: he has simultaneously expressed the violence and horror of breakdown and suggested that, if this is what our sophisticated consciousness has made of the world, it is time we returned to our primitive, pre-conscious roots. The difference is that whereas Stravinsky went on to relate the primitive, non-European elements explored in these works to a ritual, both secular and religious, relevant to Europe's past and present, Orff has, in later works, retreated still further from Europe. The oriental elements in his *Aphrodite*, for instance, extend to the investigation of elaborate melismatic melody which is far more interesting than his earlier obsession with incantatory rhythm. Orff is a minor, even a trivial, composer compared with Stravinsky; yet the success enjoyed by his music is symptomatic.* People were looking, unconsciously, for an escape from the dominance of Time and the Self. Orff offers such an escape: at a lower level than Webern or Stravinsky, but at a higher level than the jazz fanatic who expects his music to 'send' him beyond self-consciousness. Orff believes that the future, even our survival, depends on the existence of a popular religious art meaningful not to a few, but to the many. Whether the primitive and oriental features in his music can really fulfil the emotional needs of urban and industrial man is dubious indeed. But at least he is justified in thinking that an orgiastic act is religious in the sense that it puts us into direct communion with elemental forces: and to that degree with eternity.

A comparable concern with orgiastic experience and with Oriental ritual occurs in the music of a French composer of the same generation, Olivier Messiaen [b. 1908]. His orgiastic mysticism is, however, esoteric rather than popular: except in the sense that, being a zealous Roman Catholic, he presumably speaks, on behalf of his faith, to all who will listen. Whereas Webern refines away the senses, Messiaen expatiates on them, inducing a kind of auto-erotic ecstasy comparable with that found in some Catholic baroque art. The musical affinities of his early work are obviously with the sensory impressionism of Debussy: but still more, perhaps, with the obsessively 'introverted' harmony of Scriabin. Yet he carries the isolation of these

* It is relevant to note that another post-Nazi, post-war German composer, Boris Blacher [b. 1903] has created a music almost entirely reliant on rhythmic experiment. His art, however, being without Orff's deliberate primitivism, produces a curiously ascetic excitement: as though the mind were stimulating, perhaps even simulating, a vitality which the blood and heart do not possess. Perhaps it is not surprising that his music has been widely influential.

sensual moments from the idea of progression to a more extreme point than either Debussy or Scriabin. The more highly charged are the artist's sensations the more completely must they be released from the grip of the Will: so the movement of higher chromatic discords in Messiaen's earlier works is so slow as to be almost stationary, while the relationship between the chords is as disturbingly without harmonic direction as the comparable passages in the 'Rose-Croix' works of Erik Satie, which Messiaen much admires (Ex. 69). The later enormous piano

work, *Vingt Régards sur l'Enfant Jésus* is literally a series of contemplative 'looks' in the sense that the movements are without movement. Each piece tends to be built on an alternation of two or three chords, an ostinato, a pedal note, a reiterated figuration. The burden of personality dissolves into timeless contemplation. The European time-sense is no longer relevant to music which evades the concept of beginning, middle, and end: which is why Messiaen's works tend to last, chronometrically speaking, so long, if not for ever. There is no reason why they should stop.

Even in Messiaen's early works the sumptuously sensuous harmony, being non-developing, tends to proliferate into melodic arabesques related not only to mediaeval cantilation, but also to the melismatic styles of Eastern music. In his later work oriental features have become both conscious and elaborate. The sensory harmonies tend to be increasingly percussive in effect, like gongs, and virtually without harmonic meaning in the Western sense. Complementarily, the organization of such works as the *Ile de Feu* becomes almost entirely linear and rhythmic: except that Messiaen's 'series' are not completely chromatic, but are closely related to the linear ragas and rhythmic talas* of Indian music. His chord complexes are also derived from raga formations, whether traditional or (like Skryabin's) invented; in either case the 'series' are given religious, or at any rate magical, as well as technical significance. In recent years Messiaen has added to his study of oriental melodic and rhythmic techniques an equally exhaustive enquiry into the cries of birds; and has stated that the rest of his composing life will be devoted to an immense series of works wherein his humanity will be reborn through the language of birds. Fascinating though some of the piano-sounds may be, we may think that this is carrying forgetfulness of the human will a bit far; there is something in the messianic self-dedication of this most appropriately named composer that seems, in the strict sense, eccentric from—even opposed to—the needs of most twentieth-century men and women.

Yet Messiaen has created a language: which very few composers succeed in doing; and that language has made a considerable impact upon twentieth-century music. There are even affinities between it and the rival French school of Pierre Boulez [b. 1925], for Boulez has combined a completely serial, post-Webern technique with serial processes derived directly from Eastern ragas and talas. The sonorities of a work like *Le Marteau sans Maitre*, with their high, ethereal resonance, are new, yet closer to Debussy and Messiaen than to Schoenberg or even Webern. They also recall the ritualistic music of Bali: with the

* Raga: a linear pattern or series, usually with religious or magical as well as musical significance, used as the basis for improvisation in classical Indian music. Tala: a rhythmic pattern or series, similarly employed, in conjunction with the raga.

difference that the text the music sets (with a god-like exaggeration of human vocal resource!) is not a ritual celebration of the divine or the earthly, but a surrealistic poem that is, strictly speaking, nonsense. This is not a frivolous remark; for in a post-Freudian world we are, in exploring the depths below consciousness, seeking imaginative knowledge of reality. *Le Marteau* is concerned with an awareness of God, if not with an apprehension of him.

Webern and Stockhausen, Orff, Messiaen, and Boulez are, in their rejection of the West, saying something which Europe has at least partially to accept, if we are to live again. Their rejection may, however, easily become an evasion of our human responsibilities; certainly we feel more comfortable with those composers of Italy, Russia, and Britain who, while reacting against the exaggerated self-consciousness of Western civilisation, are not afraid to accept it in order to re-create it. It is interesting that in Italy—birthplace of Europe's Renaissance—some composers of both Messiaen's and of Boulez's generation have not carried the rejection of the West to anything like so extreme a point. Luigi Dallapiccola [b. 1904] has, particularly in his later works, made considerable use of serial techniques. Yet his music remains rooted in Renaissance polyphony and the unity of classical baroque texture. The forbears of his theatrical projection, his vocal lyricism, are the two great Green Men of Italian music, Monteverdi and Verdi.

While Dallapiccola is usually concerned, in his large-scale works, with religious issues, he starts not from a desire to obliterate the self in a mystical act, but from the necessity for compassion. His opera, *Il Prigioniero*, the choral *Canti di Prigionia*, stem from an awareness of the violence, suffering, and oppression which man has inflicted on man during the first half of this century. They are concerned with God because man seems impotent alone; but (like Schoenberg's music) they are in approach essentially humanistic, and it is not an accident that the central achievement of Dallapiccola's career should be a dramatization of the story of Job. This work reveals most impressively the way in which Dallapiccola's music belongs simultaneously to Italy's past, present, and future. In conception it is a *Sacra rappresentazione* in the seventeenth-century manner of Carissimi. The seventeenth-century Historicus sang in comparatively flat, emotionally uninvolved recitative. Dallapiccola's Storico speaks, but in rhythmically measured notation, his phrases being echoed by a speaking chorus, also rhythmically notated: as though a crowd of listeners (including you and me) were involving themselves in the story. This gives an extraordinary immediacy—a sense of present reality—to the setting.

The Storico recounts, impersonally. Job sings, lyrically and passionately, from within his being. Periodically the tension between the objective narration and Job's subjective passion crystallizes into operatic action; the characters in the story come alive and sing with Verdian incandescence. Various serial and contrapuntal devices are used, but in the interests of dramatic expression: for instance, the Comforters sing a double and then a triple canon, in which the processional rhythm and the contrapuntal unity suggest a girding of the loins. The climax comes in Job's desperate appeal to God, when human fortitude seems to be insufficient. The voice that replies 'out of the whirlwind' is represented by a *singing* chorus which, *largamente ma con violenza*, justifies the apparently arbitrary ways of God to man, while a brass choir blazes the Te Deum. The tortured and distraight polyphony grows gradually more sustained; but rises to a *furioso* climax as the voice from the whirlwind sings not only of man's dependence on God, but of God's dependence on man—a conclusion proudly in tune with the spirit of the Italian Renaissance and with what one takes to be Dallapiccola's attitude now. The music then fades into silence, eternity being symbolized by two flutes, one of which plays the other's part backwards. The silence seems the deeper because Dallapiccola has dared to set the profoundest imaginative statement about the nature of suffering except for Shakespeare's *King Lear*.

In Dallapiccola's music, as in Schoenberg's, the purely chromatic and serial elements seem not to deny but to extend the boundaries of the traditional elements; the exacerbated tension is never merely destructive. It is worth remarking, too, that the music of Luigi Nono [b. 1926], which is 'post-Webern' in being completely serial and extremely attenuated in sonority, also shows a quality of compassionate humanity. His works are concerned with an atom-threatened world; but the remote sighs and sobs of the dislocated choral and orchestral texture of his *Il Canto Sospeso* are intensely moving, not merely in their glimpse of a quiet beyond the harried present, but also in their response to the human suffering that must be borne in a broken, battered world.

In Dallapiccola and Nono there is, then, an embryonic religious sense combined with a social conscience.* The composers of Soviet Russia do not, of course, cultivate a religious sense, let alone the esoteric mysticism of a Webern or a Messiaen. None the less, their social conscience tends to direct attention away from a preoccupation with the self; and the official view that Soviet composers ought to study and make use of the folk traditions of the area they live in might be expected to encourage melodic and rhythmic techniques opposed to the traditions of western Europe, as it did in the case of Bartók and Szymanowsky. The paradox in the position of the Soviet composer lies, however, in the fact that he is building a new world in the interests not of a moribund peasantry, but of the proletariat: whose musical taste is still—as we saw when discussing Tchaikowsky and Rachmaninov—centred around composers of highly subjective neurosis, expressed through basically Western techniques! A Tchaikowsky 'cleaned up', rendered buoyantly extravert, seems a contradiction in terms. Yet the contradiction may have been a saving grace to Soviet composers: for it has meant that they have been able to create out of a tension between a sincere desire to affirm and an elegiac consciousness of personal frustration such as all human creatures are prone to in this state-before-Paradise (whether on earth or in Heaven). The numerous symphonies of Myaskovsky [1881–1951] are a fine example of this simultaneously optimistic and elegiac approach. The sustained melodies, the spacious proportions, the powerful rhythms lend dignity to the Tchaikowsky-like melancholy: while the melancholy reminds us of the fallible human heart.

Folk-music has no more influence on Myaskovsky's art than on Tchaikowsky's, and considerably less than it has on the work of the Big Five. He can reinvigorate nineteenth-century styles because he is, if not a great, a real composer, with something to say; and while it is true that, in Soviet Russia, much bad music has been poured into 'outdated' nineteenth-century moulds, it is equally true that a great deal of bad music has

* We should mention in this context a senior Catalan composer, Roberto Gerhard [b. 1896], who left his native country at the time of the Spanish Civil War and settled in England. His early works stemmed from impressionism and Spanish national tradition. The rhythmic energy and harmonic sensuousness of his music have survived since he has begun to explore complete serialization; and his fusion of a passionate humanism with an 'impersonal' mysticism makes his position in the European tradition more central and perhaps more important than his almost complete isolation, in his adopted country, would lead one to expect.

been created, in the West, by wilful attempts to avoid conformity. There will always be more bad music than good. Any composer starts from conditions as he knows them; what he makes of them depends on his integrity and vitality. This we can see in the work of the first two Soviet composers who have made —unlike Myaskovsky—an impact on the world outside Russia.

The fundaments of Prokofiev's art, as of Myaskovsky's, were closely related to Tchaikowsky, and still more to Rachmaninov: consider the big tune at the end of his Third Piano Concerto. In his Parisian youth, however, Sergey Prokofiev [1891–1953] learned, as an exile, to disguise the passionate heart beneath a veneer of sophistication. After the First World War it was natural enough that Paris should have fostered a deliberate cult of irresponsibility. Jean Cocteau, as mentor of the new artists, encouraged hatred of pretentiousness, love of everything supposedly simple and free of complication. Hence the cult of childhood, of Negro art, of music-hall and circus, of low life generally. Francis Poulenc [b. 1899] is the only composer of the group known as Les Six who has remained faithful to the ideals charmingly expressed in the works of his teens,* such as the *Bestiare* songs and the *Mouvements Perpétuels* for piano. These pieces are all of tiny dimensions, with aggressively diatonic themes, like nursery tunes or café songs, in regular rhythms. These banalities, however, are consciously pepped up by

* Of the other members of the group, two stopped composing and one devoted almost all his attention to film music. Of the remaining two members, Arthur Honegger [b. 1892] became a dramatic composer, dealing with large—often religious—themes on a large scale, in a re-created baroque style that is noble and ceremonial, though often sharply dissonant. Both his gravity and his 'public manner' are remote from the sophisticated banality of Les Six, but have much in common with the work of other Swiss composers such as Othmar Schoeck [b. 1886], Frank Martin [b. 1890], and Willy Burkhard [b. 1900]. It is interesting that the Swiss composers, whether their roots are German or French, seem to preserve a lucid neutrality. Comparatively uninvolved in the humanist crisis supremely represented by Wagner, they can use apparently archaic—medieval, Renaissance, and baroque—conventions with spontaneity and power. Their music is always civilized: and for that very reason, perhaps, seems rather remote from the issues that concern us most deeply.

The other member of Les Six, Darius Milhaud [b. 1892], has nothing in common with Swiss austerity. He is a composer whose uninhibited prodigality springs from his Jewish passion, his Latin (Provencal) vitality, and his prolonged sojourn in South America. From so many violent and contradictory impulses he has not achieved a coherent idiom; but in the *Concertino de Printemps* for violin and chamber orchestra, he created the most tinglingly vivacious of all pieces in the French pastoral vein, while *La Création du Monde*, though inferior to the real thing, is one of the few convincing, sophisticated evocations of Negro jazz. The value of his large-scale works—such as the immense operas on Latin-American subjects—is problematical.

sophistication: by the 'wrong' note or altered harmony; by the simultaneous (polytonal) sounding of several simple tonalities; by cheekily raucous scoring (with a prevalence of brass and woodwind). The feeling in this music is quite different from that in the music of the two composers—Chabrier and Satie—whom Les Six acknowledged as their masters. For Chabrier was a *positive* comic genius whose ironic wit was inseparable from his animal high spirits; while Satie did not play at being childish, but recovered the innocence of the child through the lucidity of his technique. In the music of Chabrier and Satie there is neither sentimentality nor nostalgia. Poulenc, on the other hand, is all sentimentality and nostalgia—for the presumed irresponsibility of childhood, for low life, for the pretty elegancies of an eighteenth-century rococo world quite distinct from Ravel's profound re-creation of the classical fairy tales. These 'regressive' qualities are Poulenc's genuine attributes, which have grown stronger with the years, as we can see from his Gounodesque church music, his Massenet-like opera, *Les Carmélites*, and his numerous, and most touching, later songs which reconcile Massenet with the malaise of the café-concert. (*Montparnasse* is perhaps the quintessential Poulenc song.)

When Prokofiev settled in Paris in the 'twenties he welcomed the debunking wit which he found in the music of Les Six, especially Poulenc; and the affecting, as well as amusing, quality of the music he wrote in this vein comes from the fact that he too loves what he laughs at. There was, moreover, a particular reason why he, as a Russian exile, should respond to the nostalgia incipient even in Poulenc's early music; in small works like the *Grandmother's Tales* for piano he gives a Russian reinterpretation of Poulenc's use of the nursery ditty. Prokofiev's themes too are short, with hypnotic repetitions; but, like so many of the modal song themes of Tchaikowsky, they invoke no urban environment, but the eternal-seeming melancholy of the Russian peasant. At the same time the haunting themes are now distanced by the disturbing relationships of the simple diatonic harmonies and the precise rhythmic patterns that accompany them. In acquiring a tender irony, their melancholy ceases to oppress.

This suggests why Prokofiev, on returning to the Soviet Union, was able to use his Parisian experience to such good effect. The sophisticated high-jinks become an element of mordant satire that can safeguard his romantic passion from hysteria and that can, at times, grow into a positive ebullience—the pride in a new world that finds expression in the finales of his symphonies and in the moto-perpetuo-like movements in his piano sonatas. (Perhaps one could not believe in these pieces if they were not, as well as vigorous, also intelligent.) Beneath the extravert gaiety, however, the tender nostalgia of Prokofiev's Russian fairy tale is always present, if never obtrusive. This is why his most moving and characteristic music tends to be lyrical. In both the early and the late violin concertos, for instance, his gaiety and nostalgia are held in equilibrium; the merriment makes the sadness supportable, and the sadness make the merriment credible. Even in his emotionally more ambitious works, when he writes under the pressure of tense, often violent, experience, he is most convincing when the lyrical basis of his art is strongest. It is not fortuitous that perhaps the finest of all his works should be a sonata for violin and piano—the mature work in F minor: wherein the interpenetration of the linear and the percussive instrument creates a piano texture that has both metallic sharpness and sonorous depth, a violin line that is at once warm and pungent.

Shostakovitch [b. 1906] made his mark at a remarkably early age with a symphony that, like Prokofiev's early music, reconciled a heartfelt Tchaikowskyan sweetness with a self-protective wit, Parisian in origin, yet growing, in the last movement, into a kind of communal frenzy. The tenderness, the cheek, the excitement, all grow to maturity in the sequence of his symphonies; but in his case the relationship to Tchaikowsky and to Parisian sophistication is complemented by another, and deeper, affinity. If Mahler seems an unexpected musician to influence a Soviet composer, we must remember that Mahler's conception of the symphony as an all-inclusive world, embracing every aspect of life, is in an obvious sense democratic. Mahler may have been an elegiac composer singing the swan-song of a once-aristocratic world; but any truly creative composer of a new world has to admit into his self-confident awareness of present and future an awareness also of the old world's death, and of the human disappointments and hopes that followed in its wake.

It is certainly not an accident that the most talented composer the Soviet Union has yet produced—perhaps her only composer of indubitable genius—should betray this affinity with a composer who, we saw, already suggested a turning away from Western traditions. And although Shostakovitch's musical materials remain Western, even nineteenth-century, the manner in which he uses them marks a radical departure from the eighteenth- and nineteenth-century notion of a symphony. Whereas for Beethoven a symphony is growth through conflict, Shostakovitch opposes the states of contemplation and of action. So although Shostakovitch described his Fifth Symphony, in Beethovenian terms, as 'the making of a man', he also said that the symphony was 'entirely lyrical'; the drama which it incarnates is not, like that in Beethoven's symphonies, subjective, but epic. Thus the work opens with an enormous melodic period that suggests, through leaping sixths in dotted rhythm, a questioning aspiration (Ex. 70). But this theme does not generate

a 'dualistic' tonal conflict; it evolves lyrically, growing cumulatively stronger, until it is transformed into a spacious cantabile theme, with a pulsing accompaniment, wherein the individual life seems to be fulfilled. Although these long, winding melodies tend to return to a nodal point, they have no relation to Russian folk-music and—like the cantabile themes of Tchaikowsky and Mahler—eclectically assimilate European elements from Italy, Austria, and France. Yet the brooding, timeless quality of this music is profoundly Russian. Its melancholy is at once introverted and impersonal. Self-contemplation leads, as in Mahler, to self-forgetfulness and liberation; in this case, because a subjective sorrow is absorbed into the vastness of the Steppes, the epic sorrow of a people.

Only at this point, after this immense lyrical paragraph, are the contradictions inherent in experience admitted. The contemplative theme is transformed, on low brass, into a sinister lament which grows into a grisly march: the lyrical fulfilment is denied, metamorphosed into horror, rather as it is in the first movement of Mahler's Ninth. So when the contemplative theme returns, it does so in a more frenzied version; and its ultimate disintegration into sweetly dreamy whimpers on flute, violin, celesta and muted trumpet leaves us feeling that the vast emptiness of the Steppes can be no assuagement for our loneliness. So the movement ends with a wistful, unresolved restatement of the apparently affirmative opening paragraph; and the scherzo that follows, although funny, is also wry. Self-forgetfulness here becomes self-mockery; the gaiety is aloof, deliberately uninvolved, as though the composer were saying that if man's aspiration is as unrewarding as the first movement suggests, there is no answer but a shrug of the shoulders. The continual modulations, the occasional acid harmony, the sharp orchestration are disturbing as well as witty.

The largo returns to the brooding contemplation of the first movement, but the questing element inherent in the leaping sixths has gone. The rhythm is level, the contours of the melody smooth; again the eternal-seeming spaciousness is emphasized by the Mahlerian, chamber-music-like nature of the scoring, the hollowness of the texture. This time there is no contradiction. The sustained lyricism gradually assimilates the introspective passion of the first movement: so that the personal contemplation can lead into a public resolution. The last movement is all kinetic energy, sometimes fierce, sometimes hilariously comic in its transformations of popular material. Shostakovitch's epic resolutions plumb less deep than Beethoven's, for their public fulfilment is juxtaposed to, not the result of, the private struggle. None the less, the personal and social aspects of Shostakovitch's music are inseparable: for although the release of power and gaiety in the external world is not the consequence of inner growth, it could not occur but for the contemplation, wherein a personal loneliness or frustration is mastered in becoming epical. It is significant that the overwhelmingly triumphant coda to the finale of this symphony is preceded by a remote reminiscence of the contemplative lyrical theme of the first movement.

Perhaps we may say that the resolution in Shostakovitch's symphonies is not so much the release of inner tensions as an act of faith. This accords with his prevailingly lyrical approach to the symphony; and although he is not, of course, a religious composer in the normally accepted sense, his communism has affinities with religious belief in that it sees personal problems in the light of an absolute. So he too manifests a turning-away from post-Renaissance principles which is not the less significant for being less obvious than that of his contemporaries in Germany, Italy, and France. It is not fortuitous that he seldom employs, either in symphonies or chamber works, the classical, dualistic first-movement sonata form. Contemplatively, he works by slow lyrical extension; dramatically, by the sharpest contradictions that remain unresolved; kinetically, by the release of rhythmic energy that sweeps all before it. We should remark too that his major piano work is a series of twenty-four preludes and fugues in all the major and minor keys—on the analogy of Bach's supreme masterpiece of baroque unity.

The conservatism of English music in the twentieth century is a more complex matter than that of Russian music because —as we saw in the chapter on Vaughan Williams—we have had to recover a spiritual heritage that our triumphant industrialism had buried. To re-create the past as Vaughan Williams did called for a passionate religious sense such as is, inevitably, rare in an industrially dominated society: so that it is not surprising that, though Vaughan Williams has had innumerable imitators, he has had only one true successor. We may say of Edmund Rubbra [b. 1901], as of Vaughan Williams, that the core of his work consists in his symphonies and his choral music, the latter being ancillary to, and in a profound sense connected with, the symphonies. These works are still more remote from the dualistic classical sonata than the symphonies of Shostakovitch, since they are in essence lyrical, contemplative—and unequivocally religious, having none of the Russian's unresolved contradictions and metrical animation. As an English composer, with a deeply mystical mind and a vocal rather than instrumental heritage, Rubbra creates melodic lines which—though they have not the pentatonic pastoralism of the imitators of Vaughan Williams—spring from the step-wise movement, the rhythms and inflexions, of the human voice in the same way as do the melodies of Dowland. From such melodic lines he builds works which are genuinely symphonic and at the same time are not opposed to the principles of vocal polyphony. This is a very different matter from writing vocal polyphony scored for instruments: for if the symphony has to be rethought in lyrical rather than dramatic terms, vocal polyphony has, in its turn, to acquire a long-range harmonic and tonal architecture.

Thus the whole first movement of his Fifth Symphony grows out of the phrase enunciated at the outset by solo oboe. The line moves 'vocally' by step: but involves too a rising augmented fourth, followed by a falling perfect fourth (Ex. 71). So the

symphony begins, like a symphony of Bruckner, as an act of praise, a 'monistic' lyrical hymn that grows spontaneously, like a tree. But as the themes expand, the tension within the augmented fourth grows increasingly dominant, reminding us of the human tensions out of which the symphonic principle had originally sprung. That the tensions are present, beneath the surface, is part of Rubbra's contemporaneity; and is the reason why he (like Bruckner) has chosen to write symphonies, rather than to express himself purely in liturgical music. In the scherzo the subterranean tensions disappear, and the structure is monistic in the most fundamental sense, being consistently contrapuntal: a deceptively simple dance tune, alternating stepwise movement with perfect fourths, glides without climax through every major key of the chromatic scale. Only the restless modulation belies the tune's tranquil gaiety and the unity of fugue. With the short slow movement the hymnic lyricism is reinstated, the pulse slower than the first movement's, the contours more spaciously serene: though it is significant that the movement makes some compromise with the sonata notion of development and recapitulation. The recapitulatory passage repeats the song-melody in a key a semitone below that of its first appearance: a transition, perhaps vocally derived, which crops up repeatedly in Rubbra's music. This restatement leads without a break into a bounding allegro in $\frac{6}{8}$, a rhythm typical of Rubbra's jubilant finales. Themes in cross-rhythm evolve from the initial phrase. Gradually a relationship is revealed between this phrase and the oboe theme with which the symphony had opened. Thus the work ends at the point where it began. The phrase has fulfilled its life-circle, and returns to its source. We may note that, for all the freedom of the modulations, the tonal sense is rooted firmly in the harmonic series. The keys in which the four movements start together make up the notes of the diatonic triad.

Since Rubbra's symphonies are basically a religious affirmation, and his vocal music is rooted in the poetry of the seventeenth century, his work may not seem to have much direct relationship to the twentieth century. Yet his 'celebrative act' has a deeper relevance to our needs than has the music of the only composer of his generation to start from an acceptance of the immediate past. William Walton [b. 1902] is an authentic successor to Elgar, as Rubbra is the natural successor to Vaughan Williams. His first works—such as the overture, *Portsmouth Point* —attempted a fusion of the materialistic vigour of the nineteenth-century symphonic poem with elements derived from earlier English traditions (the extravert aspects of Purcellian and Handelian dance-music) and with the jazzy distortions of the twentieth century. He made his reputation, however, with the brilliant parodistic or sentimental genre pieces of *Façade*, composed as accompaniment to Edith Sitwell's (spoken) poems; and although these might seem to debunk Edwardian glamour, they would not be so touching as well as funny did they not spring from love of the object laughed at. It is not therefore surprising that Walton's first considerable work—the Viola Concerto of 1925—should be prevailingly nostalgic and closely related to Elgar's elegiac 'Cello Concerto. The witty Walton of the first works is here transformed into the acid self-mockery of the scherzo; while the last movement, with its spacious marching theme over a stalking bass, hints yearningly at Elgar's public manner. But the core of the music is in the yearning, not the nobility; and the bittersweet false relations of the lyrically rhapsodic first movement return in the cadenza and valedictory epilogue. The tang of the false relations—the only element in Walton's music that harks back to our crucial seventeenth century—lends strength to the poignancy; in his later concertos for singing stringed instruments (for violin and for 'cello) Walton repeats the formula of the Viola Concerto perhaps too passively, for the retrospective nostalgia seems almost self-indulgent.

In the three concertos Walton expresses a private nostalgia which most people can share, if not always sympathize with. In *Belshazzer's Feast* he, as a North-Countryman, takes over the public manner of English oratorio, which had come to its heyday with the rise of our material prosperity. The rhythmic exuberance, the sonorous spacing, the physical excitement of the scoring have obvious affinities with the extravert animation of Handel's choral style, in its socially ceremonial vein. But the animation has turned to animus, revealing Edwardian pomp and circumstance in their true, luridly cruel colours. It is significant that this work—which is probably the last 'Handelian' oratorio—should be completely irreligious, and that the triumphant Christians should sing the same kind of music as the heathens. Now they are top dogs, they will clearly behave in exactly the same way; and this peculiarly savage irony is a logical conclusion to Walton's earlier satirical bent. *Belshazzar* 'exposes' material prosperity, the cult of power, while yearning for its personal satisfactions. The positive values in this piece are contained in the almost Delian chromaticism of the waters of Babylon episode: a heart-breaking music of elegiac lament, comparable with that of the Viola Concerto. Only once in his career has Walton attempted to create something positive from the acceptance of the violence inherent in a materialistic world. That is in the impressive (and Beethovenian) first movement of his Symphony; but it is significant that he found the work so difficult to finish, and that the last movement is a rhetorical gesture rather than a resolution.

Rubbra is essentially a religious composer, Walton an elegiacally sensuous composer; Michael Tippett [b. 1905], having both a religious sense and social awareness, perhaps touches the outside world at more points than either of them. He made his reputation with an oratorio to his own libretto, *A Child of Our Time*; and the difference between this piece and Walton's oratorio is crucial. Walton's oratorio is devastatingly negative and deliberately superficial in its public manifestations, while its positive experience is of personal lament. Tippett treats the public experience 'from within', expressing its relevance to all of us. Dramatizing a true story of the Nazi terror, the oratorio deals directly with war, oppression, persecution, and isolation. But the personal story becomes a twentieth-century myth: by relating the conception to Handel's *Messiah*, Tippett suggests some kinship with the oratorio-going British public; by substituting Negro spirituals for Bach's Lutheran chorales, he uses an oppressed people as a general symbol for the stifling of the human spirit—with the advantage that the idiom is related to the popular music with which his public is familiar. Tippett's acute awareness of the anguish inherent in experience, especially today, communicates itself to his technique which compared with Walton's assurance is in some ways strained and unfulfilled. Yet the inward immediacy and validity of the feeling conquer. Without offering any solution to our social evils, without castigating us for our wickedness, the oratorio grows into a lyrical affirmation of life. In the thrilling final chorus the polyphony swells, the solo vocal writing burgeons into ecstatic arabesque. What keeps us alive, the music tells us, is the human impulse to dance and sing, whatever man's bestiality to man.

The end of the oratorio effects 'the heart's assurance'—to quote the title of the song cycle that Tippett wrote to a series of poems about death by two young poets who were killed in the war. From this work, which deals in personal terms with the public issues involved in the oratorio, we can see how Tippett's affirmation of life entails a technical development also. Here the bounding, long-breathed melodies in their lilting 'sprung' rhythms flower into creative ornamentation (Ex. 72).

Ex. 72
O ne-ver ne-ver ne-ver ne - ver trust your pride of move-ment

Though the music is a new sound, its roots are in tradition—not so much in Renaissance music as in English music of the seventeenth century. Thus the compulsive rhythm is a more extravagant version of the Purcellian tension between vocal inflexion and physical dance movement; the polyphonically derived harmony intensifies the seventeenth-century partiality for modal variety and false relation; while the flowering of the lines into ever smaller note-values parallels the seventeenth-century technique of divisions on a ground. There is a baroque, sensuously exciting quality in the curling tendrils of Tippett's vocal line and piano texture; yet—as with such seventeenth-century masters as William Lawes and Purcell—the sustained lift of the melodies gives the music a spiritual buoyancy also. From this point of view, the contrast between Tippett's invigorating and Walton's elegiac false relations is striking.

The Heart's Assurance may have been a preludial study for Tippett's opera, *The Midsummer Marriage*: which differs from his oratorio in starting from, rather than ending with, the affirmation of life. The marriage is itself the mating of the senses' joy with the spirit's mystery; and in taking his operatic mythology from Jungian psychology Tippett has sought for imagery that will strike deep, to a twentieth-century audience, without need of intellectual explanation. Allegory is bound to be a tricky business, in a society that, believing itself to be rationalistic, has grown out of the habit of allegorical thinking. But Tippett's libretto is probably the only kind that he could have set; and its theme is closely related to the crisis in his own musical development. Technical limitations are always, perhaps, imaginative limitations; here Tippett sheds the inhibitions that partially frustrated fulfilment in earlier works. The *Ritual Dances*—if not the whole opera—are magical in the old, celebrative sense, offering not illusion, but a revelation of the deepest compulsions from which our lives draw sustenance. The difficulty of Tippett's music is evidence of the struggle most twentieth-century men must undergo in order to learn to celebrate. When once we are free, the act of celebration is itself simple. It is relevant to note that the features that make Tippett's idiom so distinctive—the sprung rhythms and lilting syncopations, the harmonic false relations, the technique of division—all have their counterparts not only in our seventeenth-century music, but also, in a cruder form, in the urban folk-music of our own day—jazz.

Both Rubbra and Tippett were slow starters. That Benjamin Britten [b. 1913] created a work of genius at the age of eighteen cannot be separated from the nature of his achievement. In so far as *A Boy was Born* was a choral work based on a traditional Christian theme, it was part of the heritage of Holst and Vaughan Williams. Where it differs from other attempts to evoke a relatively remote past is in the absence of either nostalgia or inhibition. The ripe chromaticism of Bax's or Peter Warlock's settings of mediaeval poems carries with it the knowledge that one is shut out from such single-mindedness; while Holst achieves it only by a denial of the lyrical warmth man needs to live by. The 'youthfulness' of Britten's music, on the other hand, seems to spring from a direct realization of what it felt like to live in a world dominated by faith. It is not (like a Rubbra symphony) a religious piece; it is simply about the growth of life in innocence. A boy is born indeed; and the affirmation is inseparable from the technical virtuosity which Britten (unlike Tippett) seemed to possess by natural endowment. This virtuosity is not merely a matter of contrapuntal skill. It also involves an element that one might call theatrical projection: the ability to discover, as did composers of the baroque era, a musical image that 'enacts' aurally, even physically, the visual and psychological images of the poem. (A marvellous example in this work is the simultaneously burning and freezing major and minor seconds that aurally realizes the 'bleak midwinter') (Ex. 73).

It does not follow that Britten's *A Boy was Born* is a better piece of music than Bax's *Ora Mater Filium* or Holst's *Hymn of Jesus*; but it does follow that there was in Britten's work the germ of a future evolution. In his next significant work he began to develop instrumentally the element of theatrical projection present in the choral work—its cosmopolitan, unprovincial sense of style. The *Variations for String Orchestra* on a theme of Frank Bridge represent a deliberate break from English pastoralism and are intentionally eclectic. It is not an accident that the theme should be taken from Britten's teacher, Frank Bridge [1879–1941], for as composer Bridge had been relatively impervious to Holst's and Vaughan Williams's rediscovery of our past, and had tried out his hand in most fashionable Continental techniques, from Skryabinesque chromatics, to Stravinskian percussive dissonance, to Schoenbergian atonality.

The Continental composer who has, in this work, exerted a potently meaningful influence on Britten is, however, Mahler. No doubt the voung Englishman was fascinated by Mahler's music for the same general reasons as was Shostakovitch; but there was also a particular reason for Britten's interest, in that one of the dominant themes in Mahler's work had been the search for a lost Eden, often identified with the innocence of the child. In *A Boy was Born* Britten, being still a boy himself, had expressed a childlike innocence with adult virtuosity. In the few years that had elapsed since that work he was growing up; so into the *Bridge Variations* comes an element of Mahlerian nostalgia for an innocence that is lost. The introduction, built on arpeggiated figurations in bitonal relationships, and the theme and first variation have a declamatory rhetoric and an intense pathos that recall Mahler; they have also a tender radiance that is the first unmistakable evidence of Britten's personality.

After the first variation, however, the work abruptly ceases to be a personal testament and becomes a series of genre pieces —March, Romance, Aria Italiana, Bourrée Classique, Wiener Waltz, and Moto Perpetuo—ranging from overt parody to a serious use of the 'mask' whereby the artist seeks to depersonalize his experience. The pathos, and the Mahlerian rhetoric, return with the Funeral March and Chant: until the accumulating tension is resolved in a brilliantly developed fugue. This combines the externalized vivacity of the genre pieces with the passion of the introduction: so the variations would seem to indicate, in purely musical terms, how one must lose the self in order to find it. It is as though Britten already knew that he was destined to be an operatic composer.

In the next stage of his career Britten began to explore the possibilities of operatic 'projection' by composing song cycles in the French and the Italian manner. Only when he had discovered how an English composer could exploit the heritage of European operatic style—as Purcell had exploited the Italian and French conventions of his own time—did Britten explore the possibilities of an aria and arioso relevant to the English language. The tenor *Serenade*, setting poems covering a wide range of English literature, resembles Purcell's music in being at once eclectic and almost aggressively personal. One can tabulate the derivation of Britten's mannerisms—the melodies built on arpeggiated thirds, the expansive leaps, especially of sixth and seventh, the pentatonic undulations—while knowing that his melodies have become unique, if not inimitable.

The creation of an English operatic idiom was not, however,

a purely musical matter. Purcell's failure to create an English operatic tradition in the seventeenth century was not a personal failure, but the deficiency of a society. That had something to do with the division epitomized in the Civil War; and that had something to do with the 'disassociation of sensibility' that in England split mind and matter, spirit and senses, more rapidly and more radically than elsewhere. Perhaps that breach had to be healed, and the heart reborn in innocence, before an English opera could be achieved.

However this may be, the discovery of an operatic convention involves, too, the discovery of the necessary myth. Looking back, we can see that all Britten's operas deal with the same parable: the renewal of innocence as the condition of human creativity. *A Boy was Born*—almost literally a boy's work—could with dazzling innocence create innocence in our minds and senses. The operatic works of Britten's maturity, on the other hand, are concerned with the fight between the Fool's simple heart and the corruptions of the world. *Peter Grimes* turns on the ancient myth of the Sauvage Man who in Eden would be innate goodness: whom the depravity of humanity renders destructive. Deprived of Ellen's love, Grimes's innocence turns to cruelty and he destroys the Boy who is his own soul. Then the World (thrillingly represented by the chorus) rounds on him, harries him to his death.

Though Grimes may be an unheroic hero, his predicament is genuinely tragic; and the progression from innocence to exile, to persecution, is a theme as relevant to our own times as Nahum Tate's and Purcell's rehashing of Dido's story was to theirs. Arioso—the human singing voice become dramatic enactment—is the core of Britten's opera as it is of Purcell's; and the element of theatrical projection in Britten's work now becomes reality. No opera is more evocative, yet at the same time more precise, in its creation of time and place. The tang of the sea, the hues of Suffolk light, the bustle of anonymous human activity, are revealed through that baroque instinct for the appropriate musical image that first appeared in *A Boy was Born*. And this precise realization of the external world is inseparable from the music-drama's insight into the mind and heart. Britten's music, in association with Slater's adaptation of Crabbe, achieves its deepest insight through its operatic objectivity; and its Englishness is revealed through its eclecticism.

Albert Herring has the same theme as *Grimes*, treated comically instead of tragically. Herring is again the natural fool, a pathetic if not heroic figure: and though his exile and destruction by the World turn out to be only a charade, that does not deflate the almost-tragic potency of the threnody sung over him. These two operas most convincingly attain a balance between the private and the public aspects of Britten's habitual theme. In *The Rape of Lucretia* there is much heartfelt and exquisite music; but the Christian overtones of the end strike an uncomfortable, even synthetic, note. Perhaps something the same is true of *Billy Budd*. The profound humanity of Grimes comes from the fact that the light of innocence and the dark of depravity are both within him. In *Billy Budd* the separation of Billy's light from Claggart's darkness emphasizes the personal at the expense of the universal aspects of the theme, so there is something a little neurotic, even pretentious, about the dragging in of the Crucifixion. This may explain why *Billy Budd* has not become an accepted part of operatic repertory, in the way that *Peter Grimes* has, though there is a sense in which *Billy Budd* is the more consummately realized work.

Still more completely fulfilled, imaginatively and technically, is *The Turn of the Screw*. Perhaps it is not fortuitous that this piece tackles the basic theme most directly: for Henry James's horrifying *conte* enters the world of the child to explore the corruption of innocence. Britten's tightly organized score sees the innocence of the nursery ditty—which he had entered into in his own most touching children's operas—against the ghastly machinations of human spirits that have died in losing the innocence that they, presumably, once possessed. Britten's theatrical magic has never been more insidious; we submit whether we will or not. But the private claustrophobia of the piece means that it cannot challenge the human validity of *Grimes*.

There are signs in Britten's recent work, however, that the almost pathological horror of corruption is finding its resolution. The most beautiful of all Britten's song cycles with piano, written in between *Billy Budd* and *The Turn of the Screw*, is *Winter Words*, settings of lyrics and ballads by Thomas Hardy. Britten is a highly sophisticated composer, and Hardy a notoriously unsophisticated poet. Yet Britten has used Hardy superbly for his own purposes, setting a group of poems which all deal with innocence and experience, while finding in Hardy's calm acceptance a liberation from neurosis. The first song deals with the inevitability of Time's threat to the innocence of childhood. It is a lyric poem which becomes a musical image: the bitonal chords and dislocated rhythms of the piano part suggest the wind-blustered trees and the agitation within the heart, while the intermittent unison Ds suggest a firm acceptance of the inevitable. The telescoped harmonies and dislocated rhythms continue softly in the piano while the vocal line sings sweetly, in cooing sixths and sevenths, of childhood's innocence (Ex. 74):

Ex.74
pp
And the chil - dren who
ppp
ram - ble through here con-ceive that there ne - - - ver has been a
time when no trees no tall trees grew here

only to be swept away by the winds of Time. Then follow a series of ballads which are all operatic scenas in miniature, evoked again with astonishing economy: the little boy, with his ticket stuck in his hat, travelling through the night on the hooting train, vacant, knowing nothing of his destiny; or the other little boy, playing his fiddle in ironic simplicity to the convict in the railway waiting-room; or, comically, the wagtail that flies in panic from human contagion; or, pathetically, the angelically innocent modal music that evokes the choirmaster's ghostly visitation. Only in the last song does the lyric mode reappear. The poem deals, in philosophic terms, with the birth of consciousness which is also the death of innocence; but in asking when Nescience shall be reaffirmed it admits that Eden once lost can never be recovered. Britten's long, eternally flowing vocal line marvellously creates the simplicity of primal bliss and also the longing for its return: while the regular progression of the chords, thickly grouped in the low registers of the piano, accepts the inevitability of pain.

This acceptance of reality, within the vision of innocence, finds a still richer and deeper expression in the *Nocturne* for tenor strings and a series of obbligato instruments. This work, written after *The Turn of the Screw*, carries on at the point where its companion piece, the tenor *Serenade*, left off. The *Serenade* dealt in daytime experience, while ending with Keat's invocation to sleep. The *Nocturne* deals entirely in the world of night; but sees dreams as the source of the deepest reality known to us. Thus in the introductory song from Shelley's *Prometheus Unbound* the polytonal planes on which the intrinsically simple harmonies move create an extraordinary feeling of disassociation; out of the unconscious life of dream comes the creative imagination: 'forms *more* real than living man'.

But when the first obbligato instrument enters to introduce the first 'reality' that emerges from the subconscious the experience is frightening indeed. The poem, *The Kraken*, is one of Tennyson's juvenalia; yet one wonders if a more terrifyingly aware utterance ever came from the mouth of babe or suckling. The bassoon here becomes the creature's writhings and surgings, while the strings become percussive ploppings and sea-sizzlings. As the song fades into a recurrence of the lullaby music, the nightmare is succeeded by what seems to be a pleasant dream, in the remote radiance of A major, with the obbligato instrument, a harp, playing liquid arabesques over sustained string harmonies. The unchanging tonality, the pentatonic flavour, the slow waltz rhythm, give a hypnotic quality to

Coleridge's vision of the 'lovely boy' in the wilderness. But the innocent sweetness now hides a threat. Though he is a little child (in Britten's lilting thirds and fourths), he is 'plucking fruits'; and alone in the night, he has 'no friends'.

The succeeding songs grow from the tension between the dream and the nightmare, suggesting, in the settings of Wordsworth and Wilfred Owen, the half-conscious link between the terrors within the mind and their manifestation in the external world. The final song—a setting of Shakespeare's forty-third sonnet—'When most I wink, then do my eyes best see'—fulfils the cycle's theme: that the life of dream is the gateway to reality. Musically, too, the song is consummate, for the vocal line, over-slowly moving quavers, is more lyrically sustained than in any of the previous movements, and is rooted in C major-minor—the key that seems to exert a gravitational pull on the latent, neighbouring tonalities of the other songs. And perhaps, after all, Britten's quintessential experience turns out to be religious, in a personal, not ritualistic, sense. For when, after the wide-ranging octaves of the climax, we return to the lullaby's gentle rocking, in the serenity of C major—but with other-worldly, unresolved D flat major thirds on harp and string harmonics—Britten reveals the mystical depth beneath Shakespeare's conceit of the lover who sees his love 'bright in dark directed'. It is no longer the human beloved we are seeking in the darkness of the night; it is also the Beloved, the source of life that mysteriously renews the human spirit. 'There is in God, some say a deep but dazzling darkness.' It cannot be an accident that Britten's most recent opera is also a setting of Shakespeare—an adaptation of *A Midsummer Night's Dream*: that this piece should see the human and the spirit world as complementary: and that the magic music in the opera should be closely related to the music of the unconscious in the *Nocturne*. The opera is a ritual that is life-celebrating rather than death-stricken. And although there is nothing in Britten's work to suggest that he thinks a European should, or could, escape the 'pain of consciousness', it is significant that he (like all the composers discussed in this chapter, with the partial exception of Tippett and Prokofiev) has hardly ever written a movement in sonata form: and that his recent music, especially *A Midsummer Night's Dream*, relies more on melodic arabesque over relatively static ostinati and and pedal points than on harmonic movement.

10

MUSIC IN A NEW-FOUND LAND

This book has been concerned with the history of music in Europe. We have seen that, even in Europe, the composer's approach to his art has been affected, over the past fifty or more years, by the disintegration of tradition. The American composer started from such disintegration, for he had no cultural tradition to lose. He had nothing but the old rags and bones of European culture that, imported to a new environment, soon lost their savour. Then gradually, in the pulping machine of a polyglot society, the rags and bones began to acquire a taste of their own. The process, however, took time; and perhaps for this reason the earliest American compositions to manifest a creative spark tended to be technically inexpert. William Billings [1746–1800], in the late eighteenth century, had little ambition except to produce devotional music in the tradition of the Puritan hymn. His mistakes in text-book harmony have, however, a whiff of creative genius: so that he is an original who can still move us, while the professional competence of his European-trained contemporaries and successors can move us no longer.

If the lack of a past means the loss of the wisdom that respect for tradition brings, it also offers a supreme opportunity. Potentially, the artist becomes an 'unacknowledged legislator of the world': so the first authentic American composer, Charles Ives [1874–1954], held that music was a moral force, dismissing the belief that it was primarily self-expression as 'the Byronic fallacy'. He could not be content, like his contemporary, Edward Macdowell [1861–1908], to write second-hand, if poetic, music in the German tradition, even with a piquant spice of Grieg-like chromatics. If he was to be an honest creator, he had to take his materials from the world around him. Since he was born at Danbury, Connecticut, this meant the provincial world of the hard-bitten farmer, the small business-man and trader: which in musical terms was the town band (which Ives's father directed), the corny theatre tune, the chapel hymn. The remoteness of this music from academic convention stimulated the aural imagination; and while Ives's father had given him a training in conventional harmony and counterpoint and a respect for the 'manly' classical composers, especially Beethoven, this was insignificant compared with the unpredictable sound-stuff offered to him by his environment. What excited Ives's imagination was the vast body of camp singers yelling slightly different versions of the same hymn; the horn-player who gets left behind his fellows in the town band; the four bands that, at celebration time, play different music simultaneously in the four corners of the town square; the chapel singing heard over water, mingled with the sound of wind and rustling leaves. Ives would have agreed with his father, who, when asked how he could stand hearing old John (the local stonemason) bellowing off-key at camp meetings, replied: "Old John is a supreme musician. Look into his face and hear the music of the ages. Don't pay too much attention to the sounds. If you do, you may miss the music."

Ives's empirical approach to technique relates him to Whitman; he shares the poet's all-inclusiveness, his ubiquitous love of every facet of the visible, audible, and tactile world. His gargantuan appetite 'absorbs and translates' experience as the original Leather-stocking pioneer attempted to subjugate the physical world; and techniques from conventional European music, from jazz improvisation, from chapel and bar parlour, and from the noises of Nature are to be used as experience dictates, often within the same work, and even simultaneously, since all experience is related and indivisible.

Paradoxically, these fusions of contrarieties sound purposeful, not chaotic. In *General Putman's Camp*, from the orchestral *Three Places in New England*, a diversity of military songs and ragtime tunes are played together in different rhythms and tempi, and often in different keys, mixed up with the huzzaing of the crowd and various a-rhythmic, non-tonal sounds of Nature. The music evokes, with astonishing immediacy, the physical and nervous sensation of being present at such a vast outdoor celebration; yet the flux of life becomes one through the force of the imagination. Ives tells us that the piece derives from a recollection of childhood. It is difficult to think of any art that conveys more precisely the experience—common in childhood, rarer in later years—of being at once identified with the flux of appearances and detached from it, as watching eye, as listening ear. In this sense, the essence of Ives's art is discovery: a new-found land.

The third of the *Three Places in New England—The Hausatonic at Stockbridge*—is another transient personal reminiscence that becomes a 'moment of reality'. The lovely, sinuous horn melody, with its almost Mahlerian orchestration, suggests both the chapel singing that Ives tells us he heard coming over the water, through the mist, and also the tranquil security of the love between himself and his wife (charmingly called Harmony). This melody is absorbed in a haze of floating strings that play, as from a distance, more or less independently of the rest of the orchestra. Gradually these sounds of Nature—of river, mist, and rustling leaves—grow stronger until they engulf the love-song: at which point the tumult abruptly ceases, and the song is left suspended, unresolved on a sigh. With great poignancy, the piece reveals both the centrality of human love and also its impermanence in the non-human context of the natural world.

For while Ives resembled Whitman in his appetite for experience, the obverse side of the American myth is present in his work, too: the Ego that would swallow all experience becomes progressively more aware of its isolation. The more immediate the artist's response to the external world, the more deeply he has to seek Reality beneath the flux. Ives accepted the world as it was, in all its chaos and contradiction, and for him there could be no division between the world of art and that of practical affairs. But he regarded his music and the insurance business in which he made his fortune as complementary activities. Both sought for a New World; in both the material and the spiritual were inseparable. He resembled the New England Transcendentalists in believing that he who would create a new world must first put his own house in order.

One of his most representative works—written, on and off, between 1908 and 1915—is in fact dedicated to the Transcendentalists—to those New England Heroes who lived in Concord between 1840 and 1860. The first movement of this Second Piano Sonata is a portrait of Emerson, hero of American strife; and this is a Beethovenian movement in so far as it dualistically opposes an 'epic' motive (the motto from Beethoven's Fifth) against a song-like lyric theme. But although Ives is a Beethovenian composer, he cannot share Beethoven's positives: so the opposed motives do not achieve reconciliation in tonal order. They interact; and change their identities as they are related in wildly opposed rhythms and on separate (polytonal) planes of harmony. Beethoven's transformations of themes are positively controlled by the Will; the form of the Fifth Symphony is the gradual revelation of the theme's destiny. Ives's transformations of themes are kaleidoscopic, protean like life itself, and the unity they seek becomes as much linear and serial as tonal: Ives even introduces Schoenbergian transpositions of the notes of the series to increasingly remote pitches (Ex. 75).

But the permutations of the motives do not, at the end, coalesce into a sustained melody; the music gradually disintegrates over a slowly oscillating chromatic bass: for though Ives has immense courage, he has not—perhaps no one, living in a rootless world, could have—Beethoven's assurance.

In this Emerson movement the conflict between lyric and epic forces has been largely subjective. The fight goes on within the consciousness, and the Will attempts—with only partial success—to control destiny. The second movement, however, is quite un-Beethovenian, for it deals with the subconscious life: with dreams, nightmare, and the sensory impressions of childhood. Ives says that he has not stressed the most significant aspect of Hawthorne—his Puritan sense of guilt: though guilt is closely connected with the 'phantasmal realms' in which the movement deals. In this movement there is virtually no tonality, no metre, and, one might almost say, no rhythm, since every quaver is violently syncopated off a beat that is merely implicit. Into the amorphous hurly-burly fragments of both lyric and epic motive intrude. But they have no controlling force; they are flotsam, thrown up on the waves of the unconscious.

Occasionally they provoke confused, dream-like recollections of daytime experience (the circus band episode, the tipsy ragtime, the love song that dissolves in a pianissimo haze of note-clusters, played with a strip of board).

Emerson was the life of the mind and soul, Hawthorne the life of the subconscious. With the third movement, Ives turns to everyday reality: the Allcott's house, the 'witness of Concord's common virtue'. Here both lyric and epic motive appear in simple form, realistically, for Beethoven's Fifth is being played in the parlour. The opening hymn-like version of the epic motive is a tune now unambiguously in B flat, but harmonized with telescoped tonic, dominant, and subdominant chords of E flat, so that the harmonic progression seems almost immobile, compared with the turbulence of the previous movements. But although 'the richness of not having' may provide us with tranquillity of a kind, it does not release us from the burden of the Will or the mystery of the unconscious. That can come only with a mystical act: and in the last movement Thoreau sits in his sunny doorway at Walden—"He grew in those seasons like corn in the night. He realized what the Orientals meant by contemplation and forsaking of works." The music opens barless, almost rhythmless, with a fluttering of leaves: which involves too the fluttering of human nerves in response. Gradually, the fragmentary lines grow into a long, winding melody that fuses the lyric idea with the epic. Ives directs that this melody should be played on a flute, if you happen to have one handy. This is not merely quixotic: the other-worldly colour of the instrument would emphasize the effect of the melody as the goal of the whole sonata. As the melody sings over a swaying, unmoving ostinato built out of the thirds and fifths of the epic motive, the spirit is liberated from inner strife (the Emerson movement): from nightmare (the Hawthorne movement): even from everyday reality (the Allcotts movement). The lyric and epic contrarieties have become one, in a mystical communion with Nature. Yet the end of the work is characteristic. The epic motive sounds high up, this time neither rising nor falling. This seems to suggest a final resolution into D major. Yet the C natural G complex is still audible, reminding us of the point we started from: while into the last bar the leading note, C sharp, softly obtrudes (Ex. 76): seeming to suggest how for Ives each resolution into Being is only a stage in the eternal flux

Ex.76. Ives: Concord Sonata (last movement)

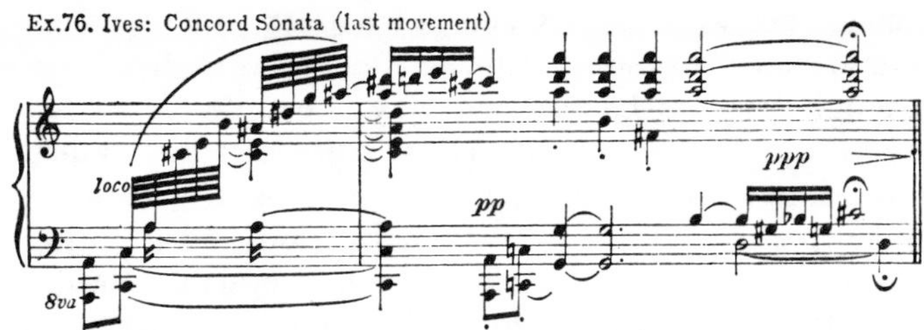

of Becoming. Experience is essentially incomplete, and never to be completed, except by death.

One might say that America has compressed its musical past, present, and potential future into the personality of Ives. The strife in his music is a still more violent development from European humanism (and the sonata principle); and its very violence leads him to a new, in part serial, search for order. That Ives anticipated by several decades the more experimental techniques of Schoenberg, Bartók, and Stravinsky (not to mention *musique concrète* and electronic music) is not in itself important; and his techniques are not always adequately realized, since he suffered—as any artist must—from working without a public. Yet in seeking order out of a polyphony not merely of lines, but also of freely evolving harmonies, rhythms, and tonalities, he may have more to suggest to the future of music than any of the European composers who are, in intrinsic achievement, greater. Nor is his significance merely 'historical'. His finest music—such as *The Hausatonic at Stockbridge*—sounds now as ripely a part of the past as the Mahler and Berg whom it fortuitously resembles. If it has also something of the rawness of a new world, the rawness brings with it an authentic note of grandeur. It is a note that is becoming rarer; we should be grateful for it.

Carl Ruggles [b. 1876], is a man of the same generation as Ives; but whereas Ives is both gregarious democrat and solitary visionary, Ruggles is unequivocally the isolated spirit. (He is almost literally a hermit; and the walls of his study, in his Vermont house, are symbolically papered with the exquisite calligraphy of his own manuscripts.) Thus the texture of Ruggles's music has nothing like the multifarious complexity of Ives's, the rag-bag into which all experience is poured helter-skelter, to be re-created. Yet although Ruggles's music contains no direct reflection of the chaos of the American scene, he is still concerned with the New: for he is a solitary in New England, where so much that went to make America is rooted.

Though Ruggles has written only a handful of works, his music is singularly consistent. His is a dedicated art, affirming the freedom of the human spirit; and his affirmation runs parallel to Schoenberg's 'free' atonal period, in the Europe of the second decade of the century. As an American, indeed, with no past, Ruggles sought freedom—from tonal bondage, from the harmonic strait-jacket—even more remorselessly than Schoenberg. The sound of his music, with its preponderance of minor seconds, major sevenths, and minor ninths, is similar to Schoenberg's; but in place of Schoenberg's density, Ruggles cultivates a clear, 'open' resonance in his singing, winging polyphony. This spacious texture and resilient rhythm are perhaps Ruggles's representatively American qualities, which have their counterpart in the polyphonic textures of Ives in, say, the Emerson movement of the 'Concord' Sonata. But Ruggles differs from Ives in his desire to refine and concentrate. Ives accepts the Universe—the tawdry and trivial along with the sublime. Ruggles is concerned with his own soul—with the 'great things' that are done 'when Men and Mountains meet'. It is revealing to compare Ruggles's *Men and Mountains* with Delius's *A Song of the High Hills*. Delius starts from the burden of his own passionate heart—the appoggiatura-laden harmony that tries to drag down the singing lines. Ruggles's chromaticism is not, historically speaking, so far from Delius's. But for him, as for Schoenberg, singing polyphony overrides harmonic tension, seeking the One in the Many. Delius is a (belated and weary) humanist; Ruggles is a mystic in a non-religious society. Paradoxically, his mysticism is a part of his Americanism: for it is also his 'newness', his search for personal integrity.

The American flavour of Harris's language centres in its 'vernacular' line and rhythm. If the opening suggests plainsong, that is not only because it is religious in feeling, but also because plainsong is close to speech. The racy vigour which the movement gradually acquires and the open texture—with a prevalence of fourths, minor sevenths, and major ninths—rejuvenate the continuous Wagnerian flow of the enharmony and the shimmer of the Sibelian moto perpetuo. So, imperceptibly, the moto perpetuo is transformed into the brusquely American fugued dance with which the work concludes. This exciting, if curious, mating of the Middle West dance-hall with the mediaeval *hoquet* is the most obviously 'contemporary' section of the score: and the closest in spirit and technique to the music of Harris's contemporary, Aaron Copland [b. 1900].

The pioneering, quasi-religious vein of Ruggles and Harris is remote from Copland's early music. In an arid machine civilization, he seems to have felt that he had to sacrifice the natural technique of lyrical growth. In the *Piano Variations* of 1930 he starts from skeletonic fragments: the ambiguous thirds, sixths, and sevenths of the Negro blues, and the declamatory leaps of Jewish synagogue music. It is significant that both Negro and Jew are dispossessed peoples who become, for Copland, symbolic of urban man's uprootedness. Since the dislocated fragments cannot grow spontaneously, they must be reintegrated in a personal vision. So the technique of the *Variations* is rigidly serial, based on a five-note figure (Ex. 77). The phrases

never grow, though they are multifarious in mood—angry, fierce, protesting, naïve, warm, tender. Yet out of these dislocated fragments a whole is created by a kind of 'cubist' reintegration; and though the piano texture, derived from the 'blue' false relations of the 'series', has the metallic hardness and precision of a machine, the music achieves, out of its minimal material, an austere but humane nobility.

If Copland felt a need to humanize his music it was not because his early works were not born of the heart; it was simply because an artist—as Ives found—cannot long subsist without an audience. The simpler style of his ballets and film music does not deny the technique of his earlier work: though the music's deliberate lack of progression is less disturbing when allied to immediately recognizable, folk-like tunes, and to physical action or visual drama. Certainly the folky vein of Copland's ballets, especially *Appalachian Spring*, is not an evasion of the steel girders—within which Copland so miraculously discovers a human warmth—of the *Piano Variations*: for he sees the prairie as symbol of the irremediable loneliness of big cities, the hymn as symbol of the religious and domestic security that urban man has lost. It is interesting that although the ballets are naturally less static, harmonically and rhythmically, than the *Variations*, they show a Stravinskian partiality for the telescoping of tonic, dominant and subdominant chords.

The identity between Copland's urban and his rustic vein is revealed by comparing *Quiet City*—a sound-image of the empty city at night—with the elegy in *Billy the Kid*; it is also worth noting that his *Music for Radio* was composed in New York, as urban music for an industrial society; the sub-title *Saga of the Prairies* being added as a result of a competition for a descriptive tag. In any case, the ultimate maturing of his talent, in the works he has written since about 1940, involves a synthesis of the implacable isolation of the *Piano Variations* with the more outward-tending humanity of his 'functional' works. This is evident in the first movement of the *Piano Sonata*, which uses the technique of the *Variations* in a richer, more direct form. Again we have the brief figures, the 'blue' false relations, the splitting up of the phrases into their component parts. Again the buoyant, upward lift of fourths, fifths, and minor sevenths is pinned down by the immense slowness of the rhythmic and harmonic design. The energetic phrases seem, against this timeless background, curiously wistful, suggesting both urban man's ant-like energy and his ineluctable loneliness. This is even more remarkable in the nagging, wedge-shaped figure on which the scherzo is built: so it is not an accident that these two movements should lead—by way of a strange bridge passage, like a sublimated hill-billy stomp—into an andante which is a quintessential expression of immobility. The tender, cool melody, with its widely spaced fifths and fourths, floats out of the material of the scherzo and trio and comes to rest in empty harmonies that pulse as unobtrusively as a heart-beat. The pendulum swings wider at the climax, when the first movement's clanging thirds return; but the regularity is never broken. The music runs down like a clock, dissolving away into space and eternity, while the grinding false relations of the opening movement echo from an immense distance (Ex. 78). The music that here stills the heart's agitation is closely related to the film score to Wilder's *Our Town*, which involves images of vast space; its serenity is the more impressive and (to most of us) moving because Copland

is not a mystic like Ruggles or a primitive like Harris. It is pertinent to note that one of his finest, most representative works is a song cycle, setting verses of that supreme poet of American isolation, Emily Dickinson.

The regional, Robert Frost-like aspects of Harris and Copland have had many imitators; yet most that is vital in American music seems to derive from the tradition of solitariness, if the paradoxical phrase be admitted. The music of Elliott Carter [b. 1908], for instance, though more controlled and sophisticated than either, has hints of both Ruggles and Ives in its sturdily independent polyphony of line and rhythm; while the impressive slow movement of his First String Quartet reveals a much more complicated form of Copland's dichotomy between the energy of the component melodic lines and the tortoise-like pace of the harmonic rhythm. Like Ives—but with a more Beethovenian awareness—Carter uses both 'dualistic' tonal techniques and 'monistic' serial methods in his attempts to create order from chaos. Other composers, notably Roger Sessions [b. 1896], have gravitated from traditional tonality to acceptance of the serial principle. The Puritan austerity common to the composers we have mentioned thus far (with the partial exception of Ives) is characteristic of Sessions too, though his music has a sensuous rhetoric that suggests Mahler and Schoenberg, though his rhythms are more kinetic than those of the Viennese school. The whirring, whirling impetus of the movement, the kaleidoscopic texture, of the allegros of his Second and Third Symphonies have a—perhaps typically

American—multifariousness and zest; and the serial unity which he seeks is, like the Reality of the poet Wallace Stevens, the truth of the imagination. The external world intrudes into his music scarcely at all; perhaps this amounts to an admission that a socially acceptable idiom is, for a 'serious' American composer, no longer a practical possibility. Certainly he and Carter have had far more influence on the younger generation of American composers than the regionalists.

It is understandable that though American music inevitably begins with an acceptance of the 'western' way of life in its most aggressive form, it also manifests, in all the composers we have discussed, a partial rejection of post-Renaissance humanism: a turning to the East comparable with, but more extreme than, that manifested in the European composers considered in the previous chapter. We shall not therefore be surprised to find that the most radically experimental tendencies we commented on in European music have their complement in American music: and that one American composer of the older generation was the pioneer of such developments on both sides of the Atlantic. Ives, in exploiting noise and non-European elements, had hinted at their abandonment. Edgar Varèse [b. 1885]—a French-American who lived and worked in Paris during the nineteen-twenties, but has now settled in the States—entirely discarded the conventional materials of melody and harmony, as well as rhythmic patterns related to harmonic tension. For him the post-Beethovenian approach to music as psychological drama was irrelevant. He rather sought a musical complement to Action painting; music should be created, like the dance, as an act of the body itself, manipulating tangible and audible material 'concretely'. So he starts from the sound-characteristics of each instrument—what he calls its density, its timbre and quality independent of pitch relationships, let alone harmony. The instrument is a sound like any other relatively accidental noise; and Varèse's music is a polyphony of timbres, each instrument having its own typical linear figure and rhythmic pattern, both of which never develop. Construction, for Varèse, is an achievement of the sense of space. Harmonically conceived music achieves this through the development of themes, the movement to and away from a central key. Varèse achieves his 'opening of space' through the addition and contrast of rhythms and timbres.

Clearly such a conception of music is more ritualistic and magical than 'expressive': and has much in common with Oriental music and with the music of primitive societies. Varèse believes that this was necessary because the hyper-self-consciousness of modern man is one of the reasons for twentieth-century chaos; art's duty is to encourage forgetfulness of self, if not in mysticism (which is accessible only to dedicated spirits), then in magic. But he has always insisted that his ritualistic approach is modern as well as primitive, being related to a machine-dominated civilization. The percussive noises and patterns in his music have affinities with the sounds of city life that have become part of our everyday consciousness. The artist's task is to help us to perceive the patterns of order and beauty that lie beneath mechanistic chaos, if we have eyes to see and ears to hear. When we can all see and hear, the artist, presumably, will be unnecessary.

Some advanced composers have, indeed, already relinquished the notion of an audience. John Cage [b. 1912], in his early works, used 'prepared' pianos to create a melodically pentatonic and harmonically percussive music closer to Balinese music than to anything in Western tradition. In later works he first subjugated the ego to completely serial processes and then—in ultimate rejection of the will—to chance (for instance, the throw of dice). Though he begins with Varèse's preoccupation with sound as such, he has no use for Varèse's physical assault on the nerves. Music becomes therapeutic, an agent of Zen Buddhism: hardly discussable in the same terms as traditional Western music. It is perhaps interesting that his work appeals strongly to those concerned with the visual arts.

Such experimental extremism seems a far cry indeed from Ives's attempt at an 'American' comprehensiveness: the dichotomy which he so profoundly distrusted would seem to be complete if we put on the one side the music of Cage and his associates, and on the other the world of common appetite, of mass-produced entertainment music. It is true that this is a situation that has developed only during the last hundred years: that up to Schubert's day (as we saw) there was a distinction in degree, but not in kind, between music written consciously to 'entertain' and music that was a testament of the human spirit: that even nineteenth-century composers such as Offenbach and

Johann Strauss [1825–1899], whose art was basically social and functional, none the less entailed a sense of values consistent with the more 'serious' art of their time. But it is a tall order to convict the twentieth century of a kind of cultural schizophrenia. Though there may be two kinds of art today, one of which preserves the integrity of the human spirit while the other debases it, we must remember that the human mind has never shown much reluctance to being debased; the difference today is that machine techniques make the process easier and more efficient. Moreover, the nature of the debasement is not fortuitous. Commercial art prostitutes our feelings in the way that seems likely to yield the biggest financial return; but even commercial techniques assume the existence of proclivities that await exploitation. Though the Hollywood Dream may be shoddy compared with the myths in the light of which great civilizations have lived, we do not preserve our precious integrity by pretending it has nothing to do with *us*. It is even possible that commercial art is beginning to develop its own inner responsibilities. *The Desert Song* is pure (or rather impure) make-believe; but the glossy American musical is unconsciously evolving codes of behaviour, even of value, which are intimately related to an industrial society. Though we may not like them, their existence cannot be gainsaid: and should make us suspicious of glib distinctions between art and commerce.

In this connexion the work of George Gershwin [1898–1937] is of particular interest. He was an instinctive musician, nurtured on the restricted diet of Tin Pan Alley. His basic material was the thirty-two-bar tune, whether in 'common' or 'three-quarter' tempo: divided into a four-bar phrase answered by a four-bar phrase, both stated twice; followed by two four-bar or four two-bar phrases of 'contrast'; rounded off by a repetition of the first eight bars. The no less machine-made harmonic vocabulary came from fifty or sixty years back—from (say) Massenet and Grieg, with a garnishing of Ravel sauce. Yet the songs which Gershwin wrote within this convention revivify cliché: whereas all his attempts to extend his range proved —with one exception—disastrous. In the *Rhapsody in Blue* or the Piano Concerto the tunes themselves are often as good—as stimulating in melodic contour, in the unexpected ellipsis or contraction of rhythm—as the best of Gershwin's commercial numbers. But the tunes are complete in themselves, and are improved neither by the spurious 'development' nor by the bits of Lisztian tinsel with which they are flimsily tied together.

Significantly, Gershwin's only successful large-scale work is his opera, *Porgy and Bess*. Here the 'numbers', as in the commercial musical, can be held together by the story: so that it is comparatively unimportant that Gershwin's technique is not much less rudimentary in his opera than in his symphonic pieces. Habitually, he resorts to ostinato basses, rhythmic patterns, alternations of two chords and mechanical sequences to keep the music going; in moments of excitement he relapses into sliding chromatics. Yet *Porgy* is a moving, deeply impressive, work; and it is so because, for all its sophisticated facilities, Gershwin's tunes have never been more spontaneous or more fetching. These tunes cohere in a dramatic intensity, not because of Gershwin's 'external' attempts at thematic interrelation, but because, working within commercial conventions, he has felt the drama deeply.

For all his urban glamour, he has created a folk-opera about a dispossessed people, with a hero who is both a Negro and a cripple. The idiom of Broadway may pollute the authenticity of his Negroid music; yet one can have no doubts as to the genuineness of the ecstatic nostalgia that pervades the score and even—in episodes such as the funeral oration in Act I—revitalizes the harmonic texture. Gershwin chose a libretto, by a Negro writer, DuBose Heywood, which dealt with corruption, oppression, isolation, and the inviolability of a radical innocence of spirit. He was not himself a Negro or a physical cripple; but he was a poor boy who made good: a Jew who knew all about spiritual isolation, and who had opportunity enough to learn about corruption. Perhaps he wrote such fresh and powerful, as opposed to cliché-ridden, music because even in the face of temptation he preserved, like Porgy, a modicum of radical innocence. Gershwin has here created a twentieth-century myth meaningful to himself: and meaningful to us, in so far as he was representative of his and our generation.

Genius does not often flourish in the environment of Tin Pan Alley. But it is not common anywhere; and Gershwin was in no way frustrated by the commercialized conventions within which he worked. When Ravel said he had nothing to teach Gershwin, he meant precisely what he said: not that Gershwin was endowed direct from heaven with a complete technical equipment, nor that he was technically past praying for; but that his technique was exactly adequate to what he had in him to do. In this connexion we may compare him with Carlo Menotti [b. 1911], who grew up a decade or so later, when the techniques of commercial music had been sophisticated by years of application to the cinema. Being intelligent and ingenious, he adapted cinematic technique to solve one of the basic problems of opera in a democratic society. Taking his cue from Hollywood and from Puccini, he has created an operatic stylization that seems almost as 'natural'—and therefore acceptable to a popular democratic audience—as realistic drama. In no discreditable sense he has also learned how to exploit subjects that go home to his public. *The Consul* is a genuinely frightening vision of the dehumanized world of officialdom, with the added advantage that it can, if need be, be imbued with political significance (on either side). *The Medium* exploits both our pseudo-scientific desire to debunk the irrational and our vague yearnings for supernatural excitement, if not satisfaction. Yet Menotti, who seems to have liberated commercial cliché in making it emotionally more malleable, is more a product of industrialized inhumanity than Gershwin: because although his musical-dramatic technique is much more complex, the music itself is neither good nor bad, but so cinematically parasitic as to be without identity. A Gershwin tune exists in its own right; Menotti's *parlando* lyricism has no existence apart from his drama.

What counts, in any field, is the quality of the music. Gershwin succeeded (and kept alive the human spirit) in his theatre music while failing, on the whole, in his concert music. Two other Jewish American composers, Marc Blitzstein [b. 1905] and Leonard Bernstein [b. 1918], started as highly sophisticated 'art' composers, but found fulfilment in a world at least allied to the commercial theatre. Blitzstein had a profound admiration for Kurt Weill [1900–1950], a German composer who wrote 'straight' music having affinities with Hindemith and Busoni, but who made his mark in such works as *Die Dreigroschenoper* (a modern version of *The Beggar's Opera*) and *Mahagonny*, wherein he expressed the malaise of the post-war years in a peculiarly haunting adaptation of the idiom of popular music. At the time of the Nazi persecution, Weill went to America and worked on Broadway and in Hollywood, where his music lost much of the evocative simplicity that had made it so memorable. But perhaps he could not be expected to 'feel' the American scene with the same authenticity as he had shown in invoking the urban Germany of his youth; certainly his example suggested to Blitzstein how the idioms of America's own popular music might be adapted to a comparably expressive purpose. His plays-in-music on social themes both refine and intensify popular idiom until it is first-hand, not mass-produced, feeling: but Blitzstein's American art is buoyant in its honesty, whereas Weill's had been pessimistic, if compassionate. The same energy is found in the work of Leonard Bernstein, who accepts the idiom of the commercial theatre more at its face value: so that his positive awareness of tenderness and compassion is perhaps suspect, when compared with Blitzstein's. Nonetheless, the musical and choreographic urgency of *West Side Story* is equated with the reality, as well as the topicality, of the human theme; and that is concerned specifically with both the herd instinct and the isolation of the individual soul.

This would seem to indicate that in American music the 'tradition of solitariness' and the social music of 'entertainment' are not as disparate as one might superficially suppose. From this point of view, the work of a minor composer, Virgil Thomson [b. 1896], has an interest more than commensurate with the intrinsic value of his compositions. He was a bright boy from Kansas whose musical legacy consisted of the kind of American bric-à-brac—hymns, parlour pieces, ragtime—that was also the background of Ives's experience. Intellectually precocious, he got himself to Harvard, and then to Paris, where, as American cosmopolitan but not expatriate, he became a member of the Gertrude Stein circle and wrote wildly experimental, often satirically debunking works as a protest against a world that had had its day. He might, given a more vigorous talent, have developed in any number of directions; yet in fact his sophistication, even his complexity, hid a peculiar naivety. His kinship with Satie is more illuminating than his association with Gertrude Stein; his bringing together of emotionally disparate elements—plainsong and café-tune, Bachian fugue and Middle West hymn—has Satie's childlike unsentimentality, while he too discovers a personal logic in unexpected relationships between triadic harmonies. Significantly, his innocence is also his most American quality. *Four Saints in Three Acts*, the Gertrude Stein opera that won him both fame and notoriety, is the first of his works to fuse the American-naïf with the Parisian-sophisticate. Although far too long for most of us, it reaches, beneath its *enfant terrible* elegance, the oddly poignant homespun humour which, on his return to the States, Thomson transplanted into his specifically American works, such as the second Stein opera, *The Mother of Us All*, and the beautiful elegiac piece for wind band, *A Solemn Music*. The vein of American feeling in these works is close to that of Blitzstein's plays in music; and it is not an accident that so much of Thomson's best music has been written for the cinema, to which medium the Satiean technique of musical *collage* admirably lends itself. The essence of Thomson is in his score to Flaherty's *Louisiana Story*: a film that, significantly enough, sees the clash between man and Nature through the eyes of a child. In the Chorale the serially related but harmonically unrelated triads that accompany the derrick's progress along the river are Satiean, yet have become at once original and indigenous. Thomson's American simplicity, which complements the American complexity of men such as Carter and Sessions—is most completely fulfilled in subservience to a function: which involves, too, a highly mechanized technique.

So if we view the amorphous, apparently chaotic American scene as a whole, it would seem that what matters most is the extremes. On the one hand stand the grand old 'progressives' —Ives, Ruggles, Varèse: with the more experimental Copland, Carter, and to a lesser degree Harris, Sessions, and some of the more recent experimentalists. On the other hand is the authentic element in jazz, as a communal, urban folk art; Gershwin when he is not writing symphonic works; Blitzstein and the Bernstein of *West Side Story*; the film music of Thomson. Comparatively, the middle-of-the-path men, even such an excellent conservative musician as Samuel Barber [b. 1910] or such a clever theatre-man as Menotti, have little vitality and not much social or artistic justification. Perhaps there is a moral in this, for a new, if not for Europe's old, community. Certainly it suggests that the split between the esoteric and the popular is not merely to be deplored. In the long run the real split may prove to be between the creatively vigorous on the one hand and the emotionally and academically safe on the other. And that split has been with us since civilization began.

The 'western hemisphere' is not, of course, confined to the United States. There is also Latin America, which is rapidly becoming an important, creatively energetic part of the modern world. Its achievements in music are not as yet comparable with those of North America, but development will inevitably be sudden and spectacular. The problems of the Latin American composer depend on the fact that he lives neither in a New World nor an old. In the background he has a very ancient Indian civilization and a still vigorous primitive culture. In the foreground he has various European elements imported by the Spanish conquest (Spanish folk-music and urban popular music of the eighteenth and nineteenth centuries); a Negroid element growing out of the slave trade; and a new, stream-lined mechanistic civilization spreading from the United States. In the music of European composers, such as Janáček, Bartók, even Stravinsky, the primitive is involved in the traditions of civilization; in Latin America the various 'layers' of culture exist alongside one another, without apparent relationship.

Thus the music of Heitor Villa-Lobos [1881–1959]—the most representative Latin American composer—has obvious affinities with the Brazilian landscape, containing the musical equivalents of the jungle, the Lost City, the skyscraper and the road-house. In his jungle-like fecundity, his appetite for experience, for life in the raw, Villa-Lobos has points in common with Ives. But whereas Ives was conscious of creating a New World, both materially and spiritually, Villa-Lobos combines a Latin exuberance with a Latin passivity. He accepts the chaos of the contemporary scene; his energy, though intermittently purposeful, is directionless. This is why he was apparently completely unself-critical: and why his music tends to be most impressive when most fortuitous.

From this point of view, it is significant that his most technically sophisticated works tend to be no more than mildly interesting. He does something with the Debussyan and Ravellian idiom he picked up in Paris in the second decade of the century; but the vein of piquant nostalgia which he distils from this style—the mood of the Latin American *saudades*—spreads thinly over so large a number of works. Almost all his memorable music is conceived in the convention of the *choros*; and this, interestingly enough, is an art-composer's adaptation of popular improvisation. Especially at Carnival time, the *choro* party is an integral part of Brazilian life: a Latin American jam-session at which any number of musicians, playing any instruments that happen to be handy, improvise empirically and episodically, with no more than a scheme of rhythmic relationships between each section to keep them going. Villa-Lobos's innumerable works called *Choros*, scored for anything from a single guitar to a mammoth symphony orchestra, are, of course, composed music, notated; but he seeks always an effect of the maximum density of detail with the maximum energy of movement. Superficially, the sharp, hard sonorities he draws from imitation of the *ad hoc choro-bands* resemble those which Stravinsky derived from popular music of the war years and the early-twenties. Whereas Stravinsky preserved, however, an almost geometric intellectual control over his unsophisticated sources, Villa-Lobos sought, and at best achieved, the white-hot immediacy of improvisation.

In the seventh *Choros*, scored for a miscellaneous instrumental ensemble, we begin, for instance, with a nostalgically impressionist prelude—the composer's own, relatively sophisticated consciousness. Out of this emerges, from the depths *below* consciousness, the primitive jungle: obsessive drum rhythms and short, screaming melodic phrases in incantatory patterns and exotic coloration. Then, with a scoop on the violin, we are in the world of nineteenth-century Spanish popular music: a waltz in which an urban nostalgia is interlaced with a savage vigour. Later, Indian incantatory elements turn Negroid, so we find ourselves in a world halfway between the jungle and the urban violence of Chicago-style jazz. At the end we return to the impressionist opening—to the composer's own sensibility that apprehends the chaotic vitality of the Brazilian scene. Yet the piece has no real structure and no development; the brief, quasi-improvisatory sections shift between the various levels of culture in a way that is exciting, but, in its rootlessness, also sad. Occasionally—as may happen in genuine jazz improvisation—the creative imagination takes complete control. Then, as in the marvellous *Nonetto* of 1923, the jungle and jazz, the primitive and the urban, become a new world of sound. That the music has no beginning, middle nor end becomes a positive quality: for the whole piece is a tremendous incremental climax that destroys consciousness, and with it the time-sense. When the chorus enters it is not as the representative of humanity, but as a terrifying animistic force. This is a twentieth-century primitivism that exposes the glibness of such a composer as Carl Orff.

While Villa-Lobos's most violent music is easily his most impressive, it is hardly surprising that, living in a world embryonically coming to birth, he should have been impelled too by a complementary yearning for 'civilization'. The most curious example of this is the sequence of works which he called *Bachianas Bresilieras*. To attempt to fuse the empirical, episodic *choros* technique with the unity and continuity of Bach's idiom would seem a forlorn hope indeed. Yet the remarkable work for eight, cellos does achieve, at least in the slow movement, a sustained line and an extraordinary depth and richness of harmony. The richness has not, of course, Bach's tense serenity; it is not a faith accepted or achieved. But in this *modinhya*—a sentimental urban song derived from eighteenth- and nineteenth-century Spanish elements—nostalgia becomes almost a positive virtue; one can understand how the miraculous new cities may rise in the midst of the jungle. Villa-Lobos felt the need for order if he could not himself create it.

The nature of the 'new order' is revealed in a Mexican composer of the next generation, Carlos Chavez [b. 1899]. The thematic and rhythmic patterns in his music are again brief, incantatory, ritualistic, related to primitive sources; the instrumental colours are hard and fierce. But he has none of Villa-Lobos's chaotic prodigality; the linear texture of his music is sharp, dry, consistent, and continuous in figuration as a baroque toccata. The unity is achieved at a cost; the linear patterns are closer to the more arid manifestations of Stravinsky's 'white note' music than to the lyrical pliancy and harmonic density of Bach—or even of the *Bachianas Bresilieras*! Yet there is a positive side to the aridity also: for this music grows from the hard light and sunbaked plain of the Mexican scene, while at the same time having affinities with the metallic urban world of the earlier works of Copland. Copland's music is discontinuous, Chavez's continuous; but while Copland's 'dislocation' is probably deeper and certainly closer to us, it is the driving motor rhythm in Chavez that builds new cities in the mountains or the jungle. There is a valid relationship between the texture and spirit of Chavez's music and the remarkable achievements of twentieth-century Mexican architecture.

Today, Latin American music seems to be trying to preserve

the geometric lucidity of Chavez without sacrificing the copious sensuality of Villa-Lobos. We can observe this in the music of the Argentinian, Alberto Ginastera [b. 1916]: for while his music has a clarity of linear contour and a rhythmic excitement characteristic of Chavez, it has also a lyrical tenderness and harmonic evocativeness more suggestive of Villa-Lobos, if we can imagine the Brazilian without the strain of banality that is part of his vigour. There is a pathos in the hollow texture of the slow movement of Ginastera's beautiful String Quartet, a plaintiveness in the bird-noises of the slow movement of his Piano Concerto, that complements the driving energy of his quick movements. There is nothing comparable with this in the hieratic, hymnic, dissonant diatonicism that Chavez exploits in his (usually brief) slow movements; and if Ginastera's melancholy embraces Villa-Lobos's nostalgia, it pierces deeper, being a sign of growing maturity.

This is in part, of course, a regional difference. An Argentinian composer—or still more a Chilean composer of the older generation, such as Domingo Santa Cruz [b. 1899]—is further removed from primitive and Indian sources than a Brazilian or Mexican composer, and so may turn spontaneously to the more 'adult' traditions of Europe. But the difference is not merely regional, for all over Latin America composers are becoming less aggressively concerned with indigenous values. As their new civilization comes to birth they remain conscious of their birthright, yet aware of their place in a community of nations. Cultural barriers, at least, are no longer unbridgeable, whatever may be true of political barriers; and a Peruvian serialist is no longer an anachronism.

11

AFTERWORD, 1988

EVERY age is inevitably an age of transition, but in some periods people have been more aware than in others of the necessity for change, and more bewildered by its pace. The seventeenth century witnessed scarifying changes of front occasioned by its scientific revolution; but not even the seventeenth century was more savagely buffeted by the winds of change and chance than we have been by *our* scientific (electronic) revolution, especially during the thirty years that have elapsed since *Man and his Music* was first published. To give an adequate account of all that has happened during these years is clearly impossible in a brief Afterword; we must be content to comment on significant later developments in composers who are now a part of history, and roughly to chart new directions that have unfolded since the mid-fifties.

Most significant in the 'historical' category is the late work of a composer who has died since the first publication of this book: Dmitri Shostakovitch. Though it was obvious in 1957 that he was a composer of genius and a major figure, his full stature has been revealed only in works of his last decade. His so-called Fourteenth Symphony was not in fact a symphony but a song cycle with orchestra which, like Mahler's *Das Lied von der Erde,* wrested affirmation out of an unflinching contemplation of death. In this work we may sense an autobiographical overtone since Shostakovitch knew that he was seriously, perhaps terminally, ill. We may, without interpreting it in crudely political terms, also think of his impending death as the death of a world that had failed: a notion supported by the extraordinary fifteenth and final symphony, written in 1972. There seems little doubt that Shostakovitch intended this symphony as an epilogic work, riddling it with quotations from his own works – presumably of autobiographical import – and from other composers. It thus becomes at once a résumé of, and a threnody for, himself and Civilization, the latter embracing not merely Soviet society but also 'Europe'. The first movement is an allegretto which, according to Shostakovitch, evokes a toyshop at night. It sounds like a touching parody of Stravinsky the Russian who 'got away': the toys come to life in sharp, tingling sonorities that recall the puppet Petrouchka. That the little soldier struts to the only tune he can play – the march from *William Tell* – is quite appropriate, for Rossini's military caper – reappearing seven times, always at the same pitch, marching but never getting anywhere – comments ironically on the trumpery bellicosities of the European nations. In the middle lurks a Mahlerian hint of psychological murk beneath the perky facade; the last return of the Rossini tune sounds clownishly pathetic.

The second movement also incorporates a march, but one that is bony in texture and funereal in pulse. Hymnic homophony for brass alternates with broken lyricism for solo cello and violin, making passing references to the adolescent First Symphony composed half a century earlier. The effect is deeply melancholy, perhaps because the hymnic music evokes the old Russia, from which a youthfully-tender lyricism emerges, yet fails to fly. The 'failure' leads without break into the short scherzo which returns to the first movement's toyshop. But it is no longer a game. The tunes, if frisky, are lopsided; modulations are incessant; the scoring is still sharp and thin, but with a Mahlerian, nightmarish acuity. Men can behave like puppets too; we are no longer merely playing with toys.

The finale, the most substantial movement, comments on the previous three. It opens with quotations from *Gotterdämmerung – Siegfried's Funeral March –* intertwined with the *Tristan* motif: the feeling of death that pervades the symphony would seem to be that of Europe, no less than that of Shostakovitch and Russia. Yet the funeral is also a celebration, and incorporates that ancient principle of unity, the chaconne: a series of variations over an unchanging ground bass. In this case the bass is another self-quotation, from the Leningrad Symphony. In its original war context it had symbolized the will of the Russian people to endure, whatever the odds; in the Fifteenth Symphony it seems rather a riposte to mortality itself. The variations encompass a lifetime's variety of mood, from Tchaikowskian balletic grace to a tremendous climax in which the dotted rhythm from the first adagio and Siegfried's funereal motif fuse in majesty and terror. A retrospective episode dreamily hints at the toyshop of the first movement; and in the long coda, constructed over a tonic pedal, the music floats away in a tinkling and clinking of toyshop percussion, into which the celesta inserts a liquid major third. The key is A major, traditionally a key of youth and innocence; the effect, far from being happy, is as though a child's Eden were distantly glimpsed beyond the weary body and sorrowing soul. The symphony, if not 'great', is strangely moving and movingly strange; for through the precision of its technique a personal predicament becomes ours also. It is an elegy – on Shostakovitch, Russia and Europe – which (just) ensures the spirit's survival, though the toyshop Eden of its close offers no clue as to the kind of world we'll find ourselves living in, if live we do. It is not fortuitous that the Fifteenth Symphony has much in common with the composer's late string quartets, which are as private, indeed hermetic, as the late quartets of Beethoven, and are occasionally (especially the magnificent eighth and twelfth) comparable in strength with them. There is rough justice in the fact that Shostakovitch, avowedly a state composer, is most consummately realized in the abstract medium that has become associated with the inner life. This spiritual transcendence is his ultimate triumph, as, in the last resort, any man's must be.

In Russia, political reaction against a moribund feudalism had led to an established musical orthodoxy based on Western models, though Soviet composers of genius, notably Shostakovitch, used these models in odd, even subversive ways. This applies also to Schnittke, the most talented Soviet composer of the generation succeeding Shostakovitch, and the closest the Soviets have come to an avant-gardist. That Schnittke is a direct heir to Shostakovitch is manifest especially in his chamber music such as the string quartets and the powerful string trio, in which his recognizable identity relates to the wryly bleak intensity of Shostakovitch's late quartets, while intensifying it with microtones, clusters, percussive effects, slides and glissandi. The 'modernity' of the music does not sever roots in ancient Russian folk and liturgical traditions; indeed the microtonal techniques make this affiliation more patent than it is in Shostakovitch.

A comparable fusion of the very new with the very old occurs in contemporary Polish music. To a degree this was already evident in the tradition running from Chopin to Szymanowski; when rebellion, political and musical, became overt it prompted concepts of freedom even more radical than those of Schnittke. Two Poles have made a decisive mark on the map of the musical avant-garde. In 1954, Witold Lutoslawski [b. 1913] wrote *Concerto for Orchestra,* a work that rivals that of Bartók in combining a show-piece with musical substance, revitalizing Western orchestral concepts with the vigour of folk tradition. His later, more representative music seeks 'freedom' by incorporating into no less complex structures aleatory techniques that allow the performers a measure of independence. The function of the improvisatory elements in *Venetian Games* (1961), is clearly defined and justifies Lutoslawski's belief that, where extreme intricacy is called for, improvisation may be more effective than notation in enhancing (not escaping from) principles of order. The growth *towards* freedom is the structural point of the work, mirroring the problems the human race has in living together, whatever the nature of individual social groups.

This is most potently revealed in *Trois Poèmes d'Henri Michaux,* for choir and instrumental ensemble, which was hailed as a masterpiece on its first performance in 1965 (and still sounds like one). The verses surreally concern not epic events in our distracted times, but what happens in our minds because of them. 'Inner' and 'outer' life are contained within the vocal and instrumental forces, which are allotted two conductors, function in partial independence of one another, and are written in proportional notation, using 'mobiles' – passages repeated and varied independently of the rest of the ensemble. This gives explicit formulation, appropriate to our times, to what must be in some degree implicit in any work of art: man's 'conscious' will and his 'unconscious' psyche interacting to induce terror and pity. Although not harmonically progressive (in the Western sense) the work has a beginning, middle and end; the latter, if mysterious, is resigned, even consolatory. Like the Third Symphony written twenty years later, this music attains a peace that passes understanding precisely because it is unafraid of hazard: 'thou mettest with things dying, I with things new born'.

Similar notions of freedom dominate the work of another Pole who achieved international celebrity in the wake of the Second World War. The music of Krzysztof Penderecki [b. 1933] calls for, and receives, instant attention – as was evident when in 1960 his *Threnody for the Victims of Hiroshima,* microtonally scored for fifty-two solo strings, startled the ears and ruffled the conscience of Europe and America. Later works, such as the *St Luke Passion* (1965) and its sequel, *Utrenja* (1971), are explicitly religious, even liturgical, but are no less theatrical in impact. Multi-divided choirs of microtonal voices and strings, many types of notated and improvised choral speech and yelling, sensationally barking brass, batteries of percussion and pyrotechnics for stratospheric solo voices make a stunning impact. These modern techniques are related to the shamanist ululations, sepulchral basses, squawking trumpets and tintinnabulating bells still active in European liturgical traditions – certainly in the wilder areas of Poland and Central Europe. Here Western art-music seems to be returning aurally and orally to the Word and the Body in ways that pervaded European music before the Renaissance, and still pervade non-European music. A similar immediacy distinguishes Penderecki's purely instrumental music, such as the Cello Concerto in which the soloist becomes a theatrical 'presence', gutsy in his virtuosity. One can understand why Polish audiences flocked to hear this piece – one might say to undergo it – no less than they did to hear performances of his *Dies Irae*, which had the adventitious pull of being dedicated to the victims of Auschwitz. Penderecki's public in his own country is proportionally as large as our public for the current pop group. This is certainly not to be deplored, though one may wonder whether the multiplicity of 'effects' in his music may not tend to trivialization. This music that excites us today may not do so, as do Lutoslawski's *Trois Poèmes*, after twenty years.

It is not by chance that remote Poland, looking to both West and East, should have become seminal to the avant-garde movement; similar ambiguities occur in the centres of European civilization. In Paris, Pierre Boulez – one-time pupil of Messiaen (who in his immense opera on St Francis has apotheosized his obsessions, from Roman Catholic and non-Western mysticism to ornithology) – has become an old master of the avant-garde. *Le Marteau sans maître*, which catapulted him to fame, still sounds like a masterpiece, releasing us, airborne, from 'the pain of consciousness' into space and eternity. But we still don't know whether what is revealed is God's will or an emptiness better than agony. There seems to have been a gradual admission that artists ought to be chary of invoking a supernatural law that is too abstract. For Boulez it is almost as though completion has become synonymous with death; today, at IRCAM, he works on and off, seeking, but perhaps never finding, a consummation of his musical metaphysics. During the years when he devoted most of his energies to conducting music by other composers he himself composed little, and what he did produce – notably the ravishingly beautiful *Pli selon Pli* (1958–1962) – usually involved aleatory elements and was usually left unfinished (in progress).

Partial indeterminacy is also found in the work of the composer's Italian contemporary, Luciano Berio [b. 1925] whose *Circles* (1960) was to spark off innumerable imitations. Berio called the piece *Circles* because its five movements set three poems in a circular ABCBA structure: a serpent eating its own tail appropriate to the poems of E. E. Cummings, which evoke an eternal *Is,* without before or after. This allows scope for the unconsciousness of improvisation, and encourages indeterminacy of pitch from both the singing-speaking-yelling voice and from the mainly percussive instrumental ensemble. Essentially about beginnings, *Circles* is musically as blessedly simple, even simple-minded, as the poems. The lovely inconclusion in which the voice embryonically surfaces through murmuring mists effects a magical act, though modern man could hardly be content, having suffered so much, childishly to live 'for ever and ever' in this paradisial present. *Circles,* like *Le Marteau,* remains, however, a crucial work; none of its many successors recaptures its pristine bloom. Over the next twenty-five years, Berio became a pioneer in the complementary activities of deconstructing articulate language into its linguistic components, and in constructing collages out of 'memory and desire' – recollections and parodies (in both the colloquial and the technical sense) of other people's music, interspersed with hopeful aspirations towards temporal 'moments' that may seem eternal, as in *Circles.* The *Sinfonia* written for the Swingle Singers and the New York Philharmonic was – and remains – a key-work in this context, while Berio has imaginatively exploited the potential of electronic tape in constructing his collages of past and present.

Contemporaneously with Berio, the German composer Karlheinz Stockhausen [b. 1928] was still more radically exploring similar techniques and areas of experience. In the first edition of this book he was mentioned as a post-Webernian serialist of fanatical rigour, who called on electronics to 'realize' his formidable metrical intricacies. Over the last twenty-five years, however, he has moved increasingly towards a synthesis of 'conscious' and 'unconscious' experience: as is aurally manifest in the remarkable *Gesang der Jünglinge*, in which pure electronic sounds mell with processed abstractions of vowel sounds and consonants, and with real children's voices, speaking and singing snatches of kiddies' runes and street songs. So the piece seems to deal with embryonic human life within the mathematical laws of the cosmos, and ends with an act of praise, sung by the Three Men in the Fiery Furnace of the Book of Daniel – the three men apparently being Boulez, Nono and Stockhausen himself as evangelists of a new world. The fiery furnace is hell, and also our post-atomic world; and though the electric gibbers and twitters get faster and fiercer while the children's voices, scattered on five loudspeakers, cry more faintly and frailly, the human voice is not obliterated. Indeed the disintegration of language into phonetics and its eventual identity with mathematics prove to be a reaffirmation of the human state.

Stockhausen in these early days, a disciple of Messiaen as well as of Webern, was a Roman Catholic. Though he has since renounced the Faith, he has increasingly become a mystical composer who, in near-Wagnerian egomania, seems to have created his own Church. (Left-wing) political rebirth seems to be implicit in some of his monumental 'circle' structures, such as *Prozession* (1967) for live instrumental ensemble and electronics, and the purely electronic *Hymnen* (1969). The most powerful of these works, *Momente*, is, however, exclusively for live resources, vocal and instrumental, employed in closed, collective, variable and multiple groups. The piece opens in the present moment, where we are: in some putative hall or concert-room, with desultory clapping scattered between four choirs and punctuated with random Bravos as well as expressions of disapproval. As the music unfolds we hear a main text, mostly allotted to soprano solo, which is timeless in being biblical, taken not from the Book of Daniel but from that erotic paean, the Song of Songs. This text must be sung in the language native to the audience, its wide-spun lyricism being an 'eternal' affirmation in the midst of the flux. Other texts are fragmentarily sung in several 'real' languages and one invented one, spoken, yelled and screamed, sometimes retaining intelligibility but more often disintegrated into syllables of pure sound (as in *Gesang der Jünglinge*). These texts, whatever their nature, were picked up by the composer at random from his reading during the period of composition. They are moments in time and history which intersect with the timeless; the ultimate point would seem to lie in Blake's aphorism:

> He who kisses a joy as it flies
> Lives in eternity's sunrise.

Although starting from 'history', in which this present moment in this concert hall is a minute point, the music transmutes 'moments' into an aural universe, in which there is no dramatic sequence and a minimum of distinction between subject and object.

It is hardly surprising that the immediacy of such moments, given the nature of the world we live in, should sometimes approach hysteria. Yet the hysteria is not the composer's but is rather what the world does to us; indeed, the composer's function may well be precisely to render us more *composed:* so that (again as in *Gesang der Jünglinge*) we may sing a love-song even from the heart of the fiery furnace. Moreover, although the sounds of the external world – laughter, sighs, whispers, croaks, wails – occur in what appears to be the random sequence in which one experiences them 'out there' in concert-hall or street, at the same time these noises are shaped by the mind of the artist. Fortuitous clapping becomes a notated metrical pattern; the heterophonic and statistically-rhythmed first section is balanced against a homophonic middle section; and that against the third section's fusion of heterophony and polyphony in more traditionally-notated metres. The recurrent magnificent refrains for chorus and brass remind us that traditional notions of the human imagination and will are not discounted in Stockhausen's discontinuous aural universe. In a strict sense this is synthetic music for our synthetic culture, for it brings together and alchemizes as many aspects as possible of experience and of sound-matter, embracing non-Western and primitive musics, as well as noise which is not strictly notatable.

Yet if the music of Stockhausen's middle years implies a social programme, even a scheme of world regeneration, it comes to do so in increasingly mystical terms. He has even devised an immense cycle of pieces with the apocalyptic title of *Aus den Sieben Tagen* (1968), in which there are no notated sounds, only an instruction that the performers should starve themselves, in solitary silence, for four days, and should then 'late at night, play single sounds, without thinking you are playing'. Some such spiritual discipline may be a necessary preparation for most of Stockhausen's later work, of which we may take *Stimmung* (1968) as representative.

The title of this work may be translated as 'tuning', and in technical terms this is what happens. Six human voices tune themselves to the pure overtone series, the voice of Nature herself (or God?), and are assisted to do so by an almost inaudible but perfect overtone series on tape. Here lies the distinction between Stockhausen and the authentic shaman; today's musician-scientist-priest offers a helping hand or rather ear to fallible humans, thereby admitting to their imperfection. The physical process of tuning is thus also a metaphysical process whereby the self becomes part of the cosmos. This simultaneously scientific and magical act is social as well as religious: for tuning to the universe is complemented by a process whereby the separate voices tune to one another in rhythm, timbre and dynamics as well as pitch, this communication between human creatures being effected by the invocation of eleven magic names and by way of the vowels of the phonetic alphabet.

Once a magic name has been called by a singer (not the composer), it is repeated until 'renewed identity is achieved'. The process is strictly comparable with the naming ceremonies among primitive peoples and today's children; with the invoking of the 'sensual speech' through a 'music of the vowels'; with the tuning ceremonies of Tibetan monks; and with the transmutations of medieval alchemy. Western music since the Renaissance has implied com-position whereby an artefact is made by 'placing together', at the instigation of the human mind, elements of experience. In this context, *Stimmung*, like most of Stockhausen's recent music – including the immense operatic festiva which when complete will outlast Wagner's *Ring* – is not composition but a ritual act that effaces consciousness in order to renew it on a 'higher' plane. Modern science and ancient magic are here no longer the opposite poles that rational enlightenment had supposed them to be. Stockhausen releases us from chronometric time not merely by reinstating mythological time but also by giving musical meaning to modern theories of space-time and relativity, of cosmological and astrological time, and to those biological and astronomical clocks that we now know to function, independent of chronometers, within the human subconscious, and apparently within the senses of animals, birds, insects, even plants. So if *Stimmung* is magic, it is magic that stems from the heart of our scientific technocracy and might be valid rather than evasive. Should this be so we might even come to believe that Stockhausen has transcended the 'failure' of Wagner's disciple Schoenberg, who in *Moses and Aaron* created an opera about the artist as priest and prophet, but left it unfinished because music, given its sensual nature, must inevitably betray the Word within the Word. If Stockhausen has found the Word that Schoenberg admitted he 'lacked', that will not make the former's intrinsic achievement greater than that of Schoenberg, let alone Wagner. It might, however, just conceivably mean that Stockhausen's estimation of himself as the most crucially significant composer of his time will be justified. Certainly the spiritual presence of *Stimmung* is still pervasive.

A conspicuous instance of this pervasive presence is in the music of György Ligeti [b. 1923], a Hungarian who has lived for the most part in Austria and Germany. His early works, such as *Nouvelles aventures, Atmosphères,* and *Lontano,* explore microtonal textures somewhat in the manner of Lutoslawski and Penderecki. From these works he gravitated into his aural 'continuum' in which pulsing beats and almost pulseless reverberations achieve a celebrative act out of atomic fragmentation; the choral and orchestral *Requiem* is an impressive instance. A similar equation between intellect and instinct distinguishes the music of the Greek composer Iannis Xenakis [b. 1922], who like Varèse and Stockhausen had training as an architect and mathematical engineer. He claims to 'construct' musical compositions on the laws of physics as well as mathematics and geometry, using computerized formulae both in writing for live instrument and for electronic sound-sources; in either case the often highly exciting *sounds* are not readily distinguishable from those of an indeterminate piece by a disciple of John Cage. Both elevate Law – whether of physics and mathematics or of chance – above human choice, though the powerfully idiosyncratic flavour of the sounds must come from the particular 'laws' selected, and the proportions in which they are combined.

Although it would be extravagant to speak of influence, we may detect preoccupations parallel to those of Stockhausen – even in traditionally conservative Britain. Benjamin Britten, in the last decade of his life, modified his Western, humanist view of opera in creating *Curlew River* which, without ceasing to be 'British Britten', draws on musical and theatrical techniques of the Japanese *Noh* play as well as on the medieval English miracle play. In so doing Britten poignantly reveals the obsessional miracle of the Boy who is born or reborn. The partly autobiographical last opera, *Death in Venice*, wondrously effaces boundaries between the conscious and the unconscious life, as we may more deeply appreciate if we consider it in relation to its purely instrumental (and marvellously pure) complement, the Third String Quartet. Michael Tippett, as early as the fifties, had delved into Jungian interrelationships between rational and irrational levels of experience in his opera, *The Midsummer Marriage*. He is still composing, and has found in that Marriage a wellspring from which most of his later work has flowed. Much of this work – for instance the Second Piano Sonata and the *Concerto for orchestra* (1963) – explores statically non-Western concepts of form which he succeeds in relating to Western, post-Beethovenian traditions. In later operas, such as *The Knot Garden* (1970) contradictory realms of experience lead to 'pluralistically' diverse techniques, as barriers are crossed between art-music, jazz, folk and rock.

The two major British composers of the Boulez-Berio-Stockhausen generation have proved to be Peter Maxwell Davies [b. 1934] and Harrison Birtwistle [b. 1934] who, while remaining sturdily indigenous, have not been impervious to Europe's new directions. The early music of Peter Maxwell Davies owed much to advanced serialism of Webernian vintage. Webern himself had been something of a medievalist, who found in serial law a manifestation of 'God's will'. Davies, congenitally imbued with the spiritual fervour of England's Middle Ages, found in serialism a revivified 'way of life', combining structural rigour stemming from medieval *cantus firmus* and proportional metre, with an incandescent purity, even innocence, of spirit. It is significant that the neo-medieval austerity typical of works like *Prolation* and *Worldes Blis* should be complemented by the modal choral music Davies wrote for children during his early composing years. *O Magnum Mysterium,* for choir and organ, is a 'great mystery' indeed, in which the unexpected transitions in the basically simple modality evoke a *precarious* wonderment – significantly comparable with the music to which Britten's Boy is reborn in *Curlew River*.

Equivocation between innocence and experience is the mainspring of Davies's art, as it is of that of so many vitally creative twentieth century composers. Not surprisingly, this is the theme of the opera *Taverner,* which stands at the centre of the composer's career: division between head and heart, spirit and flesh, the Old Faith and the humanistic Reformation are exemplified in the life and death of the sixteenth century composer. One of Davies's most well-wrought orchestral works, the *Second Fantasia on an In Nomine of John Taverner,* is closely related to the opera and although something of the 'Gothic desperation' of late medieval music survives in the sinuous lines of this work, there is little trace of the expressionist fervour of Viennese serialism. The composer's preoccupation with the darker undercurrents of our libidinal instincts is now projected into pieces with theatrical dimensions, such as the ardently lyrical *Leopardi Fragments* (in which medievalism absorbs a potent injection of High Renaissance Monteverdi), and the *Eight Songs for a Mad King* (1969), a product of the first flush of the music-theatre movement which remains, in Ezra Pound's phrase, 'news that STAYS news'. It calls on parody and collage techniques, in a manner independent of Berio and Stockhausen.

Taverner is about betrayal, and some have considered it a betrayal that Peter Maxwell Davies should have embarked on a series of three symphonies and a violin concerto, all seeking easier accessibility within the normal concert repertory. This view is counteracted by the fact that although these works behave as symphonic works are expected to – they have been compared with Sibelius – they do not abandon Davies's quasi-medieval techniques, his 'magic squares' and other mathematically extra-musical devices. Moreover, although the symphonies testify to a desire for accessibility, they are paradoxically affected by the composer's complementary need to remove himself from the hurly-burly of modern life, since they (in part) aurally image the wildness of the remote Scottish island on which he now (in part) lives. Davies's more intimate Orkney works – most of them created in collaboration with the poet George Mackay Brown – are perhaps his most profound, and certainly his most moving, statements. In them a sophisticated, formidably intelligent modern man is spontaneously responding to the pulse of a primitive folk culture, releasing – in the (literally) marvellous *From Stone to Thorn* and *Thorn Litany* – a lyricism at once tenuous and strong. Davies makes the Orkney experience part of us today, as his medievalism could never be. It is pertinent to note that during these Orkney years Davies has again begun to create music for children such as was youthfully triggered off when he was a highly idiosyncratic schoolteacher.

In this rediscovery of an ancient folk-culture Davies establishes common ground with his contemporary and one-time colleague, Harrison Birtwistle. Always the most radical of English composers, Birtwistle was aware of the continental avant-garde while remaining always his own man. Two kinds of 'awareness', which we have noted in other composers, dominate him, and prove to be complementary in their apparent contradiction. One is an obsession with intricate metrical organization, which impersonally orders the temporal dimension within which we humanly live. The other is a gut-response to primeval levels of being, manifest in the theatre-rituals of classical antiquity, in those of oriental cultures, and in English folk drama. Both categories have something in common, in philosophical concept and in sonority, with Stravinsky, though this is more an affinity than an influence. The temporal dimension, as manifest in Birtwistle's pieces about mechanical clocks and the like, is the continuum which even 'unaccommodated man' exists in; not surprisingly, their technique relates to that of Ligeti's 'continuum' works. The ritually corporeal theatre-pieces, which are more numerous, uncover man's animal nature, for instance in the searing operatic version of the *Punch and Judy* parable, and in an overt version of an English folk ritual like *Down by the Greenwood Side.* That the two distinct categories are nonetheless interdependent is revealed in one of Birtwistle's major orchestral works, *The Triumph of Time,* a 'temporal' piece which is also ritual incantation; and in the recent large-scale, one movement orchestralwork *Earth Dances,* which is indeed ferociously earthy, while being constructed on a highly intricate metrical scheme.

Every aspect of Birtwistle's music is fused in his major achievement, the opera *The Masks of Orpheus,* at which he worked, on and off, for fifteen years, before its triumphant production in 1986. That the myth of Orpheus – a poet-composer-priest of ancient Thrace who attempted, through Art and Reason, to play God and even to challenge death itself – should have haunted the human imagination over many centuries is understandable. Today, it would seem that Stockhausen regards *himself* as a modern Orpheus; Birtwistle, more English in discretion, merely re-musics his story, starting from a libretto by Peter Zinoviev that offers a version of the protean myth psychologically and philosophically pertinent to our 'pluralistic' society. No one is likely to unravel the mazes of this libretto in the theatre, nor is this necessary, since the music is stunning enough, and the visual images are dazzling enough, to absorb us utterly for nearly four hours. Birtwistle has made 'corporeal music': sounds, such as we'd long forgotten, to our bitter cost, that involve bodily action along with words so that, as with real primitive musics, one lives in the sounds while they last. The miracle is that Birtwistle's score, in alliance with visual images and mimetic movement, does function as a rite relevant to our global world. Profiting from the composer's experiments at the National Theatre, the piece evokes worlds alien to yet deeply within us. Music, decor, mime and costumes call on multifarious cultures from Australian aboriginal to the sophistications of Japanese *Noh* and *Kabuki*, with Old English fertility rites thrown in for good measure. The slowly-initiatory birth of the first act, the terrifying hurly-burly of the second act, set in hell, the introspective resolution of the third act, are sublimely simple in their complexity. Although Orpheus is annihilated, as in many versions of the legend, he is also (like Britten's Boy) reborn. Neither Greek, nor Japanese, nor Old English – since as Birtwistle points out this is a world not imitated, but made – *The Masks of Orpheus* overwhelmingly achieves, at its mysteriously serene end, that catharsis which was the end of and justification for the pity and terror of Aeschylean and Shakespearean tragedy.

Like the primitive and oriental artefactors on whom he has resourcefully drawn but not emulated, Birtwistle thinks not linearly but circularly, refashioning the myths outside Time, in ever-fluctuating permutations. This accords with the findings of our psychology, while allowing for musical recapitulations helpful to those too enmeshed in linearity to shake out of it. In any case, in the theatre dubieties don't occur, so gripped and on occasion griped are we by the vehemence of the music and the startlements of the spectacle. Birtwistle deploys his bands of percussion, woodwind and brass – one doesn't miss the strings, even over so long a stretch – in manners closer to Australian aboriginal ritual and Japanese or Javanese theatre musics than to Western symphony, yet creates sonorities that belong irresistibly to us. The vocal lines, however taxing, extend conventional *bel canto* into non-Western vocal techniques, especially in the horrendous music for black Hecate and the Oracle of the Dead. The protagonists have three identities as Man, Myth and Hero, the last being represented by awesomely gargantuan puppets; throughout, the triple identities work persuasively, perhaps because we now accept such concepts viscerally as well as intellectually. Thus the work is a breakthrough not only experientially, but in musical-theatrical techniques: *how* it is done is inseparable from *what* is done, as opera singers, not merely professional dancers, move, mime and run as to the manner born, inspired by the grandeur of Birtwistle's aural imagination. Electronics are used to auralize the voice of God (Apollo), who utters his own, to us inarticulate, language. The resort to the supernatural forces of electronics to make the numinous manifest is powerfully effectual, though Birtwistle, less convinced than most of us, has said that he won't call on electronics again. Certainly he has no need to, having in terms of 'live' music effected a *rénouvellement* of Western tradition. 'Opera' will never be the same again.

The term 'corporeal music', used in reference to *The Masks of Orpheus*, was in fact coined forty years ago by Harry Partch [1901 – 1976], that aboriginal composer who, reared in the parched and parching wastes of the deserts of Arizona, New Mexico and California, discarded the trappings of Western civilization, and along with them the accoutrements of our harmonized music. Designing his own instruments, tuned to a forty-three-tone-to-the-octave scale, Partch anticipates Stockhausen's *Stimmung* in making of Just Intonation a philosophy of man and the cosmos, expounded in his book *Genesis of a Music:* he sees the European compromise of temperament, especially equal temperament, as a fall from grace to dis-grace. There is a parallel with the Birtwistle of *Orpheus* in that all Partch's music is also mythic theatre; even purely instrumental pieces are performance-rites, in which the act of playing the very beautiful instruments is – for both player and listener – part of the experience. The difference is that whereas Birtwistle stems from, but transmutes European traditions, as to a degree do Stravinsky and Janáček, Partch is strictly speaking ab-original. Aiming at a rebirth of post-industrial man through incantation, justly intoned 'spiritual' monody and 'corporeal' rhythm, he creates, in a piece such as *The Bewitched* (1955), a cross between an American musical and a Japanese *kabuki* play. In this 'dance satyr' (the punning spelling is the composer's), four Lost Musicians consult an aged Seer, seeking a remedy for the ills of the modern world, and learn that they already possess, in being true to the moment, the only truth that is humanly apprehensible: 'truth is a sandflea; another moment must find its own flea'. Partch's 'moments' are less portentous than Stockhausen's, but not necessarily the worse for that. His musicians, outside not only 'Europe' but even American technocracy, are also clowns, fools, bums, hobos – like Partch himself, who for eight years during the forties lived by riding the rails, and made out of the experience an oddly touching theatre piece called *U. S. Highball.* When social satire and musical parody dissolve into what Partch calls slapstick, the dadaism links contemporary non-values to values so old they seem eternal. Human beings who microtonally yell, moan, shout, wail, guffaw or grunt in jazzy abandon or hysteria may become indistinguishable from hooting owls, barking foxes and the wild cats of the woods; but in returning, 'below' consciousness, to Nature, they may rediscover their true selves.

In the Prelude to scenes 8 and 10 of *The Bewitched* the wailing pentatonic chant evokes an age-old quietude that is nonetheless fraught with longing. Significantly, it is based on a chant of the Cahuilla Indians who live in the emptiness of the Californian desert. The weird incantation, sounding even more disturbing against the wavering ostinati of Partch's forty-three tone reed organs, interestingly resembles the ululating lines produced on plastic sax by Ornette Coleman, especially in *Chippaqua,* which has Amerindian associations. We are reminded simultaneously of what home means, and of how it feels to be homeless. It's pertinent to note that Partch's last and longest theatre piece, *Delusion of the Fury* [1963 – 1969], described as 'a ritual of dream and delusion', celebrates the Global Village in drawing its materials from Japanese, African, Polynesian, African and modern American sources, yet debunks it as in the last resort delusory. Partch's position is inherently paradoxical in that although he offers a programme of world-regeneration which, if less apocalyptic than Stockhausen's, concerns common men and women everywhere, his desert-based music-theatre – beyond a Birtwistle's or Stockhausen's however transmuted Europe – can only be an elitist activity since its auralization depends on his expensive and not readily transportable instruments. Invented, designed and built in supportive universities, these are now decaying under the attrition of the years. Electronics might have provided an answer had not Partch, unlike Varèse and Stockhausen, considered science the devil's ally. This philosophical muddledom will probably mean that Partch's impact, powerful though it is, will weaken.

Another old American lone wolf, who has become an increasing rather than declining force in recent years, succeeds in effecting a link between the 'head' of mathematical science and the 'body' of Afro-American jazz. Conlon Nancarrow, born in an outpost of Arkansas in 1912, moved to New York in youth, to study with those different but related props of American academicism, Walter Piston and Roger Sessions. Early works of the thirties – a piano sonatina, a string quartet, and a whirling toccata for violin and piano – transmute, indeed begin to demolish, conventional techniques through the prestidigitous speed (reflective of New York's urban frenzy?) of their articulation; recently the violin work has been dazzlingly performed with the violin part transposed upwards and the piano part taped, speeded to the vertiginous tempo the composer wanted but couldn't exact from merely human executants. There is an affinity between these early Nancarrow works and the potently original music – notably a string quartet and a hair-raising piano study in unequal rhythms – that Ruth Crawford was producing in these turbulent years. Nancarrow's career was, however, disrupted because, inspired by the social and political ferment of the thirties, he went to fight in the Spanish Civil War. On his return to the U. S. in 1939 he was subjected to political harassment, as a consequence of which he settled in Mexico City. In this pullulating if exotic conurbation Nancarrow has lived for the past forty-five years.

These biographical facts bear on the composer's status as an outsider, and this in turn relates to his abandonment of conventional instruments in favour of the player piano, for which all his music since 1948 has been composed. In youth, Nancarrow had been a jazz trumpeter, and the earlier of his pianola 'studies' relate to this alternative Big City culture, as do the studies by Charles Ives for (ostensibly) normal piano. In particular, Nancarrow's music recalls the crudest and rudest types of jazz, for both the polymetres and the clattering metallic sonorities sound like barrel house piano boogie, somewhat exoticized with touches of voice and trumpet blues, flamenco guitar and Mexican marimba band. By means of his perforated rolls, Nancarrow creates miracles of polymetrical intricacy beyond the control of human fingers, however agile the mind behind them. So the music's corporeality merges into its intellectuality.

Later studies – for which Nancarrow had more sophisticated pianolas especially designed – explore extremities of metrical proportion and disproportion, one tempo being related to another in (say) the ratio of 2 to the square root of 1; or two 'metrical canons' continuously accelerate and decelerate on overlapping planes – a mechanical fulfilment of the startlingly experimental finale of Ruth Crawford's string quartet, and an anticipation of aspects of the music of European Ligeti, who acknowledges an indebtedness to Nancarrow. If the concept is mathematically abstract, the musical consequence is of tremendous physical excitation. Body and head, for too long separated in our Western world, are reunited; and although (as we'll see) comparable complexities are now easily negotiable by electronic means, no electronic music has created such 'presence' out of 'distinguished and divided worlds', to use the phrase in which seventeenth century Sir Thomas Browne, himself both artist-theologian and putative scientist, referred to body and spirit. This is the deeper meaning of today's mating of men and machines: which explains why Nancarrow, a self-exiled loner, now occupies a crucial position in world music.

Of course there are ranges of experience – for instance, tragedy and pathos in the Greek senses – that Nancarrow's music of its nature bypasses; he cannot be a 'great' humanist composer in the same category as Charles Ives. But that is the measure of his historical import; if he embraces Black jazz within White intellect, he also anticipates those 'process' composers who seek a deliberate return to quasi-tribal 'necessity'. This takes us into areas developed since the original publication of this book, for 'minimal' and 'process' musics have become the most influential, if not the most significant, forces in the music of the last twenty years. Minimalism and process are not identical though they are related. Ultimate minimality was adumbrated in the early sixties by La Monte Young [b. 1935], for whom the 'I' loses identity in surrendering to the aural cosmos of a single tone or interval, sustained as though *in eternitatum*. This is a phenomenon related to, but not identical with, Cage's notorious silent piece *4'33"* (1962), the difference being that Cage invited the listener to become his own composer, discovering music within the world's arbitrary noises, whereas La Monte Young, a one-time pupil of Stockhausen, was encouraging the listener to participate in a mystical act – some years before *Aus den Sieben Tagen*.

Terry Riley's aural meditation less radically denies will in an oriental abnegation of works: in the sixties, through identification with a single unremittingly repeated sound-source as in the deservedly celebrated *In C;* in the seventies through mainly pentatonic, often improvised, pattern-making on electronic keyboards; in the eighties through an incantatory use of traditional resources, including the string quartet. Riley effects the transition from minimal to process music, gravitating from single sounds to endlessly reiterated patterns. The objection to this might be that although to reject Western humanism and American technocracy may be understandable and even excusable, not even West Coast Americans in fact belong to an ancient oriental culture but irremediably to Western traditions which, as Europeans like Debussy and Messiaen have demonstrated, may be modified but not denied. Young's and Riley's will-lessness in fact amounts to a prodigious exercise of will.

If a similar objection may be urged against Steve Reich's Africanism it is less damaging since the process his live performers undergo on their live instruments is indeed enlivening, calling for a high degree of skill, in which the audience participates vicariously. The body, expunged by Young and Riley, serves for Reich as a launching-pad for transcendence, as may happen in real tribal musics and in Afro-American jazz. In an hour-and-a-half Reich work such as *Drumming* (1976), the slowly exfoliating metrical and linear patterns in the tingling orchestration of percussion instruments pitched and unpitched tend to enhance, rather than to engulf, consciousness. As with Chopi xylophone bands, Mexican marimba bands and Balinese gamelan orchestras – with all of which Reich has personal acquaintance – mind, nerves, body and senses are activated as one becomes part of a ritual performance, living in the noise until it arbitrarily – for there is no beginning, middle or end – ceases. The danger is that since we, unlike the Africans or Balinese, have no clear notion as to what the ritual signifies in relation to our lives, act may degenerate into habit. Compared with Birtwistle's *Orpheus*, which embraces process within composition, the rites of Reich's process are a variously rewarding game.

Perhaps with this in mind Reich has in recent works, such as *Desert Music* and *Tehillim*, relaxed the abstraction of his pattern-making to the point of calling on melody instruments, incantatory voices, and even verbal content. Minimalist fanatics are apt to sniff at these pieces on the grounds that they betray the integrity of the abstraction which is apposite to, even as it counteracts, a mechanistic civilization. On the other hand a vast new public has found in a work like *Tehillim* a substitute tribal pop music. Momentarily and near-infantilely we live in the noise's process *as though* we were real Near-Eastern folk dancing as we chant a Hebrew version of a Psalm. An ancient way of life is rendered immediate: still a game, perhaps, but legitimate in so far as we are most of us 'alienated', like non-practising Jews in New York's urban community.

'Pure' process music might be described as a plain man's version of the metrical intricacies of Birtwistle's clock musics, while 'tribal' process music is a plain man's version of Birtwistle's corporeal rituals. In considering this distinction between 'composed' and 'processed' rites, some account of a composer often (misleadingly) allied to the processing minimalists is pertinent. He is Avro Pärt, a fifty-year-old Estonian who was creatively reborn when first 'exposed' to plainchant and the music of the Russian Orthodox Church. This was not so much a technical discovery as a discovery of spiritual identity, for all Pärt's music, whether or not it is liturgical, is concerned with the numinous. His vocal works are overtly ecclesiastical; his instrumental works seek the 'eternal silence' at the heart of sound, as is indicated by the title of his best known piece, *Tabula Rasa.* If one tries to think of points of reference in defining the nature of Pärt's music one might mention, in addition to plainsong and medieval heterophony, the liturgical music of Stravinsky, Satie's *Socrate,* the ceremonial music of Janáček, and even the children's music of Orff. These same points of reference would have general relevance to Birtwistle too, though in neither case is there any question of 'influence'. Nor, though Pärt uses few notes and much repetition, is there any real link with the minimalists, since Pärt's few notes are intimately expressive, and therefore in content not minimal at all. A five-minute *Cantus* (1976) in memory of Benjamin Britten, scored for a single bell and strings, starts from God's music of the bell's overtones and swells, bell-like, into multiple intertwining canons that function magically in palliating the finality of death. The effect has that purity of spirit which Pärt admires in Britten's music; the radiant serenity of both composers always has human relevance, and this applies even to Pärt's most abstract music, such as the second part of *Tabula Rasa,* scored monophonically or heterophonically, or in simple diatonic concords, for a solo violin with string orchestra and the intermittent, quasi-Polynesian twang of a prepared piano.

Monody and heterophony still more consistently characterize the vocal works, mostly on Latin texts. Pärt's biggest piece, *Passio domini nostri Jesu Christi secundum Joannem* (1981), at first sounds consciously archaic. The heterophonic extensions to the choral parts, often instrumentally doubled, have a savage impersonality that recalls ancient liturgical incantation, especially that with oriental affiliations, though Pärt's ritual is specifically related to humane Christian traditions. Christ is represented by a consort of voices, while even the narrator-Evangelist does not sing expressionistically, in relation to the text. Yet if the music sounds immemorially ancient, it also rings fresh as a daisy, and is as pertinent to our bruised and battered world as were the Passions of the aged Schütz to seventeenth century Germany, ravaged by a Thirty Years War which, proportionate to the population, may have exceeded in horror the two wars of our presumptively enlightened times. A parallel between the technical methods and emotional effects of the Pärt and Schütz Passions exists, though again there is no 'influence'. The blaze of harmonic homophony in Pärt's final Amen takes us by surprise, affirming the composer's chastity of heart and resilient courage in the face of odds.

Compared with Reich's *Tehillim,* Pärt's Passion is a composed rite, not a processed game, and one suspects that process music must inevitably involve an element of deceit if it pretends to be a 'way of life'. This becomes patent in the theatre music of Philip Glass, who in his early days wrote middle-of-the-road Copland-affiliated music, but arrived at a minimalism that finally bridges the narrow gulf between Process and Pop. In inviting us to surrender to the libidinal philosophy of Derrida and Lyotard, Glass attempts to abolish history, which can be achieved only by accepting Freud's equation between submission to the libido and the death instinct. This correlation has been overtly made by many pop groups, whose names (and functions) have shifted over the last twenty years from the cheerfully animalistic Beatles, Birds and Animals to Boom Town Rats, Grateful Dead, Stranglers, Sex Pistols, The Enemy, The Clash, and (ultimate irony) The Police. It is difficult to avoid seeing Glass's prodigious success in the eighties – his records sell over a hundred thousand copies, and he has had four or five operas running concurrently in capitals of the world – in relation to this fundamental negation. His music functions in the same way as that of the pop groups, both in its incremental remorselessness and in the fact that, although admitting to the existence of Western harmony, it employs it without reference to antecedence or consequence. Through electronic keyboards loudly and unremittingly playing reiteratively phased patterns it creates an aural womb that becomes a tomb. Seeking an identity of time and space, Glass offers an anti-teleological interpretation of Einstein; his later 'opera', *Ahknatan* (1984), set in ancient Egypt, with a transvestite hero, carries phased repetition to the point of mummification. Despite the splendour of the visual images achieved through dance, mime, lighting and cinematic devices, one emerges from the theatre-tomb reflecting, after four hours' submission to Glass's reiterations, that although one is for popular appeal and not against commercial success, one prefers them to be on behalf of life – as with Reich, not to mention the Beatles, Bob Dylan or Joni Mitchell – rather than on behalf of death. One cannot discount a force as potent as Glass's music; one may, however, find some of its implications alarming.

If process music has bifurcated into two streams, one abstract and elitist, the other concrete and populist, the same may be said of electronic music, the fathers of which emerged some thirty years back. They tended to be sound-engineers rather than composers, specializing either in the taped redisposition of sounds of the natural world *(musique concrète)*, or in the construction of mathematically-ordered 'pure' electronic sounds. In those days only the great Varèse (in *Deserts*) used electronics to musical ends, though his technical equipment was by later standards jejune.

The leaders of the intellectual camp were Vladimir Ussachevsky [b. 1911] and Otto Luening [b. 1900] – the latter a 'straight' composer who turned to electronics at the prompting of Busoni's theories of a New Music based on the fusion of Art and Science. Neither Luening nor Ussachevsky had enough creative impetus to make much mark; 'abstract' electronics began to matter only when taken up by a real composer, Milton Babbitt [b. 1916], who saw in them a means of bringing to fruition his ideal of total serialization, applied not only to pitch but to the minutest aspect of composition. His combinations of live instruments with electronics, in for instance *Philomel* and *Vision and Prayer*, may be distinguished by a rarefied beauty; but the purely abstract and purely electronic compositions of Babbitt and his disciples seemed to most people purely incommunicable; they are certainly the most intellectually complex music yet invented. At the heart of American democracy, though functioning within universities which financed their gadgetry, these men made a music intentionally *anti*-democratic. Babbitt himself has even maintained that the value of his music lies in its mathematically demonstrable truth, which could only be sullied by communication with any, yet alone *the*, public. That there is psychological and semantic confusion in this ivory towerism is suggested by the fact that Babbitt is passionately devoted to American musical comedy and in particular to Jerome Kern, the 'escapist' composer he would most like, at least in waggish moments, to have been. Yet the pure abstraction of electronics can only be another kind of escape from the toil and moil of living – with the further disadvantage that so few people want to escape with it. This may be why it sometimes seems that pure electronic composers are a dying breed, if breed they ever did.

Such a judgment is unacceptable because it is too early to assess the potential of what has become, with the aid of advanced computer science, a new approach to music's nature and even function. Whether the work of a Charles Dodge or John Chowning in American universities, or of Boulez and the Europeans at IRCAM in Paris, will amount to discovery as well as exploration is bound up with the future or non-future of our electronic civilization. In the interim, impure electronic composers have naturally been more prolific and – as we have noted in the case of Stockhausen – more communicative than the pure brand. For them, electronics are an enrichment of live instruments and of theatre: as we may hear, among the older American generation, in the work of the lively Robert Erikson at San Diego, for his imagination, however sensitive to new resources, maintains a recognizably humanist bias. One can say as much of some of the larger crop of composers born in the thirties, such as Roger Reynolds and Donald Erb, whose powerfully emotive music for electronics with symphony orchestras has achieved a measure of popular acclaim. Similarly accessible is the music of Morton Subotnick, whose purely electronic *Silver Apples of the Moon* creates a delicately distinctive aural universe, while his *Electric Christmas 1967* blends synthesized electronics with film and light projection to make multi-media theatre, embracing medieval cantillation and tintinnabulation along with twentieth century rock. *Return*, a piece celebrating the visit of Halley's Comet in 1985, also calls on quasi-medieval techniques, perhaps to evoke the eternity of interstellar space. In making a continuum of sound from an immensely magnified harpsichord it has something in common with Reichian process music, and more with Ligeti's continuum works. Like most pop music nowadays, it also involves a visual dimension, being intended for performance in a vast planetarium, with full-scale sky show.

It seems not improbable that the future evolution of electronic music will steer this product of highly sophisticated technology towards precisely those 'mystical' and numinous ranges of experience that science was supposed to have discredited and even obliterated. This is suggested not only by Birtwistle's use of electronics for the voice of God, but also by the deeply moving, Christianly committed, in part electronic music of Britain's Jonathan Harvey, especially in his major work *Madonna* (1986), which electronically made a virtue of the acoustics of the Albert Hall. The American Robert Eaton's famous-notorious *Mass* for microtonal Japanese soprano, clarinet and synthesizers also calls for comment in this religious context, for it offers a grotesque but not intentionally parodistic comment on God in the twentieth century. The piece, if with more (slightly scary) sociological than musical import, is weirdly fascinating; a male speaking voice declaims the Creed in American, in the portentous tones of a March of Time newscaster, while the microtonal soprano squeaks and squawks and the electronics emit their habitual bleeps, burps, gibbers and gobbles.

If, over half a century, electronic music has produced little of humanly musical substance, it may be because music as a performing art battens on human presence. We haven't yet recovered from the early 'concert' of electronic music, at which the computers owlishly winked as they bleeped, promoting hilarity or boredom. This may also be why electronic music has proved more successful – artistically as well as in terms of audience appeal – the more it has veered towards pop, which depends on synthesized sounds, if not pure electronics, for its existence. In this context, a minor, exclusively electronic composer – Jon Appleton – merits more attention than many who are both more ambitious and more esteemed. Appleton's early work, dating from the late sixties, is an extension of the primitive techniques of *musique concrète*: natural and unnatural noises of the external world are juxtaposed and 'mixed' to create ludicrous, sometimes bizarre, science fictional dreams and nightmares. The pieces – soundscapes rather than music as we have known it – are usually amusing, often stimulating, sometimes imaginative.

Appleton's later work is more conventionally musical, being composed for a digital system called the synclavier, devised by the composer in collaboration with engineers Sydney Alonso and Cameron Jones. The pieces are usually played straight at the keyboard, though the instrument stores computerized material. The synthetic sounds, even when microtonal, are clearly defined, often ripely sonorous, and the forms are not radically distinct from those of orthodox music. If the glinting sonorities remind us (as does some process music) of Balinese gamelan music, it is never in the spirit of 'the old exoticism trip', to call on Steve Reich's phrase. The music merely takes over such sonorities as part of our global birthright. The sounds are so clean, light and airy that they prompt visual analogies: a tapestry of bell sounds is a mixed metaphor that goes some way towards defining the spatial and temporal effect of a piece such as *Syntronia* (1977) – an aural analogue, perhaps, to the bright colours and sharp shapes of (tasteful) advertising boards and strip cartoons.

Although influences are not in question, there is a tie-up between the Appleton experience and the music of children (who like strip cartoons); that of the simpler exotic cultures, notably the Balinese; that of Satie both early and late; that of early (prepared piano) Cage; and perhaps, in the clean lines, open textures and non-Western modalities, of Lou Harrison. Here technology wou'ld seem to be vindicated in that it allows the new-born old-new world that Harry Partch envisaged to function in total audibility. No one, certainly not Appleton, would claim that his is 'great' music; but in that it is innocently concerned with new worlds, always sounds beautiful, and never loses its sense of humour, it does offer qualities which our beleaguered race is in need of. Jon Appleton, like Erik Satie, may be an important, little composer. By way of a modern machine, his music says something about birth and human potential; at the same time it offers a dispassionate comic assessment of our no less human limitations.

In Appleton's music, electronics, a bastion of hyper-intellectuality, join hands with a form of popular entertainment that is enlivening rather than amnesic; there is a close analogy between his lucent textures and those of Annie Lennox's *Eurythmics*. Both composers have described their music as 'soundscapes', though it is improbable that there has been mutual influence. Inversely, the dream factory of the American musical has shown signs of coming of age, or rather of catching up with that great theatre piece, Gershwin's *Porgy and Bess* (really a fully-fledged opera) and, at a somewhat lower level, with Bernstein's *West Side Story*, a Broadway musical distinguished alike by its powerfully contemporary theme and its brilliantly professional musicianship. That the generality of musicals has remained escapist pap is counteracted by the emergence of the talent of Stephen Sondheim, who has proved that the musical may still be used to adult ends. In particular, *Sweeney Todd* is a strong, subtle, funny, frightening and paradoxically *enlivening* musical that deals – by way of a sensitively-intelligent modification of Broadway conventions – with that very *death*-wish which underlies our culture, as manifest alike in (some) tribal pop and process music.

At the same time pop itself has broken the barriers. It did so twenty years ago with the Beatles' *Sergeant Pepper;* nowadays one wouldn't want to put Jon Appleton and Annie Lennox in separate categories; and one doesn't worry about where to 'place' Laurie Anderson, androgynous priestess of a tragi-comic sci-fi world in which, through sounds, mime and visual images, we alarmedly recognize the lineaments of the present, and are induced to laugh even if and as we are scared. Laurie Anderson, like Jon Appleton, may be said to update Harry Partch. Complementarily, traditionally trained jazzmen like Ornette Coleman and Keith Jarrett have embarked on notated composition and may present their music theatrically. Nor can we make sharp distinctions between artists and technicians, since the one is so dependent on the other – as men such as David Behrmann and Max Neuhaus have demonstrated.

Looking back on the thirty years surveyed in this inevitably bewildering chapter it would seem that the music we make and listen to can only add to our confusion. Confronted by so many apparently contradictory possibilities, how can we recognize the 'right' when we hear it? This is ultimately a philosophical, not a musical, question. Our world, in its instability, may baffle and frighten us; yet this is not all loss, since fear also excites, and we teeter between hazard and hope. Paradoxically, technology not only offers opportunities for complete metamorphoses in human potential, it also presents us with unwontedly efficient means of preserving the past on disc, videotape and computer. This gives us a chance to keep our options open, and so safeguards us from despair on the one hand, and on the other from a euphoric reliance on our technical expertise. As long as we keep our ears, hearts and minds open (in that order), we have a fair chance of recognizing that the words 'better than' may still mean something, or that even if they philosophically don't, we must needs act as though they did. 'Youth culture' was proven right in its realization that the Beatles were better than the Monkees, just as jazz fanatics were right to consider Duke Ellington's band better than Paul Whiteman's. In the past a fair proportion of people knew that Beethoven was better than fashionable Hummel, and that Bach was better than Telemann, even though in that case we cannot number among the wise the burghers who appointed him.

The view of the ultimate democrat of modern music, John Cage, does not really deny this, since although his silent piece invites everyone to become his own composer, he hopes that being an (even silent) composer will help people to *live better*. He is still experimentally active, and in 1976 was invited to produce a work for the Boston Symphony to perform at the American Bicentennial. He offered two different works, to be performed simultaneously. One, *Renga,* offers graphic representations to the performers, selected by chance operations from the notebooks of Cage's American Hero, Thoreau; these are to be 'realized' as the individual player's instinct suggests. The other work, *Apartment House 1776,* consists of adaptations of marches, songs and hymns of the Revolutionary period, also chosen by chance operations, played by small instrumental groups, in any order, directed by a time-beater but not 'conductor'. Vocal groups representing the people on the American continent in 1776 – Pueblo Indian, Sephardic Jew, Anglo-Saxon Protestant, Black – sing songs from their respective traditions, creating an ultimately democratic circus. The audience is supposed to stroll around and through the performers, so that whatever they hear (or don't hear) is aurally kaleidoscopic. 'Exposed' to the world, we may take our choice without having it imposed upon us.

Ultimately it is not a question of moral choice but of belief; Cage is giving positive formulation to the negatively democratic phenomenon of Muzak, the purpose of which is to destroy music itself, since it is meant to be *not listened to* – usually for some ulterior motive, such as lowering our resistance to sales pressure, or lulling our airborne nerves into insensibility. Cage, though in favour of an abnegation of the will, is not in favour of insensibility; he wants us to listen to the random sounds that reach our ears, and to be more alive in consequence. His American innocence reminds us again that although all art is in some sense propaganda, propaganda for life is preferable to propaganda for death; the point made earlier in reference to death-dealing tribal pop and the process of Philip Glass is of general application. We wait, with ears wide open, to hear whether the future will bring unimaginable marvels, submission to computerized routine, or total annihilation. This is why it is important that we should recognize life when we hear it.

COMPARATIVE CHRONOLOGY

Date	Composers	Musical events	Literature	Art and architecture	Some historical and scientific figures and events
1000	Berno of Reichenau (d. 1048). Hermannus Contractus of Reichenau (1013–54).		The *Anglo-Saxon Chronicles* continue to be compiled till after Norman Conquest.		1018 Assembly of Oxford. Danes and English under English law.
			Peter Abelard (1079–1142).	1063–92 Pisa Cathedral. 1079 Winchester Cathedral, Norman rebuilding begun. 1086–97 Tower of London.	1066 Norman Conquest. 1086 Completion of Doomsday Book.
			Bernard of Clairvaux (1090–1153). Aelred, Abbot of Rievaulx (1109?–66). John of Salisbury (*c.* 1115–80). 1135 Geoffrey of Monmouth: *Historia Regum Britanniae*.	1093 onwards, Durham Cathedral.	
1100					1147 The Second Crusade.
	1155 Bernart de Ventadorn (d.1195) visits England. *c.* 1160–80 Maître Léonin at Notre Dame, where music in two to four parts is being cultivated.	1150 Period of troubadours, trouvères, jongleurs, and ménestrels of France.	1165 Fl. Chrétien de Troyes.	1163–*c.* 1250 Notre Dame, Paris.	*c* 1167 Oxford University founded. 1169 Saladin is Sultan of Egypt. 1170 Murder of Thomas à Becket.
	c. 1180–1236 Maître Pérotin at Notre Dame.			1174–85 Canterbury Cathedral choir. 1176 Old London Bridge. 1194–1260 Chartres Cathedral.	Francis of Assisi (1182-1226). 1182 Jews banished from France. 1189 The Third Crusade.

				Ypres.	c. 1209 Cambridge University founded.
		1207 First song contests at the Wartburg.	Roger Bacon, Franciscan monk and scientific thinker, born (c. 1214–1293).		1209 The Albigensian Crusade.
					1215 *Magna Carta* signed.
					Before 1219 Bologna University founded.
				1220–88 Amiens Cathedral	1222 Padua University founded.
				1220–65 Salisbury Cathedral	1228 Frederick II leads the Sixth Crusade and takes Jerusalem.
		1226 Period of the Passion, Christmas, miracle, and Easter plays.	Thomas Aquinas (1225–1274).	Cimabue (1240?–1301?).	1237–40 Mongols conquer Russia.
	Adam de la Halle (c. 1230–c. 1288).	1230 Musical instruction at Oxford and Paris.		1246–48 Sainte Chapelle, Paris.	c. 1243 Salamanca University founded.
	1239 Death of John of Fornsete.	c. 1250 The Reading Rota: *Sumer is icumen in.*		1248 onwards Cologne Cathedral.	1244 Egyptian Sultan re-captures Jerusalem.
	Philip de Vitri (1291–1361)	1270 Adam de la Halle writes his opera, *Jeu de Robin et Marion.*	Dante Alighieri (1265–1321).	1261–1324 York Minster.	1265 Parliament summoned by Simon de Montfort.
				Giotto (c. 1266–1337)	1271 Marco Polo began his travels.
					1290 Jews expelled from England.
1300	Guillaume de Machaut (c. 1300–c. 1377)		1300 Dante: *Divina Commedia* begun.		1309 Papal Court set up at Avignon.
			Petrarch (1304–74).		
		1310 Period of transition from *ars antica* to *ars nova.*	Giovanni Boccaccio (1313–75).		1313 Berthold Schwarz, German Grey Friar, invents gunpowder.
			John Wycliff (c .1320–84).		William of Wykeham (1324–1404).
	Francesco Landini (1325–97).	1323 Jean de Muris: *Musica Speculativa*	William Langland (c. 1332–c. 1400).		1332 First record of division of Parliament into two Houses.
			Geoffrey Chaucer (c.1340–c.1400)		1338–1453 The 100 Years' War.
		1340 Secular and instrumental music increasing.	1340 The Luttrell Psalter.	Filippo Brunelleschi (1339–1446).	1340 First European paper mill.
					1347–51 The Black Death.
	John Dunstable (?–1453).		1362 Langland: *Piers Plowman.*		1348 Prague University founded.
			c. 1366 Froissart's *Chronicles.*		1362 English language used in Parliament instead of French.
		1370 Meistersingers active in Germany.	1369 Chaucer: *The Boke of the Duchesse.*	The van Eycks (1370–1441).	1381 The Peasants' Revolt.

Date	Composers	Musical events	Literature	Art and architecture	Some historical and scientific figures and events
1300 *contd.*			1387 Chaucer: *Canterbury Tales* begun.	Donatello (1386–1466). Fra Angelico (1387–1455). P. Uccello (1397–1475) (*c.* 1400 Wilton Diptych).	1386 Heidelberg University founded.
1400	Gilles Binchois (*c.* 1400–60). Guillaume Dufay (1400–74).			Roger van der Weyden (1400–64). Masaccio (*c.* 1401–28). Filippo Lippi (?1406–69) Piero della Francesca (1406–92). 1411–46 London Guildhall built. Jean Fouquet (*c.* 1415–77).	1409 Leipzig University founded. 1415 Battle of Agincourt. Jan Huss burnt at Constance.
	Johannes Ockeghem (*c.*1420–*c.*1495).		Robert Henryson (*c.* 1425–1508).	Giovanni Bellini (1428–1516). Hans Memling (1430–94).	1426–50 First printed books, in Holland and Germany.
		1436 Dufay composed his motet *Nuper rosarum.*	François Villon (b. 1431, disappeared 1463).	Andrea Mantegna (1431–1506). 1434 Jan van Eyck: *Arnolfini and his Wife.*	1431 Joan of Arc burnt at Rouen. 1431–33 First German peasant revolt near Worms.
	Jacob Obrecht (*c.* 1440–1505). Alexander Agricola (*c.* 1446–*c.* 1506)	1440–65 The Trent Codices.		Sandro Botticelli (*c.* 1445–1510). 1446–1515 King's College, Cambridge. Ghirlandaio (1449–94)	1440 Eton College founded.
		1452 *Lochamer Liederbuch,* begun.	Politian (1454–94).	Leonardo da Vinci (1452–1519).	1450 Rebellion of Jack Cade of Kent. Isabella of Castile (1451–1504). Ferdinand V of Aragon (1452–1516).
		1460 John Hambroys, Oxford's first Doctor of Music.	John Skelton (*c.* 1460–1529) William Dunbar	Filippino Lippi (1457–1504).	1453 Fall of Constantinople.

contd.	Juan de Anchieta (*c.* 1462–*c.* 1523).		Erasmus (1466–1536). Juan del Encina (*c.* 1468–*c.* 1529). Niccolo Machiavelli (1469–1527). Sir Thomas Malory, (d. 1471). 1471 *Orfeo*, by Politian, performed in Mantua. Sir Thomas More (1478–1535).	(1462–1516). Albrecht Dürer (1471–1528). Michelangelo (1475–1564). Titian (1477–1576). Giorgione (*c.* 1478–1511). *c.* 1480 Eton College frescoes. Raphael (1483–1520).	1469–92 Lorenzo de' Medici, ruler of Florence. Copernicus, Polish astronomer (1473–1543). 1476 Caxton's printing press at Westminster.
	Francisco de Peñalosa (*c.* 1470–*c.* 1528) Hugh Aston (*c.* 1480–1522).	1490–1502. Eton Choirbook collected.	1485 Malory: *Morte d'Arthur.*		1484 Parliament passes reform Acts on law, trade, and tax-collecting. 1485 Battle of Bosworth Field. Tudor dynasty. 1492 Christopher Columbus crosses Atlantic to America. Jews expelled from Spain. 1493 Maximilian I, Holy Roman Emperor. 1495 Jews expelled from Portugal.
		1495. Josquin des Prez, choirmaster at Cambrai Cathedral. 1496. Franchino Gafori: *Practica Musicae.* 1497 Petrucci of Venice prints music, etc., from movable type.	François Rabelais (1494?–1553).	1495–97 Da Vinci's *Last Supper* painted in Milan. Hans Holbein the Younger (1497–1543).	1497 The Venetians, John and Sebastian Cabot, sail from Bristol for Henry VII of England to re-discover N. America.
1500	Christopher Tye (*c.* 1500–73). Thomas Tallis (1505–85).		Sir Thomas Wyatt (1503–42).	Benvenuto Cellini (1500–71). 1503 Da Vinci: *Mona Lisa.* 1503–19 Henry VII's Chapel, Westminster. 1506–66 Bramante, Michelangelo and others: St. Peter's, Rome.	1505 A regular mail service established between Vienna and Brussels.

Date	Composers	Musical events	Literature	Art and architecture	Some historical and scientific figures and events
1500 *contd.*					1509 Henry VIII, King of England. Peter Heule of Nuremberg invents a watch.
				Michelangelo begins ceiling, Sistine Chapel.	1510 St. Paul's School, London, founded by John Colet.
				Pieter Breughel the Elder (1510-70)	1512 Selim I, Sultan of Turkey.
				1515 Hampton Court built.	
	Cypriano de Rore (*c.* 1516–65).		1516 Sir Thomas More: *Utopia.*	1516 Raphael: *Sistine Madonna.*	1517 Coffee first imported into Europe.
				Tintoretto (1518–94).	1518 Royal College of Physicians founded.
				1519–47 Chteau de Chambord.	1519 Ferdinand Magellan sails round the world.
		1520 Robert Fayrfax organizes music, etc., for Henry VIII at the Field of the Cloth of Gold in France.			1520 Chocolate first imported into Europe from Mexico.
		1522 Martin Luther reforms church service.			1521 Martin Luther at the Diet of Worms.
			Pierre de Ronsard (1524–85).		1525 Great peasant revolt in Germany suppressed.
	Palestrina (*c.* 1526–94).			1526 Holbein goes to England.	
		1527 Adrian Willaert founds a singing school in Venice. First chansons printed in Paris by Attaingnant.			1527 Sack of Rome.
				Paolo Veronese (1528–88).	
	Thomas Whythorne (*c.* 1528–91).	1528 Agricola issues his *Musica Instrumentalis.*			1529 Henry VIII summons the Reformation Parliament. Sultan Suleiman the Magnificent attacks Vienna.
	Orlando de Lassus		1532 Rabelais: *Gargantua and*		

Victoria (*c.* 1540–1613). William Byrd (1543–1623).			N. Hilliard (1537–1619).	1538 Monasteries suppressed.
	1543 Venceslaus Szamotulski composes church music in Poland. 1544 Filippo Neri (1515–95) founds the Congregation of the Oratory. 1547 Glareanus: *Dodecachordon.*	Torquato Tasso (1544–95).	El Greco (1541–1614)	
		Cervantes (1547–1616). 1548: *Book of Common Prayer.* 1549: The first English *Book of Common Prayer.* Sir Walter Raleigh (1552–1618). Edmund Spenser (1552–99). Montaigne (1553–92). Sir Philip Sidney (1554–86).	1546-1878 Palais du Louvre, Paris.	1547 Ivan IV (the Terrible), Tzar of Russia. 1549 Social and religious risings in Devon, Cornwall, Norfolk, and Yorkshire. Enclosures legalized. 1553 Accession of Mary Tudor.
G. Gabrieli (1557–1612). Thomas Morley (1557–*c.* 1603).	1554 Palestrina writes his first book of masses. 1556 de Lassus writes his first book of motets.		Isaac Oliver (*c.* 1556–1617).	1558 Jena University founded. Elizabeth I Queen of England. Manufacture of firearms begins in Carinthia.
Carlo Gesualdo (1560–1615). Jan Sweelinck (1562–1621). John Bull (1563–1628). John Dowland (1563–1626).	1563 Vincenzo Galilei: *Il Fronimo.* Byrd organist at Lincoln Cathedral.	Lope de Vega (1562–1635) Christopher Marlowe (1564–93). William Shakespeare (1564–1616).		1560 Jean Nicot imports tobacco into France. 1563 End of the Council of Trent and reform of the Catholic Church. Galileo Galilei (1564–1642).

Date	Composers	Musical events	Literature	Art and architecture	Some historical and scientific figures and events
1500 ***contd.***	John Danyel (1565–1630). Monteverdi (1568–1643).		Thomas Campion (1567–1620). Thomas Nashe (1567–1601).		1565 Manufacture of pencils begins in England. 1569 Mercator's map of the world.
		1570 A study of Greek writers on music begun in Italy.		1570 Palladio: *Treatise on Architecture*.	1572 Society of Antiquaries in London founded. Landowners in Brandenburg, Germany, allowed to expropriate their peasants.
	John Wilbye (1573–?)	1575 Elizabeth I grants Tallis and Byrd a music-publishing monopoly.	Ben Jonson (1573–1637). John Donne (1573–1631).	Inigo Jones (1573–1641). Caravaggio (1573–1610).	1576 Warsaw University founded.
	Thomas Weelkes (1577–1623?).		1577 Holinshed: *Chronicles*. 1579 Edmund Spenser: *Shepherd's Calendar*. John Fletcher (1579–1625).	Peter Paul Rubens (1577–1640).	1577–80 Drake's *Golden Hind* circumnavigates the world.
		1580 Nanini and Palestrina found a music school in Rome. 1581 Count Bardi of Vernio, Italy, founds the Florentine Camerata. Vincenzo Galilei: *Dialogo della musica antica e della moderna*.	John Webster (?1580–1625?).	Frans Hals (1580–1666).	1582 First water works in London. Edinburgh University founded.
	Orlando Gibbons (1583–1625). Frescobaldi (1583–1644).		Francis Beaumont (1584/5–1616).		1583 Sir Walter Raleigh goes to Virginia. 1584 Potatoes first imported into Europe. 1585 Shakespeare leaves Stratford for London. Cardinal Richelieu (1585–1642)
		1588 William Byrd: *Psalms, sonets and songs of sadness and pietie*.	1590 Spenser: *Faerie Queene*. Marlowe: *Tamburlaine*		1590 Janssen invents the microscope. 1591 Trinity College, Dublin, founded.

	[illegible]			Pompeii discovered.	
		1594 Peri's opera, *Dafne*, performed in Florence and Vecchi's *L'Amfiparnasso* in Modena.	George Herbert (1593–1632). René Descartes (1596–1650).	Louis Le Nain (*c.* 1593–1648). Poussin (1594–1665).	Gustavus Adolphus of Sweden (1594–1632). 1596 Galileo invents the thermometer. 1597 Acts passed for erection of workhouses and punishment of beggars (valid till 1834).
		1597 Thomas Morley: *Plaine and Easie Introduction to Practicall Musicke.*		Giovanni Bernini (1598–1690).	1598 The Bodleian Library at Oxford organized by Sir Thomas Bodley. The Edict of Nantes issued by Henry IV of France. Oliver Cromwell (1599–1658).
1600	Thomas Simpson (fl. 1600)	1600 *Euridice*, by Peri and Caccini, performed in Florence at the marriage festivities of Henry IV of France and Mary de Medicis. 1601 Thomas Morley: *Triumphes of Oriana.*		Velasquez (1599–1660). Van Dyck (1599–1641). Claude Gelée (Le Lorrain) (1600–1682).	1600 East India Company established.
	William Lawes (1602–45). Denis Gaultier (1603–1673).	1603 Thomas Robinson: *Schoole of Musicke.*			1601 Postal agreement between Germany and France. Death of Queen Elizabeth. Stuart dynasty. 1602–4. Galileo discovers laws of gravitation and oscillation. Dutch East India Company established. 1604 French East India Company established.
		1608 Frescobaldi organist at St. Peter's in Rome.	1605–15 Cervantes: *Don Quixote.* Sir William Davenant (1606–68). Pierre Corneille (1606–84). 1606 Ben Jonson: *Volpone.* John Milton (1608–74).	Rembrandt (1606–69).	1606 Virginia Company formed.

Date	Composers	Musical events	Literature	Art and architecture	Some historical and scientific figures and events
1600 *contd.*		1609 first book of catches, rounds and canons called *Pammelia* printed and published by Thomas Ravenscroft. 1609–19 Francis Tregian compiles the *Fitzwilliam Virginal Book* while imprisoned. 1611 *Parthenia*, containing music for virginals by Byrd, Bull, and Gibbons, published.	1609 Shakespeare: *Sonnets*		
			Richard Crashaw (1613?–49).	1614 Rubens: *The Descent from the Cross* in Antwerp Cathedral.	1614 Danish East India Company formed.
	Johann Jacob Froberger (1616–67). William Young (d. 1672).				1616 Serfdom of peasants established in Pomerania. Dutch and Japanese make commercial treaty. Circulation of the blood demonstrated by William Harvey.
				Peter Lely (1618–80). Charles Lebrun (1619–90).	1618 Thirty Years' War begins.
				Albert Cuyp (1620–94).	1620 *Mayflower* expedition. First negro slaves landed at Jamestown.
			Andrew Marvell (1621–78).		1621 *Corante*, first English newspaper.
			Henry Vaughan (1621–95). Molière (1622–73) 1623 Shakespeare: First Folio.		Blaise Pascal (1623–1662). George Fox (1624–91), founder of Quakers.
			Webster: *Duchess of Malfi*.	Jan Steen (1626–79).	1625–49 Charles I of England. Robert Boyle (1627–91).
		1627 *Dafne*, first German opera by Schütz, produced at Dresden.	John Bunyan (1628-88).	P. de Hooch (*c.* 1629–78).	1628 The Petition of Right against injustices of imprisonment, etc. The Taj Mahal built at Agra.

contd. Lebègue (c. 1630–1702).		John Dryden (1631–1700).	(1630–1723).	
Jean Baptiste Lully (1632–87).	1632. *Il Sant' Alessio*, opera by Stefano Landi.	Spinoza (1632–1677). John Locke (1632-1704) Samuel Pepys (1633–1703). 1634 Milton: *Comus*. 1636 Descartes: *Method*.	Jan Vermeer (1632–75).	1633 Galileo is forced by the Inquisition to renounce the theories of Copernicus. 1636 Harvard University founded. 1638 Japan closed to Europeans until 1865.
Dietrich Buxtehude (1637–1707).	1637 Teatro di San Cassiano, Venice. First public opera-house opened. 1639 Monteverdi's opera, *Adone*, performed at the above theatre. A second public opera-house opened in Venice, Santi Giovanni e Paolo.	Jean Racine (1639–99). William Wycherley (1640–1715).		1639 First American printing press built.
	1642 Theatres closed in England till 1660. Monteverdi: *L'Incoronazione di Poppaea*. 1645 Lully, violinist and kitchen-boy at French court.	Thomas Shadwell (1642–92).	1642 Rembrandt: *Night Watch*.	1642–6. Civil War between Charles I and Parliament. Isaac Newton (1642–1727). 1644 Manchus end Ming Dynasty.
Pelham Humfrey (1647–74). John Blow (1649–1708). Guiseppe Torelli (1650–1708).	Schütz: *Seven Words from the Cross*.	Earl of Rochester (1647–80).		1647 Swedish African Company formed. 1649 Charles I executed.
		Nahum Tate (1652–1715). 1652 Gerrard Winstanley: *Law of Freedom*.	c. 1650 Velasquez: *Toilet of Venus*.	
Archangelo Corelli (1653–1713). Roger North (1653–1734).	1653 Lully becomes director of the King's orchestra.	1653. Izaak Walton: *Compleat Angler*. Roger North (1653–1734).	1655 Rembrandt: *Woman Bathing in a Stream*.	1655 Cromwell organizes the conquest of Jamaica. Berlin has its first newspaper.
	1656 *The Siege of Rhodes*, first English opera performed in London, and composed by Locke, Lawes, Crooke, Colman, and Hudson, with libretto by W. Davenant.			1658 Death of Oliver Cromwell.

Date	Composers	Musical events	Literature	Art and architecture	Some historical and scientific figures and events
1600 *contd.*	A. Scarlatti (1659–1725). Henry Purcell (1659–95). Johann Kuhnau (1660–1722). Johann Ferdinand Fischer (1660-1738).	1659 *La Pastorale*, opera by Robert Cambert (1628–77), produced in France. 1660 Henry and William Lawes compose music for English masques.	1659 Samuel Pepys begins his diaries. Daniel Defoe (1661-1731).	Nicholas Hawksmoor (1661–1736). 1661–1756 Le Vau: Versailles Palace. Sir John Vanbrugh (1664–1726).	1660 Restoration of Charles II. Foundation of the Royal Society.
	François Couperin (1668–1733). Giovanni Bononcini (1670–1755).	1667 Performance in Vienna of Cesti's opera, *Il pomo d'oro*. 1671 First French opera-house opened in Paris.	Jonathan Swift (1667–1745). 1667 Milton: *Paradise Lost*. 1670 Molière: *Le bourgeois gentilhomme*. William Congreve (1670–1729).		1665–6 Great Plague and Fire of London. 1668 The East India Company acquires Bombay, India.
		1672 Académie Royale de Musique et le Danse founded in Paris.	Joseph Addison (1672–1719). 1673. Molière: *Le Malade Imaginaire*. 1674 Wycherley: *The Country Wife*.	1675–1710 Wren: St. Paul's Cathedral rebuilt after Fire.	1672 Newton propounds his law of gravitation. 1674 Nieuw Amsterdam becomes British by treaty, and is renamed New York. 1675 Royal Observatory instituted at Greenwich.
	Antonio Vivaldi (1676–1741).	1676 Thomas Mace: *Musical Grammarian*. 1676 Lebegue: *Premier livre d'orgue*.			1677 Marriage of William of Orange and Princess Mary, daughter of James, Duke of York.

	Jean-Philippe Rameau (1683–1764).	The Comédie Française established.	*and Achitophel.* 1683 William Penn: *General Description of Pennsylvania.*	1682–91 Wren: Royal Hospital, Chelsea. Antoine Watteau (1684–1721).	1682 French Protestants excluded from guilds, Civil Service, and the King's household. 1684 First attempt to light London's streets. 1685 Monmouth rebellion.
	D. Scarlatti (1685–1759). J. S. Bach (1685–1750). G. F. Handel (1685–1759). Benedetto Marcello (1686–1739)	1686 Lully: *Armide.*	Allan Ramsey (1686–1758). Alexander Pope (1688–1744).		
		c. 1689 Purcell: *Dido and Aeneas* produced in London. Kuhnau: *Clavier Studies.* Opera-house opened at Hanover.			1688 William of Orange lands at Torbay and later reaches London. 1689–1725 Peter I (the Great) Tzar of Russia. 1689 William and Mary become King and Queen of Great Britain.
	T. Roseingrave (1690–1766). Henry Carey (*c.* 1690–1743). Pietro Locatelli (1693–1764). Joseph Gibbs (1694–1788).	1692 Purcell: *Hail, bright Cecilia* and *The Fairy Queen.*	1690 Locke: *Human Understanding.* Voltaire (1694–1778).	N. Lancret (1690–1743).	1690 Battle of the Boyne in Ireland. An English factory is established in Calcutta, India. 1692 Lloyd's Coffee-house becomes an office for marine insurance. 1694 Accession of Peter the Great. Bank of England established. Greenwich Hospital founded by Queen Mary.
	Maurice Greene (1695–1755) Jean-Marie Leclair (1697–1764).	1695 Purcell: *Indian Queen.* 1696 Academy of Arts established in Berlin.	1695 Congreve: *Love for Love.*	G. B. Tiepolo (1696–1769). Canaletto (1697–1768) William Hogarth (1697–1764).	1695 End of press censorship in England.
1700	Johann Adolf Hasse (1699–1783).	1700 Sauveur measures and explains musical vibrations.		J.-B.-S. Chardin (1699–1779).	1700 Sewall: *Selling of Joseph.* First American protest against slavery.

Date	Composers	Musical events	Literature	Art and architecture	Some historical and scientific figures and events
1700 *contd.*	Gian Battista Sammartini (1701–1755).	1702 Abbé François Raguenet: *Parallèle des Italiens et des Français.*		F. Boucher (1703–70).	1701 Yale University founded. 1702 Asiento Guinea Company formed to transport Negroes to America. The first English daily newspaper appears: *Daily Courant.*
		1704 J. S. Bach writes his first cantata.			1703 Foundation of St. Petersburg. 1704 Defoe starts the weekly *Review*, first American newspaper at Boston.
		1705 Handel: *Almira*, produced in Hamburg.			Benjamin Franklin (1706–1790).
			1707 G. Farquhar: *The Beaux, Stratagem.*		1707 Empire of the Great Mogul of India, Aurungzeb, disintegrates following his death.
		1708 First German theatre in Vienna.			William Pitt the Elder (1708–78).
	William Boyce (1710–79). Thomas Arne (1710–78).	1709 Cristofori builds the first pianoforte. 1710 Handel visits England. 1711 Principle of tuning-fork discovered.	Samuel Johnson (1709–84). 1712 Pope: *Rape of the Lock.*	1709 Watteau paints military subjects at Valenciennes. 1712–19 Watteau paints in Paris.	1709 First mass emigration of Germans to America.
	C. P. E. Bach (1714–88). Christoph Willibald Gluck (1714-87).	1714 John Rich appointed Manager of Lincoln's Inn Fields Theatre. 1715 Handel: *Water Music.* 1716 François Couperin: *L'Art de toucher le clavecin.*	Jean-Jacques Rousseau (1712–78). Lawrence Sterne (1713–68).	Richard Wilson (1714–82).	1714 Death of Queen Anne. Hanoverian dynasty. Fahrenheit constructs mercury thermometer. 1715 Riot Act passed.
			1719 Defoe: *Robinson Crusoe.*	David Garrick (1717–79).	1718 Lady Mary Wortley Montagu introduces inoculation against smallpox.
		1720 D. Scarlatti: *Narciso* performed in London. 1721 J. S. Bach's Brandenburg Concertos. 1722 J. S. Bach: Book I of the *Well-tempered Clavier.* Rameau: *Traité de l'harmonie.*	Tobias Smollett (1721–71).	1721–26 James Gibbs: St-Martin-in-the-Fields. Sir Joshua Reynolds (1723–92).	
			Immanuel Kant (1724–1804).	G. Stubbs (1724–1806).	1725 Guy's Hospital founded.

contd.					
		1728 Pepusch and John Gay: *The Beggar's Opera*. Colley Cibber (1671–1757) becomes Manager of Drury Lane Theatre. 1730 Guarnerius family makes violins in Cremona.	Charles Burney (1726–1814).	(1727–88). 1728 Chardin becomes member of French Academy. Robert Adam (1728–92). Josiah Wedgwood (1730–95).	
	Joseph Haydn (1732–1809).	1733 Pergolesi: *La serva padrona*. J. S. Bach: *Kyrie* and *Gloria* of B minor Mass 1734 Empress Anne of Russia founds a permanent opera at the Imperial Court at St Petersburg.	Beaumarchais (1732–1799).	J.-H. Fragonard (1732–1806).	1732 The first Covent Garden Theatre completed.
	Joh. Christian Bach (1735–82).	1735 J. S. Bach: Italian Concerto. 1736 Pergolesi: *Stabat Mater*. 1737 Rameau: *Castor et Pollux*.		J. S. Copley (1737–1815).	
		1739 Handel: *Saul*.			1738 First spinning machines patented in England. 1739 John Wesley begins his life's work as an open-air preacher in England.
		1740 D. Scarlatti visits London and Dublin. 1741 Gluck: *Artaserse*. 1741 Rameau: *Pièces de clavecin en concert*. 1742 Handel: *Messiah*, first performance in Dublin. 1744 Bach: *Well tempered Clavier*, Book II.	James Boswell (1740–95). 1740 Richardson: *Pamela*.	1744 Hogarth: *Marriage à la Mode*.	1740 Maria-Theresa of Austria begins her reign. University of Pennsylvania founded. 1741 Empress Elizabeth of Russia begins her reign. Highway Act to improve English roads.
	Charles Dibden (1745–1810).	1745 Handel: *Belshazzar*. 1746 Handel: *Judas Maccabeus*.	1746-66 Diderot and others: *Encyclopédie*. 1748 Richardson: *Clarissa Harlowe*.	Goya (1746–1828). J. L. David (1748–1825).	1745 Last Jacobite rebellion routed at Culloden. Princeton University founded. 1747 Marggraf discovers sugar in beetroot.

Date	Composers	Musical events	Literature	Art and architecture	Some historical and scientific figures and events
1700 *contd.*			Jeremy Bentham (1748–1832).		1740 Garrick Manager of Drury Lane Theatre.
	Domenico Cimarosa (1749–1801).	1749 J. S. Bach: *Art of Fugue* 1749 Handel: *Royal Fireworks Music.*	Goethe (1749–1832). 1749 Fielding: *Tom Jones.* Richard Brinsley Sheridan (1751–1816).		
	Muzio Clementi (1752–1832). Jean Aubert (d. 1753).	1752 Gluck: *La Clemenza de Tito.*			1753 British Museum founded.
	W. A. Mozart (1756–91).	1755 Haydn composes his first string quartet. 1756 Leopold Mozart: *Violin Method.*	William Blake (1757–1827).	John Flaxman (1755–1826). Thomas Rowlandson (1757–1827).	1756–63 The Seven Years' War. 1758 Bridgewater Canal from Liverpool to Leeds begun.
			Robert Burns (1759–96). 1759 Voltaire: *Candide.* Friedrich von Schiller (1759–1805).		1759 British Museum opened. William Pitt the Younger (1759–1806). Horatio Nelson (1759–1805).
	Luigi Cherubini (1760–1842).	1761 J. C. Bach's opera, *Artaserse,* performed in Turin. 1762 Gluck: *Orfeo,* produced in Rome.	1760–7 Sterne: *Tristram Shandy.* 1761 Rousseau: *La Nouvelle Héloise.*	Hokusai (1760–1849). J. Opie (1761–1807). John Nash, architect (1762–1835). G. Morland (1763–1804).	1760 George III of Britain. Wedgwood established pottery works at Etruria, Staffs. 1762–96 Reign of Catherine the Great of Russia. 1763 Canada ceded to Britain at Peace of Paris. British dominant in India.
	Samuel Wesley (1766–1837).	1764 W. A. Mozart meets J. C. Bach in London. 1767 Mozart: *La finta semplice.*	1765 Thomas Percy: *Reliques of Ancient English Poetry.* 1766 O. Goldsmith: *Vicar of Wakefield.*	1768 Adam Brothers: the Adelphi, London.	1768–71 Captain Cook's first Pacific expedition.

contd.					
				1821).	
				T. Lawrence (1769–1830).	Napoleon Bonaparte (1769–1821).
	L. van Beethoven (1770–1827).	1770 First New York performance of *Messiah.*	W. Wordsworth (1770–1850).	1770 Gainsborough: *Blue Boy.*	
			Walter Scott (1771–1832).	J.-A. Gros (1771–1835).	
		1772 Haydn: *'Farewell' Symphony.*			1772 First division of Poland.
		1774 Gluck's *Iphigenie en Aulis* performed in Paris.	1774 Goethe: *Sorrows of Werther.*		
			Jane Austen (1775–1817).	J. M. W. Turner (1775–1851).	
		1776 Burney: *History of Music.*	1776–88 Gibbon: *Decline and Fall of the Roman Empire.*	John Constable (1776–1837).	1776 Declaration of Independence by the U.S.A.
		Sir John Hawkins: *General History of the Science and Practise of Music.*		1776–86 Chambers: new Somerset House.	
		Vienna Burg Theatre founded.	1777 Sheridan: *School for Scandal.*	1777–9 Reynolds: *Jane, Countess of Harington.*	
				1778 Reynolds: *Marlborough Family.*	
			1779–81 S. Johnson: *Lives of the Poets.*		
		1780 Paisello: *Barber of Seville*, composed for St. Petersburg.		J.-A.-D. Ingres (1780–1867).	
		1781 Series of concerts at the Gewandhaus in Leipzig inaugurated.		1780 Rowlandson produces his caricatures.	
	John Field (1782–1837).	1782 Mozart: *Seraglio.*			
	Louis Spohr (1784–1859).		1784 Beaumarchais: *Mariage de Figaro.*	1784 Reynolds: *Mrs. Siddons as the Tragic Muse.*	
		1785 Mozart: *Marriage of Figaro.*	Thomas Love Peacock (1785–1866).	1785 Gainsborough: *Mrs. Siddons.*	
	Carl Maria von Weber (1786–1826).	1786 Dittersdorf: *Doktor und Apotheker.*	1786 R. Burns: *Poems.*		
		1787 Mozart: *Don Giovanni*, performed in Prague.			1787 American Constitution passed and the Association for the abolition of Slave Trade formed in England.
		1788 Cherubini: *Demophon*, opera.	Lord Byron (1788–1824).	1788–1808 Sir John Soane: Bank of England.	

DATE	COMPOSERS	MUSICAL EVENTS	LITERATURE	ART AND ARCHITECTURE	SOME HISTORICAL AND SCIENTIFIC FIGURES AND EVENTS
1700 contd.			1789 Blake: *Songs of Innocence.*		1789 Beginning of the French Revolution.
	G. Meyerbeer (1791–1864).	1791 Mozart: *The Magic Flute.*	1791 Boswell: *Life of Johnson.*		Washington becomes President of U.S.A.
	Karl Czerny (1791–1857).		Thomas Paine: *Rights of Man.*		
	G. Rossini (1792–1865)	1792 Rouget de Lisle: *Le Marseillaise.*	P. B. Shelley (1792–1822).	1792 White House, Washington, built.	1792 France declares war on Austria. Prussia declares war on France. France becomes a republic. Coal gas is used for lighting.
					1793 Louis XVI beheaded.
		1794 Haydn makes a second journey to London.			1794 Execution of Robespierre.
		1795 Paris Conservatoire organized.	John Keats (1795–1821).		
	Franz Schubert (1797–1828).	1797 Cherubini: *Medea*, performed in Paris.		Jean-Baptiste Corot. (1796–1875).	1796 Edward Jenner proves vaccination theory.
	G. Donizetti (1797–1848).		Adam Mickiewicz (1798–1855).	Eugène Delacroix (1798–1863).	
		1799 Haydn: *Creation*, performed in Vienna.	A. Pushkin (1799–1837).	1799 Goya: *Caprichos.*	1799 Bonaparte becomes First Consul.
1800		1800 Beethoven: First Symphony (Op. 21).	Honoré de Balzac (1799–1850).	*c.* 1800 Goya: *Dr. Peral.*	1800 Bonaparte invades Austria and Italy.
		1802 St. Petersburg Philharmonic Society formed.	Victor Hugo (1802–85).	Edwin Landseer (1802–73).	1802 First protective law against child labour in England.
	Mikhail Glinka (1803–56).	1804 Beethoven: *Eroica Symphony.*	1804 Schiller: *William Tell.*		1804 Bonaparte becomes Emperor.
	Hector Berlioz (1803–69).	1805 Beethoven: *Fidelio*, presented in Vienna.	George Sand (1804–76).	Samuel Palmer (1805–81).	1805 Battle of Trafalgar. Isambard Kingdom Brunel (1806–59).
		1806 Beethoven: Violin Concerto.			
		1807 Spontini: *Vestale.*	1807 T. Moore: *Irish Melodies.* Charles and Mary Lamb: *Tales from Shakespeare.* Henry Longfellow (1807–82).		*c.* 1807. Humphry Davy: new theories of chemistry. Giuseppe Garibaldi (1807–82).

contd.	Bartholdy (1809–47).		49). Nicolai Gogol (1809–52).	*of the Defenders of Madrid.*	
	Frédéric Chopin (1810–49). Robert Schumann (1810–56). S. S. Wesley (1810–76). Franz Liszt (1811–86).	1810 Beethoven: music for *Egmont.* 1811 Weber: *Abu Hassan.*	1810 Scott: *Lady of the Lake.* 1811 Jane Austen: *Sense and Sensibility.* William Thackeray (1811–63). 1812 Grimm: *Fairy Tales.* 1812–18 Byron: *Childe Harold.* Charles Dickens (1812–70). Robert Browning (1812–89).	1811 onwards, Nash: Regent Street, Regent's Park, etc., London.	1810 Founding of Krupp Works at Essen. 1812 Napoleon retreats from Moscow. U.S.A. declare war on Britain.
	Richard Wagner (1813–83). Guiseppe Verdi (1813–1901).	1813 Philharmonic Society of London founded. 1814 Mäzel's metronome invented. John Field: *Nocturnes.* 1816 Schubert: *Erl King.* Beethoven: *An die ferne geliebte.*	1813 Shelley: *Queen Mab.* Jane Austen: *Pride and Prejudice.* Robert Owen: *A New View of Society.* Charlotte Brontë (1816–55).	1813 Turner: *Frosty Morning.* J.-F. Millet (1814–75).	1813 Elizabeth Fry begins prison reform. 1814–15 Congress of Vienna. 1815 Battle of Waterloo. Otto von Bismarck (1815–98). 1816 William Cobbett publishes his *Weekly Political Register.* 1816 Froebel founds a Kindergarten.
	Charles Gounod (1818–93).	Rossini: *Barber of Seville,* performed in Rome. 1817 Clementi: *Gradus ad Parnassum.*	1817 Byron: *Manfred.* 1818 Keats: *Endymion.* Emily Brontë (1818-48). Ivan Turgenev (1818–83).	G. F. Watts (1817–1904). 1817 Constable: *Flatford Mill.*	1817 Wartburg Festival reveals revolutionary tendencies of German students. 1818 First steamer, *Savannah,* crosses the Atlantic in twenty-six days. Karl Marx (1818–83).
		1819 Schubert: *Trout Quintet,* Op. 114.	Herman Melville (1819–1891). Walt Whitman (1819–1892). John Ruskin (1819–1900). 1819 Keats: *Eve of St. Agnes.*	W. P. Frith (1819–1909). Gustave Courbet (1819–77).	1819 Factory Act passed after campaign by Robert Owen.

DATE	COMPOSERS	MUSICAL EVENTS	LITERATURE	ART AND ARCHITECTURE	SOME HISTORICAL AND SCIENTIFIC FIGURES AND EVENTS
1800 *contd.*			Scott: *Ivanhoe*. Walt Whitman (1819–92).		
		1820 Meyerbeer: *Margherita d'Anjou*.	1820 Shelley: *Prometheus Unbound*.		Florence Nightingale (1820–1910).
		1821 Weber: *Der Freischütz*, performed in Berlin.	Feodor Dostoevsky. (1821–81). Charles Baudelaire (1821–67).	Ford Madox Brown (1821–93). 1821 Constable: *The Haywain*.	1821 Hegel: *Philosophy of Right*. 1821-5 The Stockton and Darlington Railway constructed. Mary Baker Eddy (1821–1910).
	César Franck (1822–90). Bedřich Smetana (1824–84). Anton Bruckner (1824–96).	1822 Royal Academy of Music founded in London. Schubert: '*Unfinished Symphony*' Beethoven: *Mass in D*.	Matthew Arnold (1822–88). G. Flaubert (1821–80).	1824 Delacroix: *Massacre of Chios*. Puvis de Chavannes (1824–98).	Louis Pasteur (1822–95). 1824 Byron dies in Greece.
		1825 First performance in England of Beethoven's *Choral Symphony, No.* 9, composed for the Philharmonic Society.	1825 Pushkin: *Boris Godunov*.		1825 Trade unions in Britain recognized as legal.
		1826 Weber: *Oberon*, at Covent Garden. Mendelssohn: *Overture to Midsummer Night's Dream*.	1826 Fenimore Cooper: *Last of the Mohicans*. Disraeli: *Vivian Grey*. George Meredith (1828–1909). Henrik Ibsen (1828–1906). D. G. Rossetti (1828–82). Leo Tolstoy (1828–1910).	W. Holman Hunt (1827–1910).	1827 Catholic Emancipation in England. 1828 University College, London, and King's College, London, founded.
		1829 Rossini: *William Tell*, performed in Paris. Mendelssohn conducts Bach's *St. Matthew Passion* in Berlin		J. Millais (1829–96).	

contd.		Overture *Fingal's Cave*. Auber: *Fra Diavolo*, performed in Paris.	*Hernani*. Tennyson: *Poems*. Cobbett: *Rural Rides*. Christina Rossetti (1830–94).	*Cathedral* Delacroix: *Liberty on the Barricades*.	
		1831 Bellini: *Norma* and *Sonnambula*. Chopin goes to Paris.	1831 V. Hugo: *Notre Dame de Paris*. Pushkin: *Eugene Onegin*.	Camille Pissarro (1831–1903). 1831 Constable: *Waterloo Bridge*.	1831 Faraday discovers electrical induction.
		1832 Chopin: Mazurkas, Op. 6.		Edouard Manet (1832–83).	1832 First Reform Bill in Britain.
	Johannes Brahms (1833–97).	1833 Mendelssohn goes to Düsseldorf as musical director.		Edward Burne-Jones (1833–98).	1833 Telegraph invented in Germany. First public grant for education in England. James Clerk-Maxell (1833–98).
	Alexander Borodin. (1834–87).		1834 Lytton: *Last Days of Pompeii*. Mickiewicz: *Pan Tadeusz*. William Morris (1834–96).	1834 Delacroix: *Femmes d'Alger*. James Whistler (1834–1903). Edgar Degas (1834–1917).	1834 Slavery terminated in British colonies.
	Camille Saint-Saëns (1835–1921).	1835 Donizetti: *Lucia de Lammermoor*.	1835 Dickens: *Sketches by Boz*. Georg Büchner: *Danton's Death*. Mark Twain (1835–1910).		1835 First German railway between Nuremberg and Fürth. Andrew Carnegie (1835–1919).
		1836 Glinka: *A Life for the Tzar*.	1836 Dickens: *Pickwick Papers*. Gogol: *Government Inspector*. Ranke: *History of the Popes*.		1836 First train in London (to Greenwich). 1836–48 Chartist movement in England.
		1837 Berlioz: *Benvenuto Cellini*.	1837 Carlyle: *French Revolution*. Dickens: *Oliver Twist*.		1837 Morse invents telegraphic inked tape in New York. 1837 Accession of Queen Victoria.
	Georges Bizet (1838–75).	1838 Chopin at Majorca with George Sand.		1838 National Gallery, London, opened.	1838 Regular steamship communication between England and America.

Date	Composers	Musical events	Literature	Art and architecture	Some historical and scientific figures and events
1800 *contd.*	M. Moussorgsky (1839–81).	1839 Schubert's C major Symphony produced by Mendelssohn at Leipzig. Chopin: *Twenty-Four Preludes*, Op. 28.	1839 Stendhal: *La Chartreuse de Parme*.	Paul Cézanne (1839–1906).	1839 Opium war with China. Hong Kong taken. New Zealand proclaimed a British colony.
	P. Tchaikowsky (1840–93).	1840 Schumann marries Clara Wieck. Smetana at Prague. Wagner: *Faust Overture*. Adolph Sax invents the saxophone.	George Sand: *Spiridion*. Thomas Hardy (1840–1928).	Auguste Rodin (1840–1917). Claude Monet (1840–1926). 1840–52 Charles Barry builds the Houses of Parliament.	1840 Victoria marries Prince Albert of Saxe-Coburg-Gotha. Rowland Hill introduces the penny post.
	A. Dvořák (1841–1904).	1841 Liszt: *Années de pélérinage*.		Auguste Renoir (1841–1919).	
	A. Sullivan (1842–1900).	1842 Philharmonic Society of New York founded. Verdi: *Nabucco*.	1842 R. Mayer: *Law of the conservatism of Energy*. Macaulay: *Lays of Ancient Rome*. Gogol: *Dead Souls*.		1842 Mudie's lending library opened in London. James Nasmyth invents the steam hammer.
	Edward Greig (1843–1907).	1843 Leipzig Conservatoire established by Mendelssohn. Donizetti: *Don Pasquale*. Balfe: *The Bohemian Girl* produced in London.	1843 J. S. Mill: *System of Logic*. Henry James (novelist) (1843–1916).		1843 First workmen's Co-operative Society (Pioneers of Rochdale).
	Rimsky-Korsakov (1844–1908).	1844 Mendelssohn: Violin Concerto. Berlioz: *Traité de l'Instrumentation*.	F. W. Nietzsche (1844–1900). Anatole France (1844–1924). Robert Bridges (1844–1930).	H. (Douanier) Rousseau. (1844–1910). Sarah Bernhardt (1844–1923).	
	Gabriel Fauré (1845–1924).	1845 Wagner: *Tannhäuser*. Liszt: *Les Préludes*.	1845 Disraeli: *Sybil*. F. Engels: *Situation of the Working Classes in England*.		
		1846 Mendelssohn's *Elijah* performed at Birmingham.	1846 Lear: *Book of Nonsense*. 1847 C. Brontë: *Jane*		1846 Repeal of Corn Laws. Mohl discovers protoplasm.

contd.			*Wuthering Heights.* H. Hoffman: *Struwwelpeter.*		1847–48 Irish potato famine, followed by heavy emigration.
		1848 Smetana opens a music school in Prague.	1848 Murger: *Scénes de la vie de Bohème.* Marx and Engels: *Communist Manifesto.* Thackeray: *Vanity Fair.*	Paul Gauguin (1848–1903).	1848 Public Health Act passed. First Peace Congress in Brussels under Richard Cobden. Widespread revolutionary movement throughout Europe.
		1849 Sterndale Bennett forms the London Bach Society	August Strindberg (1849–1912).		
		1850 First performance of Wagner's *Lohengrin* under Liszt at Weimar.	1850 Dickens: *David Copperfield* Tennyson: *In Memoriam.* R. L. Stevenson (1850–94).	*c.*1850. Pre-Raphaelite Brotherhood.	
		1851 Verdi: *Rigoletto.*	1851 H. Melville: *Moby Dick.* Hawthorne: *House of the Seven Gables.*	Paxton: Crystal Palace.	1851 The Great Exhibition. First submarine cable laid from Dover to Calais.
	C. V. Stanford (1852–1924).	1852 Berlioz visits London.	1852 H. Beecher Stowe: *Uncle Tom's Cabin.*		1852 Napoleon III Emperor of the French.
		1853 Schumann writes his article 'New Paths'.	1853 Mrs. Gaskell: *Cranford.*	Vincent van Gogh (1853–90).	Cecil Rhodes (1853–1902).
	Leoš Janáček (1854–1928).	1854 Berlioz: *Te Deum.* Brahms: Songs and the B major Piano Trio.	Arthur Rimbaud (1854–91).		1854–56 Crimean War.
		1855 Wagner conducts in London. Liszt plays his E flat major Piano Concerto at Weimar under Berlioz. Crystal Palace concerts start in London.	1855 Longfellow: *Hiawatha.* Walt Whitman: *Leaves of Grass.* G. B. Shaw (1856–1950). Oscar Wilde (1856–1900).	1856: Ingres: *La Source.*	1855 Alexander II Emperor of Russia. 1856 Louis Pasteur becomes Professor in University of Paris. Bessemer invents cheap process of converting iron into steel. Sigmund Freud (1856–1939).
	Edward Elgar (1857–1934).	1857 Dvořák studies in Prague. Liszt's nine symphonic poems published.	1857 Trollope: *Barchester Towers.* Flaubert: *Madame Bovary.*		1857 Indian Mutiny.

Date	Composers	Musical events	Literature	Art and architecture	Some historical and scientific figures and events
1800 *contd.*			Baudelaire: *Fleurs du Mal.*		
	G. Puccini (1858–1924). Ethel Smyth (1858–1944).		1858 Tennyson: *Idylls of the King.*		1858 Atlantic Cable completed. Property qualification for Members of Parliament removed. Alexander II begins emancipation of serfs in Russia.
		Cecil Sharp, collector of folk-songs (1859–1924). 1859 Wagner: *Tristan und Isolde.*	1859 Meredith: *Richard Feverel.* 1859 Gontcharov: *Oblomov.* C. Darwin: *Origin of Species.*	Georges Seurat (1859–91). 1859 Ingres: *Le Bain Turc.* Corot: *Macbeth.*	
	Hugo Wolf (1860–1903). Gustav Mahler (1860–1911).		Anton Chekhov (1860–1904). Rabindranath Tagore (1860–1941). 1860 George Eliot: *The Mill on the Floss.*	W. R. Sickert; P. Wilson Steer (both born and died 1860–1942). Georges Seurat (1860–91).	1860 Abraham Lincoln, President of U.S.A.
		Gounod: *Faust*, produced in Paris. Liszt leaves Weimar and goes to Rome. Dame Nellie Melba (1861–?). 1861 Royal Academy of Music founded in London.	1861 George Eliot: *Silas Marner.* Hans Andersen: *Fairy Tales.*	1861–74 Paris Opera House built.	1861 Victor Emmanuel, first King of United Italy. American Civil War.
	Claude Debussy (1862–1918). Frederick Delius (1863–1934).	Brahms: D minor Piano Concerto. 1862 Verdi's *Forza del Destino* produced at St. Petersburg.	1862 V. Hugo: *Les Misérables.*		
		1863 Bizet: *Pearl Fishers.*	1863 Renan: *Vie de Jésus.*		1863 Lincoln declares emancipation of Negroes.
	Richard Strauss (1864–1949).	1864 Tchaikowsky: Overture, *Romeo and Juliet.*		Toulouse-Lautrec (1864–1901).	1864 Geneva Convention for protection of wounded (Red Cross). Metropolitan Railway (Under-

contd.	(1865–1957). Carl Nielson (1865–1931).		*and Lilies.* 1865 Lewis Carroll: *Alice in Wonderland.* Rudyard Kipling (1865–1936). W. B. Yeats (1865–1939).		civil war; Lincoln assassinated.
		1866 Smetana: *Bartered Bride*, produced in Prague.	1866 Dostoevsky: *Crime and Punishment.* Ibsen: *Brand.* H. G. Wells (1866–1946).	*c.* 1866 Degas paints his scenes of the life and work of ballet dancers.	1866 Prussia and Italy attack Austria. First condensed milk factory in Switzerland. Federal Union of Canada.
		1867 Wagner: *Meistersinger*, produced in Munich. Verdi: *Don Carlos.* J. Strauss: *Blue Danube Waltz.* A. Sullivan: *Cox and Box.*	1867 Marx: *Capital.* Ibsen: *Peer Gynt.* 1867–69 Tolstoy: *War and Peace.* John Galsworthy (1867–1933). Arnold Bennett (1867–1931).		1867 Factory Inspector Act.
		1868 Grieg: A minor Piano Concerto. Smetana: symphonic poem, *My Fatherland.*	1868 W. Morris: *Earthly Paradise.* Haeckel: *History of Creation.*	1868–82 G. E. Street: London Law Courts.	1868 Gladstone's First Administration.
		1869 Wagner: *Das Rheingold*, produced in Munich.	1869 J. S. Mill: *Subjection of Women.* Maxim Gorky (1869–1936).	Edwin Lutyens (1869–1944). Frank Lloyd Wright (1869–1960). Henri Matisse (1869–1954)	1869 College for Women (afterwards Girton College) founded in Cambridge. Mahatma Gandhi (1869–1948).
		1870 Délibes: Ballet *Coppélia* produced in Paris.		1870 Schliemann begins to excavate Troy. Corot: *Femme à la Perle.*	1870 Franco-Prussian War. Third Republic proclaimed. Napoleon III flees to England. Compulsory education in England. Dogma of Papal Infallibility declared by Vatican Council. V. I. Lenin (1870–1924).
		1871 First performance of Verdi's *Aïda* at Cairo.	Marcel Proust (1871–1922).	1871 Whistler: *The Artist's Mother.*	1871 William I, German Emperor.

Date	Composers	Musical events	Literature	Art and architecture	Some historical and scientific figures and events
1800 *contd.*			1871–2 George Eliot: *Middlemarch.*	G. Renault (1871–1958). First Impressionist Exhibition in Paris.	
	R. Vaughan Williams (1872–1958).	Serge Diaghilev, ballet impressario (1872–1929)		Royal Albert Hall opened in London. Piet Mondrian (1872 – 1944).	1872 National Union of Agricultural Workers formed in Britain.
	S. Rachmaninov (1873–1943).	Feodor Chaliapin (1873–1938). 1873 Debussy enters the Paris Conservatoire. Enrico Caruso (1873–1921).	Walter de la Mare (1873–1956). 1873 Verne: *Round the World in Eighty days.*		1873 National Federation of Employers formed in Britain.
	Gustav Holst (1874–1934). Arnold Schoenberg (1874–1951). Charles Ives (1874–1954).	1874 Johann Strauss, Jr.: *Die Fledermaus.* Moussorgsky: *Pictures at an Exhibition.* Wagner completes his *Götterdammerung.*	W. Somerset Maugham (1874 – 1965). Gertrude Stein (1874–1946).	1874 Monet exhibits his *Impression: Soleil levant.*	1874 Disraeli's first Administration. Endowed Schools Act. Winston Churchill (1874 – 1965).
	Maurice Ravel (1875–1937).	1875 Bizet: *Carmen.*	R. M. Rilke (1875–1926). 1875 Mark Twain: *Tom Sawyer.* Robert Frost (1875 – 1963). Thomas Mann (1875–1958).		
		1876 Purcell Society founded. Grieg: music for *Peer Gynt.*	Jack London (1876–1916).	1876 Renoir: *Au Théâtre.*	1876 The telephone invented by Graham Bell.
		1877 Borodin: Symphony in B minor	1877 Tolstoy: *Anna Karenina.*		1877 Victoria proclaimed Empress of India. Edison invents the phonograph.
		1878 Beethoven's Ninth Symphony performed for the first time at Milan.	John Masefield (1878 – 1967).	Augustus John (1878–1961).	1878 German Socialists outlawed. Factory and Workshop Act in Britain.
	John Ireland (1879 – 1962).	1879 Tchaikowsky: *Eugene Onégin.*	E. M. Forster (1879 – 1970). 1879 Ibsen: *The Doll's*	Paul Klee (1879–1960). Matthew Smith (1879–1960).	

contd.	(1880 – 1959).	the Milan Conservatory. Rimsky-Korsakov: *A Night in May.* A. Sullivan: *The Pirates of Penzance.*	*Brothers Karamazov.*	(1880–1959). A. Derain (1880–1954). Franz Marc (1880–1916).	Edison and Swan.
	Béla Bartók (1881–1945). Villa-Lobos (1881–1959).	1881 Brahms: Academic Festival Overture.		1881 Monet: *Sunshine and Snow.* Pablo Picasso (1881 – 1973). Fernand Léger (1881–1955).	1881 Canadian Pacific Railway formed.
	Zoltán Kodály (1882–1967). Igor Stravinsky (1882 – 1971).	1882 Brahms: Piano Concerto in B flat. Rimsky-Korsakov: *Snow Maiden.*	James Joyce (1882–1941).	Georges Braque (1882 – 1963).	1882 Married Women's Property Act. Franklin D. Roosevelt (1882–1945).
	Karol Szymanowski (1883–1937). Arnold Bax (1883–1953).	1883 Royal College of Music opened under George Grove.	1883 Stevenson: *Treasure Island.* Nietzsche: *Zarathustra.*	1883 First skyscraper in Chicago.	1883 Britain occupies Egypt.
	Anton von Webern (1883–1945).	1884 Massenet: *Manon*, produced in Paris.		Modigliani (1884-1920)	1884 Fabian Society founded.
	Alban Berg (1885–1935).	1885 César Franck: *Variations Symphonique.* Rachmaninov studies at the Moscow Conservatory.	D. H. Lawrence (1885–1930). Ezra Pound (1885 – 1972).	1885–1911 Victor Emmanuel Monument, Rome.	1886 American Federation of Labor founded.
		1886 Improvements made in piano construction by firms of Blüthner, Bechstein and Steinway.	1886 Ibsen: *Rosmersholm*	1886 Van Gogh leaves Holland to study art in Paris. O. Kokoschka (1886 – 1980). Diego Rivera (1886–1957).	
		1887 Verdi: *Otello*, produced in Milan.	Rupert Brooke (1887–1915).	Juan Gris (1887–1927). Marc Chagall (1887 – 1985).	
		1888 Mahler directs the Budapest Opera.	T.S.Eliot (1888 – 1965). 1888 Henry James: *Aspern Papers.*	Le Corbusier (1887 – 1965) G. di Chirico (b.1888).	1888 Pasteur Institute established in Paris. 1889 London Docker's Strike. London County Council formed. Adolf Hitler (1889–1945).
			1890–1914 J. G. Frazer: *Golden Bough.*	1889 Eiffel Tower, Paris. Paul Nash (1889–1946).	1890 Free elementary education established.

Date	Composers	Musical events	Literature	Art and architecture	Some historical and scientific figures and events
1800 *contd.*			Boris Pasternak (1890–1960).		
	S. Prokofieff (1891–1953). Arthur Bliss (1891–1975). Paul Hindemith (1891–1963). Darius Milhaud (1892–1974). Walter Piston (1894–1976).	1892 Dvořák goes to New York as Director of the National Conservatory. 1893 Verdi: *Falstaff*, produced at Milan. Queen's Hall, London, built.	1891 O. Wilde: *Picture of Dorian Gray*. 1891 Hardy: *Tess of the D'Urbervilles*. Kipling: *Barrack Room Ballads*. 1891 Conan Doyle: *Adventures of Sherlock Holmes*.	Stanley Spencer (1891–1959). 1891 Gauguin goes to Tahiti. Joan Miro (1893–1983).	
		1895 Henry Wood directs concerts at Queen's Hall, London.	1895 Joseph Conrad: *Almayer's Folly*.	1895 Kiel Canal opened.	1895 X-rays discovered by Röntgen. Lumière brothers invent the cinematograph. Marconi invents wireless telegraphy.
			1896 A. E. Housman: *A Shropshire Lad*. W. W. Jacobs: *Many Cargoes*. 1896 T. Hardy: *Jude the Obscure*.	1896 National Portrait Gallery opened.	1896 Nobel Prizes established. *Daily Mail* founded.
			1897 H. G. Wells *Invisible Man*. William Faulkner (1897–1962).		1897 Workmen's Compensation Act.
		1898 Folksong Society, London, formed.	1898 G. B. Shaw: *The Perfect Wagnerite*.	Henry Moore (1898–1986).	1898 Zeppelin invents rigid airship. M. and Mme. Curie discover radium. Spanish-American War. Diesel motor first used.
	Francis Poulenc (1899–1963).		1899 Haeckel: *The Riddle of the Universe*.		1899 Boer War in South Africa. Board of Education created.
1900	Aaron Copland (1900–). Alan Bush (1900–).	1900 Elgar: *Dream of Gerontius*. Rimsky-Korsakov: *Tsar Saltan*.			1900 British Labour Party founded. Federation of Australia. The Boxer risings in China.
	Edmund Rubbra	1901 Rachmaninov:	1901 Rudyard Kipling:	1901–4 Picasso's Blue	1901 Theodore Roosevelt elected

contd.	William Walton (1901–1983).	1902 Debussy: *Pelléas et Mélisande.* 1903 Wagner's *Parsifal* performed in New York.	H. G. Wells: *First Men in the Moon.* 1903 G. B. Shaw: *Man and Superman.* G. E. Moore: *Principia Ethica* Samuel Butler: *Way of All Flesh.* Evelyn Waugh (1903–).	1903–26 A. Gaudi: Barcelona Cathedral. Barbara Hepworth (1903–1975). Graham Sutherland (1903–1980).	1902 Boer War ended. Entente Cordiale. 1903 Wright brothers achieve first powered flight by an aircraft, North Carolina.
	D. Kabelevsky (1904–1987).	1904 Phonographic studies of primitive people's music made by Berlin musicologists	1904 W. H. Hudson: *Green Mansions.* Barrie: *Peter Pan.* Romain Rolland: *Jean Christophe.*	Sal·ador Dali (1904–).	1904 Russo-Japanese War.
	A. Rawsthorne (1905–1971). M. Tippett (1905–).	1905 R. Strauss's *Salomé* produced in Dresden.	Jean-Paul Sartre (1905–1980). 1905 Wilde: *De Profundis.* H. G. Wells: *Modern Utopia.*		1905 Revolution in Russia Einstein's first theory of relativity.
	D. Shostakovitch (1906–1975).	1906 Mozart Festival held in Salzburg.	1906 John Galsworthy: *Man of Property.* Upton Sinclair: *The Jungle.* Samuel Beckett (1906–).		
	E. Maconochy (1907–).	1907 Delius: *A Village Romeo and Juliet.*	W. H. Auden (1907–1973). 1907 J. M. Synge: *Playboy of the Western World.* Gorky: *Mother.*	Cubism (1907–14). Basil Spence (1907–1976).	1907 Experimental wireless transmission by Marconi and other scientists.
	Oliver Messiaen (1908–).	1909 Vaughan Williams: *Fantasy on a Theme by Tallis.* Strauss: *Elektra.* Paderewski directs the Warsaw Conservatory.	1908 Arnold Bennett: *Old Wives' Tale.*	1909 Futurist Manifesto	1908 Old Age Pensions Bill in Britain and Australia. 1909 Blériot flies in an aeroplane from France to England. 1909 Peary discovers North Pole.

Date	Composers	Musical events	Literature	Art and architecture	Some historical and scientific figures and events
1900 *contd.*	Samuel Barber (1910 – 1981).	1910 Vaughan Williams: *A Sea Symphony.* Stravinsky: *Firebird.*	1910 G. B. Shaw: *Pygmalion.* E. M. Forster: *Howard's End.* J. Galsworthy: *Justice.*	1910–12 First London exhibitions of Post-Impressionists.	1910 Union of South Africa.
		1911 Ravel: *Daphnis et Chloë.*	1911-14 George Moore: *Hail and Farewell.*	1911-23 R. Ostberg: Stockholm Town Hall. 1911–13 Woolworth Building, New York.	1911 Italy makes war on Turkey and seizes Tripoli. Amundsen discovers South Pole
		1912 Schoenberg: *Pierrot Lunaire.*			1912 China becomes a republic. Woodrow Wilson President of U.S.A.
	Benjamin Britten (1913 – 1976).	1913 Stravinsky: *Le Sacre du Printemps.*	1913 D. H. Lawrence: *Sons and Lovers.* Proust: *Swann's Way.* Albert Camus (1913–59).	1913–40 Lutyens: Government Buildings, New Delhi.	
		1914 Vaughan Williams: *A London Symphony.* 1915 Sibelius: *Fifth Symphony.* 1916 Jazz compels interest in U.S.A.	1914 James Joyce: *Dubliners.* Dylan Thomas (1914–1953) 1916 Joyce: *Portrait of the Artist as a Young Man.*		1914 Opening of Panama Canal. Assassination of Austrian archduke. German Invasion of Belgium. First World War. 1916 Verdun; Somme; Jutland.
		1917 Salzburg Music Festival founded. Prokofiev: Classical Symphony. Respighi: *Fountains of Rome.*	1917 L. Feuchtwanger: *Jew Süss* P. Valéry: *La jeune parque.*	Sydney Nolan (1917–).	1917 Russian Revolution. U.S.A. declares war on Germany.
	Leonard Bernstein (1918–).	1918 Bartok: *Bluebeard's Castle.*		1918 Dada Manifesto	1918 Armistice.
		1919 De Falla: *Three-Cornered Hat.* Elgar: Cello Concerto.	1919 J. M. Keynes: *The Economic Consequences of the Peace.*		1919 Treaty of Versailles. Alcock and Brown's Atlantic flight.
		1921 Paul Whiteman visits Europe with orchestra. Prokofiev: *Love of Three Oranges.*			
		1922 Vaughan Williams: Classical Symphony.	Joyce: *Ulysses* Friedrich Dürrenmatt		1922 Mussolini's March on Rome. B.B.C. formed.

	1923 Honegger: *Pacific* 231.	T. S. Eliot: *The Waste Land.* Rilke: *Duino Elegies.* G. B. Shaw: *Saint Joan.*	1925 Eisenstein: *Battleship Potemkin.*	1923 First Labour government in Great Britain under J. Ramsay Macdonald.
	1924 Bloch: Piano Quintet	T. Mann: *The Magic Mountain.* E. M. Forster: *A Passage to India.*		
Pierre Boulez (1925–).		1925 Kafka: *The Trial.*	1925–6 Walter Gropius: Bauhaus, Dessau.	1925 Locarno Treaty.
	1926 Berg: *Wozzeck.* 1927 Stravinsky: *Oedipus Rex.* Weinberger: *Schwanda the Bagpiper.*		1926 First 'sound movie' in New York.	1926 General Strike in Great Britain. Amundsen's fllght over the North Pole.
Karlheinz Stockhausen (1928–).	1928 Weil and Brecht: *Beggars' Opera.* Ravel: *Bolero.*	1929 Hemingway: *Farewell to Arms.* R. Graves: *Goodbye to All That.*	John Bratby (1928–).	1929 Wall Street crash.
	1931 Walton: *Belshazzar's Feast.*	E. M. Remarque: *All Quiet on the Western Front.*	1931–39 Rockefeller Centre, New York.	1931 Statute of Westminster. 1932 Large-scale unemployment in Britain, U.S.A. and Germany.
	1933 R. Strauss: *Arabella.*	A. Malraux: *La Condition Humaine.*	1933 C. Holden, Senate House, London University.	1933 Hitler Chancellor of Germany.
Harrison Birtwistle (1934–). Peter Maxwell Davies (1934–).	1934 Hindemith: *Mathis der Mahler.* 1935 G. Gershwin: *Porgy and Bess.*	1934 A. Toynbee: *A Study of History.* 1935 T. S. Eliot: *Murder in the Cathedral.*		1935 Italian invasion of Abyssinia. 1936 Spanish Civil War.
	1937 Toscanini refuses to conduct in Europe.		1937 Picasso: *Guernica.* Paris Exhibition.	
		1938 Graham Greene: *Brighton Rock.*	1939 New York Exhibition.	1938 Austrian Anschluss. 1939 Second World War.

Date	Composers	Musical events	Literature	Art and architecture	Some historical and scientific figures and events
1900 *contd.*		1940 Stravinsky: *Symphony in C*. Webern: *Variations for Orchestra*.			
		1941 Messiaen: *Quatuor pour la Fin du Temps*. Prokofiev: *War and Peace*.			
		1942 Copland: *Rodeo*.		1943 Piet Mondrian: *Broadway Boogie-Woogie*.	1943 'Colossus' – first electronic computer – developed by Thomas Flowers.
		1944 Bartók: *Concerto for Orchestra*. Tippett: *A Child of our Time*.		1944 Barbara Hepworth: *Wave*.	
		1945 Britten: *Peter Grimes*.	1945 Osbert Sitwell: *Left Hand, Right Hand*.	1945 Kandinsky retrospective exhibition, New York.	1945 Hiroshima and Nagasaki destroyed by atom bombs. Second World War ends.
			1947 Albert Camus: *La Peste*.		1947 India gains independence from Britain.
				1948 Jackson Pollock: *Number One*. Barnett Newman: *Ornament I*.	
		1949 Messiaen: *Turangalîla*.	1949 George Orwell: *Nineteen Eighty-four*. Simone de Beauvoir: *Le Deuxième Sexe*.		1949 People's Republic of China proclaimed. 1949-50 Nato formed.
				1950 Jackson Pollock: *Lavender Mist*.	1950 Beginnings of the European Common Market.
		1951 Britten: *Billy Budd*. Stravinsky: *The Rake's Progress*. Menotti: *Amahl and the Night Visitors*.	1951 Anthony Powell: *A Question of Upbringing*.	1951 Matisse: Vence chapel, Cannes. Jean Dubuffet: *Pièce de Boucherie*.	
		1953 Britten: *Gloriana*.	1953 Samuel Beckett: *Waiting for Godot*.	1953 Francis Bacon: *Study After Velasquez's Portrait of Pope Innocent X*.	1953 Discovery of the structure of DNA.
		1954 Lutoslawski: *Concerto for Orchestra*. Varèse: *Déserts*.	1954 William Golding: *Lord of the Flies*.	1954 Mark Rothko: *Ochre and Red on Red*.	
		1955 Boulez: *Le Marteau sans Maître*. Partch: *The Bewitched*. Tippett: *The Midsummer Marriage*.	1955 Philip Larkin: *The Less Deceived*. Vladimir Nabokov: *Lolita*.	1955 Jasper Johns: *White Flag*. Le Corbusier: Notre-Dame-du-Haut, Ronchamp.	1955 Warsaw Pact set up.

contd.		*der Jünglinge.*	*Look Back in Anger.* Albert Camus: *La Chute.*	Tomorrow' exhibition, ICA, London (Pop art).	Suez crisis.
		1957 Bernstein: *West Side Story.*	1957 Boris Pasternak: *Dr. Zhivago.* Patrick White: *Voss.*		
		1958 Stravinsky: *Threni.*			1958 Algerian crisis and fall of 4th Republic in France.
		1959 Peter Maxwell Davies: *Prolation.*	1959 Harold Pinter: *The Caretaker.* Günther Grass: *Die Blechtrommel.*	1959 Robert Rauschenberg: *Monogram.*	1959 Cuban revolution.
		1960 Penderecki: *Threnody for the Victims of Hiroshima.*			
		1961 Lutoslawski: *Venetian Games.*	1961 V. S. Naipaul: *A House for Mr Biswas.*		
		1962 Boulez: *Pli selon Pli.* Cage: *4'3".* Britten: *War Requiem.* Stockhausen: *Momente.*	1962 Alexander Solzhenitsyn: *One Day in the Life of Ivan Denisovitch.*	1962 Andy Warhol: *Campbell's Soup Cans.*	1962 Cuban missile crisis. Second Vatican Council.
		1963 Tippett: *Concerto for Orchestra.*	1963 Alain Robbe-Grillet: *Pour un nouveau roman.*	1963 Roy Lichtenstein: *Drowning Girl.*	1963 Assassination of US President, J. F. Kennedy.
		1964 Britten: *Curlew River.*	1964 Saul Bellow: *Herzog.*		
		1965 Penderecki: *St Luke Passion.*		1965 James Rosenquist: *The F-111.*	1965 Chinese Cultural Revolution. US bombs North Vietnam.
		1966 Henze: *The Bassarids.*	1966 Jean Rhys: *Wide Sargasso Sea.*		
		1967 Stockhausen: *Prozession; Stimmung.* Birtwistle: *Punch and Judy.*			1967 Arab-Israeli Six-Day War.
		1968 Stockhausen: *Aus den Sieben Tagen.*	1968 Gabriel García Márquez: *A Hundred Years of Solitude.*	1968 Christo Jachareff: *56 Barrels.*	1968 Student demonstrations in Paris.
		1969 Birtwistle: *Down by the Greenwood Side.* Partch: *Delusion of the Fury.*		1969 Joseph Beuys: *The Pack.*	1969 Apollo XI lands the first men on the moon. Development of the micro-chip by Edward Hof.
		1970 Tippett: *The Knot Garden.* Penderecki: *The Devils of Loudon.*	1970 Ted Hughes: *Crow.*	1970 Robert Smithson: *Spiral Jetty.*	1970s Japan emerges as a leading industrial power.
		1971 Penderecki: *Utrenja.*	1971 Geoffrey Hill: *Mercian Hymns.*		

Date	Composers	Musical events	Literature	Art and architecture	Some historical and scientific figures and events
1900 *contd.*		1972 Shostakovitch: *15th Symphony*.	1973 Alexander Solzhenitsyn: *The Gulag Archipelago* vol. 1	1973 Jørn Utzon: Sydney Opera House.	1973 Britain enters the EEC.
					1975 Israel and Egypt sign Camp David Treaty.
		1976 Reich: *Drumming*. Pärt: *Cantus*. Cage: *Apartment House 1776*.			1976 Mao Tse-Tung dies. Viking 1 spacecraft lands on Mars.
		1977 Appleton: *Syntronia*.		1977 Walter de Maria: *The Lightning Field*.	
			1978 Iris Murdoch: *The Sea, The Sea*.		1978 Karol Wojtyla becomes Pope John Paul II. World's first test-tube baby born.
				1979 Richard Meier: The Athenaeum, New Harmony, Indiana.	1979 Moslem fundamentalist revolution in Iran. Margaret Thatcher becomes Britain's first woman Prime Minister.
			1980 William Golding: *Rites of Passage*.	1980 'The Presence of the Past' exhibition, Venice.	1980 Iran-Iraq war begins.
		1981 Pärt: *Passio domini nostri Jesu Christi secumdum Joannem*.	1981 Salman Rushdie: *Midnight's Children*.	1981 Ricardo Bofill: Les Arcades du Lac, Saint-Quentin-en-Yvelines.	1981 Assassination of President Sadat of Egypt.
			1982 Claude Simon: *La Route de Flandres*.		1982 Falklands crisis between Britain and Argentina.
					1983 The first US Cruise missiles arrive in Europe.
		1984 Glass: *Ahknatan*.	1984 Seamus Heaney: *Station Island*. Wole Soyinka: *A Play of Giants*.	1984 Philip Johnson: AT & T Building, New York.	
					1985 Mikhail Gorbachev becomes Soviet leader.
		1986 Harrison Birtwistle: *The Masks of Orpheus*.			1986 US space shuttle disaster.
			1987 V. S. Naipaul: *The Enigma of Arrival*.		1987 US-Soviet INF Treaty signed.

RECOMMENDED BOOKS

PART I
(upto *c.* 1525)

Apel, W. *Harvard Dictionary of Music* (W. & G. Foyle Ltd., 1946).

Dart, R.T. *The Interpretation of Music* (Hutchinson, 1954).

Fallows, D. *Dufay* (J. M. Dent & Sons Ltd., 1982).

Lang, P. *Music in Western Civilization* (J. M. Dent & Sons Ltd., 1942).

New Oxford History of Music, The, Vols. I – III (Oxford University Press, 1954).

Pincherle, M. *An Illustrated History of Music* (Macmillan, 1960).

Reese, G. *Music in the Middle Ages* (J. M. Dent & Sons Ltd., 1940).

Reese, G. *Music in the Renaissance* (J. M. Dent & Sons Ltd., 1954).

Westrup, J. *An Introduction to Music History* (Hutchinson, 1967).

(In addition to the above, the 'Commentary' in Davison and Apel's *Historical Anthology of Music,* Vol. I (Oxford University Press, 1949) and G. Kinsky's *A History of Music in Pictures* (J. M. Dent & Sons Ltd.) are well worth studying.

PART II
(*c.* 1525 – *c.* 1750)

Apel, W. *Harvard Dictionary of Music* (W. & G. Foyle Ltd., 1946).

Arnold, D. *Giovanni Gabrieli* (Oxford University Press, 1977).

Marenzio (Oxford University Press, 1965).

Monteverdi (J. M. Dent & Sons Ltd., 1982).

Bukofzer, M. *Music in the Baroque Era* (J. M. Dent & Sons Ltd., 1948).

Dart, R. T. *The Interpretation of Music* (Hutchinson, 1954).

Dent, E. *Alessandro Scarlatti* (Arnold Ltd., 1960).

Fellows, E. *Orlando Gibbons* (Oxford, 1925).

William Byrd (Oxford University Press, 1948).

Grew, E. and S. *Bach* (J. M. Dent & Sons Ltd., 1965).

Grout, D. *A Short History of Opera* Vol. I (Columbia University Press, 1966).

Kirkpatrick, R. *Domenico Scarlatti* (Princeton University Press, 1953).

Lang, P. *Music in Western Civilization* (Hodder & Stoughton, 1964).

New Oxford History of Music, The Vols. III – VI (Oxford University Press, 1954).

Pincherle, M. *An Illustrated History of Music* (Macmillan & Co., 1962).

Reese, G. *Music in the Renaissance* (J. M. Dent & Sons Ltd., 1954).

Talbot, M. *Vivaldi* (J. M. Dent & Sons Ltd., 1978).

Westrup, J. *An Introduction to Music History* (Hutchinson, 1967).

Purcell (J. M. Dent & Sons Ltd., 1965).

Young, P. *Handel* (J. M. Dent & Sons Ltd., 1965).

(In addition to the above, the 'Commentary' in Davison and Apel's *Historical Anthology of Music,* Vol. I (Oxford University Press, 1949) and G. Kinsky's *A History of Music in Pictures* (J. M. Dent & Sons Ltd.) are well worth studying.

PART III

(from *c.* 1750)

Anderson, E. *The Letters of Mozart and his Family* (Macmillan, 1938).

Barzun, J. *Berlioz and the Romantic Century* (1951).

Blom, E. *Mozart* (London, 1946).

Brophy, Brigid *Mozart the Dramatist* (Faber, 1963).

Brown, M. *Schubert* (1958).

Carner, Mosco *Puccini* (London, 1958).

Dean, W. *Bizet* (J. M. Dent & Sons Ltd., 1948).

Dent, E. J. *Mozart's Operas: a Critical Study* (London, 1913).

Donington, Robert *Wagner's Ring and its Symbols* (Faber, 1963).

Einstein, Alfred *Gluck* (London, 1936).

Mozart (Cassell, 1946).

Schubert (London, 1951).

The Bach Family (London, 1954).

Geiringer, K. *Haydn, a Creative Life in Music* (New York, 1946).

Goldman and Sprinchorn eds. *Wagner on Music and Drama* (Gollancz, 1970).

Greene, David B. *Temporal Processes in Beethoven's Music* (Gordon and Breach, 1982).

Hamburger, M. ed. *Ludwig van Beethoven: Letters, Journals and Conversations* (Thames & Hudson, 1952).

Jacobs, R. trans. *Three Wagner Essays* (Eulenberg, 1979).

Keller, Hans *The Great Haydn Quartets* (Dent, 1986).
Lang, P. H. *Music in Western Civilization* (J. M. Dent & Sons Ltd., 1942).
Latham, P. *Brahms* (J. M. Dent & Sons Ltd., 1948).
Mellers, Wilfrid *Bach and the Dance of God* (Faber, 1980).
Beethoven and the Voice of God (Faber, 1983).
Mitchell, D. *Gustav Mahler – the Early Years* (Barrie & Rockliff, 1958).
Newman, E. *The Life of Richard Wagner* (London 1933-47).
Redlich, H. F. *Bruckner and Mahler* (London, 1955).
Riezler, W. *Beethoven* (London, 1938).
Robins Landon, H. C. *The Collected Correspondence and London Notebooks of Joseph Haydn* (Barrie & Rockliff, 1959).
Rosen, Charles *The Classical Style* (Faber, 1971).
Schenk, E. *Mozart and his Times* trans. R. and C. Winston (Secker & Warburg, 1960).
Simpson, Robert *The Essence of Bruckner* (1967).
Tovey, D. *Essays in Musical Analysis: Beethoven* (1935 – 44).
Toye, J. F. *Guiseppe Verdi; his Life and Works* (London, 1931).
Rossini: Studies in Tragi-comedy (London, 1934).
Turner, W. J. *Berlioz, the Man and his Work* (London, 1934).
Wootton, T. *Berlioz* (Clarendon Press, 1935).

PART IV
(from 1800)

Abraham, G. *A Hundred Years of Music* (Duckworth, 1949).
Chopin's Musical Style (Oxford University Press, 1939).
Grieg Symposium (London, 1948).
Sibelius Symposium (London, 1947).
Studies in Russian Music (London, 1935).
Tchaikovsky Symposium (London, 1945).
Beecham, Sir T. *Frederick Delius* (London, 1959).
Berger, A. *Aaron Copland* (New York, 1953).
Cage, John *Silence* (Wesleyan, 1960).
Calvocoressi, M. D. *Modest Moussorgsky* (Barrie & Rockliff, 1956).
Chissell, J. *Schumann* (J. M. Dent & Sons Ltd., 1948).
Cooper, Martin *French Music from the Death of Berlioz to the Death of Fauré* (London, 1951).

Copland, Aaron and Perlis, Vivien *Aaron Copland Vol. 1* (Faber, 1984).

Cowell, H. & S. *Charles Ives* (Oxford University Press, 1955).

Craft, R. *Conversations with Stravinsky* (London, 1959).

Debussy, C. A. *M. Croche, the Dilettante-hater* (N. Douglas, 1927).

Dent, E. J. *Ferruccio Busoni* (1933).

Ewen, D. *George Gershwin: A Journey to Greatness* (New York, 1956).

Hartog, H. ed. *European Music in the Twentieth Century* (Routledge and Kegan Paul, 1957).

Hedley, A. *Chopin* (J. M. Dent & Sons Ltd., 1947).

Hindemith, Paul *A Composer's World* (Oxford University Press, 1952).

Hollander, Hans *Janáček: his Life and Works* (London, 1963).

Holst, G. and Vaughan Williams, R. *Heirs and Rebels* (Letters of Holst and Vaughan Williams) ed. I. Holst and U. V. Williams (Oxford University Press, 1959).

Howes, F. *Vaughan Williams – the Dramatic Works* (London, 1947), *– the Later Works* (London, 1945).

Hutchings, A. *Delius* (London, 1948).

Kemp, Ian *Tippett: The Composer and his Music* (Eulenberg, 1984).

Kirkpatrick, John ed. *Charles Ives: Memos* (Calder and Boyars, 1973).

Lang, Paul Henry ed. *Stravinsky, a New Appraisal* (Norton, 1963).

Lewis, Geraint ed. *Michael Tippett, A Celebration* (Baton Press, 1985).

Ley, R. trans. *Busoni: Letters to His Wife* (London, 1938).

Lockspeiser, E. *Debussy* (J. M. Dent & Sons Ltd., 1936).

Manuel, R. *Ravel* trans. C. Jolly (Dobson, 1947).

McVegh, D. *Elgar, his Life and Music* (J. M. Dent & Sons Ltd., 1955).

Mellers, Wilfrid *Music in a New Found Land* (Faber, 1987).
The Masks of Orpheus (M. U. P., 1987).

Mitchell, Donald *Gustav Mahler* 3 vols. (Faber, 1980-5).

Moreux, S. *Béla Bartók* (Richard Masse, 1949).

Northcote, S. *The Songs of Henri Duparc* (London, 1949).

Palmer, Christopher ed. *The Britten Companion* (Faber, 1984).

Partch, Harry *Genesis of a Music* (Wisconsin, 1949).

Radcliffe, P. *Mendelssohn* (J. M. Dent & Sons Ltd., 1954).

Redlich, H. F. *Alban Berg* (J. Calder, 1957).

Robertson, A. *Dvorak* (J. M. Dent & Sons Ltd., 1945).

Rockwell, John *All American Music: Composition in the Late 20th Century* (Knopf, 1983).

Rufer, J. *Composition with Twelve Notes* (Rockliff, 1954).

Schoenberg, A. *Style and Idea* (Williams & Norgate).

Schwartz, Elliott *Electronic Music* (Secker and Warburg, 1973).

Sitwell, S. *Liszt* (London, 1934).

Strauss-Hofmannsthal, *Briefwechsel*, ed. F. A. Strauss (Atlantis, 1951).

Stravinsky, I. *Chronicle of My Life* (Gollancz, 1936).

Stravinsky, I. and Craft, R. *Conversations and Journals* 3 vols. (Faber, 1982, 1984 and 1985).

Stuckenschmidt, H. H. *Arnold Schoenberg* trans. E. T. Roberts and H. Searle (Calder, 1960).

Suckling, N. *Fauré* (J. M. Dent & Sons Ltd., 1946).

Tippett, Michael *Moving into Aquarius* (Routledge and Kegan Paul, 1958).

Trend, *Manuel de Falla and Spanish Music* (London, 1929).

Vallas, L. *César Franck*, trans. H. Foss (Harrap, 1951).

Vaughan Williams, Ursula *Vaughan Williams, a Biography* (Oxford University Press, 1964).

Walker, F. *Hugo Wolf, a Biography* (London, 1951).

SELECTED MUSIC FOR PARTS I & II

So much music is now available that it is impossible to list it all. In the list below, therefore, only series, anthology titles and 'Collected Works' of individual composers are referred to. It should be noted that some series and 'Collected Works' are still in the process of completion. From the series and anthologies given the relevant music or composers can readily be found.

PART I

'Collected Works': Ciconia, Dufay, Dunstable, Isaac, Josquin des Prez, Landini, Machaut, Ockeghem, Philippe de Vitri.

Series: *see* 'Editions, historical' in Apel, *Harvard Dictionary of Music* (W. & G. Foyle Ltd., 1946).

Dessof Choir Series (Schott & Co. Ltd.).

English Gothic Music (Schott & Co. Ltd.).

Schott's Anthology of Early Keyboard Music ed. F. Dawes, Vol. I (Schott & Co. Ltd.).

Examples of Music before 1400 ed. H. Gleason (F. S. Crofts & Co.).

Fayrfax Series (Stainer & Bell Ltd.).

Geschichte der Musik in Beispielen (Breitkopf & Härtel).

Historical Anthology of Music eds. Davison and Apel, Vol. I (Oxford University Press, 1949).

Liber Usualis (Desclée & Co., Tournai).

Music Press Editions (Schott & Co. Ltd.).

PART II

'Collected Works': Albinoni, Arcadelt, J. S. Bach, Bull, Buxtehude, Byrd, Clemens non Papa, Corelli, F. Couperin, Frescobaldi, G. Gabrieli, Gesualdo, Gombert, Goudimel, Handel, Lassus, Lully, Marenzio, Monte, Monteverdi, Palestrina, Purcell, Rameau, Rore, D. Scarlatti, Scheidt, Schein, Schütz, Sweelinck, Telemann, Titelouze, Verdelot, Victoria, Vivaldi, Willaert.

Series: *see* 'Editions, historical' in Apel, *Harvard Dictionary of Music.* (W. & G. Foyle Ltd., 1946).

Buxtehude *Complete Organ Works* ed. J. Hedar (Novello).

Geschichte der Musik in Beispielen (Breitkopf & Härtel).

Historical Anthology of Music eds. Davison and Apel, Vols. I and II (Oxford University Press, 1949).

DISCOGRAPHY

COMPILED BY NICHOLAS COHU

The recordings listed in this discography have been chosen for their all-round excellence and general international availability. Preference has been given to recordings available on compact disc. This is the new medium for recordings and in its short lifespan of four years has become the yardstick by which all sound recordings are now judged. It is important to understand that, although wherever possible recordings on conventional (black vinyl) disc and cassette are also listed, many of these may soon no longer be available. The record companies are rapidly deleting records and cassettes at the rate of 25-30% of the total catalogues per year in favour of the new compact disc medium.

The discography is not intended to be an exhaustive list of all the available recordings of a particular work or works – this would not be feasible. However, whenever possible *complete* recordings of a composer's work have been given in preference to 'highlights' even if only a specific section of that work is discussed in the book.

Bearing in mind that records (the 'black disc') are rapidly disappearing and that modern trends are to record complete aspects of a composer's output rather than selected highlights (as was the case thirty years ago), it has not always been possible to include recordings of every musical example quoted in this book. However, it has been possible to include some items which were *not* available when the book was originally published.

Unless otherwise stated, the recordings listed are easily available in the UK. There are many fine retail outlets (especially in London) which will readily obtain recordings for the prospective purchaser and who can supply up-to-date advice.

PART I

CHAPTER 1

	Title	Performer	Format	Number
	GREGORIAN CHANT First Mass for Christmas & Third Mass for Christmas		CD LP MC	412 6582 412 6581 412 6584
	Requiem Mass		LP	2547 028
	Ancient Spanish Chants		LP	2533 163
	Einsiedeln Codex: First Mass for Christmas, Mass for Epiphany, Mass for Easter Sunday, Mass for Ascension Day		LP	2533 131

There are many other recordings of Gregorian chant but their availability is confined to retail outlets specialising in imports and thus they have not been included.

CHAPTER 3

There are records of troubadour and trouvère music on the TELDEC label in Germany but they are at present not imported into the UK.

Title	Performer	Format	Number
Las Cantigas de Santa Maria	Lamendier	LP MC	AL 12 KAL 12

CHAPTER 4

Title	Performer	Format	Number
Selection of 13th-century English part-songs and mediaeval English music from the 14th and 15th centuries		CD LP MC CD LP	HML 901154 HM 1154 HM 401154 HML 901106 HM 1106

CHAPTER 5

Guillaume de Machaut	Un lay de consolation & Le lay de la fontaine		LP	DSDL 705
Dufay, Briquet, De Caserta, Landini, De Insula, Brollo and Reyneau	French and Italian courtly songs of the 15th century	The Gothic Voices	CD LP MC	CDA 66144 A 66144 KA 66144

CHAPTER 6

Dufay	Complete secular music	Mediaeval Ens. of London	LP	D23706
Ockeghem	Thirty chansons (complete secular music)		LP	D254D3
	Requiem (Missa pro defunctis) & Missa Mi-mi (Missa quarti toni)	Hilliard Ens.	LP MC	EL 2700981 EL 2700984
Josquin des Prés	Motets & chansons	Hilliard Ens.	LP	ASD 1435731
	Missa faisant regretz & Missa di dadi	Mediaeval Ens. of London	LP	411 9371
	Three-part secular music	Mediaeval Ens. of London	LP	411 9381
Dunstable	Selected motets	Hilliard Ens.	LP MC	ASD 146703 TC-ASD 146703

PART II

CHAPTER 1

Composer	Work	Performers	Format	Number
	CHANSONS			
Janequin	Various chansons: A ce joly moys, Assouvy suis, L'aveugle dieu qui partout vole and 18 others	Clément Janequin Consort	LP	HM 1099
	MADRIGALS			
ITALY				
Marenzio	Madrigals	Concerto Vocale	LP	HM 1065
Gesualdo		Consort of Musicke	LP	410 1281
	Madrigals, Book 5 for 5 voices			
Monteverdi	Madrigals	Concerto Vocale	CD LP	HM 901129 HM 1129
	Madrigals: a selection by various composers including Marenzio, Gesualdo and Monteverdi	King's Singers/Consort of Musicke	LP MC	SLS 1078393 (2 LPs) TCSLS 1078395 (2 MCs)
FRANCE				
Lassus	Chansons and motets	Hilliard Ens.	LP MC	ASD 1436301 TCASD 1436304
GERMANY				
	Collection of German lieder by Lassus and Hassler		Harmonia Mundi (German import): LP	 ICo65169554

Composer	Work	Performers	Format	Number
ENGLAND				
	Collection of English madrigals by Byrd, Bennet, Morley, T. Tomkins, Gibbons, Wilbye and others	Tallis Scholars	LP MC	EMICFP 43091 TC-CFP 43091
	AYRES			
Dowland	Songs: Awake sweet love, Fine knacks for ladies, I saw my lady weepe, Shall I sue, shall I seek for grace? etc.	Partridge/Lindberg	LP	A 66095
Campion	Songs: Come cheerful day, Fire, fire, Her rosie cheeks, I care not for these ladies, The cypress curtain, etc.	Partridge/Lindberg	LP	A 66095
Morley	Ayres and madrigals	Consort of Musicke	LP	DSDL 708

CHAPTER 2

Composer	Work	Performers	Format	Number
	SACRED MUSIC			
GERMANY: LUTHERAN				
	Selected sacred music	Studio der Frühen Musik	LP	635605
GERMANY: CATHOLIC Lassus	Music for Holy Week and Easter Sunday	Pro Cantione Antiqua	LP	A 66051/2
	Missa super Bell'Amfitrit 'altera & Psalmus Poenitentialis VII	Christ Church Choir	LP MC	SA 18 SC 18
ITALY Palestrina	Missa Papae Marcelli & Tu es Petrus	Christ Church Choir	CD LP MC	1155172 1155171 4155174

Composer	Work	Performers	Format	Catalogue no.
	Stabat Mater, Magnificat à 8 voci, Litaniae de beata Virgine Maria & Hodie beata virgo senex puerum portabat	King's College Choir/Willcocks	LP	ZK 4
Gabrieli	Hodie Christus natus est, O domine Jesu Christe & O magnum mysterium	King's College Choir/Willcocks	LP	EMI EMX 2032
SPAIN Victoria	Missa ave maris stella, Motet O quam gloriosum & Missa O quam gloriosum	Westminster Cathedral Choir	CD LP MC	CDA 66114 A 66114 KA 66114
	Missa Ascendens Christus in altum & Missa O magnum mysterium	Westminster Cathedral Choir	LP MC	A 66190 KA 66190
ENGLAND: CATHOLIC Tallis	Spem in alium, Salvator mundi, Gaude gloriosa dei mater, Miserere nostri, Sancte Deus, sancte fortis, etc.	Tallis Scholars	CD LP MC	CDGIM 007 Gimell 1585-06 Gimell 1585T-06
	Lamentations of Jeremiah the Prophet. 5vv	King's College Choir	LP MC	414 3671 414 3674
Byrd	Ave verum corpus, Masses for 3, 4 and 5 voices	Tallis Scholars	CD	CDGIM 345
ENGLAND: ANGLICAN Gibbons	Tudor church music	King's College Choir	LP MC	DCA 514 ZCDCA 514

Byrd	My Ladye Nevells Booke	Hogwood	LP	D29D4 (4 LPs)
Gibbons	Keyboard music: 2 Almans, The King's jewel, Coranto, A fancy, 2 Fantasias, 4 Galliards, Italian Ground, Lord Salisbury's Pavan, Prelude, The Queen's Command, etc.	Hogwood	LP	DSLO 515
	A recital of Early English organ music including pieces by Byrd, T. Tomkins, Gibbons, Bull, Purcell and Greene	Simon Preston	CD LP MC	4156752 4156751 4156754

There are no records readily available in the UK of early instrumental music from Spain, Germany, Italy, France or the Netherlands. Until recently there were anthologies available but in reflecting modern taste for specialisation these have now been deleted. However, it is worthwhile watching out for releases on the French Harmonia Mundi label and also the German Harmonia Mundi (in UK via EMI) label for new releases covering this particular area of music history.

CHAPTER 3

ITALY Monteverdi	Orfeo	London Baroque Ens. *and others*	CD LP MC	CDS 7471428 EX 2701313 EX 2701315
		Harnoncourt	CD LP	8.35020 6.35020
Cavalli	Arias from operas	Von Stade	CD LP	ECD 88100 NUM 75183
Cesti	Orontea	Jacobs	LP	HM 1100/02

CHAPTER 3 continued

FRANCE Lully	Alceste	Malgoire	LP	CBS Import
ENGLAND Purcell	King Arthur	Gardiner	CD LP MC	ECD 880562 STU 751272 MCE 751272
	The Fairy Queen	Gardiner	LP	2742 001

CHAPTER 4

Pergolesi	La Serva Padrona	Ros-Marba	LP	9502 065
Handel	Giulio Cesare	Mackerras	LP MC	EX 2702323 EX 2702325
Rameau	Hippolyte et Aricie	Lewis	LP	D272D3

CHAPTER 5

ITALY Pergolesi	Stabat Mater	Abbado	CD LP MC	415 1032 415 1031 415 1034
Monteverdi	Vespers	Parrott	CD LP MC	CDS 747 0788 EX 2701293 EX 2701295

Lully	Dies Irae	Herreweghe	LP	HMC 1167
			MC	HMC40-1167
Couperin	Leçons de Ténèbres	Concerto Vocale	CD	HMC 901150
			LP	HM 1150
	Les Nations	Musica Antiqua Köln	LP	4109011
ENGLAND Purcell	Music for the Funeral of Queen Mary	Gardiner	CD	ECD 88071
			LP	NUM 70911
			MC	MCE 70911
Handel	Acis and Galatea	Gardiner	LP	2708038
	Dettingen Te Deum	Preston	CD	4106472
			LP	4106471
			MC	4106474
	Dixit Dominus	Willcocks	LP	SXLP30444
			MC	TC-SXLP 30444
	Samson	Leppard	LP	STU 71240
	Israel in Egypt	Preston	LP	4149771
			MC	4149774
		Gardiner	CD	ECD
	Utrecht Te Deum & Jubilate	Preston	CD	4144132
			LP	DSLO 582
			MC	KDSLC 582

Composer	Work	Conductor	Format	Number
	Coronation Anthems 1-4	Preston	CD	4100302
			LP	2534005
			MC	3311005
Handel	Ode for St. Cecilia's Day	Parrott	CD	CDC 7474902
			LP	EL 270361
			MC	EL 270364
	Messiah	Davis	CD	4125382
			LP	4125381
			MC	4125384
		Gardiner	CD	4110412
			LP	6769107
			MC	7654107
	Semele	Gardiner	LP	STU 714453
GERMANY Schütz	Psalmen Davids nos. 115, 128, 136, 150	Schneidt	CD	4152972
	Musikalische Exequien, Psalm 136, Danket dem Herren, dem er ist freudlich	Linde	LP	EL 2703421
			MC	EL 2703424
	Der Schwanengesang (Psalm 119)	Hennig	LP	EX 2702753
			MC	EX 2702755
	Deutsches Magnificat & Psalms 96, 3, 122 & 84	Norrington	LP	4145321
			MC	4145324

Composer	Work	Conductor	Format	Number
Bach, J. S.	Christmas Oratorio	Harnoncourt	CD	8.35022
			LP	6.35022
	Magnificat in D	Gardiner	CD	4114582
			LP	4114581
			MC	4114584
	Mass in B minor	Gardiner	CD	4155142
			LP	4155141
			MC	4155144
		Schreier	CD	610089 (Euro-disc)
	St. John Passion	Gardiner	CD	4193242
			LP	4193241
			MC	4193244
		Richter	CD	4136222
			LP	4139441
			MC	4139444
	St. Matthew Passion	Richter	CD	4136132
			LP	4139391
			MC	4139394
		Schreier	CD	4125272
			LP	4125271
			MC	4125274
	Masses in F, G minor, A & G	Flämig	LP	4130621

Apart from the popular numbers: 140, 147, 151, 211, 212 & 208, there are very few recordings of the Bach cantatas. However, an ambitious project has been undertaken by Teldec Schallplatten of the BRD to record all the cantatas in numerical order. To date, there are 38 volumes (two LPs per set) comprising cantatas up to BWV 160. As Teldec do not have a distributor in the UK I have not included these recordings. However, a good record shop will give further advice as to availability, and should be able to obtain copies by importing the goods themselves from Germany.

CHAPTER 6

Frescobaldi	Selected harpsichord pieces	Buckley	LP	HMC 1143
Scheidt	Tabulatura Nova Vol. I	Weir	LP	2K65
Purcell	Suites for Harpsichord 1-8	Gilbert	LP	HMC 1158
			MC	HMC 401158
	Three Elegies & music for strings	Hogwood	LP	DSLO 514
	Complete harpsichord works	Woolley	LP	SAGA 5458/9
Corelli	Concerti Grossi op. 6, nos. 1-12	Cantilena	CD	CHAN 8336/7
			LP	DBRD 3002
Albinoni	Oboe concertos op. 7, nos. 3 & 6	Rothwell	CD	PUCD 8374
	12 concertos op. 12	Solisti Venenti	LP	STU 71311
			MC	MCE 71311
Rameau	Suite in A minor, La Dauphine & Pièces en Concert	Pinnock	LP	CRD 1020
	Selected harpsichord pieces	James	CD	MK 39540
			LP	IM 39540
Couperin	Suites de Claveçin	Moroney	LP	HM 1184
			MC	HM 401184
Telemann	Recorder concertos	Petri	CD	4122152
			LP	4122151
			MC	[illegible]

Composer	Work	Performer	Format	Number
	Violin concertos	Brown	CD LP MC	411 1252 411 1251 411 1254
	Concerto for Trumpet and Strings	André	LP MC	EL 2702691 EL 2701694
	Oboe concertos	Holliger	LP MC	6514 232 7337 232
	Horn concertos	Baumann	CD LP MC	412 2262 412 2261 412 2264
	Sonata for oboe and continuo in E minor Sonata for oboe and continuo in G Minor	Holliger	LP MC	412 4041 412 4044
Buxtehude	Complete preludes and fugues, choral preludes & toccatas and fugues	Rogg	LP EMI	(German import) Ic137 16351-8 (8 LPs)
	Selected organ pieces	Hurford	LP	ZRDL 1004
Handel	Music for the Royal Fireworks & Concerti a due Cori	Pinnock	CD LP MC	415 1292 415 1291 415 1294
	Water Music	Pinnock	CD LP MC	410 5252 410 5251 410 5254
	Organ concertos op. 7	Koopman	CD LP MC	ECD 136 (3 CDs) NUM 75223 MCE 75223

Composer	Work	Performer	Format	Number
	Concerto grosso (Alexander's feast)	Pinnock	LP	4152911
			MC	4152914
	Concerti grossi op. 6, nos. 1-12	Pinnock	CD	410897-9/2
			LP	410897-9/1
			MC	410897-9/4
		Harnoncourt	CD	8.35603
			LP	6.35603
	Oboe concertos op. 3	Holliger	LP	9502113
			MC	7313113
Vivaldi	Cello concertos	Schibb	CD	4111262
			LP	4111261
			MC	4111264
	Concertos op. 8, nos. 1-4	Marriner	CD	4144862
			LP	ZRG 654
			MC	KZRC 654
	Flute concertos op. 10, nos. 1-6	Bennett	LP	EMX 2105
			MC	TC-EMX 2105
	Bassoon concertos	I Musici	CD	4163552
			LP	4163551
			MC	4163554
	Oboe concertos	Holliger	LP	4161201
	12 concertos op. 8		CD	

Composer	Work	Performer	Format	Number
	The Four Seasons	Marriner	CD	4144862
			LP	2RG 654
			MC	K2RG 654
	Concerto 'Alla Rustica'		CD	4156742
			LP	4156741
			MC	4156744
Bach, J. S.	Brandenburg Concertos 1-4	Pinnock	CD	410 500/1-2
			LP	4107081
			MC	4107084
	Violin concertos in A and E & Double concerto in D minor	Mutter/Accardo	CD	CDC 7470052
			LP	ASD 1435201
			MC	TC 1435204
	Orchestral suites 1-4	Gardiner	CD	ECD 88049/5
			LP	NUM 750762
	Violin partitas	Mintz	CD	4138102
			LP	4138101
			MC	4138104
	Cello suites	Schiff	CD	CDS 7474718
			LP	EX 2700773
			MC	EX 2700775
	Concertos for 1, 2, 3 & 4 harpsichords	Pinnock	CD	4136132
			LP	2723077
	English suites	Gould	CD	MZK 42268
		Leonhardt	LP	EX 2702433
			MC	EX 2702435

Work	Performer	Format	Number
Das wohltemperirte Klavier	Richter	CD	610277
	Gilbert	CD	4134392
		LP	4134391
		MC	4134394
Complete organ works	Hurford	LP	4142061 (25 LPs)

PART III

I

CHAPTER 1

Bach, C. P. E.	Essay on the true art of playing keyboard instruments (1753)	Hogwood	LP	DSLO 589
Bach, J. C.	Sonatas & duets	Fagius, *and others*	LP	BIS LP 273

CHAPTER 2

Haydn	String quartet op. 3, no. 5	BPO Quartet	CD	Denon C37 7094
	Symphonies 6, 7, 8	Marriner	CD	411 4412
			LP	6514 076
			MC	7337 076
	Symphony 104	CBO/Davis	CD	411 4492
		Hogwood	CD	411 8332
			LP	411 8331
			MC	411 8334
	Selected piano sonatas	Brendel	CD	416 6432 (4 CDs)
			LP	416 6431
	Last Seven Words from the Cross	Kremer, *and others*	CD	412 8782
	The Creation	Karajan	CD	410 9512
			LP	410 9511
		Marriner	CD	416 4492
			LP	6769 154
			MC	7699 154

CHAPTER 2 continued

	Nelson Mass	Willcocks	LP	ZRG 5325
			MC	KZRC 5325
		Davis	CD	416 3582
			LP	416 3581
			MC	416 3584

CHAPTER 3

Mozart	Symphony 25	Harnoncourt/Concertgebouw	CD	8.42935
			LP	6.42935
			MC	4.42935
		VPO/Levine	CD	419 2342
			LP	419 2341
			MC	419 2344
	Violin sonatas 17-28, 32, 34 & Variations K. 360	Grumiaux	CD	412 1212
	String quartets 14-23	Melos Qt.	LP	415 5871
	Serenades in C minor K. 388 & E flat K. 375	Harnoncourt	CD	8.43097
			LP	6.43097
			MC	4.43097
	Piano concerto in E flat K. 271	Perahia	CD	CBS 36584
			LP	CBS 76584
	Piano concerto in C minor K. 491	Ashkenazy	LP	SXL 6947
			MC	KSXC 6947
		Haskil	CD	412 2542
	Piano concerto in B flat K. 595	Curzon	CD	417 2882
			LP	SXL 7007
			MC	KSXC 7007

	Adagio and Fugue in C minor K. 546	Italian Qt.	LP	4120591
			MC	4120594
	String quintets 1-6	Grumiaux Trio, Gerecz *and others*	CD	4124862 (3 CDs)
	Mass in C minor K. 427	Harnoncourt	CD	8.43120
			LP	6.43120
			MC	4.43120
		Karajan	CD	4000672
			LP	2532028
			MC	3302028
	Requiem Mass in D minor K. 626	Schreier	CD	4114201
			LP	6514320
			MC	7337320
		Harnoncourt	CD	8.42756
			LP	6.42756
			MC	4.42756
	Divertimenti in E flat K. 563	Kremer/Kashkashian/ Yo-Yo Ma	CD	MK 39561
			LP	IM 39561
			MC	IMT 39561

CHAPTER 4

Mozart	Piano sonatas (complete)	Barenboim	CD	CDS 7473368
	Piano sonatas 1-7, 9, 10, 12	Barenboim	LP	EX 2703243
			MC	EX 2703245
	Piano sonatas 8, 11, 13-18 & Fantasia in C minor	Barenboim	LP	EX 2703273
			MC	EX 2703275

Composer	Work	Performer	Format	Number
	Piano sonata in C minor K. 457	Uchida	CD	412 6172
			LP	412 6171
			MC	412 6174
Beethoven	Piano sonatas (complete)	Brendel	CD	412 5752
			LP	6768 004
			MC	7699 004
	Piano sonata op. 2, no. 2	Gilels	CD	415 4812
			LP	415 4811
			MC	415 4814
	Piano sonatas op. 13, op. 27, no. 2 & op. 57	Ashkenazy	CD	410 2602
			LP	SXL 7012
			MC	KSXC 7012
	Piano sonata op. 90	Ashkenazy	CD	414 6302
	Piano sonata op. 106	Gilels	CD	410 5272
			LP	410 5271
			MC	410 5274
	Piano sonata op. 111	Michelangeli	LP	414 0651
			MC	414 0654
		Gulda	CD	412 1142
	Violin and Piano sonata op. 96	Perlman/Ashkenazy	CD	411 9482
	Violin and piano sonatas (complete)	Perlman/Ashkenazy	LP	D92D5
			MC	K92K53

Work	Performer	Format	Number
Diabelli Variations op. 120	Bishop-Kovacevich	LP	6527 178
		MC	7311 178
String quartets op. 59 nos. 1-3, op. 74 & op. 95	Alban Berg Qt.	CD	CDS 7471318
		LP	SLS 5171
		MC	TC-SLS 5171
String quartets nos. 12-16 & Grosse Fuge	Alban Berg Qt.	CD	CDS 7471358
		LP	EX 2701143
		MC	EX 2701149
Symphonies (complete)	Karajan	CD	415 0662
		LP	415 0661
		MC	415 0664
Symphony 3	Klemperer	CD	CDC 7471862
Symphony 4	Walter	CD	CBS MK 42011
Symphony 5	Kleiber	CD	415 8612
Symphony 6	Ashkenazy	CD	410 0032
Symphonies 6 & 9	Böhm	CD	413 7212
Symphony 7	Ashkenazy	CD	411 9412
	Klemperer	CD	CDC 7471892

CHAPTER 5

Composer	Work	Performer	Format	Number
Mozart	Selected lieder	Schwarzkopf	CD	CDC 7473262
Schubert	Die Schöne Müllerin	Fischer Dieskau	CD	415 1862
			LP	2530 544
	Winterreise	Fischer Dieskau	CD	415 1872
		Schreier	CD	416 2892
			LP	416 1941
			MC	416 1944
	Schwanengesang	Fischer Dieskau	CD	415 1882
	Selected lieder	Price	CD	C001811A
			LP	S0018 11A
		Norman	CD	412 6232
			LP	412 6231
			MC	412 6234
		Fischer Dieskau	LP	410 9791
		Schwarzkopf	LP	ALP 3843
			MC	TC-ALP 3843
	Symphonies (complete, including completed no. 8)	Academy of St. Martins in the Fields/Marriner	CD	412 1762
			LP	412 1761
			MC	412 1764
	Symphony 5	Solti	CD	414 372
			LP	414 3711
			MC	414 3714

Symphony 8	Sinopoli	CD	410 8622
		LP	410 8621
		MC	410 8624
Symphony 9	Solti	CD	400 0822
		LP	SXDL 7557
		MC	KSXDC 7557
	Furtwängler	CD	413 6602
String quartets 13 & 14	Alban Berg Qt.	CD	CDC 7473332
		LP	EL 2702481
String quartet 15	Italian Qt.	LP	412 4011
		MC	412 4014
Quatetsatz in C minor	Amadeus Qt.	CD	410 0242
		LP	2532 071
		MC	3302 071
String quintet in C	Cummings/Lindsay Qt.	CD	CDDCA 537
		LP	DCA 537
String quartet in G	Schiff/Alban Berg Qt.	CD	CDC 7470182
		LP	ASD 1435291
		MC	TC-ASD 1435294

CHAPTER 5 continued

	Piano quintet in A	Schiff/Hagen Qt.	CD	411 9752
			LP	411 9751
			MC	411 9754
		Brendel/Cleveland Qt.	CD	400 0782
			LP	9500 422
			MC	7300 648
	Piano trios 1 & 2, Notturno in E flat D. 897	Beaux Arts Trio	CD	412 6202
			LP	412 6201
			MC	412 6204

CHAPTER 6

Schubert	Moments Musicaux	Curzon	LP	JB 145
			MC	KJBC 145
		Brendel	LP	6527 110
			MC	7311 110
Bruckner	Mass in E minor	Best	CD	CDA 66092
	Symphony 7	BRSO/Chailly	CD	414 2902
			LP	414 4901
			MC	414 2904
	Symphony 9	CBO/Haitink	CD	410 0392
			LP	6514 191
			MC	7337 191
		CSO/Solti	CD	417 2952
			LP	417 2951
			MC	417 2954

Composer	Work	Performers	Format	Catalogue no.
Brahms	Piano concerto 1	Gilels/Jochum	CD	419 1582
	Symphony 1	Walter	CD	CBS MK 42020
		Karajan	LP	2542 166
			MC	3342 166
	Symphony 2	Walter	CD	CBS MK 42021
		Karajan	LP	2531 132
			MC	3301 132
	Symphony 3	Walter	CD	CBS MK 42022
		Haitink	LP	412 3581
			MC	412 3584
	Symphony 4	Kleiber	CD	400 0372
			LP	2532 003
			MC	3302 003
		Walter	CD	CBS MK 42023
	Clarinet quintet in B minor	King/Gabrieli Qt.	CD	CDA 66107
			LP	A 66107
			MC	KA 66107
	Selected lieder	Price	CD	C058831A
			LP	S058831A
			MC	M058831A
		Fischer Dieskau	CD	415 1892
		Norman	CD	416 4392
			LP	9500 785

Composer	Work	Performers	Format	Number
	Piano intermezzi op. 117, Four pieces op. 119	Bishop-Kovacevich	CD	411 1372
			LP	411 1371
			MC	411 1374
	Ein Deutsches Requiem	Haitink	CD	411 4362
			LP	6769 055
			MC	7654 055
		Klemperer	CD	CDC 747238
			LP	SLS 821 (EMI)
			MC	TC-SLS 821
Mahler	Symphony 1	CSO/Solti	CD	411 7312
			LP	411 7311
			MC	411 7314
	Symphony 2	NYPO/Walter	CD	CBS MK 42032
		CSO/Abbado	LP	2707 094
		PO/Sinopoli	CD	415 9592
			LP	415 9591
			MC	415 9594
	Symphony 4	VPO/Maazel	CD	CBS MK 39072
			LP	CBS IM 39072
			MC	CBS IMT 39072
		CSO/Solti	CD	410 1882
			LP	410 1881
			MC	410 1884

	Work	Performers	Format	Number
	Symphony 8	CSO/Solti	CD	414 4932
			LP	SET 534
			MC	KCET2 7006
	Symphony 9	BPO/Karajan	CD	410 7262
			LP	2707 125
			MC	3370 038
		CBO/Haitink	CD	416 4662
			LP	6700 021
	Symphony 10 (performing edition by Deryck Cooke)	CBSO/Rattle	CD	CDS 7473018
			LP	SLS 5206
			MC	TC-SLS 5206
	Das Lied von der Erde	Ferrier/Patzak/VPO/Walter	CD	414 1942
			LP	414 1941
			MC	414 1944
		Baker/King/CBO/Haitink	LP	412 9271
			MC	412 9274
		Ludwig/Wunderlich/PO/Klemperer	CD	CDC 7472312
			LP	EL 2904401
			MC	EL 2904404

II
CHAPTER 1

Gluck	Orfeo ed Euridice	Leppard	LP	NUM 750423
	Alceste	Baudo	LP	S027823F

	Iphigenie en Tauride	Gardiner	CD	416 1482
			LP	416 1481
			MC	416 1484
Mozart	Idomeneo	Harnoncourt	CD	8.35547
			LP	6.35547
			MC	4.35547
	Die Entführung aus dem Serail	Harnoncourt	CD	8.35673
			LP	6.35672
			MC	4.35673
	Le Nozze di Figaro	Solti	CD	410 1502
			LP	D267D4
			MC	K267K42
		Marriner	CD	416 3702
			LP	416 3701
			MC	416 3704
	Don Giovanni	Haitink	CD	CDS 7470378
			LP	SLS 1436653
			MC	TC-SLS 1436659
		Karajan	CD	419 1792
			LP	419 1791
			MC	419 1794
	Die Zauberflöte	Haitink	LP	SLS 5223
			MC	TC-SLS 5223

		Karajan	CD	410 9672
			LP	2741 001
			MC	3382 001
		Davis	CD	411 4592
			LP	411 4591
			MC	411 4594
	Cosi fan Tutte	Böhm	LP	SLS 5028
			MC	TC-SLS 5028
		Davis	CD	416 633
		Muti	LP	SLS 1435163
			MC	TC-SLS 1435165
		Östman	CD	414 3162
			LP	414 3161
			MC	414 3164
Beethoven	Fidelio	Klemperer	LP	SLS 5006
			MC	TC-SLS 5006
Rossini	Barber of Seville	Marriner	CD	411 0582
			LP	411 0581
			MC	411 0584
		Galliera	LP	SLS 853
			MC	TC-SLS 853
	La Cenerentola	Abbado	CD	415 6982
			LP	2709 039
	William Tell (in Italian)	Chailly	CD	417 1532

CHAPTER 1 continued

	Petite Messe Solennelle	Sawallisch	CD	610 263
		Cleobury	CD	CDS 7474328
			LP	EX 2703163
Weber	Konzertstück in F minor	Brendel	CD	412 2512
	Selected overtures	BPO/Karajan	LP	419 0691
			MC	419 0694
	Der Freischütz	Kleiber	CD	415 4322
			LP	2720 071
			MC	3371 008
		Kubelik	CD	417 1192
	Euryanthe	Janowski	LP	EX 2906983
			MC	EX 2906985
	Oberon	Kubelik	LP	419 0381
			MC	419 0384

CHAPTER 2

Wagner	Der Fliegende Holländer	Karajan	CD	CDS 7470548
			LP	EX 2700133
			MC	EX 2700139
		Solti	CD	414 5512
			LP	D240D3
			MC	K24K32
	Lohengrin	Kempe	LP	EX 2909559
			MC	EX 2909558

Tristan und Isolde	Bernstein	CD	410 4472
		LP	6769 091
		MC	7654 091
	Furtwängler	CD	CDS 7473228
		LP	EX 2906843
		MC	EX 2906849
Parsifal	Karajan	CD	413 3472
		LP	2741 002
		MC	3382 002
	Knappertsbusch	CD	416 3902
		LP	6747 250
	Goodall	MC	EX 2701785
Der Ring des Nibelungen (complete)	Solti	CD	414 1002
	Böhm	CD	413 5512

Das Rheingold, Die Walküre, Siegfried and Götterdämmerung are available separately in above performances (with Karajan) on CD and LP

Die Meistersinger von Nürnberg	Jochum	CD	415 2782
		LP	2740 149
		MC	3378 068
	Solti	LP	D13D5
		MC	K13K54
Rienzi	Hollreiser	LP	EMI (German import)
Die Feen	Sawallisch	LP	S 063833F

CHAPTER 3

Composer	Work	Performers	Format	Number
Berlioz	Symphonie Fantastique	CBO/Davis	CD	411 4252
		PO/Muti	CD	CDC 7472782
			LP	EL 2702351
			MC	EL 2702354
	Symphonie Funèbre et Triomphale	LSO/Davis	CD	416 2832
	Nuits d'Été	Kanawa	CD	410 9662
		Norman	CD	412 4932
			LP	9500 783
	Romeo et Juliette	Muti	CD	CDS 7474378
	Grande Messe des Morts	Davis	CD	416 2832
		Previn	LP	SLS 5209
			MC	TCC-SLS 5209
	Te Deum	Abbado	CD	410 6962
			LP	2532 044
	L'Enfance du Christ	Davis	LP	6700 106
			MC	7699 058
	Les Troyens	Davis	CD	416 4322
			LP	6709 002
	La Damnation de Faust	Davis	CD	416 3952
			LP	6703 042

		BPO/Karajan	CD	415 1062
			LP	415 1061
			MC	415 1064
	Carmen	Karajan	CD	410 0882
			LP	2741 025
			MC	3382 025
		Solti	CD	414 4892
			LP	D11D3
			MC	K11K33

CHAPTER 4

Bellini	Norma	Callas	CD	CDS 7473048
			LP	EX 2900663
			MC	EX 2900665
Donizetti	Lucia di Lammermoor	Sutherland	CD	410 1932
			LP	SET 528
			MC	K2L22
Verdi	Macbeth	Sinopoli	CD	412 1332
			LP	412 1331
			MC	412 1334
	Rigoletto	Sinopoli	CD	412 5922
			LP	412 5921
			MC	412 5924
		Bonygne	CD	414 2962
			LP	SET 542
	La Traviata	Bonygne	CD	410 1542
			LP	D212D3
			MC	K212K32

Work	Conductor	Format	Number
La Traviata	Kleiber	CD	415 1322
		LP	2707 103
		MC	3370 024
Aida	Karajan	LP	414 0871
		MC	414 0874
	Muti	CD	CDS 7472718
		LP	SLS 977
		MC	TC-SLS 977
Otello	Maazel	CD	CDS 7474508
		LP	EX 2704613
		MC	EX 2704615
	Barbirolli	LP	EX 2901373
		MC	EX 2901379
Falstaff	Giulini	CD	410 5032
		LP	2741 020
		MC	3382 020
	Karajan	LP	SLS 5211
		MC	TC-SLS5211
Nabucco	Sinopoli	CD	410 5122
		LP	2741 021
		MC	3382 021
Requiem Mass	Giulini	CD	CDS 7472578
		LP	SLS 909
		MC	TC-SLS 909
	Solti	CD	411 9442
		LP	SET 374

Composer	Work	Conductor/Artist	Format	Number
	Don Carlos	Abbado	CD	415 3162
			LP	415 3161
			MC	415 3164
		Giulini	CD	CDS 7473668
			LP	EX 2907123
			MC	EX 2707125
Puccini	Manon Lescaut	Sinopoli	CD	413 8932
			LP	413 8931
			MC	413 8934
		Callas	CD	CDS 7473938
	Madam Butterfly	Serafin	CD	411 6342
		Karajan	LP	SET 584
			MC	K2A1
	Tosca	Callas	CD	CDS 7471758
			LP	EX 2900393
			MC	EX 2900395
		Davis	CD	412 8852
	Il Trittico	Maazel	LP	CBS 79312
	Turandot	Mehta	CD	414 2742
			LP	SET 561
			MC	K2A2
		Karajan	CD	410 0962
			LP	2741 013
			MC	3382 013

CHAPTER 4 continued

Work	Conductor	Format	Number
La Bohème	Beecham	CD	CDS 7472358
		LP	SLS 896
		MC	TC-SLS 896
	Karajan	LP	SET 565
		MC	K2B5

PART IV
I
CHAPTER 1

Composer	Work	Performer	Format	Number
Chopin	Piano concertos 1 & 2	Zimmerman	CD	415 9702
		Agerich	LP	413 2351
			MC	413 2354
	24 Preludes op. 28	Pollini	CD	413 7962
			LP	2530 550
	Études op. 10	Ashkenazy	CD	414 1272
			LP	SXL 6710
			MC	KSXC 6710
	Ballades 1-4 & Scherzos 1-4	Rubenstein	CD	RD 89651
			LP	RL 85460
			MC	RK 85460
	Piano sonatas 2 op. 35 & 3 op. 58	Pollini	CD	415 3462
			LP	415 3461
			MC	415 3464
	Mazurkas 1-51	Rubenstein	CD	RD 85171
			LP	RL 85171
			MC	RK 85171
	Mazurkas op. 25	F. Ts'ong	LP	IM42207
			MC	IMT 42207
	Polonaises 1-7	Pollini	CD	413 7952
			LP	2530 659
			MC	3300 659

Composer	Work	Performer	Format	Number
Schumann	Papillons op. 2	Kempff	LP	413 5381
			MC	413 5384
	Carnival op. 9	Egorov	LP	ASD 4202
			MC	TC-ASD4202
	Kinderszenen op. 15	Agerich	CD	410 6532
			LP	410 6531
			MC	410 6534
	Fantasiestücke op. 12	Brendel	CD	411 0492
			LP	6514 283
			MC	7337 283
	Dichterliebe op. 48 & Liederkreis op. 39	Fischer Dieskau/Eschenbach	CD	415 1902
		Bär/Parsons	CD	CDC7473642
			LP	EL2703641
			MC	EL2703644
	Fantasia op. 17	Perahia	CD	CBS MK 42124
			LP	IM 42124
			MC	IMT 42124
	Piano Concerto op. 54	Bishop-Kovacevich	CD	412 9232
			LP	412 9231
			MC	412 9234
		Brendel	CD	412 2512
			LP	9500 677
			MC	7300 772

Mendelssohn	Lieder ohne Worte (complete)	Barenboim	LP	419 1051
			MC	419 1054
	Octet op. 20	Vienna Octet	LP	JB 138
	A Midsummer Night's Dream op. 21 & 61 (complete)	Previn	CD	CDC7471632
			LP	ASD 3377
			MC	TC-ASD3377
		Marriner	CD	411 1062
			LP	411 1061
			MC	411 1064
	Symphony 3 & Hebrides Overture	LSO/Abbado	CD	415 9732
			LP	415 9731
			MC	415 9734
	String quartets (complete)	Melos Qt.	LP	2740 267
	Organ music (Sonatas 2, 3, 6 & Preludes and Fugues op. 37)	Hurford	CD	414 4202
			LP	414 4201
			MC	414 4204

CHAPTER 2

Liszt	A Faust Symphony	CSO/Solti	CD	417 3992
			LP	417 3991
			MC	414 3994
	Piano concertos 1 & 2	Richter	CD	412 0612
		Arrau	CD	416 4612
			LP	412 9261
			MC	412 9264

CHAPTER 2 continued

	Sonata in B minor	Brendel Curzon	CD LP MC	410 0402 411 7271 411 7274
	Années de Pèlerinage (first year)	Bolet	CD LP MC	410 1602 410 1601 410 1604
	Années de Pèlerinage (second year)	Arrau	CD LP MC	4110552 6514 273 7337 273
	Totentanz	Bolet	CD LP MC	414 0792 414 0791 414 0794
	Mephisto Waltz, Les Préludes, Rhapsodies 2, 4, 5, Tasso, etc.	BPO/Karajan	CD LP MC	415 969 415 6281 415 6284

CHAPTER 3

Glinka	Russlan and Ludmilla (overture)	Salonen/BRSO	CD LP MC	412 5522 412 5521 412 5524
Balakirev	Islamey	Gavrilov	LP MC	EG 2903271 EG 2903274
Borodin	Symphonies 1-3 & In the Steppes of Central Asia	USSR,SO/Svetlanov	LP	LDX 78781/2

	Symphonies 1 & 3	USSR,SO/Svetlanov	CD	[illegible]
Mussorgsky	Boris Godunov	Karajan	LP	SET 514
	Boris Godunov (original version)	Fedoseyev	CD	412 2812
			LP	412 2821
			MC	412 2814
	The Nursery	Söderström	LP	SXL 6900
	Night on the Bare Mountain	CO/Maazel	CD	Telarc 80042
			LP	DG 10042
Tchaikovsky	Eugene Onegin	Solti	LP	SET 596
	Overtures 1812 & Romeo and Juliette	Davis	CD	411 4482
		Karajan	LP	415 8551
			MC	415 8554
	Symphonies 1-3	BPO/Karajan	CD	419 1742-1762
			LP	415 0241
			MC	415 0244
	Symphony 4	OPO/Jansons	CD	CHAN8361
			LP	ABRD1124
			MC	ABTD1124
	Symphony 5	RPO/Previn	CD	Telarc80107
			LP	DG 10107
	Symphony 6	PO/Ashkenazy	CD	411 6152
			LP	SXL 6941
			MC	KSXC 6941

CHAPTER 3 continued

	Sleeping Beauty (suite)	PO/Muti	CD	7470752
			LP	EL 2701131
			MC	EL 2701134
Rimsky-Korsakov	Scheherazade	Kondrashin	CD	400 0212
			LP	9500 681
			MC	7300 776
	Christmas Eve (suite), Le Coq d'Or, May Night, The Snow Maiden, The Tale of Tsar Sultan (suite), etc.	SNO/Järvi	CD	CHAN8327-9
			LP	DBRD 3004
			MC	DBTD 3004

CHAPTER 4

Smetana	The Bartered Bride	Kosler	CD	C37 7309/11
			LP	SUP 11163511/3
	String quartets 1 & 2	Smetana Qt.	CD	C37 7339
			LP	SUP4112130
	Ma Vlast	Kubelik	CD	(German import)
			LP	419 1111
			MC	419 1114
		Smetacek	CD	C37 7241
			LP	SUP 11103431/2
Dvořák	Cello concerto	Rostropovich	CD	413 8192
			LP	139 044

	Slavonic dances op. 46 & 72	Kubelik	LP	419 0561
			MC	419 0564
		Neumann	CD	C37 7491
		Sejna	CD	C37 004
	Symphony 8	Dohnanyi	CD	414 4222
			LP	414 4221
			MC	414 4224
		Walter	CD	CBS MK 42038
	Symphony 9	Kondrashin	CD	400 0472
			LP	SXDL 7510
			MC	KSXDC 7510
		Dohnanyi	CD	414 4212
			LP	414 4211
			MC	414 4214
	Stabat Mater	Kubelik	LP	415 1781
	Te Deum, Psalm 149, etc.	Neumann	CD	C37 7230
	Rusalka	Neumann	CD	C37 7201/3
Janáček	Sinfonietta & Taras Bulba	Mackerras/VPO	CD	410 1382
			LP	SXDL 7519
	Jenufa	Mackerras	CD	414 4832
	Glagolitic Mass	Mackerras	CD	C37 7448
	The Cunning Little Vixen	Mackerras	CD	417 1292

CHAPTER 4 continued

	String quartets 1 & 2	Smetana Qt.	CD	C37 7545

CHAPTER 5

Grieg	Lyric pieces (excerpts)	Katsaris	CD LP MC	8.42925 6.42925 4.42925
	Piano concerto	Bishop-Kovacevich	CD LP MC	412 9232 412 9231 412 92324
Granados	Goyescas (complete)	Larrocha	CD	411 9582
	Danzas Españolas op. 37	Larrocha	CD LP MC	414 5572 SXL 6980 KSXC 6980
Falla	The Three Cornered Hat & El Amor Brujo	Dutoit	CD LP MC	410 0082 SXDL 7560 KSDC 7560
	Concerto for Harpsichord and Chamber Orchestra	LS/Constable	LP	2RG 921

II

CHAPTER 1

Wolf	Goethe Lieder	Fischer Dieskau, *and others*	CD	415 1922
	[illegible]	Ameling, *and others*	LP	[illegible]

Composer	Work	Performer	Format	Number
	Spanisches Liederbuch (complete)	Schwarzkopf/Fischer Dieskau	LP MC	413 2261 413 2264
	Selected Lieder	Schwarzkopf	LP	SLS 5197
Duparc	Selected Mélodies	Baker	LP	ASD 3455
CHAPTER 2				
Franck	Symphony in D minor	Monteux	LP MC	GL 85261 GK 85261
	String quartet	Fitzwilliam Qt.	LP	DSL 046
	Piano quintet	Curzon	LP	SDD 277
	Three Chorales & Pastorale, Prélude, Fugue et Variation op. 18	Hurford	CD LP MC	411 7102 411 7101 411 7104
Chausson	Symphony in B flat	Serebrier	CD LP MC	CHAN 8369 ABRD 1135 ABTD 1135
CHAPTER 3				
Delius	A Song of the High Hills	Fenby	LP MC	DKP 9029 DKPC 9029
	A Village Romeo and Juliet	Davies	LP MC	EM 290404 EM 2904045

Composer	Work	Performer	Format	Number
	Brigg Fair, Dance Rhapsody no. 2 Fennimore and Gerda, Intermezzo, Florida Suite, On hearing the first cuckoo in spring, Sleigh Ride, Summer night on the river, etc.	Beecham	LP	EM 2903233
			MC	EM 2903235
	Sea Drift	RPO/Groves	MC	TCC2-POR54295
	Mass of Life	RPO/Groves	LP	SLS 958
Nielsen	Symphony 5	Kubelik	LP	EL 2703521
	Symphony 4	Karajan	CD	413 3132
			LP	2532 029
			MC	3302 029
Sibelius	Symphony 2	Karajan	LP	ASD 4060
			MC	TC-ASD4060
	Symphony 4 & Luonnotar	Ashkenazy	CD	400 0562
			LP	SXDL 7517
			MC	KSXDC7517
		Karajan	CD	415 107
	Symphony 7 & Tapiola	Ashkenazy	CD	411 9352
			LP	SXDL 7580
			MC	KSXDC7580
		Karajan	CD	415 1082

Composer	Work	Performer	Format	Number
Debussy	Préludes (book one)	Michelangeli	CD	413 4502
			LP	2531 200
	Nocturnes, Jeux	CBO/Haitink	CD	400 0232
			LP	9500 674
	Images & Prélude à l'après-midi d'un faune	LSO/Previn	CD	CDC7470012
			LP	ASD 3804
			MC	TC-ASD3804
	La Mer	Karajan	LP	2542 116
			MC	3342 116
		Davis	CD	411 4332
		Previn	CD	CDC7470282
			LP	ASD 1436322
			MC	TC-ASD 1436324
	Cello sonata	Rostropovich	LP	410 1681
			MC	410 1684
	String quartet	Alban Berg Qt.	CD	CDC7473472
			LP	EL 2703561
			MC	EL 2703564
	Pelléas at Mélisande	Karajan	LP	SLS 5172
			MC	TC-SLS 5172
Ravel	Gaspard de la nuit, Valses nobles et sentimentales & Pavane pour une infante défunte	Ashkenazy	CD	410 2552
			LP	410 2551
			MC	410 2554

CHAPTER 4 continued

	Daphnis et Chloé (complete)	Dutoit	CD	400 0552
			LP	SXDL 7526
			MC	KSXDC 7526
	Ma Mère l'Oye (complete)	Dutoit	CD	410 2542
			LP	410 2541
			MC	410 2544
	Shéhérazade	Ameling	CD	410 0432
			LP	6514 199
			MC	7337 199
	String Quartet	Alban Berg Qt.	CD	CDC 7473472
			LP	EL 2703561
			MC	EL 2703564
	Piano concerto in G & Piano concerto for the left hand	Collard	CD	CDC 7473862
			LP	ASD 3845
			MC	TC-ASD 8845
	L'Enfant et les Sortilèges	Previn	CD	CDC 7471692
			LP	ASD 4167

CHAPTER 5

Fauré	Mélodies	Von Stade	LP	ASD 4183
	Requiem	Rutter	CD	CDCFRA 122
			LP	CFRA 122
		Davis	CD	412 7432
			LP	412 7431

Composer	Work	Performers	Format	Number
	Piano trio	Guarneri Trio	LP	BP 201
Strauss	Tod und Verklärung, Don Juan & Till Eulenspiegel	CBO/Haitink	CD	411 4422
			LP	6514 228
			MC	7337 228
	Metamorphosen for 23 solo strings	BPO/Karajan	CD	410 8922
			LP	2532 074
			MC	3302 074
	Vier Letzte Lieder (& other songs)	Schwarzkopf	CD	CDC7470132
		Norman	CD	411 0522
			LP	6514 322
			MC	7337 322
	Elektra	Solti	CD	417 3452
			LP	SET 354
			MC	K124K22
	Der Rosenkavalier	Karajan	LP	EX 2900453
			MC	EX 2900459
		Solti	CD	418 932DH
			LP	SET 418
			MC	K3N23
	Ein Heldenleben	Karajan	CD	415 5082
			LP	415 5081
			MC	415 5084

CHAPTER 6

Composer	Work	Performers	Format	Number
Elgar	Enigma Variations & Falstaff	Mackerras	CD	CDC7474162
			LP	EL2703741
			MC	EL2703744

	Symphony 1	Boult	CD	CDC7472042
			LP	ASD 3330
			MC	TC-ASD3330
	Symphony 2	Haitink	CD	CDC7472992
			LP	EL 2701472
			MC	EL 2701474
	The Dream of Gerontius	Boult	CD	CDS7472088
			LP	SLS 987
			MC	TC-SLS 987
	Cello concerto	Pré	CD	CDC7473292
			LP	ASD 655
				TC-SLS 655
	Violin concerto	LPO/Kennedy	LP	EMX 412058-1
			MC	EMX 412058-4
Holst	The Planets	Karajan	CD	400 0282
			LP	2532 019
			MC	3332 019
Vaughan Williams	On Wenlock Edge	Tear, *and others*	LP	EL 2700591
			MC	EL 2700594
	Fantasia on a theme of Thomas Tallis & Fantasia on Greensleeves	Barbirolli	CD	CDC7475372
			LP	ASD 521
			MC	TC-ASD 521

	Job - a masque for dancing	Handley	LP MC	EMX 20561 TC-EMX 4120564
	Symphonies 3 & 5 (also available singly on LP & MC)	Boult	CD	CDC7472142
	Symphony 5 & The Wasps, etc.	Previn	CD LP MC	RD 89693 GL 89693 GK 89693
	Symphonies 4 & 6 (also available singly on LP & MC)	Boult	CD	CDC7472152
	The Pilgrim's Progress	Boult	LP MC	SLS 1435133 TC-SLS 143515
	Mass in G minor & Five Mystical Songs	King's College Choir/Willcocks	LP	ASD 2458

CHAPTER 7

Busoni	Piano concerto	Ogdon	LP	SXDW 3053
	Doktor Faustus	Leitner	LP	2740 273
Schoenberg	Verklärte Nacht & Variations for orchestra op. 31	BPO/Karajan	CD LP	415 3262 2530 627
	Pelleas und Melisande	BPO/Karajan	LP	410 9341
	Moses und Aaron	CSO/Solti	CD LP	414 2642 414 2641

CHAPTER 7 continued

Composer	Work	Performer	Format	Number
	Gurrelieder	Ozawa	CD LP MC	412 5112 6769 124 7699 124
	Quartets 1-4 (five records)	La Salle Qt.	LP	2720 029
	Pierrot Lunaire	Boulez	LP	CBS 76720
Berg	Violin concerto & Three orchestral pieces op. 6	Kremer/BRSO/Davis	CD LP MC	412 5232 412 5321 412 5234
	Lulu (completed by Cerha)	Boulez	CD	415 4892
	Wozzeck	Böhm	LP	413 8041
Hindemith	Mathis der Maler (suite)	Karajan	LP	SX 30536
	Symphonic metamorphoses on themes by Weber	Abbado	LP MC	414 4371 414 4374
	Organ sonatas	Hurford	CD	417 1592
	Mathis der Maler (complete)	Kubelik	LP	EMI ICI 6503515/7

CHAPTER 8

Composer	Work	Performer	Format	Number
Stravinsky	The Rite of Spring	Muti Karajan Abbado	CD CD LP MC	CDC7471022 415 9792 413 9751 [illegible]

	Symphony of Psalms	Chailly	CD	414 0782
			LP	414 0781
			MC	414 0784
	Oedipus Rex	Davis	LP	SO 71831
			MC	MO 71831
	The Rake's Progress	Chailly	CD	411 6442
			LP	411 6441
	Symphony in C & Symphony in three movements	Dutoit	CD	414 2722
			LP	SXDL 7543
			MC	KSXDC7543
	Agon	Atherton	LP	ZRG 937
Bartók	Duke Bluebeard's Castle	Kertesz	LP	414 1671
			MC	414 1674
		Ferencsik	CD	HCD 12254
	String quartets 1-6	Takács Qt.	CD	HCD12502/4
	Concerto for orchestra & Music for strings, percussion and celesta	BPO/Karajan	CD	415 3222

CHAPTER 9

Bloch	Schelomo & Voice in the Wilderness	Mehta	LP	414 1661
			M C	414 1664
Webern	All works with opus nos.	Boulez	LP	CBS79402(4)

Orff	Carmina Burana	Previn	CD	CDC7474112
			LP	ASD 3117
			MC	TC-ASD3117
		Mata	CD	RCD14550
			LP	RL 13925
Messiaen	L'Ascension & L'Apparition de l'Eglise Eternelle	Bates	LP	DKP 9015
	La Nativité du Seigneur	Bates	LP	DKP 9005
	Turangalîla	Salonen	CD	CBSM2K42271
	Quatour pour la fin du temps	Barenboim, *and others*	LP	2531 093
Boulez	Le Marteau sans Maître & Pli Selon Pli		LP	CBSDC40173
Prokofiev	Violin concertos 1 & 2	Mintz	CD	410 5242
			LP	410 5241
			MC	410 5244
	Violin sonata 1	Mordkovitch	CD	CHAN8398
			LP	ABRD1132
			MC	ABTD1132
Shostakovich	Symphony 5	Haitink	CD	410 0172
			LP	SXDL 7551
			MC	KSXDC7551
	Symphony 10	Karajan	CD	413 3612
			LP	2532 030

Composer	Work	Performer	Format	Number
	Piano quintet op. 57	Richter	CD LP	CDL7475072 EL2703381
Walton	Belshazzar's Feast	Previn	CD LP MC	CDRPO8001 RPO 8001 ZCRPO8001
	Violin concerto & Viola concerto	Menuhin	LP	ASD 2542
Tippett	A Child of our time	Previn	CD LP MC	CDRPO8005 RPO 8005 ZCRPO8005
	Concerto for double string orchestra & Ritual dances from The Midsummer Marriage	Barshai	CD LP MC	CDC7473302 EL2702731 EL2702734
Britten	A Boy was Born	Best	CD LP MC	CDA 66126 A 66126 KA 66126
	Variations on a theme of Frank Bridge, The Young Person's Guide to the Orchestra & Simple Symphony (also available singly on LP & MC)	Britten	CD	417 507
	Les Illuminations, Serenade for horn, tenor and strings & Nocturne (also available singly on LP & MC)	Pears	CD	417 153
	Peter Grimes	Britten	CD LP MC	414 5772 SXL 2150 K71K33

CHAPTER 9 continued

Composer	Work	Performer	Format	Number
	Sinfonia da Requiem, etc.	Rattle	CD LP MC	CDC7473432 EL2702631 EL2702634
	Billy Budd	Britten	LP	SET 379
	The Turn of the Screw	Davis	LP MC	410426-1 410426-4
	A Midsummer Night's Dream	Britten	LP	SET 338

CHAPTER 10

Composer	Work	Performer	Format	Number
Ives	Three places in New England & Symphony 4	Thomas	LP	410 9331
	Orchestral set no. 2 & Symphony 3 (The Camp Meeting)	Thomas	CD LP MC	CBSMK37823 IM37823 IMT37823
	Symphony 4	NYPO	LP	77424
Harris	Symphony 3	Bernstein	LP	CBS61681
Copland	Piano Variations	LIN	LP MC	ABR 1104 ABT 1104
	Appalachian Spring	Dorati	CD LP	414 4572 414 4571
	Piano sonata	LIN	LP	ABR 1104

Composer	Work	Conductor	Format	Number
	Billy the Kid & Rodeo	Slatkin	LP	EL2703981
			MC	EL2703984
	Dance Symphony, El Salon Mexico, Fanfare for the common man & Rodeo (four dance episodes)	Dorati	CD	414 2732
			LP	SXDL7547
			MC	KSXDC7547
Varèse	Deserts, Ecuatorial, Hyperprism, Intégrales, Octandre & Densité	Boulez	LP	CBSIM39053
			MC	CBSIMT 39053
Gershwin	Porgy and Bess	Maazel	CD	414 5592
			LP	SET 609
			MC	K3Q28
	Rhapsody in Blue	Thomas	CD	CBSMK39699
			LP	CBSIM39699
			MC	CBSIMT39699
Bernstein	West Side Story	Bernstein	CD	415 2532
			LP	415 2531
			MC	415 2534
Villa-Lobos	Bachianas Brasileiras 1, 5, 7	Hendricks	CD	CDC7474332
			LP	EL2704441
			MC	EL2904444

AFTERWORD

Composer	Work	Conductor	Format	Number
Shostakovich	Symphony 14	Haitink	CD	417 5142
			LP	SXDL7532
			MC	KSXDC7532

Composer	Work	Performer	Recording
	Symphony 15	Haitink	LP SXL 6906 MC KSXC 6906
	String quartets 1-15 & Piano quintet in G minor	Richter/Borodin Qt.	LP EX2703393(7)
Lutoslawski	Concerto for orchestra, Funeral music & Jeux venitiens	Rowicki	LP 412 3771 MC 412 3774
	Symphony 3	Lutoslawski	CD 416 3872 LP 416387-1 MC 416387-4
Penderecki	St. Luke Passion	Czyz	LP EMI (German import)
	Threnody for the victims of Hiroshima	Rowicki	LP 412 030
	Symphony 2	Penderecki	EMI Germany
Boulez	Le Marteau sans Maître & Pli Selon Pli	Boulez	LP CBSDC40173
Berio	Sinfonia & Eindrücke	Boulez	LP NUM75198 MC MCE75198
Varèse	Selected works	Boulez	LP CBSIM39053 MC CBSIMT39053
	Death in Venice	Bedford	LP SET 581
	Complete music for string quartet, etc.	Endellion Qt. *and others*	CD CDC7476942 LP EX 2705 MC EX 270502

Tippett	The Knot Garden	Davis	LP	412 7071
	Symphonies 1-4	Solti/Davis	LP MC	414 0911 414 0914
Maxwell Davies	Symphony 3	Downes	LP	BBC REGL 350
	Vesali Icones	Maxwell Davies	LP MC	KPM 7016 UKC 7016
Reich	Variations for wind, strings and keyboard	De Waart	CD LP MC	412 2142 412 2141 412 2144
	Further selections of music by Steve Reich are available on the German ECM label.			
Glass	Einstein on the beach	Riesman	CD LP MC	CBSM4K38875 CBSM438875 CBSMXT38875
	Satyagraha	Keene	CD LP MC	CBSCD39672 CBS13M39672 CBS13T39672
Bernstein	West Side Story	Bernstein	CD LP MC	415 2532 415 2531 415 2534

INDEX OF MUSIC EXAMPLES

PART I (up to *c.* 1525)

* Indicates that the music, but not necessarily the text, is complete.

PART II (*c.* 1525–*c.* 1750)

PART III (from *c.* 1750)

PART IV (from 1800)

GENERAL INDEX